CIVIL PROCEDURE 2022

THIRD CUMULATIVE SUPPLEMENT TO THE 2022 EDITION

Up to date to 1 December 2022 to the 150th CPR Update

TO ACCESS THE WHITE BOOK UPDATING SERVICE VIA HTTP://WWW.SWEETANDMAXWELL.CO.UK/WHITEBOOK YOU NEED TO ENTER THE FOLLOWING PASSWORD:
WB2022

SWEET & MAXWELL

TERS

Published in 2022 by Thomson Reuters, trading as Sweet & Maxwell.
Thomson Reuters is registered in England & Wales, Company No. 1679046.
Registered Office and address for service: 5 Canada Square, Canary Wharf, London E14 5AQ.
Typesetting by Sweet & Maxwell electronic publishing system.
Printed and bound in the UK by Hobbs The Printers Ltd.
For further information on our products and services, visit
http://www.sweetandmaxwell.co.uk.

No natural forests were destroyed to make this product; only farmed timber was used and replanted.

British Library Cataloguing in Publication Data
A CIP catalogue record for this book is available from the British Library

ISBN-978-0-41410-311-5

List of Editors

EDITOR-IN-CHIEF

THE RIGHT HONOURABLE LORD JUSTICE PETER COULSON
Lord Justice of Appeal

EMERITUS EDITOR

PROFESSOR I. R. SCOTT KC (Hon)
Emeritus Professor, University of Birmingham; Honorary Bencher of Gray's Inn

GENERAL EDITORS

SENIOR MASTER B. FONTAINE
Senior Master of the Senior Courts in the King's Bench Division and King's Remembrancer; Central Authority for the Hague Conventions on Service and Taking of Evidence; Former Member of the Civil Procedure Rule Committee
DR J. SORABJI
Barrister, 9 St John Street; Member, Civil Justice Council; Associate Professor of Law, University College London

EDITOR OF CIVIL PROCEDURE NEWS

DR J. SORABJI
Barrister, 9 St John Street; Member, Civil Justice Council; Associate Professor of Law, University College London

SENIOR EDITORIAL BOARD

THE HONOURABLE MRS JUSTICE COCKERILL
Judge of the King's Bench Division of the High Court; Formerly Judge in charge of the Commercial Court
SENIOR COSTS JUDGE A. GORDON-SAKER
Senior Courts Costs Office
HIS HONOUR NIC MADGE
A Retired Circuit Judge
DISTRICT JUDGE SIMON MIDDLETON
Truro Courts of Justice and Bodmin County Court

EDITORS

MASOOD AHMED
Associate Professor in Law, Leicester Law School, University of Leicester; Former Member of the Civil Procedure Rule Committee
JONATHAN AUBURN KC
One of His Majesty's Counsel
HIS HONOUR JUDGE SIMON AUERBACH
Senior Circuit Judge, Employment Appeal Tribunal
DR STUART BARAN
Barrister, Three New Square
JUDGE BARBER
Insolvency and Companies Court Judge
HIS HONOUR JUDGE NIGEL BIRD
Designated Civil Judge for Greater Manchester; Member of the Civil Procedure Rule Committee
MASTER BROWN
Costs Judge of the Senior Courts (Taxing Master); Master of the Senior Courts, King's Bench Division
GREG CALLUS
Barrister, 5 Raymond Buildings
MASTER CLARK
A Master of the Senior Courts, Chancery Division

MASTER DAVID COOK
A Master of the Senior Courts, King's Bench Division; Member of the Civil Procedure Rule Committee
MASTER DAGNALL
A Master of the Senior Courts, King's Bench Division
MASTER DAVISON
Admiralty Registrar and a Master of the Senior Courts, King's Bench Division
HIS HONOUR JUDGE MALCOLM DAVIS-WHITE KC
Leeds Combined Court Centre
RAJ DESAI
Barrister, Matrix Chambers
MASTER R. EASTMAN
A Master of the Senior Courts, King's Bench Division
LAURA FELDMAN
Senior Associate (Barrister), Freshfields; Lecturer in Private Law, University of Oxford
HER HONOUR JUDGE LINDSEY GEORGE
A Circuit Judge on the South Eastern Circuit; Croydon County Court
JOAN GOULBOURN
Of the Public Guardianship Office
RICHARD GRIMSHAW
Deputy Master of the Senior Courts, King's Bench Division; a Recorder of the County Court and a Recorder of the Crown Court; Barrister, No.5 Chambers
DISTRICT JUDGE MATTHEW HAISLEY
A District Judge on the Northern Circuit
PHILIPPA HOPKINS KC
One of His Majesty's Counsel
MICHAEL HOVINGTON
Former District Judge; Deputy District Judge County Court at Manchester; Former Member of the Civil Procedure Rule Committee
Y. JACOBS-JONES
Solicitor, High Court Chancery Chambers
E. JEARY
Of the Court Funds Office
THE HONOURABLE MRS JUSTICE JEFFORD DBE
Judge of the King's Bench Division of the High Court
CHRISTOPHER KNIGHT
Barrister, 11 King's Bench Walk
EMILY MACKENZIE
Barrister, Brick Court Chambers
DISTRICT JUDGE ASIF MALEK
A District Judge on the Midland Circuit
SARA MASTERS KC
One of His Majesty's Counsel
DISTRICT JUDGE SHANTI MAUGER
County Court at Central London
MASTER VICTORIA McCLOUD
A Master of the Senior Courts, King's Bench Division
ANGUS McCULLOUGH KC
One of His Majesty's Counsel
MAURA McINTOSH
Solicitor (Professional Support Consultant), Herbert Smith Freehills
JONATHAN MOFFETT KC
One of His Majesty's Counsel
JOHN O'HARE
Barrister; formerly a Master of the Senior Courts Costs Office

HIS HONOUR JUDGE RICHARD PARKES KC
A Circuit Judge on the Western Circuit; Designated Civil Judge for Hampshire, Wiltshire, Dorset and the Isle of Wight
HIS HONOUR JUDGE MARK PELLING KC
Judge in Charge, London Circuit Commercial Court
THE HONOURABLE MR JUSTICE PEPPERALL
Judge of the King's Bench Division of the High Court; a Presiding Judge of the Midland Circuit; Former Member of the Civil Procedure Rule Committee
LAURA PRINCE
Barrister, Matrix Chambers
HIS HONOUR JUDGE RICHARD ROBERTS
A Circuit Judge on the South Eastern Circuit; Former Member of the Civil Procedure Rule Committee
C. SANDERS
Solicitor
IAN SEWELL
Costs Clerk, Supreme Court of the United Kingdom
CHIEF MASTER SHUMAN
Chief Master of the Chancery Division of the High Court
DISTRICT JUDGE ANDREW SPENCER
A District Judge on the South Eastern Circuit
MASTER AMANDA STEVENS
A Master of the Senior Courts, King's Bench Division
DAVID STONE
A Deputy District Judge on the South Eastern Circuit
MASTER LISA SULLIVAN
A Master of the Senior Courts, King's Bench Division
K. TALBOT KC
One of His Majesty's Counsel; Member of the New York Bar
PAUL TEVERSON
Formerly a Master of the Senior Courts, Chancery Division; now a Deputy Master of that Division
SARAH THOMPSON-COPSEY
Non-practising Solicitor
MASTER THORNETT
A Master of the Senior Courts, King's Bench Division
HER HONOUR JUDGE WALDEN-SMITH
Senior Circuit Judge, Designated Civil Judge for East Anglia
TIM WALLIS
Mediator and Solicitor with Expedite Resolution and Trust Mediation

ADVISORY EDITORS

HIS HONOUR JUDGE NIGEL BIRD
Designated Civil Judge for Greater Manchester; Member of the Civil Procedure Rule Committee
THE RIGHT HONOURABLE LORD JUSTICE BIRSS
Deputy Head of Civil Justice
PETER HURST LLB MPhil FCIArb
39 Essex Chambers
THE RIGHT HONOURABLE SIR RUPERT JACKSON LLD
Formerly a Lord Justice of Appeal; Honorary Fellow of Jesus College, Cambridge
THE RIGHT HONOURABLE PROFESSOR SIR ROBIN JACOB
Sir Hugh Laddie Chair in Intellectual Property; Director, Institute of Brand & Innovation Law, University College, London
HIS HONOUR JUDGE MILWYN JARMAN KC
Specialist Chancery Judge, Cardiff Civil & Family Justice Centre; Member of the Civil Procedure Rule Committee; Honorary Fellow of Aberystwyth University

THE HONOURABLE SIR STEPHEN STEWART
Formerly the Judge in charge of the Queen's Bench Division Civil List; Former Member of the Civil Procedure Rule Committee

Publisher's Note

The *White Book* 2022 published in March 2022. This is the Third Cumulative Supplement to the 2022 Edition, offered as part of your *White Book* subscription, which brings both volumes of the Main Work up to date to 1 December 2022 to the 150th CPR Update.

The Third Supplement brings the White Book up to date to the elements of the Civil Procedure (Amendment No.2) Rules 2022 (SI 2022/783) and the 149th CPR Update in respect of Welsh housing procedural amendments (subsequent to the Renting Homes (Wales) Act 2016), coming into force on 1 December 2022, and to the 150th CPR Update (changes to PD 51ZB—the Damages Claims Pilot, which came into force on 15 September 2022). The supplement includes:

- amendments to Pts 55, 56 and 65 in respect of Welsh housing;
- amendments to PD 55A, PD 55B, and PD 65, and a new PD 56A in respect of Welsh housing;
- 150th CPR Update: updates to PD 51ZB—the Damages Claims Pilot;
- new editions of the Administrative Court Judicial Review Guide, Technology & Construction Court Guide and Intellectual Property Enterprise Court Guide;
- amendments to the King's Bench Court Guide;
- new and revised Practice Notes: the Remote Hand-Down of Judgments in the Chancery Division; Disclosure in the Insolvency and Companies List; and an updated Note accompanying the new edition of the Chancery Guide 2022;
- notes on Pt 4 Forms and Supreme Court Practice Directions following the death of Her Majesty Queen Elizabeth II and the accession of His Majesty King Charles III; and
- Court Funds—revised interest rates.

Civil Procedure News will continue to keep you abreast of developments for the remainder of the subscription year.

We welcome feedback from subscribers—please email *whitebook@sweetandmaxwell.co.uk* with any comments or suggestions.

The *White Book* team

November 2022

CONTENTS

TABLE OF CASES

TABLE OF STATUTES

TABLE OF INTERNATIONAL AND EUROPEAN LEGISLATION, TREATIES AND CONVENTIONS

TABLE OF UK RETAINED EU LAW

VOLUME 1

SECTION AA CORONAVIRUS (COVID-19)

REMOTE HEARINGS GUIDANCE TO HELP THE BUSINESS AND PROPERTY COURTS

Editorial note

Add new paragraph at end:

Now see the Chancery Guide 2022 Appendix Z (Remote and Hybrid Hearing Protocol), for the approach to take in the Chancery Division. **A.2.1**

ADMINISTRATIVE COURT INFORMATION FOR COURT USERS

Delete Administrative Court Information for Court Users (paragraph A.9).

Replace paragraph with:

Guidance for the Administrative Court users was issued on 24 November 2020. It was replaced by updated guidance on 27 July 2022: see para.54PN.1. **A.9.1**

CORONAVIRUS (COVID-19): IMPACT ON THE COURT FUNDS OFFICE

Delete Coronavirus (COVID-19): Impact on the Court Funds Office and editorial note (paragraphs A.12 and A.12.1).

SECTION A CIVIL PROCEDURE RULES 1998

PART 1

OVERRIDING OBJECTIVE

Add new paragraph 1.1.1.1:

Principle of finality

The long-established principle of finality of litigation is inherent in the overriding objective: *Sainsbury's Supermarkets Ltd v Visa Europe Services LLC* [2020] UKSC 24; [2020] Bus. L.R. 1196 at [238]–[239]; *AIC Ltd v Federal Airports Authority of Nigeria* [2022] UKSC 16; [2022] 1 W.L.R. 3223 at [30]–[31]. **1.1.1.1**

Encouraging use of alternative dispute resolution (ADR) procedure

To the end of the paragraph, add:

See *Sky's the Limit Transformations Ltd v Mirza* [2022] EWHC 29 (TCC) at [6]–[9] for an innovative ADR scheme that combines ENE and mediation for TCC claims, which could well be adapted more widely. **1.4.11**

Rule 1.6: Effect of rule

To the end of the paragraph, add:

Practice Direction 1A was amended, with effect from 7 June 2022, by CPR Update 147 (May 2022) to make provision, in its para.7, for the address and contact details of relevant parties to be **1.6.1** concealed for "appropriate reasons"; a derogation from open justice. On the wider general power under the inherent jurisdiction to conceal such details as a derogation from open justice, see *Axnoller Events Ltd v Brake* [2022] EWHC 1162 (Ch).

PRACTICE DIRECTION 1A—PARTICIPATION OF VULNERABLE PARTIES OR WITNESSES

Vulnerability

To the end of paragraph 7, add:

1APD.1 This may include concealing the address and/or contact details of either party or a witness for appropriate reasons.

PART 2

Application and Interpretation of the Rules

Editorial introduction

Replace the fourth and fifth paragraphs (beginning "Practice Direction 2C" and ending "of "will" and "must".") with:

2.0.1 Practice Direction 2C—Starting Proceedings in the County Court (see para.2CPD.1 below) was introduced by CPR Update 74 on 31 July 2014. It was amended and simplified by CPR Update 149 (July 2022) as from 1 October 2022. It applies to proceedings in the County Court. It provides important information on where proceedings must be issued in the County Court. Parties should always refer to the relevant provisions in the Rules and related Practice Directions and other enactments referred to in this Practice Direction.

Practice Direction 2D—References in the Rules to Actions Done by the Court was introduced by CPR Update 75 (July 2014). It came into force on 1 October 2014. It was omitted by CPR Update 149 (July 2022) as from 1 October 2022. It contained provisions relating to the meaning within the Rules of "will" and "must".

Add new r.2.1(3):

Application of the Rules[1]

2.1 **(3) These Rules apply to proceedings under—**

(a) the Companies Act 1985;

(b) the Companies Act 2005; and

(c) other legislation relating to companies and limited liability partnerships,

subject to the provisions of the relevant practice direction which applies to those proceedings.

Replace r.2.3(1) with:

Interpretation[2]

2.3 **2.3—(1) In these Rules—**

---

[1] Amended by the Civil Procedure (Amendment) Rules 1999 (SI 1999/1008), the Civil Procedure (Amendment No.2) Rules 2003 (SI 2003/1242), the Constitutional Reform Act 2005 (c.4), the Civil Procedure (Amendment No.4) Rules 2005 (SI 2005/3515), the Civil Procedure (Amendment) Rules 2007 (SI 2007/2204), the Family Procedure (Modification of Enactments) Order 2011 (SI 2011/1045), the Civil Procedure (Amendment) Rules 2014 (SI 2014/407) and the Civil Procedure (Amendment No.2) Rules 2022 (SI 2022/783).

[2] Amended by the Civil Procedure (Amendment No.4) Rules 2000 (SI 2000/2092), the Civil Procedure (Amendment No.5) Rules 2001 (SI 2001/4015), the Civil Procedure (Amendment No.2) Rules 2004 (SI 2004/2072), the Civil Procedure (Amendment) Rules 2007 (SI 2007/2204), the Civil Procedure (Amendment) Rules 2008 (SI 2008/2178), the Civil Procedure (Amendment) Rules 2009 (SI 2009/3390), the Civil Procedure (Amendment No.4) Rules 2011 (SI 2011/3103), the Civil

"child" has the meaning given by rule 21.1(2);
"civil restraint order" means an order restraining a party—

- **(a) from making any further applications in current proceedings (a limited civil restraint order);**
- **(b) from issuing certain claims or making certain applications in specified courts (an extended civil restraint order); or**
- **(c) from issuing any claim or making any application in specified courts (a general civil restraint order).**

"claim for personal injuries" means proceedings in which there is a claim for damages in respect of personal injuries to the claimant or any other person or in respect of a person's death, and
"personal injuries" includes any disease and any impairment of a person's physical or mental condition;
"claimant" means a person who makes a claim;
"CCR" is to be interpreted in accordance with Part 50;
"court officer" means a member of the court staff;
"defendant" means a person against whom a claim is made;
"defendant's home court" means—

- **(a) if a claim is proceeding in the County Court, the County Court hearing centre serving the address where the defendant resides or carries on business; and**
- **(b) if the claim is proceeding in the High Court, the district registry for the district in which the defendant resides or carries on business or, where there is no such district registry, the Royal Courts of Justice;**

"filing"means delivering a document or information, by post or otherwise, to the court office;
"judge" means, unless the context otherwise requires, a judge, Master or District Judge or a person authorised to act as such;
"judge of the County Court" has the meaning given in section 5 of the County Courts Act 1984;
"jurisdiction" means, unless the context requires otherwise, England and Wales and any part of the territorial waters of the United Kingdom adjoining England and Wales;
"justices' legal adviser" means a person nominated by the Lord Chancellor who is authorised to exercise functions under section 28(1) of the Courts Act 2003;
"legal representative" means a

- **(a) barrister;**
- **(b) solicitor;**
- **(c) solicitor's employee;**
- **(d) manager of a body recognised under section 9 of the Administration of Justice Act 1985; or**
- **(e) person who, for the purposes of the Legal Services Act 2007, is an authorised person in relation to an activity which constitutes the conduct of litigation (within the meaning of that Act),**

who has been instructed to act for a party in relation to proceedings;
"litigation friend" has the meaning given by Part 21;
"MyHMCTS" means the online case management tool managed by Her Majesty's Courts and Tribunals Service;

Procedure (Amendment) Rules 2014 (SI 2014/407), the Courts and Tribunals (Judiciary and Functions of Staff) Act 2018 (Consequential, Transitional and Saving Provision) Regulations 2020 (SI 2020/100), the Civil Procedure (Amendment No.4) Rules 2021 (SI 2021/855), the Civil Procedure (Amendment) Rules 2022 (SI 2022/101) and the Civil Procedure (Amendment No.2) Rules 2022 (SI 2022/783).

"preferred hearing centre" means, if the claim is proceeding in the County Court, the County Court hearing centre the claimant has specified in practice form N1 as the hearing centre to which the proceedings should be sent if necessary;
"protected party" has the meaning given by rule 21.1(2);
"RSC" is to be interpreted in accordance with Part 50;
"statement of case"—
- **(a) means a claim form, particulars of claim where these are not included in a claim form, defence, Part 20 claim, or reply to defence; and**
- **(b) includes any further information given in relation to them voluntarily or by court order under rule 18.1;**

"statement of value" is to be interpreted in accordance with rule 16.3;
"summary judgment" is to be interpreted in accordance with Part 24;
"tape recorded" includes (as do references to tape recording and tape recorders) recording by the use or means of any other instrument or device.

(1A) Unless the contrary is indicated, a definition that applies to a Part of these Rules applies also to a practice direction supplementing that Part.

Rule 2.3(1): Words and expressions defined

"filing"

Replace the fourth sentence (beginning "In r.2.3(1) it is") with:

2.3.9 In r.2.3(1) (as amended by the Civil Procedure (Amendment No.2) Rules 2022 (SI 2022/783)) it is stated that, in the CPR, "filing", in relation to a document or information, means "delivering it by post, or otherwise, to the court office".

Replace r.2.4 with:

Power to perform an act of the court[1]

2.4 **2.4—(1) Where these Rules provide for the court to perform any act then, except where an enactment, rule or practice direction provides otherwise, that act may be performed—**
- **(a) in relation to proceedings in the High Court, by any judge, Master, Registrar in Bankruptcy or District Judge of that Court; and**
- **(b) in relation to proceedings in the County Court, by any judge of the County Court.**

(2) A legal adviser, defined in paragraph 1.2(b) of Practice Direction 2E, may exercise the jurisdiction of the County Court specified in, and subject to, that Practice Direction.

Rule 2.4: Effect of rule

In the tenth paragraph (beginning "In various circumstances"), in the twenty-third line (beginning "judge; e.g PD 8"), replace "PD 8" with:

2.4.1 PD 49E

In the sixteenth paragraph (beginning "Claims made under"), replace "PD 8B" with:

PD 49F

[1] Amended by the Civil Procedure (Amendment) Rules 2014 (SI 2014/407), the Civil Procedure (Amendment No.3) Rules 2016 (SI 2016/788) and the Civil Procedure (Amendment No.2) Rules 2022 (SI 2022/783).

Replace r.2.4A with:

Jurisdiction of the County Court exercisable by a legal adviser[1]

2.4A [Omitted]. **2.4A**

County Court Legal Advisers

To the end of the paragraph, add:

Practice Direction 51R section 20 provides for the authorised legal advisers to exercise additional judicial functions in relation to certain claims proceeding under the Online Civil Money Claims Pilot. **2.4A.1**

In r.2.5, replace the words in brackets after (2) with:

Court staff[2]

(Rule 3.2 allows a court officer to refer a matter for judicial decision before taking any step.) **2.5**

Replace r.2.6(2) and (3) with:

Court documents to be sealed[3]

(2) The court may place the seal(GL) on the document by hand, by printing or electronically. **2.6**

(3) A document appearing to bear the court's seal(GL) shall be admissible in evidence without further proof.

Replace r.2.8(3) to (5) with:

Time[4]

(3) In this rule "clear days" means that in computing the number of days— **2.8**

(a) the day on which the period begins; and

(b) if the end of the period is defined by reference to an event, the day on which that event occurs,

are not included.

Examples—

(i) Notice of an application must be served at least 3 days before the hearing.

An application is listed to be heard on Friday 20 October.

The last date for service is Monday 16 October.

(ii) The court is to fix a date for a hearing.

The hearing must be at least 28 days after the date of notice.

If the court gives notice of the date of the hearing on 1 October, the earliest date for the hearing is 30 October.

(iii) Particulars of claim must be served within 14 days of service of the claim form.

The claim form is served on 2 October.

The last day for service of the particulars of claim is 16 October.

(4) Where the specified period—

(a) is 5 days or less; and

(b) includes—

(i) a Saturday or Sunday; or

(ii) a Bank Holiday, Christmas Day or Good Friday,

that day does not count.

---

[1] Introduced by the Civil Procedure (Amendment No.2) Rules 2018 (SI 2018/479) and omitted by the Civil Procedure (Amendment No.2) Rules 2022 (SI 2022/783).

[2] Amended by the Civil Procedure (Amendment No.2) Rules 2022 (SI 2022/783).

[3] Amended by the Civil Procedure (Amendment No.2) Rules 2022 (SI 2022/783).

[4] Amended by the Civil Procedure (Amendment No.2) Rules 2009 (SI 2009/3390) and the Civil Procedure (Amendment No.2) Rules 2022 (SI 2022/783).

Example—
Notice of an application must be served at least 3 days before the hearing.
An application is to be heard on Monday 20 October.
The last date for service is Tuesday 14 October.

(5) Subject to the provisions of Practice Direction 5C, when the period specified—

(a) by these Rules or a practice direction; or

(b) by any judgment or court order,

for doing any act at the court office ends on a day on which the office is closed, that act shall be in time under these rules if done on the next day on which the court office is open.

PRACTICE DIRECTION 2B—ALLOCATION OF CASES TO LEVELS OF JUDICIARY

Section III—The County Court

Trials and Assessments of Damages

In paragraph 11.1(1)(a), replace "Section B of Practice Direction 8A" with:

2BPD.11 Section B of Practice Direction 49E

Replace Practice Direction 2C–Starting Proceedings in the County Court with:

PRACTICE DIRECTION 2C—STARTING PROCEEDINGS IN THE COUNTY COURT

This Practice Direction supplements CPR Part 2

Scope

2CPD.1 **1.** This Practice Direction applies to Proceedings in the County Court.

Starting proceedings—general

2CPD.2 **2.** In the County Court, a claim or application may be started in any County Court hearing centre, unless any rule, practice direction or enactment provides otherwise.

Proceedings and claims which must be started in a particular County Court hearing centre or County Court Office

2CPD.3 **3.1**(1) If any rule, practice direction or enactment provides that a claim or application must be started at a particular County Court hearing centre, the claim must be started at that centre.

(2) If a claim or application is started at the wrong hearing centre, it may be sent to the correct hearing centre and issued there or returned to the claimant unissued.

3.2(1) The claim form in respect of a claim for an amount of money started under Part 7 of the Civil Procedure Rules must be sent to the County Court Money Claims Centre, unless it is a claim for which special procedures are provided in Rules or in practice directions.

(2) But a person who is permitted to start a Part 7 claim through the Production Centre pursuant to Practice Direction 7B must send the claim form to the Production Centre at the County Court Business Centre, St Katharine's House, 21-27 St Katharine's Street, Northampton, NN1 2LH. DX 702885 Northampton 7. Fax no. 0845 4085311.

(3) An application for a Part 7 claim to be issued through the Money

Claim Online scheme must be sent electronically. Any other document, application or request, other than one filed electronically, must be sent to the County Court Business Centre at St Katherine's House at the above address.

3.3(1) County Court proceedings under the Companies Acts or the Limited Liability Partnerships Act 2000 may be started either in a County Court hearing centre as permitted under any enactment or at the County Court at Central London.

3.4 A claim of a debtor or hirer for an order under section 129(1)(b) or 129(1)(ba) of the Consumer Credit Act 2006 (known as a "time order") must be made at the County Court hearing centre where the claimant debtor or hirer resides or carries on business.

3.5 The claim form in respect of an application under the Mental Health Act 1983 must be filed–

(a) in the County Court hearing centre serving the address where the patient lives; or

(b) in an application under section 30, in the court or County Court hearing centre that made the order under section 29 of the Act.

Claims and applications that may be started in any County Court hearing centre, but which will be sent or transferred to another County Court hearing centre following issue.

Claims and applications that may be started in any County Court hearing centre, but which will be sent or transferred to another County Court hearing centre following issue

4.1 Where a court officer considers that a claim or application could more appropriately be determined in a different County Court hearing centre, the claim or application may be sent to that centre. **2CPD.4**

4.2 A person wishing to find the most appropriate centre for the claim or application may consult the Court Finder tool at *https://courttribunalfinder.service.gov.uk/*, or enquire at their local County Court hearing centre.

Applications made in pre-existing claims and applications

5.1 An application made in the course of an existing claim or application must be made to the County Court hearing centre where the claim was started or to which it has been transferred. **2CPD.5**

5.2 If the parties have been notified of a fixed date for the trial, an application must be made to the court where the trial is to take place.

5.3 If the claim is started in the County Court Money Claims Centre, an application made after the claim has been started must be made to the County Court hearing centre to which the claim has been sent, or, if the claim has not been sent to a County Court hearing centre, to the County Court Money Claims Centre.

PRACTICE DIRECTION 2D—REFERENCES IN THE RULES TO ACTIONS DONE BY THE COURT

Delete Practice Direction 2D–References in the Rules to Actions Done by the Court.

PART 3

THE COURT'S CASE AND COSTS MANAGEMENT POWERS

Practice Directions

Replace the first two paragraphs with:

3.0.4 Section I of this Part is supplemented by PD 3A (Striking Out a Statement of Case) (see para.3APD.1), PD 3B (Sanctions for Non-Payment of Fees) (see para.3BPD.1) and PD 3C (Civil Restraint Orders) (see para.3CPD.1). Until 1 October 2022, Pt 3 was also supplemented by PD 3D (Mesothelioma Claims). However, as a result of the 149th CPR Update (July 2022), this practice direction has been omitted from Pt 3 and now supplements Pt 49 (Specialist Proceedings): see PD 49B (para.49BPD.1).

Section II is supplemented by PD 3E (Costs Management) (see para.3EPD.1). Practice Direction 3F (Costs Capping) supplements the rules in Section III. Following the removal of the former PD 3D to Pt 49 (see above) rr.3.12, 3.15, 3.15A and 3.20 now refer to the practice directions supplementing Sections II and III as PD 3D and PD 3E respectively. However, the titles of these practice directions have not yet been amended.

I. Case Management

Add new r.3.4(7):

Power to strike out a statement of case[1]

3.4 **(7) If a defendant applies to strike out all or part of the claim form or particulars of claim, that defendant need not file a defence before the hearing.**

Rule 3.4: Effect of rule

Replace the tenth paragraph (beginning "Applications under r.3.4") with:

3.4.1 Applications under r.3.4 should be made as soon as possible and before allocation if possible (PD supplementing r.3.4, para.5.1, see para.3APD.5). If the application is made by the defendant against the claimant's statement of case, the claimant cannot obtain a default judgment until that application is disposed of (r.12.3(3)(a)) and the defendant need not file a defence until the application is heard (r.3.4(7)).

Other forms of abuse

3.4.17 *In the list in the last paragraph, delete the last bullet point.*

Add new paragraph at end:

In *Municipio De Mariana v BHP Group Plc (UK) Ltd* [2022] EWCA Civ 951 the Court of Appeal reversed an order striking out a group action relating to a dam failure in Brazil which had been commenced on behalf of many thousands of individuals and organisations against companies alleged to be indirect polluters. Similar proceedings involving many of these claimants were already on foot in Brazil against companies alleged to be direct polluters and some high-value judgments had been obtained and some compensation had been paid out to some claimants. At first instance Turner J had ruled that the enormous overlap of issues raised in both sets of proceedings rendered the proceedings in England irredeemably unmanageable and were an abuse in that they amounted to a use of the court process for a purpose or in a way which is significantly different from the ordinary and proper use of the court process (see the quotation from *Attorney General v Barker* [2000] 1 F.L.R 759, DC set out in para.3.4.3). However, allowing the claimants' appeal, the Court of Appeal ruled that the mere fact that the litigation would place a significant burden on the courts could not be an independent basis for a finding of abuse ([184]). Even if the proceedings were

---

[1] Amended by the Civil Procedure (Amendment) Rules 2014 (SI 2014/407) and the Civil Procedure (Amendment No.2) Rules 2022 (SI 2022/783).

unmanageable due to complications arising out of parallel proceedings in Brazil, or because of other procedural complexities, that would not mean that the court process was being misused, whether vexatiously, oppressively or otherwise ([185]) unless, for example, the claimants had deliberately made the litigation unmanageable with vexatious consequences for the defendants ([187]). In any event the Court of Appeal also ruled against the learned judge's finding that the proceedings in this case were irredeemably unmanageable; no such conclusion could be reached safely at such an early stage of the proceedings ([188]).

Consequential orders after striking out

In the last paragraph, replace "and Times Travel (UK) Ltd v Pakistan International Airlines Corp [2019] EWHC 3732 (Ch)." with:

Times Travel (UK) Ltd v Pakistan International Airlines Corp [2019] EWHC 3732 (Ch) and *FCA v London Property Investments* [2022] EWHC 1041 (Ch). **3.4.22**

Consequences of non-payment

At the end of the first paragraph, replace "(Boodia v Yatsyna [2021] EWCA Civ 1705, citing r.3.10)." with:

(*Boodia v Yatsyna* [2021] EWCA Civ 1705; [2021] 4 W.L.R. 142, citing r.3.10). **3.7A1.3**

In the last paragraph, replace "Boodia v Yatsyna [2021] EWCA Civ 1705," with:

Boodia v Yatsyna [2021] EWCA Civ 1705; [2021] 4 W.L.R. 142,

Conduct complained of did not bring sanction into operation

Add new paragraph at end:

The statement by Andrew Baker J in *Cunico* (that the entry of a default judgment is not a sanction and therefore an application to set aside a default judgment can be determined without reference to the three-stage test in *Denton*) has been considered in two other High Court cases: *Ince Gordon Dadds LLP v Mellitah Oil & Gas BV* [2022] EWHC 997 (Ch) in which Hugh Sims QC (sitting as a Deputy Judge of the High Court) did not follow *Cunico* (see esp. [7] and [68]); and *C v D* [2022] 5 WLUK 99 (6 May 2022) in which Dexter Dias QC (sitting as a Deputy Judge of the High Court) followed and applied the view expressed by Andrew Baker J, both *Cunico* and *Ince Gordon Dadds* having been cited to him. **3.9.10**

Application to be supported by evidence

Replace paragraph with:

Rule 3.9(2) states that an application for relief against sanctions must be supported by evidence. Such applications are normally made under Pt 23 with a witness statement in support. However, the court has discretion to grant relief from sanctions where no formal application notice has been issued, but an application is made informally at a hearing; and also where no application is made, even informally, but the court acts of its own initiative (*Hadi v Park* [2022] EWCA Civ 581; [2022] 4 W.L.R. 61; see also *Boodia v Yatsyna* [2021] EWCA Civ 1705; [2021] 4 W.L.R. 142 noted in para.3.7A1.3; and see para.3.8.2). **3.9.24**

> "The discretion must of course be exercised consistently with the overriding objective. The court, therefore, should initially consider why there has been no formal application notice, or no application at all; whether the ability of another party to oppose the granting of relief (including, if appropriate, by the adducing of evidence in response) has been impaired by the absence of notice; and whether it has sufficient evidence to justify the granting of relief from sanctions (though the general rule in CPR r32.6 does not impose an inflexible requirement that the evidence be in the form of a witness statement). It follows, from the need for those initial considerations, that the discretion will be exercised sparingly" (*Park* at [49], which see further).

Rectifying procedural errors other than errors as to the service of claim forms

Add new paragraph at end:

In *Pitalia v NHS Commissioning Board* [2022] EWHC 1636 (QB), C purported to serve a sealed copy of the claim form on D after the time limit allowed for such service (see r.7.5) had expired. D promptly lodged an acknowledgment of service and, a few days later, applied for an order under r.3.4(2)(c) setting aside the claim form for non-compliance with r.7.5. C submitted that D's application was not an application made under CPR r.11(1) (an application for an order declaring that the court has no jurisdiction to try the claim) and therefore D had accepted the jurisdiction of the court and thereby waived the right to challenge the procedural validity of the claim (see CPR r.11(5)). D's application had been made within the time limit for an application under CPR r.11(1) and had sought an order which can be made on such an application (the setting aside of the claim form; r.11(6)) but did not refer to CPR r.11(1) and did not seek the primary order usually made on **3.10.3** such an application (a declaration that the court has no jurisdiction). HH Judge Pearce held that these errors were errors of form, not substance, which the court should rectify by the exercise of its power under r.3.10.

Replace r.3.11 with:

Orders restraining civil proceedings[1]

3.11 **3.11—(1) A "civil proceedings order" and an "all proceedings order" under section 42(1A) of the Senior Courts Act 1981 shall include provision for applying to begin, continue or make any application in any civil proceedings.**

(2) A practice direction may set out—

(a) the circumstances in which the court has the power to make a civil restraint order against a party to proceedings;

(b) the procedure where a party applies for a civil restraint order against another party; and

(c) the consequences of the court making a civil restraint order.

Civil restraint orders (CROs)

In the first paragraph, after the first sentence, add:

3.11.1 The Civil Procedure (Amendment No.2) Rules 2022 (SI 2022/783) amended the original heading to the rule to the heading shown above, inserted r.3.11(1) and numbered the subsequent text as r.3.11(2).

Threshold requirements for each type of CRO

Replace the penultimate paragraph with:

3.11.2 An application for a limited CRO may be made to any judge of the High Court or County Court in which the claim is proceeding, including Masters and district judges. An application for an ECRO or a GCRO can be made only to a Court of Appeal judge, a High Court judge or a designated civil judge (see PD 3C paras 2.7, 3.1 and 4.1), and, if necessary, the proceedings must be transferred accordingly (see PD 3C paras 3.11 and 4.11). A judge authorised to sit as a High Court judge under s.9 of the Senior Courts Act 1981 (Vol.2 para.9A-30) has jurisdiction to grant an ECRO (*Middlesborough Football and Athletic Co (1986) Ltd v Earth Energy Investments LLP* [2019] EWHC 226 (Ch)) and therefore, by parity of reasoning, jurisdiction to grant a GCRO. A contrary view was considered but not decided in *Ingeus UK Ltd v Wardle* [2021] EWHC 1268 (QB); in that case, the point was not fully argued and *Middlesborough* was not cited.

A CRO may also be made by a court acting on its own initiative. Model forms of order for each type of CRO are annexed to the practice direction (respectively, Forms **N19**, **N19A** and **N19B**).

II. Costs Management

Replace r.3.12(1) and (1A) with:

Application of this Section and the purpose of costs management[2]

3.12 **3.12—(1) This Section and Practice Direction 3D apply to all Part 7 multi-track cases, except—**

(a) where the claim is commenced on or after 22nd April 2014 and the amount of money claimed as stated on the claim form is £10 million or more; or

(b) where the claim is commenced on or after 22nd April 2014 and is for a monetary claim which is not quantified or not fully quantified or is for a non-monetary claim and in any such case the claim form contains a statement that the claim is valued at £10 million or more; or

(c) where in proceedings commenced on or after 6th April 2016 a

[1] Amended by the Civil Procedure (Amendment No.2) Rules 2022 (SI 2022/783).

[2] Introduced by the Civil Procedure (Amendment) Rules 2013 (SI 2013/262) and amended by the Civil Procedure (Amendment No.4) Rules 2014 (SI 2014/867), the Civil Procedure (Amendment) Rules 2016 (SI 2016/234), the Civil Procedure (Amendment No.3) Rules 2020 (SI 2020/747) and the Civil Procedure (Amendment No.2) Rules 2022 (SI 2022/783).

claim is made by or on behalf of a person under the age of 18 (a child) (and on a child reaching majority this exception will continue to apply unless the court otherwise orders); or

(d) where the proceedings are the subject of fixed costs or scale costs; or

(e) the court otherwise orders.

(1A) This Section and Practice Direction 3D will apply to any other proceedings (including applications) where the court so orders.

Add new paragraph 3.12.0:

Editorial note

This rule was amended by the Civil Procedure (Amendment No.2) Rules 2022 (SI 2022/783) to replace references to CPR PD 3E with references to CPR PD 3D. CPR PD Update 149 (July 2022) deleted the original PD 3D. It did not, however, renumber the subsequent PDs, e.g. it failed to renumber PD 3E as a new PD 3D. At the time of publication this error has not been rectified. References to PD 3D ought therefore be read as references to PD 3E pending correction of the Practice Direction numbering. **3.12.0**

Distinction between incurred costs and budgeted costs

To the end of the penultimate paragraph, add:

In a later case Coulson LJ described his decision in *CIP* as an extreme case in which the arithmetic was calculated following an all-day hearing at which very detailed arguments on the costs incurred had been presented (*PGI Group Ltd v Thomas* [2022] EWCA Civ 233 at [40]). **3.12.5**

In r.3.15, replace the words in brackets after (5) with:

Costs management orders[1]

(Precedent H is annexed to Practice Direction 3D.) **3.15**

Add new paragraph 3.15.0:

Editorial note

This rule was amended by the Civil Procedure (Amendment No.2) Rules 2022 (SI 2022/783) to replace the reference to CPR PD 3E with reference to CPR PD 3D. CPR PD Update 149 (July 2022) deleted the original PD 3D. It did not, however, renumber the subsequent PDs, e.g. it failed to renumber PD 3E as a new PD 3D. At the time of publication this error has not been rectified. Reference to PD 3D ought therefore be read as reference to PD 3E pending correction of the Practice Direction numbering. **3.15.0**

Replace r.3.15A(3) with:

Revision and variation of costs budgets on account of significant developments ("variation costs")[2]

(3) The revising party must— **3.15A**

(a) serve particulars of the variation proposed on every other party, using the form prescribed by Practice Direction 3D;

(b) confine the particulars to the additional costs occasioned by the significant development; and

(c) certify, in the form prescribed by Practice Direction 3D, that the additional costs are not included in any previous budgeted costs or variation.

---

[1] Introduced by the Civil Procedure (Amendment) Rules 2013 (SI 2013/262) and amended by the Civil Procedure (Amendment No.4) Rules 2014 (SI 2014/867), the Civil Procedure (Amendment) Rules 2017 (SI 2017/95), the Civil Procedure (Amendment No.3) Rules 2020 (SI 2020/747) and the Civil Procedure (Amendment No.2) Rules 2022 (SI 2022/783).

[2] Introduced by the Civil Procedure (Amendment No.3) Rules 2020 (SI 2020/747) and amended by the Civil Procedure (Amendment No.2) Rules 2022 (SI 2022/783).

Add new paragraph 3.15A.0:

Editorial note

3.15A.0 This rule was amended by the Civil Procedure (Amendment No.2) Rules 2022 (SI 2022/783) to replace references to CPR PD 3E with references to CPR PD 3D. CPR PD Update 149 (July 2022) deleted the original PD 3D. It did not, however, renumber the subsequent PDs, e.g. it failed to renumber PD 3E as a new PD 3D. At the time of publication this error has not been rectified. References to PD 3D ought therefore be read as references to PD 3E pending correction of the Practice Direction numbering.

III. Costs Capping

Section III: Effect of section

Replace the last three paragraphs (beginning "Rule 3.19(5)") with:

3.19.1 A costs capping order (CCO), if made, applies only to the costs subsequently incurred by the party subject to the cap (r.3.19(1)). Rule 3.19(5) states three pre-conditions which must each be satisfied before a CCO is made: (1) it is in the interests of justice to make a CCO; (2) there is a substantial risk that without a CCO costs will be disproportionately incurred; and (3) the court is not satisfied that the risk of disproportionate costs can be adequately controlled by costs budgeting or by detailed assessment. In *Thomas v PGI Group Ltd* [2021] EWHC 2776 (QB) Cavanagh J doubted whether pre-condition (3) could ever be met today given that the costs budgeting regime now provides a more sophisticated and nuanced way of setting a costs figure ([95]). Even if these pre-conditions are met, the court is not bound to make a CCO: it has a discretion whether or not to do so.

For case illustrations of the CCO regime see: *Tidal Energy Ltd v Bank of Scotland Plc* [2014] EWCA Civ 847 and *Black v Arriva North East Ltd* [2014] EWCA Civ 1115 (both being applications for a CCO heard by a single Lord Justice in respect of the costs of an appeal) and *PGI Group Ltd v Thomas* [2022] EWCA Civ 233 (an application to a single Lord Justice for permission to appeal). In *Tidal Energy* the applicant sought the disallowance of any costs incurred by the instruction of leading counsel for the hearing of the appeal; Arden LJ ruled that the applicant had failed to satisfy the requirement to show that such costs could not be adequately controlled by detailed assessment. The learned Lord Justice gave as an example of a case in which costs might not be adequately controlled by detailed assessment: a case in which there is evidence that the cost judge could not adequately distinguish between costs reasonably incurred and costs unreasonably incurred, for instance, in very extensive and detailed litigation on a technical matter.

In *Black v Arriva North East Ltd* [2014] EWCA Civ 1115 Christopher Clarke LJ ruled that CCOs should not be used to remedy problems of access to finance for litigation, or to counteract or minimise any substantial imbalance between the financial position of the parties. The application for a CCO in *Black* had been made in an appeal in a low value claim falling outside the QOCS regime (as to which, see rr.44.13 to 44.17); although the costs of insurance cover for the risk of losing the appeal vastly exceeded the value of the damages likely to be awarded and was not recoverable as costs, the application was dismissed.

In *PGI Group Ltd v Thomas* [2021] EWHC 2776 (QB) a claim concerning the alleged sexual abuse of 31 tea farm workers in Malawi, the defendant estimated the maximum financial value of the claim as not exceeding £310,000. Although the claimants did not accept that estimate they conceded that the financial compensation that they could expect to receive if successful would be very substantially lower than their own legal costs, but drew attention to the reputational and other benefits they would gain (the "vindication issues"). The claimants' draft costs budget showed total costs exceeding £3.1 million (£1.6 million already incurred plus estimated future costs of about £1.5 million). The defendant's draft costs budget showed total costs of about £2.25 million (£750,000 already incurred and estimated future costs of about £1.5 million). The defendant applied for a CCO limiting the future costs recoverable by the claimants to £150,000 (a sum based upon the likely costs had proceedings been taken in Malawi). Cavanagh J dismissed that application: bearing in mind the vindication issues and the claimants' right to bring this claim in this country, none of the pre-conditions required for a CCO had been satisfied: as to the interests of justice, the proposed CCO would probably stifle the claim or at the very least lead to gross inequality of arms between the parties; as to the risk that disproportionate costs would be incurred, these claims involved much more than money; as to the risk that costs could not be adequately controlled by costs budgeting or by detailed assessment, this was not a case in which a wealthy claimant was deliberately pursuing a low-value claim, at great expense, in order to harass the defendant, or to cause as much unnecessary cost to the defendant as possible. The fact that the defendant would not be able to recover its costs was irrelevant; a CCO should not be used to minimise the costs protection given to claimants falling within the QOCS regime.

At a subsequent hearing, costs budgets were set for the claimants' future costs at approximately £850,000 and the defendant's future costs at £1.75 million (see [2022] EWCA Civ 233 at [5]). The defendant applied to the Court of Appeal for permission to appeal the refusal to grant a CCO. Refusing permission, Coulson LJ ruled that there was no arguable error of principle in Cavanagh J's decision and, on the issue of proportionality, the learned judge had reached a conclusion which the vast majority of judges would also have reached. The learned judge had not ruled that a CCO could never be set at a sum lower than the amount of costs it was necessary to incur. Costs which are necessary may well be disproportionate. As to the prohibition on the citing decisions made in permission to appeal hearings see [2022] EWCA Civ 233 at [1] and see para.39MPD.2 at para.6.

Replace r.3.20(3)(a) with:

Application for a costs capping order[1]

(a) direct any party to the proceedings– 3.20

(i) to file a schedule of costs in the form set out in paragraph 3 of Practice Direction 3E–Costs capping;

(ii) to file written submissions on all or any part of the issues arising;

Add new paragraph 3.20.0:

Editorial note

This rule was amended by the Civil Procedure (Amendment No.2) Rules 2022 (SI 2022/783) to replace the reference to CPR PD 3F with reference to CPR PD 3E. CPR PD Update 149 (July 2022) deleted the original PD 3D, which necessitated the renumbering. It did not, however, renumber the subsequent PDs, e.g. it failed to renumber PD 3F as a new PD 3E. At the time of publication this error has not been rectified. Reference to PD 3E ought therefore be read as reference to PD 3F pending correction of the Practice Direction numbering. 3.20.0

Replace Practice Direction 3A–Striking Out a Statement of Case with:

PRACTICE DIRECTION 3A—STRIKING OUT A STATEMENT OF CASE

This Practice Direction supplements CPR Rule 3.4

Introductory

1.1 This practice direction sets out the procedure a party should follow if they wish to make an application for an order under rule 3.4(2)(a) (where a statement of case discloses no reasonable grounds for bringing or defending a claim); or under rule 3.4(2)(b) (where a statement of case is an abuse of the court's process or otherwise likely to obstruct the just disposal of the proceedings). 3APD.1

1.2 The following are examples of cases where the court may conclude that particulars of claim (whether contained in a claim form or filed separately) fall within rule 3.4(2)(a):

(1) those which set out no facts indicating what the claim is about, for example "Money owed £5,000",

(2) those which are incoherent and make no sense,

(3) those which contain a coherent set of facts but those facts, even if true, do not disclose any legally recognisable claim against the defendant.

1.3 A claim may fall within rule 3.4(2)(b) where it is vexatious, scurrilous or obviously ill-founded.

1.4 A defence may fall within rule 3.4(2)(a) where:

(1) it consists of a bare denial or otherwise sets out no coherent statement of facts, or

(2) the facts it sets out, while coherent, would not amount in law to a defence to the claim even if true.

1.5 A party may believe they can show without a trial that an opponent's case has no real prospect of success on the facts, or that the case is bound to succeed or fail, as the case may be, because of a point of law (including the interpretation of a document). In such a case the party concerned may make an application under rule 3.4 or apply for summary judgment under Part 24 (or both) as they think appropriate.

---

[1] Introduced by the Civil Procedure (Amendment) Rules 2013 (SI 2013/262) and amended by the Civil Procedure (Amendment No.2) Rules 2022 (SI 2022/783).

1.6 Where a rule, practice direction or order states "shall be struck out or dismissed" or "will be struck out or dismissed" this means that the striking out or dismissal will be automatic and that no further order of the court is required.

Claims which appear to fall within rule 3.4(2)(a) or (b)

3APD.2 **2.1** If a court officer is asked to issue a claim form which they believe may fall within rule 3.4(2)(a) or (b) they should issue it, but may then consult a judge (under rule 3.2) before returning the claim form to the claimant or taking any other step to serve the defendant. The judge may on their own initiative make an immediate order designed to ensure that the claim is disposed of or proceeds in a way that accords with the rules.

2.2 The judge may allow the claimant a hearing before deciding whether to make such an order.

2.3 Orders the judge may make include:

(1) an order that the claim be stayed until further order,

(2) an order that the claim form be retained by the court and not served until the stay is lifted,

(3) an order that no application by the claimant to lift the stay be heard unless they file such further documents (for example a witness statement or an amended claim form or particulars of claim) as may be specified in the order.

2.4 Where the judge makes any such order or, subsequently, an order lifting the stay they may give directions about the service on the defendant of the order and any other documents on the court file.

2.5 The fact that a judge allows a claim referred to them by a court officer to proceed does not prejudice the right of any party to apply for any order against the claimant.

Defences which appear to fall within rule 3.4(2)(a) or (b)

3APD.3 **3.1** A court officer may similarly consult a judge about any document filed which purports to be a defence and which he believes may fall within rule 3.4(2)(a) or (b).

3.2 If the judge decides that the document falls within rule 3.4(2)(a) or (b) they may on their own initiative make an order striking it out. Where they do so they may extend the time for the defendant to file a proper defence.

3.3 The judge may allow the defendant a hearing before deciding whether to make such an order.

3.4 Alternatively the judge may make an order under rule 18.1 requiring the defendant within a stated time to clarify his defence or to give additional information about it. The order may provide that the defence will be struck out if the defendant does not comply.

3.5 The fact that a judge does not strike out a defence on their own initiative does not prejudice the right of the claimant to apply for any order against the defendant.

General Provisions

3APD.4 **4.1** The court may exercise its powers under rule 3.4(2)(a) or (b) on application or on its own initiative at any time.

4.2 Where a judge at a hearing strikes out all or part of a party's statement of case he may enter such judgment for the other party as that party appears entitled to.

Applications for orders under rule 3.4(2)

3APD.5 **5.1** Attention is drawn to Part 23 (General Rules about Applications) and to Practice Direction 23A. The practice direction requires all applications to be made as soon as possible and before allocation if possible.

5.2 While many applications under rule 3.4(2) can be made without evidence in support, the applicant should consider whether facts need to be proved and, if so, whether evidence in support should be filed and served.

Applications for summary judgment

6.1 Applications for summary judgment may be made under Part 24. Attention is drawn to that Part and to Practice Direction 24. **3APD.6**

PRACTICE DIRECTION 3D—MESOTHELIOMA CLAIMS

Delete Practice Direction 3D–Mesothelioma Claims (now relocated under Part 49 as PD 49B).

PART 4

Replace Part 4–Forms with:

FORMS

Editorial introduction

With effect from 1 October 2022 Practice Direction 4 has been revoked by the 149th PD update. All forms can now be found online on the Civil Procedure Rules: Forms page (*https://www.gov.uk/guidance/civil-procedure-rules-forms* [Accessed 25 August 2022]). Prescribed forms cover the whole range of practice and procedure. Where they reflect what rules and practice directions state, they should faithfully reflect those provisions. The change was brought about partly to reduce the size of the Rules and Practice Directions and partly to ensure that the published forms did not lag behind changes to the provisions they are meant to support. **4.0.1**

4[1]—(1) Forms approved by the Civil Procedure Rule Committee, as published online by Her Majesty's Courts and Tribunals Service and available for downloading or printing, or incorporated as part of any online process specified by these Rules, must be used in the cases to which they apply. **4.1**

(2) Other forms not approved by the Civil Procedure Rule Committee, published online by Her Majesty's Courts and Tribunals Service and available for downloading, printing or other use, may be used as appropriate.

(3) A form may be varied by the court or a party if the variation is required by the circumstances of a particular case.

(4) A form must not be varied so as to leave out any information or guidance it contains.

(5) Where the court or a party produces a form with the words "Royal Arms", the form must include a replica of the Royal Arms at the head of the first page.

(6) The court must supply, on request, a paper copy of a form (with relevant explanatory material) to a person who cannot obtain access to the forms published online.

Forms approved by the Civil Procedure Rule Committee

The forms are no longer annexed in a practice direction but are to be found online on the Civil Procedure Rules: Forms page (*https://www.gov.uk/guidance/civil-procedure-rules-forms* [Accessed 25 August 2022]). Individual rules will continue to refer to forms which must be used for specific purposes and the court is now obliged to provide a paper copy of a form to any person who is unable to access the online form. **4.1.1**

Use of forms with or without variation

Subsections (3) and (4) of r.4 are self-explanatory. As stated above, many CPR provisions make express reference to specific forms, sometimes stating that a form must be used and at other times **4.1.2**

[1] Amended by the Civil Procedure (Amendment No.2) Rules 2022 (SI 2022/783).

stating that it may be used. The question whether a form must or may be used is separate from the question whether the form may or may not be varied. Subsection (4) is important as many forms contain quite elaborate guidance for those instigating the use of a certain form and for those to whom it is directed the inclusion of such guidance is mandatory.

Royal Arms

4.1.3 Where a specified online form includes a Royal Arms, the same format as is used on the online version need not be used; all that is necessary is that there is a complete Royal Arms.

Editorial note

4.1.4 The Civil Procedure Rule (CPR) Committee has approved changes to all approved forms requiring amendment following the death of HM Queen Elizabeth II and accession of HM King Charles III. Amended forms will be published in the usual way in due course. Amendments in particular include:

- all references to "Elizabeth The Second" be replaced with "Charles The Third";
- all references to "Queen" be replaced with "King";
- all references to "Queen's Bench Division" be replaced with "King's Bench Division";
- all references to "QB" be replaced by "KB"; as well as
- any other necessary and consequential amendments to reflect the change of monarch.

It is also noted that the use of the existing court seal continues until such time as another seal is prepared and authorised by His Majesty the King. Please refer to *https://www.justice.gov.uk/courts/procedure-rules/civil* [Accessed 26 September 2022] or *https://www.gov.uk/government/collections/civil-forms* [Accessed 26 September 2022] for updates.

PRACTICE DIRECTION 4—FORMS

Delete Practice Direction 4–Forms.

PART 5

Court Documents

Related sources

Replace the eighth bullet point (beginning "Practice Direction 7E") with:

5.0.3 • Practice Direction 7C (Money Claims Online), para.15.1

Rule 5.3: Effect of rule

Replace the first paragraph with:

5.3.1 For Production Centre, see now r.7.10 and note PD 5A (Court Documents) para.1 (see para.5APD.1 below). Practice Direction 7B (Production Centre) para.1.4(4) makes special provision for the signature by mechanical means of statements of truth where a party files with the Production Centre a batch of requests for the issue of claim forms (see para.7BPD.1).

Viewing the case record

Replace the first two sentences with:

5.4B.9 Other provisions, apart from r.5.4B, may provide for parties or their representatives to have access to court records. Particular examples are PD 7C (Money Claims Online) para.13.1 (see para.7CPD.13); PD 55B (Possession Claims Online) para.14.2 (see para.55BPD.14) which make provision for the viewing of case records on court-maintained websites in the proceedings to which they apply.

Rules 5.4B and 5.4C: Limits to application of rules

In the seventh paragraph (beginning "Unless the court"), at the end, replace "PD 8A." with:

5.4C.9 PD 49E

In the ninth paragraph (beginning "It is expressly"), replace "PD 8A":

PD 49E

In r.5.4D, replace the words in brackets after (3) with:

Supply of documents from court records—general[1]

(Rules 5.4, 5.4B and 5.4C are disapplied by rules 76.34, 79.30, 80.30, 82.18 and 88.33; and rule 5.4C is disapplied, and rule 5.4B applied subject to court order, by paragraph 23 of Practice Direction 49E.) **5.4D**

PRACTICE DIRECTION 5B—COMMUNICATION AND FILING OF DOCUMENTS BY E-MAIL

Scope and interpretation

Replace paragraph 1.2(b) with:

(b) only applies to claims started under Practice Direction 7C (Money Claim Online) if the claim has been sent to a County Court hearing centre. **5BPD.1**

PART 6

SERVICE OF DOCUMENTS

II. Service of the Claim Form in the Jurisdiction

In r.6.7, replace the words in brackets after (3) with:

Service on a solicitor within the United Kingdom[2]

(For Production Centre Claims see paragraph 2.3(7A) of Practice Direction 7B; for Money Claims Online see paragraph 4(6) of Practice Direction 7C; and for Possession Claims Online see paragraph 5.1(4) of Practice Direction 55B.) **6.7**

In r.6.8, replace the words in brackets after (b) with:

Service of the claim form where before service the defendant gives an address at which the defendant may be served[3]

(For Production Centre Claims see paragraph 2.3(7A) of Practice Direction 7B; for Money Claims Online see paragraph 4(6) of Practice Direction 7C; and for Possession Claims Online see paragraph 5.1(4) of Practice Direction 55B.) **6.8**

(For service out of the jurisdiction see rules 6.40 to 6.47.)

Rule 6.9: Effect of rule

Add new paragraph at end:

In *Hand Held Products, Inc v Zebra Technologies Europe Ltd* [2022] EWHC 640 (Ch), Lord Justice Nugee, sitting at first instance, gave consideration to the phrase "any place within the jurisdiction where the corporation carries on its activities" used in cl.7. He concluded that the primary purpose of this limb of cl.7 was to cater for the case of a non-trading corporation and that the phrase was the counterpart to "place of business" in limb 2 for trading companies. **6.9.1**

---

[1] Introduced by the Civil Procedure (Amendment) Rules 2006 (SI 2006/1689) and amended by the Civil Procedure (Amendment No.4) Rules 2015 (SI 2015/1569) and the Civil Procedure (Amendment No.2) Rules 2022 (SI 2022/783).

[2] Amended by the Civil Procedure (Amendment No.2) Rules 2009 (SI 2009/3390), the Civil Procedure (Amendment) Rules 2011 (SI 2011/88), the Civil Procedure (Amendment No.2) Rules 2011 (SI 2011/1979), the Civil Procedure Rules 1998 (Amendment) (EU Exit) Regulations 2019 (SI 2019/521) and the Civil Procedure (Amendment No.2) Rules 2022 (SI 2022/783).

[3] Introduced by the Civil Procedure (Amendment) Rules 2008 (SI 2008/2178) and amended by the Civil Procedure (Amendment) Rules 2011 (SI 2011/88), the Civil Procedure (Amendment No.2) Rules 2011 (SI 2011/1979), the Civil Procedure Rules 1998 (Amendment) (EU Exit) Regulations 2019 (SI 2019/521) and the Civil Procedure (Amendment No.2) Rules 2022 (SI 2022/783).

Retrospective operation—"steps already taken"

6.15.5 *Delete the fourth, fifth, sixth and seventh paragraphs (beginning "Many of the issues" and ending "photocopy claim form.").*

Replace the last five paragraphs (beginning "In Gee 7 Group") with:

In *R. (Good Law Project) v Secretary of State for Health and Social Care* [2022] EWCA Civ 355 the Court of Appeal upheld the decision of the judge not to retrospectively authorise service of a judicial review claim form in the following circumstances. The claimant filed a judicial review claim against the defendant, concerning the government's public procurement of personal protective equipment from Pharmaceuticals Direct Ltd. The claimant did not serve the sealed claim form at the defendant's designated electronic service address within the period prescribed by CPR r.54.7. It sent the unsealed claim form there on the day it was filed (but before issue) and sent the sealed claim form to the defendant's designated case officer within time. The claimant sent the sealed claim form to the designated address on the day after the deadline once the defendant communicated the error. The High Court (HC) refused to authorise service retrospectively or extend time. Good Law Project (GLP) did not challenge its refusal to remedy the error under CPR r.3.10, following *Ideal Shopping Direct Ltd v Mastercard Inc* [2022] EWCA Civ 14. Giving the lead judgment, Lady Justice Carr observed that what constitutes "good reason" is essentially a matter of factual evaluation and that over analysis and copious citation of authority will not assist. She identified the following relevant principles:

"i) The test is whether in all the circumstances, there is good reason to order that steps taken to bring the claim form to the attention of the defendant are good service;

ii) Service has a number of purposes, but the most important is to ensure that the contents of the document are brought to the attention of the person to be served. This is a critical factor. But the mere fact that the defendant knew of the existence and content of the claim form cannot, without more, constitute a good reason to make an order under CPR 6.15(2);

iii) The manner in which service is effected is also important. A 'bright line' is necessary to determine the precise point at which time runs for subsequent procedural steps. Service of the claim form within its period of validity may have significant implications for the operation of any relevant limitation period. It is important that there should be a finite limit on the extension of the limitation period;

iv) In the generality of cases, the main relevant factors are likely to be:

a) Whether the claimant has taken reasonable steps to effect service in accordance with the rules;

b) Whether the defendant or his solicitor was aware of the contents of the claim form at the time when it expired;

c) What, if any, prejudice the defendant would suffer by the retrospective validation of a non-compliant service of the claim form.

None of these factors are decisive in themselves, and the weight to be attached to them will vary with all the circumstances.

(See *Barton* at [9], [10] and [16].)"

Lady Justice Carr observed that the result might seem "harsh" but that CPR r.6.15 was not a generous provision for claimants where there are no valid obstacles to service of a claim form in time. Lord Justice Underhill, dissenting, agreed with the principles identified above but would have found a "good reason" on the facts of the case on the basis that the claimant's failure was highly technical and did not have any practical consequences.

III. Service of Documents other than the Claim Form in the United Kingdom

Replace r.6.23(1) to (3) with:

Address for service to be given after proceedings are started[1]

6.23 **6.23—(1) Unless the court orders otherwise, a party to proceedings must give an address at which that party may be served with documents relating to those proceedings. The address must include a full postcode.**

(Paragraph 2.4 of Practice Direction 16 contains provisions about postcodes.)

(2) Except where any other rule, practice direction or order makes different provision, a party's address for service must be—

[1] Introduced by the Civil Procedure (Amendment) Rules 2008 (SI 2008/2178) and amended by the Civil Procedure (Amendment No.2) Rules 2009 (SI 2009/3390), the Civil Procedure (Amendment) Rules 2011 (SI 2011/88), the Civil Procedure (Amendment No.2) Rules 2011 (SI 2011/1979), the Civil Procedure Rules 1998 (Amendment) (EU Exit) Regulations 2019 (SI 2019/521) and the Civil Procedure (Amendment No.2) Rules 2022 (SI 2022/783).

(a) the business address within the United Kingdom of a solicitor acting for the party to be served; or
(b) [Omitted]
(c) where there is no solicitor acting for the party—
(i) an address within the United Kingdom at which the party resides or carries on business;
(ii) [Omitted]

(For Production Centre Claims see paragraph 2.3(7) and (7A) of Practice Direction 7B; for Money Claims Online see paragraph 4(3A) and (6) of Practice Direction 7C, and for Possession Claims Online see paragraph 5.1(3A) and (4) of Practice Direction 55B.)

(3) Where none of sub-paragraphs (2)(a) or (c) applies, unless the court orders otherwise the party must give an address for service within the United Kingdom.

(Part 42 contains provisions about change of solicitor. Rule 42.1 provides that where a party gives the business address of a solicitor as that party's address for service, that solicitor will be considered to be acting for the party until the provisions of Part 42 are complied with.)

IV. Service of the Claim Form and other Documents out of the Jurisdiction

Brexit transitional and saving provisions

At the end of the third paragraph, replace "(see para.6.33.1 below)." with:

(see paras 6.33.1 and 6.33.9 below, and *Naftiran Intertrade Co (NICO) Sarl v GL Greenland Ltd (formerly Ferland Co Ltd)* [2022] EWHC 896 (Comm) referred to at para.6.33.9). **6.30.1**

Rule 6.30: Scope of section

In the last paragraph, replace "the court may give permission to serve an arbitration claim form" with:

an arbitration claim form may be served **6.30.2**

Summary of regimes for service of claim forms out of the jurisdiction

Replace list item (2)(b) with:

(b) under r.6.33(2B) where jurisdiction is conferred on the English court by the 2005 Hague Convention (in the conditions provided for by that Convention, summarised in para.6.33.3) or where there is otherwise a contractual choice of jurisdiction in favour of the English court (see para.6.33.4 below) or the claim is "in respect of" a contract containing such a choice (see para.6.33.4.1 below); **6.30.5**

Replace r.6.33(2B) with:

Service of the claim form where the permission of the court is not required—out of the United Kingdom[1]

(2B) The claimant may serve the claim form on the defendant outside of the United Kingdom where, for each claim made against the defendant to be served and included in the claim form— **6.33**

(a) the court has power to determine that claim under the 2005 Hague Convention and the defendant is a party to an exclusive choice of court agreement conferring jurisdiction on that court within the meaning of Article 3 of the 2005 Hague Convention;

---

[1] Introduced by the Civil Procedure (Amendment) Rules 2008 (SI 2008/2178) and amended by the Civil Jurisdiction and Judgments Regulations 2009 (SI 2009/3131), the Civil Procedure (Amendment No.7) Rules 2014 (SI 2014/2948), the Civil Jurisdiction and Judgments (Hague Convention on Choice of Court Agreements 2005) Regulations 2015 (SI 2015/1644), the Civil Procedure Rules 1998 (Amendment) (EU Exit) Regulations 2019 (SI 2019/521), the Civil Procedure (Amendment) Rules 2021 (SI 2021/117) and the Civil Procedure (Amendment No.2) Rules 2022 (SI 2022/783).

(b) a contract contains a term to the effect that the court shall have jurisdiction to determine that claim; or

(c) the claim is in respect of a contract falling within sub-paragraph (b).

Rule 6.33: Effect of rule

Replace the fourth paragraph (beginning "The rules in r.6.33") with:

6.33.1 The rules in r.6.33 provide for service out of the UK where the English court has power to determine claims in the following contexts:

(1) under provisions added to the Civil Jurisdiction and Judgments Act 1982 from IP completion day in relation to consumer and employment matters (r.6.33(2));
(2) under the 2005 Hague Convention (r.6.33(2B)(a));
(3) pursuant to a contract term conferring jurisdiction on the English court (r.6.33(2B)(b));
(4) where the claim is "in respect of" a contract which contains such a term (r.6.33(2B)(c));
(5) under other legislation (r.6.33(3)).

Replace the sixth paragraph (beginning "These transitional provisions") with:

These transitional provisions may have a relatively long tail of application, to the extent that new parties are joined after IP completion day to proceedings issued before IP completion day: see *Simon v Tache* [2022] EWHC 1674 (Comm) (HH Judge Cawson QC), in which the court confirmed that the Judgments Regulation continues to apply to "proceedings" commenced before IP completion day, including new claims added or defendants joined to such proceedings after IP completion day. See also *Benkel v East-West German Real Estate Holding* [2021] EWHC 188 (Ch); [2021] I.L.Pr. 16 (Morgan J), in which the parties were agreed on the point.

In the penultimate paragraph, replace the last sentence with:

It may be, therefore, that an application for permission to serve out is needed in those circumstances (see *Naftiran Intertrade Co (NICO) Sarl v GL Greenland Ltd (formerly Ferland Co Ltd)* [2022] EWHC 896 (Comm), referred to at para.6.33.9 below).

Add new paragraph at end:

Note that there is some uncertainty as to whether the Judgments Regulation might continue to apply to determine the court's jurisdiction in respect of proceedings which were commenced after IP completion day but which are related (pursuant to the lis pendens rules in arts 29, 30 or 31 of that Regulation) to proceedings commenced in an EU Member State court before IP completion day—though it is clear that, if the English court has jurisdiction in such a case, it will have to apply the lis pendens rules under the Judgments Regulation pursuant to the transitional provisions in the Withdrawal Agreement (art.67(1)(a)): see *Simon v Tache* [2022] EWHC 1674 (Comm) (HH Judge Cawson QC). Even if the jurisdiction rules in the Judgments Regulation do continue to apply to proceedings commenced after IP completion day in such circumstances, the transitional and saving provision for r.6.33(2) as it applied before IP completion day (as set out above) is relevant only to proceedings commenced before IP completion day.

Rule 6.33(2): Service of claim form out of the UK—permission not required where court has power to determine claim under sections 15A to 15E of 1982 Act

Add new paragraph at end:

6.33.2 CPR r.6.33(2) will not apply where a claim would have fallen within the arbitration exception to the Judgments Regulation, if that Regulation applied: see s.15A(2) of the 1982 Act and *Soleymani v Nifty Gateway LLC* [2022] EWHC 773 (Comm); [2022] Bus. L.R. 521.

Rule 6.33(2B)(a): "a claim which the court has power to determine under the 2005 Hague Convention"

Add new paragraph at end:

6.33.3 The UK's accession is subject to a declaration that it will not apply to insurance contracts save in specified cases, as set out at Sch.3FA to the 1982 Act, inserted by the Civil Jurisdiction and Judgments (2005 Hague Convention and 2007 Hague Convention) (Amendment) Regulations 2022 (SI 2022/77).

"a contract contains a term to the effect that the court shall have jurisdiction..."

In the first paragraph, replace "there is a jurisdiction clause in favour of the English court, and" with:

6.33.4 the claim falls within a jurisdiction clause in favour of the English court, but

At the end of the fourth paragraph (beginning "At the same time,"), replace "below)." with:

below)—but see para.6.33.4.1 below.

Replace the last paragraph with:

In contrast to r.6.33(2B)(a), r.6.33(2B)(b) does not state expressly that the defendant must be a party to the contractual jurisdiction clause. It is clear that the claim brought against the defendant must fall within the scope of the clause, but it is not clear whether this is sufficient to allow proceedings to be served on the defendant out of the jurisdiction under r.6.33(2B)(b) where the defendant is not party to the contractual jurisdiction clause and so has not agreed to be bound by it. The question of whether a claim against a non-party to a contract fell within the scope of such a clause has been considered in a number of cases relating to anti-suit injunctions sought on the basis of exclusive jurisdiction clause. For a case where it was held that the jurisdiction clause did extend to claims brought against an affiliate, albeit only the parent company party to the jurisdiction clause could enforce it, see *Dell Emerging Markets (EMEA) Ltd v IB Maroc.com SA* [2017] EWHC 2397 (Comm); [2017] 2 C.L.C. 417. For a case where the court decided the jurisdiction clause did not extend to claims against non-parties, see *Team Y&R Holdings Hong Kong Ltd v Ghossoub* [2017] EWHC 2401 (Comm). See also *Clearlake Shipping Pte Ltd v Xiang Da Marine Pte Ltd* [2019] EWHC 2284 (Comm); [2020] 1 All E.R. (Comm) 61 (Andrew Burrows QC) and *IBM United Kingdom Ltd v LzLabs GmbH* [2022] EWHC 2094 (TCC) (Waksman J). However, the fact that a party to a contract may be contractually obliged to refrain from suing a non-party anywhere but England, which obligation the counterparty may enforce by an anti-suit injunction, does not necessarily entail that the contracting party should be able to bring the non-party before the English court by serving proceedings on it out of the jurisdiction without the court's permission pursuant to r.6.33(2B)(b).

Add new paragraph 6.33.4.1:

A claim "in respect of" a contract falling within subparagraph (b)

As noted above, at the same time as r.6.33(2B)(b) was introduced, the former para.3.1(6)(d) of PD 6B (which provided for service out of the jurisdiction with the court's permission under r.6.36 if a claim was made in respect of a contract containing a jurisdiction clause in favour of the English court) was omitted as redundant. **6.33.4.1**

However, in the context of a review by the service subcommittee of the Civil Procedure Rule Committee in early 2022, it was noted that the differing terms of old gateway (6)(d) and CPR 6.33(2B) gave rise to a potential lacuna in cases where the claimant disputed that it (or the defendant) was party to the relevant contract, but contended that if the defendant wished to bring a claim under the contract, it must do so in England—in other words, where a claimant in such circumstances wished to obtain an anti-suit injunction to hold the defendant to the jurisdiction clause in the contract, and to serve the claim form seeking the injunction on the defendant out of the jurisdiction. The new r.6.33(2B)(c) was introduced to seek to fill this lacuna.

The rule requires that the claim against the defendant is in respect of a contract falling within r.6.33(2B)(b), i.e. a contract which contains a term to the effect that the court shall have jurisdiction to determine the claim—which (referring back to the introductory wording to r.6.33(2B)) would appear to mean the claimant's claim against the defendant. Arguably, therefore, it still requires the claimant to assert that the claimant and defendant are parties to the contract containing the jurisdiction clause (or otherwise bound by it—see para.6.33.4 above). However, this does not appear to be what was intended by the rule.

The new r.6.33(2B)(c) also appears to have the effect that a claim form can be served out of the jurisdiction without the court's permission not merely where the claim falls within a jurisdiction clause in the contract (or, as appears to be intended, would do so if the claimant and defendant were both parties to the contract) but also where the claim is "in respect of" a contract containing such a clause. This could be interpreted to apply more broadly than to claims seeking an anti-suit injunction, given the breadth of the phrase "in respect of": see *Alliance Bank JSC v Aquanta Corp* [2012] EWCA Civ 1588; [2013] 1 All E.R. (Comm) 819 and para.6HJ.14.

Brexit transitional and saving provisions

To the end of the third paragraph, add:

This "apparent oddity" was referred to in *Naftiran Intertrade Co (NICO) Sarl v GL Greenland Ltd (formerly Ferland Co Ltd)* [2022] EWHC 896 (Comm), citing the commentary in this paragraph. The deputy judge considered whether a claim which would, before IP completion day, have fallen within r.6.33(1) might now be served out of the jurisdiction without permission under r.6.33(3), which applies to claims "which the court has power to determine other than under the 2005 Hague Convention" notwithstanding that the defendant is not within the jurisdiction and the facts giving rise to the claim did not occur within the jurisdiction. That would not, however, explain why an express saving provision was included for r.6.33(2), where the court's jurisdiction is based on the Judgments Regulation. Accordingly, while noting that the position was "far from clear", the deputy judge proceeded on the basis that the claimants required permission to serve a claim form issued before IP completion day on a defendant in Switzerland where the court's jurisdiction over that defendant derived from the Lugano Convention. **6.33.9**

Rule 6.34: Effect of rule

To the end of the first paragraph, add:

A failure to file the Form **N510** does not however prevent the claim form being issued (*Chelfat v Hutchinson 3G UK Ltd* [2022] EWCA Civ 455). **6.34.1**

Rule 6.34(1)(a): "statement of the grounds"

In the penultimate paragraph, replace "Athena Capital Fund SICAV-FIS SCA v Secretariat of State for the Holy See [2021] EWHC 3166 (Comm)" with:

6.34.2 *Athena Capital Fund SICAV-FIS SCA v Secretariat of State for the Holy See* [2021] EWHC 3166 (Comm); [2022] 1 W.L.R. 1389

Rule 6.36: Effect of rule

To the end of the penultimate paragraph, add:

6.36.1 See para.6.39.1 and *Gorbachev v Guriev* [2022] EWHC 1907 (Comm) (Jacobs J) in relation to an application for non-party disclosure (cf. *Nix v Emerdata Ltd* [2022] EWHC 718 (Comm) (Cockerill J)).

Replace r.6.37(5)(b) with:

Application for permission to serve the claim form out of the jurisdiction[1]

6.37 **(b) it may give directions about the method of service.**

Rule 6.37: Effect of rule

Replace the second paragraph with:

6.37.1 In addition to the matters explained immediately below, note also the commentary to r.6.36 and the information contained in the Court Guides as follows: Chancery Guide Ch.4 paras 4.23 to 4.29 (Service out), and Ch.15 paras 15.62 and 15.63 (Applications for permission to serve out of the jurisdiction) (Vol.2 paras 1A-40 and 1A-179); Queen's Bench Guide (Service of proceedings—out of the jurisdiction) paras 5.4.1–5.4.3 and 5.4.7–5.4.10 (Vol.2 para.1B-27); Admiralty and Commercial Courts Guide para.B.8 (Service of the claim form out of the jurisdiction) and Appendix 9 paras 6 to 10 (Application for permission), and paras 13 to 14 (Practice under rule 6.36) (Vol.2 para.2A-168).

Rule 6.37(5): Directions as to service etc where court gives permission

Replace the penultimate paragraph with:

6.37.7 Where the claim form is to be served out of the jurisdiction it must be served in accordance with Section IV of Pt 6 within six months of the date of issue (r.7.5). The court may give directions about "the method of service" (para.(b) of r.6.37(5)). For general provisions as to methods of service of claim forms out of the jurisdiction, see r.6.40 below. For commentary on the question whether the court may permit service out of the jurisdiction by "an alternative method", and for relevance of r.6.37 to that issue, see para.6.40.4.

Claim form marked "not for service out of the jurisdiction"

6.37.10 *In the first paragraph, delete "See also, to similar effect, para.11.7 of the Chancery Guide (Vol.2 para.1A-72).".*

The merits of the claim ("the merits threshold")

After the penultimate paragraph, add new paragraph:

6.37.15 In *Okpabi v Royal Dutch Shell Plc* [2021] UKSC 3; [2021] 1 W.L.R. 1294, Lord Hamblen noted (at [22]) that the court will generally analyse whether there is a reasonable prospect of success on the assumption that the facts alleged in the particulars of claim are true. Unless those allegations are:

> "demonstrably untrue or unsupportable, it is generally not appropriate for a defendant to dispute the facts alleged through evidence of its own."

As Lord Hamblen put it, "Doing so may well just show that there is a triable issue."

English court the appropriate forum (forum conveniens)

Treatment of "a legitimate personal or juridical advantage"

At the end of the last paragraph, after "(Field J) at [69]", add:

6.37.17 ; and *Municipio De Mariana v BHP Group (UK) Ltd* [2022] EWCA Civ 951 at [355]

[1] Introduced by the Civil Procedure (Amendment) Rules 2008 (SI 2008/2178) and amended by the Civil Procedure (Amendment No.2) Rules 2009 (SI 2009/3390) and the Civil Procedure (Amendment No.2) Rules 2022 (SI 2022/783).

Add new paragraph at end:

In *Klifa v Slater* [2022] EWHC 427 (QB); [2022] I.L.Pr. 15 (in the context of a "service in case"), where the relevant tort took place in France before completion of the UK's withdrawal from the EU on 31 December 2021 (IP completion day) but proceedings were commenced in England after that date, the court took into account that: (i) enforcement would have to take place in England and to enforce a French judgment would require a registration process (under the Foreign Judgments (Reciprocal Enforcement) Act 1933 and Pt 74) and therefore involve cost, delay and potential opportunity for challenge; and (ii) the claimant had carried out substantial work, and incurred substantial expense, in complying with the pre-action protocol process before IP completion day (when the claimant would have been entitled to bring proceedings in England as of right under the Judgments Regulation), which would be wasted if a stay was granted.

The Cambridgeshire factor

Add new paragraph at end:

In *Samsung Electronics Co Ltd v LG Display Co Ltd* [2022] EWCA Civ 423, the Court of Appeal accepted that the Cambridgeshire factor was capable of being a powerful factor in favour of English jurisdiction, but in this case its application was not supported by evidence and it was only addressed in submissions at the appeal stage. While the evidence did not need to descend to minute detail, it had to be **6.37.18**

> "sufficient to lay a proper factual foundation for matters to which the judge is invited to give weight as supporting the exercise of jurisdiction by the English court."

Relevance of related claims

Add new paragraphs at end:

In *Abu Dhabi Commercial Bank PJSC v Shetty* [2022] EWHC 529 (Comm) at [162], the fact that one defendant had acceded to the English court's jurisdiction, so that a finding that Abu Dhabi was the most suitable jurisdiction would mean a trial in two different jurisdictions concerning the same facts, was described as "a relatively weak point". The risk of duplicated costs and inconsistent judgments arose from the claimant choosing to commence the proceedings in England and (following *Vedanta*) was not a trump card. **6.37.20**

In relation to claims for contribution under the Civil Liability (Contribution) Act 1978, in *Samsung Electronics Co Ltd v LG Display Co Ltd* [2022] EWCA Civ 423 the Court of Appeal endorsed the judge's view that, if the underlying claim is proceeding in England, that will be a powerful and sometimes overwhelming factor in favour of the court hearing the contribution claim. But if the underlying claim has been settled before the contribution claim is commenced, the only question will be whether the English court is the appropriate forum for the trial of the contribution claim. Factors going only to whether it would be the appropriate forum for the trial of the underlying claim (which will not take place) are at most of marginal relevance.

Forum non conveniens—court's power to stay proceedings on case management grounds

Add new paragraph at end:

In *Athena Capital Fund SICAV-FIS SCA v Secretariat of State for the Holy See* [2022] EWCA Civ 1051 the Court of Appeal overturned a decision granting a stay on case management grounds in light of criminal proceedings in a foreign jurisdiction, where there was an exclusive jurisdiction clause in favour of the English court. The court emphasised (at [52]) that the test is whether a stay is in the interests of justice, not whether there are "rare and compelling circumstances", despite that phrase having sometimes been treated as if it were in itself the applicable test. There was, however, no reason to doubt that it was only in rare and compelling cases that it would be in the interests of justice to grant a stay on case management grounds in order to await the outcome of proceedings abroad (see at [59]). **6.37.23**

Forum non conveniens—court's power to stay proceedings on abuse of process grounds

Replace the penultimate paragraph with:

In *Municipio de Mariana v BHP Group Plc* [2020] EWHC 2930 (TCC) (Turner J), the court struck out the claims of over 200,000 claimants against two defendants (domiciled in England and Australia respectively) arising out of the collapse of the Fundão Dam in Brazil in 2015 as an abuse of process in light of concurrent proceedings and compensation schemes in Brazil. However, that decision was overturned: [2022] EWCA Civ 951. The Court of Appeal held that the fact that proceedings may place a very heavy burden on the court's resources cannot itself constitute a ground of abuse, and further the judge was wrong to rely on forum non conveniens factors as part of his analysis on the question of abuse of process. **6.37.24**

Defamation claims

At the end of the paragraph, replace "Soriano v Forensic News LLC [2021] EWCA Civ 1952." with:

Soriano v Forensic News LLC [2021] EWCA Civ 1952; [2022] E.M.L.R. 12. **6.37.26**

Replace r.6.38 with:

Service of documents other than the claim form—permission[1]

6.38 **6.38 Any application notice issued or order made in any proceedings, or other document which is required to be served in the proceedings, may be served on a defendant out of the jurisdiction without permission where–**

(a) the claim form has been served on the defendant out of the jurisdiction with permission; or

(b) permission is or was not required to serve the claim form (whether within or out of the jurisdiction).

Rule 6.38: Effect of rule

Replace paragraph with:

6.38.1 Until 1 October 2022, the version of r.6.38 then in force (and its predecessor at paras (2) and (3) of former r.6.30, insofar as those provisions applied to documents other than claim forms) provided that, where the court's permission was required to serve the claim form out of the jurisdiction, the claimant had to obtain permission to serve any other document in the proceedings out of the jurisdiction (subject to limited exceptions set out in the rule).

The rule was amended with effect from 1 October 2022 to remove the need for permission where either the claim form has been served out with permission or permission was not required to serve the claim form (including because it was served within the jurisdiction).

The rule applies to any application notice issued or order made in any proceedings, or other document which is required to be served in the proceedings. Implicitly, this means any document other than a claim form. Under Pt 6, a claim includes an application made before action (as well as a claim made "to commence proceedings"), and claim form is "to be construed accordingly" (see r.6.2(c)). Consequently, by definition a claim form includes an application notice issued before action and such an application notice is not a document falling within r.6.38.

The rule concerns service of documents on an existing party; it does not provide a basis for service out of the jurisdiction on a non-party: see *Gorbachev v Guriev* [2022] EWHC 1907 (Comm) (Jacobs J); and see *Masri v Consolidated Contractors International Co SAL (No.4)* [2009] UKHL 43; [2009] 3 W.L.R. 385, HL (in relation to the previous r.6.30(2)). Rule 6.39 contains provisions that apply to service of an application notice out of the jurisdiction on a non-party to the proceedings.

Delete paragraphs 6.38.2, 6.38.3 and 6.38.4 (""any other document"", "Particulars of claim" and "Address for service in Scotland or Northern Ireland").

Rule 6.39: Effect of rule

Replace the penultimate paragraph with:

6.39.1 The rule does not provide that rr.6.32, 6.33, 6.36 and 6.37(1)-(4) do not apply; an application notice can only be served on a non-party out of the jurisdiction if the requirements of those provisions are satisfied. In *Gorbachev v Guriev* [2022] EWHC 1907 (Comm), Jacobs J held that this rule applied to an application for non-party disclosure, and that permission could be granted under gateway (20) relating to "Claims under various enactments" (see para.6HJ.35). Cf. *Nix v Emerdata Ltd* [2022] EWHC 718 (Comm) (Cockerill J).

Service out of the jurisdiction by an alternative method

After the sixth paragraph (beginning "In Abela v Baadarani"), add new paragraph:

6.40.4 In contrast, *Cesfin Ventures LLC v Al Qubaisi* [2021] EWHC 3311 (Ch) and *Caterpillar Financial Services (Dubai) Ltd v National Gulf Construction LLC* [2022] EWHC 914 (Comm) suggest that where an international service treaty (such as the Treaty on Judicial Assistance in Civil and Commercial Matters, entered into between the UK and the UAE in 2006) does not preclude other methods of service, exceptional circumstances may not be required before an order for alternative service could be made; "good reason" may be sufficient.

After the penultimate paragraph, add new paragraph:

In *Nokia Technologies Oy v OnePlus Technology (Shenzhen) Co Ltd* [2022] EWHC 293 (Pat); [2022] 1 All E.R. (Comm) 1384, Marcus Smith J granted an application to serve proceedings by alternative means in China where the claimant's efforts to serve under the Hague Convention had proved unsuccessful, through no fault of its own. He noted that, where there is an applicable international

[1] Introduced by the Civil Procedure (Amendment) Rules 2008 (SI 2008/2178) and amended by the Civil Procedure (Amendment No.2) Rules 2022 (SI 2022/783).

service treaty or convention, there must be special or exceptional circumstances to justify a departure from the standard rules—not just a "good reason" to order alternative service. This second stage involves balancing the importance of the due administration of justice against considerations of comity. In the instant case the effect on comity of granting the application was slight or non-existent, but the risk of prejudice to the administration of justice was considerable including because the dates fixed for trial would be disrupted unless an order was made.

Add new paragraph at end:

In *Naftiran Intertrade Co (NICO) Sarl v GL Greenland Ltd (formerly Ferland Co Ltd)* [2022] EWHC 896 (Comm), in circumstances where the court's permission was not required to serve the claim form out of the jurisdiction on D1 but was required in respect of D2, the deputy judge considered that it would not be appropriate to exercise the court's discretion to authorise service by alternative means (or extend time for service of the claim form) on D1 unless satisfied that there was a serious issue to be tried against D1. She said it would not be "principled, just or fair" to decline permission in respect of D2 on the basis that there was no serious issue that (on the facts of that case) a trust had been created, while at the same time authorising alternative service of, or an extension of time to serve, a claim on D1 for breach of that trust.

Dispensing with service

Replace "Olafsson v Gissurarson (No.2) [2008] EWCA Civ 152; [2008] 1 W.L.R. 2016 and Lonestar Communications Corp LLC v Kaye [2019] EWHC 3008 (Comm) (Teare J)," with:

Olafsson v Gissurarson (No.2) [2008] EWCA Civ 152; [2008] 1 W.L.R. 2016; *Lonestar Communications Corp LLC v Kaye* [2019] EWHC 3008 (Comm) (Teare J); and *Daiwa Capital Markets Europe Ltd v Al Sanea* [2021] EWHC 2937 (Comm) (Bryan J), **6.40.5**

Civil procedure treaties

To the end of the paragraph, add:

The UK Government has published a list of treaties on the taking of evidence and service of documents abroad, which can be found at: **6.40.7**
https://www.gov.uk/government/publications/bilateral-treaties-on-civil-procedures [Accessed 16 May 2022].

Rule 6.44: Effect of rule

After the third paragraph, add new paragraph:

Section 12(3) provides that a state which "appears in proceedings" cannot later object that s.12(1) has not been complied with. In *AELF MSN 242 LLC v De Surinaamse Luchtvaart Maatschappij NV DBA Surinam Airways* [2021] EWHC 3482 (Comm); [2022] 1 W.L.R. 2181 it was held that a defendant had submitted to the jurisdiction by applying for an extension of time to serve its defence, and that this represented an "appearance" under s.12(3). The defendant's challenge to jurisdiction by disputing the validity of service of the claim form under s.12(1) was therefore rejected. **6.44.1**

PRACTICE DIRECTION 6B—SERVICE OUT OF THE JURISDICTION

Replace paragraph 3.1 with:

Service out of the jurisdiction where permission is required

3.1 The claimant may serve a claim form out of the jurisdiction with the permission of the court under rule 6.36 where— **6BPD.3**

General grounds

(1) A claim is made for a remedy against a person domiciled within the jurisdiction within the meaning of sections 41 and 42 of the Civil Jurisdiction and Judgments Act 1982.

(1A) A claim is made against a person in respect of a dispute arising out of the operations of a branch, agency or other establishment of that person within the jurisdiction, but only if proceedings cannot be served on the branch, agency or establishment.

(2) A claim is made for an injunction ((GL)) ordering the defendant to do or refrain from doing an act within the jurisdiction.

(3) A claim is made against a person ("the defendant") on whom the claim form has been or will be served (otherwise than in reliance on this paragraph) and—

(a) there is between the claimant and the defendant a real issue which it is reasonable for the court to try; and
(b) the claimant wishes to serve the claim form on another person who is a necessary or proper party to that claim.

(4) A claim is an additional claim under Part 20 and the person to be served is a necessary or proper party to the claim or additional claim.
(4A) A claim is made against the defendant which–
(a) was served on the defendant within the jurisdiction without the need for the defendant's agreement to accept such service;
(b) falls within CPR rule 6.33; or
(c) falls within one or more of paragraphs (1A), (2), (6) to (16A) or (19) to (22A),

and a further claim is made against the same defendant which arises out of the same or closely connected facts.

Claims for interim remedies

(5) A claim is made for an interim remedy under section 25(1) of the Civil Jurisdiction and Judgments Act 1982.

Claims in relation to contracts

(6) A claim is made in respect of a contract where the contract–
(a) was (i) made within the jurisdiction or (ii) concluded by the acceptance of an offer, which offer was received within the jurisdiction;
(b) was made by or through an agent trading or residing within the jurisdiction; or
(c) is governed by the law of England and Wales.
(d) [Omitted]

(7) A claim is made in respect of a breach of contract committed, or likely to be committed within the jurisdiction.
(8) A claim is made for a declaration that no contract exists where, if the contract was found to exist, it would comply with the conditions set out in paragraph (6).
(8A) A claim for unlawfully causing or assisting in:
(a) a breach of a contract where the contract falls within one of paragraphs (6)(a) to (6)(c) above or within Rule 6.33(2B); or
(b) a breach of contract falling within paragraph (7) above.

Claims in tort

(9) A claim is made in tort where–
(a) damage was sustained, or will be sustained, within the jurisdiction;
(b) damage which has been or will be sustained results from an act committed, or likely to be committed, within the jurisdiction; or
(c) the claim is governed by the law of England and Wales.

Enforcement

(10) A claim is made to enforce any judgment or arbitral award.

Claims about property within the jurisdiction

(11) The subject matter of the claim relates wholly or principally to property within the jurisdiction, provided that nothing under this paragraph shall render justiciable the title to or the right to possession of immovable property outside England and Wales.

Claims about trusts etc.

(12) A claim is made in respect of a trust which is created by the operation

of a statute, or by a written instrument, or created orally and evidenced in writing, and which is governed by the law of England and Wales.

(12A) A claim is made in respect of a trust which is created by the operation of a statute, or by a written instrument, or created orally and evidenced in writing, and which provides that jurisdiction in respect of such a claim shall be conferred upon the courts of England and Wales.

(12B) A claim is made in respect of a trust which is created by the operation of a statute, or by a written instrument, or created orally and evidenced in writing, and which expressly or impliedly designates England and Wales as the principal place of administration.

(12C) A claim is made in respect of a trust created in the jurisdiction.

(12D) A claim is made for a declaration that no trust has arisen where, if the trust was found to have arisen, it would comply with one of the conditions set out in paragraph (12), (12A), (12B) or (12C).

(12E) A claim is made for a breach of trust where the breach is committed or likely to be within the jurisdiction.

(13) A claim is made for any remedy which might be obtained in proceedings for the administration of the estate of a person who died domiciled within the jurisdiction or whose estate includes assets within the jurisdiction.

(14) A probate claim or a claim for the rectification of a will.

(15) A claim is made against the defendant as constructive trustee, or as trustee of a resulting trust, where the claim—

(a) arises out of acts committed or events occurring within the jurisdiction;

(b) relates to assets within the jurisdiction; or

(c) is governed by the law of England and Wales.

(15A) A claim for unlawfully causing or assisting in—

(a) a breach of a trust where the trust falls within one of paragraphs (12) to (12C) above;

(b) a breach of trust falling within paragraph (12E) above; or

(c) a breach of a constructive or resulting trust where the trustee's liability would fall within paragraph (15) above.

(15B) A claim is made for breach of fiduciary duty, where—

(a) the breach is committed, or likely to be committed, within the jurisdiction;

(b) the fiduciary duty arose in the jurisdiction; or

(c) the fiduciary duty is governed by the law of England and Wales.

(15C) A claim for unlawfully causing or assisting in—

(a) a breach of fiduciary duty where the fiduciary duty falls within one of paragraph (15B)(b) or (c) above;

(b) a breach of fiduciary duty falling within paragraph (15A)(a) above.

(15D) A claim is made for a declaration that no fiduciary duty has arisen where, if the fiduciary duty was found to have arisen, it would comply with one of the conditions set out in paragraph (15B)(b) or (c).

(16) A claim is made for restitution where—

(a) the defendant's alleged liability arises out of acts committed within the jurisdiction; or

(b) the enrichment is obtained within the jurisdiction; or

(c) the claim is governed by the law of England and Wales.

Declarations of non-liability

(16A) A claim is made for a declaration that the claimant is not liable where, if a claim were brought against the claimant seeking to establish that liability, that claim would fall within another paragraph of this Practice Direction (excluding paragraphs (1) to (5), (8), (12D), (15D), (17), (22) and (24) to (25)).

Claims by HM Revenue and Customs

(17) A claim is made by the Commissioners for H.M. Revenue and Customs relating to duties or taxes against a defendant not domiciled in Scotland or Northern Ireland within the meaning of sections 41 and 42 of the Civil Jurisdiction and Judgments Act 1982.

Claim for costs order in favour of or against third parties

(18) A claim is made by a party to proceedings for an order that the court exercise its power under section 51 of the Senior Courts Act 1981 to make a costs order in favour of or against a person who is not a party to those proceedings.

(Rule 46.2 sets out the procedure where the court is considering whether to exercise its discretion to make a costs order in favour of or against a non-party.)

Admiralty claims

(19) A claim is–
- (a) in the nature of salvage and any part of the services took place within the jurisdiction; or
- (b) to enforce a claim under section 153, 154, 175 or 176A of the Merchant Shipping Act 1995.

Claims under various enactments

(20) A claim is made–
- (a) under an enactment which allows proceedings to be brought and those proceedings are not covered by any of the other grounds referred to in this paragraph.

Claims for breach of confidence or misuse of private information

(21) A claim is made for breach of confidence or misuse of private information where–
- (a) detriment was suffered, or will be suffered, within the jurisdiction; or
- (b) detriment which has been, or will be, suffered results from an act committed, or likely to be committed, within the jurisdiction;
- (c) the obligation of confidence or right to privacy arose in the jurisdiction; or
- (d) the obligation of confidence or right of privacy is governed by the law of England and Wales.

(22) A claim is made for a declaration that no duty of confidentiality or right to privacy has arisen where, if the duty or right was found to have arisen, it would comply with one of the conditions set out in paragraph (21)(c) or (d).

(23) A claim is made for unlawfully causing or assisting in–
- (a) a breach of confidence or misuse of private information where the obligation or right in question falls within paragraph (21)(c) or (d) above; or
- (b) a breach of confidence or misuse of private information falling within paragraph (21)(a) or (b) above.

Contempt applications

(24) A contempt application is made, whether or not, apart from this

paragraph, a claim form or application notice containing such an application can be served out of the jurisdiction.

Information orders against non-parties

(25) A claim or application is made for disclosure in order to obtain information—

(a) regarding:

(i) the true identity of a defendant or a potential defendant; and/or

(ii) what has become of the property of a claimant or applicant; and

(b) the claim or application is made for the purpose of proceedings already commenced or which, subject to the content of the information received, are intended to be commenced either by service in England and Wales or pursuant to CPR rule 6.32, 6.33 or 6.36.

NOTES ON HEADS OF JURISDICTION IN PARAGRAPH 3.1 OF PRACTICE DIRECTION 6B

Introduction

At the end of the third paragraph, replace "amendments." with:

amendments, including amendments made by CPR PD Update 149 (July 2022) which took effect from 1 October 2022 following a review by the service subcommittee of the Civil Procedure Rule Committee, with input from the Lord Chancellor's Advisory Committee on Private International Law. **6HJ.1**

Replace the last paragraph with:

(Note that under CPR r.62.5, there are separate grounds on which an arbitration claim form may be served out of the jurisdiction, such as where the claimant seeks to challenge an arbitration award made within the jurisdiction, or seeks some other remedy affecting an arbitration, an arbitration agreement or an arbitration award: see Vol.2 para.2E-12.)

Change title of section: **6HJ.2**

Paragraph 3.1(1) to (4A): General grounds

After "Practice Direction 6B,", replace "five" with:

six

Paragraph 3.1(1): Claim for remedy against person domiciled within the jurisdiction

At the end of the first paragraph, replace "jurisdiction"." with:

jurisdiction within the meaning of sections 41 and 42 of the Civil Jurisdiction and Judgments Act 1982". **6HJ.3**

Replace the last two paragraphs with:

In the mid-nineteenth century that hardship was remedied generally by a rule to the effect that service of a writ out of the jurisdiction was permissible with the leave of the court if, in the action begun by the writ, relief was sought "against a person domiciled or ordinarily resident within the jurisdiction" (see RSC 1965 Ord.11 r.1(1)(c)). That rule was among the rules modified (by SI 1983/1181) when the UK acceded to the European Community and the Civil Jurisdiction and Judgments Act 1982 came into force (1 January 1987). Thereafter the rule read that service of a claim form may be permitted out of the jurisdiction where a claim is made for a remedy against a person "domiciled within the jurisdiction" (but without the reference that is now found at para.3.1(1) of Practice Direction 6B to the statutory definition of domicile under the 1982 Act).

Until 31 December 2020 (the final day of the implementation period for the UK's withdrawal from the EU, as provided for in the European Union (Withdrawal Agreement) Act 2020), r.6.31(i) incorporated statutory definitions of "domicile" in the 1982 Act and the Judgments Regulation, in relation to a Convention territory or Member State, respectively. Rule 6.31(i) was however omitted by reg.4(15)(d) of the Civil Procedure Rules 1998 (Amendment) (EU Exit) Regulations 2019 (SI 2019/521). In any event, it was not clear whether the definition of "domicile" previously set out at r.6.31(i) applied to the common law head of jurisdiction based on domicile, or whether it only applied to cases falling within the Brussels/Lugano regime.

The uncertainty as to the test of domicile for the purposes of para.3.1(1) was resolved by CPR PD Update 149 (July 2022) with effect from 1 October 2022 by the addition of a reference to the statutory definition under the 1982 Act, following a review by the service subcommittee of the Rule Committee (see para.6HJ.1 above).

Add new paragraph 6HJ.3.1:

Paragraph 3.1(1A): Disputes arising out of the operations of a branch, agency or other establishment within the jurisdiction

6HJ.3.1 Paragraph 3.1(1A) of Practice Direction 6B states that a claimant may serve a claim form out of the jurisdiction with the permission of the court if the claim is made in respect of a dispute arising out of the operations of a branch, agency or other establishment of that person within the jurisdiction, but only if proceedings cannot be served on the branch, agency or establishment.

This head of jurisdiction was added to para.3.1 by CPR PD Update 149 (July 2022) and came into effect on 1 October 2022, following a review by the service subcommittee of the Rule Committee (see para.6HJ.1 above). As explained in the subcommittee's paper setting out their proposed amendments, this proposal was derived from art.7(5) of the Judgments Regulation, but (unlike art.7(5)) it makes it clear that the gateway applies when the branch, agency or establishment has ceased to operate by the time proceedings are commenced. The paper notes that, as pointed out to the subcommittee by members of the Lord Chancellor's Advisory Committee on Private International Law, where the branch, agency or other establishment is still in operation, it will not be necessary to serve proceedings out of the jurisdiction at all (as service at that place will be possible under r.6.9). There may therefore be relatively few claims which fall within this gateway and no other.

The paper also notes that the questions of what amounts to a "branch, agency or other establishment", and what is required for a claim to "arise out of the operations" of such an entity, have been considered a number of times by the CJEU (see for example *Mahamdia v Algeria* (C-154/11) EU:C:2012:491; [2014] All E.R. (EC) 96). The subcommittee therefore considered it best to keep the drafting of the gateway as close as possible to art.7(5), so as to help provide certainty and benefit from greater international recognition.

Paragraph 3.1(3): Another person a necessary or proper party to a claim

Paragraph 3.1(3)(a): "a real issue which it is reasonable for the court to try"

Replace the penultimate paragraph with:

6HJ.7 The word "try" need not involve a trial in the formal sense, or even a contested hearing for final relief or summary judgment. It does, however, denote some form of judicial determination of the claim and grant of relief as distinct from the administrative process of entering default judgment. It might be reasonable for the court to try an anchor claim despite the anchor defendant's non-participation, so long as there is some utility in doing so: see *HC Trading Malta Ltd v K. I. (International) Ltd* [2022] EWHC 1387 (Comm). See also *Satfinance Investment Ltd v Athena Art Finance Corp* [2020] EWHC 3527 (Ch) (Morgan J) at [92], in which it was held that the existence of a claim for a declaration meant there was a real issue which it was reasonable for the court to try, even though the first two defendants (the anchor defendants) did not intend to defend the claim. The critical point was that the court would not make a declaration on default of pleading but only if the court was satisfied by evidence, which would require a hearing rather than merely an administrative process of the sort involved in obtaining a default judgment. However, the court declined jurisdiction on the basis that England was not the appropriate forum.

Paragraph 3.1(4A): Claim "arises out of same or closely connected facts"

Replace the first paragraph with:

6HJ.10 Paragraph 3.1(4A) of Practice Direction 6B states that the claimant may serve a claim form out of the jurisdiction with the permission of the court under r.6.36 where a claim is made against the defendant which: (a) was served on the defendant within the jurisdiction without the need for the defendant's agreement to accept such service; (b) falls within CPR r.6.33; or (c) falls within one or more of certain subparagraphs of para.3.1, and a "further claim" is made against the same defendant which "arises out of the same or closely connected facts".

At the end of the second paragraph, replace "(2), (6) to (16), (19) and (21)." with:

(1A), (2), (6) to (16A), and (19) to (22A).

After the fourth paragraph (beginning "This head of jurisdiction"), add new paragraph:

As originally drafted, this head of jurisdiction referred to a claim made against the defendant "in reliance" on one or more of the specified heads of jurisdiction. It was amended by CPR PD Update 149 (July 2022), with effect from 1 October 2022, following a review by the service subcommittee of the Rule Committee (see para.6HJ.1 above). The amendments made it clear that the claim form need not have been served out of the jurisdiction with permission under one of the specified heads of jurisdiction: this gateway can also apply if the claim form was served within the jurisdiction (unless that was only possible because the defendant agreed to accept service in the jurisdiction) or if the claim falls within CPR r.6.33 (service out without permission). At the same time, the heads of jurisdiction specified for the purposes of gateway (4A) were expanded to include gateway (20) (claims under various enactments) and various new gateways adopted under the same CPR PD Update.

Add new paragraphs at end:

In proposing these amendments, the service subcommittee noted that there is a "degree of sensitivity" about this gateway (and the "necessary or proper party" gateways at (3) and (4)) as they necessarily involve the court taking jurisdiction over claims where it could not do so if those claims were heard by themselves. The gateways "can therefore become targets for artificial attempts to invoke the Court's jurisdiction". Given that sensitivity, the subcommittee did not consider that gateway (4A) should be amended so as to apply where the anchor claim against the defendant fell within the necessary or proper party gateways.

In *Naftiran Intertrade Co (NICO) Sarl v GL Greenland Ltd (formerly Ferland Co Ltd)* [2022] EWHC 896 (Comm), the deputy judge noted that, since the date on which the head of jurisdiction at para.3.1(4A) was added to PD 6B, the previous subparagraph of para.3.1(6) which allowed service out of the jurisdiction for claims made in respect of a contract containing a jurisdiction clause in favour of the English courts (para.3.1(6)(d)) had been deleted, having been considered redundant following the introduction of CPR r.6.33(2B)(b) (see commentary at paras 6.33.4 and 6HJ.20). On its face, therefore, para.3.1(4A) did not apply where jurisdiction over the anchor claim was based on the presence of an English jurisdiction clause, as that is not a claim made in reliance on any of the paragraphs referred to in the rule, though the deputy judge expressed the view that this was unlikely to have been the intention of the Rule Committee. The position has now been rectified by the addition of subpara.(b) which applies the gateway where the anchor claim falls within r.6.33.

Change title of section: **6HJ.12**

Paragraph 3.1(6) to (8A): Claims in relation to contracts

Replace paragraph with:

In para.3.1 of Practice Direction 6B, four particular heads of jurisdiction are marshalled under the heading "Claims in relation to contracts" in subparas (6) to (8A).

Change title of subsection: **6HJ.13**

Paragraph 3.1(6) to (8A): Claims in relation to contracts

Replace the first paragraph with:

A claimant may serve a claim form out of the jurisdiction with the permission of the court under r.6.36 where the claim: (1) is made "in respect of" a contract, being a contract satisfying one of three conditions (para.3.1(6) of PD 6B); (2) is made "in respect of" a breach of contract committed within the jurisdiction (para.3.1(7)); (3) is made for a declaration that no contract exists (para.3.1(8)); or (4) is for unlawfully causing or assisting in a breach of contract where the contract or the breach falls within para.3.1(6) or (7) or CPR r.6.33(2B). If, on the same facts, a claimant has a remedy in contract or tort, they can choose whether to seek permission for service out of the jurisdiction under the heads of jurisdiction at para.3.1(6) or (7) or on under the head of jurisdiction for claims in tort at para.3.1(9) considered at para.6HJ.23 below (*Matthews v Kuwait Bechtel Corp* [1959] 2 Q.B. 57, CA).

Paragraph 3.1(6): Claim made in respect of a contract

To the end of the fifth paragraph (beginning "In Cecil v Bayat"), add:

See also *Charterhouse Asset Management Ltd v Latchworth Ltd* [2021] EWHC 3072 (Ch). **6HJ.14**

Paragraph 3.1(6)(a): Contract made within the jurisdiction

In the first paragraph, replace the first two sentences with:

Paragraph 3.1(6)(a) of Practice Direction 6B states that the claimant may serve a claim form out **6HJ.15**
of the jurisdiction with the permission of the court under r.6.36 where a claim is made in respect of a contract where the contract "was (i) made within the jurisdiction, or (ii) concluded by the acceptance of an offer, which offer was received within the jurisdiction".

Replace the second paragraph with:

As originally drafted, this head of jurisdiction applied only where the contract was "made within the jurisdiction". The gateway was the subject of criticism, including by Lord Sumption in *Four Seasons Holdings Inc v Brownlie* [2017] UKSC 80; [2018] 1 W.L.R. 192, who commented (at [16]) that the rules of offer and acceptance, when applied to the question of when or where a contract was made, were unsatisfactory and gave rise to "serious practical difficulties". He referred in particular to the distinction between contracts made by cable or post, which are complete as soon as the letter of acceptance is put into the postbox or the cable dispatched, and contracts made by a method of instantaneous communication, e.g. by telephone, which are complete only when the acceptance is received by the offeror (see *Entores Ltd v Miles Far East Corp* [1955] 2 Q.B. 327). Lord Sumption suggested that the wording of gateway (6)(a) could profitably be re-examined by the Civil Procedure Rule Committee. These obiter remarks were cited in *Ditto Ltd v Drive-Thru Records LLC* [2021] EWHC 2035 (Ch) to support the Deputy Master's finding that there was a good arguable case that the claim fell within this gateway on the basis that the agreements in question were made both in England and in California.

In light of the criticisms made of this head of jurisdiction, it was amended by CPR PD Update 149 (July 2022) with effect from 1 October 2022, following a review by the service subcommittee of the Rule Committee (see para.6HJ.1 above), so that it applies where a contract is either: (i) made within the jurisdiction; or (ii) concluded by the acceptance of an offer where the offer was received within the jurisdiction. As explained in the subcommittee's paper setting out their proposed amendments, the intention was to broaden the gateway. The subcommittee had initially proposed an amendment to refer to a contract made as a result of an essential step being taken in the jurisdiction (in line with the applicable rules in Singapore). However, concern was expressed by members of the Lord Chancellor's Advisory Committee on Private International Law that this might lead to arguments that (for example) a board resolution authorising the making of an offer or acceptance might be sufficient, which the subcommittee accepted was broader than intended.

To the end of the last paragraph, add:

Presumably the same is true in respect of a contract concluded by the acceptance of an offer received within the jurisdiction which is then amended by an agreement made wholly outside the jurisdiction.

6HJ.17 *Change title of subsection:*

Paragraph 3.1(6)(c): Contract "governed by the law of England and Wales"

Replace the first paragraph with:

The claimant may serve a claim form out of the jurisdiction with the permission of the court under r.6.36 where a claim is made in respect of a contract where the contract "is governed by the law of England and Wales". This gateway was amended to refer to "the law of England and Wales" rather than "English law" by CPR PD Update 149 (July 2022) with effect from 1 October 2022.

The use of the governing law of a contract as a head of jurisdiction is limited to England and the Commonwealth. It plays no role in the United States, and it is not a ground of jurisdiction under the Judgments Regulation (recast) scheme or the Lugano Convention. A number of cases have stressed the exorbitance of this head of jurisdiction as an important factor to be placed in the balance against the grant of permission, where it is the sole head relied on (see e.g. *Amin Rasheed Shipping Corp v Kuwait Insurance Co (The Al Wahab)* [1984] A.C. 50). In *Novus Aviation Ltd v Onur Air Tasimacilik AS* [2009] EWCA Civ 122; [2009] 1 Lloyd's Rep. 576, CA at [72] et seq, Lawrence Collins LJ reviewed the authorities and considered the principles, noting that the fact that a contract was governed by English law would have a different weight in different circumstances. Factors which might weigh in favour of granting permission would include the fact that issues of English public policy may be involved (as in *EI du Pont de Nemours & Co v Agnew* [1987] 2 Lloyd's Rep. 585, *Mitsubishi Corp v Alafouzos* [1988] 1 Lloyd's Rep. 191) or that the foreign court may apply its own law despite an express choice of English law (*Coast Lines v Hudig & Veder Chartering NV* [1972] 2 Q.B. 34).

Contract with English jurisdiction clause (formerly para.3.1(6)(d))

Replace the second paragraph with:

6HJ.20 Paragraph 3.1(6)(d) was omitted by the 127th CPR Practice Direction Update (February 2021), as it was considered to be redundant upon the amendment of r.6.33(2B) to introduce a new subpara.(b) with effect from 6 April 2021 by r.6 of the Civil Procedure (Amendment) Rules 2021 (SI 2021/117). That amendment removed the need for the court's permission to serve the claim form outside the jurisdiction where a contract contains a term to the effect that the court shall have jurisdiction to determine that claim. In other words, the amendment means that there is no need for permission to serve out where the claim falls within a jurisdiction clause in favour of the English court, even if that jurisdiction clause does not fall within the 2005 Hague Convention. (There would in any event have been no need for permission to serve out of the jurisdiction where the jurisdiction clause fell within that Convention, as that was the circumstance addressed by r.6.33(2B) before its amendment.) See para.6.33.4 above. Rule 6.33(2B) was however further amended with effect from 1 October 2022 to fill a perceived lacuna resulting from the omission of para.3.1(6)(d): see para.6.33.4.1 above.

Paragraph 3.1(7): Claim for breach of contract within the jurisdiction

In the first paragraph, after "breach of contract", replace "committed" with:

6HJ.21 committed, or likely to be committed,

Replace the fourth paragraph (beginning "When RSC Ord.11") with:

When RSC Ord.11 was brought into Pt 6 of the CPR (with effect from 2 May 2000) the formulation was enacted (as r.6.20(6)) to refer simply to a breach of contract committed within the jurisdiction. That wording does not capture the point that this head of jurisdiction is available to a claimant where the contract is made outside the jurisdiction as well as within it, but nothing turns on that. It also does not capture the point of the remedial amendment made in 1921.

The head of jurisdiction was amended by CPR PD Update 149 (July 2022) with effect from 1 October 2022, following a review by the service subcommittee of the Rule Committee (see para.6HJ.1 above), to add reference to a breach of contract "likely to be committed" within the jurisdiction. As explained in the subcommittee's paper setting out their proposed amendments, the aim was to capture claims for quia timet injunctions to restrain an anticipated breach of contract, in line with the then wording of gateway (9) in respect of tort claims and gateway (21) in respect of claims for breach of confidence or misuse of private information.

Add new paragraph 6HJ.22.1:

Paragraph 3.1(8A): Claim for unlawfully causing or assisting in a breach of contract

A claimant may serve a claim form out of the jurisdiction with the permission of the court under r.6.36 where the claim is for unlawfully causing or assisting in: (a) a breach of a contract where the contract falls within one of para.3.1(6)(a) to (6)(c) above or within r.6.33(2B); or (b) a breach of contract falling within para.3.1(7). **6HJ.22.1**

This head of jurisdiction was added by CPR PD Update 149 (July 2022) with effect from 1 October 2022, following a review by the service subcommittee of the Rule Committee (see para.6HJ.1 above). It is one of a number of similar amendments introducing new gateways in respect of claims against third parties where the cause of action is for unlawfully interfering with a legal relationship which is considered to be jurisdictionally significant. Corresponding gateways have been introduced relating to breaches of trust (gateway (15B)), breaches of fiduciary duty (gateway (15C)), and breaches of confidence or misuse of private information (gateway (23)) (see para.6HJ.36 below).

As explained in the subcommittee's paper setting out their proposed amendments, the subcommittee had originally proposed addressing claims for unlawful interference with qualifying contracts by extending gateway (6) to claims "which relate to" such contracts (rather than claims "in respect of" such contracts). However, following concerns expressed by members of the Lord Chancellor's Advisory Committee on Private International Law at the potential breadth of such wording, it sought to address the issue more directly. The paper notes that the gateway:

> "has been framed with a view to capturing causes of action for what (in broad terms) might be termed the unlawful interference with a qualifying contract (or other relevant relationship), whatever their governing law" .

It therefore uses neutral language, rather than tracking the language of relevant English law causes of action (most obviously a claim for inducing a breach of contract).

Paragraph 3.1(9): Claims in tort

Replace the first paragraph with:

In para.3.1 of Practice Direction 6B, under the heading "Claims in tort", one particular head of jurisdiction is listed in subpara.(9). This provides that a claimant may serve a claim form out of the jurisdiction with the permission of the court under r.6.36 where the claim "is made in tort" and: **6HJ.23**

> "(a) damage was sustained, or will be sustained, within the jurisdiction; (b) damage which has been or will be sustained results from an act committed, or likely to be committed, within the jurisdiction; or (c) the claim is governed by the law of England and Wales."

If, on the same facts, a claimant has a remedy in contract or tort, they can choose whether to seek permission for service out of the jurisdiction under this head of jurisdiction or under the heads of jurisdiction at para.3.1(6) or (7) considered at paras 6HJ.13 et seq. above (*Matthews v Kuwait Bechtel Corp* [1959] 2 Q.B. 57, CA).

In the second paragraph, after the penultimate sentence, add:

It was further broadened by CPR PD Update 149 (July 2022), with effect from 1 October 2022, by the addition of subpara.(c) referring to claims governed by English law.

After the second paragraph, add new paragraph:

In determining whether the claim is one which is "made in tort", difficult issues of characterisation may arise. In *Tulip Trading Ltd v Bitcoin Association for BSV* [2022] EWHC 667 (Ch) at [165] Falk J expressed the view (obiter) that there was a good arguable case that a claim for breach of fiduciary duty fell within the scope of this gateway, where it rested on a form of voluntary assumption of duty which it was alleged had not been (or would not be) performed (but now see gateway (15B)). Issues of characterisation may be further complicated where the cause of action is governed by foreign law (see below).

In the third paragraph, in the second sentence, replace "recast Brussels Regulation" with:

recast Judgments Regulation

To the end of the fourth paragraph (beginning "With regard to subpara.(b)"), add:

Similarly, the making of a conspiratorial agreement in England has been found to amount to a substantial and efficacious act sufficient to bring the claim within this gateway: *Tugushev v Orlov* [2019] EWHC 645 (Comm), *Chep Equipment Pooling BV v ITS Ltd* [2022] EWHC 741 (Comm); [2022] 4 W.L.R. 47.

Replace the last two paragraphs with:

With regard to subpara.(c) in para.3.1(9), in proposing the expansion of the tort gateway to claims governed by English law, the service subcommittee of the Rule Committee noted that there were gateways for contracts governed by English law (gateway (6)(c)), trusts governed by English law (gateway (12)) and restitution claims governed by English law (gateway (16)(c)) but not other types of claim. The subcommittee considered that the same rationale underpinning the existing gateways supported their extension to all English law claims. However, rather than proposing a general gateway in respect of all causes of action governed by the law of England and Wales, it recommended specific new gateways to fill the perceived lacunas for tort and certain other causes of action, namely those relating to: constructive or resulting trusts; breaches of fiduciary duty; and breaches of confidence and misuse of private information (see gateways (15(c)), (15B(c)) and (21)(d)).

As for the rules the English court will apply to determine the applicable law for a tort claim, where the event giving rise to damage occurred on or after 11 January 2009, Regulation (EC) No.864/2007 on the law applicable to non-contractual relations (the Rome II Regulation) applies, so that the general rule is that the applicable law is the law of the country in which the damage occurs (though this general rule is displaced if the tort is manifestly more closely connected with a different country). For events giving rise to damage on or after 1 January 2021, the court will apply the UK version of the Rome II Regulation, i.e. the Rome II Regulation as it has been implemented into UK law with amendments (see ss.3 and 20 of the European Union (Withdrawal) Act 2018 and reg.11 of the Law Applicable to Contractual Obligations and Non-Contractual Obligations (Amendment etc.) (EU Exit) Regulations 2019 (SI 2019/834)). Where the act or omission giving rise to the claim occurred between 1 May 1996 and 11 January 2009, the Private International Law (Miscellaneous Provisions) Act 1995 applies to determine the applicable law, the general rule (under s.11) being the law of the country in which the events constituting the tort occur (though that rule is displaced, by s.12, if in all the circumstances it appears that it is substantially more appropriate for the applicable law to be the law of another country).

Where, applying any of these provisions (as relevant), the court determines that the law applicable to a claim is the law of a foreign country, it seems that country's law (to the extent it is pleaded, and is shown to differ from English law) must be relevant in characterising the claim as one in tort (or otherwise) and considering where in substance it has been committed (cf. *Vidal-Hall v Google Inc* [2015] EWCA Civ 311; [2015] 3 W.L.R. 409, CA at [39]).

Before 1 May 1996 the so-called "double actionability rule" applied so that, in deciding whether a tort had been committed in this or another country, the court would exclusively apply English law (and, if the tort was in substance committed abroad, the English court's jurisdiction would be limited to where the relevant acts would give rise to a tort actionable both in the foreign jurisdiction and in English law: see *Metall v Rohstoff*, op cit). That rule was abolished by the 1995 Act.

Contribution claims

Replace paragraph with:

6HJ.23.7 In *Samsung Electronics Co Ltd v LG Display Co Ltd* [2021] EWHC 1429 (Comm); [2022] 1 All E.R. 717 it was held that a claim in tort for the purposes of this gateway included a claim for contribution under the Civil Liability (Contribution) Act 1978, even though it was a claim by a joint tortfeasor rather than by the original victim. The tests of where the damage was sustained, or whether the damage sustained resulted from an act committed within the jurisdiction, were to be applied to the underlying tort (but the tests were also satisfied on the facts of the case if, contrary to the court's view, it were necessary to look at the contribution claim itself). There was no challenge to this finding on appeal: *Samsung Electronics Co Ltd v LG Display Co Ltd* [2022] EWCA Civ 423.

Paragraph 3.1(11): Claims about property within the jurisdiction

In the penultimate paragraph, replace "Fetch.ai Ltd v Persons Unknown Category A [2021] EWHC 2254 (Comm)" with:

6HJ.25 *Fetch.ai Ltd v Persons Unknown Category A* [2021] EWHC 2254 (Comm); 24 I.T.E.L.R. 566

After the penultimate paragraph, add new paragraph:

The question of whether a cryptoasset is located within the jurisdiction appears to depend on whether the person or company who owns the cryptocurrency is resident within the jurisdiction. In *Ion Science Ltd v Persons Unknown*, 21 December 2020, unrep., Butcher J suggested that the relevant question was where the owner was domiciled, referring to the analysis by Professor Andrew Dickinson in David Fox and Sarah Green (eds), *Cryptocurrencies in Public and Private Law* (Oxford: Oxford University Press, 2019). However, in *Tulip Trading Ltd v Bitcoin Association for BSV* [2022] EWHC 667 (Ch) Falk J observed that the distinction between domicile and residence or place of business appeared not to have been material in *Ion Science*, and that Professor Dickinson's textbook in fact referred to residence. Falk J did not need to decide the point but would have preferred the test of residency, not domicile.

Change title of section: **6HJ.26**

Paragraph 3.1(12) to (16): Claims about trusts, etc.

In the first paragraph, replace "six" with:
fourteen

Replace the second paragraph with:
These heads of jurisdiction were expanded significantly by CPR PD Update 79, with effect from 6 April 2015, which replaced the then subpara.(12) with two new provisions, subparas (12) and (12A), and by CPR PD Update 149 (July 2022), with effect from 1 October 2022, which added new subparas (12B) to (12E), (15)(c) and (15A) to (15D).

Change title of subsection: **6HJ.27**

Paragraph 3.1(12) and (12A) to (12E): Claims made in respect of a trust

Replace the first paragraph with:
A claimant may serve a claim form out of the jurisdiction with the permission of the court under r.6.36 where a claim is made in respect of a trust which is created by the operation of a statute, or by a written instrument, or created orally and evidenced in writing, and which (under the head of jurisdiction at para.3.1(12) of Practice Direction 6B) "is governed by the law of England and Wales"; or (under (12A)) "provides that jurisdiction in respect of such a claim shall be conferred upon the courts of England and Wales"; or (under (12B)) "expressly or impliedly designates England and Wales as the principal place of administration". A claimant may also serve a claim form out of the jurisdiction with the permission of the court under r.6.36 where a claim is made which is: (under the head of jurisdiction at para.3.1(12C)) "in respect of a trust created in the jurisdiction"; or (under (12D)):

> "for a declaration that no trust has arisen where, if the trust was found to have arisen, it would comply with one of the conditions set out in paragraph (12), (12A), (12B) or (12C)" ;

or (under (12E)) "for a breach of trust where the breach is committed or likely to be [committed] within the jurisdiction". (The second instance of "committed" does not appear in gateway (12E) but no doubt this is what is intended.)

Add new paragraphs at end:
By CPR PD Update 149 (July 2022), with effect from 1 October 2022, following a review by the service subcommittee of the Civil Procedure Rule Committee (see para.6HJ.1 above), the heads of jurisdiction for claims relating to trusts were expanded significantly with the addition of new subparas (12B) to (12E), in the terms referred to above.

With regard to para.(12B), which applies to a trust which expressly or impliedly designates England and Wales as the principal place of administration, the service subcommittee's paper explaining its proposals noted that this new gateway had been suggested by a member of the Lord Chancellor's Committee on Private International Law. As the paper stated, the 2019 Hague Judgments Convention (the Hague Convention on the Recognition and Enforcement of Foreign Judgments in Civil or Commercial Matters 2019), permits enforcement of a judgment concerning the validity, construction, effects, administration or variation of a trust created voluntarily and evidenced in writing, where the state of origin of the judgment was expressly or impliedly designated as the principal place of administration. It is also a factor relevant to ascertaining the law with which a trust is most closely connected, for the purposes of ascertaining the law governing the trust in the absence of a choice, under art.7 of the Hague Trusts Convention (the Hague Convention on the Law Applicable to Trusts and on their Recognition 1985). The subcommittee's paper states that both tests are jurisdictionally significant, "the former directly so, given it sets out the circumstances in which foreign courts will recognise and enforce an English judgment" (although the UK has not yet signed up to the 2019 Hague Judgments Convention). The subcommittee therefore considered it appropriate to introduce a new gateway mirroring that test.

With regard to para.(12C)), which applies to a trust created in the jurisdiction, the subcommittee's paper said it could be argued that the same rationale as exists for gateway (6) (broadly, contracts made within the jurisdiction: see para.6HJ.15 above) applies also to certain other legal relationships arising in the jurisdiction, including trusts, fiduciary duties and obligations of confidence and rights of privacy. The subcommittee therefore recommended introducing the new gateway at (12C) (and corresponding gateways for the other legal relationships referred to in this paragraph: see gateways (15B(b)) and (21(c))).

With regard to para.(12D), which applies to a declaration that no trust has arisen where (if it was found to have arisen) it would comply with one of the conditions set out in subparas (12) to (12C), the subcommittee's paper noted that an equivalent gateway existed in respect of claims that a qualifying contract did not exist, but not other jurisdictionally-significant legal relationships. It recommended expanding this approach to cover trusts, with the introduction of new gateway (12D) (and similar new gateways for fiduciary duties and duties of confidence or rights to privacy: see gateways (15D) and (22)).

With regard to para.(12E), which applies to a breach of trust committed (or likely to be committed) within the jurisdiction, the service subcommittee's paper noted that, while a number of other gateways were premised on relevant events occurring in the jurisdiction (e.g. the breach of contract and tort gateways), there was an apparent lacuna in that there was no equivalent gateway for claims for trust or breach of fiduciary duty. The subcommittee considered whether there should be a general gateway which would apply whenever a substantial part of a cause of action had occurred or was likely to occur in the jurisdiction (with or without retaining the existing more specific gateways for claims of this sort), but rejected that approach in favour of the "lacuna-filling" approach with the new gateway (12C) (and the similar new gateways for breaches of fiduciary duty and obligations of confidence or rights of privacy).

6HJ.30 *Change title of subsection:*

Paragraph 3.1(15): Claims against trustees

Replace the first paragraph with:

Paragraph 3.1(15) of Practice Direction 6B states that a claimant may serve a claim form out of the jurisdiction with the permission of the court under r.6.36 where a claim is made against the defendant as constructive trustee, or as trustee of a resulting trust, in three circumstances: first, where the claim arises out of acts committed or events occurring within the jurisdiction; secondly, where the claim relates to assets within the jurisdiction; and thirdly, where the claim is governed by the law of England and Wales.

To the end of the third paragraph, add:

It was further broadened by CPR PD Update 149 (July 2022), with effect from 1 October 2022, to apply also where there are no relevant events, acts or assets within the jurisdiction but the claim is governed by English law. This followed a review by the service subcommittee of the Rule Committee, with input from the Lord Chancellor's Advisory Committee (see para.6HJ.1 above). Similar gateways were introduced for other causes of action governed by English law, namely: tort (see para.6HJ.23 above); breaches of fiduciary duty (see para.6HJ.30.2 below); and breaches of confidence and misuse of private information (see para.6HJ.36 below).

Replace the last paragraph with:

In *Ion Science Ltd v Persons Unknown*, 21 December 2020, unrep., Butcher J found there was a good arguable case that an equitable proprietary claim for the return of cryptocurrency could be served out of the jurisdiction under the head of jurisdiction at para.3.1(15) on the basis that (inter alia) the claim related to assets (the cryptocurrency) within the jurisdiction. In the absence of a decided case as to the *lex situs* of a cryptoasset, the court referred to the analysis by Professor Andrew Dickinson in *Cryptocurrencies in Public and Private Law* (Oxford University Press) which suggests that the *lex situs* is the place where the person or company who owns the cryptocurrency is domiciled. See also *Fetch.ai Ltd v Persons Unknown Category A* [2021] EWHC 2254 (Comm); 24 I.T.E.L.R. 566 (HH Judge Pelling QC) at [14] and [23]. But see *Tulip Trading Ltd v Bitcoin Association for BSV* [2022] EWHC 667 (Ch) in which Falk J expressed the view (obiter) that the relevant test is residency, not domicile. She observed that the distinction between domicile and residence or place of business appeared not to have been material in *Ion Science*, and that Professor Dickinson's textbook in fact referred to residence rather than domicile.

The second limb of this gateway, referring to "assets within the jurisdiction" may not be available if there are no assets within the jurisdiction at the time of the application for permission to serve out, even if the claim relates to assets that were previously in the jurisdiction: *Denisov v Delvecchio* [2022] EWHC 377 (Comm).

Add new paragraphs 6HJ.30.1 and 6HJ.30.2:

Paragraph 3.1(15A): Accessory liability

6HJ.30.1 Paragraphs 3.1(15A) of Practice Direction 6B states that a claimant may serve a claim form out of the jurisdiction with the permission of the court under r.6.36 where a claim is made for "unlawfully causing or assisting in": (a) a breach of a trust where the trust falls within one of subparas (12) to (12C); or (b) a breach of trust falling within subpara.(12E); or (c) a breach of a constructive or resulting trust where the trustee's liability would fall within subpara.(15).

This head of jurisdiction was added by CPR PD Update 149 (July 2022) with effect from 1 October 2022, following a review by the service subcommittee of the Rule Committee (see para.6HJ.1 above). As noted at para.6HJ.22.1 above, it is one of a number of similar amendments introducing new gateways in respect of claims against third parties where the cause of action is for unlawfully interfering with a legal relationship which is considered to be jurisdictionally significant, the others being breaches of contract (gateway 8A), breaches of fiduciary duty (gateway (15C)), and breaches of confidence or misuse of private information (gateway (23)).

Paragraph 3.1(15B) to (15D): Claims made in respect of fiduciary duties

6HJ.30.2 Paragraphs 3.1(15B) to (15D) of Practice Direction 6B state that a claimant may serve a claim form out of the jurisdiction with the permission of the court under r.6.36 where a claim is made (under (15B)) for breach of fiduciary duty, where:

"(a) the breach is committed, or likely to be committed, within the jurisdiction; (b) the fiduciary duty arose in the jurisdiction; or (c) the fiduciary duty is governed by the law of England and Wales" ;

(under (15C)) for unlawfully causing or assisting in a breach of fiduciary duty where the breach, or the duty, falls within (15B) (the reference to (15A)(a) at (15C)(b) is no doubt erroneous); or (under (15D) for a declaration that no fiduciary duty has arisen where, if it was found to have arisen, it would comply with one of the conditions set out in (15B)(b) or (c).

These heads of jurisdiction were added by CPR PD Update 149 (July 2022) with effect from 1 October 2022, following a review by the service subcommittee of the Rule Committee (see para.6HJ.1 above). Previously, there was no specific head of jurisdiction for claims for breach of fiduciary duty. In *Twin Benefits Ltd v Barker* [2017] EWHC 1412 (Ch) (Marcus Smith J), the judge explained ([110]-[114]) that a claim for breach of fiduciary duty may sometimes be regarded as contractual (potentially falling within para.3.1(6)), or tortious (potentially falling within para.3.1(9)), or as giving rise to a claim against a defendant as constructive trustee (potentially falling within para.3.1(16)). The question in each case was what, in substance, was the nature of the claim being asserted. And see *Tulip Trading Ltd v Bitcoin Association for BSV* [2022] EWHC 667 (Ch) at [165], referred to at para.6HJ.23 above. The addition of the specific heads of jurisdiction at para.3.1(15B) to (15D) means that it will no longer be necessary to seek to characterise claims in respect of fiduciary duties as falling within some other category.

The various connecting factors introduced in gateway (15B) for claims for breach of fiduciary duty generally reflect those relating to other causes of action, such as in contract and tort. So, the gateway will apply if the breach is committed (or likely to be committed) within the jurisdiction or the fiduciary duty arose in the jurisdiction (see para.6HJ.27 above for corresponding additions to the gateway in respect of claims for breach of trust), or the fiduciary duty is governed by the law of England and Wales (see para.6HJ.23 above for a corresponding addition to the gateway in respect of tort claims).

Gateway (15C) is one of a number of new gateways in respect of claims against third parties where the cause of action is for unlawfully interfering with a legal relationship which is considered to be jurisdictionally significant, the others being breaches of contract (gateway 8A), breaches of trust (gateway (15A)), and breaches of confidence or misuse of private information (gateway (23)).

Similarly, gateway (15D) is one of a number of new gateways in respect of claims for a declaration that a particular qualifying relationship does not exist, modelled on the pre-existing gateway for claims for a declaration that no contract exists (gateway (8)). (There are similar new gateways relating to trusts and duties of confidence or rights to privacy: see paras 6HJ.27 and 6HJ.36 below.)

Paragraph 3.1(16): Claim for restitution

In the last paragraph, replace "Fetch.ai Ltd v Persons Unknown Category A [2021] EWHC 2254 (Comm)" with:

Fetch.ai Ltd v Persons Unknown Category A [2021] EWHC 2254 (Comm); 24 I.T.E.L.R. 566 **6HJ.31**

Add new paragraph 6HJ.31.1:

Paragraph 3.1(16A): Declarations of non-liability

In para.3.1 of Practice Direction 6B, under the heading "Declarations of non-liability", one **6HJ.31.1**
particular head of jurisdiction is listed in subpara.(16A). That provision states that the claimant may serve a claim form out of the jurisdiction with the permission of the court under r.6.36 where a claim is made for a declaration that the claimant is not liable where, if a claim were brought against the claimant seeking to establish that liability, that claim would fall within another paragraph of Practice Direction 6B (excluding paragraphs (1) to (5), (8), (12D), (15D), (17), (22) and (24) to (25)).

This head of jurisdiction was added by CPR PD Update 149 (July 2022) with effect from 1 October 2022, following a review by the service subcommittee of the Rule Committee (see para.6HJ.1 above). The subcommittee's paper explaining the proposed amendments noted that there was an existing gateway (gateway (8)) which expressly addressed claims for negative declaratory relief in relation to the existence of a qualifying contract, but no other gateways addressing claims for negative declarations. The paper stated that, while it might well be possible to fit such claims within the existing gateways, the subcommittee could see benefit in adding an express provision, which it said would be in keeping with the significant change in the attitude of the English court to claims for negative declarations, which were commonplace under the Brussels/Lugano regimes.

The new gateway excludes from its ambit claims which would have fallen within certain of the other gateways, as listed above. The subcommittee's paper explained that this was intended to avoid the undesirable and unintended consequence of allowing a claimant to seek a negative declaration in the courts of its domicile simply because it could have been sued there, as well as excluding gateways where the possibility of negative declarations would not seem to be engaged or which already address some other form of declaratory relief.

Paragraph 3.1(17): Claims by HM Revenue and Customs

Replace paragraph with:

In para.3.1 of Practice Direction 6B, under the heading "Claims by HM Revenue and Customs", **6HJ.32** one particular head of jurisdiction is listed in subpara.(17). That provision states that a claim form may be served out of the jurisdiction with the permission of the court under r.6.36 where a claim is made by HMRC relating to duties or taxes against a defendant not domiciled in Scotland or Northern Ireland within the meaning of ss.41 and 42 of the Civil Jurisdiction and Judgments Act 1982 (para.3.1(17) of PD 6B).

The reference to the statutory definition of domicile under the 1982 Act was added by CPR PD Update 149 (July 2022), with effect from 1 October 2022, following a review by the service subcommittee of the Rule Committee (see para.6HJ.1 above). This resolves any uncertainty as to the test of domicile for the purposes of para.3.1(17) (and see para.6HJ.3 above for a similar amendment to para.3.1(1)).

Paragraph 3.1(20): Claims under various enactments

Replace the fifth paragraph (beginning "In subpara.(a) of") with:

6HJ.35 In *ED&F Man Capital Markets LLP v Obex Securities LLC* [2017] EWHC 2965 (Ch); [2018] 1 W.L.R. 1708 (Catherine Newman QC) it was held that in subpara.(a) of para.3.1(20), "proceedings" is not confined to proceedings in which a claim form has been issued and may include proceedings in the form of an application for pre-action disclosure under r.31.16. In *Gorbachev v Guriev* [2022] EWHC 1907 (Comm), Jacobs J held that the same applied to an application for non-party disclosure, disagreeing with the contrary conclusion of Cockerill J in *Nix v Emerdata Ltd* [2022] EWHC 718 (Comm). (As noted in those cases, however, in general, applications for disclosure from overseas third parties should be made using the letter of request regime under r.34.13 and PD 34A.)

6HJ.36 *Change title of section:*

Paragraph 3.1(21) to (23): Claims for breach of confidence or misuse of private information

Replace the first paragraph with:

In para.3.1 of Practice Direction 6B, under the heading "Claims for breach of confidence or misuse of private information", three particular heads of jurisdiction are listed in subparas (21) to (23). These provisions state that a claimant may serve a claim form out of the jurisdiction with the permission of the court under r.6.36 where:

- (under subpara.(21)) a claim is made for breach of confidence or misuse of private information where: (a) detriment was suffered, or will be suffered, within the jurisdiction; (b) detriment which has been, or will be, suffered results from an act committed, or likely to be committed, within the jurisdiction; (c) the obligation of confidence or right to privacy arose in the jurisdiction; or (d) the obligation of confidence or right of privacy is governed by the law of England and Wales;
- (under subpara.(22)) a claim is made for a declaration that no duty of confidentiality or right to privacy has arisen where, if the duty or right was found to have arisen, it would comply with one of the conditions set out in para.(21)(c) or (d).
- (under subpara.(23)) a claim is made for unlawfully causing or assisting in: (a) a breach of confidence or misuse of private information where the obligation or right in question falls within para.(21)(c) or (d) above; or (b) a breach of confidence or misuse of private information falling within (21)(a) or (b) above.

The head of jurisdiction at subpara.(21) was inserted in para.3.1 by CPR Update 81 (August 2015) with effect from 1 October 2015, for the purpose of making, for the first time, express provision for service out of the jurisdiction with the court's permission where a claim form makes claims for breach of confidence or misuse of private information. At that time, the gateway applied only where the connecting factors were detriment within the jurisdiction, or detriment resulting from an act within the jurisdiction (i.e. subparas (21)(a) and (b) of the provision).

This gateway was expanded, and the new gateways at (22) and (23) were added, by CPR PD Update 149 (July 2022) with effect from 1 October 2022, following a review by the service subcommittee of the Rule Committee (see para.6HJ.1 above). The aim of the expansion was to fill various lacunae the subcommittee had identified in the operation of the gateway relating to claims for breach of confidence or misuse of private information compared to other causes of action. So, gateway (21), for claims for breach of confidence or misuse of confidential information, has been expanded to apply if the obligation of confidence arose in the jurisdiction or is governed by English law (see paras 6HJ.27 and 6HJ.30.2 above for corresponding additions to the gateways in respect of claims for breaches of trust and fiduciary duty). Gateway (22) is one of a number of new gateways in respect of claims for a declaration that a particular qualifying relationship does not exist, modelled on the pre-existing gateway for claims for a declaration that no contract exists (gateway (8)). (There are similar new gateways relating to trusts and fiduciary duties: see paras 6HJ.27 and 6HJ.30.2 above.) Gateway (23) is one of a number of new gateways in respect of claims against third parties where the cause of action is for unlawfully interfering with a legal relationship which is considered to be jurisdictionally significant, the others being breaches of contract (gateway 8A), breaches of trust (gateway (15A)), and breaches of fiduciary duty (gateway (15C)).

At the start of the penultimate paragraph, replace "Not long before this subparagraph came into effect," with:
Not long before subpara.(21) came into effect,

In the last paragraph, replace "Fetch.ai Ltd v Persons Unknown Category A [2021] EWHC 2254 (Comm)" with:
Fetch.ai Ltd v Persons Unknown Category A [2021] EWHC 2254 (Comm); 24 I.T.E.L.R. 566

Add new paragraphs 6HJ.37 and 6HJ.38:

Paragraph 3.1(24): Contempt application

In para.3.1 of Practice Direction 6B, under the heading "Contempt applications", one particular head of jurisdiction is listed in subpara.(24). This provisions states that a claimant may serve a claim form out of the jurisdiction with the permission of the court under r.6.36 where a contempt application is made, whether or not, apart from that paragraph, a claim form or application notice containing such an application can be served out of the jurisdiction. **6HJ.37**

This head of jurisdiction was added by CPR PD Update 149 (July 2022) with effect from 1 October 2022, following a review by the service subcommittee of the Rule Committee (see para.6HJ.1 above). The subcommittee's paper explaining the proposed amendments noted that difficulties had arisen where it was necessary to serve a non-party out of the jurisdiction in order to engage the court's prescriptive powers. In particular, the lack of an express gateway for an application for contempt had caused difficulties where a party wished to serve a contempt application on a director, who was outside the jurisdiction, of a company which was subject to the court's jurisdiction. Where contempt is alleged against both the company and the directors, it may be possible to serve the director as a necessary or proper party to the proceedings against the company, but that is not always the case. The subcommittee therefore proposed the creation of this additional gateway, which was adapted from the Singapore Rules of Court.

Paragraph 3.1(25): Information orders against non-parties

In para.3.1 of Practice Direction 6B, under the heading "Information orders against non-parties", one particular head of jurisdiction is listed in subpara.(25). This provision states that a claimant may serve a claim form out of the jurisdiction with the permission of the court under r.6.36 where a claim or application is made for disclosure in order to obtain information: (a) regarding: (i) the true identity of a defendant or a potential defendant; and/or (ii) what has become of the property of a claimant or applicant; and (b) for the purpose of proceedings already commenced or which, subject to the content of the information received, are intended to be commenced either by service in England and Wales or pursuant to CPR rr.6.32, 6.33 or 6.36. **6HJ.38**

This head of jurisdiction was added by CPR PD Update 149 (July) with effect from 1 October 2022, following a review by the service subcommittee of the Rule Committee (see para.6HJ.1 above). The subcommittee's paper explaining the proposed amendments noted that the increasing prevalence of digital transactions had brought into sharp relief the limitations of the then existing gateways in facilitating service out of applications for information orders from third parties, for example where money or cryptoassets were stolen and a bank or exchange could provide information which might assist the innocent party in tracking and recovering the asset or in identifying the wrongdoers.

The paper noted that there was some tension in the authorities as to whether it was possible to serve such application outside the jurisdiction. In particular, in *AB Bank Ltd v Abu Dhabi Commercial Bank PJSC* [2016] EWHC 2082 (Comm); [2017] 1 W.L.R. 810, Teare J held that a claim for *Norwich Pharmacal* relief could not be served outside the jurisdiction using the necessary or proper party gateway, though in subsequent cases, the courts had been willing to permit service out of *Bankers' Trust* applications, where there is a substantive proprietary claim against a wrongdoer (see the discussion at para.6HJ.8 above).

To address this unsatisfactory situation, the subcommittee recommended the addition of a discrete gateway directed at applications for information of the relevant sort. It noted that the addition of such a gateway would be consistent with the approach which appeared to be developing in other parts of the common law world to international digital frauds, citing a judgment of the Singapore High Court in which disclosure orders were made against parties: (i) incorporated outside of the jurisdiction and; (ii) against whom no substantive cause of action was advanced (*CLM v CLN* [2022] SGHC 46), and commenting that it was also aware of such an order being made by the Isle of Man Court.

To avoid the gateway applying too widely, the subcommittee recommended limiting the gateway to applications for information regarding the identity of a potential defendant, or what has become of the claimant's property, where the information is required for the purposes of proceedings which have been or are to be bought in England and Wales. This is reflected in subpara.(25) as adopted.

PART 7

HOW TO START PROCEEDINGS—THE CLAIM FORM

Editorial introduction

In the firth paragraph (beginning "In the majority"), replace "(para.7BPD.1)." with:
7.0.1 (para.49CPD.1).

Related sources

To the end of the list, add:
7.0.3 • Practice Direction 51ZB—The Damages Claims Pilot

Practice Directions

Replace paragraph with:
7.0.5 Following the 149th PD Update (July 2022), there are now only three practice directions to Pt 7. The first (PD 7A—How to Start Proceedings—The Claim Form) contains provisions of general application. The second (PD 7B) deals with Production Centre claims under r.7.10 and the third (PD 7C) deals with Money Claims online. It does not supplement any particular rule in Pt 7. It provides for a scheme enabling claimants to start certain types of county court claims by requesting by electronic means the issue of claim forms. As amended by CPR PD Update 57 (September 2011) (with effect from 1 September 2011) para.4 of this practice direction stipulates (amongst other things) that the claimant's address for service must be within the UK (but not elsewhere in the EU, cf. r.6.7) and that the defendant's address for service must be within England and Wales. (This practice direction also provides for the filing of certain other documents by such means.) Rule 7.12 states that a practice direction may make provision for a claimant to start a claim by requesting the issue of a claim form electronically; see further commentary following that rule.

The former PD 7B and PD 7D are now to be found in Pt 49 as PDs 49C and 49D respectively.

In addition to the Practice Directions to this Part, Practice Direction 51ZB establishes a pilot to test an online claims process in respect of claims for damages only. All claims issued on or after 4 April 2022 which meet the conditions set out in subpara.(3) of the Practice Direction must be issued in accordance with the pilot procedure. The pilot will run from 28 May 2021 to 30 April 2024.

Practice Direction

Replace "para.4 of PD 7B (see para.7BPD.4 below)." with:
7.1.1 para.4 of PD 49C in respect of Consumer Credit matters.

Rule 7.2: Effect of rule

Replace the second paragraph with:
7.2.1 For the procedure in relation to money claims online see the note to PD 7C—Money Claims Online (para.7CPD.13.1).

Starting a claim in the County Court Money Claims Centre

After the first paragraph, add new paragraph:
7.2.2 The requirement to send the claim form to the CCMCC is modified by Practice Direction 51ZB which establishes a pilot to test an online claims process for the issue of claims for damages only. All claims issued on or after 4 April 2022 which meet the conditions set out in subpara.(3) of the Practice Direction must be issued in accordance with the pilot procedure. It should be noted that the pilot only applies to claims by claimants who are legally represented by a legal representative who has been registered with MyHMCTS and has been granted access to the Damages Claims Portal. The pilot will run from 28 May 2021 to 30 April 2024.

"Claims which can be conveniently disposed of in the same proceedings" (the convenience test)

In the second paragraph, replace the last sentence with:
7.3.5 The court has recently been confronted with extreme attempts to bring claims on behalf of multiple claimants, or to sue multiple defendants, in one action. See *Abbott v Ministry of Defence* [2022] EWHC 1807 (QB) and *Thurrock Council v Stokes* [2022] EWHC 1998 (QB). In both cases the court concluded that the convenient disposal test was conclusively failed.

Replace r.7.4(3) with:

Particulars of claim[1]

(3) Where the claimant serves particulars of claim on the defendant, the claimant must, within 7 days of service on the defendant, file a copy of the particulars unless a copy has already been filed. 7.4

(4) The claimant need not file a copy of the particulars of claim under paragraph (3) if the claim is being dealt with at the Production Centre (under rule 7.10) or the County Court Business Centre (under Practice Direction 7C) and is not transferred to another court.

(Part 16 sets out what the particulars of claim must include.)

(Part 22 requires particulars of claim to be verified by a statement of truth.)

Delete paragraph 7.4.2, "Particulars of claim".

Replace the table in r.7.5(1) with:

Service of a claim form[2]

Method of service	***Step required***	
First class post, document exchange or other service which provides for delivery on the next business day	**Posting, leaving with, delivering to or collection by the relevant service provider**	7.5
Delivery of the document to or leaving it at the relevant place	**Delivering to or leaving the document at the relevant place**	
Personal service under rule 6.5	**Completing the relevant step required by rule 6.5(3)**	
Electronic method	**Sending the e-mail or other electronic transmission**	

Rule 7.5: Effect of rule

After the third paragraph, add new paragraph:

It should be noted that what must be served is a sealed claim form, not an unsealed one, re-emphasised in *Ideal Shopping Direct Ltd v Mastercard Inc* [2022] EWCA Civ 14; [2022] 1 W.L.R. 1541. 7.5.1

Rule 7.6(2): Applications under rule

Replace paragraph with:

In *ST v BAI (SA) (t/a Brittany Ferries)* [2022] EWCA Civ 1037 at [62] Lady Justice Carr conveniently summarised the general principles as follows: 7.6.2

"i) The defendant has a right to be sued (if at all) by means of originating process issued within the statutory period of limitation and served within the period of its initial validity of service. It follows that a departure from this starting point needs to be justified;

ii) The reason for the inability to serve within time is a highly material factor. The better the reason, the more likely it is that an extension will be granted. Incompetence or oversight by the claimant or waiting some other development (such as funding) may not amount to a good reason. Further, what may be a sufficient reason for an extension of time for service of particulars of claim is not necessarily a sufficient reason for an extension for service of the claim form;

iii) Where there is no good reason for the need for an extension, the court still retains a discretion to grant an extension of time but is not likely to do so;

iv) Whether the limitation period has or may have expired since the commencement of proceedings is an important consideration. If a limitation defence will or may be

---

[1] Amended by the Civil Procedure (Amendment) Rules 2008 (SI 2008/2178), the Civil Procedure (Amendment No.3) Rules 2008 (SI 2008/3327), Civil Procedure (Amendment No.2) Rules 2009 (SI 2009/3390), the Civil Procedure (Amendment No.4) Rules 2015 (SI 2015/1569) and the Civil Procedure (Amendment No.2) Rules 2022 (SI 2022/783).

[2] Amended by the Civil Procedure (Amendment) Rules 2008 (SI 2008/2178) and the Civil Procedure (Amendment No.2) Rules 2022 (SI 2022/783).

prejudiced by the granting of an extension of time, the claimant should have to show at the very least that they have taken reasonable steps (but not all reasonable steps) to serve within time;

v) The discretionary power to extend time prospectively must be exercised in accordance with the overriding objective."

The following older cases may remain of use to practitioners.

Rule 7.6(3): Applications under rule

Add new paragraph at end:

7.6.3 These cases are often very fact-specific. In *Walton v Pickerings Solicitors* [2022] EWHC 2073 (Ch) the claimant waited until the final day of the limitation period before seeking to issue his claim. The court then appears to have lost it. He was slow in chasing this up. On balance, the court concluded that he failed to satisfy the threshold conditions of CPR r.7.6(3)(c) and his application for an extension failed.

Fixed date actions

Replace the second paragraph with:

7.9.1 The Practice Directions which supplement r.7.9 relate only to claims under the Consumer Credit Act 1974; see para.49CPD.1. For the Recovery of Taxes and Duties see para.49DPD.1, for bulk claims issued at the Production Centre see para.7BPD.1, and for money claims issued online at Northampton see para.7CPD.1. Claims by mortgages and landlords seeking recovery of property are now covered by Pts 55 and 56.

Replace r.7.10(2) and (3) with:

Production Centre for claims[1]

7.10 **(2) Practice Direction 7B makes provision for—**

(a) which claimants may use the Production Centre;

(b) the type of claims which the Production Centre may issue;

(c) the functions which are to be discharged by the Production Centre;

(d) the place where the Production Centre is to be located; and

(e) other related matters.

(3) Practice Direction 7B may disapply or modify these Rules as appropriate in relation to claims issued by the Production Centre.

Practice Direction

Replace paragraph with:

7.10.2 Practice Direction 7B—Production Centre supplements r.7.10 (see para.7BPD.1). The Practice Direction modifies the effects of certain CPR provisions. For example, para.1.4(4) enables a claimant to attach a single statement of truth to a batch of claim forms, and para.5.2 (a provision introduced by amendments on 6 April 2009 via CPR Update 49) makes special arrangements for the situation where a claimant wishes to serve particulars of claim separately from the claim forms to which they relate (modifying r.7.4). Claims which may not be issued through the Centre are listed in para.2 of PD 7B. That list (as amended with effect from 1 September 2011 by CPR Update 57 (September 2011)) includes a claim where the claimant's address for service as it appears on the claim form is not in the UK, and a claim where the where the defendant's address for service as it appears on the claim form is not in England and Wales (see para.7BPD.2 below). See further, r.6.8 (Service of claim form where before service the defendant gives an address for service), and r.6.23 (Address for service to be given after proceedings are started).

Replace r.7.12 with:

Electronic issue of claims[2]

7.12 **7.12—(1) A practice direction may permit or require a claimant to start a claim by requesting the issue of a claim form electronically.**

---

[1] Amended by the Civil Procedure (Amendment No.2) Rules 2009 (SI 2009/3390) and the Civil Procedure (Amendment No.2) Rules 2022 (SI 2022/783).

[2] Introduced by the Civil Procedure (Amendment No.5) Rules 2003 (SI 2003/3361) and amended by the Civil Procedure (Amendment No.2) Rules 2009 (SI 2009/3390) and the Civil Procedure (Amendment No.2) Rules 2022 (SI 2022/783).

(2) The practice direction may, in particular–
(a) specify–
(i) the types of claim which may be issued electronically; and
(ii) the conditions which a claim must meet before it may be issued electronically;
(b) specify–
(i) the court where the claim will be issued; and
(ii) the circumstances in which the claim will be transferred to another court;
(c) provide for the filing of other documents electronically where a claim has been started electronically;
(d) specify the requirements that must be fulfilled for any document filed electronically; and
(e) provide how a fee payable on the filing of any document is to be paid where that document is filed electronically.

(3) The practice direction may disapply or modify these Rules as appropriate in relation to claims started electronically.

Practice Direction

To the end of the paragraph, add:

Practice Direction 51ZB establishes a pilot to test an online claims process for the issue of claims for damages only. All claims issued on or after 4 April 2022 which meet the conditions set out in subpara.(3) of the Practice Direction must be issued in accordance with the pilot procedure. The pilot will run from 28 May 2021 to 30 April 2024. **7.12.1**

Replace Practice Direction 7A–How to Start Proceedings–The Claim Form with:

PRACTICE DIRECTION 7A—HOW TO START PROCEEDINGS—THE CLAIM FORM

This Practice Direction supplements CPR Part 7

General

1. Subject to the following provisions of this practice direction, proceedings where both the High Court and the County Court have jurisdiction may be started in the High Court or in the County Court. **7APD.1**

Where to start proceedings

2.1 Proceedings (whether for damages or for a specified sum) may only be started in the High Court if the value of the claim is more than £100,000. **7APD.2**

2.2 Proceedings which include a claim for damages in respect of personal injuries may only be started in the High Court if the value of the claim is £50,000 or more (paragraph 9 of the High Court and County Courts Jurisdiction Order 1991 (S.I. 1991/724 as amended) describes how the value of a claim is to be determined).

2.3 A claim must be issued in the High Court or the County Court if an enactment so requires.

2.4 Subject to paragraphs 2.1 and 2.2 above, a claim should be started in the High Court if by reason of–

(1) the financial value of the claim and the amount in dispute, and/or
(2) the complexity of the facts, legal issues, remedies or procedures involved, and/or
(3) the importance of the outcome of the claim to the public in general,

the claimant believes that the claim ought to be dealt with by a High Court judge.

(CPR Part 30 and Practice Direction 30 contain provisions relating to the transfer to the County Court of proceedings started in the High Court and vice-versa.)

2.5(1) A claim in the County Court under Part 7 may be made at any County Court hearing centre, unless any enactment, rule or practice direction provides otherwise.

(2) If a claim which is required to be made at a particular County Court hearing centre is made at the wrong hearing centre, a court officer will send the claim to the correct hearing centre before it is issued.

2.6 A claim relating to Business and Property work (which includes any of the matters specified in paragraph 1 of Schedule 1 to the Senior Courts Act 1981) and which includes any work under the jurisdiction of the Business and Property Courts, may, subject to any enactment, rule or practice direction, be dealt with in the High Court or in the County Court. The claim form should, if issued in the High Court, be marked in the top right hand corner "Business and Property Courts" and, if issued in the County Court, be marked "Business and Property work" (except, in the County Court, for those areas listed as exceptions in paragraph 4.2 of Practice Direction 57AA (Business and Property Courts).

(For the equity jurisdiction of the County Court, see section 23 of the County Courts Act 1984.)

2.7 A claim relating to any of the matters specified in sub-paragraphs (a) and (b) of paragraph 2 of Schedule 1 to the Senior Courts Act 1981 must be dealt with in the High Court and will be assigned to the Queen's Bench Division.

2.8 Practice directions applying to particular types of proceedings, or to proceedings in particular courts, will contain provisions relating to the commencement and conduct of those proceedings.

2.9 The following proceedings may not be started in the County Court unless the parties have agreed otherwise in writing—

(1) a claim for damages or other remedy for libel or slander, and

(2) a claim in which the title to any toll, fair, market or franchise is in question.

2.10(1) Subject to paragraph 2.9, a claim relating to media and communications work (which includes any work which would fall within the jurisdiction of the Media and Communications List if issued in the High Court) may be started in the County Court or High Court; and paragraph 2.1 shall not apply to such a claim.

(2) Such a claim should be started in the High Court if, by reason of the factors set out in paragraph 2.4(1) to (3), the claimant believes that the claim ought to be dealt with by a High Court judge.

(3) If a claimant starts such a claim in the High Court and the court decides that it should have been started in the County Court, the court will normally transfer it to the County Court on its own initiative. This is likely to result in delay.

2.11(1) The normal rules apply in deciding in which court and specialist list a claim that includes issues under the Human Rights Act 1998 should be started. They also apply in deciding which procedure to use to start the claim; this Part or CPR Part 8 or CPR Part 54 (judicial review).

(2) The exception is a claim for damages in respect of a judicial act, which should be started in the High Court. If the claim is made in a notice of appeal then it will be dealt with according to the normal rules governing where that appeal is heard.

(The County Court cannot make a declaration of incompatibility in accordance with section 4 of the Human Rights Act 1998. Legislation may direct that such a claim is to be brought before a specified tribunal.)

The claim form

3.1 A claimant must use form **N1** to start a claim under Part 7. **7APD.3**

3.2 Other practice directions may require other forms to be used to start types of proceedings, or proceedings in particular courts.

3.3 Where a claim form to be served out of the jurisdiction is one which the court has power to deal with under–

(a) the Civil Jurisdiction and Judgments Act 1982; and

(b) the Judgments Regulation (Regulation (EU) No 1215/2012 of the European Parliament and of the Council of 12 December 2012 on jurisdiction and the recognition and enforcement of judgments in civil and commercial matters),

the claim form must, under rule 6.34, be filed and served with the notice referred to in that rule and paragraph 2.1 of Practice Direction 6B.

3.4 If a claim for damages or for an unspecified sum is started in the High Court, the claim form must–

(1) state that the claimant expects to recover more than £100,000 (or £50,000 or more if the claim is for personal injuries); or

(2) state that some enactment provides that the claim may only be started in the High Court and specify that enactment; or

(3) state that the claim is to be in one of the specialist High Court lists (see CPR Parts 49 and 58-62) and specify that list.

3.5 If a claim for damages for personal injuries is started in the County Court, the claim form must state whether or not the claimant expects to recover more than £1000 in respect of pain, suffering and loss of amenity.

3.6 If a claim for housing disrepair which includes a claim for an order requiring repairs or other work to be carried out by the landlord is started in the County Court, the claim form must state–

(1) whether or not the cost of the repairs or other work is estimated to be more than £1000, and

(2) whether or not the claimant expects to recover more than £1000 in respect of any claim for damages.

If either of the amounts mentioned in (1) and (2) is more than £1000, the small claims track will not be the normal track for that claim.

Title of proceedings

4.1 The claim form and every other statement of case, must be headed with the title of the proceedings. The title should state– **7APD.4**

(1) the identifying number given to the proceedings;

(2) the court or Division in which they are proceeding;

(3) the full name of each party;

(4) each party's status in the proceedings (i.e. claimant/defendant).

(Paragraph 2.4 of Practice Direction 16 sets out what is meant by a full name in respect of each type of claimant.)

4.2 Where there is more than one claimant and/or more than one defendant, the parties should be described in the title as follows–

1. [Name of first claimant]
2. [Name of second claimant, etc]

and

1. [Name of first defendant]
2. [Name of second defendant, etc]

Editorial note

Paragraph 4.1(3) does not preclude using a suitable descriptive title for a party where its actual name is not known. See *Farah v Abdullah* [2018] EWHC 738 (QB). **7APD.4.1**

Starting a Part 7 Claim in the County Court

7APD.5 **5.1**(1) Subject to subparagraph (2), if a claim–
- (a) is started in the County Court under Part 7;
- (b) is a claim only for an amount of money, whether specified or unspecified; and
- (c) is not a claim for which special procedures are provided in the Civil Procedure Rules or practice directions, form **N1** must be sent to: County Court Money Claims Centre, PO Box 527, M5 0BY.

(2) For the purpose of this practice direction, the procedure in Practice Direction 49D is not a special procedure.

5.2 In proceedings referred to in paragraph 4A.1, the claimant must specify the preferred hearing centre on form **N1**.

Start of proceedings

7APD.6 **6.1** Proceedings are started when the court issues a claim form at the request of the claimant (see rule 7.2) but where the claim form as issued was received in the court office on a date earlier than the date on which it was issued by the court, the claim is "brought" for the purposes of the Limitation Act 1980 and any other relevant statute on that earlier date.

6.2 The date on which the claim form was received by the court will be recorded by a date stamp either on the claim form held on the court file or on the letter that accompanied the claim form when it was received by the court.

6.3 An enquiry about the date on which the claim form was received by the court should be directed to a court officer.

6.4 Parties proposing to start a claim which is approaching the expiry of the limitation period should recognise the potential importance of establishing the date the claim form was received by the court and should themselves make arrangements to record the date.

6.5 Where a person seeks to start proceedings against the estate of a deceased defendant where probate or letters of administration have not been granted, the claimant should issue the claim against "the personal representatives of A.B. deceased". The claimant should then, before the expiry of the period for service of the claim form, apply to the court for the appointment of a person to represent the estate of the deceased.

Claims by and against partnerships within the jurisdiction

7APD.7 **7.1** Paragraphs 7 and 8 apply to claims that are brought by or against two or more persons who–
- (1) were business partners; and
- (2) carried on that partnership business within the jurisdiction,

at the time when the cause of action accrued.

7.2 For the purposes of this paragraph, "partners" includes persons claiming to be entitled as partners and persons alleged to be partners.

7.3 Where that partnership has a name, unless it is inappropriate to do so, claims must be brought in or against the name under which that partnership carried on business at the time the cause of action accrued.

Partnership membership statements

7APD.8 **8.1** In this paragraph a "partnership membership statement" is a written statement of the names and last known places of residence of all the persons who were partners in the partnership at the time when the cause of action accrued, being the date specified for this purpose in accordance with paragraph 8.3.

8.2 If the partners are requested to provide a copy of a partnership membership statement by any party to a claim, the partners must do so within 14 days of receipt of the request.

8.3 In that request the party seeking a copy of a partnership membership statement must specify the date when the relevant cause of action accrued.

(Signing of the acknowledgment of service in the case of a partnership is dealt with in CPR rule 10.5(5).)

Persons carrying on business in another name

9.1 This paragraph applies where– **7APD.9**

(1) a claim is brought against an individual;

(2) that individual carries on a business within the jurisdiction (even if not personally within the jurisdiction); and

(3) that business is carried on in a name other than that individual's own name ("the business name").

9.2 The claim may be brought against the business name as if it were the name of a partnership.

Statement of truth

10.1 The form of a statement of truth is specified in paragraph 2.1 of Practice Direction 22. **7APD.10**

10.2 Attention is drawn to rule 32.14 which sets out the consequences of verifying a statement of case containing a false statement without an honest belief in its truth.

Extension of time

11.1 An application under rule 7.6 (for an extension of time for serving a claim form under rule 7.6(1)) must be made in accordance with Part 23 and supported by evidence. **7APD.11**

11.2 The evidence should state–

(1) all the circumstances relied on,

(2) the date of issue of the claim,

(3) the expiry date of any rule 7.6 extension, and

(4) a full explanation as to why the claim has not been served.

(For information regarding (1) written evidence see Part 32 and Practice Direction 32 and (2) service of the claim form see Part 6 and Practice Directions 6A and 6B.)

Notes on Practice Direction 7A (see Practice Direction 1A para.7 et seq.)

Not all cases over the financial limits specified by paras 2.1 and 2.2 will be suitable for trial in the High Court and some will be transferred elsewhere. The guidelines in this paragraph will assist the court in this exercise. **7APD.11.1**

This refers to writs of habeas corpus (except applications for a writ of habeas corpus for release relating to a minor, which are assigned to the Family Division), claims for judicial review, and certain other proceedings.

Almost all of the RSC and CCR Orders preserved in Schs 1 and 2 of the CPR have been replaced by Parts inserted in the CPR in the years since (see Vol.2 paras 12-27+ and 12-28+).

These paragraphs were added in October 2006 when Ord.81 was revoked from Sch.1, to give effect to rr.1, 2 and 9 of that Order.

5A The name of the firm—This must be the name at the time the cause of action accrued, not the name at the date of the proceedings. If the firm has been dissolved before proceedings are issued the claim can still be made against the former partners in the name of the dissolved firm. **7APD.11.2**

5B Partnership membership statements—This provision enables the other party to obtain information on the partners that may be necessary for security for costs or enforcement. The old rule specifically gave the court the power to order the provision of the statement. Presumably if the partnership fails to provide the statement in accordance with a request under the PD the party could make an application under Pt 23 seeking an order for compliance. **7APD.11.3**

5C Persons carrying on business in another name—This provision enables proceedings to be brought against a business even if the name of the individual or company who carry on that business is not known, providing the trading name is known. **7APD.11.4**

PRACTICE DIRECTION 7B—CONSUMER CREDIT ACT 2006—UNFAIR RELATIONSHIPS

Delete Practice Direction 7B–Consumer Credit Act 2006–Unfair Relationships (now relocated under Part 49 as PD 49C).

Change title of Practice Direction 7C–Production Centre:

PRACTICE DIRECTION 7B—PRODUCTION CENTRE

Renumber paragraphs 7CPD.1 to 7CPD.5.1 as paragraphs 7BPD.1 to 7BPD.5.1.

PRACTICE DIRECTION 7D—CLAIMS FOR THE RECOVERY OF TAXES AND DUTIES

Delete Practice Direction 7D–Claims for the Recovery of Taxes and Duties (now relocated under Part 49 as PD 49D).

Change title of Practice Direction 7E–Money Claims Online:

PRACTICE DIRECTION 7C—MONEY CLAIMS ONLINE

Renumber paragraphs 7EPD.1 to 7EPD.14 as paragraphs 7CPD.1 to 7CPD.14.

Editorial note on Practice Direction—Money Claim Online and Online Civil Money Claims Pilot Scheme

In the last paragraph, replace "PD 7E" with:
7CPD.14 PD 7C

PART 8

ALTERNATIVE PROCEDURE FOR CLAIMS

Editorial introduction

Replace the fifth paragraph (beginning "Rule 8.1 and para.3.1") with:
8.0.1 There are two distinct types of claim in which the Pt 8 procedure may be followed. The first category is where the claim seeks the court's decision on a question which is unlikely to involve a substantial dispute of fact. These claims will normally be heard and disposed of on written evidence. Claims for declarations as to the construction of documents, questions of law and administration of estates are usually appropriate for this procedure.

Replace the sixth paragraph (beginning "The second category") with:
The second category is where an Act, rule or practice direction requires or permits the use of alternative procedure, e.g. claims under the Inheritance (Provision for Family and Dependants) Act 1975 (CPR r.57.16(1)) or under s.50 of the Administration of Justice Act 1985 (CPR r.64.3). Claims in this category often require substantial disputes of fact to be resolved, so that disclosure and oral evidence may be needed, or in appropriate cases, a direction that the claim continue as a Pt 7 claim, e.g. *Havering LBC v Persons Unknown* [2021] EWHC 2648 (QB); [2021] 4 W.L.R. 135, a claim for an injunction under s.187B of the Town and Country Planning Act 1990 (required by PD 49E para.4.1 to be brought by Pt 8) against over 100 parties, in which the documentary evidence ran to thousands of pages–use of the Pt 8 procedure risked real unfairness.

At the end of the twelfth paragraph (beginning "Modifications to Pt 8"), replace "Admiralty and Commercial Courts Guide, Part B4." with:
Commercial Court Guide, Parts B4.45, B9.2(a) and B10.2(a).

Appeals

8.0.2 *After "Under", delete "the latest version of".*

Change title of paragraph: 8.0.3

Practice Direction 49E

Replace paragraph with:

Part 8 is supplemented by three Practice Directions. The first of them, PD 49E (Alternative Procedure for Claims) (see para.49EPD.1 and following below), replacing PD 8A with effect from 1 October 2022, is divided into three Sections. Section A (para.3) contains general provisions about claims and applications to which Pt 8 applies. As is explained in para.2.1, Section B (para.4) includes a table (following para.4.4) listing claims, petitions and applications under various enactments which must be made under Pt 8 and sets out specific procedural provisions for them, modifying those that would otherwise apply (generally directions indicating whether the appropriate originating process is by way of Pt 8 claim or Pt 23 application or by some other method, and in some instances indicating the person or body upon whom service of such process should be effected). Section C (paras 5.1 to 25.9) contains certain additions and modifications to the Pt 8 procedure that apply to the particular claims and applications identified in addition to those applied by directions in Section B.

Amendments, generally by way of adding directions to take account of proceedings under new or amended statutory provisions, or to remedy procedural difficulties that have emerged, are made to Sections B and C of PD 49E from time to time.

Change title of paragraph: 8.0.5

Practice Direction 49F: RTA and EL/PL Protocols Practice Direction

Replace "para.8BPD.0" with:

para.49FPD.0

Managing the claim

Replace the first paragraph with:

All Pt 8 claims are treated as allocated to the multi-track. Directions questionnaires are not 8.0.7
required in Pt 8 claims. In the Business and Property Courts in London, the claim is reviewed by the assigned Master after the time for acknowledgment of service has expired, or, if the time for filing the defendant's evidence has been extended, after the expiry of that period. If a defendant has not acknowledged service, the assigned Master will typically make an order in the form of **CH44**. Defendants who acknowledge service but do not intend to file evidence should notify the court in writing when they file their acknowledgment of service that they do not intend to file evidence. This enables the court to know what each defendant's intention is when it considers the file and avoids delay. If the claim is urgent or requires a hearing before a certain date, then on issue, the claimant should file a letter explaining this, and asking for the claim to be referred to the Master for review immediately on issue. The court may give directions immediately after the review in an appropriate case, or order a directions hearing.

In the Insolvency and Companies Court List ("ICL"), Pt 8 claims will be listed on issue for an initial hearing with a time estimate of 15 minutes, unless the claimant requests a longer hearing or invites the court to consider the claim on paper. The court will only determine Pt 8 claims on paper in clear cases in which the other parties have stated that they will not oppose the relief sought. The first hearing will take place before an ICC Judge, unless otherwise directed, at which the ICC Judge may decide some or all of the claim or give directions as to its future conduct.

Company directors' disqualification proceedings in the ICL follow a modified procedure. See Chancery Guide Ch.21 and Practice Direction: Directors Disqualification Proceedings.

In the B&PCs District Registries, local practice as to triage and case management may differ from that provided for in the Chancery Guide. See Practice Note: Business and Property Courts in Leeds, Liverpool, Manchester and Newcastle—
https://www.judiciary.uk/announcements/the-chancery-guide-2022/ [Accessed 11 August 2022]. Requests for an early review or guidance from a specialist B&PC District Judge should be sent to the court in question.

In *Kershaw v Roberts* [2014] EWHC 1037 (Ch); [2015] 1 All E.R. 734; [2014] 3 Costs L.R. 536 the court held that Pt 29 does not apply to Pt 8 claims that are not specifically allocated by the court to the multi-track, that CPR r.8.9(c) does not automatically allocate Pt 8 claims to the multi-track but merely provides that such claims are treated as so allocated, and that the express power in CPR r.29.3(1) to fix a case management conference is only triggered by the court's allocation to the multi-track.

Replace the last paragraph with:

Where a claim made under the Pt 8 procedure is a claim arising under the "Stage 3 procedure" provided for by the RTA Pre-Action Protocol or the E/PL Pre-Action Protocol the management of the claim is affected by the modifications made to Pt 8 by PD 49F (previously PD 8B). Parts 26 to 29 do not apply.

Disclosure

Replace paragraph with:

The disclosure pilot scheme (PD 57AD) applies to all claims issued in the B&PCs, but does not 8.0.7.1

directly apply to Part 8 claims. Part 8 has its own regime under which the documents relied upon by the parties are exhibited to their witness statements.

The only statement of case in a Part 8 claim is the claim form. Paragraph 5.1 of PD 57AD provides there is no obligation to give Initial Disclosure with the Part 8 claim form.

The court has power to make an order for extended disclosure under the pilot scheme in a Part 8 claim. It will adopt such elements of PD 57AD as are appropriate to the case and the scope of disclosure that is sought. The party requesting disclosure will need to identify the issues for disclosure and the Model or Models that apply. The full procedure for extended disclosure, including completion of all elements of the Disclosure Review Document, will not normally be required. See *Chief Master's Note: Disclosure Pilot and Part 8 Claims* (27 March 2019) para.5.

In the Queen's Bench Division, disclosure, if ordered, is governed by CPR Pt 31.

Costs management

Replace the first paragraph with:

8.0.8 The Civil Procedure (Amendment No.4) Rules 2014 (SI 2014/867) expressly provide that CPR r.3.12 and PD 3E apply, with exceptions, to all Pt 7 multi-track cases commenced on or after 22 April 2014. The effect of these provisions is to clarify that Pt 8 claims will not be subject to costs management unless there is a specific direction. Practice Direction 3E gives examples of types of non Pt 7 claims where the parties and the court should consider whether a costs management order should be sought or made. These include applications under the Trusts of Land and Appointment of Trustees Act 1996 and claims under the Inheritance (Provision for Family and Dependants) Act 1975 and, importantly, Pt 8 claims or applications involving a substantial dispute of fact and/or likely to require oral evidence and/or extensive disclosure; such cases are more appropriate to Pt 7 anyway.

In the second paragraph, replace the first sentence with:

Paragraph 5 of PD 3F contains detailed provisions in relation to costs capping orders in relation to trust funds (and "trust fund" includes the estate of a deceased person).

Determination of the claim

Replace the first sentence with:

8.0.9 The final hearing of a Pt 8 claim is referred to as a "disposal hearing".

Related sources

Replace list with:

8.0.10
- CPR r.79.5 (Modification of Part 8)
- Practice Direction 49E (Alternative Procedure for Claims)
- Practice Direction 49F (Pre-Action Protocols for Low Value Personal Injury Claims in Road Traffic Accidents and Low Value Personal Injury (Employers' Liability and Public Liability) Claims—Stage 3 Procedure)
- Practice Direction 54D (Planning Court Claims and Appeals to the Planning Court)
- **N208** Part 8 claim form
- **N208A** Part 8 notes for claimants
- **N208C** Part 8 notes for defendant
- **N209** Part 8 notice of issue
- Part 8 acknowledgment of service (**N210**)
- Stage 3 Procedure acknowledgment of service (**N201B**)
- Costs—Only Part 8 Claim (**N210A**)
- Chancery Guide (Chs 13, 21; Vol.2 paras 1A-136 and 1A-206)
- Queen's Bench Guide (paras 5.50 to 5.55; Section 8; Vol.2 para.1B-49)
- Commercial Court Guide (Parts B.5, B9.2(a), B10.2(a)) (see Vol.2 paras 2A-46, 2A-50 and 2A-51)
- Pre-Action Protocol for Low Value Personal Injury Claims in Road Traffic Accidents
- *Chief Master's Note: Disclosure Pilot and Part 8 Claims* (27 March 2019)
- Practice Note: Business and Property Courts in Leeds, Liverpool, Manchester and Newcastle—*https://www.judiciary.uk/announcements/the-chancery-guide-2022/*

Replace r.8.1 with:

Types of claim in which the Part 8 procedure is used[1]

8.1 **8.1—(1) The Part 8 procedure is the procedure set out in this Part.**

[1] Amended by the Civil Procedure (Amendment) Rules 2008 (SI 2008/2178), the Civil Procedure (Amendment) Rules 2011 (SI 2011/88), the Civil Procedure (Amendment) Rules 2014 (SI 2014/

(2) A claimant may, unless any enactment, rule or practice direction states otherwise, use the Part 8 procedure where they seek the court's decision on a question which is unlikely to involve a substantial dispute of fact.

(3) In the County Court, a claim under the Part 8 procedure may be made at any County Court hearing centre unless an enactment, rule or practice direction states otherwise.

(4) The court may at any stage order the claim to continue as if the claimant had not used the Part 8 procedure and, if it does so, the court may give any directions it considers appropriate.

(5) Where the claimant uses the Part 8 procedure, they may not obtain default judgment under Part 12.

(6) A rule or practice direction may, in relation to a specified type of proceedings, disapply or modify any of the rules set out in this Part as they apply to those proceedings.

(Rule 8.9 provides for other modifications to the general rules where the Part 8 procedure is being used.)

Change title of paragraph: 8.1.1

Rule 8.1: Effect of rule (as amended 1 October 2022)

Add new paragraph at start:

Rule 8.1 is amended by the Civil Procedure (Amendment No.2) Rules 2022 (SI 2022/783) with effect from 1 October 2022.

In the second paragraph, replace "Rule 8.1(2)(a)" with:

Rule 8.1(2)

Delete the third paragraph.

Replace the fourth paragraph (beginning "Rule 8.1(3) permits") with:

Rule 8.1(4) permits the court to order a claim to continue as if the Pt 8 procedure had not been used, for example in a case where a Pt 8 claim has been issued in the erroneous belief that there would be no substantial dispute of fact. In such a case the court will order that the claim continues as a Pt 7 claim, allocate to track and give directions. However, Sections B and C of Practice Direction 49E provide for the mandatory use of the Part 8 procedure for claims under certain statutes even where substantial disputes of fact may be involved, although by the nature of such claims this is unlikely.

Delete the fifth paragraph (beginning "The other types").

Replace the sixth paragraph (beginning "Paragraph (2A) was") with:

Rule 8.1(6) is important as setting out the authority of the practice direction by providing that such direction can require or permit the use of the Pt 8 procedure and that the practice direction may disapply or modify any Pt 8 rule. This is given effect in, for example, Section C of PD 49E.

At the start of the seventh paragraph (beginning "Prior to 31 December"), replace "Prior to" with:

Before

Replace the eighth paragraph (beginning "A claim made") with:

A claim made under the Stage 3 Procedure where the parties have followed the Pre-Action Protocol for Low Value Personal Injury Claims in Road Traffic Accidents is made under PD 49F where the procedure is set out (see para.8.0.5 and para.49FPD.0 below). The claim is made pursuant to Pt 8 as modified by PD 49F.

Costs-only proceedings

In the second paragraph, replace "PD 8B" with:

PD 49F 8.1.2

407), the Civil Procedure Rules 1998 (Amendment) (EU Exit) Regulations 2019 (SI 2019/521) and the Civil Procedure (Amendment No.2) Rules 2022 (SI 2022/783).

Contents of the claim form

Replace the penultimate paragraph with:

8.2.1 A Pt 8 claim form must be in practice form **N208**: PD 7A para.3.1. The claim form must state that Pt 8 applies: r.8.2(a); and either that the claimant wishes the claim to proceed under Pt 8 or the claim is required to proceed under Pt 8: PD 7A para.3.3. The burden is on the claimant to show that the claim is suitable for Pt 8 procedure.

At the end of the last paragraph, replace "(Johnson J), and para.4.1 of PD 8A." with:

(Johnson J).

No party to be served

Replace the first paragraph with:

8.2A.1 Rule 8.2A accommodates a previous gap in Pt 8 procedure for cases in which it is wished to issue a claim without naming a defendant, e.g. where there is no person to be served, such as applications for payment or transfers of monies into court, or where the court is asked to make an order to assist executors who are unable to locate beneficiaries named in a will.

Where permission is needed, it should be sought by application notice in accordance with Pt 23, before issuing the claim. The application should be listed before a Master. The evidence should carefully explain why the order is appropriate and be accompanied by the proposed claim form. In a simple case the Master may be willing to deal with it on paper. The Master will give directions for the future conduct of the case on the application. See Chancery Guide para.13.38.

No practice direction having general application has been made pursuant to r.8.2A(1). However, there are specific rules and practice directions which set out the circumstances in which a claim form may be issued under Pt 8 without naming a defendant. These are set out at para.13.36 of the Chancery Guide.

Replace the last two paragraphs with:

In *Barking and Dagenham LBC v Persons Unknown* [2022] EWCA Civ 13; [2022] 2 W.L.R. 946, the Court of Appeal reviewed and clarified the safeguards in claims for wide injunctions against "persons unknown" (typically aimed at the travelling community) prohibiting unauthorised occupation or use of land.

Rule 8.3

At the end of the paragraph, replace "acknowledgment of service (PD 8A para.5.3)." with:

8.3.1 acknowledgment of service.

Responding to claim

In the last paragraph, replace "[Accessed 3 February 2022]" with:

8.4.1 [Accessed 11 August 2022]

Add new paragraph at end:

A defendant who files their acknowledgment of service out of time may not rely upon the 14-day period in CPR r.11(4)(a) to make an application challenging the court's jurisdiction in order to delay a disposal hearing of a Part 8 claim: *Mansard Mortgages 2007-2 Plc v Beyat Holdings Ltd* [2021] EWHC 3355 (Ch).

Replace r.8.5 with:

Filing and serving written evidence[1]

8.5 **8.5—(1) When the claimant files the claim form, they must also file any written evidence on which they intend to rely.**

(2) The claimant must serve their written evidence on the defendant with the claim form.

(3) A defendant who wishes to rely on written evidence must file it when they file their acknowledgment of service.

(4) If they do so, they must also, at the same time, serve a copy of their evidence on the other parties.

(5) The claimant may, within 14 days of service of the defendant's evidence on them, file further written evidence in reply.

[1] Amended by the Civil Procedure (Amendment No.2) Rules 2022 (SI 2022/783).

(6) If they do so, they must also, within the same time limit, serve a copy of their evidence on the other parties.

(7) The claimant may rely on the matters set out in the claim form as evidence under this rule if the claim form is verified by a statement of truth.

(8) A party may apply to the court for an extension of time to serve and file evidence or for permission to serve and file additional evidence under rule 8.6(1).

(9) The parties may agree in writing on an extension of time of not more than 14 days for serving and filing evidence from the defendant and of not more than 28 days for serving and filing evidence in reply.

(10) Any such agreement must be filed with the court with the acknowledgement of service or, if it relates to evidence in reply, within 48 hours of the agreement.

Filing and serving written evidence

Add new paragraph 8.5.0:

Rule 8.5 is amended by the Civil Procedure (Amendment No.2) Rules 2022 (SI 2022/783) with effect from 1 October 2022. **8.5.0**

Defendant's evidence

Replace the first paragraph with:

Similarly, the defendant must file and serve their evidence with their acknowledgment of service. Rule 8.5(4) gives 14 days in which the claimant can serve evidence in reply. Rule 8.5(8) provides that any party may apply for an extension of time to serve and file evidence and r.8.5(9) makes provision for the parties agreeing between themselves an extension of time for serving and filing evidence under r.8.5(3) or 8.5(5). Rule 8.5(9) imposes time limits to such agreement and r.8.5(10) requires any agreement extending time to be filed with the court by the defendant with their acknowledgment of service, or, if it relates to evidence in reply, within 48 hours of the agreement. This is consistent with the court managing the case. Attention is drawn to section E in Form **N210**. This section must be completed in order to assist the court in managing the claim. **8.5.2**

If an extension cannot be agreed, or a longer extension than is permitted by agreement is required, an application should be made to the court. In substantial matters the court will normally be willing to grant a reasonable extension.

Timings

Replace paragraph with:

Timings are important and are set out in this rule. In summary the claimant must be ready to serve all their evidence with their claim form. The defendant then has 14 days from service on them to file and serve their acknowledgment of service, and any evidence in reply by the claimant must be filed and served within 14 days of service of the acknowledgment of service by the defendant. Attention is drawn to the provisions of r.8.5(9) concerning the limits on agreements to extend time. A defendant who does not intend to file evidence should expressly notify the court of that in the acknowledgment of service. **8.5.3**

Procedure where defendant objects to use Part 8 procedure

In the second paragraph, after "issues of fact, and", replace "incurs a defendant in costs will be likely to be the subject to an order for summary assessment of costs." with:

causes a defendant to incur costs that are wasted will be likely to be the subject to an order to pay those costs. **8.8.1**

Editorial note

Replace "(r.12.2)" with:

(r.8.1(5)) **8.9.1**

PRACTICE DIRECTION 8A—ALTERNATIVE PROCEDURE FOR CLAIMS

Delete Practice Direction 8A–Alternative Procedure for Claims (now relocated under Part 49 as PD 49E).

PRACTICE DIRECTION 8B—PRE-ACTION PROTOCOL FOR LOW VLAUE PERSONAL INJURY CLAIMS IN ROAD TRAFFIC ACCIDENTS AND LOW VALUE PERSONAL INJURY (EMPLOYERS' LIABILITY AND PUBLIC LIABILITY) CLAIMS—STAGE 3 PROCEDURE

Delete Practice Direction 8B–Pre-Action Protocol for Low Value Personal Injury Claims in Road Traffic Accidents and Low Value Personal Injury (Employers' Liability and Public Liability) Claims–Stage 3 Procedure (now relocated under Part 49 as PD 49F).

PART 9

RESPONDING TO PARTICULARS OF CLAIM—GENERAL

Rule 9.1: Effect of rule

At the end of the paragraph, replace "claim." with:

9.1.1 claim once they have been served on them.

Irregular default judgment

Replace paragraph with:

9.1.2 Unfortunately, r.9.1(2) is still not as widely known as it should be. A claimant who has not served particulars of claim is in error in entering judgment because the defendant has not acknowledged the claim form (see also r.10.3(1)). The defendant would have an unanswerable application to set aside such a default judgment (likely with costs) under r.13.2.

Electronic communication and filing of documents

Replace paragraph with:

9.2.3 For special provisions dealing with the filing by electronic means, in particular circumstances, of documents to which Pt 9 applies, see PD 7B—Production Centre (para.7BPD.1), PD 7C—Money Claims Online (para.7CPD.1), PD 51O—The Electronic Working Pilot Scheme (para.51OPD.1) and PD 51ZB—The Damages Claims Pilot (para.51ZBPD.1).

PART 10

ACKNOWLEDGMENT OF SERVICE

Forms

Replace the second sentence with:

10.0.3 In most cases this will be Form N9 but there are other equivalent forms used in specialist proceedings. See the Civil Procedure Rules: Forms page at *https://www.gov.uk/guidance/civil-procedure-rules-forms* [Accessed 25 August 2022].

"Filing"

Add new paragraph at end:

10.1.1 Where the claim has been issued via the Damages Claims Portal pursuant to PD 51ZB (The Damages Claims Pilot), acknowledgment must be given through the Damages Claim Portal (see PD 51ZB para.5(2)).

PART 11

DISPUTING THE COURT'S JURISDICTION

Rule 11(2) and (4): Filing acknowledgment of service and making application

In the first paragraph, after the second sentence, add:

11.1.4 Where the claim has been issued via the Damages Claims Portal pursuant to PD 51ZB (The

Damages Claims Pilot), acknowledgment must be given through the Damages Claim Portal (see PD 51ZB para.5(2)).

Jurisdiction agreements—relevance to a Pt 11 application

In the fourth paragraph, replace list items 1. to 3. with:

1. Where there is a jurisdiction agreement in favour of the English court, that court will almost certainly have jurisdiction pursuant to the Judgments Regulation provided that proceedings were commenced before the end of the implementation period established by the Withdrawal Agreement (which ended on 31 December 2020) (unless for example it is not a civil or commercial matter and therefore falls outside the scope of the Regulation, but that will be rare in a case where a jurisdiction agreement is concerned) and will be bound to give effect to the clause regardless of whether it considers there is a more appropriate forum for the dispute to be heard. In those circumstances, if the defendant is outside the jurisdiction, it can be served with proceedings without the need for the court's permission. Where the claimant has invoked the English court's jurisdiction on the basis of an English jurisdiction agreement falling within the Judgments Regulation, and regardless of whether proceedings have been served within or without the jurisdiction, an application under Pt 11 is likely to turn on whether the dispute is indeed subject to a valid English jurisdiction agreement falling within the Judgments Regulation. There may also be arguments that, if the English court does have jurisdiction on that basis, the court should not exercise that jurisdiction, pursuant either to the "lis pendens–related actions" rules under arts 29 to 31 of the Judgments Regulation (particularly where the clause is non-exclusive) or the broadly similar (but not identical) rules under arts 27 to 30 of the Lugano Convention, or under some residual discretion. See further paras 6.33.2, 6.33.9, 6JRx.34+ to 6JRx.37+, 6JRx.40+ to 6JRx.46+. **11.1.11**
2. If there is a jurisdiction agreement in favour of the English court but the Judgments Regulation does not apply (and nor does either of its predecessors, the Brussels I Regulation or Brussels Convention: see para.6.30.4 above) so that the case is subject to the common law rules on jurisdiction, the existence of the jurisdiction agreement will be relevant to the question of whether there is a good arguable case that the claimant's claim falls within para.3.1(6)(d) of PD 6B (see para.6HJ.20), and also as a factor relevant to the question whether England is the forum conveniens. This is considered further at para.11.1.14 below.
3. Where there is an exclusive jurisdiction agreement in favour of an EU Member State court, again, that court will almost certainly have jurisdiction pursuant to the Judgments Regulation (if proceedings were commenced before the implementation period established by the Withdrawal Agreement) and will have jurisdiction pursuant to the Hague Convention if the proceedings have been commenced subsequently and those proceedings fall within its scope. In either case, the English court will be bound to give effect to the clause regardless of whether it considers the English court to be a more appropriate forum. In these circumstances, if the claimant has invoked the jurisdiction of the English court despite such a clause, and regardless of whether proceedings have been served within or without the jurisdiction and with or without the court's permission, the defendant may bring an application under Pt 11 to challenge the court's jurisdiction on that basis. The application will turn on whether the dispute is indeed subject to a valid exclusive jurisdiction agreement in favour of an EU Member State court falling within the Judgments Regulation or the Hague Convention. However, if proceedings have been, or are subsequently, commenced in the chosen forum and the Judgments Regulation applies, the English court will not determine the question of jurisdiction; it will be bound to stay its proceedings, under art.31(2) of the Judgments Regulation, unless and until the chosen court declares that it has no jurisdiction under the agreement. See further paras 6JRx.34+ to 6JRx.37+.

PART 12

DEFAULT JUDGMENT

Revision of Part 12

In the first sentence, replace "Civil Procedure Rules 1998 (Amendment) (EU Exit) Regulations" with:

Civil Procedure Rules 1998 (Amendment) (EU Exit) Regulations 2019 (SI 2019/521) **12.0.2**

Scope of provision

Replace the last sentence with:

Examples (previously listed in the now deleted PD 12) include admiralty proceedings, arbitration **12.2.1** proceedings, contentious probate proceedings, claims for provisional damages and (see r.55.7(4)) possession proceedings.

Replace r.12.3(3)(b) with:

Conditions to be satisfied[1]

12.3 **(b) the defendant has satisfied the whole claim (including any claim for costs) on which the claimant is seeking judgment;**

(c) (i) the claimant is seeking judgment on a claim for money; and

(ii) the defendant has filed or served on the claimant an admission under rule 14.4 or 14.7 (admission of liability to pay all of the money claimed) together with a request for time to pay; or

"judgment in default of an acknowledgment of service"

Replace the second paragraph with:

12.3.1 In r.12.3(1) the words "at the date on which judgment is entered" were originally introduced by the Civil Procedure (Amendment) Rules 2020 (SI 2020/82) with effect from 6 April 2020. They make it clear that a default judgment may only be obtained where, at the time judgment is entered, no acknowledgment of service or defence has been filed and the time for acknowledging service has expired. This resolves the previously uncertain construction of r.12.3(1) which had been capable of different interpretations, notably summarised in *Cunico Resources NV v Daskalakis* [2018] EWHC 3382 (Comm). The same new wording was also introduced into r.12.3(2) in relation to judgments in default of defence (see para.12.3.3 below). Rule 12.3(2) now qualifies "defence" with the words "or any document intended to be a defence", as in r.12.1(b) (see para.12.1.1 above). It is not clear if r.12.3(1)(a) should be read in the same way, but there would seem little purpose in the rule making any distinction.

In the third paragraph, delete the second sentence.

"strike out or summary judgment"

In the first sentence, after "out under r.3.4", replace "and/or" with:

12.3.4 or

"a specified amount of money"

Replace the second paragraph with:

12.4.3 A common example is a claim arising out of a road traffic accident where no personal injury ensued. Claiming the cost of, e.g. repairs and/or hire-car charges as "a specified amount of money" enables a claimant to obtain a default judgment for that sum thus avoiding a "disposal hearing" held in accordance with PD 26 para.12.4. It is the better practice to claim a specified sum in such cases. Similarly, in *Merito Financial Services Ltd v Yelloly* [2016] EWHC 2067 (Ch) it was held on an application under r.12.4(2)(a) (replaced by what is now r.12.4(3)(a)), in which the claimant relied on r.12.11(1) (replaced by what is now r.12.12(1)), that there was nothing to prevent loss and damage caused by a breach of duty from being claimed as "a specified amount of money" for the purposes of Pt 12.

Defendant's date of birth

Replace paragraph with:

12.4.8 Under r.12.4(3), the claimant is required to provide the defendant's date of birth (if they know it) when they apply under Pt 23 for a default judgment (as is also now required under r.12.4(2) in requests under r.12.4(1)—see para.12.4.1 above). This could be of particular relevance to any directions the court might give as to service of the application or subsequent enforcement.

---

[1] Amended by the Civil Procedure (Amendment) Rules 2000 (SI 2000/221), the Civil Procedure (Amendment No.2) Rules 2001 (SI 2001/1388), the Civil Procedure (Amendment) Rules 2008 (SI 2008/2178), the Civil Procedure (Amendment No.5) Rules 2013 (SI 2013/1571), the Civil Procedure Rules 1998 (Amendment) (EU Exit) Regulations 2019 (SI 2019/521), the Civil Procedure (Amendment) Rules 2020 (SI 2020/82), the Civil Procedure (Amendment) Rules 2022 (SI 2022/101) and the Civil Procedure (Amendment No.2) Rules 2022 (SI 2022/783).

Replace r.12.7(1)(b) with:

Interest[1]

(b) where interest is claimed under section 35A of the Senior Courts Act 1981 or section 69 of the County Courts Act 1984, the rate is no higher than the rate of interest payable on judgment debts at the date when the claim form was issued; and **12.7**

Rule 12.9: Effect of rule

In the second paragraph, replace the second sentence with:

Accordingly, where a claimant has a claim against a number of defendants, not in the alternative but on a several basis, the case falls not within r.12.9(2)(b), but within r.12.9(2)(a) (*Otkritie International Investment Management Ltd v Urumov* [2012] EWHC 890 (Comm) (Flaux J)). **12.9.1**

Replace r.12.11(a) with:

Default judgment obtained by making an application[2]

(a) the claim is— **12.11**

(i) a claim against a child or protected party; or

(ii) a claim in tort by one spouse or civil partner against the other;

Rule 12.11: Effect of rule

Replace the penultimate paragraph with:

Prior to 31 December 2020, r.12.10(b)(i) and (ii) (now r.12.11(b)(i) and (ii)) made reference to provisions in r.6.33(1) and (2) concerning cases where the court's permission was not required to serve a claim form out of the jurisdiction under the Judgments Regulation or the Brussels or Lugano Conventions. These provisions were deleted by reg.6(3) of the Civil Procedure Rules 1998 (Amendment) (EU Exit) Regulations 2019 (SI 2019/521) as amended by the Civil, Criminal and Family Justice (Amendment) (EU Exit) Regulations 2020 (SI 2020/1493), which contains the transitional provisions in relation to CPR Pt 12. Regulation 19 provides: **12.11.1**

> "Where before IP completion day a claim was served out of the jurisdiction without requiring permission of the court under any of the provisions of rule 6.33, rules 12.10 and 12.11 [now rr.12.11 and 12.12] apply on and after IP completion day in relation to an application for default judgment as if the amendments made to those rules by these Regulations had not been made."

Replace r.12.12(8)(c) with:

Supplementary provisions where applications for default judgment are made[3]

(c) where paragraph (8)(b) permits a judgment or an application notice to be served out of the jurisdiction, the procedure for serving the judgment or the application notice is the same as for serving a claim form under Section III of Part 6 except where an alternative method of service has been agreed under section 12(6) of the State Immunity Act 1978. **12.12**

---

[1] Amended by the Civil Procedure (Amendment) Rules 2022 (SI 2022/101) and the Civil Procedure (Amendment No.2) Rules 2022 (SI 2022/783).

[2] Amended by the Civil Procedure (Amendment No.2) Rules 2000 (SI 2000/940), the Civil Procedure (Amendment No.5) Rules 2001 (SI 2001/4015), the Civil Procedure (Amendment No.3) Rules 2005 (SI 2005/2292), the Civil Jurisdiction and Judgments Regulations 2007 (SI 2007/1655), the Civil Procedure (Amendment) Rules 2007 (SI 2007/2204), the Civil Procedure (Amendment) Rules 2008 (SI 2008/2178), the Civil Jurisdiction and Judgments Regulations 2009 (SI 2009/3131), the Civil Jurisdiction and Judgments (Hague Convention on Choice of Court Agreements 2005) Regulations 2015 (SI 2015/1644), the Civil Procedure Rules 1998 (Amendment) (EU Exit) Regulations 2019 (SI 2019/521), the Civil Procedure (Amendment) Rules 2021 (SI 2021/117), the Civil Procedure (Amendment) Rules 2022 (SI 2022/101) and the Civil Procedure (Amendment No.2) Rules 2022 (SI 2022/783).

[3] Introduced by the Civil Procedure (Amendment) Rules 2022 (SI 2022/101) and amended by the Civil Procedure (Amendment No.2) Rules 2022 (SI 2022/783).

Scope of provision

Replace the first paragraph with:

12.12.1 Rule 12.12 should be read in conjunction with the new r.12.11. It is a new and largely self-explanatory rule which helpfully amalgamates provisions from the old r.12.11 and the now deleted PD 12 as to the nature and requirements of applications for default judgment, including those made against defendants who are outside the jurisdiction of England and Wales. It reflects the transitional "Brexit" provisions contained in the Civil Procedure Rules 1998 (Amendment) (EU Exit) Regulations 2019 (SI 2019/521) as amended by the Civil, Criminal and Family Justice (Amendment) (EU Exit) Regulations 2020 (SI 2020/1493) (see para.12.11.1 above).

PART 13

SETTING ASIDE OR VARYING DEFAULT JUDGMENT

Rule 13.3(2): need to act promptly

In the eighth paragraph (beginning "In Khan v Edgbaston Holdings"), replace "Regency Rolls Ltd v Carnall (Security for Costs) 22 June 2000, unrep.," with:

13.3.3 *Regency Rolls Ltd v Carnall* [2000] EWCA Civ 379,

PART 14

ADMISSIONS

Editorial introduction

Replace paragraph with:

14.0.1 Part 14 now covers three separate situations. First, "formal" admissions (typically an admission made in a defence); secondly, pre-action admissions made after 6 April 2007 either after receipt of a letter of claim under one of the three pre-action protocols listed in PD 14 para.1.1(2) or, if made before a letter of claim is received, stated to be made under Pt 14; and thirdly a debtor's admission of a debt (usually accompanied by an offer to pay by instalments) on a form provided by the court and served with the claim form. In the first case the appropriate judgment can be obtained by an application to the court under r.14.3. In the second case judgment can be obtained on the pre-action admission by an application made under Pt 23. In both instances the application will be heard by a District Judge or, if in the High Court in London, by a Master. In the third case there is usually no judicial input and judgment is obtained administratively. Rule 14.1B was introduced upon the coming into effect on 30 April 2010 of the Pre-action Protocol for Low Value Personal Injury Claims in Road Traffic Accidents. It was amended, first when the Pre-action Protocol for Low Value Personal Injury (Employers' Liability and Public Liability) Claims was introduced in 30 July 2013, and again after the introduction of the RTA Small Claims Protocol with effect from 31 May 2021.

"claimant has a right to enter judgment"

Replace paragraph with:

14.1.7 The claimant's right to enter judgment on an admission pursuant to r.14.1(4) is subject only to the usual requirement pursuant to r.21.10, where the defendant is a child or protected party, or the claimant is a child or protected party and the admission is under r.14.5 or r.14.7 (but note that if the admission is under r.14.4 or r.14.6 in a case involving a child or protected party, an application to the court is still necessary: see Pt 21—Children and Protected Parties, and Pt 23—General Rules about Applications for Court Orders). Otherwise—i.e. in the vast majority of cases—the claimant has a right to enter judgment. Judgment is obtained merely by completing the appropriate court form (see rr.14.4(3), 14.5(6), 14.6(4) and 14.7(5)). Judgment is entered administratively by a member of the court staff without any judicial input.

Examples of the approach in different cases

Replace the third paragraph with:

14.1.9 In *Co-operative Group Ltd v Carillion JM Ltd* [2014] EWHC 837 (TCC), Akenhead J refused an application for permission under r.14.1(5) to withdraw an admission made by the defendant on expert advice, where the defence had since been taken over by the third party who was seeking to alter the terms of the defence in its own interests so as to avoid having to indemnify the defendant under the terms of a settlement agreement. In addition, the application was made far too late in the proceedings.

Pre-action admissions made after 6 April 2007

At the start of the paragraph, replace "The new rule was implemented" with:

This rule was implemented in April 2007 **14.1A.1**

Rule 14.1A

In the second paragraph, after "strictly r.14.1A(3)-(5) only", replace "applies" with:

apply **14.1A.3**

Rule 14.1B: Effect of rule

Replace the second paragraph with:

Details of these Protocols can be found in Section C below in Vol.1. They describe the behaviour **14.1B.1** the court expects of the parties before the start of proceedings in each of the types of claim covered. The pre-action processes prescribed by the RTA Protocol and the EL/PL Protocol are structured in the same way, in that each is divided into Stage 1 and Stage 2. Where those Stages are exhausted and court proceedings are commenced, the claim enters Stage 3, that is to say, proceedings may be started in accordance with the modified Pt 8 procedure provided for in PD 49F. Rules in Pt 14 make provision for admissions generally, whether before or after the commencement of proceedings. Rule 14.1B makes special provision for the withdrawal, either before or after the "commencement of proceedings", of certain pre-commencement admissions made by defendants in the course of progress through the Stage 1 and Stage 2 stages of the RTA Protocol and the EL/PL Protocol. The rule draws a distinction between admissions "of causation" and other admissions (which may include admissions of liability). In this context, "proceedings" obviously includes proceedings started under the Stage 3 Procedure, but it also includes proceedings commenced under Pt 7. As is explained in commentary on PD 49F, provisions in that practice direction and in the RTA Protocol and EL/PL Protocol state that, in the case of a claim to which either Protocol applies, a claimant may start proceedings under Pt 8 where compliance by the parties with the relevant Protocol may not be possible before the expiry of the primary limitation period (see para.49FPD.16.1 above). It would seem that proceedings commenced in this way and for those purposes are not "proceedings" within the meaning of r.14.1B.

Rule 14.3: Effect of rule

After the first paragraph, add new paragraph:

It appears that the dismissal of an application for judgment on an admission does not in itself **14.3.2** prevent the applicant from pursuing a claim for judgment for the same remedy at trial. In *Valley View Health Centre v NHS Property Services Ltd* [2022] EWHC 1393 (Ch) the claimants had been unsuccessful in their applications under r.14.3 for declarations based on the defendant's admissions in the defences but later sought the same remedies (among others) at trial. After reviewing the principles governing the ability of a party to relitigate an issue ("res judicata") (*Virgin Atlantic Airways Ltd v Premium Aircraft Interiors UK Ltd* [2013] UKSC 46; [2014] A.C. 160 referred to), Edwin Johnson J held (at [562]-[587]) that although the claimants' earlier applications had been dismissed, the claim itself had not been dismissed and it was therefore not an abuse of process to pursue declarations at trial. At trial the court was in a fundamentally different position to that of the court hearing the interim applications: at the interim stage, the applications were not treated as the hearing of a preliminary issue and the parties were not required, and could not reasonably be expected, to deploy all the evidence and arguments on which they might wish to rely at trial. Nor, it was held for the same reasons, had any cause of action estoppel arisen in this case: although the applications for judgment on admissions had failed, the causes of action had not been struck out nor had summary judgment to the defendant been awarded. On the facts of this case, therefore (i.e. where the original applications had been solely for judgment on admissions and not for, e.g. judgment on a preliminary issue), it was open to the claimants to pursue the remedies again at trial.

"specified amount of money"

Replace the last sentence with:

In this case, or indeed any other where the claimant claims a "specified amount of money", if **14.4.2** the defendant admits not only the claim but also the specified sum they can make an admission and r.14.4 applies.

"the court will serve a notice"

Replace the second sentence with:

14.5.5 It is therefore the court's task to notify the claimant of the partial admission by sending a Form **N225A**.

Acceptance of partial admission

Replace paragraph with:

14.5.6 If the claimant accepts the partial admission, note that it is not sufficient to merely return the notice in accordance with r.14.5(3) and (4). They must also file "a request in the relevant practice form" in accordance with r.14.5(6) in order to obtain judgment. The relevant form is **N225**.

"filing an admission"

Replace paragraph with:

14.6.3 As in r.14.5(2) but in contrast with r.14.4(2), the rule requires the defendant to file the admission with the court and the court to serve a copy on the claimant.

Disposal hearing

Replace paragraph with:

14.6.6 Paragraph 12.2 of PD 26 (see para.26PD.12) enables the court to order a disposal hearing. At a disposal hearing the court may give directions or decide the amount payable (see para.26PD.12 para.12.4). See further, para.12.8.6.

Scope of provision

Replace paragraph with:

14.8.1 Rules 14.6 and 14.7 apply where the claim is for an "unspecified amount of money" and the defendant admits liability. One of the permutations which can arise is a judgment for an amount to be decided by the court. Rule 14.8 requires the court to give appropriate directions for trial of the issue of damages. In particular the court will have to consider the need for disclosure, exchange of witness statements and permission for either party to call expert evidence or rely on an expert's report. (See generally, Pt 31—Disclosure and Inspection of Documents, Pt 32—Evidence and Pt 35—Experts and Assessors.) Clearly the giving of directions is important. As r.14.8(b) recognises it may not always be appropriate to allocate the case to a specific track. Allocation could be important, however, as it can have costs consequences. For the scope of each track see r.26.6. For example, a case will normally only be allocated to the fast-track if within the financial limits (see r.26.6(4)) and if it can be concluded in one day (r.26.6(5)). There will be costs limitations if the case is allocated to the small claims track (see r.27.14). However, the court does have some discretion as to the choice of track (see rr.26.7 and 26.8). See generally Pt 26, and, in particular, at para.26PD.12. Cases within the financial limits of the small claims track are usually allocated to that track (the court considering it "appropriate" pursuant to r.14.8(1)(b)) so as to keep the costs within the very limited costs regime of that track.

"request for time to pay"

Replace paragraph with:

14.9.1 A request by the defendant for time to pay an admitted claim is a very common occurrence in practice. Rule 14.9 applies to three distinct situations which all have the common feature of a defendant's request for time to pay, namely under r.14.4 (admission of whole of claim for a specified amount of money); under r.14.5 (admission of part of claim for a specified amount of money which the claimant is accepting in full settlement of the claim); and under r.14.7 (admission of liability in a claim for an unspecified amount of money where the defendant also offers a sum in satisfaction of the claim which the claimant is accepting). A "request for time to pay" is defined in r.14.9(2).

Scope of provision

Replace paragraph with:

14.9.2 Rule 14.9 applies to the three situations specified in r.14.9(1) (see commentary above) where the defendant has made a request for time to pay and the claimant is agreeing to that request (if they are not agreeing to it, r.14.10 will apply). The rule enables judgment to be obtained administratively without the need for a hearing or any judicial input.

"time and rate of payment determined by the court"

Replace paragraph with:

14.10.5 In most cases this is done by a court officer, not a judge (see r.14.11). The court officer works to prescribed guidelines. For the right to have the payment rate re-determined by a judge see r.14.13.

For variation of orders to pay by instalments see CCR Ord.22 r.10 (contained in Sch.2 to the CPR) and para.14PD.6. Note also r.40.11 (Time for complying with a judgment or order) and commentary following that rule.

Variation

Replace paragraph with:
Variation of an order is governed by CCR Ord.22 r.10 (see Sch.2 to the CPR) and by PD 14 para.6.1. **14.11.3**

With a hearing

In the first sentence, replace "at least 7 days notice" with:
at least 7 days' notice **14.12.3**

Scope of provision

Replace the last paragraph with:
Rule 14.13 does not apply to a determination by a judge at a hearing pursuant to r.14.12(2) or (2A). In such a case a dissatisfied party must accept the decision or appeal. For variation of an order see CCR Ord.22 r.10 (contained in Sch.2 to the CPR) and PD 14 para.6.1. **14.13.1**

"defendant's home court"

In the second paragraph, replace "For "preferred court" see" with:
For "preferred hearing centre" see **14.13.3**

Evidence of means

Replace "a claimant's plea that" with:
a claimant's plea that, e.g. **14.13.4**

"Judgment under rule 14.4"

In the last sentence, delete "reasonable". **14.14.4**

PART 15

DEFENCE AND REPLY

Editorial introduction

Add new paragraph at end:
The Civil Procedure (Amendment No.2) Rules 2022 (SI 2022/783), in force from 1 October 2022, provide an entirely new and substituted Pt 15 (and remove the former PD 15 on the basis it did not add anything). A significant new rule makes clear that a defendant who applies for summary judgment or to strike out a claim need not file a defence before the application is heard. This is already the case for summary judgment but the rules were unclear if the application was only for strike out. **15.0.1**

Related sources

Delete the first bullet point ("Practice Direction (Defence and Reply), see para.15PD.1, below"). **15.0.2**

Delete paragraph 15.0.3, "Practice Direction".

Replace r.15.1 with:

Part not to apply where claimant uses Part 8 procedure[1]

15.1 This Part does not apply where the claimant uses the procedure set out in Part 8. **15.1**

[1] Amended by the Civil Procedure (Amendment No.2) Rules 2022 (SI 2022/783).

Replace r.15.2 with:

Filing a defence[1]

15.2 **15.2 A defendant who wishes to defend all or part of a claim must file a defence.**

(Part 14 contains further provisions which apply where the defendant admits a claim.)

Replace r.15.3 with:

Consequence of not filing a defence[2]

15.3 **15.3 If a defendant fails to file a defence, the claimant may obtain default judgment if Part 12 allows it.**

Replace r.15.4 with:

The period for filing a defence[3]

15.4 **15.4—(1) The general rule is that the period for filing a defence is—**

(a) 14 days after service of the particulars of claim; or

(b) if the defendant files an acknowledgment of service under Part 10, 28 days after service of the particulars of claim.

(2) The general rule is subject to rules 3.4(7), 6.12(3), 6.35, 11 and 24.4(2).

Replace r.15.5 with:

Agreement extending the period for filing a defence[4]

15.5 **15.5—(1) The defendant and the claimant may agree to extend the period for filing a defence specified inrule 15.4 by up to 28 days.**

(2) Where the defendant and the claimant agree to extend the period for filing a defence, the defendant must notify the court in writing.

Replace r.15.6 with:

Service of copy of defence[5]

15.6 **15.6 A copy of the defence must be served on every other party.**

(Part 16 sets out what a defence must contain.)

"a copy of the defence must be served"

Add new paragraph at end:

15.6.1 Where the claim has been issued via the Damages Claims Portal pursuant to PD 51ZB (The Damages Claims Pilot), a defendant who wishes to defend the claim must submit their defence through the Damages Claim Portal and upload any documents which the defendant wishes or is required to file with the defence. (See PD 51ZB para.6(5).)

Replace r.15.7 with:

Making a counterclaim[6]

15.7 **15.7 Part 20 applies to a defendant who wishes to make a counterclaim. Where a defendant serves a counterclaim the defence and counterclaim should normally form one document with the counterclaim following the defence.**

---

[1] Amended by the Civil Procedure (Amendment No.2) Rules 2022 (SI 2022/783).

[2] Amended by the Civil Procedure (Amendment No.2) Rules 2022 (SI 2022/783).

[3] Amended by the Civil Procedure (Amendment No.2) Rules 2000 (SI 2000/940), the Civil Procedure (Amendment) Rules 2008 (SI 2008/2178) and the Civil Procedure (Amendment No.2) Rules 2022 (SI 2022/783).

[4] Amended by the Civil Procedure (Amendment No.2) Rules 2022 (SI 2022/783).

[5] Amended by the Civil Procedure (Amendment No.3) Rules 2000 (SI 2000/1317), the Civil Procedure (Amendment No.2) Rules 2009 (SI 2009/3390), the Civil Procedure (Amendment No.7) Rules 2013 (SI 2013/1974) and the Civil Procedure (Amendment No.2) Rules 2022 (SI 2022/783).

[6] Amended by the Civil Procedure (Amendment No.2) Rules 2022 (SI 2022/783).

"counterclaim"

Replace paragraph with:

This term is defined in the glossary (see Section E below). A defendant may make a counterclaim against a claimant by filing particulars of the counterclaim (r.20.4). Rule 15.8 provides that the counterclaim should appear in the same document as any reply, providing the dates for each falling due are the same. **15.7.1**

Time for defence to a counterclaim

Replace paragraph with:

The period for filing a defence to counterclaim is not expressly stipulated the revised Pt 15, as incorporated by the Civil Procedure (Amendment No.2) Rules 2022 (SI 2022/783), but it is submitted the logical period would be the same 14-day period as stipulated at r.15.4(1)(a), thus treating both counterclaim and particulars of claim as statements of case. Rule 15.8 however does expressly contemplate a defence to counterclaim in the context of forming part of a reply to defence, if one is relied upon, clarifying that both should form one document with the reply coming first. The possibility of reply and defence to counterclaim being separate documents is contemplated at r.15.8(b) if "the dates on which they are due to be filed differ from one another". It is suggested that a claimant that wants to rely upon a reply but not serve it alongside any defence to counterclaim (instead filing with the directions questionnaire per r.15.8(a)) should make this clear to other parties to avoid later misunderstanding. **15.7.3**

Replace r.15.8 with:

Reply to defence and defence to counterclaim[1]

15.8 If a claimant files a reply to the defence— **15.8**

(a) the claimant must—

(i) file the reply with a directions questionnaire; and

(ii) serve the reply on the other parties at the same time as it is filed; and

(b) the reply should form one document with any defence to counterclaim, with the defence to counterclaim following the reply, unless the dates on which they are due to be filed differ from one another.

Time for reply

Replace the second paragraph with:

Rule 15.8(b) expressly states who is to serve the reply, i.e. the claimant not the court. **15.8.2**

Replace the last paragraph with:

The time limit for serving a reply in certain specialist proceedings, such as the Commercial Court, TCC and Admiralty, is 21 days from the service of the defence.

Serving a reply and defence to counterclaim

Replace paragraph with:

If the reply falls due later than defence to counterclaim, then they will need to feature as separate documents. However, if they fall due at the same time (either by consequence of the date for direction questionnaire, agreement or other direction of the court) then they should form part of the same document with the reply coming first: r.15.8(b). **15.8.3**

Replace r.15.9 with:

No statement of case after a reply to be filed without court's permission[2]

15.9 A party may not file or serve any statement of case after a reply without the permission of the court. **15.9**

---

[1] Amended by the Civil Procedure (Amendment No.7) Rules 2013 (SI 2013/1974) and the Civil Procedure (Amendment No.2) Rules 2022 (SI 2022/783).

[2] Amended by the Civil Procedure (Amendment No.2) Rules 2022 (SI 2022/783).

Replace r.15.10 with:

Claimant's notice where defence is that money claimed has been paid[1]

15.10 **15.10—(1) Where—**

- **(a) the only claim (apart from a claim for costs and interest) is for a specified amount of money; and**
- **(b) the defendant states in his defence that he has paid to the claimant the amount claimed,**

the court will send notice to the claimant requiring the claimant to state in writing whether the claimant wishes the proceedings to continue.

(2) A copy of the claimant's response must be served on the defendant at the same time as it is filed.

(3) If the claimant fails to respond within 28 days after service of the court's notice the claim shall be stayed.

(4) Any party may apply under Part 23 for the stay to be lifted. The application must include an explanation for the delay in proceeding with or responding to the claim.

(5) If the claimant files a notice stating a wish that the proceedings should continue, the procedure set out in Part 26 shall apply.

Replace r.15.11 with:

Claim stayed if it is not defended or admitted[2]

15.11 **15.11—(1) Where—**

- **(a) at least 6 months have expired since the end of the period for filing a defence specified in rule 15.4;**
- **(b) no defendant has served or filed an admission or filed a defence or counterclaim; and**
- **(c) no party has entered or applied for judgment under Part 12 (default judgment), or Part 24 (summary judgment); and**
- **(d) no defendant has applied to strike out all or part of the claim form or particulars of claim,**

the claim shall be stayed.

(2) Any party may apply under Part 23 for the stay to be lifted. The application must include an explanation for the delay in proceeding with or responding to the claim.

Rule 15.11: Effect of rule

Replace the second paragraph with:

15.11.1 *Bank of America Europe DAC (formerly Merrill Lynch International Bank Ltd) v Citta Metropolitana Di Milano* [2022] EWHC 1544 (Comm) concluded that the automatic stay of a claim following failure by a claimant to ensure it had remained subject to judicial management or a further stay (either of which might be achieved by agreement with other part(ies) or direction from the court) should, as a matter of ordinary language, be described as a "sanction". Such a claimant loses the unfettered right to pursue its claim, and must instead obtain the exercise of a court's discretion in its favour, which might be refused or granted on unfavourable terms. The court approached the application by utilising the test in *Denton* but, in observing the variety of conflicting obiter observations whether *Denton* had to apply, expressed the need for flexibility in approach if it does, given r.15.11 can be distinguished from more conventional cases of default and instead is a combination of the failure of both parties to take a particular step which brings the automatic stay into operation.

Delete the penultimate paragraph.

---

[1] Amended by the Civil Procedure (Amendment No.2) Rules 2022 (SI 2022/783).

[2] Amended by the Civil Procedure (Amendment No.2) Rules 2022 (SI 2022/783).

PRACTICE DIRECTION 15—DEFENCE AND REPLY

Delete Practice Direction 15–Defence and Reply.

PART 16

STATEMENTS OF CASE

Editorial introduction

To the end of the second paragraph (after "exceeds 25 pages."), add:

Pending anticipated formal rule changes, it is suggested that exceptionally long statements of case are preceded by an appropriate short summary. **16.0.1**

Replace r.16.2 with:

Contents of the claim form[1]

16.2—(1) The claim form must— **16.2**

(a) contain a concise statement of the nature of the claim;

(b) specify the remedy which the claimant seeks;

(c) contain a statement of value in accordance with rule 16.3, where the claimant is making a claim for money;

(d) contain a statement of the interest accrued on that sum, where the only claim is for a specified sum; and

(e) contain such other matters as may be set out in a practice direction.

(1A) In civil proceedings against the Crown, as defined in rule 66.1(2), the claim form must also contain—

(a) the names of the government departments and officers of the Crown concerned; and

(b) brief details of the circumstances in which it is alleged that the liability of the Crown arose.

(2) If the particulars of claim specified in rule 16.4 are not contained in, or are not served with the claim form, the claimant must state on the claim form that the particulars of claim will follow.

(3) If the claimant is claiming in a representative capacity, the claim form must state what that capacity is.

(4) If the defendant is sued in a representative capacity, the claim form must state what that capacity is.

(5) The court may grant any remedy to which the claimant is entitled, even if that remedy is not specified in the claim form.

(Part 22 requires a claim form to be verified by a statement of truth.)

"such other matters as may be set out in a practice direction"

Replace the penultimate paragraph with:

Practice Direction 49B (Mesothelioma Claims) (para.49BPD.3) provides that, in any claim for compensation for mesothelioma, the claim form and every statement of case must be marked with the title "Living Mesothelioma Claim" or "Fatal Mesothelioma Claim" as appropriate. Paragraph 5.2 of that Practice Direction (see para.49BPD.5, above) states that claims marked "Living Mesothelioma Claim" will be given priority when fixing a case management conference. The practice of heading asbestos exposure claims to identify other medical conditions sustained is accordingly wholly unnecessary and misconceived. **16.2.4**

---

[1] Amended by the Civil Procedure (Amendment No.3) Rules 2000 (SI 2000/1317), the Civil Procedure (Amendment No.4) Rules 2005 (SI 2005/3515), the Civil Procedure (Amendment No.2) Rules 2009 (SI 2009/3390), the Civil Procedure (Amendment No.7) Rules 2013 (SI 2013/1974) and the Civil Procedure (Amendment No.2) Rules 2022 (SI 2022/783).

Replace r.16.3 with:

Statement of value to be included in the claim form[1]

16.3 **16.3—(1) This rule applies where the claimant is making a claim for money.**

(2) The claimant must, in the claim form, state—

(a) the amount of money claimed;

(b) that the claimant expects to recover—

(i) not more than £10,000; or

(ii) more than £10,000 but not more than £25,000; or

(iii) more than £25,000; or

(c) that the claimant cannot say how much is likely to be recovered.

(3) Subject to paragraphs (3A) and (3AA), in a claim for personal injuries, the claimant must also state in the claim form whether the amount which they expect to recover as general damages for pain, suffering and loss of amenity is—

(a) not more than £1,500; or

(b) more than £1,500.

(3A) Where—

(a) a claim for personal injuries arises from a road traffic accident which occurred on or after 31st May 2021; and

(b) rules 26.5A, 26.6A or 26.6B do not apply to that claim,

the claimant must state in the claim form whether the amount which they expect to recover as general damages for pain suffering and loss of amenity is—

(i) not more than £5,000; or

(ii) more than £5,000.

(3AA) Where—

(a) a claim for personal injuries arises from a road traffic accident; and

(b) rule 26.6A applies to that claim,

the claimant must state in the claim form whether the amount which the claimant expects to recover as general damages for pain, suffering and loss of amenity is—

(i) not more than £1,000; or

(ii) more than £1,000.

(3B) "Road traffic accident" has the meaning ascribed to it by rule 26.6(2A).

(4) Where a tenant of residential premises, or a contract-holder of an occupation contract of a dwelling under section 7 of the Renting Homes (Wales) Act 2016, claims an order against a landlord requiring the landlord to carry out repairs or other work, the claimant must also state in the claim form—

(a) whether the estimated costs of those repairs or other work is—

(i) not more than £1,000; or

(ii) more than £1,000; and

(b) whether the value of any other claim for damages is—

(i) not more than £1,000; or

(ii) more than £1,000.

(5) If the claim form is to be issued in the High Court it must, where this rule applies—

(a) state that the claimant expects to recover more than £100,000;

---

[1] Amended by the Civil Procedure (Amendment) Rules 1999 (SI 1999/1008), the Civil Procedure (Amendment No.3) Rules 2008 (SI 2008/3327), the Civil Procedure (Amendment) Rules 2013 (SI 2013/262), the Civil Procedure (Amendment) Rules 2014 (SI 2014/407), the Civil Procedure (Amendment No.2) 2021 (SI 2021/196), the Civil Procedure (Amendment) Rules 2022 (SI 2022/101) and the Civil Procedure (Amendment No.2) Rules 2022 (SI 2022/783).

(b) state that some other enactment permits or requires the claim to be brought in the High Court and specify that enactment;
(c) if the claim is for personal injuries, state that the claimant expects to recover £50,000 or more; or
(d) state that the claim is to proceed in one of the specialist High Court lists and state which list.

(6) When calculating how much the claimant expects to recover, the claimant must disregard any possibility—
(a) that the court may make an award of—
  (i) interest;
  (ii) costs;
(b) that the court may make a finding of contributory negligence;
(c) that the defendant may make a counterclaim or that the defence may include a set-off; or
(d) that the defendant may (under section 6 of the Social Security (Recovery of Benefits Act 1997) be liable to pay direct to the Secretary of State part of any award of money made by the court to the claimant against the defendant.

(7) The statement of value in the claim form does not limit the power of the court to give judgment for an amount which it finds the claimant is entitled to.

Replace r.16.4 with:

Contents of the particulars of claim[1]

16.4—(1) Particulars of claim must include— 16.4
(a) a concise statement of the facts on which the claimant relies;
(b) if the claimant is seeking interest, a statement to that effect and the details set out in paragraph (2);
(c) if the claimant is seeking aggravated damages(GL) or exemplary damages(GL), a statement to that effect and the grounds for claiming them;
(d) if the claimant is seeking provisional damages, a statement to that effect and the grounds for claiming them; and
(e) such other matters as may be set out in a practice direction.

(2) If the claimant is seeking interest they must—
(a) state whether they are doing so—
  (i) under the terms of a contract;
  (ii) under an enactment and, if so, which; or
  (iii) on some other basis and, if so, what that basis is; and
(b) if the claim is for a specified amount of money, state—
  (i) the percentage rate at which interest is claimed;
  (ii) the date from which it is claimed;
  (iii) the date to which it is calculated, which must not be later than the date on which the claim form is issued;
  (iv) the total amount of interest claimed to the date of calculation; and
  (v) the daily rate at which interest accrues after that date.

(Part 22 requires particulars of claim to be verified by a statement of truth.)

"such other matters as may be set out in a practice direction"

Replace list items (5) and (6) with:

(5) mesothelioma claims (see para.49BPD.3); 16.4.4

[1] Amended by the Civil Procedure (Amendment No.2) Rules 2022 (SI 2022/783).

(6) Consumer Credit Act claims (see para.49CPD.7);

Particulars of claim served separately from the claim form

Replace the penultimate paragraph with:

16.4.5 In claims to which PD 7B or PD 7C apply, that is to say claims issued in the Production Centre or started using Money Claim Online, the place for filing copy particulars is the court to which the claim is sent or transferred and the deadline for doing so is seven days from the date the centre in question served a notice that the proceedings have been sent or transferred elsewhere (PD 7B para.5.2(3) and PD 7C para.6.3). In these cases there is no requirement to file a copy of the particulars unless and until the centre serves such a notice or serves an order requiring them to be filed (PD 7B para.5.2(4) and PD 7C para.6.4).

Replace r.16.5 with:

Contents of defence[1]

16.5 **16.5—(1) In the defence, the defendant must deal with every allegation in the particulars of claim, stating—**

(a) which of the allegations are denied;

(b) which allegations they are unable to admit or deny, but which they require the claimant to prove; and

(c) which allegations they admit.

(2) Where the defendant denies an allegation—

(a) they must state their reasons for doing so; and

(b) if they intend to put forward a different version of events from that given by the claimant, they must state their own version.

(3) If a defendant—

(a) fails to deal with an allegation; but

(b) sets out in the defence the nature of their case in relation to the issue to which that allegation is relevant,

the claimant is required to prove the allegation.

(4) Where the claim includes a money claim, the claimant must prove any allegation relating to the amount of money claimed, unless the defendant expressly admits the allegation.

(5) Subject to paragraphs (3) and (4), a defendant who fails to deal with an allegation shall be taken to admit that allegation.

(6) If the defendant disputes the claimant's statement of value under rule 16.3 they must—

(a) state why they dispute it; and

(b) if they are able, give their own statement of the value of the claim.

(7) If the defendant is defending in a representative capacity, they must state what that capacity is.

(8) If the defendant has not filed an acknowledgment of service under Part 10, they must give an address for service.

(Part 22 requires a defence to be verified by a statement of truth.)

(Rule 6.23 makes provision in relation to addresses for service.)

Filing a defence and counterclaim

Replace the first paragraph with:

16.5.7 A defendant who wishes to defend must file a defence (r.15.2) and a copy of it must be served on every other party (r.15.6). A defendant may make a counterclaim against a claimant by filing particulars of the counterclaim (r.20.4). Rule 15.8 states that:

> "the reply should form one document with any defence to counterclaim, with the defence to counterclaim following the reply, unless the dates on which they are due to be filed differ from one another."

---

[1] Amended by the Civil Procedure (Amendment) Rules 2008 (SI 2008/2178), the Civil Procedure (Amendment) Rules 2011 (SI 2011/88) and the Civil Procedure (Amendment No.2) Rules 2022 (SI 2022/783).

Replace r.16.6 with:

Defence of set-off[1]

16.6 Where a defendant– **16.6**

(a) contends that they are entitled to money from the claimant; and

(b) relies on this as a defence to the whole or part of the claim,

the contention may be included in the defence and set off against the claim, whether or not it is also an additional claim.

Replace r.16.7 with:

Reply to defence[2]

16.7–(1) If a claimant does not file a reply to the defence, the defendant must prove the matters raised in the defence. **16.7**

(2) If a claimant–

(a) files a reply to a defence; but

(b) fails to deal with a matter raised in the defence,

the defendant must prove that matter even though it is not dealt with in the reply.

(Part 22 requires a reply to be verified by a statement of truth.)

Serving a reply and defence to counterclaim

Replace the first paragraph with:

A claimant who wishes to rely on a reply must file it and serve copies on the other parties (r.15.8). A claimant who wishes to defend a counterclaim must file a defence and a copy of it must be served on every other party. Whilst Pt 15 does not expressly stipulate the date for defending a counterclaim, it would seem to be the 14-day period as stipulated at r.15.4(1)(a), thus treating both counterclaim and particulars of claim as statements of case. Rule 15.8 provides that if both reply and defence to counterclaim fall due at the same time, they should be in the same document with the reply first. **16.7.4**

Replace Practice Direction 16–Statements of Case with:

PRACTICE DIRECTION 16—STATEMENTS OF CASE

This Practice Direction supplements CPR Part 16

General

1.1 Where special provisions about statements of case apply to particular types of proceedings, Part 16 and this practice direction only apply in so far as consistent with those rules and practice directions. **16PD.1**

1.2 Examples of proceedings with special provisions about statements of case include–

(1) media and communications claims (Part 53 and Practice Direction 53B);

(2) possession claims (Part 55); and

(3) probate claims (Part 57).

1.3 If a statement of case exceptionally exceeds 25 pages (excluding schedules) it must include an appropriate short summary at the start.

The claim form

2.1 The claim form must include an address (including the postcode) at which the claimant lives or carries on business, even if the claimant's address for service is the business address of their solicitor. **16PD.2**

2.2 Where the defendant is an individual, the claimant should (if able to do so) include in the claim form an address (including the postcode) at which the defendant lives or carries on business, even if the defendant's solicitors have agreed to accept service on the defendant's behalf.

[1] Amended by the Civil Procedure (Amendment No.2) Rules 2022 (SI 2022/783).

[2] Amended by the Civil Procedure (Amendment No.2) Rules 2022 (SI 2022/783).

2.3 If the claim form does not include a full address, including postcode, for all parties the claim form will be issued but retained by the court and not served until the claimant has supplied a full address, including postcode, or the court has dispensed with the requirement to do so. The court will notify the claimant.

2.4 The claim form must be headed with the title of the proceedings, including the full name of each party, where it is known—

(1) for an individual, the full name and title by which the person is known;

(2) for an individual carrying on business other than in their own name, the full name of the individual, the title by which they are known, and the full trading name (for example, Jane Smith "trading as" or "T/as" "JS Autos");

(3) for a partnership (other than a limited liability partnership (LLP))—

(a) where partners are sued in the name of the partnership, the full name by which the partnership is known, together with the words "(a Firm)"; or

(b) where partners are sued as individuals, the full name of each partner and the title by which each is known;

(4) for a company or limited liability partnership registered in England and Wales, the full registered name, including suffix (plc, Limited, LLP, etc), if any;

(5) for any other company or corporation, the full name by which it is known, including suffix where appropriate.

(For information about how and where a claim may be started see Part 7 and Practice Direction 7A.)

Particulars of claim

16PD.3 **3.1** If practicable, the particulars of claim should be set out in the claim form. If not, they may be served with the claim form or later, within the periods specified in rule 7.4 and 7.5.

3.2 Particulars of claim which are not included in the claim form must be verified by a statement of truth, in the form specified in paragraph 2.1 of Practice Direction 22.

3.3 Particulars of claim served separately from the claim form must also contain—

(1) the name of the court in which the claim is proceeding;

(2) the claim number;

(3) the title of the proceedings; and

(4) the claimant's address for service.

Matters which must be included in the particulars of claim in certain types of claim

Personal injury claims

16PD.4 **4.1** The particulars of claim must contain—

(1) the claimant's date of birth; and

(2) brief details of the claimant's personal injuries.

4.2 The claimant must attach to his particulars of claim a schedule of details of any past and future expenses and losses which he claims.

4.3 Where the claimant is relying on evidence from a medical practitioner, the claimant must attach a report from the medical practitioner about the claimant's personal injuries.

4.3A(1) In a soft tissue injury claim, the claimant may not proceed unless the medical report is a fixed cost medical report. Where the claimant files more than one medical report, the first report obtained must be a fixed cost medical report from an accredited medical expert selected via the MedCo Portal (website at: *www.medco.org.uk*) and any further report from an expert in any of the following disciplines must also be a fixed cost medical report–

(a) Consultant Orthopaedic Surgeon;
(b) Consultant in Accident and Emergency Medicine;
(c) General Practitioner registered with the General Medical Council;
(d) Physiotherapist registered with the Health and Care Professions Council.

(1A) The cost of obtaining a further report from an expert not listed in paragraph (1)(a) to (d) is not subject to rule 45.29(2A)(b), but the use of that expert and the cost must be justified.

(2) In this paragraph, "accredited medical expert", "fixed costs medical report", "MedCo" and "soft tissue injury claim" have the same meaning as in paragraph 1.1(A1), (10A), (12A), and (16A), respectively, of the Pre-Action Protocol for Low Value Personal Injury Claims in Road Traffic Accidents.

4.3B(1) In a claim for a whiplash injury, whether or not it is part of a claim for other injuries–

(a) the claimant may not proceed in respect of the claim for the whiplash injury unless the medical report is a fixed cost medical report;
(b) where the claimant files more than one medical report, the first report obtained in respect of the whiplash injury must be a fixed cost medical report from an accredited medical expert selected via the MedCo Portal;
(c) where the claimant lives outside England and Wales, but chooses to be examined for the purposes of a medical report in England or Wales, paragraphs (a) and (b) apply; and
(d) any further report in respect of the claim for the whiplash injury only must also be a fixed cost medical report from an expert in any of the following disciplines–
  (i) Consultant Orthopaedic Surgeon;
  (ii) Consultant in Accident and Emergency Medicine;
  (iii) General Practitioner registered with the General Medical Council;
  (iv) Physiotherapist registered with the Health and Care Professions Council.

(2) Where the claimant obtains a medical report in respect of a more serious injury suffered on the same occasion as the whiplash injury, the claimant may use that report instead of a fixed costs medical report under paragraph (1) provided that–

(a) the report is from a doctor who is listed on the General Medical Council's Specialist Register; and
(b) the report provides evidence of the whiplash injury.

(3) Unless paragraph (1)(c) applies, in any other case where the claimant lives outside England and Wales, the medical report in respect of the claim for the whiplash injury (or, if there is more than one report, the first report) must be from a person who is recognised by the country in which they practise as–

(i) being a medical expert; and
(ii) having the required qualifications for the purposes of diagnosis and prognosis of a whiplash injury.

(4) The cost of obtaining a further report from an expert not listed

in paragraph (4)(a) to (d) is not subject to rule 45.29I(2A)(b), but the use of that expert and the cost must be justified.

(5) In this paragraph, "fixed cost medical report", "accredited medical expert", "MedCo", and "whiplash injury" have the same meaning as in paragraph 1.2(1), (17), (19) and (38), respectively, of the Pre-Action Protocol for Personal Injury Claims Below the Small Claims Limit in Road Traffic Accidents.

4.4 In a provisional damages claim the claimant must state in the particulars of claim—

(1) that they are seeking an award of provisional damages under either section 32A of the Senior Courts Act 1981 or section 51 of the County Courts Act 1984;
(2) that there is a chance that at some future time the claimant will develop some serious disease or suffer some serious deterioration in their physical or mental condition; and
(3) specify the disease or type of deterioration in respect of which an application may be made at a future date.

(Part 41 and Practice Direction 41A contain information about awards for provisional damages.)

Fatal accident claims

16PD.5 **5.1** In a fatal accident claim the claimant must state in the particulars of claim—

(1) that it is brought under the Fatal Accidents Act 1976;
(2) the dependants on whose behalf the claim is made;
(3) the date of birth of each dependant; and
(4) details of the nature of the dependency claim.

5.2 A fatal accident claim may include a claim for damages for bereavement.

5.3 In a fatal accident claim the claimant may also bring a claim under the Law Reform (Miscellaneous Provisions) Act 1934 on behalf of the estate of the deceased person.

(For information on apportionment under the Law Reform (Miscellaneous Provisions) Act 1934 and the Fatal Accidents Act 1976 or between dependants see Part 37 and Practice Direction 37.)

Hire purchase claims

16PD.6 **6.1** Where the claim is for the delivery of goods let under a hire-purchase agreement or conditional sale agreement to a person other than a company or other corporation, the claimant must state in the particulars of claim—

(1) the date of the agreement;
(2) the parties to the agreement;
(3) the number or other identification of the agreement;
(4) where the claimant was not one of the original parties to the agreement, the means by which the rights and duties of the creditor passed to the claimant;
(5) whether the agreement is a regulated agreement, and if it is not a regulated agreement, the reason why;
(6) the place where the agreement was signed by the defendant;
(7) the goods claimed;
(8) the total price of the goods;
(9) the paid-up sum;
(10) the unpaid balance of the total price;
(11) whether a default notice or a notice under section 76(1) or 98(1) of the Consumer Credit Act 1974 has been served on the defendant, and if it has, the date and method of service;

(12) the date when the right to demand delivery of the goods accrued;
(13) the amount (if any) claimed as an alternative to the delivery of goods; and
(14) the amount (if any) claimed in addition to–
  (a) the delivery of the goods; or
  (b) any claim under (13) above

with the grounds of each claim.

(If the agreement is a regulated agreement the procedure set out in Practice Direction 49C should be used.)

6.2 Where the claim is not for the delivery of goods, the claimant must state in the particulars of claim–
(1) the matters set out in paragraph 6.1(1) to (6) above;
(2) the goods let under the agreement;
(3) the amount of the total price;
(4) the paid-up sum;
(5) the amount (if any) claimed as being due and unpaid in respect of any instalment or instalments of the total price; and
(6) the nature and amount of any other claim and how it arises.

Hire of replacement motor vehicle following a road traffic accident

6.3 Where the claim includes the cost of hire of a replacement motor vehicle following a road traffic accident, the claimant must state in the particulars of claim–
(1) the need for the replacement vehicle at the relevant time;
(2) the period of hire claimed (providing the start and end of the period);
(3) the rate of hire claimed;
(4) the reasonableness of the period and rate of hire; and
(5) if the claim relates to credit hire, whether the claimant could afford to pay in advance to hire a replacement car, and, if not, why not ("impecuniosity").

6.4 In paragraph 6.3–
(1) "relevant time" means at the start of the hire and throughout the period of hire;
(2) the obligation to state the matters in paragraph (3) includes an obligation to state relevant facts.

Other matters to be included in particulars of claim

7.1 Where a claim is made for an injunction or declaration relating to any land or the possession, occupation, use or enjoyment of any land the particulars of claim must– **16PD.7**
(1) state whether or not the injunction or declaration relates to residential premises, and
(2) identify the land (using a plan where necessary).

7.2 Where a claim is brought to enforce a right to recover possession of goods the particulars of claim must contain a statement showing the value of the goods.

7.3 Where a claim is based upon a written agreement–
(1) a copy (or copies) of the contract or documents constituting the agreement should be attached to or served with the particulars of claim and the original(s) should be available at the hearing, and
(2) any general conditions of sale incorporated in the contract should also be attached (but where the documents are bulky it is acceptable to attach or serve only the relevant parts of the contract or documents).

7.4 Where a claim is based upon an oral agreement, the particulars of claim should set out the contractual words used and state by whom, to whom, when and where they were spoken.

7.5 Where a claim is based upon an agreement by conduct, the particulars of claim must specify the conduct relied on and state by whom, when and where the acts constituting the conduct were done.

7.6 In a claim issued in the High Court relating to a Consumer Credit Agreement, the particulars of claim must contain a statement that the action is not one to which section 141 of the Consumer Credit Act 1974 applies.

Matters which must be specifically set out in the particulars of claim

16PD.8 **8.1** A claimant who wishes to rely on evidence–

(1) under section 11 of the Civil Evidence Act 1968 of a conviction of an offence, or

(2) under section 12 of the above-mentioned Act of a finding or adjudication of adultery or paternity,

must include in the particulars of claim a statement to that effect and give the following details–

(a) the type of conviction, finding or adjudication and its date;

(b) the court or Court-Martial which made the conviction, finding or adjudication; and

(c) the issue in the claim to which it relates.

8.2 The claimant must specifically set out the following matters in the particulars of claim where they wish to rely on them in support of the claim–

(1) any allegation of fraud;

(2) the fact of any illegality;

(3) details of any misrepresentation;

(4) details of all breaches of trust;

(5) notice or knowledge of a fact;

(6) details of unsoundness of mind or undue influence;

(7) details of wilful default; and

(8) any facts relating to a claim for mitigation expenditure.

General

16PD.9 **9.1** Where a claim is for a sum of money expressed in a foreign currency it must state–

(1) that the claim is for payment in a specified foreign currency,

(2) why it is for payment in that currency,

(3) the Sterling equivalent of the sum at the date of the claim, and

(4) the source of the exchange rate relied on to calculate the Sterling equivalent.

9.2 A subsequent statement of case must not contradict or be inconsistent with an earlier one; for example a reply to a defence must not bring in a new claim. Where new matters have come to light a party may seek the court's permission to amend their statement of case.

9.3 In clinical negligence claims, the words "clinical negligence" should be inserted at the top of every statement of case.

Statement of truth

16PD.10 **10.1** The defence must be verified by a statement of truth in the form specified in paragraph 2.1 of Practice Direction 22.

Matters which must be included in the defence

Personal injury claims

11.1 Where the claim is for personal injuries and the claimant has attached a medical report in respect of the alleged injuries, the defendant should— **16PD.11**

(1) state in the defence whether the defendant—
  (a) agrees;
  (b) disputes; or
  (c) neither agrees nor disputes but has no knowledge of,

  the matters contained in the medical report;
(2) where the defendant disputes any part of the medical report, give in the defence their reasons for doing so; and
(3) where the defendant has obtained their own medical report, attach it to the defence.

11.2 Where the claim is for personal injuries and the claimant has included a schedule of past and future expenses and losses, the defendant should include in or attach to the defence a counter-schedule stating—

(1) which of those items the defendant—
  (a) agrees;
  (b) disputes; or
  (c) neither agrees nor disputes but has no knowledge of; and

(2) where any items are disputed, supplying alternative figures where appropriate.

11.3 The defendant must give details of the expiry of any relevant limitation period relied on.

Other matters

12.1 Rule 37.3 and paragraph 2 of Practice Direction 37 contains information about a defence of tender. **16PD.12**

12.2 A party may in a statement of case—

(1) refer to any point of law;
(2) give the name of any witness they propose to call,

and may attach to it a copy of any document necessary to their case (including any expert's report under Part 35).

Competition Act 1998

13 A party who relies on a finding of the Competition and Markets Authority must include in the statement of case a statement to that effect and identify the finding. **16PD.13**

Human Rights

14.1 A party who relies on any provision of or right arising under the Human Rights Act 1998 or seeks a remedy under that Act must state that fact in their statement of case, and must— **16PD.14**

(a) give details of the Convention right infringed and details of the infringement;
(b) specify the relief sought;
(c) state if the relief sought includes—
  (i) a declaration of incompatibility under section 4 if that Act, or
  (ii) damages in respect of a judicial act to which section 9(3) of that Act applies;

(d) where the relief sought includes a declaration of incompatibility, give details of the legislative provision and the alleged incompatibility;

(e) where the claim is founded on a finding of unlawfulness by another court or tribunal, give details of the finding; and

(f) where the claim is founded on a judicial act alleged to have infringed a Convention right of the party as provided by section 9 of the Human Rights Act 1998, the judicial act complained of and the court or tribunal that made it.

(Practice Direction 19A provides for notice to be given and parties joined in the circumstances referred to in (c), (d) and (f).)

14.2 A party seeking to amend a statement of case to include the matters referred to in paragraph 14.1 must, unless the court orders otherwise, do so as soon as possible.

(Part 17 provides for the amendment of a statement of case.)

NOTES ON AWARDS OF INTEREST

A. Introduction

1. Rates of interest

In list item (a), replace the last four sentences (beginning "Base rate is set") with:

16AI.2 Base rate is set by the Bank of England. Following an unprecedented period of a low stable rate, reaching as low as 0.10%, the rate has climbed in recent months and is 2.25% as of 22 September 2022. In the past the rate has changed frequently. The Bank's website at *http://www.bankofengland.co.uk/boeapps/database/Bank-Rate.asp* [Accessed 31 October 2022] records all rates since 20 January 1975 so all relevant rates are readily ascertainable.

PART 17

AMENDMENTS TO STATEMENTS OF CASE

Practice on amendment

After the fourth paragraph (beginning "Where a statement"), add new paragraph:

17.1.2 The fact a proposed amendment is arguable and advances a permissible case is relevant but not necessarily decisive. Such an amendment may still well be refused if its unjustified lateness is prejudicial to the other party. See the remarks of the Court of Appeal in *ABP Technology Ltd v Voyetra Turtle Beach Inc* [2022] EWCA Civ 594 at [27]-[30], [33]-[34], [38]-[39] and [41] in holding that the amendment could have been raised far earlier and its timing was only really to seek to deprive the opposing party of a course of action they might have had if the amendment had been proposed earlier.

To the end of the last paragraph, add:

Mann J further decided that CPR r.17.1 does not permit amendment of a claim form to add other claimants to the proceedings between the issue and service of the claim form since CPR r.17.1(1) is available only to an existing claimant and, secondly, that, in any event, CPR r.19.4(4) is not satisfied merely by completion of a statement of truth on an amended claim form signed by the solicitor acting for a claimant added by the amendment. This decision was qualified in *Rawet v Daimler AG* [2022] EWHC 235 (QB) which ruled that CPR r.17.1 was to be interpreted as allowing additional claimants to be added to a claim form *prior* to service of the form but confirmed that the requirements in CPR r.19.4(4) applied after service of the claim form.

Applications to amend only to be dealt with upon a formal application

Replace paragraph with:

17.1.4 In *Magdeev v Tsvetkov* [2019] EWCA Civ 1802 at [26]-[27] the Court of Appeal remarked upon the need for a party formally to apply for an amendment if they were seeking a decision from the court. Accordingly, the judge had been wrong to reach a decision based upon merely a proposed or mooted amendment. An application to amend ordinarily should be by way of a completed, issued and served **N244** and the court may require explanation from a party that chooses instead only orally to apply to amend. Even then, such application is to be formally treated as if issued. The

Court of Appeal listed various reasons why applications to amend must not be merely mentioned or proposed: (i) only orders, not judgments, can be appealed and orders follow applications; (ii) decisions from the court when there has been no formal application create procedural confusion; (iii) a formal application enables the respondent to consider and court to determine whether it is competent to deal with the application, to know what it is to decide and then to determine that identified issue; and (iv) it ensures the appropriate fee for the application is paid. The need for formal application does not mean, however, that the court (whether on submission from another party or of its own motion) cannot utilise its general case management powers to oblige a party to focus on the issue(s) that might merit amendment.

PART 18

Further Information

Editorial introduction

Replace the fourth paragraph (beginning "Part 18 is concerned") with:

Part 18 is concerned with the provision by parties of information for the purpose of clarifying matters in dispute in the proceedings. In *HRH Prince Khaled Bin Abdulaziz Al Saud v Gibbs* [2022] EWHC 706 (Comm) the defendants were ordered to provide further information on their defence, even though competing applications for summary judgment by the claimants and the defendants were pending. In doing so, however, the court emphasised (at [35]) that the information sought must relate to a "matter which is in dispute in the proceedings", and that the requirement of the Practice Direction that any request must be strictly confined to matters which are reasonably necessary and proportionate for one or other of the stated purposes, are threshold conditions. If those conditions are not satisfied, the court has no jurisdiction to make an order under CPR Pt 18. The court added that in the event a dispute arises as to the adequacy of the replies, the better course is not simply to ask the court to oblige a response to the original requests but to ask the court to specify in its order precisely what further enquiries the party responding to the Pt 18 request should carry out, so that the issue of what proper compliance requires is plainly defined from the outset ([48]). **18.0.1**

The object and function of Pt 18 should be distinguished from three other circumstances in which, for other purposes, the parties may or must provide the court with information. First, where a party files a directions questionnaire under Pt 26, they may take advantage of PD 26 (Case Management—Preliminary Stage), para.2.2 and give the court "extra information" relevant to the allocation of the case to an appropriate case management track or to case management. Secondly, when the court has considered the statements of case and directions questionnaire responses filed, before making a decision about allocation, it may serve on the parties an "order for further information" in Form **N156**; see CPR r.26.5(3) and PD 26 para.4.2(2) requiring them to provide information about particular matters relevant to allocation. Thirdly, where a party has access to information which is not reasonably available to the other party, the court may direct the former party to provide the latter with that information (CPR r.35.9). The expression "further information" is used in some other contexts within the CPR where no confusion with Pt 18 is at all likely (e.g. CPR r.75.10 (further information to be provided on application for enforcement of traffic penalty)).

Judicial review

To the end of the paragraph, add:

However, see Lang J in *R. (KBL) v Secretary of State for the Home Department* [2022] EWHC 1545 (Admin) ("*KBL*") at [30]. In deciding what is "reasonably necessary and proportionate in order to resolve the matter fairly", the court may properly have regard to the context in which the application under CPR Pt 18 is made. If the context is a claim for judicial review, it is relevant that the duty of candour applies, unlike in private law proceedings. See also the general reviews of the legal framework of Pt 18 in such proceedings in *R. (JZ) v Secretary of State for the Home Department* [2022] EWHC 1708 (Admin) from [21] and in *R. (KBL) v Secretary of State for the Home Department* [2022] EWHC 1545 (Admin) from [25]. **18.1.7**

PART 19

Parties and Group Litigation

Multiplicity of parties

In the first paragraph, replace the third sentence with:

The claims included in a claim form issued under Pt 7 must be "claims which can be conveni- **19.1.1** ently disposed of in the same proceedings" (r.7.3; as to the application of this rule to a claim form issued under Pt 8, consider PD 49E para.4.1; para.49EPD.4).

In the penultimate paragraph, replace "para.3.1.10," with:
para.3.1.9

19.1.4 *Change title of paragraph:*

Same party as claimant and defendant—same party as claimant and defendant in different capacities

Replace paragraph with:
The same party cannot, generally, be both claimant and defendant in proceedings. This follows from the nature of causes of action, which are, as held in, for instance, *Letang v Cooper* [1965] 1 Q.B. 232 at 243, the "factual situation the existence of which entitles one person to obtain from the court a remedy against another person". They are the means by which one party may obtain from the court a remedy from another party. In *Re Cwmni Rheoli Pentref Marina Conwy Cyfynedig (Conwy Marina Village Management Co)* [2021] EWHC 1275 (Ch) the court considered a Part 8 claim issued with the same party as claimant and defendant. While no commentary was cited in support of the proposition, it did not permit the claim to go forward on that basis or without naming a defendant. Pre-CPR authority, however, supports the proposition that the same person cannot be both claimant and defendant. See, for instance, *Ellis v Kerr* [1910] 1 Ch. 529 at 537 and *Re Phillips* [1931] W.N. 109. The pre-CPR authorities also supported the proposition that the same person could not be both claimant and defendant in different capacities. In obiter, Morgan J in *Conwy* said that a party holding more than one capacity may be a claimant and a defendant, in a different capacity, in the same proceedings. No authority was cited for this. In principle, such an approach is consistent with the nature of causes of action. See further para.57.16.1.1, on parties holding different capacities in the same proceedings in respect of claims under the Inheritance (Provision for Family and Dependants) Act 1975.

I. Addition and Substitution of Parties

Rule 19.2(2)(a): Adding a party to resolve all issues in dispute

In the last paragraph, after "[2018] EWHC 2017,", replace "Mann J." with:
19.2.2 Mann J).

Rule 19.2(4): Adding a party by way of substitution

Add new paragraph at end:
19.2.5 In *Power v Bernard Hastie & Co Ltd* [2022] EWHC 1927 (QB) it was held that where a provisional damages order in an asbestos claim had been made in favour of the claimant who had then died, before renewing their claim, the executor of the now-deceased claimant could be substituted under CPR r.19.2(4). It was held that the cause of action survived the death of the claimant and could vest in their estate. The doctrine of merger of judgments did not prevent this vesting.

Joinder or substitution after judgment

Add new paragraph at end:
19.2.6 In *Hotel Portfolio II UK Ltd (in Liquidation) v Ruhan* [2022] EWHC 1695 (Comm) an application to join a new defendant was made after judgment, and refused; it would have been unfair to join a party so as to bind them in relation to findings which had been made but in relation to which the proposed party had been given no opportunity to be heard ([25]).

"The court's permission is required"

Replace the first paragraph with:
19.4.1 CPR r.19.4 provides that addition, substitution or removal of a party can take place without permission of the court before service of the claim form. This includes the addition of a new claimant–see further para.19.4.4 below. Parties may be removed, added or substituted in existing proceedings either on the court's own initiative (r.3.3(4)) or, as r.19.4(2) states, on the application of either an existing party or a person who wishes to become a party (PD 19A para.1.1). The application may be considered with or without a hearing where all the existing parties and the proposed new party are in agreement (as above para.1.2). All applications must be supported by evidence—either in the form of a completed Part C to Form **N244** or in a separate witness statement (PD 19A para.1.3). Where the applicant is not already a party, the application notice must include their address for service (PD 23 para.2.1(4)). The court should deal with as many aspects of the case as it can on the same occasion (CPR r.1.4(i)); the court may consider giving case management directions

on joining a new party. On the other hand, the interests of justice may require that the new party have the opportunity of making representations before directions are given (see generally CPR Pt 3).

Rule 19.4(4): "Nobody may be added or substituted as a claimant unless...he has given his consent in writing"

After the first paragraph, add new paragraph:

In *Rawet v Daimler AG* [2022] EWHC 235 (QB) the Divisional Court granted a declaration expressly disagreeing with the High Court decision in *Various Claimants v G4S Plc* [2021] EWHC 524 (Ch) on the question of whether the consent of the claimant is necessary before the addition of a new claimant after issue of the claim, but before service. The Divisional Court held that such consent was not necessary, that CPR r.17.1 applied (amendment without permission before service) and that CPR r.19.4 was relevant only after service of the claim form. **19.4.4**

To the end of the second paragraph (after the list), add:

This aspect of the *G4S* case was approved by the Divisional Court in *Rawet v Daimler AG* [2022] EWHC 235 (QB).

Rule 19.5(3)(a): The Sardinia Sulcis test for mistake

In the fourth paragraph (beginning "The following cases"), replace the last bullet point with:

- *Rosgosstrakh Ltd v Yapi Kredi Finansal Kiralama AO* [2017] EWHC 3377 (Comm) (claim as an insurer); and **19.5.4**
- *Cameron Taylor Consulting Ltd v BDW Trading Ltd* [2022] EWCA Civ 31 (construction—design).

II. Representative Parties

Change title of paragraph: **19.6.9**

Previous and subsequent case law

Add new paragraphs at end:

The power of the judge managing the case to impose a requirement to notify members of the class of the proceedings and to establish a simple procedure for opting out of representation, cannot cause the "same interest" test to be re-defined, stretched or widened. If the members of a class have conflicting interests, and not merely divergent interests, it would be an error to permit a representative action to proceed on the basis of that class, whatever requirements as to notice were imposed: *Genius Sports Technologies Ltd v Soft Construct (Malta) Ltd* [2021] EWHC 3200 (Ch).

In *BT Group Plc v Le Patourel* [2022] EWCA Civ 593 the Court of Appeal upheld the decision of the Competition Appeal Tribunal to order that a claim should proceed on an opt-out, rather than opt-in, basis under the Competition Act 1998 Pt 1 s.47B. This arose in the context of collective proceedings. The relative benefits of different types of opt-in and opt-out proceedings other than representative proceedings under CPR r.19.6 were considered by the Supreme Court in *Google LLC v Lloyd*.

Rule 19.7: Effect of rule

General approach

Add new paragraph at end:

Careful consideration needs to be given as to whether it is appropriate for one law firm to act for a trustee applicant as well as for representative classes of beneficiaries. This may be appropriate whether the court's approval of a settlement is being sought affecting represented persons and approval of the settlement is not opposed by any other party. The possible perception by persons who were not parties to the claim that there might have been collusion in allowing the claim to proceed undefended is an important consideration. The instruction of a law firm which had no prior involvement in the underlying transaction provides a degree of added stringency: *South Downs Trustees Ltd v GH* [2018] EWHC 1064 (Ch). **19.7.3**

Rule 19.8 has no role to play where proceedings are a nullity at the time of issue

Replace the penultimate paragraph with:

In *Haastrup v Okorie* [2016] EWHC 12 (Ch) the court struck out a claim regarding the alleged misuse by a defendant of a power of attorney before the death of her former husband. At the date the claim was issued the claimant was subject to a Nigerian Court injunction restraining him from relying on letters of administration granted to him in Nigeria. The grant, as resealed in England, **19.8.2** had been recalled by the probate registry pending further investigation. An application by the claimant for an order under r.19.8(1)(a) or (b) was dismissed. It was stated to be part of the ratio of the Court of Appeal in *Millburn-Snell* that the words "[Where] a person who had an interest in a claim has died" in r.19.8(1) apply only to the case where the claim in question had already commenced, and then the claimant or some other person having an interest in it, died. This summary of the ratio is over-concise. It was recognised by Rimer LJ in his judgment in *Milburn-Snell* at [28]-[30] that the phrase doesn't refer exclusively to a deceased person who was a party to the claim and that r.19.8(1) enables the joinder during the currency of the proceedings of someone to represent the interests of a deceased person who had an interest in the claim, but who may not have been a party to it. That does not assist a claimant without title to sue when the claim is issued.

Rule 19.8A: History and effect of this rule

To the end of the last paragraph, add:

19.8A.1 Note: existing PD 4—Court Forms is deleted with effect from 1 October 2022 by CPR Practice Direction 149th Update (July 2022).

Derivative claims

Rule 19.9: Scope of rule

To the end of the last paragraph, add:

19.9.1 See also *McGaughey v Universities Superannuation Scheme Ltd* [2022] EWHC 565 (Ch) at [10] and [17] and *Prinse v Landmasters (Overseas) Ltd* [2022] EWHC 1921 (Ch) at [48].

PART 20

COUNTERCLAIMS AND OTHER ADDITIONAL CLAIMS

Claim by defendant against co-defendant

Replace paragraph with:

20.6.1 In *Kazakhstan Kagazy Plc v Zhunus* [2016] EWCA Civ 1036; [2017] 1 W.L.R. 1360, the claimants alleged fraud against three defendants, each of whom denied liability. The second and third defendants sought permission to make an additional claim seeking a contribution against the first defendant in the event that, contrary to their primary case, they were found to have acted fraudulently. In the contribution notice, they relied on the claimant's case against the first defendant and set out no other positive case of fraud against the first defendant. The claimant and first defendant compromised the claim so that the claimant's allegations of fraud against the first defendant were stayed. The Court of Appeal (overturning the first instance decision of Leggatt J—as he then was—[2016] EWHC 1048 (Comm); [2016] 4 W.L.R. 86) granted permission. They referred to s.1(3) of the Civil Liability (Contribution) Act 1978 which expressly allows a contribution notwithstanding settlement.

PART 21

CHILDREN AND PROTECTED PARTIES

Rule 21.2: Effect of rule

To the end of the last paragraph, add:

21.2.1 The litigation friend does not have a broader duty to act in the party's best interests. Their obligation is only to fairly and competently conduct the proceedings in question. That includes a duty to help the court further the overriding objective (see *Bushby v Galazi* [2022] EWHC 136 (Ch), *Shirazi v Susa Holdings Establishment* [2022] EWHC 477 (Ch) and also *CDE v Buckinghamshire CC* [2022] EWHC 738 (QB)).

Editorial note

Add new paragraph at end:

21.4.1 A defendant's litigation friend may be ordered to pay the costs that the child or protected party would have to pay where the litigation friend has breached their duty to fairly and competently conduct the proceedings, or where the litigation friend has taken steps for a purpose unrelated to the proceedings. The jurisdiction to make such an order is derived from s.51 of the Senior Courts Act 1981 (*Bushby v Galazi* [2022] EWHC 136 (Ch)).

Rule 21.7: Effect of rule

To the end of the last paragraph, add:

Applications by the other party to a claim to change a litigation friend or prevent a person from acting as a litigation friend should be exceptional. The question is whether the person satisfies the conditions in r.21.4(3), there is no broader requirement that the court consider whether the litigation friend is acting in the party's best interest generally, or to look at their conduct with a counsel of perfection (see *Shirazi v Susa Holdings Establishment* [2022] EWHC 477 (Ch)). **21.7.1**

Costs

In the last paragraph, replace "PD 8B" with:

PD 49F **21.10.2**

PART 22

Statements of Truth

Related sources

In the list, replace from the eighteenth bullet point (beginning "Practice Direction 7A") to the end with:

- Practice Direction 7A (How to Start Proceedings), para.7 (see para.7APD.7) **22.0.1**
- Practice Direction 16 (Statements of Case), para.11 (see para.16PD.11)
- Practice Direction 20 (Counterclaims and Other Part 20 Claims), para.4.1 (see para.20PD.4)
- Practice Direction 18 (Further Information), para.3 (see para.18PD.3)
- Practice Direction 35 (Experts and Assessors) (see para.35PD.1)
- Practice Direction 40B (Judgments and Orders) (see para.40BPD.1)
- Practice Direction 52 (Appeals), para.5.23 (see para.52CPD.27)
- Practice Direction 61 (Admiralty Claims), para.4.2(3) (see Vol.2, para.2D-95)
- Practice Direction 5A (Court Documents), para.1 (Signature of documents by mechanical means) (see para.5APD.1)
- Practice Direction 5B (Electronic Communication and Filing of Documents), para.5 (Statement of truth in documents filed electronically) (see para.5BPD.5)
- Practice Direction 7B (Production Centre), para.1.4(4) (Modification of Pt 22) (see para.7BPD.1)
- Practice Direction 7C (Money Claims Online), paras 9 and 10 (Statement of truth and signature) (see paras 7CPD.9 and 7CPD.10)
- Practice Direction 55B (Possession Claims Online), paras 8 and 9 (Statement of truth and signature) (see paras 55BPD.8 and 55BPD.9)

Rule 22.1: Effect of rule

In the fourth paragraph (beginning "Many of the forms"), replace the first sentence with:

Many of the forms to be used in civil proceedings to which the CPR apply have to be verified in whole or in part by persons completing them. **22.1.1**

Replace the last paragraph with:

In PD 7C (Money Claims Online) it is provided that certain types of county court claim may be started by requesting the issue of claim forms electronically through Her Majesty's Courts and Tribunals Service website. In such cases, r.22.1(6) is satisfied if the person verifying the document types their name underneath the statement of truth: see PD 7C para.10. Also see PD 51R (Online Court Pilot) paras 67 and 68 (see para.51RPD.9); PD 51S (The County Court Online Pilot) para.14 (see para.51xSPD.4).

Defence

Delete the last paragraph. **22.1.4**

RTA Protocol and EL/PL Protocol claims

Replace paragraph with:

The Claim Notification Form (CNF) must be verified by a statement of truth as provided for in **22.1.18** that Form; see RTA Protocol paras 1.4 and 6.6, and EL/PL Protocol paras 1.3 and 6.5. For the required verification of a prognosis statement filed by a child claimant for a settlement hearing in proceedings to which those Pre-Action Protocols apply, see PD 49F (Pre-Action Protocol for Low Value Personal Injury Claims in Road Traffic Accidents—Stage 3 Procedure) para.6.5 (para.49FPD.6).

Form of statement of truth

Replace the first two paragraphs with:

22.1.19 The form of statement of truth verifying a statement of case should be as stated in PD 22 (Statements of Truth) para.2.1 (see para.22PD.2); see also PD 7A (How to Start Proceedings—The Claim Form) para.7 (see para.7APD.7), PD 16 (Statements of Case) para.13 (see para.16PD.5), and PD 20 (Counterclaim and Other Pt 20 Claims) para.4.1 (see para.20PD.1).

In certain circumstances, claim forms may be issued through the Production Centre. Practice Direction 7B (Production Centre) (see para.7BPD.1) modifies PD 22 (Statements of Truth) op. cit. in a manner which facilitates the preparation of statements of truth where a party files with the Centre a batch of requests for the issue of claim forms (ibid. para.1.4(4)).

In the third paragraph, replace "PD 7E (Money Claim Online)" with:

PD 7C (Money Claims Online)

Statement of truth in documents filed and applications made by electronic means

Replace paragraph with:

22.1.22 Where a document is filed or sent to the court by electronic means other than facsimile, as permitted by a practice direction made under r.5.5, and the document is verified by a statement of truth, the practice direction will contain special provisions indicating how the signature requirements of r.22.1(6) shall be satisfied; e.g. PD 7C (Money Claims Online) paras 9 and 10 (see paras 7CPD.9 and 7CPD.10), and PD 5B (Electronic Communication and Filing of Documents by E-Mail) para.5 (see para.5BPD.5). Other practice directions now making special provision for the making of statements of truth in documents filed by electronic means, or forms completed on court websites, include PD 55B (Possession Claims Online) paras 8 and 9 (see paras 55BPD.8 and 55BPD.9). Note also PD 5A (Court Documents) para.1 (Signature of documents by mechanical means) (see para.5APD.1) and PD 7B (Production Centre) para.1.4(4) (Modification of PD 22) (see para.7BPD.1).

PART 24

SUMMARY JUDGMENT

Editorial introduction

Replace the last paragraph with:

24.0.1 In certain types of case, proceedings which are akin to summary judgment proceedings are provided automatically as a filter so as to ensure that only those cases which have a real prospect of defence go forward to trial (the Show Cause procedure under Practice Direction 49B (Mesothelioma Claims) as to which, see para.49BPD.6.2, above; and the first hearing under Pt 55 (Possession Claims) as to which, see para.55.8.1, below and *Forcelux Ltd v Binnie* [2009] EWCA Civ 854; [2009] 5 Costs L.R. 825; [2010] H.L.R. 20, noted in para.3.1.17.2, above).

Adjudication decisions in favour of a company in liquidation

Replace paragraph with:

24.3.5 An adjudication decision in favour of a company in insolvent liquidation will not generally be enforced by way of summary judgment: *Bouygues UK Ltd v Dahl-Jensen UK Ltd* [2001] 1 All E.R. (Comm) 1041 (see also on this point *Bresco Electrical Services Ltd (In Liquidation) v Michael J Lonsdale (Electrical) Ltd* [2019] EWCA Civ 27; [2019] 3 All E.R. 337).

Depending on the facts, following *Bresco*, the position might be different where summary enforcement was being sought by a company that was subject to a Company Voluntary Arrangement rather than being in insolvent liquidation: in such a scenario the court had jurisdiction to grant summary enforcement (see *FTH Ltd v Varis Developments Ltd* [2022] EWHC 1385 (TCC), the decision of Adrian Williamson QC sitting as a High Court judge). The proper approach is to decline to grant summary enforcement if there is a real risk that granting it would deprive the defendant of security for its cross-claim: *John Doyle Construction Ltd (In Liquidation) v Erith Contractors Ltd* [2020] EWHC 2451 (TCC); [2021] 2 All E.R. (Comm) 955.

In *John Doyle Construction Ltd (In Liquidation) v Erith Contractors Ltd* [2021] EWCA Civ 1452 the Court of Appeal, considering *Bresco*, held, obiter, that a company in liquidation with an adjudication decision on its final account claim in its favour, but facing a continuing set-off and counterclaim, was not entitled to summary judgment. Coulson LJ, further, gave guidance on the burden on a claimant in an application to enforce the decision of an Adjudicator at [28]–[32]: any undertakings offered by a claimant company in liquidation needed to be clear, evidenced and unequivocal.

Replace r.24.4(2) with:

Procedure[1]

(2) If a party applies for summary judgment before a defendant has filed a defence, the defendant by or against whom the application is made need not file a defence before the hearing. **24.4**

Contents of an application notice

In the first paragraph, replace list item (6) with:

(6) draw the attention of the respondent to r.24.5(1) (see para.2(5) of the Practice Direction supplementing Pt 24 (at para.24PD.2 below)). **24.4.9**

Evidence in support of the application

In the first paragraph, replace "Practice Direction supplementing Pt 8 para.5.2 (see para.8APD.5)." with:

Practice Direction 49E para.5.2 (see para.49EPD.5). **24.4.10**

An order dealing with costs

In the second paragraph, replace "Practice Direction 7B" with:

Practice Direction 49C **24.6.8**

PART 25

INTERIM REMEDIES AND SECURITY FOR COSTS

Forms

After the first bullet point, replace "use (see Practice Direction (Forms) Tables 1 and 3):" with:

use: **25.0.4**

In the last paragraph, delete the second sentence.

I. Interim Remedies

Rule 25.1(1)(a): Interim injunction

Unnamed defendants

In the third paragraph, replace "Practice Direction 8A para.20 (para.8APD.20)." with:

Practice Direction 49E para.20 (para.49EPD.20). **25.1.12.3**

Replace the fifth paragraph (beginning "See also the") with:

In *Barking & Dagenham LBC v Persons Unknown* [2022] EWCA Civ 13, the Court of Appeal clarified that injunctions against persons unknown, whether interim or final, can bind newcomers who become aware of the order made and "make themselves" a party by violating such order. State-

[1] Amended by the Civil Procedure (Amendment) Rules 2000 (SI 2000/221), the Civil Procedure (Amendment No.3) Rules 2005 (SI 2005/2292) and the Civil Procedure (Amendment No.2) Rules 2022 (SI 2022/783).

ments to the contrary in *Canada Goose UK Retail Ltd v Persons Unknown* [2020] EWCA Civ 303; [2020] 1 W.L.R. 2802, at [89]-[92], were inconsistent with earlier decisions of the Court of Appeal and were not to be regarded as good law.

Form of order for interim injunction

In the second paragraph, replace "use (see Practice Direction (Forms), Table 3):" with:

25.1.13 use:

Rule 25.4(1)(a): Interim remedy order in support of foreign proceedings

In the penultimate paragraph, replace "(see para.8BPD.1)." with:

25.4.2 (see para.49FPD.1).

II. Security for Costs

"A defendant to any claim may apply"

Application to set aside a recognition order

25.12.4.1 *In the first sentence, delete "an action entitled".*

How to apply

In the third paragraph, replace "Practice Direction 8A para.5.2, see para.8APD.5." with:

25.12.5 Practice Direction 49E para.5.2, see para.49EPD.5.

Ideal time for applying

In the first paragraph, replace "discretion to order security." with:

25.12.6 discretion to order security (see *Everwarm Ltd v BN Rendering Ltd* [2019] EWHC 1985 (TCC), Cockerill J, at [15]-[16]).

Replace the last paragraph with:

In *Owners of the Panamax Alexander v Registered Owners of the NYK Falcon* [2022] EWHC 478 (Admlty) (Andrew Baker J), it was held appropriate to weigh in the balance the degree to which, if at all, the lateness of the application will cause any prejudice to the claimant. On the facts of that case there were none. This was even allowing for the argument that the reason that security for costs applications should be brought sooner rather than later was to give the claimant a meaningful opportunity to decide whether to pursue the claim or drop it, paying the costs, prior to the more substantial costs being incurred that will be incurred after whatever earlier point was the time when, all things being equal, a security for costs application could have been brought.

Amount of security

After the first paragraph, add new paragraph:

25.12.7 In *Pisante v Logothetis* [2020] EWHC 3332 (Comm); [2020] Costs L.R. 1815 (Henshaw J) and *Tulip Trading Ltd v Bitcoin Association for BSV* [2022] EWHC 141 (Ch) (Master Clark) the principles were summarised as follows:

"(i) The appropriate quantum is a matter for the court's discretion, the overall question being what is just in all the circumstances of the case. In approaching the exercise, the court will not attempt to conduct an exercise similar to a detailed assessment, but will instead approach the evidence as to the amount of costs which will be incurred on a robust basis and applying a broad brush (see also *Excalibur Ventures v Texas Keystone* [2012] EWHC 975 (QB) § 15).

(ii) In some cases, the court may apply an overall percentage discount to a schedule of costs having regard to (a) the uncertainties of litigation, including the possibility of early settlement and (b) the fact that the costs estimate prepared for the application may well include some detailed items which the claimant could later successfully challenge on a detailed assessment between litigants. There is no hard and fast rule as to the percentage discount to apply. Each case has to be decided upon its own circumstances and it is not always appropriate to make any discount.

(iii) In deciding the amount of security to award, the court may take into account the 'balance of prejudice' as it is sometimes called: a comparison between the harm the applicant would suffer if too little security is given and the harm the claimant would suffer if the amount secured is too high. The balance usually favours the applicant: an under-secured applicant will be unable to recover the balance of the costs which is unsecured whereas, if the applicant is not subsequently awarded costs, or if too much security is given, the claimant may suffer only the cost of having to put up security, or the excess amount of security, as the case may be (see also *Excalibur* § 18).

...

(v) In determining the amount of security, the court must take into account the amount that the respondent is likely to be able to raise. The court should not normally make continuation of their claim dependent upon a condition which it is impossible for them to fulfil."

Security on an indemnity basis

To the end of the paragraph, add:

In *Tulip Trading* Master Clark refused to order security for costs on the indemnity basis commenting, inter alia, that the approach urged by the defendants would require her to consider the merits of the claim, without having heard any detailed argument on them (see [11]–[20]). **25.12.7.2**

Manner and time within which security must be given

In the second paragraph, delete "Waller LJ considered it preferable to adopt instead the practice of the Commercial Court (as to which, see para.25.12.10 below).". **25.12.8**

In the last paragraph, replace the last sentence with:

Coulson J, as he then was, granted a freezing injunction against the director and his wife in order to maintain the status quo pending the appeal.

Add new paragraph at end:

In *Saurympper v Fishman Brand Stone (A Firm)* [2022] EWHC 752 (Ch) Master Teverson held that it was open to the court in its discretion to accept security for costs in the form of a charge over property if satisfied that the property provided adequate security and that it would not be just to require the claimant to sell the property in order to pursue their claim. However, the claimant was in a position to provide security in a conventional form and the balance of injustice to the claimant in having to tie up some of their cash until trial and the injustice to the defendant in being without readily realisable security fell in favour of the defendant.

Effect of legal expenses insurance on applications for security for costs

Replace the second paragraph with:

Even at the jurisdictional stage of considering security for costs, defendants are entitled to some assurance that the insurances are not liable to be avoided for misrepresentation or non-disclosure; see *Premier Motorauctions* (above) in particular at [27] and [29]. Akenhead J in *Michael Phillips Architects Ltd v Riklin* [2010] EWHC 834 (TCC) held, when summarising the relationship between security and ATE, that: **25.12.9**

> "it is necessary where reliance is placed by a claimant on an ATE insurance policy to resist or limit a security for costs application for it to be demonstrated that it actually does provide some security. Put another way, there must not be terms pursuant to which or circumstances in which the insurers can readily but legitimately and contractually avoid liability to pay out for the defendants costs."

For a further consideration of ATE policy terms in this context, see *Lewis Thermal Ltd v Cleveland Cable Co Ltd* [2018] EWHC 2654 (TCC) in which O'Farrell J held that an ATE insurance policy did not provide the defendant with adequate security and payments in were ordered. Subsequently a deed from the claimant's ATE insurers indemnifying the defendant for any costs awarded against the claimant at the case's conclusion was held to give the defendant adequate security for its costs and was substituted for the order for payment into court, see [2018] EWHC 3033 (TCC).

As to other issues concerning ATE policies, including the creditworthiness and reputation of the insurer and the effect which overseas insolvency proceedings taken against the insured claimant may have on policy enforcement, see further, *Verslot Dredging BV v HDI Gerling Versicherung AG* [2013] EWHC 658 (Comm) and *Harlequin Property (SVG) Ltd v Wilkins Kennedy (A Firm)* [2015] EWHC 1122 (TCC).

Policy terms which do not include any anti-avoidance clause

In the second paragraph, after "It is now", delete "firmly". **25.12.9.1**

Replace the third paragraph with:

In *Infinity Distribution Ltd (In Administration) v Khan Partnership LLP* [2021] EWCA Civ 565; [2021] 1 W.L.R. 4630, reversing the decision at first instance, it was held that a relevant factor to be taken into account that allowing C to give security by way of increasing the cover on a pre-LASPO

ATE policy would potentially expose D to possible liability for the cost of the premium: *Infinity Distribution Ltd (In Administration) v Khan Partnership LLP* [2021] EWCA Civ 565; [2021] 1 W.L.R. 4630, instead, the Court of Appeal ordered that security be given by payment into court.

The absence of any anti-avoidance clause can sometimes be remedied by the insurer executing a deed of indemnity in favour of the defendants (*Premier Motorauctions* (above) at [29] and see also *Verslot Dredging BV v HDI Gerling Versicherung AG* [2013] EWHC 658 (Comm)). Such a deed can also overcome difficulties in accessing the benefits of the policy if the insured becomes insolvent, as discussed in *Ure Energy Ltd v Notting Hill Genesis* [2021] EWHC 2695 (Comm) at [45] and *Re Ingenious Litigation* [2020] EWHC 235 (Ch).

Alternatively, the insurer may make a policy endorsement which provides that any costs ordered to be paid to the defendant would be paid directly, without set-off (*Harlequin Property (SVG) Ltd v Wilkins Kennedy (A Firm)* [2015] EWHC 1122 (TCC) at [37] and see also, *Recovery Partners GB Ltd v Rukhadze* [2018] EWHC 95 (Comm); [2018] 1 W.L.R. 1640 and *Lewis Thermal Ltd v Cleveland Cable Co Ltd* [2018] EWHC 3033 (TCC) (O'Farrell J), mentioned in para.25.12.14).

Discretionary power to order security for costs

The merits

25.13.1.2 *In the first sentence, after "It has", delete "clearly and recently".*

Discretionary factors where both claims and counterclaims are raised

Add new paragraph 25.13.2.4:

25.13.2.4 *Trustees in bankruptcy*—Security for costs would only be ordered against a trustee in bankruptcy in an exceptional case: *Trustees in Bankruptcy v Li Shu Chung* [2021] 11 WLUK 462. Although *Li Shu Chung* was decided under the Cross-Border Insolvency Regulations 2006 (SI 2006/1030), the principle of exceptionality was held by Falk J to apply at common law (applying *Cowell v Taylor* (1885) 31 Ch. D. 34), see *Kireeva v Bedzhamov* [2022] EWHC 1047 (Ch). In *Kireeva* Falk J granted a Russian national's application for security for his costs of the remittal of an application by his Russian trustee in bankruptcy for recognition of the bankruptcy order in England and Wales. The case was held to be exceptional; the trustee had no assets in England and Wales against which an order for costs could be enforced, there was a real risk of non-enforcement in Russia, and there was no assurance that the trustee's litigation funder would fund an adverse costs order if the application for recognition failed.

No discrimination against claimants resident in other States

In the first paragraph, after "cannot be made", add:

25.13.6 (absent any other relevant gateway/provision)

Rule 25.13(2)(g): Taking steps as to assets which hinder enforcement

After the second paragraph, add new paragraph:

25.13.16 This guidance has been cited with approval in *Kolyada v Yurov* [2014] EWHC 2575 (Comm), [27], *Al Jaber v Al Ibrahim* [2019] EWHC 1136 (Comm), [4] and *Re Tonstate Group Ltd* [2020] EWHC 328 (Ch), [11]. It has also been held that it can also be important to note the extent of the effect of the steps taken by the respondent upon the ability of the applicant to enforce the following or subsequent cost judgment, because that effect is relevant to the exercise of the discretion. For example, if the steps taken have a minimal effect on the ability of the applicant subsequently to enforce a judgment, then the court is much less likely to make an order. See *Stavrinides v Cyprus Popular Bank Public Co Ltd* [2018] EWHC 313 (Ch), [58]–[60] (Master Bowles) referred to by HH Judge Paul Matthews, sitting as High Court judge in *Axnoller Events Ltd v Brake* [2021] EWHC 2640 (Ch).

Rule 25.14(2)(b): Financing claimant's costs in return for a share of any fruits of proceedings

Add new paragraph at end:

25.14.3 When considering a claim for security for costs against solicitors acting for the opposing party, Ritchie J held that that recovery of hourly rates for legal work on winning a case could not be categorised as "a share of any money or property which the claimant may recover": although successful claimants recovered their lawyers' costs, such costs were not their own winnings, *Edwards v Slater and Gordon UK Ltd* [2022] EWHC 1091 (QB).

PART 26

CASE MANAGEMENT—PRELIMINARY STAGE

Replace r.26.2A(6)(c) with:

Transfer of money claims within the County Court[1]

(c) if the claim falls within Practice Direction 49D– **26.2A**

(i) the defence is filed; or

(ii) enforcement of a default judgment other than by a warrant of control is requested,

whichever occurs first.

Rule 26.2A: Effect of rule

Replace the last paragraph with:

Practice Direction 49D, referred to in para.(6), deals with claims for the recovery of taxes and **26.2A.3** duties (see para.49DPD.1). As directions questionnaires are not required in relation to claims by HM Revenue and Customs for the recovery of taxes and duties (see PD 49D) such claims should be sent to the relevant County Court hearing centre on the filing of a defence and listed for hearing in accordance with para.2.1 of PD 49D.

Rule 26.8: Effect of rule

After the penultimate paragraph, add new paragraphs:

"Any amount not in dispute" includes in relation to a claim of an admission made by the **26.8.4** defendant prior to allocation that reduces the amount in dispute: *Akhtar v Boland* [2014] EWCA Civ 872.

In *Williams v Santander UK Plc* [2015] EW Misc B37(CC), a PPI claim, an application was unsuccessfully made to re-allocate a case allocated to the small claims track to the fast track to take into account the complexity of the matters being argued. The district judge determined that the costs on any other track than small claims would be completely disproportionate to the disputed sums.

The value of any counterclaim or other Part 20 Claim

Add new paragraph at end:

A case allocated to the multi-track as a consequence of an inflated counterclaim may result in **26.8.5** the defendant being penalised in costs: *Peakman v Linbrooke Services Ltd* [2008] EWCA Civ 1239.

PART 27

THE SMALL CLAIMS TRACK

Rule 27.9: Effect of rule

Replace the second paragraph with:

If a party gives notice under r.27.9(1) and does not attend the hearing the district judge will **27.9.1** prepare a written note of the reasons for the decision and send a copy to each party (PD 27A para.5.4). The requirement for the district judge to prepare a written note of reasons is mandatory, and failure to do so may result in a successful appeal: *Mohammad v Churchill Insurance Co Ltd* [2022] 2 WLUK 182 per HH Judge Hassall.

---

[1] Introduced by the Civil Procedure (Amendment No.4) Rules 2011 (SI 2011/3103) and amended by the Civil Procedure (Amendment) Rules 2013 (SI 2013/262), the Civil Procedure (Amendment) Rules 2014 (SI 2014/407), the Civil Procedure (Amendment No.4) Rules 2014 (SI 2014/867) , the Civil Procedure (Amendment No.5) Rules 2015 (SI 2015/1881), the Civil Procedure (Amendment No.3) Rules 2016 (SI 2016/788) and the Civil Procedure (Amendment No.2) Rules 2022 (SI 2022/783).

Parties in person cannot give written notice of their non-attendance but then attend the hearing by way of a representative appearing on their behalf.

PART 28

THE FAST TRACK

Editorial introduction

In the second paragraph, after "residential premises against", replace "his landlord for damages" with:

28.0.1 their landlord for damages

In the second paragraph, replace "district judges and circuit judges" with:

District Judges and Circuit Judges

Replace the last paragraph with:

(Note that the provisions below, like those relating to the other litigation tracks, were subject to the emergency provisions of Practice Directions 51Y, 51Z and 51ZA introduced in March 2020 in response to the Coronavirus pandemic. Only PD 51Y remains in force, until 25 March 2023.)

Pre-action protocols

Replace the second paragraph with:

28.2.2 There are currently 17 pre-action protocols (set out at para.C1A-003). However, the spirit of the protocols applies to all cases, and paras 3-13 of the Practice Direction–Pre-Action Conduct and Protocols impose specific obligations on the proposed parties (see paras C1-002 et seq.).

"the court will fix the trial date or fix a period ... within which the trial is to take place"

Replace the first paragraph with:

28.2.3 In practice it is more likely that the court will fix a trial period (often referred to as a "trial window") of one, two or three weeks rather than give a fixed trial date. However some courts do fix a trial date when giving case management directions. If that is not the practice of the particular court, it can be asked to fix a trial date at the allocation stage if there is a particular reason why it should do so. Early fixing of the trial date or trial period–and insisting upon it–is of the essence of the fast track.

Split trial

Replace paragraph with:

28.2.5 One consequence of the fast track regime has been an increase in the number of cases where liability is ordered to be tried separately from and before the issue of quantum. The power to order a split trial is found in r.3.1(2)(i). If the claimant fails on liability, a significant costs saving is invariably achieved and the case is concluded at a much earlier stage. If the claimant succeeds on liability, quantum may be agreed without a further hearing. Often, due to non-availability of experts, it will not be possible to fix a trial date within the 30-week period and ordering a trial on liability only is one way to overcome this difficulty. Furthermore, a case is allocated to the fast track only if the trial is likely to last for no longer than one day and oral expert evidence is limited to one expert per party in relation to any expert field and to two fields only (see r.26.6(5)). By narrowing the issues for trial, the court will be able to allocate to the fast track a case that might otherwise have had to be allocated to the multi-track. It must be anticipated that, where a case is within the financial limits of the fast track, the court will make every effort to allocate it to the fast track.

Scope of provision

Replace paragraph with:

28.3.1 In a fast track case, the only matters which need to be addressed when giving directions are the fixing of the trial date or trial period and the three matters mentioned in r.28.3(1): disclosure, witness statements, expert evidence. Standard directions are contained in and encouraged by PD 28 para.2.7 and Appendix A. Parties will have to undertake more pre-issue preparation than was formerly the case (see above commentary on "Pre-action protocols" and "Split trial" at paras 28.2.2 and 28.2.5 respectively). Standard disclosure (defined in r.31.6) may be ordered (PD 28 para.3.9), but disclosure should be limited to what is required in each case having regard to what is proportionate: the court may order a limited form of disclosure and leave it to the parties to seek specific disclosure if required. Exchange of witness statements will always be ordered. If either party is relying on expert evidence (note the limitations in r.26.6(5) and see generally Pt 35), the court will have to give directions as to service of experts' reports. Permission is always required to adduce expert evidence (r.35.4(1)). Usually a single joint expert will be directed as this is a proportionate and cost-effective way to proceed and so in accordance with the overriding objective. The court will bear in mind that normally trial of a fast track case "is likely to last for no longer than one day" (see r.26.6(5)).

Rule 28.4: Effect of rule

Replace paragraph with:

A case management timetable, once set, should be complied with. The aim of the rules is to set a **28.4.1** realistic timetable which all must then honour. It should be noted that orders for directions should have a warning at the top as to compliance with its terms and the imposition of sanctions in the event of default. However, minor variations (e.g. extending by a few days the time for exchange of witness statements) can be agreed by the parties in writing without troubling the court: see rr.2.11 and 3.8(4) which allow parties to agree to vary dates for compliance with directions by up to 28 days as long as any such variation does not put at risk any hearing date (note that, under para.2 of PD 51ZA which was in force under the Coronavirus provisions until 30 October 2020, this extension period was up to 56 days). There is no requirement to file such an agreement (see para.4.5(1) of PD 28) although it may be sensible to do so. However, it is made clear in r.28.4(1) that the trial date (or trial period if the trial date is not yet fixed: see r.28.2 above) and the date for return of the pre-trial checklist (formerly the "listing questionnaire") cannot be varied simply by agreement, so a party who wishes to vary any of these dates must apply to the court. (See Pt 23 for general rules regarding applications.) It must be anticipated that the court will not be pre-disposed to delaying the trial and very cogent arguments and reasons will be required in order to achieve it:

> "Litigants and lawyers must be in no doubt that the court will regard the postponement of a trial as an order of last resort. The court may exercise its power to require a party as well as his legal representative to attend court at a hearing where such an order is to be sought" , per para.5.4(6) of PD 28.

In the unlikely event of the court granting an adjournment costs sanctions must be anticipated.

Rule 28.5: Effect of rule

Replace the first paragraph with:

The court will have fixed a trial date or (more likely) a trial period of one, two or three weeks **28.5.1** when it gave directions upon allocation (see r.28.2). The trial date or end of the trial period will be not more than 30 weeks from the directions. The court needs to make final listing arrangements (especially where a fixed date has not yet been given) as the period draws to a close. Further, it is anticipated that a significant proportion of cases will have been settled during the trial preparation period and will not now require a trial (settlement rate of fast-track cases is very high). Rule 28.5 therefore requires the court to send out a "pre-trial check list". This will be done about 10 weeks before the trial date or beginning of the trial period. The precise date for the return of the pre-trial check list is specified in the notice of allocation and that date "will not be more than 8 weeks before the trial date or beginning of the trial period".

"fix the date for trial"

Replace "a trial window" with:

a trial period **28.6.2**

"trial timetable"

Replace paragraph with:

Rule 26.6(5) provides that the fast track is the normal track for cases within its financial limit **28.6.4** ("not more than £25,000") "only if the court considers that the trial is likely to last for no longer than one day". Paragraph 9.1(3)(a) of the Practice Direction supplementing Pt 26 states that "one day" means five hours (i.e. 10.30 to 16.30 or thereabouts, including one hour for lunch). It has always been envisaged that, for fast track cases, in addition to the case management rules, some firm judicial control of the trial itself will be required. Parties—and especially advocates—need to know in advance how much time has been allocated to the case. Accordingly, a trial timetable is necessary and will be given at the listing stage. Rule 28.6(1) requires the court to give a trial timetable. See also Pt 39 and in particular note that r.39.4 provides that when the court sets a timetable for trial, it will do so in consultation with the parties; in practice, this is normally updated at the commencement of the trial. Practice Direction 28 (see para.28PD.18) contains the format for a trial timetable.

28.6.6 *Change title of paragraph:*

Summary assessment of costs at fast track trial

PART 29

THE MULTI-TRACK

Fixing the trial date

In the second paragraph, replace the last sentence with:

29.2.6 Target dates which are even shorter are provided for some cases governed by PD 49B (Mesothelioma Claims) as to which see para.49BPD.7.

PART 30

TRANSFER

Rule 30.3(1)(a): "transfer between the High Court and the county court"

To the end of the second paragraph, add:

30.3.1 It was held in *Lappett Manufacturing Co Ltd v Rassam* [2022] EWHC 1412 (Ch) that the High Court would retain a low-value intellectual property claim where significant non-monetary relief was sought.

Chancery Division

In the first paragraph, after "out in r.30(3)(2)", add:

30.3.14 (and see *Lappett Manufacturing Co Ltd v Rassam* [2022] EWHC 1412 (Ch) where the High Court would retain a low-value intellectual property claim where significant non-monetary relief was sought)

After the penultimate paragraph, add new paragraph:

Circumstances may exist where claims in the Chancery Division should be transferred to the Family Division to be heard with overlapping or related claims, although questions of timing may be important—see *Aldridge v O'Leary* [2022] EWHC 420 (Ch).

Intellectual property claims

To the end of the penultimate paragraph, add:

30.3.21 In *Lappett Manufacturing Co Ltd v Rassam* [2022] EWHC 1412 (Ch) the High Court retained a low-value intellectual property claim where significant non-monetary relief was sought within the Shorter Trials scheme on the basis that the defendant's financial resources were not so low as to require a transfer to IPEC; while in *Cook (UK) Ltd v Barton Scientific Ltd* [2022] EWHC 2060 (Pat) a claim was transferred out of the Shorter Trials scheme when it had become apparent that the trial estimate was to be lengthened.

PART 31

DISCLOSURE AND INSPECTION OF DOCUMENTS

31.0.0 *Change title of paragraph:*

Relationship with PD 57AD—Disclosure Pilot Scheme

Replace paragraph with:

For cases in the Business and Property Courts, see the disclosure pilot scheme in Practice Direction 57AD. This was introduced (originally as PD 51U) on 1 January 2019 without transitional provisions, and so applies to all existing proceedings, including even where an initial disclosure order has already been made before that date: *UTB LLC v Sheffield United Ltd* [2019] EWHC 914 (Ch); [2019] 3 All E.R. 698 at [16]-[17] per Vos C. Where the pilot applies, CPR Pt 31 is disapplied in its entirety and issues of disclosure and inspection are governed by Practice Direction 57AD. See paras 51.2.7, 57ADPD.1, and 57AB.4, and following for details of the pilot scheme and its application.

Delete paragraph 31.0.1.1, "Brexit".

(2) Litigation privilege

Solicitors and non-professional agent or third party

To the end of the penultimate paragraph, add:

Whether the identity of a person communicating with a lawyer is protected by the privilege **31.3.8** depends on whether the underlying communication is protected by the privilege, and whether that privilege would be undermined by the disclosure of the identity of the person in issue: *Loreley Financing (Jersey) No 30 Ltd v Credit Suisse Securities (Europe) Ltd* [2022] EWHC 1136 (Comm).

(3) Legal professional privilege generally

Subsequent litigation

After the second paragraph, add new paragraph:

As to the effect of disclosure in earlier foreign proceedings, the effect of a loss of privilege in a **31.3.17** foreign jurisdiction on disclosure in English litigation is resolved by applying English law: *Rochester Resources Ltd v Lebedev* [2014] EWHC 2185 (Comm); *Bourns Inc v Raychem Corp (No.3)* [1999] 3 All E.R. 154; *Suppipat v Willkie Farr & Gallagher (UK) LLP* [2022] EWHC 381 (Comm). It is relevant to ask whether the document and its information remained confidential, in the sense of being not available for use in the English litigation: *Suppipat v Willkie Farr & Gallagher (UK) LLP*.

Waiver or loss of privilege

To the start of the eighth paragraph (beginning "Where legal professional"), add:

If there has been a waiver of privilege, the court must then consider the scope of the waiver: **31.3.24** *PJSC Tatneft v Bogolyubov* [2020] EWHC 3225 (Comm); [2021] 1 W.L.R. 1612, at [48] per Moulder J.

After the eighth paragraph, add new paragraphs:

Voluntary disclosure of a privileged document may result in waiver of privilege in other material, but not necessarily all documents in the same category, or relating to all issues upon which the disclosed document touches, however a broader waiver may result where the voluntary disclosure is partial or selective such that unfairness or misunderstanding may result if there is not a broader waiver: *R. (Jet2.Com Ltd) v Civil Aviation Authority* [2020] EWCA Civ 35; [2020] Q.B. 1027 at [111]; *Paragon Finance Plc (formerly National Home Loans Corp) v Freshfields* [1999] 1 W.L.R. 1183, CA, at 1188D per Lord Bingham CJ.

It is necessary to identify the issue in relation to which the voluntary disclosure has been deployed, with waiver being limited to documents relating to that "transaction", subject to overriding requirements of fairness: *R. (Jet2.Com Ltd) v Civil Aviation Authority* [2020] EWCA Civ 35; [2020] Q.B. 1027 at [113]; *General Accident Fire & Life Assurance Corp Ltd v Tanter (The Zephyr)* [1984] 1 W.L.R. 100 at 113D per Hobhouse J. To identify the "transaction", one looks to what it is in essence that the waiving party was seeking to disclose, and to this end, the purpose of the disclosure may in some cases provide a realistic, objectively determinable definition of the transaction: *Fulham Leisure Holdings Ltd v Nicholson Graham & Jones (A Firm)* [2006] EWHC 158 (Ch); [2006] 2 All E.R. 599, at [18]. The purpose of the voluntary disclosure is an important consideration in the assessment of what constitutes the relevant transaction. The identification of the transaction must be approached realistically to avoid either artificially narrow or wide outcomes: *R. (Jet2.Com Ltd) v Civil Aviation Authority* [2020] EWCA Civ 35; [2020] Q.B. 1027 at [114]; *PCP Capital Partners LLP v Barclays Bank Plc* [2020] EWHC 1393 (Comm), at [85].

It is not open to the waiving party to say that the transaction is simply what that party chose to disclose; the court determining for itself what the real transaction is, and thus the scope of the waiver: ibid. Once the transaction has been identified and proper disclosure made of that, then the additional principles of fairness may come into play if it is apparent from the disclosure that has been made that it is in fact part of some bigger picture (not necessarily part of some bigger "transaction") and fairness, and the need not to mislead, requires further disclosure: ibid, at [19].

Moulder J summarised the relevant principles in *E20 Stadium LLP v Allen & Overy LLP* [2022] EWHC 1808 (Comm) at [28] as follows:

"i) it is for the court to determine objectively what the real transaction is so the scope of the waiver can be determined;
ii) one has to look at what it is in essence that the waiving party is seeking to disclose;
iii) in some cases the purpose of the disclosure may provide a realistic, objectively determinable definition of the transaction in question;
iv) once the transaction has been identified and proper disclosure made of that, then the additional principles of fairness may come into play if it is apparent from the disclosure that has been made that it is in fact part of some bigger picture (not necessarily part of some bigger transaction) and fairness, and the need not to mislead, requires further disclosure."

(4) Other grounds of privilege

Without prejudice communications

To the start of the thirteenth paragraph (beginning "The test for loss"), add:

31.3.39 The without prejudice privilege continues after settlement has been reached, and can be asserted in subsequent proceedings: *Rush & Tompkins Ltd v Greater London Council* [1989] A.C. 1280, HL, at 1301 per Lord Griffiths; *Avonwick Holdings Ltd v Webinvest Ltd* [2014] EWCA Civ 1436, at [22] per Lewison LJ; *EMW Law LLP v Halborg* [2017] EWHC 1014 (Ch), at [37].

Description-privileged documents

In the second paragraph, replace the first sentence with:

31.10.3 This is the long-established and widespread practice of the profession, confirmed in case law, e.g. *Tonstate Group Ltd v Wojakovski*, 11 February 2022, unrep., ChD (Sir Alastair Norris).

Privileged documents mentioned in witness statements

Add new paragraph at end:

31.14.6 Where the content of specific conversations is mentioned in a witness statement, disclosure and inspection may be ordered of any attendance note of the relevant conversations: *Scipharm Sarl v Moorfields Eye Hospital NHS Foundation Trust* [2021] EWHC 2079 (Comm). Where the meeting was with lawyers, whether the privilege has been waived will depend on whether there had been a sufficiently direct allusion to an attendance note, and in the absence of an express explanation as to how the information had come to be included in the witness statement, an inference may be drawn that it must have been by way of reliance on attendance notes: *Schipharm.*

Scope of documents covered by pre-action disclosure

In the last paragraph, replace "PD 51U:" with:

31.16.3 PD 57AD:

"The court may make an order ..."

31.17.2.1 *Delete the second paragraph.*

"hearing ... held in public"

Add new paragraph at the start:

31.22.2 An order made by the court without a hearing, following the submission by the parties of an agreed draft order, was not one made as in "a hearing ... held in public": *UXA v Merseycare NHS Foundation Trust* [2021] EWHC 3455 (QB); [2022] 4 W.L.R. 30, at [31] per Fordham J.

PRACTICE DIRECTION 31C—DISCLOSURE AND INSPECTION IN RELATION TO COMPETITION CLAIMS

Delete paragraph 31CPD.0, "Introduction".

PART 32

EVIDENCE

Rule 32.1: Effect of rule

In the fourth paragraph (beginning "Where proceedings, having"), replace "Practice Direction 8B" with:

32.1.1 Practice Direction 49F

Proof by oral evidence at trial

In the first paragraph, replace "(Practice Direction 8A (Alternative Procedure for Claims), para.5.2 (see para.8APD.5))." with:

(Practice Direction 49E (Alternative Procedure for Claims) para.5.2 (see para.49EPD.5)). **32.2.1**

Delete paragraph 32.4.19, "References to written evidence in practice forms".

Rule 32.9: Effect of rule

In the second paragraph, after the first sentence, add:

The standard directions from the court ordering service of witness statements or any notices or summaries by a particular date do not give permission to serve summaries instead of witness statements. Express permission to serve witness summaries must be sought in accordance with this rule (*Otuo v Watch Tower Bible and Tract Society of Britain* [2019] EWHC 346 (QB)). **32.9.1**

Rule 32.15: Effect of rule

Delete the last paragraph. **32.15.1**

Rule 32.16: Effect of rule

Replace paragraph with:

For form and swearing of affidavits, see further Practice Direction 32 (Evidence) paras 2 et seq. and Annex 1 (see paras 32PD.2 and 32PD.27, below). **32.16.1**

PRACTICE NOTE: WITNESSES GIVING EVIDENCE REMOTELY

Add new paragraph 32PN.0.1:

Editorial introduction

This Practice Note was issued in May 2021. It was retained by the Chancery Practice Note 2022, issued by the Chancellor in July 2022. **32PN.0.1**

PART 34

WITNESSES, DEPOSITIONS AND EVIDENCE FOR FOREIGN COURTS

Forms

After the eighth bullet point (beginning "No.37 Order"), add:

- **PF120A** Witness Summons in the High Court issued by special order of the High Court under section 36(1) of the Senior Courts Act 1981 **34.0.6**

I. Witnesses and Depositions

"witness summons"

After the first paragraph, add new paragraph:

For witnesses within the jurisdiction a Form **N20** must be used, but if the proposed witness is out of the jurisdiction the **PF120A** procedure must be used, which requires the consent of the court before it is issued. Parties must apply to the High Court for witness summonses for all inferior courts and tribunals: see r.34.4. **34.2.1**

II. Evidence for Foreign Courts

Distinction between evidence for trial or for pre-trial purposes

After the penultimate paragraph, add new paragraph:

In *Sakab Saudi Holding Co v Al Jabri* [2021] EWHC 3390 (QB) (Senior Master Fontaine), a request was refused in part on the basis that it appeared to be an impermissible fishing expedition. **34.21.5**

PART 35

EXPERTS AND ASSESSORS

Types of cases raising particular considerations

35.1.5 *Change title of subparagraph:*

Professional negligence

Replace paragraph with:

In *Pantelli Associates Ltd v Corporate City Developments Number Two Ltd* [2010] EWHC 3189 (TCC) ([17]), it was held (subject to certain exceptions) to be standard practice that a pleaded allegation of professional negligence must be supported, in writing, "by a relevant professional with the necessary expertise". However, in *ACD (Landscape Architects) Ltd v Overall* [2012] EWHC 100 (TCC); [2012] P.N.L.R. 407 ([17]), Akenhead J held that, whilst a party must have "sufficient" to enable the statement of case in question to be verified with a statement of truth, the foregoing standard practice did not constitute an immutable rule, setting out various circumstances in which it may not apply.

As to the treatment of a defendant's opinion evidence in professional negligence cases, in *DN v Greenwich LBC* [2004] EWCA Civ 1659 at [25]-[26], Brooke LJ said:

> "It very often happens in professional negligence cases that a defendant will give evidence to a judge which constitutes the reason why he considers that his conduct did not fall below the standard of care reasonably to be expected of him ... it is certainly admissible ... Of course, a defendant's evidence on matters of this kind may lack the objectivity to be accorded to the evidence of an independent expert, but this consideration goes to the cogency of the evidence, not to its admissibility."

Add new paragraphs 35.1.6.1 and 35.1.6.2:

35.1.6.1 *Foreign law*—As to the flexibility of adducing evidence of the content of foreign law and the fact that:

> "The old notion that foreign legal materials can only ever be brought before the court as part of the evidence of an expert witness is outdated" ,

see *FS Cairo (Nile Plaza) LLC v Lady Brownlie* [2021] UKSC 45, [148] per Leggatt JSC.

35.1.6.2 *Acoustic shock*—In *Storey v British Telecommunications Plc* [2022] EWCA Civ 616, the Court of Appeal noted that acoustic shock is different from, and unrelated to, noise-induced hearing loss. As such, and depending upon the circumstances, it may be possible for a claim to proceed to trial without expert evidence from an acoustic engineer.

Application of Pt 35 to judicial review

Add new paragraph at end:

35.1.9 In *R. (Gardner) v Secretary of State for Health and Social Care* [2021] EWHC 2946 (Admin), Bean LJ noted that the practice in the TCC of factual witnesses often giving technical and expert opinions accorded with the practice in, for example, professional negligence cases and personal injury claims arising out of factory accidents, where:

> "it is common for witnesses of fact to express a view that a particular practice was not unsafe. The judge, while making the appropriate discount for the fact that the witness is not independent, may have regard to such evidence. If the witness's evidence is contentious the opposing party can cross examine on it."

However, he noted that judicial review claims are not treated in the same way for the reasons given in the *Law Society* case and because, except in rare cases, cross-examination is not permitted in judicial review cases ([8]-[9]).

Public procurement

Replace the first paragraph with:

35.1.10 The principles governing the adducing of expert evidence in public procurement cases are summarised in *Atos Services UK Ltd v Secretary of State for Business, Energy and Industrial Strategy* [2022] EWHC 42 (TCC).

Add new paragraphs 35.1.12 and 35.1.13:

35.1.12 *Intellectual property*—In claims concerning common consumer goods in registered design cases expert evidence as to consumer "eye appeal" is not necessary to assist the court (*Thermos Ltd v Aladdin Sales & Marketing Ltd* [2000] F.S.R. 402, Ch D).

As to whether trade evidence is expert evidence, see *Fenty v Arcadia Group Brands Ltd (t/a Topshop)* [2013] EWHC 1945 (Ch), as applied and further considered in *Lifestyle Equities CV v Royal County of Berkshire Polo Club Ltd* [2022] EWHC 1244 (Ch).

Construction law—In *Multiplex Constructions (UK) Ltd v Cleveland Bridge UK Ltd* [2008] EWHC 2220 (TCC) at [671], Jackson J made reference to the decision in *DN v Greenwich LBC* (see above) and noted that, as a matter of practice in the TCC, technical and expert opinions were often given by factual witnesses in the course of their narrative evidence, without objection. Though such opinion evidence did not have the same standing as that of independent experts called pursuant to CPR Pt 35, it was usually valuable and saved costs. **35.1.13**

Add new paragraph 35.3.2.1:

Expert witness immunity

Expert witnesses were, for several centuries, immune from suit in respect of the evidence they gave. That immunity, a particular application of witness immunity from suit, was considered by the UK Supreme Court in *Jones v Kaney* [2011] UKSC 13; [2011] 2 A.C. 398. While it maintained expert witness immunity from defamation claims, it abolished it in respect of claims for negligence. As a result, experts are now at risk of proceedings for negligence brought by the party instructing them in respect of advice given prior to proceedings being issued and in respect of the evidence they give; see *Hersi & Co Solicitors v Lord Chancellor* [2018] EWHC 946 (QB), at [95]. **35.3.2.1**

However an expert's duty does not extend to protecting a party from the risk of adverse credibility findings: *Radia v Marks* [2022] EWHC 145 (QB) at [61].

Independence issues in relation to experts

After the second paragraph, add new paragraph:

In *Radia v Marks* [2022] EWHC 145 (QB), a negligence claim brought against a medical expert who had previously been instructed to act as a single joint expert, Lambert J held that the scope of the duty of care owed by a medical expert where the tribunal had made adverse credibility findings about the claimant, did not extend to protecting the claimant from the risk of an adverse credibility finding, or a finding of dishonesty. **35.3.4**

The joint statement

After the sixth paragraph (beginning "In BDW Trading"), add new paragraph:

Serious breach of this guidance in *Andrews v Kronospan Ltd* [2022] EWHC 479 (QB) resulted in the revocation of permission for a claimant to rely upon certain expert evidence in group litigation. **35.12.2**

Delete paragraph 35.12.4, "Expert witness immunity".

PART 36

OFFERS TO SETTLE

Related sources

Replace the fourth bullet point with:

- Practice Direction 49F—The Pre-Action Protocols for Low Value Personal Injury Claims in Road Traffic Accidents and Low Value Personal Injury (Employers' Liability and Public Liability) Claims—Stage 3 Procedure (see para.49FPD.0) **36.0.5**

Replace r.36.1(3) with:

Scope of this Part[1]

(3) Section II of this Part contains rules about offers to settle where the parties have followed the Pre-Action Protocol for Low Value Personal Injury Claims in Road Traffic Accidents ("the RTA Protocol") or the Pre-Action **36.1**

[1] Introduced by the Civil Procedure (Amendment No.8) Rules 2014 (SI 2014/3299) and amended by the Civil Procedure (Amendment No.2) Rules 2022 (SI 2022/783).

Protocol for Low Value Personal Injury (Employers' Liability and Public Liability) Claims ("the EL/PL Protocol") and have started proceedings under Part 8 in accordance with Practice Direction 49F.

I. Part 36 Offers to Settle

Nature of a Part 36 offer

To the end of the first paragraph, add:

36.2.2 In *O'Grady v B15 Group Ltd* [2022] EWHC 67 (QB), Master Thornett held that the common-law doctrine of mistake could apply where the offeree appreciated that a clear and obvious mistake had been made.

36.3.2 *Change title of paragraph:*

Rule 36.3(g): "the relevant period"

To the end of the paragraph, add:

As Pt 36 is a self-contained code, the court has no power either under Pt 36 or under r.3.1(2)(a) to vary the 21-day time period: *Begum v Barts Health NHS Trust* [2022] EWHC 1668 (QB) at [10]-[11].

II. RTA Protocol and EL/PL Protocol Offers to Settle

Replace r.36.24(2) with:

Scope of this Section[1]

36.24 **(2) This Section applies to an offer to settle where the parties have followed the RTA Protocol or the EL/PL Protocol and started proceedings under Part 8 in accordance with Practice Direction 49F ("the Stage 3 Procedure").**

History of Section II

The RTA Protocol

Replace "Practice Direction 8B." with:

36.24.1 Practice Direction 49F.

Effect of Section II

Replace the first paragraph with:

36.24.4 The RTA and the EL/PL Protocols describe the processes which the court will normally expect parties to follow prior to the start of proceedings for low-value personal injury claims arising out of a road traffic accident or employer's or public liability. For the details of the Protocols and the Stage 3 process, see para.C13A-001 (for the RTA Protocol), para.C15A-001 (for the EL/PL Protocol) and para.49FPD.0 (for Practice Direction 49F). Both Protocols state that, where the parties do not reach an agreement on the amount of damages, the claimant must send the Court Proceedings Pack (Part A and Part B) Form to the defendant. That Form must contain (amongst other things) the final offer and counteroffer from the Stage 2 Settlement Pack Form (see para.7.64 of the RTA Protocol; para.7.48 of the EL/PL Protocol). Where, having followed the Stage 1 and Stage 2 processes as stipulated in the Protocol, but having not succeeded in agreeing the amount of damages payable at the end of Stage 2, the claimant may start court proceedings against the defendant under the Stage 3 Procedure as set out in Practice Direction 49F for the purpose of determining quantum. Proceedings under the Stage 3 Procedure are subject to the fixed costs regime contained in Section III of Pt 45 (r.45.16). These pre-issue offers made during the pursuit of the RTA or the EL/PL Protocol processes are known as "Protocol offers" (r.36.25).

In the last paragraph, replace "(para.6.1 of Practice Direction 8B, at para.8BPD.6)." with:

(para.6.1 of Practice Direction 49F at para.49FPD.6).

Withdrawal of a Protocol offer

Replace "Practice Direction 8B and not Pt 36 (see para.8BPD.10)." with:

36.25.1 Practice Direction 49F and not Pt 36 (see para.49FPD.10).

---

[1] Introduced by the Civil Procedure (Amendment No.8) Rules 2014 (SI 2014/3299) and amended by the Civil Procedure (Amendment No.2) Rules 2022 (SI 2022/783).

Deemed date of offer

Replace paragraph with:

A "Part 36 offer", made in accordance with Section I of Pt 36, is made when it is served on the offeree (r.36.7(1)). A "Protocol offer" as defined in r.36.25 is not an offer served by one party on another during Stage 2 of the Protocol process, but an offer made using the Court Proceedings Pack (Part B) Form (r.36.25(2)(a)). The Court Proceedings Pack Form is prepared by the claimant after the parties have failed to reach agreement under Stage 2 and should include (in Part B) the parties' final offers. Court proceedings under the Stage 3 Procedure as set out in Practice Direction 49F are started by a claim form. The claim form must (amongst other things) state the date when the Court Proceedings Pack (Part B) Form, containing the final offer and counter offer, was sent to the defendant (para.5.2(2) of Practice Direction 49F at para.49FPD.5). It would not be wholly accurate to say that a final offer is made at the time when the Form is sent by the claimant to the defendant. Rather it is recorded there after negotiations between the parties have been completed for the purposes of any court proceedings under the Stage 3 procedure as set out in Practice Direction 49F, and thereby becomes a "Protocol offer". Rule 36.26(2) was inserted into Section II by the Civil Procedure (Amendment No.8) Rules 2014 (SI 2014/3299), with effect from 6 April 2015, in order to supply the missing wording to make para.(1) work. **36.26.1**

Offers and appeal costs

In the first paragraph, replace "Practice Direction 8B." with:

Practice Direction 49F. **36.27.1**

Rule 36.28: Effect of rule

Replace "Practice Direction 8B," with:

Practice Direction 49F, **36.28.1**

PART 38

DISCONTINUANCE

Rule 38.2: Effect of rule

Replace the last paragraph with:

It is not entirely clear from rr.38.3(1) and 38.5(1) whether a notice of discontinuance is required where the court's permission to discontinue must be obtained. On its face, r.38.3 requires the filing and service of a notice for a discontinuance to take place, whatever the circumstances may be. This is reinforced by r.38.5 which specifies that discontinuance takes effect on service of the notice on the relevant defendant or defendants, and by the fact that there is a prescribed Form **N279** and mandatory requirements (see r.38.3). The terms of the rule are explicit and it is hard to avoid the conclusion that the filing and service of a notice of discontinuance is required in every case. Obtaining the court's permission, where it is required, is a preliminary step to discontinuance which takes place by filing and service of the notice. Unless and until notice has been filed and served there has not been a discontinuance. However, it may well be, in practice, that the court often implicitly waives the requirement for a notice and deals with costs and any other issues that arise on the permission hearing. In *Galazi v Christoforou* Chief Master Marsh held that this was a sensible pragmatic approach, albeit not one which can be found in the existing rule; and a similar approach seems to have been taken in *Pycom Ltd v Campora* [2022] 7 WLUK 114. The CPRC have, with effect from 1 October 2022, amended r.38.3 to add a new subrule (5) requiring a notice of discontinuance to be in the Form **N279**, unless the court otherwise permits, in order to emphasise the need for a specific judicial decision and direction. **38.2.1**

Permission to discontinue

To the end of the last paragraph, add:

For an example of a case where the court regarded it as appropriate to refuse permission and instead to dismiss the claim, see *Vale SA v Steinmetz* [2022] EWHC 343 (Comm). **38.2.2**

In *Wilson v Bayer Pharma AG* [2022] EWHC 670 (QB) the requirement for other claimants to consent in writing was waived in a group action case for reasons of practicality.

Add new r.38.3(5):

Procedure for discontinuing[1]

38.3 **(5) The notice of discontinuance must be in Form N279 unless otherwise permitted by the court.**

Notice of discontinuance

Replace "in Form N279." with:

38.3.1 in Form **N279** (and from 1 October 2022 there is inserted a new subrule (5) requiring use of that form unless the court otherwise permits, thus emphasising the need for a judicial decision if the mandatory form is not being used).

Rule 38.6: Effect of rule

After the second paragraph, add new paragraph:

38.6.1 In *Galazi v Christoforou* [2019] EWHC 670 (Ch) it was held that the removal of a cause of action by way of a CPR Pt 17 amendment could amount to a deemed discontinuance of that part of the case and so r.38.6 applied. A similar approach was adopted in *Pycom Ltd v Campora* [2022] 7 WLUK 114. The CPRC has questioned whether Pt 38 should have any direct application in the Pt 17 context and has referred the point to its general reviewing subcommittee.

In the penultimate paragraph, replace "Hewson v Wells [2020] EWHC 2722 (Ch); and GREP London Portfolio II Trustee 3 Ltd v BLFB Ltd [2021] EWHC 1850 (TCC) (issuing claim in order to preserve limitation and to conduct equivalent to a Pre-Action Protocol process was not there sufficient to displace the rule)." with:

Hewson v Wells [2020] EWHC 2722 (Ch); *GREP London Portfolio II Trustee 3 Ltd v BLFB Ltd* [2021] EWHC 1850 (TCC) (issuing claim in order to preserve limitation and to enable conduct equivalent to a Pre-Action Protocol process to occur was not there sufficient to displace the rule); *Countrywide Signs Ltd v Blueprometheus Ltd* [2022] EWHC 573 (Ch) (defendant's unreasonable conduct resulted in no order as to costs); and *Epoq Legal Ltd v DAS Legal Expenses Insurance Co Ltd* [2022] EWHC 1577 (Comm) (not unreasonable for defendant to exercise contractual right to be refer to mediation).

Basis for costs

To the end of the paragraph, add:

38.6.2 In *Epoq Legal Ltd v DAS Legal Expenses Insurance Co Ltd* [2022] EWHC 1577 (Comm) where a defendant had exercised a contractual right to refer to mediation and the claimant had discontinued, only standard basis costs were awarded as it was held that the defendant had delayed and acted tactically. In *Pycom Ltd v Campora* [2022] 7 WLUK 114 partial indemnity costs were awarded where the claimant should have realised the weakness of their case and discontinued at an earlier point.

Rule 38.7: Effect of rule

Replace the second, third and fourth paragraphs with:

38.7.1 Where the conditions stated in paras (a) and (b) of this rule apply, a claimant who wishes "to make another claim" requires the permission of the court. In terms the rule imposes no fetter on the court's discretion but the court will require a sufficient explanation for what has happened "to overcome its natural disinclination to permit a party to re-introduce" a previously discontinued claim (*Hague Plant Ltd v Hague* [2014] EWCA Civ 1609; [2015] C.P. Rep. 14, at [61] per Briggs LJ). The court is likely to give permission, for example, where the claimant was misled or tricked by the defendant, where important new evidence has come to light or where there has been a retrospective change in the law (e.g. a Supreme Court case overruling a Court of Appeal decision which had led the claimant to discontinue). All these examples are, of course, unusual cases and assume that the limitation period has still not expired. However, in *Western Power Distribution (South West) Plc v South West Water Ltd* [2020] EWHC 3747 (TCC) it was held, apparently, that the court is to look at the matter and all the circumstances in the round, and it is for the defendant to show why it is manifestly unfair to allow the second claim to proceed especially where the first claim had been discontinued at an early stage and there was a sufficient explanation; but that and some other elements of the reasoning of that decision (but not its outcome) were not accepted in *Astley v Mid-Cheshire* (below). There is a distinction between a previous claim being "dismissed" (which may well prevent the claim being raised again) and being "discontinued"; see *Spicer v Tuli* [2012] EWCA Civ 845; [2012] 1 W.L.R. 3088, CA, where the making of an order that a claim be "dismissed" rather than "discontinued" was said to be a technical error of which it would be unconscionable to allow

[1] Amended by the Civil Procedure (Amendment No.2) Rules 2022 (SI 2022/783).

the defendant to take advantage. A useful summary of the principles appears in both *Wickham v Riley* [2020] EWHC 3711 (Fam) at [41], where a claimant was allowed to bring a second claim where he had discontinued the first when he was a vulnerable 18-year old, and in *Astley v Mid-Cheshire Hospitals NHS Foundation Trust* [2022] EWHC 337 (QB) where an incremental clarification of the law was regarded as insufficient in the circumstances of that case.

It was held in *King v Kings Solutions Group Ltd* [2020] EWHC 2861 (Ch) (not following *Ward v Hutt* on this point) that, whether or not r.38.7 applied, it might be and there was an abuse of process for the claimant, after having discontinued a previous claim, to, in effect, bring the claim again, applying *Henderson v Henderson* [1843–60] All E.R. Rep. 378 and *Johnson v Gore Wood & Co (No.1)* [2002] 2 A.C. 1 principles (and see also "Attempts to re-litigate issues which were raised, or should have been raised, in previous proceedings", para.3.4.5 above); and that such an abuse of process might arise even if a claim did not fall within r.38.7 because either (i) it did not arise from the same or substantially the same facts of; or (ii) it was against a different person from the defendant to, the previous discontinued claim. However, in *Astley v Mid-Cheshire* the judge applied the broad-based test as set out in *Hague v Hague* and regarded matters such as potential for abuse (and also consideration of the merits) as merely factors to be taken into account rather than as being elements of the test itself.

The rule is silent as to how or when the claimant seeks permission. Chief Master Marsh has held, although obiter, that an application has to be made for permission prior to issue of the second claim—see *Saulawa v Abeyratne* [2018] EWHC 2463 (Ch) basing himself on the previous text of this paragraph which indicated that a specific Part 23 application would be required for permission and inferring that this should be prior to the issue of the claim form. However, the rule says nothing as to how or when the permission needs to be sought (and as to whether it might or might not be sought in a statement of case or by a post-issue Part 23 application) and the contrary can be argued from the court's approach in other contexts and the general power of waiver in CPR r.3.10. The CPRC has expressed some dissatisfaction with the *Saulawa* dicta, and their updating subcommittee is consulting with regard to amending the rule to provide that permission should be sought in the claim form itself, and also as to its application to the Part 8 procedure.

PART 39

MISCELLANEOUS PROVISIONS RELATING TO HEARINGS

Impact of COVID-19 on public hearings

Replace the first paragraph with:

From 25 March 2020, Practice Direction 51Y (March 2020) has provided an additional procedure to that contained in CPR r.39.2 for holding wholly audio or video hearings in public or in private; *Teesside Gas Transportation Ltd v Cats North Sea Ltd* [2020] EWCA Civ 503 at [93]–[96]. And see *Gubarev v Orbis Business Intelligence Ltd* [2020] EWHC 2167 (QB) on the need to maintain a clear distinction between wholly and partially audio or video hearings: see para.51.2.11. **39.2.0.1**

Rule 39.2: "hearing to be in public"

At the end of the fourth paragraph (beginning "The rule, as"), replace "at [21(7)]." with:

at [21(7)] and see also *R. (Public and Commercial Services Union) v Secretary of State for the Home Department* [2022] EWHC 823 (Admin). **39.2.1**

Rule 39.2(3)(c): "confidential information" and "personal financial matters"

After the second paragraph, add new paragraph:

The Court of Appeal in *CDE v NOP* [2021] EWCA Civ 1908 considered whether the judge at first instance had erred in holding a case management conference in private in Commercial Court proceedings involving allegations which had been the subject of arbitration proceedings and had resulted in an award which the claimants wanted to be in the public domain. The Court of Appeal reaffirmed that a hearing could only be conducted in private if the court was satisfied of one or more of the matters set out in r.39.2(3)(a) to (g) and that it was necessary to sit in private to secure the proper administration of justice. The court noted that arbitral confidentiality is recognised by English law as significant and worthy of protection and that the fact that the arbitration and/or the award is confidential was sufficient to demonstrate confidentiality. However, when the court comes to consider at a later stage whether it is necessary to sit in private to secure the proper administration of justice, the absence of other detriment may be relevant. The Court of Appeal explained that, although the case management conference clearly involved confidential information, confidentiality itself was not a trump card and the critical question was whether it had been neces- **39.2.3.1** sary to sit in private to secure the administration of justice. Although the court will take into account various factors, including the stage that the proceedings had reached and the nature of the hearing, it must have in mind the reasons why proceedings are in general required to be subject to "the full glare of a public hearing" (see Lord Woolf in *R. v Legal Aid Board Ex p. Kaim Todner* [1999] Q.B. 966). In the instant case, once it had been shown that r.39.2(3)(c) applied, a debate was required about whether the court should sit in private at the case management conference. The Court of Appeal held that the tension between the principle of open justice and the confidentiality of the award had to be addressed and because of publicity concerning the case, that debate could only take place in private and, therefore, it had been necessary for the judge to sit in private to secure the proper administration of justice.

Rule 39.2(4): Anonymity of party or witness

In the second paragraph, replace the sentence after the list with:

39.2.13 See *R. (Newsquest Media Group Ltd) v Police Misconduct Tribunal* [2022] EWHC 299 (Admin). See also *R. (CHF) v Headteacher and Governing Body of Newick Church of England Primary School* [2021] EWCA Civ 613 for the approach to be taken in amending an anonymity order in favour of children so that it extends to their parents.

Replace the last paragraph with:

In *Pink Floyd Music Ltd v EMI Records Ltd* [2010] EWCA Civ 1429; [2011] 1 W.L.R. 770, Lord Neuberger MR stated that party anonymisation (whether or not granted by the court below) will be granted in the Court of Appeal only if, and only to the extent that, a member of the court is satisfied that it is necessary for the proper administration of justice and gave guidance as to the correct procedure to be adopted where a party to an appeal wants anonymisation ([62]-[69]). See also Practice Guidance—Anonymisation of Parties to Asylum and Immigration Cases in the Court of Appeal (Vos MR, Underhill LJ (VP), dated 22 March 2022) (see para.52PG.2), which replaced *Practice Note (Court of Appeal: Asylum and Immigration Cases)* [2006] 1 W.L.R. 2461. For anonymity orders (and reporting restrictions) in relation to proceedings in the Supreme Court (and continuation of orders made by court below), see Vol.2, paras 4A-10.1.1 and 4A-20.8.1. See also para.40.2.13 (Judgments and anonymity orders), and Vol.2, para.15-42 below.

Add new Practice Guidance: Open Justice–Remote Observation of Hearings–New Powers:

PRACTICE GUIDANCE: OPEN JUSTICE—REMOTE OBSERVATION OF HEARINGS—NEW POWERS

Introduction

39PG.3 **1.** From 28 June 2022, courts and tribunals will have new powers to allow reporters and other members of the public to observe hearings remotely. The purpose of this Practice Guidance is to help judicial office holders understand and apply the new law.

Background and sources

2. Open justice has been a fundamental principle for centuries. The principle is a broad one, but at its core has always been a right of access to a public hearing. Historically, this has meant access for reporters and other members of the public to the court or other room in which the hearing takes place. Recently, there has been a move towards remote access.

3. Remote observation of public hearings was first allowed by temporary provisions enacted by the Coronavirus Act 2020. Those provisions applied only to wholly video or wholly audio hearings. The temporary provisions are repealed and replaced by a new and permanent regime with expanded powers. Courts and tribunals are now able to give directions to allow remote observation of in-person and hybrid hearings as well.

4. The primary legislation is contained in section 85A of the Courts Act 2003 as inserted by section 198 of the Police, Crime, Sentencing and Courts Act 2022. The regime is implemented by the Remote Observation and Recording (Courts and Tribunals) Regulations 2022. Judicial office holders will need to familiarise themselves with the statutory text. Fortunately this is relatively concise and clear. What follows is a summary of the main features of the legislation.

Nature, purpose and scope of the new power

5. The power is to "direct that images or sounds of the proceedings be transmitted electronically". It is to be exercised "for the purpose of enabling persons not taking part in the proceedings to watch or listen to" them. So it is not designed for those taking part in the proceedings. Other powers cover remote participation.

6. This power is given to any "court", but in this context that term has the expanded meaning of "any tribunal or body exercising the judicial power of the state". This Guidance adopts that meaning. The power can be exercised in "proceedings of any type" that are (a) in public or (b) not open to the general public but "specific categories of person, or specific individuals, who are not taking part in the proceedings are entitled to be present by virtue of provision made by or under any enactment or of being authorised by the court." The second category would include youth court proceedings, family proceedings to which the media or researchers are admitted under FPR 27.11(2), and other hearings in private, where the court has allowed a non-participant to attend.

7. There are two kinds of direction that can be made. The first is a direction for transmission to "premises" designated by the Lord Chancellor as live-streaming premises. The second option is a direction for transmission "to which individuals are given access". The first option might be used in a case that generates a high level of public interest, to enable proceedings to be watched from a second court room or a room in some external premises. This would require a designation. The second option can be used alongside the first. Or it can be used as a stand-alone measure, which is likely to be more common. If this option is used, the individuals must first identify themselves to the court. It is not a form of broadcasting.

8. There are two straightforward threshold criteria for giving a direction. Before making a direction the court must be satisfied that (a) it would be in the interests of justice to make it; (b) there is capacity and technological capability to enable transmission and giving effect to the direction would not create an unreasonable administrative burden.

9. There is a list of mandatory considerations. The court must take into account the need for open justice; the timing of any access request and its impact on the business of the court; the extent to which the resources necessary for effective remote observation are or can be made available; any statutory limitation on those entitled to observe; any issues that might flow from observation by people outside the UK; and any impact which the making or withholding of such a direction, or its terms, might have upon (i) the content and quality of the evidence; (ii) public understanding; (iii) the ability of the media and public to observe and scrutinise; and (iv) the safety and right to privacy of any person involved with the proceedings. This is a useful checklist of matters which a court would be likely to consider in any event.

The form of a "direction"

10. For over two years, courts have been making directions for remote access under the temporary provisions, with varying degrees of formality. The Regulations do not require any fundamental changes of practice, but they do prescribe some minimum requirements.

11. Any direction other than an order for live-streaming to designated premises must require those who want to watch or listen to (a) identify themselves to the court by providing their full name and email address beforehand, unless the court dispenses with the requirement to provide their full name and email address and (b) conduct themselves appropriately, and in accordance with the court's directions, during the transmission. These twin requirements need not burden judicial office holders. They can be built into standard forms of messaging, via email or on the platform being used to give remote access. Those standard messages will also need to make plain that unauthorised recording or transmission of the hearing is a contempt of court.

12. Where the proceedings are only open to certain categories of person the direction must contain provision for them to demonstrate their right to attend and it must prohibit observation by those who are not authorised. Again, these standard requirements can be built into standard forms.

13. Responsibility for the fair and lawful processing of personal data required for these limited purposes will lie with HMCTS or the other public authority responsible for court administration.

14. A direction can also include other provisions, for instance about the manner of the transmission, and about who can watch or listen. A direction can impose conditions or limits on access. Conditions could, where appropriate, include deadlines by which to apply for access, restrictions on the numbers given access, or enhanced requirements for identification to enable the court to be confident that a person seeking remote access will not risk impeding or prejudicing the administration of justice. The requirement that those who wish to observe remotely must identify themselves remotely cannot be relaxed, but the court could expressly dispense with the default requirement for names and email addresses—for instance, where a family group attends from home. In such cases those wishing to observe remotely must identify themselves by other means.

Principles

15. Judicial office holders must consider the prescribed factors and apply the statutory test. What follows is no substitute for the statutory provisions, nor is it intended to be exhaustive, but it is a list of general factors that courts will wish to keep in mind, assuming the threshold requirement of technological capability is met. More detailed guidance or protocols may be developed in particular jurisdictions.

16. *The decision whether to make any and if so what direction for remote observation will always be a judicial decision not an administrative one.* In order to minimise the burden on judicial office holders the judiciary will help HMCTS develop effective operating procedures. It is likely that a degree of standard practice will develop. This may include standing access arrangements for those who regularly report on proceedings. But the ultimate power and responsibility for a decision on remote access lies with the judicial office holder in the individual case.

17. *Decision-makers must give due weight to the importance of open justice.* This is a mandatory consideration. Open justice serves the key functions of exposing the judicial process to public scrutiny, improving public understanding of the process, and enhancing public confidence in its integrity. Remote observation can promote all those purposes. Access for reporters, legal commentators and academics is likely to do so. Judicial office holders may take as a starting point that remote access for other observers is desirable if they would be entitled in principle to have access to a courtroom in which the hearing was taking place, and giving them remote access is both operationally feasible and compatible with the interests of justice.

18. *Timing and impact on the business of the court must be considered.* Media applications and others that are timely and uncontroversial may pose no difficulty. On occasion, however, applications may be late, or numerous, or raise complex issues. Judicial office holders might properly guillotine the process, limit the numbers given access, or decline to deal with an application if they would otherwise be disabled or impeded from administering justice in the case itself, or diverted from other pressing judicial duties.

19. *Decision makers must give due weight to all the relevant circumstances, including the factors identified in the Regulation.* The Regulation is not an exhaustive list, other factors may arise too. Nor do the matters listed in the Regulation operate necessarily as trump cards in every case. All circumstances have to be considered. For example, taking into account the impact on a right of privacy of a person involved, in relation to the remote observation of a hearing which is to be in open court, does not necessarily mean remote observation should always be refused. Whether to do so or not will depend on the circumstances.

20. *Remote observation should be allowed if and to the extent it is in the interests of justice; it should not be allowed to jeopardise the administration of justice in the case before the court.* The primary duty of any court is to administer justice in the case before it. In some circumstances, remote observation could jeopardise that aim. For example, a witness might be reluctant to give evidence under remote observation by an unknown number of unseen persons, or the quality of the evidence might be impaired by the prospect. Remote observers may be more likely than someone watching in a court room to breach a reporting restriction or the ban on filming or photography or to engage in witness intimidation. They may be harder to observe, identify and hold to account if they do. For observers outside the jurisdiction these risks may be greater, and it is unlikely that sanctions for disobedience could in practice be imposed. Judicial office holders should consider whether any such risks exist in the case that is before them when assessing whether remote access would be in the interests of justice. They should reflect the answer in their decisions and in the content of any directions they make.

21. *Issues about remote observation should not undermine the court's ability to meet the needs of other cases.* Decision-makers are required to satisfy themselves that giving effect to a direction would not unreasonably burden the court or its staff. In some cases the parties may provide the means of remote access. Otherwise, the facilities and personnel will be provided by HMCTS or another public sector body. Provision varies. Most salaried judicial office holders will know very well what facilities and personnel are available to them. Others may be reliant on information from those responsible for their court. The court must bear in mind the need to allocate its scarce resources in an appropriate way between the cases that come before it. Open justice has been and still can be achieved without remote access.

22. *Any derogations from open justice should apply equally to remote observers.* It is sometimes necessary to derogate from open justice, for instance by restricting public access to aspects of the evidence or restricting reporting of what takes place in open court. In such a case it is very likely that the court will need to impose equivalent restrictions on remote observers. That may have practical implications which will need consideration. For example, if screens are used to prevent a witness being seen in court, steps will be needed to make sure that restriction applies to remote observers. Reporting restriction orders may need to be communicated to remote observers by email.

23. *The ultimate decision will inevitably depend on the nature of the jurisdiction, the particular resources available at the relevant time, and the specific facts and circumstances of the case.* The work undertaken in courts and tribunals covers a vast spectrum. The turnover of work, the technical facilities and available staff resources vary greatly geographically and over time. These are all matters that can properly influence a decision.

24. *It will not usually be necessary to give more than the briefest reasons.* These are multi-factorial assessments which will often have to be made at speed by judicial office holders who are best placed to identify and evaluate the considerations relevant to the application before them and to reach robust decisions in the interests of justice.

Unauthorised recording

25. Remote observers must be warned that they must not record or transmit what they see and hear and may be punished if they do. The statutory bans on filming and photography and audio recording in the courtroom remain in place. The new s 85B of the Courts Act 2003 makes it both a summary offence and a contempt of court for a person remotely attending court proceedings to make or attempt to make an unauthorised recording or transmission of an image or sound that is being transmitted to them. The maximum sentence is therefore two years' imprisonment.

26. Some established systems contain written warnings. Examples are here. If the method they are using does not do this, judicial office holders will need to give an oral warning. It may be wise to do so in any event. Judicial office holders need not assume that in all instances a warning will be enough to deter such misconduct.

June 2022

Lord Burnett of Maldon	Sir Keith Lindblom
Lord Chief Justice	Senior President of Tribunals

PART 40

JUDGMENTS, ORDERS, SALE OF LAND ETC.

I. Judgments and Orders

Effect of judgment before entry—altering judgment

To the end of the first paragraph, add:

40.2.1 The *Re Barrell* jurisdiction does not, however, create jurisdiction where none existed: see *Preston v Beaumont* [2022] EWHC 440 (Ch) (no jurisdiction to deal with an application for costs where there was non-compliance with the mandatory requirements of PD 40E).

Recalling and reconsidering judgment

Replace the first paragraph with:

40.2.1.1 In *AIC Ltd v Federal Airports Authority of Nigeria* [2022] UKSC 16; [2022] 1 W.L.R. 3223 at [30]–[40] the Supreme Court reviewed the court's jurisdiction, including its prior decision in *Re L-B (Children) (Care Proceedings: Power to Revise Judgment)* [2013] UKSC 8; [2013] 1 W.L.R. 634, SC, to recall and reconsider a judgment before it is perfected. In considering whether to do so, a judge is required to do justice according to the overriding objective. The principle of finality is an inherent part in the overriding objective. Given that, a judge approaching such a question must not do so from a position of neutrality: the scales are not evenly balanced. If it is clear that a judgment should not be re-opened, i.e. an application to re-open has no real prospect of success, it may be refused without a hearing. A two-stage test or process to an application to re-open should not be adopted. The discretionary jurisdiction to re-open is essentially flexible, with the judge essentially asking themselves whether they should set aside their order and replace it with a new one. In considering whether to re-open, the principle of finality, which applies when an order is made, not when it is sealed, will always be a weighty matter in assessing that question. The weight to be given to it will necessarily depend on the judgment or order to potentially be re-opened. It will be of greater weight where a final order or judgment is concerned, and will be of less weight where the order is an interim one or a case management order. Reference to the need for "exceptional circumstances" or similar terms to refer to the weight given to finality is, however, to be avoided. Ultimately,

> "[39] ... The question is whether the factors favouring re-opening the order are, in combination, sufficient to overcome the deadweight of the finality principle on the other side of the scales, together with any other factors pointing towards leaving the original order in place.
>
> [40] It would also be wrong to attempt to identify a list of factors prima facie qualifying for inclusion as being in principle sufficient to displace the finality principle. Subsequent cases will always reveal that the list has proved to be inadequate, and the peculiarities of the present case could hardly have been imagined in advance. Some, such as judicial change of mind, have already been the subject of analysis in the authorities, but even they are of widely variable weight. It is perhaps easier to advance factors that will have no significant weight, such as a desire by counsel to re-argue a point lost at trial in a different way."

Delete the sixth, seventh, eighth, ninth, tenth and eleventh paragraphs (beginning "In Bank St Petersburg" and ending "abuse of process).").

Replace the twelfth paragraph (beginning "In Heron Bros") with:

For an explanation of the practice in Patents Court proceedings which enables a patentee to make an application after judgment, not simply to delete claims which have been held invalid, but rather to make what are contended to be validating amendments to some or all of the claims and to seek a second trial of the amended claims, see *Generics (UK) Ltd v Warner-Lambert Co LLC* [2015] EWHC 3370 (Pat) (Arnold J) (where it was held that the amendment sought amounted to an abuse of process).

Altering draft judgment

Replace the first paragraph with:

Modern practice in the High Court and the Court of Appeal is that judges, on a confidential basis, routinely make available their written judgments to legal advisers in advance of the handing down hearing (see further para.40.2.6.1 below). The duties of counsel in these circumstances were stressed and explained in *Crown Prosecution Service v P* [2007] EWHC 1144 (Admin); [2008] 1 W.L.R. 1024 (see further para.40.2.6 below). If a judge sends their written judgment to the advisers in draft, and they are able to agree the consequential orders, the judge may be able to excuse their attendance when delivering the judgment formally in court, thereby making it available to the public and the media (if interested), but cannot dispense completely with the formality of handing down the judgment in open court (*Owusu v Jackson* [2002] EWCA Civ 877; cf. *Williams Corporate Finance Plc v Holland* [2001] EWCA Civ 1526). In such circumstances, the judgment may be formally delivered by another judge. A draft judgment may be as good as a judgment signed and sealed for the purpose of enforcing it (*Birmingham City Council v Yardley* [2004] EWCA Civ 1756). **40.2.1.2**

Handing down written judgments—public and private judgments

Delete the last seven paragraphs (beginning "Generally where judgment"). **40.2.6**

Add new paragraphs 40.2.6.1 and 40.2.6.2:

Circulation and confidentiality of draft judgments

Generally, where judgment is reserved in the Court of Appeal or in the High Court, the written judgment will be given to the parties' legal advisers on a confidential basis before the handing down hearing. In a given case, on application a court by order may permit wider circulation. The principle of confidentiality in this context extends to communications with the court in response (*R. (Mohamed) v Secretary of State for Foreign and Commonwealth Affairs* [2010] EWCA Civ 158; [2011] Q.B. 218). Breach of this confidence may be contempt of court. The particular advantages of this practice are that it enables counsel in advance of the handing down hearing: (1) to draw to the attention of the court any minor corrections or amendments that should be made to the judgment before it is handed down; (2) to prepare drafts of consequential orders (whether agreed or not) that will have to be made upon handing down; and (3) to prepare their submissions as to summary assessment of costs and for permission to appeal. The judge is not bound by the terms of the draft judgment as circulated under this practice; the opportunity for correction is available, not only on the application of one of the parties, but also on the judge's personal initiative if, on re-reading their draft, they think it appropriate to do so (*R. (Mohamed) v Secretary of State for Foreign and Commonwealth Affairs*, op cit). The procedure is particularly useful in cases where it is very important that consequential orders be settled quickly (*Re M (Child Abduction: Delay) Times*, 28 August 2007). It may be appropriate for an appellate court to arrange for a written judgment to be given before handing down to an appellant in person (*Perotti v Collyer-Bristow (A Firm) (Vexatious Litigant: Directions: Corrections)* [2004] EWCA Civ 1019). Under this practice the attendance of counsel at the handing down may be unnecessary and, where attendance is unnecessary the costs of attendance may be disallowed. Provisions reflecting and amplifying the points made immediately above are found in various places. **40.2.6.1**

Practice Direction 40E (Reserved Judgments) (see para.40EPD.1 below) contains provisions that apply to all reserved judgments which the court intends to hand down in writing and which regulate the availability of such judgments before handing down, corrections to the draft judgment, orders consequential on judgment, and attendance at handing down. This is designed to take account of the fact that before handing down, routinely draft written judgments are circulated by electronic methods, and to deal with the concerns expressed in *Crown Prosecution Service v P* [2007] EWHC 1144 (Admin); [2008] 1 W.L.R. 1024, and elsewhere. As a consequence, because they were no longer required, provisions dealing with the matter in the practice direction then supplementing Pt 52 (Appeals) were omitted. Earlier provisions dealing with this matter are found in *Practice Statement (Sup Ct: Judgments) (No.1)* [1998] 1 W.L.R. 825, as modified by *Practice Statement (Sup Ct: Judgments) (No.2)* [1999] 1 W.L.R. 1 (see paras 40PS.1 and 40PS.2). It is presumed that these earlier provisions were impliedly revoked by PD 40E.

Practice Direction 40E sets out the normal practice for the circulation in confidence of draft judgments before handing down. In a given case a court may make other arrangements, in particular in cases where national security issues are involved and in which special advocates have been appointed. In *R. (Mohamed) v Secretary of State for Foreign and Commonwealth Affairs* [2010] EWCA Civ 158; [2011] Q.B. 218, Sir Anthony May referred to the practice under which the intelligence services, through the Foreign Secretary, are permitted in such cases:

> "to comb through a draft open judgment before it is published to request redactions which they consider to be required for national security reasons" (at [259]).

His lordship added that this practice can have unsatisfactory procedural consequences and suggested that it may need re-examination before it becomes an entrenched procedure.

Following upon the coming into effect of Practice Direction 40E (Reserved Judgments) (see above), principally for the purpose of ensuring that journalists understand the risks, it was stressed that, unless a specific order is made by the court, all "draft" judgments are embargoed and cannot be published until the "official" judgment is handed down; the publication of a draft judgment would be regarded as a contempt of court and the consequences of a breach of the practice direction might be severe (*Baigent v Random House Group Ltd* [2006] EWHC 1131 (Ch) (Peter Smith J)). In *Crown Prosecution Service v P* [2007] EWHC 1144 (Admin); [2008] 1 W.L.R. 1024, a Divisional Court stressed that, under the Practice Direction, disclosure of a draft judgment to solicitors is limited to the solicitors directly involved in the case. Such solicitors should not disclose a draft to other members of their firms or organisations (e.g. the CPS or government departments), save to the extent necessary for the taking of instructions in respect of the instant case. Any solicitor in doubt as to the propriety of a particular disclosure should request permission from the judge concerned (by email if that is convenient). Further guidance on the circulation of draft judgments was given by the Court of Appeal in *R. (Counsel General for Wales) v Secretary of State for Business, Energy and Industrial Strategy* [2022] EWCA Civ 181 and *Public Institution for Social Security v Banque Pictet & Cie SA* [2022] EWCA Civ 368. In both cases, the court was at pains to stress that compliance with the requirements of the Practice Direction was essential and that any breach should be reported to the court immediately. In *R. (Counsel General for Wales)* at [31], the approach to be taken by barristers was summarised as:

> "... (i) it is not appropriate for persons in the clerks' rooms or offices of Chambers to see the draft judgment or to be given a summary of its contents, (ii) drafting press releases to publicise Chambers is not a legitimate activity to undertake within the embargo, (iii) it should be sufficient for one named clerk to provide the link between the court and the barrister or barristers, (iv) proper precautions and double-checks need to be in place in barristers' Chambers and solicitors offices to ensure that errors come to attention before the embargo is breached, and (v) in future, those who break embargoes can expect to find themselves the subject of contempt proceedings as envisaged in paragraph 2.8 of CPR PD40E."

In *Public Institution for Social Security* at [18] it was stressed that draft judgments should not be circulated for any purpose other than the following legitimate purposes:

> "the making of suggestions for the correction of errors, preparing submissions, agreeing orders on consequential matters and preparation for the publication of the judgment."

Moreover, they should only be circulated to lawyers who were involved in the conduct of the litigation for the purpose of carrying out those legitimate purposes. And see *Match Group LLC v Muzmatch Ltd* [2022] EWHC 1023 (IPEC) at [40], where it was additionally stressed that courts are "likely to look with a very critical eye" at cases where breach of the embargo arose from a party's desire to manage publicity concerning the litigation.

For alteration, either before or after handing down, of a judgment circulated to counsel before handing down as a result of counsel's further submissions, see para.40.2.1, above.

Settlement and hand down of draft judgment

40.2.6.2 The court has responsibilities wider than its duties to the parties. One obvious example is the duty to exercise its power to hand down judgment if to do so is in the public interest, even where parties have settled and do not want the judgment published (*R. (Mohamed) v Secretary of State for Foreign and Commonwealth Affairs* [2010] EWCA Civ 65; [2010] 3 W.L.R. 554, CA, at [178] per Lord Neuberger MR). In *Prudential Assurance Co Ltd v McBains Cooper* [2000] 1 W.L.R. 2000, CA, after the judge had circulated his draft written judgment but before he had handed it down, the parties agreed a settlement and lodged with the court a draft Tomlin order containing a term to the effect that the judge would not publish the judgment. The Court of Appeal upheld the judge's ruling that, in these circumstances, he had a discretion to hand down the judgment notwithstanding the parties' agreement. The court stated: (1) that the parties' agreement is just one factor which a judge should take into account in exercising his discretion in the public interest; and (2) that the purpose of the practice of circulating draft judgments is not to make available to the parties more material to help them settle their dispute. Generally, if a draft judgment has not been sent to parties by the time they compromise, the court (particularly a trial court) will not publish that judgment (*Gurney Consulting Engineers v Gleeds Health & Safety Ltd (No.2)* [2006] EWHC 536 (TCC); 108 Con. L.R. 58 (Judge Peter Coulson QC)). See also *R. (Lodhi) v Secretary of State for the Home Department*, 11 March 2010, unrep., DC (where it was held that it was appropriate for the court to give a substantive, narrative judgment on the merits of an extradition appeal despite the appellant's death in the period between the appeal hearing and the court delivering its reserved judgment).

That a draft judgment had been finalised and circulated prior to settlement does not create a presumption in favour of handing down the judgment (*Beriwala v Woodstone Properties (Birmingham) Ltd* [2021] EWHC 609 (Ch) at [19]–[21], explaining *Prudential Assurance Co Ltd* on this point). In *Barclays Bank Plc v Nylon Capital LLP* [2011] EWCA Civ 826; [2012] 1 All E.R. (Comm) 912, CA,

Lord Neuberger MR at [74]–[75] identified a number of factors that could point towards exercising the discretion to hand down a draft judgment, viz., the judgment dealt with a point concerning which there is a public interest in it being considered in a judgment because, for instance, it raises a point of law of potential general interest, where an appellate court departs from the decision of the court below, where the case involves wrongdoing or an activity that ought to be brought to public attention, or where the case is a matter of legitimate public interest. The last factor was not held as being a "powerful reason" for handing down the draft judgment. In *F&C Alternative Investments (Holdings) Ltd v Barthelemy* [2011] EWHC 1851 (Ch); [2012] Bus. L.R. 884, at [7], Sales J outlined a number of additional relevant factors to be taken account of when considering the discretion to hand down a draft judgment following settlement. Those were: the public interest in conserving court time and resources by bringing the proceedings to an end; whether the dispute concerned the conduct of a range of regulated individuals or entities; whether witness honesty and credibility had been attacked during the trial and would be vindicated in the judgment; and whether there were legal questions that the judgment would develop or on which it would provide guidance. In *Jabbar v Aviva Insurance UK Ltd* [2022] EWHC 912 (QB), it was confirmed that *Prudential Assurance Co Ltd* did not require there to be exceptional circumstances to justify handing down a draft judgment in a private law case. It also affirmed that the approach to handing down was the same whether settlement occurred prior to or after the hand down process had commenced. Circulation of a draft judgment is also not intended to be a means to assist in facilitating settlement: see *R. (S) v General Teaching Council for England* [2013] EWHC 2779 (Admin) at [26]–[27], in which Foskett J considered the relevant authorities and material considerations affecting the exercise of the discretion.

See further *Glaxo Group Ltd v Genentech Inc* [2008] EWCA Civ 23; [2008] Bus. L.R. 888, CA, *R. (Williams) v Secretary of State for Energy and Climate Change* [2015] EWHC 1202 (Admin); [2015] J.P.L. 1257, *Beriwala v Woodstone Properties (Birmingham) Ltd* [2021] EWHC 609 (Ch), *Kingsley Napley LLP v Harris* [2021] EWHC 1641 (QB), *Tecoil Shipping Ltd v Neptune EHF* [2021] EWHC 1582 (Admlty).

II. Sale of Land etc. and Conveyancing Counsel

Permission to bid

Replace paragraph with:

Under a sale directed by the court any party to the claim, desiring to purchase, should obtain permission to bid before the sale; but the sale will not necessarily be set aside because such permission has not been obtained: see CPR PD 40D para.3.1. Bid includes tender or offer: para.3.4. In an appropriate case, the court may order an immediate sale to one of the parties, but should exercise extreme care before doing so; such an order is draconian and unusual: *Kotak v Kotak* [2014] EWHC 3121 (Ch). **40.16.6**

Change title of paragraph: **40.18.1**

Jurisdiction

Replace paragraph with:

Both the High Court and the County Court can refer any matter of title to conveyancing counsel. Part 2 of Practice Direction 40D deals with the mechanism of such references. This procedure is rarely used in practice. The court is more likely to direct expert evidence on any issues relating to title.

Reference to conveyancing counsel

Replace paragraph with:

The usual practice is that the court when making an order does not specify the name of the conveyancing counsel (under PD 40D para.6.1 (see para.40DPD.6)) but refers to "conveyancing counsel of the court". The solicitor concerned will then write to the Chief Master enclosing a copy of the order and asking for nomination of a particular counsel (PD 40D paras 6.2 and 6.3 (see para.40DPD.6). The Chief Master will nominate and write to them, sending them a copy of the order (PD 40D para.6.3 (see para.40DPD.6)), and making such other directions as are appropriate in relation to the provision of documents or otherwise. At the same time the Chief Master will write back to the solicitor concerned, informing them of the name and address of the nominated counsel. **40.18.2**

Conveyancing counsel are appointed under s.131 of the Senior Courts Act 1981 by the Lord Chancellor with the concurrence of the Lord Chief Justice. There are currently no appointed conveyancing counsel of the court.

Add new paragraph 40.18.3:

Fees of conveyancing counsel

Paragraph 5.2 of Practice Direction 44 states that, where the court refers a matter to the conveyancing counsel of the court, the fees payable to counsel in respect of the work done or to be done will be assessed in accordance with r.44.2. **40.18.3**

Delete paragraph 40.19.1, "Jurisdiction".

PRACTICE DIRECTION 40B—JUDGMENTS AND ORDERS

Examples of forms of trial judgment

40BPD.14 *In paragraph 14.3, delete "The forms referred to in this practice direction are listed in Practice Direction 4.".*

Add new Practice Note: Remote Hand-down of Judgments:

PRACTICE NOTE: REMOTE HAND-DOWN OF JUDGMENTS

40PN.1 During the COVID-19 pandemic, reserved judgments in the Chancery Division were in most cases handed down remotely. The procedure worked well, and it seems sensible to retain it in most cases notwithstanding that the Courts have resumed routine sitting at the Rolls Building. The practice from now on will be as follows:

1. Unless otherwise directed, reserved judgments in the Chancery Division will be handed down remotely, in accordance with the procedure at paragraphs 2–4 below.
2. Notice of hand-down of reserved judgments will be given in the published daily cause list, as follows:

   "*Remote hand-down*: This judgment will be handed down remotely by circulation to the parties or their representatives by email and release to The National Archives. A copy of the judgment in final form as handed down should be available on The National Archives website shortly thereafter but can otherwise be obtained on request by email to the Judicial Office (*press.enquiries@judiciary.uk*)."
3. At the published date and time, the judgment will be sent by the clerk to the Judge, Master or ICC Judge attached to an e-mail in the following terms:

   "In accordance with the Practice Guidance dated 5 October 2022, I attach the judgment in this case by way of hand-down, which will be deemed to have occurred at [Listed Time and Date]."
4. At the same time a copy will be sent to The National Archives.
5. The final/approved version of the judgment will have this wording on the front page:

   "*Remote hand-down*: This judgment was handed down remotely at [time] on [date] by circulation to the parties or their representatives by email and by release to The National Archives."
6. If the Court decides that judgment should be handed down in open Court rather than remotely, the cause list will so indicate; and the parties or their representatives will be informed by the clerk to the Judge, Master or ICC Judge whether or not their attendance is required and of any matters on which their submissions may be required.
7. This guidance affects only the mode of hand-down. It does not affect anything in Practice Direction 40E.

The Rt. Hon. Sir Julian Flaux
Chancellor of the High Court
5 October 2022

PART 42

CHANGE OF SOLICITOR

Effect of change on lien

Add new paragraph at end:

In *Higgins v TLT LLP* [2017] EWHC 3868 (Ch), it was held by Barling J that very serious negligence by a solicitor in the conduct of litigation was capable of amounting to "misconduct" so as to justify that solicitor's lien for unpaid costs. **42.2.5**

CPR COSTS RULES

POST- AND PRE-1 APRIL 2013

A Short Guide to the Costs Rules

In the third paragraph, delete "Section IV provides for scale costs in the Intellectual Property Enterprise Court.". **43.0**

To the end of the fourth paragraph (beginning "Part 46 contains"), add:

Section VII provides for scale costs in the Intellectual Property Enterprise Court. Section VIII provides that there should be no orders for costs in claims for environmental review except in the case of unreasonable or improper conduct.

PART 44

GENERAL RULES ABOUT COSTS

I. General

Costs orders—order displacing the general rule—"a different order"

To the end of the fourth paragraph (beginning "In some cases"), add:

Where the court decided not to determine an application, because it would not be possible to do so proportionately, the applicant should pay the costs as it was unsuccessful. This was different to the kind of case identified in *BCT*, where the settlement of the substantive dispute left the court with no proper basis for determining the winner: *Deepchand v Sooben* [2020] EWCA Civ 1409. **44.2.6**

Costs where regulatory body unsuccessful party

To the end of the first paragraph, add:

However the Supreme Court has explained that there is no general principle that public bodies should be protected from costs orders merely because they have exercised their public functions in the public interest. Rather, the important factor will be whether there would be a chilling effect on the conduct of the public body if costs orders were routinely made against it. In the types of case referred to above there was a general risk of a chilling effect: *Competition and Markets Authority v Flynn Pharma Ltd* [2022] UKSC 14. **44.2.16**

Summary assessment—procedure

After the second paragraph, add new paragraph:

It was appropriate to make a summary assessment of the costs of a claim which had been struck out for failure to comply with an order for security for costs. The defendant's costs were substantial, but the further costs of a lengthy detailed assessment risked throwing good money after bad. It is likely that an important factor in the decision was that the defendant was willing to have the costs assessed in the sum which the claimant had already been ordered to pay on account and which was about only 44% of the total claimed: *Roman Pipia v BGEO Group Ltd Plc* [2022] EWHC 846 (Comm). **44.6.3**

Form for summary assessment (Form N260)

Replace the last sentence with:

44.6.4 From 1 April 2019 until 31 March 2022, Practice Direction 51X permitted the use of alternative model forms **N260A** and **N260B** in paper/pdf form and electronic spreadsheet form.

Summary assessment—quantum

Add new paragraph at the start:

44.6.7 If an hourly rate in excess of the guideline rate is claimed, a clear and compelling justification must be provided: *Samsung Electronics Co Ltd v LG Display Co Ltd (Costs)* [2022] EWCA Civ 466. For the guideline hourly rates see para.44SC.31.

Signing the bill of costs

Replace the last paragraph with:

44.6.8 The certificates on the bill required by para.5.21 of Practice Direction 47 must be signed by the receiving party or that party's solicitor. If signed by the solicitor, the signatory must be identified in the bill. Paper bills must identify the status of and the hourly rate claimed in respect of each individual fee earner. "Status" includes the fee earner's professional qualification and either their grade (by reference to the Guide to the Summary Assessment of Costs (see para.44SC.29) or their number of years of post-qualification experience). Electronic bills must disclose the name, grade and status of each fee earner: *AKC v Barking, Havering and Redbridge University Hospitals NHS Trust* [2022] EWCA Civ 630.

Editorial note

Add new paragraph at end:

44.11.1 The court has no power under the rule to reduce the amount of fees due to a solicitor in an assessment between solicitor and client under s.70 of the Solicitors Act 1974: *John Poyser & Co Ltd v Spencer* [2022] EWHC 1678 (QB).

PRACTICE DIRECTION 44—GENERAL RULES ABOUT COSTS

Costs budgets

Replace paragraph 3.1 with:

44PD.3 **3.1** In any case where the parties have filed budgets in accordance with Practice Direction 3D but the court has not made a costs management order under rule 3.15, the provisions of this subsection shall apply.

PART 45

FIXED COSTS

Editorial introduction

Replace the fifth paragraph (beginning "As re-enacted by") with:

45.0.1 As re-enacted by the Civil Procedure (Amendment) Rules 2013 (SI 2013/262), Section V replicated Section VIII as it stood before 1 April 2013. By the Civil Procedure (Amendment No.2) Rules 2022 (SI 2022/783), Section IV (Scale Costs for Claims in the Intellectual Property Enterprise Court) was moved to Section VII of Pt 46.

I. Fixed Costs

In r.45.1, replace the words in brackets after (2) with:

Scope of this Section[1]

45.1 **(Practice Direction 49C sets out the types of case where a court will give a fixed date for a hearing when it issues a claim.)**

[1] Amended by the Civil Procedure (Amendment) Rules 2013 (SI 2013/262) and the Civil Procedure (Amendment No.2) Rules 2022 (SI 2022/783).

III. The Pre-Action Protocols for Low Value Personal Injury Claims in Road Traffic Accidents and Low Value Personal Injury (Employers' Liability and Public Liability) Claims

Replace r.45.16(1) with:

Scope and interpretation[1]

45.16—(1) This Section applies to claims that have been or should have been started under Part 8 in accordance with Practice Direction 49F ("the Stage 3 Procedure"). 45.16

The Stage 3 procedure and fixed costs

Replace the first paragraph with:

Practice Direction 49F sets out the procedure, referred to in the RTA Protocol and in the EL/PL Protocol as "the Stage 3 Procedure", for a claim in which the parties have followed the Stage 1 process and (liability having been admitted) the Stage 2 process as set out in the Protocols but were unable, at the end of Stage 2, to agree the amount of damages payable. The claim is made pursuant to Pt 8 as modified by PD 49F. The Stage 3 Procedure also applies where the parties were able to reach agreement at the end of Stage 2 but, because the claimant was a child, the approval of the court is required in relation to the settlement in accordance with r.21.10(2) (see further rr.45.21 to 45.23). 45.16.2

Fixed costs—when payable

Replace the first paragraph with:

Rule 45.16 states that this Section applies to claims that have been or should have been started under Practice Direction 49F. Where court proceedings are started under Part 8 in accordance with Practice Direction 49F the claimant must file the claim form and must file with it certain documents (para.6.1). Complying with that requirement represents the start of the Stage 3 Procedure for the purposes of fixed costs (para.6.2). The fixed costs in r.45.18 apply in relation to a claimant only where a claimant has a legal representative (see para.4.6 of the RTA Protocol and para.4.4 of the EL/PL Protocol). Where, in proceedings to which Section III applies, a child is a party (whether claimant or defendant) the court will not make an order for detailed assessment of the costs payable to the child, but will assess the costs in the manner set out in Section VI (r.21.10(3) (see further rr.45.21 to 45.23)). 45.18.2

In the last paragraph, replace "(Practice Direction 8B para.7.3)." with:

(Practice Direction 49F para.7.3).

Rule 45.20: Effect of rule

Replace "Practice Direction 8B para.3.4," with:

Practice Direction 49F para.3.4, 45.20.1

Rule 45.21: Effect of rule

Replace paragraph with:

As to the payment of costs in accordance with r.45.21 where there has been a settlement at Stage 2 of the RTA Protocol processes and the claimant is a child, see further Practice Direction 49F paras 12.1 to 12.3. As to meaning of a "settlement hearing", see Practice Direction 49F para.3.3, and commentary following r.45.22 below. 45.21.1

Rule 45.22: Effect of rule

In the first paragraph, replace "Practice Direction 8B paras 13.1 to 13.3." with:

Practice Direction 49F paras 13.1 to 13.3. 45.22.1

[1] Amended by the Civil Procedure (Amendment) Rules 2013 (SI 2013/262), the Civil Procedure (Amendment No.6) Rules 2013 (SI 2013/1695) and the Civil Procedure (Amendment No.2) Rules 2022 (SI 2022/783).

In the second paragraph, replace "(Practice Direction 8B para.3.3)." with:
(Practice Direction 49F para.3.3).

Replace the last paragraph with:
A "Stage 3 hearing" means a final hearing under the Stage 3 Procedure as set out in Practice Direction 49F to determine the amount of damages in a claim to which the relevant Protocol applies, or after, and the claimant is a child (Practice Direction 49F para.3.4).

Rule 45.23: Effect of rule

In the first paragraph, replace "Paragraph 12.5 of Practice Direction 8B" with:
45.23.1 Paragraph 12.5 of Practice Direction 49F

In the second paragraph, replace "see Practice Direction 8B" with:
see Practice Direction 49F

Rule 45.24: Effect of rule

In the first paragraph, replace "(Practice Direction 8B para.9.1)." with:
45.24.1 (Practice Direction 49F para.9.1).

In the last paragraph, replace "Practice Direction 8B" with:
Practice Direction 49F

Replace r.45.25(1) with:

Where the parties have settled after proceedings have started[1]

45.25 **45.25—(1) This rule applies where an application is made under rule 45.29 (costs-only application after a claim is started under Part 8 in accordance with Practice Direction 49F).**

Rule 45.25: Effect of rule

In the first paragraph, replace "Practice Direction 8B," with:
45.25.1 Practice Direction 49F,

In the second paragraph, replace "Practice Direction 8B" with:
Practice Direction 49F

Costs on adjournment of hearings

Replace "Practice Direction 8B" with:
45.27.1 Practice Direction 49F

Replace r.45.29 with:

Costs-only application after a claim is started under Part 8 in accordance with Practice Direction 49F[2]

45.29 **45.29—(1) This rule sets out the procedure where—**
- **(a) the parties to a dispute have reached an agreement on all issues (including which party is to pay the costs) which is made or confirmed in writing; but**
- **(b) they have failed to agree the amount of those costs; and**
- **(c) proceedings have been started under Part 8 in accordance with Practice Direction 49F.**

(2) Either party may make an application for the court to determine the costs.

---

[1] Amended by the Civil Procedure (Amendment) Rules 2013 (SI 2013/262), the Civil Procedure (Amendment No.6) Rules 2013 (SI 2013/1695) and the Civil Procedure (Amendment No.2) Rules 2022 (SI 2022/783).

[2] Amended by the Civil Procedure (Amendment) Rules 2013 (SI 2013/262) and the Civil Procedure (Amendment No.2) Rules 2022 (SI 2022/783).

(3) Where an application is made under this rule the court will assess the costs in accordance with rule 45.22 or rule 45.25.

(4) Rule 44.5 (amount of costs where costs are payable pursuant to a contract) does not apply to an application under this rule.

Rule 45.29: Effect of rule

Replace the first paragraph with:

Before the re-enactment of the CPR Costs Rules by SI 2013/262, with effect from 1 April 2013, this rule was r.44.12C (Costs-only application after a claim is started under Part 8 in accordance with Practice Direction 49F). The rule was inserted by the Civil Procedure (Amendment) Rules 2010 (SI 2010/621), and came into effect on 30 April 2010. That statutory instrument made amendments to the CPR consequential upon the making of the Pre-Action Protocol for Low Value Personal Injury Claims in Road Traffic Accidents and Practice Direction 49F. **45.29.1**

Replace the last paragraph with:

Practice Direction 49F (Pre-action Protocols for Low Value Personal Injury Claims in Road Traffic Accidents and Low Value Personal Injury (Employers' Liability and Public Liability) Claims—Stage 3 Procedure) deals with the position where the parties have followed the relevant pre-action protocol, but are unable to agree the amount of damages payable at the end of stage 2 of the protocol. The Practice Direction also applies where the claimant is a child, the damages have been agreed, but the approval of the court is required; and where compliance with the relevant protocol is not possible before the expiration of a limitation period and proceedings are commenced. The above rule applies where the parties have reached an agreement on all issues, including which party is to pay the costs, which is confirmed in writing, but have failed to agree the amount of those costs and proceedings have been started under Pt 8 in accordance with Practice Direction 49F. Under this rule the court will assess the costs under Section III of Pt 45.

IIIA. Claims Which No Longer Continue Under the RTA or EL/PL Pre-Action Protocols and Claims to Which the Pre-Action Protocol for Resolution of Package Travel Claims Applies—Fixed Recoverable Costs

Replace r.45.29A(1)(a) with:

Scope and interpretation[1]

(a) to a claim started under— **45.29A**

(i) the Pre-Action Protocol for Low Value Personal Injury Claims in Road Traffic Accidents ("the RTA Protocol"); or

(ii) the Pre-Action Protocol for Low Value Personal Injury (Employers' Liability and Public Liability) Claims ("the EL/PL Protocol"),

where such a claim no longer continues under the relevant Protocol or the Stage 3 Procedure in Practice Direction 49F; and

Section IIIA: Effect of Section

Replace "Practice Direction 8B." with:

Practice Direction 49F. **45.29A.1**

Add new paragraph 45.29B.4:

Cases where the parties have agreed to a detailed assessment

Where, in a claim which would have fallen within Section IIIA, the consent order which concluded the claim provided that the defendant was to pay the claimant's costs subject to a detailed assessment if not agreed, the claimant was entitled to costs to be assessed on the standard basis rather than the fixed recoverable costs provided under the section: *Doyle v M&D Foundations & Building Services Ltd* [2022] EWCA Civ 927. **45.29B.4**

---

[1] Introduced by the Civil Procedure (Amendment No.6) Rules 2013 (SI 2013/1695) and amended by the Civil Procedure (Amendment No.2) Rules 2018 (SI 2018/479) and the Civil Procedure (Amendment No.2) Rules 2022 (SI 2022/783).

Replace Section IV (paragraphs 45.30 to 45.32.1) with:

IV. [Omitted]

Scope and interpretation[1]

45.30 **45.30 [Omitted].**

Amount of scale costs[2]

45.31 **45.31 [Omitted].**

Summary assessment of the costs of an application where a party has behaved unreasonably[3]

45.32 **45.32 [Omitted].**

VII. Costs Limits in Aarhus Convention Claims

Aarhus Convention claims

Add new paragraph at end:

45.41.2 Where a ground which is within the scope of the Convention is included in a claim in good faith, it is not appropriate to distinguish between the costs attributable to that ground and those attributable to other grounds which are not within the scope of the Convention. Provided that part of the claim falls within the definition in r.45.41(2)(a) the cap will apply to the whole claim: *R. (Lewis) v Welsh Ministers* [2022] EWHC 450 (Admin).

The nature of the claimant

Add new paragraph at end:

45.43.1 A claimant pursuing a claim with the benefit of crowdfunding was still claiming only as an individual and not on behalf of others: *R. (Lewis) v Welsh Ministers* [2022] EWHC 450 (Admin).

PRACTICE DIRECTION 45—FIXED COSTS

In the Table of Contents, replace the entry for Section IV (including the entry for para.3) with:

Contents of this Practice Direction

Change title of Section IV:

Section IV—[Omitted]

Replace paragraph with:

45PD.3 **3** [Omitted.]

PART 46

COSTS—SPECIAL CASES

I. Costs Payable by or to Particular Persons

Editorial note

In the last paragraph, replace "Practice Direction 8B" with:

46.4.1 Practice Direction 49F

[1] Omitted by the Civil Procedure (Amendment No.2) Rules 2022 (SI 2022/783).
[2] Omitted by the Civil Procedure (Amendment No.2) Rules 2022 (SI 2022/783).
[3] Omitted by the Civil Procedure (Amendment No.2) Rules 2022 (SI 2022/783).

II. Costs Relating to Legal Representatives

Editorial note

Replace the third paragraph with:

See paras 6.4 to 6.19 of Practice Direction 46 as to the procedure to be adopted. An assessment under s.70 of the Solicitors Act 1974 is not a detailed assessment for the purposes of Pt 47: *John Poyser & Co Ltd v Spencer* [2022] EWHC 1678 (QB). **46.10.2**

IV. Costs-Only Proceedings

Editorial note

In the eighth paragraph (beginning "Rule 45.29 sets"), replace "Practice Direction 8B" with:

Practice Direction 49F **46.14.1**

In the penultimate paragraph, replace "Practice Direction 8B" with:

Practice Direction 49F

Add new Sections VII and VIII:

VII. Scale Costs for Claims in the Intellectual Property Enterprise Court

Scope and interpretation[1]

46.20—(1) Subject to paragraph (2), this Section applies to proceedings in the Intellectual Property Enterprise Court. **46.20**

(2) This Section does not apply where—

(a) the court considers that a party has behaved in a manner which amounts to an abuse of the court's process; or

(b) the claim concerns the infringement or revocation of a patent or registered design or registered trade mark the validity of which has been certified by a court or by the Comptroller-General of Patents, Designs and Trade Marks in earlier proceedings.

(3) The court will make a summary assessment of the costs of the party in whose favour any order for costs is made. Rules 44.2(8), 44.7(b) and Part 47 do not apply to this Section.

(4) "Scale costs" means the costs set out in Table A and Table B of the Practice Direction supplementing this Part.

Section VII: Transitional provisions

By the Civil Procedure (Amendment No.2) Rules 2010 (SI 2010/1953), Section VII (Scale Costs for Claims in a Patents County Court) was added to Pt 45 and it was provided that the Patents County Court will make a summary assessment of the costs of the party in whose favour any order for costs is made according to a "scale of costs" regime. **46.20.1**

By the Civil Procedure (Amendment No.7) Rules 2013 (SI 2013/1974), with effect from 1 October 2013, the Patents County Court was reconstituted as a specialist list of the Chancery Division, named the Intellectual Property Enterprise Court ("IPEC"). Transitional provisions in CPR PD Update 66 stated that the increases to the scales provided in Tables A and B in para.3 of Practice Direction 45 would apply only to cases started in IPEC; the earlier scales of costs applicable to proceedings in the Patents County Court would apply to Patents County Court cases continued in IPEC.

By the Civil Procedure (Amendment No.2) Rules 2022 (SI 2022/783) the rules in what had become Section IV of Pt 45 were moved to Section VII of Pt 46. By CPR PD Update 146, Practice Direction 46 was amended to incorporate Tables A and B, at para.11, and the scale costs were increased. By the transitional provisions, the increases apply only in relation to claims made on or after 1 October 2022. For claims made before that date, the maximum amounts are those set out in Tables A and B in para.3 of Practice Direction 45, as in force until 30 September 2022.

Rule 46.20: Effect of rule

Section VII of Pt 46 sets out the scale costs for claims in the Intellectual Property Enterprise Court. The provisions do not apply where the court considers that a party has behaved in a manner **46.20.2**

[1] Introduced by the Civil Procedure (Amendment No.2) Rules 2022 (SI 2022/783).

which amounts to an abuse of the court's process (r.46.20(2)(a)) or the claim concerns the infringement or revocation of a patent or registered design, the validity of which has been certified by a court in earlier proceedings (r.46.20(2)(b)). For the effect of offers made under Pt 36: see para.2F-17.19.3.

The exceptions to the application of Section VII set out in r.46.20(2) are self-explanatory. The exceptions are limited and narrow, and there is no doubt that they are intended to be so, for otherwise the certainty of the scheme would be defeated. For example unreasonable behaviour is not a reason ordinarily for raising or disregarding the scale costs. However, where a party had advanced an implausible case on evidence found to be dishonest and had attempted to obscure the effect of its infringements, such conduct amounted to an abuse of the court's process so that scale costs were disapplied and costs awarded against it on the indemnity basis: *Link Up Mitaka Ltd (t/a thebigword) v Language Empire Ltd (Costs)* [2018] EWHC 2728 (IPEC) (Judge Clarke). See in particular the judge's comments on this rule at [12]-[16].

The court will make a summary assessment of the costs of the party in whose favour any order for costs is made. Rules 44.2(8), 44.7(b) and Pt 47 do not apply to Section IV: r.46.20(3).

The court will reserve the costs of an application to the conclusion of the trial when they will be subject to summary assessment. However, where a party has behaved unreasonably, the court may make an order for costs at the conclusion of the hearing. Where the court makes a summary assessment of costs it will do so in accordance with Section VII of Pt 46 (r.63.26).

Paragraph 11 of Practice Direction 46 sets out the maximum amount of scale costs which the court will award for each stage of the claim. There are two tables. Table A sets out the scale costs for each stage of the claim up to determination of liability. Table B sets out the scale costs for each stage of an enquiry as to damages or account of profits.

The Intellectual Property Enterprise Court could depart from the overall caps on costs and scale costs only in truly exceptional circumstances. It was, however, possible not to apply scale costs for one or more of the earlier stages of the claim provided the total award remained within the overall cap: *FH Brundle v Perry* [2014] EWHC 979 (IPEC) (Judge Hacon).

Where the claimant's conduct did not amount to abuse and the circumstances were not truly exceptional, but the claimant had failed to formulate its case properly leading to a striking-out application which was withdrawn by consent, the court awarded an extra £5,000 over the IPEC application cap. The overall cap for the claim could not be disturbed: *Skyscape Cloud Services Ltd v Sky Plc* [2016] EWHC 1340 (IPEC) (Judge Hacon).

Amount of scale costs[1]

46.21 **46.21—(1) Subject to rule 46.22, the court will not order a party to pay total costs of more than—**

(a) £60,000 on the final determination of a claim in relation to liability; and

(b) £30,000 on an inquiry as to damages or account of profits.

(2) The amounts in paragraph (1) apply after the court has applied the provision on set off in accordance with rule 44.12(a).

(3) The maximum amount of scale costs that the court will award for each stage of the claim is set out in Practice Direction 46.

(4) The amount of the scale costs awarded by the court in accordance with paragraph (3) will depend on the nature and complexity of the claim.

(5) Subject to assessment where appropriate, the following may be recovered in addition to the amount of the scale costs set out in Practice Direction 46—Costs—Special Cases—

(a) court fees;

(b) costs relating to the enforcement of any court order; and

(c) wasted costs.

(6) Where appropriate, VAT may be recovered in addition to the amount of the scale costs and any reference in this Section to scale costs is a reference to those costs net of any such VAT.

Rule 46.21: Effect of rule

46.21.1 The figures for total costs of £60,000 and £30,000 in r.46.21(1) were increased from £50,000 and £25,000 by the Civil Procedure (Amendment No.2) Rules 2022 (SI 2022/783) and apply only to claims made on or after 1 October 2022.

The scale costs for each stage are set out in Tables A and B under para.11 of Practice Direction

[1] Introduced by the Civil Procedure (Amendment No.2) Rules 2022 (SI 2022/783).

46 in respect of claims made on or after 1 October 2022. For claims made before that date, the scale costs are those set in Tables A and B under para.3 of Practice Direction 45, as it was in force up to 30 September 2022.

Table A sets out the scale costs for each stage of a claim up to determination of liability, and Table B for each stage of an inquiry as to damages or account of profits.

The rules in Section V of Pt 63 (Intellectual Property Claims) (rr.63.17 to 63.28) apply to claims started in or transferred to the Intellectual Property Enterprise Court. Where the court makes a summary assessment of costs, it will do so in accordance with Section VII of Part 46 (r.63.26(3)). The court will reserve the costs of an application to the conclusion of the trial, when they will be subject to summary assessment (r.63.26(1)); however, where a party has behaved unreasonably, the court may make an order for costs at the end of the hearing (r.63.26(2)) and any costs awarded to a party in those circumstances are in addition to the total costs that may be awarded to that party under r.46.21 (r.46.22). See, further, commentary on r.63.26 in Vol.2 para.2F-17.19.1.

The scale costs provided for by the Tables are maximum costs. In some cases lower sums will be appropriate, and indeed r.46.21(4) makes this plain.

Rule 46.21(1) imposes a maximum of £60,000 and the court is unable to award any larger sum in costs, even where there were multiple defendants who had filed separate pleadings and evidence and were separately represented. A claimant is not permitted to share out its single costs bill as between two or more defendants and thereby recover more than the maximum (*Gimex International Groupe Import Export v Chill Bag Co Ltd* [2012] EWPCC 34; [2012] 6 Costs L.R. 1069 (Judge Birss QC); and see *Liversidge v Owen Mumford Ltd* [2012] EWPCC 40; [2012] 6 Costs L.R. 1076 (Judge Birss QC)). Where a defendant had succeeded on its counterclaim but part of the claim had been adjourned, the defendant asked for its costs of the counterclaim to be assessed. The court held that it could not assess the costs until all of the issues, including the adjourned claim, had been resolved: *Global Flood Defence Systems Ltd v Johan Van Den Noort Beheer BV* [2016] EWHC 189 (IPEC).

Where appropriate, VAT may be recovered in addition to the amount of scale costs (r.46.21(5)). However the figures for total costs provided in r.46.21(1) are inclusive of VAT: *Response Clothing Ltd v Edinburgh Woollen Mill Ltd* [2020] EWHC 721 (IPEC).

As to the effect of Part 36 offers, see the commentary under r.63.26 at para.2F-17.19.3.

Assessment

There is no need to take too narrow a view of the scope of the stages in Table A. Although the stages are broadly chronological, they are not limited in that way, so that if, for example, work is done pre-action which could, when proceedings are commenced, properly be regarded as part of the defence and counterclaim stage, the costs of that work ought potentially to be recoverable. Stages 1 to 4 in Table A simply refer to a particular statement of case. It is legitimate to include within the costs of any of those stages the costs of considering the other parties' statement of case, although that does not mean that such costs would be recoverable in every case (*Westwood v Knight* [2011] EWPCC 11; [2011] F.S.R. 37 (Judge Birss QC)). **46.21.2**

Since the definition of costs included (under r.43.2(1)(a) as it stood before 1 April 2013) any additional liability, ATE premiums and CFA success fees were subject to r.45.41(1) (now r.46.21(1)). For the court to exercise its discretion to depart from a cap in anything other than a truly exceptional case would undermine the point of the costs capping system, which was to favour certainty, as opposed to a fully compensatory approach to costs: *Henderson v All Around the World Recordings Ltd (Costs)* [2013] EWPCC 19 (Judge Birss QC). Where the claimant argued that it was entitled to costs both in respect of the determination of liability and a decision on quantum, the total of which exceeded the overall cap of £50,000, the court held that the two costs caps could not be aggregated together. The case had been conducted as a single proceeding, with one set of statements of case, one case management conference and one trial, therefore only one cap should apply: *Azzurrin Communications Ltd v International Telecommunications Equipment Ltd (t/a SOS Communications)* [2013] EWPCC 22 (Judge Birss QC).

Summary assessment of the costs of an application where a party has behaved unreasonably[1]

46.22 Costs awarded to a party under rule 63.26(2) are in addition to the total costs that may be awarded to that party under rule 46.21. **46.22**

VIII. Environmental Review Costs

Environmental review costs[2]

46.23—(1) In this Section, "party" includes an intervener or interested party. **46.23**

[1] Introduced by the Civil Procedure (Amendment No.2) Rules 2022 (SI 2022/783).
[2] Introduced by the Civil Procedure (Amendment No.2) Rules 2022 (SI 2022/783).

(2) Subject to paragraph (3), no party to a claim for environmental review (for which see Section III of Part 54) is entitled to an order for costs against any other party.

(3) The court may make an order for costs against a party if satisfied that the conduct of a party or that party's legal representative, before or during the proceedings, was unreasonable or improper.

(4) Where–

(a) the court makes an order under paragraph (2) against a legally represented party; and

(b) the party is not present when the order is made,

the party's legal representative must notify that party in writing of the order no later than 7 days after the legal representative receives notice of the order.

Editorial note

46.23.1 Section VIII was added by the Civil Procedure (Amendment No.2) Rules 2022 (SI 2022/783) with effect from 1 October 2022. A "claim for environmental review" means a claim made by the Office for Environmental Protection under s.38 of the Environment Act 2021 (see r.54.25(2)(a)).

PRACTICE DIRECTION 46—COSTS SPECIAL CASES

Add new paragraph 11.1:

Scale costs for proceedings in the Intellectual Property Enterprise Court—rule 46.20(4)

11.1 Tables A and B

46PD.11 (a) Tables A and B set out the maximum amount of scale costs which the court will award for each stage of a claim in the Intellectual Property Enterprise Court;

(b) Table A sets out the scale costs for each stage of a claim up to determination of liability; and

(c) Table B sets out the scale costs for each stage of an inquiry as to damages or account of profits.

Table A

Stage of a claim	*Maximum amount of costs*
Particulars of claim	£9,000
Defence and counterclaim	£8,000
Reply and defence to counterclaim	£7,000
Reply to defence to counterclaim	£3,500
Attendance at a case management conference	£6,000
Making or responding to an application	£4,000
Providing or inspecting disclosure or product/process description	£6,000
Performing or inspecting experiments	£3,000
Preparing witness statements	£8,000
Preparing experts' report	£9,000
Preparing for and attending trial and judgment	£20,000
Preparing for determination on the papers	£5,500

Table B

Stage of a claim	*Maximum amount of costs*
Points of claim	£4,000
Points of defence	£4,000
Attendance at a case management conference	£5,000
Making or responding to an application	£3,000
Providing or inspecting disclosure	£3,000
Preparing witness statements	£6,000
Preparing experts' report	£7,000
Preparing for and attending trial and judgment	£10,000
Preparing for determination on the papers	£3,000

SENIOR COSTS JUDGE PRACTICE NOTE: APPROVAL OF COSTS SETTLEMENTS, ASSESSMENTS UNDER CPR 46.4(2) AND DEDUCTIONS FROM DAMAGES: CHILDREN AND PROTECTED PARTIES

Add new paragraph 46PN.5.1:

Editorial note

In paragraph 12, the reference to para.2.1 of Practice Direction 47 should be to para.2.1 of Practice Direction 46. **46PN.5.1**

PART 48

PART 2 OF THE LEGAL AID, SENTENCING AND PUNISHMENT OF OFFENDERS ACT 2012 RELATING TO CIVIL LITIGATION FUNDING AND COSTS: TRANSITIONAL PROVISION IN RELATION TO PRE-COMMENCEMENT FUNDING ARRANGEMENTS

Order for recovery of costs insurance in clinical negligence claims

Replace the penultimate paragraph with:

Regulation 3 of the 2013 Regulations provides that: **48.0.4**

> "a costs order made in favour of a party to clinical negligence proceedings who has taken out a costs insurance policy may include provision requiring the payment of an amount in respect of all or part of the premium of that policy" .

It has been held, at costs judge level, that (subject to the normal principles of the assessment of costs) a premium will be recoverable under any order for costs (whether deemed or actual) without any need for the order to make specific provision: *Dance v East Kent University Hospitals NHS Foundation Trust* [2022] EWHC B9 (Costs).

PART 49

Replace Part 49–Specialist Proceedings with:

SPECIFIC PROCEEDINGS

Editorial introduction

This Part originally concerned "specialist proceedings". It was amended, as from 1 October 2022, by the Civil Procedure (Amendment No.2) Rules 2022 (SI 2022/783), which substituted a **49.0.1** new Pt 49 for the one previously in force from 2009 (Civil Procedure (Amendment) Rules 2009 (SI 2009/2092)). It now concerns "specific proceedings" and makes provision for Practice Directions to be made under it for that purpose. Practice Direction 49A—Applications under the Companies Acts and Related Legislation (see Vol.2 Section 2G)—see CPR PD Update 50 (with effect from 1 October 2009)—remains in force, as dealing with specific proceedings, under the new Pt 49. Practice Direction 49B—Order Under Section 127 Insolvency Act 1986 was omitted as from 1 October 2022 via CPR PD Update 149 (July 2022), it having been otiose since the introduction of the Practice Direction on Insolvency Proceedings (see Vol.2 para.3E-1). That PD Update also, as from 1 October 2022, revised and moved a number of Practice Directions into Pt 49. Practice Direction 3D—Mesothelioma Claims became a new PD 49B. Practice Direction 7B—Consumer Credit Act 2006—Unfair Relationships became PD 49C. Practice Direction 7D—Claims for the Recovery of Taxes and Duties became PD 49D. Practice Direction 8A—Alternative Procedure for Claims became PD 49E. Practice Direction 8B—Pre-Action Protocol for Low Value Personal Injury Claims in Road Traffic Accidents and Low Value Personal Injury (Employers' Liability and Public Liability) Claims—Stage 3 Procedure became PD 49F.

For detailed commentary on this rule's previous content, see Vol.2 Section 12 (CPR: Application, Amendments and Interpretation), Sections C2 and D2 (paras 12-19+ and 12-30+).

Practice directions for specific proceedings[1]

49.1 **49.1 The practice directions made under this Rule apply to proceedings of the types described in them.**

Add new Practice Direction 49B–Mesothelioma Claims:

PRACTICE DIRECTION 49B—MESOTHELIOMA CLAIMS

This Practice Direction supplements CPR Part 49

Scope

49BPD.1 **1.** This Practice Direction applies to claims for compensation for mesothelioma.

"Mesothelioma"

49BPD.1.1 Mesothelioma is a highly aggressive cancer. The majority of cases originate in the pleura, but it is sometimes peritoneal or pericardial. It is a rare cancer in persons who have not been exposed to the inhalation of asbestos dust. Characteristically there is a long latency period between the first exposure to asbestos dust and the first clinical signs of mesothelioma, more than 30 years in most cases, but intervals of as little as 10 years are found and less in rare cases. There is no upper limit to the latency period. That period is not the same as the period in which the tumour grows, which period is thought to commence on average 10 years before clinical signs of the tumour appear.

All types of asbestos fibres can cause mesothelioma but they differ in potency. Crocidolite (blue asbestos) is thought to be the most potent, then amosite (brown or grey asbestos) and chrysotile (white asbestos) is thought to be the least potent. The cancer may occur after low levels of exposure but the risk of contracting it increases in proportion to the dose received, though the severity of the cancer does not. Successive periods of exposure each increase the risk that the cancer will occur and consequently, Mesothelioma is characterised as an "indivisible" disease.

The rate of occurrence of mesothelioma in the UK has been characterised as an epidemic. In 2004 the authors of a paper in the British Medical Journal (Treasure et al, *Radical Surgery for Mesothelioma* (31 January 2004) stated that there were at that time over 1,800 deaths per year in Britain (that is, about 1 in 200 of all deaths in men and 1 in 1,500 in women) and that the number was still increasing. They predicted that the peak of the epidemic was to be expected in 2015 to 2020 when the death rate was likely to be 2,000 a year in the UK. Experience to date does not challenge that prediction.

In May 2002 a special list for asbestos-related illness claims was set up at the Royal Courts of Justice (RCJ), which is now conducted by Master Eastman, Master Fontaine, Master Davison, Master Gidden, Master Thornett and some Deputy Masters of the Queen's Bench Division, and administered by staff there (contact: *qb.asbestos@hmcts.gsi.gov.uk*). Over the years, an efficient practice has been developed in that list to resolve claims for damages for mesothelioma (most of which are made against former employers) quickly and wherever possible, to provide compensation during the lifetime of the victim of exposure either by interim payment or full assessment of damages. Experience in that list has shown that in a very high percentage of claims, there is no real prospect of success of any defence and that if liability can be eliminated as an issue at an early stage, by pro-active use of the court's case management powers, then almost all claims can be quickly timetabled and managed to settlement of the issue of quantum. Experience has also shown

[1] Amended by the Civil Procedure (Amendment) Rules 2009 (SI 2009/2092) and the Civil Procedure (Amendment No.2) Rules 2022 (SI 2022/783).

that in many claims in which life expectancy is short and which need to be dealt with expeditiously, where there is some probability of a real prospect of a defence being shown which relates to exposure and breach of duty, the alleged victim's evidence should be taken on deposition and recorded on a DVD and a transcript made available, in case death occurs before any sort of trial can be arranged and the victim's evidence is lost.

In 2007 the Civil Justice Council brought together the RCJ and other courts where these claims are issued and representative claimant and defendant lawyers, to establish by consensus a standard method of resolving these claims based on the system in use at the RCJ. This Practice Direction, in force from 6 April 2008 is the result. For an up-to-date description of the procedure in the asbestos disease court at the RCJ see the judgment of Master McCloud in *Yates v Commissioners for Her Majesty's Revenue & Customs* [2014] EWHC 2311 (QB); [2014] P.I.Q.R. P24; [2014] B.T.C. 39 at [10]-[21]. As mentioned at [1] of the judgment in this case, it should be noted that it is the established practice of the Asbestos List in the RCJ to apply provisions of the Practice Direction to all asbestos disease cases, not just mesothelioma claims. Parties should not, however, seek to bring other lung disease claims, such as those for silicosis or berylliosis, in the Asbestos List.

CE Filing is now the appropriate vehicle for issuing and filing documents for asbestos claims, as with all others. Further there is a dedicated email address, *qb.asbestos@justice.gov.uk*, which should be used as the continuing point of contact for claims issued in the RCJ as well as emailing direct to the relevant Masters.

The Compensation Act 2006

In ss.16 and 17, this Act establishes two basic principles which modify the law as laid down by the House of Lords in *Barker v Corus (UK) Plc* [2006] UKHL 20 and which apply to all mesothelioma claims: **49BPD.1.2**

(1) a person who has exposed a victim in circumstances amounting to a breach of duty, who has consequently contracted mesothelioma, will be liable for all the damage flowing and will not be able to reduce that liability by reference to any other exposure:
  (a) by any other person whether it was tortious or non-tortious or
  (b) by the victim, of themself, unless that exposure can found a defence of contributory negligence;

(2) where more than one person has exposed the victim in breach of duty the liability of each such person will be for all the damage and will be joint and several.

The Mesothelioma Act 2014

This Act received Royal Assent on 30 January 2014. Its purpose is to establish a payment scheme for victims of mesothelioma (and their eligible dependants) where their employer or employers' liability insurance company cannot be traced, and to make provision about the resolution of certain insurance disputes. The scheme is to be funded by a levy on insurance companies that are currently active in the employers' liability insurance market. The provisions of the Act resulted from a prior public consultation, which also led to a government decision not to introduce a dedicated protocol for Mesothelioma claims. The diseases protocol and this PD therefore remain the primary sources of procedural guidance. The "Diffuse Mesothelioma Payment Scheme" set up under this Act came into effect from 1 July 2014. **49BPD.1.3**

Pre-Action disclosure of HMRC work records of deceased parties

With the passing of s.85 of the Deregulation Act 2015, the need for the *Yates v Commissioners for Her Majesty's Revenue & Customs* [2014] EWHC 2311 QB applications has passed and such records should be provided by HMRC upon proper request. **49BPD.1.4**

Definitions

2. In this Practice Direction— **49BPD.2**

"show cause procedure" means (without prejudice to the court's general case management powers in Part 3 of the CPR) the procedure set out in paragraph 6;

"outline submissions showing cause" means an outline or skeleton argument of the defendant's case within the show cause procedure; and

"standard interim payment" means the standard payment in respect of interim damages, and (if appropriate) interim costs and disbursements as determined from time to time by the Head of Civil Justice. The amount of this payment is currently £50,000.

"show cause procedure"

See the notes to para.6 below. **49BPD.2.1**

"standard interim payment"

The making of a standard interim payment order in the majority of cases avoids the expense of a separate application and prolonged argument over the correct level of payment during CMCs **49BPD.2.2** that are usually allocated no more than half an hour of the court's time. The payment also provides early interim payment to living victims in cases in which liability is no longer in issue. The practice at the RCJ is that the standard payment is seldom exceeded though it may be cut back in low value claims where the standard level of payment would far exceed a reasonable proportion of the damages likely to be payable. The figure is currently £50,000 and it is usually determined by the lower level of damages for mesothelioma in the JSB Guide to Damages.

Starting proceedings

49BPD.3 **3.1** The claim form and every statement of case must be marked with the title "Living Mesothelioma Claim" or "Fatal Mesothelioma Claim" as appropriate.

3.2 In order for the court to adopt the show cause procedure in the first case management conference, the claimant must file and serve any witness statements about liability (as are available)—

(1) either—

(a) at the same time as filing and serving the claim form and (where appropriate) the particulars of claim; or

(b) as soon as possible after filing and serving the claim form and (where appropriate) the particulars of claim; and

(2) in any event not less than 7 days before the case management conference.

3.3 Any witness statement about liability must identify as far as is possible—

(1) the alleged victim's employment history and history of exposure to asbestos;

(2) the identity of any employer where exposure to asbestos of the alleged victim is alleged;

(3) details of any self employment in which the alleged victim may have been exposed; and

(4) details of all claims made and payments received under the Pneumoconiosis etc. (Workers' Compensation) Act 1979.

3.4 The claimant must also attach to the claim form—

(1) a work history from H M Revenue and Customs (where available); and

(2) any pre-action letter of claim.

"adopt ... in the first case management conference"

49BPD.3.1 It is a key part of the process of these claims that a CMC is called as early as possible and certainly as soon as possible after a defence has been filed. The court may not wait for all defences to be filed in a multi-defendant claim as in most such claims in relation to mesothelioma there will be defendants who will not respond. Unless it is able to concede liability or has already done so before the first CMC, the defendant may be called on to do so at that conference. Some defendants at that CMC will consent to judgment. Some will not be able to consent, but will not oppose and judgment may then be entered. Others will ask for more time to investigate liability or obtain factual or expert evidence. In many cases, where sufficient time for investigation has passed since the receipt of the pre-action protocol letter, defendants will be unable to produce any (or any relevant) factual evidence of their own and there will be no reason on the face of the claimant's expert medical evidence to allow a defendant to obtain its own such evidence. However, unless judgment is consented to or not opposed, the court will not normally enter judgment in those circumstances without seeing the claimant's evidence. In some cases the totality of the evidence will be available at the first CMC. The court will decide the matter as far as possible on the material that would be available at a trial and in particular the factual and expert evidence. Hence the requirement here for the claimant to ensure that that evidence is before the court at the first CMC if the show cause procedure is to be invoked at that time. This paragraph of the PD sets out what material should be included where possible. In some cases, where the defendant is an extant company known to have contemporary evidence, the claimant may wish the normal procedure of simultaneous exchange of evidence to be followed and then seek to invoke the show cause procedure at a later stage in the proceedings. In para.2 of the PD it is made clear that the show cause procedure is without prejudice to the court's general case management powers in Pt 3 of the CPR.

Claimants with severely limited life expectancy

49BPD.4 **4.1** Where the claimant believes that the claim is particularly urgent then on issue of the claim form, the claimant—

(1) may request in writing that the court file is placed immediately before a judge nominated to manage such cases in order to fix a case management conference; and

(2) must explain in writing to the court why the claim is urgent.

4.2 Where the court decides that the claim is urgent (and notwithstanding that a claim has not yet been served or a defence has not yet been filed) it will—

(1) fix the date for the case management conference to take place within a short period of time; and

(2) give directions as to the date by which the claimant must serve the claim form if it has not been served already.

"Claimants with a severely limited life expectancy ... the claim is particularly urgent"

The default trigger of the case management process in mesothelioma claims is the filing of any defence or the making of a default judgment (see para.5 below). In some claims in which the alleged victim is still alive, the prognosis is such that the claim should be case managed by the court with extreme urgency and a date fixed for a CMC without waiting for the time for acknowledgment and defence to expire. This paragraph explains that in such cases the claimant's solicitor may request an urgent CMC when the claim is issued, giving an explanation in writing (which includes email where such communication is accepted by the court in question) and the file will then be referred to the judge or Master. If the court accepts that there is such urgency, it may fix a CMC and require the claim form to be served, if it has not already been served and set a timetable for acknowledgment and defence or it may simply order a CMC. Experience in the RCJ list has shown that frequently (notwithstanding the terms of the pre-action protocol) little or no investigation of liability has been carried out by defendants before the issue of proceedings and in cases where the alleged victim is still alive and has an uncertain prognosis, urgent case management is not only beneficial but also necessary if the aim of bringing living claims to either a trial on assessment of damages or a trial of liability as a preliminary issue, followed by the standard interim payment, can be achieved within 16 weeks of service of proceedings (see para.7.1 below). It is however to be noted that the court will use this discretion sparingly—all living mesothelioma claims are urgent which is why the procedure exists in the first place—and so applications should only be made in extreme cases, and costs sanctions could be imposed if the judge considers such an application to be unnecessary, or indeed tactical. **49BPD.4.1**

Fixing the case management conference for other claims

5.1 Where paragraph 4 does not apply and— **49BPD.5**

(1) a defence is filed by the defendant or one of the defendants (where there is more than one); or

(2) the claimant has obtained a default judgment,

the court file will be referred to a judge nominated to manage such cases and the judge will give directions for the date of the case management conference.

5.2 Claims marked "Living Mesothelioma Claim" will be given priority when fixing a case management conference.

"where paragraph 4 does not apply"

Paragraph 5 applies (a) to claims by alleged victims who are alive but whose life expectancy is such that the normal period for acknowledgment and defence (as extended by agreement by the parties if appropriate) will be acceptable, and (b) to claims in which the alleged victim has died before proceedings were commenced. Both types of claim are covered by the PD because the methods that can be used for expeditious resolution of mesothelioma claims are the same for both living and fatal claims, the difference being that there is not the same need for an urgent timetable in fatal claims. Nevertheless it has been the aim at the RCJ to dispose of fatal claims, where possible, within six months of service of proceedings. **49BPD.5.1**

Living mesothelioma claims given priority when fixing CMC

Paragraph 7.1 of the PD aims for a period of 16 weeks from service of the claim form to a trial (if necessary of liability as a preliminary issue) or assessment of damages in claims where the alleged victim is still alive therefore even in the case of less urgent live claims under this paragraph there will be a need to set a case management conference within weeks in order for this to be achievable. In such cases the normal notice requirement for CMCs will often have to be abridged. Fatal claims lack the urgency of living claims but the aim of the PD to eliminate the issue of liability at an early stage where possible means that as early a CMC date as possible should be set after any defence has been filed. **49BPD.5.2**

However, it must be stressed that priority listing is not to be requested from QB Asbestos, especially not before the defence, simply on the basis that the claim concerns a living claimant.

Costs budgeting at the CMC in mesothelioma and other asbestos disease cases

The convention of dispensing with costs budgeting in asbestos disease cases has been reinforced by the introduction of PD 3E para.2(b) which indicates that in all cases where there is limited or **49BPD.5.3** severely impaired life expectation (five years or less remaining) the court will ordinarily disapply cost management.

The show cause procedure

49BPD.6 **6.1** The show cause procedure is a requirement by the court, of its own initiative and usually on a "costs in the case" basis, for the defendant to identify the evidence and legal arguments that give the defendant a real prospect of success on any or all issues of liability. The court will use this procedure for the resolution of mesothelioma claims.

6.2 At the first case management conference, unless there is good reason not to do so, the defendant should be prepared to show cause why—

(1) a judgment on liability should not be entered against the defendant; and

(2) a standard interim payment on account of damages and (if appropriate) costs and disbursements should not be made by the defendant by a specified date.

6.3 At the first case management conference if liability remains in issue the court will normally order that the defendant show cause within a further given period.

6.4 The order requiring the defendant to show cause within a further given period will direct—

(1) that the defendant file and serve on the claimant by a specified date outline submissions showing cause and—

(a) if the outline submissions are not filed and served by a specified date, judgment, for a sum to be determined by the court, will be entered against the defendant without the need for any further order and the defendant will be ordered to make a standard interim payment by a specified date; or

(b) if the outline submissions are filed and served by the specified date, the claim will be listed for a show cause hearing; or

(2) that the defendant show cause at a hearing on a date fixed by the court.

6.5 At the first case management conference the court will—

(1) fix the date or trial window for the determination of damages and give any other case management directions as appropriate where the defendant admits liability or judgment is entered;

(2) fix the date or trial window for the determination of damages and give any other case management directions as appropriate where an order to show cause under paragraph 6.3 has been made (if the defendant subsequently shows cause then the determination date or trial window may be utilised for the trial of any issue); or

(3) in cases in which there is to be a trial on liability, give directions including the date or window for the trial.

6.6 Where the defendant fails to show cause on some issues, the court will normally enter judgment on those issues.

6.7 Where the defendant fails to show cause on all issues, the court will enter judgment for a sum to be determined and will normally order that a standard interim payment be made.

6.8 Where the defendant succeeds in showing cause on some or all issues, the court will order a trial of those issues. The court may also require the issue of quantum or apportionment (as appropriate) to be dealt with at the trial provided that it does not delay the date for the fixing of the trial.

"show cause procedure"

49BPD.6.1 This is defined as a requirement by the court, of its own initiative and usually on a "costs in the case" basis, for the defendant to identify the evidence and legal arguments that give the defendant a real prospect of success. Applying the test for summary judgment, the burden of showing that the defendant has no real prospect of success remains on the claimant. Further, at a show cause hearing it is for the claimant to adduce credible evidence in support of their case, and it is only if they do so that the defendant becomes subject to an evidential burden to show cause: *Revenue and Customs Commissioners v Silcock* [2009] EWHC 3025 (QB). The justification for the court imposing this filter rather than requiring a full blown application under Pt 24 to be initiated by the claimant, is the fact that the RCJ experience has shown that in many claims there is no such defence and a summary judgment application simply duplicates work and increases costs unnecessarily. The requirement to "show cause" may be imposed on successive occasions, i.e. at the first CMC and then at a later substantive "show cause hearing"' if the defendant is able to persuade the court to allow more time. The court's order is to show cause not only as to liability but also as to why the usual standard interim payment should not be made.

Any subsequent application for judgment should be made under Pt 24, not under this procedure.

"The show cause procedure ... usually on a costs in the case basis"

This is a summary judgment filter imposed by the court which utilises the documents and evidence prepared in the normal course of the interlocutory process, thus avoiding the need for the preparation of a specific Pt 24 application and supporting evidence. By this method the court ensures that only cases with a real prospect of a defence on any issue go forward to use trial listing resources. In those circumstances the practice at the RCJ has been to order the costs of any "show cause hearings" to be "in the case" whatever the outcome. There is overall fairness in this approach because the procedure is imposed by the court and not by choice of the parties and if a defendant is able to go to trial there is nothing unfair in that defendant losing the costs of having shown cause if it fails at trial or in gaining them from the claimant if it succeeds at trial. The practice also avoids lengthy argument over costs at show cause hearings which are seldom given more than one hour of the court's time, or at CMCs which are seldom given more than half an hour. **49BPD.6.2**

"unless there is good reason not to do so"

Good reason usually consists of some acceptable reason for allowing a defendant more time to investigate or to obtain and rely on further evidence, either from factual witnesses, forensic engineers or medical witnesses. It will not usually be a good reason to allow more time (or at least to allow more than a week or two) that there has been a failure by the defendant to investigate liability and find witnesses in the period following the pre-action protocol letter. In the case of a company which is extant and trading, it is the responsibility of that company as defendant to investigate (either themselves or through solicitors) and not to leave it to brokers or insurers once they have been traced, sometimes several weeks later. There is nothing unacceptable in trying to trace insurers who can respond to the claim, but not at the expense of urgent investigation of liability. **49BPD.6.3**

"within a further given period" "The order requiring the defendant to show cause"

The RCJ practice is to order *either* (1) that unless the defendant files (this may, in courts which accept it, be done by email) and serves outline submissions by a certain date, judgment on the issue of liability will be entered without need for further order and the standard interim payment will be made within 14 days and if submissions are filed the court will conduct a "show cause hearing" *or* (2) simply, that the defendant will show cause at a hearing the date of which is fixed there and then. The latter course is the one usually taken where it is clear that the defendant is likely to want to show cause. **49BPD.6.4**

"At the first case management conference the court will ..."

It is the practice in all mesothelioma claims for the court not only to order an early CMC but also at that first CMC wherever possible to set the date for (and timetable to) an assessment of damages, on the supposition that the defendant will not be, or has not been, able to show cause. If the defendant does show cause that date or one as near to it as possible can be used for a trial. Directions will be issued based upon **PF 52A** (April 2016 edition) and no other standard form. **49BPD.6.5**

"Where the defendant fails to show cause"

If this happens at the first CMC or at a later hearing set for showing cause, the court will enter judgment and make the interim payment order. Where the "unless" form of show cause order has been made, the judgment will normally have been ordered to be entered automatically without need for further order. **49BPD.6.6**

"Where the defendant succeeds in showing cause"

What happens at this stage will depend on a number of factors; the urgency of the claim, the delay in obtaining further expert evidence if necessary, etc. In claims by living victims, where there is nothing more to do in relation to liability except have a trial, either because there is only a factual dispute or there is a dispute on the expert opinions but the evidence is ready, then a trial will often be ordered to take place within weeks, so that an interim payment can be made if the claimant succeeds. If quantum can be assessed at that early time as well then the court will order a full trial rather that the trial of a preliminary issue. **49BPD.6.7**

Setting the trial date

7.1 In Living Mesothelioma Claims the date of the determination of damages or the trial will generally not be more than 16 weeks following service of the claim form. **49BPD.7**

7.2 In Fatal Mesothelioma Claims the hearing date may be more than 16 weeks following service of the claim form.

"16 weeks following service of the claim form"

49BPD.7.1 This is a reference to either a full trial if that is possible or a trial of liability only followed by an interim payment. Where it is necessary to obtain expert evidence, particularly expert engineering/health and safety evidence, it will not always be possible to have a trial, even of liability only within such a time limit, because of the shortage of experts in this field. However, generally the 16-week timetable for disposal should be the aim and this requires efficient listing of CMCs and trials if it is to be achieved.

Taking evidence by deposition

49BPD.8 **8** Any party who for good reason wishes evidence to be taken by deposition may apply to the court at any time for such an order. However, the court will normally expect that such a request is made at a case management conference. The order will include a direction for the recording of such evidence on DVD and for the provision of a transcript. The parties must also be prepared to arrange for the provision of equipment to view the DVD by the court.

(Part 34 contains provisions for evidence to be taken by deposition.)

"who for good reason wishes evidence to be taken by deposition"

49BPD.8.1 At the first CMC where the alleged victim is still alive, the court should always consider making an order that the claimant's evidence be taken on deposition by a certain date or that the claimant's solicitors have permission to have it taken on short notice if the claimant's health deteriorates. The importance of a live victim as a primary source of evidence cannot be over stressed, particularly in cases where the defendant is likely to be able to put forward its own live witnesses at a trial. The live victim is also a valuable source of information for the defendants for them to assess their chances of success on liability and to be able to take an early decision thereon. Many disputes on liability are conceded after evidence is taken on deposition. If there is any likelihood that the claimant might be lost as a source of evidence then that claimant's evidence should be taken as soon as possible so that the defendant can also cross-examine as to its case. The invariable practice at the RCJ is to order the evidence to be recorded on a DVD as well as having the usual transcript made available. The DVD medium is readily useable on judicial laptops. This evidence is most likely to be used at a trial after the alleged victim has died or is too ill to attend trial and often when the defendants are able to call witnesses. The deployment of this evidence on DVD "levels the playing field" as much as possible in those circumstances. It is particularly useful to order evidence to be taken on deposition, where possible, after the closing date in the court's order for the production of witness statements although in particularly urgent cases it may be done earlier. If the evidence has been taken and the claimant then dies or is too ill to give further evidence or assistance, it would be unusual for the court to consider allowing the defendants to put in further evidence.

Compliance with pre-action protocols

49BPD.9 **9** In Living Mesothelioma Claims the court may decide not to require strict adherence to Practice Direction (Pre-Action Conduct) and any relevant pre-action protocol.

"strict adherence to any relevant pre-action protocol"

49BPD.9.1 Although a specific pre-action protocol for mesothelioma claims is under discussion it is not likely to be promulgated for some time. The protocol that applies to these and other asbestos induced illness claims is the Disease and Illness Protocol in which mesothelioma is specifically mentioned at para.2.5 where it is made clear that in cases where a claimant has mesothelioma the timescales of the protocol may be too long. In claims where the alleged victim is still alive, if it seems that the defendant is not investigating liability after the pre-action protocol letter has been sent, that fact will often justify the immediate issue of proceedings so that the court can set an urgent timetable.

Add new Practice Direction 49C–Consumer Credit Act 2006–Unfair Relationships:

PRACTICE DIRECTION 49C—CONSUMER CREDIT ACT 2006—UNFAIR RELATIONSHIPS

This Practice Direction supplements CPR Part 49

Interpretation

49CPD.1 **1.1** In this practice direction "the Act" means the Consumer Credit Act 1974, a section referred to by number means the section with that number in the Act, and expressions which are defined in the Act have the same meaning in this practice direction as they have in the Act.

1.2 "Consumer Credit Act procedure" means the procedure set out in this practice direction.

When to use the Consumer Credit Act procedure

2.1 A claimant must use the Consumer Credit Act procedure where they make a claim under a provision of the Act to which paragraph 3 of this practice direction applies. **49CPD.2**

2.2 Where a claimant is using the Consumer Credit Act procedure the CPR are modified to the extent that they are inconsistent with the procedure set out in this practice direction.

2.3 The court may at any stage order the claim to continue as if the claimant had not used the Consumer Credit Act procedure, and if it does so the court may give any directions it considers appropriate.

2.4 This practice direction also sets out matters which must be included in the particulars of claim in certain types of claim, and restrictions on where certain types of claim may be started.

The provisions of the Act

3.1 Subject to paragraph 3.2 and 3.3 this practice direction applies to claims made under the following provisions of the Act— **49CPD.3**

(1) section 141 (claim by the creditor to enforce regulated agreement relating to goods etc),
(2) section 129 (claim by debtor or hirer for a time order),
(3) section 90 (creditor's claim for an order for recovery of protected goods),
(4) section 92(1) (creditor's or owner's claim to enter premises to take possession of goods),
(5) section 140B(2)(a) (debtor's or surety's application for an order relating to an unfair relationship);
(6) creditor's or owner's claim for a court order to enforce a regulated agreement relating to goods or money where the court order is required by—
  (a) section 65(1) (improperly executed agreement),
  (b) section 86(2) (death of debtor or hirer where agreement is partly secured or unsecured),
  (c) section 111(2) (default notice etc not served on surety),
  (d) section 124(1) or (2) (taking of a negotiable instrument in breach of terms of section 123), or
  (e) section 105(7)(a) or (b) (security not expressed in writing, or improperly executed).

3.2 This practice direction does not apply to any claim made under the provisions listed in paragraph 3.1 above if that claim relates to the recovery of land.

3.3 This practice direction also does not apply to a claim made by the creditor under section 141 of the Act to enforce a regulated agreement where the agreement relates only to money. Such a claim must be started by the issue of a Part 7 claim form.

Restrictions on where to start some Consumer Credit Act claims

4.1(1) If a claim which includes a claim to recover goods to which a regulated hire purchase agreement or conditional sale agreement relates is made at a County Court hearing centre which does not serve the address at which the debtor, or one of the debtors— **49CPD.4**
  (a) resides or carries on business, or
  (b) resided or carried on business at the date when the defendant last made a payment under the agreement, the claim will be issued by the hearing centre where the claim is made and sent to the hearing centre serving the address in (1)(a) or (b) as appropriate.

(2) A claimant should consider the potential delay which may result if a claim is not made at the County Court hearing centre in subparagraph (1)(a) or (b) in the first instance.

4.2(1) In any other claim to recover goods, if the claim is made at a County Court hearing centre which does not serve the address at which—

(a) the defendant, or one of the defendants, resides or carries on business, or

(b) the goods are situated, the claim will be issued by the hearing centre where the claim is made and sent to the County Court hearing centre serving the address in (a) or (b), as appropriate.

(2) A claimant should consider the potential delay which may result if a claim is not made the County Court hearing centre in subparagraph (1)(a) or (b) in the first instance.

4.3 A claim of a debtor or hirer for an order under section 129(1)(b) or 129(1)(ba) of the Act (a time order) must be made at the County Court hearing centre where the claimant debtor or hirer resides or carries on business.

(Costs rule 45.1(2)(b) allows the claimant to recover fixed costs in certain circumstances where such a claim is made.)

(Paragraph 7 sets out the matters the claimant must include in his particulars of claim where he is using the Consumer Credit Act procedure.)

The Consumer Credit Act procedure

49CPD.5 **5.1** Subject to paragraph 5.2, in the types of claim to which paragraph 3 applies the court will fix a hearing date on the issue of the claim form.

5.2(1) In the types of claim to which paragraph 4.1 applies, if the claim is made at a County Court hearing centre which does not serve the address at which the debtor, or one of the debtors—

(a) resides or carries on business, or

(b) resided or carried on business at the date when the defendant last made a payment under the agreement,

the hearing date will be fixed by the hearing centre serving the address at (1)(a) or (b), as appropriate, upon receipt of the claim from the hearing centre where the claim was made.

(2) In the types of claim to which paragraph 4.2 applies, if the claim is made at a County Court hearing centre which does not serve the address at which—

(a) the defendant, or one of the defendants, resides or carries on business, or

(b) the goods are situated, the hearing date will be fixed by the hearing centre serving the address at (2)(a) or (b), as appropriate, upon receipt of the claim from the hearing centre where the claim was made.

5.3 The particulars of claim must be served with the claim form.

5.4 Where a claimant is using the Consumer Credit Act procedure, the defendant to the claim is not required to—

(1) serve an acknowledgment of service, or

(2) file a defence, although he may choose to do so.

5.5 Where a defendant intends to defend a claim, the defence should be filed within 14 days of service of the particulars of claim. If the defendant fails to file a defence within this period, but later relies on it, the court may take such a failure into account as a factor when deciding what order to make about costs.

5.6 Part 12 (default judgment) does not apply where the claimant is using the Consumer Credit Act procedure.

5.7 Each party must be given at least 28 days' notice of the hearing date.

5.8 Where the claimant serves the claim form, he must serve notice of the hearing date at the same time, unless the hearing date is specified in the claim form.

Powers of the court at the hearing

6.1 On the hearing date the court may dispose of the claim. **49CPD.6**

6.2 If the court does not dispose of the claim on the hearing date—

(1) if the defendant has filed a defence, the court will—

(a) allocate the claim to a track and give directions about the management of the case, or

(b) give directions to enable it to allocate the claim to a track,

(2) if the defendant has not filed a defence, the court may make any order or give any direction it considers appropriate.

6.3 Rule 26.5 (3) and (4) and rules 26.6 to 26.10 apply to the allocation of a claim under paragraph 6.2.

Matters which must be included in the particulars of claim

7.1 Where the Consumer Credit Act procedure is used, the claimant must state in his particulars of claim that the claim is a Consumer Credit Act claim. **49CPD.7**

7.2 A claimant making a claim for the delivery of goods to enforce a hire purchase agreement or conditional sale agreement which is—

(1) a regulated agreement for the recovery of goods, and

(2) let to a person other than a company or other corporation, must also state (in this order) in his particulars of claim—

(a) the date of the agreement,

(b) the parties to the agreement,

(c) the number or other identification of the agreement (with enough information to allow the debtor to identify the agreement),

(d) where the claimant was not one of the original parties to the agreement, the means by which the rights and duties of the creditor passed to him,

(e) the place where the agreement was signed by the defendant (if known),

(f) the goods claimed,

(g) the total price of the goods,

(h) the paid up sum,

(i) the unpaid balance of the total price,

(j) whether a default notice or a notice under section 76(1) or section 88(1) of the Act has been served on the defendant, and, if it has, the date and the method of service,

(k) the date on which the right to demand delivery of the goods accrued,

(l) the amount (if any) claimed as an alternative to the delivery of goods, and

(m) the amount (if any) claimed in addition to—

(i) the delivery of the goods, or

(ii) any claim under sub paragraph (l) above with the grounds of each such claim.

7.3 A claimant who is a debtor or hirer making a claim for an order under section 129(1)(b) or 129(1)(ba) of the Act (a time order) must state (in the following order) in the particulars of claim—

(1) the date of the agreement,

(2) the parties to the agreement,

(3) the number or other means of identifying the agreement,

(4) details of any sureties,
(5) if the defendant is not one of the original parties to the agreement then the name of the original party to the agreement,
(6) the names and addresses of the persons intended to be served with the claim form,
(7) the place where the claimant signed the agreement,
(8) details of the notice served by the creditor or owner giving rise to the claim for the time order,
(9) the total unpaid balance the claimant admits is due under the agreement, and—
 (a) the amount of any arrears (if known), and
 (b) the amount and frequency of the payments specified in the agreement,

(10) the claimant's proposals for payments of any arrears and of future instalments together with details of his means;
(11) where the claim relates to a breach of the agreement other than for the payment of money the claimant's proposals for remedying it.

7.4 A claimant who is a debtor or hirer making a claim for an order under section 129(1)(ba) of the Act must attach to the particulars of claim a copy of the notice served on the creditor or owner under section 129A(1)(a) of the Act.

7.5(1) This paragraph applies where a claimant is required to obtain a court order to enforce a regulated agreement by—
 (a) section 65(1) (improperly executed agreement),
 (b) section 105(7)(a) or (b) (security not expressed in writing, or improperly executed),
 (c) section 111(2) (default notice etc. not served on surety),
 (d) section 124(1) or (2) (taking of a negotiable instrument in breach of terms of section 123), or
 (e) section 86(2) of the Act (death of debtor or hirer where agreement is partly secured or unsecured).

(2) The claimant must state in his particulars of claim what the circumstances are that require the claimant to obtain a court order for enforcement.

Admission of certain claims for recovery of goods under regulated agreements

49CPD.8 **8.1** In a claim to recover goods to which section 90(1) applies—
(1) the defendant may admit the claim, and
(2) offer terms on which a return order should be suspended under section 135(1)(b).

8.2 The defendant may do so by filing a request in practice form **N9C**.

8.3 The defendant should do so within the period for making an admission specified in rule 14.2(b). If the defendant fails to file his request within this period, and later makes such a request, the court may take the failure into account as a factor when deciding what order to make about costs.

8.4 On receipt of the admission, the court will serve a copy on the claimant.

8.5 The claimant may obtain judgment by filing a request in practice form **N228**.

8.6 On receipt of the request for judgment, the court will enter judgment in the terms of the defendant's admission and offer and for costs.

8.7 If—
(1) the claimant does not accept the defendant's admission and offer, and
(2) the defendant does not appear on the hearing date fixed when the claim form was issued,

the court may treat the defendant's admission and offer as evidence of the facts stated in it for the purposes of sections 129(2)(a) and 135(2).

Additional requirements about parties to the proceedings

9.1 The court may dispense with the requirement in section 141(5) (all parties to a regulated agreement and any surety to be parties to any proceedings) in any claim relating to the regulated agreement, if– **49CPD.9**

(1) the claim form has not been served on the debtor or the surety, and
(2) the claimant either before or at the hearing makes an application (which may be made without notice) for the court to make such an order.

9.2 In a claim relating to a regulated agreement where–

(1) the claimant was not one of the original parties to the agreement, and
(2) the former creditor's rights and duties under the agreement have passed to him by–
    (a) operation of law, or
    (b) assignment,

the requirement of section 141(5) (all parties to a regulated agreement and any surety to be parties to any proceedings) does not apply to the former creditor, unless the court otherwise orders.

9.3 Where a claimant who is a creditor or owner makes a claim for a court order under section 86(2) (death of debtor or hirer where agreement is partly secured or unsecured) the personal representatives of the deceased debtor or hirer must be parties to the proceedings in which the order is sought, unless no grant of representation has been made to the estate.

9.4 Where no grant of representation has been made to the estate of the deceased debtor or hirer, the claimant must make an application in accordance with Part 23 for directions about which persons (if any) are to be made parties to the claim as being affected or likely to be affected by the enforcement of the agreement.

9.5 The claimant's application under paragraph 9.4:

(a) may be made without notice, and
(b) should be made before the claim form is issued.

Notice to be given to re-open a consumer credit agreement

10.1 Paragraph 10.2 applies where– **49CPD.10**

(1) a debtor or any surety intends to seek an order relating to an unfair relationship between a creditor and that debtor, arising out of a credit agreement (taken together with any related agreement);
(2) a claim relating to that agreement or any related agreement has already begun; and
(3) section 140B(2)(b) or section 140B(2)(c) applies.

10.2 The debtor or surety must serve written notice of intention on the court and every other party to the claim within 14 days of service of the claim form.

10.3 A debtor or surety (as the case may be) who serves a notice under paragraph 10.2 will be treated as having filed a defence for the purposes of the Consumer Credit Act procedure.

Editorial note

By CPR PD Update 44, paras 3.1(5), 10.1 and 10.2 of this Practice Direction were amended as a consequence of amendments made to the Consumer Credit Act 1974 by the Consumer Credit Act 2006, having the effect of replacing provisions on extortionate credit bargains (ss.137 to 140) with new provisions about unfair relationships (ss.140A to 140D). By CPR PD Update 49, the Practice Direction was further amended, with effect from 6 April 2009, by the deletion of para.10.2A and a consequential amendment was made to para.10.3 accordingly. (This deletion reflected a transitional provision permitting the continued application of s.139 to agreements made before 6 April 2007 **49CPD.10.1** for a period of one year.) For text and commentary on the 1974 Act (as amended), see Vol.2, Section 3H.

Add new Practice Direction 49D–Claims for the Recovery of Taxes and Duties:

PRACTICE DIRECTION 49D—CLAIMS FOR THE RECOVERY OF TAXES AND DUTIES

This Practice Direction supplements CPR Part 49

Scope

49DPD.1 **1.1** This practice direction applies to claims by HM Revenue and Customs for the recovery of–

(a) Income Tax,
(b) Corporation Tax,
(c) Capital Gains Tax,
(d) Interest, penalties and surcharges on Income Tax, Corporation Tax or Capital Gains Tax which by virtue of section 69 of the Taxes Management Act 1970 are to be treated as if they are taxes due and payable,
(e) National Insurance Contributions and interest, penalties and surcharges thereon,
(f) student loan repayments deducted by and recoverable from an employer under Part IV of the Education (Student Loans) (Repayment) Regulations 2000 (S.I. 2000/944),
(g) Value added tax and interest and surcharges thereon,
(h) Insurance premium tax and interest and penalties thereon,
(i) Stamp duty land tax and interest and penalties thereon,
(j) the following environmental taxes–
 (i) landfill tax and interest and penalties thereon,
 (ii) aggregates levy and interest and penalties thereon, and
 (iii) climate change levy and interest and penalties thereon,
(k) the following duties of customs and excise–
 (i) amusement machine licence duty and penalties thereon,
 (ii) air passenger duty and interest and penalties thereon,
 (iii) beer duty and penalties thereon,
 (iv) bingo duty and penalties thereon,
 (v) cider and perry duty,
 (vi) excise and spirits duty,
 (vii) excise wine duty,
 (viii) gaming duty and penalties thereon,
 (ix) general betting duty,
 (x) lottery duty and penalties thereon,
 (xi) REDS (registered excise dealers and shippers) duty,
 (xii) road fuel duty and penalties thereon,
 (xiii) tobacco duty, and
 (xiv) wine and made-wine duty.

1.2 This practice direction also applies to claims by the Welsh revenue Authority for the recovery of a devolved tax (as defined by section 116A(4) of the Government of Wales Act 2006) and interest and penalties thereon.

(Section 116A(4) of the Government of Wales Act 2006 defines a devolved tax as a tax which is specified in Part 4A of that Act as a devolved tax. For example, section 116L of the 2006 Act specifies as a devolved tax a tax which is charged on a Welsh land transaction and complies with the requirements of that section.)

Procedure

2.1 If a defence is filed, the court will fix a date for the hearing. **49DPD.2**

2.2 Part 26 (Case management–preliminary stage) with the exception of rules 26.2 and 26.2A, does not apply to claims to which this practice direction applies.

At the hearing

3.1 On the hearing date the court may dispose of the claim. **49DPD.3**

(Section 25A(1) and (2) of the Commissioners for Revenue and Customs Act 2005 ("the 2005 Act") provides that a certificate of an officer of Revenue and Customs that, to the best of that officer's knowledge and belief, a sum payable to the Commissioners under or by virtue of an enactment or by virtue of a contract settlement (within the meaning of section 25(6) of the 2005 Act) has not been paid, is sufficient evidence that the sum mentioned in the certificate is unpaid.)

(Section 168(1) of the Tax Collection and Management (Wales) Act 2016 ("the 2016 Act") provides that a certificate of Welsh Revenue Authority that a relevant amount (as defined by section 164 of the 2016 Act) has not been paid to Welsh Revenue Authority is sufficient evidence that the sum mentioned in the certificate is unpaid unless the contrary is proved.)

3.2 But exceptionally, if the court does not dispose of the claim on the hearing date it may give case management directions, which may, if the defendant has filed a defence, include allocating the case.

Editorial note on Practice Direction—Claims for the Recovery of Taxes and Duties

The 2005 Act (see para.3.1) provides that if an Inspector of Taxes issues a certificate of tax due in relation to an unpaid amount of a tax within a defined category of taxes and duties, in effect a defence to an issued claim cannot generally be pursued to a contested trial. Paragraph 1.1 of the Practice Direction lists the defined taxes and duties. This list was significantly extended from 6 April 2009—note that student loans repayable by an employer are included although they are neither a tax nor a duty, but certain taxes, including tax credits, are not included. **49DPD.3.1**

When a claim is issued for a payment of a "tax" in the list in para.1.1 and a "defence" is filed, the Practice Direction provides for the case to be issued for a short disposal hearing (in a similar way to most Pt 8 claims). The court nonetheless exceptionally (not defined) has the power at that hearing, under para.3.2 of the Practice Direction, to allocate the case to track and give directions to trial, presumably either when no certificate has been issued, or there is prima facie evidence that the certificate may be incorrect.

In April 2009 the list of taxes in para.1.1 was extended; (f) to (xiv) were the new additions. Note that (f), a student loan, is not a tax but where an employer is deducting the repayments they are under a statutory obligation to pass the payments to the Inland Revenue.

Paragraph 4A.1(2) of PD 7A provides that for the purposes of that Practice Direction the obligation under para.2.2 of PD 49D to fix a hearing date upon the filing of a defence does not constitute a "special procedure". This resolves the former uncertainty as to whether it was necessary for claims to which this Practice Direction applies to be issued through the County Court Money Claims Centre. It is now clear that such claims are to be issued at the CCMCC in the same way as any other Pt 7 money claim. On the filing of a defence the file will be sent to the appropriate County Court hearing centre for a hearing to be fixed. In the event of a defence being filed, directions questionnaires are not required (as r.26.3 does not apply), rather the claim is listed for hearing. If the claim has been issued against an individual defendant at a hearing centre which is not the defendant's home court, then the case will be sent to the defendant's home court in accordance with r.26.2 (High Court) or r.26.2A (County Court).

Add new Practice Direction 49E–Alternative Procedure for Claims:

PRACTICE DIRECTION 49E—ALTERNATIVE PROCEDURE FOR CLAIMS

This practice direction supplements CPR Part 49

Terminology

1.1 This practice direction is made under Part 49 of the Civil Procedure Rules. **49EPD.1**

1.2 In this practice direction, "Schedule rules" means provisions contained in the Schedules to the CPR, which were previously contained in the Rules of the Supreme Court (1965) or the County Court Rules (1981).

Application of this Practice Direction

49EPD.2 **2.1** Section A contains general provisions about claims and applications to which Part 8 applies. Section B comprises a table listing claims, petitions and applications under various enactments which must be made under Part 8. Section C contains certain additions and modifications to the Part 8 procedure that apply to the particular claims and applications identified.

2.2 Some of the claims and applications listed in the table in Section B are dealt with in the Schedule Rules in the CPR. The table in Section B contains cross-reference to the relevant Schedule Rules.

Section A General Provisions Applicable to Part 8 Claims

49EPD.3 **3.1** Where a claim is listed in the table in Section B and is identified as a claim to which particular provisions of Section C apply, the Part 8 procedure shall apply subject to the additions and modifications set out in the relevant paragraphs in Section C.

3.2 The Part 8 procedure must also be used for any claim or application in relation to which an Act, rule or practice direction provides that the claim or application is brought by originating summons, originating motion or originating application.

3.3 Where it appears to a court officer that a claimant is using the Part 8 procedure inappropriately, the court officer may refer the claim to a judge for the judge to consider the point.

Section B Claims and Applications That Must Be Made under Part 8

49EPD.4 **4.1** The claimant must use the Part 8 procedure if the claim is listed in the table below.

4.2 Section C of this Practice Direction contains special provisions modifying the Part 8 procedure, and where it does so, those provisions should be followed. The table below refers to the relevant paragraph of Section C where it applies.

4.3 Some of the claims and applications listed in the table below are dealt with in the Schedule Rules, and those rules modify the Part 8 procedure. A cross-reference to the relevant Schedule Rule is contained in the table below.

4.4 For applications that may or must be brought in the High Court, where no other rule or practice direction assigns the application to a Division of the court, the table specifies the Division to which the application is assigned.

Type of Claim or Application	***Paragraph of Section C***	***Division***	***Schedule Rule***
Application under section 14 of the Bills of Sale Act 1878 (Rectification of register)	Paragraph 10A	Queen's Bench Central Office	
Application under section 15 of the Bills of Sale Act 1878 (Entry of satisfaction)	Paragraph 11	Queen's Bench Central Office	
Application under section 16 of the Bills of Sale Act 1878 (Search of the bills of sale register)	Paragraph 11A	Queen's Bench Central Office	
Application under the proviso to section 7 of the Bills of Sale Act (1878) Amendment Act 1882 (Restraining removal or sale		Queen's Bench Central Office	

Type of Claim or Application	*Paragraph of Section C*	*Division*	*Schedule Rule*
of goods seized)			
Application under the Public Trustee Act 1906 (free-standing proceedings)	Paragraph 12	Chancery	
Application under section 7 of the Deeds of Arrangement Act 1914 (Rectification of register)	Paragraph 12A	Queen's Bench Central Office	
Proceedings under the Trustee Act 1925		Chancery	
Applications under section 2(3) of the Public Order Act 1936	Paragraph 13	Chancery	
Proceedings under jurisdiction conferred by section 1 of the Railway and Canal Commission (Abolition) Act 1949	Paragraph 14	Chancery	
Administration of Justice Act 1960 (Applications under the Act)		Divisional Court	RSC O.109, r.1(3)
Administration of Justice Act 1960 (Appeals under section 13 of the Act)		Divisional Court	RSC O.109, r.2(4)
Proceedings under section 14 of the Commons Registration Act 1965		Chancery	
Application under the Mines (Working Facilities and Support) Act 1966	Paragraph 15	Chancery	
Proceedings under section 21 or 25 of the Law of Property Act 1969		Chancery	
Local Government Act 1972 (claims under section 92—proceedings for disqualification)		Queen's Bench Central Office	
Application under article 10 of the Mortgaging of Aircraft Order 1972 (Rectification of register)	Paragraph 15A	Chancery	
Application to register an assignment of book debts (section 344 of the Insolvency Act 1986)	Paragraph 15B	Queen's Bench Central Office	
Proceedings under the Control of Misleading Advertisements Regulations 1988		Chancery	
Application under section 42	Paragraph 16	Administrative	

Type of Claim or Application	*Paragraph of Section C*	*Division*	*Schedule Rule*
of the Senior Courts Act 1981		Court	
Proceedings in the High Court under the Representation of the People Acts	Paragraph 17A	Queen's Bench Central Office	
Applications under Part II of the Mental Health Act 1983	Paragraph 18	Administrative Court	
Applications under section 13 of the Coroners Act 1988	Paragraph 19	Administrative Court	
Application for an injunction to prevent environmental harm under section 187B or 214A of the Town and Country Planning Act 1990; section 44A of the Planning (Listed Buildings and Conservation Areas) Act 1990; or section 26AA of the Planning (Hazardous Substances) Act 1990	Paragraph 20	Queen's Bench	
Confiscation and forfeiture in connection with criminal proceedings (I. Drug Trafficking Act 1994 and Criminal Justice (International Co-operation) Act 1990—Application for a confiscation order)		Queen's Bench	RSC O.115, r.2B(1)
Confiscation and forfeiture in connection with criminal proceedings (I. Drug Trafficking Act 1994 and Criminal Justice (International Co-operation) Act 1990—Application for a restraint order or charging order)		Queen's Bench	RSC O.115, r.3(1)
Confiscation and forfeiture in connection with criminal proceedings (I. Drug Trafficking Act 1994 and Criminal Justice (International Co-operation) Act 1990—Realisation of property)		Queen's Bench	RSC O.115, r.7(1)
Criminal Procedure and Investigations Act 1996 (Application under section 54(3))		Administrative Court	

Type of Claim or Application	*Paragraph of Section C*	*Division*	*Schedule Rule*
Confiscation and forfeiture in connection with criminal proceedings (III. Terrorism Act 2000—Application for a restraint order)		Queen's Bench	RSC O.115, r.26(1)
Proceedings under the Financial Services and Markets Act 2000	Paragraph 21	Chancery	
Application for an injunction under section 12 or 26 of the Energy Act 2008	Paragraph 20	Queen's Bench	
Stakeholder applications—mode of application, unless there are existing proceedings (Rule 86.2(3))		Chancery or Queen's Bench	RSC O.17, r.3(1)
Criminal proceedings (estreat of recognizances)		Queen's Bench	RSC O.79, r.8(2
Criminal proceedings (bail)		Queen's Bench	RSC O.79, r.9(2)
Application under an enactment giving the High Court jurisdiction to quash or prohibit any order, scheme, certificate or plan, any amendment or approval of a plan, any decision of a Minister or government department or any action on the part of a Minister or government department	Paragraph 22	Administrative Court	
Application under section 66 of the Anti-Social Behaviour, Crime and Policing Act 2014 to question the validity of a public spaces protection order or variation of such an order	Paragraph 22	Administrative Court	
Proceedings under The Telecommunications Restriction Orders (Custodial Institutions) (England and Wales) Regulations 2015	Paragraph 23	N/A (County Court)	N/A
Proceedings under the Drug Dealing Telecommunications Restriction Orders Regulations 2017	Paragraph 24	N/A (County Court)	N/A
Proceedings transferred to the High Court from the Magistrates' Court under section 303R of the Proceeds of Crime Act 2002 or under	Paragraph 25	Queen's Bench	N/A

Type of Claim or Application	*Paragraph of Section C*	*Division*	*Schedule Rule*
paragraph 10J of Part 4A of Schedule 1 to the Anti-terrorism, Crime and Security Act 2001			

Section C Special Provisions

49EPD.5 **5.1** The following special provisions apply to the applications indicated.

Applications under section 14 of the Bills of Sale Act 1878

49EPD.6 **6.1** This paragraph applies to an application under section 14 of the Bills of Sale Act 1878 for an order to rectify an omission or mis-statement in relation to the registration, or renewal of the registration, of a bill of sale—

(1) by inserting in the register the true name, residence or occupation of a person; or
(2) by extending the time for registration of the bill of sale or an affidavit of its renewal.

6.2 The application must be made—

(1) by claim form under Part 8; or
(2) by witness statement.

6.3 Where the application is made by witness statement—

(1) Part 23 applies to the application;
(2) the witness statement constitutes the application notice under that Part;
(3) the witness statement does not need to be served on any other person; and
(4) the application will normally be dealt with without a hearing.

6.4 The application must set out—

(1) the particulars of the bill of sale and of the omission or mis-statement; and
(2) the grounds on which the application is made.

6.5 The application must be made to a Master of the Queen's Bench Division and accompanied by payment of the prescribed fee.

Applications under Section 15 of the Bills of Sale Act 1878

49EPD.7 **7.1** This paragraph applies where an application is made under section 15 of the Bills of Sale Act 1878 for an order that a memorandum of satisfaction be written on a registered copy of a bill of sale.

7.2 If the person entitled to the benefit of the bill of sale has not consented to the satisfaction, the claim form—

(1) must be served on that person; and
(2) must be supported by evidence that the debt (if any) for which the bill of sale was made has been satisfied or discharged.

7.3 If the person entitled to the benefit of the bill of sale has consented to the satisfaction, the application may be made by—

(1) claim form under Part 8; or
(2) witness statement.

7.4 Where paragraph 11.3 applies and the application is made by Part 8 claim form, the claim form—

(1) must contain details of the consent;
(2) must be supported by a witness statement by a person who witnessed the consent verifying the signature on it; and

(3) must not be served on any person other than the person entitled to the benefit of the bill of sale.

7.5 Where paragraph 11.3 applies and the application is made by witness statement—

(1) Part 23 will apply to the application;
(2) the witness statement will constitute the application notice under that Part;
(3) the witness statement does not need to be served on any other person; and
(4) the application will normally be dealt with without a hearing.

Applications under section 16 of the Bills of Sale Act 1878

8.1 This paragraph applies to an application under section 16 of the Bills of Sale Act 1878 for a search of the bills of sale register and for a certificate of the results of the search. **49EPD.8**

8.2 The application must be made—

(1) by claim form under Part 8; or
(2) by written request.

8.3 The application must give sufficient information to enable the relevant bill of sale to be identified.

8.4 The application must be made to a Master of the Queen's Bench Division and accompanied by payment of the prescribed fee.

Application under the Public Trustee Act 1906

9.1 An application under the Public Trustee Act 1906 must be made— **49EPD.9**

(1) where no proceedings have been issued, by a Part 8 claim;
(2) in existing proceedings, by a Part 23 application.

9.2 Without prejudice to sections 10(2) and 13(7) of the Public Trustee Act 1906, the jurisdiction of the High Court under the Act is exercised by a single judge of the Chancery Division sitting in private.

Applications under section 7 of the Deeds of Arrangement Act 1914

10.1 This paragraph applies to an application under section 7 of the Deeds of Arrangement Act 1914 for an order to rectify an omission or mis-statement in relation to the registration of a deed of arrangement— **49EPD.10**

(1) by inserting in the register the true name, residence or description of a person; or
(2) by extending the time for registration.

10.2 The application must be made—

(1) by claim form under Part 8; or
(2) by witness statement.

10.3 Where the application is made by witness statement—

(1) Part 23 applies to the application;
(2) the witness statement constitutes the application notice under that Part;
(3) the witness statement does not need to be served on any other person; and
(4) the application will normally be dealt with without a hearing.

10.4 The application must set out—

(1) the particulars of the deed of arrangement and of the omission or mis-statement; and
(2) the grounds on which the application is made.

10.5 The application must be made to a Master of the Queen's Bench Division and accompanied by payment of the prescribed fee.

Application under section 2(3) of the Public Order Act 1936

49EPD.11 **11.1** The Attorney General may determine the persons who should be made defendants to an application under section 2(3) of the Public Order Act 1936.

11.2 If the court directs an inquiry under section 2(3), it may appoint the Official Solicitor to represent any interests it considers are not sufficiently represented and ought to be represented.

Proceedings under section 1 of the Railway and Canal Commission (Abolition) Act 1949

49EPD.12 **12.1** Paragraphs 15.3 to 15.14 apply, with appropriate modifications, to proceedings in which jurisdiction has been conferred on the High Court by section 1 of the Railway and Canal Commission (Abolition) Act 1949, except to the extent that–

(1) an Act;
(2) a rule;
(3) a practice direction,

provides otherwise.

Application under the Mines (Working Facilities and Support) Act 1966

49EPD.13 **13.1** In this paragraph–

(1) "the Act" means the Mines (Working Facilities and Support) Act 1966;
(2) "the applicant" means the person who has applied for the grant of a right under the Act.

13.2 This paragraph applies where the Secretary of State refers an application to the High Court under any provision of the Act.

13.3 The Secretary of State must–

(1) file a reference signed by him or a person authorised to sign on his behalf in the Chancery Division of the High Court;
(2) file, along with the reference, any documents and plans deposited with him by the applicant in support of his application; and
(3) within 3 days of filing the reference, give notice to the applicant that the reference has been filed.

13.4 Within 10 days of receiving the notice referred to in paragraph 15.3(3), the applicant must issue a claim form.

13.5 The claim form–

(1) must identify the application under the Act and the remedy sought; and
(2) need not be served on any other party.

13.6 Within 7 days of the claim form being issued, the applicant must–

(1) apply for the claim to be listed for a hearing before a Master; and
(2) give notice of the hearing date to the Secretary of State.

13.7 The applicant must, not less than 2 days before the date fixed for a hearing, file at court–

(1) a witness statement in support of the claim, giving details of all persons known to the applicant to be interested in, or affected by, the application; and
(2) a draft of any proposed advertisement or notice of the application.

13.8 At the hearing, the Master will–

(1) fix a date by which any notice of objection under paragraph 15.9 must be filed;
(2) fix a date for a further hearing of the claim; and
(3) give directions about–
    (a) any advertisement that is to be inserted or notice of the application and hearing date that is to be given; and

(b) what persons are to be served with a copy of the application or any other document in the proceedings.

13.9 Any person who wishes to oppose the application must, within the time fixed by the court under paragraph 15.8, serve notice of objection on the applicant, stating–

(a) his name and address;
(b) the name and address of his solicitor, if any;
(c) the grounds of his objection;
(d) any alternative method for effecting the objects of the application that he alleges may be used; and
(e) the facts on which he relies.

13.10 Any document that is required to be served on the person who has given notice of objection ("the objector") may be served by posting it to the following address–

(1) where the notice of objection gives the name and address of a solicitor, to the solicitor;
(2) in any other case, to the objector at the address stated in the notice of objection.

13.11 The objector may appear, or be represented at any further hearing, and may take such part in the proceedings as the court allows.

13.12 The applicant must, not less than two days before the date set for the further hearing, file at court–

(1) any notices of objection served on him;
(2) a list of objectors, together with–
  (a) their names and addresses;
  (b) the names and addresses of their solicitors, if any; and
  (c) a summary of their respective grounds of objection.

13.13 If the objector does not appear, or is not represented, at the further hearing–

(1) his notice of objection will have no effect; and
(2) he will not be entitled to take any further part in the proceedings unless the court orders otherwise.

13.14 At the further hearing, the court will–

(1) give directions about the future conduct of the claim, including–
  (a) any further information the applicant is required to give in relation to any of the grounds or facts relied on in support of the application;
  (b) any further information the objector is required to give in relation to any of the grounds or facts relied on in opposition to the application;
  (c) whether the applicant may serve a reply to any notice of objection;
  (d) whether any particular fact should be proved by a witness statement;
  (e) whether any statements of case or points of claim or defence are to be served; and

(2) adjourn the claim for hearing before a judge.

Applications under article 10 of the Mortgaging of Aircraft Order 1972

14.1 This paragraph applies to an application under article 10 of the Mortgaging of Aircraft Order 1972 for an order to amend the Register of Aircraft Mortgages. **49EPD.14**

14.2 The application must be made by claim form under Part 8.

14.3 Every person (other than the claimant) who appears in the register as mortgagor or mortgagee of the aircraft concerned must be made a defendant to the claim.

14.4 A copy of the claim form must be sent to the Civil Aviation Authority.
14.5 The application will be assigned to the Chancery Division.
14.6 The Civil Aviation Authority is entitled to be heard in the proceedings.

Applications under section 344 of the Insolvency Act 1986 for registration of assignments of book debts

49EPD.15 **15.1** This paragraph applies to an application under section 344 of the Insolvency Act 1986 to register an assignment of book debts.

15.2 The application must be made—
(1) by claim form under Part 8; or
(2) by witness statement.

15.3 The application must be made to a Master of the Queen's Bench Division and accompanied by payment of the prescribed fee.

15.4 Where the application is made by witness statement—
(1) Part 23 applies to the application;
(2) the witness statement constitutes the application notice under that Part;
(3) the witness statement does not need to be served on any other person; and
(4) the application will normally be dealt with without a hearing.

15.5 The application—
(1) must have exhibited to it a true copy of the assignment and of every schedule to it;
(2) must set out the particulars of the assignment and the parties to it; and
(3) must verify the date and time of the execution of the assignment, and its execution in the presence of a witness.

15.6 Upon the court being satisfied, the documents so exhibited will be filed and the particulars of the assignment and of the parties to it entered in the register.

Application under section 42 of the Senior Courts Act 1981

49EPD.16 **16.1** An application under section 42 of the Senior Courts Act 1981 is heard and determined by a Divisional Court.

16.2 The claim form must be filed at the Administrative Court and—
(1) be accompanied by a witness statement in support; and
(2) be served on the person against whom the order is sought.

Application for detailed assessment of a returning officer's account

49EPD.17 **17.1**(1) An application by—
(a) the Secretary of State under section 30 of the Representation of the People Act 1983 or paragraph 4 of Schedule 1 to the Recall of MPs Act 2015;
(b) the Welsh Ministers under article 24 of the National Assembly for Wales (Representation of the People) Order 2007; or
(c) the Electoral Commission under paragraph 17 of Schedule 3 to the European Union Referendum Act 2015,

for the detailed assessment of a returning officer's account must be made by claim form.

(2) In this paragraph and paragraphs 17.3 to 17.5 and 17.8, references to the returning officer are to be read—
(a) for applications under the Recall of MPs Act 2015, as references to the petition officer;
(b) for applications under the National Assembly for Wales (Representation of the People) Order 2007, as references to—
(i) the constituency returning officer, in relation to a constituency election; and

(ii) the constituency and regional returning officer, in relation to a regional election; and

(c) for applications under the European Union Referendum Act 2015, as references to the counting officer or Regional Counting Officer.

17.2 When it issues the claim form, the court will fix a date for the hearing of the detailed assessment to be dealt with if the application is granted.

17.3 The returning officer may, on the application, apply to the court to examine any claim made against him in respect of matters charged in the account.

17.4 To make an application under paragraph 17.3, the returning officer must file an application within 7 days of being served with a copy of the application for detailed assessment.

17.5 When an application is filed under paragraph 17.3, the court will–

(a) fix a date for the hearing;

(b) give notice of the hearing date to the returning officer; and

(c) serve a copy of the application and notice of hearing on the claimant.

17.6 The examination and detailed assessment may take place on the same day, provided that the examination is determined before the detailed assessment is concluded.

17.7 The district judge may hear and determine–

(a) an application for detailed assessment;

(b) any application under paragraph 17.3.

17.8 The court will serve a copy of the order made in the application on–

(a) the Secretary of State;

(b) the returning officer; and

(c) in an application under paragraph 17.3, the claimant.

Other proceedings under the Representation of the People Acts

18.1(1) This paragraph applies to proceedings under the Representation of the People Acts (other than proceedings under section 30 of the Representation of the People Act 1983) and the European Union Referendum (Conduct) Regulations 2016 ("the 2016 Regulations"). **49EPD.18**

(2) The jurisdiction of the High Court under those Acts in matters relating to Parliamentary and local government elections, or under the 2016 Regulations, will be exercised by a Divisional Court except that–

(a) any jurisdiction, under a provision of any of those Acts, or under the 2016 Regulations, exercisable by a single judge will be exercised by a single judge;

(b) any jurisdiction, under any such provision, exercisable by a Master will be exercised by a Master; and

(c) where the court's jurisdiction in matters relating to Parliamentary elections is exercisable by a single judge, that jurisdiction in matters relating to local government elections is also exercisable by a single judge.

Application under Mental Health Act 1983

19.1 In this paragraph– **49EPD.19**

(1) a section referred to by a number refers to the section so numbered in the Mental Health Act 1983 and "Part II" means Part II of that Act;

(2) "hospital manager" means the manager of a hospital as defined in section 145(1) of the Act; and

(3) "place of residence" means, in relation to a patient who is receiving treat-

ment as an in-patient in a hospital or other institution, that hospital or institution.

19.2 The claim form must be filed–

(1) in the County Court hearing centre serving the patient's place of residence is situated; or

(2) in the case of an application under section 30, in the court or County Court hearing centre that made the order under section 29 which the application seeks to discharge or vary.

19.3 Where an application is made under section 29 for an order that the functions of the nearest relative of the patient are to be exercisable by some other person–

(1) the nearest relative must be made a respondent, unless–

  (a) the application is made on the grounds that the patient has no nearest relative or that it is not reasonably practicable to ascertain whether he has a nearest relative; or

  (b) the court orders otherwise; and

(2) the court may order that any other person shall be made a respondent.

19.4 Subject to paragraph 18.5, the court may accept as evidence of the facts relied upon in support of the application, any report made–

(1) by a medical practitioner; or

(2) by any of the following acting in the course of their official duties–

  (a) a probation officer;

  (b) an officer of a local authority;

  (c) an officer of a voluntary body exercising statutory functions on behalf of a local authority; or

  (d) an officer of a hospital manager.

19.5 The respondent must be informed of the substance of any part of the report dealing with his fitness or conduct that the court considers to be material to the determination of the claim.

19.6 An application under Part II shall be heard in private unless the court orders otherwise.

19.7 The judge may, for the purpose of determining the application, interview the patient. The interview may take place in the presence of, or separately from, the parties. The interview may be conducted elsewhere than at the court. Alternatively, the judge may direct the district judge to interview the patient and report to the judge in writing.

Applications under section 13 of the Coroners Act 1988

49EPD.20 **20.1** An application under section 13 of the Coroners Act 1988 is heard and determined by a Divisional Court.

20.2 The application must, unless made by the Attorney General, be accompanied by the Attorney General's fiat.

20.3 The claim form must–

(1) state the grounds for the application;

(2) be filed at the Administrative Court; and

(3) be served upon all persons directly affected by the application within six weeks of the grant of the Attorney General's fiat.

Application for injunction to prevent environmental harm or unlicensed activities

49EPD.21 **21.1** This paragraph relates to applications under–

(1) section 187B or 214A of the Town and Country Planning Act 1990;

(2) section 44A of the Planning (Listed Buildings and Conservation Areas) Act 1990;

(3) section 26AA of the Planning (Hazardous Substances) Act 1990; or
(4) section 12 or 26 of the Energy Act 2008.

21.2 An injunction may be granted under those sections against a person whose identity is unknown to the applicant.

21.3 In this paragraph, an injunction refers to an injunction under one of those sections and "the defendant" is the person against whom the injunction is sought.

21.4 In the claim form, the applicant must describe the defendant by reference to–
(1) a photograph;
(2) a thing belonging to or in the possession of the defendant; or
(3) any other evidence.

21.5 The description of the defendant under paragraph 20.4 must be sufficiently clear to enable the defendant to be served with the proceedings.

(The court has power under Part 6 to dispense with service or make an order permitting service by an alternative method or at an alternative place).

21.6 The application must be accompanied by a witness statement. The witness statement must state–
(1) that the applicant was unable to ascertain the defendant's identity within the time reasonably available to him;
(2) the steps taken by him to ascertain the defendant's identity;
(3) the means by which the defendant has been described in the claim form; and
(4) that the description is the best the applicant is able to provide.

21.7 When the court issues the claim form it will–
(1) fix a date for the hearing; and
(2) prepare a notice of the hearing date for each party.

21.8 The claim form must be served not less than 21 days before the hearing date.

21.9 Where the claimant serves the claim form, he must serve notice of the hearing date at the same time, unless the hearing date is specified in the claim form.

(CPR rules 3.1(2) (a) and (b) provide for the court to extend or shorten the time for compliance with any rule or practice direction, and to adjourn or bring forward a hearing)

21.10 The court may on the hearing date–
(1) proceed to hear the case and dispose of the claim; or
(2) give case management directions.

Proceedings under the Financial Services and Markets Act 2000

22.1 This paragraph applies to proceedings in the High Court under the Financial Services and Markets Act 2000. **49EPD.22**

22.2 Proceedings in the High Court under the Act (other than applications for a mandatory order) and actions for damages for breach of a statutory duty imposed by the Act shall be assigned to the Chancery Division.

22.3 Such proceedings and actions must be begun by claim form (except for applications by petition by the Financial Conduct Authority or the Prudential Regulation Authority under section 367 of the Act).

22.4 The Financial Conduct Authority or the Prudential Regulation Authority may make representations to the court where there is a question about the meaning of any rule or other instrument made by, or with the approval or consent of, the Financial Conduct Authority or the Prudential Regulation Authority.

22.5 When the court makes a voting rights suspension order under section

89NA of the Act, the Financial Conduct Authority must within 7 days, or such period as the Court may direct, serve a copy of the order on the company which issued the shares to which it relates

Proceedings under The Telecommunications Restriction Orders (Custodial Institutions) (England and Wales) Regulations 2015

49EPD.23 **23.1** This paragraph applies to proceedings under The Telecommunications Restriction Orders (Custodial Institutions) (England and Wales) Regulations 2015 ("the TRO Regulations").

23.2 An application under regulation 3(1) for a Telecommunications Restriction Order ("TRO") must be made at the Clerkenwell and Shoreditch County Court hearing centre.

23.3 If the claimant indicates in the claim form that the claimant is also applying for a non-disclosure order under regulation 8 of the TRO Regulations, the claimant's evidence in respect of the TRO application must not be served until the court has determined the non-disclosure application. If the non-disclosure application is not granted, the court must give the claimant an opportunity to withdraw the TRO application. If the non-disclosure application is not granted and the claimant withdraws the claim, then the court must return the TRO claim form, and any documents submitted in connection with the TRO application, to the claimant.

23.4 The court must when it issues the claim form fix a date for hearing of the application for a TRO, which must unless the court orders otherwise be no later than 21 days after the date of issue.

23.5 In accordance with regulation 10 of the TRO Regulations, if a hearing is held, it must be held in private unless the court orders otherwise.

23.6 Rule 44.2(2)(a) (the general rule on costs) does not apply to proceedings to which this paragraph applies.

(Regulation 6 of the TRO Regulations makes specific provision for costs in relation to an application for a TRO.)

23.7 Rule 5.4B (supply of court documents to a party) applies subject to any order made by the court under regulation 5(2) of the TRO Regulations.

23.8 Unless the court orders otherwise, rule 5.4C (supply of court documents to a non-party) does not apply to any proceedings to which this paragraph applies.

Proceedings under the Drug Dealing Telecommunication Restriction Orders Regulations 2017

49EPD.24 **24.1** This paragraph applies to proceedings under The Drug Dealing Telecommunication Restriction Orders Regulations 2017 ("the DDTRO Regulations"); and references in this paragraph to a regulation by number alone are to a regulation in the DDTRO Regulations.

24.2 An application under regulation 3(1) for a Drug Dealing Telecommunication Restriction Order ("DDTRO") must be made at one of the following County Court hearing centres–

- Clerkenwell and Shoreditch
- Manchester
- Liverpool
- Birmingham
- Newcastle
- Bristol.

24.3 The court must when it issues the claim form fix a date for hearing of the application for a DDTRO, which must unless the court orders otherwise be no later than 21 days after the date of issue.

24.4 In accordance with regulation 4(2), an application for a DDTRO must be made and heard without notice of the application or hearing having been given to an affected person or their legal representative and be heard and determined in the absence of an affected person or their legal representative.

24.5 Rule 5.4B (supply of court documents to a party) applies subject to any order made by the court under regulation 9(1) of the DDTRO Regulations.

24.6 Unless the court orders otherwise, rule 5.4C (supply of court documents to a non-party) does not apply to any proceedings to which this paragraph applies.

24.7 In accordance with regulation 9(4), an application for a non-disclosure order may be determined in advance of, or at the same time as, a DDTRO application or appeal.

24.8. In accordance with regulation 9(7), if the claimant indicates in the claim form that the claimant is also applying for a non-disclosure order under regulation 9 of the DDTRO Regulations, the claimant's evidence in respect of the DDTRO application must not be served until the court has determined the non-disclosure application. If the non-disclosure application is not granted, the court must give the claimant an opportunity to withdraw the DDTRO application. If the non-disclosure application is not granted and the claimant withdraws the claim, then the court must return the DDTRO claim form, and any documents submitted in connection with the DDTRO application, to the claimant.

Proceedings under Chapter 3A of Part 5 of the Proceeds of Crime Act 2002 and Part 4A of Schedule 1 to the Anti-terrorism, Crime and Security Act 2001

25.1 This paragraph applies to applications which are transferred from a magistrates' court to the High Court under Section 303R of the Proceeds of Crime Act 2002 or paragraph 10J of Schedule 1 to the Anti-terrorism Crime and Security Act 2001 ("transferred forfeiture applications"). **49EPD.25**

25.2 The Part 8 procedure applies to transferred forfeiture applications with the following modifications.

25.3 Rules 8.2 and 8.2A(2)–(4), and paragraphs 4.1, 4.2, and paragraphs 7.1 to 7.5 of this practice direction, do not apply, and—

(1) the application made to the magistrates' court ("the MC document") shall be treated as equivalent to a Part 8 claim form (whether or not any defendant is named in it);
(2) no separate claim form is to be issued;
(3) the applicant to the magistrates' court shall be "the claimant";
(4) the address of the claimant given in the MC document shall be the claimant's address for service;
(5) any person named in the MC document as being a person the application was being brought against or who has sought to oppose or who has failed or refused to agree to the application whilst it was in the magistrates' court shall be a defendant; and
(6) any evidence filed by the claimant with the magistrates' court prior to the transfer of the application to the High Court shall be treated as evidence filed by the claimant in support of the Part 8 Claim; and any evidence so filed by any defendant or other person shall be treated as evidence filed in relation to the Part 8 Claim.

25.4 On receipt of a transferred forfeiture application—

(1) the court shall give the proceedings a number;
(2) the proceedings are to be heard in the Queen's Bench Division unless the court shall otherwise order;
(3) if the court considers it is necessary, the court shall order that the claimant must provide the court with any of the information listed in rule 8.2(b) to (e), and with the names (or other means of identification) of the defendant(s), where that information is not otherwise provided in the MC document; and

(4) the court shall order a directions hearing to be listed on the first available date after twenty-eight days after the end of the service period (see paragraph 25.5), at which the court will–
  (i) fix a date for the hearing of the application or for a further directions hearing;
  (ii) give directions as to the exchange of evidence between the parties;
  (iii) give directions as to any other matters which are required in advance of that hearing, for example regarding the joinder of or service upon any further persons.

25.5 Rule 7.5 shall not apply and, subject to any direction made by the Court in accordance with paragraph 25.6 (or order made under rules 6.15, 6.16, 6.27 or 6.28), the claimant shall serve (in like manner as provided by Part 6 of the Rules in relation to service of claim forms or as provided by any enactment) upon the defendant the following documents within two months of the date of the order made under paragraph 25.4 ("the service period")–

(1) the transferred application, and any evidence described in paragraph 25.3(6);
(2) a statement of who are the defendants (unless such is apparent from the MC document) which must also be filed at court;
(3) the order transferring the application to the High Court under Section 303R of the Proceeds of Crime Act 2002 or paragraph 10J of Schedule 1 to the Anti-terrorism Crime and Security Act 2001 (as appropriate);
(4) the order made under paragraph 25.4; and
(5) an acknowledgment of service form.

25.6 The court may extend the service period by making a direction of its own initiative or on application of any party, whether before or after the expiry of the period described in paragraph 25.5. An application for a direction to extend the service period is to be supported by evidence, with the court having a general discretion (and, for the avoidance of doubt, no sanction is imposed by paragraph 25.5), and rule 3.1(2)(a) shall apply and rules 7.6 and 7.7 shall not apply.

25.7 Rule 8.3 applies with the modification that the acknowledgment of service must be filed not more than 14 days after service of the documents listed in paragraph 25.5.

25.8 Rule 8.5 does not apply, and, except as provided by paragraphs 25.3(6) above, the parties–

(1) may (but without any obligation to do so) file and serve evidence not less than 7 days before the first directions hearing; and
(2) must file and serve evidence in accordance with the directions given by the court, and any such evidence must (unless the court otherwise directs) be in the form of a witness statement or an affidavit.

25.9 Rule 8.6 applies with the modification that no written evidence may be relied on at the hearing of the claim unless–

(1) it is as described in paragraphs 25.3(6) or 25.8(1) or it has been filed and served in accordance with the court's directions; or
(2) the court gives permission (for which any party may apply).

Add new Practice Direction 49F–Pre-Action Protocol for Low Value Personal Injury Claims in Road Traffic Accidents and Low Value Personal Injury (Employers' Liability and Public Liability) Claims–Stage 3 Procedure:

PRACTICE DIRECTION 49F—PRE-ACTION PROTOCOL FOR LOW VALUE PERSONAL INJURY CLAIMS IN ROAD TRAFFIC ACCIDENTS AND LOW VALUE PERSONAL INJURY (EMPLOYERS' LIABILITY AND PUBLIC LIABILITY) CLAIMS—STAGE 3 PROCEDURE

This Practice Direction supplements CPR Part 49

Editorial introduction

The Pre-Action Protocol for Low Value Personal Injury Claims in Road Traffic Accidents ("the RTA Protocol") (see para.C13-001 below) and the Pre-Action Protocol for Low Value Personal Injury (Employers' Liability and Public Liability) Claims ("the EL/PL Protocol") (see para.C15-001 below) describe the behaviour the court will normally expect of the parties prior to the start of proceedings where a claimant claims damages valued at no more than £25,000 as a result of a personal injury sustained by that person in a road traffic accident, employers' liability or public liability claim. It should be noted that for claims in relation to accidents occurring in England and Wales on or after 31 May 2021 where the total value of the claim is less than £10,000 and the damages for injury are no more than £5,000 the Pre-Action Protocol for Personal Injury Claims below the Small Claims Limits in Road Traffic Accidents ("the RTA Small Claims Protocol") may apply (see para.C18-001) rather than the RTA Protocol. The commentary that follows applies to claims which do not fall under the RTA Small Claims Protocol. **49FPD.0**

The pre-action processes which the parties are expected to follow are set out in detail in the Protocols and are divided into two consecutive stages, Stage 1 and Stage 2 (the second coming into play where there has been an admission of liability by the defendant under the first). Fixed costs, as provided for in CPR Pt 45 Section III are recoverable by the claimant at various points during these processes, and under Stage 2 the claimant is entitled to interim payments of damages.

In relation to the type of claim to which it relates, these two Protocols supplant the Pre-Action Protocol for Personal Injury Claims. A claimant wishing to start court proceedings for a claim of the type covered by either Protocol would normally start those proceedings by issuing a claim form under CPR Pt 7, and the Protocols provide that, in various circumstances, before the parties have exhausted the processes set out therein, the claimant may start proceedings in this way (see, in the RTA Protocol, paras 7.26, 7.28, 7.40, 7.46, 7.60 and 7.75). However the Protocols further provide that, where the parties have followed the negotiating processes set out therein but are unable to agree the amount of damages payable at the end of Stage 2, court proceedings to determine the amount of damages should be started, not under Pt 7, but "under Part 8 in accordance with Practice Direction 8B" (now PD 49F). In both Protocols and in PD 49F, this modified Pt 8 procedure is referred to as "the Stage 3 Procedure". The Stage 3 Procedure builds on the Protocol processes. In various ways the procedure restricts the issues that can be contested and the evidence that may be adduced. See *Wickes Building Supplies Ltd v Blair* [2019] EWCA Civ 1934 where a witness statement not served pursuant to the Protocol was not admitted. In effect the steps taken by the parties during Stage 1 and Stage 2 are treated as if they had been taken during the post-issue and pre-trial stages of a claim brought under Pt 7.

The Stage 3 Procedure is also to be followed where a claim is made by a child and the parties have reached a settlement at the end of Stage 2 of the Protocol and the approval of the court is required in relation to the settlement in accordance with r.21.10(2). (The Protocols do not apply where the claimant or defendant is a protected party as defined in r.21.2.)

Paragraph 4.1 of PD 49F states that the court may "at any stage" order a claim that has been started under Pt 7 to continue under the Pt 8 procedure as modified by that Practice Direction. In the circumstances provided for in para.7.2 the court may order that a claim started under the Stage 3 procedure should be continued under Pt 7, and where, in the circumstances provided for in para.9.1, the defendant opposes the claim, the court will dismiss the claim, leaving the claimant with the option of starting proceedings under Pt 7.

Both protocols and PD 49F recognise that compliance with the Protocol's terms may not be possible before the expiry of the limitation period relevant to the claimant's claim (generally three years from the date of accident). It is provided (in para.5.7 of each Protocol and in para.16 of PD 49F) that, in this event, the claimant may start court proceedings and apply to the court for an order to stay the proceedings "while the parties take steps to follow this Protocol" (see further commentary in para.49FPD.16.1 below).

The RTA Protocol and the EL/PL Protocol differ in significant respects from the other Pre-Action Protocols. The fact that they are linked (as explained above) to a bespoke court procedure for claims to which it applies is but one example. Another is that, where at the end of Stage 2 the parties are unable to agree the amount of damages payable, and the prospect of proceedings being started under the Stage 3 procedure looms, the Protocols provide that defendants must pay the claimant (except where the claimant is a child) their final offer of damages together with disbursements (reasonable if not agreed) and the fixed costs payable under the Protocol provisions. (Such payment is referred to as "a non-settlement payment"; see para.7.70 in the RTA Protocol and para.7.53 in the EL/PL Protocol.)

The claim under PD 49F must be started in the County Court. The defendant is required to acknowledge service in a form specially designed for that purpose (Form **N210B**) (para.8.1). The claim will not be allocated to a case management track; Parts 26 to 29 do not apply (para.17.1). Normally the claim will be heard by a District Judge (para.1.2). A determination of the claim may be made on paper or at "a Stage 3 hearing" (para.11.1).

In court proceedings started under the Stage 3 procedure the rules in Section II of CPR Pt 36 (RTA Protocol and EL/PL Protocol Offers to Settle) apply. Rule 36.29 states the costs consequences of a "Protocol offer". An admission made by a party during the Protocol processes is a pre-action admission for the purposes of CPR Pt 14 (Admissions). Rule 14.1B deals with the circumstances in which such an admission may be withdrawn.

Court proceedings started under the Stage 3 procedure are subject to the fixed costs regime contained in Section III of Pt 45 (Fixed Costs) (see r.45.16). The only costs allowed are prescribed by r.45.17.

The RTA and EL/PL Protocols differ from all the other Pre-Action Protocols. Normally the rules themselves are paramount and are supplemented by Practice Directions and, pre-issue, by protocols. But here the process is reversed. The Protocols are paramount and PD 49F should be seen as part of the process. Various rules (r.14.1B, Section II of Pt 36 and Section III of Pt 45) further support the process.

It is worth emphasising that the process is intended for relatively straightforward cases where liability is not in dispute.

For cases which do exit the process for any reason (the most common reason being that liability is in dispute) there is now a fixed costs regime (see Section IIIA of Pt 45).

The Pre-Action Protocol for Resolution of Package Travel Claims applies to all claims notified on or after 7 May 2018. Claims for "gastric illness" now fall within the portal procedure and the fixed costs regime that applies to public liability claims.

General

49FPD.1 **1.1** This Practice Direction sets out the procedure ("the Stage 3 Procedure") for a claim where–

(1) the parties–

(a) have followed the Pre-Action Protocol for Low Value Personal Injury Claims in Road Traffic Accidents ("the RTA Protocol") or the Pre-Action Protocol for Low Value Personal Injury (Employers' Liability and Public Liability) Claims ("the EL/PL Protocol"); but

(b) are unable to agree the amount of damages payable at the end of Stage 2 of the relevant Protocol;

(2) (a) the claimant is a child;

(b) a settlement has been agreed by the parties at the end of Stage 2 of the relevant Protocol; and

(c) the approval of the court is required in relation to the settlement in accordance with rule 21.10(2); or

(3) compliance with the relevant Protocol is not possible before the expiry of a limitation period and proceedings are started in accordance with paragraph 16 of this Practice Direction.

1.2 A claim under this Practice Direction must be started in the County Court and will normally be heard by a District Judge.

Editorial note

49FPD.1.1 A claim is started (or proceedings are started) by the issue of a claim form, not (as para.1.2 states) "under this practice direction", but more accurately (as CPR rules related to such a claim state) "under Part 8 in accordance with Practice Direction 8B" (now PD 49F) (see e.g. r.36.24 and r.45.16(1)). Paragraph 2.1 speaks of a claim "made under the Part 8 procedure as modified by this Practice Direction". The procedure is called, simply, "the Stage 3 Procedure" (as in paras 7.2, 8.3 and 8.4 of PD 49F), provided it is remembered that the procedure may be applied in circumstances other than where the parties have engaged in the Protocol processes (see para.4.1 of PD 49F). Under either Protocol, "claim" means a claim, prior to the start of proceedings, for payment of damages under the process set out in that Protocol (para.1.1(6)). Where a claim is made, not only by a child (as para.1.1(5) envisages), but also against a child, no settlement is valid without the approval of the court (r.21.10(1)).

Modification of Part 8

49FPD.2 **2.1** The claim is made under the Part 8 procedure as modified by this Practice Direction and subject to paragraph 2.2.

2.2 The claim will be determined by the court on the contents of the Court Proceedings Pack. The following rules do not apply to a claim under this Practice Direction—

(1) rule 8.2A (issue of a claim form without naming defendants);
(2) rule 8.3 (acknowledgment of service);
(3) rule 8.5 (filing and serving witness evidence);
(4) rule 8.6 (evidence—general);
(5) rule 8.7 (Part 20 claims);
(6) rule 8.8 (procedure where defendant objects to use of the Part 8 procedure); and
(7) rule 8.9(c).

Editorial note

Where the parties do not reach agreement in Stage 2 of the Protocol process, the claimant must send the Court Proceedings Pack (Part A and Part B) to the defendant. Generally, where the Pt 8 procedure is followed, the claim is treated as allocated to the multi-track (r.8.9(c)). Obviously, this would be inappropriate for proceedings to which PD 49F applies and for which the procedures in it are intended. **49FPD.2.1**

Definitions

3.1 References to "the Court Proceedings Pack (Part A) Form", "the Court Proceedings Pack (Part B) Form" and "the CNF Response Form" are references to the forms used in the Protocols. **49FPD.3**

3.2 "Protocol offer" has the meaning given in rule 36.17.

3.3 "Settlement hearing" means a hearing where the court considers a settlement agreed between the parties (whether before or after proceedings have started) and the claimant is a child.

3.4 "Stage 3 hearing" means a final hearing to determine the amount of damages that remain in dispute between the parties.

3.5 "Accredited medical expert", "fixed costs medical report", "MedCo" and "soft tissue injury claim" have the same meaning as in paragraph 1.1(A1), (10A), (12A), and (16A), respectively, of the RTA Protocol.

Editorial note

As to contents of the Pack, see para.7.64 of the RTA Protocol and para.7.48 of the EL/PL Protocol. The expression "Protocol offer" is not a term of art within the Protocol, and its only use in PD 49F is in para.10.1 (Withdrawal of the Protocol offer). Where a judgment is given in proceedings under the Stage 3 procedure set out in PD 49F, a Protocol offer will have the costs consequences set out in r.36.29, and it is in that context that the meaning of the expression as given in r.36.25 (Form and content of Protocol offer) becomes important. For further information on the nature of such offers and the possible consequences, see commentary following r.36.29. **49FPD.3.1**

Types of claim in which this modified Part 8 procedure may be followed

4.1 The court may at any stage order a claim that has been started under Part 7 to continue under the Part 8 procedure as modified by this Practice Direction. **49FPD.4**

Editorial note

The heading to this paragraph is misleading. In various circumstances, a claim may no longer continue under the Protocol processes and proceedings may be started under Pt 7. Claims which no longer continue under the Protocol cannot subsequently re-enter the process. In terms, para.4.1 (by providing that the court "may at any stage order a claim") appears to apply to any claim that has been started under Pt 7 and in any circumstances. **49FPD.4.1**

The costs provisions in Section III of Pt 45 apply to claims that have been started, or should have been started, under PD 49F (see r.45.16(1)), and, presumably, to claims that had been started under Pt 7 but are continued under the Pt 8 procedure as modified by this Practice Direction by an order made under this paragraph.

An application to the court to determine the amount of damages

5.1 An application to the court to determine the amount of damages must be started by a claim form. **49FPD.5**

5.2 The claim form must state—

(1) that the claimant has followed the procedure set out in the relevant Protocol;
(2) the date when the Court Proceedings Pack (Part A and Part B) Form was sent to the defendant. (This provision does not apply where the claimant is a child and the application is for a settlement hearing);
(3) whether the claimant wants the claim to be determined by the court on the papers (except where a party is a child) or at a Stage 3 hearing;
(4) where the claimant seeks a settlement hearing or Stage 3 hearing, the dates which the claimant requests should be avoided; and
(5) the value of the claim.

Editorial note

49FPD.5.1 Paragraphs 5.1 to 8.5 clearly apply where the Stage 3 Procedure has been invoked for a claim in which the parties have followed the Protocol processes, but were unable to agree the amount of damages payable at the end of Stage 2 of those processes. A claim made under the Stage 3 procedure in those circumstances is aptly described as "an application to the court to determine the amount of damages" (para.5.1). However, that description is not apt where the circumstances are that the claimant is a child and the Stage 3 procedure applies for the purpose of obtaining the court's approval of a settlement agreed by the parties during Stage 1 or Stage 2 of the Protocol processes (r.21.10(2)). (In other circumstances, application for approval is made under r.21.10, using the procedure set out in Pt 8.) Nevertheless, it would seem that the procedures set out in paras 5.1 to 8.5 apply as far as may be to an application for approval made in this way (see in particular para.6.5). Protocol offers must be set out in Court Proceedings Pack (Part B) Form. The fixing of the date on which the Form was sent to the defendant (para.5.2(2)) is important for the purposes of determining the costs consequences following judgment under the Stage 3 Procedure of a Protocol offer and calculating interest thereon (see further r.36.29).

Filing and serving written evidence

49FPD.6 **6.1** The claimant must file with the claim form—
(1) the Court Proceedings Pack (Part A) Form;
(2) the Court Proceedings Pack (Part B) Form (the claimant and defendant's final offers) in a sealed envelope. (This provision does not apply where the claimant is a child and the application is for a settlement hearing);
(3) copies of medical reports;
(4) evidence of special damages; and
(5) evidence of disbursements (for example the cost of any medical report) in accordance with rule 45.19(2).

6.2(1) In a soft tissue injury claim, the claimant may not proceed unless the medical report is a fixed cost medical report. Where the claimant includes more than one medical report, the first report obtained must be a fixed cost medical report from an accredited medical expert selected via the MedCo Portal (website at: *www.medco.org.uk*) and any further report from an expert in any of the following disciplines must also be a fixed cost medical report—
(a) Consultant Orthopaedic Surgeon;
(b) Consultant in Accident and Emergency Medicine;
(c) General Practitioner registered with the General Medical Council;
(d) Physiotherapist registered with the Health and Care Professions Council.

(2) The cost of obtaining a further report from an expert not listed in paragraph (1)(a) to (d) is not subject to rule 45.19(2A)(b), but the use of that expert and the cost must be justified.

6.3 The filing of the claim form and documents set out in paragraph 6.1 represent the start of Stage 3 for the purposes of fixed costs.

6.4 Subject to paragraph 6.5 the claimant must only file those documents in paragraph 6.1 where they have already been sent to the defendant under the relevant Protocol.

6.5 The claimant's evidence as set out in paragraph 6.1 must be served on the defendant with the claim form.

6.6 Where the claimant is a child the claimant must also provide to the court the following in relation to a settlement made before or after the start of proceedings–

(1) the draft consent order;
(2) the advice by counsel, solicitor or other legal representative on the amount of damages; and
(3) a statement verified by a statement of truth signed by the litigation friend which confirms whether the child has recovered in accordance with the prognosis and whether there are any continuing symptoms. This statement will enable the court to decide whether to order the child to attend the settlement hearing.

6.7 Where the defendant is uninsured and the Motor Insurers' Bureau ("MIB") or its agents have consented in the CNF Response Form to the MIB being joined as a defendant, the claimant must name the MIB as the second defendant and must also provide to the court a copy of the CNF Response Form completed by or on behalf of the MIB.

6.8 Where this Practice Direction requires a step to be taken by the defendant, it will be sufficient for this step to be taken by the MIB.

Editorial note

Where the parties do not reach an agreement under Stage 2 of the Protocol processes as to the amount of damages, the claimant must send the Court Proceedings Pack (Part A and Part B) Form, referred to in para.6.1(1) and (2), to the defendant. The Pack must contain supporting comments from both parties on disputed heads of damages. Whether other documents of the type referred to in para.6.1 have been sent to the defendant will depend on the circumstances of the case. **49FPD.6.1**

Paragraph 6.5 applies where the claimant is a child and a settlement has been agreed by the parties "before or after the start of proceedings". The provision clearly applies where a settlement was agreed by the parties at the end of Stage 2 of the Protocol, and the Stage 3 Procedure was invoked for the purposes of obtaining the court's approval of the settlement. However it may also apply where that was not the case, and the procedure was invoked because the parties were unable to reach agreement at Stage 2, but managed to do so after proceedings had been started under the Stage 3 Procedure. The material that the child claimant is required to provide for the court under para.6.5 may be contrasted with that required under PD 21 (Children and Patients) para.5.

Evidence—general

7.1 The parties may not rely upon evidence unless– **49FPD.7**

(1) it has been served in accordance with paragraph 6.4;
(2) it has been filed in accordance with paragraph 8.2 and 11.3; or
(3) (where the court considers that it cannot properly determine the claim without it), the court orders otherwise and gives directions.

7.2 Where the court considers that–

(1) further evidence must be provided by any party; and
(2) the claim is not suitable to continue under the Stage 3 Procedure,

the court will order that the claim will continue under Part 7, allocate the claim to a track and give directions.

7.3 Where paragraph 7.2 applies the court will not allow the Stage 3 fixed costs.

Editorial note

Paragraphs 7.1 to 7.3 demonstrate that, under the Stage 3 procedure, the material that the court will consider in determining the amount of damages is restricted. The procedure builds on the Stage 2 process. The process is designed to enable the parties to narrow and limit the issues in dispute. The Stage 3 process is not designed to give the parties the opportunity to put forward new material or to raise new issues that were not exchanged or raised previously. See *Wickes Building Supplies Ltd v Blair* [2019] EWCA Civ 1934 and *Islington LBC v Bourous* [2022] EWCA Civ 1242. Where the defendant opposes the claim because the claimant has filed and served additional or new evidence with the claim form that had not been provided under the Protocol, the court will dismiss the claim (para.9.1). The power of the court to order that the claim is not suitable to continue under the Stage 3 process is a power the court may exercise on its own initiative. However, in *Phillips v Willis* [2016] EWCA Civ 401 the court set aside an order of the District Judge, made **49FPD.7.1** on his own initiative, to transfer a credit hire claim (all other claims having been settled) from the Stage 3 procedure to Pt 7 proceedings allocated to the small claims track. No further evidence was necessary and the directions given would have required parties to incur costs grossly disproportionate to the damages at stake.

Acknowledgment of Service

49FPD.8 **8.1** The defendant must file and serve an acknowledgment of service in Form **N210B** not more than 14 days after service of the claim form.

8.2 The defendant must file and serve with the acknowledgment of service, or as soon as possible thereafter, a certificate that is in force.

("Certificate" is defined in rule 36.15(1)(e)(i).)

8.3 The acknowledgment of service must state whether the defendant–

(1) (a) contests the amount of damages claimed;
(b) contests the making of an order for damages;
(c) disputes the court's jurisdiction; or
(d) objects to the use of the Stage 3 Procedure;

(2) wants the claim to be determined by the court on the papers or at a Stage 3 hearing.

8.4 Where the defendant objects to the use of the Stage 3 Procedure reasons must be given in the acknowledgment of service.

8.5 The acknowledgment of service may be signed and filed by the defendant's insurer who may give their address as the address for service.

Dismissal of the claim

49FPD.9 **9.1** Where the defendant opposes the claim because the claimant has–

(1) not followed the procedure set out in the relevant Protocol; or
(2) filed and served additional or new evidence with the claim form that had not been provided under the relevant Protocol,

the court will dismiss the claim and the claimant may start proceedings under Part 7.

(Rule 45.24 sets out the costs consequences of failing to comply with the relevant Protocol.)

Editorial note

49FPD.9.1 A dismissal of the claim under para.9.1 on the basis of the defendant's objections is a dismissal otherwise than on the merits and is, in effect, a procedural sanction (but presumably not one from which CPR r.3.9 relief may be sought), designed to ensure that claimants follow Stage 2 of the Protocol processes conscientiously. The alternative of starting proceedings under Pt 7 may be of no use to the claimant where the limitation period has run. See further para.49FPD.16.1 below.

Withdrawal of the Protocol offer

49FPD.10 **10.1** A party may only withdraw a Protocol offer after proceedings have started with the court's permission. Where the court gives permission the claim will no longer continue under the Stage 3 Procedure and the court will give directions. The court will only give permission where there is good reason for the claim not to continue under the Stage 3 Procedure.

Editorial note

49FPD.10.1 As to Protocol offers, see commentary in CPR Pt 36 Section II, especially on rr.36.24 to 36.30.

Consideration of the claim

49FPD.11 **11.1** The court will order that damages are to be assessed–

(1) on the papers; or
(2) at a Stage 3 hearing where–
(a) the claimant so requests on the claim form;
(b) the defendant so requests in the acknowledgment of service (Form **N210B**); or
(c) the court so orders,

and on a date determined by the court.

11.2 The court will give the parties at least 21 days notice of the date of the determination on the papers or the date of the Stage 3 hearing.

11.3 Where further deductible amounts have accrued since the final offer was made by both parties in the Court Proceedings Pack (Part B) Form, the defendant must file an up to date certificate at least 5 days before the date of a determination on the papers.

11.4 Where the claim is determined on the papers the court will give reasons for its decision in the judgment.

("Deductible amount" is defined in rule 36.15(1)(d).)

Settlement at Stage 2 where the claimant is a child

12.1 Paragraphs 12.2 to 12.5 apply where– **49FPD.12**

(1) the claimant is a child;

(2) there is a settlement at Stage 2 of the Protocol; and

(3) an application is made to the court to approve the settlement.

12.2 Where the settlement is approved at the settlement hearing the court will order the costs to be paid in accordance with rule 45.21(2).

12.3 Where the settlement is not approved at the first settlement hearing and the court orders a second settlement hearing at which the settlement is approved, the court will order the costs to be paid in accordance with rule 45.21(4) to (6).

12.4 Where the settlement is not approved at the first settlement hearing and the court orders that the claim is not suitable to be determined under the Stage 3 Procedure, the court will order costs to be paid in accordance with rule 45.23 and will give directions.

12.5 Where the settlement is not approved at the second settlement hearing the claim will no longer continue under the Stage 3 Procedure and the court will give directions.

Settlement at Stage 3 where the claimant is a child

13.1 Paragraphs 13.2 and 13.3 apply where– **49FPD.13**

(1) the claimant is a child;

(2) there is a settlement after proceedings have started under the Stage 3 Procedure; and

(3) an application is made to the court to approve the settlement.

13.2 Where the settlement is approved at the settlement hearing the court will order the costs to be paid in accordance with rule 45.22(2).

13.3 Where the settlement is not approved at the settlement hearing the court will order the claim to proceed to a Stage 3 hearing.

Adjournment

14.1 Where the court adjourns a settlement hearing or a Stage 3 hearing it **49FPD.14** may, in its discretion, order the costs to be paid in accordance with rule 45.27.

Appeals—determination on the papers

15.1 The court will not consider an application to set aside a judgment **49FPD.15** made after a determination on the papers. The judgment will state the appeal court to which an appeal lies.

Limitation

16.1 Where compliance with the relevant Protocol is not possible before the **49FPD.16** expiry of a limitation period the claimant may start proceedings in accordance with paragraph 16.2.

16.2 The claimant must–

(1) start proceedings under this Practice Direction; and
(2) state on the claim form that–
(a) the claim is for damages; and
(b) a stay of proceedings is sought in order to comply with the relevant Protocol.

16.3 The claimant must send to the defendant the claim form together with the order imposing the stay.

16.4 Where a claim is made under paragraph 16.1 the provisions in this Practice Direction, except paragraphs 1.2, 2.1, 2,2 and 16.1 to 16.6, are disapplied.

16.5 Where–
(1) a stay is granted by the court;
(2) the parties have complied with the relevant Protocol; and
(3) the claimant wishes to start the Stage 3 Procedure,

the claimant must make an application to the court to lift the stay and request directions.

16.6 Where the court orders that the stay be lifted–
(1) the provisions of this Practice Direction will apply; and
(2) the claimant must–
(a) amend the claim form in accordance with paragraph 5.2; and
(b) file the documents in paragraph 6.1.

16.7 Where, during Stage 1 or Stage 2 of the relevant Protocol–
(1) the claim no longer continues under that Protocol; and
(2) the claimant wishes to start proceedings under Part 7,

the claimant must make an application to the court to lift the stay and request directions.

Editorial note

49FPD.16.1 The Limitation Act 1980 s.11 states that an action in respect of personal injuries "shall not be brought" after the expiration of the period of three years from the date on which the cause of action accrued or the date of knowledge (if later) of the person injured. Once the limitation period in relation to a cause of action to which either Protocol applies starts to run, nothing can stop it. According to CPR r.7.2, "proceedings are started" when the court issues a claim form at the request of the claimant. A claim form is issued on the date entered on the form by the court (r.7.2(2)). However, to save a party who lodges the claim form in time but the claim form is issued by the court out of time, para 5.1 of PD 7A provides that the claim is "brought" for the purposes of the Limitation Act 1980 when the claim form was received in the court office. Where that date is after the expiration of the three-year period the action falls foul of s.11; where it is not, it does not. (In the former instance, the defendant may plead limitation. If that plea is successful, the claimant's cause of action is not extinguished; but encounters a permanent procedural bar preventing it from being pursued.) CPR r.7.5 states that, where (as will normally be the case where an action is brought in respect of personal injuries) the claim form is to be served within the jurisdiction, the "step required" appropriate to the method of service must be completed before 12.00 midnight on the calendar day four months after the date of issue of the claim form. This time limit may be varied by the written agreement of the parties (unless the court orders otherwise) (r.2.11), and, in restricted circumstances, may be extended by order of the court (r.7.6).

Both Protocols prescribe the behaviour the court will normally expect of the parties "prior to the start of proceedings" (para.2.1). The Protocol and PD 49F anticipate that, in a given case, the compliance by the parties with the Protocol processes may not be possible before the expiry of the primary limitation period, and concede (they could hardly do otherwise) that the claimant, in order to ensure that the action is brought within that period, may have to "start proceedings" before those processes have been commenced or completed. Paragraph 16.2 of PD 49F states that a claimant taking this step must "start proceedings under this Practice Direction" (para.16.2(1)). That is misleading as it suggests that, in these circumstances, proceedings are started under the Stage 3 Procedure. It would be more accurate to say that, where proceedings are started for limitation protection purposes, they are started "under Part 8 in accordance with Practice Direction 8B" (now PD 49F, see para.49FPD.1.1 above), and specifically in accordance with para.16 (this is reinforced by para.16.4, disapplying most of PD 49F). The procedure stands apart from the Stage 3 procedure and has its effects before that procedure comes into play.

A court order staying proceedings may be granted in various circumstances and for various purposes and may contain terms distinguishing between those procedural steps that the parties may or may not take, or should or should not take, whilst the stay subsists. Paragraph 16.2 is inelegant. It states that, where a claimant seeks a stay what is sought is a stay "in order to comply with the Protocol". Presumably what is meant is that a stay granted in these circumstances is a stay generally, preventing either party from taking a further step in the proceedings without the permission of the court. The principal significance of such an order in this context is that it suspends the normal CPR procedures that would follow upon the issue of a claim form (in particular, those dealing with the service by the claimant of the claim form and the particulars of claim in accordance with rr.7.4 and 7.5). For obvious reasons, it is expressly provided that a claimant starting proceedings under para.16.2 must immediately notify the defendant accordingly (para.16.3). Where a claimant takes advantage of para.16.2, proceedings are started by the issue of a claim form and any question as to whether the action has been brought before the expiry of the limitation period that might arise subsequently will fall to be determined on the basis that it was brought on the date of issue (or earlier presentation to the court—see above). The starting of proceedings under para.16.2 and the imposing of a stay on those proceedings do not have the effect of suspending the running of the limitation period.

By para.16.2, the claimant is required to "state on the claim form that ... a stay of proceedings is sought". In effect, by issuing the claim form the claimant starts the proceedings and makes an application without notice for a stay. (The stay application is not a pre-action application.)

The terms of para.16.1 are permissive, not mandatory. However a claimant anticipating that compliance with the Protocol was not possible before the expiry of the limitation period would be wise to take advantage of it. The court fees payable "where proceedings are started as a result of a limitation period that is about to expire" is a disbursement recoverable by the claimant (r.45.29I(2)(d)).

Where a stay has been granted and, subsequently, the claimant wishes "to start the Stage 3 Procedure", the parties having complied with the Protocol since the stay was granted, their proceedings are already on foot and there is no need for them to issue a claim form, but they must amend their claim form (issued for the purpose of obtaining the stay) so that it complies with para.5.2. In *Grant v Dawn Meats (UK)* [2018] EWCA Civ 2212 it was held that the period of a stay of proceedings does not count towards the time limit required for service of a claim form. Paragraph 16.7 is odd. It assumes circumstances (which may arise readily enough) in which a claimant has a claim falling within the scope of either Protocol but which no longer continues under it, leaving them with the prospect of having to launch proceedings under Pt 7 in order to assert their claim. It is not obvious why it should be assumed that in these circumstances the lifting of the stay on the Pt 8 proceedings should be a prerequisite for that. The Pt 7 proceedings will be fresh proceedings, and almost certainly for a cause of action now exposed to a limitation defence. However, in these circumstances, provided after the stay was imposed on their Pt 8 proceedings the claimant had complied conscientiously with the Protocol processes until their claim no longer continued under those processes, it is highly unlikely that the defendant would be able to resist an application by the claimant under s.33 of the 1980 Act. But the defendant would be able to resist such an application where the claimant has not conscientiously complied with the Protocol. Paragraph 16.7 does not expressly say that the court can lift the stay on the Pt 8 proceedings but then go on to order that they continue as if begun under Pt 7. However, note r.8.1(3). In *Lyle v Allianz Insurance Plc*, 21 December 2017, unrep., HH Judge Pearce held that r.8.1(3) does apply so that the court could lift the stay and then give directions that the case proceed under Pt 7 (but on the facts he declined to do so).

Modification to the general rules

17.1 The claim will not be allocated to a track. Parts 26 to 29 do not apply. **49FPD.17**

PART 51

TRANSITIONAL ARRANGEMENTS AND PILOT SCHEMES

Online Civil Money Claims Pilot Scheme

To the end of the last paragraph, add:

CPR Update 146 (May 2022) extended the pilot scheme's application so that claims up to £25,000 could be brought through it by legally represented parties and where there are up to three parties. The amendment took effect on 25 May 2022. **51.2.5**

The County Court Online Pilot

Replace paragraph with:

Practice Direction 51S was made in accordance with r.51.2 and was published in CPR Update 91 **51.2.6**

(September 2017); see para.51xSPD.1. The Direction established a pilot scheme, called "County Court Online", which applied in the County Court for the purpose of testing a procedure that enabled legal representatives to file claims online at the CCMCC, using the County Court Online website, and for the claims to be issued to those legal representatives electronically, for the claimant then to serve. The pilot ran on an invitation-only basis. It ran from 12 September 2017 to 1 March 2022, when it was omitted by CPR PD Update 141 (March 2022) albeit it remained in force, via transitional provisions, for claims commenced under it prior to its omission.

Disclosure Pilot Scheme for the Business and Property Courts

Replace paragraph with:

51.2.7 Practice Direction 51U made in accordance with r.51.2 was published in CPR Update 100 (September 2018). Its purpose was to establish, as from 1 January 2019, a new scheme for disclosure operative in the Business and Property Courts only. The pilot scheme was omitted from Pt 51 by CPR Update 149 (July 2022) as from 1 October 2022 when the scheme was formally incorporated into the CPR as Practice Direction 57AD—Disclosure for the Business and Property Courts.

New Statement of Costs for Summary Assessment Pilot

Replace paragraph with:

51.2.10 Practice Direction 51X made in accordance with r.51.2 was published in CPR Update 104 (February 2019). Its purpose was to provide a new Statement of Costs for Summary Assessment. The pilot scheme commenced on 1 April 2019 and was to run until 31 March 2021. It was extended to run until 31 March 2022 by CPR Update 127 (February 2021). It applied to all claims where "costs are to be summarily assessed, whenever they were commenced"; para.2(b). It provided a model Form **N260A** (for costs incurred on an interim application) and Form **N260B** (for costs incurred up to trial), as model statements of costs for use under the pilot scheme. It is no longer in force and was omitted from CPR Pt 51 from 31 March 2022.

Video or Audio Hearings Pilot during the Coronavirus Pandemic—Pilot Scheme

Replace the first two sentences with:

51.2.11 Practice Direction 51Y made in accordance with r.51.2 was published in CPR Update 116 (March 2020); see para.51YPD.1. Its purpose was to provide, from 25 March 2020 until the Coronavirus Act 2020 ceased to have effect on 25 March 2022 (see s.89 of the Coronavirus Act 2020), a pilot scheme to supplement the power to direct that proceedings may take place wholly by way of a video or audio hearing, in circumstances where the audio or video recording cannot be broadcast live in a court building (see para.9A-928.12 and s.85A of the Courts Act 2003). The first sentence of its third paragraph continues in force until 25 March 2023 in virtue of amendments to the pilot scheme by CPR Update 143 (March 2022).

The Damages Claims Pilot Scheme

To the end of the paragraph, add:

51.2.14 It was amended by CPR Update 142 (March 2022) to require claimants who are legally represented to use the pilot scheme where it is applicable to their claim. It was further amended by CPR Update 144 (March 2022) to clarify that it only applies to legally represented parties and that it is not mandatory for multi-party claims. All claims issued on or after 4 April 2022 by legal representatives registered with MyHMCTS and which meet the conditions set out in subpara.(3) of the Practice Direction must be issued in accordance with the Damages Claim Pilot scheme. It was to be further amended as from 2 June 2022 (subject to transitional provisions) by CPR Update 145 (May 2022). The amendment provided, amongst other things, that legally represented defendants must use the pilot scheme's damages claims portal. Before the amendment came into effect CPR PD Update 145 was revoked by CPR PD Update 148 (June 2022), which came into effect on 1 June 2022. Those amendments were reintroduced by CPR Update 150 (September 2022) and came into effect on 15 September 2022, subject to transitional provisions.

Add new paragraph 51.2.15:

The Small Claims Paper Determination Pilot Scheme

51.2.15 Practice Direction 51ZC made in accordance with r.51.1 was published in CPR Update 143 (March 2022). The Practice Direction is in force from 1 June 2022 until 1 June 2024. It applies in the County Court hearing centres (incorrectly referred to in the Practice Direction as "County Courts") at Bedford, Luton, Guildford, Staines, Cardiff and Manchester. It applies to all small claims in those court centres, including claims transferred to them, except those claims where the parties have followed the process set out in the Pre-Action Protocol for Personal Injury Claims below the Small Claims Limit in Road Traffic Accidents and have commenced proceedings under Practice Direction 27B, and those for housing disrepair. It provides a power to direct, without the consent of the parties, that such claims be determined entirely on the papers, i.e. without a hearing.

PRACTICE DIRECTION 51R—THE ONLINE CIVIL MONEY CLAIMS PILOT

Section 2—Scope of the Pilot

Scope of this Pilot

In paragraph 2.1, replace list items (3), (4) and (5) with:

(3) A claim is only suitable for the pilot if all the following conditions are met– **51RPD.2**

- (a) the claim is a claim for a specified amount of money only not exceeding the amount specified in paragraph 2.1(6) including interest;
- (b) the claim would not ordinarily follow the Part 8 procedure;
- (c) the claim is not being brought under the Consumer Credit Act 1974, unless it is brought under section 141 of that Act, to enforce a "regulated agreement" (as defined) relating only to money;
- (d) either–
  - (i) the claimant will not be getting help with bringing the claim from a "legal representative" (as defined) and the claimant believes that the defendant will not be getting help with defending the claim from a "legal representative"; or
  - (ii) the claimant and the defendant are each represented by a legal representative;
- (e) the claim is not for personal injury
- (f) where–
  - (i) paragraph 2.1(3)(d)(i) applies, there is only one claimant making the claim, and the claimant informs the court that there is only one defendant; or
  - (ii) paragraph 2.1(3)(d)(ii) applies, the claim is brought by one claimant against either one or two defendants, or is brought by two claimants against one defendant;
- (g) if an individual, the claimant is aged 18 years or older;
- (h) the claimant is not a "protected party" (as defined);
- (i) the claimant's postal address for service is within the United Kingdom;
- (j) the claimant has an email address which can be used for the case;
- (k) [Omitted]
- (l) the claim is conducted in English;
- (m) the claimant does not have in force against them–
  - (i) a "civil proceedings order" (as defined);
  - (ii) an "all proceedings order" (as defined); or
  - (iii) a "civil restraint order" (as defined);
- (n) the claimant believes that the defendant–
  - (i) [Omitted]
  - (ii) has a postal address for service within England and Wales;
  - (iii) if an individual, is aged 18 years or older;
  - (iv) is not a "protected party" (as defined); and
  - (v) is not the Crown.

(4) If the claimant decides to use Online Civil Money Claims, the claimant may also volunteer their claim to be used to test "new features" (as defined) in the pilot. If the claimant volunteers their claim, "HMCTS" (as defined) may select the claim to test the new features, but does not have to. The court must tell the claimant straight away if the claim has been selected. It must also tell the defendant that the claim has been

selected, the first time that any communication is sent by the court to the defendant.

(5) If the claimant decides to use Online Civil Money Claims, this practice direction applies. This practice direction contains provisions that apply generally to claims in the pilot, and also specific provisions that apply to claims selected to test new features. Where provisions in this practice direction conflict with other provisions in the Civil Procedure Rules or other practice directions, this practice direction takes precedence until the claim is sent out of the pilot. Once the claim is sent out of the pilot, this practice direction will no longer apply. The rest of the Civil Procedure Rules and practice directions, however, will continue to apply to the claim, along with any changes to the Civil Procedure Rules or other practice directions made by this practice direction or orders made by the court to enable the claim to be sent out of the pilot successfully.

(6) The amount specified is–
  (a) £10,000 if paragraph 2.1(3)(d)(i) applies; or
  (b) £25,000 if paragraph 2.1(3)(d)(ii) applies.

Section 5—Defendant's Response Online—General

Defendant to complete directions questionnaire online (form OCON180), to tell the court about their hearing requirements

In paragraph 5.2, replace list item (1) with:

51RPD.5 (1) This paragraph applies where the defendant is not legally represented and–
  (a) the defendant wishes to defend the whole of the claim, and will be using form OCON9B to make the response; or
  (b) the defendant wishes to defend part of the claim and admit part of the claim and uses form OCON9A and OCON9B to make the response.

Add new paragraphs 5.3, 5.4 and 5.5:

Represented defendant to complete directions questionnaire online

5.3(1) This paragraph, and paragraph 5.4, only apply where the defendant is legally represented and the defendant wishes to defend the whole of the claim.

(2) The defendant must submit the directions questionnaire by completing the relevant screens, and selecting the "submit response" button, on the OCMC website.

(3) The defendant's response must include the information required by CPR 16.5.

Initial case management

5.4 Paragraphs 7.1 to 7.4 of Practice Direction 51ZB shall apply, as if references to "the DCP" were references to "the OCMC website".

Represented defendant indicates that they admit the claim in whole or part or admit part and defend the rest of the claim

5.5 Where the defendant is legally represented and indicates electronically that they wish to admit the whole or part of the claim, or admit part and defend the rest of the claim, the court must–

(a) notify the claimant; and
(b) transfer the claim out of OCMC to the CTSC.

PRACTICE DIRECTION 51S—THE COUNTY COURT ONLINE PILOT

Renumber paragraphs 51SPD.0 to 51SPD.5 as 51xSPD.0 to 51xSPD.5.

Replace paragraph with:

This Practice Direction was omitted as from 1 March 2022 by CPR Update 141 (March 2022). It remains in force, however, under transitional provisions for claims that commenced under it prior to its omission. **51xSPD.0**

PRACTICE DIRECTION 51U—DISCLOSURE PILOT FOR THE BUSINESS AND PROPERTY COURTS

Delete Practice Direction 51U–Disclosure Pilot for the Business and Property Courts (now relocated under Part 57A as PD 57AD).

DISCLOSURE PILOT PRACTICE NOTE

Delete Disclosure Pilot Practice Note (now relocated under Part 57A).

MESSAGE FROM THE CHIEF INSOLVENCY AND COMPANIES COURT JUDGE

Delete Message from the Chief Insolvency and Companies Court Judge (now relocated under Part 57A as Practice Note on Disclosure in the Insolvency and Companies List (ChD)).

PRACTICE DIRECTION 51X—NEW STATEMENT OF COSTS FOR SUMMARY ASSESSMENT PILOT

Delete Practice Direction 51X–New Statement of Costs for Summary Assessment Pilot and editorial note.

PRACTICE DIRECTION 51Y—VIDEO OR AUDIO HEARINGS DURING CORONAVIRUS PANDEMIC

Replace paragraph 1 with:

1. This practice direction, made under rule 51.2 of the Civil Procedure Rules ("CPR"), makes provision in relation to audio or video hearings. With the exception of the first sentence of paragraph 3, it ceases to have effect on the date on which the Coronavirus Act 2020 ceases to have effect in accordance with section 89 of that Act. The first sentence of paragraph 3 ceases to have effect on 25 March 2023. **51YPD.1**

Insert Practice Direction 51ZA–Extension of Time Limits and Clarification of Practice Direction 51Y–Coronavirus:

PRACTICE DIRECTION 51ZA—EXTENSION OF TIME LIMITS AND CLARIFICATION OF PRACTICE DIRECTION 51Y—CORONAVIRUS

This Practice Direction supplements Part 51

1. This practice direction is made under rule 51.2 of the Civil Procedure Rules ("CPR"). It is intended to assess modifications to the rules and Practice Directions that may be necessary as a temporary measure during the Coronavirus pandemic to ensure that the administration of justice is carried out so as not to endanger public health. As such it **51ZAPD.1**

(a) makes provision for parties to agree extensions of time to comply with procedural time limits in the CPR, Practice Directions and court orders; and

(b) provides guidance to the court when considering applications for extensions of time and adjournments.

It further makes provision to clarify the meaning of paragraph 4 of Practice Direction 51Y. It ceases to have effect on 30 October 2020.

2. During the period in which this Direction is in force CPR rule.3.8 has effect as if in substitution for the reference to 28 days there was a reference to 56 days.

3. Any extension of time, whether agreed by the parties or on application by a party, beyond 56 days requires the permission of the court. An application for such permission will be considered by the court on the papers. Any order made on the papers must, on application, be reconsidered at a hearing.

4. In so far as compatible with the proper administration of justice, the court will take into account the impact of the Covid-19 pandemic when considering applications for the extension of time for compliance with directions, the adjournment of hearings, and applications for relief from sanctions.

5. In paragraph 4 of Practice Direction 51Y, the reference to 'application' in the final sentence is to be read as 'request'. As such any person seeking permission to listen to or view a recording of a hearing is not required to make a formal application under CPR Part 23.

PRACTICE DIRECTION 51ZB—THE DAMAGES CLAIMS PILOT

Section 1—Scope of the Damages Claims Pilot

Replace paragraph 1.2 with:

51ZBPD.1 **1.2**(1) This Practice Direction—

(a) establishes a pilot to test an online claims process called "Damages Claims". Damages Claims are managed using the Damages Claims Portal ("DCP"); and

(b) sets out the circumstances in which the DCP must be used.

(2) The pilot applies in the county court.

Replace paragraph 1.6 with:

1.6(1) The conditions for using the pilot are set out in sub-paragraph (3).

(2) If all of the conditions in sub-paragraph (3) are met—

(a) the claimant's legal representative must register with MyHMCTS and secure access to the DCP before the claim is started;

(b) the claimant must give the defendant the notice referred to in paragraph 1.9(2)(a) unless it is impractical to do so; and

(c) the claim must be started using the procedure set out in this Practice Direction.

(3) The conditions referred to in sub-paragraph (1) are—

(a) the claim is a claim for damages only;

(b) the claim would not ordinarily follow the Part 8 procedure;

(c) the claim is not made under one of the provisions of the Consumer Credit Act 1974 specified in CPR PD 7B paragraph 3.1;

(d) the claimant is represented by a legal representative;

(e) if an individual, the claimant is aged 18 years or over, or is under 18 and has a litigation friend (in which case a statement of suitability must be provided);

(f) the claimant is not a protected party within the meaning of CPR 21.1(2)(d);

(g) the fee for issuing the claim is paid in full using the "Payment By Account" system;

(h) the claim is conducted in English;

(i) the claimant does not have in force against them—

(i) a civil proceedings order;

(ii) an all proceedings order; or

(iii) a civil restraint order;

(j) the claimant believes that the defendant–
(i) has a postal address for service within England and Wales;
(ii) if an individual, is aged 18 years or older; and
(iii) is not a protected party; and
(iv) is not the Crown;
(k) the claim is not one to which Practice Direction 27B applies; and
(l) the claim–
(i) is brought by one claimant against either one or two defendants; or
(ii) is brought by two claimants against one defendant.

Add new paragraph 1.9:

1.9(1) If all of the conditions in sub-paragraph (2) are met–
(a) the defendant's legal representative must–
(i) register with MyHMCTS and secure access to the DCP before the claim is started;
(ii) notify the claimant that they are instructed; and
(iii) provide the claimant with their email address for claim notifications; and
(b) the claimant must–
(i) provide the defendant's legal representative's email address for claim notifications to the court using the DCP when starting the claim under section 2 of this Practice Direction; and
(ii) notify the claim to the defendant using the procedure set out in section 3 of this Practice Direction.

(2) The conditions referred to in sub-paragraph (1) are–
(a) the claimant gives the defendant at least 14 days' notice of their intention to bring a claim using the DCP; and
(b) the defendant has instructed a legal representative before the claim is started.

Section 2—Starting a Claim

In paragraph 2.2, replace list item (6) with:

(6) If the defendant is not represented by a legal representative who is registered with MyHMCTS, the claim will be automatically transferred out of the DCP, immediately after it is issued, to the CCMCC. **51ZBPD.2**

Section 7—Initial Case Management

Replace paragraph 7.5 with:

7.5 In those claims to which the provisions of Section II of CPR Part 3 and Practice Direction 3D apply, CPR 3.13(1)(a) is disapplied and all parties except litigants in person must file and exchange budgets in accordance with CPR 3.13(1)(b), namely not later than 21 days before the first case management conference. **51ZBPD.7**

Add new Practice Direction 51ZC–The Small Claims Paper Determination Pilot:

PRACTICE DIRECTION 51ZC—THE SMALL CLAIMS PAPER DETERMINATION PILOT

1. General

1.1 This Practice Direction is made under rule 51.2 and provides for a pilot scheme to be called the "Small Claims Paper Determination Pilot" to test a procedure which will enable the court to direct that a small claim will be determined without a hearing without requiring the agreement of all parties, as is currently required under rule 27.10 ("the Pilot"). **51ZCPD.1**

1.2 The Pilot will commence on 01 June 2022 ("the Commencement Date") and will terminate on 01 June 2024 unless extended (the "Pilot Period"). Evaluation may be undertaken as the pilot proceeds and an interim report or reports may be made before the end of the pilot.

1.3 Subject to paragraph 1.4 below, the Pilot shall apply to all small claims in the County Court sitting at Bedford, Luton, Guildford, Staines, Cardiff and Manchester (each a "Pilot Court" and together the "Pilot Courts") which are issued after the Commencement Date and shall not apply to existing proceedings.

1.4 The Pilot shall not apply to small claims–

(a) where the parties have followed the Pre-Action Protocol for Personal Injury Claims below the Small Claims Limit in Road Traffic Accidents and proceedings have been started under Practice Direction 27B; or

(b) for housing disrepair.

1.5 The Pilot will continue to apply after the end of the Pilot Period to any proceedings listed for determination without a hearing during the Pilot Period.

1.6 For the purposes of the Pilot, where the provisions of this Practice Direction conflict with other provisions of the rules or other Practice Directions, including rule 27.10, this Practice Direction shall take precedence.

2. Transfers in and out of Pilot Courts

51ZCPD.2 **2.1** If a small claim which does not fall within sub-paragraph 1.4 is transferred into a Pilot Court from a court which is not a Pilot Court, the Pilot will apply, and the court may direct that the small claim will be determined without a hearing.

2.2 If a small claim is transferred out of a Pilot Court into a court which is not a Pilot Court, any order listing the matter for determination on paper made under the Pilot will remain in force, unless the transferee court makes a different order.

3. Re-allocation

51ZCPD.3 **3.1** Where a small claim is listed for determination without a hearing pursuant to the Pilot and is subsequently re-allocated from the small claims track to another track, the listing for determination without a hearing will no longer apply and the court will make case management directions to trial.

4. Suitability for determination without a hearing

51ZCPD.4 **4.1** A determination without a hearing can be a proportionate and efficient means of determining a small claim in cases where it is not necessary to hear oral evidence or oral advocacy to determine the issues justly.

4.2(1) Form **N180** (Directions Questionnaire (Small Claims)) shall be amended before the Commencement Date to include a section requiring each party to indicate–

(a) whether they consider that the claim is suitable for determination without a hearing; and

(b) if not, why not;

("the Amended Form **N180**").

(2) The Amended Form **N180** shall remain in use by the County Court throughout the Pilot Period.

4.3 During the Pilot Period, a Pilot Court may direct that a small claim which falls within the Pilot should be determined without a hearing–

(a) if all parties agree; or

(b) if, having considered the completed directions questionnaires in Amended Form **N180**, the court considers it is suitable for determination without a hearing.

4.4 Whether a small claim is suitable for determination without a hearing is a matter for judicial discretion to be exercised in accordance with the Overriding Objective. The types of small claims which may be suitable include—

(a) a claim for compensation for flight delay or denial of boarding pursuant to EU Regulation 261/2004 and/or The Air Passenger Rights and Air Travel Organisers' Licensing (Amendment) (EU Exit) Regulations 2019;
(b) a claim arising out of the issuance of a parking ticket on private land; and
(c) any other claim of £1000 or less by value where there is no significant factual dispute which requires oral evidence, and the issues are not of such complexity as to require oral advocacy.

5. Determination

5.1 A Pilot Court will give the parties at least 21 days' notice of the date of the determination of a small claim without a hearing ("date of determination"). **51ZCPD.5**

5.2 Where a direction is made pursuant to sub-paragraph 4.3(b), any party may file at the Pilot Court short written submissions objecting to that direction no less than 7 days before the date of determination, which will be put before the judge at the time listed for the paper determination. The judge will consider the suitability of the small claim for paper determination afresh and may either continue with the paper determination or direct that it be listed for a hearing instead.

5.3 Where the judge determines a small claim without a hearing under the Pilot, the judge will prepare a note of reasons (which shall include reasons for determining that it is suitable for determination without a hearing, if a party has objected pursuant to sub-paragraph 5.2) and the Pilot Court will send a copy to each party.

5.4 For the purposes of the Pilot, rule 5.4C(1) shall be read as if it included a new sub-section (c) as follows—

"*5.4C*

(1) The general rule is that a person who is not a party to proceedings may obtain from the court records a copy of—
   (a) ...;
   (b) ...;
   (c) a copy of a note of reasons prepared pursuant to PD 51ZC."

6. Appeals

6.1(1) A party who is dissatisfied with a determination without a hearing under the Pilot may not apply to set aside a judgment under rule 27.11 but may seek permission to appeal it pursuant to rule 52.3. **51ZCPD.6**

(2) In considering such an appeal, the appeal court will take into account the summary nature of the note of reasons produced following a determination without a hearing.

PART 52

APPEALS

Appeals are against orders, not reasoned judgments

Replace paragraph with:

In a number of cases it has been stated that the function of an appeal court, in particular of the Court of Appeal, is to deal with "judgments", "orders" or "determinations", that is to say, to deal with the "result" or "outcome" (to use non-technical terms) of the hearing in the lower court, and not with "findings" or "reasons" given in the judgment; see, e.g. *Compagnie Noga d'Importation et d'Exportation SA v Abacha (No.3)* [2002] EWCA Civ 1142; [2003] 1 W.L.R. 307, CA; *Morina v* **52.0.6**

Secretary of State for Work and Pensions [2007] EWCA Civ 749; [2007] 1 W.L.R. 3033, CA, at [6] per Maurice Kay LJ. The law in this respect restricts "winner's appeals" and is in part based on the Senior Courts Act 1981 s.16 (Appeals from High Court). In *Anwer v Central Bridging Loans Ltd* [2022] EWCA Civ 201 at [15]-[21], Coulson LJ confirmed that "determination" under the County Courts Act 1984 s.77(1) and "decision" did not differ materially from judgment or order. Coulson LJ further confirmed that a party did not, therefore, need to obtain a sealed order before seeking permission to appeal (at [22]). He further confirmed that appeals are brought against "outcomes" and that difference in terminology (judgment, order, direction determination) may once have been important but was no longer so under the CPR (at [16]).

In *Re W (A Child) (Care Proceedings: Non Party Appeal)* [2016] EWCA Civ 1140; [2017] 1 W.L.R. 2415, CA, where witnesses were subject to serious criticism in a judgment in family proceedings, it was unnecessary to assess whether they sought to challenge a judgment or the findings in the judgment. On the contrary, as the criticism, or possibility of such criticism, had not been put to them by the judge during the hearing they had not been afforded a fair process, to which they were entitled at common law and under the European Convention on Human Rights art.6. They could thus appeal from the decision in order to assert that the court had acted unlawfully by virtue of s.6(1) of the Human Rights Act 1998. For extended commentary on the subject and references to relevant authorities, see the commentary on that provision in Vol.2 para.9A-59.3.

I. Scope and interpretation

Add new paragraph 52.1.18:

Asylum and immigration—open justice

52.1.18 The principle of open justice applies to appeal proceedings. In so far as asylum and immigration appeals are concerned the Court of Appeal's approach is to maintain anonymity where that was ordered in the proceedings subject to appeal. It will, however, assess whether to maintain anonymity at the permission to appeal stage and, if maintained whether to continue anonymity when handing down judgment. Hearings will be in open court. See Practice Guidance—Anonymisation of Parties to Asylum and Immigration Cases in the Court of Appeal (23 March 2022) (see para.52PG.2), which replaced Practice Note (Anonymisation In Asylum and Immigration Cases In the Court of Appeal) [2006] EWCA Civ 1359.

II. Permission to Appeal—General

Exceptions to rule that permission is required

After the second paragraph, add new paragraph:

52.3.4 The continued existence of the right to appeal from committal decisions has been criticised: see *Al-Rawas v Hassan Khan & Co (A Firm)* [2022] EWCA Civ 671 at [17]-[20] (noting that there are two routes to control contempt appeals: (i) through, as noted above, distinguishing between an appeal from a committal order, for which permission is not needed, and from an ancillary order (*Masri v Consolidated Contractors International Co SAL* [2011] EWCA Civ 898; [2012] 1 W.L.R. 223); and (ii) the imposition of conditions on the right of appeal, albeit an appeal court would rarely take this route (*X Ltd v Morgan Grampian (Publishers) Ltd* [1991] 1 A.C. 1; *JSC BTA Bank v Ablyazov* [2012] EWCA Civ 639).

IV. Additional Rules

Obligation on respondents in appeals to Court of Appeal

In the fourth paragraph (beginning "Paragraph 8(1) and (2)"), after "an appeal notice", replace "(as distinct from a respondent's notice)" with:

52.13.2 (on which see PD 52C para.1)

Rule 52.13(4) and (5): Time for filing respondent's notice

Replace the last sentence with:

52.13.3 Such an application is application under r.3.1(2)(a) and not under r.3.9, but the same principles, e.g. those in *Denton v TH White Ltd* [2014] EWCA Civ 906; [2014] 1 W.L.R. 3926, apply (*Salford Estates (No.2) Ltd v Altomart Ltd (Practice Note)* [2014] EWCA Civ 1408; [2015] 1 W.L.R. 1825 and *Unite the Union v Alec McFadden* [2021] EWCA Civ 199; [2021] I.R.L.R. 354 at [44]; the latter decision stressing at [43] the importance of filing a respondent's notice when required to do so by r.52.13).

Replace r.52.14 with:

Transcripts at public expense[1]

52.14—(1) Subject to paragraph (2), the lower court or the appeal court may direct, on the request of a party to the proceedings, that an official transcript of the judgment of the lower court, or of any part of the evidence or the proceedings in the lower court, be obtained at public expense for the purposes of an appeal. **52.14**

(2) Before making a direction under paragraph (1), the court must be satisfied that—

(a) the requesting party qualifies for fee remission or is otherwise in such poor financial circumstances that the cost of obtaining a transcript would be an excessive burden; and

(b) it is necessary in the interests of justice for such a transcript to be obtained.

(3) A request under paragraph (1) must be made on the approved form.

Rule 52.14: Effect of rule

Replace paragraph with:

This rule was enacted by r.8(c) of the Civil Procedure (Amendment No.6) Rules 2014 (SI 2014/2044) and came into effect on 1 October 2014. It is designed to ensure a uniform practice for the providing of transcripts at public expense in appeals to the Civil Division of the Court of Appeal, the High Court and the County Court. Any request for a transcript at public expense should be made in the appellant's notice (Practice Direction 52B para.4.3 and Practice Direction 52C para.6(2)). A request for a transcript at public expense is not an application for the purposes of a standard civil restraint order, and would not therefore be subject to any restriction on making applications under such an order: *Anwer v Central Bridging Loans Ltd* [2022] EWCA Civ 201 at [32]-[37]. The rule was amended by r.20 of the Civil Procedure (Amendment No.2) Rules 2022 (SI 2022/783) to render the language of the rule consistent with that used in the form used to request transcripts. **52.14.1**

Asylum and immigration appeals

To the end of the first paragraph, add:

On anonymisation of asylum and immigration appeals in the Court of Appeal, see paras 52.1.18 and 52PG.2. **52.15.6**

Rule 52.18: Effect of rule

Add new paragraph at end:

On imposing conditions on an appeal where permission is not required, e.g. in appeals from committal orders, see para.52.3.4. **52.18.1**

Appeal in the absence of one of the parties

Replace paragraph with:

Until *General Medical Council v Theodoropolous* [2017] EWHC 1984 (Admin); [2017] 1 W.L.R. 4794, there was an absence of authority on the question of an appellate court's jurisdiction to hear an appeal in the absence of one of the parties. Neither CPR r.3.1(2)(m) nor r.39.3 provided a jurisdictional basis for the court to proceed in such circumstances. Moreover, there was no specific provision in CPR Pt 52 to enable the court to that effect. However, Lewis J held that an appellate court could proceed to hear and determine an appeal in the absence of one of the parties under the inherent jurisdiction, as a court that has a specific jurisdiction, i.e. an appellate jurisdiction, has powers necessary "to enable it to act effectively within such jurisdiction", see *Connelly v DPP* [1964] A.C. 1254, HL, at 1301. **52.21.6**

In order to assess whether to proceed in a party's absence, the following guidance was then given: first, it might be appropriate to proceed where the appellant or respondent had received notice of the hearing and there was no record of any attempt by them to inform the court of their non-attendance or to seek an adjournment. To determine that question the court could take account of any evidence of contact between the parties or between the absent party and the court office in reaching its decision; secondly, where the party has contacted the court and indicated their

[1] Introduced by the Civil Procedure (Amendment No.6) Rules 2014 (SI 2014/2044) and amended by the Civil Procedure (Amendment No.3) Rules 2016 (SI 2016/788) and the Civil Procedure (Amendment No.2) Rules 2022 (SI 2022/783).

non-attendance the starting point to determine whether to proceed in their absence was *General Medical Council v Adeogba* [2016] EWCA Civ 162; [2016] 1 W.L.R. 3867 and criteria, adapted for the present appellate context, it endorsed. As such, it was necessary to consider: the nature and circumstances leading to the party's absence, particularly whether the absence was deliberate or voluntary; the likelihood of the absent party attending any adjourned hearing; the length of any likely adjournment; whether the absent party is or wished to be legally represented or, by conduct, had waived a right to representation; whether the absent party had had an opportunity to give their legal representative instructions before or during the hearing; the extent of any disadvantage to the absent party accruing from non-attendance; the general public interest; and the effect any delay might have on witness memory, where that was relevant, in the rare case, to the appeal or any future potential hearing. In *Leave.EU Group Ltd v Information Commissioner* [2022] EWCA Civ 109 at [18]-[21], the Court of Appeal affirmed that the inherent jurisdiction also provides the power to dismiss an appeal in the absence of one of the parties.

VII. Reopening Final Appeals

Scope of the rule

After the second paragraph, add new paragraph:

52.30.2 In *R. (Nicholas) v Upper Tribunal (Administrative Appeals Chamber)* [2013] EWCA Civ 799, CA, the Court of Appeal were asked to reopen an appeal because of mistakes made by previous lawyers. The Court of Appeal concluded that the jurisdiction was not intended to cater for such mistakes, however reasonable and understandable they may be. As Longmore LJ put it, "mistakes are, regrettably, not exceptional at all".

Where permission to appeal has been granted on some issues only

To the end of the first paragraph, add:

52.30.4 Such an application for permission to reopen had to be brought "as soon as possible". If the facts that formed the basis of the application to reopen are known then that application should generally (i.e. unless there are reasons justifying delay) be brought "well before" the hearing of the substantive appeal: see *Ingenious Games LLP v Commissioners for Her Majesty's Revenue and Customs* [2022] EWCA Civ 1015 at [18]-[19].

Delete the last paragraph.

PRACTICE DIRECTION 52B—APPEALS IN THE COUNTY COURT AND HIGH COURT

Section IV—Initiating an appeal

Documents to be filed with the appellant's notice:

Replace paragraph 4.2(b) with:

52BPD.5 (b) a copy of the sealed order or determination under appeal;

Section VI—Conduct of the appeal

Documents relevant to the appeal:

Replace paragraph 6.4(1)(d) with:

52BPD.11 (d) a copy of the order or determination under appeal;

PRACTICE DIRECTION 52C—APPEALS TO THE COURT OF APPEAL

Section II—Starting an appeal to the Court of Appeal

Filing the appellant's notice and accompanying documents

Replace paragraph 3(3)(a) with:

52CPD.2 (a) the sealed order or other determination being appealed;

Add new Practice Guidance (Anonymisation of Parties to Asylum and Immigration Cases in the Court of Appeal):

PRACTICE GUIDANCE (ANONYMISATION OF PARTIES TO ASYLUM AND IMMIGRATION CASES IN THE COURT OF APPEAL)

1. This guidance replaces the Practice Note issued on 31 July 2006. **52PG.2**

2. The starting point for the consideration of anonymity orders is open justice. This principle promotes the rule of law and public confidence in the legal system. Given the importance of open justice, appellants should generally expect to be named in proceedings in the Court of Appeal. Any departure from this principle will need to be justified.

3. The Court will apply CPR 39.2(4) which provides that the court must order that the identity of a party shall not be disclosed if, but only if, it considers non-disclosure necessary to secure the proper administration of justice and in order to protect the interests of that party.

4. This may require the weighing of the competing interests of a party and their rights (for example, under Articles 3 or 8 of the ECHR or their ability to present their case in full without hindrance) against the need for open justice. The interests of children and the effect of them being identified should be considered.

5. The Court of Appeal will continue its long-standing practice of anonymising judgments in most appeals raising asylum or other international protection claims, provided it is satisfied that the publication of the names of appellants in such cases may create avoidable risks for them in the countries from which they have come.

6. Judgments will also be anonymised where there is a statutory prohibition on naming an individual, for example, a victim of a sexual offence or a victim of trafficking (sections 1 and 2 of the Sexual Offences Amendment Act 1992, as amended) or a child subject to family law proceedings (section 97(2) of the Children Act 1989).

7. When a new immigration or asylum case is issued in the Court of Appeal, it will initially be anonymised if it was anonymised in the lower court or Tribunal or involves a protection claim. Where a decision is required on permission to appeal the judge granting permission will consider whether the initial anonymisation should be continued.

8. Hearings will continue to take place in open court unless the court otherwise directs. Where judgment is given in an anonymised appeal (or a permission to appeal application where the judgment is released from the usual restriction on citation), the Court will reassess at that stage whether continued anonymity is required.

9. Where the case was anonymised in the lower court or Tribunal any continued anonymisation in the Court of Appeal will be in the same form. Otherwise, anonymised cases will be assigned three random initials and the country of origin, for example, XYZ (Turkey), unless a judge gives a specific direction to contrary effect. Such cases will then be listed and referred to solely by reference to this "name" and the reference number allocated to them in the Civil Appeals Office.

The Rt. Hon. Sir Geoffrey Vos, The Master of the Rolls
Underhill LJ
22 March 2022

PART 53

[ISSUED FROM 1 OCTOBER 2019] MEDIA AND COMMUNICATIONS CLAIMS

Sources of information

Replace "1981." with:

53.6.1 1981, as recently demonstrated in *Vardy v Rooney* [2022] EWHC 1209 (QB).

PRACTICE DIRECTION 53B—MEDIA AND COMMUNICATIONS CLAIMS

Specifying the meaning to be proved true

In the penultimate paragraph, replace "para.29.6" with:

53BPD.18 para.29.006

Honest opinion

To the end of the third paragraph, add:

53BPD.21 The factual basis of the stated opinion must be true: *Riley v Murray* [2022] EWCA Civ 1146.

Publication on a matter of public interest

To the end of the second paragraph, add:

53BPD.23 For the practical difficulties that may arise in proving reasonable belief that publishing a statement was in the public interest, see *Lachaux v Independent Print Ltd* [2021] EWHC 1797 (QB); [2022] E.M.L.R. 2.

Determination of meaning

To the end of the second paragraph, add:

53BPD.40 It will usually also be asked to determine whether the words are (or include) a statement of fact or expression of opinion, and whether they are, in any meaning found, defamatory of the claimant at common law. This is now conventional: see e.g. *Duke of Sussex v Associated Newspapers Ltd* [2022] EWHC 1755 (QB).

Whether the words complained of are defamatory at common law

To the end of the paragraph, add:

53BPD.44 See also the Queen's Bench Guide 2022 para.17.34:

> "The court will be slow to direct a preliminary issue as to serious harm involving substantial evidence: any continuing dispute as to serious harm should ordinarily be left to trial."

Whether the words complained of are a statement of fact or opinion

To the end of the paragraph, add:

53BPD.45 Increasingly, it has become conventional to resolve the issue at an early stage: see most recently *Duke of Sussex v Associated Newspapers Ltd* [2022] EWHC 1755 (QB).

Tribunal

To the end of the paragraph, add:

53BPD.48 See the Queen's Bench Guide 2022 paras 17.41–17.42.

Editorial note

Replace paragraph with:

53BPD.54 The course of conduct relied upon (para.10.3) must involve conduct on at least two occasions if one person is involved, and if two or more people are claimants, it must involve conduct on at least one occasion with respect to each person: Protection from Harassment Act 1997 s.7(3). "Conduct" includes speech: s.7(4). But claims for harassment by publication are likely to be rare, because to comply with s.3 of the Human Rights Act 1998, the courts will hold that a course of conduct in the form of journalistic speech is reasonable under s.1(3)(c) of the 1997 Act unless the course of conduct is so unreasonable that it is necessary and proportionate to interfere with that speech in pursuit of one of the aims listed in art.10(2): *Trimingham v Associated Newspapers Ltd* [2012] EWHC 1296 (QB). In pleading a claim for harassment by publication, it will be essential to have that test in mind. See also *McNally v Saunders* [2021] EWHC 2012 (QB); [2022] E.M.L.R. 3, where the defendant was a "citizen journalist" whose art.10 rights protected his postings from liability in harassment even though their tone was "puerile and abrasive". Indeed, nothing short of a conscious or negligent abuse of media freedom by a media defendant is likely to justify a finding of harassment, and such a case would be exceptional: *Sube v News Group Newspapers Ltd* [2020] EWHC 1125 (QB); [2020] E.M.L.R. 25. Two cases where that threshold was crossed are *Hourani v Thomson* [2017] EWHC 432 (QB) and *Ware v McAllister* [2015] EWHC 3068 (QB) (a case involving online publication by a community "activist" and online journalist).

PART 54

JUDICIAL REVIEW AND STATUTORY REVIEW

Practice Directions

Replace paragraph with:

CPR Pt 54 is currently supplemented by four Practice Directions: Practice Direction 54A makes general provision for claims for judicial review, Practice Direction 54B makes provision for urgent applications and applications for interim remedies, Practice Direction 54C deals with the venue at which claims should be commenced and administered, and Practice Direction 54D is concerned with the Planning Court. With effect from 1 October 2022, there will be an additional Practice Direction, Practice Direction 54E, which makes provision for environmental review claims brought by the Office for Environmental Protection under s.38 of the Environment Act 2021. There is also a Practice Direction on termination of proceedings: see *Practice Direction (Administrative Proceedings)* [2008] 1 W.L.R. 1377. **54.0.2**

Administrative Court Guide and E-Bundle Guidance

Replace paragraph with:

A guide to practice and procedure in the Administrative Court has been produced: see Vol.2 para.1BA-1. The Court has also issued a document entitled "Information for Court Users", which includes guidance on the preparation and use of electronic bundles and on the filing of documents electronically, which took effect on 27 June 2022: see Vol.1 para.54PN.1. **54.0.4**

Administrative Court Listing Policy

Replace "[Accessed 7 February 2022]." with:

[Accessed 21 July 2022]. **54.0.4.1**

Add new paragraph 54.0.4.2:

Hearings will take place in person

The default position for Administrative Court hearings is that they will be held in person: for the general position, see the Administrative Court's Information for Court Users section G para.2 (see para.54PN.1); for specific guidance on the position in Wales and on the Midland, Northern, North-Eastern and Western Circuits, see para.54PN.2. **54.0.4.2**

I. Judicial Review

The Administrative Court in Wales and the regions of England (see Practice Direction 54D)

Replace the second paragraph with:

Proceedings should be commenced at the Administrative Court Office for the region with which the claim is most closely connected, having regard to the subject matter of the claim, the locations of the claimant and defendant, and any other relevant circumstances (including those set out in Practice Direction 54C para.2.5): Practice Direction 54C paras 2.1 and 2.5. The fact that a defendant exercises its functions across the country is of itself unlikely to justify a matter being dealt with in London when other factors point towards it being dealt with elsewhere: *R. (Fortt) v Financial Services Compensation Scheme Ltd* [2022] EWHC 152 (Admin), [5] per Fordham J. **54.1.1.1**

Those matters which are not handled in the regional courts, namely the "excepted classes of claim" are set out in Practice Direction 54C para.3.1 to which reference should be made. It should be stressed that the regional courts can and do have Divisional Courts when the need arises; albeit not as frequently as occurs in London.

Is the measure, action or omission challenged one that is amenable to judicial review?

In the third paragraph, replace "R. (Unison) v Lord Chancellor [2017] UKSC 51; [2017] 3 W.L.R. 409." with:

R. (Unison) v Lord Chancellor [2017] UKSC 51; [2020] A.C. 869. **54.1.3**

Court's discretion

Add new paragraphs at end:

54.1.10 A court should only grant a remedy (including a declaration) if there is a finding that the defendant public body has acted, or is proposing to act, unlawfully, unless an advisory declaration is sought and it is an appropriate case in which to grant such a declaration: *R. (Richards) v Environment Agency* [2022] EWCA Civ 26; [2022] 1 W.L.R. 2593, [81]-[86] per Lewis LJ.

Where a court grants a quashing order in a claim that was commenced on or after 14 July 2022, it has the power to include in that order provision for the quashing not to take effect until a date specified in the order, or provision removing or limiting any retrospective effect of the quashing: Senior Courts Act 1981 s.29A (inserted by the Judicial Review and Courts Act 2022 s.1); see further para.54.2.1.

Standing: Who may apply for judicial review

Replace the last two sentences with:

54.1.11 Although the courts have generally adopted an increasingly liberal approach to questions of standing over recent years, there is a recent example of the Divisional Court adopting a stricter approach (*R. (Good Law Project) v Prime Minister* [2022] EWHC 298 (Admin)). The courts will consider a number of factors in deciding whether bodies have sufficient interest to bring a challenge including the merits of the challenge, the importance of vindicating the rule of law, the importance of the issue raised, the likely absence of any other responsible challenger, the nature of the breach and the role played by the group or body in respect of the issues in question (*R. v Secretary of State for Foreign and Commonwealth Affairs Ex p. World Development Movement Ltd* [1995] 1 W.L.R. 386).

Judicial review remedies

Replace the third paragraph with:

54.2.1 Where a court grants a quashing order in a claim that was commenced on or after 14 July 2022, it has a power to include in that order provision for the quashing not to take effect until a date specified in the order (a so-called "suspended quashing order"), or provision removing or limiting any retrospective effect of the quashing (a "so-called prospective-only quashing order"): Senior Courts Act 1981 s.29A (inserted by the Judicial Review and Courts Act 2022 s.1). That section specifies the matters to which a court must have regard when exercising its discretion whether to exercise this power, including: the nature and circumstances of the defect in the impugned decision or act; any detriment to good administration that would result from exercising or failing to exercise the power; the interests or expectations of persons who would benefit from the quashing of the impugned decision or act; the interests or expectations of persons who have relied on the impugned decision or act; and, insofar as it appears to the court to be relevant, any action taken or proposed to be taken, or undertaking given, by a person with responsibility in connection with the impugned act.

Discretion

To the end of the paragraph, add:

54.4.4 Permission may also be refused if the claim raises an abstract question that would have to be decided on the basis of hypothetical facts: see *R. (Counsel General for Wales) v Secretary of State for Business, Energy and Industrial Strategy* [2022] EWCA Civ 118, [26]-[33] per Nicola Davies LJ.

Time limits and delay

In the fifth paragraph, replace "[88]-[94]" with:

54.5.1 [88]-[94]; *R. (All the Citizens) v Secretary of State for Digital, Culture, Media and Sport* [2022] EWHC 960 (Admin), [155]-[156];

Editorial note

Replace paragraph with:

54.7.1 The claimant must file the claim form in the Administrative Court Office. The claimant must also serve the claim form on the defendant and, unless the court otherwise directs, on any person that the claimant considers to be an interested party within seven days of the issue of the claim form. In order for there to be valid service of a claim form under CPR r.54.7, the claim has to have been issued; there cannot be service of non-existence proceedings: see *R. (Good Law Project) v Secretary of State for Health and Social Care* [2021] EWHC 1782 (TCC); [2021] B.L.R. 599. As to the correct approach to an application retrospectively to extend time for serving a claim form, see *R. (Good Law Project) v Secretary of State for Health and Social Care* [2022] EWCA Civ 355; *R. (Karanja) v University of the West of Scotland* [2022] EWHC 1520 (Admin), [33]-[42] per Michael Ford QC. On the definition of the parties see para.54.1.12 above. See further Practice Direction 54A paras 5.1-5.2.

Rule 54.7A: Effect of rule

To the end of the paragraph, add:

Section 11A of the Tribunals, Courts and Enforcement Act 2007 (inserted by the Judicial Review and Courts Act 2022 s.2) excludes judicial review of decisions of the Upper Tribunal to refuse permission to appeal that were taken on or after 14 July 2022 altogether. **54.7A.1**

Consequences

Replace "R. (Nur) v Birmingham City Council [2020] EWHC 3526 (Admin)." with:

R. (Nur) v Birmingham City Council [2020] EWHC 3526 (Admin); [2021] H.L.R. 23. **54.9.1**

Skeleton arguments

Replace the last paragraph with:

Practice Direction 54A para.14.4 warns that any skeleton argument that does not comply with the requirements above may be returned to its author by the Administrative Court Office and may not be re-filed unless and until it complies with those requirements; the lead judge of the Administrative Court has indicated that this practice will be followed: *R. (SSE Generation Ltd) v Competition and Markets Authority* [2022] EWHC 865 (Admin), [76]-[78] per Swift J. Practice Direction 54A also warns that the court may disallow the cost of preparing a skeleton argument which does not comply with these requirements. **54.16.5.1**

Add new paragraph 54.19.3:

Suspended and prospective-only quashing orders

Where a court grants a quashing order in a claim that was commenced on or after 14 July 2022, it has the power to include in that order provision for the quashing not to take effect until a date specified in the order, or provision removing or limiting any retrospective effect of the quashing: Senior Courts Act 1981 s.29A (inserted by the Judicial Review and Courts Act 2022 s.1); see further para.54.2.1. **54.19.3**

Add new Section III:

III. Environmental Review under the Environment Act 2021

Scope and interpretation[1]

54.25—(1) This Section contains rules about environmental review. **54.25**

(2) In this Section—

(a) "claim for environmental review" means a claim made by the Office for Environmental Protection ("OEP") under section 38 of the Environment Act 2021;

(b) "the environmental review procedure" means the Part 8 procedure as modified by this Section;

(c) "interested party" means any person (other than the claimant and defendant) who is directly affected by the claim; and

(d) "court" means the High Court.

Environmental review

Section VII of Part 54, comprising rr.54.25 to 54.35, is inserted with effect from 1 October 2022. It makes provision for "environmental review" under the Environment Act 2021, i.e. a claim for environmental review brought by the Office for Environmental Protection under s.38 of that Act. Section VII of Part 54 is supplemented by Practice Direction 54E, which also takes effect on 1 October 2022. **54.25.1**

Who may exercise the powers of the High Court[2]

54.26—(1) Rule 54.1A (excluding paragraph (3)(a) of the rule) applies to a claim for environmental review. **54.26**

---

[1] Introduced by the Civil Procedure (Amendment No.2) Rules 2022 (SI 2022/783).

[2] Introduced by the Civil Procedure (Amendment No.2) Rules 2022 (SI 2022/783).

(2) A claim for environmental review shall be assigned to the Planning Court.

When this Section must be used[1]

54.27 **54.27—(1) The environmental review procedure must be used where a claim for environmental review is made.**

(2) Practice Direction 54E applies to the environmental review procedure.

Time limit for filing claim form[2]

54.28 **54.28—(1) The claim form must be filed not later than 6 months from the date by which a response to a decision notice was required under section 36(3) of the Environment Act 2021.**

(2) The time limit in paragraph (1) may be extended, but only upon application to the court by the claimant and if the court is satisfied that it is reasonable to do so.

Claim form[3]

54.29 **54.29—(1) In addition to the matters set out in rule 8.2 (contents of the claim form) the claimant must also state—**

(a) the name of the public authority, the defendant, against whom the claim for environmental review is brought;

(b) the name and address of any person the claimant considers to be an interested party; and

(c) any remedy (including any interim remedy) sought by the claimant.

(2) The claim form must be accompanied by the documents required by Practice Direction 54E.

Service of claim form[4]

54.30 **54.30 The claim form must be served on—**

(a) the defendant; and

(b) unless the court otherwise directs, any person the claimant considers to be an interested party,

within 7 days after the date of issue.

Acknowledgment of service[5]

54.31 **54.31—(1) Any person served with the claim form who wishes to take part in the environmental review must file an acknowledgment of service in the relevant practice form in accordance with the following provisions of this rule.**

(2) Any acknowledgment of service must be—

(a) filed not more than 35 days after service of the claim form; and

(b) served on—

(i) the claimant; and

(ii) subject to any direction under rule 54.30(b), any other person named in the claim form,

as soon as practicable and, in any event, not later than 7 days after it is filed.

(3) The time limits under this rule may not be extended by agreement between the parties.

(4) The acknowledgment of service—

(a) must state the name and address of any person the person filing it considers to be an interested party; and

---

[1] Introduced by the Civil Procedure (Amendment No.2) Rules 2022 (SI 2022/783).
[2] Introduced by the Civil Procedure (Amendment No.2) Rules 2022 (SI 2022/783).
[3] Introduced by the Civil Procedure (Amendment No.2) Rules 2022 (SI 2022/783).
[4] Introduced by the Civil Procedure (Amendment No.2) Rules 2022 (SI 2022/783).
[5] Introduced by the Civil Procedure (Amendment No.2) Rules 2022 (SI 2022/783).

(b) may include or be accompanied by an application for directions.

(5) Rule 10.3(2) does not apply.

Detailed grounds and evidence[1]

54.32—(1) A defendant and any other person served with the claim form who wishes to contest the claim or support it on additional grounds must file and serve with the acknowledgement of service— 54.32

(a) detailed grounds for contesting the claim or supporting it on additional grounds; and

(b) any written evidence.

(2) Rule 8.6(1) does not apply.

(3) No written evidence may be relied on unless—

(a) it has been served in accordance with any—

(i) rule in this Section; or

(ii) direction of the court; or

(b) the court gives permission.

Failure to file acknowledgment of service[2]

54.33—(1) Where a person served with the claim form has failed to file an acknowledgment of service in accordance with rule 54.31 or to comply with 54.32, they may not take part in the hearing of the claim unless the court allows them to do so and they comply with rule 54.31 or any other direction of the court regarding the filing and service of— 54.33

(a) detailed grounds for contesting the claim or supporting it on additional grounds; and

(b) any written evidence.

(2) Where that person takes part in the hearing of the environmental review, the court may take their failure to file an acknowledgment of service into account when deciding whether an order as to costs should be made.

(3) Rule 8.4 does not apply.

Where claimant seeks to rely on additional grounds[3]

54.34 The court's permission is required if the claimant seeks to rely on grounds other than those set out in the original claim. 54.34

Other procedural rules[4]

54.35 Rules 54.10 and 54.16–54.20 shall apply to the environmental review procedure, except that— 54.35

(a) references to "permission to proceed" shall be disregarded; and

(b) the reference in rule 54.19 to "the decision to which the claim relates" shall be read as referring to "the matter to which the claim relates".

Add new Practice Direction 54E–Environmental Review Claims:

PRACTICE DIRECTION 54E—ENVIRONMENTAL REVIEW CLAIMS

This practice direction supplements Part 54

Section I—General

1.1 This Practice Direction supplements Part 54. It applies to claims for environmental review. 54EPD.1

[1] Introduced by the Civil Procedure (Amendment No.2) Rules 2022 (SI 2022/783).
[2] Introduced by the Civil Procedure (Amendment No.2) Rules 2022 (SI 2022/783).
[3] Introduced by the Civil Procedure (Amendment No.2) Rules 2022 (SI 2022/783).
[4] Introduced by the Civil Procedure (Amendment No.2) Rules 2022 (SI 2022/783).

1.2 In this Practice Direction the term "environmental review" has the same meaning as in rule 54.25(2).

Section II—Environmental review

The Claim Form

54EPD.2 **2.1**(1) The Claim Form must include or be accompanied by the following documents–

(a) a clear and concise statement of the facts relied on set out in numbered paragraphs–"the Statement of Facts"; and

(b) a clear and concise statement of the grounds for bringing the claim–"the Statement of Grounds". The Statement of Grounds should: identify in separate, numbered paragraphs each ground of challenge; identify the relevant provision or principle of law said to have been breached; and provide sufficient detail of the alleged breach to enable the parties and the court to identify the essential issues alleged to arise. The Statement of Grounds should succinctly explain the claimant's case by reference to the Statement of Facts and state precisely what relief is sought.

(2) The Statement of Facts and the Statement of Grounds may be contained in a single document.

(3) The Statements of Facts and Grounds should be as concise as possible. The two documents together (or the single document if the two are combined) shall not exceed 40 pages. In many cases the court will expect the documents to be significantly shorter than 40 pages. The court may grant permission to exceed the 40-page limit.

2.2 Any application (a) to extend the time limit for filing the Claim Form; and/or (b) for directions in the claim, should be included in or contained in a document that accompanies the Claim Form.

2.3(1) In addition, the Claim Form must be accompanied by–

(a) any written evidence in support of the claim (in this regard, see also rules 8.5(1) and 8.5(7)).

(b) any written evidence in support of any other application contained in the Claim Form;

(c) a copy of any order or decision that the claimant seeks to have quashed;

(d) where the claim relates to a decision of a public authority an approved copy of the reasons for reaching that decision and a copy of any record of the decision under challenge;

(e) copies of any documents on which the claimant proposes to rely;

(f) copies of any relevant statutory material; and

(g) a list of essential documents for advance reading by the court (with page references to the passages relied on).

(2) Where it is not possible to file all the above documents, the claimant must indicate which documents have not been filed and the reasons why they are not currently available.

The claim bundle

54EPD.3 **3.1**(1) The claimant must prepare a paginated and indexed bundle containing all the documents referred to in paragraphs 2.1 and 2.3. An electronic version of the bundle must also be prepared in accordance with the Guidance on the Administrative Court website.

(2) The claimant shall (unless otherwise requested) lodge the bundle with the Court in both electronic and hard copy form. For Divisional

Court cases the number of hard copy bundles required will be one set for each judge hearing the case.

Devolution issues

4.1(1) In this Practice Direction "devolution issue" has the same meaning as in paragraph 1, Schedule 9 to the Government of Wales Act 2006, paragraph 1, Schedule 10 to the Northern Ireland Act 1998; and paragraph 1, Schedule 6 to the Scotland Act 1998. **54EPD.4**

(2) Where the claimant intends to raise a devolution issue, the Claim Form must: (a) specify that the claimant wishes to raise a devolution issue and identify the relevant provisions of the Government of Wales Act 2006, the Northern Ireland Act 1998 or the Scotland Act 1998; and (b) contain a summary of the facts, circumstances and points of law on the basis of which it is alleged that a devolution issue arises.

Service of Claim Form

5.1 Part 6 contains provisions about the service of Claim Forms. **54EPD.5**

5.2 Where the defendant or interested party to the claim is the Crown, service of the Claim Form must be effected on the solicitor acting for the relevant government department as if the proceedings were civil proceedings as defined in the Crown Proceedings Act 1947. Practice Direction 66 gives the list published under section 17 of the Crown Proceedings Act 1947 of the solicitors acting in civil proceedings (as defined in that Act) for the different government departments on whom service is to be effected, and of their addresses.

Acknowledgment of Service and Detailed Grounds

6.1 The Acknowledgment of Service must contain the information specified in rules 8.3(2) and 10.5. See also the requirements set out in Practice Direction 10. **54EPD.6**

6.2(1) If a defendant or other party chooses to file an Acknowledgement of Service, the Detailed Grounds referred to in CPR 54.32(1)(a) should meet the following requirements.

(2) The Detailed Grounds should identify succinctly any relevant facts. Material matters of factual dispute (if any) should be highlighted.

(3) The Detailed Grounds should (again succinctly) explain the legal basis of that party's response to the claimant's case, by reference to relevant facts.

(4) The Detailed Grounds should be as concise as possible, and shall not exceed 40 pages. The court may grant permission to exceed the 40-page limit.

(5) Where a party filing Detailed Grounds intends to rely on written evidence or on documents not already filed, the party must prepare a paginated and indexed bundle containing that evidence and those documents. An electronic version of the bundle shall also be prepared in accordance with the Guidance on the Administrative Court website.

6.3 The party shall file and serve electronic and hard copy versions of the bundle when filing and serving the Detailed Grounds.

Evidence

7.1 In accordance with the duty of candour, the defendant should, in its Detailed Grounds or evidence, identify any relevant facts, and the reasoning, underlying the matter the subject of the claim for environmental review. **54EPD.7**

7.2 Disclosure is not required unless the court orders otherwise.

7.3 It will rarely be necessary in an environmental review for the court to hear oral evidence. Any application under rule 8.6(2) for permission to adduce oral evidence or to cross-examine any witness must be made promptly, in accordance with the requirements of Part 23, and be supported by an explanation of why the evidence is necessary for the fair determination of the claim.

Rule 54.34—Where Claimant Seeks to Rely upon Additional Grounds

54EPD.8 **8.1** Where the claimant intends to apply for environmental review on grounds additional to those set out in the Claim Form, the claimant must make an application to the court for permission to amend the Claim Form. The application should be made in accordance with the requirements of Part 23.

8.2 The application must be made promptly and should include, or be accompanied by, a draft of the amended grounds and be supported by evidence explaining the need for the proposed amendment and any delay in making the application for permission to amend.

8.3 The application, the proposed additional grounds and any written evidence, must be served on the defendant and any interested party named in the Claim Form or an Acknowledgement of Service.

8.4 For the purposes of determining an application to rely on additional grounds, rules 17.1 and 17.2 shall apply. Where permission to rely on additional grounds is given, the court may give directions as to amendments to be made to the defendant's Detailed Grounds and/or such other case management directions as appropriate.

Rule 54.17 and 54.35—Court's Powers to Hear Any Person

54EPD.9 **9.1** An application for permission to intervene under rules 54.17 and 54.35 should be made by application in the relevant proceedings, in accordance with the provisions of Part 23.

9.2 Any such application must be made promptly. The Court is unlikely to accede to an application to intervene if it would have the consequence of delaying the hearing of the relevant proceedings.

9.3 The Application Notice must be served on all parties to the proceedings.

9.4(1) The duty of candour applies. The Application Notice should explain who the applicant is and indicate why and in what form the applicant wants to participate in the hearing.

(2) If the applicant requests permission to make representations at the hearing, the application should include a summary of the representations the applicant proposes to make.

(3) If the applicant requests permission to file and serve evidence in the proceedings a copy of that evidence should be provided with the Application Notice. The application should explain the relevance of any such evidence to the issues in the proceedings.

9.5 Where the court gives permission for a person to file evidence or make representations at the hearing of the claim for environmental review (whether orally or in writing), it may do so on conditions and may give case management directions.

9.6 Where all the parties consent, the court may deal with an application under rules 54.17 and 54.35 without a hearing.

Skeleton arguments, the hearing bundle and the authorities bundle

54EPD.10 **10.1** Paragraphs 14.1 to 15.5 of Practice Direction 54A shall apply to the environmental review procedure, save that references to "judicial review" shall be read as referring to "environmental review".

Agreed final order

54EPD.11 **11.1** Paragraphs 16.1 to 16.4 of Practice Direction 54A shall apply to the environmental review procedure.

Replace Administrative Court–Electronic Bundle Guidance with:

ADMINISTRATIVE COURT INFORMATION FOR COURT USERS

The following practical measures will remain in place until further notice, to assist the court to deal with its business as efficiently as possible. **54PN.1**

Sections A and B apply to all Administrative Court claims. Compliance with Section A is required by Practice Directions 54A and 54B.

Sections C to H also apply to claims, appeals and applications administered by the Administrative Court; but where arrangements differ depending on which Administrative Court office is dealing with the matter, this is explained in the text below.

Arrangements for electronic working

A. Electronic Bundles

(Practice Direction 54A, §§ 4.5 and 15; Practice Direction 54B, §1.3)

Electronic bundles must be prepared as follows and be suitable for use with all of Adobe Acrobat Reader and PDF Expert and PDF Xchange Editor. **54PN.1.1**

1. A bundle must be a single PDF.
2. If the bundle is filed in support of an urgent application (i.e., an application made using Form **N463**) it must not exceed 20mb, and (unless the court requests otherwise) should be filed by email
3. If the papers in support of any claim or appeal or non-urgent application exceed 20mb, the party should file:
   a. a core bundle (no larger than 20mb) including, as a minimum, the Claim Form and Grounds or Notice of Appeal and Grounds, or Application Notice and Grounds; documents regarded as essential to the claim, appeal, or application (for example the decision challenged, the letter before claim and the response, etc.); any witness statements (or primary witness statement) relied on in support of the claim, appeal or application; and a draft of the order the court is asked to make; and
   b. a further bundle containing the remaining documents.

   Bundles should be filed using the Document Upload Centre.
4. All bundles must be paginated in ascending order from start to finish. The first page of the PDF will be numbered "1", and so on. (Any original page numbers of documents within the bundle are to be ignored.) Index pages must be numbered as part of the single PDF document, they are not to be skipped; they are part of the single PDF and must be numbered. If a hard copy of the bundle is produced, the pagination on the hard copy must correspond exactly to the pagination of the PDF.
5. Wherever possible pagination should be computer-generated; if this is not possible, pagination must be in typed form.
6. The index page must be hyperlinked to the pages or documents it refers to.
7. Each document within the bundle must be identified in the sidebar list of contents/bookmarks, by date and description (e.g., "email 11.9.21 from [x] to [y]"). The sidebar list must also show the bundle page number of the document.
8. All bundles must be text based, not a scan of a hard copy bundle. If documents within a bundle have been scanned, optical character recognition should be undertaken on the bundle before it is lodged. (This is the process which turns the document from a mere picture of a document to one in which the text can be read as text so that the document becomes

word-searchable, and words can be highlighted in the process of marking them up.) The text within the bundle must therefore be selectable as text, to facilitate highlighting and copying.

9. Any document in landscape format must be rotated so that it can be read from left to right.
10. The default display view size of all pages must always be 100%.
11. The resolution on the electronic bundle must be reduced to about 200 to 300 dpi to prevent delays whilst scrolling from one page to another.
12. If a bundle is to be added to after the document has been filed, it should not be assumed the judge will accept a new replacement bundle because he/she may already have started to mark up the original. Inquiries should be made of the judge as to what the judge would like to do about it. Absent a particular direction, any pages to be added to the bundle as originally filed should be provided separately, in a separate document, with pages appropriately sub-numbered.

For guidance showing how to prepare an electronic bundle, see (as an example) this video prepared by St Philips Chambers, which explains how to create a bundle using Adobe Acrobat Pro *https://st-philips.com/creating-and-using-electronic-hearing-bundles/*

Any application filed by a legal representative that does not comply with the above rules on electronic bundles may not be considered by a Judge. If the application is filed by a litigant in person the electronic bundle must if at all possible, comply with the above rules. If it is not possible for a litigant in person to comply with the rules on electronic bundles, the application must include a brief explanation of the reasons why.

B. The Document Upload Centre

54PN.1.2 Whenever possible, file documents electronically. This includes claims, responses, interlocutory applications, and hearing bundles. Unless stated otherwise below, file documents using the Document Upload Centre (DUC).

Requests to upload documents to the DUC should be sent to the email addresses referred to below in Sections D, E and F. After uploading a document, you must email the relevant court office to confirm the upload.

For guidance on how to use the DUC, see the HMCTS "Professional Users Guide" for detailed information about the Document Upload Centre[1], and the DUC video guide on YouTube[2].

Arrangements for filing and responding to claims, appeals and applications

C. Applications for Urgent Consideration

Administrative Court, London (Royal Courts of Justice)

54PN.1.3 Urgent applications (i.e. applications within the scope of Practice Direction 54B) should be filed either electronically (preferred wherever possible), or by post or DX. Until further notice, urgent applications may not be filed over the counter at the Royal Courts of Justice.

The process explained below should be used for any urgent interlocutory application that is filed electronically.

1. Applications must be filed by email to: *immediates@administrativecourtoffice.justice.gov.uk* accompanied with either a PBA number, receipt of pay-

[1] *https://assets.publishing.service.gov.uk/government/uploads/system/uploads/attachment_data/file/887109/Document_Upload_Centre_-_Professional_User.pdf*

[2] *https://www.youtube.com/watch?v=rbYBhdPNr5E*

ment by debit/credit card or a fee remission certificate (see below, Section G).

2. This inbox will be monitored Monday to Friday between the hours of 9:30am and 4:30pm. Outside of these hours the usual QB out of hours procedure should be used.
3. Your application must be accompanied by an electronic bundle containing only those documents which it will be necessary for the court to read for the purposes of determining the application—see Practice Direction 54B at §§1.3, and 2.2–2.3. The bundle must be prepared in accordance with the guidance at Section A; it must not exceed 20mb.
4. Any other urgent queries should be sent by email to: *generaloffice@administrativecourtoffice.justice.gov.uk*, marked as high priority, and with "URGENT" in the subject line. Any such emails will be dealt with as soon as possible.

If you are not legally represented and do not have access to email, you should contact the Administrative Court Office by telephone on 020 7947 6655 (option 6) so that details of your application may be taken by telephone and alternative arrangements made if permitted by the senior legal manager or the duty judge.

Other Administrative Court Offices

Out of London, urgent applications may be filed between 10am and 4pm, Monday to Friday. Urgent applications may also be filed in person. If you wish to file in person, you should contact the relevant office by phone to arrange to attend the public counter. The phone numbers are as follows

Birmingham	0121 681 4441—pick option 2 then option 5.
Cardiff	02920 376460
Leeds	0113 306 2578
Manchester	0161 240 5313

If filing an urgent application by email, the arrangements at 1–4 above apply, save that: (a) see Section H below for how to pay the application fee; and (b) please use the following email addresses.

Birmingham:
birmingham@administrativecourtoffice.justice.gov.uk
Cardiff:
cardiff@administrativecourtoffice.justice.gov.uk
Leeds:
leeds@administrativecourtoffice.justice.gov.uk
Manchester:
manchester@administrativecourtoffice.justice.gov.uk

D. Non-urgent Work: Civil Claims and Appeals

All other civil business (i.e. non-urgent claims, appeals and applications) **54PN.1.4**
should be filed electronically (preferred wherever possible) or by post or DX. There may be a slight delay before claims/applications are issued, but the date the Claim Form or Notice of Appeal is received by the Administrative Court office will be recorded as the date of filing. It remains the responsibility of the party making an application or claim to ensure that it is filed within the applicable time limit.

If a decision on an interlocutory application is time-sensitive, please state (both in the Application Notice and in a covering letter) the date by which a decision on the application is required.

Filing claims, appeals and non-urgent applications

1. Wherever possible, claims for judicial review, statutory appeals, planning matters, and non-urgent interlocutory applications are to be filed electronically using the Document Upload Centre.
2. Requests to upload documents should be sent
   for London cases to: *DUC@administrativecourtoffice.justice.gov.uk*
   for other offices, use the appropriate email address at Section C above.

   You will receive an invitation by email to upload your documents. You should then upload the claim/appeal/application bundle (prepared in accordance with Section A).
3. If you are commencing a claim or appeal please upload a further PDF document comprising an additional copy of the Claim Form or Notice of Appeal and the decision document challenged. If filing in London include a PBA number or proof of payment by debit/credit card or a fee remission certificate (see Section H); if you are filing the claim at any office out of London, also see Section H.
4. Documents being uploaded must be in PDF format, no other format will be accepted by the system. If the papers in support of an application for judicial review or an appeal or an application exceed 20mb, the claimant/appellant/applicant should file:
   a. a core bundle (no larger than 20mb) including, as a minimum, the Claim Form and Grounds or Notice of Appeal and Grounds, or Application Notice and Grounds; documents regarded as essential to the claim, appeal, or application (for example the decision challenged, the letter before claim and the response, etc.); any witness statements (or primary witness statement) relied on in support of the claim, appeal or application; and a draft of the order the court is asked to make; and
   b. a further bundle containing the remaining documents.
5. All electronic bundles must be prepared/formatted in accordance with the guidance at Section A.
6. Once a claim or appeal has been issued, Administrative Court staff will provide the case reference number to the parties by email.
7. Interlocutory applications should be sent by email
   for London cases to: *generaloffice@administrativecourtoffice.justice.gov.uk*
   for other offices, use the appropriate email address at Section C above.

   If filing in London include a PBA number or receipt of payment by debit/credit card (see Section H); if filing at an office out of London, also see Section H.
8. If you are not legally represented and do not have access to email, contact the Administrative Court office by telephone so that alternative arrangements can be made. For London claims the number is 020 7947 6655 (option 6). For claims at other offices use the appropriate phone number at Section C above.

Responding to claims, appeals or application notices

1. Wherever possible, any response to a claim or appeal or application notice should be filed electronically. This will include Acknowledgements of Service, Respondent's Notices, responses to interlocutory applications, and any supporting bundles.
2. File smaller documents (less than 50 pages or less than 10mb) by email. In London these should be sent to *caseprogression@administrativecourtoffice.*

justice.gov.uk, for other offices use the appropriate email address at Section C above.

3. For all larger documents use the Document Upload Centre. Any request to upload documents must be made by the professional representative by email:

    for London cases to: *DUC@administrativecourtoffice.justice.gov.uk*
    for other offices, use the appropriate email address at Section C above.

4. The requirements for the preparation of bundles at Section A and Section D (filing claims) apply and must be followed. Please note the provisions on file size.
5. If you are not legally represented and do not have access to email, you should contact the Administrative Court office by telephone so that alternative arrangements can be made. For London claims the number is 020 7947 6655 (option 6). For claims at other offices use the appropriate phone number at Section C above.

E. Non-urgent Work: Claims in Criminal Causes or Matters, Appeals by Case Stated

Filing claims and issuing applications and case stated appeals

1. Wherever possible, non-urgent claims for judicial review in criminal causes or matters and appeals by case stated are to be filed electronically using the Document Upload Centre. **54PN.1.5**
2. Requests to upload documents should be sent

    for London cases to: *crimex@administrativecourtoffice.justice.gov.uk*
    for other offices, use the appropriate email address at Section C above.

3. You will receive an invitation by email to upload your documents. You should then upload the claim/appeal/application bundle (prepared in accordance with Section A). If you are commencing a claim or appeal please also upload a further PDF document comprising an additional copy of the Claim Form or Notice of Appeal and the decision document challenged. If filing in London include a PBA number or proof of payment by debit/credit card or a fee remission certificate (see Section H); if filing at any of the out of London offices, also see Section H.
4. Once a claim or appeal has been issued, Administrative Court staff will provide the case reference number to the parties by email.
5. Interlocutory applications should be sent by email

    for London cases to: *crimex@administrativecourtoffice.justice.gov.uk*
    for other offices, please use the appropriate email address referred to at Section B above.

For London include a PBA number or receipt of payment by debit/credit card (see Section H); if you are filing the claim in one of the out of London offices, also see Section H.

6. The requirements for the preparation of bundles at Section A and Section D (filing claims) apply and must be followed. Please note the provisions on file size.
7. If you are not legally represented and do not have access to email, you should contact the Administrative Court office by telephone on 020 7947 6655 (option 6) so that alternative arrangements can be made.

Responding to claims and case stated appeals

1. Wherever possible, any response to a claim or appeal or application notice should be filed electronically. This includes Acknowledgements of

Service, Respondent's Notices, responses to interlocutory applications, and any supporting bundles.

2. File smaller documents (less than 50 pages or less than 10mb) by email. In London, use *crimex@administrativecourtoffice.justice.gov.uk*, and for other offices use the appropriate email address at Section C above.
3. For all larger documents use the Document Upload Centre. Requests to upload documents should be sent

   for London cases to: *crimex@administrativecourtoffice.justice.gov.uk*

   for other offices, use the appropriate email address at Section C above.

4. The requirements the preparation of bundles at Section A and Section D apply and must be followed. Please note the provisions on file size.
5. If you are not legally represented and do not have access to email, you should contact the Administrative Court Office by telephone on 020 7947 6655 (Option 6) so that alternative arrangements can be made.

F. Extradition Appeals

Filing appeals and issuing Application Notices

54PN.1.6 1. Wherever possible, extradition appeals and interlocutory applications in extradition appeals must be sent electronically to:

crimex@administrativecourtoffice.justice.gov.uk

Include a PBA number or proof of payment by debit/credit card (see Section H). If you are not legally represented and do not have access to email, you should contact the Administrative Court office by telephone 020 7947 6655 (Option 6) so that alternative arrangements can be made.

2. After the period for lodging amended grounds of appeal has expired the Appeal Bundle must be lodged. Please use the Document Upload Centre. Any request to upload documents must be made by the professional representative by email to:

crimex@administrativecourtoffice.justice.gov.uk

Litigants in person without access to email should contact the Court to make alternative arrangements—see paragraph 1 above.

3. Any further bundles (whether for renewed application for permission to appeal or for the hearing of the appeal) shall also be lodged in by the methods stated at paragraph 2 above.
4. All bundles for the appeal or (if heard other than at the permission to appeal hearing or the appeal hearing), for any application in the appeal must be prepared in accordance with the requirements at Section A above. If the papers in support of an appeal or application exceed 20mb, the Appellant/Applicant should file:
   a. a core bundle (no larger than 20mb) including, as a minimum, the Notice of Appeal and Grounds, or Application Notice and grounds; documents regarded as essential to the appeal, or application (for example the extradition request, the judgment of the District Judge, the Respondent's Notice etc.); any witness statements (or primary witness statement) relied on in support of the appeal or application; and a draft of the order the court is asked to make; and
   b. a further bundle containing the remaining documents.

Responding to appeals and Application Notices

1. Wherever possible, responses to appeals and Application Notices should be filed electronically with the Administrative Court.
2. File smaller documents (less than 50 pages or less than 10mb) by email, to *Crimex@administrativecourtoffice.justice.gov.uk.*

3. Larger documents should be filed using the Document Upload Centre. Any request to upload documents must be made by email to
   crimex@administrativecourtoffice.justice.gov.uk
4. Litigants in person without access to email should contact the Administrative Court office by phone on 020 7947 6655 (Option 6) so that alternative arrangements can be made.
5. Any documents for the hearing of the appeal or application must be prepared in accordance with the requirements at Section A, and be lodged in the manner described above in the paragraphs concerning the filing of appeals.

Other arrangements

G. Determination of Claims

Paper applications

Applications for permission to apply for judicial review, applications for permission to appeal, and interlocutory applications will continue to be considered on the papers, as usual. **54PN.1.7**

Orders

Orders will be served on all parties by email or, if service by email is not possible, they will be served by post.

Hearings

1. All matters for hearing will appear in the Daily Cause List. The list may be subject to change at short notice.
2. Hearings will ordinarily take place either in person (in court).
3. A judge may, on application by the parties, permit a different mode of hearing: either a hybrid hearing, or a remote hearing. A hybrid hearing is when some participants in court and others present by video. At a remote hearing all participants are present by video or phone. Hybrid hearings are conducted using the Cloud Video Platform (CVP) for persons attending by video. Remote hearings are by Cloud Video Platform (CVP) or Microsoft Teams (video), or BT Meet Me (phone). If a hearing takes place by video and/or phone, the arrangements will be made by the court.
4. If an application is made that the hearing take place as a hybrid hearing or a remote hearing, the application will be determined by a judge who will decide whether it is in the interests of justice to grant the application. Whenever possible the judge will make this decision taking account of the views of the parties.
5. If it appears a hearing may need to be vacated (e.g. by reason of illness) or the arrangements for the hearing may need to be changed (e.g. because a party is required to self-isolate), please inform the court as soon as possible.

H. Fees (Applies to All Claims)

Payment by debit or credit card (by phone or email)

You can pay a court fee for a London claim by debit or credit card by contacting the Fees Office on 020 7073 4715 between the hours of 10:00am and 16:00pm, Monday to Friday (except bank holidays) or by emailing *RCJfeespayments@justice.gov.uk* Once the payment has been processed you will receive a receipt which you should submit with the claim form and/or application form. **54PN.1.8**

Court fees for claims at other offices can also be paid by debit or credit card—please provide your contact telephone number in the email/letter that accompanies the claim or application, you will be contacted to make payment by phone.

Payment by PBA

If you have a PBA account, then you must include the reference number in a covering letter with any claim form and/or application you lodge so the fee can be deducted from this account.

Payment by cheque

Cheques should be made payable to HMCTS. The cheque should be sent together with the Claim Form or Application Notice, either by post or DX.

For London claims cheques can be sent via the drop box at the main entrance in the Royal Courts of Justice. For claims at other offices, if you have arranged to file the claim/application in person, you may bring the cheque with you.

Attending the Fees Office counter (Royal Courts of Justice, London only)

The Fees Office counter is open to the public Monday to Friday 10:00am to 4:30pm (except Bank Holidays). **Access to the Fees Office counter is on an appointment only basis. There is no walk-in facility.** To make an appointment to attend the counter contact the Fees Office, Monday to Friday 10.00am to 4.00pm (except Bank Holidays), by phone (020 7947 6527) or by email (*feesofficecounterbooking@justice.gov.uk*). Do not attend without a confirmed appointment.

Once the fee has been taken or the fee remission form completed the Claim Form, or Notice of Appeal or Application Notice may be sent and will be forwarded to the relevant Administrative Court office for processing.

Help with fees

To apply for fee remission, go to the Help with Fees website *http://www.gov.uk/get-help-withcourt-fees* and complete the step-by-step application process.

If your claim is in London forward your "HWF" reference to the Fees Office *feesrcj@justice.gov.uk* along with a copy of your Claim Form and/or application form. Please note, the number is confirmation of applying and is not confirmation of Remission entitlement. The Fees Office will process your application and contact you with the outcome of the Help with Fees application and will advise your next steps. For the out of London offices send your HWF reference along with the Claim Form and/or application form.

Add new Practice Note: The Administrative Court in Wales and on the Midland, Northern, North-Eastern and Western Circuits:

PRACTICE NOTE: THE ADMINISTRATIVE COURT IN WALES AND ON THE MIDLAND, NORTHERN, NORTH-EASTERN AND WESTERN CIRCUITS

54PN.2 With effect from 26 April 2022, the general default position in the Administrative Court in Wales and on the Midland, Northern, North-Eastern and Western Circuits will be that hearings will be in person. Any party wishing to apply for a different mode of hearing will be required to file and serve an application notice (using form **N244**, and paying the relevant fee).

The Court retains the ability of its own motion to list a hearing to be heard remotely where appropriate in accordance with the overriding objective (e.g. if a judge authorised to sit in the Planning Court is not available to hear a 30 minute oral renewal hearing in a particular centre, such a hearing may be listed for a remote hearing).

A different arrangement applies in respect of applications to extend interim orders imposed on health or social work professionals. The default position is that these hearings will be heard remotely (via a video hearing platform). However, it is open to either party to invite the Court to list the hearing in person, which request may be made by email (cc'd to the other parties) and need not be in the form of a formal application notice.

Mr Justice Fordham
Administrative Court Liaison Judge for the Northern and North-Eastern Regions

Mrs Justice Steyn
Liaison Judge for the Administrative Court in Wales, the Midland and Western Circuits

11 April 2022

PART 55

POSSESSION CLAIMS

I. General Rules

Renting homes in Wales

In the penultimate paragraph, replace the second sentence with:
Implementation of the Renting Homes (Wales) Act 2016 is now expected in December 2022. **55.2.6**

The claim form

In the first paragraph, replace the second sentence with:
The claim form must be in prescribed form (PD 55A para.1.5) and must be verified by a statement of truth (r.22.1). **55.3.4**

Case management where claim genuinely disputed on grounds which appear to be substantial

In the second paragraph, replace "Global 100 Ltd v Laleva [2021] EWCA Civ 1835," with:
Global 100 Ltd v Laleva [2021] EWCA Civ 1835; [2022] H.L.R. 20, **55.8.2**

The Debt Respite Scheme

To the end of the paragraph, add:
For examples of the operation of the scheme, see *Axnoller Events Ltd v Brake* [2021] EWHC 2308 (Ch) (mental health crisis moratorium) and *Lees v Kaye* [2022] EWHC 1151 (QB). **55.8.12**

Add new Sections IV and V:

IV. Renting Homes Wales—General Rules

Interpretation[1]

55.30 In this Section of this Part— **55.30**

- **(a) "the 2016 Act" means the Renting Homes (Wales) Act 2016;**
- **(b) "a contract-holder" is the person who makes an occupation contract with a landlord and is a contract-holder under sections 7 and 48 of the 2016 Act;**
- **(c) "Convention rights" has the meaning provided by the Human Rights Act 1998;**
- **(d) "a dwelling" means a dwelling let under an occupation contract;**

[1] Introduced by the Civil Procedure (Amendment No.2) Rules 2022 (SI 2022/783).

(e) "an extended possession order" means an order for possession against a sub-holder under section 65 of the 2016 Act;
(f) "an occupation contract" is a tenancy or licence that is an occupation contract under section 7 of the 2016 Act;
(g) "a prohibited conduct standard contract order claim" means a claim under section 116 of the 2016 Act;
(h) "a Renting Homes possession claim" means a claim for the recovery of possession of a dwelling under the 2016 Act;
(i) "a sub-holder" has the meaning provided by section 59 of the 2016 Act;
(j) "a standard contract" has the meaning provided by section 8 of the 2016 Act.

Scope[1]

55.31 55.31—(1) The procedure set out in this Section of this Part must be used where the claim is a Renting Homes possession claim.

(Where a prohibited conduct standard contract order claim is made in the same claim form in which a Renting Homes possession claim is made, this Section of this Part applies. Where the claim is a prohibited conduct standard contract order claim only, Section III of Part 65 applies.)

(2) This Section of this Part—
(a) is subject to any enactment or practice direction which sets out special provisions with regard to any particular category of claim;
(b) does not apply where the claimant uses the procedure set out in Section V of this Part;
(c) applies irrespective of whether an application for an extended possession order may be made in the course of the Renting Homes possession claim.

Starting the claim[2]

55.32 55.32—(1) In the County Court—
(a) the claimant may make the claim at any County Court hearing centre, unless paragraph (2) applies or an enactment provides otherwise;
(b) the claim is to be issued by the hearing centre where the claim is made; and
(c) if that hearing centre does not serve the address where the dwelling is situated, the claim is to be sent, after issue, to the hearing centre serving that address.

(Practice Direction 55A includes further direction in respect of claims which are not made at the County Court hearing centre which serves the address where the dwelling is situated.)

(2) The claim may be started in the High Court if the claimant files with their claim form a certificate stating the reasons for bringing the claim in that court verified by a statement of truth in accordance with rule 22.1(1).

(3) The claim form and form of defence sent with it must be in the forms specified in Practice Direction 55A.

Particulars of claim[3]

55.33 55.33 The particulars of claim must be filed and served with the claim form.

---

[1] Introduced by the Civil Procedure (Amendment No.2) Rules 2022 (SI 2022/783).
[2] Introduced by the Civil Procedure (Amendment No.2) Rules 2022 (SI 2022/783).
[3] Introduced by the Civil Procedure (Amendment No.2) Rules 2022 (SI 2022/783).

(Part 16 and Practice Direction 55A provide details about the contents of the particulars of claim.)

Hearing date[1]

55.34—(1) Subject to paragraph (2), the court is to fix a date for the hearing when it issues the claim form. 55.34

(2) If the claim has been sent on to the hearing centre which serves the address where the dwelling is situated, that hearing centre is to fix a date for hearing when it receives the claim.

(3) In all Renting Homes possession claims—

- (a) the hearing date is to be not less than 28 days from the date of issue of the claim form;
- (b) the standard period between the issue of the claim form and the hearing is to be not more than 8 weeks; and
- (c) the defendant must be served with the claim form and particulars of claim not less than 21 days before the hearing date.

Defendant's response and adding of sub-holder as a party[2]

55.35—(1) An acknowledgment of service is not required and Part 10 does not apply. 55.35

(2) Where, in any Renting Homes possession claim, the defendant does not file a defence within the time specified in rule 15.4, the defendant may take part in any hearing but the court may take their failure to do so into account when deciding what order to make about costs.

(3) Part 12 (default judgment) does not apply in a claim to which this Section applies.

(4) Where a sub-holder applies to the court to be added as a party to proceedings, the court must add them as a defendant if they are entitled to be a party under section 65(4) of the 2016 Act.

The hearing[3]

55.36—(1) At the hearing fixed in accordance with rule 55.34 or at any adjournment of that hearing, the court may— 55.36

- (a) decide the claim; or
- (b) give case management directions.

(2) Where the claim is genuinely disputed on grounds which appear to be substantial, case management directions given under paragraph (1)(b) will include the allocation of the claim to a track or directions to enable it to be allocated.

(3) Except where—

- (a) the claim is allocated to the fast track or the multi-track; or
- (b) the court orders otherwise,

any fact that needs to be proved by the evidence of witnesses at a hearing referred to in paragraph (1) may be proved by evidence in writing.

(4) All witness statements must be filed and served at least 2 days before the hearing.

(5) Where the claimant serves the claim form and particulars of claim, the claimant must produce at the hearing a certificate of service of those documents and rule 6.17(2)(a) does not apply.

---

[1] Introduced by the Civil Procedure (Amendment No.2) Rules 2022 (SI 2022/783).
[2] Introduced by the Civil Procedure (Amendment No.2) Rules 2022 (SI 2022/783).
[3] Introduced by the Civil Procedure (Amendment No.2) Rules 2022 (SI 2022/783).

Allocation[1]

55.37 **55.37—(1) When the court decides the track for a Renting Homes possession claim, the matters it must consider include—**

(a) the matters set out in rule 26.8 as modified by the relevant practice direction;

(b) the amount of any arrears of rent;

(c) the importance to the defendant of retaining possession of the dwelling;

(d) the importance of vacant possession to the claimant; and

(e) if applicable, the alleged conduct of the defendant.

(2) The court may only allocate Renting Homes possession claims to the small claims track if all the parties agree.

(3) Where a Renting Homes possession claim has been allocated to the small claims track the claim must be treated, for the purposes of costs, as if it were proceeding on the fast track except that trial costs are to be in the discretion of the court and must not exceed the amount that would be recoverable under rule 45.38 (amount of fast track costs) if the value of the claim were up to £3,000.

(4) Where all the parties agree the court may, when it allocates the claim, order that rule 27.14 (costs on the small claims track) applies and, where it does so, paragraph (3) does not apply.

Electronic issue of certain Renting Homes possession claims[2]

55.38 **55.38—(1) A practice direction may make provision for a claimant to start certain types of Renting Homes possession claim in certain courts by requesting the issue of a claim form electronically.**

(2) The practice direction may, in particular—

(a) provide that only particular provisions apply in specific courts;

(b) specify—

(i) the type of claim which may be issued electronically;

(ii) the conditions that a claim must meet before it may be issued electronically;

(c) specify the court where the claim may be issued;

(d) enable the parties to make certain applications or take further steps in relation to the claim electronically;

(e) specify the requirements that must be fulfilled in relation to such applications or steps;

(f) enable the parties to correspond electronically with the court about the claim;

(g) specify the requirements that must be fulfilled in relation to electronic correspondence;

(h) provide how any fee payable on the filing of any document is to be paid where the document is filed electronically.

(3) The practice direction may disapply or modify these Rules as appropriate in relation to claims started electronically.

[1] Introduced by the Civil Procedure (Amendment No.2) Rules 2022 (SI 2022/783).
[2] Introduced by the Civil Procedure (Amendment No.2) Rules 2022 (SI 2022/783).

V. Renting Homes Wales—Accelerated Possession Claims of Dwellings Let on a Standard Contract

Interpretation[1]

55.39 The definitions set out in rule 55.30 apply to this Section also. **55.39**

When this Section may be used[2]

55.40—(1) The claimant may bring a Renting Homes possession claim under this Section of this Part where— **55.40**

(a) the claim is brought under—

(i) section 170 of the 2016 Act to recover possession of a dwelling let under a periodic standard contract (following contract-holder's notice);

(ii) section 178 of the 2016 Act to recover possession of a dwelling let under a periodic standard contract (landlord's notice);

(iii) section 186 of the 2016 Act to recover possession of a dwelling let under a fixed term standard contract (landlord's notice at end of fixed term);

(iv) section 191 of the 2016 Act to recover possession of a dwelling let under a fixed term standard contract (following contract-holder's break clause); or

(v) section 199 of the 2016 Act to recover possession of a dwelling let on a fixed term standard contract (landlord's break clause); and

(b) all the conditions listed in rule 55.41 are satisfied.

(2) The claimant may make the claim at any County Court hearing centre, unless an enactment provides otherwise.

(3) The claim is to be issued by the hearing centre where the claim is made.

(4) If the hearing centre where the claim is made does not serve the address where the dwelling is situated, the claim is to be sent, after issue, to the hearing centre serving that address.

Conditions[3]

55.41 The conditions referred to in rule 55.40(1)(b) are that— **55.41**

(a) the only purpose of the claim is to recover possession of the dwelling and no other claim is made;

(b) the claim relates to an occupation contract which is a standard contract; and

(c) a prescribed notice in accordance with any of the following sections of the 2016 Act was given to the contract-holder—

(i) section 171 (if the claim is brought under section 170 of that Act);

(ii) section 173 (if the claim is brought under section 178 of that Act);

(iii) section 186 (if the claim is brought under that section);

(iv) section 192 (if the claim is brought under section 191 of that Act); or

(v) section 194 (if the claim is brought under section 199 of that Act).

---

[1] Introduced by the Civil Procedure (Amendment No.2) Rules 2022 (SI 2022/783).
[2] Introduced by the Civil Procedure (Amendment No.2) Rules 2022 (SI 2022/783).
[3] Introduced by the Civil Procedure (Amendment No.2) Rules 2022 (SI 2022/783).

Claim form[1]

55.42 **55.42—(1) The claim form must—**

(a) be in the form specified in Practice Direction 55A; and

(b) contain all information and be accompanied by all documents as are required by that form.

(2) The court is to serve the claim form by first class post (or an alternative service which provides for delivery on the next working day).

Defence[2]

55.43 **55.43—(1) A defendant who wishes to—**

(a) oppose the claim; or

(b) seek a postponement of possession in accordance with rule 55.47,

must file a defence within 14 days after service of the claim form.

(2) The defence must be in the form specified in Practice Direction 55A.

Claim referred to judge[3]

55.44 **55.44—(1) On receipt of the defence the court must—**

(a) send a copy to the claimant; and

(b) refer the claim and defence to a judge.

(2) Where the period set out in rule 55.43 has expired without the defendant filing a defence—

(a) the claimant may file a written request for an order for possession; and

(b) the court must refer that request to a judge.

(3) Where the defence is received after the period set out in rule 55.43 has expired but before a request is filed in accordance with paragraph (2), paragraph (1) still applies.

(4) Where—

(a) the period set out in rule 55.43 has expired without the defendant filing a defence; and

(b) the claimant has not made a request for an order for possession under paragraph (2) within 3 months after the expiry of the period set out in rule 55.43,

the claim must be stayed.

Consideration of the claim[4]

55.45 **55.45—(1) After considering the claim and any defence, the judge may—**

(a) make an order for possession under rule 55.46 without requiring the attendance of the parties;

(b) strike out the claim if the claim form discloses no reasonable grounds for bringing the claim; or

(c) where paragraphs (2) or (3) apply—

(i) direct that a date be fixed for a hearing; and

(ii) give any appropriate case management directions.

(2) This paragraph applies where the judge is not satisfied either that the claim form was served or that the claimant has established that they are entitled to recover possession from the defendant.

(3) This paragraph applies where—

(a) an application under section 36 (incomplete written statement) or section 37 (incorrect statement: contract-holder's application to the court) of the 2016 Act has been made (and not disposed of) in con-

---

[1] Introduced by the Civil Procedure (Amendment No.2) Rules 2022 (SI 2022/783).

[2] Introduced by the Civil Procedure (Amendment No.2) Rules 2022 (SI 2022/783).

[3] Introduced by the Civil Procedure (Amendment No.2) Rules 2022 (SI 2022/783).

[4] Introduced by the Civil Procedure (Amendment No.2) Rules 2022 (SI 2022/783).

nection with the occupation contract of the dwelling in respect of which the possession claim has been brought;

(b) the claim is a claim under section 178 or section 199 of the 2016 Act, where the issue of retaliatory possession has been raised under section 217 of the 2016 Act;

(c) the claim is a claim under section 170, section 178, section 186, section 191 or section 199 of the 2016 Act, where a defence based on the defendant's Convention rights is raised.

(5) The court is to give all parties not less than 14 days' notice of a hearing fixed under paragraph (1)(c)(i).

(6) Where a claim is struck out under paragraph (1)(b)—

(a) the court is to serve its reasons for striking out the claim with the order; and

(b) the claimant may apply to restore the claim within 28 days after the date the order was served on them.

Possession order[1]

55.46 Except where rules 55.45(1)(b) or (c) apply, the judge must make an order for possession without requiring the attendance of the parties. **55.46**

Postponement of possession[2]

55.47—(1) Where the defendant seeks postponement of possession on the ground of exceptional hardship under section 219 of the 2016 Act, the judge may direct a hearing of that issue. **55.47**

(2) Where the judge directs a hearing under paragraph (1)—

(a) the hearing must be held before the date on which possession is to be given up; and

(b) the judge must direct how many days' notice the parties must be given of that hearing.

(3) Where the judge is satisfied, on a hearing directed under paragraph (1), that exceptional hardship would be caused by requiring possession to be given up by the date in the order of possession, the judge may vary the date on which possession must be given up.

Application to set aside or vary[3]

55.48 The court may— **55.48**

(a) on application by a party within 14 days of service of the order; or

(b) of its own initiative,

set aside or vary any order made under rule 55.46.

PRACTICE DIRECTION 55A—POSSESSION CLAIMS

Section I—General Rules

55.3—Starting the claim

Replace paragraph 1.5 with:

1.5 The claimant must use the appropriate claim form and particulars of claim form. The defence must be in form **N11**, **N11B**, **N11M** or **N11R**, as appropriate. **55APD.1**

[1] Introduced by the Civil Procedure (Amendment No.2) Rules 2022 (SI 2022/783).
[2] Introduced by the Civil Procedure (Amendment No.2) Rules 2022 (SI 2022/783).
[3] Introduced by the Civil Procedure (Amendment No.2) Rules 2022 (SI 2022/783).

Add new Section V:

Section V—Renting Homes Wales Possession Claims

55APD.15 **11.1** Subject to paragraph 11. 3 and the modifications in this Section, Sections I, II and IV of this Practice Direction apply in relation to Renting Homes possession claims.

11.2 In Sections I, II and IV—

(a) any reference to land or property (unless the context otherwise requires) includes reference to a dwelling;

(b) any reference to a possession claim includes reference to a Renting Homes possession claim;

(c) any reference to a tenancy includes reference to an occupation contract and any reference to a tenant includes reference to a contract-holder; and

(d) any reference to a demotion claim includes reference to a prohibited conduct standard contract order claim and any reference to a demotion order includes reference to a prohibited conduct standard contract order under section 116 of the 2016 Act.

11.3 Paragraphs 2.1(2), 2.4, 2.5, 2.5A, 2.6, 4.1, 7.1 and 7.2 do not apply.

11.4 In paragraph 1.5—

(a) reference to the appropriate claim form and particular of claim is to the following forms as appropriate—

(i) **N5 (W)** claim for possession of property;

(ii) **N5B (W)** claim for possession of property—Accelerated;

(iii) **N121 (W)** claim form (Trespassers);

(iv) **N120 (W)** Claim Form (Mortgaged residential premises);

(v) **N119 (W)** POC (residential possession); and

(b) reference to the applicable defence form in connection with a Renting Homes possession claim is to Form **N11 R (W)** defence form (Rented Premises); and

(c) a claim for an extended possession order must be in the relevant claim form listed in paragraph (a) and be accompanied by the notice required under section 65(3)(b) of the 2016 Act.

11.5 Paragraph 2.1(4) is to be read as referring only to details about any occupation contract.

11.6 Paragraph 2.7 has effect that if the claim is a Renting Homes possession claim under section 178 or section 181 of the 2016 Act in relation to an occupation contract which is a prohibited conduct standard contract or introductory standard contract (provided for under section 16 of that Act), the particulars of claim must have attached to them a copy of the notice provided to the contract-holder in accordance with section 173 or section 182 of that Act.

11.7 In paragraphs 8.1, 8.3 and 8.4 reference to section 89 of the Housing Act 1980 includes reference to section 219 of the 2016 Act.

11.8 Paragraph 10.1 has effect as including reference to sections 211(2) and (3) of the 2016 Act.

PRACTICE DIRECTION 55B—POSSESSION CLAIMS ONLINE

Claims Which May Be Started Using Possession Claims Online

In paragraph 5.1, replace list items (1) and (2) with:

55BPD.5 (1) it is brought under Sections I or IV of Part 55;

(2) it includes a possession claim for residential property or a Renting homes possession claim by—

(a) a landlord against a tenant or contract holder, solely on the ground of arrears of rent (but not a claim for forfeiture of a lease); or

(b) a mortgagee against a mortgagor, solely on the ground of default in the payment of sums due under a mortgage,

relating to land the address for which is served by a County Court hearing centre;

Starting a Claim

Replace paragraph 6.2 with:

6.2 The particulars of claim must be included in the online claim form and may not be filed separately. It is not necessary to file a copy of the tenancy agreement, occupation contract, mortgage deed or mortgage agreement with the particulars of claim. **55BPD.6**

Replace paragraph 6.2A with:

6.2A In the case of a possession claim for residential property or a renting homes possession claim that relies on a statutory ground or grounds for possession, the claimant must specify, in section 4(a) of the online claim form, the ground or grounds relied on.

In paragraph 6.3, replace list item (1) with:

(1) the dates and amounts of all payments due and payments made under the tenancy agreement, occupation contract, mortgage deed or mortgage agreement either from the first date of default if that date occurred less than two years before the date of issue or for a period of two years immediately preceding the date of issue; and

In paragraph 6.3A, replace list item (1) with:

(1) details of the dates and amounts of all payments due and payments made under the tenancy agreement, occupation contract, mortgage deed or mortgage account—
   (a) for a period of two years immediately preceding the date of commencing proceedings; or
   (b) if the first date of default occurred less than two years before that date, from the first date of default; and

In paragraph 6.3B, replace list item (1) with:

(1) the amount of arrears—
   (a) as stated in the notice served—
      (i) under section 83 of the Housing Act 1985;
      (ii) under section 8 of the Housing Act 1988; or
      (iii) under section 159, 182 or 188 of the Renting Homes (Wales) Act 2016; or
   (b) as at the date of the claimant's letter before action,

as appropriate;

In paragraph 6.3C, replace the last paragraph with:

(Rules 55.8(4) and 55.36(4) require all witness statements to be filed and served at least 2 days before the hearing.)

Electronic Applications

Replace paragraph 11.1 with:

11.1 Certain applications in relation to a possession claim or Renting Homes possession claim started online may be made electronically ("online applications"). An online application may be made if a form for that application is published on the PCOL website ("online application form") and the application is made at least five clear days before the hearing. **55BPD.11**

PART 56

Change title of Part:

LANDLORD AND TENANT CLAIMS AND MISCELLANEOUS PROVISIONS ABOUT LAND AND CLAIMS UNDER THE RENTING HOMES (WALES) ACT 2016

Add new Section III:

III. Applications and Claims to the Court under the Renting Homes (Wales) Act 2016

Scope and interpretation[1]

56.5 **56.5—(1) In this Section of this Part—**

(a) "the 2016 Act" means the Renting Homes (Wales) Act 2016;

(b) "Renting Homes (Wales) claim" means a claim or application under the 2016 Act other than a claim —

(i) for possession;

(ii) for a prohibited conduct standard contract order under section 116 of the 2016 Act;

(iii) to which the Pre-Action Protocol for Housing Disrepair Cases applies; or

(iv) brought in the same proceedings as a claim under rule 56.5(a) to (c); and includes an appeal under section 78 of the 2016 Act;

(c) "the claimant" meansthe person making the Renting Homes (Wales) claim, irrespective of whether it is a claim or application under the 2016 Act.

Making the Renting Homes (Wales) claim[2]

56.6 **56.6 In the County Court, the Renting Homes (Wales) claim—**

(a) may be made at any County Court hearing centre;

(b) is to be issued by the hearing centre where the claim is made; and

(c) if not made at the County Court hearing centre which serves the address where the land is situated, is to be sent to the hearing centre serving that address.

Further provision for Renting Homes (Wales) claims[3]

56.7 **56.7 A practice direction may set out provisions with regard to Renting Homes (Wales) claims.**

After Practice Direction 56–Landlord and Tenant Claims and Miscellaneous Claims about Land, add new Practice Direction 56A–Renting Homes (Wales) Claims:

PRACTICE DIRECTION 56A—RENTING HOMES (WALES) CLAIMS

This practice direction supplements CPR Part 56

Introduction

56APD.1 **1.1** In addition to any relevant definitions in Part 56, particularly those in rule 56.5, which all apply to this practice direction in any event, terms defined in the 2016 Act have the same meaning in this practice direction.

1.2 This practice direction makes provision for the bringing of Renting

[1] Introduced by the Civil Procedure (Amendment No.2) Rules 2022 (SI 2022/783).
[2] Introduced by the Civil Procedure (Amendment No.2) Rules 2022 (SI 2022/783).
[3] Introduced by the Civil Procedure (Amendment No.2) Rules 2022 (SI 2022/783).

Homes (Wales) claims. Where a claim for possession, the making of a prohibited conduct standard contract order, or a claim for damages for disrepair is made at the commencement of proceedings Section III of Part 56 does not apply and the procedure for those particular claims should be followed.

Starting the claim

2.1(1) "Permission to make an out of time application" means an application for permission to make an application out of time under the following provisions of the 2016 Act— **56APD.2**

(a) section 14(4);
(b) paragraph 16(4) of Schedule 2;
(c) paragraph 5(4) of Schedule 4; or
(d) paragraph 6(4) of Schedule 7.

(2) Where permission to make an out of time application is sought before the substantive application is made, it should be sought by written request.

(3) Where permission to make an out of time application is sought at the same time as the substantive application is made it should be sought as part of substantive claim using the procedure appropriate for that claim.

2.2 Renting Homes (Wales) claims should normally be brought in the county court. Only exceptional circumstances justify starting a claim in the High Court even if the High Court has jurisdiction.

2.3 If a claimant starts a claim in the High Court and the court decides that it should have been started in the County Court, the court will normally either strike the claim out or transfer it to the County Court on its own initiative. This is likely to result in delay and the court will normally disallow the costs of starting the claim in the High Court and of any transfer.

2.4 Circumstances which may, in an appropriate case, justify starting a claim in the High Court are if—

(a) there are complicated disputes of fact; or
(b) there are points of law of general importance.

2.5 The value of the property and the amount of any financial claim may be relevant circumstances, but these factors alone will not normally justify starting the claim in the High Court.

2.8 A Renting Homes (Wales) claim started in the High Court must be brought in the Chancery Division.

Contents of the claim form in all cases

3.1 The claim form must contain details of— **56APD.3**

(a) the dwelling to which the claim relates;
(b) the particulars of the current occupation contract (including date, parties and duration) insofar as the claimant is able to confirm the same;
(c) any notice relevant to the claim;
(d) the provisions of the 2016 Act under which the claim is brought.

Particular Renting Homes (Wales) claims

Application under section 14(2) of the 2016 Act (review of the landlord's decision to give notice of standard contract)

4.1 The evidence in support of the Renting Homes (Wales) claim must include a copy of the notice given by the landlord under section 13 of the 2016 Act. **56APD.4**

Applications under sections 34, 36 and 37 of the 2016 Act (application for declaration about an occupation contract: missing, incomplete or incorrect contract terms)

4.2 The claim form or evidence in support of the Renting Homes (Wales) claim must give details of any fundamental or supplementary provision which the claimant claims was not incorporated into the occupation contract or was incorporated with modification and identify such modifications.

Application under section 44 of the 2016 Act (application for order to return security)

4.3 The claim form must give details of the security that has been given and the person who appears to be holding the property constituting that security.

Application under section 66 of the 2016 Act (application by sub-holder to end contract-holder's occupation contract)

4.4 The claim form must give details of the landlord and the evidence in support of the Renting Homes (Wales) claim must include a copy of the notice given under section 66(3) of the 2016 Act and proof that such notice was given to both the contract-holder and to the contract-holder's landlord.

Appeal under section 78 of the 2016 Act (appeal as to who is to succeed to an occupation contract)

4.5 The claim form must give details of all relevant successors and any reasons given by the landlord for the selection made by the landlord.

Application under section 85 of the 2016 Act (application for declaration or order about a landlord's refusal, or conditions of, giving consent)

4.6 The claim form must give details of the request for consent and the evidence in support of the Renting Homes (Wales) claim must include the landlord's written statement giving reasons for refusing consent or consenting subject to conditions.

Application under section 87 of the 2016 Act (compensation for failure relating to provision of written statements)

4.7 Where a Renting Homes (Wales) claim is made for compensation under section 87 of the 2016 Act whether on its own or in combination with other claims under the 2016 Act the proceedings should normally be commenced under Part 7. The claim form must provide details of the rent payable under the occupation contract and the amount of compensation claimed.

Application under section 140 of the 2016 Act (application for order requiring a joint contract-holder to join a transfer)

4.8 The evidence in support of such a Renting Homes (Wales) claim must include a copy of the occupation contract or give full details of the terms relied upon and the reasons why a copy of the contract cannot be provided.

Claim under section 208 of the 2016 Act (claim for misrepresentation or concealment of facts used to obtain order for possession)

4.9 If the Renting Homes (Wales) claim for compensation is not made in the original proceedings the claim should normally be commenced under Part 7.

Application under sections 222, 226 and 228 of the 2016 Act (remedies against the landlord: order or declaration of the court)

4.10 The claim form must give details of the grounds on which the claimant relies and the evidence in support of the Renting Homes (Wales) claim must include copies of any notices given to the contract-holder under sections 220, 225 or 227 of the 2016 Act.

Application under paragraph 16 of Schedule 2 of the 2016 Act (review of decision to extend the period of a licence or tenancy that is not an occupation contract)

4.11 The evidence in support of the Renting Homes (Wales) claim for a review must include a copy of the landlord's notice of extension.

Application under paragraph 5 of Schedule 4 of the 2016 Act (review of decision to confirm extension of introductory period)

4.12 The evidence in support of the Renting Homes (Wales) claim for a review must include copies of the landlord's notice of extension of the introductory period and the landlord's notice after review confirming their decision to give a notice of extension of the introductory period.

Application under paragraphs 2 or 3 of Schedule 5 of the 2016 Act (applications in relation to deposit schemes)

4.13 The Renting Homes (Wales) claim should normally be commenced under Part 7 and the particulars of claim must confirm—

(a) the amount of the deposit paid; and
(b) the ground or grounds on which the application is made.

Application under paragraph 6 of Schedule 7 of the 2016 Act (review of decision to extend probation period)

4.14 The evidence in support of the Renting Homes (Wales) claim for a review must include copies of the landlord's notice of extension of the probation period and the landlord's notice after review confirming their decision to give a notice of extension of the probation period.

Application under paragraph 7 of Schedule 7 of the 2016 Act (application for order to end a probation period early)

4.15 The claim form must identify the ground or grounds on which the Renting Homes (Wales) claim is made. The evidence in support of such application must include a copy of the order made under section 116 of the 2016 Act imposing the periodic standard contract and confirm that the landlord had not made an appropriate programme of social support available to the contract-holder and that it is unlikely that such support will be made available if paragraph 7(3)(b) of Schedule 7 of the 2016 Act is relied upon.

PART 57

PROBATE, INHERITANCE, PRESUMPTION OF DEATH AND GUARDIANSHIP OF MISSING PERSONS

I. Probate Claims

Editorial note

Add new paragraph at end:

Original testamentary documents may be released by the court for examination by an expert. An **57.5.1** application for their release should be made under CPR Pt 23. In the case of a represented party, the court will require an undertaking by that party's solicitor to return the documents to the court by a specific date. In the case of an unrepresented party, the court will require an undertaking from that party. For a form of order see Form **CH27**.

III. Substitution and Removal of Personal Representatives

Editorial note

Replace the last paragraph with:

Note the requirements at PD 57 para.13.2 to file with the claim form a signed consent to act and **57.13.1** written evidence as to the fitness (suitability) of the proposed substitute personal representative to act as such. The written evidence as to the fitness of the proposed substitute personal representative to act should be provided by an independent person and not by the proposed substitute personal representative themselves. It should state for how long they have known the person proposed to act and confirm the person proposed to act is of good character and a suitable person to administer the estate.

IV. Claims under the Inheritance (Provision for Family and Dependants) Act 1975

Procedure

Add new paragraph 57.16.1.1:

57.16.1.1 *Parties*—Where a grant has been obtained, the personal representatives are necessary parties to the claim. The taking of a grant by the claimant is no bar to an application under the Act. An application under the Act does not impugn the validity of the grant or the will (if any). There is no need for a spouse or civil partner to renounce probate or the right to letters of administration if such a person wishes to claim under the Act. The personal representative may in that situation be the claimant. There is no need for the same person also to be joined as a defendant in their capacity as personal representative. For the possibility of a person bringing proceedings in one capacity against themselves in a different category, see *Re Cwmni Rheoli Pentref Marina Conwy Cyfynedig (Conway Marina Village Management Co)* [2021] EWHC 1275 (Ch) and commentary at para.19.1.4 above.

Any other personal representative should be joined as a defendant. At least one of the main beneficiaries should be joined at the outset. In a simple case where there are two or three beneficiaries equally entitled to the estate under the will or intestacy, they should all be joined at the outset. If the beneficiaries are numerous, a representation order may be asked for under r.19.7(1)(d) or the court asked to direct that notice of the claim be given to them under r.19.8A.

VI. Proceedings under the Guardianship (Missing Persons) Act 2017

Editorial note

To the end of the fifth paragraph (beginning "Under s.1 of"), add:

57.25.1 Section 3(2)(b) of the Act provides that the court may make a guardianship order where a person has been missing throughout the period of 90 days ending with the day on which the application was made ("the absence condition"). Where the absence condition is not met, the court may make a guardianship order if satisfied that a decision is needed, or is likely to be needed, in relation to property or financial affairs of the missing person ("the urgency condition") under s.3(3)(b). Where the absence condition is not met, the witness statement in support of the application must provide reasons why the claimant considers the urgency condition is met, and attach any supporting evidence: PD 57C para.1.3.

PRACTICE DIRECTION 57—PROBATE

Annex

A Form of Witness Statement or Affidavit about Testamentary Documents (CPR Rule 57.5)

Replace the penultimate paragraph with:

57PD.19 [I believe that the facts stated in this witness statement are true] [I understand that proceedings for contempt of court may be brought against anyone who makes, or causes to be made, a false statement in a document verified by a statement of truth without an honest belief in its truth.] [*or jurat for affidavit*]

PRACTICE DIRECTION 57C—PROCEEDINGS UNDER THE GUARDIANSHIP (MISSING PERSONS) ACT 2017

Practice Direction 8A (alternative procedure for claims)

Replace paragraph 7.1 with:

57CPD.7 **7.1** [Omitted].

PART 57A

BUSINESS AND PROPERTY COURTS

Practice Guidance in the Business and Property Courts

Replace "(see para.51UPD.1)." with:
(see para.57ADPD.1). **57A.0.2**

Pilot Schemes operating in the Business and Property Courts

Replace paragraph with:
For pilot schemes specifically operative in the Business and Property Courts, see the Electronic Working Pilot Scheme (paras 51.2.3 and 51OPD.1). **57A.0.3**

Change title of paragraph: **57A.0.4**

Electronic bundles in remote hearings

PRACTICE DIRECTION 57AB—SHORTER AND FLEXIBLE TRIALS SCHEMES

Suitability for Shorter Trials Scheme

Replace paragraph with:
In determining whether a claim was suitable for the shorter trial scheme it was appropriate to consider the extent of disclosure; the nature of any expert evidence; the likely trial length, and particularly if the trial could be expected to be no more than four days in length. In doing so it was important to focus on the nature of the shorter trial scheme, such that even where statements of case disclosed a degree of complexity that might suggest the dispute was outside its scope, the overall nature of the dispute, i.e. the extent of the evidence, disclosure and likely trial length, could still justify proceeding under the scheme. **57ABPD.5.1**

It is essential that the decision to allocate a claim to the shorter trial scheme is kept under continuous review. The scheme must not be used to cut corners in the resolution of proceedings consistently with the overriding objective. A decision to transfer a claim to or keep a claim on the shorter trial scheme may be revisited in the light of developments in the course of case management. The court has jurisdiction under CPR r.3.1(2)(m) to transfer a claim out of the scheme: see *EMFC Loan Syndications LLP v Resort Group Plc* [2021] EWCA Civ 844; [2022] 1 W.L.R. 717 at [111], *Excel-Eucan Ltd v Source Vagabond System Ltd* [2018] EWHC 3864 (Ch). Also see *Sprint Electric Ltd v Buyer's Dream Ltd* [2019] EWHC 1853 (Ch), noted at para.57ABPD.4.1.

PRACTICE DIRECTION 57AC—TRIAL WITNESS STATEMENTS IN THE BUSINESS AND PROPERTY COURTS

Editorial note

To the end of the paragraph, add:
Where parties make oppressive or disproportionate applications for sanctions, particularly strike out sanctions, they are at risk of adverse costs being awarded on an indemnity basis. When assessing what steps to take in respect of alleged non-compliance by another party, common sense and proportionality should guide parties: *Curtiss v Zurich Insurance Plc* [2022] EWHC 1514 (TCC) at [19]-[21]. **57ACPD.0.1**

Add new Practice Direction 57AD–Disclosure in the Business and Property Courts:

PRACTICE DIRECTION 57AD—DISCLOSURE IN THE BUSINESS AND PROPERTY COURTS

This practice direction supplements CPR Part 57A

Editorial introduction

Practice Direction 57AD was introduced by CPR Update 149 (July 2022). It substantively reproduced and brought within the CPR PD 51U–The Disclosure Pilot Scheme and came into force on 1 October 2022. The disclosure pilot scheme, which ran from January 2019 to October 2022 was the result of concerns that reforms to CPR Pt 31 introduced in 1999 and then in 2013 had failed to introduce a more proportionate, economical and efficient approach to disclosure. **57ADPD.0.1**

Those concerns resulted in the formation of a Disclosure Working Group in 2016. It identified a number of problems with Pt 31, including a failure on the part of both the courts and parties to use the full range of disclosure options, set out in CPR r.31.5. Standard disclosure too often remained the default. Additionally, Pt 31 was noted to be insufficiently able to deal with e-disclosure.

The pilot scheme was intended to remedy the various problems with disclosure, and not least to ensure that a new, proportionate, culture of disclosure was embedded into the litigation process. It was intended to operate "along different lines driven by reasonableness and proportionality" (*UTB LLC v Sheffield United Ltd* [2019] EWHC 914 (Ch); [2019] 3 All E.R. 698, at [75]). Under the pilot, disclosure was to be focused on the key Issues for Disclosure In this way it was intended to strike a better balance between wider disclosure, where and only where that is appropriate, and the aim of reducing the amount of unnecessary documentary disclosure, either because it is irrelevant or peripheral to the issues in dispute. To effect the necessary culture change the court was required to take a more pro-active approach to the case management of the disclosure process and parties had to ensure that they acted consistently with the Disclosure Duties contained in pilot scheme. The pilot scheme was subject to a number of significant revisions aimed at improving its operation. Practice Direction 57AD is expected to operate consistently with the approach taken to the pilot scheme's operation, i.e. to maintain the more proportionate and targeted approach to disclosure effected by the scheme.

Application of the Practice Direction

57ADPD.0.2 The Practice Direction applies to existing and new proceedings in the Business and Property Courts of England and Wales and those courts in Birmingham, Bristol, Cardiff, Leeds, Liverpool, Manchester and Newcastle. It does not apply in the County Court. Where orders for disclosure were made prior to its commencement date (1 October 2022) or before proceedings are transferred to the Business and Property Courts, they remain in place unless varied or set aside. Where proceedings are transferred out of the Business and Property Courts, any disclosure order made under this Practice Direction remains in place unless and until further order: see PD 57AD paras 1.2 and 1.3. Paragraphs 1.4, 1.5, 1.8, 1.11 and 1.12 make further provision for its application, including guidance on the application of the Practice Direction to claims brought under CPR Pt 8.

Where provisions of the Practice Direction conflict with other parts of the CPR and its Practice Directions, those in this Practice Direction take precedence: para.1.6.

Relationship with pre-action disclosure under CPR r.31.16

57ADPD.0.3 In *A v B* [2019] 10 WLUK 65 Knowles J considered and refused an application for pre-action disclosure. In the course of his judgment he noted that the proposed approach to disclosure, post-issue, was that of standard disclosure. He expressed the view that the approach to disclosure under the disclosure pilot scheme, with its focus on the court working with the parties to define the issues and apply the most appropriate disclosure model under the scheme, was preferable, and that this was particularly the case where disclosure was sought of communications.

Party co-operation

57ADPD.0.4 The disclosure pilot scheme is intended to introduce a new culture of disclosure. In *McParland & Partners Ltd v Whitehead* [2020] EWHC 298 (Ch), Vos C at [4], [53]-[54] and [58] stressed that party co-operation was imperative. Party co-operation, carried out constructively in order to identify those documents required to enable claims to be resolved fairly, is an essential means by which disproportionate disclosure cost could be avoided. He specifically deprecated use of the pilot scheme to derive procedural or tactical advantage. Serious adverse cost sanctions ought to be expected by parties who adopt such meretricious tactics. Given that PD 57AD was intended to formalise the disclosure pilot scheme in the CPR and substantively reproduces it, his guidance ought to apply, mutatis mutandis, to PD 57AD.

Inherent jurisdiction to direct disclosure

57ADPD.0.5 The court's inherent jurisdiction, codified in CPR r.3.1(2)(m) to direct disclosure should not be applied inconsistently with PD 57AD: *Patisserie Holdings Plc (In Liquidation) v Grant Thornton UK LLP* [2021] EWHC 3022 (Comm) at [37]. The same approach ought to apply under PD 57AD.

Residual power to order specific disclosure

57ADPD.0.6 In *White Winston Select Asset Funds LLC v Mahon* [2019] EWHC 1014 (Ch) at [11]-[13], Edwin Johnson QC, sitting as a deputy judge of the High Court, held that the court could order specific disclosure in a case to which the disclosure pilot scheme applied under its general case management powers in CPR Pt 3. It could do so in circumstances where there had been non-compliance with standard disclosure, which had been ordered prior to commencement of the pilot scheme. The court could in this way, and in such circumstances, make an order equivalent to that which would otherwise be available under CPR r.31.12. It appeared inapt to rely upon para.18 of the pilot scheme, which is substantively reproduced as para.18 of PD 57AD, as that applied where there had been an order for extended disclosure. In *Revenue and Customs Commissioners v IGE USA Investments Ltd* [2020] EWHC 1716 (Ch); [2021] Bus. L.R. 424 at [25]-[31], James Pickering QC sitting as a deputy judge of the High Court held that the court could order specific disclosure where there was no agreed or approved list of issues. While there was no provision equivalent to CPR r.31.12, the pilot scheme contained powers analogous to it, albeit they were materially different from it, in paras 17 and 18 of the pilot scheme and now those paras in PD 57AD. And see *UTB*

LLC v Sheffield United Ltd [2019] EWHC 914 (Ch); [2019] 3 All E.R. 698, and *Maher v Maher* [2019] EWHC 3613 (Ch).

1. General

1.1 This Practice Direction provides for disclosure in the Business and Property Courts. **57ADPD.1**

1.2 The Commencement Date is 1 October 2022. This Practice Direction applies to existing and new proceedings in the Business and Property Courts of England and Wales and the Business and Property Courts in Birmingham, Bristol, Cardiff, Leeds, Liverpool, Manchester and Newcastle. For the avoidance of doubt, it does not apply in the County Court. This Practice Direction is substantially in the form of (and replaces) Practice Direction 51U.

1.3 This Practice Direction shall not disturb an order for disclosure made before the Commencement Date or before the transfer of proceedings into a Business and Property Court, unless that order is varied or set aside. If proceedings are transferred out of one of the Business and Property Courts into a court that is not one of the Business and Property Courts, any order for disclosure made under this Practice Direction will stand unless and until any other order is made by the transferee court.

1.4 This Practice Direction shall not, unless otherwise ordered, apply to proceedings which are—

(1) a Competition claim as defined in Practice Direction 31C;
(2) a Public Procurement claim;
(3) within the Intellectual Property and Enterprise Court;
(4) within the Admiralty Court;
(5) within the Shorter and Flexible Trials Schemes;
(6) within a fixed costs regime or a capped costs regime; or
(7) claims proceeding under Part 8.

1.5 In the Patents Court, PD63 paragraphs 6.1 to 6.3 will continue to apply under this Practice Direction with the following modification: unless the court expressly orders otherwise, no provision in this practice direction nor any disclosure order made under this Practice Direction will take effect as requiring disclosure wider than is provided for in PD 63 paragraph 6.1.

1.6 For the purposes of this Practice Direction, where its provisions conflict with other provisions of the rules or other Practice Directions, this Practice Direction shall take precedence.

1.7 Terms in Section I of this Practice Direction shall have the meaning given to them in the schedule of definitions at Appendix 1.

1.8 Save for those provisions of CPR Part 31 that are set out in Section II, and the related provisions of Practice Directions 31A and 31B, CPR Part 31 and Practice Directions 31A and 31B shall not apply to any proceedings falling within this Practice Direction.

1.9 Save that references in Section II to an Electronic Documents Questionnaire should be treated as references to the Disclosure Review Document, nothing in this Practice Direction is intended to change the application or working of those provisions of CPR Part 31 that are set out in Section II and the related provisions of Practice Directions 31A and 31B, and CPR Part 31 as a whole should still be used to interpret those provisions.

1.10 Provisions relating to Extended Disclosure in Less Complex Claims are contained in Appendix 5. Less Complex Claims are defined in paragraph 1.9 of Appendix 1 to this Practice Direction.

1.11 This Practice Direction applies in multi-party cases. However, the court may order that the timetable and procedure is to be varied so as to provide a bespoke timetable and procedure to meet the needs of the individual multi-party case. Any application to the court in this connection should be made at an early stage.

1.12 A party seeking an order for disclosure in a Part 8 claim shall serve and file a List of Issues for Disclosure in relation to which disclosure is sought and the Models that are to be adopted for each issue. The court may adapt the provisions of this Practice Direction in such manner as may be appropriate when making an order for disclosure in a Part 8 claim.

Application to claims in the Business & Property Courts

57ADPD.1.1 Practice Direction 57AD, like the disclosure pilot scheme, is intended to provide a mechanism to secure proportionate disclosure for all applicable types of claims within the Business & Property Courts. It ought therefore to apply to small claims as it does to large claims. In lower value cases, and also in higher value cases, parties should avoid an unduly granular and complex approach to disclosure (see *McParland & Partners Ltd v Whitehead* [2020] EWHC 298 (Ch), Vos C at [3]-[4] and [55]) (see further para.57ADPD.6.1).

Section I

2. Principles, "document", "adverse" and "known adverse documents"

57ADPD.2 **2.1** Disclosure is important in achieving the fair resolution of civil proceedings. It involves identifying and making available documents that are relevant to the issues in the proceedings.

2.2 For the purpose of disclosure, the term "document" includes any record of any description containing information. The term is further defined below.

2.3 The court expects the parties (and their representatives) to cooperate with each other and to assist the court so that the scope of disclosure, if any, that is required in proceedings can be agreed or determined by the court in the most efficient way possible.

2.4 The court will be concerned to ensure that disclosure is directed to the issues in the proceedings and that the scope of disclosure is not wider than is reasonable and proportionate (as defined in paragraph 6.4) in order fairly to resolve those issues, and specifically the Issues for Disclosure (as defined in paragraph 7.6).

2.5 A "document" may take any form including but not limited to paper or electronic; it may be held by computer or on portable devices such as memory sticks or mobile phones or within databases; it includes e-mail and other electronic communications such as text messages, webmail, social media and voicemail, audio or visual recordings.

2.6 In addition to information that is readily accessible from computer systems and other electronic devices and media, the term "document" extends to information that is stored on servers and back-up systems and electronic information that has been 'deleted'. It also extends to metadata, and other embedded data which is not typically visible on screen or a printout.

2.7 Disclosure extends to "adverse" documents. A document is "adverse" if it or any information it contains contradicts or materially damages the disclosing party's contention or version of events on an issue in dispute, or supports the contention or version of events of an opposing party on an issue in dispute, whether or not that issue is one of the agreed Issues for Disclosure.

2.8 "Known adverse documents" are documents (other than privileged documents) that a party is actually aware (without undertaking any further search for documents than it has already undertaken or caused to be undertaken) both (a) are or were previously within its control and (b) are adverse.

2.9 For this purpose a company or organisation is "aware" if any person with accountability or responsibility within the company or organisation for the events or the circumstances which are the subject of the case, or for the conduct of the proceedings, is aware. For this purpose it is also necessary to take reasonable steps to check the position with any person who has had such accountability or responsibility but who has since left the company or organisation.

Principles and known adverse documents

57ADPD.2.1 In *Obaid v Al-Hezaimi* [2019] EWHC 1953 (Ch), Falk J at [43] accepted that "known adverse documents" (CPR PD 51U para.2.8, now PD 57AD para.2.8) was a broad concept that could encompass matters not dealt with in statements of case. The judge also noted that important considerations in ensuring that disclosure was reasonable and proportionate such that a fair resolution of civil proceedings could be achieved (see para.2.1) were the need to avoid ambush and to enable parties a proper opportunity to respond to allegations. At [44], Falk J held that the provisions in the pilot scheme concerning adverse documents did not require the court to admit such documents. The pilot scheme and its provisions, and hence now, and now PD 57AD, were subject to the general power set out in CPR r.32.1 to exclude otherwise admissible evidence.

In *Castle Water Ltd v Thames Water Utilities Ltd* [2020] EWHC 1374 (TCC) at [10]–[13], Stuart-Smith J provided guidance on the nature of the obligation placed on a party to discover whether it had any known adverse documents. It was clear that a party had to take reasonable steps to ascertain if it had such documents. This required a reasonable and proportionate check to be undertaken to ascertain if it had such documents and a reasonable and proportionate search to locate them. Paragraph 2.9 of PD 51U, replicated as para.2.9 of PD 57AD, requires the steps taken to check to be fact and context specific. In a case:

> "... of any complexity at all or an organisation of any size, reasonable steps to check whether a company or organisation has 'known adverse documents' will require more than a generalised question that fails to identify the issues to which the question and any adverse documents may relate. Similarly, it will not be sufficient simply to ask questions of the leaders or controlling mind of an organisation, unless the issue in question is irrelevant to others" (see [10]).

The continuing duty to disclose such documents does not imply that once a party has discharged its initial obligation to search for such documents it is required on a continuing basis to carry out further searches in the absence of a change of circumstances in the litigation. Where circumstances change, e.g. a party's claim changes in a material manner, that may require a further search for such documents to be carried out and disclosed.

3. Duties in relation to disclosure

3.1 A person who knows that it is or may become a party to proceedings that have been commenced or who knows that it may become a party to proceedings that may be commenced is under the following duties ("the Disclosure Duties") to the court– **57ADPD.3**

(1) to take reasonable steps to preserve documents in its control that may be relevant to any issue in the proceedings;
(2) by no later than the time(s) set out in paragraphs 9.1 to 9.3, to disclose known adverse documents, unless they are privileged. This duty exists regardless of whether or not any order for disclosure is made;
(3) to comply with any order for disclosure made by the court;
(4) to undertake any search for documents in a responsible and conscientious manner to fulfil the stated purpose of the search;
(5) to act honestly in relation to the process of giving disclosure and reviewing documents disclosed by the other party; and
(6) to use reasonable efforts to avoid providing documents to another party that have no relevance to the Issues for Disclosure in the proceedings.

3.2 Legal representatives who have the conduct of litigation on behalf of a party to proceedings that have been commenced, or who are instructed with a view to the conduct of litigation where their client knows it may become a party to proceedings that have been or may be commenced, are under the following duties to the court–

(1) to take reasonable steps to preserve documents within their control that may be relevant to any issue in the proceedings;
(2) to take reasonable steps to advise and assist the party to comply with its Disclosure Duties;
(3) to liaise and cooperate with the legal representatives of the other parties to the proceedings (or the other parties where they do not have legal representatives) so as to promote the reliable, efficient and cost-effective conduct of disclosure, including through the use of technology;
(4) to act honestly in relation to the process of giving disclosure and reviewing documents disclosed by the other party; and
(5) to undertake a review to satisfy themselves that any claim by the party to privilege from disclosing a document is properly made and the reason for the claim to privilege is sufficiently explained.

3.3 The duties under paragraphs 3.1 and 3.2 above are continuing duties that last until the conclusion of the proceedings (including any appeal) or until it is clear there will be no proceedings.

3.4 Where there is a known adverse document but it has not been located, the duty to disclose the document is met by that fact being disclosed, subject to any further order that the court may make.

Explanation of duty to retain documents

57ADPD.3.1 It is particularly important for solicitors to explain the nature and application of the disclosure rules and obligations to clients unfamiliar with them to ensure they fully understand the duties imposed upon them by those rules: *Provimi France SAS v Stour Bay Co Ltd* [2022] EWHC 218 (Comm) at [32]-[33].

4. Preservation of documents

57ADPD.4 **4.1** Documents to be preserved in accordance with the duties under paragraphs 3.1(1) and 3.2(1) above include documents which might otherwise be deleted or destroyed in accordance with a document retention policy or in the ordinary course of business. Preservation includes, in suitable cases, making copies of sources and documents and storing them.

4.2 The duty under paragraph 3.1(1) and 3.2(1) includes—

(1) an obligation to suspend relevant document deletion or destruction processes for the duration of the proceedings;

(2) in accordance with paragraph 4.3 below, an obligation to send a written notification in any form to relevant employees and former employees of the party where there are reasonable grounds for believing that the employee or former employee may be in possession of disclosable documents which are not also in the party's possession; and

(3) an obligation to take reasonable steps so that agents or third parties who may hold documents on the party's behalf do not delete or destroy documents that may be relevant to an issue in the proceedings.

4.3 A written notification under paragraph 4.2 above should—

(1) identify the documents or classes of documents to be preserved; and

(2) notify the recipient that they should not delete or destroy those documents and should take reasonable steps to preserve them.

4.4 Legal representatives who have the conduct of litigation on behalf of a party to proceedings that have been commenced, or who are instructed with a view to the conduct of litigation where their client knows it may become a party to proceedings that have been or may be commenced, must within a reasonable period of being instructed—

(1) notify their client of the need to preserve documents and of their obligations under paragraph 3.1 above; and

(2) obtain written confirmation from their client or an appropriate representative of their client that their client has taken the steps required under paragraphs 4.2 and 4.3 above.

4.5 Each party must confirm in writing (and may do so by their legal representative) when serving their particulars of claim or defence (as appropriate), that steps have been taken to preserve relevant documents in accordance with the duties under paragraph 3.1(1) and 3.2(1) above, and as required by paragraph 4.1 to 4.4 above.

5. Initial Disclosure

57ADPD.5 **5.1** Save as provided below, and save in the case of a Part 7 claim form without particulars of claim, each party must provide to all other parties at the same time as its statement of case an Initial Disclosure List of Documents that lists and is accompanied by copies of—

(1) the key documents on which it has relied (expressly or otherwise) in sup-

port of the claims or defences advanced in its statement of case (and including the documents referred to in that statement of case); and

(2) the key documents that are necessary to enable the other parties to understand the claim or defence they have to meet.

5.2 This form of disclosure is known as "Initial Disclosure".

5.3 Initial Disclosure is not required where—

(1) the parties have agreed to dispense with it (see paragraph 5.8 below);

(2) the court has ordered that it is not required (see paragraph 5.10 below); or

(3) a party concludes and states in writing, approaching the matter in good faith, that giving Initial Disclosure would involve it or any other party providing (after removing duplicates, and including documents referred to at paragraph 5.4(3)(a)) more than (about) whichever is the larger of 1000 pages or 200 documents (or such higher but reasonable figure as the parties may agree), at which point the requirement to give Initial Disclosure ceases for all parties for the purposes of the case.

Documents comprising media not in page form are not included in the calculation of the page or document limit at (3) but, where provided pursuant to a requirement to give Initial Disclosure, should be confined strictly to what is necessary to comply with paragraph 5.1 above.

5.4 A party giving Initial Disclosure—

(1) is under no obligation to undertake a search for documents beyond any search it has already undertaken or caused to be undertaken for the purposes of the proceedings (including in advance of the commencement of the proceedings);

(2) need not provide unless requested documents by way of Initial Disclosure if such documents—

(a) have already been provided to the other party, whether by disclosure before proceedings start (see CPR 31.16) or through pre-action correspondence or otherwise in the period following intimation of the proceedings (and including when giving Initial Disclosure with a statement of case that is being amended); or

(b) are known to be or have been in the other party's possession;

(3) need not disclose adverse documents by way of Initial Disclosure.

5.5 Unless otherwise ordered, or agreed between the parties, copies of documents shall be provided in electronic form for the purpose of Initial Disclosure. The Initial Disclosure List of Documents should be filed but the documents must not be filed.

5.6 In proceedings where a statement of case is to be served on a defendant out of the jurisdiction Initial Disclosure is not required in respect of that defendant unless and until that defendant files an acknowledgement of service that does not contest the jurisdiction, or files a further acknowledgement of service under CPR 11(7)(b).

5.7 For the avoidance of doubt, Initial Disclosure does not require any document to be translated.

5.8 The parties may agree in writing, before or after the commencement of proceedings, to dispense with, or defer, Initial Disclosure. They may also agree to dispense with the requirement to produce an Initial Disclosure List of Documents. Each party should record its respective reasons for any agreement, so that those reasons may be available to the court, on request, at any case management conference. The court may set aside an agreement to dispense with or defer Initial Disclosure if it considers that Initial Disclosure is likely to provide significant benefits and the costs of providing Initial Disclosure are unlikely to be disproportionate to such benefits.

5.9 The court shall disregard any prior agreement to dispense with Initial Disclosure when considering whether to order Extended Disclosure.

5.10 A party may apply to the court for directions limiting or abrogating the obligation to provide Initial Disclosure. In particular, if a party is requested but does not agree to dispense with Initial Disclosure, the requesting party may apply to the court with notice to the other party for directions limiting or abrogating the obligation to provide Initial Disclosure if it considers compliance with the obligation will incur disproportionate cost or be unduly complex. Such an application must be made by application notice, supported by evidence where necessary, and, save in exceptional cases, will be dealt with without a hearing or at a short telephone hearing.

5.11 In an appropriate case the court may, on application, and whether or not Initial Disclosure has been given, require a party to disclose documents to another party where that is necessary to enable the other party to understand the claim or defence they have to meet or to formulate a defence or a reply.

5.12 A complaint about Initial Disclosure shall be dealt with at the first case management conference unless, exceptionally and on application, the court considers that the issue should be resolved at an earlier hearing.

5.13 A significant failure to comply with the obligation to provide Initial Disclosure may be taken into account by the court when considering whether to make an order for Extended Disclosure and the terms of such an order. It may also result in an adverse order for costs.

5.14 For the avoidance of doubt, nothing in this paragraph affects the operation of paragraph 7.3 of Practice Direction 16.

Key documents

57ADPD.5.1 In *Breitenbach v Canaccord Genuity Financial Planning Ltd* [2020] EWHC 1355 (Ch) the court held that documents that went beyond enabling a defence to be understood were not key documents. As such documents that were said to be necessary to evaluate and weigh the defence's prospects of success were not key documents for the purpose of para.5.1(1) and (2) of PD 51U, now para.5.1(1) and (2) of PD 57AD.

Limited focus of Initial Disclosure

57ADPD.5.2 Initial disclosure is "very tightly focused", i.e. it is limited to key documents necessary to enable the case that is to be met to be understood. Examples are key documents relied upon such as a contract or those documents that potentially evidence a contract was made or specific representation made: *Qatar v Banque Havilland SA* [2020] EWHC 1248 (Comm) at [16].

Disclosure "necessary to enable the other party to understand the claim or defence"

57ADPD.5.3 Practice Direction 57AD para.5.11 (previously PD 51U para.5.11) must be given a narrow interpretation given the Practice Direction's purpose of introducing a proportionate approach to disclosure: *Patisserie Holdings Plc (In Liquidation) v Grant Thornton UK LLP* [2021] EWHC 3022 (Comm) at [30].

6. Extended Disclosure

57ADPD.6 **6.1** A party wishing to seek disclosure of documents in addition to, or as an alternative to, Initial Disclosure must request Extended Disclosure. No application notice is required. However, the parties will be expected to have completed the Disclosure Review Document pursuant to paragraphs 7 and following below.

6.2 Save where otherwise provided, Extended Disclosure involves using Disclosure Models (see paragraph 8 below) in respect of Issues for Disclosure which have been identified (see paragraph 7 below).

6.3 The court will only make an order for Extended Disclosure that is search-based (ie Models C, D and/or E) where it is persuaded that it is appropriate to do so in order fairly to resolve one or more of the Issues for Disclosure.

6.4 In all cases, an order for Extended Disclosure must be reasonable and proportionate having regard to the overriding objective including the following factors—

(1) the nature and complexity of the issues in the proceedings;
(2) the importance of the case, including any non-monetary relief sought;
(3) the likelihood of documents existing that will have probative value in supporting or undermining a party's claim or defence;
(4) the number of documents involved;
(5) the ease and expense of searching for and retrieval of any particular document (taking into account any limitations on the information available and on the likely accuracy of any costs estimates);
(6) the financial position of each party; and
(7) the need to ensure the case is dealt with expeditiously, fairly and at a proportionate cost.

6.5 A request for search-based Extended Disclosure (ie Models C, D and/or E) must specify which of the Disclosure Models listed in paragraph 8 below is proposed for each Issue for Disclosure defined in paragraph 7 below. It is for the party requesting Extended Disclosure to show that what is sought is appropriate, reasonable and proportionate (as defined in paragraph 6.4).

6.6 The objective of relating Disclosure Models to Issues for Disclosure is to limit the searches required and the volume of documents to be disclosed. Issues for Disclosure may be grouped. Disclosure Models should not be used in a way that increases cost through undue complexity.

6.7 It is important that the parties consider what types of documents and sources of documents there are or may be, including what documents another party is likely to have, in order that throughout a realistic approach may be taken to disclosure.

Court control over disclosure

6.8 The court will determine whether to order Extended Disclosure at the first case management conference or, if directed by the court, at another hearing convened for that purpose or without a hearing.

6.9 The court may determine any point at issue between the parties about disclosure including the application or effect of any provision in this Practice Direction or an order made by the court and about the scope of searches, the manner in which searches are to be carried out and the use of technology. The parties may, at any time, apply to the court to seek the determination of an issue concerning disclosure by issuing an application notice.

6.10 The court may also provide disclosure guidance in accordance with paragraph 11.

6.11 Upon the application of the parties/a party, or on its own motion, the court may vary any period of time for a party/the parties to complete a step in disclosure. If the variation is agreed between the parties and will not affect the date set for the Case Management Conference or trial (as appropriate), court approval is not required.

Consideration of factors to determine whether to order Extended Disclosure

One of the problems identified by the Disclosure Working Party with CPR Pt 31 was that standard disclosure was too often adopted as a default form of order. Care should be taken by both the court and parties to ensure that a similar approach is not taken to Extended Disclosure, i.e. that ordering Extended Disclosure and "Model D" Disclosure, under PD 51U para.8.3 (now PD 57AD para.8.3), does not become a "default" approach. **57ADPD.6.1**

When considering whether it is "reasonable and proportionate having regard to the overriding objective" to grant an application for extended disclosure, each of the factors set out in para.6.4 of PD 57AD (previously para.6.4 of PD 51U) are to be given weight. Those factors highlight the fact that the disclosure pilot scheme applies to all cases, from the lowest to the highest value, from the most complex and document heavy to the least complex and document light, in the Business & Property Courts (see *McParland & Partners Ltd v Whitehead* [2020] EWHC 298 (Ch), Vos C at [3]–[4]).

In a complex and important case, the third, fourth and seventh factors are likely to have particular importance (*UTB LLC v Sheffield United Ltd* [2019] EWHC 914 (Ch); [2019] 3 All E.R. 698, at [76]). In *Merck Sharp & Dohme Ltd v Wyeth LLC* [2019] EWHC 1692 (Pat), Arnold J, in considering an application for disclosure, accepted that a wide-ranging search would be both costly and disproportionate. In the circumstances, disclosure on a specific issue was justified. He also noted that a further application for wider disclosure could be made in the future, if justified.

Disclosure review document

57ADPD.6.2 Requests for Model C disclosure must not be in general terms, see the guidance concerning the predecessor to para.6.1 in PD 51U, in *Pipia v BGEO Group Ltd* [2020] EWHC 402 (Comm); [2020] 1 W.L.R. 2582 at [66]-[67] and *Sheeran v Chokri* [2021] EWHC 3553 (Ch) at [2].

7. Identifying the Issues for Disclosure and Models

57ADPD.7 **7.1** Within 28 days of the final statement of case each party should state, in writing, whether or not it is likely to request search-based Extended Disclosure to include one or more of Models C, D or E (see paragraph 8 below) on one or more Issues for Disclosure in the case. At this point it should not particularise the Model(s) or the issue(s) in the case.

7.2 Where one or more of the parties has indicated it is likely to request search-based Extended Disclosure (i.e. Models C, D and/or E), the claimant must within 42 days of the final statement of case prepare and serve on the other parties a draft List of Issues for Disclosure unless an agreed list of issues for trial already exists and the parties agree that it is suitable (with or without adaptation) to be used for disclosure. The draft List of Issues for Disclosure should be set out in Section 1A of the Disclosure Review Document.

7.3 At the same time as serving a draft List of Issues for Disclosure, the claimant shall identify for each Issue for Disclosure which Model of Extended Disclosure it proposes for each party. If the claimant proposes Model C Disclosure for any Issue for Disclosure it should indicate, using Section 1B of the Disclosure Review Document, how the particular documents or narrow class of documents it proposes should be defined for that purpose (see paragraph 8 below).

7.4 If the claimant fails to prepare and serve a List of Issues for Disclosure within 42 days of the final statement of case any defendant may prepare and serve its own draft List of Issues for Disclosure on the other parties together with its proposed Models including any Model C requests.

7.5 A List of Issues for Disclosure is not required if the parties are agreed that Extended Disclosure is to be confined to Models A and B.

7.6 The List of Issues for Disclosure should be as short and concise as possible. "Issues for Disclosure" means for the purposes of disclosure only those key issues in dispute, which the parties consider will need to be determined by the court with some reference to contemporaneous documents in order for there to be a fair resolution of the proceedings. It does not extend to every issue which is disputed in the statements of case by denial or non-admission. For the purposes of producing a List of Issues for Disclosure the parties should consider what matters are common ground but should only include the key issues in dispute in the list.

7.7 When drafting Issues for Disclosure the parties should have regard to the primary functions of those Issues namely (i) to help the parties to consider, and the court to determine, whether Extended Disclosure is required and, if so, which Model or Models should be used; (ii) to assist the parties in identifying documents and categories of documents that are likely to exist and require to be disclosed; (iii) to assist those carrying out the disclosure process to do so in a practical and proportionate way including, in the case of search-based disclosure, to help define and guide the searches; (iv) to assist with the process of reviewing documents produced by searches; and (v) to avoid the production of documents that are not relevant to the issues in the proceedings.

7.8 The claimant should seek to ensure that the draft List of Issues for Disclosure provides a fair and balanced summary of the key areas of dispute identified by the parties' statements of case and in respect of which it is likely that one or other of the parties will be seeking search-based Extended Disclosure.

7.9 A party served with a draft List of Issues for Disclosure and proposals on Models shall, as soon as practicable but in any event no later than 21 days from service, indicate using Section 1A (and, if applicable, 1B) of the Disclosure Review Document whether it agrees with the proposals (including any proposals as to how Model C Disclosure should be defined). If the party served with the proposals does not agree, or wishes to propose alternative or additional Issues for Disclosure, other Models and/or other Model C proposals, it should set out its alternative or additional proposals in Sections 1A and 1B of the Disclosure Review Document.

7.10 In advance of the first case management conference, the parties must discuss and seek to agree the draft List of Issues for Disclosure, the Models identified for each Issue for Disclosure, and the wording of any Model C proposals. They should consider whether any draft Issue for Disclosure can be removed.

7.11 Whilst reasonable and proportionate efforts are required to agree the List of Issues for Disclosure, if agreement cannot be reached after such efforts the List should be concluded by showing the areas of disagreement. The parties should consider seeking Disclosure Guidance from the court at an early stage as a means to help resolve the differences between them. One situation in which Disclosure Guidance should be considered is where one party believes the other is proposing a list of issues that is far too complex to serve as a List of Issues for Disclosure.

7.12 The List of Issues for Disclosure does not bind the parties at trial. The List of Issues for Disclosure need not contain / include a list of all the issues in the case and the issues in the case may develop or be refined as the case proceeds. The List of Issues for Disclosure may be revised or supplemented at any time prior to or following the case management conference, including as a result of statements of case or amended statements of case subsequently served or discussions between the parties in relation to the Disclosure Review Document.

7.13 If the parties are (subject to the court) agreed that there are preliminary issues suitable for determination before other issues in the case, or that the case should be divided into stages, the parties may apply to the court before any case management conference for an order for the trial of those issues or for trial in stages (and related directions), and they may agree in writing to limit the work towards disclosure required by this Practice Direction until that application has been heard.

7.14 In an appropriate case where the claimant is acting in person and a defendant is not the court may request the legal representatives of the defendant to lead on the preparation of the List of Issues for Disclosure.

7.15 The parties may agree a revised timetable for completion of the Disclosure Review Document (including the List of Issues for Disclosure, Models and Model C requests) where appropriate, provided always that any such revision to the timetable does not affect the date set for the Case Management Conference.

7.16 In a multi-party case, where the risk of undue complexity in Lists of Issues for Disclosure is heightened, while the provisions of this Practice Direction remain the default arrangement, an application may be made under paragraph 1.11 above to request that the Court order for a bespoke timetable and procedure to be set in order to meet the needs of the multi-party case.

Identification of issues

In *McParland & Partners Ltd v Whitehead* [2020] EWHC 298 (Ch), Vos C at [44]-[49] provided guidance on the approach to take to issue identification. The starting point is the documentation that is, or is likely to be, in each party's possession. It should not be a mechanical exercise based on identifying issues from the pleadings that will arise at trial. Identification should arise from assessing the relevance of categories of documents to contested issues that are in the parties' possession. Issues for disclosure may thus be different from issues for trial. The former are: **57ADPD.7.1**

"... issues to which undisclosed documentation in the hands of one or more of the parties is likely to be relevant and important for the fair resolution of the claim."

Hence PD 57AD para.7.6 (previously PD 51U para.7.3) provides that issues for disclosure are only the "key issues in dispute, which the parties consider will need to be determined by the court with some reference to contemporaneous documents ...". In many cases, therefore the issues for disclosure are unlikely to be numerous and, in any event, will almost never be legal issues. Nor will they involve factual issues that can be resolved by reference to such documents as are available via initial disclosure (see PD 57AD para.5). The identification of issues for disclosure also serve to enable the review of documents following a case management conference to be carried out more clinically, and hence in a more orderly and principled manner, than was previously the case under standard disclosure. *Lonestar Communications Corp LLC v Kaye* [2020] EWHC 1890 (Comm) at [32] explained that it followed Vos C's analysis at [47]-[49] of *McParland and Partners Ltd v Whitehead* [2020] EWHC 298 (Ch), and issues for disclosure must be issues that are "crystallised in the statements of case". Where an issue is not a pleaded issue it cannot be an issue for disclosure. That approach was, however, doubted and not followed in *Revenue and Customs Commissioners v IGE USA Investments Ltd* [2020] EWHC 1716 (Ch) at [48] and following, where it was held that the scope of issues for sisclosure was not limited to issues pleaded in the statements of case. While it did not resolve the different approaches taken in the two judgments, *Curtiss v Zurich Insurance Plc* [2021] EWHC 1999 (TCC) at [18] adopted the view that the approach in *Lonestar* was the appropriate one for "most case management conferences".

The absence of a reply to a defence was not determinative of the nature of the factual issues in dispute: *Performing Right Society Ltd v Qatar Airways Group QCSC* [2021] EWHC 869 (Ch) at [33].

8. The Extended Disclosure Models

57ADPD.8 **8.1** Extended Disclosure may take the form of one or more of the Disclosure Models set out below.

8.2 There is no presumption that a party is entitled to search-based Extended Disclosure (Extended Disclosure Models C, D and/or E). No Model will apply without the approval of the court.

8.3 The court may order that Extended Disclosure be given using different Disclosure Models for different Issues for Disclosure in the case. It is important that there is moderation in the number of Models used and the way in which they are applied to the Issues for Disclosure so that the disclosure process that will follow, using the Models and the Issues for Disclosure, will be practical. In the interests of avoiding undue complexity the court will rarely require different Models for the same set or repository of documents. The court may also order that Extended Disclosure be given by only one party, or that different Models are to apply to each party's Disclosure on a particular Issue for Disclosure. In some cases, it may be appropriate, practical and proportionate for different Models to be applied to different types of documents (e.g. one Model for physical documents and another Model for electronic documents).

Model A: Disclosure confined to known adverse documents

The court may order that the only disclosure required in relation to some or all of the Issues for Disclosure is of known adverse documents in accordance with the (continuing) duty under paragraph 3.1(2) above.

Model B: Limited Disclosure

(1) The court may order the parties to disclose (where and to the extent that they have not already done so by way of Initial Disclosure, and without limit as to quantity)—
- (a) the key documents on which they have relied (expressly or otherwise) in support of the claims or defences advanced in their statement(s) of case; and
- (b) the key documents that are necessary to enable the other parties to understand the claim or defence they have to meet;

and in addition to disclose known adverse documents in accordance with their (continuing) duty under paragraph 3.1(2) above.

(2) A party giving Model B Disclosure is under no obligation to undertake a search for documents beyond any search already conducted for the

purposes of obtaining advice on its claim or defence or preparing its statement(s) of case. Where it does undertake a search however then the (continuing) duty under paragraph 3.1(2) will apply.

Model C: Disclosure of particular documents or narrow classes of documents

(1) The court may order a party to give disclosure of particular documents or narrow classes of documents relating to a particular Issue for Disclosure, by reference to requests set out in or to be set out in Section 1B of the Disclosure Review Document or otherwise defined by the court.

(2) If the parties cannot agree that disclosure should be given, or the disclosure to be given, pursuant to a request, then the requesting party must raise the request at the case management conference. The court will determine whether the request is reasonable and proportionate and may either order the disclosing party to search for the documents requested, refuse the request, or order the disclosing party to search for a narrower class of documents than that requested. Any appropriate limits to the scope of the searches to be undertaken will be determined by the court using the information provided in the Disclosure Review Document. A party may address Model C requests not only to the other party or parties, but also propose that Model C be used in respect of documents which it may propose searching for and disclosing.

(3) For the avoidance of doubt, a party giving Model C Disclosure must still comply with the duty under paragraph 3.1(2) above to disclose known adverse documents; these will include any arising from the search directed by the court.

Model D: Narrow search-based disclosure, with or without Narrative Documents

(1) Under Model D, a party shall disclose documents which are likely to support or adversely affect its claim or defence or that of another party in relation to one or more of the Issues for Disclosure.

(2) Each party is required to undertake a reasonable and proportionate search in relation to the Issues for Disclosure for which Model D disclosure has been ordered. Any appropriate limits to the scope of the searches to be undertaken will be determined by the court using the information provided in the Disclosure Review Document.

(3) The court may order the parties to include or exclude Narrative Documents. In the absence of an order, the parties are encouraged to take reasonable steps to exclude Narrative Documents where it is reasonable and proportionate to do so with a view to reducing the overall volume and the cost of any subsequent review by the party receiving the disclosure.

(4) For the avoidance of doubt, a party giving Model D Disclosure must still comply with the duty under paragraph 3.1(2) above to disclose known adverse documents; these will include any arising from the search directed by the court.

Model E: Wide search-based disclosure

(1) Under Model E, a party shall disclose documents which are likely to support or adversely affect its claim or defence or that of another party in relation to one or more of the Issues for Disclosure or which may lead to a train of inquiry which may then result in the identification of other documents for disclosure (because those other documents are likely to support or adversely affect the party's own claim or defence or that of another party in relation to one or more of the Issues for Disclosure).

(2) Model E is only to be ordered in an exceptional case.

(3) Each party is required to undertake a reasonable and proportionate search in relation to the Issues for Disclosure for which Model E Disclosure has been ordered. The scope of the search will be determined by the court using the information provided in the Disclosure Review Document and is likely to be broader than that ordered for Model D Disclosure.

(4) Narrative Documents must also be searched for and disclosed, unless the court otherwise orders.

(5) For the avoidance of doubt, a party giving Model E Disclosure must still comply with the duty under paragraph 3.1(2) above to disclose known adverse documents; these will include any arising from the search directed by the court.

Approach to determining choice of disclosure model

57ADPD.8.1 In *McParland & Partners Ltd v Whitehead* [2020] EWHC 298 (Ch), Vos C at [50]–[52] provided guidance on the approach to be taken determining the appropriate disclosure model under the disclosure pilot scheme. The same approach will apply to PD 57AD. Where a party had made a reasonable request for further documentation and disclosure could not be agreed, Model C disclosure was appropriate. Where parties did not trust each other, Model D disclosure was likely to be the simplest, most appropriate choice. Care should also be taken to consider if different disclosure models should apply to different parties. There is no reason in principle why the same issue might not be subject to disclosure Model D for one party, while it is subject to disclosure Models B or C for another party. Model D disclosure may also be appropriate in respect of issues that are central to a party's pleaded case: *Lombard North Central Plc v Airbus Helicopters SAS* [2020] EWHC 3819 (Comm), Bryan J, at [20]–[30] following *McParland* at [51].

Narrative documents

57ADPD.8.2 Disclosure of narrative documents should only be directed where there is:

"(1) a real (as opposed to a fanciful) prospect that in connection with a particular issue a document exists which is relevant only to the background or context of material facts or events, and not directly to the Issue, but which would none the less be sufficiently important to the parties' cases that it merit searches, analysis and the other costs of disclosure and

(2) no real likelihood that such a document will emerge as a result of the disclosure exercise in respect of any other Issue."

Such disclosure is also likely to be more appropriate for fraud claims and those that involve "secret meetings, obscure processes or hidden participants". It is unlikely to be suitable for building disputes or other disputes where the court is required to carry out an objective analysis of a defendant or third party's conduct. See *Bouygues (UK) Ltd v Sharpfibre Ltd* [2020] EWHC 1309 (TCC) at [40]–[41].

Scoping Model C Extended Disclosure

57ADPD.8.3 Model C Extended Disclosure is, in one sense, the implicitly preferred model for Extended Disclosure. Model D and E are only appropriate where Model C is neither appropriate nor sufficient: see *Lonestar Communications Corp LLC v Kaye* [2020] EWHC 1890 (Comm) at [54] and para.8.2 of PD 57AD (previously para.8.2 of PD 51U). Where documents are requested in respect of Model C Extended Disclosure they must be capable of being described with precision, either individually or by class. A disclosing party must be able to understand what is to be disclosed, and be readily able to recognise disclosable documents without too much difficulty when a search is carried out: see Section 1B of the Disclosure Review Document set out in Appendix 2 to PD 51U, now of Appendix 2 to PD 57AD: *Lonestar Communications Corp LLC* at [58].

Limited use of Model E Extended Disclosure

57ADPD.8.4 It was apparent that the pilot scheme intended Model E (train of inquiry) Extended Disclosure to be exceptional. It was and is, given that PD 57AD para.8.3 replicates para.8.3 of PD 51U, thus clear that such disclosure will be ordered in fewer cases than it will be ordered under CPR Pt 31. It is to be expected that more demanding circumstances than those in *Berezovsky v Abramovich* [2010] EWHC 2010 (Comm) will be required to justify such an order. It will also not therefore be the case that such disclosure must follow where it is said, without more, that there is a serious case involving conspiracy: *Qatar v Banque Havilland SA* [2020] EWHC 1248 (Comm) at [22]–[24], and also see the approach in *McParland and Partners Ltd v Whitehead* [2020] EWHC 298 (Ch) and *Kings Security Systems Ltd v King* [2019] EWHC 3620 (Ch).

9. Other provisions concerning Disclosure Models

57ADPD.9 **9.1** Where an order for Model B, C, D or E Extended Disclosure is made on one or more Issues for Disclosure, any known adverse documents to be disclosed in compliance with the duty under paragraph 3.1(2) above and not already disclosed must be disclosed at the time ordered for that Extended Disclosure.

9.2 In a case where no order for Extended Disclosure is made in respect of a party on any Issue for Disclosure, that party must still disclose all known adverse documents within 60 days of the first case management conference and provide a Disclosure Certificate certifying that this has been done.

9.3 The provisions of paragraph 8 and this paragraph 9 do not affect the fact that the duty under paragraph 3.1(2) above is a continuing duty as provided by paragraph 3.3 above: if adverse documents in the control of a party come to its knowledge at a later date they must (unless privileged) be disclosed without delay.

9.4 The court may make an order for Extended Disclosure in stages.

9.5 When it is necessary to decide any question of what is reasonable and proportionate under a particular Disclosure Model, the court will consider all the circumstances of the case including the factors set out in paragraph 6.4 above and the overriding objective.

9.6 Where the Disclosure Model requires searches to be undertaken, the parties must discuss and seek to agree, and the court may give directions, on the following matters with a view to reducing the burden and cost of the disclosure exercise—

(1) that the scope of the searches which the disclosing parties are required to undertake be limited to—
   (a) particular date ranges and custodians of documents;
   (b) particular classes of documents and/or file types;
   (c) specific document repositories and/or geographical locations;
   (d) specific computer systems or electronic storage devices;
   (e) documents responsive to specific keyword searches, or other automated searches (by reference, if appropriate, to individual custodians, creators, repositories, file types and/or date ranges, concepts);

(2) if Narrative Documents are to be excluded, how that is to be achieved in a reasonable and proportionate way;

(3) the use of—
   (a) software or analytical tools, including technology assisted review software and techniques;
   (b) coding strategies, including to reduce duplication.

(4) prioritisation and workflows.

9.7 In making an order for Extended Disclosure, the court may include any provision that is appropriate including provision for all or any of the following—

(1) requiring the use of specified software or analytical tools;
(2) identifying the methods to be used to identify duplicate or near-duplicate documents and remove or reduce such documents;
(3) requiring the use of data sampling;
(4) specifying the format in which documents are to be disclosed;
(5) identifying the methods that the court regards as sufficient to be used to identify privileged documents and other non-disclosable documents;
(6) the use of a staged approach to the disclosure of electronic documents;
(7) excluding certain classes of document from the disclosure ordered.

9.8 In considering Extended Disclosure as well as when complying with an order for Extended Disclosure the parties should have regard to the guidance set out in Section 3 of the Disclosure Review Document.

9.9 In an appropriate case, the court may order that the question of which party bears the costs of disclosure is to be given separate consideration at a later stage rather than the costs being treated automatically as costs in the case;

9.10 For the avoidance of doubt, Extended Disclosure does not require any document to be translated.

Extended disclosure on agreed issue

57ADPD.9.1 Party agreement on an issue and on the fact that documents went to that issue did not, on its own, justify the making of an order under para.9.4 of the Practice Direction. The court is required to actively manage disclosure under the Practice Direction. Making such an order on that basis prior to the first case management conference would run contrary to that case management role: *Patisserie Holdings Plc (In Liquidation) v Grant Thornton UK LLP* [2021] EWHC 3022 (Comm) at [32]-[36].

10. Completion of the Disclosure Review Document

57ADPD.10 **10.1** The Disclosure Review Document is the document by which the parties must identify, discuss and seek to agree the scope of any Extended Disclosure sought of Model C, D or E, and provide that information in due course to the court.

10.2 The Disclosure Review Document may be modified (shortened or lengthened) as required in order that key information is exchanged and in due course provided to the court in an efficient, convenient and helpful format. This may include revising some of the questions asked in Section 2 of the DRD or adding others relevant to the particular disclosure exercise to be undertaken. In cases where there is likely to be limited disclosure or the identification and retrieval of documents is straightforward, not every section of the Disclosure Review Document will need to be completed. For such cases, the parties should consider whether it would be more appropriate to use the Less Complex Claims regime.

10.3 The parties' obligation to complete, seek to agree and update the Disclosure Review Document is ongoing. If a party fails to co-operate and constructively to engage in this process the other party or parties may apply to the court for an appropriate order at or separately from the case management conference, and the court may make any appropriate order including the dismissal of any application for Extended Disclosure and/or the adjournment of the case management conference with an adverse order for costs.

10.4 Where Model C is proposed for any Issue(s) for Disclosure, these should be limited in number, focused in scope and concise so that the responding party may be clear as to the particular document(s) or narrow classes of document relating to a particular Issue for Disclosure for which it is being asked to undertake searches. Broad and wide-ranging formulations such as "any or all documents relating to..." should not be used. Model C requests should not be used in a tactical or oppressive way.

10.5 Having sought to agree the List of Issues for Disclosure, proposals on Model(s) for Extended Disclosure and the wording of any Model C requests, the parties should prepare and exchange drafts of Section 2 of the Disclosure Review Document (including costs estimates of different proposals, and where possible estimates of likely amount of documents involved) as soon as reasonably practicable and in any event not later than 14 days before the case management conference. Section 2 of the Disclosure Review Document should be completed only if any party is seeking an order for search-based Extended Disclosure (i.e. Models C, D and/or E).

10.6 The parties must seek to resolve any disputes over the scope of any Extended Disclosure sought in advance of the first case management conference. Any disputes which have not been resolved will normally be decided by the court at the first case management conference.

10.7 A finalised single joint Disclosure Review Document should be filed by the claimant not later than 5 days before the case management conference. Related correspondence and earlier drafts should not ordinarily be filed.

10.8 The parties must each file and serve a signed Certificate of Compliance substantially in the form set out in Appendix 3 not less than two days before the case management conference. A Certificate of Compliance is not required for cases where a Disclosure Review Document has been dispensed with under paragraph 10.5.

10.9 In an appropriate case where the claimant is acting in person and a defendant is not the court may request the legal representatives of the defendant to lead on the preparation and filing of the Disclosure Review Document.

No power to direct party to evidence steps taken to fulfil disclosure obligations

In *Eurasian Natural Resources Corp Ltd v Qajygeldin* [2021] EWHC 462 (Ch) at [54]-[60] and [82]-[86] Master Clark held that there was no power either under paras 10.3 or 17.1 of PD 51U, now paras 10.3 and 17.1 of PD 57AD, for the court to order a party to disclose documents evidencing their compliance with their disclosure obligation. The court did, however, retain a discretion under its inherent jurisdiction to order such disclosure, however it should be very sparingly. **57ADPD.10.1**

11. Disclosure Guidance

11.1 A party may seek guidance from the court on any point concerning the operation of this Practice Direction in a particular case, where— **57ADPD.11**

(1) there is a significant difference of approach between the parties;

(2) the parties require guidance from the court in order to address the point of difference between them without a formal determination; and

(3) the point is suitable for guidance to be provided either on the papers or, other than in substantial claims, within the maximum hearing length and maximum time for pre-reading provided at paragraph 11.2.

11.2 Disclosure Guidance may be obtained by issuing an application notice. The application notice should contain a statement identifying the point upon which guidance is sought and confirming the matters at (1) to (3) of paragraph 11.1 above. Evidence will not normally be required for Disclosure Guidance. If a hearing is requested, or is fixed by the court, the application will ordinarily have a maximum hearing length of 60 minutes and a maximum time of 30 minutes for pre-reading. However, where suitable the Court may decide to deal with the application on the documents and without an oral hearing. The Court may also direct a longer maximum hearing length or time for pre-reading, if it is required.

11.3 At a hearing the court will generally expect a legal representative with direct responsibility for the conduct of disclosure to be the person who participates on behalf of each party in the discussion.

11.4 The guidance given by the court will be recorded in a short note, to be approved by the court. Whilst the primary function of Disclosure Guidance is to provide guidance (see paragraph 11.1(2) above), for the avoidance of doubt the court may, where it considers it is appropriate to do so, make an order.

11.5 Unless otherwise ordered, the costs of an application for Disclosure Guidance are costs in the case and no order from the court to that effect is required.

11.6 The provisions in this paragraph do not affect or limit the court's jurisdiction to determine any point about the scope of disclosure, the application of any provision in this Practice Direction or the effect of any order made by the court. A party may apply to the court seeking the determination of an issue about disclosure at any time (see paragraphs 6.8 to 6.11 above).

When to seek court guidance

In *Vannin Capital PCC v RBOS Shareholders Action Group Ltd* [2019] EWHC 1617 (Ch), Joanna Smith QC, sitting as a deputy High Court judge, was critical of the parties' failure to seek guidance from the court on the question whether an application for further searches under CPR PD 51U para.17, now PD 57AD para.17, fell within the scope of an existing order for extended disclosure. Such guidance could have narrowed issues between the parties. As the parties had explored the issues in correspondence and not resolved the issues between them, such guidance from the court was particularly pertinent and ought to have been sought. If guidance had been sought it could have saved court and party time and costs. As such it would have furthered the aims of the pilot scheme. **57ADPD.11.1**

12. Complying with an order for Extended Disclosure

57ADPD.12 **12.1** An order for Extended Disclosure is complied with by undertaking the following steps—

(1) service of a Disclosure Certificate substantially in the form set out in Appendix 4 signed by the party giving disclosure, to include a statement supported by a statement of truth signed by the party or an appropriate person at the party that all known adverse documents have been disclosed;

(2) service of an Extended Disclosure List of Documents (unless dispensed with, by agreement or order); and

(3) production of the documents which are disclosed over which no claim is made to withhold production or (if the party cannot produce a particular document) compliance with paragraph 12.3.

12.2 The order for Extended Disclosure will not have been complied with until each step specified in paragraph 12.1 has taken place.

12.3 If a party cannot produce a particular document (because the document no longer exists, the party no longer has it in its possession or for any other reason) the disclosing party is required to describe each such document with reasonable precision and explain with reasonable precision the circumstances in which, and the date when, the document ceased to exist or left its possession or the other reason for non-production. If it is not possible to identify individual documents, the class of documents must be described with reasonable precision.

12.4 In the case of a company, firm, association or other organisation, or where the Disclosure Certificate is signed by a party on behalf of other parties, the certificate must—

(1) identify the person signing the Disclosure Certificate; and

(2) explain why she or he is considered to be an appropriate person to sign it.

12.5 A party may not without the permission of the court or agreement of the parties rely on any document in its control that it has not disclosed at the time required for Extended Disclosure (or within 60 days after the first case management conference in a case where there will be no Extended Disclosure). For the avoidance of doubt the party and its legal representatives remain under the duties under paragraph 3.1 (the Disclosure Duties) and 3.2 above.

12.6 A Disclosure Certificate may be signed by the legal representative for the party concerned, provided always that the legal representative has explained the significance of the Disclosure Certificate to his or her client(s) and has been given written authority to sign the Disclosure Certificate on the client(s) behalf. In such cases, the party will be deemed to have agreed to and be bound by the certifications given by its legal representative.

13. Production of documents

57ADPD.13 **13.1** Save where otherwise agreed or ordered, a party shall produce—

(1) disclosable electronic documents to the other parties by providing electronic copies in the documents' native format, in a manner which preserves metadata; and

(2) (save as provided by paragraph 5.5 above in the case of Initial Disclosure) disclosable hard copy documents by providing scanned versions or photocopied hard copies.

13.2 Electronic documents should generally be provided in the form which allows the party receiving the documents the same ability to access, search, review and display the documents (including metadata) as the party providing them.

13.3 A party should provide any available searchable OCR versions of electronic documents with the original, unless they have been redacted. If OCR versions are provided, they are provided on an "as is" basis, with no assurance to the other party that the OCR versions are complete or accurate.

13.4 A party should not disclose more than one copy of a document unless additional copies contain or bear modifications, obliterations or other markings or features which of themselves cause those additional copies to fall within a party's Initial or Extended Disclosure obligations.

13.5 In multi-party cases, the parties should discuss and seek to agree whether it is appropriate for all of the disclosing party's documents to be given to all of the other parties or to some only. In the event of disagreement, the parties may seek Disclosure Guidance from the Court pursuant to paragraph 11 or, if appropriate, apply by application notice to the court for directions.

14. Right to withhold production of documents (other than public interest immunity)

14.1 A person who wishes to claim a right or duty (other than on the basis of public interest immunity) to withhold disclosure or production of a document, or part of a document, or a class of documents which would otherwise fall within its obligations of Initial Disclosure or Extended Disclosure may exercise that right or duty without making an application to the court subject to— **57ADPD.14**

(1) describing the document, part of a document or class of document; and
(2) explaining, in the Disclosure Certificate, the grounds upon which the right or duty is being exercised.

A claim to privilege may (unless the court otherwise orders) be made in a form that treats privileged documents as a class, provided always that paragraph 3.2(5) is complied with.

14.2 A party who wishes to challenge the exercise of a right or duty to withhold disclosure or production must apply to the court by application notice supported where necessary by a witness statement.

14.3 The court may inspect the document or samples of the class of documents if that is necessary to determine whether the claimed right or duty exists or the scope of that right or duty.

15. Confidentiality

If there are material concerns over the confidentiality of a document (whether the confidentiality benefits a party to the proceedings or a third party), the court may order disclosure to a limited class of persons, upon such terms and subject to such conditions as it thinks fit. The court may make further orders upon the request of a party, or on its own initiative, varying the class of persons, or varying the terms and conditions previously ordered, or removing any limitation on disclosure. **57ADPD.15**

16. Redaction

16.1 A party may redact a part or parts of a document on the ground that the redacted data comprises data that is— **57ADPD.16**

(1) irrelevant to any issue in the proceedings, and confidential; or
(2) privileged.

16.2 Any redaction must be accompanied by an explanation of the basis on which it has been undertaken and confirmation, where a legal representative has conduct of litigation for the redacting party, that the redaction has been reviewed by a legal representative with control of the disclosure process. A party wishing to challenge the redaction of data must apply to the court by application notice supported where necessary by a witness statement.

Editorial note

Except where privilege is claimed data may be redacted where the data is both irrelevant to any issue in a proceedings and is confidential: *Astra Asset Management UK Ltd v Musst Investments LLP* **57ADPD.16.1**

[2020] EWHC 1871 (Ch) at [18]-[20]. Where data is redacted an explanation must be given as to the basis on which it was made. In cases where there are multiple documents and redactions, separate explanations for each redaction need not be given where they would be repetitive or would risk identifying the redacted data. Explanations should however provide an accurate and complete explanation of the rationale for redaction.

17. Failure adequately to comply with an order for Extended Disclosure

57ADPD.17 **17.1** Where there has been or may have been a failure adequately to comply with an order for Extended Disclosure the court may make such further orders as may be appropriate, including an order requiring a party to—

(1) serve a further, or revised, Disclosure Certificate;
(2) undertake further steps, including further or more extended searches, to ensure compliance with an order for Extended Disclosure;
(3) provide a further or improved Extended Disclosure List of Documents;
(4) produce documents; or
(5) make a witness statement explaining any matter relating to disclosure.

17.2 The party applying for an order under paragraph 17.1 must satisfy the court that making an order is reasonable and proportionate (as defined in paragraph 6.4).

17.3 An application for any order under paragraph 17.1 should normally be supported by a witness statement.

Editorial note

57ADPD.17.1 In *Agents' Mutual Ltd v Gascoigne Halman Ltd (t/a Gascoigne Halman)* [2019] EWHC 3104 (Ch) at [11], Marcus Smith J held that there was a clear difference between the test applicable to applications under paras 17 and 18 of PD 51U, now PD 57AD. Under para.17 "the order must be 'appropriate', which requires the applicant to satisfy the court that making an order is 'reasonable and proportionate'", whereas under para.18 "making the order is 'reasonable and proportionate', but also that varying the original order 'is necessary for the just disposal of the proceedings'". The latter test is a more difficult one to satisfy. This can be contrasted with the approach taken by Richard Salter QC sitting as a deputy judge of the High Court in *Ventra Investments Ltd v Bank of Scotland* [2019] EWHC 2058 (Comm) at [35], where he held there was no practical difference in the circumstances of that case between the applicable tests. It is suggested that the approach in *Agents' Mutual* ought to be taken as expressing the general rule, with that in *Ventra* applying where applications are made in close proximity to the trial date. See para.57ADPD.10.1 and *Eurasian Natural Resources Corp Ltd v Qajygeldin* [2021] EWHC 462 (Ch) on the absence of a power to direct a party to disclose evidence of their compliance with the disclosure obligation under para.17.1. Also see *Astra Asset Management UK Ltd v Musst Investments LLP* [2020] EWHC 1871 (Ch) at [22] which reiterated the approach taken by Marcus Smith J, emphasising the difference between the two rules and stressing that the test under para.18 was more onerous than that under para.17. In *Sheeran v Chokri* [2021] EWHC 3553 (Ch) at [4], Meade J approached para.17 as a two stage test: first, to assess whether there had been non-compliance with para.17.1; and secondly, whether it was reasonable and proportionate to make one of the orders set out in para.17.1(1)-(5). He went on, at [5], to note that he needed more than a general suspicion that there had been non-compliance to make an order under para.17. Also see *Berkeley Square Holdings Ltd v Lancer Property Asset Management Ltd* [2021] EWHC 849 (Ch) at [61]-[68].

In *AAH Pharmaceuticals Ltd v Jhoots Healthcare Ltd* [2020] EWHC 2524 (Comm) HH Judge Worster at [34]-[39] considered Marcus Smith J's approach to the carrying out of electronic searches as part of the disclosure process. The judge endorsed Marcus Smith J's view that parties ought not to conduct such searches unilaterally. The pilot scheme requires party co-operation. Unilateral action is contrary to that requirement. Where one party deliberately refuses to agree to sensible proposals put forward by the other party in respect of such searches, the proper approach is to apply to a Disclosure Guidance hearing to seek to vary the disclosure order. In *Berkeley Square Holdings Ltd v Lancer Property Asset Management Ltd* [2021] EWHC 849 (Ch), Robin Vos, sitting as a deputy judge of the High Court, at [82] stated that, notwithstanding the need for a party's solicitor to supervise the disclosure process, they were not required to be in direct contact with all those, whether individuals or organisations, who were asked to search for documents further to the process, the nature of any such contact depending on the circumstances.

On the court's approach to an application for disclosure under PD 51U, now PD 57AD, paras 17 and/or 18 of expert reports from other proceedings in a case where disclosure had been ordered under CPR Pt 31, see *Byers v Samba Financial Group* [2020] EWHC 2591 (Ch).

Paragraphs 17 and 18 of PD 51U, now PD 57AD, provide powers analogous to, albeit materially different from, those concerning specific disclosure contained in CPR r.31.12: *Revenue and Customs Commissioners v IGE USA Investments Ltd* [2020] EWHC 1716 (Ch) at [26]-[31].

Remedying non-compliance

In *Berkeley Square Holdings Ltd v Lancer Property Asset Management Ltd* [2021] EWHC 849 (Ch) Robin Vos, sitting as a deputy judge of the High Court, set out guidance on the approach to be taken to applications that sought to remedy non-compliance with extended disclosure. **57ADPD.17.2**

Control

In *Pipia v BGEO Group Ltd* [2020] EWHC 402 (Comm); [2020] 1 W.L.R. 2582 at [8]-[13], Andrew Baker J considered the concept of "control" for the purposes of both CPR r.31.8 and PD 51U, now PD 57AD, and its document review process. It was implicit in the extended disclosure process that "control" set the limits ("fixes the universe of documents") within which such disclosure was to be generated. He went on to consider the approach to take to control as between a parent company and its subsidiary. **57ADPD.17.3**

In *Berkeley Square Holdings Ltd v Lancer Property Asset Management Ltd* [2021] EWHC 849 (Ch) Robin Vos, sitting as a deputy judge of the High Court, further considered the concept of "control". A sworn statement that documents are not under the control of a non-compliant party did not preclude the court from making an order under para.17 of the pilot scheme, now para.17 of PD 57AD. In this respect para.17 was analogous to the approach taken to specific disclosure under CPR r.31.12: see [17]-[26]. "Control" for the purposes of the pilot scheme was the same as that set out in CPR r.31.8(2). As such the authorities concerning "control" under CPR Pt 31 were applicable to "control" under the pilot scheme (see para.31.8.0 above): see [27]-[28], [40] and the summary of the principles derived from the authorities at [46]. Furthermore, there was no reason in principle why a subsidiary company could not have control over documents in the custody of their parent company or a shareholder (at [40]).

18. Varying an order for Extended Disclosure; making an additional order for disclosure of specific documents

18.1 The court may at any stage make an order that varies an order for Extended Disclosure. This includes making an additional order for disclosure of specific documents or narrow classes of documents relating to a particular Issue for Disclosure. **57ADPD.18**

18.2 The party applying for an order under paragraph 18.1 must satisfy the court that varying the original order for Extended Disclosure is necessary for the just disposal of the proceedings and is reasonable and proportionate (as defined in paragraph 6.4).

18.3 An application for an order under paragraph 18.1 must be supported by a witness statement explaining the circumstances in which the original order for Extended Disclosure was made and why it is considered that order should be varied.

18.4 The court's powers under this paragraph include, but are not limited to, making an order for disclosure in the form of Models A to E and requiring a party to make a witness statement explaining any matter relating to disclosure.

Variation of order for extended disclosure

In *Vannin Capital PCC v RBOS Shareholders Action Group Ltd* [2019] EWHC 1617 (Ch), Joanna Smith QC sitting as a deputy High Court judge, considered applications to vary an order for extended disclosure (CPR PD 51U para.18.1, now PD 57AD para.18.1) and for further searches (CPR PD 51U, now PD 57AD para.17). The judge was critical of the approach to the applications taken by the parties, which was noted to be contrary to the spirit of the pilot scheme. A more co-operative manner was required by the culture change inherent in the pilot scheme's approach. The judge further held at [8]-[10] that the power to vary orders under CPR r.3.1(7) did not apply to applications to vary orders for extended disclosure: that general power gave way to the specific power to vary set out in CPR PD 51U, now PD 57AD paras 18.1 and 18.2. As such, the criteria applicable to applications to vary under CPR r.3.1(7) set out in *Tibbles v SIG Plc* [2012] EWCA Civ 518; [2012] 1 W.L.R. 2591, CA, were not applicable to applications to vary extended disclosure under the pilot scheme. While the power to vary under paras 18.1 and 18.2 was focused more clearly on applications to expand the scope of an order, the judge considered that the power to vary could be applied to reduce the scope of an extant disclosure order. The question to determine, as in this case, where a reduction in the scope of an extant order was sought was whether it was reasonable and proportionate to reduce the scope of the existing order: see [11]-[13]. Also see *AAH Pharmaceuticals Ltd v Jhoots Healthcare Ltd* [2020] EWHC 2524 (Comm) at [21], where on an application to vary an extended disclosure order following the parties being unable to reach agreement on keyword searches, the judge explained that it was not appropriate for one party to cease to engage with the other on the issue. The proper, and properly co-operative approach further to the disclosure pilot scheme, required the parties to continue their dialogue. Attempts should be made to persuade the **57ADPD.18.1** other that the approach proposed is the right one and worth attempting. If that comes to nothing the proper approach is to then seek the court's guidance at a Disclosure Guidance hearing.

Threshold condition for varying an order for extended disclosure

57ADPD.18.2 In *Re Stay in Style (In Liquidation)* [2020] EWHC 538 (Ch), HH Judge Matthews sitting as a judge of the High Court held that on an application to vary an order for extended disclosure under para.18.1 of PD 51U, now of PD 57AD, had to be supported by a witness statement as required by para.18.3. This was a threshold condition that had to be satisfied for the court to be able to consider whether to exercise its discretion to vary the order. It was necessary as the court had to be placed in the position of being able to consider whether the original order should be maintained or whether it could properly be varied.

19. Restriction on use of a privileged document which has been inadvertently produced

57ADPD.19 **19.1** Where a party inadvertently produces a privileged document, the party who has received the document may use it or its contents only with the permission of the court.

19.2 Where a party is told, or has reason to suspect, that a document has been produced to it inadvertently, that party shall not read the document and shall promptly notify the party who produced it to him. If that party confirms that the document was produced inadvertently, the receiving party shall, unless on application the court otherwise orders, either return it or destroy it, as directed by the producing party, without reading it.

20. Sanctions

57ADPD.20 **20.1** Throughout disclosure the court retains its full powers of case management and the full range of sanctions available to it.

20.2 If a party has failed to comply with its obligations under this Practice Direction including by—

(1) failing to comply with any procedural step required to be taken;
(2) failing to discharge its Disclosure Duties; or
(3) failing to cooperate with the other parties, including in the process of seeking to complete, agree and update the Disclosure Review Document,

the court may adjourn any hearing, make an adverse order for costs or order that any further disclosure by a party be conditional on any matter the court shall specify. This provision does not limit the court's power to deal with the failure as a contempt of court in an appropriate case.

21. Documents referred to in evidence

57ADPD.21 **21.1** A party may at any time request a copy of a document which has not already been provided by way of disclosure but is mentioned in—

(1) a statement of case;
(2) a witness statement;
(3) a witness summary;
(4) an affidavit; or
(5) an expert's report.

21.2 Copies of documents mentioned in a statement of case, witness evidence or an expert's report and requested in writing should be provided by agreement unless the request is unreasonable or a right to withhold production is claimed.

21.3 A document is mentioned where it is referred to, cited in whole or in part or there is a direct allusion to it.

21.4 Subject to rule 35.10(4), the court may make an order requiring a document to be produced if it is satisfied such an order is reasonable and proportionate (as defined in paragraph 6.4).

Paragraph 21.2: Scope of "mentioned"

57ADPD.21.1 On the scope of "mentioned", see *Hoegh v Taylor Wessing LLP* [2022] EWHC 856 (Ch) at [40] (document not "mentioned" unless reference alludes to it or its contents directly. Reference by inference and reference to the effect of document is not sufficient, nor is a "mere opinion" on the balances of probabilities that a transaction had been effected by a document). And see the authorities cited at para.31.14.2.

22. Cost

22.1 The parties are required to provide an estimate of what they consider to be the likely costs of giving the disclosure proposed by them in the Disclosure Review Document, and the likely volume of documents involved, in order that a court may consider whether such proposals on disclosure are reasonable and proportionate (as defined in paragraph 6.4). These estimated costs may be used by the court in the cost budgeting process. **57ADPD.22**

22.2 In cases where the cost budgeting scheme applies, if it is not practical to complete the disclosure section of Form H in relation to disclosure prior to the court making an order in relation to disclosure at the case management conference, the parties may notify the court that they have agreed to postpone completion of that section of Form H until after the case management conference. If they have agreed to postpone they must complete the disclosure section within such period as is ordered by the court after an order for disclosure has been made at the case management conference. Where possible the court will then consider (and if appropriate, approve) that part of the cost budget without an oral hearing.

23. False Disclosure Certificates

23.1 Proceedings for contempt of court may be brought against a person who signs, or causes to be signed by another person, a false Disclosure Certificate without an honest belief in its truth. **57ADPD.23**

Section II

Disclosure before proceedings start

31.16—(1) This rule applies where an application is made to the court under any Act for disclosure before proceedings have started. **57ADPD.24**

(2) The application must be supported by evidence.

(3) The court may make an order under this rule only where—

- **(a) the respondent is likely to be a party to subsequent proceedings;**
- **(b) the applicant is also likely to be a party to those proceedings;**
- **(c) if proceedings had started, the respondent's duty by way of standard disclosure, set out in rule 31.6, would extend to the documents or classes of documents of which the applicant seeks disclosure; and**
- **(d) disclosure before proceedings have started is desirable in order to—**
  - **(i) dispose fairly of the anticipated proceedings;**
  - **(ii) assist the dispute to be resolved without proceedings; or**
  - **(iii) save costs.**

(4) An order under this rule must—

- **(a) specify the documents or the classes of documents which the respondent must disclose; and**
- **(b) require him, when making disclosure, to specify any of those documents—**
  - **(i) which are no longer in his control; or**
  - **(ii) in respect of which he claims a right or duty to withhold inspection.**

(5) Such an order may—

- **(a) require the respondent to indicate what has happened to any documents which are no longer in his control; and**
- **(b) specify the time and place for disclosure and inspection.**

Orders for disclosure against a person not a party

31.17—(1) This rule applies where an application is made to the court under any Act for disclosure by a person who is not a party to the proceedings.

(2) The application must be supported by evidence.

(3) The court may make an order under this rule only where—

(a) the documents of which disclosure is sought are likely to support the case of the applicant or adversely affect the case of one of the other parties to the proceedings; and

(b) disclosure is necessary in order to dispose fairly of the proceedings or to save costs.

(4) An order under this rule must—

(a) specify the documents or the classes of documents which the respondent must disclose; and

(b) require the respondent, when making disclosure, to specify any of those documents—

(i) which are no longer in his control; or

(ii) in respect of which he claims a right or duty to withhold inspection.

(5) Such an order may—

(a) require the respondent to indicate what has happened to any documents which are no longer in his control; and

(b) specify the time and place for disclosure and inspection.

Rules not to limit other powers of the court to order disclosure

31.18 Rules 31.16 and 31.17 do not limit any other power which the court may have to order—

(a) disclosure before proceedings have started; and

(b) disclosure against a person who is not a party to proceedings.

Claim to withhold inspection or disclosure of a document (public interest immunity)

31.19—(1) A person may apply, without notice, for an order permitting him to withhold disclosure of a document on the ground that disclosure would damage the public interest.

(2) Unless the court orders otherwise, an order of the court under paragraph (1)—

(a) must not be served on any other person; and

(b) must not be open to inspection by any person.

...

(8) This Part does not affect any rule of law which permits or requires a document to be withheld from disclosure or inspection on the ground that its disclosure or inspection would damage the public interest.

Subsequent use of disclosed documents and completed Electronic Documents Questionnaires

31.22—(1) A party to whom a document has been disclosed may use the document only for the purpose of the proceedings in which it is disclosed, except where—

(a) the document has been read to or by the court, or referred to, at a hearing which has been held in public;

(b) the court gives permission; or

(c) the party who disclosed the document and the person to whom the document belongs agree.

(2) The court may make an order restricting or prohibiting the use of a document which has been disclosed, even where the document has been read to or by the court, or referred to, at a hearing which has been held in public.

(3) An application for such an order may be made—

(a) by a party; or

(b) by any person to whom the document belongs.

(4) For the purpose of this rule, an Electronic Documents Questionnaire which has been completed and served by another party pursuant to Practice Direction 31B is to be treated as if it is a document which has been disclosed.

Appendix 1 to Practice Direction 57AD

Definitions for the purpose of Section I

1.1 "Control" in the context of disclosure includes documents: (a) which are or were in a party's physical possession; (b) in respect of which a party has or has had a right to possession; or (c) in respect of which a party has or has had a right to inspect or take copies. **57ADPD.25**

1.2 "Copy" means a facsimile of a document either in the same format as the document being copied or in a similar format that is readable by the recipient, and in all cases having identical content.

1.3 "Data Sampling" means the process of checking data by identifying and checking representative individual documents.

1.4 "Disclose" comprises a party stating that a document that is or was in its control has been identified or forms part of an identified class of documents and either producing a copy, or stating why a copy will not be produced.

1.5 "Disclosure Certificate" means a certificate that is substantially in the form set out in Appendix 3 and signed in accordance with the Practice Direction.

1.6 "Disclosure Review Document" means as the case may be the Disclosure Review Document at Appendix 2, or in the case of Less Complex Claims the Disclosure Review Document at Appendix 6, which is to be completed by the parties pursuant to the Practice Direction, in respect of any application for Extended Disclosure.

1.7 "Electronic Image" means an electronic representation of a paper document.

1.8 "Keyword Search" means a software-aided search for words across the text of an electronic document.

1.9 "Less Complex Claim" means a claim which the parties have agreed or the Court has ordered is one that meets the criteria for the Less Complex Claims regime as set out in Appendix 5 of this Practice Direction.

1.10 "List of Documents" means a list of documents in chronological order (or if appropriate classes of documents in chronological order), identifying each document with a clear description including the date and, where applicable any author, sender or recipient. Where appropriate the list must distinguish between documents which exist and those that no longer exist.

1.11 "Metadata" means data about data. In the case of an electronic document, metadata is typically embedded information about the document which is not readily accessible once the native electronic document has been converted into an electronic image or paper document. It may include (for example) the date and time of creation or modification of a word-processing file, or the author and the date and time of sending an e-mail. Metadata may be created automatically by a computer system or manually by a user.

1.12 "Narrative Document" means a document which is relevant only to the background or context of material facts or events, and not directly to the Issues for Disclosure; for the avoidance of doubt an adverse document (as defined at paragraph 2.6) is not to be treated as a Narrative Document

1.13 "Native Electronic Document" or "Native Format" means an electronic document stored in the original form in which it was created by a computer software program;

1.14 "Optical Character Recognition" (OCR) means the computer-facilitated recognition of printed or written text characters in an electronic image in which the text-based contents cannot be searched electronically.

1.15 "Technology Assisted Review" includes all forms of document review that may be undertaken or assisted by the use of technology, including but not limited to predictive coding and computer assisted review.

Appendix 2 to Practice Direction 57AD

Disclosure Review Document

Section 1A: Issues for Disclosure and proposed Disclosure Models

			Issue agreed?		***Proposed Model of Extended Disclosure (A–E)***		***Decision (for the court)***
	Brief description of the Issue for Disclosure[2]	***Reference to statement of case***	***Yes***	***No (party not agreeing)***	***To be completed by claimant***	***To be completed by defendant***	
	[Alternative proposed wording, if not agreed][1]						

[1] *If the wording of any Issue for Disclosure cannot be agreed, the alternative wording proposed should be included immediately under the claimant's formulation.*

57ADPD.27

Section 1B: Model C requests for Disclosure

Claimant / Defendant (delete as appropriate)				
	Issue for Disclosure	*Request for document or narrow classes of documents relating to the Issue for Disclosure*	*Response*	*Decision (for the court)*
1.	**Issue [ ]:**			
2.				
3.				
4.				
5.				
6.				
7.				
8.				
9.				
10.				

[Note: Parties should refer to the guidance on 'Completion of section 2 of the DRD' in the 'Explanatory notes for the DRD' when completing this section]

57ADPD.28

Section 2: Questionnaire

Claimant / Defendant (delete as appropriate)		
	Question	*Details*
1.	**Hard copy documents / files** Confirm whether hard copy documents (for example, notebooks, lever arch files, note pads, drawings/plans and handwritten notes) that are not originally electronic files should be included in the collection of documents which you propose to search. Please propose an approach for the production of hard copy documents: if they will be scanned and made searchable or if they will be disclosed and made available for inspection in hard copy only.	
2.	**Electronic files: data sources/locations** Please set out details on data sources to be considered at collection which you propose to search. Please include details of any sources that are unavailable but may host relevant documents or which may raise particular difficulties due to their location, format or any other reason. Examples of sources to be considered may include the following: (1) Document repositories and/or geographical locations (2) Computer systems or electronic storage devices (3) Mobile phones, tablets and other handheld devices (4) Document management systems (5) Email servers (6) Cloud based data storage (7) Webmail accounts e.g. Gmail, Hotmail, Instant Messaging / collaboration systems	

Claimant / Defendant (delete as appropriate)		
	Question	***Details***
	(8) Back-up systems (9) Social media accounts (10) Third parties who may have relevant documents which are under your control (e.g. agents or advisers). The list above is not intended to be exhaustive, and it may be appropriate to consider other relevant data sources. If a data source is likely only to host documents relevant to particular Issues for Disclosure, this should be noted in this section.	
3.	Please identify and provide details of any bespoke or licensed proprietary software in which relevant documents have been created or stored which may not be available to the other party but without which it is not possible to review the relevant data (e.g. Microsoft Project, Lotus Notes, Bloomberg Chat etc.).	
4.	**Custodians and date ranges** Please set out a list of custodians whose files you propose to search and the date range(s) within which you would propose to search for documents which are relevant to Issues for Disclosure for which any party seeks Extended Disclosure. If a custodian or range of dates is only relevant to certain Issues for Disclosure, or if a certain date range is only relevant to a particular custodian, please indicate this next to their name if this might allow the scope of the search to be narrowed. If the list is extensive, please set out a proposal to prioritise key custodians.	

Claimant / Defendant (delete as appropriate)		
	Question	***Details***
5.	*(For completion after discussions between the parties)* Are the proposals at 4. agreed? If not, set out any areas of disagreement.	
6.	**Search proposals** Please list any searches and methods of searching (including any automated searches or techniques other than keyword searches) you have identified at this stage that you may use to search the data to identify documents that may need to be disclosed. If a certain method of searching, proposed search or keyword is relevant only to a particular Issue for Disclosure, please indicate this if it might allow the scope of the search to be narrowed. Note: The use of initial keywords may assist the parties to identify the likely volume of data that may need to be reviewed. However, keywords will need to be tested and refined during the disclosure process. Accordingly, any keywords proposed at this stage are for the purposes of discussion only. The fact that a party may propose a keyword at this stage should not be taken as an acceptance that the keyword should ultimately be used, particularly if, on testing the keyword against the available data, it provides false positive results. If it is not practicable to provide a list of keywords prior to the CMC, the parties should engage and seek to co-operate following the CMC to identify and agree the key words they propose using and thereafter test those key words against the data to determine whether or not they	

Claimant / Defendant (delete as appropriate)		
	Question	***Details***
	are appropriate.	
7.	*(For completion after discussions between the parties)* Are the proposals at 6. agreed? If not, set out areas of disagreement.	
8.	**Irretrievable documents** Please state if you anticipate any documents being irretrievable due to, for example, their destruction or loss, the destruction or loss of devices upon which they were stored, or other reasons.	
9.	**Technology / computer assisted review** Parties are to consider the use of technology to facilitate the efficient collection of data and its further use for data review. This may include the use of some of the more sophisticated forms of technology / computer assisted review software (TAR / CAR / analytics). If the parties are in a position to propose the use of any technology or computer assisted review tools in advance of the CMC, those proposals should be set out in this section. Where parties have considered the use of such tools but decided against this at this stage (particularly where the review universe is in excess of 50,000 documents), they should explain why such tools will not be used, particularly where this may mean that large volumes of data will have to be the subject of a manual review exercise. Parties should update this form and draw any material updates to the attention of all parties and the Court if they later determine it would be appropriate to use such tools.	

Claimant / Defendant (delete as appropriate)		
	Question	***Details***
10.	**Estimates of costs** Where the parties have agreed searches to be undertaken, state the estimated cost of collection, processing, search, review and production of your Extended Disclosure.	
11.	Where any aspect of the approach to Disclosure is not agreed, estimate your costs of collection, processing, search, review and production of your documents based on Extended Disclosure (Models and scope of any search required) requested by the claimant(s).	
12.	Where any aspect of the approach to Disclosure is not agreed, estimate your costs of collection, processing, search, review and production of your documents based on Extended Disclosure (Models and scope of any search required) requested by the defendant(s).	

Explanatory notes for Disclosure Review Document

Introduction

57ADPD.29 **1.** The Disclosure Review Document ("DRD") is intended to:

(1) facilitate the exchange of information and provide a framework for discussions about the scope of Extended Disclosure;

(2) help the parties to agree a sensible and cost-effective approach to disclosure and identify areas of disagreement; and

(3) provide the court with parties' proposals on disclosure, agreed or otherwise, so the court can make appropriate case management decisions at the case management conference.

2. The explanatory notes provide guidance. While not all of this guidance will be suitable for every claim, parties are nevertheless encouraged to follow this guidance unless there are good reasons not to do so.

3. Unless otherwise stated, references to paragraph numbers in the DRD are to the paragraph numbers in Practice Direction 57AD. If there is a conflict between the DRD and the Practice Direction, the Practice Direction will prevail.

4. The DRD does not need to be completed in cases where an order for only Models A and/or B Extended Disclosure is sought. Section 1A and Section 2 of the DRD only need to be completed if the parties are seeking an order for Extended Disclosure involving a search-based Disclosure Model (i.e. Models C, D and/or E). Where Model C Extended Disclosure is proposed, Section 1B of the DRD will also need to be completed.

5. The DRD may be modified (shortened or lengthened) as required to ensure that key information is provided to the court in a convenient and helpful format. This may include revising some of the questions asked in Section 2 of the DRD or adding others relevant to the particular disclosure exercise to be undertaken.

6. In some proceedings, not every section of the DRD will need to be completed, particularly if the proceedings are likely to require limited disclosure and/or if the identification and retrieval of documents is expected to be straightforward.

7. The DRD should be completed and submitted electronically as a single document to the court by the parties. The claimant will be responsible for doing this.

8. The timetable for completion of the DRD is set out in paragraphs 7 and 10 of the Practice Direction. The parties may agree a revised timetable for completion of the Disclosure Review Document (including the List of Issues for Disclosure, Models and Model C requests) where appropriate, provided always that any such revision to the timetable does not affect the date set for the Case Management Conference. For convenience the timetable is summarised below as follows:

	Stage to be completed	*PD Ref.*	*Deadline*
Step 1	Each party should state, in writing, whether or not it is likely to request search-based Extended Disclosure to include one or more of Models C, D or E on one or more issues in the case. At this point it should not particularise the Model(s) or the issue(s) in the case.	Para 7.1	Within 28 days of the closure of statements of case
Step 2	Where one or more of the parties has indicated it is likely to request search-based Extended Disclosure	Para 7.2	Within 42 days of the closure of statements of case

	Stage to be completed	*PD Ref.*	*Deadline*
	(i.e. Models C, D and/or E), the claimant must prepare and serve on the other parties a draft List of Issues for Disclosure unless the equivalent of such a list has already been agreed between the parties (for example, as part of a fuller list of issues). At the same time, the claimant shall identify for each Issue for Disclosure which Model of Extended Disclosure it proposes for each party. If the claimant proposes Model C Disclosure for any Issue for Disclosure it should indicate, using Section 1B of the Disclosure Review Document, the particular documents or narrow class of documents it proposes should be defined for that purpose. If the claimant fails to take these steps, the defendant may, but is not obliged to, prepare and serve its own draft List of Issues for Disclosure on the other parties together with its proposals on Models and any Model C requests.		
Step 3	A party served with a draft List of Issues for Disclosure and proposals on Models shall indicate using Section 1A (and, if applicable, 1B) of the Disclosure Review Document whether it agrees with the proposed Issues for Disclosure and corresponding Model(s) for Extended Disclosure (including any proposals as to how Model C Disclosure should be defined). If the party does not agree, or wishes to propose alternative or additional Issues for Disclosure, other Models and/or other Model C proposals, it should set out its alternative or additional proposals in Sections 1A and 1B of the Disclosure Review Document.	Para 7.9	As soon as practicable but in any event no later than 21 days after service of the draft List of Issues for Disclosure
Step 4	The parties must discuss and seek to agree the draft List of Issues for Disclosure, the Models identified for each Issue for Disclosure, and the wording of any Model C proposals. They should consider whether any draft Issue for Disclosure can be removed.	Paras 7.10 and 10.6	In advance of the first case management conference

	Stage to be completed	*PD Ref.*	*Deadline*
Step 5	Having sought to agree the List of Issues for Disclosure, proposals on Model(s) for Extended Disclosure and the wording of any Model C requests, the parties should prepare and exchange drafts of Section 2 of the Disclosure Review Document (including costs estimates of different proposals, and where possible estimates of the likely amount of documents involved). Section 2 of the Disclosure Review Document should be completed only if the parties are seeking an order for Extended Disclosure involving a search-based Disclosure Model (i.e. Models C, D and/or E).	Para 10.5	As soon as reasonably practicable and in any event not later than 14 days before the case management conference.
Step 6	A finalised single joint Disclosure Review Document should be filed by the claimant. Related correspondence and earlier drafts should not ordinarily be filed.	Para 10.7	Not later than 5 days before the case management conference
Step 7	The parties must independently file a signed Certificate of Compliance substantially in the form set out in Appendix 3 to the Practice Direction	Para 10.8	Not less than two days before the case management conference

Completing Section 1A of the DRD

57ADPD.30 **1.** The purpose of Section 1A of the DRD is to provide a concise summary of the parties' proposals in relation to Extended Disclosure by identifying the Issues for Disclosure and the proposed Models for Disclosure in respect of such issues. The list of Issues for Disclosure must be completed in accordance with paragraphs 7 and 10 of the Practice Direction[1].

2. Issues for Disclosure are defined at paragraph 7.6 of the Practice Direction as only those key issues in dispute, which the parties consider will need to be determined by the court with some reference to contemporaneous documents in order for there to be a fair resolution of the proceedings. It does not extend to every issue which is disputed in the statements of case by denial or non-admission.

3. The Issues for Disclosure are a point of reference for further discussions between the parties about the manner and scope of disclosure to be given. They are not a statement of case. Nor are they intended to replace the List of Issues, which the parties may be required to prepare and file in advance of the case management conference, although the two documents should ultimately be consistent with each other.

4. The List of Issues for Disclosure should:

(1) state whether each Issue for Disclosure is agreed or opposed and, if so, by whom;

[1] It is to be competed as a Word Document, with any amendments proposed in redline by the parties during period when it is being discussed and finalised. A clean version should ultimately be provided to the court.

(2) seek to avoid any duplication of issues, by using consolidated wording for any overlapping Issues for Disclosure where possible.

5. In accordance with paragraph 7.9 of the Practice Direction, if a particular Issue for Disclosure has not been included in Section 1A by the claimant, or is described in a manner that is unacceptable to the defendant, using Section 1A of the DRD the defendant should provide the claimant with its proposed wording or alternative wording for inclusion in the draft list of Issues for Disclosure as soon as reasonably practicable but in any event no later than 21 days after service of the draft List of Issues for Disclosure.

6. If the parties cannot agree whether certain issues should be included as an Issue for Disclosure, such issues should be included with a tick in the "No" section of the "Issue Agreed?" column, along with an indication of the party not agreeing to it (C for claimant, D for defendant, D1 etc. for each defendant in cases with multiple defendants).

7. Where the parties disagree as to the need for Extended Disclosure or seek Extended Disclosure on different Models in relation to an Issue for Disclosure, that should be recorded in the "Proposed model of Extended Disclosure" column.

Specifying Disclosure Models in Section 1A of the DRD

8. The Disclosure Models under paragraph 8 are:

Model A:	Disclosure confined to known adverse documents[1]
Model B:	Limited Disclosure
Model C:	Disclosure of particular documents or narrow classes of documents
Model D:	Narrow search-based Disclosure, with or without Narrative Documents
Model E:	Wide Search-based Disclosure

9. In addition to completing a List of Issues for Disclosure in Section 1A of the DRD, the parties should also specify which of the above Disclosure Models is proposed in respect of particular Issues for Disclosure.

10. If a party proposes that a different Disclosure Model should apply to each party in the case of a particular Issue for Disclosure, this should be noted (e.g. "Model B for C" (Claimant), "Model D for D" (Defendant)).

11. The claimant must update and re-circulate Section 1A of the DRD to identify areas of agreement and disagreement following the discussions required by paragraph 7.

Updating the Issues for Disclosure

12. The scope of disclosure may require ongoing review, discussion and co-operation between the parties.

13. The fact that a party has not included a particular Issue for Disclosure in the DRD, does not prevent that party from later proposing that a new Issue for Disclosure should be added to the list. For example, new factual issues relevant to the parties' statements of case may be identified because of documents disclosed or evidence exchanged during the proceedings, or because of amendments to a statement of case. In the usual way, if the issues in dispute change during the proceedings, then it may well be appropriate to update the Issues for Disclosure and, as a consequence, Section 2 of the DRD.

14. The parties may agree changes to the Issues for Disclosure after the first

[1] Under Model A, the only further disclosure that is required is to disclose any known adverse documents in relation to the relevant Issue for Disclosure (without the need for any search), in accordance with the duty under paragraph 3.1(2) of the Practice Direction.

CMC without having to seek the court's approval, unless the effect of such changes will be to materially change an order already made, or impact in a material way on the procedural timetable, costs and/or trial date.

Completion of Section 1B of the DRD

(Disclosure of particular documents or narrow classes of documents—Model C)

57ADPD.31 **1.** In accordance with paragraph 10.5, any party proposing Model C Extended Disclosure must complete Section 1B of the DRD.

2. Any party provided with a completed Section 1B in this way must respond within 21 days by completing the "response" column either agreeing to the request or giving concise reasons for not agreeing to the request.

3. Model C requests are not intended to be used to replicate the approach sometimes taken in arbitration with Redfern schedules where parities may include a large number of broad requests for disclosure from the other side, addressing all issues in dispute and all potential data sources. As described in paragraph 8.3 of the Practice Direction, the approach envisaged with Model C is very different.

4. The parties' requests should be limited in number, focused in scope and concise in order that the responding party may be clear as to the particular document(s) or narrow classes of documents relating to a particular Issue for Disclosure for which it is being asked to undertake searches. Broad and wide-ranging formulations such as "any or all documents relating to..." should not be used.

5. In addition, Model C requests should not be used where extensive search-based disclosure is sought other than "to give disclosure of particular documents or narrow classes of documents relating to a particular Issue(s) for Disclosure".[1] In such cases, it may well be more efficient to use a combination of Models A, B and D. It will rarely be appropriate to have a large number of Model C requests in respect of the same data set, because that is likely to (a) make it more difficult for the parties to agree what the Model C requests should be; and b) increase the complexity, costs and time required to undertake the subsequent review exercise. Further, using multiple Model C requests can, in fact, undermine rather than facilitate the use of technology / computer assisted review tools and should therefore be avoided.

6. Model C should not be used in a tactical or oppressive way.

Completion of Section 2 of the DRD

57ADPD.32 **1.** Section 2 of the DRD only needs to be completed if the parties are seeking an order for Extended Disclosure involving a search-based Disclosure Model (i.e. Models C, D and/or E). This is because Models A and B do not require mandatory searches to be undertaken.

2. In cases where a search-based Disclosure Model (Models C, D or E) is proposed by the parties, the purpose of Section 2 of the DRD is to provide the court with information about the data held by each party, including:

(1) where and how the data is held;

(2) how the parties propose to process and search the data where a search-based Disclosure Model (Models C, D and E) is sought in relation to particular Issues for Disclosure); and

(3) whether there are any points that the parties have not been able to agree through discussions and which they therefore need the court to determine at the case management conference.

---

[1] See paragraph 8 of the Practice Direction

3. Section 2 of the DRD should also be used to identify data that can be excluded from the review process, for example, particular custodians, data ranges and back up data to ensure that the data pool is it is reasonable and proportionate, having particular regard to the factors in section 6.4 of the Practice Direction.

4. In cases where no documents are held by a party, that party may confirm this in writing rather than complete Section 2 of the DRD.

5. In Section 2 of the DRD, the parties should seek to provide information about how they intend to approach disclosure so that the court is then in a position to decide what, if any, orders for Extended Disclosure should be made.

6. The parties should include in Section 2 any information that will assist the court in determining the appropriate scope of disclosure for each Issue for Disclosure. The information listed in Section 2 should be treated as a guide and not an exclusive list of the information that should be provided. The DRD may be adapted to meet the needs of the particular case and the parties are not required to answer all of the questions. In particular:

(1) In cases where the disclosure exercise is likely to be complex and substantial with multiple sources of data, it may be necessary to raise additional questions and to provide other information. Conversely, it may not in fact be possible to answer all of the questions in Section 2 of the DRD questionnaire in advance of the case management conference because that information may not yet be available.

(2) In cases where the disclosure exercise is likely to be less complex or involving a very limited number of documents or sources of data, the parties may complete only those parts of Section 2 which are relevant or helpful for a particular case.

(3) The parties are expected to take a reasonable and proportionate approach in completing Section 2 and to seek to agree upon on any such changes to achieve that outcome as far as possible.

7. The parties must confer and seek to agree the contents of Section 2 of the DRD as it applies to their disclosure, in advance of the case management conference. The parties are expected to do this by phone, video conference or in person. Extensive correspondence in relation to the DRD is unlikely to be efficient or helpful. Where particular points cannot be agreed, they should be recorded, in a summary form in the relevant sections of the DRD after discussions between the parties.

8. For the avoidance of doubt, if only one party considers that disclosure of certain materials is required, the other party must nevertheless state its proposals as to how the disclosure of such materials should be effected, without prejudice to its position that no order for disclosure should be made.

9. The provision of information about the data that might be relevant to a request for Extended Disclosure shall not be treated as a concession that Extended Disclosure is appropriate.

10. In advance of the production of documents, parties should consider and discuss whether in a case involving multiple parties, it will be appropriate for the entirety of a party's disclosure to be provided to all parties or only to those parties to whom the disclosure is relevant.

Who has responsibility for incorporating the parties' comments on the DRD?

11. Unless otherwise agreed or ordered, the claimant is to be responsible for updating the DRD throughout the proceedings to ensure that it reflects the parties' combined comments and discussions. Where the claimant is unrepresented, it may be appropriate for the defendant's advisers to assist the claimant and/or take responsibility for completion of the DRD by agreement.

12. When a party other than the claimant is completing Section 2 of the

DRD, it may do so by completing and sending across just Section 2 of the DRD completed (i.e. there is no need for the party to carry across any text already discussed and agreed in relation to Sections 1A and 1B). The claimant should then ensure that the information provided to it in Section 2 by the other party is incorporated into the latest draft of the DRD, over which it has ultimate carriage.

Estimates as to costs

13. In accordance with paragraph 22 of the Practice Direction, the parties are required to provide an estimate of what they consider to be the likely costs of giving the disclosure proposed by them in the DRD, and the likely amount of documents involved, in order that a court may consider whether such proposals on disclosure are reasonable and proportionate. This information is to be provide in answer to questions 10 to 12 of Section 2.

14. If the approach to Extended Disclosure is not fully agreed, the parties should be ready to provide more detailed information at the CMC as to how their global estimates were arrived at and the impact upon them of particular requests for Extended Disclosure.

15. In cases where the costs budgeting scheme applies, if it is not practical to complete the disclosure section of Form H in relation to disclosure prior to the court making an order in relation to disclosure at the case management conference, the parties may notify the court that they have agreed to postpone completion of that section of Form H until after the case management conference (see paragraph 22.2 of the Practice Direction).

Guidance on process after any order for Extended Disclosure has been made

57ADPD.33 **1.** Where the court orders the parties to give Extended Disclosure, the parties will need to consider the appropriate methodology for the disclosure exercise, which includes the collection, processing, review and production of documents.

2. The parties and their advisers are reminded of their Disclosure Duties to the court to discuss and endeavour to agree the approach to be taken to disclosure, always with a view to reducing the burden and cost of this process.

3. Although the parties are under a duty to liaise and cooperate with the legal representatives of the other parties to the proceedings (or the other parties where they do not have legal representatives) so as to promote the reliable, efficient and cost-effective conduct of disclosure, including through the use of technology, there may be points which cannot be agreed despite the best efforts of the parties, in which case the parties should request the assistance of the court in a Disclosure Guidance Hearing as set out paragraph 11 of the Practice Direction.

4. This guidance identifies various forms of analytics, and technology or computer assisted review software which are currently available and in use. The parties should not, however, feel constrained from proposing new forms of processing and review software, which may be developed in the future and which may be appropriate for use in any given case.[1]

Appropriate methodology

5. Although the parties may approach the disclosure exercise in different ways and using different technology, an appropriate methodology for a case involving electronic documents should always include the following:

(1) Electronic documents should be collected in a format that preserves and

[1] The onus is on the parties to ensure they engage appropriate IT forensic expertise to assist with this process if they or their legal advisers do not have such expertise in house.

does not alter the underlying document metadata (where possible)[3] thereby allowing the party receiving the documents the same ability to access, search, review and display the documents as the party giving disclosure. This approach should generally be taken unless a document has been redacted.

(2) A record should be kept of each stage of the process so that the methodology can be explained to the court if necessary after the event (see Methodology record below).

(3) To the fullest extent practicable, deduplication of the data set (for example by using the hash values of the documents) should be undertaken during processing and prior to giving disclosure of data to the other side.

Agreeing aspects of methodology

6. To the extent that this has not already been agreed between the parties or determined by the court, the parties should seek to agree the following as early in the process as possible:

(1) How the collection data set is to be identified and collected.

(2) Data culling measures applied at collection (i.e. date range, custodians, search terms).

(3) Any limitations that will be applied to the document collection process and the reasons for such limitations.

(4) Data exclusion measures applied during or post-collection (e.g. Domains such as @ CompanyA.com).

(5) How each party intends to use analytics to conduct a proportionate review of the data set.

(6) How each party intends to use technology assisted review to conduct a proportionate review of the data set (particularly where the review data set is likely to be in excess of 50,000 documents).

(7) The approach and format for production. This will have an impact on the approach to the review exercises, so parties should endeavour to agree this point at an early stage.

(8) Format of documents to be exchanged—parties are encouraged to exchange documents in native format unless there is a reasonable justification not to do so (e.g. redacted documents). Electronic documents should generally be made available in the form which allows the party receiving documents the same ability to access, search, review and display the documents as the party giving disclosure.

(9) Management of document groups for production—parties should describe and agree the approach they will adopt for document groups (families). Often, it will be appropriate to agree not to break document groups (families) and to review a document group as a whole.

(10) If documents within a group are to be withheld at the production stage the parties should consider and agree whether to use placeholders indicating the reasons for document being withheld (e.g. Withheld for Privilege).

(11) Format for electronic exchange—parties are encouraged to agree database load file format and details to be included in load file/document index. All documents to be produced should be assigned a Disclosure Identification/Number. There is no need to produce a typed list of documents in the traditional sense, unless that will be of assistance to the parties.

(12) Methodology record

7. The parties should keep records of their methodology during the disclosure exercise, to include the following:

(1) Document sources not considered at collection and why.

(2) The deduplication[1] method applied.
(3) Any DeNISTing[2] applied.
(4) Approach to non-text searchable items.
(5) Approach with encrypted/password protected items (i.e. what measures were applied to decrypt).
(6) Search terms, including the number of search term responsive documents and search term responsive documents plus family members.
(7) Any use of clustering, concept searching, e-mail threading, categorisation and any other form of analytics or technology assisted review.

Appendix 3 to Practice Direction 57AD

Certificate of Compliance (represented parties)

57ADPD.34 By submitting the disclosure review document to the court, I hereby confirm that I have discussed, explained and advised my client on the following:

1. The alternative orders that can be made by the court in relation to disclosure, including the question of whether or not an order for Extended Disclosure should be sought at all and, if so, what the Issues for Disclosure should be and which of the Disclosure Models are appropriate to achieve a fair determination of those Issues for Disclosure;
2. The duties that I and my client are under in relation to disclosure pursuant to paragraph 3 of Practice Direction 57AD;
3. The overriding objective in all cases to seek to ensure that the burden and costs of disclosure are reasonable and proportionate in the context of the proceedings.
4. The likely costs that will be incurred in respect of the disclosure orders sought.

I further confirm that the information provided in this disclosure review document is, to the best of my knowledge and belief, true and accurate.

Name: ....
Position: ....
[Claimant / Defendant]

Certificate of Compliance (unrepresented parties)

By submitting the disclosure review document to the court, I hereby confirm as follows:

1. I understand the duties that I am under in relation to disclosure pursuant to paragraph 3 of Practice Direction 57AD.
2. I am aware of the overriding objective in all cases to seek to ensure that the burden and costs of disclosure are reasonable and proportionate in the context of the proceedings.
3. The information provided in this DRD is, to the best of my knowledge and belief, true and accurate.

Name: ....
Position: ....

---

[1] The options for deduplication are as follows; (A) Global—where documents across the entire processed data set are deduplicated against each other. This means that where a document exists in any location within the data set only one copy of it is retained; (B) Custodian—where documents held by the same custodian are deduplicated against each other only or (C) Custom—specific to the project.

[2] "DeNISTing" is a method of reducing the number of documents subject to lawyer or computer review by removing file types that are highly unlikely to have evidentiary value. DeNISTing" is the National Institute of Standards and Technology and the process of DeNISTing is based on a list of file types maintained by the agency.

[Claimant / Defendant]

Appendix 4 to Practice Direction 57AD

Disclosure Certificate

Notes: This Disclosure Certificate is for use in all claims where Practice Direction 57AD (Disclosure in the Business and Property Courts) applies. **57ADPD.35**

In the	
Claim No.	
Claimant (including ref)	
Defendant (including ref)	
Date	
Party returning form	

Initial Disclosure

Either:

On [date] [party], [with its Statement of Case] [or state if the parties agreed to defer the time for provision of Initial Disclosure] , provided [to party/ parties] by way of Initial Disclosure [a List, and/or] copies of the following:

- the key documents on which it has relied (expressly or otherwise) in support of the claims or defences advanced in its statement of case (and including the documents referred to in that statement of case); and
- the key documents that are necessary to enable the other parties to understand the claim or defence they have to meet.
  (These comprise Initial Disclosure as defined at paragraphs 5.1 and 5.2 of Practice Direction 57AD.)

[The Initial Disclosure List is found at [at Appendix A]] or [The parties agreed to dispense with the requirement to produce an Initial Disclosure List of Documents, as permitted by paragraph 5.8 of Practice Direction 57AD.]

Or

[No Initial Disclosure was required because [the parties agreed to dispense with it] [the Court ordered that it was not required] [it would involve [name of party] providing (after removing duplicates, and including documents referred to at paragraph 5.4(3)(a)) more than (about) whichever is the larger of 1000 pages or 200 documents (or such higher but reasonable figure as the parties may agree)].

Where the parties agreed to dispense with Initial Disclosure, please set out here your reasons for this agreement.

Extended Disclosure

Please list the orders made in the proceedings that have imposed Extended Disclosure obligations (together, "the Disclosure Order/s"):

Please state if the Extended Disclosure List of Documents has been dispensed with, by agreement or order.

Unless already particularised in the Disclosure Review Document or in any Extended Disclosure List of Documents, if any of Models C, D or E (search-based Extended Disclosure) were ordered in respect of any Issues for Disclosure, set out here the limits of the search conducted, by reference to custodians, date ranges, locations, document types, keyword searches and any relevant limits specified.

To the extent any of these limits were not contained in the Disclosure Order/s or recorded in an agreement in writing between the parties either in the Disclosure Review Document or elsewhere, please identify them and explain why they were necessary and why they were not agreed with the other part[y/ies]

I, [name] certify [for and on behalf of the above-named Party] that I am aware of and, to the best of my knowledge and belief, have complied with [my / Party's] duties under Practice Direction 57AD, including having:

A) taken and caused to be taken reasonable steps to preserve documents in [the Party's] control that may be relevant to any issue in the proceedings;
B) disclosed documents I am aware (or, in the case of a company or organisation, of which the company or organisation is aware, within the meaning of paragraph 2.9 of Practice Direction 57AD) are or have been in [my] or [the Party's / company's] control and adverse to [my/the Party's] case on any issue in the proceedings, unless they are privileged;
C) [*in the case of an order for Extended Disclosure of Model C, D or E only*] undertaken and caused to be undertaken any search for documents in a responsible and conscientious manner to fulfil the stated purpose of the search and in accordance with [my/the Party's] obligations as set out in Practice Direction 57AD and [the Disclosure Order/s];
D) acted honestly in relation to the process of giving disclosure;
E) used reasonable efforts to avoid providing documents to another party that have no relevance to the Issues for Disclosure in the proceedings.
F) produced electronic copies of documents in their native format, in a manner which preserves metadata and produced disclosable hard copy documents by providing scanned versions or photocopied hard copies.

I certify [on behalf of the Party] that I am aware of and, to the best of my knowledge and belief, have complied with the Disclosure Order.

I understand that I [and Party] must inform the court and the other parties if any further document required to be disclosed (whether under Practice Direction 57AD or the Disclosure Order/s) comes into [the Party's] control at any time before the conclusion of the case.

I wish to withhold production of the following [document, part of a document, or class of documents] which would otherwise fall within [my/the Party's] obligations:

Description of document, part of a document or class of documents	***Grounds upon which production is being withheld***
	e.g. Privilege, already in other party's possession (inter-partes correspondence etc)
	Documents no longer within party's control

I am aware that proceedings for contempt of court can be brought against me if I sign a false Disclosure Certificate without an honest belief in its truth.

Signed		**Date**	
	(Party) (Party's representative or legal representative)		

If the party making disclosure is a company or other organisation, the person signing this Disclosure Certificate should be someone from within the organisation with appropriate authority and knowledge of the disclosure exercise or the party's legal representative. This person will have received confirmation from all those people with accountability or responsibility within the company or organisation either for the events or circumstances the subject of the case or for the conduct of the litigation that they have provided for disclosure all adverse documents of which they are aware, and will have taken reasonable steps to check the position with any such person who has since left the company or organisation. Identify here who the person making the disclosure statement is and why he or she is the appropriate person to make it:

Name:
Role and explanation of why you are the appropriate person to sign this Certificate:

Appendix A

List/s of Documents

Please either attach copies of any Initial Disclosure and/or Extended Disclosure Lists of Documents, or incorporate the text of the lists here. **57ADPD.36**

Appendix 5 to Practice Direction 57AD

Less Complex Claims

1. This appendix contains provisions for a simplified disclosure regime for Less Complex Claims. All the provisions of the main body of Practice Direction 57AD on disclosure in the Business and Property Courts apply to Less Complex Claims, including the provisions relating to Initial Disclosure in accordance with paragraph 5 of Practice Direction 57AD, unless they are expressly varied by this appendix or are required to be applied with appropriate changes as a consequence of its provisions. **57ADPD.37**

2. Parties to a dispute should always consider whether a dispute or claim is suitable for the Shorter Trials Scheme rather than being treated as a Less Complex Claim.

Designating claims as Less Complex Claims

3. A Less Complex Claim is a claim which by virtue of its nature, value, complexity and the likely volume of Extended Disclosure may not benefit from the full procedure set out in the main body of Practice Direction 57AD. The value of a claim means a reasonable estimate, made in good faith, of the total financial value at risk in the claim taken with the value, so far as ascertainable, of any non-financial relief sought.

4. If the value of a claim is less than £1,000,000 then unless the other factors specified in paragraph 3 above indicate to the contrary, the claim should be treated as a Less Complex Claim. The fact that the value of a claim may exceed £1,000,000 does not, of itself, mean that the claim should not be treated as a Less Complex Claim if the other factors specified in paragraph 3 above indicate that it should be.

5. A claim may be treated as a Less Complex Claim for the purposes of Extended Disclosure either by an agreement made between all the parties to the claim or by order of the court.

6. An agreement to treat a claim as a Less Complex Claim may be made between parties before or after a claim is issued and these provisions may be used in respect of existing as well as new proceedings. If an agreement is reached before a claim is issued it takes effect upon service of the claim on the parties to the agreement. An agreement between the parties may not vary the provisions for Extended Disclosure contained in this appendix, unless approved by court order.

7. If there is no agreement between the parties before the claim is issued, the claimant may by letter or in its particulars of claim notify the defendant that it wishes the claim to be treated as a Less Complex Claim. If no such notification is given by the claimant, a defendant may by letter or in its defence notify the claimant that it wishes to treat the claim as a Less Complex Claim.

8. A request to treat a claim as a Less Complex Claim must include brief reasons for believing that the claim meets the criteria specified in paragraph 3 of this appendix.

9. If the parties acting reasonably and in good faith do not agree to the claim being treated as a Less Complex Claim, the provisions of this appendix shall not apply unless the court makes an order to the contrary. The court may make such an order of its own volition or upon determining an application made by application notice. The application notice must contain or be accompanied by a fair summary of the parties' competing contentions in relation to the application of the criteria specified in paragraph 3 of this appendix and copies of any relevant correspondence. Where possible, the court will make a determination in writing without a hearing.

Simplified procedure for Less Complex Claims

10. Where the parties have agreed that this appendix shall apply to the claim, or the court has so ordered, the provisions in the main body of Practice Direction 57AD shall be varied and shall operate as follows:

10.1 Extended Disclosure will be given using only Models A, B or D. Models C and E are not available for use in a Less Complex Claim.

10.2 The parties shall complete a disclosure review document in the form set out in Appendix 6 in accordance with the timetable contained within paragraphs 7 and 10 of Practice Direction 57AD and Appendix 7.

10.3 As provided for in paragraphs 7.1 and 10.1 of Practice Direction 57AD, if none of the parties are requesting search-based Extended Disclosure (ie Model D), but instead are only proposing Models A and/or B, then the provisions in Appendices 5, 6 and 7 shall not apply (unless the court orders to the contrary) and there shall be no requirement to identify the Issues for Disclosure or to complete a Disclosure Review Document, although the parties may agree to do so if they consider this will assist.

10.4 "Issues for Disclosure" has the same meaning as in paragraph 7.6 of Practice Direction 57AD. However, the definition is to be applied with the following additional guidance. Issues for Disclosure in a Less Complex Claim must be brief and be drafted at a high level of abstraction. Only rarely should the number of Issues for Disclosure exceed five and they should not be defined by reference to sub-issues if that will materially increase the length and complexity of the List of Issues for Disclosure.

10.5 When drafting Issues for Disclosure the parties should have regard to the primary functions of those Issues namely (i) to help the parties to consider, and the court to determine, whether Extended Disclosure is required and, if so, which Model or Models should be used; (ii) to assist the parties in identifying documents and categories of documents that are likely to exist and require to be disclosed; (iii) to assist those carrying out the disclosure process to do so in a practical and proportionate way including, in the case of search-based disclosure, to help define and guide the searches; (iv) to assist with the process of reviewing documents produced by searches; and (v) to avoid the production of documents that are not relevant to the issues in the proceedings.

10.6 The parties may use issues for trial as a starting point for defining Issues for Disclosure but it is not the function of Issues for Disclosure to replace issues for trial.

10.7 The parties must discuss and seek to agree the draft List of issues for Disclosure in advance of the date fixed for the first case management conference.

10.8 The parties must at all times have regard to their duties under paragraph 3 (in particular the duty placed upon legal representatives under paragraph 3.2(3)) of Practice Direction 57AD and their duty to assist the court to further the overriding objective, in particular to deal with the claim at proportionate cost. The parties should recognise that there may be genuine differences of view about whether Extended Disclosure should be ordered and, if so, what order should be made. If the parties are unable to agree the terms of an order for Extended Disclosure after reasonable engagement between them, brief submissions on the differences of approach should be made to the court at the case management conference and the court requested to make a determination.

11. For the avoidance of doubt, all provisions in the main body of Practice Direction 57AD regarding Known Adverse Documents apply to Less Complex Claims.

57ADPD.38

Appendix 6 to Practice Direction 57AD

Disclosure Review Document for Extended Disclosure in Less Complex Claims

1.	**Issues for Disclosure and disclosure Model proposals**	**Issue for Disclosure**	**Proposed Disclosure Models**	**Issue agreed?**[1]	**Model Agreed?**[7]
		1. *[Concise description of the issue for disclosure]* **[Alternative proposed wording of the Claimant(s)/ Defendant(s):]**	*[B / D]*	*[Y/N]*	*[Y/N]* **[Alternative proposed disclosure model of the Claimant(s)/ Defendant(s):]**
		2.			
		3.			
		4.			
		5.			
2.	**Data collection sources to be searched by the parties** Each party should confirm whether there are any data sources or locations, or categories of hard copy or electronic documents (as applicable) which should be included in the collection of documents which are likely to be relevant to the Issues for Disclosure and which the party proposes to search for the disclosure. Please set out details of the data sources,				

	locations and categories which are proposed to be included.	
3.	**Unavailable sources or irretrievable/inaccessible documents** Please identify and briefly set out details for any documents likely to be relevant to Issues for Disclosure which it is known or anticipated may be irretrievable or otherwise unavailable or difficult to access in order to be searched for the purpose of the disclosure (e.g. due to destruction or loss, or the need for bespoke or licenced software to review the data)	
4.	**Search proposals** Please set out any initial search proposals to identify any documents which may need to be disclosed (including any automated searches or techniques other than keyword searches, as applicable). The proposals should indicate any custodians' files the parties propose to search, any applicable date ranges for the searches, and which particular	

	Issues for Disclosure the custodians or date ranges are relevant to. Parties should also set out proposals to use technology to facilitate the disclosure exercise if the parties consider the use of technology to be appropriate. When considering the use of technology parties should have regard to the following factors: (i) whether it would be efficient and proportionate to use technology, (ii) the number of documents in the potential pool of documents to be searched and potentially reviewed for the proposed disclosure, (iii) the estimated cost of the disclosure (including estimated costs of using technology compared with not using technology), (iv) the value of the claim, (v) the complexity of the claim, (vi) the nature of the claim, and (vii) any other relevant factors.	
5.	**Costs estimates** Where the parties have agreed / sought to agree for searches to be undertaken, please state	

	the estimated cost of collection, processing, search, review and production of each parties' Extended Disclosure (as applicable).	
6.	**Areas of disagreement** Please indicate any areas of disagreement between the parties in respect of any of the matters set out in sections 1–5 of this form and briefly set out the reasons for any areas of disagreement and for any alternative wording proposed for Issues for Disclosure or alternative Models proposals. Where any aspect of the approach to Extended Disclosure is not agreed, each party should indicate their estimated costs of collection, processing, search, review and production of their documents based on the Extended Disclosure (Models and scope of any search required) requested: (i) by the claimant(s) and (ii) by the defendant(s).	*[E.g. Description of area of disagreement]* *Claimant'(s') position:* *Defendant'(s') position:]*

[7] If the parties cannot agree the wording of any issue and/or any disclosure model proposals, the parties who disagree with the formulation of an issue for disclosure or model proposal should include alternative proposals or wording under the formulation. The parties should also briefly outline the areas of disagreement and state the reasons for the disagreement and for any alternative proposals in section 6 of this form.

Appendix 7 to Practice Direction 57AD

Explanatory notes for the Disclosure Review Document for Extended Disclosure in Less Complex Claims

57ADPD.39 **1.** The Less Complex Claims Disclosure Review Document ("LCCDRD") is intended to:

a. facilitate the exchange of information and provide a framework for discussions about the scope of Extended Disclosure;
b. help the parties to agree a sensible and cost-effective approach to Extended Disclosure for Models A, B and/or D and identify areas of disagreement; and
c. provide the court with parties' proposals on Extended Disclosure for Models A, B and/or D, agreed or otherwise, so that the court can make appropriate case management decisions at the case management conference.

2. These explanatory notes provide guidance. While not all of this guidance will be suitable for every claim, parties are nevertheless encouraged to follow this guidance unless there are good reasons not to do so.

3. Unless stated otherwise below, the explanation and guidance in the Introduction of the Explanatory notes for Disclosure Review Document in Appendix 2 will apply for the completion of this form. If an order for Extended Disclosure is made by the court, the parties may also find it helpful to refer to the "Guidance on process after any order for Extended Disclosure has been made", which is also in Appendix 2.

4. References to paragraph numbers in the LCCDRD are to the paragraphs in Appendix 5 to Practice Direction 57AD (the "Practice Direction") unless stated otherwise and if there is a conflict between the LCCDRD and the Practice Direction, the Practice Direction will prevail.

5. The LCCDRD only needs to be completed where one or more of the parties are seeking Extended Disclosure in a Less Complex Claim. Parties do not need to complete a LCCDRD in Less Complex Claims where only Model A or B or no Extended Disclosure is sought by the parties. Where only Model B is requested, if the parties consider that it would nevertheless assist to identify and seek to agree upon a List of Issues for Disclosure or to complete any other sections of the LCCDRD, the parties may agree to do so.

6. Unless agreed by the parties or ordered otherwise by the court, the claimant(s) will be responsible for ensuring that the form is completed and a single agreed version is filed with the court. If the claimant(s) is not seeking any search-based Disclosure (i.e. Model D disclosure) but one or more of the defendants is, the parties may agree that the defendant(s) shall be responsible for producing the LCCDRD and ensuring that the form is filed with the court. If there is more than one defendant, the parties should seek to agree which defendant shall bear this responsibility for the form.

7. The parties must seek to agree and complete a List of Issues for Disclosure. Apart from the List of Issues for Disclosure in section 1, which must be completed in all cases where a LCCDRD is required under paragraph 10.1 of Appendix 5 to the Practice Direction, the parties are not required to complete all of the other sections of the form. They only should complete the sections which are applicable and relevant to the disclosure being requested in the particular case. This should as a minimum include the key information which the parties consider would assist the court in deciding what disclosure to order in the case.

8. If the parties agree that any of the sections in the form are not applicable or relevant at all to the case, they should leave the response box next to those sections blank. If the parties cannot agree on whether a section is not applicable or is irrelevant, or if a section is only not applicable to a particular party or to a particular extent, they should include the wording "Not applicable" next to that section and a brief explanation, in order to assist the court in understanding the parties' positions and in its review of the form.

9. The parties are encouraged to confer (in person or by phone or video conference) and seek to agree the contents of the LCCDRD as it applies to their disclosure, in advance of the case management conference. Extensive correspondence in relation to the LCCDRD is unlikely to be efficient or helpful.

10. If the parties cannot agree on any aspects of the LCCDRD (including the List of Issues for Disclosure) this should be recorded in summary form in section 6. The parties may also apply if appropriate for guidance from the court under paragraph 11 of the Practice Direction in order to seek to resolve any differences in advance of the case management conference.

11. The fact that a party may propose initial searches (including keyword searches) at the stage of completing the LCCDRD should not be taken as acceptance by that party that those searches should ultimately be used (particularly if, on testing the keyword searches against the available data, it provides false positive results).

12. If it is not practicable to provide a list of keywords for searches prior to the case management conference, the parties should engage and seek to co-operate following the case management conference to identify and agree the key words they propose using and thereafter test those key words against the data to determine whether or not they are appropriate.

Timetable for completing the LCCDRD

13. The timetable for completion of the LCCDRD is set out in paragraphs 7 and 10 of the Practice Direction. The parties may agree a revised timetable for completion of the LCCDRD (including the List of Issues for Disclosure and Models) where appropriate, provided always that any such revision to the timetable does not affect the date set for the Case Management Conference. For convenience the timetable is summarised below as follows:

	Stage to be completed	*Deadline*
Step 1	Each party should state, in writing, whether or not it is likely to request Extended Disclosure Models A, B and/or D on one or more issues in the case. At this point it should not particularise the Model(s) or the issue(s) in the case.	Within 28 days of the closure of statements of case
Step 2	Where one or more of the parties has indicated it is likely to request search-based Extended Disclosure (i.e. Models D), unless the parties agree otherwise, the claimant must prepare and serve on the other parties a draft List of Issues for Disclosure unless the equivalent of such a list has already been agreed between the parties (for example, as part of a fuller list of issues). At the same time, the claimant shall identify for each Issue for Disclosure which Model of Extended Disclosure	Within 42 days of the closure of statements of case

	Stage to be completed	*Deadline*
	it proposes for each party. If the claimant fails to take these steps, the defendant may, but is not obliged to, prepare and serve its own draft List of Issues for Disclosure on the other parties.	
Step 3	A party served with a draft List of Issues for Disclosure and proposals on Models shall indicate within section 1 of the LCCDRD whether it agrees with the proposed Issues for Disclosure and corresponding Model(s) for Extended Disclosure by completing the "Issue Agreed" and "Model Agreed" columns in section 1. If the party does not agree, or wishes to propose alternative or additional Issues for Disclosure or other Models, it should set out its alternative or additional proposals in section 1 of the LCCDRD and briefly explain and set out in section 6 of the LCCDRD the reasons why it disagrees with the Issues for Disclosure or Models proposals of the other party the reasons for the alternative proposals it is proposing.	As soon as practicable but in any event no later than 21 days after service of the draft List of Issues for Disclosure
Step 4	Having sought to agree the List of Issues for Disclosure and proposals on Model(s) for Extended Disclosure, the parties should prepare and exchange drafts of the LCCDRD (with all applicable sections of the document completed) in accordance with the guidance in Appendix 7.	As soon as reasonably practicable and in any event not later than 14 days before the case management conference
Step 5	The parties must seek to resolve any disputes over the scope of any Extended Disclosure sought or any other aspect of the completion of the LCCDRD.	In advance of the first case management conference
Step 6	Unless otherwise agreed by the parties or ordered by the court, the claimant(s) shall be responsible for ensuring that the form is completed and a single agreed version is filed with the court. Related correspondence and earlier drafts should not ordinarily be filed.	Not later than 5 days before the first case management conference
Step 7	The parties must independently file a signed Certificate of Compliance	Not less than two days before the case management

	Stage to be completed	*Deadline*
	substantially in the form set out in Appendix 3 to the Practice Direction.	conference

Add new Disclosure Pilot Practice Note:

DISCLOSURE PILOT PRACTICE NOTE

Editorial introduction

This Practice Note was initially issued to supplement PD 51U—The Disclosure Pilot Scheme. That pilot scheme was incorporated into the CPR as PD 57AD, as from 1 October 2022 (CPR Update 149, July 2022). The Practice Note was retained by the Chancery Guide Practice Note 2022, issued by the Chancellor in July 2022. It did not, however, rename the Disclosure Pilot Practice Note, which was identified in the 2022 Practice Note by its citation from *Civil Procedure* 2022: para.51UPN.1 **57ADPN.1.0.1**

1. This note applies to claims in the following lists in the Business and Property Courts of England and Wales: **57ADPN.1**

- Business List (ChD) (and its sub-lists)
- Insolvency and Companies List
- Intellectual Property List
- Property Trusts and Probate List
- Revenue List

2. Practitioners have expressed uncertainty about whether the disclosure pilot applies to Part 8 claims. This note is intended to provide guidance. It is not, however, authoritative about the meaning of the Practice Direction.

3. The pilot does not directly apply to Part 8 claims because Part 8 contains its own regime for the disclosure of documents that are relied on by the parties.

4. The only statement of case in a Part 8 claim is the claim form. Paragraph 5.1 of the Practice Direction says there is no obligation to give Initial Disclosure with the Part 8 claim form. This is to ensure that the provisions relating to Initial Disclosure do not overlap with, and duplicate, the provisions in Part 8.

5. The court has power to make an order for extended disclosure under the pilot in a case proceeding under Part 8. It will adopt such elements of the Practice Direction as are appropriate to the case and the scope of disclosure that is sought. The party requesting disclosure will need to identify the issues for disclosure and the Model or Models that apply. It is not expected that the full procedure for extended disclosure, including completion of all elements of the Disclosure Review Document, will normally be required.

Chief Master Marsh
27 March 2019

Add new Practice Note on Disclosure in the Insolvency and Companies List (ChD):

PRACTICE NOTE ON DISCLOSURE IN THE INSOLVENCY AND COMPANIES LIST (CHD)

Editorial introduction

This Practice Note was issued on 6 October 2022 by the Chief Insolvency and Companies Court Judge. It replaced the Practice Note in relation to the operation of PD51U—Disclosure Pilot for the Business and Property Courts as a consequence of the pilot scheme being incorporated formally into the CPR as PD 57AD as from 1 October 2022 (CPR Update 149, July 2022). **57ADPN.2.0.1**

This practice note replaces the practice note in relation to the operation of PD51U—Disclosure Pilot for the Business and Property Courts, issued in February 2019, following the coming into force of PD57AD—Disclosure in the Business and Property Courts on 1st October 2022. **57ADPN.2**

1. PD57AD does not directly apply to Part 8 claims because Part 8 contains its own regime for the disclosure of documents that are relied on by the parties.
2. Forms of originating process familiar to users of the Insolvency and Companies List, such as petitions and Insolvency Act applications, are not "statements of case" for the purpose of PD57AD.
3. The only statement of case in a Part 8 claim is the claim form. The parties attention is drawn to Paragraph 1.4 (7) and 5.1 of the Practice Direction.
4. PD57AD Paragraph 1.12 provides the court with a power to apply the Practice Direction in proceeding under Part 8.
5. The Court may, as part of its case management powers, consider it appropriate to order disclosure in accordance with PD57AD.
6. Petitions issued for relief under section 994 of the Companies Act 2006 will be subject to disclosure.
7. Where a party requests disclosure they will need to identify the issues for disclosure and the Model or Models that apply. It is not expected that the full procedure for extended disclosure, including completion of all elements of the Disclosure Review Document, will be required.
8. Standard disclosure is no longer available.

Chief Insolvency and Companies Court Judge Briggs
6 October 2022

Add new Practice Note: Business and Property Courts in Leeds, Liverpool, Manchester and Newcastle:

PRACTICE NOTE: BUSINESS AND PROPERTY COURTS IN LEEDS, LIVERPOOL, MANCHESTER AND NEWCASTLE

Editorial introduction

57ADPN.3.0.1 This Practice Note was issued by the Supervising Judge of the Business and Property Courts for the Northern & North-Eastern Circuits in May 2022. It was retained by the Chancery Guide Practice Note 2022, issued by the Chancellor in July 2022.

Introduction

57ADPN.3 **1.** This Practice Note and the Chancellor's Practice Note: The Chancery Guide 2022 apply to all cases in Chancery lists in the B&PC District Registries in Liverpool, Manchester, Leeds and Newcastle.

2. They come into force on 29 July 2022 and apply to existing and future cases.

3. The guidance in the Chancery Guide applies to cases in the Chancery lists in the B&PCs London and in the B&PC District Registries alike, save where local guidance is different. This Practice Note adopts the abbreviations generally used in the Chancery Guide.

4. It is recognised that there are differences in the way that the Chancery lists and courts work outside London. In particular, Chancery Masters and ICC Judges only sit in London. HCJs sit in B&PC District Registries from time to time, as needed.

5. Outside London, most of the work done by Masters and ICC Judges is done instead by specialist BPC District Judges and section 9 Judges, but without replicating the particular ways that Masters and ICC Judges work.

6. It is therefore appropriate to provide guidance where local practices are materially different and where guidance is needed. The Chancery Guide is to be applied in B&PC District Registries as it applies in the B&PC London, subject only to this guidance and otherwise making all necessary adjustments, so that the substance of the Guide applies to serve the overriding objective notwithstanding the differences: see para 6.2 of the Chancery Guide.

Case Management

7. Part 7 claims issued in Manchester, Leeds and Newcastle District Registries are not triaged by a judge prior to the filing of directions questionnaires, except where an earlier application brings the claim before the court for a decision. Paras 6.41 and 6.42 of the Chancery Guide therefore do not apply. Accordingly, if the parties consider that an early review is required they should request it by email.

8. In Liverpool, Part 7 and Part 8 claims are triaged by a BPC District Judge upon issue. They will be referred to a section 9 Judge or transferred, if appropriate.

9. The default management track in B&PC District Registries is case management by a BPC District Judge and trial by HCJ, section 9 Judge or Deputy High Court Judge, as appropriate. However, the court may direct instead case management and trial by a BPC District Judge, a section 9 Judge or (with the approval of the Vice-Chancellor) a HCJ, where appropriate. A request for a different case management track must be made before the first CMC or CCMC.

10. Requests for an early review, a different case management track or guidance from a specialist BPC District Judge should be sent to *bpc.manchester@justice.gov.uk*, *bpc.leeds@justice.gov.uk*, *newcastlebpc@justice.gov.uk* or *LiverpoolBPC@justice.gov.uk* as appropriate.

11. Although there is no formal procedure for docketing cases to a particular judge, this may be considered, if justified, on the first review of a case following directions questionnaires, at a CMC or at any stage, on application.

Hearings

12. All CMCs and CCMCs before a judge will be listed for a remote hearing of 1½ hours, unless the court otherwise directs.

13. Any request for a different mode of hearing or a different estimated length of hearing should be included in the directions questionnaire or, if later, sent by email to the relevant email address given above.

14. In Liverpool, first hearings of Part 8 claims are listed for 45 minutes plus 15 minutes of pre-reading time, to take place remotely unless the judge orders otherwise.

15. In addition to the electronic bundle, a hard copy bundle must also be prepared for a CMC or CCMC and delivered to the court not less than 3 clear days before the hearing, unless the court otherwise directs. A CMC/CCMC bundle should also include a short chronology where this is likely to be helpful in resolving issues at the CMC/CCMC.

16. Subject to any direction to the contrary, trial bundles must be filed in accordance with paragraphs 6 and 14 of Appendix X to the Chancery Guide.

17. Skeleton arguments must be provided for a CMC/CCMC unless there is no issue of any substance in dispute.

18. Listing trial windows will be fixed by the court at the CMC/CCMC. At hearings before the section 9 Judge in Newcastle an attempt will be made to list the trial itself at the hearing and parties should attend with dates of availability within an agreed 6 month trial window.

19. District Judges robe for trials and, in Manchester, when hearing winding up petitions.

20. Pre-trial checklists are not required to be filed in Manchester.

21. The pre-trial review, if any, will be conducted by the trial judge where possible.

22. All trials will be listed with a fixed start date. Parties' dates of availability must be filed by email to *bpc.leeds.listing@justice.gov.uk*, for the attention of the Case Progression Officer, to *bpc.manchester@justice.gov.uk* for the attention of the BPC Listing Officer, to *Newcastle.bpc@justice.gov.uk* or to *LiverpoolBPC@justice.*

gov.uk as appropriate, by the date specified at the first CMC/CCMC once the trial window has been identified. A party who fails to return availability dates in time will be deemed available throughout the listing window.

23. In Liverpool, for trials of 3 days or more, or trials in which there is likely to be contested oral expert evidence, the parties must agree and the Claimant must send three proposed fixtures within the trial window: these should be filed by email to *LiverpoolBPC@justice.gov.uk* by the date specified at the first CMC/CCMC.

24. Skeleton arguments must be CE-filed in accordance with Appendix Y to the Chancery Guide and also emailed to an HCJ's clerk, where their identity is known in time, and in all other cases emailed to *bpc.manchester@justice.gov.uk*, *bpc.leeds.skeletons@justice.gov.uk*, *newcastle.bpc@justice.gov.uk* or *LiverpoolBPC@justice.gov.uk* as appropriate.

25. Draft orders must be filed only through CE-file unless the judge directs otherwise.

Applications

26. An application may be reviewed by a judge before it is listed and the court may give directions before or in addition to listing it.

27. In Liverpool, applications before a BPC District Judge of 2 hours or less (excluding reading time) will be listed as remote hearings, unless the judge otherwise directs. Electronic bundles for an application hearing in Liverpool must be filed upon CE file not less than 3 clear days before the hearing, unless the court otherwise directs, and should include a non-controversial case summary and a draft order.

28. Urgent applications to be heard by a HCJ, section 9 Judge or Deputy High Court Judge must be certified as urgent business and listing arranged with the Case Progression Officer or BPC Listing Officer where the Friday Applications List procedure does not apply. The certificate should provide a realistic time estimate and state which other parties are to be served.

Friday Applications List (Manchester and Leeds)

29. Applications suitable for the Friday Applications List are those which require to be heard by a HCJ, s.9 Judge or Deputy HCJ and meet the requirements of paragraph 31 below.

30. Arrangements for the listing of an application in the Judge's Friday Applications List must be made with the BPC Listing Officer in Manchester (*bpc.manchester@justice.gov.uk*) and the Applications List Officer in Leeds (*bpc.leeds@justice.gov.uk*).

31. The time required for pre-reading, oral argument, judgment and dealing with costs and consequential matters (including any application for permission to appeal) must not exceed 2 hours in total.

32. Insolvency and Company applications are frequently listed in the Friday Applications List, including applications for:

a. Administration orders and administration extensions;
b. Injunctions to restrain presentation of a winding up petition or to restrain advertisement of such a petition;
c. Appointment of an interim receiver;
d. Appointment of a provisional liquidator;
e. Search and seize orders pursuant to Insolvency Act 1986, s.365;
f. Validation order

and other applications that meet the requirements of paragraph 31 above.

33. Applications in the Friday Applications List will normally be heard in person: see *Practice Note: Business and Property Courts in Manchester and Leeds* (26 May 2022). Any person seeking a direction that the application be heard fully remotely or on a hybrid basis must apply at the earliest possible time by email to *bpc.manchester@justice.gov.uk* or *bpc.leeds@justice.gov.uk* (in Leeds, marked for the attention of the Applications List Officer) for a direction. The application must be copied to any respondent (or to the applicant).

34. All applications are listed for 10:30am and the judge hearing the list will decide at 10:30 in which order to hear them. Parties must arrive at court and sign in with the clerk at least 10 minutes before the court sits (or 15 minutes before in the case of any person attending remotely).

35. A hard copy bundle must also be filed if requested by the court.

36. The court must be notified by email and a consent order CE-filed by no later than 4.00pm on the working day before the hearing if the parties agree the disposal of the application or terms on which it is to be adjourned. Otherwise, attendance is required.

Insolvency and Companies List

37. Insolvency and companies work will be allocated between HCJs, s.9 Judges and District Judges in accordance with paragraph 3 of the Insolvency Practice Direction. Such cases will be listed before a HCJ, section 9 Judge or Deputy High Court Judge in the same way as other cases are listed (see above), and before a District Judge as directed by the court.

38. District Judges will ordinarily only hear matters of up to 3 days' duration but may occasionally hear longer cases.

39. In Leeds, winding up petitions are listed for a first hearing in a general list on the second and fourth Tuesday or each month. Petitions are block listed to be heard at 10.30am and will be heard in list order. Applications to rescind winding up orders are heard in the afternoon on the same days. All bankruptcy petitions are listed with a fixed appointment.

40. In Manchester, winding up petitions are heard every other Tuesday and are block listed to be heard at 10.00am. The unopposed petitions are heard first. The Official Receiver's list is heard from 11am and the bankruptcy list from 11.30am, both on an individual hearing basis. Applications to rescind winding up orders are listed individually as ordinary applications, not in the fortnightly list.

41. In Newcastle, winding up petitions listed for a remote hearing are given a fixed hearing time on Tuesday and Friday of each week. Those listed to be heard in person are listed at 10am and 2pm each Tuesday and Friday and are heard in list order. Bankruptcy petitions are also listed on Tuesday and Friday of each week and given a fixed appointment, whether listed for a remote or in person hearing.

42. In Liverpool, winding up petitions are listed on Tuesdays for a first hearing in a general list. Petitions are all listed to be heard at 10.30am and the judge decides the order in which to hear them.

43. Winding up petitions and bankruptcy petitions are heard in person save in Newcastle (see paragraph 41 above) and in Liverpool, where bankruptcy petitions may be heard remotely. A bundle should be filed electronically by no later than 10am on the working day before the hearing.

44. In Leeds, District Judges maintain a District Judges' Companies and Insolvency List on the afternoon of the second and fourth Tuesday of each month, when short Companies and Insolvency Applications may be heard. This is separate from the Friday Applications List.

Orders

45. Draft orders filed after a hearing should not bear the word "Draft" in the heading and should be emailed to *bpc.manchester@justice.gov.uk*, *bpc.leeds@justice.gov.uk*, *newcastle.bpc@justice.gov.uk* or *LiverpoolBPC@justice.gov.uk* as appropriate. Draft winding up or bankruptcy orders need only be filed if the order contains non-standard provisions.

46. For all applications, a draft of the proposed order should be filed in editable Word format by the applicant at the same time as they file their application. Where a judge directs the parties to file an agreed draft order for the judge's approval, that must be filed in editable Word format, with confirmation that the draft has been agreed between the parties.

47. In Newcastle, if time permits, the judge will seal and provide the order to the parties at the hearing. Parties should include in their draft the email addresses to which electronic copies can be sent. Where orders are provided in this way, there is no further requirement to serve the order on those parties.

The Hon Mr Justice Fancourt

Vice-Chancellor of the County Palatine of Lancaster

PART 64

ESTATES, TRUSTS AND CHARITIES

Related sources

In the first list, replace the last two bullet points with:

64.0.3 • Chancery Guide Ch.23 paras 23.50–23.56, Ch.25, Ch.26 (pensions) (Vol.2 paras 1A-240—1A-241, 1A-243 and 1A-259)

I. Claims Relating to the Administration of Estates and Trusts

Rule 64.2(a): Applications under rule to determine any question arising in the administration of the estate of a deceased person or execution of a trust

Replace the second paragraph with:

64.2.1 If the trustees consider it appropriate they may apply to the court under r.8.2A for permission to issue the claim form without naming any defendants (PD 64B para.4.2 (see para.64BPD.4); Chancery Guide paras 13.35—13.39 (see Vol.2 para.1A-147)). Guidance as to the procedure for applying to the court for directions in relation to the administration of a trust is given in Practice Direction 64B.

Rule 64.2(a): Prospective costs orders in relation to applications under rule

Replace paragraph with:

64.2.2 See PD 64A paras 6.1 to 6.8 at para.64APD.6. Prospective costs orders may be made in favour of beneficiaries who are joined as defendants to claims brought by trustees raising questions of construction relating to a trust, will or pension scheme documentation. Proceedings of the same type brought by a beneficiary and which would have justified an application by the trustees may also qualify: see *Re Buckton (Costs)* [1907] 2 Ch. 406 at 413–417. Such an order will only be made if it is considered inevitable that the trial judge would order the beneficiaries' costs out of the estate (*McDonald v Horn* [1995] 1 All E.R. 961; [1995] I.C.R. 685). The court may order the costs to be paid from time to time on an interim basis. An application for a prospective costs order, which should be made by Part 23 Application Notice supported by evidence given by witness statement, will be dealt with on paper in an ordinary case (PD 64B para.6.5). Trustees should in every case consider whether the application is suitable to be dealt with without a hearing. If a hearing is considered necessary the Part 23 Application Notice should seek a hearing and in Part C or in the evidence explain the position. Detailed guidance on the procedure to be followed is given in PD 64A para.6, to which is annexed a model form of order. See also Chancery Guide paras 25.30-25.32. Unlike *Beddoe* applications (see para.64.2.3), applications for prospective costs orders are made by Pt 23 application in the substantive proceedings. It is possible to apply for a prospective costs order in relation to part only of proceedings, where for example there is a costs agreement in place in relation to the remainder of the proceedings: (*HR Trustees v German (No.2)* [2010] EWHC 321 (Ch); [2010] 3 Costs L.R. 443). For further commentary on the position of representative beneficiaries in pension claims, see the Chancery Guide at paras 26.21-26.30 (Vol.2 paras 1A-263—1A-264).

Costs apart from prospective costs orders

To the end of the last paragraph, add:

64.2.2.1 In *Royal Commonwealth Society for the Blind v Beasant* [2021] EWHC 351 (Ch), a will construction case, the court refused to order the parties' costs to be borne by the estate and instead joined the solicitors firm who drafted the will as a party and made an indemnity costs order against the firm.

Rule 64.2(a): Beddoe applications under rule

Replace paragraph with:

Trustees or executors may bring applications for directions as to whether or not to bring or defend proceedings: *Re Beddoe* [1893] 1 Ch. 547. Although a trustee or executor is entitled to an indemnity out of the trust fund against all charges and expenses properly incurred by them, they will be deprived of their indemnity if it is held that the expenses were not properly incurred. Therefore an executor or trustee is at risk of being deprived of their costs of defending or bringing a claim if they do so without either the consent of all the beneficiaries, or in default of such consent, the direction of the court. The application must be made by Part 8 claim, independently of the main litigation, to a Master other than the assigned Master. Following the changes to PD 2B (Allocation of Cases to Levels of Judiciary), which came into force on 6 April 2015, Masters now have the same jurisdiction as High Court Judges to deal with all *Beddoe* applications. Paragraph 7.11 of PD 64B remains out of date. The application will normally be heard by a Master, unless the Master releases it to a High Court Judge. District Judges, however, may only deal with such applications with the consent of their Supervising Judge (PD 2B para.7B.2(c)). In an appropriate case relief may only be granted in stages, for example, up to a certain stage of the proceedings such as disclosure and inspection, with permission to restore for further directions. All *Beddoe* applications must be supported by evidence given by witness statement including the advice of a suitably qualified lawyer as well as, in summary form, an estimate of the significance to the trust estate of the issues in the proceedings, the likely costs, and other relevant factors (PD 64B paras 7.1–7.6). The evidence must also state whether the PD (Pre-Action Conduct) or any relevant Pre-Action Protocol has been complied with, and whether the trustees have proposed or undertaken, or intend to propose, mediation by ADR, and (in each case) if not, why not (PD 64B para.7.5). The evidence should not generally be served on a beneficiary who is a defendant, unless no harm would be done by the disclosure (PD 64B para.7.6). A draft order must be filed. No separate application notice is necessary for the claim to be decided. **64.2.3**

The need to consider whether Beddoe proceedings are necessary

At the end of the paragraph, replace "issue (see Chancery Guide para.29.89 on pensions claims, but relevant also to private trust claims)." with:

issue. **64.2.3.2**

Applications for permission to distribute the estate of a deceased Lloyd's name

Replace "Chancery Guide paras 9.2, 29.13, 29.41-29.42" with:

Chancery Guide paras 25.61–25.62 **64.2.5**

Rule 64.2(c): Variation of Trusts Act 1958

At the end of the paragraph, replace "applies (see Chancery Guide paras 21.18 and 29.23)." with:

applies. **64.2.7**

Confidentiality orders

Replace the second paragraph with:

The practice concerning the way in which the initial stages of Variation of Trusts claims are handled in the light of the decision in *V v T* [2014] EWHC 3432 (Ch), the change to Masters' jurisdiction in April 2015, and the guidance contained in the Chancery Guide paras 25.37–25.48 (Vol.2 para.1A-252), is stated in Practice Note (Variation of Trusts: Confidentiality Orders Pending the Hearing of Application), 9 February 2017, unrep. (see para.64PN.1). The Practice Note is published on the *judiciary.gov* website with a draft confidentiality order, also available on the *http://www.gov.uk* website under form **CH43**. **64.2.7.1**

Evidence

In the first paragraph, delete "(See also Chancery Guide, paras 29.23-29.28).". **64.2.7.2**

At the end of the second paragraph, replace "para.29.25)." with:

para.25.46).

Rule 64.2(d): Administration of Justice Act 1985 s.48

Replace the last sentence with:

If the Master directs service of notices under r.19.8A and any acknowledgment of service is **64.2.8** received, the claimant should apply to the Master, on notice to the parties who acknowledged service, for directions (see Chancery Guide paras 25.49-25.58 and in relation to pensions cases see paras 26.35-26.37).

PRACTICE NOTE: VARIATION OF TRUSTS

Add new paragraph 64PN.0.1:

Editorial introduction

64PN.0.1 This Practice Note was issued in February 2021 by the Chief Chancery Master. It was retained by the Chancery Practice Note 2022, issued by the Chancellor in July 2022.

Editorial note

To the end of the paragraph, add:

64PN.1.1 Paragraphs 29.22 to 29.27 of the Chancery Guide, referred to above, are now found at paras 25.38 to 25.45.

PART 65

PROCEEDINGS RELATING TO ANTI-SOCIAL BEHAVIOUR AND HARASSMENT

Replace r.65.1(c) with:

Scope of this Part[1]

65.1 **(c) in Section III, about claims for demotion orders under the Housing Acts 1985 and 1988, and for prohibited conduct standard contract orders under the Renting Homes (Wales) Act 2016, and related proceedings;**

Change title of Section III:

III. Demotion Claims, Prohibited Conduct Standard Contract Order Claims (in Wales), Related Proceedings and Applications (in England) to Suspend the Right to Buy

Replace r.65.11 with:

Scope of this Section and interpretation[2]

65.11 **65.11—(1) This Section applies to—**

(a) claims by a landlord for an order under section 82A of the Housing Act 1985 or under section 6A of the Housing Act 1988 ("a demotion order");

(aa) claims by a landlord for an order under section 121A of the Housing Act 1985 ("a suspension order");

(b) proceedings relating to a tenancy created by virtue of a demotion order; and

(c) claims by a landlord for an order under section 116 of the Renting Homes (Wales) Act 2016.

---

[1] Introduced by the Civil Procedure (Amendment) Rules 2004 (SI 2004/1306) and amended by the Civil Procedure (Amendment) Rules 2007 (SI 2007/2204), the Civil Procedure (Amendment) Rules 2008 (SI 2008/2178), the Civil Procedure (Amendment) Rules 2009 (SI 2009/2092), the Civil Procedure (Amendment No.2) Rules 2010 (SI 2010/1953) and the Civil Procedure (Amendment No.2) Rules 2022 (SI 2022/783).

[2] Introduced by the Civil Procedure (Amendment) Rules 2004 (SI 2004/1306) and amended by the Civil Procedure (Amendment No.3) Rules 2005 (SI 2005/2292) and the Civil Procedure (Amendment No.2) Rules 2022 (SI 2022/783).

(2) In this Section—

(za) "the 2016 Act" means the Renting Homes (Wales) Act 2016;

(a) "a demotion claim" means a claim made by a landlord for a demotion order;

(b) "a demoted tenancy" means a tenancy created by virtue of a demotion order;

(ba) "a dwelling" means a dwelling let under an occupation contract;

(bb) "a prohibited conduct standard contract" has the meaning provided by section 116(6) of the 2016 Act;

(bc) "a prohibited conduct standard contract order" is an order imposed under section 116 of the 2016 Act;

(bd) "a prohibited conduct standard contract order claim" means a claim for a prohibited conduct standard contract order;

(be) "a Renting Homes possession claim" means a claim for the recovery of possession of a dwelling under the 2016 Act;

(c) "suspension claim" means a claim made by a landlord for a suspension order; and

(d) "suspension period" means the period during which the suspension order suspends the right to buy in relation to the dwelling house.

Replace r.65.12 with:

Demotion claims, prohibited conduct standard contract order claims or suspension claims made in the alternative to possession claims[1]

65.12—(1) Where a demotion order or suspension order (or both) is claimed in the alternative to a possession order, the claimant must use the Part 55 procedure and Section I of Part 55 applies, except that the claim must be made in accordance with rule 55.3(1). **65.12**

(2) Where a prohibited conduct standard contract order is claimed in the alternative to a possession order, the claimant must use the Part 55 procedure and Section IV of Part 55 applies.

Replace r.65.13 with:

Other demotion claims, prohibited conduct standard contract order claims or suspension claims[2]

65.13 Where a demotion claim or suspension claim (or both), or a prohibited conduct standard contract order claim is made other than in a possession claim or a Renting Homes possession claim, rules 65.14 to 65.19 apply. **65.13**

[1] Introduced by the Civil Procedure (Amendment) Rules 2004 (SI 2004/1306) and amended by the Civil Procedure (Amendment No.3) Rules 2005 (SI 2005/2292), the Civil Procedure (Amendment) Rules 2014 (SI 2014/407) and the Civil Procedure (Amendment No.2) Rules 2022 (SI 2022/783).

[2] Introduced by the Civil Procedure (Amendment) Rules 2004 (SI 2004/1306) and amended by the Civil Procedure (Amendment No.3) Rules 2005 (SI 2005/2292) and the Civil Procedure (Amendment No.2) Rules 2022 (SI 2022/783).

Replace r.65.14 with:

Starting a demotion claim, prohibited conduct standard contract order claim or suspension claim[1]

65.14 **65.14—(1) (a) The claim may be made at any County Court hearing centre;**

(b) the claim will be issued by the hearing centre where the claim is made; and

(c) if the claim is not made at the County Court hearing centre which serves the address where the property or dwelling is situated, the claim, when it is issued, will be sent to that hearing centre.

(Practice Direction 65 makes further provision in respect of claims which are not made at the County Court hearing centre which serves the address where the property or dwelling is situated.)

(2) The claim form and form of defence sent with it must be in the forms set out in Practice Direction 65.

(Part 16 and Practice Direction 65 provide details about the contents of the particulars of claim).

Replace r.65.20 with:

Proceedings relating to demoted tenancies and prohibited conduct standard contract order claims[2]

65.20 **65.20 A practice direction may make provision about proceedings relating to demoted tenancies or to prohibited conduct standard contracts.**

V. Proceedings under the Protection from Harassment Act 1997

General approach

After the penultimate paragraph, add new paragraph:

65.27.2 The Court of Justice of the European Communities has provided useful guidance in cases alleging psychological harassment. See *KF v European Investment Bank* (T-299/20) EU:T:2022:171 and *KU v EEA* (T-425/60).

PRACTICE DIRECTION 65—ANTI-SOCIAL BEHAVIOUR AND HARASSMENT

I. Housing Act 1996, Policing and Crime Act 2009 and Anti-Social Behaviour, Crime and Policing Act 2014

Issuing the Claim

In paragraph 1.1(1), replace "Practice Direction 8A" with:

65PD.1 Part 8

65PD.5 *Change title of Section III:*

III. Demotion Claims, Prohibited Conduct Standard Contract Order Claims or Suspension Claims

Suspension Claims Made in the Alternative to Possession Claims

Add paragraph at start:

65PD.5A (Suspension claims may be made in England, but may not be made in Wales.)

[1] Introduced by the Civil Procedure (Amendment) Rules 2004 (SI 2004/1306) and amended by the Civil Procedure (Amendment No.3) Rules 2005 (SI 2005/2292), the Civil Procedure (Amendment No.2) Rules 2009 (SI 2009/3390), the Civil Procedure (Amendment) Rules 2014 (SI 2014/407) and the Civil Procedure (Amendment No.2) Rules 2022 (SI 2022/783).

[2] Introduced by the Civil Procedure (Amendment) Rules 2004 (SI 2004/1306) and amended by the Civil Procedure (Amendment No.2) Rules 2022 (SI 2022/783).

Add new paragraph 5B.1:

Prohibited Conduct Standard Contract Order Claims made in the Alternative to Possession Claims

5B.1 If the claim relates to a residential dwelling in Wales, let under an occupation contract and if the claim includes a prohibited conduct standard contract order claim, the particulars of claim must– **65PD.5B**

(1) state that the prohibited conduct standard contract order claim is a claim under section 116 of the 2016 Act;
(2) state whether the claimant is a community landlord or registered charity;
(3) provide details of any agreement reached between the landlord and the contract-holder as to the terms of the periodic standard contract, pursuant to paragraph 2 of Schedule 7 to the 2016 Act; and
(4) state particulars of the conduct alleged.

Change title of paragraph: **65PD.6**

Other Demotion Claims, Prohibited Conduct Standard Contract Order Claims or Suspension Claims

Replace paragraph 6.2 with:

6.2 The claimant must use the relevant approved claim form and particulars of claim form. The defence must be in form **N11D** or **N11D (W)** as appropriate.

Particulars of Claim

Add new paragraph 7.1A:

7.1A In a prohibited conduct standard contract claim the particulars of claim must– **65PD.7**

(a) state that the prohibited conduct standard conduct claim is a claim under section 116 of the 2016 Act;
(b) state whether the claimant is a community landlord or a registered charity;
(c) identify the dwelling to which the claim relates;
(d) provide the following details about the occupation contract to which the prohibited conduct claim relates–
 (i) the parties to the occupation contract;
 (ii) the period of the occupation contract;
 (iii) the amount of the rent;
 (iv) the dates on which the rent is payable; and
 (v) details of any agreement reached between the landlord and the contract-holder as to the terms of the periodic standard contract; and
(e) state details of the conduct alleged.

The Hearing

In paragraph 9.2, after "the 1996 Act", add:

or section 55 of the 2016 Act **65PD.9**

Change title of Section III: **65PD.10**

III. Proceedings Relating To Demoted Tenancies; Proceedings Against a Contract Holder of a Prohibited Conduct Standard Contract for Possession

Change title of paragraph 10.1:

Proceedings for the Possession of a Demoted Tenancy; Proceedings Against a Contract Holder of a Prohibited Conduct Standard Contract for Possession

Replace paragraph 10.1 with:

10.1 Proceedings against a tenant of a demoted tenancy or a contract-holder of a prohibited conduct standard contract for possession must be brought under the procedure in Part 55 (Possession Claims).

PART 67

PROCEEDINGS RELATING TO SOLICITORS

The nature of Pt 8 proceedings under the Solicitors Act 1974

To the end of the paragraph, add:

67.2.1 However, on an application for the detailed assessment of a bill under s.70 of the Solicitors Act 1974, the court does not have a general jurisdiction to set aside the retainer agreement, for example, on the basis of undue influence: *Jones v Richard Slade & Co Ltd* [2022] EWHC 1968 (QB).

Add new paragraph at end:

In an appropriate case, the court may order disclosure under Pt 31 and the provision of further information under Pt 18: *Edwards v Slater and Gordon UK Ltd* [2022] EWHC 1091 (QB).

PART 69

COURT'S POWER TO APPOINT A RECEIVER

Related sources

Replace list with:

69.0.2
- Chancery Guide (paras 14.88 to 14.91)
- Queen's Bench Guide (Receivers and equitable execution, paras 22.89 to 22.96)

Editorial note

Replace the penultimate paragraph with:

69.2.1 Injunctions: although the bar on the grant of injunctions by Masters and District Judges in the High Court has been removed in the revised PD 2B, the guidance at para.14.12 of the Chancery Guide means that in practice where application is made for an injunction to restrain disposal of assets and to appoint a receiver on an interim basis, application should be made to a judge. This would not apply to an injunction in aid of appointment of a receiver by way of equitable execution which is not an interim order in this sense, or other cases where the *American Cyanamid* principles are not in play.

Editorial note

In the first paragraph, in the penultimate sentence, replace "Operational" with:

69.5.1 Operations

PART 70

GENERAL RULES ABOUT ENFORCEMENT OF JUDGMENTS AND ORDERS

Enforcement of decisions of tribunals, etc.

Add new paragraph at end:

No application under r.70.5(4) is required where a local authority wishes to apply under r.73.3 for a charging order in respect of a council tax liability order made in a Magistrates' Court. (See the Council Tax (Administration and Enforcement) Regulations 1992 (SI 1992/613) reg.50 and r.73.2.) **70.5.1**

PART 71

ORDERS TO OBTAIN INFORMATION FROM JUDGMENT DEBTORS

Should a committal order be made

Add new paragraph at end:

In *Farrer & Co LLP v Meyer* [2022] EWHC 362 (QB) Kerr J confirmed that the jurisdiction to find a person in contempt for non-compliance with an order under Pt 71 is: (a) separate from the power to make a finding of contempt on an application made under Pt 81 ([163]); and (b) is dependent upon a failure to comply by a person against whom an order has been made under r.71.2 ([164]). **71.8.2**

PART 73

CHARGING ORDERS, STOP ORDERS AND STOP NOTICES

Charging order on matrimonial home

Replace list item (4) with:

(4) Where an interim order has been made after a petition for divorce the court will usually order that the application for a final order is heard alongside the financial remedy proceedings in the divorce and if necessary transfer the application to the divorce court for that purpose (*Harman v Glencross* [1986] Fam. 81). **73.0.4**

I. Charging Orders

Add new r.73.3(6):

Application for charging order[1]

(6) Where paragraph (1) or (5) requires service of the application notice, interim charging order and any documents filed in support of the application on a person who is outside the jurisdiction, the permission of the court is not required for service. **73.3**

Council Tax (Administration and Enforcement) Regulations 1992

Replace paragraph with:

Under these regulations a local authority can obtain a "liability order" from the magistrates' court in respect of unpaid council tax. That order can then be enforced by obtaining a charging **73.3.4**

[1] Introduced by the Civil Procedure (Amendment No.4) Rules 2001 (SI 2001/2792) and amended by the Civil Procedure (Amendment No.2) Rules 2009 (SI 2009/3390), the Civil Procedure (Amendment) Rules 2012 (SI 2012/505), the Civil Procedure (Amendment) Rules 2014 (SI 2014/407), the Civil Procedure (Amendment) Rules 2016 (SI 2016/234) and the Civil Procedure (Amendment No.2) Rules 2022 (SI 2022/783).

order under Pt 73. As the Regulations expressly provide for enforcement by way of a charging order, it is not necessary for the local authority to apply for an order under r.70.5(4) before submitting an application for a charging order. The application for a charging order must be made to the County Court Money Claims Centre. If the application is transferred from the Centre under r.73.4(6)(b) or r.73.10(3), the claim will be sent to the County Court Hearing Centre for the district in which the property in respect of which the liability order has been made is situated.

Service

To the end of the paragraph, add:

73.7.4 In *Cesfin Ventures LLC v Al Qubaisi* [2021] EWHC 3311 (Ch), the High Court (Master Kaye) granted (retrospectively and prospectively) an application for service of an interim charging order by alternative means on a third-party creditor in the United Arab Emirates (UAE) under a treaty between the government of the United Kingdom of Great Britain and Northern Ireland (UK) and the UAE, taking into account, in particular, that the third-party creditor was not a party to the proceedings and that the giving of notice of a charging order application to a creditor was not the same as a typical application for service out of the jurisdiction on a party or prospective party.

PART 74

ENFORCEMENT OF JUDGMENTS IN DIFFERENT JURISDICTIONS

I. Enforcement in England and Wales of Judgments of Foreign Courts

Judgments on judgments

Replace the last sentence with:

74.6.12 However, it contrasts with the position under the recast Brussels regime (see *J v H Ltd* (C-568/20) EU:C:2022:264; [2022] I.L.Pr. 21 in which the CJEU interpreted arts 2(a) and 39 of the Judgments Regulation as meaning that an order for payment, made by an EU Member State court on the basis of final judgments delivered in a third state, constitutes a "judgment" and is enforceable in other Member States, and said that its decision in *Owens Bank Ltd v Bracco* (C-129/92) EU:C:1994:13, decided under the Brussels Convention, did not mean have the contrary effect).

Editorial note

In the last paragraph, replace "Windhorst v Levy [2021] EWCA Civ 1802," with:

74.8.1 *Windhorst v Levy* [2021] EWCA Civ 1802; [2022] B.P.I.R. 626,

Public policy

In the last paragraph, replace "London Steam-Ship Mutual Insurance Association Ltd v Spain [2021] EWHC 1247 (Comm)," with:

74x.10.5 *London Steam-Ship Mutual Insurance Association Ltd v Spain* [2021] EWHC 1247 (Comm); [2022] 1 W.L.R. 99,

Add new paragraph at end:

In a later decision in the same case, following a reference from the English High Court (which was later set aside by the Court of Appeal, but which the CJEU determined in any event), the CJEU held that, if art.34(3) of the previous Judgments Regulation (art.45(1)(c) of the Judgments Regulation) does not apply to a judgment enforcing an arbitration award (see para.74x.10.8 below), the recognition or enforcement of a judgment from another Member State cannot be refused as being contrary to public policy under art.34(1) (art.45(1)) on the grounds that it would disregard the principle of res judicata in the judgment enforcing the arbitration award: *London Steam-Ship Owners' Mutual Insurance Association Ltd v Spain* (C-700/20) EU:C:2022:488 (20 June 2022).

Irreconcilable with a judgment in a dispute between the same parties in State in which recognition sought

Add new paragraph at end:

74x.10.8 The CJEU has held that, although a judgment enforcing an arbitration award is not disqualified from being a judgment within the meaning of art.34(3) of the previous Judgments Regulation (art.45(1)(c) of the Judgments Regulation) by the arbitration exception, it will only be a judgment for these purposes if the adoption of a judgment resulting in the same outcome as the award would not infringe the provisions and fundamental objectives of the Regulation: *London Steam-Ship Owners' Mutual Insurance Association Ltd v Spain* (C-700/20) EU:C:2022:488 (20 June 2022).

PART 75

PRACTICE DIRECTION 75—TRAFFIC ENFORCEMENT

Interpretation and scope

In paragraph 1.1 replace list items (7), (8) and (9) with:

(7) "the Civil Enforcement of Road Traffic Contraventions (England) Regulations" means the Civil Enforcement of Road Traffic Contraventions (Approved Devices, Charging Guidelines and General Provisions) (England) Regulations 2022; **75PD.1**

(8) "the Civil Enforcement of Road Traffic Contraventions (Wales) Regulations" means the Civil Enforcement of Road Traffic Contraventions (General Provisions) (Wales) Regulations 2013;

(9) "the Representations and Appeals (England) Regulations" means the Civil Enforcement of Road Traffic Contraventions (Representations and Appeals) (England) Regulations 2022;

In paragraph 1.2, replace list item (8) with:

(8) increased penalty charges provided for in charge certificates issued under regulation 21 of the Civil Enforcement of Road Traffic Contraventions (England) Regulations;

In paragraph 1.3(2), replace list item (f) with:

(f) a charge certificate issued under regulation 21 of the Civil Enforcement of Road Traffic Contraventions (England) Regulations; or

In paragraph 1.3(3), replace list items (h), (i) and (j) with:

(h) regulation 22 of the Civil Enforcement of Road Traffic Contraventions (England) Regulations;

(i) regulation 21 of the Civil Enforcement of Road Traffic Contraventions (Wales) Regulations;

(j) regulation 16(1) of the Representations and Appeals (England) Regulations for any amount which is payable under an adjudicator's adjudication;

Functions of court officer

In paragraph 4.1(1), replace list item (d) with:

(d) regulations 23(4) and 23(5)(d) of the Civil Enforcement of Road Traffic Contraventions (England) Regulations; **75PD.4**

Application for longer period for filing of statutory declaration or witness statement

In paragraph 5.1(2), replace list item (a) with:

(a) regulation 23(3) of the Civil Enforcement of Road Traffic Contraventions (England) Regulations; **75PD.5**

PART 77

PROVISIONS IN SUPPORT OF CRIMINAL JUSTICE

Section 2

Replace the fifth paragraph (beginning "Where a court") with:

77.0.3 Where a court makes an order under s.54(2) certifying that an acquittal was tainted, an application may be made to the High Court for an order quashing the acquittal (s.54(3)). The provisions in Section 2 of Pt 77 govern the procedure to be followed on such an application. The application is to be made by the individual or body which acted as prosecutor in the proceedings which led to the acquittal (r.77.6(2)), and must be made to the Administrative Court by filing a claim form pursuant to Pt 8 (rr.77.8(2) and 77.9(1)). Applications under s.54(3) are listed in the table following para.9.4 of Practice Direction 49E (Alternative Procedure for Claims) (see para.49EPD.9 above). Consequently, the provisions of Pt 8 and the general provisions applicable to Pt 8 claims as stated in Section A of Practice Direction 49E apply, subject to any modifications and additional procedural requirements imposed for the purposes of such applications by the rules in Section 2.

PART 81

APPLICATIONS AND PROCEEDINGS IN RELATION TO CONTEMPT OF COURT [FROM 1 OCTOBER 2020]

Relationship with pre-2020 Pt 81

To the end of the paragraph, add:

81.0.2 This approach was endorsed by the Court of Appeal in *AAA v CCC* [2022] EWCA Civ 479 at [7]. For a fuller discussion of the extent of changes introduced (or not introduced) by the new CPR Pt 81, see Nicklin J in *MBR Acres Ltd v Maher* [2022] EWHC 1123 (QB).

Add new paragraph 81.1.3:

Relationship between Pt 52 (Appeals) and Pt 81

81.1.3 On the relationship between Pts 52 and 81, generally see *AAA v CCC* [2022] EWCA Civ 479. On the power to attach conditions to an appeal from committal for contempt see para.52.3.4 and *Al-Rawas v Hassan Khan & Co (A Firm)* [2022] EWCA Civ 671 at [17]-[20].

Form of application

To the end of the paragraph, add:

81.3.9 Where the application is made under Pt 23, the form **N600**—and not the usual **N244**—should be used unless there are compelling reasons not to do so: *MBR Acres Ltd v Maher* at [19].

Test for permission—generally

Add new paragraph at end:

81.3.10 In *MBR Acres Ltd v McGivern* [2022] EWHC 2072 (QB) at [100]-[103], Nicklin J concluded that the court had the power to impose a permission requirement, under its case management powers, in respect of contempt applications arising from injunctions that enjoin persons unknown. Such a permission requirement is not a form of limited civil restraint order. It is a requirement that protects the courts' process from being abused and resources being wasted. Where such a permission requirement is imposed, an applicant must satisfy the court that the proposed contempt application: (i) has a real prospect of success; (ii) does not rely upon wholly technical or insubstantial breaches; and (iii) is supported by evidence that the respondent had actual knowledge of the terms of the injunction they are alleged to have breached.

Costs of committal applications

Replace paragraph with:

81.3.17 Generally, on the factors relevant to the costs of committal applications see *Symes v Phillips (Costs)* [2005] EWCA Civ 663; [2006] 4 Costs L.R. 553 at [7]. When determining the costs of a withdrawn committal application the merits of the application can be considered where either the breaches were admitted or there was no real scope for them to be denied: *Loveridge v Loveridge* [2021] EWCA

Civ 1697; [2021] Costs L.R. 1429. While political protest contempt applications are not a different category, the approach to costs may be somewhat "tempered" by proportionality considerations when Convention rights are engaged: *Secretary of State for Transport v Cuciurean* [2022] EWCA Civ 661 at [50]-[68].

Rule 81.4: Effect of rule

To the end of the second paragraph, add:

It was understood to be fundamental to the new Pt 81 regime (2020 Consultation at 13). In *MBR Acres Ltd v Maher* at [50]-[105], Nicklin J confirmed that r.81.4(2)(c) and (d) operated on the basis that the underlying order which is sought to be enforced by a contempt application (not just the contempt application itself) was personally served, and that this was a requirement of the substantive law of contempt which survived the introduction of the new CPR Pt 81. CPR r.81.4(2) was a requirement engaging CPR r.6.22. Furthermore, at [106]-[119], the test for retrospective alternative service or dispensing with service in the case of an injunction order was akin to the similar tests for claim forms in CPR rr.6.15 and 6.16, and will not be granted merely on the basis of expediency. **81.4.1**

Add new paragraph 81.4.3.1:

Service

CPR r.81.4(2)(c) requires injunction orders to be served via personal service, except where alternative service is required or where service is dispensed with by the court. An order to dispense with service will only be made exceptionally. The requirement to effect personal service is part of the substantive law of contempt, hence it is not set out within CPR Pt 81: *MBR Acres Ltd v Maher* [2022] EWHC 1123 (QB) at [102]-[105]. **81.4.3.1**

Penal notice

To the end of the last paragraph, add:

The continued power of the court to dispense with a penal notice and the requirements of personal service under the new CPR Pt 81, and the consistency of the applicable test for the exercise of that power with the authorities under the old CPR Pt 81, was confirmed by Miles J in *Business Mortgage Finance 4 Plc v Hussain* [2022] EWHC 449 (Ch) at [43]-[58]. **81.4.4**

Legal aid—legal representation

Add new paragraph at end:

In *Liverpool Victoria Insurance Co Ltd v Khan* [2022] 3 WLUK 261, Costs Judge Leonard, sitting in the High Court, Senior Courts Costs Office, held that: **81.4.7**

(a) there was no implied disapplication of the indemnity principle, and solicitors acting under a legal aid certificate were limited in recovery to the hourly rates under Sch.4 para.7 of the Criminal Legal Aid (Remuneration) Regulations 2013 (SI 2013/435); and

(b) the proceedings (involving both criminal and civil contempts) were civil proceedings and (notwithstanding their characterisation for the purposes of legal aid under LASPO) not "criminal proceedings" for the purposes of ss.58 and 58A of the Courts and Legal Services Act 1990, and so the Conditional Fee Agreement was not unlawful and unenforceable.

Change title of paragraph: **81.6.2**

"the court on its own initiative shall consider"—Form N601

To the end of the paragraph, add:

Form **N601** is the standard form applicable where the court brings contempt proceedings on its own initiative.

Right to remain silent

In the last paragraph, replace "[2018] EWHC 2979 (Comm)." with:

[2018] EWHC 2979 (Comm) and the discussion of Peel J in *Helene v Bailey* [2022] EWFC 5 at [10]-[18]. **81.7.5**

Replace r.81.8(8) with:

Hearings and judgments in contempt proceedings[1]

81.8 **(8) The court shall be responsible for ensuring that where a sentence of imprisonment (immediate or suspended) is passed in contempt proceedings under this Part, that judgment is transcribed and published on the website of the judiciary of England and Wales.**

Rule 81.8: Effect of rule

To the start of the penultimate paragraph, add:

81.8.1 Rule 81.8(8) was amended by the Civil Procedure (Amendment No.2) Rules 2022 (SI 2022/783), as from 1 October 2022. The amendment clarified that judgments need only be transcribed and published where the committal concluded with a sentence of imprisonment, including one that was suspended.

Custodial sentence combined with a fine

In the first paragraph, after "credit must be given at all:", replace "Su v Lakatamia Shipping Co Ltd [2021] EWCA Civ 1355" with:

81.9.1 *Su v Lakatamia Shipping Co Ltd* [2021] EWCA Civ 1355; [2022] 4 W.L.R. 2

PRACTICE GUIDANCE: COMMITTAL FOR CONTEMPT OF COURT—OPEN COURT, 24 JUNE 2015, UNREP.

Editorial note—Annex 1

Replace paragraph with:

81PG.1.1 The form annexed to this Practice Guidance can be found in the Forms in the online *Civil Procedure Forms Volume* (see **PG 81 Form**).

PART 82

CLOSED MATERIAL PROCEDURE

Editorial introduction

Procedures to which Part 82 applies

Replace the last paragraph with:

82.0.2 As observed by Cobb J in *Re R (Closed Material Procedure: Special Advocates: Funding)* [2017] EWHC 1793 (Fam); [2018] 1 W.L.R. 163, at [17]:

> "Currently, there are no family procedural rules equivalent to Part 82 of the Civil Procedure Rules 1998 ('CPR') dealing with these situations in family cases; Part 82 was inserted into the CPR in 2013, at the time of the implementation of the Justice and Security Act 2013 to deal with Closed Material Procedure issues. Nonetheless, procedures have been adapted in the family court to replicate as appropriate the arrangements for a closed material process, to achieve fairness, and ensure the protection of the Article 6 rights of the parties."

See also *Sheffield City Council v M* [2022] EWHC 128 (Fam) at [19]-[20].

[1] Introduced by the Civil Procedure (Amendment No.3) Rules 2020 (SI 2020/747) and amended by the Civil Procedure (Amendment No.2) Rules 2022 (SI 2022/783).

PART 83

PRACTICE DIRECTION 83—WRITS AND WARRANTS—GENERAL PROVISIONS

Section III—Writs

Forms of writs

Replace paragraphs 3.1, 3.2 and 3.3 with:

3.1 A writ of control must be in Forms 53 to 57 as appropriate. **83PD.3**

3.2 A writ of delivery must be in Form 64 or 65, whichever is appropriate.

3.3 A writ of possession must be in Form 66 or 66A, whichever is appropriate.

PART 84

ENFORCEMENT BY TAKING CONTROL OF GOODS

IV. Proceedings in Relation to Certificates Under Section 64 of the 2007 Act

Replace r.84.18(2) with:

Application for issue of a certificate under section 64 of the 2007 Act[1]

(2) The application must be made to the County Court Business Centre, using the approved form. **84.18**

Replace r.84.20(2) with:

Complaints as to fitness to hold a certificate[2]

(2) The complaint must be submitted to the County Court hearing centre at which the certificate was issued, using the approved form. **84.20**

PRACTICE DIRECTION 84—ENFORCEMENT BY TAKING CONTROL OF GOODS

Interrelationship of rules on taking control of goods with other legislation

Replace paragraph 1.1 with:

1.1 The provisions in this Practice Direction and Part 84 on taking control of goods are closely linked to, and need to be read with– **84PD.1**

(1) Part 3 of and Schedule 12 to the Tribunals Courts and Enforcement Act 2007 (The Act), which can be found at *http://www.legislation.gov.uk*;

(2) the Taking Control of Goods Regulations 2013, which can be found at *http://www.legislation.gov.uk*; and

(3) the Taking Control of Goods (Fees) Regulations 2013, which can be found at *http://www.legislation.gov.uk*.

Replace paragraph 1.3 with:

1.3 [Omitted].

---

[1] Introduced by the Civil Procedure (Amendment No.2) Rules 2014 (SI 2014/482) and amended by the Civil Procedure (Amendment No.2) Rules 2022 (SI 2022/783).

[2] Introduced by the Civil Procedure (Amendment No.2) Rules 2014 (SI 2014/482) and amended by the Civil Procedure (Amendment No.2) Rules 2022 (SI 2022/783).

PART 87

APPLICATIONS FOR WRIT OF HABEAS CORPUS

Forms

87.0.2 *In the first paragraph, delete the second sentence.*

II. Applications to the High Court for a Writ of Habeas Corpus for Release

Rules 87.2 to 87.7: Effects of rules

87.2.1 *In the third paragraph, delete the second sentence.*

Replace r.87.8(1) with:

Forms and directions as to the return to the writ[1]

87.8 **87.8—(1) A writ of habeas corpus for release must be in Practice Form No. 89.**

III. Writ of Habeas Corpus to Give Evidence or to Answer a Charge

Replace r.87.12(2) and (3) with:

Writ of habeas corpus to give evidence or to answer a charge[2]

87.12 **(2) A writ of habeas corpus to give evidence must be in Practice Form No. 91.**

(3) A writ of habeas corpus to answer a charge must be in Practice Form No. 92.

SCHEDULE 1—RSC PROVISIONS

RSC ORDER 79—CRIMINAL PROCEEDINGS

Forms

Replace "Ord.79. These forms are included in Table 2 (Practice Forms) attached to Practice Direction (Forms):" with:

sc79.0.3 Ord.79:

Replace r.9 with:

Bail[3]

sc79.9 9.—(1) Subject to the provisions of this rule, every application to the High Court in respect of bail in any criminal proceeding—

(a) where the defendant is in custody, must be made by claim form to a judge to show cause why the defendant should not be granted bail;

[1] Amended by the Civil Procedure (Amendment No.2) Rules 2022 (SI 2022/783).

[2] Amended by the Civil Procedure (Amendment No.2) Rules 2022 (SI 2022/783).

[3] Amended by the Civil Procedure (Amendment) Rules (SI 1999/1008), the Civil Procedure (Amendment) Rules (SI 1999/1008), the Civil Procedure (Amendment No.2) Rules 2009 (SI 2009/3390), the Civil Procedure (Amendment No.6) Rules 2013 (SI 2013/1695) and the Civil Procedure (Amendment No.2) Rules 2022 (SI 2022/783).

(b) where the defendant has been admitted to bail, must be made by claim form to a judge to show cause why the variation in the arrangements for bail proposed by the applicant should not be made.

(2) Subject to paragraph (5), the claim form (in Form **No. 97** or **No. 97A**) must, at least 24 hours before the day named therein for the hearing, be served—

(a) where the application was made by the defendant, on the prosecutor and on the Director of Public Prosecutions, if the prosecution is being carried on by him;

(b) where the application was made by the prosecutor or a constable under section 3(8) of the Bail Act 1976, on the defendant.

(3) Subject to paragraph (5), every application must be supported by witness statement or affidavit.

(4) Where a defendant in custody who desires to apply for bail is unable through lack of means to instruct a solicitor, he may give notice in writing to the court stating his desire to apply for bail and requesting that the Official Solicitor shall act for him in the application, and the court may assign the Official Solicitor to act for the applicant accordingly.

(5) Where the Official Solicitor has been so assigned the court may dispense with the requirements of paragraphs (1) to (3) and deal with the application in a summary manner.

(6) Where the court grants the defendant bail, the order must be in Form **No.98** and a copy of the order shall be transmitted forthwith—

(a) where the proceedings in respect of the defendant have been transferred to the Crown Court for trial or where the defendant has been committed to the Crown Court to be sentenced or otherwise dealt with, to the appropriate officer of the Crown Court;

(b) in any other case, to the designated officer for the court which committed the defendant.

(6A) The recognizance of any surety required as a condition of bail granted as aforesaid may, where the defendant is in a prison or other place of detention, be entered into before the governor or keeper of the prison or place as well as before the person specified in section 8(4) of the Bail Act 1976.

(6B) Where under section 3(5) or (6) of the Bail Act 1976the court imposes a requirement to be complied with before a person's release on bail, it may give directions as to the manner in which and the person or persons before whom the requirement may be complied with.

(7) A person who in pursuance of an order for the grant of bail made by the court under this rule proposes to enter into a recognizance or give security must, unless the court otherwise directs, give notice (in Form **No.100**) to the prosecutor at least 24 hours before he enters into the recognizance or complies with the requirements as aforesaid.

(8) Where in pursuance of such an order as aforesaid a recognizance is entered into or requirement complied with before any person, it shall be the duty of that person to cause the recognizance or, as the case may be, a statement of the requirement complied with to be transmitted forthwith—

(a) where the proceedings in respect of the defendant have been transferred to the Crown Court for trial or where the defendant has been committed to the Crown Court to be sentenced or otherwise dealt with, to the appropriate officer of the Crown Court;

(b) in any other case, to the designated officer for the court which committed the defendant,

and a copy of such recognizance or statement shall at the same time be sent to the governor or keeper of the prison or other place of detention in which the defendant is detained, unless the recognizance was entered into or the requirement complied with before such governor or keeper.

(10) An order varying the arrangements under which the defendant has been granted bail shall be in Form **98A** and a copy of the order shall be transmitted forthwith—

(a) where the proceedings in respect of the defendant have been transferred to the Crown Court for trial or where the defendant has been committed to the Crown Court to be sentenced or otherwise dealt with, to the appropriate officer of the Crown Court;

(b) in any other case, to the designated officer for the court which committed the defendant.

(11) Where in pursuance of an order of the High Court or the Crown Court a person is released on bail in any criminal proceeding pending the determination of an appeal to the High Court or the Supreme Court or an application for a quashing order, then, upon the abandonment of the appeal or application, or upon the decision of the High Court or Supreme Court being given, any justice (being a justice acting for the same petty sessions area as the magistrates' court by which that person was convicted or sentenced) may issue process for enforcing the decision in respect of which such appeal or application was brought or, as the case may be, the decision of the High Court or Supreme Court.

(12) If an applicant to the High Court in any criminal proceedings is refused bail, the applicant shall not be entitled to make a fresh application for bail to any other judge or to a Divisional Court.

(13) The record required by section 5 of the Bail Act 1976 to be made by the High Court shall be made by including in the file relating to the case in question a copy of the relevant order of the Court and shall contain the particulars set out in Form **No.98** or **98A**, whichever is appropriate, except that in the case of a decision to withhold bail the record shall be made by inserting a statement of the decision on the Court's copy of the relevant claim form and including it in the file relating to the case in question.

(14) In the case of a person whose return or surrender is sought under the Extradition Act 1989, this rule shall apply as if references to the defendant were references to that person and references to the prosecutor were references to the State seeking the return or surrender of that person.

(15) In the case of a prosecutor's appeal to the High Court against the grant of bail under section 1(1A) or (1B) of the Bail (Amendment) Act 1993 ("the 1993 Act")—

(a) the appeal proceedings are to be commenced by the prosecutor filing a copy of the written notice of appeal required by section 1(5) of the 1993 Act in the High Court; and

(b) paragraphs (1) to (14) do not apply to such appeals.

RSC ORDER 109—THE ADMINISTRATION OF JUSTICE ACT 1960

Replace r.4(4) with:

Release of appellant on bail by the Court of Appeal[1]

sc109.4 (4) When granting bail under this rule in a case of civil contempt of court,

[1] Introduced by the Civil Procedure (Amendment) Rules 2000 (SI 2000/221) and amended by the Civil Procedure (Amendment No.2) Rules 2009 (SI 2009/3390) and the Civil Procedure (Amendment No.2) Rules 2022 (SI 2022/783).

the Court of Appeal may order that the recognisance or other security to be given by the appellant or the recognisance of any surety shall be given before any person authorised by virtue of section 119(1) of the Magistrates' Court Act 1980 to take recognisance where a magistrates' court having power to take it has, instead of taking it, fixed the amount in which the principal and his sureties, if any, are to be bound. An order by the Court of Appeal granting bail as aforesaid must be in Form **No. 98** with the necessary adaptations.

RSC ORDER 115—CONFISCATION AND FORFEITURE IN CONNECTION WITH CRIMINAL PROCEEDINGS

Related sources

Replace the penultimate bullet point with:

- Practice Direction (CPR Pt 8 and Sch.1 and Sch.2 to the CPR) (see para.49EPD.1 above) **sc115.0.7**

I. Drug Trafficking Act 1994 and Criminal Justice (International Co-operation) Act 1990

Practice

Replace the last two sentences with:

Rules 2B and 3(1) are listed in the table at para.4.4 of PD 49E (see para.49EPD.4). Consequently, Section B of PD 49E takes effect where claims are brought under r.2B and r.3(1). **sc115.3.7**

Practice

Replace paragraph with:

Applications under r.7 should be made by claim form if there are no proceedings in the High Court against the defendant (for example a restraint order) otherwise the prosecutor should commence the application by application notice. The application should be supported by written evidence dealing with all the matters stated in para.(3) of this rule. Rule 7(1) is listed in the table at para.4.4 of PD 49E (see para.49EPD.4). Consequently, Section B of PD 49E takes effect where application is made by claim form. See also para.sc115.3.7 above. **sc115.7.4**

III. Terrorism Act 2000

Practice

Replace paragraph with:

Paragraph 5(4) of Sch.4 to the 2000 Act states that an application for a restraint order (see further para.sc115.27.1 below) "may be made to a judge in chambers without notice". Applications under r.26 should be made by claim form or by application notice. The application should be supported by written evidence dealing with all the matters stated in para.(2) of this rule. Rule 26(1) is listed in the table at para.4.4 of PD 49E (see para.49EPD.4). Consequently, Section B of PD 49E takes effect where application is made by claim form. See also para.sc115.3.7 above. **sc115.26.3**

PRACTICE DIRECTION RSC 115—RESTRAINT ORDERS AND APPOINTMENT OF RECEIVERS IN CONNECTION WITH CRIMINAL PROCEEDINGS AND INVESTIGATIONS

Editorial note—Appendix 1—Example of a restraint order prohibiting disposal of assets

After "Forms prescribed by PD", delete "(other than PD 4)". **scpd115.10**

SECTION C PRE-ACTION CONDUCT AND PROTOCOLS

PRE-ACTION PROTOCOL FOR THE RESOLUTION OF CLINICAL DISPUTES

Editorial note—Annex B—Form for Requesting Health Records

After "Requesting Health Records", replace "can" with:
C3-016 could, until 30 September 2022,

THE PROTOCOL FOR LOW VALUE PERSONAL INJURY CLAIMS IN ROAD TRAFFIC ACCIDENTS

The Stage 3 procedure

In the first paragraph, replace "Practice Direction 8B" with:
C13A-003 Practice Direction 49F

In the third paragraph, replace "Practice Direction 8B" with:
Practice Direction 49F

In the sixth paragraph (beginning "For further information"), replace "Practice Direction 8B," with:
Practice Direction 49F,

Limitation period and RTA Protocol processes

In the first paragraph, replace "Practice Direction 8B" with:
C13A-004 Practice Direction 49F

In the second paragraph, replace "Practice Direction 8B" with:
Practice Direction 49F

In the third paragraph, replace "PD 8B (para.8BPD.16.1 above)." with:
PD 49F (para.49FPD.16.1 above).

Rules, practice direction and pre-action protocol

Replace the second paragraph with:
C13A-005 Normally, CPR rules are supplemented directly by practice directions and indirectly by pre-action protocols. Here these relationships are reversed. The RTA Protocol is the primary source governing party behaviour in the claims to which it applies; Practice Direction 49F builds on the Protocol Stage 2 processes and provides special and limited court procedures for the purpose of determining the claim if settlement is not achieved (and for some other purposes); and Section II of CPR Pt 36 (RTA Protocol Offers to Settle) and Section VI of Pt 45 (Fixed Costs) provide the legal framework, not only for the Stage 3 procedure but also for the pre-action negotiating processes, in effect supplementing Practice Direction 49F and the RTA Protocol.

In the last paragraph, replace "Practice Direction 8B (supplementing Pt 8) (see paras 8BPD.0 et seq, above)," with:
Practice Direction 49F (supplementing Pt 49—previously PD 8B supplementing Pt 8) (see paras 49FPD.0 et seq, above),

Forms

Replace paragraph with:
C13A-006 Several forms have been specially designed for use by parties engaged in the RTA Protocol processes (the "RTA Forms"). They are listed in para.1.4 of the RTA Protocol and are available on the HMCTS website through the address given there. Where court proceedings are commenced under Practice Direction 49F, or under Pt 7, in relation to claims to which the Protocol processes have been applied, the usual forms for commencing court proceedings as referenced in those Pts 7

and 8 are used. Where, under para.8.1 of Practice Direction 49F, a defendant files and serves an acknowledgment of service the appropriate form is Form **N210B**, a form specially provided for this procedural purpose.

The 2014 amendments

In the first paragraph, replace "(PD 8B)" with:
(PD 49F) **C13A-008**

The 2015 amendments

In the second paragraph, replace "(see PD 8A)." with:
(see PD 49F). **C13A-009**

THE PROTOCOL FOR LOW VALUE PERSONAL INJURY (EMPLOYERS' LIABILITY AND PUBLIC LIABILITY) CLAIMS

Editorial introduction

In the third paragraph, replace the last sentence with:
Stage 3 proceedings are commenced under CPR Pt 8 and are governed by Practice Direction 49F (which has streamlined the former PD 8B and provides for the Stage 3 procedure under both the RTA Protocol and this Protocol). **C15A-001**

Disease claims

In the first paragraph, replace the third sentence (beginning "Mesothelioma claims are") with:
Mesothelioma claims are expressly excluded (para.4.3(10)) and are dealt with in the separate dedicated Practice Direction 49B, which replicates PD 3D which was in force until 30 September 2022. **C15A-002**

Claims by children

Replace the last sentence with:
Application for approval of a settlement is governed from 1 October 2022 by para.6.1 of PD 49F (supplementing CPR Pt 8). **C15A-005**

Stage 3

Replace the second paragraph with:
Proceedings in Stage 3 are governed by Practice Direction 49F with effect from 1 October 2022 in substitution for the former PD 8B. They must be issued in the county court and will normally be heard by a district judge. Though either party can request an oral hearing no further evidence is permitted so it is intended that they will be paper hearings. The court will always give at least 21 days' notice of the date of determination. See further the commentary on PD 49F. **C15A-007**

Limitation

Replace the first sentence with:
Paragraph 5.7 of the Protocol and para.16 of PD 49F, from 1 October 2022 in place of the former PD 8B, apply where compliance with the Protocol is not possible before the expiry of the limitation period. **C15A-008**

PRE-ACTION PROTOCOL FOR LOW VALUE PERSONAL INJURY (EMPLOYERS' LIABILITY AND PUBLIC LIABILITY) CLAIMS

Section I—Introduction

Scope

After paragraph 4.1(4), replace the words in brackets with:
(Rule 26.6 provides that the small claims track is not the normal track where the value of any claim for damages for personal injuries (defined as compensation for pain, suffering and loss of amenity), other than a claim arising from a road traffic accident, is more than £1,500.) **C15-004**

Section II—General Provisions

Claimant's reasonable belief of the value of the claim

Replace paragraph 5.9 with:

C15-005 **5.9** Where the claimant reasonably believes that the claim is valued at between £1,500 and £25,000 but it subsequently becomes apparent that the value of the claim is less than £1,500, the claimant is entitled to the Stage 1 and (where relevant) the Stage 2 fixed costs.

THE PROTOCOL FOR DEBT CLAIMS

Editorial introduction

In the first paragraph, replace "CPR PD 7D." with:

C16A-001 CPR PD 49D which from 1 October 2022 replaces the identical wording formerly contained in PD 7D.

PRE-ACTION PROTOCOL FOR RESOLUTION OF PACKAGE TRAVEL CLAIMS

Section I—Introduction

Scope

After paragraph 4.1(5), replace the words in brackets with:

C17-004 (Rule 26.6 provides that the small claims track is not the normal track where the value of any claim for damages for personal injuries (defined as compensation for pain, suffering and loss of amenity), other than a claim arising from a road traffic accident, is more than £1,500.)

VOLUME 2

SECTION A1 PROCEDURAL GUIDES

5. Case Management and Sanctions

5.1 Track Allocation: Rules

Scope of the three case management tracks

The small claims track

Replace table with:

CPR r.26.6(1)(a)	The small claims track is the normal track for: (a) any claim for damages for personal injuries which is not more than– £5,000 in a claim for personal injuries arising from a road traffic accident, except where (per r. 26.6A): (i) the accident occurred before 31 May 2021, or (ii) when the accident occurred, the claimant was using a motor cycle or was a pillion passenger on, or a passenger in a sidecar attached to, a motor cycle or was using a wheelchair, a powered wheelchair or a mobility scooter, a bicycle or other pedal cycle, riding a horse, or was a pedestrian (see rule 26.6A), or (iii) save in whiplash cases (for which see rule 26.6B) the claimant is a child or protected party when proceedings are started, or (iv) save in whiplash cases (for which see rule 26.6B) the claimant is an undischarged bankrupt, the claimant or defendant acts as a personal representative of a deceased person, or (v) save in whiplash cases (for which see rule 26.6B) on the date of the accident, the defendant's vehicle was registered outside the United Kingdom. £1,000 in a claim for personal injuries arising from a road traffic accident, in any of the circumstances specified in points (i)-(v) above (see rr.26.6A and 26.6B); or £1,500 in any other claim for personal injuries	**A1.5-001**
CPR r.26.6(1)(b)	(b) any claim which includes a claim by a tenant of residential premises against his landlord where (i) the tenant is seeking an order requiring the landlord to carry out repairs or other work to the premises (whether or not the tenant is also seeking some other remedy); (ii) the cost of the repairs or other work to the premises is estimated to be not more than £1,000; and (iii) the financial value of any other claim for damages is not more than £1,000.	
CPR r.26.7(4)	(c) certain claims in respect of harassment and unlawful eviction will *not* be allocated to the small claims track.	
CPR r.26.6(3)	(d) save as above, the small claims track is the normal track for any claim which has a financial value of not more than £10,000.	

15. Insolvency

Replace list with:

1. winding up petitions presented in the period 27 April 2020 to 30 September 2021 are subject to temporary restrictions imposed by (the original) Sch.10 to the Corporate Insolvency and Governance Act 2020 ("CIGA"). For the procedure to be applied in relation to winding up petitions presented in the period 27 April 2020 to 30 September 2021, see **A1.15-000**

the Insolvency Practice Direction relating to the Corporate Insolvency and Governance Act 2020 ("the CIGA IPD"), as reproduced at para.3E-21.1.0 of section 3E and *Petitioner v Company* [2022] EWHC 1690 (Ch); and

2. winding up petitions presented in the period 1 October 2021 to 31 March 2022 are subject to the temporary restrictions imposed by (the new) Sch.10 to CIGA, introduced by the Corporate Insolvency and Governance Act 2020) (Coronavirus) (Amendment of Schedule 10) (No.2) Regulations 2021 (SI 2021/1091). The CIGA IPD does not apply to petitions presented on or after 1 October 2021. Petitions presented on or after 1 October 2021 may be advertised in the usual way and are listed in the usual winding up list, without a non-attendance pre-trial review or preliminary hearing.

SECTION 1 COURT GUIDES
SECTION 1A CHANCERY GUIDE

Add new Chancery Court Practice Note:

CHANCERY COURT PRACTICE NOTE — CHANCERY GUIDE 2022

Editorial introduction

1APN-0 The Chancery Practice Note 2022 was issued by the Chancellor in July 2022 (and reissued in October 2022). It accompanied the publication of The Chancery Guide 2022. It provides that, apart from Practice Notes and Directions specified in its Schedule all other Chancery Practice Notes and Directions are revoked. This statement has to be read with care. As a Practice Note, which does not have the force of law, it cannot revoke Practice Directions. Only another Practice Direction, and one issued by the Master of the Rolls concerning civil proceedings, can revoke a Practice Direction concerning civil proceedings. The 2022 Chancery Practice Note ought therefore to be read as revoking, apart from those specified, all other Practice Notes, Practice Statements and Practice Guidance that were not issued under the Practice Direction-making power.

1APN-1 **1.** The new Chancery Guide was published on 29 July 2022. This Practice Note accompanies the first update published in October 2022.

2. The Chancery Guide is now available online with hyperlinks on the *Courts and Tribunals Judiciary website*. It has been substantially rewritten and revised compared with previous versions of the Chancery Guide and so merits careful reading by judges and practitioners alike.

3. The new Chancery Guide seeks so far as possible to bring the practice in the Chancery Division into line with the practice in the other Business and Property Courts. The new Chancery Guide also applies in the District Registries out of London, save where local guidance is necessary.

4. Apart from the Practice Notes, Guidance and Directions listed in the Schedule attached to this Practice Note, all other Chancery Division Practice Notes, Guidance and Directions are revoked, on the basis that so far as relevant they are otherwise incorporated in the new Chancery Guide.

5. Practice Notes, Guidance and Directions may be issued from time to time by the Chancellor, Supervising Judges, Chief ICC Judge or Chief Master and will take effect from the date they are issued.

6. Nothing in this Practice Note or the Chancery Guide substitutes or overrides the CPR including relevant Practice Directions.

The Rt. Hon. Sir Julian Flaux
Chancellor of the High Court
July 2022
Reissued October 2022

SCHEDULE

Schedule

The following Practice Notes and Directions will remain in force:

1. PN: Companies Court: Company Restoration 12 November 2012

See Appendix D of the *Company Restoration Guide*

2. PN: Companies Court: *Unfair Prejudice Petition Direction* 1 May 2015
3. PN: Variation of Trusts 9 February 2017
4. PN: Chief Master and the Senior Master's joint Practice Note 30 September 2017
5. PN: Witnesses Giving evidence remotely 11 May 2021
   Practice Note: Giving Evidence Remotely
6. Practice Statement: Patents Court trial listing issued by Meade J
   Practice Statement: Listing of Cases for Trial in the Patents Court 1 February 2022
7. PN: Remote hand-down of judgments 5 October 2022
   Chancellor's Practice Note Remote hand-down of judgments
8. PN: Disclosure in the Insolvency and Companies Court List (ChD) 6 October 2022
   Chief ICC Judge's Practice Note

Practice Notes, Guidance and Directions issued by the Supervising Judges:

PN: Business and Property Courts in Leeds, Liverpool, Manchester, and Newcastle: 29 July 2022
VC Practice Note July 2022
PN: Business and Property Courts in Manchester and Leeds 27 October 2022
Applications Lists: VC Practice Note Applications Lists

Replace The Chancery Guide with "The Business and Property Courts of England & Wales Chancery Guide 2022":

THE BUSINESS AND PROPERTY COURTS OF ENGLAND & WALES CHANCERY GUIDE 2022

CONTENTS

Chapter 1 Introduction

ABOUT THE BUSINESS & PROPERTY COURTS

1.1 The Business & Property Courts ('B&PCs') comprise the Chancery Division, the Commercial Court and Admiralty Court and the Technology and Construction Court. The B&PCs became operational on 2 October 2017. The Chancellor of the High Court (the 'Chancellor'), currently Sir Julian Flaux, has oversight of the day-to-day running of the B&PCs in consultation with the President of the Queen's Bench Division. Details about the operation of the B&PCs can be found in CPR PD 57AA. **1A-1**

1.2 The B&PCs are part of the High Court. In **London** they are based in the Rolls Building at 7 Rolls Buildings, Fetter Lane, London EC4A 1NL. Contact details for the B&PC Judges in London can be found at Appendix B. The Chancery Division in London is referred to in this Guide as "ChD B&PCs London".

1.3 Business and Property Courts District Registries ('B&PC District Registries') have been established in **Birmingham, Bristol, Cardiff, Leeds, Liverpool, Manchester and Newcastle**. Cases that fall within the ambit of the B&PC District Registries are heard there by specialist Business and Property judges.

1.4 The Chancellor supervises the Chancery lists in the B&PCs in London and on the South Eastern Circuit. A Chancery Division High Court Judge ('HCJ') supervises the Chancery work including the Business and Property lists outside the South-East ('Supervising Judge'). Mr Justice Fancourt is the Vice-Chancellor of the County Palatine of Lancaster and Supervising Judge for the Northern and North-Eastern Circuits. Mr Justice Zacaroli is the Supervising Judge for the Midlands, Wales and Western Circuits.

1.5 There were previously an additional 3 regional Chancery District Registries: Caernarfon, Mold and Preston. Since the advent of electronic working, no new Chancery Business and Property Courts claims are issued in these District Registries, though B&PC specialist judges may hear cases at them. Contact details for each of the B&PC District Registries (and the former Chancery District Registries) are at Appendix C. Further details can be found on the judiciary website.

1.6 The work of the Chancery Division is divided up between several specialist lists, sub-lists and courts. A complete list of the Chancery Division lists and sub-lists and courts (together with a non-exhaustive description of the types of cases dealt with in each list, sub-list and court) is found at Appendix F.

1.7 A claim should be issued in the list and/or sub-list and/or court with which its subject-matter has the closest connection. In addition to the Chancery Division, lists, sub-lists and courts in the B&PCs include the Commercial Court, the Admiralty Court, the Circuit Commercial Court (formerly known as the Mercantile Court) and the Technology and Construction Court. The Financial List is a joint list of the Chancery Division and the Commercial Court. Cases issued in the ChD B&PCs London will be assigned to and heard in the relevant list, sub-list or court by a B&PCs judge.

1.8 Cases in the B&PC District Registries issued in the specialist lists, sub-lists and courts will be listed in the Business and Property lists and heard by specialist B&PC judges. Further details can be found on the Judiciary website including links to any local guidance.

1.9 In addition to the ChD B&PCs London and the 7 B&PC District Registries some specialist work of the type undertaken in the B&PCs is undertaken in specialist Business and Property lists by the County Court at 9 of its hearing centres around the country: Birmingham, Bristol, Cardiff, Leeds, Liverpool, Central London, Manchester, Newcastle and Preston (as defined in CPR PD

57AA, para 4.2). In London that work is undertaken in the County Court sitting at Central London. The County Court at Central London has its own Guide to Business & Property Work at Central London.

1.10 Contact details for each of the County Court hearing centres are at Appendix C. Further details can be found on the gov.uk website.

ABOUT THE CHANCERY DIVISION

1A-2 **1.11** The Chancery Division is based in the Rolls Building and in the B&PC District Registries. The Rolls Building is the largest court centre for handling specialist financial, business and property cases in the world. The Chancery Division undertakes a broad range of civil work, much of which is business and property litigation. There is a strong international element to much of the work and many claims are high value and complex. See Appendix F for a brief description of each specialist list, sub-list and court.

1.12 There are currently 17 HCJs (including the Chancellor) attached to the Chancery Division. Other HCJs may sit in retirement. They generally sit in London (other than the Supervising Judges, who regularly sit on circuit) but will be deployed to B&PC District Registries as required to try the most substantial cases. There are also currently 4 Judges called 'Masters' (one of whom is the Chief Master) and 6 Insolvency and Companies Court Judges ('ICC Judge(s)') (one of whom is the Chief ICC Judge), who sit in the Rolls Building. A list of the judges and their clerks is in Appendix B.

1.13 In addition to the HCJs, ICC Judges and Masters, the business of the Chancery Division is conducted in the B&PC District Registries by specialist civil judges authorised to sit as judges in the High Court pursuant to section 9(1) of the Senior Courts Act 1981 ('Section 9 Judges') and by specialist District Judges. The work of these specialist civil judges is supplemented by fee-paid deputy HCJs appointed pursuant to section 9(4) of the Senior Courts Act 1981 ('Deputy HCJs'), deputy ICC Judges, deputy Masters and, in the B&PC District Registries, by Recorders and deputy District Judges. All such deputies are approved specialist judges.

ABOUT THIS GUIDE

1A-3 **1.14** This is the first new edition of the Chancery Guide (the 'Guide') since February 2016. Much has changed since that time and the Guide has been wholly re-written to take account of changes in the way that the Chancery Division courts operate, technological changes, and new practices that have evolved, particularly during the Covid-19 pandemic.

1.15 Work has been carried out to seek to align the content of this Guide, the Commercial Court Guide and the Technology and Construction Court Guide where practices in the Chancery Division and in those courts should be substantially the same, though there are many areas of practice that are different and where different guidance is appropriate. There has also been alignment of guidance on work of the Masters and deputy Masters with guidance on work of the HCJs, Section 9 Judges and Deputy HCJs. To that end, this Guide uses the term 'judge' to refer to Masters, ICC Judges, HCJs Deputy HCJs and Section 9 Judges alike. Where it is necessary to distinguish between them, the terms 'Master', 'ICC Judge', 'Section 9 Judge' 'Deputy HCJ' and 'High Court Judge' or 'HCJ' are used.

1.16 In the B&PC District Registries there are specialist B&PC District Judges and deputy District Judges. The allocation of work between the Section 9 Judges and the District Judges in the B&PC District Registries is a matter of local practice and may be the subject of local guidance. However, where appropriate, references to 'judge' in this Guide includes District Judge and deputy District Judge.

1.17 This Guide applies in general to cases in the Chancery lists in all the B&PCs (including the B&PC District Registries). Some chapters, sections and particular guidance are, however, specific to the working of the lists in the Rolls Building in London. Where that is so, any local guidance or established practice in the B&PC District Registries should be followed. Links to current regional guidance can be accessed through Appendix C and/or may be found on the judiciary website which has separate pages for each B&PC District Registry.

1.18 Where there is no specific local guidance, parties should apply the Guide in an analogous way that is most likely to serve the overriding objective and, if in doubt, consult the local court.

1.19 The distribution of cases between judges in the Chancery Division in London and in the B&PC District Registries is governed by the practice of the court in which the case is being conducted, the availability of judicial resources and any limits on jurisdiction set out in PD2B 'Allocation of cases to level of the Judiciary'. Further guidance is provided in relation to the distribution of business between different levels of judge in the ChD B&PCs London throughout this Guide, with links where appropriate to information concerning the distribution of business between different levels of judge in the B&PC District Registries.

1.20 For guidance on the distribution of business for Insolvency and Companies List ("ICL") cases, see Chapter 21 and the Insolvency PD paragraph 3. Much of the work in the ICL is done by ICC Judges in London, though very large or complex cases are heard by HCJs, Section 9 Judges and Deputy HCJs. In the B&PC District Registries, the District Judges deal with shorter hearings and Section 9 Judges with longer hearings and most trials. Allocation and distribution of business between the judges and as between the B&PC District Registries and the County Court outside London is a matter for the local judges and/or as provided for in the Insolvency PD.

1.21 This is the first digital edition of the Guide. The Guide is written so as to be clear and easily used and navigated online. There is substantial use of hyperlinks to other parts of the Guide and its appendices and to related content, such as the Civil Procedure Rules (the 'CPR'), Practice Notes and other relevant statutory material. The Guide accordingly does not rehearse or repeat the content of these materials unless in giving guidance it is helpful to do so. A direct link is provided instead. The editors have aimed, in consequence, to shorten some of the narrative content, where possible. There are however some new chapters, and some existing material has been merged or relocated.

1.22 The reader will see that after this introductory chapter:

(a) Part 1 of the Guide follows a chronological line from the issue of the proceedings and the parties to them, through statements of case, case management and the procedures leading up to trial, whether of a Part 7 or Part 8 claim;

(b) Part 2 deals with applications and orders;

(c) Part 3 addresses in turn the work carried out in the various Chancery lists in the B&PCs and gives guidance on specialist Chancery work; and

(d) Part 4 deals with matters after the trial and ancillary issues.

1.23 There is a Glossary, which sets out the defined terms and abbreviations used frequently in this Guide. All terms and abbreviations are also defined when used for the first time in each chapter, even if also defined in the Glossary, to make this Guide more accessible to users. Where a defined term or abbreviation is used only infrequently in this Guide, it is defined in the relevant chapters or sections only and omitted from the Glossary.

1.24 The Chancery Guide is intended to promote the efficient conduct of litigation in the Chancery lists. The Guide does not however provide a complete blueprint for litigation and should be seen as providing guidance, which should be adopted flexibly (where appropriate) and adapted to the circumstances of the particular case. The Guide does not substitute or override the CPR, including relevant Practice Directions ('PDs'), and all litigants are expected to familiarise themselves and comply with the rules and PDs. In the event of inconsistency between this Guide and any rule or PD the provisions of the CPR must prevail. It is not the function of the Guide to provide legal advice.

1.25 The CPR, its PDs and pre-action protocols are found on the gov.uk website. Example forms and orders which can be used for Chancery cases can be found in Chancery Forms.

1.26 The Guide is published on the gov.uk website and on the Judiciary website. The Guide will continue to be kept under review in the light of practical experience and changes made to the CPR and PDs. Amendments will be made from time to time as necessary. The Guide is also printed in the main procedural reference books.

1.27 Suggestions for improvements to this Guide or the practice or procedure of the Chancery Division are welcome, as are any corrections and comments on the text of the Guide. These should be addressed to the Chancellor's Private Office at *ChancellorsPO@judiciary.uk.*

CE-FILE AND ELECTRONIC FILING

1.28 Proceedings issued in the B&PCs are stored by the court as an electronic case file, currently known as CE-File. Electronic filing is mandatory for professional court users and is strongly encouraged for litigants in person. It is the principal mode of communication with the court about a claim and the B&PCs increasingly expect all court users who have internet access and the means to send emails with attachments to register for CE-File. **1A-4**

1.29 The system is easy to use. To file a document using electronic filing, a party should register for an account, enter the case details, upload the appropriate document and pay any required fee. Both professional court users and litigants in person are able to pay court fees through CE-File either by account or card payment. If a party wishes to apply for Help With Fees, they must contact the relevant court office to process their application for Help With Fees before filing a document using electronic filing. Details on how to register for the HMCTS e-filing service can be found at HMCTS E-Filing service for citizens and professionals - GOV.UK (*www.gov.uk*). Please also see PD 51O for more information about electronic working.

1.30 The electronic file contains those documents the court is required to hold under the CPR, and contains notes, emails and letters added by court users or court staff, as did the previous paper file. All documents lodged with the court are held on CE-File. Documents accepted in paper form will in general be restricted to (i) original wills or similar documents, where it is necessary to lodge an original; and (ii) cases where the court has expressly directed that particular bundles or documents are to be filed in hard copy format (for more information about CE-File see Appendix E). For the position with litigants in person, see paragraphs 2.44 to 2.54 below.

1.31 Parties e-filing a claim form or an application notice with supporting documents should not file them as a single pdf. Each document should be clearly labelled (see PD 51O paragraph 5.1). For example, an application notice, witness statement and exhibit should be filed in pdf together with a draft order in Word and should each be filed and labelled separately, as four documents. This makes it easier for a judge and court staff to identify documents and, if necessary, to comply with any request under CPR 5.4C.

1.32 A party to the case may make a request for copies of documents to which they are entitled under CPR 5.4B. A non-party may make a request for copies of documents to which they are entitled as set out in CPR 5.4C.

GENERAL INFORMATION

1A-5 **1.33** For contact details for staff in the Rolls Building, please see Appendix A. Contact details for the B&PC District Registries are given in Appendix C.

CHANCERY DIVISION COURT USERS' COMMITTEES

1A-6 **1.34** The Chancery Division is keen to hear the concerns and views of the litigation community, particularly in times of continuous improvement and change. Several user committee groups exist to allow a steady flow of information and constructive suggestions between the court, litigants and professional advisers. The committees usually meet three times a year or more often as necessary. A list of the Chancery Division's current court user committees and their contact details, in London and the B&PC District Registries, is found at Appendix D.

ASSISTANCE FOR LITIGANTS IN PERSON

1A-7 **1.35** Many forms of help are available to the increasing numbers of individuals who, for various reasons, bring and defend claims without legal representation. An individual who exercises their right to conduct legal proceedings on their own behalf is known as a 'litigant in person'. It is important for litigants in person to be aware that the CPR (the rules of procedure and practice) apply to them in the same way as to lawyers. The court will however have regard to the fact that a party is unrepresented, so that the party is treated fairly. Further guidance can also be found in Chapter 2 Parties and representation.

1.36 Appendix H provides a non-exhaustive list of sources of assistance for litigants in person such as CAS, and Support Through Court.

1.37 Neither the court staff nor the judges can provide advice or assistance in relation to the conduct of a claim or defence.

1.38 There are voluntary schemes to provide assistance to litigants in person in respect of applications in the Judges' Applications List (which list is described in Chapter 15) and corporate insolvency in the winding up court.

CHAPTER 2 PARTIES AND REPRESENTATION

GENERAL

1A-8 **2.1** A claimant who issues a claim must give an address for service within the United Kingdom in compliance with CPR 6.23. The same applies to other parties to the proceedings. Where any party's address for service changes, the party must notify the other parties and the court in compliance with CPR 6.24.

2.2 In all claims, the claimant must consider carefully which parties are necessary to the proceedings before issuing the claim. Any number of claimants or defendants may be named: CPR 19.1 but no person should be named more than once, even if having more than one capacity.

2.3 In the case of a claimant or claimants seeking a joint remedy, attention is drawn to CPR 19.3.

2.4 It is usually necessary for at least one defendant or respondent to be named in any proceedings or application. However, in some limited circumstances it may be possible or appropriate to issue a claim or application without naming another party. For further guidance see CPR 8.2A and Chapter 13.

2.5 The claimant should comply with the relevant pre-action protocol or procedure in respect of all defendants to the claim, except where compliance is not appropriate, for example in trust cases where consultation under CPR PD 64B paragraph 7.7 is preferred or where an urgent without notice application is made in accordance with the guidance in Chapter 15.

2.6 Parties can be added or substituted at any time need the court's permission will be needed unless the claim form has not yet been served: CPR 19.2 and CPR 19.4. Special considerations apply where a relevant limitation period has expired: CPR 19.5.

2.7 Where a defendant is out of the jurisdiction consideration must be given to whether permission is required to serve the claim form on that defendant (CPR 6.12 and CPR 6.30 - CPR 6.37). If it is, the claimant should apply for permission in advance of service. The application should be supported by evidence, and will usually be considered on paper, without notice, or at a hearing of any pre-issue interim relief application (see Chapter 3 and Chapter 15 for further guidance).

REPRESENTATIVE PARTIES

1A-9 **2.8** In claims brought in the Chancery Division parties sometimes act or seek permission to act in a representative capacity. Attention is drawn generally to CPR 19.6 to 19.8A.

2.9 This most commonly occurs in the case of trusts and estates. Further guidance can be found in Chapter 25 Trusts paragraphs 25.10 to 25.14 and Chapter 26 Pensions paragraphs 26.21 to 26.29 and in CPR 19.7 and 19.7A.

2.10 Particular considerations arise where a party dies during ongoing proceedings. Where there is a personal representative, whether an executor with or without a grant of probate, or an administrator pursuant to a grant of representation, the personal representative should be substituted for the deceased person under CPR 19.2 to represent the deceased's estate. Where there is no such representative, CPR 19.8(1) applies, and the court may order the claim to proceed in the absence of a person representing the estate of the deceased or may order that a person be appointed to represent the estate of the deceased. Such an order is for the purposes of the proceedings only. It is not a grant of representation, nor does it entitle the person appointed to obtain a grant of representation.

2.11 Orders that the claim may proceed in the absence of a person representing the estate of the deceased are very rare. The best person to represent the estate of the deceased is likely to be the person, or a person, entitled to a grant of representation. However, the court is very unlikely to order somebody to represent the estate of the deceased if that person is unwilling to do so.

2.12 In cases where the parties cannot find a person willing to act as representative of the estate of a deceased party, an application for directions should be made to the court under CPR 19.8. The court will consider what steps can be taken in light of evidence concerning attempts to locate a representative. The court will also consider what costs order is just in the event of such an application being made.

GROUP LITIGATION INCLUDING GROUP LITIGATION ORDERS

2.13 Where numerous claims may or will give rise to common or related issues of facts or law, **1A-10**
parties must consider carefully whether to apply for a group litigation order ('GLO') or whether another form of bespoke case management such as managed claims or a representative claim would be suitable.

2.14 The specific rules in relation to GLOs are set out in CPR 19.10 to 19.14, together with PD 19B. The rules relating to representative parties with the same interest are set out in CPR 19.6.

2.15 Parties are expected to collaborate to identify any common or related issues of fact or law as early as possible and to have considered whether to apply for a GLO or whether bespoke case management or conjoined case management of the claims up to a certain stage is more appropriate and cost and resource efficient. Examples of case management techniques that can be used within or outside the GLO regime include the use of preliminary issues, sampling or test cases. In such cases the court is likely to wish to identify common issues or test cases for early trial.

2.16 If the parties in a claim involving multiple claimants or defendants seek bespoke case management, including for example sampling or test cases, other than as part of a GLO they should inform the court as early as possible and apply to defer the application of cost budgeting and PD51U until after a first case management conference (for further guidance on docketing and case management see Chapter 6).

2.17 An application for a GLO must be made by application notice under Part 23 in accordance with the requirements of CPR PD 19B (Group Litigation). The application should be made to the Chief Master, or in a specialist list, to the judge in charge of that list. The making of a GLO requires the approval of the Chancellor, who will usually docket such a case to a HCJ or a HCJ and Master in partnership for case management. A draft GLO can be found in Chancery Forms at CH6.

2.18 An applicant considering applying for a GLO may wish to 'mention' the matter to the Chief Master in advance of issue and seek guidance. In such circumstances an email addressed to the Chief Master should be sent to *chancery.mastersappointments@justice.gov.uk*

2.19 Where a GLO has been made, a claimant wishing to join the group register should issue the claim and apply to the lead solicitors to be joined on the register, or as may be required by the terms of the GLO.

2.20 A list of GLOs is published on the gov.uk website.

CAPACITY AND LITIGATION FRIENDS

2.21 Attention is drawn to CPR 21 where a party is a child or protected party. In insolvency **1A-11**
cases attention is drawn to Insolvency Rules 12.23 to 12.26.

2.22 A child must have a litigation friend to conduct proceedings on their behalf unless the court otherwise orders: CPR 21.2(2) and CPR 21.2(3).

2.23 A person lacks capacity to litigate, and so is a protected party, when they do not have capacity within the meaning of the Mental Capacity Act 2005 (the 'MCA 2005'), see in particular sections 2 and 3.

2.24 The MCA 2005 contains an assumption that a person has capacity unless it is established that they do not: section 1(2). A person is not to be treated as unable to make a decision unless all practicable steps to help them to do so have been taken without success: section 1(3). Even where a person lacks capacity, regard must be had to whether the purpose for any act taken on the person's behalf can be as effectively achieved in a way that is less restrictive of the person's rights and freedom of action: section 1(6). Special attention is drawn to these and the other principles contained in section 1 of the MCA 2005.

2.25 Capacity, including the capacity to conduct proceedings, may fluctuate. Under section 4(3) and 4(4) of the MCA 2005, any person, including the court, determining a protected party's bests interests, or the bests interests of somebody who it is reasonable to believe may be a protected party (see section 4(8)(b)), must consider whether it is likely that the person will at some time have capacity in relation to the matter in question; and must, so far as reasonably practicable, permit and encourage the protected party to participate, or to improve their ability to participate, as fully as possible in any act done for them and any decision affecting them.

2.26 Where a party lacks capacity when proceedings are issued, a litigation friend must be appointed: CPR 21.2. Those representing a protected party must ensure that a litigation friend is appointed in accordance with CPR 21.

2.27 Where a party loses capacity during proceedings, no step in the proceedings concerning the protected party has any effect unless the court orders otherwise: CPR 21.3(4). A litigation friend must be appointed, whether by the prospective litigation friend filing a certificate of suitability under CPR 21.5, or by application to the court for an order under CPR 21.6.

2.28 In the case of a certificate of suitability, attention is drawn to CPR PD 21, paragraph 2. In the case of an application for an order, attention is drawn to CPR PD 21, paragraph 3. In either case, the court will expect there to be cogent evidence that the person lacks capacity to conduct proceedings, by way of a medical report from a suitably qualified medical professional.

2.29 The Court of Protection may exercise powers in respect of those who lack capacity. The Court of Protection may appoint a deputy with power to conduct proceedings on behalf of a person who lacks such capacity, in which case the deputy is entitled to act as the person's litigation friend in any proceedings to which his power extends: CPR 21.4(2). An application may be made to the Court of Protection for the appointment of a deputy. Attention is drawn to section 19 of the MCA 2005, and to the Court of Protection Rules 2017.

2.30 If no litigation friend can be found to act, the Official Solicitor may act as litigation friend. The Official Solicitor is, however, a litigation friend of last resort. In such circumstances, provision must be made in any order for the payment of the Official Solicitor's charges: CPR PD 21, paragraph 3.4.

2.31 Where a party has reason to believe that another party lacks capacity to conduct proceedings, considerable care should be taken. The question of capacity engages rights safeguarded by the European Convention on Human Rights. Where a party is reasonably concerned that another party does or may lack capacity, the issue should be raised with the court promptly, and fully investigated. The court will also investigate capacity of its own motion where there is reason to believe it is lacking. Attention is drawn to *Masterman-Lister v Brutton & Co (Nos 1 and 2)* [2003] 1 WLR 1511.

2.32 Where the person whose capacity is in doubt is unrepresented, the other party should write to that person setting out in clear language the nature of their concerns and inviting the person whose capacity is in doubt to obtain and disclose a medical report addressing their capacity to conduct proceedings. If that person refuses, or if the medical report shows that the person lacks relevant capacity, but no litigation friend is appointed, the other party should apply to the court for directions.

2.33 Where an unrepresented litigation friend purports to be acting for a protected party, but another party has reason to believe that the protected party in fact has capacity, the other party should write to the litigation friend and the protected party setting out in clear language the nature of their concerns and inviting the litigation friend and the person whose capacity is in doubt to obtain and disclose a medical report addressing their capacity to conduct proceedings. If that person refuses, or if the medical report shows that the protected person retains relevant capacity, the other party should apply to the court for directions.

VULNERABILITY

1A-12 **2.34** Where a party or witness may be vulnerable even if no capacity issue arises the parties should consider the application of PD1A 'Participation of Vulnerable Parties or Witnesses'. The parties should seek to identify any vulnerable party or witness at an early stage and assist the court to take proportionate measures to address any issues of vulnerability where necessary, and to make such directions about their participation as may be appropriate, consistent with the overriding objective.

RIGHTS OF AUDIENCE AND REPRESENTATION

1A-13 **2.35** The conduct of litigation and the exercise of a right of audience (such as the right to appear before and address the court at a hearing) is a reserved activity under section 12 of the Legal Services Act 2007. Subject to limited exceptions only a person authorised under the Legal Services Act 2007 may exercise a right of audience.

2.36 Who has an automatic right of audience to appear before and address the court at a hearing depends on the type of hearing and the level of court. For all hearings before a HCJ in the High Court only counsel, or a solicitor or a registered European lawyer who have successfully completed the appropriate higher courts advocacy qualification may appear.

2.37 Counsel, solicitors and registered European lawyers generally have rights of audience in all other types of hearing. Legal executives who are members of CILEX, costs lawyers, patent attorneys and trade mark attorneys have rights of audience for some types of hearings. Trainees, paralegals, and agents may also have a limited right to represent a party at some types of hearing.

2.38 Those representing a party should satisfy themselves that they have the requisite right of audience to appear before and address the court at any hearing they attend and if there is any doubt seek permission to address the court at the outset of the hearing. Anyone representing a party at a hearing should be in a position to direct the judge to the relevant provisions that provide them with a right of audience for the hearing.

2.39 Alternatively, parties are entitled to represent themselves in any court proceedings (see paragraph 2.44).

LEGAL REPRESENTATIVES

2.40 Usually, parties find it helpful to instruct authorised legal representatives to assist them in the conduct of litigation and at court hearings. **1A-14**

2.41 If a party instructs an authorised legal representative to commence a claim or acknowledge a claim on their behalf that legal representative will be on the court file as the party's address for service and as representing the party until a Notice of Change [N434] is filed under CPR 42.

2.42 If a party instructs an authorised legal representative after either issuing a claim or filing an acknowledgment of service or defence, that legal representative will have to file a Notice of Change to notify the court of their instruction. They will then be on the court record and their address will be the address for service in the jurisdiction for the party to the proceedings.

2.43 A legal representative remains on the court record until either a Notice of Change is filed either by the party stating they are no longer represented or by a new legal representative on behalf of that party stating that they are the new representative, or the existing legal representative makes a successful application to be removed. Particular attention is drawn to CPR 42 where there is a change of legal representation and the need to comply with CPR PD 42.5. Where a party ceases to be legally represented attention is drawn to the requirements set out in CPR 6.23 and CPR 6.24.

LITIGANTS IN PERSON

2.44 Individuals who conduct legal proceedings on their own behalf are known as a 'litigants in person'. A company can also conduct legal proceedings on its own behalf but will need to obtain permission for an authorised employee to represent it at a hearing: CPR 39.6. **1A-15**

2.45 An authorised employee of a company should ensure that they are able to provide evidence of such authorisation by the board of the company or evidence that they are a sole director if requested by the judge.

2.46 Unless an individual or a company is acting as a litigant in person, anyone exercising a right of audience on their behalf (for example addressing the court at a hearing) must be authorised to exercise a right of audience (see paragraphs 2.35 to 2.38 above).

2.47 The rules and practice directions in the CPR apply to litigants in person in the same way as to represented parties.

2.48 Proceedings issued in the B&PCs are stored by the court as an electronic case file, currently known as CE-File. Electronic filing is strongly encouraged for litigants in person. It is easy to use for anyone with an email address and access to the internet, and is the principal mode of communication with the court about a claim.

2.49 Fees can be paid online when using CE-File, using a credit or debit card or by providing a Help With Fees number. See paragraphs 1.28 to 1.32 and Appendix E for further information about the use of CE-File.

2.50 Litigants in Person who are unable to use CE-File can submit paper copies of forms or documents to the court by post together with payment for any fees or a completed Help With Fees Form.

2.51 Alternatively, litigants in person can submit paper copies of forms or documents to the court in person. Payment in person can be made by cheque or card or by using Help With Fees.

2.52 Any forms or documents submitted as paper copies will be uploaded to CE-File. No paper file will be retained. See Appendix E.

2.53 The court will not accept forms and documents by email. Any correspondence, forms or documents should be uploaded to CE-File, not sent by email. If that is not possible it should be sent by post or delivered by hand.

2.54 Litigants in person should consider carefully the time it might take for documents to be delivered to the court by post when considering using post rather than CE-File.

MCKENZIE FRIENDS

2.55 A litigant who is acting in person may be assisted at a hearing by another person, often referred to as a 'McKenzie Friend' (see *McKenzie v McKenzie* [1971] P 33). The litigant must be present at the hearing. If the hearing is in private, it is a matter of discretion for the court whether such an assistant is allowed to attend the hearing. That may depend, among other things, on the nature of the proceedings. **1A-16**

2.56 The McKenzie Friend is allowed to help by taking notes, quietly prompting the litigant and offering advice and suggestions to the litigant.

2.57 The court can, and sometimes does, permit the McKenzie Friend to address the court on behalf of the litigant, by making an order to that effect under schedule 3 paragraph 2 of the Legal Services Act 2007. Although applications are considered on a case by case basis, the Chancery Division will usually follow the guidance contained in *Practice Note (McKenzie Friends: Civil and Family Courts)* [2010] 1 W.L.R. 1881.

2.58 Different considerations may apply where the person seeking the right of audience is acting for remuneration, and any litigant should be prepared to disclose whether the proposed McKenzie Friend is acting for remuneration and, if so, how the remuneration is calculated.

2.59 Where a litigant wants assistance at a hearing from a McKenzie Friend, they and their McKenzie Friend will be asked to complete a McKenzie Friend Notice (Appendix J).

2.60 The completed Notice will be provided to the judge who will consider it at the start of the hearing.

2.61 A new Notice will need to be completed for each hearing at which assistance is required and the request will be considered by the judge afresh. The completed Notice will be retained on the electronic court file.

2.62 Further guidance for unrepresented parties can be found in Chapter 1 and Appendix H.

CHAPTER 3 COMMENCEMENT AND TRANSFER (PART 7)

STARTING A CLAIM

1A-17 **3.1** The Civil Procedure Rules ('CPR') permit claims to be issued by following one of two different procedures that are governed respectively by CPR 7 and Part 8. This chapter addresses claims brought under Part 7, which is usually appropriate where the claim is likely to involve a substantial dispute of fact. For Part 8 claims see Chapter 13.

3.2 Parties are referred to Part 7 and Practice Direction ('PD') 7A (How to start proceedings - the claim form) as well as the provisions of Part 16 and PD 16 (Statements of case) in relation to the contents of the claim form and particulars of claim (and see Chapter 4).

3.3 Additional claims may also be brought in existing proceedings using the procedure set out at CPR 20.

3.4 Some specialist Companies Act and insolvency proceedings are required to be issued by petition or originating application rather than by Part 7 or Part 8 claim form (see Chapter 21).

PRE-ACTION BEHAVIOUR

1A-18 **3.5** The Practice Direction - Pre-Action Conduct and Protocols applies to cases in the Chancery Division where they are begun as a Part 7 or Part 8 claim. It does not apply to claims which are started by some other means (e.g. petition).

3.6 This PD and any relevant Pre-Action Protocol should ordinarily be observed, although it is sometimes necessary or proper to start proceedings without following the relevant procedures, for example where telling the other party in advance would defeat the purpose of the application (e.g. an application for a freezing order).

3.7 Subject to complying with the PD and any applicable Pre-Action Protocol, the parties are not required, or generally expected, to engage in elaborate or expensive pre-action procedures, and restraint is encouraged.

3.8 Thus, the letter of claim should be concise, and it is usually sufficient to explain the proposed claim(s), identifying key dates, so as to enable the potential defendant to understand and to investigate the allegations. Only key documents need be supplied. Any period specified for a response should be reasonable and comply with any applicable Pre-Action Protocol.

3.9 A potential defendant should acknowledge a letter of claim promptly and then respond in detail within any reasonable time specified or in accordance with the relevant Pre-Action Protocol. A potential defendant who needs longer should explain the reasons when acknowledging the letter of claim. Only key documents need be supplied with the response.

3.10 The court has the power to impose sanctions for substantial non-compliance with the PD or any applicable Pre-Action Protocol.

PLACE OF ISSUE

1A-19 **3.11** The claimant should consider carefully whether the Chancery Division, as part of the Business and Property Courts of England and Wales ('B&PCs'), is the appropriate court in which to issue the claim, and if so whether the Rolls Building in London ('ChD B&PCs London') or one of the Business and Property Courts District Registries (the 'B&PC District Registries') is the right venue. The principal considerations are:

(a) Does paragraph 1 of Schedule 1 to the Senior Courts Act 1981 require the claim to be issued in the Chancery Division?

(b) Does any other statute, regulation or provision of the CPR, including PD 7A (How to start proceedings - the claim form) or PD 57AA (Business and Property Courts) require the claim to be brought in a particular venue? Note that even if the value of the claim exceeds the minimum £100,000 High Court threshold (see paragraph 2.1 of PD 7A), it may nevertheless be more appropriate to issue the claim in the County Court. The value of the claim is only one of several criteria which should be considered and as a general starting point the ChD B&PCs London will scrutinise a claim with a value of less than £500,000 to see if it should remain in the High Court.

(c) Do the issues raised by the claim suggest that it would be preferable to issue it in another Division of the High Court?

(d) Does the claim have significant links to one of the regional circuits, such that it should be issued in the relevant B&PC District Registry (paragraph 2.3 of PD 57AA). The value of the claim or, with certain exceptions, the perceived need for a specialist judge is not of itself a good reason to issue in the ChD B&PCs London. That is because the appropriate judge will where necessary travel to hear the claim or deal with case management (where it is not appropriate to hold a case management hearing remotely). The exceptions are certain Competition List claims, the Financial List, and the Patents Court sub-list of the Intellectual Property List, where claims must be issued in the ChD B&PCs London (see Chapter 19, Chapter 20 and Chapter 22).

3.12 The claimant must take care to issue the claim in the correct list or sub-list. This will depend on the principal subject matter of the dispute. For example, if the dispute involves land, even if the land is for commercial use, it should be assigned to the Property, Trusts and Probate List. Similarly, a dispute about pensions should be assigned to the Business List, Pensions sub-list, even if professional negligence is involved. Where different aspects of the dispute indicate that the claim may be issued in different courts, lists or sub-lists, the claimant must consider whether there are aspects requiring the expertise of a specialist judge and, if so, must select the court, list or sub-list in which the relevant specialist judges sit (for information as to the availability of specialist judges, contact the relevant Listing Office). Only one court, list or sub-list may be chosen.

3.13 See Appendix F for details of the available lists and sub-lists for claims in the Chancery Division (and the B&PCs generally). If claimants are in doubt as to which list or sub-list is appropriate, they should seek guidance from a Master. This should be by letter sent to *chancery.mastersappointments@justice.gov.uk* setting out briefly what the issue is. The Master will either address the request for guidance on paper or fix a short without notice hearing. In the B&PC District Registry the guidance should be sought from a specialist B&PC District Judge.

3.14 All Part 7 claims issued in London are triaged by a Master upon the particulars of claim being filed. At this stage the Master will consider the value and nature of the claim and whether any early case management is necessary, including for example consideration of docketing or transfer (see paragraphs 3.23 to 3.27 below), or dealing with early applications that do not require a hearing (see Chapter 15), or making any directions that appear appropriate, such as for the filing of compliant particulars of claim or the listing of a hearing to consider striking out the claim of the court's own motion. Practice in the B&PC District Registries may vary.

FINANCIAL LIST

3.15 The Financial List is a single specialist list defined in CPR 63A and PD 63AA. Claims in the Financial List may be commenced in either the Chancery Division in London or the Commercial Court (See Chapter 20). **1A-20**

SHORTER TRIALS SCHEME

3.16 The claimant may start a claim in the Shorter Trials Scheme in the B&PCs including any B&PC District Registry if the trial will not exceed 4 days, including judicial reading time and time for preparing and delivering closing submissions, and if the claim is otherwise appropriate for the Scheme. Claims may also be transferred into the Shorter Trials Scheme in some circumstances (See PD 57AB (Shorter and Flexible Trials Schemes) and Chapter 17). **1A-21**

ARBITRATION CLAIMS

3.17 Applications to the court under the Arbitration Acts 1950 - 1996 and other applications relating to arbitrations are known as 'arbitration claims'. The procedure applicable to arbitration claims is set out in CPR 62 and PD 62. Arbitration claims relating to partnership or landlord and tenant disputes must be issued in the Chancery Division. **1A-22**

TITLES AND NUMBERING OF CLAIMS

3.18 See paragraph 16.15 and Appendix F for information on titles and numbering of claims. **1A-23**

EXPEDITION

3.19 The court may expedite the trial of a claim in cases of sufficient urgency and importance. **1A-24**

3.20 A party seeking an expedited trial should make an application on notice to all parties at the earliest possible opportunity. This will normally be on the hearing of an early interim application on notice or after issue and service of the claim form and particulars of claim but before service of a defence (see Chapter 15). The application to expedite must be made to a HCJ in London (see paragraph 4.1 of PD 2B (Allocation of cases to levels of judiciary)) and to a Section 9 Judge in the B&PC District Registries.

3.21 If the court makes an order for expedition, it will ordinarily fix a date for trial and refer the case to a Master for an urgent case management conference ('CMC') or costs and case management conference ('CCMC'), but in an appropriate case the court may consider giving case management directions at the same time as making the order for expedition. Exceptionally and where necessary, the court may order that the case shall proceed without the filing or service of particulars of claim or defence or of any other statement of case.

3.22 If directions are given for an urgent CMC or CCMC, it is the responsibility of the parties to provide the Master's clerk or the District Judge (via CE-File) with: (a) a combined list of dates to avoid; (b) a realistic time estimate for the hearing and any pre-reading; (c) a copy of the order for expedition; and (d) (if known) the date or window for the trial. The urgent case management conference is unlikely to be listed until this information is provided. The parties should file a bundle for the case management conference in accordance with this Guide.

DOCKETING

1A-25 **3.23** See Chapter 6 paragraphs 6.19 to 6.23 for a description of the four alternative case management tracks used to manage claims in the ChD B&PCs London, and the procedure to be followed where the parties wish to request that a case be docketed to a HCJ or made subject to an order for partnership management (i.e. case management by a HCJ and a Master, with trial by a HCJ).

TRANSFER

1A-26 **3.24** As noted at paragraph 3.14 above, all Part 7 claims are reviewed by a Master upon the particulars of claim being filed. If (at that stage or subsequently) it is considered that the Chancery Division in the Rolls Building is not the appropriate venue, or that the claim has been issued in an inappropriate list, an order for transfer will be made of the court's own motion, with or without notice to the parties (but once the order for transfer is made, the parties will be notified: see CPR 30.4(1)). An order may be made transferring the case:

(a) To the County Court.
(b) To another list or sub-list within the Chancery Division.
(c) To a B&PC District Registry having regard to the factors in paragraph 3.1 of PD 57AA (Business and Property Courts)).
(d) To the Commercial Court or Technology and Construction Court (subject to the consent of the Chancellor and the judge in charge of the receiving court).
(e) To another Division of the High Court outside the B&PCs, whether in London or a District Registry.

A party may also apply for an order transferring the case as set out in any of (a) to (e) above. In cases (c) and (d), the application should be accompanied by confirmation that the applicant has obtained the consent of the receiving court (and for this purpose see the contact details for the B&PC District Registries at Appendix C). See CPR 30 (Transfer) and PD 57AA (and CPR 63.18 in relation to transfers to the Intellectual Property Enterprise Court).

3.25 Sometimes a party to a claim in one of the Chancery B&PC lists such as the Business List will also be a party to a related claim/petition in the Insolvency and Companies List (the 'ICL' see Chapter 21). It is not always possible to *issue* a Part 7 claim in the ICL and it is not possible to present a Petition in the Business List. Such proceedings will usually relate to the same dispute and will feature the same parties, or some of them.

3.26 The parties should consider carefully whether the substance of the claim indicates that one list should be preferred for the future conduct of the claims and, if so, lodge a consent order for transfer in the list out of which transfer is sought as soon as possible. Where consent is not possible and a party considers that both claims should be heard in the same list, this should be raised at the first hearing when either claim comes before the court and, at the latest, at the first CMC listed in either claim.

3.27 The bundle for that hearing should include the statements of case and other relevant documents in both sets of proceedings to enable the ICC Judge or Master (or District Judge outside London) to consider whether to make an order for transfer of the proceedings into the same list for effective case management.

APPLICATIONS MADE PRE-ISSUE OR AT POINT OF ISSUE

1A-27 **3.28** Some types of application may be made pre-issue or at the point of issue of the claim form (see Chapter 15).

3.29 For guidance on applications to issue proceedings without naming defendants, or for anonymity and/or confidentiality see paragraphs 13.35 to 13.39 and paragraph 3.31 onwards below.

3.30 If a pre-issue application is made (eg for service out of the jurisdiction or anonymity/

confidentiality), when the claim to which the application relates is subsequently issued it will be given a separate claim number by CE-File. The claimant must file a letter on CE-File when issuing the claim requesting that the claim be assigned to the same Master who dealt with the pre-issue application (in London) and that the two be linked together.

PRIVACY, ANONYMITY AND CONFIDENTIALITY

3.31 Open justice is a fundamental principle of common law. Any derogation from the principle of open justice should be the minimum strictly necessary in the interests of justice and for the proper administration of justice. **1A-28**

3.32 Applications for part or all of a hearing to take place in private, or for anonymity and/or confidentiality in respect of some or all of the court file must be supported by evidence. Applications for anonymity and/or to limit access to the court file are often made in the same application but may be made as separate applications. In all cases the evidence in support must justify the derogation from the principle of open justice. Such applications are often made before issue or at the point of issue although they can be made at any stage including after judgment. Further guidance can be found in CPR 39.2, Chapter 15 (Urgent Applications), Chapter 25 (Trusts) and Chapter 26 (Pensions) of this Guide.

PRIVACY

3.33 As a general rule hearings take place in public. The circumstances in which a hearing must be held in private are set out in CPR 39.2(3). **1A-29**

3.34 Even if the parties are in agreement, the court will have to be satisfied that one or more of the matters set out in CPR 39.2 (3 (a) to (g)) applies and that it is necessary to hold part or all of the hearing in private to secure the proper administration of justice. An order that a hearing to be held in private will rarely be made without a hearing. It will usually be considered at the commencement of the hearing in respect of which privacy is sought. However if, unusually, an order is made on paper or an interim order has been made, even if not contentious between the parties, it will be considered afresh at the start of the hearing. Any order for privacy once made shall be published on the judiciary website unless the court orders otherwise (see CPR 39.2(5) and the Practice Guidance: Publication of Privacy and Anonymity Orders). Even if part or all of a hearing takes place in private the court may consider it appropriate to publish any judgment, if necessary in redacted form.

ANONYMITY

3.35 In an appropriate case the court may order that the identity of a party or witness is not disclosed where this is necessary to secure the proper administration of justice and in order to protect the interests of that party or witness (CPR 39.2(4)). It most commonly arises where additional safeguards may be needed to protect the identity of children or protected parties or where an application for a freezing injunction or search order is issued. Further guidance on anonymity applications can be found at paragraphs 15.64 to 15.68 (Urgent Applications) and paragraphs 25.39 to 25.45 (Trusts). In some circumstances it may be considered appropriate to issue an application to seek permission to anonymise some or all of the identities of the parties to a claim prior to issue. In such a case the applicant should have regard to the guidance in paragraph 13.39. In a simple case the judge may be willing to deal with such an application on paper. **1A-30**

CONFIDENTIALITY

3.36 CPR 5.4B, 5.4C and 5.4D set out the rules on the provision of documents from the court file (upon payment of the prescribed fee) to parties and non-parties with and without permission of the court. Where permission is required the party or non-party should apply using form N244. Although the application can be made without notice the court may direct that notice should be given to any person who may be affected by the decision. **1A-31**

3.37 However, CPR 5.4C(4) enables the court to restrict who can access documents and what documents (individually or as classes) may be accessed by non-parties. In every case the court will need to consider the balance between the importance of open justice, the risk of harm and the legitimate interests of others.

CHAPTER 4 STATEMENTS OF CASE AND SERVICE (PART 7)

STATEMENTS OF CASE: FORM AND CONTENT

4.1 Parties are referred to Part 16 of the Civil Procedure Rules ('CPR') and Practice Direction 'PD' 16 (Statements of Case) which must be complied with in all cases brought under Part 7. **1A-32**

4.2 The following principles apply to all statements of case as defined in CPR 2.3, i.e. particulars of claim (including where set out in the claim form and in any additional claim form issued pursuant to Part 20), defence, counterclaim, reply to defence, defence to counterclaim and any further information given in relation to any of them:

(a) The document must be as concise as possible.

(b) The document must be set out in separate consecutively numbered paragraphs and sub-paragraphs.
(c) The document must deal with the case on a point by point basis to allow a point by point response. In particular, each separate cause of action, or defence, should be pleaded separately wherever possible.
(d) So far as possible each paragraph or sub-paragraph should contain no more than one allegation.
(e) Special care should be taken to set out only those factual allegations which are necessary to establish the cause of action, defence, or point of reply being advanced, to enable the other party to know what case it has to meet. Evidence should not be included, and a general factual narrative is neither required nor helpful (and is likely to contravene paragraphs (f), (h) and/or (k) below).
(f) Particulars of primary allegations should be stated as particulars and not appear as if they are primary allegations.
(g) A party wishing to advance a positive case must set that case out; and reasons must be set out for any denial of an allegation.
(h) Where particulars are given of any allegation or reasons are given for a denial, the allegation or denial should be stated first and the particulars or reasons for it listed one by one in separate numbered sub-paragraphs.
(i) Where they will assist:
 i. headings should be used; and
 ii. abbreviations and definitions should be established and used.

(j) Contentious headings, abbreviations and definitions should not be used. Every effort should be made to ensure that headings, abbreviations and definitions are in a form that will enable them to be adopted without issue by the other parties.
(k) In rare cases where it is necessary to give lengthy particulars of an allegation, these should be set out in schedules or appendices.
(l) A response to particulars set out in a schedule should be set out in a corresponding schedule.
(m) In a rare case where it is necessary for the proper understanding of the statement of case to include substantial parts of a lengthy document the passages in question should be set out in a schedule rather than in the body of the statement of case.
(n) Contentious paraphrasing should be avoided.
(o) The document must be signed by the individual person or persons who drafted it. If drafted by a solicitor it must be signed in the name of the firm PD 5A 2.1. The requirement for a signature on a document can be satisfied by a printed name in accordance with CPR 5.3.

4.3 The document must be accompanied by a Statement of Truth: see CPR 22, which must always be signed in the name of an individual.

4.4 A statement of case should be no longer than is necessary, should generally not exceed 25 pages and, save in exceptional circumstances should not exceed 40 pages. The court will expect a party to be able to justify the need for any statement of greater length.

4.5 Where, exceptionally, a statement of case is longer than 40 pages a summary of the statement of case (of no more than 5 pages) must also be served. The summary should be a concise summary of the statement of case and should not include any matters not set out in the statement of case. It does not form part of the statement of case and does not need to be responded to separately by any other party. Where a statement of case is longer than 40 pages, it must also be accompanied by a brief note explaining why the greater length is appropriate.

4.6 For these purposes a statement of case includes schedules and appendices annexed to it or served with it, and for all the documents referred to in this paragraph a minimum 12 point font and 1.5 line spacing must be used.

THE PURPOSE OF STATEMENTS OF CASE

1A-33 **4.7** A statement of case serves three purposes (as summarised by Cockerill J in *King v Stiefel* [2021] EWHC 1045 (Comm): see paragraph 145 et seq), which should also be borne in mind by parties preparing any statement of case in the Chancery Division:
(a) It enables the other side to know the case it has to meet.
(b) It ensures that the parties can properly prepare for trial - and that unnecessary costs are not expended and court time required chasing points which are not in issue or which lead nowhere.
(c) The process of preparing the statement of case operates (or should operate) as a critical audit for the claimant or defendant and its legal team that it has a complete cause of action or defence.

SETTING OUT ALLEGATIONS OF FRAUD

1A-34 **4.8** Paragraph 8.2 of PD 16 requires the claimant specifically to set out any allegation of fraud relied on. Parties must ensure that they state:

(a) full particulars of any allegation of fraud, dishonesty, malice or illegality; and
(b) where any inference of fraud or dishonesty is alleged, the facts on the basis of which the inference is alleged.

4.9 A party should not make allegations of fraud or dishonesty unless there is credible material to support the contentions made. Setting out such matters without such material being available may result in the particular allegations being struck out and may result in wasted costs orders being made against the legal advisers responsible.

DEFENCE TO COUNTERCLAIM AND REPLY

4.10 Where a party serves a defence to counterclaim and reply, the defence to counterclaim is due to be filed 14 days after the defence and counterclaim (see CPR 15.4, 20.3 and 20.4(3)), subject to the parties' agreement to extend that period by up to 28 days (see CPR 15.5). However, the reply is due to be filed only with the directions questionnaire (see CPR 15.8), which is likely to be some time later. **1A-35**

4.11 Where that is the case, the parties should cooperate and seek to agree that the reply and defence to counterclaim should be filed and served at the same time. This may either be by agreeing that the reply is to be filed and served early and at the same time as the defence to counterclaim or, if there is no particular urgency for the defence to counterclaim, by seeking to agree an extension of time to serve the defence to counterclaim (and where necessary file a consent order to obtain the court's approval to such an extension) so that the defence to counterclaim and reply are due to be filed at the same time at some agreed later date.

4.12 Despite the deadline set out at CPR 15.8, claimants should if possible file and serve any reply (and, where the above applies, any defence to counterclaim) before they file their directions questionnaire. This will enable other parties to consider the defence to counterclaim and reply before they file their directions questionnaire.

INITIAL DISCLOSURE

4.13 Parties are referred to paragraph 5 of PD 51U (Disclosure Pilot for the Business and Property Courts) which requires parties to give Initial Disclosure at the same time as serving a statement of case (subject to the exceptions set out in that PD). Chapter 7 provides further guidance on disclosure. **1A-36**

SERVICE

SERVICE OF CLAIM FORM BY CLAIMANT

4.14 Parties are referred to CPR 6 in relation to the service of claim forms (and other documents) **1A-37**

4.15 The current practice in the ChD B&PCs London is that *all* claim forms are served by the claimant and not the court. Claimants must ensure that they serve a sealed copy of the claim form (downloading the sealed copy from CE-file) rather than the unsealed copy as submitted to the court to be issued (see *Ideal Shopping Direct Ltd v Mastercard Incorporated* [2022] EWCA Civ 14). Any other document filed electronically using CE-File shall be served by the parties unless the court orders otherwise CPR PD51O paragraph 8.2.

4.16 A claim form must be served within 4 months of issue (6 months if it is served out of the jurisdiction): see CPR PD 7.5.

4.17 In most cases the claim should be served promptly and, if necessary, an application for an order for alternative service or to dispense with service under CPR 6.15 or 6.16 should be made without delay.

EXTENSION OF TIME FOR SERVICE

4.18 The parties may agree to the period of time for service of the claim form being extended by an agreement in writing. **1A-38**

4.19 The court may grant an extension of time for service of a claim form on an application by the claimant under CPR 7.6, and subject to the requirements of that rule. Such an application is invariably made without notice, and any order granted is vulnerable to being set aside on an application made later by the defendant under CPR 23.10, which may be a particular risk if an extension is granted at or towards the end of the limitation period.

ADDRESS FOR SERVICE

4.20 A claim when issued must include an address at which the claimant resides or carries on business which need not be the same as the address for service (PD 16.2.2). Where the defendant is an individual the claim form should also provide an address at which the defendant resides or carries on business (PD 16.2.3). **1A-39**

4.21 All parties, whether represented or not, must give an address for service in the United Kingdom: see CPR 6.23. For the claimant, the address will be in the claim form or other document by which the proceedings are brought. For the defendant, it will be in either the defence or the acknowledgment of service form filed under Part 10. A failure by either party to comply with this requirement is likely to result in sanctions, such as a stay of the action (for a claimant's failure) or an unless order (for a defendant's failure).

4.22 It is essential that the court should be notified promptly of any change of address. A letter notifying the new address should be filed via CE-File and served on all other parties: see CPR 6.24.

SERVICE OUT

1A-40 **4.23** Applications for service out of the jurisdiction are normally made before or when the claim is issued. However, the claim form may be issued even though one or more defendants is resident outside the jurisdiction without first obtaining permission to serve out of the jurisdiction. In that case the claimant may apply for permission to serve out after the claim form has been issued. The procedure for the application is the same as an application made before issue of the claim: see Chapter 15.

4.24 A claim form can be served out of the jurisdiction without the court's permission under CPR 6.32 or 6.33. A claim form cannot otherwise be validly served out of the jurisdiction without permission of the court (see CPR 6.36 and 6.37 and PD 6B).

4.25 An application for service out of the jurisdiction must show that (i) the applicant has a good arguable case that the application comes within one of the jurisdictional gateways set out in PD6B, (ii) there is a serious issue to be tried in respect of each cause of action for which permission to serve out is sought and (iii) the courts of England and Wales are the *forum conveniens.*

4.26 The applicant has a duty of full and frank disclosure (see paragraph 15.33) to draw to the attention of the court in evidence all relevant matters whether they help or hinder the application.

4.27 A draft form of order can be found in Chancery Forms at CH5. Note that orders permitting service out of the jurisdiction do not include provision to apply to set aside or vary in accordance with CPR 23.10. Applications to challenge the jurisdiction are governed by a separate regime set out in CPR 11.

4.28 For service of a claim form on a State see CPR 6.44 and section 12 of the State Immunity Act 1978.

4.29 An application to challenge the court's jurisdiction (whether it is a challenge to the grant of permission to serve out of the jurisdiction, a challenge to the court's jurisdiction or exercise of jurisdiction on another ground, or a challenge to the effectiveness of service) must be made under CPR 11.

CHAPTER 5 JUDGMENT IN DEFAULT

GRANTING A DEFAULT JUDGMENT

1A-41 **5.1** Default judgment may be available in Part 7 claims where, at the date at which a judgment is entered, a defendant (or defendant to counterclaim/Part 20 claim) has failed to file an acknowledgment of service (CPR 10) or, having filed an acknowledgement of service, has failed to file and serve a defence (CPR 15), and the time for doing so has expired. The default judgment may be sought in a Request for Default Judgment or an Application for Default Judgment (CPR 12.1 and CPR 12.3).

REQUEST FOR DEFAULT JUDGMENT

1A-42 **5.2** A Request for Default Judgment is an administrative process which can only be used where a claim is a money claim for a specified amount or for damages to be assessed. If the request satisfies the requirements of CPR 12.3 judgment will be entered either for the specified amount (plus interest, if validly claimed) or for damages to be assessed (CPR 12.4).

5.3 If a claim is for both a money claim and another remedy (for example an injunction) default judgment for the money claim only may be entered following a request under CPR 12.1 if the other remedies are waived (CPR 12.4(3) and (4).

APPLICATION FOR DEFAULT JUDGMENT

1A-43 **5.4** An Application for Default Judgment (CPR 12.3), which should be supported by evidence, will rarely be suitable for determination on paper. A hearing will usually be necessary. Applications for Default Judgment are usually determined by a Master or District Judge.

5.5 An application will be necessary either if the defendant falls within the class of defendants identified in CPR 12.10 or if the claim seeks any other remedy (CPR 12.4(2)). This includes any discretionary relief such as a declaration, rectification or an injunction.

5.6 Default judgment shall be such judgment as it appears to the court that the claimant is entitled to. If the claimant seeks discretionary relief the judge will need to be satisfied that the relief is necessary and ought to be granted.

5.7 Declaratory relief and relief by way of rectification will not be granted without evidence and will not ordinarily be appropriate for resolution by way of default judgment.

5.8 A claimant may not obtain default judgment if the defendant has applied to strike out the claim (CPR 3.4) or for summary judgment (CPR 24) and/or if any of the other provisions of CPR12.3(3) apply.

5.9 Default judgment is not available in Part 8 claims (CPR 12.2) or where the CPR otherwise provides, for example in a Probate Claim (CPR 57.10).

SETTING ASIDE A DEFAULT JUDGMENT

5.10 An application to set aside or vary a default judgment should be made promptly and served on the claimant, supported by evidence and (if possible and where appropriate) include a draft defence. A hearing will usually be necessary. **1A-44**

5.11 Where a default judgment has been wrongly entered (because the conditions for granting it were not properly complied with or the whole of the claim was satisfied before judgment was entered) the court must set it aside, regardless of the merits (CPR 13.2).

5.12 In any other case the court **may** set aside or vary a default judgment where the defendant has a real prospect of successfully defending the claim or there is some other good reason to set aside or vary the judgment or allow the defendant to defend (CPR 13.3 and 13.4). A defendant must apply promptly.

CHAPTER 6 CASE AND COSTS MANAGEMENT IN PART 7 CLAIMS

GENERAL

6.1 This chapter applies to all Part 7 claims issued in the Chancery lists of the Business and Property Courts in London (as set out in Appendix F - the 'ChD B&PCs London'), except for those claims in: **1A-45**

(a) the Patents Court;
(b) the Shorter and Flexible Trials Schemes (see PD 57AB (Shorter and Flexible Trials Schemes) and Chapter 17); or
(c) the Financial List (see Chapter 20).

Guidance about case and costs management for claims issued in 6.1(a) to (c) above can be located using the hyperlinks provided.

6.2 The practice in B&PC District Registries will be broadly similar, though with some differences, in particular as regards the time at which a District Judge first reviews the court file, triage, case management by District Judges alone, and the practice for listing a CMC or CCMC. Where there is no specific local guidance this Chapter applies to costs and case management in the B&PC District Registries directly or by analogy in a way most likely to serve the overriding objective. Links to any local guidance can be found in Appendix C.

6.3 For case management in Part 8 claims, see Chapter 13.

BEFORE THE FIRST CASE MANAGEMENT CONFERENCE ('CMC') / COSTS AND CASE MANAGEMENT CONFERENCE ('CCMC')

ALLOCATION

6.4 All cases appropriately issued in the ChD B&PCs London will automatically be allocated to the multi-track. Once all defences have been filed, a court officer will serve on each party a Notice of Proposed Allocation in Form N149C confirming this allocation and providing a date for the filing of Directions Questionnaires (N181). **1A-46**

6.5 If any defendant does not file a defence, the sending of the Notice of Proposed Allocation may not be triggered on CE-File. Accordingly, if a Notice of Proposed Allocation has not been received within 21 days of the last deadline for filing a defence, the claimant should contact the court by letter filed on CE-File to request that a Notice of Proposed Allocation be sent to the parties.

DIRECTIONS QUESTIONNAIRES ('DQS')

6.6 Form N149C requires the parties to file and serve DQs and attempt to agree directions (see paragraphs 6.17 to 6.18 below) by the deadline specified therein. The parties may extend the deadline for a period or periods of up to 28 days, provided that in such event the parties agree and file a consent order recording the extension of time before the expiry of the relevant deadline, and that order is approved by the court (even if that approval occurs after the deadline has passed). For guidance on consent orders see paragraphs 16.35 to 16.40. **1A-47**

6.7 A failure to file the documents specified in Form N149C by the original or the revised deadline may lead to the claim, or the defence, being struck out or some other sanction being imposed.

6.8 If the CMC / CCMC is likely to require a hearing of more than 1½ hours plus 1 hour pre-reading when filing the DQs the parties should provide: (i) an agreed realistic time estimate for the hearing; (ii) estimated pre-reading time; (iii) if appropriate the proposed format for the hearing with brief reasons (see paragraph 6.44)); and, (iv) dates to avoid for a period of 3 months following the filing of the DQs if they want the court to take them into account when considering the listing of the CCMC or CMC.

6.9 Parties must not, however, expect that a CMC / CCMC will be delayed for a substantial length of time in order to accommodate the advocates' availability, and it is a matter for the court to decide whether the hearing is listed taking dates to avoid into account, particularly where the availability of counsel is limited.

PRELIMINARY ISSUES AND SPLIT TRIALS

1A-48 **6.10** Costs and time can sometimes be saved by identifying decisive issues, or potentially decisive issues, and ordering that they are tried first. A trial of a preliminary issue may also be appropriate where its determination, although not itself decisive of the whole case, may enable the parties to settle the remainder of the dispute or otherwise shorten the proceedings. An example would be a relatively short question of law which can be tried without significant delay (or much in the way of disclosure or witness evidence) but which would be determinative of one of more of the key issues in dispute.

6.11 Parties should actively consider at the earliest opportunity, and certainly in advance of the first CMC / CCMC, whether there are any issues which are suitable for determination as a preliminary issue, or which should be tried separately such as a split between liability and quantum. If possible, parties should indicate when filing DQs whether a preliminary issue or split trial is under consideration and provide a summary of the proposed approach in Section I of the DQ. Parties should give careful consideration to the approach to costs budgeting where a preliminary issue or split trial is proposed or agreed (see paragraph 6.36).

6.12 If a party considers a preliminary issue or split trial would be appropriate, the matter should ideally first be discussed, and where possible agreed, in correspondence between the parties.

6.13 An application for a preliminary issue or split trial should be made in accordance with Chapter 14 and CPR 23. The application would normally be determined at the first CMC / CCMC. Parties are not, however, precluded from bringing an application following the first CMC / CCMC should they consider it desirable for the effective conduct of the litigation.

6.14 The court will expect the application to explain the precise scope of the issue or issues proposed to be determined separately, why that is proposed and why a preliminary issue or split trial would be in furtherance of the overriding objective to deal with cases justly and at proportionate cost. In the case of proposals for split trial, very careful consideration must be given as to where the issues to be determined are split, including whether the proposed split will genuinely assist the efficient case management of the proceedings and whether the issue(s) to be considered first would assist in the resolution of the remaining issues to be determined.

6.15 Parties should also consider the level of judge required to try the preliminary issue. Relevant considerations would be whether the issue is of great substance and/or great complexity and/or of public importance (which may make it more suitable for determination by a High Court Judge ('HCJ'), a specialist civil judge authorised to sit as a judge in the High Court pursuant to section 9(1) of the Senior Courts Act 1981 (a 'Section 9 Judge'), or a Deputy HCJ), and how long the preliminary issue trial is likely to be, and whether examination of witnesses and/or experts is likely to be required.

6.16 The court may make an order for a preliminary issue or split trial of its own motion. However, any such order will not usually be made without the agreement of at least one of the parties.

DRAFT DIRECTIONS

1A-49 **6.17** Draft case management directions suitable for claims in the Chancery Division are available in Chancery Forms and these should be used or varied as appropriate, in all cases. They are designed to be a list of possible directions covering a wide range of possibilities. Many of the directions on the menu will not apply in the majority of cases and care needs to be taken to avoid compiling a list of draft directions which is overly complicated if the claim does not warrant it. Parties in cases in the B&PC District Registries should check for any local practices and guidance: see Appendix C.

6.18 The parties' proposed draft directions must include a time estimate for trial and a trial window - see paragraphs 6.75 to 6.78 below.

CASE MANAGEMENT ALLOCATION AND DOCKETING

1A-50 **6.19** Cases in the ChD B&PCs London will be managed in accordance with one of four management tracks:

(a) Case management by Master and trial by High Court Judge (HCJ), Section 9 Judge or Deputy HCJ (which is the most common track);
(b) Case management and trial by docketed HCJ (full docketing);
(c) Case management and trial by Master; and
(d) Case management by a docketed HCJ and Master or ICC Judge and trial by the docketed HCJ (partnership management).

6.20 For distribution of business between judges in proceedings commenced in the Insolvency and Companies Court List ('ICL') see Chapter 21 paragraphs 21.26 to 21.28.

6.21 The parties may, before the CMC / CCMC, request that a case be made subject to full docketing or partnership management, providing reasons why and indicating whether they consider that it would be helpful for the docketed HCJ to have any particular specialist knowledge.

6.22 A request may be made by correspondence to the Master or in section I ('Other information') of the parties' DQs, and may be made by the parties jointly or, if the parties are not agreed, separately. The Master may request written submissions or direct that a hearing take place to resolve the issue.

6.23 Alternatively, the Master may, without any application, consider whether full docketing or partnership management would be appropriate.

6.24 The parties will be informed of the Master's decision and, if the Master considers that the case should be subject to full docketing (or partnership management), the Master will ask the Chancellor to nominate a HCJ to take charge of the case. The Chancellor, or the HCJ to whom the case has been docketed, may direct that the case should be subject to partnership management.

6.25 The following factors are to be taken as pointing towards full docketing or partnership management:

(a) The heaviest claims where the trial is estimated to last 15 days or more and there is the potential for reducing the length of the trial process by active case management by the trial judge;

(b) Claims involving numerous pre-trial applications which have been or will in any event be required to be dealt with by a HCJ;

(c) Claims where there will be a particular advantage in pre-trial applications being heard by the trial judge;

(d) Claims which by their subject matter require the specialist knowledge of a specialist HCJ such as the more complex IP claims, and those commercial claims whose subject matter is highly involved or technical such as sophisticated types of commercial instrument or securitisation, complex trust claims and some large multi-jurisdiction trust and estate claims;

(e) Cases that are subject to a Group Litigation Order (GLO) and other substantial group claims requiring active case management by a HCJ assigned to try them;

(f) Urgent claims requiring expedition and determination by a HCJ within weeks or a few months;

(g) Claims where one or more parties are litigants in person, and it is considered that full docketing or partnership management would: (i) best serve the needs of the parties and (ii) be consistent with the efficient administration of justice.

6.26 A decision about docketing may be reconsidered at the CMC / CCMC.

6.27 A Deputy Master will not make a decision about full docketing or partnership management but will refer it to a Master.

COSTS MANAGEMENT AND BUDGETING

6.28 All Part 7 claims shall be subject to costs management in accordance with Section II of CPR 3 and PD 3E, except where different rules or guidance apply such as in the Patents Court, the Shorter or Flexible Trials schemes or the Financial List or where the circumstances set out at sub-paragraphs (a) to (c) apply: **1A-51**

(a) The claim is stated or valued at £10 million or more (CPR 3.12). However, subject to 6.28(c) below, where there is no statement of value on the claim form costs management will apply, even if the potential value of the claim is £10 million or more.

(b) The court orders otherwise, typically following an application by the parties (CPR 3.12). If the parties agree that the court should exercise its case management powers to direct that a costs management order will not be made, a consent order should be lodged in advance of the CCMC, with a short explanation of why the order is sought. If the order has not yet been approved, the parties must still exchange costs budgets in advance of the CCMC in accordance with CPR 3.13.

(c) The parties have been unable to agree whether the value of the claim should be assessed at £10 million or more and therefore whether costs management shall apply (and the court has not determined the issue) (see paragraphs 6.29 and 6.30).

6.29 Where the defendant disagrees with the claimant's assessment of the value of the claim as stated in the claim form (or considers that the claim form should have included a statement that the claim is valued at £10 million or more), and therefore disagrees with the claimant's assessment as to whether costs management applies in accordance with Section II of CPR 3 and PD 3E, the parties should seek to resolve the issue by agreement.

6.30 If the parties are unable to reach agreement by the time the DQs are filed, the issue should be raised with the court when filing the DQs. In those circumstances, the requirements for filing and exchanging costs budgets will not apply until the matter is resolved by either agreement between the parties or determination by the court. If the parties have agreed that the claim is valued at £10 million or more, but that is not stated on the face of the claim form, a consent order should be lodged in advance of the CMC / CCMC disapplying Section II of CPR 3 and PD 3E, with a short explanation of why the order is sought. If the parties have agreed that the claim is not valued at £10 million or more, they should proceed to file budgets in accordance with CPR 3.13. A claim form which seeks non-monetary relief falls within CPR 3.13(1)(b).

6.31 It is the court's experience that it is often helpful for costs budgets to be exchanged in cases in the ChD B&PCs London even if costs budgeting would not otherwise apply. Parties should consider exchanging costs budgets or opting into costs management even in cases which are outside the costs management regime. If the parties agree that a costs management order should be made, a consent order should be lodged in advance of the CMC including proposed directions for costs management.

LITIGANTS IN PERSON

1A-52 **6.32** Litigants in person are not required to file costs budgets, unless otherwise ordered by the court, but may do so. The court may order litigants in person to file costs budgets where the litigant is likely to incur substantial costs or disbursements. Litigants in person should have regard to CPR 46.5 and PD 46 paragraph 3.

6.33 Litigants in person are encouraged to participate in the costs management process and are able to agree or challenge cost budgets.

UPDATING BUDGETS BEFORE COSTS MANAGEMENT ORDER MADE

1A-53 **6.34** In the B&PCs where costs budgets are required (see CPR 3.12 and 3.13), they must be filed and exchanged not later than 21 days before the first CMC / CCMC (CPR3.13(1)(b)) unless the court orders otherwise.

6.35 However, costs budgets may become out of date if a CMC / CCMC is relisted or adjourned. In such cases, if permission has not already been given, it may be appropriate to seek permission to serve an updated costs budget before any CMC / CCMC or relisted CMC / CCMC. (See also paragraphs 6.67 and 6.74 in relation to budget revisions after a costs management order has been made.)

6.36 Parties may seek an order for part or all of the costs management to be adjourned to a later date to enable them to revisit their costs budgets in light of case management directions made at the CMC / CCMC (for example as to the scope of disclosure, a direction for a split trial or preliminary issues, whether the court gives permission for experts, and trial length).

6.37 Parties should also note paragraph 22.2 of PD 51U which allows the parties to agree to postpone completion of the disclosure phase of their costs budgets until after the CMC.

DISCLOSURE

1A-54 **6.38** Further information regarding the approach to disclosure in proceedings issued in the B&PCs is set out in Chapter 7.

6.39 Parties are reminded that proceedings issued in the ChD B&PCs London, and in the District Registries in Birmingham, Bristol, Cardiff, Leeds, Liverpool, Manchester and Newcastle (the 'B&PC District Registries') are all subject to the Disclosure Pilot Scheme set out in PD 51U.

6.40 If PD 51U does not apply, the parties should approach disclosure in accordance with CPR 31. However, consistent with the overriding objective, the court will still expect the parties to approach the disclosure exercise having regard to the duties set out in PD51U and to adopt the high degree of cooperation expected under PD51U.

TRIAGE BY THE MASTER

1A-55 **6.41** After DQs are filed and before the first CMC / CCMC, the Master will review the DQs and the draft directions, and consider:

(a) Whether the claim should remain in the ChD B&PCs London (see Chapter 3 for further guidance).

(b) Whether a listing of more than 1½ hours is required for a CCMC or CMC.

(c) The appropriate hearing format for the CMC / CCMC.

(d) Whether cost management applies (if the parties disagree about that: see paragraphs 6.28 and 6.29 above) and whether or not a costs management order is required.

(e) (If requested) whether there should be a stay of proceedings, or a continuation of an existing stay.

6.42 The Master may make an order in respect of any of matters (a) to (e) above in advance of the CMC / CCMC.

THE CMC / CCMC

1A-56 **6.43** The CMC / CCMC is a very significant stage in the proceedings, and its importance should not be underestimated. Parties are expected to liaise and cooperate to promote the efficient preparation for and conduct of the CMC / CCMC.

PREPARATION FOR THE CMC / CCMC

1A-57 **6.44** The court will fix a date for a CMC / CCMC after DQs have been filed, with a time estimate of 1½ hours and 1 hour pre-reading unless the parties provide a different agreed time estimate for both the CMC / CCMC and pre-reading. A CMC / CCMC with a time estimate of half a day or less (and no more than 90 mins pre-reading) will take place remotely unless the court orders otherwise (see paragraphs 6.8 and 6.9 above). For further guidance on the preparation and conduct of remote and hybrid hearings see Appendix Z.

6.45 Wherever possible, an advocate instructed or expected to be instructed to appear at the trial should attend the CMC / CCMC. Where a party has retained more than one advocate (e.g. leading and junior counsel), there is no requirement that all of them attend. The experience of the court is that on many case management issues, junior advocates within a team may be well placed to assist the court. Parties should consider in every case (a) whether attendance by the more (or most) senior advocate instructed in the case is reasonably required, and (b) whether, even where that is the position, at least some of the matters arising may appropriately be dealt with by the more (or most) junior advocate.

6.46 If the parties wish the court to have regard to the availability of counsel when fixing the CMC / CCMC, dates to avoid may be provided with the DQs (see paragraphs 6.8 and 6.9 above).

6.47 Before the first CMC / CCMC, and before any subsequent CMC / CCMC at which disclosure is to be considered, the parties shall have regard to their disclosure obligations, including the information required pursuant to PD 51U and necessary for the completion of the Disclosure Review Document ('DRD') or Less Complex Claims DRD (the 'LCCDRD'), as applicable (see PD51U and Chapter 7 for further guidance).

6.48 If the parties are required to complete a DRD, the parties should ensure they complete, or substantially complete, Section 2 of the DRD before the hearing. A failure to do so may restrict the ability of the court to determine any disclosure matters in dispute between the parties and may result in costs sanctions being imposed.

6.49 The parties should also consider who is the most appropriate person to assist the court when seeking Disclosure Guidance pursuant to PD51U, or a determination of any disputed disclosure issue. The solicitor with conduct of the disclosure exercise or a junior advocate may be best placed to deal with some or all of the matters in respect of which guidance is sought.

6.50 A case management bundle is needed at every CMC / CCMC. See Appendix X for further guidance regarding the preparation of bundles. The bundle should be in electronic form unless otherwise ordered (and the court may order, or the parties may agree, that some or all of the CMC/CCMC bundle should be filed in hard copy in addition). The bundle should contain only the following (unless, exceptionally, additional documents are essential to the CMC / CCMC):

(a) An agreed case summary (not normally exceeding 2 pages). The case summary should contain:
   i. a short and uncontroversial description of what the case is about; and
   ii. a short and uncontroversial summary of the material procedural history of the case.

(b) An agreed list of issues for trial (not normally exceeding 3 pages).
(c) An agreed list of issues to be resolved at the CMC / CCMC.
(d) Statements of case.
(e) Orders.
(f) DQs.
(g) Draft directions.
(h) The DRD (including section 2) or the LCCDRD, where applicable, prepared in accordance with PD51U.
(i) Costs budgets (if applicable).
(j) Budget discussion reports in the form of Precedent R (if applicable, and if a costs management order is to be made). If the budget discussion reports are not available at the time the bundle is filed, they should be added as soon as possible in advance of the hearing.
(k) Any application notice(s) and supporting evidence returnable for the CMC / CCMC.
(l) Correspondence between the parties (but only where it is essential for the court to have regard to it).

6.51 The parties are referred to Appendix X for general guidance on the preparation of bundles. They should prepare the bundle in such a way as to avoid duplication of documents. In appropriate cases exhibits or parts of exhibits and other documents can be removed to reduce the overall size of the bundle where they are not essential for the hearing.

6.52 A separate landscape bundle should be filed, whether in hard copy or electronic format, containing the DRD, costs budgets (if applicable) and Precedent Rs and any other landscape documents relevant for the CMC / CCMC.

6.53 Unless (exceptionally) the parties wish to request a CMC / CCMC on the documents (see paragraph 6.61 below), the case management bundle should be filed at court at least 2 clear days before the hearing of the first and any subsequent CMC / CCMC. (If for example the CMC / CCMC is on the Friday, the case management bundle should be filed by 4.30 pm on the Tuesday.) For a definition of clear days see CPR 2.8.

6.54 The claimant shall be responsible for the preparation (and upkeep) of the case management bundle, including producing and filing the case summary, list of issues for trial, and list of issues for the CMC / CCMC, and (where appropriate) updating those documents.

6.55 The parties shall endeavour to agree the contents of the bundle. If the parties cannot agree the case summary, list of issues for trial, list of issues for the CMC / CCMC, or draft directions, the parties should consider the best way of clearly setting out the differences between them for the court. This will ordinarily involve the preparation of composite versions of these documents setting out (if necessary, in different colours or highlighting) the elements which are not agreed. The parties shall, by 4pm the working day before the hearing, file with the court any updated draft directions indicating those directions which are agreed and not agreed.

6.56 Short notes or skeleton arguments from each party will almost invariably be essential and shall be filed with the court at least 2 clear days before the CMC / CCMC (see example at paragraph 6.53 above) in Microsoft Word format (or similar). If the parties require further time to prepare skeleton arguments, they shall seek to agree any revised timetable for exchange and filing between them and seek the consent of the judge.

6.57 Skeleton arguments should be no longer than is necessary and should not exceed 25 pages (including any appendices and schedules). Should a party wish to file a longer skeleton argument, the senior legal representative whose name appear at the end of the skeleton argument must file a letter along with the skeleton argument explaining why this has been necessary. If the Master or HCJ is not satisfied by the explanation the party may be required to re-draft the skeleton argument and/or costs sanctions may be imposed. For further guidance on skeleton arguments generally see Appendix Y.

FIXED TRIAL DATES

1A-58 **6.58** Trials are normally listed with a commencement date floating within a 3-5 day period, referred to as a trial window, but the court may (exceptionally) consider listing the trial for a fixed start where certain criteria are met. These will include such matters as the length of the trial, the number of parties and witnesses, and the need for parties or witnesses to travel from abroad to attend trial. Further guidance on the procedure for listing can be found at paragraphs 12.16 to 12.22.

6.59 Where any party wishes the court to consider directing that the trial be listed for a fixed start date, this should be raised with the court for consideration at the CMC / CCMC. Any such direction will be subject to approval by the court officer responsible for listing and confirmation by the trial judge at the pre-trial review ('PTR'), if there is one - (see further Chapter 11).

THE HEARING

1A-59 **6.60** In general, the most important matters to be discussed at the CMC will be: the issues and how they are best to be tried, where and by whom; proposals for Alternative Dispute Resolution ('ADR'); the DRD/LCCDRD and the terms in which permission for any expert evidence will be granted. The court will want to:

(a) Discuss the issues in the case, having first reviewed: the case summary, the list of issues for trial, the list of issues for the CMC/CCMC and the notes or skeleton arguments filed by the parties.

(b) Discuss the requirements of the case with the parties / their advocates.

(c) Review and approve, amend or reject as may be appropriate the parties' proposals for disclosure;

(d) In light of those matters consider whether the trial judge will be assisted by a core bundle of key documents or a narrative chronology;

(e) Fix the pre-trial timetable to the fullest extent possible, having regard to (a) and (b) above, and any draft directions proposed and/or agreed by the parties.

(f) (If appropriate) make a costs management order, alternatively direct that a separate costs management hearing take place.

(g) (If appropriate) make an order staying the proceedings to permit the parties time to engage in ADR.

(h) (If appropriate) discuss with the parties the use of information technology to assist with case management, including the use of information technology at trial (see Chapter 12 paragraph 12.32: IT at Trial).

6.61 There may be exceptional cases where a CMC / CCMC can take place on the documents, if for example, the issues are straight-forward, and the costs of an oral hearing cannot be justified. If the parties wish to request a CMC / CCMC on the documents, they must file the case management bundle together with an agreed draft order at least one week before the date listed for the CMC / CCMC. It is unlikely that any case involving extended disclosure (other than on Models A or B (as explained in PD 51U)), expert evidence or preliminary issues will be suitable for a CMC / CCMC on the documents.

6.62 The costs incurred by the parties in preparation for and the conduct of the CMC / CCMC will usually be costs in the case. However, the court has a broad discretion in relation to costs and if a party has failed to comply with any procedural step required to be taken and/or has failed to cooperate with the other parties in preparation for the CMC / CCMC (including, for the avoidance of doubt, in the provision and preparation of the hearing bundle) the court may adjourn the CMC / CCMC and/or may make an adverse costs order.

INTERIM APPLICATIONS AT THE CMC

1A-60 **6.63** CMCs are intended to consider and manage the future procedural conduct of the case. They are not an opportunity to make controversial interim applications without appropriate notice to the opposing party and an appropriate time allowance.

6.64 If, however, a party wishes to make an application to be heard at the CMC / CCMC, such an application should be made in accordance with CPR 23 and have regard to the provisions of PD 29 paragraph 5.8. Parties should also have regard to the provisions of paragraphs 14.38 to 14.40.

6.65 Where parties fail to comply with those provisions, or the time available is inadequate, it is highly unlikely that the court will entertain, other than by consent, an application which is not of a routine nature.

6.66 If a party making such an application considers that the time allowed for the CMC / CCMC is likely to be insufficient for the application to be heard they should inform the court at once. If this is done either before the listing of, or sufficiently in advance of, the CMC / CCMC, it may be possible, and the court may consider it appropriate, to extend the time estimate to allow the application to be heard at the CMC/CCMC. Otherwise, the application will be listed as considered appropriate by the court. This may require the CMC / CCMC to be vacated and/or for the application to be heard in place of the CMC/CCMC, or separately at a later date.

COSTS MANAGEMENT ORDERS

6.67 At the CMC / CCMC the court will normally consider directions (including disclosure) first and costs management afterwards. **1A-61**

6.68 However, the directions made by the court are likely to be informed by the costs budgets and the court's consideration of the costs budgets will be informed by for example the scope of disclosure. The court will wish to form an overall view about proportionality taking into account the factors in CPR 44.3(5) and may wish to be addressed on this subject before considering the disputed budget phases.

6.69 The parties shall endeavour to discuss and agree costs budgets before the CCMC. If elements of the filed costs budgets have not been agreed, the court will consider the phases in respect of which costs have not been agreed and hear submissions from the parties. The court will then determine and approve a figure for the budgeted costs (i.e. those not yet incurred) for each disputed phase.

6.70 Subject to CPR 3.15A (where there is an application to revise an approved costs budget: see paragraph 6.73 and 6.74 below), costs up to and including the date of any CCMC are not subject to the court's approval (CPR 3.17(3)). The court may record its comments on those costs which have already been incurred for any phase and take those costs into account when considering the reasonableness and proportionality of all budgeted costs for each phase. However, the power to make comments about incurred costs is likely to be used sparingly.

6.71 In practice given that costs budgets are necessarily prepared in advance of the CCMC, and the parties do not stop all work when costs budgets are filed, a small proportion of the budgeted costs approved by the court may in fact have been incurred by the time of the hearing.

6.72 The outcome of costs management in the ChD B&PCs London will typically be recorded by setting out all the budget phases, agreed and approved by the court, in an appendix to the costs management order (see form CH40 here, to be adapted as appropriate to the circumstances).

6.73 In some cases, the court may direct a party to file a revised budget to reflect decisions at the CMC / CCMC in accordance with CPR 3.15(7).

6.74 Parties should also note CPR 3.15A which requires budgeted costs to be revised upwards or downwards if warranted by significant developments in the litigation after the costs budget has been approved, and for the revised budget to be submitted promptly to the other parties for agreement and subsequently to the court.

TRIAL TIME ESTIMATE

6.75 All claims in ChD B&PCs London and the B&PCs District Registries are tried on the basis that the trial time estimate, which includes judicial reading time before the trial starts, is fixed. Estimates for judicial pre-reading must be realistic and regard should be had to any pre-reading that may be required before the commencement of trial, or following opening submissions, or in respect of witnesses who are to give evidence at trial (having regard, in particular, to the approach to witness evidence set out in PD 57AC). Estimates do not need to make provision for judgment writing. **1A-62**

6.76 It will only be possible in exceptional circumstances for the time estimate to be exceeded. It is therefore essential that careful thought is given, both before and at the CMC / CCMC, to the length of the trial. The advocates will need to have considered the number of witnesses who will be called, the likely length of cross-examination, the need for expert evidence and how far it is likely to be controversial. In substantial cases it may be obvious that the court and the advocates will benefit from a break between the end of the evidence and closing speeches; if so, this time must be included within the trial estimate.

6.77 Inevitably there will be some uncertainties about the time estimate. It will generally be desirable for the order for directions to specify a date by which the parties are to review the time estimate and seek the court's approval for any revised time estimate. If the change is minor and sufficient notice is given, a revised time estimate will usually be accommodated. The review date should typically be 4 weeks after the exchange of witness evidence, or alternatively expert evidence.

6.78 If there is a PTR the time estimate will be reviewed again at that stage, but if a substantial revision is needed the case may lose its trial date.

TRIAL DATE

6.79 The standard directions are required to include a listing trial window. Listing trial windows for trial by HCJ are set by the Chancery Judges' Listing Office ('Judges' Listing') and are updated **1A-63**

monthly. The current listing trial windows can be found at Trial date windows for Chancery Division. Listing trial windows or dates for trial by a Master are set by Masters. The dates vary depending upon the length of the trial.

6.80 Following the CMC / CCMC, the parties are to liaise with Judges' Listing for trial by HCJ (as well as by a Section 9 Judge or a Deputy HCJ and) and Chancery Masters' Appointments for trial by Master in order to fix a date for trial within the listing trial window. Parties are reminded that all communication with the court is to be filed using CE-File unless otherwise directed. The parties should provide the court with (a) a combined list of dates to avoid, (b) a time estimate for the trial, and (c) a copy of the case management order. Typically, this is dealt with by counsel's clerks (see Chapter 12 paragraphs 12.16 to 12.22).

6.81 Normally, for trial by HCJ, once provided with the information set out at paragraph 6.76 above, Judges Listing will provide a narrower trial window, with a commencement date usually floating within a 3-5 day period. In limited circumstances, Judges Listing may provide a fixed start date: see paragraphs 6.58 to 6.59 above. For trial by a Master Chancery Masters Appointments will provide a fixed start date.

6.82 In every claim with a trial time estimate of 5 days or more (including judicial reading time) a PTR will be held approximately 4-6 weeks before the trial is due to commence. The date will be fixed when the trial date is fixed. In cases due to last 9 days or more the PTR will be conducted by the trial judge where possible. A PTR of half a day or less (and no more than 90 mins pre-reading) will take place remotely unless the court orders otherwise. If the parties propose a different format for the PTR this should be raised at the CMC / CCMC when the trial window is fixed. See Chapter 11 for further information about PTRs.

TRIAL CATEGORY

1A-64 **6.83** Trials before judges in the ChD B&PCs London may come before:

(a) A HCJ (or retired HCJ);

(b) A Section 9 Judge; or

(c) A Deputy HCJ, Master, deputy Master, ICC Judge, or deputy ICC Judge.

6.84 Cases are listed by reference to the following listing categories:

A Cases of great substance and/or great difficulty or of public importance, suitable for trial only by a HCJ.

B Cases of substance and/or difficulty suitable for trial either by a HCJ, a Section 9 Judge or a Deputy HCJ.

C Cases of lesser substance and/or difficulty than category B cases, suitable for trial by a Section 9 Judge, a Deputy HCJ, a Master, a deputy Master, and ICC Judge or a deputy ICC Judge.

6.85 The order for directions must specify the listing category approved by the court.

6.86 Masters will not normally try cases where the trial is estimated to last more than 5 days and will not normally try cases other than those which fall within listing category C but may do so in an appropriate case. For guidance in respect of ICL trials see Chapter 21.

TRIAL VENUE

1A-65 **6.87** Consideration will be given at the CMC / CCMC to whether London is a suitable trial venue, having regard to the links that the case, the parties and their representatives and the witnesses have with any circuit or region within any circuit in England and Wales. If it is suitable, the order must specify '*Trial in London*'.

6.88 Even if the advocates are all based in London, for the convenience of the parties and witnesses it may be desirable to direct that a claim is transferred immediately to a B&PC District Registry for further case management and trial. A category A case should not be transferred out of London for trial without prior consultation with the relevant Supervising Judge. No such prior consultation is required in the case of category B or C cases.

6.89 If a claim is to be transferred out of London but case management of the claim is to remain in London until shortly before the trial, the claim must be formally transferred at that stage. If the claim is being transferred out of London for trial:

(a) the PTR shall be ordered to take place before the trial judge in the relevant B&PC District Registry; or

(b) if there is no PTR, the parties shall jointly liaise with the trial venue so that any directions for trial are appropriate for the trial venue.

For guidance on general listing arrangements in the B&PC District Registries see Appendix C and follow the links for any local guidance.

OTHER GUIDANCE

1A-66 **6.90** Follow the hyperlinks below for further guidance in relation to:

(a) Disclosure (Chapter 7)

(b) Witness statements (Chapter 8)

(c) Expert evidence (Chapter 9)

(d) Alternative dispute resolution (Chapter 10)
(e) PTR (Chapter 11)
(f) Trial (Chapter 12)
(g) Part 8 (Chapter 13)
(h) Cases within the Insolvency and Companies List (Chapter 21)
(i) Appeals including Arbitration Appeals (Chapter 30)

CHAPTER 7 DISCLOSURE

GENERAL

7.1 Disclosure and production of documents in the Business and Property Courts (the 'B&PCs') is conducted in accordance with the Disclosure Pilot contained in Practice Direction ('PD') 51U of the Civil Procedure Rules ('CPR'), as amended, save where one of the exceptions set out in paragraph 1 of PD 51U applies. **1A-67**

7.2 The Pilot is due to run until 31 December 2022. It substantially replaces CPR 31. Feedback regarding the pilot should be sent by email to *DWG@justice.gov.uk.*

PD 51U

7.3 PD 51U applies to all relevant proceedings in the B&PCs, whether started before or after 1 January 2019, even in a case where a disclosure order was made before 1 January 2019 under CPR 31: see *UTB LLC v Sheffield United & Ors* [2019] EWHC 914 (CH). **1A-68**

7.4 If proceedings are transferred out of the BP&Cs into a court that is not one of the B&PCs, any order for disclosure made under PD 51U will stand unless and until any other order is made by the transferee court.

7.5 For the avoidance of doubt unless one of the exceptions applies CPR 31 does not apply to any claim issued in the B&PCs and any order for disclosure will be made in accordance with the principles and approach set out in PD51U.

7.6 The duties of parties and their lawyers are set out in paragraphs 3 and 4 of PD 51U. These are important and breach of any of the duties will be treated as a serious matter by the court and may result in sanctions.

7.7 Unless dispensed with by agreement or order, or an exception applies, the parties must give Initial Disclosure in accordance with paragraph 5 of PD 51U.

7.8 An application to dispense with Initial Disclosure under paragraph 5.10 of PD 51U will, save in exceptional circumstances, be dealt with on paper and without a hearing but should be made by application notice using an N244 (CPR 23) on notice to the other parties and be supported by evidence explaining why the applicant considers that compliance will incur disproportionate cost or will be unduly complex.

7.9 A party wishing to seek disclosure of documents in addition to, or as an alternative to, Initial Disclosure must request Extended Disclosure in accordance with paragraph 6 of PD 51U. The Disclosure Models for Extended Disclosure are set out in paragraph 8 of PD 51U.

7.10 Unless Extended Disclosure is to be restricted to non-search-based models i.e. Models A and B, the parties and their advisers must discuss and complete a joint Disclosure Review Document ('DRD') (including completing section 2) before the first case management conference / costs and case management conference ('CMC' / 'CCMC') in accordance with paragraph 10 of PD 51U. In a less complex claim the parties must complete a Less Complex Claim DRD ('LCCDRD') (see Appendix 5 PD51U).

7.11 The parties are obliged to cooperate: paragraph 3.2 of PD 51U; they should not allow the settling of the DRD or the LCCDRD to become contentious, time consuming or expensive. The court has power to impose sanctions including costs orders if a party fails to engage constructively.

7.12 The DRD (where applicable) should be kept simple and concise. In particular, the Issues for Disclosure should be limited by the definition contained in paragraph 7.3 of PD 51U. See also paragraph 10.5 of Appendix 5, which has general application in relation to the parties' approach to drafting Issues for Disclosure. The proliferation of different Models for Extended Disclosure should be avoided where possible and kept to a minimum where it cannot be reasonably avoided.

7.13 Parties must cooperate and seek to resolve any issues over the scope of Extended Disclosure in advance of the CMC / CCMC including those relating to documents held by third parties and/or documents said to have been lost or destroyed and/or where retrieval may still be possible. A narrow point on the scope of Extended Disclosure may be suitable for Disclosure Guidance in advance of a CMC / CCMC (see paragraph 7.19 below).

7.14 There is no obligation on a disclosing party to obtain translations of documents that are wholly or partially not in English when giving Extended Disclosure unless the court orders otherwise. They must, however, disclose such translations as they have already obtained as part of their Extended Disclosure.

7.15 Where it is known or becomes apparent that Extended Disclosure will include a substantial number of documents which are wholly or partially not in English the parties should cooperate at an early stage to seek to agree proposals for the identification of documents for which translation may be necessary. This should be considered by the parties in advance of the CMC / CCMC. In some cases, it may be appropriate to seek directions at the CMC / CCMC.

7.16 Parties should give careful consideration in every case, whatever its financial value or general complexity, to whether it may properly be treated as a Less Complex Claim, as defined in paragraph 1.8A of Appendix 1 of PD 51U. Issues for Disclosure in a Less Complex Claim must be brief, drafted at a high level of abstraction, and rarely exceed five in number.

7.17 Explanatory notes for the DRD are set out in Appendix 2 of PD 51U and, for a LCCDRD, in Appendix 7 of PD 51U. The notes at paragraph 8 of Appendix 2 of PD 51U include a summary of the timeline of steps to be completed in advance of the first CMC, unless otherwise agreed between the parties or ordered by the court. Some sections of the DRD do not need to be completed where there is likely to be limited disclosure, or the identification and retrieval of documents is straightforward. See paragraph 13 of Appendix 7 for the timeline in relation to a LCCDRD.

7.18 Further disclosure, for example for specific documents or where there has been or may have been a failure to comply adequately with an order for Extended Disclosure, may be sought in accordance with paragraphs 17 and 18 of PD 51U.

7.19 A party may seek Disclosure Guidance in accordance with paragraph 11 of PD 51U for guidance from the court at any time (before or after the first CMC / CCMC) on any point concerning the operation of PD51U to address differences between the parties, including in relation to settling Issues for Disclosure and the selection of Extended Disclosure Models, without a formal determination.

7.20 The provisions relating to Disclosure Guidance do not affect or limit the court's power to determine any point about disclosure at any time by application of a party in a hearing convened for that purpose ('Disclosure Hearing') or without a hearing (see paragraph 6A of PD 51U).

7.21 The court will not typically list a Disclosure Hearing in advance of the CMC / CCMC though it may list an application for Disclosure Guidance to encourage cooperation and agreement in respect of the DRD or LCCDRD in advance of the CMC / CCMC.

7.22 However, the court will expect to be able to determine whether to order Extended Disclosure, and to deal with any issues arising from and to approve the DRD or LCCDRD (where applicable), within the time estimate allowed for the CMC / CCMC. Parties should carefully consider the time estimate for the CMC / CCMC. If the issues raised by disclosure are likely to take up more than 1 hour of the court's time the parties should consider whether a longer time estimate or separate Disclosure Hearing may be appropriate (see Chapter 6 paragraphs 6.8 and paragraphs 6.44 to 6.46).

7.23 Where the judge considers it would be beneficial to the parties, the court will seek to list any Disclosure Hearing before the same judge who dealt with any Disclosure Guidance Hearing or CMC/CCMC.

7.24 Parties should consider who is the most appropriate person to assist the court when seeking Disclosure Guidance or a determination in relation to any disclosure issues. The solicitor with conduct of the disclosure exercise or junior advocates may be best placed to deal with some or all of the matters in respect of which guidance is sought.

7.25 The steps for compliance with an order for Extended Disclosure are set out in paragraph 12 of PD51U.

CONTINUED APPLICATION OF CPR 31 TO CASES SUBJECT TO PD51U

1A-69 **7.26** CPR 31.16 (disclosure before proceedings start), CPR 31.17 (orders for disclosure against a person not a party), CPR 31.18 (rules not to limit other powers of the court to order disclosure), CPR 31.19 (claim to withhold inspection of a document (public interest immunity)) and CPR 31.22 (subsequent use of disclosed documents and completed Electronic Disclosure Questionnaire) continue to apply and are set out in section II of PD51U.

WHERE PD51U DOES NOT APPLY

1A-70 **7.27** Paragraph 1 of PD 51U sets out those claims which are excluded from the operation of PD51U. In such claims CPR 31 will continue to apply. (Note that CPR 31 is modified in intellectual property cases: see CPR 63.9 and 63.24.)

7.28 Even in claims to which PD 51U does not apply, the court will have regard to the principles and general duties set out in paragraphs 2 and 3 of PD 51U and have regard to the overriding objective when considering the appropriate form of disclosure in accordance with CPR 31 including which of the options in CPR 31.5.(7) is appropriate.

PRE-ACTION AND NON-PARTY DISCLOSURE

1A-71 **7.29** An order for disclosure before proceedings have started is made in accordance with CPR 31.16 in Section II of CPR PD 51U. It comprises a two-stage test:

- (a) Parties must first satisfy the four-part jurisdictional test set out in CPR 31.16(3). This includes consideration of whether such disclosure is desirable in order to dispose fairly of the anticipated proceedings, or to assist the parties to avoid litigation, or to save costs; and
- (b) If the court is satisfied that the application meets the jurisdictional threshold, it will then consider whether it is appropriate to make an order for pre-action disclosure as a matter of discretion, which has to be considered on all of the facts and not merely in principle but in

detail: see *Black v Sumitomo* [2001] EWCA Civ 1819; [2002] 1WLR 1562; [2003] 3 All ER 643.

7.30 The jurisdictional criteria in CPR 31.16 still require consideration of whether the documents would fall within the scope of 'standard disclosure' under CPR 31.6. However, when considering whether to make an order, the court should take into account that if proceedings are brought they are likely to be subject to PD 51U, where the court would work with the parties to define the issues for disclosure and apply the most appropriate disclosure model (paragraph 8 of PD 51U): see also *Willow Sports Ltd v SportsLocker24.com Ltd* [2021] EWHC 2524 (Ch).

7.31 An order for disclosure against a person who is not a party is made in accordance with CPR 31.17 (see Section II of CPR PD 51U and Chapter 14).

7.32 For applications for disclosure pursuant to *Norwich Pharmacal v Customs and Excise Commissioners* [1974] AC 133 see Chapter 14.

7.33 Applications pursuant to CPR 31.16 and CPR 31.17 should be made by application notice in accordance with CPR 23 (see also Chapter 14). They should be issued to be heard by a Master or an Insolvency and Companies Court Judge (as applicable) unless, exceptionally, the weight and complexity of the application warrants it being released to be dealt with by a HCJ, Section 9 Judge or Deputy HCJ. For further guidance on applications see Chapter 14 and Chapter 15.

PART 8 CLAIMS

7.34 There is no automatic disclosure in a Part 8 claims but where it is ordered PD51U will apply and any disclosure ordered or given in a Part 8 claim in the B&PCs should be consistent with the principles and approach in PD51U. The parties can request and the court has power to order Extended Disclosure in accordance with paragraph 6 of PD 51U in a Part 8 claim, as set out in the Disclosure Pilot Practice Note (51UPN.1). See also Chapter 13. **1A-72**

INSOLVENCY AND COMPANIES LIST (ICL)

7.35 The provisions of PD51U apply to the Insolvency and Companies List unless excluded. See Chapter 21 for further guidance and the Chief ICC Judge's Practice Note. **1A-73**

CHAPTER 8 WITNESS EVIDENCE

FORM AND CONTENT OF WITNESS STATEMENTS

8.1 Witness statements must be prepared in accordance with Part 32 (Evidence) of the Civil Procedure Rules ('CPR')) and CPR 22 (Statements of Truth) and their practice directions ('PDs'), including in particular paragraphs 17 to 22 of PD 32, and (for trial witness statements for use in the Business and Property Courts ('B&PCs')) in accordance with PD 57AC (which applies to all Part 7 and Part 8 claims except those specifically excluded at paragraph 1 of PD 57AC). For these purposes, a 'trial witness statement' is one falling within the definition in paragraph 1.2 of PD 57AC which includes written evidence filed in accordance with either CPR 8.5 or 8.6. **1A-74**

8.2 These rules and practice directions contain a detailed code for the preparation of witness statements. PD 57AC was introduced in the light of consistent failure by parties in B&PCs cases to prepare trial witness statements that contained only the evidence that the witness would be able and allowed to give orally. Failure to comply with these provisions can have serious consequences. See, for example, CPR 32.10, paragraph 25 of PD 32 and paragraph 5 of PD 57AC.

8.3 When preparing *trial* witness statements in any claim, careful thought therefore needs to be given to compliance with (or dispensation from) the requirements of PD 57AC.

8.4 Parties should note, in addition, that under CPR 32.2(3) the court may give directions:

(a) identifying or limiting the issues to which factual evidence may be directed;
(b) identifying the witnesses who may be called or whose evidence may be read; or
(c) limiting the length or format of witness statements.

8.5 In all cases parties should give careful thought to whether in addition to witness statements the judge would be assisted at trial by an agreed bundle of key documents and an agreed narrative chronology with reference where appropriate to those key documents. If so, appropriate directions should be sought at the CMC / CCMC.

8.6 Where there is disagreement between the parties, the narrative chronology should identify each of the parties' respective positions, making clear there is divergence between them on a particular issue. The bundle of key documents and the narrative chronology (in Word format) should be provided to the trial judge by the PTR and/or with skeleton arguments.

DOCUMENTS REFERRED TO IN WITNESS STATEMENTS

8.7 Paragraph 3.4 of the Appendix to PD 57AC provides that a trial witness statement should refer to documents, if at all, only where necessary. Where it does so, the document should not be exhibited, but a reference should be given enabling the document to be identified. The same approach should generally be adopted for trial witness statements where PD 57AC does not apply. **1A-75**

8.8 For these purposes, the disclosure numbers assigned on disclosure should be used (defaulting to the claimant's disclosure if a document is disclosed by more than one party) unless otherwise agreed.

8.9 If a document has not previously been made available on disclosure, it may be helpful for the document to be exhibited to the witness statement. However, the claim form, statements of case, other witness statements, orders of the court, and judgments should not be exhibited, nor should documents already before the court.

8.10 Where documents are exhibited, the exhibit should not be included in the trial bundles in that form. The documents in the exhibit should be included in the trial bundles in an appropriate location (or locations) which should be cross-referenced from the witness statement in the trial bundles. See also Chapter 12 and Appendix X.

WITNESS STATEMENT AS EVIDENCE IN CHIEF

1A-76 **8.11** Where a witness is called to give oral evidence, the witness statement of that witness is to stand as the witness's evidence in chief unless the court orders otherwise: CPR 32.5(2).

8.12 The trial judge may direct that the whole or any part of a witness's evidence in chief is to be given orally, either on the judge's own initiative or on application by a party. Any application for such an order should normally be notified in good time before, and made at, the pre-trial review ('PTR') (or, if there is no PTR, as early as possible before the start of the trial).

8.13 Any objection to the court treating some or all of the content of a witness statement as evidence in chief at trial should be raised when the case is next before the court following service of the statement in question. If there is no further hearing before the trial, then the objection should be notified to the other parties as soon as possible and raised in the objecting party's skeleton argument for trial.

HEARSAY, SUPPLEMENTAL STATEMENTS, CORRECTIONS AND AMPLIFICATION

1A-77 **8.14** Parties must ensure that the statements of all factual witnesses intended to be called, or whose statements are to be tendered as hearsay statements, are exchanged simultaneously (unless otherwise ordered) by the date the court has directed for the service of witness statements. Witnesses additional to those whose statements have been initially exchanged may only be called with the permission of the court, which will not normally be given unless prompt application is made supported by compelling evidence explaining the late introduction of that witness's evidence.

8.15 Where a party has served a witness statement and later decides not to call that witness to give oral evidence at trial, prompt notice of this decision should be given to all other parties indicating whether the party proposes to put, or seek to put, the witness statement in as hearsay evidence: see CPR 32.5(1). Parties should note that, if they do not put the witness statement in as hearsay evidence, CPR 32.5(5) allows any other party to put it in as hearsay evidence.

8.16 Where a witness proposes materially to add to, alter, correct or retract from what is in the witness's original statement, a supplemental witness statement should be served. Permission will be required for the service of a supplemental statement, unless the content of the statement falls within the terms of a direction already given for the service of evidence in reply or all parties consent to the service of the supplemental statement. Any supplemental or reply witness statements must be served in accordance with any directions given for them.

8.17 A party should not seek the court's permission for service of a supplemental statement unless it has first provided a copy of the statement to all other parties and sought their consent to service. The request for consent should be made without delay. Where an application for permission is necessary, the application should be made at the PTR or, if there is no PTR, as early as possible before the start of the trial. If the application is made at any later stage, the applicant must provide compelling evidence explaining its delay in adducing such evidence.

8.18 Witnesses are expected to have re-read their witness statements shortly before they are called to give evidence. If any corrections are needed, a list of such corrections should be provided to the court and to all other parties at least 24 hours before the witness is called.

8.19 CPR 32.5 provides that a witness giving oral evidence at trial may, with the court's permission, amplify the witness statement and give evidence in relation to new matters which have arisen since the witness statement was served. Permission will be given only if the court considers that there is good reason not to confine the evidence of the witness to the contents of the witness statement. Any proposal for amplification or new evidence should be discussed between advocates for each party before the witness is called.

WITNESS STATEMENTS FOR APPLICATIONS

1A-78 **8.20** Witness statements in support of applications should be prepared in accordance with CPR 32 and PD 32. PD 57AC applies only to *trial* witness statements.

8.21 In some cases, it may be convenient for the evidence in support of an application to be given by way of a witness statement from a party's legal representative, based on instructions, rather than serving statements from those with direct knowledge of the matters in question. Such a statement must however comply strictly with paragraph 18.2 of PD 32, which requires a witness statement to indicate which of the statements in it are made from the witness's own knowledge and which are matters of information or belief, and the source for any matters of information or belief.

WITNESS SUMMARIES

8.22 A party who is required to serve a trial witness statement but cannot obtain one may apply without notice for permission to serve a witness summary instead: see CPR 32.9. **1A-79**

8.23 In considering whether to grant permission, the court will consider various factors including the extent to which the witness is likely to be able to give relevant evidence, whether the proposed witness summary satisfies the requirements of CPR 32.9, and whether permitting service of the witness summary is likely to further the overriding objective.

OTHER GUIDANCE

8.24 Follow the hyperlinks below for further guidance in relation to witness evidence: **1A-80**

(a) Expert Evidence (Chapter 9)
(b) Trial (Chapter 12)
(c) Business List rectification (Chapter 18)

CHAPTER 9 EXPERT EVIDENCE

GENERAL

9.1 The use of expert evidence is governed by Part 35 of the Civil Procedure Rules ('CPR'). Expert evidence is restricted to that which is reasonably required to resolve the proceedings (CPR 35.1 and see *British Airways Plc v Spencer* [2015] EWHC 2477 (Ch) [68-69]). **1A-81**

9.2 No party may rely on expert evidence at any stage during the proceedings without the permission of the court (CPR 35.4).

9.3 Expert evidence is generally limited to opinion evidence of a suitably qualified expert. Permission for such evidence is only given where the court is satisfied that there is a sufficiently recognised body of expertise on which to draw and that the court would be assisted by such evidence in determining one or more issues in the proceedings.

9.4 Permission should be sought only for expert evidence on identified issues, not generally.

DUTIES OF AN EXPERT

9.5 Attention is drawn to the Practice Direction ('PD') to CPR 35, and in particular to the Civil Justice Council Guidance for the instruction of experts in civil claims which provides guidance on best practice in complying with CPR 35 and PD35 for both those instructing experts and for experts. PD35 sets out the duties of an expert and the form and content of an expert's report. **1A-82**

9.6 PD 35 paragraph 2.1 provides that expert evidence should be the independent product of the expert, uninfluenced by the pressures of litigation.

9.7 The primary duty of an expert witness is to provide independent unbiased and objective assistance to the court. They should not assume the role of advocate or judge.

9.8 An expert witness is personally responsible for the content of their report, regardless of whether others have assisted in its preparation.

9.9 An expert report must be verified by a statement of truth in the form set out in PD 35 paragraph 3.3.

9.10 Experts are reminded in particular of the seriousness with which the court will view any false statement contained in a written report (*Liverpool Victoria Insurance Co.Ltd v Zafar* [2019] EWCA Civ 392).

9.11 Other sanctions may be imposed on parties if their experts do not comply with their duties to the court or the directions given by the court - see for example *Dana UK Axle Ltd v Freudenberg FST GMBH* [2021] EWHC 1413 (TCC).

9.12 Where the evidence of an expert is to be relied upon for the purpose of establishing primary facts, as well as for the purpose of expressing an opinion on any matter related to or in connection with the primary facts, that part of the evidence which is to be relied upon to establish the primary facts is to be treated as factual evidence to be incorporated into a factual witness statement to be exchanged in accordance with the order for the exchange of factual witness statements. The purpose of this practice is to avoid postponing disclosure of a party's factual evidence until service of expert reports.

CASE MANAGEMENT CONFERENCE

9.13 Draft case management directions which include suitable directions for both single joint experts and separate experts are available at Chancery Forms and should be adapted as appropriate. **1A-83**

9.14 The question of whether expert evidence is necessary or likely to be of assistance to the trial judge, the scope of the evidence and the timing and sequence of the provision of reports, will usually be considered at a case management conference ('CMC') (see Chapter 6).

9.15 The court will expect the parties to have discussed in advance of the CMC the scope of any expert evidence they think appropriate and, if possible, to have agreed the list of issues to be addressed by the experts (whether the parties seek the appointment of separate experts or a single joint expert).

9.16 When parties apply for permission for expert evidence, they must identify the relevant field of expertise or experience and the issues for expert evidence and be able to justify the need for expert evidence on those issues. Where practicable, they should identify the name of the proposed expert (CPR 35.4). They must also provide an estimate of the costs of the proposed expert evidence (whether or not there is a requirement to file costs budgets in the case).

9.17 The exchange of expert evidence will normally take place simultaneously after both disclosure and the exchange of witness evidence. However, in an appropriate case, the parties and the court should consider earlier exchange of expert evidence and/or sequential exchange.

9.18 Sequential reports may be appropriate if the service of the first expert's report would help to define and limit the issues on which such evidence may be relevant or help the second party to understand the first party's case. For example, sequential exchange may sometimes be appropriate where the court gives permission for forensic accountancy or foreign law expert evidence.

9.19 Where experts are proposed in several disciplines, it may assist with overall case management for the experts in one discipline to exchange their reports ahead of experts in other disciplines.

9.20 Parties should be aware that the court discourages the practice of 'expert shopping', in the sense of casting around for a more favourable expert opinion in place of one already obtained. The court can, and ordinarily will, require a party to waive privilege in a previous expert's report as a condition of granting permission to adduce evidence from a different expert (see, for example, *Edwards-Tubb v J D Wetherspoon* [2011] EWCA Civ 136).

SINGLE JOINT EXPERT

1A-84 **9.21** The court will consider the appointment of a single joint expert ('SJE') where it is reasonable and proportionate to do so and consistent with the overriding objective.

9.22 Factors the court will take into account in deciding whether there should be a SJE include those listed in PD 35 paragraph 7. SJEs are often appropriate to assist the court on lower value and/or less complex claims. They may also be appropriate where issues of quantum or valuation arise, but where the primary issues to be determined are ones of liability. A SJE may provide assistance to the court where expert evidence is required on matters of expert fact such as technical evidence, as opposed to opinion.

9.23 It is not a sufficient objection to an order for a SJE that the parties have already appointed experts to assist them. An order for a SJE does not prevent a party from appointing their own expert to advise them, but they are unlikely to be able to recover the cost of doing so in the litigation.

9.24 Where a SJE is to be appointed the parties will be expected to cooperate to seek to agree the terms of reference, identify any documentary material the SJE is to be asked to consider and specify any assumptions the SJE is to be asked to make.

SEPARATE EXPERTS

1A-85 **9.25** In cases where liability will turn on expert opinion evidence or quantum will be a primary issue; it is more likely to be appropriate for the parties to be permitted to instruct their own experts. For example, in cases where an issue for determination is whether a party acted in accordance with proper professional standards, it is likely to be of assistance to the court to hear expert evidence from separate experts who will be likely to represent the range of opinion, which can then be tested in cross-examination. However, it is not an invariable practice and in all cases the court will consider what is reasonable and proportionate.

EXCHANGE OF REPORTS

1A-86 **9.26** Whilst the most common order is for expert reports to be exchanged simultaneously, in an appropriate case the court will direct that experts' reports are delivered sequentially (see paragraphs 9.17 and 9.19 above).

JOINT MEETINGS AND STATEMENTS OF ISSUES AGREED AND DISAGREED

1A-87 **9.27** Where the court gives permission to rely on expert evidence, it will usually give directions for the experts to meet and prepare a joint statement of those matters that are agreed or not agreed between them - see CPR 35.12 and PD 35 paragraph 9.

9.28 The court may also direct discussion between experts before reports are exchanged, particularly where there is a need to refine the issues on which the expert evidence may assist the court, or to identify the extent of any disagreement between the experts in relation to the issues.

9.29 Unless the court orders otherwise, the structure and content of the joint meeting (or meetings) are matters solely for the experts and should not be controlled by the parties. The meetings may be held in person or remotely, as the experts find most convenient.

9.30 The discussions between the experts are without prejudice, to enable a free-flowing discussion. The content of the discussions will not be referred to at trial unless the parties agree (CPR 35.12(4)).

9.31 Parties must not seek to restrict their expert's participation in any discussion, or the preparation of a joint statement, directed by the court.

9.32 The joint statement is to be the work of the experts alone. Whilst the parties' legal advisers may assist in identifying issues which the statement should address, they must not be involved in either negotiating or drafting the statement.

9.33 The experts may provide a draft of the joint statement to the parties' legal advisers, but the legal advisers should not suggest amendments to the draft statement save in exceptional circumstances, for example where there are serious concerns that the court may misunderstand or be misled by the terms of that joint statement, where a party has sought to introduce new issues into a statement which were not in the agreed list of issues to be addressed by the experts or were not in their report, or where issues have been overlooked by the experts.

WRITTEN QUESTIONS TO EXPERTS

9.34 A party can seek clarification of either a SJE's report or another party's expert report. **1A-88**
Written questions that are more than clarificatory can only be raised by agreement of the parties or with the permission of the court - see CPR 35.6 and PD 35 paragraph 6.

9.35 The court has the power to disallow some or all of the written questions and impose sanctions in relation to costs, for example if the questions are oppressive in number or content, or if they extend beyond clarification without permission of the court or agreement between the parties.

9.36 This procedure is separate to, and should not interfere with, the joint expert meeting, discussions or statement.

REQUEST BY AN EXPERT TO THE COURT FOR DIRECTIONS

9.37 An expert may seek directions from the court (CPR 35.14). Unless the court orders **1A-89**
otherwise the expert must provide a copy of the request to all parties. The expert should guard against accidentally informing the court about communications that are without prejudice or privileged.

ROLE OF EXPERTS AT TRIAL

9.38 The trial judge may disallow expert evidence which is not relevant to the issues to be **1A-90**
determined at trial or which the judge regards as excessive or disproportionate in all the circumstances, even though permission for the evidence has been given.

9.39 The trial judge may order the experts to meet and attempt to agree further issues during the trial, with the aim of reducing the length of the trial or narrowing the issues for cross-examination.

9.40 The trial judge may direct that the evidence be given on an issue-by-issue basis, so that each party calls its expert to give evidence on a particular issue, followed by the other parties' experts on that same issue (see PD 35 paragraph 11.2). The experts should therefore be available throughout the trial period.

9.41 The unavailability of an expert or the late introduction of new expert evidence will rarely be a sufficient ground for varying a trial date or window.

CONCURRENT EXPERT EVIDENCE: 'HOT TUBBING'

9.42 Parties should consider in advance of the CMC and/or any pre-trial review ('PTR') **1A-91**
whether concurrent expert evidence, sometimes referred to as 'hot tubbing', would assist the court in the determination of the issues for trial - see PD 35 paragraph 11.

9.43 In an appropriate case the court may direct a mixture of approaches with the experts giving evidence and being cross examined on some issues before being asked to give concurrent expert evidence on other issues.

9.44 Concurrent expert evidence can be useful when there are a large number of issues of disagreement between experts of like discipline. The court can hear the evidence on each issue in turn, with questions being raised by the judge and the advocates. This can often achieve a clearer view of the extent of agreement and disagreement on a particular issue.

9.45 As an alternative to concurrent expert evidence the court may hear evidence from all parties' experts of like discipline or those dealing with one particular area of expertise together in turn. So for example hearing all the expert valuation evidence and then all the expert accounting evidence in an appropriate case.

EXPERT EVIDENCE OF FOREIGN LAW

9.46 Foreign law is a matter of fact to be proved by evidence, but CPR 32.1(b)/(c), 35.1, 35.3 (1) **1A-92**
and 35.5(1) give the court flexibility in determining how it is to be proved at trial.

9.47 The parties should consider and, if possible, agree in advance of the CMC what issues of foreign law are or may be disputed such that they may be issues for determination at trial.

9.48 The parties should consider and, if possible, agree in advance of the CMC what approach to invite the court to take, if there are foreign law issues to be determined. Various approaches can be adopted, including but not limited to the following:

(a) The court may make directions as set out above, treating an expert of foreign law in the same way as other experts providing evidence in the proceedings.
(b) The court may direct an exchange of expert reports and other procedural steps as set out above, but on the basis that the foreign law experts will not give evidence at trial, either at all or only on limited issues, although their evidence is not agreed. The trial advocates may make submissions at trial by reference to the reports and foreign law materials filed.
(c) The parties may agree the nature and importance of sources of foreign law, but choose not to file expert evidence, leaving the matter to submissions by the trial advocates, referring to source materials they have obtained from their own research.
(d) If the parties have retained foreign lawyers to advise them on issues of foreign law, they may agree it is not necessary to instruct a separate foreign law expert to provide the expert evidence, and instead their foreign lawyer may be directed to assist the court with source documents and /or witness evidence on relevant legal principles (see Chapter 8 on witness evidence).
(e) The court may limit the expert evidence to identification of the relevant sources of foreign law and relevant legal principles, with the trial advocates making submissions based on such materials.

9.49 It will be open to the court at the CMC to defer any decision on whether, and if so on what issues, the foreign law experts are to give evidence at trial.

9.50 Where there is a PTR and there is a previous direction of the court for foreign law expert evidence to be adduced at trial, the parties should consider in advance of the PTR whether, and if so to what extent, such evidence is still reasonably required for the trial (see Chapter 11 PTR).

EXPERT EVIDENCE FOR USE IN INTERIM APPLICATIONS

1A-93 **9.51** No party may rely on expert evidence in support of an interim application without permission of the court.

9.52 Where an applicant considers that expert evidence is reasonably necessary for the fair disposal of their application they should, at the same time as issuing their application, apply for permission to rely on expert evidence.

9.53 If the respondent considers that expert evidence is reasonably necessary for the fair disposal of the application they should, at the same time as filing their evidence in response, apply for permission to rely on expert evidence.

9.54 Such an application may be dealt with on paper and without a hearing, in an appropriate case.

9.55 Parties should where possible seek to agree the scope of any expert evidence which may be reasonably necessary for the fair disposal of the application. If the expert evidence sought is expert evidence of foreign law, parties should have regard to paragraphs 9.46 to 9.50 which should be applied analogously.

ASSESSORS

1A-94 **9.56** Under CPR 35.15 and PD 35 10 the court may appoint an assessor to assist it in relation to any matter in which the assessor has skill and experience. An assessor provides advice and assistance to the judge not the parties and cannot be cross examined or give evidence. However, any report of the assessor prepares for the court is made available to the parties.

9.57 It is rarely used both because parties often have their own experts whose duty is to assist the court and because save in exceptional cases the additional cost would be prohibitive. However, assessors have been used by the court to provide scientific or technical advice, assistance on complex costs disputes and in nautical collision cases.

9.58 The remuneration of the assessor is determined by the court and forms part of the costs of the proceedings.

CHAPTER 10 ALTERNATIVE DISPUTE RESOLUTION ('ADR')

GENERALLY

1A-95 **10.1** ADR is a broad umbrella term for alternative types of dispute resolution and includes, but is not confined to, mediation, negotiation, early neutral evaluation, arbitration, adjudication, expert determination and financial dispute resolution. Parties should consider carefully whether ADR will be of assistance in resolving their dispute before the issue of any claim.

10.2 This chapter is focussed on those types of ADR that are primarily used to facilitate settlement before a trial or appeal in claims that have already been issued in the B&PCs.

10.3 The settlement of disputes by means of ADR can:
(a) save significant expense;
(b) provide a resolution expeditiously;
(c) preserve existing commercial relationships and market reputation;
(d) provide a wider range of solutions than those offered by the determination of the issues in the claim; and

(e) ensure confidentiality.

10.4 In all cases, legal representatives should consider with their clients and the other parties concerned the possibility of attempting to resolve the dispute or particular issues by ADR and they should ensure that their clients are fully informed about points (a) - (e) above.

10.5 ADR should be considered before issue and at all stages of a claim. At the case management conference ('CMC'), parties should be prepared for a discussion about what steps have already been taken to try to resolve the claim, and in appropriate cases the parties will be invited to consider whether their dispute, or particular issues in it, could be resolved by ADR, and when that should take place.

STAYS FOR ADR

10.6 Parties who consider that ADR might be an appropriate means of resolving the dispute may apply for a stay at any stage, including before the first CMC. The court will readily grant a stay at an early stage in proceedings if the parties are agreed that there should be one. This can be dealt with by lodging a consent order, which should also specify the steps that the parties must take once the stay has expired (see form CH12 which can be adapted as appropriate to the circumstances). **1A-96**

10.7 A stay for ADR will normally be for a fixed period and include a provision that the parties may agree to extend the stay for periods not exceeding a total of 3 months from the date of the order without reference to the court, provided they notify the court in writing. Any request for a further extension after 3 months must be referred to the court. At the end of the stay the parties should be in a position to tell the court what steps have been taken or are proposed to be taken.

10.8 The court may also stay the case or adjourn a hearing of its own motion to encourage and enable the parties to use ADR. The stay will be for a specified period and may include a date by which representatives of the parties with authority to settle and their legal advisers are required to meet, or a requirement for parties to exchange lists of neutral individuals who are available to carry out ADR and seek to agree on one. If agreement cannot be reached, the CMC can be restored for the court to facilitate agreement. Although the court may strongly recommend mediation, it cannot order that a mediation takes place and will not recommend an individual or body to facilitate ADR.

10.9 For information and example only, but not by way of recommendation, a list of mediators and mediation providers can be found at *https://civilmediation.org/mediator-search/*.

10.10 Any order staying the case for ADR may (but is not required to) include an order as to the liability of the parties for the costs they incur in using or attempting to use ADR. Such order will usually be (a) costs in the case or (b) each side to bear its own costs.

10.11 Once directions have been given and a trial date fixed, a stay or further stay for ADR may be inappropriate if it will interfere with the directions timetable. ADR can take place without a stay of the proceedings and in parallel with the continuing case management directions timetable, so as not to endanger the trial date.

10.12 Where an application is made for permission to appeal, the court may adjourn that application to allow the opportunity for ADR. Failing settlement within a specified period, the application for permission to appeal will be restored.

HIGH COURT APPEALS MEDIATION SCHEME

10.13 Where a High Court Judge ('HCJ') grants permission to appeal against a decision of the County Court or adjourns the application for permission to appeal or permission to appeal out of time, or both, for a hearing, the appeal will be recommended for mediation unless the HCJ otherwise directs. **1A-97**

10.14 All parties will be notified of the recommendation, as will the Centre for Effective Dispute Resolution ('CEDR'), which operates the scheme. The recommendation will be accompanied by a letter explaining the operation of the scheme. CEDR will liaise with the parties to facilitate the mediation (further information about the scheme can be found on the CEDR website).

10.15 The recommendation is not compulsory, though a failure to mediate following a recommendation may well have consequences for any order for costs at the end of the appeal.

10.16 There is no stay of the appeal proceedings where a recommendation to mediate is made. The parties are expected to agree suitable extensions of time for any procedural steps required, to allow time for the mediation to take place.

EARLY NEUTRAL EVALUATION ('ENE')

10.17 ENE is a simple, independent evaluation of the merits of a dispute or a particular issue, by a judge or someone with relevant expertise. This evaluation is non-binding and without prejudice unless the parties agree otherwise. It is given after time-limited consideration of core materials, the judge having read or listened to concise submissions. **1A-98**

10.18 The court may order ENE at a case management conference if it deems it appropriate. Following *Lomax v Lomax* [2019] EWCA Civ 1467, this may be ordered even if one or more party does not consent.

10.19 There is no one type of case which is suitable, though complex factual and legal disputes are generally unsuited to ENE. It can be particularly effective where the claim turns on an issue of interpretation or an issue of law, where the case involves the court forming an impression about infringement of intellectual property rights, or where the case is an appeal against a decision of a lower court, tribunal or office holder.

10.20 ENE may be provided by appropriate third parties or by the court pursuant to its powers under rule CPR 3.1(2)(m) of the Civil Procedure Rules ('CPR'). If it is provided by the court, the ENE will generally be conducted by a judge of the same level as would be allocated to hear the trial (or appeal), but the parties may agree otherwise.

10.21 There are no set procedures for ENE. The judge who is to conduct the ENE will give such directions for its preparation and conduct as they consider appropriate. The court will usually direct the parties to provide and exchange written position papers and to agree a bundle of core documents. The ENE can be on paper but in some cases the judge will direct a short hearing of up to half a day (2.5 hours).

10.22 Unless the parties have agreed that the ENE will be binding, the court will not retain on the court file any of the papers lodged for the ENE or a record of the judge's evaluation.

10.23 The judge conducting the ENE will have no further involvement with the claim unless both parties agree otherwise.

10.24 A draft ENE order can be found at Appendix K.

CHANCERY FINANCIAL DISPUTE RESOLUTION ('CH FDR')

1A-99 **10.25** Ch FDR is a form of ADR in which the court facilitates negotiations and may provide the parties with an opinion about the claim or elements of it. It is without prejudice and non-binding and will not be ordered unless all parties' consent.

10.26 Ch FDR has been particularly effective in resolving disputes about shares in property, business partnerships, probate and inheritance.

10.27 Ch FDR will usually be undertaken in London by a Master or an Insolvency and Companies Court Judge and in the B&PC District Registries by specialist B&PC District Judges, or where the case warrants it by a Section 9 Judge.

10.28 Ch FDR is a dynamic process. There will be a Ch FDR meeting in which the court plays the role of both facilitator and evaluator. Parties must be present at this meeting. The court will try to lead the parties to agree terms but will not make a determination. If the parties request it, the court may express an opinion about an issue or the claim as a whole.

10.29 In advance of the Ch FDR meeting the court will give directions which may include directing the parties to exchange and file without prejudice position papers (and direct what is to be addressed) and to lodge a bundle. If expert evidence is likely to be required or helpful for the Ch FDR, the court may permit that evidence to be filed and exchanged for the purposes of the Ch FDR without the need for a CPR compliant report.

10.30 The court will allocate time for initial discussions between the parties before the commencement of the Ch FDR meeting.

10.31 Unless the parties have agreed otherwise, the court will not retain on the court file any of the papers lodged for the Ch FDR or a record of the judge's opinion.

10.32 The judge conducting the Ch FDR will have no further involvement with the claim.

10.33 A draft Ch FDR order can be found at Appendix L.

CHAPTER 11 PRE-TRIAL REVIEW AND TRIAL TIMETABLE

TIMING AND ATTENDANCE

1A-100 **11.1** Pre-trial reviews ('PTRs') are typically held in all cases where the trial is estimated to last 5 days or more (including time for pre-reading and writing closing submissions). PTRs are not typically held in cases where the trial is estimated to last less than 5 days (inclusive). Where a PTR would not normally be held it is the responsibility of the parties to consider whether the trial or any part of it should be conducted remotely or as a hybrid hearing and to raise the matter with the court (by way of a letter sent via CE-File) in good time; the court may then direct a short PTR if necessary.

11.2 Where a case with a time estimate of at least 5 days is fixed for final hearing, the Chancery Judges' Listing Office (or Masters Appointments) will at the same time fix a PTR before an appropriate judge. A PTR will usually be fixed to take place about 4-6 weeks before the start of the trial. A PTR will usually be listed for half a day (2.5 hours). A PTR of half a day or less (and no more than 90 mins pre-reading) will take place remotely unless the court orders otherwise. For guidance on the preparation and conduct of remote and hybrid hearings see Appendix Z.

11.3 For guidance on PTR listing arrangements in the B&PC District Registries follow the links in Appendix C. For guidance on PTR listing arrangements before ICC Judges see paragraph 21.35.

11.4 If the trial judge has already been nominated, the PTR will, if possible, be heard by that judge.

11.5 A PTR should be attended by at least one of the advocates who are to represent each party at the trial. Any unrepresented party should also attend.

DOCUMENTS

LIST OF MATTERS TO BE CONSIDERED AT THE PTR

11.6 In cases where there is to be a PTR, the parties must attempt to agree a list of matters to be considered at the PTR, including: **1A-101**

(a) any outstanding procedural matters, directions or steps still to be taken, including the status of the trial bundle (but note paragraph 11.18 below);
(b) proposals as to how the case should be tried, including all questions of timetabling of witnesses (see paragraphs 11.9 to 11.12 below), the use of technology and whether any parts of the trial should be heard remotely or by a hybrid hearing;
(c) any possible changes in the time estimate for the trial (see further paragraph 11.17 below and paragraphs 12.13 to 12.15 of Chapter 12); and
(d) any arrangements for witnesses to give evidence remotely. Where such evidence is to be given from out of the jurisdiction, parties will be expected to provide confirmation that any necessary permissions have been obtained (see paragraph 33 of Appendix Z).

11.7 The parties should be prepared to update the court on the state of preparedness of the trial bundle and should consider whether, in an appropriate case, the court would be assisted by the provision of the trial bundle at a time earlier than that provided for at paragraph 12.37.

11.8 Unless the court orders otherwise, the list of matters to be considered at the PTR should be prepared and provided to the court according to the following timetable:

(a) not less than 7 clear days before the PTR, the claimant must provide the other parties with a draft list of matters for their consideration;
(b) not less than 3 clear days before the PTR, the other parties should provide their comments on the draft list of matters to the claimant;
(c) by 10 am two clear days before the PTR, the claimant must provide the draft list of matters, agreed, if possible, to the court (using CE-File, as part of the PTR bundle - see paragraph 11.13 below).

TRIAL TIMETABLE

11.9 The parties must attempt to agree a timetable for the trial. In cases where a PTR has been fixed, timetables (agreed if possible) must be included in the PTR bundle (see paragraph 11.13 below). In cases where a PTR has not been fixed, the trial judge will determine the timetable at trial. The parties should co-operate to seek to agree a draft timetable, which should be filed at court at the same time as skeleton arguments when required by paragraph 12.49 of Chapter 12. The advocates for the parties should be ready to assist the court in this respect if so required. See further paragraph 12.5 of Chapter 12. **1A-102**

11.10 Trial timetables are always subject to any further order by the trial judge.

11.11 The timetable should allow a realistic time for pre-reading by the judge as well as opening and closing submissions, witnesses of fact and experts. If written closing submissions are contemplated, the timetable must allow time for the parties to prepare and lodge them, and for the judge to have read them before oral closing submissions. It is not usually necessary to allow time for judgment.

11.12 Where the parties put forward rival timetables, any differences of view should be clearly identified and briefly explained in a neutral manner using the template set out below (which includes space for the court to record its decision on the disputed matters):

Trial day	*Claimant's proposed timetable*	*Defendant's proposed timetable*	*Explanation of parties' difference*	*Court's decision*
Day 1 - am	Judge's pre-reading	Judge's pre-reading		
Day 1 - pm	Claimant's opening	Judge's pre-reading		
Day 2 - am	Witness A	Claimant's opening		
Day 2 - pm	Witness B	Defendant's opening		
Etc				

PTR BUNDLE

11.13 The claimant, or another party if so directed by the court, must deliver to the court, using CE-File, by 10 am two clear days before the PTR, a bundle including: **1A-103**

(a) the list of matters to be dealt with (whether agreed or not), a list of agreed proposals and the parties' respective proposals for matters which are not agreed;
(b) the trial timetable, with any differences of view clearly identified and briefly explained using the template set out in paragraph 11.12 above;
(c) all current statements of case;
(d) all orders made in the proceedings;
(e) all witness statements filed for the trial (without exhibits);
(f) all experts' reports filed for the trial (without exhibits);

(g) any core bundle intended to be used for the trial; and
(h) such other documents (not generally more than 100 pages in total at most) as the parties consider are reasonably necessary for the PTR.

11.14 Unless the court orders otherwise, the PTR bundle should be electronic, not hard copy. It should be prepared and provided to the court in accordance with the guidelines in Appendix X.

11.15 If there are any substantial matters in dispute, the parties must file skeleton arguments with the PTR bundle. If not, a short note to explain the agreed proposals will suffice.

AT THE PTR

1A-104 **11.16** At the PTR the court will review the state of preparation of the case, and deal with outstanding procedural matters, not limited to those apparent from the lists of matters lodged by the parties. The extent to which information technology may be used may be considered at this stage if it has not already been discussed at an earlier stage - see paragraph 6.60 of Chapter 6 (Case Management) and paragraph 12.32 Chapter 12 (IT at Trial).

11.17 The court may give directions as to how the case is to be tried, including directions as to the order in which witnesses are to be called (for example all witnesses of fact before all expert witnesses), whether the trial judge will be assisted by the provision of a core bundle of key documents and/or a narrative chronology, whether and the extent to which expert evidence (particularly foreign law evidence) is still reasonably required at trial, the time to be allowed for particular stages in the trial or matters relating to the trial bundle requiring the court's direction (see paragraph 12.36 of Chapter 12 (Documents for trial). The judge conducting the PTR will be particularly concerned to ensure that the time estimate for the trial is appropriate and that the parties have agreed a realistic trial timetable. If the trial timetable is not agreed, the court will impose one.

PRE-TRIAL APPLICATIONS

1A-105 **11.18** It is sometimes the case that there are still outstanding steps to be taken at the time of the PTR. This may be due to one or more parties' failure to comply with an earlier direction of the court. In such cases, the court is likely to require prompt compliance, and may make adverse costs orders to reflect the delays.

11.19 Parties should, where possible, avoid making applications with a view to their being heard at the same time as the PTR. It is preferable for applications to be made and heard well in advance of the PTR.

11.20 If it is not practicable to make an application before the PTR, the court should be asked to allocate additional time for the PTR in order to accommodate specific applications. If additional time is not available, such applications will not generally be entertained.

11.21 Urgent applications in the run up to trial but after the PTR should be made to the trial judge if known. If the trial judge is unidentified or unavailable, such an application should be made to the assigned Master, who will if possible or appropriate determine it on an urgent basis or refer it to the Judges' Applications List (described in Chapter 15) to be heard by a HCJ. Alternatively, such an application may be made directly to the Judges' Applications List if the application needs to be heard by a HCJ.

VACATING THE PTR

1A-106 **11.22** In some cases it may be possible to obtain agreement from the judge to vacate the PTR if the parties are able to certify that the trial time estimate and the timetable are agreed, the trial will be completed within the time estimate the court has approved, and there are no outstanding issues. The judge may consider, however, that a PTR will still be helpful, and in that situation will indicate to the parties those issues that should be addressed at the PTR.

CHAPTER 12 TRIAL

PROCEDURAL AND PRELIMINARY MATTERS

1A-107 **12.1** A trial is a final hearing of any claim (under Part 7 or Part 8 of the Civil Procedure Rules ('CPR')), petition or other originating application, in whole or in part, whether with or without live evidence. Trials in the Chancery Division may be conducted by High Court Judges ('HCJs'), specialist civil judges authorised to sit as judges in the High Court pursuant to section 9(1) of the Senior Courts Act 1981 ('Section 9 Judges'), fee paid deputy HCJs appointed pursuant to section 9(4) of the Senior Courts Act 1981 ('Deputy HCJs'), Masters and deputy Masters and Insolvency and Companies Court Judges ('ICC Judges') and deputy ICC Judges - see Chapter 6 (Case Management) at paragraph 6.83 and Chapter 21 (Insolvency and Companies List) at paragraphs 21.7 to 21.9. In the B&PCs District Registries trials may be conducted by B&PC District Judges.

12.2 Parties should also have regard to other parts of this Guide potentially relevant to trials, including the Shorter and Flexible Trials Schemes (Chapter 17 - see also CPR Practice Direction ('PD') 57AB and Chapter 3 at paragraph 3.16), expedition (Chapter 3, at paragraphs 3.19 to 3.22), and trials of preliminary issues (Chapter 6 at paragraphs 6.10 to 6.16).

PROPER PREPARATION FOR TRIAL

12.3 Parties will be expected to have taken all reasonable steps to ensure that their cases are adequately prepared in sufficient time to enable a trial which has been fixed to proceed. This covers, among other things: **1A-108**

(a) the timely production of any document (including written evidence) required to be served on any other party in sufficient time to enable the other party to be adequately prepared;
(b) the preparation and exchange of skeleton arguments in accordance with this Chapter and Appendix Y, chronologies and other documents to assist the trial judge;
(c) compiling and filing bundles of documents in accordance with this Chapter and Appendix X (Preparation of bundles);
(d) dealing out of court with queries that need not concern the court;
(e) giving consideration to the use of information technology at trial where this would save time and cost or increase accuracy (as addressed further at paragraphs 12.32 to 12.34 below);
(f) compliance as appropriate with Appendix Z where the court has directed that part or all of the trial take place as a remote or hybrid hearing; and
(g) the identification, and where possible agreement, of the main issues in dispute.

12.4 A failure to provide the court or other parties with documents in accordance with the relevant provisions of the CPR and this Guide or a court order may result in sanctions which could include the matter not being heard on the fixed date, the costs of preparation being disallowed, and an adverse costs order being made. See also paragraphs 12.27 to 12.31 below in relation to adjournments.

TRIAL TIMETABLE

12.5 See paragraphs 11.9 to 11.12 of Chapter 11 for an explanation of the process by which a timetable for the trial is set at the pre-trial review ('PTR') (if there is one) or at the start of trial. During the course of the trial, the parties should check each day whether the timetable is being adhered to and, if it is not, be ready to assist the trial judge with proposals (agreed if possible) for revisions which will enable the trial to finish within the fixed trial period. If necessary, the court will impose a revised timetable. See also paragraphs 12.13 to 12.15 below for guidance on time estimates for trial and the importance of their accuracy. **1A-109**

COURT DRESS FOR JUDGES AND ADVOCATES

12.6 HCJs, Section 9 Judges and Deputy HCJs wear robes for all trials except fully remote hearings. Masters wear robes for all trials and disposal hearings in court rooms (but not in hearing rooms) except fully remote hearings. They do not robe for the oral examination of a debtor. ICC Judges robe for hearings when sitting in a hearing room or court. **1A-110**

12.7 Where the judge is robed, advocates, whether counsel or solicitor advocates, wear court dress for trials, appeals and committal applications.

12.8 Court dress is worn by barristers and other advocates in accordance with the updated guidance issued by the Bar Council (2020). The judge may dispense (in advance or at the hearing) with any requirement for advocates to be robed.

LISTING

12.9 This section of the Guide applies to trials in the Business and Property Courts at the Rolls Building in London (ChD B&PCs in London'). The same general approach applies in the B&PCs District Registries, however for any local guidance on listing arrangements follow the links in Appendix C. **1A-111**

RESPONSIBILITY FOR LISTING

12.10 The listing of trials before Masters is dealt with by Masters' Appointments in the manner described at paragraph 12.16 below. For guidance on listing trials before an ICC Judge see Chapter 21. **1A-112**

12.11 The Chancery Judges' Listing Officer is responsible for listing trials before HCJs (which may also be heard by Section 9 Judges or Deputy HCJ's). The Listing Officer is supported by a team in the Chancery Judges' Listing Office ('Judges' Listing').

12.12 Any party dissatisfied with a decision of the Listing Officer may apply to the Judges' Applications List following the procedure set out in Chapter 14.

ESTIMATED LENGTH OF TRIAL

12.13 A time estimate for trial is usually fixed at a case management conference ('CMC') and confirmed at any PTR and when skeleton arguments are lodged. It is vital that the time estimates are kept under review and are updated (and the court informed) as soon as it becomes apparent that a change is required; the parties should also keep each other informed of any changes (see also Chapter 6 (Case Management) at paragraphs 6.75 to 6.78). **1A-113**

12.14 Only in exceptional circumstances will a trial be permitted to continue beyond the period allocated to it at the time of listing. Paragraph 12.16 below sets out the procedure to be followed in the event of a change in the time estimate after the trial date has been fixed.

12.15 Paragraphs 11.9 - 11.12 of Chapter 11 set out further considerations which should inform the parties' time estimates.

PROCEDURE FOR LISTING

1A-114 **12.16** The procedure for listing a trial before a HCJ or Master has two stages.

12.17 Fixing of trial window

At an early stage in the claim, usually at a CMC or other directions hearing (see Chapter 6 (Case Management) paragraphs 6.79 - 6.82), for trials before a HCJ (as well as trials to be heard by a Section 9 Judge or a Deputy HCJ) the court will specify a listing trial window, usually of 3 months, during which the trial is to take place. This is known as the listing trial window. The listing trial window will usually be fixed by reference to the estimated length of the trial: the listing trial window for a shorter trial will normally be sooner than the window for a longer trial. This is to allow the parties sufficient time to complete their preparations for trial. Parties should note that a listing trial window, once fixed, will not readily be altered. A list of current listing trial windows is available online at Trial date windows for Chancery Division. For a trial before a Master the Master will specify the listing trial window, if applicable, when giving listing directions.

Fixing of trial date

(a) At the time the listing trial window is fixed, the court will usually set a date by which the parties must co-operate to allow the claimant to provide an agreed list of dates within the window to avoid when fixing the date on which the trial window will begin. In practice:
   i. For trials before a HCJ (as well as trials to be heard by a Section 9 Judge or a Deputy HCJ), the date by which agreed dates to avoid must be provided to the court is known as the 'appointment to fix'. The claimant should send an email (copying the other parties) to Judges' Listing at ChanceryJudgesListing@Justice.gov.uk. Judges' Listing will then proceed to fix a date for the start of the narrower trial window (usually a period of 3-5 days) within which the trial will commence and will communicate this to the parties. Where one or more of the parties is represented by counsel, it is normal for their clerks to liaise with Judges' Listing. In limited circumstances the court may provide a fixed start date: see paragraphs 6.58 - 6.59.
   ii. For trials before a Master, the claimant should send the agreed list of dates to avoid to the court by CE-File and notify the other parties that it has done so. The dates to avoid and any other important information should also be included in the filing comments box on CE-File. Failure to do this may result in a delay in listing. Masters' Appointments will then proceed to fix a date for the start of trial and will communicate this to the parties.

12.18 For the procedure for fixing and listing trials before an ICC Judge, see Chapter 21 (Insolvency and Companies List).

12.19 In all cases, the court officer responsible for listing (whether within Judges' Listing or Masters' Appointments) will take into account, insofar as it is practical to do so, the times at which counsel, experts and witnesses are available. The officer will, though, try to ensure the speedy disposal of the matter by fixing a trial date as early as possible in the listing trial window. If, exceptionally, it appears to the officer responsible for listing that a trial date cannot be provided within the listing trial window, they may fix the trial date outside the listing trial window at the first available date.

12.20 In all cases with a time estimate of 5 days or more including judicial pre-reading, the officer responsible for listing will fix a date for a PTR at the same time the trial date is fixed (see Chapter 11).

12.21 When the trial date is fixed, the court will specify the date by which the parties must file a pre-trial checklist (Form N170) and the trial fee - see further CPR 29.6.

12.22 A trial fee (where payable) must be paid by either the claimant or if the claim proceeds only by counterclaim, by the counterclaimant. Where the claimant files a pre-trial checklist via CE-File they will be required to pay the trial fee when the pre-trial checklist is filed. In any other case the claimant or counterclaimant must arrange to pay the trial fee by the date specified. A claim or counterclaim will be automatically struck out without further order if the trial fee is not paid unless the court orders otherwise (CPR 3.7A1 and CPR 3.7AA).

12.23 A trial date, once fixed, will only rarely be altered or vacated. Paragraphs 12.27 to 12.31 below set out the procedure to be followed where a party seeks an adjournment.

PART 8 CLAIMS

1A-115 **12.24** In most Part 8 claims, it will not be necessary to call oral evidence and a trial will be listed before the relevant level of judge as directed by a Master or ICC Judge.

12.25 In Part 8 claims which require a trial with oral evidence, the applicable procedures set out in paragraph 12.16 above for fixing a trial date before the relevant level of judge should be followed.

CHANGES TO ESTIMATED TRIAL LENGTH AND SETTLEMENT OF CASE

1A-116 **12.26** If, after a case is listed, the estimated length of the trial needs to be varied the parties must immediately inform Judges' Listing or ICC Judges' Hearings, preferably by email, or Masters'

Appointments through CE-File. Failure to do so may result in an adverse costs order. Unless the parties have agreed a reduction in the estimated trial length, a direction from the court will usually be required.

12.27 If the case is settled before the trial begins, a consent order should be filed on CE-File for approval by: (i) a docketed HCJ, if there is one; or (ii) the trial judge, if known; or (iii) the assigned Master, or (iv) an ICC Judge. The parties must also notify Judges' Listing, ICC Judges' Hearings or Masters' Appointments, as the case may be, by email or by telephone, in order that the case can be taken out of the list.

ADJOURNMENTS

12.28 Once a trial date has been fixed, it will rarely be adjourned. An application for adjournment should only be made where there has been a change of circumstances not known at the time the trial was fixed. The application should be made as soon as possible and never, unless unavoidable, immediately before the start of trial. **1A-117**

12.29 Any application to adjourn, whether agreed or not, should be made on notice under CPR 23 and in accordance with the guidance in Chapter 14 and Chapter 15. Depending on how close to the trial date an application is made, it will be dealt with, on paper or at a hearing as may be directed, by:

(a) the docketed HCJ, if there is one; or
(b) the trial judge, if known; or
(c) the assigned Master or an ICC Judge; or
(d) the HCJ hearing the Judges' Applications List (described in Chapter 15).

12.30 Where an adjournment is sought on medical grounds, the applicant must, subject to any contrary direction by the court, provide medical evidence which satisfies the criteria set down in the judgment of Norris J in *Levy v Ellis-Carr* [2012] EWHC 63 (Ch).

12.31 If a failure by a party to take reasonable steps necessitates an adjournment, the court may impose sanctions which could include: disallowing costs as between solicitor and client; ordering the person responsible to pay the costs under CPR 46.2 or CPR 46.8; dismissing the application; or making any other order (including an order for the payment of costs on the indemnity basis).

12.32 The court may order an adjournment of its own motion where, at a prior hearing, it becomes apparent that the trial date cannot stand without injustice to one or both parties.

INFORMATION TECHNOLOGY ('IT') AT TRIAL

12.33 Parties and their legal representatives should seek to minimise the use of paper at trial. In any event, no hard copy trial bundle, only electronic trial bundles, should be lodged for use by the court, unless specifically requested at any stage by the court. See Appendix X for details on electronic bundles. **1A-118**

12.34 Parties are strongly encouraged to consider the use of IT at, or in preparation for, trial beyond just the use of electronic bundles. This will range from consideration of the provision of transcripts to a full trial support package. The court will expect proposals to be made, or an explanation of why it is not proposed to make wider use of IT at trial, at the PTR, if there is one, and in the parties' pre-trial checklists. This will not be necessary if directions for the use of IT in the case, including at trial, have been made at an earlier stage (see Chapter 6 paragraph 6.60) and there is no proposal to alter those directions.

12.35 In deciding whether and to what extent IT should be used at the trial, the court will have regard to the financial resources of the parties and the value of the claim. Where financial resources are unequal, it will consider whether it is appropriate for the party applying for the use of such IT to bear the cost initially, subject to the court's ultimate orders as to the overall costs of the case following judgment.

DOCUMENTS FOR TRIAL

12.36 Documents to be referred to at trial must be filed in one or more bundles of documents. Bundles of documents for the trial, including bundles of authorities, must be prepared in accordance with Appendix X (Preparation of bundles). **1A-119**

12.37 It is the responsibility of the claimant's legal representative to prepare and provide the agreed trial bundles: see CPR PD 32 paragraph 27.7. If the claimant is unrepresented, the court may direct that another party must prepare and provide the trial bundles. The preparation of bundles requires a high level of co-operation between the legal representatives for all parties. It is the duty of all legal representatives to co-operate to the necessary level. Where a party is a litigant in person it is also that party's duty to co-operate with the other parties' legal representatives.

12.38 The trial bundles should be prepared as follows, unless the court directs, or the parties agree, otherwise:

(a) the claimant must submit proposals to all other parties at least 6 weeks before the date fixed for trial;
(b) the other parties must provide the claimant with details of any additions they require or revisions they suggest at least 4 weeks before the date fixed for trial (and in any event before the PTR, if there is one); and

(c) preparation of the trial bundles must be completed no later than 10 days before the date for service of skeleton arguments.

12.39 The number, content and organisation of the trial bundles must be approved by the advocates with the conduct of the trial. The court and the advocates should all have exactly the same bundles (see CPR PD 32 paragraph 27.13).

12.40 If hard copy trial bundles are to be provided, in no case must a bundle contain more than 300 sheets of paper (i.e. 600 pages if double-sided) see Appendix X ?Preparation of bundles'.

FILING AND DELIVERY

1A-120 **12.41** The general rule (which may be modified by the court) is that the claimant must ensure that the full set of properly prepared trial bundles is delivered in accordance with the guidance set out in Appendix X paragraphs 15 to 18 for electronic bundles and/or that any hard copy trial bundles are delivered at the same time to Judges' Listing (for trials before HCJs, Section 9 Judges and Deputy HCJ's) or Masters' Appointments (for trials before Masters) or ICC Judges' Hearings (for trials before an ICC Judge) not less than 3 clear days (and not more than 7 clear days) before the start of the trial or, if applicable, not less than 3 clear days (and not more than 7 clear days) before the start of the designated pre-reading period. For a definition of clear days see CPR 2.8.

12.42 Appendix X (Preparation of bundles) provides further information about the filing and delivery of both electronic and hard copy bundles to the court.

12.43 A bundle delivered to the court should always be in final form and parties should not make a request to alter the bundle after it has been delivered to the court, except for good reason. Appendix X explains how changes to electronic bundles should be made.

12.44 Where oral evidence is to be given at trial, and if, exceptionally, the entire trial bundle is in hard copy, the claimant should bring to court at the start of the trial an unmarked copy of the bundle for the use of the witnesses (see CPR PD 32 paragraph 27.13). Unless otherwise ordered by the court, the claimant is responsible for ensuring that these bundles are kept up to date throughout the trial.

12.45 Where a witness has access to the hearing bundle only in electronic form, and the witness is asked a question about a document appearing in the bundle, the court and the advocates should ensure that the witness is given a proper opportunity to orientate or familiarise themselves with the document (for instance by being shown the front page, or the pages before/after the section they are being asked about) before answering.

12.46 The parties are expected to cooperate in respect of the arrangements for witnesses to give evidence remotely and are referred to Appendix Z paragraphs 36 and 39. Where a witness who will be giving evidence remotely requires a hard copy bundle in addition to or in place of an electronic bundle it will be the responsibility of the party for whom the witness is giving oral evidence to arrange for a hard copy bundle to be available to the witness.

12.47 Any party preparing a trial bundle should provide all other parties who are to take part in the trial with an electronic copy free of charge, and, if a hard copy is required, one copy at the cost of the receiving party. Further copies should be supplied on request, again at the cost (if there is a cost) of the receiving party.

PHYSICAL EXHIBITS

1A-121 **12.48** Some cases involve a number of physical exhibits. The parties should try to agree the exhibits in advance and their system of labelling. Where it would be desirable, they should agree a scheme of display (e.g. on a board with labels readable from a distance). Where witness statements refer to these, a note in the margin (which can be handwritten) of the exhibit number should be added.

SKELETONS, READING LISTS AND AUTHORITIES

SKELETON ARGUMENTS AT TRIAL

1A-122 **12.49** Written skeleton arguments should be prepared by each party. Guidelines on the preparation and filing of skeleton arguments are set out at Appendix Y (Skeleton arguments).

12.50 Unless otherwise ordered, skeleton arguments (and any other documents - see paragraphs 12.51 and 12.55 below) should be served on all other parties and provided to the court, via CE-File and, if the name of the trial judge is known, by email to their clerk, not less than 2 clear days before the date or the first date on which the trial is due to come on for hearing; or, if earlier, one clear day before the trial judge is due to begin pre-reading. For a definition of clear days see CPR 2.8.

12.51 Trial skeleton arguments should not be no longer than is necessary and should not exceed 50 pages in length, including appendices and schedules (minimum font size of 12 point and 1.5 line spacing) save in exceptional circumstances. They are skeleton arguments, not advance closing arguments. Where the advocates for trial consider that it is not reasonably possible to comply with that limit given the complexity of the claim, and so certify in the skeleton, or with permission given at the PTR, that page limit may be exceeded.

LISTS OF ISSUES, LISTS OF PERSONS, CHRONOLOGIES AND INDICES

1A-123 **12.52** In most trials, a list of the persons involved in the facts of the case, a chronology and a list of the main issues for decision will be required. In certain cases, the use of indices (i.e. documents that collate key references on particular points, or a substantive list of the contents of a particular bundle or bundles) may also be helpful for the court. Unless otherwise ordered, the claimant is responsible for preparing and delivering these documents to the court with their skeleton argument.

12.53 These documents should be non-contentious and agreed between the parties, if possible. If there is a material dispute about a particular event or description, it should be stated in neutral terms and the competing versions shortly stated.

12.54 Once prepared, these documents can be easily updated and may be of continuing usefulness throughout the case.

12.55 The documents should be no longer than is necessary and should be cross-referenced to the trial bundles and core bundle.

READING LISTS

12.56 The documents which the trial judge should, if possible, read before the trial may be identified in a skeleton argument, but must in any event be listed in a separate reading list, if possible agreed between the advocates. **1A-124**

12.57 The reading list must be lodged at court with the trial bundles, together with a realistic estimate, if possible agreed, of the time required for the reading. Advocates should remember, when specifying the time estimate, that the trial judge may have no familiarity with the case.

12.58 If any party objects to the trial judge reading any document, witness statement or expert report in advance of the trial, the objection and its grounds should be clearly stated in a letter accompanying the trial bundles and in the skeleton argument of that party. In the absence of objection, the trial judge will be free to read the witness statements and documents in advance. The parties may agree that the trial judge should read a witness statement or document in advance on the basis that argument objecting to the witness statement or document will be heard in due course and, if that objection is upheld, the trial judge will reach their decisions in the case without taking the witness statement or document into account.

AUTHORITIES

12.59 An agreed, single joint bundle of the authorities cited in the parties' skeleton arguments should be provided to the court by 4.00 pm on the day before the start of the trial or, if the pre-reading includes any authorities, at least one clear day before the start of the pre-reading. The authorities bundle should be filed using CE-File and, where the trial judge has requested a hard copy, by delivery to Judges' Listing or Masters' Appointments, as appropriate. **1A-125**

12.60 Unless otherwise agreed or directed, the preparation of the bundles of authorities for trial is the responsibility of the claimant, who should provide copies to all other parties. Advocates should liaise to ensure that the same authority does not appear in more than one bundle.

12.61 Excessive citation of authority should be avoided and practitioners must have full regard to *Practice Direction (Citation of Authorities)* [2012] 1 WLR 780. In particular, the citation of authority should be restricted to the expression of legal principle rather than the application of such principle to particular facts. Citations should comply with *Practice Direction (Judgments: Neutral Citations)* [2002] 1 WLR 346.

ORAL OPENING STATEMENTS, APPLICATIONS DURING TRIAL AND CLOSING SUBMISSIONS

ORAL OPENING STATEMENTS

12.62 Subject to any direction to the contrary by the trial judge, there should be an oral opening statement on behalf of the claimant. The appropriate length of that opening statement will depend on the nature of the claim. At the conclusion of the claimant's opening statement, the trial judge will invite short opening statements on behalf of the other parties. The trial timetable should set out the time allowed for oral openings (see paragraphs 11.9 to 11.12 of Chapter 11 for guidance on the trial timetable). **1A-126**

12.63 Oral opening statements should, so far as possible, be uncontroversial and no longer than the circumstances require. Their purpose is to explain the party's case, on the key issues for trial, introduce the trial judge to the significant facts of the case, including any important documents, and to identify the points of contention expected to arise; they are not an opportunity to repeat the parties' skeleton arguments or to make closing submissions on questions of law.

12.64 Unless notified otherwise, advocates should assume that the trial judge will have read their skeleton arguments and the principal documents referred to in the reading list lodged in advance of the hearing. The trial judge will state at an early stage, and in any event before any oral opening statement, how much they have read and what arrangements are to be made to read any documents not already read, for which an adjournment of the trial after opening speeches may be appropriate. Sometimes it is more helpful for a judge to read witness statements and expert reports shortly before the relevant witness is called. If the trial judge needs to read any documents additional to those mentioned in the reading list lodged in advance of the hearing, a list should be provided during the opening.

12.65 It is normally convenient for any outstanding procedural matters to be dealt with in the course of, or immediately after, the opening statements.

ORAL ADVOCACY

1A-127 **12.66** The court may indicate the issues on which it wishes to be addressed and those on which it wishes to be addressed only briefly.

12.67 Where a party is represented by more than one advocate at the trial, the advocates may share the oral advocacy, though no more than one advocate for each party may address the court on the same issue without the court's permission. The court's permission is also required for more than one advocate for a party to cross-examine the same witness and will rarely be granted. The court however encourages oral advocacy to be undertaken by junior advocates.

EVIDENCE

1A-128 **12.68** When agreeing bundles for trial, the parties are reminded that pursuant to CPR 32.19 documents disclosed in the course of any claim are deemed to be authentic unless a notice to prove has been served. Parties should establish through their legal representatives, whether the deemed agreement that the documents in the bundles are authentic includes agreement that the documents may be treated as evidence of the facts stated in them.

12.69 The court will normally expect parties to agree that the documents, or at any rate the great majority of them, may be treated as evidence of the facts stated in them. A party not willing to agree should, when the trial bundles are lodged, write a letter to the court (via CE-File), with a copy to all other parties, stating that it is not willing to agree, and explaining why.

12.70 Even where it is agreed that the documents may be treated as evidence of the facts stated in them the fact that a document is in an agreed bundle does not mean that every such document is (without more) part of the evidence given to the trial judge. It is the responsibility of a party to identify any documentary evidence on which it relies. An advocate should avoid, so far as reasonably possible, identifying a document relied on as evidence for the first time in their closing submissions. Failure to comply with this guidance may well lead to an adverse costs or wasted costs order if time and costs are incurred dealing with an objection.

DOCUMENTS AND AUTHORITIES

1A-129 **12.71** Only the key part of any document or authority should be read aloud in court.

12.72 At any hearing, handing in written material designed to reduce or remove the need for the court to take a manuscript note will assist the court and save time. Such material may include a note, in narrative or chronological form, of the factual case that a party invites the court to accept, which should if possible be cross-referenced to documents in the bundle and oral evidence. Any such material should also be available to the trial judge in electronic form.

APPLICATIONS DURING TRIAL

1A-130 **12.73** It will not normally be necessary for an application notice to be issued for an application which is to be made during the course of the trial, but all other parties should be given adequate notice of the intention to apply.

12.74 Unless the trial judge directs otherwise, the parties should prepare skeleton arguments for the hearing of the application.

CLOSING SUBMISSIONS AT TRIAL

1A-131 **12.75** After the evidence is concluded, and unless the trial judge directs otherwise, oral closing submissions will be made on behalf of the claimant first, followed by the defendant(s) in the order in which they appear on the claim form, followed by a reply on behalf of the claimant.

12.76 In a lengthy and complex case each party should provide written summaries of their closing submissions. Advocates should be ready to discuss with the court, in advance of their preparation, the form, scope and length of any written closing submissions. Any court time to prepare written submissions should have been included in the trial timetable fixed at the PTR or at the start of trial.

RECORDINGS AND TRANSCRIPTS

RECORDINGS

1A-132 **12.77** Hearings in the B&PCs, whether the hearing is held in person or remotely, are recorded.

12.78 Hearings in private will also be recorded, but a note will be made by the court to the effect that the hearing, or part of it as the case may be, was in private. If any party wishes different arrangements to be made, they should raise the issue with the court by way of letter sent via CE-File and, for trials before HCJs and where the name of the HCJ is known, to the HCJ's clerk.

12.79 No party or member of the public may record or transmit any part of court proceedings, however the relevant hearing is conducted, without the court's permission. Parties should note carefully and comply with the provisions of Appendix Z (the remote and hybrid hearings protocol) in relevant cases.

REAL-TIME OR DAILY TRANSCRIPTS

1A-133 **12.80** Various services are available for the transcription of proceedings at trial on either a real-time basis or in a transcript delivered at the end of each day. The use of transcripts in trials is always of assistance if they can be justified on the ground of cost, and in long cases they are almost a necessity.

12.81 If a real-time service is proposed, the matter should be raised at the PTR, if there is one. Otherwise, inquiries should be made of the trial judge (via Masters' Appointments, ICC Judges' Hearings, Judges' Listing or, where the trial judge is a known HCJ through their clerk) and sufficient time for the installation of the equipment necessary and for any familiarisation on the part of the trial judge with the system should be found. In all cases, the requesting party must complete and provide to the court a completed Form EX107OFC. Parties should also familiarise themselves with the relevant provisions of Appendix Z (the remote and hybrid hearings protocol) in relevant cases. If special transcript-handling software is to be used by the parties, consideration should be given to making the software available to the trial judge, though it will not be possible to load software (as opposed to the text of transcripts) on the trial judge's computer.

12.82 If the shorthand writers make transcripts available in digital form (as nearly all do) the trial judge should be provided with a digital version of the transcripts as they become available, if they require them.

TRANSCRIPTS PREPARED AFTER THE TRIAL

12.83 A party wishing to obtain a transcript of the judgment must make a request to the Court Recording and Transcription Unit using Form EX107. Parties should consult the Guidance Notes to Form EX107 which sets out the procedure to be followed and contains details of the different transcription services available and the names of authorised court transcribers. **1A-134**

12.84 Any party asking for a transcript should be ready to assist the transcribers by providing copies of documents and authorities referred to in the judgment.

JUDGMENTS AND CONSEQUENTIAL ORDERS

12.85 Unreserved judgments (which is to say judgments that are given immediately or shortly after oral argument has concluded) and some reserved judgments are delivered orally. A party wishing to obtain a transcript of the judgment must make a request to the Court Recording and Transcription Unit, following the procedure set out in paragraph 12.82. The transcriber will supply a copy once it has been approved by the trial judge. **1A-135**

12.86 Most reserved judgments are delivered by the trial judge handing down the written text without reading it out in open court. Where this course is adopted, the procedure set out in PD 40E will be followed. That includes, unless otherwise directed in a particular case, providing the parties in confidence with a draft of the judgment proposed to be handed down. The requirement stated on the front of the draft to treat the draft judgment as confidential must be strictly observed. Failure to do so amounts to a contempt of court. Draft judgments so provided are generally confidential to the parties and their legal representatives only, but in an appropriate case the judge may approve provision to an additional person, such as an insurer, on confidential terms. This must be specifically requested in writing (via CE-File and, in the case of a HCJ, by email to the HCJ's clerk) and approved by the trial judge before the draft is shared with such a person.

12.87 Advocates should inform the trial judge in the manner set out on the draft judgment or otherwise via Judges' Listing, Masters' Appointments, ICC Judges' Hearings or the clerk to a HCJ within the time specified or (where no time is specified) not later than 12 noon on the business day before the judgment is to be handed down of any typographical or other obvious errors of a similar nature which the trial judge may wish to correct. This is not to be used as an opportunity to attempt to persuade the trial judge to change the decision on matters of substance.

12.88 The judgment does not take effect until formally delivered in court, unless it is marked as having been handed down remotely by circulation to the parties and upload to The National Archives, 'Find Case law' website.

12.89 The parties should seek to agree any consequential orders: see PD 40E, paragraph 4.1. If the parties have agreed the form of the order and any consequential orders, and have supplied the trial judge with a draft, it is not necessary for the parties to attend any hearing at which the judgment is to be handed down.

12.90 If the parties are not agreed on the form of order or consequential orders, they should inform the court by written submissions by 12 noon on the working day before the judgment is to be handed down (see PD 40E paragraph 4.4), indicating (subject to any direction that the judge has already given) whether they wish such matters to be dealt with on written submissions or at a hearing (see PD 40E paragraph 4.5), and if at a hearing whether on hand down or at a later date.

12.91 Parties are reminded that if permission to appeal is to be sought from the trial judge such an application must be made when judgment is handed down unless the parties have obtained an extension of time for doing so. Such an extension if granted will usually be up to the date of any later consequentials hearing.

12.92 Any application or renewed application for permission to appeal a judgment must be made to a single HCJ or the Court of Appeal within 21 days of the date on which the judgment was handed down by the trial judge (and not the date of any later hearing to consider consequential matters unless the time for doing so has been extended). A party wishing to extend the period in which permission to appeal may be sought either from the trial judge or from a HCJ or the Court of Appeal must make an application in good time to the trial judge. See further the judgment in *McDonald v Rose* [2019] EWCA Civ 4.

CHAPTER 13 PART 8 CLAIMS

1A-136 **13.1** The alternative procedure for claims under Part 8 of the Civil Procedure Rules ('CPR') is flexible and is used for a range of disputes. As a general rule the procedure will lead to a final hearing, typically referred to as a 'disposal hearing', far more quickly than a Part 7 claim. In ChD B&PCs London the majority of Part 8 claims are dealt with by Masters and Insolvency and Companies Court Judges ('ICC Judges'). In the B&PCs District Registries specialist B&PC Circuit Judges and District Judges deal with Part 8 claims.

WHEN PART 8 IS APPROPRIATE

1A-137 **13.2** Part 8 claims are appropriate in particular where there is no substantial dispute of fact, such as where the case raises only questions of the construction of a document or a statute. Additionally, PD 8A section B lists a large number of claims which must be brought under Part 8. Other rules, and the practice of the court, also require the Part 8 procedure to be used for certain types of claim, of which the following are commonly seen:

(a) Claims under CPR 64. See Chapter 25.
(b) Claims under the Inheritance (Provisions for Family and Dependants) Act 1975. See Chapter 23.
(c) Claims for the removal of trustees and personal representatives where the guidance in *Schumacher v Clarke* [2019] EWHC 1031 (Ch) applies. See Chapter 23.
(d) Certain applications under the Companies Act 2006 which are governed by CPR PD 49A. See Chapter 21.

13.3 In cases in which both Part 7 and Part 8 could be used, caution should be exercised to avoid the inappropriate use of Part 8, and attention is drawn to the guidance given in *Cathay Pacific Airlines Ltd v Lufthansa Technik AG* [2019] EWHC 484 (Ch) 6 March 2019 unrep. (at paragraphs 31-42) and in particular that generally in such cases:

(a) the proposed defendant ought to be notified that the use of CPR 8 is being contemplated;
(b) a brief explanation ought to be provided as why CPR 8 is considered to be more appropriate than CPR 7 in the particular circumstances of the case;
(c) a draft of the precise issue or question which the claimant is proposing to ask the court to decide ought to be supplied to the defendant for comment; and
(d) any agreed facts relevant to the issue or question ought to be identified.

13.4 The Shorter Trials Scheme or the Flexible Trials Scheme may well be suitable for the determination of a limited factual dispute if Part 8 is unsuitable: see Chapter 17.

INITIAL STEPS

1A-138 **13.5** A claimant who wishes to commence a claim under CPR 8 must use Form N208.

13.6 Attention is drawn to the requirements in CPR 8.2(a) and PD 7A paragraph 3.3 including that the claim form must state that Part 8 applies and either that the claimant wishes the claim to proceed under Part 8 or that the claim is required to proceed under Part 8. These requirements ensure that anyone commencing Part 8 claims has given proper thought to whether or not Part 8 properly applies.

13.7 Defendants who wish to contest a Part 8 claim or to take part in the proceedings, even if neither contesting nor agreeing to the relief sought, should complete and file the acknowledgment of service in Form N210 not more than 14 days after service of the claim form (CPR 8.3). A defendant should state in the acknowledgment of service any different remedy that they seek. A failure to file an acknowledgement of service has serious consequences: a defendant may only attend the hearing(s) but may not take part without the court's permission (CPR 8.4). Where an acknowledgement of service has not been filed within the time limit, the court will normally fix a hearing date and make an order for a hearing for disposal of the claim, or further directions (Form CH 44).

13.8 There is no requirement to file a defence to a Part 8 claim and therefore various rules of the CPR are disapplied to such claims (CPR 8.9).

EVIDENCE

1A-139 **13.9** Part 8 provides a strict set of rules regarding the evidence which may be relied upon by the parties. Attention is drawn to CPR 8.5 and 8.6.

13.10 It is not unusual for an extension of time to be agreed between the parties for the service of evidence. Attention is drawn to CPR PD 8A paragraph 7.5. Any agreement to extend time must be filed with the court. If an extension cannot be agreed, or a longer extension than is permitted by agreement is required, an application should be made to the court. In substantial matters the court will normally be willing to grant a reasonable extension.

13.11 Parties should note that PD 57AC applies to *trial* witness statements (as defined in PD 57AC paragraph 1.2) filed in Part 8 proceedings (see paragraph 13.25 below).

CASE MANAGEMENT

13.12 Part 8 claims will generally be disposed of on written evidence without cross-examination. The witness statements together with the claim form should be sufficient in most cases to define the issues. **1A-140**

13.13 Claims issued under the Part 8 procedure are treated as having been allocated to the multi-track and CPR 26 does not apply (CPR 8.9(c)). The claimant does not need to serve particulars of claim and the defendant does not need to serve a defence. No directions questionnaires are required. Judgment cannot be granted in default.

13.14 The court file will generally be considered by the assigned Master after the time for acknowledgment of service has expired, or, if the time for serving the defendant's evidence has been extended, after the expiry of that period. If a defendant has not acknowledged service, the assigned Master will typically make an order in the form of CH44. Defendants who acknowledge service but do not intend to file evidence should notify the court in writing when they file their acknowledgment of service that they do not intend to file evidence. This enables the court to know what each defendant's intention is when it considers the file and avoids delay.

13.15 If 21 days after the expiry of any extended period for service of evidence no notice of a directions hearing has been received, the claimant should contact the court by letter filed on CE-File together, if appropriate, with a draft order substantially in form CH44, requesting either a directions or disposal hearing. The letter should provide dates to avoid, and a realistic time estimate for both the hearing and any pre-reading.

13.16 The procedure adopted by ICC Judges is set out at paragraph 13.22 below.

13.17 The Master will then consider the claim and decide:

(a) Whether the claim may be capable of being dealt with 'on paper'.

  i. Disposal without a hearing is exceptional. If the claimant considers that a hearing is not required, and the defendant has filed an acknowledgement of service saying the claim will not be defended, the claimant may ask the court to consider whether the claim may be dealt with on paper.

  ii. Examples of Part 8 claims which are dealt with on paper include some *Norwich Pharmacal* applications, some claims for relief where the court has directed that the claim need not name a defendant, and some unopposed applications for relief such as applications for a vesting order.

(b) If not, whether directions may be given without a hearing. In most Part 8 claims, the Master will either make an order for directions at the point of initial review or direct that a hearing is fixed. If directions are given at that stage they will usually give notice of a disposal hearing and give directions concerning further evidence to be filed. The court will give notice of the hearing to all the parties, and the notice or order will specify to whom the notice has been sent.

(c) Whether the claim is likely to be referred to a different level of judge for disposal.

13.18 A directions hearing with a time estimate of half a day or less (and no more than 90 mins pre-reading) will take place remotely unless the court orders otherwise. If a party considers that the directions hearing should take place using a format other than the default format, they should CE-File and serve on the other parties a letter setting out their alternative proposal, together with brief reasons, within 7 days of receipt of the Notice of Hearing. For further guidance on the preparation and conduct of remote or hybrid hearings see Appendix Z.

13.19 At a directions hearing the court will generally wish to establish whether:

(a) the court has all the evidence it will need (including expert evidence)

(b) the claim is ready for a disposal hearing;

(c) any witnesses will need to attend the final hearing for cross-examination, in which case the court will give directions with a view to fixing the period during which the case will be heard;

(d) the disposal hearing should be dealt with by a Master or by a HCJ, Section 9 Judge or Deputy HCJ.

13.20 Some Part 8 claims are by virtue of their subject matter exceptions to this general approach. Pension claims and Inheritance Act claims (see Chapter 26 and Chapter 23) are examples.

13.21 Some Part 8 claims are complex and raise a number of issues. In such cases, the parties should prepare an agreed list of issues, stating briefly the position that each party will take. The court may, in appropriate cases, direct such an agreed list of issues to be prepared.

13.22 In the Insolvency and Companies Court List ('ICL'), Part 8 claims will be listed on issue for an initial hearing with a time estimate of 15 minutes, unless the claimant requests a longer hearing or invites the court to consider the claim on paper. The court will only determine Part 8 claims on paper in clear cases in which the other parties have stated that they will not oppose the relief sought. The first hearing will take place before an ICC Judge, unless otherwise directed, at which the ICC Judge may decide some or all of the claim or give directions as to its future conduct.

13.23 Company Directors' Disqualification Proceedings follow a modified procedure. See Chapter 21 and Practice Direction: Directors Disqualification Proceedings.

DISCLOSURE

1A-141 **13.24** Attention is drawn to the Disclosure Pilot Practice Note (51UPN.1) and Chief ICC Judge's Practice Note concerning the application of PD 51U to Part 8 claims and ICL claims including Part 8 claims. PD51U applies to all claims issued in the B&PCs unless excluded. PD51U does not directly apply to Part 8 claims when issued, and it is rare for an order for disclosure to be made in a Part 8 claim. However, if any form of disclosure is ordered the court will adopt such parts of PD 51U as are appropriate (and CPR 31 does not apply). For further guidance on disclosure, see Chapter 7.

WITNESS STATEMENTS

1A-142 **13.25** PD 57AC applies to Part 8 claims unless the type of proceedings is excluded pursuant to PD 57AC paragraph 1.3. For further guidance on witness statements see Chapter 8.

OBJECTION TO THE PART 8 PROCEDURE

1A-143 **13.26** In some claims it becomes clear that the Part 8 procedure is not appropriate because there are substantial issues of fact to be tried and the Part 7 procedure is more suitable. The defendant may also object to proceedings being brought within the Part 8 procedure in the acknowledgment of service (CPR 8.8). The parties are encouraged to try to reach agreement on the use of Part 8 where possible. Use of the steps suggested in *Cathay Pacific Airlines Ltd v Lufthansa Technik AG* [2019] EWHC 484 (Ch) at paragraph 42 will help to identify and resolve issues with the use of Part 8.

13.27 If the court accepts the objection, it may direct the claimant's evidence to stand as particulars of claim, or direct that the claimant must file particulars of claim or short points of claim. The court will wish to avoid adopting a procedure which incurs unnecessary expense. Part 8 is flexible and the court can adopt a hybrid procedure under which limited factual disputes requiring oral evidence or disclosure can be accommodated within Part 8 proceedings - see *Vitpol Building Service v Samen* [2008] EWHC 2283 (TCC) (paragraph 18). However, it is unsatisfactory in a case of complexity for the claimant's case to be pleaded informally in a witness statement.

CONTINUING UNDER PART 7

1A-144 **13.28** The court may at any stage order a claim started under Part 8 to continue as if commenced under Part 7 if it becomes clear that there are significant issues of fact which make the Part 8 procedure inappropriate: see *Canary Wharf (BP4) T1 Ltd v European Medicines Agency* [2019] EWHC 335 (Ch) (paragraph 47) and *Cathay Pacific Airlines Ltd v Lufthansa Technik AG* [2019] EWHC 484 (Ch). It is a matter of judgment whether one or more issues of fact will make the claim unsuitable for Part 8, but it should not be assumed that the existence of any factual issue is sufficient to require conversion to Part 7. This provision only applies where the claim could have been issued under either Part 8 or Part 7.

COSTS AND COSTS MANAGEMENT

1A-145 **13.29** Costs management does not apply to Part 8 claims unless the court orders otherwise (CPR 3.12). PD 3E paragraph 2 gives examples of the type of Part 8 claim in which costs management may be appropriate.

13.30 A party seeking an order that costs management should apply to a Part 8 claim should give notice to the other parties and the court well in advance of the directions hearing, and explain, preferably in a witness statement, why such an order is sought.

13.31 Attention is drawn to PD 3F (Costs Capping), Section II which affects all claims in which a party is intending to seek an order for costs out of a 'trust fund', including Part 8 claims. For further guidance see Chapter 25 Trusts.

LISTING PART 8 CLAIMS

1A-146 **13.32** The final hearing of a Part 8 claim that does not involve oral evidence, known as a disposal hearing, should be listed in accordance with the guidance set out in Chapter 12. This will apply to most Part 8 claims. Where a Part 8 claim will involve oral evidence at the final hearing and directions have been given, it should be listed as a trial in accordance with the guidance in Chapter 12.

13.33 The final hearing of a Part 8 claim is usually listed before a Master however when directed to be tried by a HCJ, Section 9 Judge or Deputy HCJ they will be listed in the appropriate Chancery list by the Chancery Judges' Listing Office (see Chapter 12 for further guidance).

13.34 Part 8 claims in the ICL directed to be heard by an ICC Judge should be listed in accordance the guidance in Chapter 21 and Chapter 12.

ISSUING CLAIM FORM WITHOUT NAMING DEFENDANT

1A-147 **13.35** CPR 8.2A permits a Part 8 claim form to be issued without naming a defendant, where this is provided for in a practice direction. In some cases, the permission of the court will be required in advance.

13.36 The following practice directions or rules permit the issue of a Part 8 claim form without naming a defendant and do not require permission of the court to do so:

(a) **PD 57B 1.1-1.5:** Claims for declaration of presumed death (see Chapter 23 Probate);
(b) **CPR 57.16 (3A):** Claims under the Inheritance (Provision for Family and Dependants) Act 1975 where no grant has been obtained (see Chapter 23 Probate);
(c) **PD 64A paragraphs 1A.1 & 1A.2:** Claims for an order approving any sale, purchase, compromise or other transaction by a trustee (see Chapter 25);
(d) **CPR 64:** Application for permission to distribute the estate of a deceased Lloyd's name (see Chapter 25 and Chancery Form CH 38);
(e) **PD 64A paragraph 5:** Application by trustees under section 48 of the Administration of Justice Act 1985 for authority to act in reliance on a legal opinion (see Chapter 25);
(f) PD Application for Warrant under Enterprise Act 2002, paragraph 2.3; and
(g) PD Application for Warrant under the Competition Act 1998, paragraph 2.3.

13.37 PD 64B, paragraph 4 permits a Part 8 claim form to be issued without naming a defendant in cases concerning an application to the court by a trustee for directions as to which persons should be defendants but requires permission to be sought from the court in advance.

13.38 Where permission is needed, it is to be sought by application notice in accordance with Part 23, in advance of issuing the claim. The application should be listed before a Master. The evidence should carefully explain why the order is appropriate and be accompanied by the proposed claim form. In a simple case the Master may be willing to deal with it on paper. The Master will give directions for the future conduct of the case on the application.

13.39 If a pre-issue application is made (e.g. for permission to issue a claim form without naming a defendant or for anonymity/confidentiality) when the claim to which the application relates is subsequently issued it will be given a separate claim number by CE-File. The claimant must file a letter on CE-File when issuing the claim requesting that the claim be assigned to the same Master who dealt with the pre-issue application and that the two be linked together.

CHAPTER 14 GENERAL APPLICATIONS

INTRODUCTION

14.1 Applications are governed by Part 23 of the Civil Procedure Rules ('CPR') and Practice Direction 23A ('PD 23A') which contain detailed rules about how applications should be made. This chapter contains guidance in respect of general applications (whether ordinary or heavy, as explained further below). Urgent applications are dealt with in Chapter 15. The operation of this chapter in respect of applications within the Insolvency and Companies List ('ICL'), as well as the ICL Interim Applications List, is addressed in Chapter 21. **1A-148**

14.2 This Chapter provides guidance on the practice in the ChD B&PCs in London. The guidance applies generally or by analogy to the B&PC District Registries subject to any necessary local variations or guidance. For any local guidance follow the links in Appendix C.

14.3 Applications are usually supported by evidence in the form of a witness statement. Where convenient the written evidence relied on in support of an application may be included in the application notice itself rather than in a separate witness statement. Even where no specific requirement for evidence is set out in the CPR the court will in practice often need to be satisfied by evidence of the facts that are relied on in support of, or in opposition to, the application.

14.4 Applications may be dealt with at a hearing either in person or remotely (which includes telephone and video hearings) or without a hearing (on paper) (see paragraphs 14.59 to 14.66 below).

14.5 An application made in existing proceedings is called an interim application. In certain cases, applications may be made before a claim has been commenced. Except where a CPR rule or PD specifically requires otherwise, applications should be made by application notice form N244 (or form N244(CHFL) for the Chancery Division Financial List).

14.6 The party (or parties) making the application is called the applicant and the party (or parties) against whom the application is made is called the respondent. References in this section to 'parties' are to the applicant(s) and respondent(s) to the application unless otherwise specified.

14.7 In the ChD B&PCs London the court reviews all applications before they are listed for a hearing and may give directions before listing, in particular in heavy applications referred to at paragraphs 14.44 to 14.58 below. A deputy Master will refer a heavy application to a Master. An application will not be referred to a judge, and will not otherwise be heard, until the necessary court fee has been paid and a Word version of the order sought has been filed in accordance with the requirements of Chapter 16 paragraphs 16.15 to 16.21.

14.8 Normally, applications are made on notice to the respondent. At least 3 clear days' notice to the respondent is required before any hearing. However, in cases of urgency or for other good reason the application can be made without giving notice at all or on short notice. Permission to serve on short notice may be obtained on application without notice to the Judges' Applications List in the case of applications to a HCJ, or a Master, and will generally be dealt with on paper. For a definition of clear days see CPR 2.8.

14.9 For further guidance on urgent and without notice applications, and the Judges' Applications List, see Chapter 15.

14.10 The remainder of this chapter deals with non-urgent applications on notice to a respondent.

14.11 Applications will be heard in public in accordance with CPR 39.2, except where otherwise ordered. For further guidance on hearings in private see Chapter 3 and Chapter 15.

DIVISION OF RESPONSIBILITY FOR APPLICATIONS BETWEEN HCJS, ICC JUDGES AND MASTERS

1A-149 **14.12** There is now a significant overlap between the responsibilities of HCJs, Insolvency and Companies Court Judges ('ICC Judges') and Masters. There are relatively few matters which *may not* be dealt with by either a Master (see PD 2B, and PD 25A, paragraphs 1.1-1.4) or an ICC Judge (see Insolvency PD, paragraph 3.2 and Chapter 21). These include the grant of freezing injunctions, search and imaging orders, extended civil restraint orders, contempt applications and applications made pursuant to CPR 25.1(1)(g). In each case the parties should indicate clearly that the application is an HCJ application when issued. Masters may grant all types of interim injunctions including interim injunctions which are secondary to the main relief sought. However, they will not generally hear applications for interim injunctions where the court needs to consider the American Cyanamid principles.

14.13 Some claims are docketed to be case managed and tried by a HCJ (see Chapter 6 paragraphs 6.19 to 6.27). In docketed cases all applications are to be heard by the docketed HCJ and should be provided to the HCJ's clerk at the same time as being issued on CE-File.

14.14 In claims that are being managed in partnership, applications may be heard by either the docketed HCJ or the assigned Master, or when appropriate the HCJ and Master may sit together. Applications should initially be issued on CE-File for consideration by the Master, however, where appropriate or necessary, they should be emailed to the HCJ's clerk at the same time.

14.15 For more information about the procedure for making applications to HCJs and ICC Judges in the ICL, see Chapter 21 paragraphs 21.41 to 21.56.

14.16 General applications should be made to a Master or District Judge unless there is a special reason for making the application to a HCJ or Section 9 Judge. If an application which should have been made to a Master is made to a HCJ without following the procedure in paragraph 14.20 below, the HCJ (or Section 9 Judge or Deputy HCJ) may refuse to hear it.

14.17 If an application can or should only be dealt with by a HCJ, the application notice should indicate that it is considered to be a HCJ application. In all other cases where a Master has jurisdiction, but a party wishes an application to be heard by a HCJ, the process and principles set out in paragraphs 14.20 to 14.23 below apply.

14.18 In the rest of this chapter other than paragraphs 14.77 and 14.87 'HCJ' includes a Section 9 Judge and a Deputy HCJ.

14.19 The allocation of general applications between Section 9 Judges and District Judges in the B&PC District Registries is determined locally. Please see Appendix C and follow the links for guidance on any local practice.

RELEASE OF APPLICATIONS TO A HCJ

1A-150 **14.20** Except for cases which have been docketed to a HCJ, applications in the Judges' Applications List and urgent applications to a HCJ (see Chapter 15), a party wishing an application to be heard by a HCJ should apply to the Master for the application to be released to a HCJ. The application to release the substantive application should be made by letter and filed on CE-File at the same time as the application notice. The letter requesting release must be copied to the respondent.

14.21 The following criteria will point to the application being heard by a HCJ:

(a) Complex legal issues, particularly where there are conflicting authorities.
(b) Complex issues of construction.
(c) Substantial media interest.
(d) Claims which by their subject matter require the specialist knowledge of a HCJ, such as the more complex intellectual property claims and those commercial claims whose subject matter is highly involved or technical (such as sophisticated types of commercial instrument or securitization), complex trust claims and some large multi-jurisdiction trust and estate claims.
(e) Difficult cases involving litigants in person.
(f) Particularly lengthy applications (2 days or more).

14.22 In exceptional circumstances, the refusal to release an application to a HCJ may be informally reviewed by the HCJ hearing the Judges' Applications List on an application by letter (see Chapter 15).

14.23 There will be occasions when it will be natural to seek approval from a HCJ for a HCJ to hear the application, for example if a HCJ is dealing with directions following a hearing in the Judges' Applications List.

TIME ESTIMATES

1A-151 **14.24** Parties must be realistic about the length of time required to determine applications. The court's experience is that parties under-estimate the time required for pre-reading, for the hearing, or both, far more often than they over-estimate time. Where pre-reading or hearing time is under-estimated, the hearing may be adjourned and/or there may be costs sanctions.

14.25 If at any time either party considers that there is a material risk that the hearing of the application will exceed the time allowed, it must inform the court immediately.

ORDINARY APPLICATIONS

14.26 Applications to be listed for a hearing (including oral argument, the delivery of judgment, dealing with costs and/or other consequential matters, including any application for permission to appeal) of half a day (2.5 hours) or less, with additional time for pre-reading of no more than 90 minutes, are regarded as 'ordinary' applications. **1A-152**

14.27 An application should not be treated or listed as an ordinary application unless the parties reasonably expect to require no more than one and a half hours to one and three quarter hours to argue the application. The application notice should state the total time required for the hearing.

PROCEDURE TO BE FOLLOWED IN RESPECT OF ORDINARY APPLICATIONS

14.28 Ordinary applications will be listed as remote hearings unless the court orders otherwise. **1A-153** For further guidance on the preparation and conduct of remote and hybrid hearings see Appendix Z. If the parties consider that an alternative format is more appropriate, the applicant (if the position is agreed) or the relevant party, should file a letter on CE-File setting out brief reasons why they consider that the alternative format is appropriate or necessary, at the same time as providing dates to avoid (see paragraph 14.32).

14.29 Before issuing an application, the applicant and the respondent should, if possible, agree a realistic time estimate for both the hearing and pre-reading and dates to avoid.

14.30 A timetable for ordinary applications directed under PD23A, paragraph 9 will typically be as follows:

(a) Evidence in support must be filed and served with the application;
(b) Evidence in response must be filed and served within 14 days thereafter;
(c) Evidence in reply (if any) must be filed and served within 7 days thereafter.

14.31 This timetable may be abridged or extended by agreement between the parties provided that the date fixed for the hearing of the application is not affected. The parties should file a consent order for approval.

14.32 At the time of issuing the application, the applicant should, wherever possible, provide to the court the agreed time estimate for the hearing and pre-reading, dates to avoid, any agreed directions and any request for an alternative format. The applicant should add a note to the comment box on CE-File saying 'Ordinary Application' and, where necessary, indicate the date by which the agreed dates to avoid and time estimate will be provided. This will assist the court staff when processing the application. If no comment saying 'Ordinary Application' is added to CE-File it may delay when the application is processed.

14.33 If appropriate the applicant must, at the same time, also file any request for the application to be released to be heard by a HCJ, following the process set out in paragraph 14.20 and 14.21 above, indicating whether or not this is agreed.

14.34 If it is not possible to agree the time estimate or dates to avoid promptly, and by the date provided in the comment box on CE-File, the applicant should file a letter on CE-File (adding a note to the comment box) which sets out, briefly and in neutral terms, why it has not been possible to agree the time estimate or dates to avoid.

14.35 The application will not be referred to the Master to be reviewed and/or listed for hearing until the information or letter referred to above has been received.

14.36 The court will list the application for hearing on the first available date before a Master or a HCJ as appropriate having regard to the parties' time estimate and dates to avoid and, if approved, provide the applicant with a sealed order reflecting the terms of any agreed directions.

14.37 In an appropriate case, the court may refuse to list the hearing of an application until further information has been provided or listing issues have been raised with the respondent which may include consideration of the format of the hearing.

14.38 Where the time estimate for pre-reading or hearing the application(s) has been underestimated, the hearing may be vacated or adjourned and/or there may be costs sanctions.

14.39 Where an application has been listed for hearing and an additional application is then made, the approval of a Master must be obtained if the additional application is to be heard at the same time as the first. In the case of an additional application made in a claim with a docketed HCJ, the approval of the docketed HCJ, and not a Master, is required.

14.40 The applicant wishing to make the additional application must:

(a) Seek to agree with the respondent: (i) a separate time estimate for the extra time required to hear the additional application (including additional pre-reading, oral argument, the delivery of judgment and dealing with costs and other consequential matters, including any application for permission to appeal); (ii) that the additional application will not affect the overall time estimate for the hearing (if that is the case); or (iii) that the determination of the application issued earlier will necessarily determine the additional application or the matters raised in the additional application are not contested; and, (iv) that the additional application will not affect the format of the hearing or if the parties agree that a different format is now more appropriate a request should be made to change format.

(b) At the time of issuing the additional application, write to the court confirming the matters set out in paragraph 14.40(a) above.

14.41 The Master (or HCJ) will then either list the additional application for the hearing, give directions or (in the case of applications to a HCJ) refer the matter to the HCJ.

SKELETON ARGUMENTS FOR ORDINARY APPLICATIONS

1A-154 **14.42** Skeleton arguments must be provided by all parties in accordance with the guidance at Chapter 12 and Appendix Y. They must be provided to the court in Word version in accordance with Appendix Y and served on the advocates for all other parties by 10am on the working day before the date fixed for the hearing.

14.43 Skeleton arguments for ordinary applications should be no longer than is necessary and should not exceed 15 pages (including any appendices and schedules). Should a party wish to file a longer skeleton argument, the legal representatives whose names appear at the end of the skeleton argument must file a letter along with the skeleton argument explaining why this has been necessary. If the Master or HCJ is not satisfied by the explanation the party may be required to re-draft the skeleton argument and/or costs sanctions may be imposed.

HEAVY APPLICATIONS

1A-155 **14.44** Applications to be listed for a hearing longer than half a day (2.5 hours) (including oral argument, delivery of judgment, costs and/or other consequential matters including any application for permission to appeal) and/or with pre-reading of more than 90 minutes are regarded as 'heavy' applications. Heavy applications normally involve a greater volume of evidence and other documents and more extensive issues. They accordingly require serious co-operation between the parties.

14.45 Heavy applications will be listed as in person hearings unless the court orders otherwise. If the parties consider that an alternative format is more appropriate, the applicant (if the position is agreed) or the relevant party, should file a letter on CE-File setting out brief reasons why they consider that an alternative format is appropriate or necessary, at the same time as providing dates to avoid (see paragraph 14.32).

14.46 A timetable for service of evidence in heavy applications directed under PD23A, paragraph 9 will typically be as follows:

(a) Evidence in support must be filed and served with the application;
(b) Evidence in response must be filed and served within 28 days thereafter;
(c) Evidence in reply (if any) must be filed and served as soon as possible, and in any event within 14 days of service of the evidence in response.

PROCEDURE TO BE FOLLOWED IN RESPECT OF ALL NON-URGENT, ON NOTICE, HEAVY APPLICATIONS

1A-156 **14.47** In all heavy applications the applicant and the respondent should, either before or promptly after the issue of the application notice, seek to agree the time estimate and dates to avoid for the hearing.

14.48 The agreed time estimate must identify separately the time for the judge to pre-read any documents required to be pre-read; the hearing time of the application; and the time to give any judgment at the conclusion of the hearing. The time for judgment should also take into account any further time that may be required for the judge to assess costs, and deal with consequential matters including any application for permission to appeal.

14.49 When a heavy application is issued the applicant should add a note in the comment box on CE-File saying 'Heavy Application'. When issuing the application, the applicant should provide the agreed time estimate for the hearing and pre-reading, dates to avoid, any draft directions and any request for an alternative format to the court or add a note to the comment box on CE-File indicating the date by which that information will be provided. This will assist the court staff when processing the application. If no comment saying 'Heavy Application' is added to CE-File it may delay when the application is processed.

14.50 If appropriate the applicant must also file any request for the application to be heard by a HCJ, following the process set out in paragraphs 14.20 and 14.21 above, indicating whether or not this is agreed.

14.51 If it is not possible to agree the time estimate or dates to avoid promptly, the applicant should file a letter on CE-File (adding a note to the comment box) which sets out, briefly and in neutral terms, why it has not been possible to agree the time estimate or dates to avoid.

14.52 The application will not be referred to the Master to be reviewed and/or listed for hearing until the information or letter referred to above have been received.

14.53 The court will list the application for hearing on the first available date before a Master or a HCJ as appropriate having regard to the parties' time estimate and dates to avoid and, if approved, provide the applicant with a sealed order reflecting the terms of any agreed directions.

14.54 In an appropriate case, the court may refuse to list the hearing of an application until further information has been provided or listing issues have been raised with the respondent which may include consideration of the format of the hearing.

14.55 Where the time estimate for pre-reading or hearing the application(s) has been under-estimated, the hearing may be vacated or adjourned and/or there may be costs sanctions.

14.56 Paragraphs 14.36 to 14.40 above apply equally to heavy applications.

SKELETON ARGUMENTS FOR HEAVY APPLICATIONS

14.57 Skeleton arguments must be provided by all parties in accordance with the guidance at Chapter 12 and Appendix Y. They must be provided to the court in accordance with the guidance in Appendix Y and served on the advocates for all other parties by 12pm two clear days before the date fixed for the hearing. For a definition of clear days see CPR 2.8. **1A-157**

14.58 Skeleton arguments for heavy applications should be no longer than is necessary and should not exceed 25 pages (including any appendices and schedules). Should a party wish to file a longer skeleton argument, the legal representatives whose names appear at the end of the skeleton argument must file a letter along with the skeleton argument explaining why this has been necessary. If the Master or HCJ is not satisfied by the explanation the party may be required to re-draft the skeleton argument and/or costs sanctions may be imposed.

APPLICATIONS WITHOUT A HEARING

14.59 Although contested applications are usually best determined at an oral hearing, some applications may be suitable for determination on documents (i.e. without a hearing). CPR 23.8 makes provision for applications to be dealt with without a hearing. This is not generally appropriate for contentious matters but may be appropriate for instance in cases where the parties consent to the terms of the order sought, or agree that a hearing is not necessary (often filing written representations, by letter or otherwise). It is also a useful provision in a case where, although the parties have not agreed to dispense with a hearing and the order is not consented to, the order sought by the application is, in reality, unopposed. In the latter case, the order made will be treated as being made on the court's own initiative and will set out the right of any party affected by the application who has not been heard to apply to vary or set aside the order. **1A-158**

14.60 If a party inappropriately seeks a determination on paper and without a hearing this is likely to result in delay since the court will order a hearing on notice in any event. It may also give rise to adverse costs orders. It is not usually appropriate to seek an order which imposes sanctions, in the event of non-compliance, without notice and without a hearing. An application seeking such an order may well be dismissed.

14.61 Whether an application is suitable to be determined without a hearing should be considered by the parties before filing an application notice. A heavy application and/or one which requires more than 90 mins pre-reading will not generally be suitable for determination without a hearing.

14.62 If the applicant and the respondent agree that the application is suitable for determination without a hearing and agree a timetable for exchange of evidence and written submissions, the applicant should file the application notice together with any supporting evidence. At the same time, the applicant should inform the court by letter that the parties have agreed the application is suitable for determination without a hearing and of the agreed timetable. If the judge concludes that, despite the agreement of the parties, a hearing is required, the court will inform the parties.

14.63 If either the applicant or the respondent considers that the application is suitable for determination without a hearing but the other does not agree:

(a) The applicant should file the application notice together with any supporting evidence and a brief letter setting out whether the application is suitable for determination without a hearing;

(b) Within 3 clear days of service of the application notice and the other documents referred to in paragraph 14.63(a) above, the respondent should file a brief letter setting out whether the application is suitable for determination without a hearing.

14.64 If the court determines that the application is suitable for determination without a hearing, it will give directions for the service of evidence and submissions.

14.65 If the court determines that the application is not suitable for determination without a hearing, the procedure for ordinary applications or heavy applications, as appropriate, is to be adopted.

14.66 For consent orders, see Chapter 16, paragraphs 16.35 to 16.40.

CONSENT TO RELIEF BEYOND THE SCOPE OF AN APPLICATION NOTICE

14.67 It is commonly the case on an interim application that the respondent does not appear either in person or by solicitors or counsel, but the applicant seeks a consent order based upon a letter of consent from the respondent or their solicitors or a draft statement of agreed terms signed by the respondent's solicitors. This causes no difficulty where the agreed relief falls wholly within the relief claimed in the application notice. **1A-159**

14.68 If, however, the agreed relief goes outside that which is claimed in the application notice (or even in the claim form), or when undertakings are offered, then difficulties can arise. A procedure has been established for this purpose to be applied to all applications in the Chancery Division.

14.69 Subject always to the discretion of the court, no order will be made in such cases unless a written consent, signed by or on behalf of the respondent to an application, is put before the court in accordance with the following provisions:

(a) Where there are solicitors on the record for the respondent, the court will normally accept as sufficient a written consent signed by those solicitors on their headed notepaper.

(b) Where there is a written consent signed by a respondent acting in person, the court will not normally accept it as sufficient unless the court is satisfied that the signature is that of the respondent, and that the respondent understands the effect of the order, either by reason of the circumstances or by means of other material (for example, the respondent's consent is given in reply to a letter explaining in simple terms the effect of the order).

14.70 Where the respondent offers any undertaking to the court: (a) the document containing the undertaking must be signed by the respondent personally; (b) solicitors must certify on their headed notepaper that the signature is that of the respondent; and (c) where appropriate, the solicitors must certify that they have explained to the respondent the consequences of giving the undertaking and that the respondent appeared to understand. If the respondent is acting in person, the court will usually require the respondent to attend to give the undertaking in person, so that the importance of the undertaking can be explained to them.

APPLICATION BUNDLES AND EVIDENCE

1A-160 **14.71** For guidance on the preparation of bundles (including electronic bundles) for both ordinary and heavy applications, see Chapter 12 and Appendix X.

14.72 An electronic bundle should be lodged in all cases. Whilst for most applications electronic bundles and documents will be sufficient, the parties should consider whether a hard copy of the bundle, part of a bundle, core documents, skeleton arguments or other documents would be of particular assistance to the court. The court may request hard copies of some or all of these documents, and the parties (normally the applicant) should provide these promptly to the court on request.

14.73 Bundles should be filed 2 clear days before the hearing of an ordinary or heavy application unless the court orders otherwise.

14.74 If no bundle has been filed it is very likely the hearing will be adjourned to the next available date. This may result in the imposition of sanctions including as to costs.

REMOTE HEARINGS

1A-161 **14.75** For remote hearings, including telephone and video hearings, see Appendix Z.

SPECIFIC APPLICATIONS

1A-162 **14.76** For applications generally made without notice, including for permission to serve out of the jurisdiction, see Chapter 15.

VACATION ARRANGEMENTS

1A-163 **14.77** There is a Chancery HCJ available to hear urgent applications in vacation. This is always a HCJ not a Section 9 Judge or a Deputy HCJ. In the long vacation, two vacation HCJs sit each day to hear vacation business. In other vacations there is one vacation HCJ. Tuesdays and Thursdays are made available for urgent interim applications on notice. The vacation HCJ is available on the remaining days for business so urgent that it cannot wait until the next Tuesday or Thursday.

14.78 There is no distinction between term time and vacation so far as business before Masters is concerned or in the B&PCs District Registries. They will deal with all types of business throughout the year.

PRE-ACTION DISCLOSURE AND NON-PARTY DISCLOSURE

1A-164 **14.79** Applications made pursuant to CPR 31.16 and CPR 31.17 may be made by application notice using N244 and will be heard by a Master unless exceptionally the weight and complexity of the application warrants it being released to be dealt with by a HCJ, in accordance with the procedure at paragraph 14.20 above.

14.80 The application must be supported by a witness statement and the scope of disclosure, whether as to specific documents or classes of documents, should be carefully described and should be no wider than is strictly necessary (see also Chapter 7).

NORWICH PHARMACAL ORDERS

1A-165 **14.81** Applications for disclosure pursuant to *Norwich Pharmacal v Customs and Excise Commissioners* [1974] AC 133, [1973] 2 All ER 943, HL should be made by Part 8 claim form. An application under Part 23 is likely to be rejected.

14.82 The *Norwich Pharmacal* jurisdiction is an exceptional jurisdiction and careful scrutiny will be given both to the need for an order and to the scope of the order which is sought. In principle it should be no wider than is strictly necessary to enable the applicant to pursue its proposed claims.

14.83 Applications should be made in the first instance to a Master. The application will be referred to a HCJ if the complexity and/or importance of the application warrants it. If the applicant wishes to apply direct to a HCJ, release from a Master should be sought in accordance with the procedure at paragraph 14.20 above.

SUMMARY JUDGMENT/STRIKE-OUT

14.84 Applications for summary judgment under CPR Part 24 or for a statement of case to be struck out under CPR 3.4 should generally be heard by a Master (see PD paragraph 24.3). It is commonly the case that a Part 24/strike out application will constitute a heavy application and in a weighty or important matter may be released to be heard by a HCJ. **1A-166**

14.85 Requests for an application for summary judgment or strike-out to be released to a HCJ should be made in accordance with the practice set out at paragraph 14.20 above.

APPLICATIONS FOR EXPEDITION

14.86 For applications for expedition of claims, see Chapter 3, paragraph 3.19 to 3.22. **1A-167**

CONTEMPT APPLICATIONS

14.87 Contempt applications are governed by CPR 81 and must be dealt with by a HCJ or a Section 9 Judge or, with the permission of the Chancellor, a Deputy HCJ (PD 2B, paragraph 3.1). Because the liberty of the respondent is potentially at stake, great care must be taken to comply with the procedural requirements set out in CPR 81. **1A-168**

APPOINTMENT OF RECEIVERS

14.88 It is often appropriate to make applications for the appointment of receivers under CPR 69 and PD 69 to a HCJ in the Judges' Applications List if the matter is urgent and/or weighty. However, the Masters and ICC Judges have jurisdiction to appoint receivers and an application should otherwise be listed before a Master or ICC Judge who may release the application to a HCJ in accordance with the procedure at paragraph 14.20 above. **1A-169**

14.89 Where an order is made appointing a receiver it is generally necessary to apply for directions. This can either be at the same time as the appointment or immediately after the appointment but the receiver may apply at any time during the receivership for further directions.

14.90 The court may give directions in relation to the matters set out in PD 69 paragraph 6 and 7. An order appointing a receiver will usually include directions in relation to security, remuneration and accounts. The court is likely to require a receiver to either give security by guarantee or bond or satisfy the court that they already have sufficient security in force to cover any liability for their own acts of omissions before they begin to act or within a specified period of time after appointment (see CPR 69.5 and PD 69 paragraph 7). The court may terminate a receivers' appointment if there is any failure to provide security to the satisfaction of the court in accordance with CPR 69.5.

14.91 When a receiver has completed their duty, they or any party should apply for an order discharging the receiver and cancelling the security.

POSSESSION CLAIMS AGAINST TRESPASSERS

14.92 For guidance regarding possession claims against trespassers, see Chapter 27. **1A-170**

CHAPTER 15 APPLICATIONS WITHOUT NOTICE AND URGENT APPLICATIONS

15.1 Any application to the ChD B&PCs London which the parties consider cannot wait its due turn to be heard and which needs to be heard on an expedited basis (i.e. urgently and ahead of other general applications in the list) should be issued and listed for hearing in accordance with the guidance provided in this chapter rather than the guidance in Chapter 14. **1A-171**

15.2 This chapter also provides guidance in relation to applications without notice including when they may be appropriate and the procedures to be followed. Whether an application is genuinely urgent, and whether or not an application should be made on notice, are separate questions both of which must carefully be considered.

15.3 Separate guidance applies to urgent applications in the Insolvency and Companies List ('ICL') in London including applications in the ICC Judges' Applications List. For further guidance see Chapter 21.

15.4 Whilst the general guidance in this chapter applies equally to the B&PC District Registries, separate local guidance applies to the listing of urgent applications. For further guidance on urgent applications in the B&PC District Registries please follow the links in Appendix C or contact the relevant B&PC District Registry as appropriate.

15.5 If the court is not satisfied that an application is urgent, or should be without notice, the judge may direct that it be listed as a normal ordinary or heavy application in accordance with the procedure in Chapter 14. This is likely to result in a delay in listing the application.

15.6 Failure to comply with the procedures and guidance set out below may result in the Master or a High Court Judge ('HCJ') refusing to hear the application and/or an adverse costs order being made.

15.7 In this chapter, other than in connection with the Judges' Applications List and out of hours emergency arrangements, HCJ includes a Section 9 Judge and a Deputy HCJ.

URGENT APPLICATIONS

1A-172 **15.8** Any urgent applications (whether on notice or without notice) which can or should *only* be dealt with by a HCJ must be certified as urgent business (see paragraph 15.12(a)). Arrangements for listing the application should be made with the Chancery Judges' Listing Office ('Judges' Listing').

15.9 If the overall time required to deal with the urgent application (including pre-reading, oral argument, the delivery of judgment, costs and/or consequential matters (including any application for permission to appeal)) is less than 2 hours, the application should be listed in the Judges' Applications List. See paragraphs 15.16 to 15.27 below for guidance on cases that are suitable for the Judges' Applications List and its operation.

15.10 While the provisions for ordinary and heavy applications in Chapter 14 will not automatically apply to urgent applications, other than for applications in the Judges Applications List the default format for urgent applications will be as set out in Chapter 14 unless the court orders otherwise. A judge may direct that the format of or procedures for such applications, or a modified version of such procedures, shall apply before or at the hearing of, the application as appropriate.

15.11 All urgent applications other than those which can or should only be dealt with by a HCJ or which can be listed in the Judges' Applications List should be made to a Master. When issuing the application the applicant should add 'Urgent Application' to the comment box on CE-File to assist the court staff with processing the application promptly. This includes urgent applications before trial unless they are properly brought at a PTR. The procedure at paragraph 15.12 below should be followed. In an appropriate case an applicant may consider it necessary to take steps to have an urgent application heard in private, anonymise parties or seek to protect confidentiality in advance of or at the time of issue of the application (see paragraph 15.46, paragraphs 15.66 to 15.68, and paragraphs 3.31 to 3.37).

15.12 Where an urgent application is made to a Master:

(a) Applicants must certify the following on the application notice when issued: 'I hereby certify that this is urgent business and cannot await a hearing before the assigned Master in its due turn because [specify reasons]. [signed] [dated].' If appropriate, the certification and reasons for urgency may be attached in a covering letter which should be CE-filed and (unless the application is without notice) copied to the proposed respondent.

(b) Upon receipt of an application stated to be urgent, a Master will first consider whether that appears to be the case on the basis of the application, the evidence in support and any reasons for urgency provided by the applicant. If the Master is not satisfied as to the urgency of the application, the applicant will be directed to follow the ordinary or heavy applications procedures in Chapter 14 in the usual way.

(c) If the Master considers that the application is on its face urgent the Master may:

  i. List the application for an urgent hearing before a Master if the overall time required to deal with the application is two hours or less and a Master has both jurisdiction and the capacity to hear the application on an urgent basis: the two hour maximum includes pre-reading, oral argument, the delivery of judgment and dealing with costs and/or consequential matters (including any application for permission to appeal);

  ii. Direct that the application be referred to the Judges' Applications List if the Master considers that it should be heard by a HCJ and the overall time required to deal with the application is two hours or less, including pre-reading, oral argument, the delivery of judgment and dealing with costs and/or consequential matters (including any application for permission to appeal);

  iii. Release the application to a HCJ to be listed by Judges' Listing (whether because the overall time estimate exceeds two hours or for any other reason);

  iv. Refer the question as to how the application is to be disposed of to a HCJ or to the Judges' Applications List; and/or

  v. Make other directions for the disposal of the application by a Master (including where the overall time estimate exceeds two hours).

15.13 In cases of genuine urgency where it is not considered practicable to make an urgent application to a Master, the applicant should file a letter with the court explaining why it is not practicable to do so. The letter must be filed on CE-file and, unless the application is made without notice, copied to the respondent. The court will either list the application to be heard in the Judges' Applications List, or refer the issue to a HCJ for directions, which directions may include referral to a Master.

15.14 In respect of urgent applications to a Master or a HCJ:

(a) Application notices should be filed and served in the usual way except for applications where it is appropriate or necessary to proceed without notice or upon short notice (as addressed further at paragraphs 15.29 to 15.35 below);

(b) The directions set out in Appendix X, Appendix Y and Chapter 12 in relation to the delivery of bundles and skeleton arguments will apply unless otherwise directed.

(c) The application will not be referred to a Master or HCJ, and will not otherwise be heard, until the necessary court fee has been paid and a Word version of the order sought has been filed in accordance with the requirements of Chapter 16.

(d) Where the application is to be heard as a remote or hybrid hearing Appendix Z applies.

15.15 Further guidance in relation to particular urgent and without notice applications is set out at paragraphs 15.42 to 15.68 below.

JUDGES' APPLICATIONS LIST

15.16 The Judges' Applications List in London is only for applications which are urgent and which need to be dealt with by a HCJ, as well as applications where a Master has made a direction in accordance with paragraph 15.12(c) above. In each case the time required for pre-reading, oral argument, the delivery of judgment and dealing with costs and/or consequential matters (including any application for permission to appeal) must not exceed two hours. The procedure for listing such an application is set out at paragraphs 15.8 to 15.14 above. **1A-173**

15.17 Judges' Applications List sits in person in Court 10 in the Rolls Building unless, at the discretion of the HCJ hearing the Judges' Applications List, an alternative format is considered appropriate.

15.18 If the applicant considers that an alternative format may be appropriate they should file a letter on CE-File setting out brief reasons why they consider that the alternative format is appropriate or necessary when making arrangements with Judges' Listing to list the application. If the court directs that the application should proceed as a remote or hybrid hearing the applicant should prepare for and conduct the hearing in accordance with the provisions of Appendix Z as modified by any directions from the HCJ or as appropriate for the urgency of the application.

15.19 The HCJ hearing the Judges' Applications List sits each working day in term except for the last day of term and is always a HCJ. However, if the volume of applications requires it, any other HCJ, Section 9 Judge or Deputy HCJ who is available to assist will hear such applications as the HCJ hearing the Judges' Applications List may direct.

15.20 At the beginning of each day's hearing, the HCJ hearing the Judges' Applications List calls on each of the applications to be made that day in turn. This enables the HCJ to establish the identity of the parties, their state of readiness, their estimates of the duration of the hearing, and (where relevant) the degree of urgency of the case. The HCJ will hear at that stage from any CLIPS representative on duty as to their need for any additional time. On completion of this process, the HCJ decides the order in which the applications will be heard and gives any other directions that may be necessary. Sometimes cases are released in accordance with the procedure described in paragraph 15.12(c) above.

15.21 If a case is likely to take more than 2 hours (including pre-reading, oral argument, the delivery of judgment and dealing with costs and/or consequential matters (including any application for permission to appeal)), the HCJ will either refer it to Judges' Listing to find another HCJ, Section 9 Judge or Deputy HCJ to hear it urgently or give directions for it to be heard as an application by order (either as an ordinary application or a heavy application) on a subsequent date and hear any application for interim relief to last until the application is heard fully.

15.22 In respect of in person and hybrid hearings, parties and/or their representatives should arrive at least ten minutes before the court sits. If the hearing is fully remote, parties and/or their representatives should attend the hearing, using the link provided by the court, at least 15 minutes before the court sits. This will assist the usher to take a note of the names of those proposing to address the court and any revised estimate of the hearing time which will be given to the HCJ before they sit, as well as to allow any technical difficulties to be resolved.

15.23 Where agreement has been reached as to how the application should be disposed of, or is likely to be reached, the parties should also allow time before the court sits to agree a form of order with any other party if this has not already been done. If the form of the order is not agreed before the court sits, the parties may have to wait until there is a convenient break in the list before they can ask the court to make an agreed order.

15.24 If an application is adjourned the Associate in attendance will notify Judges' Listing of the date to which it has been adjourned so that it may be re-listed for the new date.

15.25 If all parties to an application listed in the Judges' Applications List agree, it can be adjourned for not more than 14 days by notifying Judges' Listing and (if it is known which HCJ is listed to hear the application) the HCJ's clerk, at any time before 4.00pm on the day before the hearing of the application and producing consents signed by solicitors or counsel for all parties agreeing to the adjournment. This procedure may not be used for more than two successive adjournments and no adjournment may be made by this procedure on the last two days of any term or the first day of any term.

15.26 Undertakings given to the court may be continued unchanged over any adjournment. If, however, on an adjournment an undertaking is to be varied or a new undertaking given that must be dealt with by the court.

15.27 The B&PC District Registries in Leeds and Manchester each have Urgent Applications lists on Friday which are heard by a Section 9 Judge or the Vice-Chancellor, when sitting. They operate in a similar way to the Judges' Applications List in the ChD B&PCs London. However, they may be used for both urgent and non-urgent applications which need to be heard by a Section 9 Judge rather than a District Judge, where the time estimate is 2 hours or less (including pre-reading, judgment and costs). For local guidance on listing applications in these Urgent Applications lists please follow the links in Appendix C.

WITH OR WITHOUT NOTICE APPLICATIONS FOR AN EXTENSION OF TIME

1A-174 **15.28** An application for an extension of time for compliance with a time limit set by the CPR or a time limit in an Order should be made to a Master using the urgent applications procedure set out in paragraphs 15.11 to 15.14 but does not need to be certified as urgent business. When issuing the application the applicant should add 'Urgent Application EOT' to the comment box on CE-File to assist the court staff to process the application promptly.

WITHOUT NOTICE APPLICATIONS TO HCJS AND MASTERS

1A-175 **15.29** The guidance in this section applies to all without notice applications to a Master or a HCJ except for procedural applications to a Master addressed at paragraphs 15.36 to 15.37 below. Parties should be aware that certain applications may not be made to a Master as set out in Chapter 14.

15.30 Applications must usually be made on notice to the other parties (and the usual rule is that 3 clear days' notice must be given). There are, however, exceptions such as:

(a) Applications where the giving of notice might frustrate the order (e.g. a freezing or search order).

(b) Where there is such urgency that it is truly not possible to give the requisite notice. Even in such a case, however, the applicant should give the respondent informally as much notice of the application as is possible. This is known as short notice.

(c) Some procedural applications normally made without notice relating to such matters as service out of the jurisdiction, service, extension of the validity of claim forms, permission to issue writs of possession etc.

15.31 An application made without giving notice which does not fall within the classes of cases where absence of notice is justified may be dismissed or adjourned until proper notice has been given. PD25A paragraph 3.4 requires that the evidence in support of an application without notice should explain why no notice was given.

15.32 Except for procedural applications to a Master addressed at paragraphs 15.36 to 15.37 below, on all applications made in the absence of the respondent, including applications made on paper, the applicant and their legal representatives owe a duty to the court to disclose all matters relevant to the application. This includes all matters of fact or law, whether known to the applicant or which would have been known had proper enquiries been made, which are or may be adverse to the applicant.

15.33 This requirement is known as the 'duty of full and frank disclosure', and parties are expected to familiarise themselves with that duty before making a without notice application. If made orally, the full and frank disclosure must be confirmed by witness statement or affidavit. The applicant or their legal representatives must specifically direct the court to passages in the evidence which disclose matters adverse to the application. The duty of full and frank disclosure also applies to litigants in person, who are also expected to familiarise themselves with this duty before making a without notice application. If there is a failure to comply with this duty and an order is made, the court may subsequently set aside the order on this ground alone regardless of the merits.

15.34 In cases where orders are sought without notice (except for orders sought on procedural applications to a Master addressed at paragraphs 15.36 to 15.37 below), parties' attention is also drawn to CPR 23.9 (service of application where application made without notice). Unless a rule or PD provides otherwise the draft order must comply with that provision, including a statement of the right to make an application to set aside or vary the order under CPR 23.10.

15.35 In the case of urgent and without notice applications, the parties and their legal representatives should ensure they provide realistic time estimates and reading lists. In both cases, care should be taken to ensure that sufficient time has been allowed to ensure that important material is brought to the attention of the court. It will often be better to take the judge hearing the application to such material in the hearing, rather than to expect it to be read, and time should be allowed for doing so. If the time estimate is under-estimated for either pre-reading or the hearing, the hearing may be adjourned or vacated.

PROCEDURAL APPLICATIONS TO A MASTER

1A-176 **15.36** Straight-forward procedural applications may be made to a Master without notice in respect of matters that are capable of being disposed of within 15 minutes or on paper and which do not require significant reading or investigation into the substance of the case. Examples of suitable matters might be an application for permission to serve a witness summary or to issue a Part 8 claim form without naming defendants (addressed further at paragraphs 15.64 to 15.65 below). Such applications should not be used for matters which should be dealt with on notice, without notice applications of the types addressed in paragraphs 15.29 to 15.35 above or applications which would be likely to be contentious if notice were to be given.

15.37 For procedural applications of this nature, the requirements of full and frank disclosure and other procedural safeguards referred to in paragraphs 15.32 to 15.33 above do not apply.

OUT OF HOURS EMERGENCY ARRANGEMENTS

15.38 An application should not be made out of hours unless it is essential. An explanation will be required as to why it was not made or could not be made during normal court sitting hours. It should be noted that normal sitting hours for court hearings before judges are 10.30 am to 1.00 pm and 2.00 pm to 4.15 pm. Applications made during legal vacations must also be certified as being vacation business (i.e. being of such urgency they cannot await the start of term to be heard). **1A-177**

15.39 There is always a Duty Chancery HCJ available to hear urgent out of hours applications that are High Court Chancery business. The following is a summary of the procedure:

(a) All requests for the Duty Chancery HCJ to hear urgent matters are to be made through the HCJ's clerk. There may be occasions when the Duty Chancery HCJ is not immediately available. The clerk will be able to inform the applicant of the Duty Chancery HCJ's likely availability.

(b) Initial contact must be through the Royal Courts of Justice (tel: 020 7947 6000/6260), who should be requested to contact the Duty Chancery HCJ's clerk.

(c) When the clerk contacts the applicant, the clerk will need to know:
   i. the name of the party on whose behalf the application is to be made;
   ii. the name of the person who is to make the application and their status (counsel or solicitor);
   iii. the nature of the application;
   iv. the degree of urgency; and
   v. contact telephone numbers for the persons involved in the application.

(d) The Duty Chancery HCJ will indicate to their clerk whether he or she is prepared to deal with the matter remotely (whether by telephone or video) or whether it will be necessary for the matter to be dealt with at an in person hearing. The clerk will inform the applicant and make the necessary arrangements. The Duty Chancery HCJ will also indicate how any necessary papers are to be delivered (whether physically, by email, or by CE-file).

(e) Save in exceptional circumstances applications for interim injunctions will only be heard remotely where the applicant is represented by counsel or solicitors (PD 25A paragraph 4.5 (5)).

(f) Which HCJ will, in appropriate cases, hear an out of hours application varies according to when the application is made.
   - **Weekdays.** Out of hours duty, during term time, is the responsibility of the HCJ hearing the Judges' Applications List who is normally available from 4.15pm until 10.15am Monday to Thursday.
   - **Weekends.** A different Duty Chancery HCJ is on duty for weekends, commencing 4.15pm Friday until 10.15am Monday.
   - **Vacation.** The Vacation HCJ also undertakes out of hours applications.

15.40 If it is not possible to issue a sealed order electronically out of hours the HCJ may direct the applicant to email the draft order to their clerk by 10am on the following working day. The HCJ's clerk will then seal it manually if necessary.

15.41 Similar arrangements exist for making urgent applications out of hours in High Court matters proceeding in the B&PC District Registries. The pager numbers for regional urgent business officers are given in Appendix C.

SPECIFIC URGENT AND/OR WITHOUT NOTICE APPLICATIONS

FREEZING INJUNCTIONS AND SEARCH ORDERS

15.42 The grant of freezing injunctions (both domestic and world-wide) and search and imaging orders is an important feature of the work of the Chancery Division. Such orders are of the utmost seriousness and exceptional by nature. Freezing and search orders, including orders made under CPR 25.1(g), will only be made by a HCJ, a Section 9 Judge or a Deputy HCJ. Masters can vary or discharge such orders by consent. **1A-178**

15.43 Attention is drawn to CPR 25, including PD 25A. In particular where the application is made without notice, the evidence in support must explain why no notice was given to the respondent (PD25A paragraph 3.4).

15.44 Where such an application is to be heard, the order sought, together with the application notice, should be sent to the clerk to the HCJ or Section 9 Judge hearing the application and copied to Judges' Listing by email (or in the case of a deputy HCJ, sent to Judges' Listing only). Alternatively, CE-file may be used if steps to protect confidentiality have been taken in advance or the application is for hearing on notice.

15.45 The applicant should consider whether providing hard copies of some or all of the documents (in addition to an electronic bundle) would be of particular assistance to the court. In cases of exceptional urgency, where it is not possible to lodge the application notice in advance of the hearing, the applicant will need to undertake to issue the application notice, and pay the relevant court fee, within a specified period of time.

15.46 Applications for such orders are often made without notice in the first instance. In a proper case the court will sit in private in order to hear such applications. If the application is to be made in private, it will be listed as 'application without notice' without naming the parties. The court will consider, in each case, whether publicity might defeat the object of the hearing and whether it is necessary to hear the application in private and, if satisfied, will hear the application in private: CPR 39.2.

15.47 When an application for an injunction is heard without notice, and the court decides that an injunction should be granted, it will normally be granted for a limited period only and a return date will be given - usually in 7 or 14 days.

15.48 If it is not practicable to issue the claim form before the application is made, the party making the application must give an undertaking to the court to issue the claim form forthwith even if the court makes no order, unless the court orders otherwise.

15.49 The standard form of wording for a freezing injunction is set out in Appendix M. A standard form of imaging order can be found at PD25A Annex B. Standard forms of wording for delivery up and non-disclosure orders are set out in Appendix N and Appendix P. The standard wording may be modified as appropriate in any particular case. But any modification to the standard form should be tracked on the standard form; identified and explained individually in a skeleton argument for the application and expressly drawn to the court's attention at the application hearing.

15.50 When seeking a freezing injunction, an applicant must consider what form of relief is necessary and appropriate, particularly where the application is without notice, and not simply apply for the widest possible terms and hope that the court does not question it. In particular, an applicant will always be expected to justify the factual basis for and need to freeze interests under trusts or assets of subsidiaries of, or entities controlled by, the respondent. An applicant should not without good reason (which must be explained to the judge) seek to expand the definition of assets that are to be captured by the freezing injunction.

15.51 An applicant for a search order is expected to consider what type of order is the minimum necessary to protect its interests, which in many cases will be an imaging order: see *TBD (Owen Holland) Ltd v Simons* [2020] EWCA Civ 1182; [2021] 1 WLR 992.

15.52 Full and frank disclosure is of the utmost importance on applications for freezing injunctions and search or imaging orders. For further guidance see paragraphs 15.32 to 15.33 above.

15.53 The applicant who is granted an injunction without notice is always required to provide to the respondent either a transcript or a detailed note of the without notice hearing, together with the evidence and any skeleton argument and/or other documents relied upon in support of the application.

15.54 Often the party against whom an injunction is sought gives to the court an undertaking which avoids the need for the court to grant the injunction. In these cases, there is an implied undertaking in damages by the applicant in favour of the respondent. The position is less clear where the applicant also gives an undertaking to the court. The parties should consider and, if necessary, raise with the court whether the party in whose favour the undertaking is given must give a cross-undertaking in damages in those circumstances. Consideration should also be given to whether a cross-undertaking should be given in favour of a person who is not a respondent to the application.

15.55 The applicant must ensure that an application notice for continuation of the injunction on the return date is issued (and the appropriate fee paid) and served on the other parties (normally at least 3 clear days before the return date). There will usually need to be an undertaking to this effect in the order granting the injunction. In the meantime the respondent will be entitled to apply, though generally only after giving notice to the applicant, for the order to be varied or discharged (for a definition of clear days see CPR 2.8).

15.56 For the return date the applicant must lodge an up to date hearing bundle in accordance with Chapter 12 and Appendix X. This bundle must include copies of the interim injunction or order, the issued application notice for the relief originally granted, the transcript or note of the without notice hearing, and the issued application notice for the return date. Failure to comply with these requirements may lead to delay in dealing with the application or costs sanctions or both.

15.57 An order, the effect of which is to continue an injunction granted by an earlier order, may be drawn up in either of the following ways:

(a) by writing out in full in the new order the terms of the injunction granted by the earlier order, amended to give effect to a new expiry date or event; or

(b) by ordering in the new order that the injunction contained (in a specific paragraph or paragraphs) in the annexed earlier order is to continue until the new expiry date or event (and annexing the earlier order).

15.58 In general, the better practice is the first alternative set out above, as it expresses in the clearest possible way by reference to a single document exactly what it is that the party restrained is prevented from doing in the period of the continuation.

15.59 The second alternative is also acceptable where the terms of the injunction are not substantially changed, but can be confusing, particularly where an order is continued several times or where the earlier order is detailed and much of it no longer relevant.

15.60 In drafting the new order, consideration should always be given to whether a penal notice should be included. A penal notice is added by the party, not by the court (see paragraphs 16.29 to 16.34).

15.61 It is good practice to recite in the new order the making of any earlier orders, including their dates and by whom they were made.

APPLICATIONS FOR PERMISSION TO SERVE OUT OF THE JURISDICTION

15.62 Applications for permission to serve out of the jurisdiction are usually dealt with on paper, by the assigned Master unless the Master considers a short hearing would be of assistance. Such an application will only be referred to a HCJ in exceptional circumstances. **1A-179**

15.63 Applicants are reminded of the need to comply with the obligation of full and frank disclosure addressed in paragraphs 15.32 to 15.33 above. A failure to comply with this obligation may lead to an order giving permission to serve out of the jurisdiction being set aside regardless of the merits. It will usually be appropriate for the applicant to file a short skeleton argument dealing with the relevant legal issues. For further guidance see paragraphs 4.23 to 4.29.

APPLICATION TO ISSUE PART 8 CLAIM FORM WITHOUT NAMING DEFENDANTS

15.64 CPR 8.2A permits the court to make an order in relation to a Part 8 claim (not a Part 7 claim) entitling the claimant to issue the claim without naming defendants. An order might be appropriate, for example, where the court is asked to make an order to assist executors who are unable to locate beneficiaries named in a will. For further guidance see Chapter 13. **1A-180**

15.65 These applications are often dealt with on paper by the assigned Master. Where the Master considers that a short hearing may be of assistance, in a simple case, they may be willing to deal with it in accordance with the procedure set out at paragraph 15.36 to 15.37 above (Procedural Applications to a Master).

APPLICATIONS TO ISSUE THE CLAIM FORM WITH ANONYMOUS PARTIES

15.66 In some cases the court will permit a claim form to be issued without the claimant and/or the defendant being identified. This is an exceptional order and must be fully justified with evidence. **1A-181**

15.67 An application for such an order should initially be made to a judge on paper. In a simple case the judge may be prepared to deal with such an application on paper. However, most cases are likely to require a short hearing. Only if it is urgent and non-contentious should the application be made to a Master in accordance with the procedure set out at paragraphs 15.36 to 15.37 above (procedural applications to a Master).

15.68 If it is appropriate to make an order preventing a party being identified the applicant may also wish to consider whether to apply under CPR 5.4C (4) for an order preventing a non-party from obtaining the statements of case, or perhaps any document, from the court file without permission. For further guidance see Chapter 3 and Chapter 25.

CHAPTER 16 ORDERS

RESPONSIBILITY FOR PREPARATION AND SERVICE

16.1 Parties are generally responsible for providing the court with an order in a form which may be approved and sealed without amendment. The claimant or the party seeking the order ('the applicant'), as appropriate, will be responsible for providing the order to the court for approval unless the court orders otherwise. **1A-182**

16.2 A nominated party (usually the claimant or applicant) will then be required to serve an order once it has been sealed. An unrepresented party will not generally be nominated as the serving party. Where an order is required to be served personally, the party who seeks that order will be responsible for service.

16.3 The court will send the serving party one sealed copy of the order. It is the responsibility of the serving party to ensure that the text of the order and the court seal are legible in copies served on the other parties.

16.4 A number of editable procedural orders are available on the gov.uk website for the use of parties. See Chancery Forms.

DRAFT ORDERS OTHER THAN THOSE FOLLOWING HEARINGS

16.5 A draft order in the form sought by an applicant must always be filed by CE-File in Word format when an application is filed to enable minor changes to be made without either the court re-typing the order or it being returned to the legal representative for amendment. It must be drafted in accordance with this guidance. **1A-183**

16.6 Only where required by this guidance or requested by the court should a draft order in Word format also be provided by email to the clerk to the relevant High Court Judge ('HCJ') or Insolvency and Companies Court Judge ('ICC Judge').

16.7 In this chapter reference to a HCJ includes a Section 9 Judge and a Deputy HCJ.

DRAFT ORDERS SUBMITTED FOLLOWING HEARINGS

16.8 The responsibility for producing an accurate draft order reflecting in neutral terms the orders made by the court at a hearing will rest with either (a) the claimant, (b) the applicant or (c) the party nominated by the judge. **1A-184**

16.9 If there remains doubt about who bears responsibility for producing a draft order (for example in the case of multiple applications or where no direction is given by the court), it is to be produced by the claimant unless the claimant is a litigant in person, in which case it will be a represented party who will have responsibility. Where all parties are unrepresented, the court will draw up the order.

16.10 The terms of any order made must be noted by the legal representatives present and, in case of doubt about the terms of any order, they must be clarified with the court at the hearing.

16.11 The draft order should be filed on CE-File and sent by email as a Word document to the relevant HCJ's clerk or ICC Judge's clerk within two working days of the hearing (unless otherwise directed) and must be copied to the other parties. For a Master, the Word document should only be filed through CE-File within two working days unless the Master directs otherwise.

16.12 Before filing the draft order, the parties should attempt to agree it. If (exceptionally) there is a genuine problem that the parties think can be resolved with a little extra time, they should communicate with the court to seek a short extension.

16.13 The person lodging the draft should confirm if it is agreed by the other parties. If there are significant differences of view about the correct terms of the order, alternative versions should be recorded on the draft and the judge will determine the points in issue.

16.14 The judge who heard the hearing will settle the terms of the order and give instructions for it to be sealed. It will be then sent by the court to the serving party.

GENERAL CONTENT AND FORMAT OF AN ORDER

1A-185 **16.15** An order must include:

(a) the correct title and number of the proceedings;
(b) the title and name of the judge at the hearing: Mr/Mrs Justice [name]/Master[name]/ICC Judge [name];
(c) if the judge sat in private the words 'sitting in private' should be added after the judge's name;
(d) the date the order was made;
(e) if the order was made at a hearing, the names of the advocates and/or those given permission to address the court;
(f) the order should not recite that the court has read the documents recorded on the court file as having been read. There is no such record.
(g) the service note: see paragraphs 16.20 and 16.21 below;
(h) The order should not include internal references (for example in the footer) or logos.

16.16 Normally all the parties should be listed. There is generally no need to recite statutes, deeds etc in the title.

16.17 On an application without notice there should be a recital of the evidence before the court. Where more than one witness statement or affidavit was read, a list of what was read should usually be set out in a schedule to the order.

16.18 On an application without notice the order must usually include a statement of the right of the parties to make an application to set aside or vary the order under CPR 23.10. For further guidance see paragraph 15.34.

16.19 If the order directs a payment into or out of court, after that direction the words *'as directed in the attached payment/lodgment schedule'* should appear. In such a case a payment or lodgment schedule should be drawn by the Associate.

16.20 Back sheets are no longer used and must not be included. Instead, the names and addresses of the parties to whom the order has been sent, including any reference, should be recorded immediately below the last paragraph of the order in the format shown in the example form of order below. This is referred to below as 'the service note'.

16.21 Where an order is drawn and served by the court the service note will be in a similar format, replacing *'The court has provided a sealed copy of this order to the serving party'* with *'The court has sent sealed copies of this order to:'* followed by the identity of the parties to whom the order has been sent.

EXAMPLE FORM OF ORDER

1A-186 **16.22** Orders should adopt the following format:

IN THE HIGH COURT OF JUSTICE
BUSINESS AND PROPERTY COURTS OF ENGLAND AND WALES
PROPERTY TRUSTS AND PROBATE LIST (ChD)*
**This is an example only. It will vary depending on the appropriate Chancery list and/or sub-list*
MR/MRS JUSTICE [NAME] *or* **MASTER [NAME]** *or* **ICC JUDGE [NAME]**
[DAY, MONTH, YEAR]
[IN THE MATTER OF [*insert any required reference to statute***]]**
[IN THE ESTATE OF [NAME, DECEASED]]

BETWEEN:

[NAME]

Claimant

-and-

(1) [NAME]

(2) [NAME]

Defendants

ORDER

UPON the application of [party] by [notice] dated .....*

[**AND UPON HEARING** [names of the advocates and/or those given permission to address the court] for the Claimant and the first Defendant and the second Defendant in person]

IT IS ORDERED that:

1. ....
2. ....
3. This order shall be served by the Claimant on the Defendants

Service of the order

The court has provided a sealed copy of this order to the serving party:

ABC Solicitors LLP at [address] [reference] (solicitors for the Claimant)

**To be adapted as appropriate. Where, for example, an application has been made by a Part 8 claim form, the recital should read:*

'**UPON** the application of [party] by Part 8 Claim Form dated .....'

An order made following the trial of a Part 7/Part 8 claim should recite:

'**UPON THE TRIAL** of this claim'.

Where a declaration has been made it should normally be the first part of the order which should recite:

' IT IS DECLARED THAT:

1....*followed by:*

AND IT IS ORDERED THAT

UNLESS ORDERS

16.23 These orders are made by the court under CPR 3.1(3) and 3.4(2)(c), which together give the court power to strike out a statement of case without further order if a procedural order it has made is not complied with by a specified date. The order is normally in the following terms: **1A-187**

> 'unless the [party] (*details of procedure to be complied with*) on or before (*time and date*) their/its claim/defence/counterclaim/defence to counterclaim shall be struck out and stand dismissed without further order [and the claimant/counterclaimant shall be entitled to apply for judgment]'

16.24 The party against whom the order is sought will usually be ordered to pay the costs of any application for an unless order.

16.25 This is a serious sanction and will be used sparingly by the court, usually as a last resort. Such an order will rarely be made on paper and/or without notice, except in connection with applications for permission to appeal where there is a persistent failure to comply with procedural requirements.

PERMISSION/REFUSAL OF PERMISSION TO APPEAL

16.26 It is important to include the correct wording in an order following the grant or refusal of permission to appeal. No distinction is now made between interim and final decisions and in general all appeals now lie to the next tier of the judiciary (see Chapter 30). **1A-188**

16.27 All appeals from Masters and ICC Judges, both interim and final, are to the High Court, to be heard by a HCJ, rather than the Court of Appeal, (Table 1 in PD 52A) unless the decision of the ICC Judge was itself made on appeal from the County Court, in which case the appeal will be to the Court of Appeal.

16.28 The order giving or refusing permission to appeal must state:

1. whether an appeal lies from the substantive decision and, if so, to which appeal court, with an indication of the appropriate division of the High Court where the High Court is the appeal court;
2. whether the court gives or refuses permission to appeal; and
3. if refused, the appropriate appeal court (including the appropriate division, where relevant) to which any further application for permission may be made.
4. The form of words to be used in an order is:

   'This is an order from which an appeal lies to [a single judge of the High Court, Chancery Division] [the Court of Appeal]. [Permission to appeal is granted][Permission to appeal is refused].

   A further application for permission may be made to [a single judge] [the Court of Appeal]'. (deleting as appropriate).'

PENAL NOTICES

16.29 If a party considers that enforcement of an order by an order for committal may be needed, the order must be served with a penal notice endorsed upon it. CPR 81.4(2)(e) requires **1A-189**

evidence that any order breached or disobeyed included a penal notice, except where such a notice was inapplicable. The standard form of penal notice is described in CPR 81.2, but any wording to substantially the same effect is sufficient.

16.30 A penal notice is not required in an order that records an undertaking given by a person to the court. Although Part 81 no longer says so expressly, it is not considered to have changed the procedural requirements in this respect.

16.31 It is not necessary to obtain the consent of the court before a penal notice is endorsed on an order *before* service.

16.32 Most orders are now drafted by a party nominated by the court. If the drafting party wishes to include a penal notice in the order to be sealed by the court, it should be added to the draft so that it is part of the sealed order. If the party who is not given responsibility for drafting the order wishes it to contain a penal notice, the terms of the penal notice should be provided to the drafting party.

16.33 It is, however, always open to the party wishing to enforce the order to endorse a penal notice on the copy of the order to be served. It is not essential that the penal notice forms part of the order when it is sealed.

16.34 If the order is being drafted by the court, and the penal notice has not been included in the order, it should be endorsed on the copy of the order to be served.

CONSENT ORDERS (INCLUDING TOMLIN ORDERS)

1A-190 **16.35** Parties can enter into consent orders both in relation to procedural matters and in respect of the substantive relief sought. The substantive relief sought in the body of a consent order must be within the scope of the relief claimed in the claim form; otherwise the court has no jurisdiction to grant it.

16.36 If the parties wish the order to deal with other matters outside the scope of the claim, then an order in 'Tomlin' form may be appropriate (see paragraphs 16.42 to 16.44 below).

16.37 All consent orders, whether procedural or substantive, must be CE-filed. Only if requested by the court or it is necessary for them to be considered urgently (for example where a hearing is imminent) should they also be emailed to the clerk to the relevant HCJ or ICC Judge at the same time as they are filed on CE-File.

16.38 Any applicable court fee must be paid on filing or sending the order, or an appropriate undertaking given by a legal representative that the court fee will be paid within two working days. An order will not be referred for approval until the fee has been paid or an appropriate undertaking given.

16.39 A version signed by the parties or their legal representatives confirming that they consent to an order in those terms must be filed in PDF format, together with a 'clean' copy of the order in Word format. The documents will not be referred for approval unless they comply with the following requirements:

(a) the title and preamble must be in the correct format;
(b) the draft must bear the words 'BY CONSENT' before the words 'IT IS ORDERED THAT';
(c) the word 'draft' or 'minute' must not appear;
(d) the signature provisions must not be included in the Word version of the order;
(e) the draft must specify the party who will serve the order;
(f) a service note must be included in the correct format.

16.40 If a consent order requires amendment because the terms of the order are not approved by the court, the order will normally be returned for re-drafting. If the changes are minor the court may choose to make the necessary amendments and approve the order.

ORDERS FOR A TIME LIMITED STAY OF PROCEEDINGS

1A-191 **16.41** Where the parties seek an order staying a claim during the course of the proceedings they must specify the period of the stay and the trigger for lifting the stay, including the next steps to be undertaken by the parties to notify the court (see for example CH12).

FORM OF TOMLIN ORDER

1A-192 **16.42** All Tomlin Orders must be headed 'Tomlin Order' (not simply 'consent order'). A correct form of Tomlin Order (i.e. where proceedings are stayed on agreed terms scheduled to the order) will include the following provisions after any other necessary recitals:

> ... '**AND UPON** the parties having agreed to the terms set out in [the attached schedule] [a [confidential] agreement] dated........, [copies of which are held by the parties' solicitors/the solicitors for the (*party*)] ('the Agreement') and to the terms of this Order
>
> **BY CONSENT IT IS ORDERED** that
>
> 1. All further proceedings in this claim [and counterclaim/Part 20 claim] be stayed upon the terms set out in the Agreement except for the purposes of enforcing those terms. Each party shall have permission to apply to the court to enforce those terms without the need to bring a new claim.

2. There be no order as to costs [or such other costs order as the parties have agreed]
3. This order shall be served by the [party]
[*Service note etc*]"

16.43 If the parties intend the settlement terms to remain confidential, they should not be filed with the court and the order must clearly identify the agreement (including its date) and where it is held.

16.44 It is not the normal practice when Tomlin Orders are approved for the court to inspect the settlement terms, but it may do so, particularly in claims pursuant to CPR 57. If sight of the settlement terms is requested, they should be sent separately, by email as directed. By approving a Tomlin order the court undertakes no responsibility for the settlement terms and cannot be taken to have approved them.

COPIES OF ORDERS

16.45 Copies of orders may be obtained upon payment of the appropriate fee. **1A-193**

CHAPTER 17 SHORTER AND FLEXIBLE TRIALS SCHEMES

SHORTER TRIALS SCHEME

17.1 The claimant may start a claim in the Shorter Trials Scheme in any of the Business and Property Courts ('B&PCs') if the trial will not exceed 4 days, including judicial reading time and time for preparing and delivering closing submissions, and if the claim is otherwise appropriate for the Scheme: see Civil Procedure Rules ('CPR')Practice Direction ('PD') 57AB (Shorter and Flexible Trials Scheme). **1A-194**

17.2 The aim of the Shorter Trials Scheme is to enable some shorter trials to be tried within a year from the service of the claim form and, so far as sensible, case managed by the designated trial judge.

17.3 A case management conference ('CMC') is fixed for about 12 weeks after acknowledgment of service is due, and then a trial date is fixed for not more than 8 months after the CMC. Statements of case and witness statements are subject to limits in length and there is only a limited disclosure procedure: PD 51U does not apply. Oral expert evidence is limited to permitted issues.

17.4 The Shorter Trials Scheme is particularly suitable for cases where there are only limited factual disputes: see PD 57AB, paragraph 2.2. It has been successfully used in intellectual property disputes that are not suitable for the Intellectual Property Enterprise Court but may be equally suitable for other types of case.

17.5 A party may apply for a claim to be transferred into or out of the Shorter Trials Scheme: see paragraphs 2.9 to 2.15 of PD 57AB. The application must be made promptly and, in any event, not later than the first CMC. The court may, of its own initiative, suggest that a case be transferred into the Shorter Trials Scheme.

17.6 The court hearing the CMC and pre-trial review ('PTR') will ensure that the case is sensibly capable of trial within the 4 days allowed. The appropriateness of the allocation to the Shorter Trials Scheme needs to be kept under review and the court can, when appropriate, transfer a claim out of the scheme: *EMFC Loan Syndications LLP v The Resort Group plc, Practice Note* [2021] EWCA Civ 844; [2022] 1 WLR 717 at [111].

17.7 Specific procedural rules apply within the Shorter Trials Scheme: see paragraphs 2.16 onwards of PD 57AB.

FLEXIBLE TRIALS SCHEME

17.8 The Flexible Trials Scheme applies to a claim started in any of the B&PCs: see paragraph 3 of PD 57AB. The aim of the Flexible Trials Scheme is to enable the parties by agreement to adopt a procedure to try their dispute, or identified issues in it, with limited disclosure and oral evidence. **1A-195**

17.9 Unlike the Shorter Trials Scheme, a claim may not be issued under the Flexible Trials Scheme: the parties have to agree after issue to adopt it. There are standard Flexible Trial directions that apply, subject to variation agreed by the parties: paragraph 3.9 of PD 57AB. These are designed to shorten the process of preparing for and conducting a trial. The disclosure process is limited and PD 51U does not apply.

17.10 If the parties agree to use the Flexible Trials Scheme, they should inform the court in advance of the first CMC: see Chapter 6. The court will then direct that the Flexible Trials Scheme procedure or any variation of it that the parties have agreed will apply, unless there is good reason to order otherwise.

17.11 The parties may agree to use the Flexible Trials Scheme to have identified issues determined on the basis of written evidence and submissions: paragraph 3.4 of PD 57AB.

17.12 The Flexible Trials Scheme has been little used in practice. It is well suited to non-confrontational litigation where parties agree that there is an issue or issues that need to be resolved quickly and efficiently. It may also be used as an alternative to directing that a Part 8 claim continue as a Part 7 claim, where there are limited but important factual issues in dispute: see paragraph 13.4 of Chapter 13.

CHAPTER 18 BUSINESS LIST (BL)

GENERAL

1A-196 **18.1** The types of dispute which are suitable for the Business List are numerous and include all types of business dispute for which there is no specific list as set out in Appendix F.

18.2 Claims in the Business List can be commenced using the procedures within either Part 7 or Part 8 of the Civil Procedure Rules ('CPR') depending on the nature of the claim and the remedies sought. The general procedures set out in the CPR, its Practice Directions ('PDs') and this Guide should be followed in all Business List claims issued in the Business and Property Courts.

18.3 There are two specialist sub-lists:

(a) The Financial Services and Regulatory List (FS) (Appendix F) and,
(b) The Pensions List (PE) (Chapter 26)

18.4 This chapter provides particular guidance in relation to partnership claims and Business List rectification claims.

PARTNERSHIP

1A-197 **18.5** This guidance relates to claims concerning partnerships under the Partnership Act 1890.

18.6 Partnership disputes which may require a trial include (but are not limited to) disputes as to:

(a) the existence of a partnership (whether it is claimed that there never was a partnership or that the partnership is still continuing and has not been dissolved);
(b) the terms of the partnership (e.g. as to the profit sharing ratios);
(c) whether assets constitute partnership assets;
(d) the true status of a partner;
(e) allegations of fraudulent misappropriation of partnership assets;
(f) whether a '*Syers v Syers*' order should be granted (an order that the majority partners buy out the minority on the dissolution of a partnership);
(g) liability for annuities;
(h) partnership indemnities or contributions.

18.7 Allocation of claims for trial as between Masters and High Court Judges ('HCJs') will be decided in accordance with the guidance in Chapter 3 and Chapter 6.

18.8 The taking of accounts will typically follow on from a trial concerning issues of liability or deciding matters of principle, such as those outlined above. Partnership accounts and related issues (including following a trial) will usually be undertaken by a Master.

18.9 In claims for or arising out of the dissolution of a partnership where the only matters in dispute between the partners are matters of accounting, there will be no trial of the claim. The court will, if appropriate, make a summary order under PD 24 paragraph 6 for the taking of an account by the Master (see PD 40A Accounts, Inquiries etc.).

18.10 The expense of taking an account in court may be disproportionate to the amount at stake. Partnership claims are often suitable for alternative dispute resolution (see Chapter 10). Parties are strongly encouraged to consider referring disputes on accounts to a jointly instructed accountant for determination, acting as an expert or an arbitrator.

18.11 Where resolution without the court's intervention is not possible, the parties must work with the court to identify the points in dispute and how each issue is best determined.

18.12 In many cases and in order to reduce costs, it may still be appropriate for the parties to invite the Master to determine discrete factual issues in advance of the taking of an account, e.g. issues as to terms of the partnership or assets comprised in it. The court will not simply order accounts and inquiries without identifying the issues.

18.13 At any case management conference, it will be particularly important to identify the issues to be determined before an effective account or inquiry can be made.

18.14 See Chapter 29 (Accounts and Inquiries), paragraphs 29.10 to 29.12, which provide guidance on directions for the taking of an account and the use of a Scott Schedule to identify the issues between the parties and facilitate early discussion about how the issues may be resolved. Cost budgeting for accounts and inquiries is considered at paragraph 29.16 to 29.17 of Chapter 29.

18.15 The parties should seek to agree a way in which the value of the partnership business and assets can be preserved. If this is not possible, the court has power to appoint a receiver and manager and confer powers on them to manage the ongoing partnership business where it considers it necessary to do so (see Chapter 14 paragraphs 14.88 to 14.91). The functions of a receiver in a partnership claim are, however, usually limited. Unlike a company liquidator, it is not the receiver's duty to wind up the partnership. The receiver's primary function is to get in the debts and preserve the assets pending winding up by the court. The receiver has no power of sale without the permission of the court.

RECTIFICATION

18.16 Claims for rectification of documents are assigned to the Chancery Division by Schedule 1 to the Senior Courts Act 1981. **1A-198**

18.17 The court may in appropriate circumstances rectify the following classes of documents.

(a) Documents made by agreement between two or more parties, such as contracts. The scope of this remedy is quite general, although parties should be aware that it does not apply to certain specialised types of documents such as the articles of association of companies. Claims for rectification of consensual documents should be issued in the Business List.

(b) Voluntary documents, such as trusts (including pension trusts) - see Chapter 25 and Chapter 26. Claims to rectify pension documents should be issued in the Pensions sub-list of the Business List. Claims to rectify trust documents should be issued in the Property, Trusts and Probate List.

(c) Wills. This power is granted by section 20 of the Administration of Justice Act 1982, and is dealt with in Chapter 23 (Probate) and CPR 57. Claims to rectify testamentary documents should be issued in the Property, Trusts and Probate List.

18.18 Rectification is an equitable, discretionary remedy, and it has been said that it is a jurisdiction which is to be treated with caution: see *Racal Group Services Ltd v Ashmore* [1995] STC 1151.

18.19 Rectification as a remedy is distinct from the processes of construction and implication of terms and from the remedy of rescission, and parties should consider carefully before issuing proceedings whether and to what extent they need to seek the remedy of rectification (as opposed to some other remedy).

18.20 Rectification claims will be case managed and determined by a Master save in exceptional cases. In particular, the Master will only refer to a HCJ a claim which is consented to or not opposed if it raises issues of particular complexity or difficulty.

18.21 The parties should give careful consideration to whether the claim should be brought under the Part 7 or Part 8 procedure: attention is drawn to Chapter 13 (Part 8 Proceedings).

18.22 Where a claim is brought under Part 8, there will be no particulars of claim. The claimant should therefore consider whether to prepare a document which summarises the claim to be provided to the court and the parties with the claim form. This document, or the draft particulars of claim in an anticipated Part 7 claim, may usefully be provided to other potential parties in advance of issuing the claim in order to establish whether they will in clear cases not oppose a summary judgment application (in a Part 7 case) or a disposal application (in a Part 8 case).

18.23 It is not the practice of the court to make an order for rectification by default or by consent or without a hearing save in exceptional cases.

18.24 In all cases, even if unopposed, the court will not make an order without being satisfied that it is justified by the evidence. The court will therefore wish to scrutinise carefully the changes that are proposed and the reasons for them.

18.25 The evidence in support must establish the common or unilateral mistake on which the claim in rectification is based even where the parties consent to, or do not oppose, the claim. The court may direct that oral evidence be given even where all relevant parties consent (or do not oppose), with or without cross-examination. The court may also wish to hear argument on all relevant matters and may direct that arguments against the remedy are put, including if appropriate by directing that a party take such a role.

18.26 If there are fiscal consequences which will arise from the changes to the document, HMRC (or any appropriate foreign tax body or bodies) should be notified, preferably before the claim is issued, and invited to confirm whether they wish to be joined as a party to the claim in order to make representations. The evidence in support of the claim should include such notification, and the position of HMRC (or any appropriate foreign tax body or bodies).

18.27 Claimants (and any parties agreeing or consenting to the claim) are encouraged to consider carefully the form of order sought in advance of issuing the claim. The court is likely to wish to make the minimum possible changes in order to rectify the document in question. Claimants (and any parties agreeing or consenting to the claim) should also consider in advance of issuing the claim how the document in respect of which rectification is sought is intended be treated (i.e. whether the order will be indorsed on the document to be rectified, and, if so, how).

18.28 When preparing *trial* witness statements in a rectification claim, careful thought needs to be given to compliance with (or dispensation from) the requirements of PD 57AC. This is a particularly important consideration in rectification claims where the passage of time or the nature of the rectification sought may mean that there is no witness able to give evidence as to the relevant events and/or where it is necessary for a witness to express a belief as to whether there has been a mistake and/or to explain what happened.

18.29 In all rectification claims whether proceeding under Part 7 or Part 8 the parties should consider whether it may be of assistance to the court (and the parties) in addition to any witness evidence to seek a direction for a narrative chronology with key documents. If such an order is made the parties should seek to identify and agree the key documents and a narrative chronology with reference where appropriate to those key documents. Where there is disagreement, the narrative chronology should set out each of the parties' positions making clear where there is a divergence between them on a particular issue. A bundle containing that narrative chronology and the key documents should be made available to the judge by any PTR and/or provided with skeleton arguments for trial or final hearing.

18.30 For further guidance in relation to claims for rectification of trusts or pension documents see Chapter 25 and Chapter 26.

CHAPTER 19 COMPETITION LIST (CHD)

INTRODUCTION

1A-199 **19.1** In this Guide, "competition law" has the same meaning as in paragraph 2(1) of Schedule 8A to the Competition Act 1998 and "competition claim" has the same meaning as paragraph 2(2) of Schedule 8A of the Competition Act 1998.

19.2 Proceedings before the High Court relating to the application of competition law must be brought either in the Competition List in the Chancery Division or in the Commercial Court, if they fall within CPR 58.1(2). The transfer of competition claims is governed by rule 30.8 of the Civil Procedure Rules ('CPR') and Practice Direction ('PD') 30.

19.3 High Court Judges ('HCJs') assigned to the Chancery Division and some Commercial Court HCJs also sit in the Competition Appeal Tribunal ('CAT') in the capacity of a chairman of the CAT. This Guide discusses the jurisdiction of the CAT only insofar as it is relevant to the transfer of competition law claims between the High Court and the CAT. Further information about the CAT is available on its website at *www.catribunal.org.uk.*

NATURE OF COMPETITION LAW CLAIMS

1A-200 **19.4** Claims relating to the application of competition law brought in the Chancery Division typically take the form of injunction applications seeking to restrain alleged breaches of competition law, or private actions for damages for alleged breaches of competition law.

19.5 Private actions for damages may be characterised as 'follow-on' claims, 'stand-alone' claims or a hybrid of both types of claims. So-called 'follow-on' claims follow on from a pre-existing finding which is binding upon the court, by a competition authority (or by a court or tribunal on appeal from a competition authority), that there has been an infringement of competition law. In contrast, 'stand-alone' claims are claims in which the court is asked to make a finding of infringement. Claims that include allegations of infringement that 'follow on' from a decision and some that are 'stand-alone' are referred to as 'hybrid claims'.

19.6 Competition law claims are by their nature complex and frequently involve consideration of economic or technical issues.

PRACTICE DIRECTION – COMPETITION LAW

1A-201 **19.7** The Practice Direction on Competition Law (Claims relating to the application of Chapters I and II of Part I of the Competition Act 1998) sets out certain requirements in relation to competition law claims that raise Chapter I or Chapter II issues.

19.8 In addition to transfers of competition law claims (discussed in further detail below), the Competition PD covers the following matters relevant to claims raising Chapter I or II issues:

- (a) The requirement to serve a copy of the statement of case on the Competition and Markets Authority at the same time as it is served on the other parties to the claim; and
- (b) The procedure by which a competition authority may submit observations to the court on issues relating to the application of Chapter I or II.

19.9 Claims that raise Chapter I or Chapter II issues must be issued in the High Court in London and will be assigned to the Competition List (ChD) except where the claim falls within CPR 58.1(2), when it may be issued in the Commercial Court.

19.10 A competition law claim may be issued in a B&PC District Registry pursuant to PD 57AA 2.5(2). Such claims should be referred to a B&PC Section 9 Judge on issue for triage.

TRANSFER OF COMPETITION LAW CLAIMS TO THE COMPETITION LIST FROM OTHER DIVISIONS OF THE HIGH COURT OR THE COUNTY COURT

1A-202 **19.11** Where a party's statement of case raises an issue relating to the application of competition law under Chapter I or Chapter II of Part I of the Competition Act 1998 and the claim has not been commenced in the ChD B&PCs London (or, where applicable, the Commercial Court), the claim **must** be transferred to the Competition List (ChD) at the Royal Courts of Justice (CPR 30.8). However, where CPR 30.8 (4) applies a party may apply for the claim to be transferred to the Commercial Court but if the application is refused the claim must be transferred to the Competition List.

19.12 The claim, or part of the claim, may subsequently be transferred to another court if the issue relating to the application of competition law has been resolved, or the court considers that the claim or part of the claim to be transferred does not involve any issue relating to the application of competition law.

19.13 In an appropriate case, competition law claims may be transferred between the Competition List and the Commercial Court. The High Court may order a transfer on its own initiative or on application by the claimant or defendant. In accordance with CPR 30.5(4), such an order may only be made with the consent of the Chancellor and the Judge in Charge of the Commercial Court.

TRANSFER OF COMPETITION LAW CLAIMS TO OR FROM THE CAT

19.14 In an appropriate case, competition claims may, in whole or in part, be transferred from the Competition List to the CAT pursuant to section 16(1) of the Enterprise Act 2002 and the Section 16 Enterprise Act 2002 Regulations 2015 (S.I. 2015 No. 1643), and/or section 16(4) of the Enterprise Act 2002 (CPR 30.8 and PD 30, paragraph 8). When deciding whether to make an order, the court must consider all the circumstances of the case including the wishes of the parties. Barling J in *Sainsbury's Supermarkets Ltd v MasterCard Incorporated and Others* [2015] EWHC 3472 (Ch) considered the reasons why such a transfer might be appropriate. **1A-203**

19.15 In *Unwired Planet International Ltd v Huawei Co Ltd* [2016]EWHC 958 (Pat), Birss J explained that where not all issues in the case could be transferred to the CAT, the extent to which dividing the issues may cause difficulties in the proceedings was an important factor. In *Sainsbury's Supermarkets Ltd v Mastercard Incorporated and Others* [2018] EWCA Civ 1536, the Court of Appeal said at paragraph 357 that competition claims 'should in normal circumstances be transferred to the CAT'.

19.16 The CAT may, in an appropriate case, direct that all or part of a claim before it be transferred to the Competition List, pursuant to section 16(5) of the Enterprise Act 2002 (PD 30, paragraphs 8.7-8.9). Upon transfer the claim will be listed for a case management conference or costs and case management conference ('CMC' / 'CCMC') before a HCJ, Section 9 Judge or Deputy HCJ. For this purpose, the claimant should take out a listing appointment by emailing Judges Listing in the ChD B&PCs London. The parties should provide a time estimate which should include a realistic time estimate for both pre-reading and the hearing (which should as far as possible be agreed) and dates to avoid (See Chapter 14).

19.17 In all Competition List claims issued in the ChD B&PCs London, when a CMC / CCMC is to be listed consideration should be given as to whether the issues raised are of sufficient specialist complexity that it is appropriate to seek to have the claim docketed to a specialist HCJ for further case management. The parties are referred to the discussion of docketing in Chapter 3 for further guidance.

DISCLOSURE IN RELATION TO COMPETITION LAW CLAIMS

19.18 PD 51U does not apply to competition claims unless otherwise ordered. Specific rules apply to some aspects of disclosure. These are set out in PD 31C and in many cases include the need to make any relevant competition authority a party to any application for disclosure. A failure to take the relevant procedural steps before the first CMC / CCMC may result in sanctions. Disclosure in competition law claims is otherwise subject to CPR Pt 31 and the parties to such claims are encouraged to further the overriding objective by adopting a co-operative, constructive and sensible approach. **1A-204**

CHAPTER 20 FINANCIAL LIST

20.1 The Financial List is a single specialist list defined in Part 63A of the Civil Procedure Rules ('CPR') and Practice Direction ('PD') 63AA. Claims in the Financial List may be commenced in either the Chancery Division in London or the Commercial Court. **1A-205**

20.2 There is a separate Financial List Guide, which is the primary source of guidance for proceedings in the Financial List. The Financial List Guide states that, for matters it does not address (and which are not dealt with in CPR 63A or PD 63AA), the Admiralty and Commercial Court Guide will apply. For any other issues not dealt with in those sources, this Guide will apply.

CHAPTER 21 INSOLVENCY AND COMPANIES LIST (ICL)

INTRODUCTION AND APPLICATION OF THE GUIDE

21.1 The Insolvency and Companies List ('ICL') is a specialist list within the Chancery Division. It comprises two sub-lists: 'Insolvency' and 'Companies'. The work of the ICL covers both corporate and individual insolvency pursuant to the Insolvency Act 1986 ('IA 1986') and the Insolvency (England and Wales) Rules 2016 ('IR 2016'), as well as matters of company law outside the insolvency context, such as shareholder disputes, in claims or petitions under the Companies Act 2006 ('CA 2006'). It also includes claims for the disqualification of company directors under the Company Directors Disqualification Act 1986 ('CDDA 1986'). **1A-206**

21.2 Proceedings are usually commenced in the ICL by petition, by an application under the IA 1986 or IR 2016 (an 'IA Application') or by a claim form pursuant to Part 8 of the Civil Procedure Rules ('CPR'), depending on the nature of the proceedings. Some proceedings under the CA 2006 are required to be commenced under Part 7 of the CPR; however, more commonly, Part 7 claims are not commenced in the ICL but will be transferred to the ICL from another list.

21.3 In the ICL in the ChD B&PCs London, Chapters 3 to 6 will not apply and the Insolvency and Companies Court Judge ('ICC Judge') will give directions as to the future conduct of all such proceedings, whether issued in the ICL or transferred to it.

21.4 However, in the B&PC District Registries, where a Part 7 claim is issued in the ICL, or a Part 8 claim is ordered to proceed as a Part 7 claim, Chapters 3 to 6 will apply unless modified by any local guidance.

21.5 In all cases, however, statements of case including points of claim, points of defence or points of reply should comply with the guidance in Chapter 4 of this Guide.

21.6 The remaining parts of this Guide apply to proceedings commenced in or transferred to the ICL as relevant, subject to the modifications in this chapter.

THE JUDGES

1A-207 **21.7** In London, the judges who hear insolvency or companies cases are HCJs, Section 9 Judges, Deputy HCJs, ICC Judges and Deputy ICC Judges. In this chapter "HCJ" includes Section 9 Judges and Deputy HCJs unless specified otherwise.

21.8 As explained in Chapter 30, both HCJs and ICC Judges hear appeals from the County Court on corporate insolvency matters, as well as exercising first instance jurisdiction in respect of applications and trials. ICC Judges also hear appeals in respect of claims under the CA 2006.

21.9 In B&PC District Registries, insolvency or companies work will be assigned between the visiting Chancery HCJs, Section 9 Judges and specialist B&PC District Judges as part of their general Chancery work. The allocation of work in the B&PC District Registries between judges will be a matter of local practice. For any local guidance, follow the links in Appendix C.

COURT RULES AND PRACTICE DIRECTIONS

1A-208 **21.10** Insolvency proceedings, whether personal or corporate, are governed by the IR 2016, as amended. The CPR apply as provided for by Rule 12.1, IR 2016. Those provisions are supplemented by the Practice Direction on Insolvency Proceedings (IPD). The IPD provides further general guidance and explains the requirements for particular applications.

21.11 Claims under the CDDA 1986 have their own prescribed rules, namely the Insolvent Companies (Disqualification of Unfit Directors) Proceedings Rules 1987 (SI 1987/2023), as amended. The CPR will apply to such claims, except when inconsistent with these rules. Regard should also be had to the Practice Direction: Directors Disqualification Proceedings.

21.12 Unfair prejudice petitions under section 994 CA 2006 are governed by the Companies (Unfair Prejudice Applications) Proceedings Rules 2009 (SI 2009/2469), as amended. The CPR apply, except when inconsistent with these rules or the CA 2006. Attention is drawn to PD 49B, which warns against seeking alternative winding up relief as a matter of course, and requires the petitioner in a contributory's petition (where the relief sought includes a winding up order) to indicate whether the petitioner consents or objects to a validation order under section 127 IA 1986 in the standard form and makes consequential provision.

21.13 The CPR apply to all other companies cases. Attention is drawn to PD 49A, which sets out certain requirements for applications under companies legislation generally and also specific requirements in particular cases.

21.14 Reference should also be made to PD 57AA - Business and Property Courts.

21.15 The distribution of business between the ChD B&PCs London, the B&PC District Registries and their associated County Court hearing centres, the County Court at Central London, Specialist County Court hearing centres for non-local business and County Court hearing centres with insolvency jurisdiction is set out in paragraphs 3.6 and 3.7 of the IPD. The County Court hearing centres not located at B&PCs which are specialist for the purposes of the IPD are currently Brighton, Croydon, Medway, Preston and Romford.

ISSUING PROCEEDINGS AND TRANSFER OF RELATED CLAIMS

1A-209 **21.16** In order to start proceedings it is necessary to file a petition, an IA Application or a claim form. This cannot be done without payment of the required fee, unless the relevant party has obtained remission of fees. A fee is also payable on filing an interim application within proceedings.

21.17 A file will be created when proceedings are started. Cases will be opened electronically using the CE-File. Electronic filing of documents is compulsory for parties with legal representation and may be used by unrepresented parties. Attention is drawn to PD 51O of the CPR with regard to the operation of the electronic filing system. The CE-File can be accessed online through the HMCTS E-Filing service for citizens and professionals webpage.

21.18 Requests to inspect the court file are made in insolvency proceedings by application under Rule 12.39, IR 2016 and, in company matters, under CPR 5.

21.19 It sometimes happens that a party to proceedings in the ICL will issue proceedings in another list of the B&PCs that are closely related to the proceedings in the ICL. Such proceedings usually relate to the same dispute and feature the same parties, or some of them.

21.20 The parties should consider carefully whether the substance of the claim indicates that one list should be preferred to another for the future conduct of the claims and, if so, lodge a consent order for transfer in the list out of which transfer is sought as soon as possible. Where consent is not possible and a party considers that both sets of proceedings should be heard in the same list, this should be raised at the first hearing in time when either claim comes before the court and, at the latest, at the first case management conference in time.

21.21 The bundle for that hearing should include the statements of case and other relevant documents in both sets of proceedings, to enable the ICC Judge or Master (or District Judge outside London) to consider whether to make an order for transfer of the proceedings into the same list for effective case management.

21.22 The party who starts the proceedings is responsible for serving them on every other party.

EVIDENCE

21.23 The parties should note that PD 57AC - Trial Witness Statements in the Business and Property Courts applies to Part 8 claims, unfair prejudice petitions under section 994 CA 2006 and a contributory's just and equitable winding up petition under section 122(1)(g) IA 1986. (For further guidance, including exclusions, see Chapter 8 and PD 57AC paragraph 1.3.) **1A-210**

21.24 It does not apply, unless otherwise ordered, to an application for an order under the IA 1986 (other than a contributory's just and equitable winding up petition, as above), under the IR 2016, or under certain other insolvency provisions. Nor does it apply to a claim made under the CA 2006 listed in Part II of PD 49A or applications for an order under Part 26A CA 2006.

21.25 There are other exceptions and reference should be made to PD 57AC accordingly. Where the evidence in support of proceedings to which PD 57AC applies is necessarily of a formal and technical nature, an application can be made to dispense with some or all or the requirements of that practice direction.

DISTRIBUTION OF BUSINESS BETWEEN JUDGES

PERSONAL AND CORPORATE INSOLVENCY

21.26 Paragraph 3 of the IPD sets out the level of judge required to hear certain applications and the criteria for transfer between levels of judge. **1A-211**

COMPANIES (NON-INSOLVENCY)

21.27 The ChD B&PCs London, the B&PC District Registries and the County Court have power to hear all non-insolvency corporate matters unless otherwise provided for in the CPR. In the ChD B&PCs London all shareholder disputes, schemes of arrangement, capital reductions. **1A-212**

21.28 If a derivative claim brought under sections 261-264 CA 2006 by a shareholder/member of a company in respect of a cause of action vested in the company is made in the ChD B&PCs London or in the B&PC District Registries, then the application for permission to bring the derivative claim must be decided by a HCJ. Reference should be made to PD 19C as to the practice of the court.

LISTING OF HEARINGS

21.29 Hearings before a HCJ will be listed as part of the general listing jurisdiction of the Chancery Judges' Listing Office ('Judges' Listing') (addressed further in Chapter 12, Chapter 14 and Chapter 15 of this Guide). **1A-213**

21.30 Listing before an ICC Judge will take place as directed by the court. Listing queries in relation to ICC Judges should be directed to a member of ICL listing team. Listing of cases outside London will take place in accordance with local practice.

21.31 ICC Judges will ordinarily hear matters of up to 10 days' duration but longer hearings may sometimes be accommodated. Queries in relation to any hearings taking place before an ICC Judge should be directed to ICC Judges' Hearings at *rolls.icl.hearings1@justice.gov.uk*.

21.32 Bankruptcy and winding up petitions are listed for hearing in a general list in the first instance. These hearings take place in person.

21.33 Unfair prejudice petitions made for relief under section 994 CA 2006 have automatic directions that will be sent to the parties by the court on issuing the petition.

21.34 For all other matters before an ICC Judge, the listing team will list according to a time estimate provided by the issuing party and, if no time estimate is provided, it is likely that an initial hearing of 15 minutes will be listed for directions. Where possible, the parties should seek to agree directions before issue and file a consent order with the documents filed for issue.

21.35 The court may direct the filing of listing certificates before a final hearing or trial is listed and will list the case for hearing at a non-attendance pre-trial review, at which the court will consider the documents and the listing certificates filed by the parties and give appropriate directions. The ICC listing certificate form appears as Schedule 1 to this chapter. If the parties consider that an attended pre-trial review may be necessary, they should seek a direction for one when case management directions are given. The listing team may make use of a trial window if appropriate but trials and final hearings before ICC Judges will usually be directed to be listed on the first available date after completion of all other procedural steps.

21.36 The ICC Judges maintain an ICC Judges' Applications List in which urgent applications may be made (see paragraphs 21.44 to 21.53). This is separate from the ChD B&PCs London Judge's Applications List addressed further in Chapter 15.

21.37 Follow the links in Appendix C for any guidance issued in the B&PC District Registries in respect of local listing arrangements and applications lists.

COSTS AND CASE MANAGEMENT

1A-214 **21.38** Case management directions will usually be given at the first hearing of the proceedings, except in the case of unfair prejudice petitions where standard directions are automatically given by the court when the petition is issued. Parties should seek to agree directions in advance of the hearing and, if agreed, these can be submitted in advance of the hearing so that, if approved, the hearing may be vacated.

21.39 Costs management under CPR 3 and PD 3E does not usually apply to proceedings in the ICL but is routinely ordered for unfair prejudice petitions. In other cases, the court may make provision for the preparation of budgets and costs management if it sees fit. A party seeking costs management should request it at the first opportunity.

DISCLOSURE

1A-215 **21.40** PD 51U - Disclosure Pilot for the Business and Property Courts applies to proceedings in the ICL to the extent set out therein. Petitions and IA Applications do not constitute 'statements of case' for the purposes of the practice direction and so many of the triggers for a step to be taken under it do not arise. In general, therefore, the obligation to provide Initial or Extended disclosure does not arise unless otherwise ordered. Such an order is made on issue of unfair prejudice petitions and the points of claim, points of defence and points of reply should be treated as statements of case for the purposes of the practice direction. Further guidance on disclosure, including the process of Initial and Extended Disclosure, can be found in Chapter 7.

INTERIM APPLICATIONS AND IA APPLICATIONS

1A-216 **21.41** For interim applications in proceedings under the Companies Acts (or related legislation) governed by the CPR, Chapter 14 should be followed, except that references to a Master should be construed as a reference to an ICC Judge and the first two sentences of paragraph 14.7 do not apply.

21.42 In IA Applications (whether applications starting proceedings or interim applications in insolvency proceedings), Chapter 14 should be followed except that -

(a) Applications will be made in accordance with the IR 2016 and, in the case of any inconsistency between the IR 2016 or the IPD and this Guide, the provisions of the Rules or IPD must be followed. This is particularly relevant to allocation of cases to different levels of the judiciary and the period of notice that must be given to the respondent.

(b) The first two sentences of paragraph 14.7 and paragraphs 14.27, 14.44 and 14.76 do not apply. Applications will be listed for an initial hearing of 15 minutes before an ICC Judge unless the applicant requests a longer hearing, directions for the conduct of the case have been agreed and filed with the application, the case is appropriate for release to a HCJ or the court otherwise directs. The applicant should attempt to agree directions with the other parties before issuing the application.

21.43 The guidance in relation to applications to the HCJs' Applications List in paragraphs 15.1 to 15.10 and paragraphs 15.13 to 15.61 of Chapter 15 apply to applications to HCJs in ICL cases. The provisions relating to applications to Masters in Chapter 15 do not apply. Urgent and without notice applications to ICC Judges are dealt with below.

THE ICC JUDGES' APPLICATIONS LIST

1A-217 **21.44** The ICC Judges maintain an applications list for urgent applications. It takes place on Thursdays and Fridays of each week and every other Monday. The ICC Judges' listing team should be contacted if an urgent application needs to be heard on any other day.

21.45 The ICC Judges' Applications List operates in the same way as the HCJs' Applications List (see Chapter 15). Applications that may be brought in the ICC Interim Applications List may also be heard in the HCJs' Applications List if it is not possible to accommodate an urgent hearing before an ICC Judge or if the nature of the application warrants it.

21.46 The ICC Judges' Applications List sits in person in the Rolls Building unless, at the discretion of the ICC Judge hearing the ICC Judges' Applications List, an alternative format is considered appropriate.

21.47 If the applicant considers that an alternative format may be appropriate they should file a letter on CE-File setting out brief reasons why they consider that the alternative format is appropriate or necessary when contacting the ICC Judges' listing team. If the court directs that the application should proceed as a remote or hybrid hearing the applicant should prepare for and conduct the hearing in accordance with the provisions of Appendix Z as modified by any directions from the ICC Judge or as appropriate for the urgency of the application.

21.48 The ICC Judge's Applications List is used to hear applications for:
(a) administration orders;
(b) urgent injunctions to restrain presentation of a petition to wind up a company or to restrain advertisement of such a petition;
(c) appointment of an interim receiver under section 286 IA 1986;
(d) appointment of a provisional liquidator under section 135 IA 1986;
(e) search and seizure orders pursuant to section 365 IA 1986;
(f) validation orders; and
(g) other orders that might, depending on the circumstances, be urgently required, such as those made pursuant to section 125 CA 2006.

21.49 Unless otherwise directed a certificate of urgency is required, which must be signed by counsel or other advocate appearing or by a litigant acting in person. The form of the certificate should be as follows: '*I hereby certify that this is urgent business, and cannot await a hearing before the ICC Judge in its due turn, because [specify reasons]. [signed] [dated].*' Where practicable, the certificate should be included in the application notice.

21.50 Parties appearing in the ICC Judges' Applications List should report to the ICC Judges' clerks on the first floor of the Rolls Building before 10:30 am if the hearing is taking place in person. The ICC Judges will work from bundles provided by the applicant and not from CE-File. Bundles and skeleton arguments complying with Appendix X and Appendix Y should be provided to the ICC Judges' clerks no later than 10am on the day before the hearing unless otherwise directed. These should be CE-Filed and provided to ICC Judges' Hearings at *rolls.icl.hearings1@justice.gov.uk* (or the ICC Judge's clerk, if known). Paper bundles must not be provided unless requested.

21.51 The applications will be called on together. The ICC Judge will go through the list and ask whether the hearing is effective and for a time estimate. The ICC Judge will then decide the order in which to hear the applications.

21.52 Applications with a time estimate of more than two hours (including pre-reading time, judgment and consequential arguments) are not usually suitable for the ICC Judges' Applications List and will generally be listed by order, that is to say listed for a longer hearing on a fixed time and date.

21.53 For guidance on preparation for and hearing of urgent applications in the B&PC District Registries, follow the links in Appendix C.

WITHOUT NOTICE APPLICATIONS

21.54 Paragraphs 15.43 to 15.62 of Chapter 15 apply to without notice applications to ICC Judges as if the reference to the assigned Master were a reference to an ICC Judge. **1A-218**

APPLICATIONS FOR VALIDATION ORDERS

21.55 A validation order is a court order which allows a company to continue trading or a debtor to deal with their property notwithstanding a winding up petition/bankruptcy petition being made against the applicant. Section 127 IA 1986 is applicable in relation to a company and section 284 IA 1986 is applicable to an individual debtor. **1A-219**

21.56 It is imperative that the provisions for validation orders as set down in paragraphs 9.11 and 12.8 of the IPD are strictly complied with in order to allow the court to deal with the application in a timely manner. If those provisions are not complied with, the application will need to be adjourned to another day and a costs sanction may be imposed.

THE WINDING UP COURT

21.57 The Winding Up Court sits in person at the Rolls Building each Wednesday during term time. The court deals with a large number of cases in a short timeframe and it will usually be inappropriate to file a skeleton or a bundle for the hearing of a winding up petition. The court will have before it the winding up petition and verifying statement and the judge's directions from any previous hearing. Where, exceptionally, a bundle or additional document is essential it must be lodged before 12 noon on the Monday of the week of the hearing at the latest or it is unlikely to reach the judge. The Winding Up Court is not the proper forum for extended argument or prolonged consideration of documents, and the costs of preparation of unnecessary documents or bundles are likely to be disallowed. **1A-220**

21.58 The City Law School's Company Insolvency Pro Bono Scheme (CO.IN) was set up in 2015 to provide free legal advice and representation to assist litigants in person (including a company or corporation that is not represented by a lawyer) in the Winding Up Court in the Rolls Building. Further guidance in relation to CO.IN may be found at Appendix H.

21.59 It should be noted that a company must be represented by a barrister or solicitor with a right of audience, or by a director or an employee of the company duly authorised by the board of directors, to whom the court gives permission to be heard. Evidence of such authorisation must be supplied, except where the company is represented by its sole director.

21.60 Petitions will be listed to be heard 'not before' a certain time and will be heard in turn. If, exceptionally, the court requires further submissions or evidence, the ICC Judge may direct that the petition be taken 'second time around', which means that the petition will be put to the back of that day's winding up list.

21.61 Applications to rescind winding up orders are heard in the Winding Up Court once all the petitions have been heard. A bundle and skeleton arguments complying with Appendix X and Appendix Y are required.

21.62 Winding up petitions are also heard by District Judges in the B&PC District Registries, usually on a fortnightly or monthly basis. For any guidance on how they are listed follow the links in Appendix C.

GENERAL PROVISIONS AS TO HEARINGS BEFORE AN ICC JUDGE

1A-221 **21.63** Accurate time estimates must be given for all hearings, including for judicial pre-reading. If a time estimate proves inadequate it is likely that a hearing will be adjourned and a costs sanction applied.

21.64 Hearings with a time estimate of half a day or less (2.5 hours) (and no more than 90 mins pre-reading) will take place remotely unless the court orders otherwise. Hearings with a time estimate of over half a day (and/or more than 90 mins pre-reading) will be heard in person unless the court orders otherwise. If the parties consider that an alternative format is more appropriate, the applicant (if the position is agreed) or the relevant party, should file a letter on CE-File setting out brief reasons why they consider that an alternative format is appropriate or necessary.

21.65 A hearing bundle must be lodged for all hearings before an ICC Judge, apart from hearings of winding up petitions in the Winding Up Court. In respect of bankruptcy petitions all the necessary procedural documents demonstrating compliance with the IA 1986 and the IR 2016 must be produced and contained in the bundle.

21.66 The person seeking a remedy at the hearing is responsible for the preparation, filing and service of the bundle but the parties should liaise and reach agreement as to content whenever practicable.

21.67 The bundle must be in electronic format, complying with the provisions of Appendix X to this Guide. If a satisfactory bundle is not lodged, the hearing is likely to be adjourned and a costs order made against the defaulting party. A paper bundle should not be provided to the court unless requested by the ICC Judge's clerk, except in the case of bankruptcy petitions in the general list. Draft orders should be lodged in Word format.

21.68 Skeleton arguments must comply with Appendix Y.

21.69 Bundles and skeleton arguments must be CE-Filed and provided to ICC Judges' Hearings at *rolls.icl.hearings1@justice.gov.uk* (or the ICC Judge's clerk, if known). Further guidance on the filing and delivery of electronic bundles can be found in Appendix X.

21.70 The court will inform the parties whether the hearing is to be fully remote, hybrid or fully in person. Reference should be made to Appendix Z in relation to remote or hybrid hearings. Parties for an in-person hearing in the ChD B&PCs London should report to the counter on the first floor of the Rolls Building at least 15 minutes before the hearing.

21.71 Chapter 12 and the Appendices X, Y and Z apply to trials before ICC Judges. Where a PTR is ordered, the guidance in Chapter 11 should be followed.

21.72 ICC Judges robe for hearings when sitting in a hearing room or court room. The occasions when court dress is worn by barristers and other advocates is set out in the updated guidance issued by the Bar Council (2020).

ORDERS

1A-222 **21.73** Attention is drawn to Chapter 16, which must be complied with. Draft minutes of orders filed after a hearing must be in Word format and should be emailed to *rolls.icl.hearings1@justice.gov.uk*. The order should not include the word 'draft' or 'minute' and need not include the case number as this will be added automatically on sealing, provided that the file name includes the case number and short title of the case.

21.74 The court office will produce winding up and bankruptcy orders. Counsel need only draft such orders where they contain non-standard provisions.

21.75 The judge's judicial title and the date of the order should appear below the court details. 'Chief ICC Judge', 'ICC Judge' or 'Deputy ICC Judge', as appropriate, are acceptable abbreviations of the titles of the ICC Judges and their deputies in orders and other documents.

21.76 Where the parties wish a consent order to be approved, the signed consent order must be lodged in PDF format together with a copy for sealing in Word format without the signature block signifying the parties' agreement. Attention is drawn to the provisions of Chapter 16 relating to consent orders (including Tomlin Orders).

21.77 Parties are reminded that in insolvency cases or substantial company cases, multiple applications by various parties may have been filed under the same case number. When filing a consent order in any case the filing party should always submit a covering letter stating the date of the application to which the consent order relates and the reasons for the order. Where the consent order varies existing case management directions, it should explain whether the variation may have an impact on any hearing listed.

APPEALS

21.78 ICC Judges have jurisdiction in appeals from District Judges in the County Court in relation to applications under the CA 2006 and in relation to corporate insolvency under the IA 1986. This includes proceedings under the CDDA 1986. Reference should be made to Chapter 30 of this Guide and Section III of PD52A of the CPR. **1A-223**

COURT-TO-COURT COMMUNICATIONS IN CROSS-BORDER INSOLVENCY CASES

21.79 Communication between courts in different jurisdictions may be of assistance in the efficient conduct of cross-border insolvency cases. Reference should be made to: **1A-224**

(a) The American Law Institute/International Insolvency Institute's *Guidelines for Court-to-Court Communications in International Insolvency Cases*
(b) The EU Cross-Border Insolvency Court-to-Court Cooperation Principles
(c) The Judicial Insolvency Network Conference's *Guidelines For Communication And Cooperation Between Courts In Cross-Border Insolvency Matters*

21.80 In a cross-border insolvency case, the insolvency practitioner involved, together with any other interested parties, should consider at an early stage in the proceedings whether the court should be invited to adopt one of these sets of guidelines for use in the proceedings, with such modifications as the circumstances of the case may require.

SCHEDULE 1

IN THE HIGH COURT OF JUSTICE

Case number:

BUSINESS AND PROPERTY COURTS OF ENGLAND AND WALES
INSOLVENCY AND COMPANIES LIST (ChD)

LISTING CERTIFICATE LODGED BY THE PETITIONER / RESPONDENT*

For the Non-Attendance Pre-Trial Review on: [. . . . . .20]

I / We .... of .... (name & address) confirm on behalf of the Petitioner / Respondent* as follows:-

EITHER:

A: that this case is ready for hearing ☐ (tick if case is ready)

1. The following witness statement(s) has / have* been filed:

Name of witness	*Date of witness statement*	*Date filed*
(a)		

2. The time estimate for judicial pre-reading is .... hours .... minutes
3. The time estimate for the hearing (including judgment) is .... day(s) .... hours .... minutes
4. My / our dates to avoid are:
5. I / we intend / do not intend* to instruct counsel who is: .... of ....
6. Oral evidence will / will not be required (give reasons if an order for cross-examination is sought).
7. This case is / is not suitable for a remote hearing.
8. Number of people expected to attend hearing on your behalf:

OR:

B: that this case is not ready for hearing ☐ (tick if case is not ready)

This case is not ready because:

Signed: .... Solicitor / Litigant in Person* Date: ....

Note: If the case is not ready and/or this form has not been completed on time the court may fix an appointment for further directions. The party who has not complied with any directions given may be ordered to pay any costs unnecessarily incurred.

If a party considers that further directions other than those for the listing of a final hearing are required, a draft order should be submitted with this form .

*Delete as appropriate

CHAPTER 22 INTELLECTUAL PROPERTY LIST

INTRODUCTION

22.1 Intellectual property proceedings are dealt with, under Part 63 of the Civil Procedure Rules ('CPR') and Practice Direction ('PD') 63, within the Chancery Division depending on their subject matter and value. There are two specialist courts: the Patents Court and the Intellectual **1A-225**

Property Enterprise Court ('IPEC'). The assignment of cases involving different intellectual property rights to specific lists or courts or as part of the general Chancery jurisdiction is set out in CPR 63.2 and CPR 63.13.

22.2 Although all intellectual property matters are assigned to the Intellectual Property List, some types of intellectual property claims must be dealt with in either the Patents Court or the IPEC. General intellectual property claims must be dealt with in either the Intellectual Property List or IPEC. As set out in CPR 63 Section I, higher value or more complex claims involving patents and registered designs are allocated to the Patents Court. Lower value or less complex claims falling with Section V of CPR 63 are allocated to the IPEC.

22.3 General intellectual property cases are assigned to Masters on a rota basis when issued in the same way as other types of claims. However, if the parties consider that their intellectual property claim requires specialist intellectual property knowledge, they can apply to the assigned Master copied to the Chief Master by letter filed on CE-File with brief reasons, asking for the claim to be re-assigned to Master Clark. To apply to have a claim docketed to a specialist High Court Judge ('HCJ') the parties should follow the guidance on docketing set out in Chapter 3. The majority of claims will remain with the assigned Masters. This procedure is only intended to be used for the most complex technical intellectual property claims where the knowledge of a specialist in the area may assist with case management.

22.4 Intellectual property cases are commenced by either Part 7 or Part 8 claim form and the provisions of this Guide apply.

THE PATENTS COURT

1A-226 **22.5** The procedure of the Patents Court is broadly that of the Chancery Division as a whole, but there are important differences, as set out in the Patents Court Guide, which must be consulted for guidance as to the procedure in the Patents Court. In particular Masters have limited jurisdiction in respect of Patent Court claims (see PD2B).

THE INTELLECTUAL PROPERTY ENTERPRISE COURT, INCLUDING SMALL CLAIMS TRACK

1A-227 **22.6** The IPEC has a significantly adapted procedure as set out in CPR 63 and PD 63. It has its own Intellectual Property Enterprise Court guide. The small claims track in the IPEC also has its own Court Guide, the Intellectual Property Enterprise Court: a guide to small claims. These Guides must also be consulted for guidance as to the procedure in the IPEC and the IPEC small claims track.

22.7 Both multi-track and small claim IPEC claims can be issued and heard in the B&PCs District Registries. Multi-track cases in the B&PCs District Registries are heard by HHJ Hacon or by one of the Deputy IPEC Judges or, where appropriate, by an HCJ nominated to hear IPEC cases.

APPEALS

1A-228 **22.8** Most appeals from decisions of the Intellectual Property Office as well as the Patents Court and IPEC are governed by CPR Part 52 as stipulated by CPR 63.16. A reference to the Court by the Appointed Person is governed by paragraph 25 of PD 63. Chapter 30 provides guidance on the general procedure as regards such appeals and parties should also consult the Patents Court Guide and the IPEC Guide as appropriate.

For further guidance see:

- Appendix F (Lists and Sub Lists)
- Chapter 3 (Commencement)
- Chapter 6 (Case Management)
- Chapter 29 (Accounts and Inquiries)

CHAPTER 23 PROBATE, INHERITANCE, PRESUMPTION OF DEATH AND GUARDIANSHIP OF MISSING PERSONS

1A-229 **23.1** The claims covered by this chapter fall within the Property Trust and Probate List (PT) and are generally governed by Part 57 of the Civil Procedure Rules ('CPR'), and, as applicable, Practice Directions ('PDs') 57, 57B, and 57C.

23.2 The court will generally expect a claim made under CPR 57 or CPR 64 to include an approximate value of the estate, fund or property in issue. This should be stated in the claim form.

PROBATE CLAIMS

1A-230 **23.3** The rules relating to contentious probate claims are contained in CPR 57.2 to 57.11 and PD 57, paragraphs 1 to 8. A probate claim is defined in CPR 57.1(2). Probate claims broadly follow the same procedure as Part 7 claims. Further guidance on general case management for Part 7 claims can be found at Chapter 6. However, there are important differences which are set out in CPR 57 and PD 57 with which parties are expected to be familiar.

23.4 Parties should bear in mind that a probate claim is akin to a claim in rem where the court undertakes an investigative role and makes declarations binding on the world at large.

23.5 All probate claims are allocated to the multi-track and are issued using Form N2.

23.6 The claimant must also file and serve written evidence about testamentary documents (see CPR 57.5(3)) and lodge with the court any original testamentary documents held by them. A specimen form is annexed to PD 57. This is an important requirement because the information provided by the parties enables the court to decide whether it is necessary for other parties either to be joined or given notice of the claim under CPR 19.8A.

23.7 Similarly, every defendant who files an acknowledgement of service must lodge any original testamentary documents held by them, and file and serve their written evidence about testamentary documents.

23.8 Unless PD 57, paragraph 3.3 applies, if a claim or acknowledgment of service is filed electronically using CE-file, the claimant or defendant must file written confirmation that the original 'testamentary documents' (see the definition in CPR 57.1(2)(c)) will be lodged within 5 working days, or an explanation as to why they cannot be lodged.

23.9 Original documents must be filed physically with the court. The will, and other original documents, must be clearly marked as an original document, with a front sheet marked in a font of not less than 14 point:

> **'CLAIM NO. XXXXXX**
> **ORIGINAL DOCUMENT – NOT TO BE DESTROYED'**

23.10 In every case, the court will write to the Leeds District Probate Registry to ask if it holds any testamentary documents; and if it does, to send them to the court. Original testamentary documents are securely stored by the court.

23.11 Where a probate claim is transferred to or from the Rolls Building, any Business and Property Courts District Registry or the County Court at Central London, Business and Property List, any original testamentary documents will remain securely stored at the transferring court until requested by the receiving court. The receiving court may call for the original testamentary documents at any stage after the transfer has been effected.

23.12 In all cases where the original testamentary documents were filed with the transferring court it is the responsibility of the party preparing the court bundle to write to the transferring court at least four weeks in advance of the trial to request that the original testamentary documents be forwarded to the receiving court if they have not already been requested by the receiving court. Such a request should be filed on CE-File where appropriate. Failure to request the original testamentary documents be sent to the receiving court may result in sanctions which could include an adverse costs order should that failure affect the trial date. This paragraph does not apply to cases that have been transferred to the County Court at Central London.

23.13 Original testamentary documents may be released to be sent to an expert for examination if a judge gives permission. An application should be made under CPR Part 23. The court will have to be satisfied that the examiner is suitably qualified, and generally that the proposed methods of examination will not unnecessarily damage the will. Normally, the court will require an undertaking by the solicitor or expert to preserve and return the documents to the court by a specific date (for guidance on the form of order see Form CH 27).

23.14 When the court orders the trial of a contentious probate claim on written evidence under PD 57 paragraph 6.1(1), or where the court is asked to pronounce in solemn form under CPR Part 24, it is normally necessary for an attesting witness to sign a witness statement of due execution of any will or codicil sought to be admitted to probate.

23.15 If the attesting witness has not signed a witness statement of due execution of any will or codicil before the original testamentary documents are lodged at court, a party may request a certified photocopy of the original will or codicil in question. The witness statement must in that case state that the exhibited document is a certified copy of the original document signed in the witness' presence.

23.16 In exceptional cases it may be necessary for the original testamentary documents to be inspected before the attesting witness is able to sign a witness statement of due execution. Where a party is legally represented, their solicitor may seek the release of the testamentary documents by application or by consent. The court will require the solicitor to provide an undertaking to the court and an order in substantially the same form as CH27 (but adapted for the circumstances) before releasing the original testamentary documents.

23.17 In such exceptional cases unrepresented parties whose attesting witnesses need to inspect the original testamentary documents rather than a certified copy will need to attend the court in which the original testamentary documents are held in order to inspect them in the presence of an officer of the court before signing their witness statement.

SETTLEMENT OF PROBATE CLAIMS

23.18 Where a claimant or defendant seeks discontinuance or dismissal, attention is drawn to CPR 57.11. Particular care is needed in the compromise of probate claims. In particular the court will not approve an arrangement unless it is satisfied that the order will lead to a grant where one has not yet been made or an existing one is to be revoked. **1A-231**

23.19 The approach to be adopted in the order settling the claim will depend upon what is in issue in the claim, whether there are competing wills and who might benefit under the will(s) or on an intestacy. Orders compromising probate claims must be drawn up carefully to ensure that any substantive orders to be made by consent, including the making of grants, are included in the substantive order and not in the schedule. For further guidance see CH26.

23.20 The compromise may be on any of the bases set out in PD 57, paragraph 6.1. Attention is also drawn to PD 57, paragraph 6.2. A settlement sought under section 49 of the Administration of Justice Act 1985, requires the consents of all the relevant beneficiaries. The class of relevant beneficiaries may be very wide, and it may not be possible to obtain all the consents which are needed.

DEFAULT JUDGMENT IS NOT AVAILABLE IN PROBATE CLAIMS

1A-232 **23.21** Default judgment cannot be obtained in a probate claim. Where, however, no defendant acknowledges service or files a defence, the claimant may apply for an order that the claim proceeds to trial and seek a direction that the claim be tried on written evidence.

APPLICATION FOR AN ORDER TO BRING A WILL ETC

1A-233 **23.22** An application under sections 122 and 123 of the Senior Courts Act 1981 should be made in an existing probate claim if it has been commenced. Where a probate claim has not been commenced, an application should be made to the Principal Registry pursuant to section 50(2) Non-Contentious Probate Rules.

RECTIFICATION OF WILLS

1A-234 **23.23** CPR 57.12 and PD 57, paragraphs 9 to 11 contain provisions which apply where a claim is made to rectify a will under section 20 of the Administration of Justice Act 1982. In particular the parties must ensure that any grant of representation is lodged with the court when the claim is issued (PD 57.10).For general guidance on rectification see Chapter 18 and Chapter 26.

SUBSTITUTION AND REMOVAL OF PERSONAL REPRESENTATIVES

1A-235 **23.24** Applications made under section 50 of the Administration of Justice Act 1985 are governed by CPR 57.13 and PD 57, paragraphs 12 to 14. The information specified in paragraph 13.1 of PD 57 is essential and must be set out fully. The application should include a draft order in Form CH41, adapted as appropriate to the circumstances.

23.25 Parties should consider the requirements of PD 57, paragraph 13.2 which apply where the claim is for the appointment of a substituted personal representative. The court will not be able to make an appointment without a signed consent to act from the proposed substitute personal representative and written evidence of fitness. Evidence of fitness must come from a person independent of the proposed substituted personal representative, which should generally not include employees or partners in the same firm as the proposed substituted personal representative.

23.26 In applications under section 50 of the Administration of Justice Act 1985 it is only in exceptional cases that oral evidence and cross examination will be required. The nature of the applications is such that they can usually be determined without issues of fact being resolved.

23.27 The original grant of representation must be lodged with the court by the personal representative at the final hearing. If the beneficiary does not have the original grant, they can lodge an office copy (PD 57.14).

ADMINISTRATION PENDING DETERMINATION OF A PROBATE CLAIM

1A-236 **23.28** Applications made under section 117 of the Senior Courts Act 1981 for the appointment of an administrator pending the determination of a probate claim are governed by PD 57, paragraph 8.

INHERITANCE (PROVISION FOR FAMILY AND DEPENDANTS) ACT 1975

1A-237 **23.29** Claims made under the Inheritance (Provision for Family and Dependants) Act 1975 in the Chancery Division are issued by way of a Part 8 claim in the Property Trust and Probate List. They are governed by CPR 57.14 to 57.16 and PD 57, paragraphs 15 to 18.

23.30 Attention is drawn to CPR 57.15, and to section 25 of the County Courts Act 1984. Careful thought should be given to whether a claim should be commenced in the High Court, and, if so, whether it should be commenced in the Chancery Division or the Family Division. Ordinarily claims commenced in the Chancery Division in London will be tried by a Master unless an order is made transferring the claim to the County Court for trial.

23.31 On the hearing of a claim under the 1975 Act, the personal representatives must comply with PD 57, paragraph 18.1 and produce the original grant of representation. The original grant of representation cannot be filed using electronic working but must be filed physically with the court. The grant must be clearly marked as an original document, with a front sheet marked in a font of not less than 14 point:

'CLAIM NO. XXXXXX
ORIGINAL DOCUMENT - NOT TO BE DESTROYED'

PRESUMPTION OF DEATH ACT 2013

23.32 Claims made under the Presumption of Death Act 2013 are governed by CPR 57.17 to 57.24 and PD 57B. **1A-238**

23.33 The claim must be issued by Part 8 claim form (CPR 57.19(1)), which must include the information required by PD 57B, paragraphs 1.1 or 1.2. A claimant may seek permission to issue a claim form without serving notice on any person (CPR 57.19(3) and PD 57B, paragraph 1.3). Such an application should be made at the same time as the claim is issued and be supported by evidence.

23.34 In addition to the information required by PD 57B, the Registrar General, who maintains a register of presumed deaths, also requires information as to the time of presumed death. A draft order in form CH42 should always be attached to the claim form, with Annex A (a Schedule of prescribed information for the General Register Office) completed which includes this requirement.

23.35 The claimant must give notice of the claim (CPR 57.20) and advertise (CPR 57.21 and PD 57B, paragraph 2.1). A copy of the advertisement and confirmation of the date of publication must be filed at least 5 days before the hearing.

23.36 A directions hearing will invariably be required; the role of the court in these proceedings is quasi-inquisitorial and the court must satisfy itself that the requirements of the Presumption of Death Act 2013 are fulfilled before making a declaration. It may for example (under section 12) at any stage require a non-party to provide information that it considers relevant to the question whether the missing person is alive or dead.

23.37 The claim should be listed for a directions hearing not less than 28 days (and where practicable not more than 56 days) after issue, allowing time for response to notice or advertisement of the claim by persons who may be entitled to intervene (CPR 57.22 and PD 57B, paragraph 3). Exceptionally, if all the papers are in order at the first directions hearing, the court may be prepared to treat the hearing as a final disposal hearing.

23.38 Where the court makes a declaration of presumed death a copy of the declaration will be sent to the Public Guardian.

23.39 Further information for litigants may be found on the gov.uk website at Get a declaration of presumed death.

GUARDIANSHIP (MISSING PERSONS) ACT 2017

23.40 Claims under the Guardianship (Missing Persons) Act 2017 (the '2017 Act') are governed by CPR 57.25 to 57.30 and by PD 57C. The 2017 Act contains detailed provisions that need to be considered carefully before the claim is issued. The claim must be issued by Part 8 claim form (CPR 57.27(1)), which must include the information required by PD 57C, paragraph 1.1 and be accompanied by a witness statement containing the information required by PD 57, paragraph 1.2 and, where appropriate, PD57C, paragraph 1.3. **1A-239**

23.41 The missing person is named as the defendant. However, the usual service requirements are varied by CPR 57.27(4). Notice of the claim must be given, and the claim must be advertised in accordance with CPR 57.29 and PD 57C, paragraphs 3.1 and 4.1.

23.42 The court will fix a directions/disposal hearing when the claim is issued to establish that: (1) the claim and the evidence provide the information that is required by the 2017 Act and the CPR; and (2) that the claim has been notified and advertised. Any applications to intervene will also be dealt with at the directions hearing. In a straightforward case, the court may be able to make an order appointing a guardian at the first hearing.

23.43 If there is a dispute about the appointment, or further steps are required, directions will be given, and a disposal hearing date will be fixed. It is very unlikely the court will permit a trial of disputed issues of fact other than in exceptional circumstances.

23.44 The court may hear an urgent application to appoint a guardian if the 'urgency condition', as it is defined in section 3(3) of the 2017 Act, is met (PD 57C, paragraphs 1.1(4) and 1.3).

23.45 Applications (made in accordance with CPR 23) may be made after the appointment of a guardian to vary or revoke the order and for other orders (CPR 57.28 and 57.30 and PD 57C, paragraph 2).

23.46 All claims and applications in respect of the 2017 Act made in the ChD B&PCs London, including urgent claims, are dealt with by Masters unless, exceptionally, they are released to be heard by a High Court Judge.

23.47 The court will send copies of orders made in such a claim to the Public Guardian in accordance with CPR 57.32.

23.48 If there is real doubt about whether the missing person is alive or the missing person is found to have died, parties should consider the provisions of CPR 57.33.

23.49 Attention is drawn to the Code of Practice issued by the Ministry of Justice in June 2019 pursuant to section 22 of the 2017 Act. It provides a useful summary of the legislative provisions and examples of how they may operate in particular circumstances. Useful guidance on managing a missing person's finances and property can be found on the gov.uk website at Manage a missing person's finances and property.

CPR 64 CLAIMS IN RELATION TO THE ADMINISTRATION OF ESTATES

1A-240 **23.50** In some circumstances personal representatives and beneficiaries will wish to use the procedure under CPR 64 to seek directions from the court before distributing the assets of the estate of the deceased. For further guidance on the use of CPR 64 generally see Chapter 25 (Trusts) and Chapter 26 (Pensions).

23.51 In cases where historic child abuse claims are being made against an estate, or where there is more than a remote concern that such claims may be made it may be appropriate for executors or administrators to seek directions from the court under CPR 64. Parties are referred to *Re Studdert, deceased* [2020] EWHC 1869 (Ch). Although the court will approach each case on its individual facts, it is expected that the court will consider the appropriateness or not of the steps identified at [22(2) and (3)], [30], [31], [35] of *Re Studdert*, and any person seeking directions should address the applicability of such directions in the evidence filed with the claim form. The personal representative(s), any beneficiary, or any claimant may seek the court's directions.

OVERSEAS PROPERTY AND MINOR CHILDREN

1A-241 **23.52** Where an application is made for permission to enter into a contract for the sale of land in another jurisdiction on behalf of a minor child habitually resident in England it should be referred to the Chief Master on issue.

23.53 A Part 8 claim should be made by the minor child acting through a litigation friend. Others with an interest in the immoveable property should be defendants.

23.54 Whilst the English court would have jurisdiction over the child, the capacity to deal with immoveable property is governed by the lex situs (where the property is) so the court would have to apply the law of the immoveable property.

23.55 The evidence in support should address the law which applies, why it is in the best interests of the child to sell the immoveable property, and the proposed application of the proceeds.

23.56 In *Re Shanavazi* [2021] EWHC 1832 (Ch) Master Clark considered the approach to such applications in the Chancery Division. However, cases relating to the a child's interest in immoveable property in another jurisdiction are also sometimes brought in the Family Division (see *In Re B (A Child)* [2022] EWFC 7, [2022] 4 WLR 34).

CHAPTER 24 NON-CONTENTIOUS PROBATE

GENERAL

1A-242 **24.1** Non-Contentious or common form probate business relates to obtaining probate and administration for estates both testate and intestate where the validity of a will is not in issue and/or there is no dispute about who is entitled to probate.

24.2 Any application made pursuant to the Non-Contentious Probate Rules 1987 and the Non-Contentious Probate (Amendment) Rules 2020 should be made to the relevant Probate Registry.

24.3 There are district probate registries undertaking non-contentious probate work in Brighton, Cardiff, Liverpool, Leeds, Oxford, Newcastle, and Winchester.

24.4 Applications should not be made to the B&PCs.

CHAPTER 25 TRUSTS

1A-243 **25.1** This chapter contains guidance on a number of aspects of proceedings concerning trusts, the estates of deceased persons (other than probate claims), and charities. Claims in relation to trusts generally concern matters which should be issued in the Property Trusts and Probate List (PT). A non-exhaustive description of the types of cases included in this list may be found in Appendix F.

25.2 Most claims relating to trusts, estates, and charities will be disposed of by a Master. The Master will only release a claim to be heard by a High Court Judge ('HCJ') if, exceptionally, the claim is of particularly high value, complexity, or legal novelty.

25.3 In this chapter unless indicated otherwise reference to a HCJ includes a Section 9 Judge and a Deputy HCJ.

25.4 The court will generally expect the evidence in support of the claim and/or the claim form to include an approximate value of the estate, fund or property in issue.

25.5 For further guidance on probate claims see Chapter 23 and for matters specific to pensions claims see Chapter 26.

TRUSTEES' APPLICATIONS FOR DIRECTIONS

1A-244 **25.6** Applications to the court by trustees for directions in relation to the administration of a trust or charity, or by personal representatives in relation to a deceased person's estate, are to be brought by Part 8 claim form, and are governed by Part 64 of the Civil Procedure Rules ('CPR'), and its Practice Directions ('PDs') (see in particular PD 64B).

25.7 When applying to the court for directions under CPR 64 it may be appropriate to seek permission to issue a claim form without naming a defendant (CPR 8.2A). Further guidance on such applications can be found in Chapter 13 paragraphs 13.35 to 13.39.

25.8 Such an application for directions may include applications under *Public Trustee v Cooper* [2001] WTLR 901, in particular category 2 cases where the blessing of the court is sought, applications for *Benjamin* orders, and applications for permission to distribute the estates of deceased Lloyd's names (addressed further below).

PROCEEDING WITHOUT A HEARING

25.9 Once the defendant has acknowledged service the Master will consider the papers on the court file (Chapter 13, paragraph 13.17). Where the claim is for approval of a sale, purchase, compromise or other transaction by a trustee, provided the claimant is able to satisfy the court that there is no conflict of interest or prejudice to beneficiaries, the court may deal with the claim on paper and without a hearing. **1A-245**

PARTIES

25.10 CPR 64.4 sets out the general rules about parties in trust claims. Where a claim is between trustees or personal representatives and third parties, consideration should be given to CPR 19.7A. **1A-246**

25.11 Where the claim relates to the internal affairs of the trust or estate it may be appropriate for a representation order to be made so that the interests of all classes of beneficiaries are represented and protected but they are also all bound by the decision (CPR 19.7).

25.12 Alternatively, where appropriate the court may direct either of its own motion or on the application of the claimant that notice of either the claim or any judgment is served on a non-party pursuant to CPR 19.8A.

25.13 A non-party who subsequently files an acknowledgement of service within the time specified becomes a party to the claim. A non-party who does not file an acknowledgment of service will still be bound by the court's decision. Further guidance on representative parties can be found in Chapter 26 (Pensions) paragraph 26.21 to 26.29.

25.14 In some cases it may be entirely appropriate and proper for one firm of solicitors to represent more than one party. However, particular attention is drawn to *South Downs Trustees Limited v GH* [2018] EWHC 1064 (Ch) where the parties are considering that course of action.

COSTS

25.15 Although the general costs rules apply equally to claims involving disputes about trusts or estates, the court retains a broad discretion in relation to costs. However, the general rule in relation to the costs incurred by trustees' and personal representatives' is set out in CPR 46.3 and CPR PD 46, paragraph 1. The costs of beneficiaries joined as defendants may in appropriate circumstances be paid from the trust fund or estate (see *Re Buckton* [1907] 2 Ch 406). **1A-247**

25.16 Attention is also drawn to PD 3F, paragraph 5 which applies where any party intends to seek an order for the payment of costs out of a trust fund (which includes the estate of a deceased person). The court may also consider alternative costs orders having regard to *Spiers v English* [1907] P 122 in an appropriate case.

BEDDOE APPLICATIONS

25.17 Trustees or personal representatives should consider whether they may need to apply, under CPR 64.2(a), for directions as to whether or not to bring or defend proceedings. This is known as a *Beddoe* application (*Re Beddoe, Downes v Cottam* [1893] 1 Ch. 547). **1A-248**

25.18 If costs or expenses are incurred in bringing or defending the proceedings without the approval of the court or the consent of all the beneficiaries, it may not be possible to recover them from the trust fund or estate.

25.19 If trustees are adequately indemnified against costs in any event, applying for *Beddoe* relief is likely to be unnecessary; there are also cases in which it is likely to be so clear that the trustees should proceed as they intend to do that the costs of making the application may not be justified in comparison with the size of the fund or the significance of the matters in issue.

25.20 Where a claim by a third party may exhaust the trust fund or estate, consideration must be given to joining that third party to the application for a *Beddoe* order.

25.21 Where a third party has been joined as a party to the application for a *Beddoe* order, it may be necessary to redact or not serve privileged material on the third party and/or to exclude the third party from those parts of the hearing during which the privileged material is discussed (see *Re Moritz* [1960] Ch. 251), even when that third party is a beneficiary or potential beneficiary of the trust or estate. This material will generally consist of legal advice obtained by the trustees regarding the merits of the third party's claim or defence. This procedure does not breach the third party's human rights (*Three Professional Trustees v Infant Prospective Beneficiary* [2007] EWHC 1922 (Ch)), although the third party will generally be allowed to participate as fully as possible in the *Beddoe* application.

25.22 The Court may also need to consider whether, when a beneficiary of the trust or estate is on the other side of the third party claim, the claim should be continued by the trustee or PR, or by other beneficiaries by way of a derivative claim, and whether it should be funded by and at the risk of the trust or estate or the other beneficiaries personally.

25.23 The *Beddoe* application must be made by separate Part 8 claim form, with a request that it be assigned to a Master other than the Master assigned to the main proceedings which are the subject matter of the Beddoe application.

25.24 The applicant will therefore need to know the name of the Master assigned to the main claim and should add a note to the CE-File when issuing the claim so as to ensure that it is not allocated to the assigned Master on issue.

25.25 In some cases it may be necessary to issue a without notice application in advance of or at the same time as the substantive *Beddoe* application to seek directions in relation to any privileged material, confidentiality, redactions, or participation in and exclusion from the *Beddoe application* hearing before service.

25.26 *Beddoe* applications are usually heard in private, and will be listed in private in the first instance. A hearing in private always needs to be justified on an individual basis, however: CPR 39.2. Even if heard in private, the court may think it appropriate to publish the judgment, if necessary, in a redacted form: see e.g. *Spencer v Fielder* [2014] EWHC 2768 (Ch). For further Guidance see Chapter 3 'Privacy, Anonymity and Confidentiality'.

TRUSTEES SEEKING COURT APPROVAL

1A-249 **25.27** Where trustees need to seek the court's approval of a decision under Category 2 of *Public Trustee v Cooper* [2001] WTLR 901, careful thought should be given by the trustees to the question of who should be joined as defendants. They should ensure that the defendants, so far as practicable, represent the range of different views available which the court should consider.

25.28 Representation orders should be sought as appropriate for categories of beneficiary with concurrent interests. In such cases, the court will only be looking to confirm that the decision for which approval is sought is one which is within the scope of the trustees' powers, reasonable in the light of relevant considerations, and not vitiated by any conflict of interest.

25.29 The applicants should provide full and candid evidence, in order that the court can reach a fully informed view. A failure to supply all relevant evidence could lead to an order not being made at all or a risk of the order failing to protect the applicants from later challenge by disgruntled beneficiaries. The trustees' evidence should normally include details of their consultation with the relevant beneficiaries, and of any expert advice they have taken.

PROSPECTIVE COSTS ORDERS (CPR PD 64A.6)

1A-250 **25.30** The court has power to make a prospective costs order in limited circumstances. Such an order directs that the beneficiaries' costs are to be paid out of the trust fund in any event (both costs incurred by them and any costs which they may be ordered to pay to any other party): see *McDonald v Horn* [1995] 1 All ER 961.

25.31 Applications for prospective costs orders by beneficiaries should be made on notice to the trustees. The court will need to be satisfied that there are matters which need to be investigated, and that any order is made for the benefit of the trust. How far the court will wish to go into that question, and in what way it should be done, will depend on the circumstances of the particular case, and attention is drawn in particular to PD 64A, paragraph 6.5.

25.32 The order may provide for payments out of the trust fund from time to time on account so that the beneficiaries' costs may be paid on an interim basis. The order may be expressed to cover costs incurred only up to a particular stage in the proceedings, so that the application has to be renewed, if necessary, and reconsidered in the light of the position at the time of that application. A model form of order is appended to PD 64A, 6.8.

RECTIFICATION AND RESCISSION

1A-251 **25.33** Applications for the rectification of trust instruments, and other voluntary transactions, are brought in the Property, Trusts and Probate List. Further general guidance about rectification can be found at Chapter 18 (Business List Rectification) and Chapter 26 (Pensions) paragraphs 26.16 to 26.20.

25.34 The same principles also apply to the court's power to rescind for mistake the exercise of powers or the making of voluntary dispositions under the principles set out in *Pitt v Holt* [2013] 2 AC 108. Parties will be expected to approach claims for rescission in the same way as claims for rectification. In particular, attention is drawn to the court's practice not to make orders for rescission (as with rectification) by default or consent without a hearing, save in exceptional circumstances; and the need to notify HMRC (or any appropriate foreign tax body or bodies) where rescission (as with rectification) will have fiscal consequences.

25.35 When preparing witness statements in any claim for rectification or rescission careful thought should be given to compliance with (or dispensation from) the requirements of PD 57AC. This is a particularly important consideration in rectification and rescission claims where the passage of time often means that there is no witness who able to give evidence as to the relevant events and/or where it is necessary for a witness to express a belief as to whether there has been a mistake and/or to explain what happened.

25.36 Claims to rescind trusts and other voluntary transactions on grounds other than mistake, such as fraud, undue influence, duress, or misrepresentation, are not subject to the guidance above. They will almost invariably be made by way of Part 7 claim in the usual way.

VARIATION OF TRUSTS ACT 1958

25.37 An application for an order under the Variation of Trusts Act 1958 ('VTA') should be made by a Part 8 claim form (see PD 64A, paragraph 4). **1A-252**

25.38 Following the decision by Morgan J in *V v T* [2014] EWHC 3432 (Ch) it will be unusual for Variation of Trust cases to be heard in private. However, the Master will consider at the hearing whether parts of the evidence should not be available for inspection on the court file and whether additional safeguards are needed to protect children, born and unborn, as to which attention is drawn to *MN v OP* [2019] EWCA Civ 679. Attention is also drawn to the Practice Note: Variation of Trusts dated 9 February 2017.

25.39 Where the parties consider that a question of confidentiality or anonymity arises, they should, when they issue proceedings, include a covering letter together with an application for confidentiality or anonymity if sought, requesting that the assigned Master consider the application before any other step is taken. Further guidance on applications relation to privacy, anonymity and confidentiality can be found at paragraphs 3.31 to 3.37 and paragraphs 15.66 to 15.68.

25.40 In some circumstances it may be considered appropriate to issue an application to seek permission to anonymise some or all of the identities of the parties and/or for confidentiality in relation to some of the documents that would be on the court file before the claim is issued.

25.41 If the parties wish to apply for confidentiality or anonymity before the claim is issued, the application together with any covering letter requesting that the assigned Master consider the application on paper should be issued on CE-File as a pre-issue application and marked confidential. A note should be added to the Comment Box on CE-File so that the nature of the application is clear to the court staff. In an appropriately sensitive case in may be considered appropriate for the application and covering letter to be emailed to the Master's clerk to seek the order before even the application for anonymity and confidentiality is issued on CE-File. Such a course of action will be exceptional. However, as set out in Chapter 3 and Chapter 15 any derogation from the principles of open justice will be the minimum necessary.

25.42 If an order is made, when the claim is subsequently issued, the claimant must write to the court requesting that the claim be assigned to the same Master who dealt with the confidentiality or anonymity application and case managed with the application (the application and claim form will have been given separate case numbers).

25.43 The covering letter should propose case management directions so that the claim (whether issued or not) can be progressed following disposal of the confidentiality or anonymity application.

25.44 It will be unusual for a confidentiality or anonymity order to made without a hearing. The Master must be satisfied that it is necessary and in the interests of justice for an order to be made. Any order made will be the minimum necessary to achieve that purpose. Any order exceptionally made on the papers will be reviewed at the first directions hearing of the claim.

25.45 The orders may include anonymising some or all of the parties, listing the first hearing in private, listing the hearing in public but with a reporting restrictions order, managing how the parties and key facts are referred to in court. The court may order that parts of the court file, that might otherwise be available, will only be released to non-parties upon written application on notice and a hearing is likely to be listed. A Variation of Trusts Confidentiality Order is at Form CH43.

25.46 Applications under the VTA will require the court to consider the current trusts that are to be varied. It will assist the court and save time if the parties' representatives can agree a single summary of the trusts (and their tax effects) and where appropriate, a summary of the documents and events that have led to the current trusts. Such summaries might appear in or be appended to the claimant's (or some other) witness statement, or be contained in a separate document filed with the skeleton arguments. If other summaries appear in the documents (e.g. in opinions prepared for litigation friends) which the court need not consider in light of the agreed summaries, their location should be identified in a pre-reading list with an indication that they need not be considered.

25.47 For cases involving children or unborn beneficiaries, and unless the court orders otherwise, a written opinion from the advocate representing the children or the unborn beneficiaries must be filed. For further guidance see PD 64A paragraph 4.1 to 4.4. Where a written opinion has been put in evidence and no additional matters beyond those appearing from the instructions or the opinion are to be relied on, a skeleton argument may not be needed. Where the Master considers it appropriate, they may dispense with the need for a written opinion.

25.48 Deputy Masters may only deal with VTA claims with permission of the Chief Master.

APPLICATIONS UNDER SECTION 48 OF THE ADMINISTRATION OF JUSTICE ACT 1985

25.49 The jurisdiction conferred on the High Court by section 48 of the Administration of Justice Act 1985 to authorise action based on a written legal opinion about an issue of construction of a trust document may be invoked by trustees where such a question has arisen out of the terms of a trust. **1A-253**

25.50 Whilst the jurisdiction is particularly well suited to construction issues arising in relation to a trust of modest value where a conventional inter partes application would be prohibitively expensive, it may be (and has been) successfully invoked in other cases. It is intended to be used in clear cases only.

25.51 Applications under section 48 of the Administration of Justice Act 1985 should be made by Part 8 claim form (PD 64A 5).

25.52 The claim should be supported by a witness statement to which are exhibited: (a) copies of all relevant documents; (b) instructions to a person with a 10-year High Court qualification within the meaning of the Courts and Legal Services Act 1990 (the 'qualified person'); (c) the qualified person's opinion; and (d) draft terms of the desired order.

25.53 The application is for an order to authorise the trustees to act on the basis of a legal opinion, which may deal with construction issues; it should not seek a binding decision of the court itself on the construction of any instrument.

25.54 The court may consider that, as a matter of discretion, it would be preferable to have the issue finally and bindingly resolved at a substantive hearing, as opposed to its merely being made the subject of directions to the trustees. This is more likely where conflicting opinions have been expressed by different counsel advising the trustees: see *Greenwold v Pike* [2007] EWHC 2202 (Ch).

25.55 The witness statement (or exhibits thereto) should set out: (a) the reason for the application; (b) the names of all persons who are, or may be, affected by the order sought; (c) all surrounding circumstances admissible and relevant in construing the document; (d) the date of qualification of the qualified person and his or her experience in the construction of trust documents; (e) the approximate value of the fund or property in question; (f) whether it is known to the applicant that a dispute exists and, if so, details of such dispute; and (g) what steps are proposed to be taken in reliance on the opinion.

25.56 The Master will consider the claim, and, if necessary, direct service of notices under CPR 19.8A or request further information. It is important that the evidence explains how those potentially affected have been identified, and what steps have been taken to consult them on the order sought. If the court is satisfied that the order sought is appropriate, it will be made without a hearing and sent to the claimant.

25.57 If following service of notices under CPR 19.8A any acknowledgment of service is received, the claimant must apply to the Master (on notice to the parties who have so acknowledged service) for directions. The Master will ordinarily direct that the case proceeds as a Part 8 claim.

25.58 If on the hearing of the claim the court is of the opinion that any party who entered an acknowledgment of service has no reasonably tenable argument contrary to the qualified person's opinion, in the exercise of the court's discretion it may order such party to pay all or part of any costs thrown away.

VESTING ORDERS – PROPERTY IN SCOTLAND

1A-254 **25.59** In applications for vesting orders under the Trustee Act 1925 any investments or property situate in Scotland (which cannot be the subject of such an order: see the Trustee Act 1925, section 56) should be set out in a separate schedule to the claim form, and the claim form should ask that the trustees have permission to apply for a vesting order in Scotland in respect of them.

25.60 The form of the order to be made in such cases will (with any necessary variation) be as follows:

> '*It is ordered that the [..........] as Trustees have permission to take all steps that may be necessary to obtain a vesting order in Scotland relating to [the securities] specified in the schedule hereto.*'

ESTATES OF DECEASED LLOYD'S NAMES

1A-255 **25.61** The procedure concerning the estates of deceased Lloyd's Names is governed by a *Practice Statement* [2001] 3 All ER 765.

25.62 If personal representatives need the court's permission to distribute the estate of a deceased Lloyd's Name, they should apply by Part 8 claim form headed *'In the Matter of the Estate of [..........] deceased (a Lloyd's Estate) and In the Matter of the Practice Direction dated May 25 2001'* for permission to distribute the estate. Ordinarily, the claim form need not name any other party and may be issued without a separate application for permission under CPR 8.2A (see the *Practice Statement*). Further guidance can be found in Chapter 13 at paragraphs 13.35 to 13.39.

25.63 The claim should be supported by a witness statement together with a form of order examples of both can be found in Chancery Forms at CH38 and CH39. The application will be considered by the Master who, if satisfied that the order should be made, may make the order on paper and without a hearing. If not, the Master may give directions for the further disposal of the application or list a directions hearing.

JUDICIAL TRUSTEES AND SUBSTITUTE PERSONAL REPRESENTATIVES

1A-256 **25.64** Judicial trustees may be appointed by the court to replace existing trustees or personal representatives under the Judicial Trustees Act 1896, in accordance with the Judicial Trustee Rules 1983.

25.65 An application for the appointment of a judicial trustee should be made by Part 8 claim form (or, if in an existing claim, by an application notice in that claim) which must be served on every existing trustee or personal representative who is not an applicant and on such of the beneficiaries as the applicant thinks fit. It should include a draft order.

25.66 Once appointed, a judicial trustee may obtain non-contentious directions from the assigned Master informally by letter, without the need for a Part 23 application (unless the court directs otherwise).

25.67 In practice the appointment of judicial trustees is no longer sought. Instead application is made, under section 50 of the Administration of Justice Act 1985, for the removal of a personal representative and the appointment of a substitute; or an application for replacement of a trustee, under section 41 of the Trustee Act 1925 and/or the court's inherent jurisdiction.

25.68 Applications under section 50 are dealt with in Chapter 23 (Probate). Applications under section 41 or the inherent jurisdiction will usually be made by Part 8 claim form, unless it is made within an existing claim, in which case it may be made by Part 23 application: see *Schumacher v Clark* [2019] EWHC 1031 (Ch).

25.69 Although such applications are required to be brought in the High Court, and are assigned to the Chancery Division, jurisdiction can be conferred upon the County Court by transfer out in an appropriate case.

25.70 Where the disability of a trustee or personal representative is alleged, there must be medical evidence showing incapacity to act as a trustee or personal representative at the date of issue of the claim form and that the incapacity is continuing at the date of signing the witness statement or swearing the affidavit.

25.71 The witness statement should also show incapacity to execute transfers, where a vesting order of stocks and shares is asked for.

25.72 The trustee or personal representative under disability should be made a defendant to the claim but need not be served unless he or she is sole trustee or has a beneficial interest.

BONA VACANTIA AND TRUSTS

25.73 Where the property of a deceased person or a dissolved company is bona vacantia, the relevant Crown department to be joined to legal proceedings is the Attorney General. In practice it is still the Treasury Solicitor that considers the evidence, but the relevant representative of the Crown that should be joined to such an application is the Attorney General: see *Orwin v A-G* [1998] FSR 415, 419. **1A-257**

25.74 Where the deceased or the company held assets on trust, they are not bona vacantia: see *Re Strathblaine Estates Ltd* [1948] Ch 228. In such a case a vesting order may be sought under the Trustee Act 1925.

25.75 Where a company owning property overseas is dissolved and the property escheats, the correct defendants are the Crown Estate Commissioners (see *UBS Global Asset Management (UK) Limited v Crown Estate Commissioners* [2011] EWHC 3368 (Ch)) and *Lizzium Ltd v The Crown Estate Commissioners* [2021] EWHC 941 (Ch)).

25.76 Responsibility for dealing with bona vacantia and escheat lies with the Duchy of Cornwall or Duchy of Lancaster where the relevant property or registered office address of any dissolved company is in either of the Duchies. There is no substantive difference in the procedures that apply to any application.

CHARITY TRUSTEES' APPLICATIONS FOR PERMISSION TO BRING PROCEEDINGS

25.77 In the case of a charitable trust, the trustees should first apply to the Charity Commission for permission to commence charity proceedings. If the Charity Commission refuses its consent to the trustees applying to the court for directions under the Charities Act 2011 section 115(2), and also refuses to give the trustees the directions under its own powers, for example under sections 105 or 110, the trustees may apply to the court under section 115(5). **1A-258**

25.78 An application should be made in accordance with the provisions of CPR 64.6 and PD 64A, paragraphs 7 to 10. An application for permission to commence proceedings is made to a HCJ: section 115(5) Charities Act 2011. In straightforward cases where all the papers are in order the HCJ may be prepared to deal with the application for permission on paper. However, the HCJ may request a statement from the Charity Commission setting out its reasons for refusing permission, if not already apparent from the papers (CPR 64.6(4) and PD 64A, paragraph 9.2).The court may require the trustees to attend a hearing before deciding whether to grant permission for the proceedings. The court may, if appropriate, require notice of the hearing to be given to the Attorney General (PD 64A, paragraph 7).

CHAPTER 26 PENSIONS

INTRODUCTION

26.1 This chapter provides guidance in respect of claims brought in the Pensions sub-list. A description of the types of claims covered by the Pensions sub-list can be found in Appendix F. Claims in the Pensions sub-list relate to pension schemes, particularly occupational pension schemes, which are established under trust. **1A-259**

26.2 For claims which concern the trust aspects of pension schemes, parties should also consider the guidance provided in both Chapter 25 (Trusts), Part 64 of the Civil Procedure Rules ('CPR') and Practice Directions ('PDs') 64A and 64B.

26.3 Claims by trustees and/or employers relating to occupational pension schemes in the Pension sub-list include professional negligence claims against former advisers, or action taken under statutory powers, for example by the Pensions Regulator, or statutory appeals, for example from the Pensions Ombudsman.

26.4 Claims issued in the Pensions sub-list should be entitled *'In the Matter of the [ ] Pension Scheme'.*

26.5 Pension cases are assigned to Masters on a rota basis when issued in the same way as other types of claims. However, if the parties consider that their pension claim requires specialist knowledge of pensions, they can apply to the assigned Master copied to the Chief Master by letter filed on CE-File with brief reasons, asking for the claim to be re-assigned to either the Chief Master or a master with specialist knowledge of pensions. This procedure is only intended to be used for the most complex technical pensions claims where the knowledge of a specialist in the area may assist. Deputy Masters may only deal with pension scheme rectification claims with the permission of the Chief Master.

26.6 Pensions cases issued in a B&PC District Registry should be referred to a B&PC Specialist Circuit Judge on issue for triage.

STARTING PROCEEDINGS

1A-260 **26.7** Many pension claims are brought under Part 8. For further guidance on Part 8 claims see Chapter 13. This is suitable where there is unlikely to be a substantial dispute of fact, and is required by CPR 64.3 where the claim is for the determination of any question arising in the execution of a trust or under section 48 of the Administration of Justice Act 1985. For further guidance on CPR 64 applications for directions see Chapter 25 (Trusts) paragraph 25.6.

26.8 The trustees are usually the claimants, applying to court for the determination of questions of construction, or seeking directions, but questions arising in the execution of the trusts can be brought before the court by any party with a sufficient interest. If the trustees are not the claimants, they should be joined as defendants even if no specific relief is sought against them.

26.9 Usually, the trustees will wish to ensure that all those potentially interested in the question, which will very often be both the employer(s) and the members, are made parties or represented. See below, paragraph 26.21, for Representative Beneficiaries and Chapter 2, paragraphs 2.8 to 2.12.

26.10 Some claims may be capable of being issued without naming any defendants under CPR rule 8.2A (for further guidance on how to apply see Chapter 13, paragraphs 13.35 to 13.39 and Chapter 25, paragraph 25.7). Given the nature of members' interests under a pension scheme, this is likely to be quite rare (the only reported example being *Owens Corning Fibreglass UK Ltd* [2002] Pens LR 323).

26.11 It may be necessary to consider the potential impact of the litigation on the Pension Protection Fund: see the comments of Sir Andrew Morritt C in *Capita ATL Ltd v Zurkinskas* [2010] EWHC 3365 (Ch) at [22].

26.12 Where a claim commenced under Part 8 turns out to involve substantial factual issues the court will give directions for its future case management which may involve statements of case or continuation under Part 7. For further guidance see Chapter 13 (Part 8 claims). The parties could alternatively agree to continue the claim under the Flexible Trial Scheme: see Chapter 17.

26.13 Some pensions claims are more suited to and should be issued under Part 7. Examples include actions by trustees and/or employers against former advisers for professional negligence, and actions to recover trust property paid away in breach of trust. No special provisions apply to such claims and parties should consider the guidance in Chapter 3 to Chapter 12 in respect of the conduct of Part 7 claims generally.

26.14 Sometimes the outcome of litigation is relevant to a separate professional negligence claim against advisers. There are several options to consider to avoid the risk of points being re-argued in separate proceedings. The advisers can agree to be bound by the outcome of the litigation, or joined as defendants for the purpose of being bound (as in *Shannan v Viavi Solutions UK Ltd* [2016] EWHC 1530 (Ch)). An alternative route is an application under CPR 19.8A for the court to direct notice of the claim to be served on the adviser (see Chapter 2 (Parties and Representatives) and Chapter 25 (Trusts)).

BEDDOE APPLICATIONS

1A-261 **26.15** Pension Trustees who are proposing to sue third parties, or who are sued by them and wish to defend the action at the expense of the trust fund, may wish to apply for directions in accordance with the re Beddoe procedure. For further guidance see Chapter 25 (Trusts), paragraphs 25.17 to 25.26, and PD 64B, paragraphs 7.1 to 7.12.

RECTIFICATION CLAIMS

1A-262 **26.16** Claims for rectification of a scheme's trust deed or other governing documentation, if likely to be contentious, must be commenced by Part 7 claim. However, in an appropriate case they may still be suitable for summary judgment under CPR Part 24.

26.17 Some rectification cases are in practice uncontentious and can be commenced using Part 8 enabling the parties to seek an early or summary disposal hearing under PD8A, paragraph 8.1(1) (see *Sovereign Trustees Ltd v Lewis* [2016] EWHC 2593 (Ch)).

26.18 When preparing witness statements in any claim for rectification or rescission careful thought should be given to compliance with (or dispensation from) the requirements of PD 57AC. This is a particularly important consideration in pension rectification claims where the passage of time often means that there is no witness who able to give evidence as to the relevant events and/or where it is necessary for a witness to express a belief as to whether there has been a mistake and/or to explain what happened.

26.19 The court has power to impose terms protective to members (or some of them) on which the scheme's governing documentation is rectified: see *Konica Minolta Business Solutions (UK) Ltd v Applegate* [2013] EWHC 2536 (Ch) at [49]-[63].

26.20 Further guidance on rectification claims generally can be found in Chapter 18 (Business List Rectification) and Chapter 25 (Trusts).

REPRESENTATIVE BENEFICIARIES

26.21 The use of one or more representative beneficiaries to represent the interests of members under CPR 19.7(2) is a common feature of most pension claims. The number of representatives and classes represented should be kept to the minimum necessary to enable the court to be satisfied that it has heard full argument on behalf of all those interested. It is often convenient to make an 'issue-based' representation order, that is for the representative to be appointed to represent all those interested in an issue being resolved in a particular way: see *Capita ATL Ltd v Zurkinskas* [2010] EWHC 3365 (Ch). If the trustees are in doubt as to who to join, an application in accordance with PD 64B paragraph 4.3 may be sensible. See also Chapter 2 (Parties and Representatives) and Chapter 25 (Trusts). **1A-263**

26.22 CPR 19.7(2) does not specifically require that the representative be a member of the class represented, although this is usually the case. The court's overriding concern is that the interests of all those represented are protected. The court will be willing to appoint a non-member of the class if the circumstances warrant it: see e.g. *Sovereign Trustees v Glover* [2007] EWHC 1750 (Ch) and *Walker Morris Trustees Ltd v Masterson* [2009] EWHC 1955 (Ch), in each of which solicitors were appointed as representatives.

26.23 In some cases the interests of some classes of members are aligned with those of the employer(s), and an employer can properly be appointed to represent their interests. In other cases, the trustees, (who would normally be neutral, but may sometimes be joined as a co-claimant: see, e.g., *Saga Group Ltd v Paul* [2016] EWHC 2344 (Ch)) may agree to be appointed to represent the members or some class of them to save costs. See e.g. *Premier Foods v RHM Pension Trust Ltd* [2012] EWHC 447 (Ch) and *Arcadia Group Ltd v Arcadia Group Pension Trust Ltd* [2014] EWHC 2683 (Ch). This procedure can be useful, particularly when the claim concerns pure questions of construction or law where there are only two possible outcomes. It is not suitable for cases for example where the issue is likely to be a divisive one among the members or employers, or there are questions as to what the trustees did, particularly if there is any criticism of the trustees' conduct. It is, though, equally capable of being adopted in a case involving the cross-examination of witnesses: see *BIC UK Ltd v Burgess* [2018] EWHC 785 (Ch).

26.24 In cases involving questions of construction or law where there are only two possible outcomes on a given issue, it may be appropriate to seek an 'issue based' representation order under which the employer represents the members whose interests are aligned with those of the employer and where the trustees agree to represent all those members whose interests are opposed to the interests of the employer on the issue or issues raised.

26.25 In such cases and where directions are agreed the parties may invite the court to give case management directions without the need for a hearing which include a direction for representation orders of this type to be made. To enable the Master to consider the proposed case management directions on paper, the parties should file (on CE-File) with their proposed directions, a joint letter with which includes: (i) an agreed concise summary of the issues in the claim and their possible outcomes; and (ii) confirms that they agree it is not necessary for a representative beneficiary to be separately appointed to represent the interests of any class of members.

26.26 If a compromise is proposed in proceedings in which a representative is to be or has been appointed under CPR 19.7, the court's approval is required, and the court may only approve the compromise where it is for the benefit of the represented persons (CPR 19.7(5) and (6)). The court will require an opinion on the merits of the proposed compromise from counsel instructed on behalf of the represented class. Such an opinion is normally confidential and not served on or shown to the other parties.

26.27 Whilst the parties may make an application for a hearing to be heard in private (see CPR 39.2) any derogation from the principles of open justice should be the minimum required, and an application for the court's approval should generally be in public. However, a discussion of the merits of the proposed compromise from the perspective of the represented class will, where necessary and appropriate, take place in private and in the absence of the other parties.

26.28 A similar practice of having part of the hearing in private in the absence of the other parties is often adopted where a defendant acting as a representative does not consider it appropriate to oppose the relief sought. This can arise in claims for rectification of pension scheme rules. In such unopposed applications for summary judgment, the hearing will be held in open court, but submissions on behalf of the representative party as to the merits of the summary judgment application may be held in private and in the absence of the claimant. Any opinion provided for that purpose will normally be treated as confidential and not be served on or shown to the other parties.

26.29 Whilst the court may adopt this approach in many cases, see as one example the decision of Chief Master Marsh in *SPS Technologies Ltd v Moitt & Ors* [2020] EWHC 2421 (Ch) at [6] it should be noted that it is not an invariable approach and different procedures may be appropriate in different cases.

PROSPECTIVE COSTS ORDERS

1A-264 **26.30** If no costs agreement is reached with the employer, representative beneficiaries will usually be funded at the expense of the scheme. In such cases it will usually be necessary to obtain a prospective costs order. Details of a proposed order are usually agreed by the trustees' solicitors and solicitors for the proposed representative and put before the Master for approval at the first hearing. For the procedure generally see Chapter 25 (Trusts), paragraphs 25.30 to 25.32 and the model order annexed to PD 64A. See also Chapter 25 (Trusts) paragraph 25.16 in respect of payments of costs out of a trust fund and the court's power to make a costs capping order (see Chapter 13 paragraph 13.31).

CONSULTATION OR NOTIFICATION

1A-265 **26.31** Although there is no requirement to consult with or notify members of a pension scheme when it is proposed that a person be appointed under CPR 19.7(2) to represent their interests, in the context of unopposed summary judgment applications it has been said that notification to affected members is desirable or good practice. *Industrial Acoustics Company Ltd v Crowhurst* [2012] EWHC 1614 (Ch) at [60] and *CitiFinancial Europe Plc v Davidson* [2014] EWHC 1802 (Ch) at [7].

26.32 The scheme's trustees would ordinarily be the appropriate persons to notify members of what is proposed and it is sensible to agree the terms of any notice(s) with the representative beneficiary's legal representatives. Two notices are commonly sent, one explaining the nature of the proceedings and a second, later notice informing members of the date and place of any hearing. One or other notice should explain the stance proposed to be adopted by the representative beneficiary. A failure to consult, or to consult in a manner the court regards as adequate, risks the matter being adjourned for this purpose.

26.33 The same considerations would also apply where the court's approval is sought under CPR 19.7(6) to the settlement of a claim.

26.34 Where members have not been notified and are unaware of the proposed compromise, the court might decide to postpone the effective date of any order for a short period to allow any person affected by it to apply to the court if they consider that, due to circumstances which are particular to them, they should not be bound. (see *Smithson v Hamilton* [2008] EWCA Civ 996 at [13]-[15] (period 28 days), and *Archer v Travis Perkins PLC* [2014] EWHC 1362 (Ch) at [26]-[28] (period 42 days).

S 48 ADMINISTRATION OF JUSTICE ACT 1985

1A-266 **26.35** Section 48 of the Administration of Justice Act has been successfully invoked in cases involving occupational pension schemes of substantial size where the question concerned has been sufficiently clear so as to be an appropriate one to deal with under section 48. For further guidance on the procedure and approach to such an application see Chapter 25 (Trusts), paragraphs 25.49 to 25.58.

26.36 In the case of a pension scheme, the employer is not a necessary party to the application, nor will any order made either be directed to it (as opposed to, and affording protection to, the applicant trustees) or prevent a member from subsequently asserting a claim, either by legal proceedings or before the Pensions Ombudsman, which is inconsistent with an order made under section 48. The effect of an order under section 48 is to protect the trustees against any complaint that they have wrongly administered the scheme but it does not bind any of the members or potential beneficiaries of the scheme: see *re BCA Pension Plan* [2015] EWHC 3492 (Ch) at [36].

26.37 Where the court makes an order, it may require the trustees to notify the members in some suitable fashion: see generally *re BCA Pension Plan* [2015] EWHC 3492 (Ch) at [37]-[43].

APPEALS FROM THE PENSIONS OMBUDSMAN

1A-267 **26.38** Appeals from determinations or directions of the Pensions Ombudsman lie on a point of law to the High Court under s.151(4) of the Pension Schemes Act 1993, and are assigned to the Chancery Division by PD 52D, paragraph 5.1(8). The permission of the High Court is required for such appeals under CPR 52.29. For further guidance on appeals generally see Chapter 30.

26.39 The Ombudsman has given a general direction for England and Wales that a person wishing to appeal must lodge the appeal within 28 days after the date of an Ombudsman determination, instead of the usual period of 21 days. A different direction could be given by the Ombudsman in an individual case.

26.40 The appellant's notice *must* name the other party to the underlying original complaint as the Respondent to the appeal.

26.41 The appellant must serve the appellant's notice on the Ombudsman as well as the Respondent (PD 52D, paragraph 3.4(1)). Although there is no obligation to do so, the Ombudsman's Office often finds it helpful to be kept informed of the progress of the appeal and copied into relevant correspondence.

26.42 Where scheme members appeal, they are frequently unrepresented. In such a case the respondent (trustees or employer or other as the case may be) should ensure that the Ombudsman has been served with the appellant's notice and that the material put before the court includes all material that was before the Ombudsman and is potentially relevant to the appeal. Failure to do so may result in an adjournment of the hearing.

26.43 The court has power under CPR 52.19 to make an order to limit the recoverable costs in such an appeal. Any application asking the court to exercise that power should be made as soon as practicable: see *Coats UK Pension Scheme Trustees Ltd v A Styles & Others* [2019] EWHC 35 (Ch).

26.44 It is desirable that the order made on appeal from a determination of the Pensions Ombudsman is clear about which aspects of the determination are upheld, set aside or remitted back to the Pensions Ombudsman for further determination. Therefore, where parties propose to compromise such an appeal, they should, where possible, liaise with the office of the Pensions Ombudsman about the wording of any consent order.

26.45 For Further Guidance see

(a) Chapter 3 (Commencement)
(b) Chapter 6 (Case Management)
(c) Chapter 13 (Part 8 claims)
(d) Chapter 18 (Business List Rectification)
(e) Chapter 25 (Trusts)
(f) Chapter 30 (Appeals)

CHAPTER 27 PROPERTY

GENERAL

27.1 As the names 'Business and Property Courts of England and Wales' ('B&PCs') and 'Property, Trusts & Probate List' suggest, property litigation is conducted in the Chancery lists in the High Court, as it always has been. Less valuable or complex property cases are, however, better suited to resolution in the County Court. Some property cases are statutorily required to be issued in the First-tier Tribunal (Property Chamber) or in the Upper Tribunal (Lands Chamber). Nevertheless, where an appropriate case exists, the judge will either retain it in the B&PCs or transfer it in from the County Court when asked to do so. **1A-268**

27.2 The B&PCs have judges at all levels with expertise in real property, personal property and landlord and tenant law.

27.3 There are, however, various inhibitions on bringing claims relating to property in the Chancery lists in the B&PCs. These can be summarised as follows:

(a) General jurisdiction limits for claims issued in the High Court;
(b) Part 55 and Part 56 of the Civil Procedure Rules ('CPR'), which apply to possession claims and certain types of statutory landlord and tenant claim;
(c) CPR Practice Direction ('PD') 57AA, which describes the specialist work conducted in the B&PCs and excludes certain work, including some property work;
(d) The availability of specialist Circuit Judges (including three Senior Circuit Judges) in the County Court at Central London, which runs a Business and Property List. Even when the value threshold for the High Court is exceeded, a case in London or the South-East that does not raise an important question of practice or law is often more suitable for resolution by a specialist judge of the County Court with property expertise.
(e) The suitability of the Queen's Bench Division for straightforward money claims relating to property.

27.4 The relevant factors for determining if a case should be brought in the High Court are the financial value of the claim or amount in dispute; complexity of the factual or legal issues; and the degree of public interest or importance of the outcome of the claim (which may include the need for an authoritative ruling setting a precedent) (PD 7A, paragraph 2.4).

27.5 The County Court has jurisdiction to hear equitable claims where the value of the property, mortgage or charge, estate or trust in issue does not exceed £350,000, or higher by agreement of the parties in writing (County Courts Act 1984, s.23, as amended). In the case of a claim for damages and in relation to money claims (for example outstanding rent), a claim with a value below the £100,000 threshold for High Court jurisdiction will prevent the claim being issued in the High Court (PD 7A, paragraph 2.1; PD8A, paragraph 4.1(1); CPR 20.3(1)) unless exceptionally the claimant is able to satisfy the criteria in PD7A paragraph 2.4.

27.6 High value is not of itself a good reason for bringing a claim in the High Court, if the issues raised are straightforward. Conversely, a low value claim that raises an important point of practice or law, or where there is real urgency, may be suitable to be issued in the High Court.

27.7 A claimant is expected to consider whether there are good reasons for bringing a claim in the High Court before doing so, and if so whether the Chancery Division or the Queen's Bench Division is the more appropriate Division. Except where the Practice Note on Possession Claims against Trespassers applies (see under CPR 55, below), there is no requirement to obtain prior approval from a Master to issue a property claim in the ChD B&PCs London, though a Master is always willing to give informal advice about such matters.

27.8 However, PD 57AA specifies that the following categories of claim (among others) are not specialist work of the type undertaken in the B&PCs:

(a) Claims for possession of domestic property, rent and mesne profits;
(b) Claims in respect of domestic mortgages;
(c) Claims for possession of commercial premises or disputes arising out of business tenancies that are routine in nature;
(d) Claims falling under the Trusts of Land and Appointment of Trustees Act 1996, unless combined with other specialist claims;
(e) Boundary and easement disputes involving no conveyancing issues;
(f) Applications under the Access to Neighbouring Land Act 1992.

27.9 It follows that claims of this kind may not generally be issued in the lists of the B&PCs unless they raise points of particular novelty or complexity.

CLAIMS UNDER CPR 55

1A-269 **27.10** Where a claim for possession of non-domestic property (or relief against forfeiture) falling within CPR 55 is sought to be issued in the High Court, the procedure in CPR 55.3(2) requiring certification of the appropriateness of issuing in the High Court must be followed. Guidance on the exceptional circumstances justifying issue in the High Court is given in PD 55A. These circumstances may be claims against trespassers where there is real urgency, and claims involving complicated disputes of fact or points of law of general importance. 'Exceptional' in this context means out of the normal run of cases, rather than very rare. However, the value of the property and the amount of any financial claim may be relevant circumstances, although these factors alone will not normally justify starting a claim in the High Court.

27.11 To deal with a particular problem of aggressive fly-tipping, the Chief Master and the Senior Master issued a joint Practice Note on 30 September 2017 which is set out in full at 55APN.1 of the White Book. It applies only to claims in the High Court in London and provides that in cases of real urgency the court may fix a hearing very soon after issue and give permission for short service of the claim.

27.12 Practice Note 55A provides that an applicant in such cases should, before issuing the application, speak first to the Chief Master or, if unavailable, to another Master. An applicant wishing to contact the Chief Master in relation to such an application should send an email to chancery.mastersappointments@justice.gov.uk marked as Urgent and referring to the Practice Note. The Master will consider the certificate and witness statement and decide whether the claim should be issued in the High Court, and whether short service is appropriate. If the Master agrees to the claim being listed urgently a date will be fixed straight away. The defendants must be notified and be told that they will have an opportunity to put their case if they attend the hearing. Form CH 47 (a tailor-made order for possession) should be used, if appropriate.

27.13 Accelerated possession claims against an assured shorthold tenant and a claim including a demotion claim must be issued in the County Court (CPR 55.11(2); PD 55, paragraph 1.9).

CLAIMS UNDER CPR 56

1A-270 **27.14** If the claim is a statutory landlord and tenant claim falling within CPR 56, the procedure in CPR 56.2(2) requiring the certification of the appropriateness of issuing the claim in the High Court must be followed. Guidance on exceptional circumstances justifying issue in the ChD B&PCs London is given in PD 56. These may be where the claim involves complicated disputes of fact or points of law of general importance. Again, 'exceptional' here means out of the normal run of cases, rather than very rare. Note that some landlord and tenant statutes require claims to be issued in the County Court, or in a tribunal, and in those cases, claims cannot be issued in the High Court.

27.15 In addition to the above restrictions, claimants should bear in mind, before issuing a property claim in the ChD B&PCs London, that there is a body of expertise in real property and landlord and tenant law among the judges sitting in the County Court at Central London. The need (or wish) for an expert judge to hear the case will therefore rarely justify starting the claim in the High Court, given the existence of the Business and Property List in Central London. However, a case of substantial importance that raises an issue that should be decided by a court of record may properly be brought in the B&PCs. In case of doubt, the appropriateness of issuing in the High Court can be raised informally with the Chief Master before issue, or a letter may be filed with the claim form explaining why it is considered to be suitable for the High Court.

27.16 Parties are generally discouraged from bringing claims for rent or other money sums relating to property in the B&PCs: see paragraph 27.8(a) above. Simple debt claims falling within the High Court's jurisdiction (including claims against sureties for damages) are generally more appropriately issued in the Queen's Bench Division. However, if it is known that the apparently straightforward claim will give rise to a more complex issue by way of defence, e.g. relating to the validity of a disclaimer, the effect of an authorised guarantee agreement or an individual or corporate voluntary arrangement, it is likely to be appropriate to issue the claim in the Property, Trusts & Probate List in the B&PCs.

BONA VACANTIA, CROWN DISCLAIMER AND ESCHEAT

27.17 Responsibility for dealing with bona vacantia, Crown disclaimer and escheat lies with the Crown, the Duchy of Cornwall or the Duchy of Lancaster. **1A-271**

27.18 Any application for a vesting order should be made using Part 8 and be supported by evidence.

27.19 Where the legal estate in property has been terminated due to the dissolution of a company, the court may order the creation of a corresponding estate and then vest it in the person who would have been entitled to the estate had it continued to exist (section 181 Law of Property Act 1925).

27.20 Alternatively it may be possible to apply for a vesting order under the Companies Act or the Insolvency Act. Further guidance on bona vacantia and escheat generally can be found in Chapter 25 (Trusts) at paragraphs 25.73 to 25.76.

27.21 Further guidance on Part 8 claims can be found in Chapter 13.

27.22 Further guidance on vesting orders in an insolvency context can be found in Chapter 21 (Insolvency and Companies List).

REFERENCE TO CONVEYANCING COUNSEL

27.23 CPR 40.18 and PD 40D paragraph 6 provide that the court may direct conveyancing counsel to prepare a report on title of any land or draft any document. Conveyancing Counsel's fees are governed by PD 44 paragraph 5.2. **1A-272**

27.24 It should now be extremely rare for this procedure to be used and the court is more likely to direct expert evidence on any issues relating to title.

27.25 If exceptionally it is necessary to invoke this procedure under CPR 40.18 any order directing the appointment of conveyancing counsel to determine an issue pursuant to CPR 40.18 must be notified to the Chief Master.

27.26 The Chief Master will then nominate one of the conveyancing counsel of the court and provide them with a copy of the court order and make such other directions as are appropriate in relation to the provision of documents or otherwise.

CHAPTER 28 REVENUE LIST (RL)

GENERAL

28.1 The purpose of the Revenue List is to determine major points of principle where HMRC are a party. **1A-273**

28.2 The Revenue List should *not* be used for claims in respect of disputed tax liabilities, recovery of taxes or duties, which should either be brought in the First-tier Tribunal (Tax Chamber) ('FTT') or the Business List as appropriate.

28.3 The Revenue List should *not* be used for claims which can and should be raised by way of an appeal to the FTT under the statutory scheme. See for example *Revenue and Customs v MCX Dunlin (UK) Ltd* [2021] EWCA Civ 186.

28.4 Parties should consider carefully whether the proposed claim should be brought in the Revenue List at all and if so whether it should be by way of Part 7 or Part 8.

28.5 The general provisions of the Civil Procedure Rules, Practice Directions and this Guide apply to claims issued in the Revenue List.

CHAPTER 29 ACCOUNTS AND INQUIRIES

29.1 Proceedings for an account or an inquiry in the Chancery Division are regulated by the Civil Procedure Rules ('CPR')Practice Direction ('PD') 40A (Accounts, Inquiries etc.). **1A-274**

INQUIRY AS TO DAMAGES

29.2 Where issues of causation and/or quantum are not addressed at the same time as issues of liability, the court may order an inquiry as to the level of damages or equitable compensation for loss suffered that is to be paid in a wide variety of circumstances. The provisions set out in PD 40A, as well as the additional guidance set out below, are of general application in relation to such **1A-275**

inquiries. Issues arising in the intellectual property context are dealt with at paragraph 29.18 below. An inquiry may also be ordered in respect of undertakings as to damages given when obtaining an interim injunction or similar relief, as set out at paragraph 29.20 below.

ACCOUNT

1A-276 **29.3** This is a discretionary remedy and may also be ordered in a wide variety of circumstances, with the following being the more common instances with cross-references to further parts of this Guide where appropriate:

ACCOUNTING FOR PROPERTY HELD IN A FIDUCIARY CAPACITY:

1A-277 **29.4** This form of account will commonly be ordered against trustees, executors, agents, receivers, guardians and others who hold property for others in a fiduciary custodial capacity, as well as those required to account as a constructive trustee in respect of the receipt of trust property. There are two types of account for property held in a fiduciary capacity. They are distinct from one another in principle. It is crucial that any party seeking either account against a custodial fiduciary should clearly plead on what basis the account is sought.

i. The first is an account in common form. On such an account the fiduciary must account only for the fund they have received. Where the fiduciary has misapplied any property, that misapplication will be disallowed, and the fiduciary required to make good any loss by way of a payment of equitable compensation.
ii. The second is an account on the footing of wilful default. That is available where the fiduciary has failed by their default to bring into the fund property which they should have brought in. In such a case the account will be surcharged with the property which ought to have been included, and the fiduciary will be required to make the loss good by payment of equitable compensation.

29.5 The court may decide, in a suitable case, either to order an account only of particular assets or transactions, on either the common basis or on the basis of wilful default and/or to order that an account of only some particular assets or transactions on one basis and some on another basis.

29.6 Following the taking of the account the court may order the accounting party to restore any shortfall found to exist, or in an appropriate case to make a direct payment to the party seeking the account.

PARTNERSHIP ACCOUNTS:

1A-278 **29.7** Particular considerations that arise between partners, including accounting for the assets and liabilities of a partnership upon dissolution, are addressed further at Chapter 18 (Business List: Partnership).

ACCOUNTS OF PROFITS:

1A-279 **29.8** This form of account will commonly be ordered following a finding of breach of fiduciary duty or confidence with the purpose of establishing the true measure of the profit or benefit obtained. However, even if a claimant elects as their remedy an account of profits this may only be ordered at the court's discretion in connection with disputes involving the infringement of intellectual property rights (see paragraph 29.18 below).

CO-OWNERSHIP ACCOUNTS:

1A-280 **29.9** Accounts may be ordered in respect of the income, capital, expenses and dealings with co-owned property, primarily land. In the context of land where one co-owner has occupied exclusively, the account will also establish the quantum of any occupation rent to which other co-owners are entitled, and any allowance to be made upon sale in respect of improvements or liabilities repaid, enhancing the value of the land. Co-ownership accounts will usually be ordered only after the parties' respective beneficial interests in the property concerned have been established.

DIRECTIONS

1A-281 **29.10** Where a judgment or order directs the taking of an account or inquiry, it will usually give directions as to how the account or inquiry is to be conducted.

FOR ACCOUNTS

1A-282 **29.11** The process of taking an account requires the accounting party to first render an account, with the party seeking the account then obliged to raise its objections to the same. Accordingly, the court will commonly give directions as to:

(a) who is to lodge the account and within what period, and how the same is to be verified;
(b) within what period objection is to be made, and how any notice of objection is to be verified;
(c) arrangements for inspection of books of account, vouchers or other relevant documents, and whether the relevant books of account are to be evidence of their contents; and

(d) whether statements of case (usually points of claim and points of defence) shall be served and filed, and if so, within what time period.

29.12 The parties are encouraged to consider whether the use of an adapted form of Scott Schedule may assist the parties and the court to identify issues between the parties in order to facilitate consideration with the court at an early stage as to how any issues should be addressed.

FOR INQUIRIES

29.13 An inquiry as to damages/equitable compensation will usually commence with the claimant particularising and evidencing the loss and damage that is said to have been suffered, and proceed with the defendant challenging the same. The court will commonly give directions as to: **1A-283**

(a) whether the inquiry is to proceed on written evidence or with statements of case, usually points of claim, points of defence, points of reply, and whether schedules are to be produced for each party to comment upon;
(b) directions for service of such evidence, statements of case and schedules; and
(c) directions as to disclosure.

29.14 If directions are not given in the judgment or order, an application should be made to the assigned Master or ICC Judge as soon as possible to specify the directions sought. Before making the application, applicants should write to the other parties setting out the directions they seek and inviting their response within 14 days. The application to the court should not be made until after the expiry of that period unless there is some special urgency. The application must state that the other parties have been consulted and attach copies of the applicant's letter to the other parties and of any response from them. The Master or ICC Judge will then consider what directions are appropriate. In complex cases the Master or ICC Judge may direct a case management conference.

29.15 If any inquiry is estimated to last more than two days and involves very large sums of money or strongly contested issues of fact or difficult points of law, the Master or ICC Judge may direct that it be heard by a HCJ. The parties are under an obligation to consider whether, in any particular case, the inquiry is more suitable to be heard by a HCJ and should assist the Master or ICC Judge in this. Accounts, however long they are estimated to take, will normally be heard by the Master or ICC Judge, other than in intellectual property cases.

COSTS BUDGETING

29.16 Where proceedings are for an account, costs budgeting (where applicable - see Chapter 6) includes the costs of taking the account. If accounts and inquiries follow as a separate process after the trial in which issues of liability or any points of principle relating to the account are addressed, costs budgeting in relation to the account and inquiries should usually be deferred until after liability and issues of principle have been determined, and addressed as part of the directions before commencement of that later stage. **1A-284**

29.17 If the parties are unable to reach agreement as to whether costs budgeting in relation to the taking of the account should be included in the costs budget for the first trial, the parties should seek the input of the court at an early stage. Consideration should be given as to the utility of the parties having an understanding of the likely costs of taking the account as part of the first costs budget.

INTELLECTUAL PROPERTY CASES

29.18 In intellectual property infringement cases there is usually a split trial. Only after liability has been established will directions be given for a hearing to assess the quantum of loss or damage. The defendant's disclosure for the trial on liability will not usually include many documents relating to the quantity or value of sales of infringing products or services or to the cost of producing those goods or services. Where there is to be a split trial and there are likely to be alternative remedies if liability is established, it will rarely be useful to provide costs budgets for all those alternative remedies at the liability stage. Parties should therefore consider carefully the approach to be adopted in such cases (see paragraphs 29.16-29.17 above and Chapter 6). **1A-285**

29.19 Consequently, claimants typically seek either an inquiry as to loss and damage or an account of profits as alternative remedies. If so, then an election will usually need to be made as to which of the two the claimant wishes to proceed with, once liability has been established. In order for a successful claimant to have sufficient relevant information to enable such an election to be made, the court will usually make an order (following *Island Records Ltd v Tring International plc* [1996] 1 WLR 1256)for the defendant to give disclosure of financial information. The order then provides for the claimant to make the election within a short time period. Once the election has been made, the court will give directions for the further conduct of the account or inquiry, as above.

INTERIM INJUNCTIONS ETC.

29.20 Where an interim injunction, search order or freezing order is granted, the applicant is required to give a cross-undertaking in damages to compensate the respondent if the court **1A-286**

subsequently determines that the applicant was not entitled to the relief granted. In those circumstances an inquiry as to loss or damage suffered by the respondent may be ordered to assess the quantum, following the procedure set out in PD 40A, as well as the additional guidance set out in this Chapter 29.

CHAPTER 30 APPEALS

GENERAL

1A-287 **30.1** This chapter provides guidance about how to commence and pursue an appeal in the Chancery Division.

30.2 It should be read in conjunction with the detailed procedure for appeals is set out in CPR 52 and its Practice Directions 52A, 52B and 52D.

30.3 A High Court Judge ('HCJ') of the Chancery Division has jurisdiction to consider the following types of appeals:

(a) appeals from decisions of Circuit Judges and Recorders in the County Court (except where the decision was on an appeal from the decision of a District Judge);
(b) appeals from decisions of District Judges in the County Court in personal and corporate insolvency proceedings and proceedings brought pursuant to the Companies Act 2006 (appeals from decisions of District Judges in the County Court in other civil matters are considered by Circuit Judges);
(c) appeals from decisions of Chancery Masters;
(d) appeals from decisions of Insolvency and Company Court Judges ('ICC Judges') (where those decisions are not themselves made on appeal from the County Court);
(e) appeals from decisions of B&PC District Judges in a B&PC District Registry;
(f) appeals and applications arising from arbitration awards, pursuant to section 67 to 70 of the Arbitration Act 1996;
(g) specialist statutory appeals, such as appeals under section 217(1)of the Pensions Act 2004 and the Pension Schemes Act 1993.

30.4 Where the appeal is from the decision of a District Judge in the County Court made in proceedings pursuant to the Companies Acts, the appeal will be made to an ICC Judge where the appeal centre is the Royal Courts of Justice, and to a HCJ, Section 9 Judge or Deputy HCJ elsewhere.

30.5 ICC Judges also have an appellate jurisdiction in relation to decisions of District Judges sitting in the County Court on the South Eastern Circuit in corporate insolvency proceedings. Schedule 10 of the Insolvency (England and Wales) Rules 2016 sets out whether an appeal in such proceedings lies to a HCJ or Section 9 Judge in a District Registry or to an ICC Judge in the Rolls Building. Such proceedings also include appeals in claims under sections 6 to 8A or 9A of the Company Directors Disqualification Act 1986 and certain applications made under section 17 of that Act for permission to act notwithstanding a disqualification order or undertaking.

30.6 Details relating to appeals and routes of appeal in insolvency proceedings are found in the Practice Direction on Insolvency Proceedings and in relation to company directors disqualification claims in the Practice Direction on Company Directors Disqualification Proceedings.

30.7 For further guidance on where to make an application for permission to appeal in respect of intellectual property claims: see CPR 63.16.

30.8 For further guidance on appeals in respect of the Pensions Ombudsman see Chapter 26 (Pensions).

30.9 Further guidance on the destination of appeals can be found at CPR 52.3(5) which sets out in two tables where to issue an application for permission to appeal on first appeals. There is no difference between an interim and final decision.

30.10 Further guidance on the destination of statutory appeals can be found in PD 52D. Where such an appeal is to be made to a HCJ in the Chancery Division, the procedures and time limits in this chapter apply except as varied by PD 52D or any specific statute.

30.11 Applications for permission to appeal a decision of a Master, Deputy Master or District Judge sitting in the Queens Bench Division should not be issued in the ChD B&PCs London nor should an appeal from the County Court that by its subject matter is more suited for consideration in the Queens Bench Division.

30.12 Applications for permission to appeal from a relevant decision of the County Court outside London and the South Eastern Circuit should be issued in the relevant B&PC District Registry.

APPLICATION FOR PERMISSION TO APPEAL

1A-288 **30.13** Permission to appeal is required in all cases except appeals against committal orders and certain statutory appeals. Permission to appeal will be granted only where the court considers that the appeal would have a real prospect of success or there is some other compelling reason why the appeal should be heard (CPR 52.6(1)).

30.14 Any party wishing to appeal a decision of the lower court (known as the appellant) must file an Appellant's Notice on Form N161 within the time limit set out in CPR 52 (21 days) or as varied in any order whether or not the judge of the lower court has granted permission to appeal, and must pay the appropriate fee. There are sometimes different time limits for statutory appeals and care should be taken to ensure that the party seeking to file an Appellants Notice complies with the relevant prescribed time limit. The time to file the N161 is counted from the date the decision of the lower court was made, *not* from the date that the formal order recording the decision was issued (CPR 52.12 (2)(b)) unless that time limit is varied by any order of the court.

30.15 Any application for an extension of time to issue the application for permission to appeal should be made in the N161. An explanation of why an extension of time should be granted must be provided.

30.16 An application for permission to appeal should usually first be made to the judge who made the decision against which the appellant wants to appeal. This should be made either at the conclusion of the hearing at which the decision is made or when a judgment is handed down. If the judgment is handed down on a non-attendance basis, any application for permission to appeal should be made or notified in writing in advance of the time at which the judgment or order is to be handed down. If the parties require a hearing of the application, the court should be requested to adjourn the hearing of the application for permission to appeal, for written submissions or a hearing, and to extend the time for filing an N161: *McDonald v Rose* [2019] EWCA Civ 4 at [21].

30.17 If the lower court refuses permission to appeal, or permission is not applied for at the conclusion of the hearing or when judgment is handed down or at any adjourned hearing, the application for permission to appeal must then be made to the appeal court, by filing the N161, and paying the appropriate fee at the appeal court within the time permitted.

30.18 Applications for permission to appeal to a HCJ are filed through CE-File. A new file will be opened for the appeal and the parties must thereafter use the new reference for any filing in respect of the appeal, not the underlying case reference or file.

30.19 The use of CE-File is mandatory for professional court users and is strongly encouraged for litigants in person. Further guidance on the use of CE-File can be found in Chapter 2 and Appendix E. There is further general guidance for unrepresented parties in Appendix H.

30.20 If an unrepresented party is unable to use CE-File they may file their application for permission to appeal in person at the Chancery Judges' Listing Office ('Judges' Listing'), which in the Rolls Building is located on the ground floor, or by post.

30.21 The application for permission to appeal will then be uploaded to CE-File and an electronic court file will be created. Enquiries relating to such applications should be made through the CE File. If an unrepresented party is unable to access CE-File, they should make their enquiry by letter to Judges' Listing.

30.22 Applications for permission to appeal for hearing by an ICC Judge are filed through CE-File or, as an alternative for unrepresented parties unable to use CE-File, in person to the ICC Issue Team, also located on the ground floor of the Rolls Building.

STAY OF LOWER COURT'S DECISION

30.23 Unless the lower court or the appeal court orders otherwise, an appeal does not operate as a stay of any order or decision of the lower court. An application for a stay of execution or enforcement of the lower court's decision should be made in the N161. Evidence in support, setting out the reasons for seeking the stay, should be included. The application is dealt with on the papers, without notice, unless the court requires a hearing. Any person affected by the without notice decision may apply to set aside or vary the order made: PD 52B, paragraph 7. **1A-289**

DOCUMENTS TO BE FILED WITH FORM N161

30.24 The appellant must lodge a copy of the sealed order appealed against and the grounds of appeal with Form N161, together with the documents as set out in PD 52B paragraph 4.2, and pay the appropriate court fee (unless exempt). A skeleton argument must be filed within 14 days of filing the N161. The remaining documents required to make up the appeal bundle, including a copy of judgment of the decision under appeal, must be filed within 35 days of filing the N161, or within any extended period ordered by the court. **1A-290**

30.25 If the judge handed down a written judgment setting out the decision which the appellant seeks to appeal, there is no need to obtain a transcript, but a copy of the written judgment must be included in the appeal bundle.

30.26 If a written judgment is not available, the appellant must obtain a transcript of the judgment or the decision which they seek permission to appeal. Where a judgment has been officially recorded, the appellant must apply for an approved transcript within 7 days of filing an N161. To obtain a transcript the appellants should complete Form EX107; a fee is required to be paid. In most cases only the judgment itself will be required, not a full transcript of the hearing.

30.27 An application for permission to obtain a copy of the transcript at public expense must be made in the N161, accompanied by a completed Form EX105. Before directing that the transcript be provided at public expense the court must be satisfied that the applicant qualifies for fee remission or is otherwise in such poor financial circumstances that the cost of obtaining a transcript would be an excessive burden and that the interests of justice require a transcript to be provided at public expense.

30.28 If there is a delay in obtaining a transcript of the decision, an application for an extension of time to lodge the appeal bundle must be made to a judge as soon as possible and in any event before the time for lodging the bundle has expired. The judge will usually grant a first extension of time and may grant a further extension, if sufficient explanation of the reasons for the delay and the steps taken by the appellant to obtain the transcript are provided, supported by evidence of the attempts made to obtain it. If a transcript has proved difficult to obtain, the appellant should try to obtain a note of the decision to be appealed that has been approved by the judge or lawyers representing any party at the hearing below.

30.29 If a PD 52B compliant appeal bundle has not been lodged by the expiry of any permitted extension of time, the application for permission to appeal may be struck out without further warning, or the court may make an order that unless it is lodged by a specified time and date the application will be automatically struck out.

PERMISSION TO APPEAL TO THE HIGH COURT

1A-291 **30.30** An application for permission to appeal will usually be determined by a HCJ on the papers without an oral hearing. A Section 9 judge and a Deputy HCJ have no jurisdiction to decide the permission to appeal application, but if permission is granted some appeals may be heard by Section 9 judges and Deputy HCJs: see CPR PD 52A paras 4.3 to 4.4. If permission is refused on paper, the appellant is normally entitled to request that it be reconsidered at an oral hearing. The request may be made by letter and must be filed within 7 days after service of the notice that permission has been refused; see CPR 52.4(6). No further fee is payable.

30.31 However, a judge who refuses permission to appeal, and considers that the application is totally without merit, they may refuse permission for the application to be reconsidered at an oral hearing; see CPR 52.4(3).

30.32 Sometimes, the application for permission to appeal, or for permission to appeal out of time, is adjourned to be heard in court, on notice to the respondent. It may also be listed to be heard immediately before the appeal hearing which will follow on if permission is granted.

HIGH COURT APPEALS MEDIATION SCHEME

1A-292 **30.33** Where permission to appeal against an order of the County Court is granted or the application is adjourned to be heard in court, the matter will be referred to mediation unless the judge considers that the appeal is unsuitable for mediation. Mediation is not compulsory and the parties have up to 14 days in which to agree to mediate. Details of the mediation scheme can be found on the CEDR website. No stay of the appeal is granted: it will be listed for a date that allows time for a mediation. The parties must inform the court if the appeal has been settled. The parties are expected to agree sensible extensions of time for steps that need to be taken before the appeal hearing, including for service of a respondent's notice.

RESPONDENT'S NOTICE

1A-293 **30.34** A respondent to an appeal may seek permission to appeal the whole or part of the decision of the lower court, or they may ask the appeal court to uphold the order of the lower court for reasons different from or additional to those given by the lower court. In either case, the respondent must file a respondent's notice using an N162. The N162 must be filed in accordance with CPR 52.13 (4) and (5) (generally, within 14 days after the respondent is notified that the appeal will be heard) or within any extended time agreed or permitted.

APPEALS TO THE COURT OF APPEAL: PERMISSION TO APPEAL

1A-294 **30.35** An appeal from a decision of a HCJ (and of a Section 9 Judge or a Deputy HCJ) is to the Court of Appeal (unless an enactment or order makes it final and unappealable). Permission is required in all cases except where the order is for committal. Permission may be sought at the conclusion of the hearing or when judgment is handed down, or from the Court of Appeal in the N161. This is a first appeal. See CPR PD 52C for the specific requirements for first appeals to the Court of Appeal.

30.36 If the decision which is sought to be appealed was itself made in relation to an appeal (other than an appeal from the Comptroller of Patents), permission for a second appeal may only be granted by the Court of Appeal: CPR 52.7. See CPR 63.16 in relation to appeals from the Comptroller of Patents and registrars of trade marks and registered designs.

30.37 An appeal from the decision of an ICC Judge (where the ICC Judge's decision was itself made on an appeal from the County Court) is a second appeal and also lies to the Court of Appeal, and permission to appeal may only be granted by the Court of Appeal.

DISMISSAL BEFORE DETERMINATION OF AN APPLICATION OR AN APPEAL

1A-295 **30.38** PD 52A, paragraphs 6.1 to 6.3 set out the procedure for all appeals where an appellant no longer wishes to pursue an application for permission to appeal or an appeal.

30.39 An application for permission to appeal may be struck out if the appellant fails to file an appeal bundle including a transcript of the decision of the lower court within the time specified by the court. An appeal may be struck out if an appellant fails to pay any security ordered for the costs of the appeal or to comply with any condition subject to which permission to appeal was granted.

EXHAUSTION OF REMEDIES

30.40 Where a party has exhausted their remedies available through the domestic courts and they want to pursue their rights in the European Court of Human Rights (ECtHR) they will first need to obtain a certificate of the exhaustion of their domestic remedies. **1A-296**

CHAPTER 31 ENFORCEMENT

GENERAL

31.1 It is not the purpose of this Guide to provide Judgment Creditors or Judgment Debtors with legal or procedural advice on post judgment methods of enforcement nor is it the purpose of this Guide to provide a comprehensive list of enforcement options. This Guide is intended to provide guidance on the practice of the court in relation to post judgment methods of enforcement. **1A-297**

ENFORCEMENT OF JUDGMENTS IN OTHER JURISDICTIONS

31.2 Whether a judgment of the courts of England and Wales can be enforced in a foreign state depends on the law of that foreign state. **1A-298**

31.3 Many foreign states require a certified copy of a judgment. An application for a certified copy of the judgment should be made to the Master within the existing proceedings in which the judgment was obtained, in accordance with CPR 74.12, 74.13 and PD 74A. If the relevant enforcement regime requires a wet signature from a judge on the certificate or other enforcement form or document, the Judgment Creditor must complete the relevant forms and upload them to CE-File as a separate document and not as part of a general exhibit, to enable them to be printed for signature by the judge.

ENFORCEMENT OF FOREIGN JUDGMENTS IN ENGLAND AND WALES (CPR 74)

31.4 Whether a foreign judgment is enforceable in England and Wales will depend on where the judgment originates from and what the relevant enforcement regime is for that foreign state. **1A-299**

31.5 In the case of foreign judgments from EU member states it will also depend on whether the judgment was obtained in proceedings instituted before or after 31 December 2020.

31.6 Some foreign judgments need to be registered before they can be enforced.

31.7 Applications for registration of a judgment pursuant to CPR 74.3 should be made to the Central Office of the Senior Courts, Royal Courts of Justice, Strand, London WC2A 2LL and *not* to the B&PCs.

31.8 Enforcement between United Kingdom jurisdictions is governed by CPR 74.14 to 74.18.

ENFORCEMENT OF JUDGMENTS

31.9 This chapter considers the most common forms of enforcement in the Chancery Division. **1A-300**

31.10 Examination of a Judgment Debtor, Charging Orders and Third Party Debt Orders each have their own procedural regime and forms. In each case the court will consider the initial application on paper and without notice to the Judgment Debtor and if satisfied that the papers are in order will make an order on paper as the first stage in the enforcement process. This will be drawn up by the court and sent to the Judgment Creditor for service. Parties should ensure that they comply with the requirements of each procedural regime.

EXAMINATION OF A JUDGMENT DEBTOR (DEBTOR QUESTIONING) (CPR 71)

31.11 A Judgment Creditor may apply for an order requiring a Judgment Debtor or, if the Judgment Debtor is a company, an officer of that company, to attend court to provide information about the Judgment Debtor's means or other information needed to enforce the Judgment Debt (CPR 71.2). **1A-301**

31.12 An application for Debtor Questioning should be issued in the court in which the judgment or order giving rise to the Judgment Debt was made. The application is made on paper and without notice in Form N316 which should include the information required by CPR 71.2 and PD 73 1 and any additional questions or requests for documents that the Judgment Creditor seeks.

31.13 If the court is satisfied that the papers are in order it will make an order specifying the amount of the debt and directing that the Judgment Debtor attend court at the time and place specified in the order to answer such questions as the court may require on oath and to provide the documents described in the application. Unless the court orders otherwise the questions will be those in EX140 or EX141 as appropriate.

31.14 The Order for Debtor Questioning once made is provided to the Judgment Creditor for them to effect personal service (CPR 71.3).

31.15 The court will usually direct that the Debtor Questioning take place in the County Court local to the Judgment Debtor. The court officer or District Judge in the Judgment Debtor's local County Court will undertake the Debtor Questioning on behalf of the ChD B&PCs London.

31.16 The underlying claim to which the Judgment Debt relates is not transferred to the County Court and any further enforcement action or other steps in the underlying claim will continue to be undertaken in the B&PCs where the claim remains. This may include enforcement action for non-compliance with the Debtor Questioning order (see paragraphs 31.21 to 31.23), which will be remitted back to the B&PCs.

31.17 The Judgment Creditor may request that the Debtor Questioning take place before a judge in the B&PCs but will have to provide compelling reasons why such an order should be made. This should be provided by letter filed on CE-File as the same time as the application.

31.18 If the Debtor Questioning takes place before a judge the questioning will be conducted by the Judgment Creditor or his legal representative rather than a court officer.

31.19 In either case any documents produced at court pursuant to the Debtor Questioning order will be retained by the court. The Judgment Creditor can inspect them and take copies unless the court orders otherwise.

31.20 The Judgment Creditor must comply with CPR 71.5.

31.21 If the Judgment Debtor fails to attend for questioning at the time and place indicated in the order, refuses to answer any questions, or fails to comply with the order in some other way such as failing to provide the documents identified by the order, the Judgment Debtor may be considered to be in contempt of court.

31.22 If the Debtor Questioning was being undertaken by a court officer or District Judge in the County Court or a Master or District Judge in the B&PCs they will certify the non-compliance in accordance with CPR 71.8 and PD 71 6 and the non-compliance will be referred to a HCJ or Section 9 Judge in the B&PC (not the County Court in which the Debtor Questioning was undertaken).

31.23 The HCJ or Section 9 Judge will then consider whether to make a final order to comply, a suspended committal order or a committal order (see CPR 71.8, PD 71 7 and PD 71 8).

CHARGING ORDERS (CPR 73)

1A-302 **31.24** A Charging Order can be sought to secure a judgment debt and may be made in relation to an interest in land or securities.

31.25 An application for an Interim Charging Order ('ICO') in the ChD B&PCs London should be made within the same proceedings in which the relevant judgment was obtained. It should identify the nature of the Judgment Debtor's interest in the asset to be charged and any other creditors or those who may have a beneficial interest.

31.26 The ICO application may be made using form N379 for an interest in land or N380 for an interest in securities. The ICO application may include more than one asset (PD 71 1.3). The ICO application is made without notice to the Judgment Debtor and is considered on paper. If the papers are in order an ICO will be made substantially in form CH45 and returned to the Judgment Creditor for service. The court will list a hearing to determine if an ICO should be made Final (an 'FCO').

31.27 CPR 73.7(7) identifies all those including creditors or other parties to whom notice of the Final hearing should be given, and CPR 73.7.5 sets out what must be served and by when.

31.28 CPR 6 and the rules relating to service out of the jurisdiction apply to Charging Orders. Although an existing permission to serve all documents out of the jurisdiction may extend to the Judgment Debtor, it will not extend to a creditor or other party who must be given notice under CPR 73.7.7. Permission should be sought (if required) on paper by way of a separate application notice (using an N244 under CPR 23) at the same time as an application is made for an ICO.

31.29 If the application for an ICO relates to land and the Judge considers it appropriate (for example where the ICO is over the Judgment Debtor's main residential home) the judge may transfer the Final hearing to consider whether the ICO should be made final to the Judgment Debtor's home court, including their local county court.

31.30 The claim itself is not transferred and any subsequent applications within the claim should still be made to court in which the claim is based.

31.31 A separate FCO will be needed for each property or security over which a Charging Order is sought, except where an application for a Charging Order seeks an ICO against all legal owners of the same property. An FCO if made should be substantially in Form CH46.

31.32 If the court adjourns the FCO hearing, the Judgment Creditor should ensure that any draft order extends the ICO to the adjourned FCO hearing.

31.33 An FCO in respect of securities may, at the Judgment Creditor's request and if considered appropriate, include a Stop Notice. For Stop Notices generally see CPR 73.17 to 73.21.

31.34 Unless the court orders otherwise, the Judgment Creditor is only entitled to Fixed Costs in accordance with the Table in CPR 45.8 together with reasonable disbursements, which are usually limited to: the court fee, fees for obtaining official copy entries of title and Land Registry fees as appropriate.

THIRD PARTY DEBT ORDER (CPR 72)

31.35 Third Party Debt Orders follow the same procedure as Charging Orders. **1A-303**

31.36 An application for an Interim Third Party Debtor Order (ITPDO) is made on paper and without notice, using form N349.

31.37 If the papers are in order the court will issue an ITPDO which will include a hearing date. It will also include an amount for the Fixed Costs to which the Judgment Creditor would be entitled under CPR 45.8 (together with any relevant court fee) if the whole balance of the judgment debt were recovered.

31.38 The Judgment Creditor must serve the ITPDO on the Third Party and the Judgment Debtor.

31.39 A Third Party bank or building society must provide the information set out in CPR 72.6 (1) to (3) to the court and the Judgment Creditor within 7 days of being served with the ITPDO. A Third Party other than a bank or building society must provide the information set out in CPR 72.6 (4) to the court and the Judgment Creditor within 7 days of being served with the ITPDO.

31.40 In either case the Third Party must not make any payment which reduces the amount they owe/hold for the Judgment Debtor to less than the amount specified in the ITPDO. They should not pay the money to the Judgment Creditor or the court.

31.41 An ITPDO cannot be made against money held in court for the credit of the Judgment Debtor, instead the procedure set out in CPR 72.10 must be followed.

31.42 A Judgment Debtor who is an individual who suffers hardship in meeting their ordinary living expenses as a result of the ITPDO may apply using N244 under CPR 23 for a hardship payment under CPR 72.7. The application must be supported by evidence.

31.43 If the Third Party or the Judgment Debtor object to the ITPDO being made final, for example because the Third Party does not accept that they owe the Judgment Debtor any money or they say that another person has a claim to the money, they must file and serve written evidence as soon as possible and, in any event, not less than 3 days before the hearing. The Judgment Creditor must also file and serve any evidence disputing the Third Party's case as soon as possible and, in any event, not less than 3 days before the hearing where possible.

31.44 In either case if the court is notified that some other person may have an interest in the money specified in the ITPDO it will direct that the Judgment Creditor give them notice. At the hearing the court will consider whether to make the ITPDO final. If the ITPDO is made final the Final Third Party Debt Order is enforceable as an order for the payment of money as against the Third Party and the Third Party can pay the money held to the Judgment Creditor. The court may discharge the ITPDO and dismiss the application and is likely to do so if the ITPDO has not secured any money belonging to the Judgment Debtor, for example if a bank cannot identify any accounts in the name of the Judgment Debtor or any such accounts as are identified held no money at the time of the ITPDO.

31.45 In the event of a dispute the court will determine the issues at the hearing, where possible, adjourn the hearing, or direct a trial of the issues and give directions. In such circumstances the court will consider whether any substantive hearing should be transferred to the county court where the Judgment Debtor resides. In such cases any order should include continuation of the ITPDO pending resolution of the dispute unless the court orders otherwise. Fixed Costs apply to any application for a Third Party Debtor Order (CPR 45.8) together with any relevant court fee, unless the court orders otherwise. An HMCTS leaflet EX325 provides advice on Third Party Debt Orders and Charging Orders.

ORDER FOR SALE (CPR 73.10C)

31.46 Proceedings to enforce a FCO over land by way of an Order for Sale are new proceedings **1A-304**
and should be commenced in the court in which the FCO was made, in the Property Trusts and Probate List using Part 8. For guidance on Part 8 see Chapter 13.

31.47 The Judgment Creditor should consider carefully the evidential requirements set out in CPR 73.10C and PD 73 4.3. The court is unlikely to make an order for sale if there is little or no equity in the property and/or no actual benefit to the claimant.

31.48 If the Judgment Debtor does not respond to the claim, the Judgment Creditor should follow the procedure set out in paragraphs 13.14 to 13.15. Form CH44 should be adapted as appropriate. The final hearing/disposal hearing will be on written evidence.

31.49 The Judgment Creditor has no statutory power of sale nor a legal title that they can convey. The order for sale must therefore either include a vesting order or an order giving power to convey. This will depend on whether the Judgment Debtor is the sole owner of the land or a joint owner.

31.50 PD 73 has specimen orders annexed to it. Forms CH36 and CH37 may also be used, adapted as necessary for the particular circumstances.

PERMISSION TO ENFORCE A WRIT OF POSSESSION

31.51 In certain circumstances a party with the benefit of a possession order may not enforce it **1A-305**
without permission of the court (see CPR 83).

31.52 An application for permission to issue and/or enforce a writ of possession may be made without notice and on paper (unless the court directs otherwise). It must be supported by evidence including a copy of the underlying order in respect of which permission is sought. In most cases Fixed Costs apply see CPR 45.8.

WRITS

1A-306 **31.53** Requests to issue writs of execution and writs of control relating to enforcement of B&PC judgments should generally be made in the High Court or District Registry where the underlying claim took place. Further guidance can be found in CPR 83 and PD 83.

CHAPTER 32 COURT FUNDS (PAYMENTS INTO AND OUT OF COURT)

1A-307 **32.1** Reference should be made to Part 37 of the Civil Procedure Rules ('CPR') and CPR Practice Direction ('PD') 37, as well as the Court Funds Rules 2011, in relation to making an application for payment out of court funds.

PAYMENTS INTO COURT

1A-308 **32.2** Any trustee (including personal representatives) who wishes to make a payment into court should follow the procedure set out in CPR 37. The evidence in support should comply with PD37, paragraph 6.1. If the trustee is a mortgagee the evidence in support should include additional information as set out in paragraph 32.3 below.

MORTGAGEES

1A-309 **32.3** Mortgagees wishing to lodge surplus proceeds of sale in court under section 63 of the Trustee Act 1925 must in their witness statement, in addition to the matters set out in PD 37, paragraph 6.1:

(a) set out the steps they have taken to fulfil their obligation under section 105 of the Law of Property Act 1925 to pay other prior chargees (if any) and the mortgagor, and why those steps have not been successful; and

(b) exhibit official copies of the title of the mortgaged property.

32.4 Failure to set out what steps have been taken and why they were unsuccessful will usually result in the application being rejected by the court.

PAYMENTS OUT OF COURT FUNDS

APPLICATION

1A-310 **32.5** Applications under PD 37 for payment out of money held in court must be made by CPR 23 application notice (Form N244). The application notice and the court fee should be sent to the Miscellaneous Payments Team in the ChD B&PCs London; the application notice can also be CE-filed.

32.6 The following details must be included in Part 10 of the application notice:

(a) the reasons why the payment should be made;

(b) a statement confirming that no-one else has any claim to the money (or if there is another claimant providing details of that person and their interest);

(c) bank details of the person to whom the payment out of court should be made including the name and address of the bank/building society branch, its sort code, and the account title and number; and

(d) the Statement of Truth must be completed and signed.

32.7 Copies of documents which show an entitlement to the money in court and proof of identity (see paragraphs 32.23 to 32.28 below) must be exhibited to the application notice. The court may, in some cases, require certified copies or the original documents. Documents may be certified by a solicitor or any other person on the list of persons who may approve a passport application as long as the certifier provides his/her name and status, and legibly signs each copy; or copies may be certified at a Post Office. Where an original document is sent, this should be stated in the covering letter and its return requested.

32.8 Approval is shown not by a formally drawn order, but by the court signing the payment schedule in Form CFO 200.

APPLICATION BROUGHT ON BEHALF OF A DISSENTIENT SHAREHOLDER

1A-311 **32.9** In the case of an application for payment out of funds by or on behalf of a dissentient shareholder (a shareholder who did not consent to the acquisition of their company), the best evidence to be provided is the relevant share certificate(s). If the share certificate is unavailable, then the court will consider other documents showing communications with the shareholder such as a dividend notice, emails or other correspondence.

32.10 In cases where the application for payment out is brought by a personal representative long after the date the funds were paid into court, such direct evidence may be lacking. In such cases the court may consider the following documents to establish a link between the dissentient shareholder and the funds in court:

(a) evidence of the address of the shareholder as shown on the share register of the company;
(b) evidence of the address of the shareholder as shown on the schedule lodged in court when the dissentient shareholder's funds were paid in;
(c) the address shown in a will or grant of probate/administration; and/or
(d) evidence from a tracing agency or similar establishing the link between the dissentient shareholder and their address as set down in the share register of the company/lodgement schedule.

32.11 The above list is not intended to be prescriptive, other evidence establishing the requisite evidential link between the applicant and the funds in court will be considered. Please see paragraph 32.23 below for more details.

APPLICATION BROUGHT IN RESPECT OF SURPLUS FUNDS IN COURT FOLLOWING A SALE OF PROPERTY

32.12 In the case of an application made by a proprietor or co-proprietor for surplus funds following the sale of a property, evidence must be provided to show a link between the applicant and the property. The court may consider the following documents to establish a link between the applicant and the surplus property funds in court: **1A-312**

(a) conveyancing documents or official copies of the title. However the court is unlikely to accept historical official copies of the title alone as evidence of connection to the property;
(b) court documents or correspondence relating to the repossession of the property;
(c) other documents directed to the applicant at the property before repossession; and/or
(d) evidence from a tracing agency establishing the applicant at his or her current address was connected to the subject property.

32.13 In the case where an applicant makes an application for surplus funds as a chargee, the burden is on the applicant to establish entitlement to the funds as against all others who may have a claim on the funds in court. The applicant must establish that any prior charges have been released or discharged or that there is sufficient money in court so that they can establish entitlement to an identified balance; the court will not conduct any enquiries and applications that do not address prior charges or establish an entitlement notwithstanding the existence of prior charges will be dismissed.

32.14 Where the applicant claims surplus funds as a chargee, the court may consider the following documents to establish a link between the applicant and the surplus property funds in court:

(a) official copies of the title showing the charge; and/or
(b) any legal documents establishing the charge such as orders creating a charge over a proprietor's interest in the property.

32.15 Where an applicant seeking surplus funds as a proprietor or a chargee is unable to contact a prior chargee or is unable to identify the extent of prior liability, they should demonstrate in the application that reasonable steps have been taken to do so. This includes the steps taken to effect service/alternative service of the application on the prior chargee. The court will then consider what next steps should be taken.

32.16 Where the application for surplus funds is made by one of a number of joint proprietors of the subject property, then in addition to establishing their own entitlement to the funds, it will be for the joint proprietor to establish their entitlement as against co-owners. The applicant co-owner should produce evidence that the other co-owner(s) consent to the application and to the share of the surplus funds in court sought by the applicant.

32.17 Where consent has not been obtained from the other co-owner(s) for the division of surplus funds, the applicant should support the application with a witness statement setting out the circumstances of joint purchase, any agreements or assurances as to shares or other evidence that might bear on the parties' shares. All relevant documents should be exhibited to the application.

32.18 In the case where a co-owner has failed to respond to a proposed consent order for the division of funds or where, after diligent enquiries they cannot be traced, the applicant should include in the application evidence of the steps that have been taken to trace the co-owner with evidence regarding the co-owner's lack of response. The court will then give directions in respect of the application.

32.19 Where consent by a co-owner has been refused, the applicant should include that information and any supporting documents in their application. The court will then consider any directions for further disposal of the application, including whether the matter ought to be transferred to the County Court.

32.20 If a bankruptcy order has been made against the applicant, even if it has been discharged, the name of Trustee in Bankruptcy should be included in the application. The applicant will also need to explain why the funds being claimed belong to them and not the Trustee in Bankruptcy.

32.21 If an application is being made on behalf of a person who has died, the information regarding the deceased person must be provided to the best of the applicant's knowledge and belief.

DETERMINATION OF THE APPLICATION BY THE COURT

1A-313 **32.22** If there is a dispute as to entitlement to money in court, the Master will generally transfer the matter to the County Court. If, exceptionally, it is appropriate for the case to be retained in the High Court (for example if significant sums are involved or there are other linked proceedings) the Master may order it to proceed by Part 8 claim form (see Chapter 13) and may list it for disposal or directions.

EVIDENCE OF ENTITLEMENT

1A-314 **32.23** The person claiming to be entitled to funds held in court must produce evidence of their entitlement to the fund; failure to provide evidence may result in the application being dismissed.

32.24 This may be one or more of the following documents:

(a) Sealed copy of court order;
(b) Where the person entitled to the funds has died, a sealed copy of the grant of representation (grant of probate or letters of administration);
(c) Where there is more than one personal representative the written consent (or death certificate, if deceased) of every other representative (together with evidence of their identity - see below);
(d) Where the value of the estate is less than £5,000, a copy of the will (or written declaration of kinship if the person died intestate) and death certificate of the deceased, rather than a copy of the grant of representation;
(e) In the case of money paid in by a bank or building society (as mortgagee), or by a trustee, the paying-in witness statement or affidavit; and/or
(f) Where the applicant is the former landowner in an application for payment of monies paid into court following a compulsory purchase, documents evidencing title to the land at the relevant time and notice of the compulsory purchase order.

EVIDENCE OF IDENTITY

1A-315 **32.25** The person claiming entitlement must normally produce evidence of their identity.

32.26 This may be one or more of the following documents:

(a) passport;
(b) driving licence;
(c) UK identity card for foreign nationals, residence permit or travel documents issued by the Home Office;
(d) European Community or European Economic Area identity card;
(e) a birth or adoption certificate may be provided, but this is not absolute proof of identity and must be accompanied by one other supporting document;
(f) National insurance card or a letter from the Department of Work and Pensions showing NI number;
(g) The front page of a benefits book or a letter concerning state pension and showing NI number;
(h) P45, P60 or payslip;
(i) Student union card;
(j) Marriage certificate;
(k) Decree nisi or decree absolute; and/or
(l) Bank or building statement issued in the last 3 months.

EVIDENCE OF NAME OR ADDRESS CHANGE

1A-316 **32.27** Where the person claiming entitlement has changed their name, they must also produce one of the following (as appropriate):

(a) a marriage or civil partnership certificate;
(b) a decree nisi or decree absolute;
(c) a deed poll declaration; and/or
(d) An adoption certificate.

32.28 Where the person claiming entitlement has changed their address, they must produce:

(a) 2 of the following documents evidencing their previous address: utilities or council tax bill, or bank/building society statement from the relevant time; and
(b) A utilities bill or bank/building society statement issued within the last 3 months for their current address.

GLOSSARY

1A-317

Term	*Definition*
ADR	Alternative Dispute Resolution including (but not limited to) mediation, negotiation, early neutral evaluation (ENE), arbitration, adjudication and Chancery financial dispute resolution. See further Chapter 10.

Term	*Definition*
B&PCs	The Business and Property Courts of England and Wales comprising the Commercial Court, the Admiralty Court, the Circuit Commercial Court (formerly the Mercantile Court), the Technology and Construction Court, and the Chancery Division. The various B&PC lists and sub-lists are set out in Appendix F.
B&PC District Registry/ Registries	The district registries of the Business and Property Courts in Birmingham, Bristol, Cardiff, Leeds, Liverpool, Manchester and Newcastle. Further details about, and contact details for, the B&PC District Registries may be found in Appendix C.
Chancery District Registry/ Registries	The regional Chancery District Registries in Preston, Mold and Caernarfon. Further details about, and contact details for, the Chancery District Registries may be found in Appendix C.
ChD B&PCs London	The Chancery lists of the Business and Property Courts in London (as further set out in Appendix F).
ChFDR	Chancery financial dispute resolution, a form of alternative dispute resolution further described in Chapter 10.
CMC / CCMC	Case management conference at which directions will be given for the conduct of proceedings. Where costs management pursuant to Section II of CPR 3 and PD 3E is to be considered at the same conference, this is referred to as a costs and case management conference or CCMC. See further the guidance in Chapter 6.
Chancellor	The Chancellor of the High Court.
CLIPS	The Chancery Bar Litigants in Person Support Scheme providing assistance to litigants in person in the Judges' Application List as further described at Appendix H.
CO.IN	The Company Insolvency Pro Bono Scheme providing assistance to litigants in person (including unrepresented companies or corporations) in the winding up court as further described at Appendix H.
County Court	Pursuant to s.A1 of the County Court Act 1984 (as amended) there is now a single county court for England and Wales sitting in locations designated by the Lord Chancellor including the former locations of discrete county courts.
CPR	The Civil Procedure Rules (including CPR practice directions (PDs)).
Deputy HCJ	Fee paid deputy High Court Judges appointed pursuant to Section 9(4) of the Senior Courts Act 1981, as described at paragraph 1.13.
DQ	Directions Questionnaire to be filed before the first case management conference (CMC) in accordance with the guidance in Chapter 6.
DRD	Disclosure review document required to be prepared in connection with extended disclosure pursuant to CPR PD 51U and the guidance in Chapter 7.
ENE	Early neutral evaluation, a form of alternative dispute resolution further described in Chapter 10.
CE-File	The electronic case file kept in respect of proceedings in the Business and Property Courts, as described further at paragraphs 1.28.
GLO	A group litigation order in relation to which guidance is given at paragraphs 2.13 to 2.20.
Guide	The Chancery Guide
HCJ	High Court Judge.
Hot Tubbing	A term sometimes used to describe the practice of concurrent expert evidence addressed in paragraphs 9.42 to 9.44.
ICL	The Insolvency and Companies List described further in Chapter 21.
ICC Judge	A judge of the Insolvency and Companies Court.
IT	Information technology. For guidance on the use of IT at trial, see paragraphs 12.32 to 12.34.
IP	Intellectual property. For guidance in relation to claims within the intellectual property list, see Chapter 22.
Judge's Application List	The daily list of interim applications heard by Chancery High Court Judges and other authorised judges as further described in Chapter 15.
Judges' Listing	The Chancery Judges' Listing Office, contact details for which may be

Term	Definition
	found in Appendix A.
LCCDRD	The disclosure review document for to be prepared in connection with extended disclosure pursuant to CPR PD 51U and the guidance in Chapter 7 for less complex claims.
Masters' Appointments	Chancery Masters Appointments which deals with the listing of hearings before, and other logistical matters concerning, Chancery Masters. Contact details are provided in Appendix A.
McKenzie Friend	A person permitted to assist a litigant in person at a hearing in accordance with the guidance in paragraphs 2.55 to 2.62.
PD	Practice Directions within the Civil Procedure Rules (CPR).
PTR	The pre-trial review to be conducted in accordance with the guidance in Chapter 11.
Section 9 Judges	Specialist civil judges authorised to sit as judges in the High Court pursuant to s.9(1) of the Senior Courts Act 1981.

APPENDIX A

CONTACT DETAILS

1A-318 (all telephone numbers to be preceded by 020 and by 7947, except where indicated)

IN THE ROLLS BUILDING

Issue Section

Issue of all Chancery process including High Court Patents and IPEC claims. Issue Clerks (7783)

Email: *chancery.issue@justice.gov.uk.*

Chancery Masters' Appointments

Issue of all Masters' applications.
Clerks to Chancery Masters (7391)
Email: *chancery.mastersappointments@justice.gov.uk.*

Chancery Masters' Clerks

Clerks to Chancery Masters (7391).

Chancery High Court Judges' Listing

Chancery Judges' Listing, general enquiries & High Court Appeals (6690/7717)
Email: *ChanceryJudgesListing@justice.gov.uk*
Please see Appendix B for details of all judges and their clerks.

Chancery Associates

Team Leader, In Court Support/Usher (6322)
Associates (6733)

Insolvency and Companies Court

For general queries relating to the issue of Creditors' Bankruptcy Petitions, Applications to set aside Statutory Demands and other matters in the Insolvency and Companies List (6294/6102)
Insolvency and Companies Court Delivery Manager (7472)
Companies Schemes and Reductions of Capital (6727)
Email: *Rcjcompanies.orders@justice.gov.uk*
For general queries relating to case management and hearings (6731)
Email: *Rolls.ICL.Hearings1@justice.gov.uk*

Intellectual Property Enterprise Court

The IPEC is supervised by His Honour Judge Hacon. His clerk can be reached on *IPEC@justice.gov.uk*

Miscellaneous Payments out of Court Funds

Applications for payment out of money held in the Court Funds Office
Clerks (7929)
Email: *chancery.miscellaneouspayments@justice.gov.uk*

Court Recording and Transcription Unit
Clerks (6148)
Email: *TranscriptRequest.Rolls@justice.gov.uk*

Additional numbers at the Rolls Building (prefaced by 020 7947 unless otherwise specified)
RCJG Switchboard (6000)
Rolls Security Office (7000)
Rolls First Aid (7000)
Consultation Room requests (6585)

At the Royal Courts of Justice Main Building, Strand
(Prefaced by 020 7947 unless otherwise specified)
RCJG switchboard (6000)
RCJ Advice Bureau (0203 475 4373) Email: *admin@rcjadvice.org.uk*
RCJ Support through Court (7701) Email: *London@supportthroughcourt.org*
RCJ Security Office (6260)
Emergency Out of Hours contact (6260)

Outside of London Offices
See Appendix C for the court addresses, telephone and email addresses of the courts sitting outside London

Appendix B

ChD Chancellor, HCJs, Masters, ICCJs contact information

(Prefaced by 020 7947 unless otherwise specified)

HIGH COURT JUDGES' CLERKS

1A-319

Judge	*Clerk*	*Telephone*	*Email*
Chancellor of the High Court, the Rt Hon Sir Julian Flaux	Olivia Jay	6171	*Olivia.Jay@justice.gov.uk*
	Adam Davis, Diary Secretary		*ChancellorsPO@judiciary.uk*
	Iain Prest, Legal Adviser		*ChancellorsPO@judiciary.uk*
	Amy Jabbal, Private Secretary		*ChancellorsPO@judiciary.uk*
	[ ], Assistant Private Secretary		*ChancellorsPO@judiciary.uk*
Mr Justice Roth	Ava Tranter	6396	*Ava.Tranter1@justice.gov.uk*
Mr Justice Hildyard	Salma Begum	6039	*Salma.Begum@Justice.gov.uk*
Mr Justice Marcus Smith	Wendy Simpson	7767	*Wendy.Simpson@justice.gov.uk*
Mr Justice Zacaroli	Gwilym Morris	6775	*Gwilym.Morris2@justice.gov.uk*
Mr Justice Fancourt	Steven Brilliant	6251	*Steven.Brilliant@justice.gov.uk*
Mrs Justice Falk	Supriya Saleem	6044	*Supriya.Saleem@justice.gov.uk*
Mr Justice Trower	Jas Kahlon	6339	*Jas.Kahlon@justice.gov.uk*
Mr Justice Miles	Hannah Wood	7624	*Hannah.Wood@justice.gov.uk*
Mr Justice Meade	Pauline Drewett	0314 / 07971062200	*Pauline.Drewett@justice.gov.uk*
Mr Justice Adam Johnson	Casey Ford	6401	*Casey.Ford@justice.gov.uk*

Judge	Clerk	Telephone	Email
Mrs Justice Bacon	Wendy Simpson	7767	*Wendy.Simpson@justice.gov.uk*
Mr Justice Michael Green	Olivia Jay	6397	*Olivia.Jay@justice.gov.uk*
Mr Justice Mellor	Susan Woolley	7964	*Susan.Woolley@justice.gov.uk*
Mrs Justice Joanna Smith	Caroline Reid	6419	*Caroline.Reid@justice.gov.uk*
Mr Justice Edwin Johnson	Lewis Hill	0304	*Lewis.Hill@justice.gov.uk*
Mr Justice Leech	Paul Byrne	6485	*Paul.Byrne1@justice.gov.uk*

For a list of judges in the Chancery Division of the High Court and judges sitting in the Patents Court, including details of their clerks and contact details please also visit: *https://www.gov.uk/guidance/chancery-judges*

JUDGES' LISTING

1A-320 Chancery Judges' Listing, general enquiries & High Court Appeals Office 6690/7717
Email: *chanceryjudgeslisting@justice.gov.uk*

INTELLECTUAL PROPERTY ENTERPRISE COURT ('IPEC')

1A-321

Judge	Clerk	Telephone	Email
His Honour Judge Hacon	Rachel Morgan	6265	*Rachel.morgan3@justice.gov.uk*

CHANCERY MASTERS

1A-322

Judge	Clerk	Telephone	Email
Chief Master Shuman	Hearing Room 3	Dani Ince	*Dani.Ince@justice.gov.uk*
Master Clark	Hearing Room 6	Mohammed Choudhury	*Mohammed.Choudhury5@justice.gov.uk*
Master Kaye	Hearing Room 4	Jeremy Jules	*Jeremy.Jules@justice.gov.uk*
Master Pester	Hearing Room 1	Alison Gaby	*Alison.Gaby@justice.gov.uk*
Vacant Master	Hearing Room 2	Jack Gunby	*Jack.Gunby@justice.gov.uk*
Vacant Master 2	Hearing Room 5	Chyna Gibbs	*Chyna.Gibbs@justice.gov.uk*

Masters' Clerks' Telephone: (7391)
Email: *chancery.mastersappointments@justice.gov.uk*

INSOLVENCY AND COMPANIES COURT JUDGES:

1A-323

Judge	Hearing Room
Chief ICC Judge Briggs	7
ICC Judge Barber	any
ICC Judge Jones	any
ICC Judge Prentis	any
ICC Judge Mullen	any
ICC Judge Burton	any

Insolvency and Companies Court Judges' Clerks telephone (6731)
Email: *Rolls.ICL.Hearings1@justice.gov.uk*

APPENDIX C

CHANCERY BUSINESS OUTSIDE THE ROLLS BUILDING

1. Outside the Rolls Building there are seven Business and Property Courts District Registries. The B&PC District Registries are located at Court centres in Birmingham, Bristol, Cardiff, Leeds, Liverpool, Manchester and, Newcastle-upon-Tyne. The additional three Chancery District Registries were Preston, Mold and Caernarfon. Chancery business outside London is divided into two broad geographical areas each with a supervising High Court Judge, one comprising the Midlands, Western and Wales Circuits and the other the Northern and North Eastern Circuits. **1A-324**

2. Disputes in Chancery cases in the B&PC District Registries are determined by a High Court Judge, a specialist civil Section 9 Circuit Judge or a specialist Business and Property Court District Judge, depending upon the complexity, value and length of the proceedings. The names of the current specialist B&PC judges in each District Registry are provided below.

3. The Chancery Guide applies in general to the Chancery lists in the B&PC District Registries. However, as explained in Chapter 1, some sections or guidance are specific to the working of the lists in the ChD B&PCs London, such as the differences that arise from having Masters and ICC Judges in the ChD B&PCs London. The work done by Masters and ICC Judges is allocated between District Judges and Section 9 Judges in the B&PC District Registries. The allocation of that work is determined locally. The Guide should nonetheless be applied by analogy and in substantially the same way as it applies to the ChD B&PC London. However, there are some local practices particularly in relation to case management procedures, listing and hearings. Please follow the links below for further information about local practices.

4. Specialist Chancery work is also carried on in lists in the County Court sitting at Birmingham, Bristol, Cardiff, Central London, Liverpool, Leeds, Manchester, Newcastle and Preston: see CPR PD57AA paragraphs 4.1 to 4.4. This work will be conducted by local Section 9 Judges, specialist Recorders or specialist District Judges.

5. The court addresses, telephone and email addresses for the Business and Property Courts and other courts that deal with Chancery work outside the Rolls Building are listed below.

6. For any local guidance, consult the B&PC pages of the Judiciary website follow the links for each of the B&PCs District Registries. Each B&PC District Registry has its own page on the Judiciary Website links to which are set out below. The information and links on the Judiciary Website will be updated from time to time with any local guidance and Practice Notes issued by the Supervising Judge.

BUSINESS & PROPERTY COURTS DISTRICT REGISTRIES:

1A-325

Birmingham Business & Property Court	The Priory Courts, 33 Bull Street, Birmingham B4 6DS *Judge in Charge:* HHJ David Worster The specialist B&PC Circuit Judges (including Senior Circuit Judges) and specialist B&PC District Judges based in Birmingham are set out below: HHJ David Worster HHJ Richard Williams HHJ Brian Rawlings HHJ Sarah Watson HHJ Emma Kelly (DCJ) HHJ James Tindall HHJ Abbas Mithani HHJ Delia Truman HHJ Jane Ingram HHJ Stephen Murch DJ Ashwin Mody DJ Chloë Phillips DJ Anthony Rich DJ Augustine Rouine DJ Daryl Shorthose DJ Saira Singh DJ Robert Talog-Davies Switchboard: 0121 681 3181 Email: *bpc.birmingham@justice.gov.uk* Contact for request for consent to transfer cases: Mark Farley *mark.farley@justice.gov.uk* Urgent court business officer number for out of hours applications: Birmingham (Midland Region): West Side - 07748 542966 East Side - 07748 613886 More information about the B&PC District Registry in Birmingham including

	any local guidance can be found on the judiciary.uk website. The County Court at Birmingham has both a Business and Property list and undertakes non-local insolvency business: The contact details for Business and Property List work in the County Court at Birmingham are: 0300 123 5577 and *enquiries.birmingham.countycourt@justice.gov.uk*
Bristol Business & Property Court	2 Redcliff Street, Bristol BS1 6GR *Judge in Charge of the Business & Property List:* His Honour Judge Paul Matthews There are a total of 2 specialist B&PC Circuit Judges and 4 specialist B&PC District Judges based in Bristol: HHJ Paul Matthews HHJ Jonathan Russen QC DJ Tony Woodburn DJ Chris Taylor DJ Jan Markland DJ Matthew Wales Switchboard: 0117 366 4800 Specialist Team: 0117 366 4860 Email: *bristolspecialist@justice.gov.uk* Email: *bristolchancerylisting@justice.gov.uk* Contact for request for consent to transfer cases: Eddie Hunt (Specialist Team leader) *edward.hunt@Justice.gov.uk* Chancery Listing: Anne Steel (Chancery Clerk) More information about the B&PC District Registry in Bristol including any local guidance can be found on the judiciary.uk website. The County Court at Bristol has both a Business and Property list and undertakes non-local insolvency business: The contact details for Business and Property List work in the County Court at Bristol are: 0117 366 4850 and *e-filing.bristol.countycourt@justice.gov.uk*
Leeds Business & Property Court	The Court House, 1 Oxford Row, Leeds LS1 3BG *Judge in Charge of the Business & Property List:* His Honour Judge Davis-White QC There are a total of 4 specialist B&PC Circuit Judges and 6 specialist B&PC District Judges based in Leeds: HHJ Malcolm Davis-White QC HHJ Jonathan Klein HHJ Claire Jackson HHJ Siobhan Kelly DJ Kelly Bond DJ Joanna Geddes DJ Jeff Goldberg DJ Sarah Greenan DJ Anesh Pema DJ Alison Shepherd Switchboard: 0113 306 2460 Email: *bpc.leeds@justice.gov.uk* Contact for request for consent to transfer cases: Please call the BPC team on 0113 306 2460 Urgent court business officer number for out of hours applications: 07810 181828 More information about the B&PC District Registry in Leeds including any local guidance can be found on the judiciary.uk website. The County Court at Leeds has both a Business and Property list and undertakes non-local insolvency business: The contact details for Business and Property List work in the County Court at Leeds are: 0113 306 2401 and *enquiries.leeds.countycourt@Justice.gov.uk*
Liverpool Business & Property Court	35 Vernon Street, Liverpool, Merseyside L2 2BX *Judge in Charge of the Business & Property List:* His Honour Judge Cadwallader There are 3 specialist B&PC District Judges based in Liverpool: DJ Charlie Deane DJ Samantha Johnson DJ Mark Lampkin Switchboard: 0151 296 2200 Direct Line: 0151 296 2483 Email: *LiverpoolBPC@justice.gov.uk* Contact for request for consent to transfer cases: Kevin Fitzmaurice

	kevin.fitzmaurice@justice.gov.uk Urgent court business officer pager number for out of hours applications: Cheshire & Merseyside - 07876 034775 Liverpool - 0151 296 2483 More information about the B&PC District Registry in Liverpool including any local guidance can be found on the judiciary.uk website. The County Court at Liverpool has both a Business and Property list and undertakes non-local insolvency business: The contact details for Business and Property List work in the County Court at Liverpool are: 0151 296 2200 and *LiverpoolBPC@justice.gov.uk*
Manchester Business & Property Court	1 Bridge Street West, Manchester M60 9DJ *Judge in Charge of the Business & Property List:* His Honour Judge Hodge QC There are currently 5 specialist B&PC Circuit Judges and 6 specialist B&PC District Judges based in Manchester: HHJ David Hodge QC HHJ Stephen Davies HHJ Richard Pearce HHJ Mark Halliwell HHJ Mark Cawson QC DJ Araba Obodai DJ Paul Richmond DJ Ranj Matharu DJ Adrian Bever DJ Joanne Woodward DJ Richard Carter In addition, HHJ Charles Khan is a specialist Chancery judge who sits in Manchester from time to time. Switchboard: 0161 240 5307 Email: *bpc.manchester@justice.gov.uk* Contact for request for consent to transfer cases: bpc.manchester@justice.gov.uk Urgent court business officer number for out of hours applications: 07554 459 626 More information about the B&PC District Registry in Manchester including any local guidance can be found on the judiciary.uk website. The County Court at Manchester has both a Business and Property list and undertakes non-local insolvency business: The contact details for the Business and Property List work in the County Court at Manchester are: 0161 240 5027 and *manchestercivil@Justice.gov.uk*
Newcastle Business & Property Court	Barras Bridge, Newcastle-upon-Tyne, NE1 8QF *Judge in Charge of the Business & Property List:* His Honour Judge Kramer There are in addition 3 specialist B&PC District Judges based in Newcastle: DJ Michelle Temple DJ Terry Phillips DJ David Hambler Switchboard: 0191 205 8750 Email: *NewcastleBPC@justice.gov.uk* Contact for request for consent to transfer cases: *NewcastleBPC@justice.gov.uk* Urgent court business officer number for out of hours applications: 07562 431 182 More information about the B&PC District Registry in Newcastle including any local guidance can be found on the judiciary.uk website. The County Court at Newcastle has both a Business and Property list and undertakes non-local insolvency business: The contact details for the Business and Property List work in the County Court at Newcastle are: 0191 2058750 and *NewcastleBPC@justice.gov.uk*

WALES/CYMRU

1A-326

Business & Property Courts in Wales	Under the Welsh Language (Wales) Measure 2011 the Welsh language has official status in Wales and under the Welsh Language Act 1993 in any legal proceedings in Wales the Welsh language may be used by anyone wishing to use it. By CPR 1.5(2) parties are required to assist the court to put into effect those principles. The practice direction on the use of the Welsh language can be found at *https://www.justice.gov.uk/courts/procedure-rules/civil/rules/welshpd*

Llysoedd Busnes ac Eiddo yng Nghymru	O dan Fesur yr Iaith Gymraeg (Cymru) 2011 mae gan yr iaith Gymraeg statws swyddogol yng Nghymru ac o dan Ddeddf yr Iaith Gymraeg 1993, mewn unrhyw achos cyfreithiol yng Nghymru, gellir defnyddio'r iaith Gymraeg gan unrhyw un sy'n dymuno ei defnyddio. Yn ôl CPR 1.5(2) mae'n ofynnol i'r partïon gynorthwyo'r llys i weithredu'r egwyddorion hynny. Gellir dod o hyd i'r cyfarwyddyd ymarfer ar ddefnyddio'r iaith Gymraeg yn *https://www.justice.gov.uk/courts/procedure-rules/civil/rules/welshpd* Cardiff Civil and Family Justice Centre 2 Park Street, Cardiff CF10 1ET Canolfan Cyfiawnder Sifil a Theuluol Caerdydd 2 Stryd y Parc Caerdydd CF10 1ET Caernarfon Justice Centre Llanberis Road Caernarfon LL55 2DF Canolfan Cyfiawnder Caernarfon Ffordd Llanberis Caernarfon LL55 2DF Mold Justice Centre Wrexham Law Courts Bodhyfryd Wrexham, LL12 7BP Canolfan Cyfiawnder Yr Wyddgrug Y Llysoedd Barn Wrecsam Bodhyfryd Wrecsam. LL12 7BP *Judge in Charge of the Business & Property List:* His Honour Judge Jarman QC *Barnwr â Chyfrifoldeb am y Rhestr Busnes ac Eiddo:* Ei Anrhydedd y Barnwr Jarman CF The judges of the Business and Property Court in Wales, some of whom are Welsh speakers are: Barnwyr Llysoedd Busnes ac Eiddo Yng Nghymru, gan cynnwys siaradwr Cymraeg, yw: **Specialist B&PC Circuit Judges:** His Honour Judge Milwyn Jarman QC/Ei Anrhydedd y Barnwr Milwyn Jarman CF His Honour Judge Andrew Keyser QC/ Ei Anrhydedd y Barnwr Andrew Keyser CF His Honour Judge Robert Harrison/Ei Anrhydedd y Barnwr Robert Harrison **Cardiff/ Caerdydd:** District Judge Robert Vernon/Y Barnwr Rhanbarth Robert Vernon District Judge Clare Coates/Y Barnwr Rhanbarth Clare Coates District Judge David Morgan/Y Barnwr Rhanbarth David Morgan **Swansea, Haverfordwest and Aberystwyth/Abertawe, Hwlfforddd and Aberystwyth:** District Judge Jake Pratt/Y Barnwr Rhanbarth Jake Pratt **Caernarfon:** District Judge Merfyn Jones-Evans/Y Barnwr Rhanbarth Merfyn Jones-Evans **Prestatyn:** District Judge Rachel Watkins/Y Barnwr Rhanbarth Rachel Watkins **Wrexham:** District Judge Gareth Humphries/Y Barnwr Rhanbarth Gareth Humphries **Switchboard/Switsfwrdd:** 02920 376 430 (Cardiff/Caerdydd) 01286 669 700 (Caernarfon) 029 2037 6412(Mold/Yr Wyddgrug) Email/contact and for consent to transfer cases: E-bost/Cyswllt ar gyfer ceisiadau am ganiatâd i drosglwyddo achosion: *bpc.cardiff@justice.gov.uk* (Cardiff/Caerdydd) *enquiries.cardiff.countycourt@justice.gov.uk* (Cardiff/Caerdydd) *enquiries.caernarfon.countycourt@justice.gov.uk* (Caernarfon) *northwalescivillisting@justice.gov.uk* (Mold/Yr Wyddgrug) Out of hours: Allan o oriau: North/Gogledd: 07760 285792 South/De: 07500 779433 Mid & West/Canol: 07970 363991

	For more information visit: Am ragor o wybodaeth, ewch i: More information about the B&PC District Registry in Wales including any local guidance in both English and Welsh can be found on the judiciary.uk website. Mae rhagor o wybodaeth am Gofrestrfa Ddosbarthol B&PC yng Nghymru gan gynnwys canllawiau lleol yn y Gymraeg a'r Saesneg ar wefan judiciary.uk. The County Court at Cardiff has both a Business and Property list and undertakes non-local insolvency business. Mae Llys Siriol Caerdydd yn delio gyda rhestr Busnes ac Eiddo a hefyd gyda busnes ansolfedd ddim lleol. The contact details for the Business and Property List work in the County Court in Wales are set out above.

OTHER COUNTY COURT HEARING CENTRES WITH A BUSINESS AND PROPERTY LIST

COUNTY COURT AT CENTRAL LONDON **1A-327**

County Court at Central London	County Court at Central London, Royal Courts of Justice, Thomas More Building, Strand, London WC2A 2LL Central London is a County Court hearing centre with a Business and Property List, a centre for non-local insolvency business for the South-Eastern Circuit. *Judge in Charge of the Business & Property List:* His Honour Judge Dight CBE There are 6 specialist Circuit Judges (including 3 Senior Circuit Judges) who undertake work in the Business and Property List. His Honour Judge Marc Dight CBE (Senior CJ) His Honour Judge Nigel Gerald His Honour Judge Alan Johns QC (Senior CJ) His Honour Judge Simon Monty His Honour Judge Parfitt His Honour Judge Mark Raeside QC (Senior CJ) There are 4 specialist District Judges District Judge Charlotte Hart District Judge Shanti Mauger District Judge Carla Revere District Judge Wilkinson Call Centre: 0300 123 5577 Email: *enquiries.centrallondon.countycourt@justice.gov.uk* Users can contact either HHJ Dight CBE or HHJ Johns QC in connection with transfers to the Business & Property List by email to: Sanna Mirza, clerk to HHJ Dight CBE, at sanna.mirza@justice.gov.uk Diane Morris, clerk to HHJ Johns QC, at diane.morris@justice.gov.uk For more information including further contact details please see the Guide to Business & Property Work at Central London: BP Guide 2nd (judiciary.uk)

PRESTON COMBINED COURT CENTRE

Preston Combined Court Centre	The Law Courts, Openshaw Place, Ring Way, Preston PR1 2LL Preston is a Chancery District Registry (but not a B&PC District Registry), a County Court hearing centre with a Business and Property List and a specialist County Court hearing centre for the purposes of non-local insolvency work. *Judge in Charge of the Business & Property List:* HHJ Jacqueline Beech There are additionally one specialist Circuit Judge and two specialist District Judges undertaking Chancery work who sits from time to time in Preston: HHJ Charles Khan DJ Michael Anson DJ Bradley Burrow Switchboard: 01772 844 700 Email: *centralisedcivilli@Justice.gov.uk* Contact for request for consent to transfer cases: Stephen Craig/Angela Moizer on *preston.cmb.dm@justice.gov.uk*

	More information about Preston Combined Court Centre can be found on the gov.uk website.

APPENDIX D

CHANCERY USERS' COMMITTEES

CHANCERY COURT USERS' COMMITTEE

1A-328 **1.** The Chancery Court Users' Committee's function is to review the practice and procedure of all courts forming part of the Chancery Division, and to ensure that they continue to provide a just, economical and expeditious system for the resolution of disputes. The Chancellor is the chairman. Its membership includes the Chief Master, barristers and solicitors, and other representatives of court staff and users. Suggestions for discussion should be sent to the Chief Master at *ChiefMaster.Shuman@ejudiciary.net* or to Amy Jabbal at *ChancellorsPO@judiciary.uk.*

INSOLVENCY AND COMPANIES COURT USERS' COMMITTEE

1A-329 **2.** The Insolvency and Companies Court Users' Committee's function is to review the practice and procedure of the Insolvency and Companies Court. The Chief ICC Judge is the Chairman. Its membership includes the Chancellor, specialist judges, insolvency practitioners, the Official Receiver, the insolvency service (policy), HMRC, and barristers and solicitors who practise in the field. Suggestions for discussion should be sent to the Chief ICC Judge.

FINANCIAL LIST USERS' COMMITTEE

1A-330 **3.** The Financial List Users' Committee's function is to review the practice and procedure of the Chancery and the Commercial Court in the Financial List as a joint enterprise. The Chancellor is the chair. Its membership includes barristers and solicitors and representatives from legal or financial professional associations and financial institutions. Suggestions for discussion should be sent to the Secretary to the Committee, Amy Jabbal at *ChancellorsPO@judiciary.uk.*

INSOLVENCY RULES COMMITTEE

1A-331 **4.** The Insolvency Rules Committee's function is to review any changes to the Insolvency (England and Wales) Rules 2016 and to consult on those changes. The chair of the Insolvency Rules Committee, Mr Justice Zacaroli. Proposals for changes in the Rules should be sent to the Insolvency Service at *insolvency.enquiryline@insolvency.gov.uk,* with a copy to the clerk to Mr Justice Zacaroli or the Chief ICC Judge.

INTELLECTUAL PROPERTY COURT USERS' COMMITTEE

1A-332 **5.** The Intellectual Property Users' Committee's function is to consider any issues regarding intellectual property litigation generally. Mr Justice Meade is the chair. Membership of the committee includes members the Patent Bar Association, the Intellectual Property Lawyers Association, the Chartered Institute of Patent Attorneys, the Institute of Trade Mark Attorneys and the Trade Marks Designs and Patents Federation. Suggestions for discussion should be sent to the Secretary to the committee, Michael Burdon at *Michael.burdon@simmons-simmons.com.*

INTELLECTUAL PROPERTY ENTERPRISE COURT USERS' COMMITTEE

1A-333 **6.** The IPEC Users' Committee's function is to consider concerns raised by intellectual property litigators in the IPEC. His Honour Judge Hacon is the chairman. Its membership includes those in the Intellectual Property Users' Committee. Suggestions for discussion should be sent the Secretary to the committee, Luke Maunder, at luke.maunder@bristows.com.

PENSION LITIGATION COURT USERS' COMMITTEE

1A-334 **7.** The Pensions Litigation Court Users' Committee's function is to consider issues concerning pensions litigation. Mr Justice Trower is the chairman. Its membership consists of a Master (currently Chief Master Shuman), barristers and solicitors who are current members of the Association of Pension Lawyers. Any suggestions for discussion should be sent to the Secretary to the committee, David Grant at *David.GrantQC@outertemple.com.*

COURT USERS' GROUPS/COMMITTEES OUTSIDE LONDON:

1A-335 **8.** There are several Court Users' Committees relating to chancery work based outside the Rolls Building. Each of these Committees meets twice a year (unless otherwise stated), and its membership includes judges, court staff, barristers and solicitors:

(a) **Northern and North-Eastern Circuit:** Each of the 4 principal BPC centres (Liverpool, Manchester, Leeds and Newcastle) has a Users' Group that meets at least twice a year. Each has a membership including local judges, court staff, barristers and solicitors. The Vice-Chancellor of the County Palatine of Lancaster chairs the Committees, and the Vice-Chancellor's clerk acts as secretary to each Committee. All communications should be sent to the clerk to Mr Justice Fancourt, Steven Brilliant, at *Steven.Brilliant@justice.gov.uk*.

(b) **South-Western Region:** HHJ Paul Matthews chairs the committee in Bristol (or Mr Justice Zacaroli when there). All communications should be addressed to the secretary, Anne Steel at *anne.steel@Justice.gov.uk*.

(c) **Wales:** HHJ Jarman QC chairs the committee in Cardiff (or Mr Justice Zacaroli when there). Meetings are held annually and Vanessa Kam acts as secretary. All communications should be addressed to her at *vanessa.kam2@Justice.gov.uk*.

(d) **Midland Region:** HHJ David Worster chairs the committee in Birmingham (or Mr Justice Zacaroli when there). All communications should be addressed to the secretary, Dot Byrne at *bpc.birmingham@justice.gov.uk*.

APPENDIX E

CE-FILE

1. The electronic file ('CE-File') contains those documents which the court is required to hold pursuant to the Civil Procedure Rules 'CPR', whether they are documents created by the court or filed by the parties. It also contains notes, emails and letters added by the court staff and the judiciary, as did the previous paper file. All claims are now managed from the CE-File. **1A-336**

2. CE-File is used to start, or continue, Part 7, Part 8 and Part 20 claims and pre-action applications and also for petitions and applications commenced in the Insolvency and Companies Court List.

3. Further guidance can be found in Chapter 1 paragraphs 1.28 – 1.32 and CPR Practice Direction 51O and on the.gov.uk website.

4. All documents lodged with the court are held on CE-File, and routine case management is generally carried out using that file unless the volume of documents makes it impractical. If paper copies are required by the court a direction will be given to lodge further paper copies, usually in the form of a bundle (see below). The parties may be asked on occasions to file a .pdf version of long documents to assist the court.

5. Other parties to proceedings are able to inspect electronically all documents on the CE-File which are available to them under CPR 5.4B once they have been granted access to the system.

6. The court file is not and is not intended to be a complete record of all documents created by the parties during the life of the claim. It is not usually necessary to CE-file disclosure or disclosure lists, or trial witness statements when exchanged and served unless the court orders otherwise.

7. The court file is not a repository for correspondence between the parties. Before corresponding with the court, other than in relation to purely administrative matters, parties should consider carefully whether an application is more appropriate. Any correspondence with the court should be copied to the other parties in any event.

8. No paper file is maintained for claims. Any paper documents lodged with the court, after having been scanned to the file, are retained in day files for a period of 6 months. They will be available during this period only if scanning errors need to be corrected. They are destroyed at the end of the period.

9. The only exception is original documents that are required to be lodged with the court pursuant to an order or a provision of the CPR (such as original wills). Original documents are retained in a separate secure storage area. Original documents must be clearly marked as such with a front sheet marked in a font of not less than 14 point, as follows:

'CLAIM NO. XXXXXX
ORIGINAL DOCUMENT - NOT TO BE DESTROYED'

APPENDIX F

COURT LISTS OF THE BUSINESS AND PROPERTY COURTS

1. The categories listed alphabetically include all of those within the Business and Property Courts ('B&PCs'). Those marked QBD are not within the Chancery Division. **1A-337**

2. When a case is issued in a list or sub-list its case number will first identify the list it has been issued in and then the year it has been issued before giving a 6-digit number (For example BL-2022-000000). If a claim has been issued in one of the Business and Property Courts District Registries it will include a 3-letter abbreviation for the relevant court centre (for example MAN for Manchester and so on). This will appear immediately before the 6-digit number.

3. Each case number is unique and enables the court to identify the case quickly. You should always have it available when contacting the court by any means.

4. For each of the Chancery Division lists set out below the initials for the relevant list are in () after its name.

5. The various examples of cases dealt with in each category are not exhaustive:

ADMIRALTY COURT (QBD) (AD)

1A-338 **6.** The Admiralty Court deals with shipping and maritime disputes and with claims brought against the owner of a ship ('in personam' claims) and claims brought against the ship itself ('in rem' claims). This list also deals with cases such as collisions between ships, disputes over the transport of cargo and claims by ship-owners to limit liability for loss or damage.

BUSINESS LIST (BL (CH))

1A-339 **7.** The scope of the Chancery Business List is broad. It includes a wide range of national and international business disputes concerning a business structure (company, LLP, LP, partnership etc), sale and purchase of businesses, claims for professional negligence, claims for breach of contract and rectification as well as other equitable remedies. If a claim does not fall within any other list or sub-list it should be issued in the Business List.

8. The Business List has two sub-lists:

(a) **Financial Services and Regulatory (FS)** Financial claims where the Financial Conduct Authority (FCA) is a party, claims under the Financial Services and Markets Act 2000 and claims involving regulators (other than the Pensions Regulator).

(b) **Pensions (PE)** This List covers all claims where pensions are the subject matter of the dispute and includes claims relating to pensions trusts and claims unrelated to trusts law, such as claims for professional negligence against former advisers. Claims arising from actions taken under statutory powers, such as those of the Pensions Regulator, also come within this List, as do Pensions Ombudsman appeals.

CHANCERY APPEALS (CH)

1A-340 **9.** This list comprises appeals against decisions of the County Court if the decision being appealed is one where any appeal lies to the High Court, appeals against decisions of Masters, Insolvency and Companies Court Judges, B&PC District Judges and certain statutory appeals.

10. An appeal or application for permission to appeal must always be a commenced as a new file in this list, even if the underlying proceedings are in a different B&PCs list.

COMMERCIAL COURT (QBD) (CL)

1A-341 **11.** The Commercial Court deals with complex cases arising out of business disputes, both national and international, encompassing all aspects of commercial disputes, in the fields of banking and finance, shipping, insurance and reinsurance and commodities. The Court is also the principal supervisory court for London arbitration.

CIRCUIT COMMERCIAL COURT (QBD) (FORMERLY THE MERCANTILE COURT) (LM OR CC)

1A-342 **12.** Formerly known as the Mercantile Court, it deals with commercial business disputes of all kinds apart from those which, because of their size, value or complexity, will be heard by the Commercial Court. In London it is known as the London Circuit Commercial Court (LM). Outside London it is the Circuit Commercial Court (CC) whichever B&PC District Registry a claim is issued in.

COMPETITION LIST (CP)

1A-343 **13.** This list deals with claims previously brought under Article 101 and Article 102 of the Treaty on the Functioning of the European Union ('TFEU') and claims brought under the corresponding provisions of UK domestic law contained in Chapters I and II of Part 1 of the Competition Act 1998. This includes cases that prevent, restrict or distort competition and includes cases dealing with abuse of dominant position, the imposition of unfair prices, unfair trading arrangements and breaches of competition rules.

FINANCIAL LIST (CHD/COMMERCIAL COURT - QBD) (FL)

1A-344 **14.** The Financial List is a specialist cross-jurisdictional list set up to address the particular business needs of parties litigating on financial matters. Disputes that are eligible for inclusion are those that principally relate to financial disputes of over £50m or equivalent, or which require particular market expertise, or raise issues of general market importance.

INSOLVENCY AND COMPANIES LIST (ICL)

1A-345 **15. The Insolvency and Companies List comprises two sub-lists:**

(a) **Insolvency (BR)** Insolvency work includes bankruptcy petitions where a creditor is owed

£50,000 or more, insolvency administration orders, winding up petitions, and applications and claims relating to individual and corporate insolvency under the Insolvency Act 1986, the Insolvency (England and Wales) Rules 2016 and related legislation.

(b) **Companies (CR)** Companies work includes claims and applications made under the Companies Act 2006 and related legislation, including unfair prejudice petitions and other forms of shareholder dispute. Claims and applications made under the Company Directors Disqualification Act 1986 are also included in this list.

INTELLECTUAL PROPERTY LIST (IL)

16. Claims in the Intellectual Property List include those brought under the Trade Marks Act 1994, copyright issues, passing off, and other intellectual property claims. Large or complex intellectual property claims or patents claims valued over £500,000 are heard in Intellectual Property List or **Patents Court (HP)**. Lower value simpler intellectual property claims (including patents) are issued and heard in the **Intellectual Property Enterprise Court (IPEC) (IP)**. **1A-346**

INTERIM APPLICATIONS LIST

17. This list is a daily list of applications to be heard in the Applications Court. It is not a substantive list of the B&PCs and cases in which applications are to be heard retain their reference in a different B&PCs list. **1A-347**

PROPERTY, TRUSTS AND PROBATE LIST (PT)

18. This list covers a large amount of the work of the Chancery Division. It is separate from the Business List. The property work includes all disputes about land ownership or development, commercial mortgages and leases, receivership, orders for sale to enforce charging orders and resulting and constructive trusts. The trusts work includes removal of trustees, claims against trustees, issues of construction/rectification, disputes concerning trust property and applications for approval or administration orders. The probate work includes contentious probate claims, rectification of wills, substitution or removal of Personal Representatives and cases involving the Presumption of Death Act 2013 and the Guardianship (Missing Persons) Act 2017. **1A-348**

REVENUE LIST (RL)

19. This List covers claims involving major points of principle where HMRC is a party. This List does *not* include claims for the recovery of taxes or duties or where a taxpayer disputes liability to pay tax; such claims generally fall within the jurisdiction of the Upper Tribunal (Tax and Chancery Chamber), or otherwise within the Business List. **1A-349**

TECHNOLOGY & CONSTRUCTION COURT (QBD) (HT)

20. The general work of the Technology and Construction Court List includes complex building and engineering disputes, environmental claims and claims by and against local authorities regarding land/building, construction and procurement disputes. The List also deals with claims brought under the Arbitration Act 1996, engineering disputes and/or application for permission to appeal and appeals in such cases. **1A-350**

APPENDIX G

TITLES AND FORMS OF ADDRESS

1. There are a various different types of judges in the High Court and County Court with different names and different titles. **1A-351**

2. Some judges are addressed in different ways depending on the type of hearing they are conducting.

3. This appendix provides some helpful information about how to address judges in court and some of the more common titles.

4. If you are in any doubt about how to address the judge at a hearing you should ask the court staff, the usher or the judge's clerk or the judge at the commencement of the hearing.

HIGH COURT

5. A High Court Judge is generally known and Mr or Mrs Justice [Surname]. They should be addressed in court as My Lord or My Lady (or as your Lordship or Ladyship) as appropriate. **1A-352**

6. Any judge conducting a hearing in the High Court sitting as a High Court Judge or Deputy High Court Judge (whatever their title) should be addressed in court as My Lord or My Lady (or as your Lordship or Ladyship) as appropriate.

7. Insolvency and Companies Court Judges should be addressed in court as Judge.

8. Masters should be addressed in court as either Master or Judge.

BUSINESS AND PROPERTY COURT DISTRICT REGISTRIES

1A-353 **9.** In the Business and Property Courts District Registries a Senior Circuit Judge and Circuit Judge is known as His or Her Honour [Surname]. Recorders are known as Recorder [Surname].

10. A Senior Circuit Judge, Circuit Judge or Recorder when sitting as a judge of the High Court in one of the BPC District Registries should be addressed in court as My Lord or My Lady (or as your Lordship or Ladyship). They should be addressed as His or Her Honour or Your Honour when they sit as a judge of the County Court.

11. In the BPC District Registries hearings are also conducted by District Judges. They are known as District Judge [Surname]. District Judges should be addressed as Sir or Ma'am or Judge.

APPENDIX H

PRACTICAL ASSISTANCE FOR LITIGANTS IN PERSON

1A-354 It is important to note that neither the court staff nor the judges are in a position to give advice about the conduct of a claim. There is however a great deal of practical help available for litigants in person.

All claims issued in the Business and Property Courts are stored on an electronic file on CE-File. Advice about how to use CE-File can be found at HMCTS E-Filing service for Citizens and Professionals and in Chapter 1 and Appendix E. You are encouraged to use CE-File wherever possible.

Advice about How to apply for Help With Fees can be found on the gov.uk website.

URGENT APPLICATIONS:

1A-355 There are two schemes providing help with urgent applications in either the Judges' Applications List or the winding up list. For information about local schemes that may be available in the B&PC District Registries or other courts follow the links in Appendix C.

THE CLIPS SCHEME: HELP WITH APPLICATIONS IN THE JUDGES' APPLICATIONS LIST

1A-356 'CLIPS' is the acronym of the Chancery Bar Litigants In Person Support scheme. Under the scheme, barristers provide free legal assistance on the day to litigants in person appearing in the Judges' Applications List, where HCJs typically hear applications for an urgent interim remedy such as an injunction or other order made in or before a claim is issued. The scheme is run by the Chancery Bar Association in conjunction with the RCJ Advice Bureau and Advocate and is available to any litigant in person party to an application within the Judges' Applications List without any means testing.

Under the scheme one or two barrister volunteers are available each applications day during the legal term (and in the long vacation on applications days) from 10am. Initially they will be outside Court 10 in the Rolls Building to meet a litigant in person; at 10.30 they will go into court and the HCJ will invite any litigant in person to consider whether they would like to make use of the free advice or representation available.

The barrister may give advice and may, if appropriate and possible, represent the litigant. If the barrister is not needed in court they will return to their place of work at about 11am but will be contactable by telephone up to 4.30 pm.

If hearings in the Judges' Applications List are being heard remotely, there will generally be one barrister volunteer available remotely between 10am and 4:30pm on the day of volunteering. In such cases, the litigant in person will contact the barrister volunteer in private, by email or telephone as advised by the court.

COMPANY INSOLVENCY PRO BONO SCHEME

1A-357 The City Law School's Company Insolvency Pro Bono Scheme (CO.IN) was set up in 2015 to provide free legal advice and representation to assist litigants in person (including a company or corporation that is not represented by a lawyer) facing corporate insolvency in the winding up court.

CO.IN can assist with the following:

- Advice on the law and procedure in the winding up court
- How to respond to a winding up petition
- Representation before the winding up court
- How to apply for a validation order, rescission of or an appeal against a winding up order

The CO.IN scheme runs on Wednesday during term time from 10am in consultation room 17 on the 2nd floor of the Rolls Building, where a litigant in person will be able to speak to the scheme's volunteers. Litigants in person can also contact CO.IN at *companyinsolvency@city.ac.uk*.

OTHER ASSISTANCE

Further help and advice is available to unrepresented parties from a number of sources both online and in person. The list below is non-exhaustive: **1A-358**

1. *Citizen's Advice Service.* There is no Citizen's Advice Service ('CAS') in the Rolls Building, but there is an RCJ Advice Service located off the main hall in the Royal Courts of Justice, London. CAS is run by lawyers to deliver free legal advice to people who cannot afford a solicitor and need assistance with preparing or dealing with a court case. Currently appointments are being conducted over the telephone on 0203-475-4373; please see *https://www.rcjadvice.org.uk/* for further information. You can also find a local CAS on *https://www.citizensadvice.org.uk/*.
2. *Advicenow.* Advicenow is a not-for-profit, independent website providing accurate and practical information on rights and the law of England and Wales. Advicenow also has links to organisations who can offer information, advice and support to help everyday legal problems; Advicenow also provides links to a wide range of materials on law and procedure that can be found here: *www.advicenow.org.uk.*
3. Litigants in person who may be eligible for legal aid can find information about the Civil Legal Advice (CLA) on *https://www.gov.uk/civil-legal-advice.* The CLA can be contacted on 0345 345 4345.
4. *Support Through Court* (formerly the Personal Support Unit) provides emotional and practical support to litigants throughout the court process, ensuring those facing court alone can represent themselves and fully take part in court. It is based in the several courts around the country and appointments can be made for face-to-face appointments or appointments over the telephone on 03000 810 006. For further information, see *https://www.supportthroughcourt.org/*
5. *Advocate* (formerly the Bar Pro Bono Unit) provides free legal assistance from volunteer members of the bar for those who are unable to obtain legal aid and cannot afford to pay for legal advice and support. For more information go to Advocate: Finding free legal help from barristers (*weareadvocate.org.uk*).
6. The *Direct Access Portal* provides direct contact with barristers who are qualified to work under the direct access scheme. This is *not* a free legal advice scheme but enables litigants to instruct a barrister directly to assist them for example with a court hearing. Further details can be found through the Bar Council.
7. Further sources of advice for litigants in person can be found on the judiciary.uk website.

APPENDIX I

[Deliberately blank] **1A-359**

APPENDIX J

MCKENZIE FRIEND NOTICE

IN THE HIGH COURT OF JUSTICE **1A-360**
BUSINESS AND PROPERTY COURTS OF ENGLAND AND WALES
MCKENZIE FRIEND

To be completed by the Claimant/Applicant or the Defendant/Respondent and their proposed McKenzie Friend

Please fill in the form and hand it to the court usher before the hearing starts

By completing this form you are letting the Judge know that you wish to have a McKenzie Friend provide you with reasonable assistance. The Judge will consider this at the start of the hearing.

Claim Number: ....

Parties: ....

Claimant: ....

Defendant: ....

Applicant: ....

Respondent: ....

Other: ....

I am the (please tick any which apply)

Claimant:

Defendant:

Applicant:

Respondent:

Other:

(if you have ticked Other please say who you are)

I wish to have a McKenzie Friend with me at the hearing. I understand that my McKenzie Friend:

1. may provide moral support, take notes, help with case papers and quietly give advice on any aspect of the conduct of the case;
2. may not address the court, make oral submissions or examine witnesses unless the Judge gives permission to do so.

The McKenzie Friend is (please tick):

3. A relative (please give relationship) ....
4. A friend/neighbour/colleague/other (please specify) ....
5. A free advice agency worker (name of agency) ....
6. A person I am paying to help in this case (name of agency, organisation or association the person belongs to) ....

Name and Address of McKenzie Friend (use business address if 3) or 4) above has been ticked)

....

....

....

The McKenzie Friend must complete below:

7.	Have you read the Practice Guidance issued on the 12 July 2010 by the Head of Civil Justice? It is available online here: *https://www.judiciary.uk/wp-content/uploads/JCO/Documents/Guidance/mckenzie-friends-practice-guidance-july-2010.pdf*	Yes/No
8.	Do you agree to comply with it?	Yes/No
9.	Do you have a legal qualification? If yes, please specify	Yes/No
10.	Do you have any interest in the outcome of this case?	Yes/No
11.	Have you previously acted as a McKenzie Friend for anyone else?	Yes/No
12.	Do you confirm that you understand the role of a McKenzie Friend and the duty of confidentiality?	Yes/No

The Judge may ask you questions about your answers to satisfy themself that your answers are accurate and when considering whether to give permission for you to assist the Claimant/Applicant or Defendant/Respondent at this hearing.

....

A new form must be completed for each hearing. The form will be retained electronically by the court.

Signature of Claimant/Applicant or Defendant /Respondent ....

Signature of McKenzie Friend ....

Date: ....

APPENDIX K

DRAFT ENE ORDER

1A-361 Upon the parties requesting at a CMC the Hon Mr(s) Justice / Master/ Insolvency and Companies Court Judge ("the Judge") to provide an opinion about the likely outcome of the claim [or the issue defined in the appendix]

IT IS ORDERED THAT:

1. The Claimant and Defendant shall exchange position papers by 4pm on [date].
2. The parties shall agree a core bundle of documents for the Judge/Master which shall be lodged by 4pm on [date].
3. The parties shall attend before the Judge/Master [in private] at 10.30 on [date].
4. The parties estimate the judicial pre-reading to be [x] hours.
5. The Judge/Master shall consider the submissions made by the parties and provide an informal non-binding opinion about the likely outcome of the claim [or the issue].
6. The opinion shall be without prejudice to the claim and the opinion shall remain confidential to the parties.
7. The court shall not retain any papers filed for the ENE hearing or any record of the opinion provided by the Judge/Master. No non-party shall be entitled to obtain a transcript of the hearing.
8. The Judge/Master shall have no further involvement with this claim or any associated claim.

9. The costs incurred by the ENE shall be costs in the case.

APPENDIX L

DRAFT CH FDR ORDER

Upon the parties requesting that the Master / Insolvency and Companies Court Judge ("the Judge") should conduct an FDR hearing **1A-362**

IT IS ORDERED THAT:

1. The claim shall be listed before the Master/Judge for a without prejudice financial dispute resolution ('FDR') appointment in private on [date] [or a date to be fixed in consultation with counsel's clerks] with a time estimate of [x] hours commencing at 11.00. Judicial pre-reading is estimated to take [x] hours.
2. The parties and their representatives shall attend one hour beforehand for the purpose of seeking to narrow issues and negotiation.
3. The FDR appointment must be treated as a meeting held for the purposes of discussion and negotiation. Parties attending the FDR appointment must use their best endeavours to reach agreement on all matters in issue between them.
4. The parties must personally attend the FDR appointment unless the court directs otherwise.
5. Not less than 7 days before the FDR appointment, the claimant must file with the court a bundle for the FDR appointment. Copies of all offers and proposals, and responses to them whether made wholly or partly without prejudice should be included in the bundle. The disclosure of offers to the court does not amount to a waiver of privilege.
6. At the conclusion of the FDR appointment, the court may make an appropriate consent order.
7. At the conclusion of the FDR appointment, any documents filed under paragraph (3), and any filed documents referring to them, must be returned to that party and not retained on the court file and the court will not retain a record of the hearing. No non-party will be entitled to obtain a transcript of the hearing.
8. The judge hearing the FDR appointment must have no further involvement with the claim, other than to conduct any further FDR appointment or to make a consent order or a further directions order.
9. The costs of and associated with the FDR hearing shall be costs in case.

APPENDIX M

FORM OF FREEZING ORDER[1]

Adapted for use in the Chancery Division

Claim No: [. . . . .] **1A-363**

Name of Court[2]

IN THE HIGH COURT OF JUSTICE

BUSINESS AND PROPERTY COURTS [OF ENGLAND AND WALES *or* **IN** [*insert name of regional Business and Property Courts District Registry, e.g. Birmingham / Manchester*]]

[*insert name of list, e.g. Business List / Competition List / Financial List / Insolvency and Companies List / Intellectual Property List / Property, Trusts and Probate List / Revenue List*] **(ChD)**

or

IN THE HIGH COURT OF JUSTICE

IN THE [*insert name of Chancery District Registry*] **DISTRICT REGISTRY CHANCERY DIVISION]**

or

IN THE COUNTY COURT AT [*insert*]

CHANCERY BUSINESS/BUSINESS AND PROPERTY LIST

---

[1] This form of order assumes that the freezing order is made on an application which has been made without notice to the Respondent(s) (for guidance on making without notice applications in the Chancery Division see: CPR rule 25.3; CPR PD 25A and Chapter 15 paragraphs 15.42-15.61 of the Chancery Guide). Where a freezing order is continued by the Judge at a return date or is made at a hearing at which the Respondent(s) is/are present and on notice the order will need to be suitably adapted.

[2] Freezing orders may be granted in both the High Court and the County Court, although see note [3] below in relation to the types of Judge in each court who may make a freezing order.

*** Name of Judge and date of order***

Before [*insert the level and name of the Judge who made the order, e.g. The Honourable Mr/Mrs Justice xxxxxx His / Her Honour Judge xxxxxx*][1] **[(sitting in private)]**
[*insert date of order*]
BETWEEN:

[*insert name of Applicant(s)*]
Applicant(s)

-and-

[*insert name(s) of Respondent(s)*][2]
Respondent(s)

PENAL NOTICE[3]

IF YOU [. . . . .][4] DISOBEY THIS ORDER YOU MAY BE HELD TO BE IN CONTEMPT OF COURT AND MAY BE IMPRISONED, FINED OR HAVE YOUR ASSETS SEIZED.
ANY OTHER PERSON WHO KNOWS OF THIS ORDER AND DOES ANYTHING WHICH HELPS OR PERMITS THE RESPONDENT TO BREACH THE TERMS OF THIS ORDER MAY ALSO BE HELD TO BE IN CONTEMPT OF COURT AND MAY BE IMPRISONED, FINED OR HAVE THEIR ASSETS SEIZED.

THIS ORDER

1. This is a Freezing Injunction made against [. . . . .][5] (**"the Respondent"**) on [. . . . .] by Mrs/Mr Justice[6] [. . . . .] on the application of [. . . . .] (**"the Applicant"**). The Judge read the Affidavits listed in Schedule A and accepted the undertakings set out in Schedule B at the end of this Order.

2. This order was made at a hearing without notice to the Respondent [at which the Court was satisfied that it was in the interests of justice to sit in private].[Pursuant to CPR rule 39.2(5), in the interests of justice this order is not to be published on the judiciary website.][7] The Respondent has a right to apply to the Court to vary or discharge the order— see paragraph 13 below.

3. There will be a further hearing in respect of this order on [. . . . .] (**"the Return Date"**).[8]

4. If there is more than one Respondent:-

(1) unless otherwise stated, references in this order to "the Respondent" mean both or all of them; and

(2) this order is effective against any Respondent on whom it is served or who is given notice of it.

---

[1] There are restrictions on the judges who may grant a freezing order. In the High Court a freezing order may only be made by a Judge (not including Insolvency and Companies Court Judges): Practice Direction 2B, paragraph 2 and Practice Direction - Insolvency Proceedings, paragraph 3.2(2). In the County Court a freezing order may only be made by a Circuit Judge authorised for the purpose by the Master of the Rolls or the Deputy Head of Civil Justice: Practice Direction 2B, paragraph 8.4.

[2] It is possible to make a single freezing order against more than one respondent, and the wording of the standard order caters for this. In general, however, the better practice is for a separate order to be made in relation to each respondent, particularly if any of the wording in the order is intended to cater specifically for, or apply specifically to, a particular respondent.

[3] This wording may need to be suitably adapted where the Respondent is a corporate entity, e.g. to remove the reference to imprisonment of the entity and to include reference to any director to whom notice of the freezing order is to be given and the potential consequences to that director if the corporate entity disobeys the order.

[4] Insert name of Respondent(s).

[5] Insert name of Respondent(s).

[6] If made by a suitably authorised Circuit Judge, the correct title is "His/Her Honour Judge".

[7] The Court will sit in private where satisfied under CPR rule 39.2 that it is necessary to do so. In such circumstances, it may also be necessary to dispense with publication of the order on the Judiciary website.

[8] The timing of the return date is in the discretion of the Judge granting the Order but will usually be either 7 or 14 days after the freezing order was first granted.

FREEZING INJUNCTION

[FOR AN INJUNCTION LIMITED TO ASSETS IN ENGLAND AND WALES]

5. Until after the Return Date or further order of the Court, the Respondent must not remove from England and Wales or in any way dispose of, deal with or diminish the value of any of its, her or his assets which are in England and Wales up to the value of £ [. . . . .].

[FOR A WORLDWIDE INJUNCTION]

5. Until the Return Date or further order of the Court, the Respondent must not:-

(1) remove from England and Wales any of its, her or his assets which are in England and Wales up to the value of £[. . . . .]; or

(2) in any way dispose of, deal with or diminish the value of any of its, her or his assets whether they are in or outside England and Wales up to the same value.

[FOR EITHER FORM OF INJUNCTION]

6. Paragraph 5 applies to all the Respondent's assets whether or not they are in its, her or his own name, whether they are solely or jointly owned [and whether the Respondent is interested in them legally, beneficially or otherwise[1]]. For the purpose of this order the Respondent's assets include any asset which it, she or he has the power, directly or indirectly, to dispose of or deal with as if it were its, her or his own. The Respondent is to be regarded as having such power if a third party holds or controls the asset in accordance with its, her or his direct or indirect instructions.

7. [This prohibition includes the following assets in particular –

(1) the property known as [title/address] or the net sale money after payment of any mortgages if it has been sold;

(2) the property and assets of the Respondent's business [known as [name]] [carried on at [address]] or the sale money if any of them have been sold; and

(3) any money standing to the credit of any bank account including the amount of any cheque drawn on such account which has not been cleared; and

(4) the Respondent's beneficial interest in [property] held under a trust [give details].][2]

[FOR AN INJUNCTION LIMITED TO ASSETS IN ENGLAND AND WALES]

8. If the total value free of charges or other securities (**"unencumbered value"**) of the Respondent's assets in England and Wales exceeds £[. . . . .], the Respondent may remove any of those assets from England and Wales or may dispose of or deal with them so long as the total unencumbered value of its, her or his assets still in England and Wales remains above £[. . . . .].

[FOR A WORLDWIDE INJUNCTION]

8.(1) If the total value free of charges or other securities (**"unencumbered value"**) of the Respondent's assets in England and Wales exceeds £[. . . . .], the Respondent may remove any of those assets from England and Wales or may dispose of or deal with them so long as the total unencumbered value of the Respondent's assets still in England and Wales remains above £[. . . . .].

(2) If the total unencumbered value of the Respondent's assets in England and Wales does not exceed £[. . . . .], the Respondent must not remove any of those assets from England and Wales and must not dispose of or deal with any of them. If the Respondent has other assets outside England and Wales, she, he or it may dispose of or deal with those assets outside England and Wales so long as the total unencumbered value of all its, her or his assets whether in or outside England and Wales remains above . . . . £[. . . . .].

---

[1] Whether this wider wording (which could capture assets held by a respondent on trust for someone else) should be included in relation to the Order and/or the provision of information will be considered on a case by case basis and, if sought, must be justified. Vested beneficial interests under a trust may appropriately be frozen but should, if possible, be identified specifically under para 7 below.

[2] The standard form of injunction at paragraph 5 will apply to the Respondent's assets whether or not they are individually identified in the order. It may be desirable, however, to list for the avoidance of doubt specific assets of which the Applicant is aware at the time the order is made. Some example wording for different types of assets has been included here. Note that the reference to the "Respondent's business" in paragraph 7.2 is intended to refer to a business which is that of the Respondent personally but carried on under a trading or business name. It is neither designed nor intended to cover the business of a company with separate personality which is owned by the Respondent (where the Respondent's property and assets comprise its/her/his shareholding or debt in the company rather than the property and assets of the company.)

PROVISION OF INFORMATION

9.(1) Unless paragraph (2) applies, the Respondent must [within [. . . . .] hours/ days] of service of this order][1] and to the best of his ability inform the Applicant's solicitors of all its, her or his assets [in England and Wales / worldwide][2] [exceeding £ . . . . in . . . . value][3] whether in its, her or his own name or not and whether solely or jointly owned, giving the value, location and details of all such assets.

(2) If the provision of any of this information is likely to incriminate the Respondent, she or he may be entitled to refuse to provide it, but is recommended to take legal advice before refusing to provide the information. Wrongful refusal to provide the information is contempt of Court and may render the Respondent liable to be imprisoned, fined or have its, her or his assets seized.

10. Within [. . . . .] working days after being served with this order, the Respondent must swear and serve on the Applicant's solicitors an affidavit setting out the above information.[4]

EXCEPTIONS TO THIS ORDER

11.(1) This order does not prohibit the Respondent from spending £[. . . . .] a week towards its, her or his ordinary living expenses and also £[. . . . .] [or a reasonable sum] on legal advice and representation. [But before spending any money the Respondent must tell the Applicant's legal representatives where the money is to come from.[5]]

(2) This order does not prohibit the Respondent from dealing with or disposing of any of its, her or his assets in the ordinary and proper course of business, [but before doing so the Respondent must tell the Applicant's legal representatives[6]].

(3) The Respondent may agree with the Applicant's legal representatives that the above spending limits should be increased or that this order should be varied in any other respect, but any agreement must be in writing.

(4) The order will cease to have effect if the Respondent—

(a) provides security by paying the sum of £[. . . . .] into Court, to be held to the order of the Court; or

(b) makes provision for security in that sum by another method agreed with the Applicant's legal representatives.

COSTS

12. The costs of this application are reserved to the Judge hearing the application on the Return Date.

VARIATION OR DISCHARGE OF THIS ORDER

13. Anyone served with or notified of this order may apply to the Court at any time to vary or discharge this order (or so much of it as affects that person), but they must first inform the Applicant's solicitors. If any evidence is to be relied upon in support of the application, the substance of it must be communicated in writing to the Applicant's solicitors in advance.

INTERPRETATION OF THIS ORDER

14. A Respondent who is an individual who is ordered not to do something must not do it herself or himself or in any other way. She or he must not do it through others acting on her or his behalf or on her or his instructions or with her or his encouragement.

15. A Respondent which is not an individual which is ordered not to do something must not do it itself or by its directors, officers, partners, employees or agents or in any other way.

---

[1] The time period in which a Respondent is required to provide this information should be a realistic one having regard to the nature and volume of information which may be involved.

[2] Delete as appropriate.

[3] Careful consideration must be given to inserting a realistic lower limit below which value assets need not be disclosed.

[4] In an appropriate case paragraphs 9 and 10 may be amalgamated so as to require only one disclosure exercise, verified by Affidavit.

[5] The proviso requiring advance notice should only be included in a without notice order where really necessary. It should not be included otherwise.

[6] The proviso requiring advance notice should only be included in a without notice order where really necessary. It should not be included otherwise.

PARTIES OTHER THAN THE APPLICANT AND RESPONDENT

16. Effect of this order

It is a contempt of Court for any person notified of this order knowingly to assist in or permit a breach of this order. Any person doing so may be imprisoned, fined or have their assets seized

17. Set off by banks

This injunction does not prevent any bank from exercising any right of set of it may have in respect of any facility which it gave to the respondent before it was notified of this order

18. Withdrawals by the Respondent

No bank need enquire as to the application or proposed application of any money withdrawn by the Respondent if the withdrawal appears to be permitted by this order.

[FOR A WORLDWIDE INJUNCTION]

19. Persons outside England and Wales

(1) Except as provided in paragraph (2) below, the terms of this order do not affect or concern anyone outside the jurisdiction of this Court.

(2) The terms of this order will affect the following persons in a country or state outside the jurisdiction of this Court–

(a) the Respondent or its officer or its, her or his agent appointed by power of attorney;

(b) any person who -

(i) is subject to the jurisdiction of this Court;

(ii) has been given written notice of this order at its, her or his residence or place of business within the jurisdiction of this Court; and

(iii) is able to prevent acts or omissions outside the jurisdiction of this Court which constitute or assist in a breach of the terms of this order; and

(c) any other person, only to the extent that this order is declared enforceable by or is enforced by a Court in that country or state.

[FOR A WORLDWIDE INJUNCTION]

20. Assets located outside England and Wales

Nothing in this order shall, in respect of assets located outside England and Wales, prevent any third party from complying with:-

(1) what it reasonably believes to be its obligations, contractual or otherwise, under the laws and obligations of the country or state in which those assets are situated or under the proper law of any contract between itself and the Respondent; and

(2) any orders of the Courts of that country or state, provided that reasonable notice of any application for such an order is given to the Applicant's solicitors.

COMMUNICATIONS WITH THE COURT

All communications to the court about this order should be sent to -

[Chancery Judges' Listing, Ground Floor, The Rolls Building, 7 Rolls Buildings, Fetter Lane, London EC4A 1NL quoting the case number. The telephone number is 020 7947 6690.]

Or

[*Insert address and telephone number of appropriate Business and Property Courts District Registry, Chancery District Registry or County Court*]

The offices are generally open between 10 a.m. and 4.30 p.m. Monday to Friday.

SCHEDULE A – AFFIDAVITS

The Applicant relied on the following affidavit(s)[1]:

(1) [. . . . .]

(2) [. . . . .]

SCHEDULE B – UNDERTAKINGS GIVEN TO THE COURT BY THE APPLICANT

(1) If the Court later finds that this order has caused loss to the Respondent, and decides that the Respondent should be compensated for that loss, the Applicant will comply with any order the Court may make.

---

[1] For each affidavit state the name of person who swore it, the number of the affidavit (e.g. First, Second, Third etc), the date on which it was sworn and the name of the applicant on whose behalf it was filed.

(2) [The Applicant will-
   (a) on or before [date] cause a written guarantee in a form satisfactory to the Court in the sum of £ to be issued from a bank with a place of business within England or Wales, in respect of any order the Court may make pursuant to paragraph (1) above [and (7) below]; and
   (b) immediately upon issue of the guarantee, cause a copy of it to be served on the Respondent.][1]

(3) [As soon as practicable the Applicant will issue and serve a claim form [and/or application notice] [in the form of the draft produced to the Court] [claiming the appropriate relief] and pay the appropriate fee.][2]

(4) The Applicant will [swear and file an affidavit] [cause an affidavit to be sworn and filed] [substantially in the terms of the draft affidavit produced to the Court] [confirming the substance of what was said to the Court by the Applicant's advocate].[3]

(5) The Applicant will serve upon the Respondent [together with this order] [as soon as practicable]-
   (a) copies of the affidavits and exhibits containing the evidence relied upon by the Applicant, and any other documents provided to the Court on the making of the application;
   (b) the claim form;
   (c) an application notice for continuation of the order; and
   (d) a transcript of the hearing on [. . . . .] (if available) or otherwise a full note of the hearing.

(6) [Anyone notified of this order will be given a copy of it by the Applicant's legal representatives.]

(7) The Applicant will pay the reasonable costs of anyone other than the Respondent which have been incurred as a result of this order including the costs of finding out whether that person holds any of the Respondent's assets and if the Court later finds that this order has caused such person loss, and decides that such person should be compensated for that loss, the Applicant will comply with any order the Court may make.

(8) If this order ceases to have effect (for example, if the Respondent provides security or the Applicant does not provide a bank guarantee as provided for above) the Applicant will immediately take all reasonable steps to inform in writing anyone to whom he has given notice of this order, or who she, he or it has reasonable grounds for supposing may act upon this order, that it has ceased to have effect.

(9) [The Applicant will not without the permission of the Court use any information obtained as a result of this order for the purpose of any civil or criminal proceedings, either in England and Wales or in any other jurisdiction, other than this claim.]

(10) [The Applicant will not without the permission of the Court seek to enforce this order in any country outside England and Wales [or seek an order of a similar nature including orders conferring a charge or other security against the Respondent or the Respondent's assets].]

NAME AND ADDRESS OF THE APPLICANT'S LEGAL REPRESENTATIVES:

The Applicant's legal representatives are: -
[*Name, address, reference, fax and telephone numbers both in and out of office hours and e-mail*]

APPENDIX N

FORM OF DELIVERY UP ORDER[4]

Adapted for use in the Chancery Division

1A-364 **Claim No: [. . . . .]**

Name of Court

---

[1] This paragraph need only be included where fortification of the undertaking given in paragraph (1) is to be provided.

[2] This paragraph is only required where, at the time the order is made, the Applicant has not yet issued and/or served a claim form.

[3] This paragraph is only required where, owing to reasons of urgency, an Applicant was unable to produce affidavit evidence to the Court at the hearing of the application and relied instead upon either a draft affidavit or upon submissions made by the Applicant's advocate at the hearing.

[4] General Notes:

(i) 'Delivery up' covers a wide range of relief which the Court can grant to an applicant on

IN THE HIGH COURT OF JUSTICE
BUSINESS AND PROPERTY COURTS [OF ENGLAND AND WALES or IN [*insert name of Business and Property Courts District Registry, e.g. Birmingham / Manchester*]]
[*insert name of list, e.g. Business List / Competition List / Financial List / Insolvency and Companies List / Intellectual Property List / Property, Trusts and Probate List / Revenue List*] **(ChD)**
or
IN THE HIGH COURT OF JUSTICE
IN THE [*insert name of Chancery District Registry*] **DISTRICT REGISTRY**
CHANCERY DIVISION]
or
IN THE COUNTY COURT AT [*insert*]
CHANCERY BUSINESS/BUSINESS AND PROPERTY LIST
*** Name of Judge and date of order***
Before [*insert the level and name of the Judge who made the order, e.g. The Honourable Mr/Mrs Justice xxxxxx His or Her Honour Judge xxxxxx*]
[*insert date of order*]
BETWEEN:

[*insert name of Applicant(s)*]

Applicant(s)

- and -

[*insert name(s) of Respondent(s)*]

Respondent(s)

PENAL NOTICE[1]

IF YOU [. . . . .][2] DISOBEY THIS ORDER YOU MAY BE HELD TO BE IN CONTEMPT OF COURT AND MAY BE IMPRISONED, FINED OR HAVE YOUR ASSETS SEIZED.
ANY OTHER PERSON WHO KNOWS OF THIS ORDER AND DOES ANYTHING WHICH HELPS OR PERMITS THE RESPONDENT TO BREACH THE TERMS OF THIS ORDER MAY ALSO BE HELD TO BE IN CONTEMPT OF COURT AND MAY BE IMPRISONED, FINED OR HAVE THEIR ASSETS SEIZED.

---

an interim basis, in relation to specific property or information (see e.g. the types of orders referred to in CPR rules 25.1(c), (d), (i) and (j)). Each order will therefore need to be tailored to the particular relief being sought by the applicant. The example provided here may be suitable for the delivery up of specific materials to be held pending trial or further order.

(ii) Although the forms of relief set out under CPR rules 25.1(c), (d), (i) and (j) are not termed as an injunctions, insofar as they require a Respondent to carry out mandatory action or actions it will often be appropriate to include within any order made the provisions and safeguards that are commonly found within injunctions (as to which see CPR PD 25A). In particular, paragraph 8 of practice direction 25A provides that where it is likely that an order for delivery up or preservation of property will be executed at the premises of the respondent or a third party, the court shall consider whether to include in the order for the benefit or protection of the parties similar provisions to those specified in Practice Direction 25A relation to injunctions and search orders.

[1] This wording may need to be suitably adapted where the Respondent is a corporate entity, e.g. to remove the reference to imprisonment of the entity and/or to include reference to any director to whom notice of the order is to be given and the potential consequences to that director if the corporate entity disobeys the order.

[2] Insert name of Respondent(s).

ABOUT THIS ORDER

1. This is an order for delivery up made against [. . . . .] ("**the Respondent**") which was made by [. . . . .][1] on the application of [. . . . .] ("**the Applicant**"). The Judge read the evidence listed in Schedule A and accepted the undertakings from the Applicant set out in Schedule B.

[IF THE ORDER WAS MADE ON NOTICE]

2. [The Application was attended by [. . . . .] for the Applicant and [. . . . .] for the Respondent.]

[IF THE ORDER WAS MADE WITHOUT NOTICE]

2. This order was made at a hearing without notice to the Respondent. As a result:

(1) The Respondent has a right to apply to the Court to vary or discharge the order—see paragraph [6] below.

(2) There will be a further hearing in respect of this order on [. . . . .] (**"the Return Date"**).[2]

3. If there is more than one Respondent: -

(1) unless otherwise stated, references in this order to "the Respondent" mean both or all of them; and

(2) this order is effective against any Respondent on whom it is served or who is given notice of it.

THE DELIVERY UP ORDER

4. The Respondent must [by no later than [. . . . .][3] or within [24 hours] of service of this Order] deliver up the materials identified in Schedule C (**"the Materials"**) to [. . . . .][4] pending the trial of this action or until further order.

VARIATION OR DISCHARGE OF THIS ORDER

5. The Respondent may agree with the Applicant's solicitors that this Order should be varied, but any agreement must be in writing and filed at the court.

6. The Respondent [or any third party affected by this Order] may apply to the Court at any time to vary or discharge this Order, but anyone wishing to do so must first inform the Applicant's solicitors in writing.

COSTS OF THE APPLICATION AND COMPLIANCE WITH THE ORDER

7. [. . . . .][5].

SERVICE OF THIS ORDER

8. This Order shall be served by the [Applicant(s)] on the [Respondent(s)].[6]

The Court has provided a sealed copy of this order to the serving party:

[*insert name, postal address and email address of the serving party or, if they are legally represented, the name, postal address and email address of their solicitors*].

SCHEDULE A – AFFIDAVITS

The Court [read / considered] on the following evidence(s)[7]:

(1) [. . . . .]

---

[1] Insert the name and appropriate title of the Judge who made the order.

[2] The timing of the return date is in the discretion of the Judge granting the Order but will usually be either 7 or 14 days after the freezing order was first granted.

[3] Insert the time and date by which the delivery up must take place.

[4] Insert the person to whom the Materials must be delivered up, e.g. the Applicant's solicitors, the Applicant (if not legally represented), or a suitable third party (where that third party - for example a bank or warehousing agent - has so agreed to act).

[5] This paragraph of the draft should set out the order the Applicant is asking the Court to make in respect of the costs of the application and, if different, the costs of the Respondent and/any third parties in complying with the order.

[6] This provision, and the provision under the heading "Service of this order", should be included unless - exceptionally in the High Court - the Court itself is to serve the order.

[7] For each piece of evidence (e.g. witness statement or affidavit) state the name of person who made it, the number of the statement / affidavit (e.g. First, Second, Third etc), the date on which it

(2) [. . . . .]

SCHEDULE B – UNDERTAKINGS GIVEN TO THE COURT BY THE APPLICANT

(1) If the Court later finds that this order has caused loss to the Respondent, and decides that the Respondent should be compensated for that loss, the Applicant will comply with any order the Court may make.

(2) [The Applicant will-
  (a) on or before [date] cause a written guarantee in a form satisfactory to the Court in the sum of £ to be issued from a bank with a place of business within England or Wales, in respect of any order the Court may make pursuant to paragraph (1) above; and
  (b) immediately upon issue of the guarantee, cause a copy of it to be served on the Respondent.][1]

(3) [Upon their delivery up, the Applicant will preserve [the Materials / a copy of the Materials] in a form capable of being returned to the Respondent if the Court should later decide they should be returned to the Respondent.]

(4) [As soon as practicable the Applicant will issue and serve a claim form [and/or application notice] [in the form of the draft produced to the Court] [claiming the appropriate relief] and pay the appropriate fee.][2]

(5) [The Applicant will [make and file a witness statement] [cause a witness statement to be made and filed] [substantially in the terms of the draft witness statement produced to the Court] [confirming the substance of what was said to the Court by the Applicant's advocate].[3]]

(6) [The Applicant will serve upon the Respondent together with this order as soon as practicable-
  (a) copies of the evidence and exhibits containing the evidence relied upon by the Applicant, and any other documents provided to the Court on the making of the application;
  (b) the claim form;
  (c) an application notice for continuation of the order; and
  (d) a transcript of the hearing on [. . . . .] (if available) or otherwise a full note of the hearing.]

SCHEDULE C – THE MATERIALS

For the purposes of paragraph [4] of this Order, "the Materials" to be delivered up are the following:[4]
(1) [. . . . .]

NAME AND ADDRESS OF THE APPLICANT'S LEGAL REPRESENTATIVES:

The Applicant's legal representatives are: -
[*Name, address, reference, fax and telephone numbers both in and out of office hours and e-mail*]

APPENDIX O

[Deliberately blank] **1A-365**

---

was made/sworn and the name of the party on whose behalf it was prepared.

[1] This paragraph need only be included where fortification of the undertaking given in paragraph (1) is to be provided.

[2] This paragraph is only required where, at the time the order is made, the Applicant has not yet issued and/or served a claim form.

[3] This paragraph is only required where, owing to reasons of urgency, an Applicant was unable to produce written evidence to the Court at the hearing of the application and relied instead upon either a draft written evidence or upon submissions made by the Applicant's advocate at the hearing.

[4] This schedule should identify the Materials which the Respondent is obliged to deliver up, and should do so with sufficient detail and precision so that the Respondent is not left in any doubt as to what it, she or him is obliged to deliver up.

APPENDIX P

FORM OF NON-DISCLOSURE ORDER[1]

Adapted for use in the Chancery Division

1A-366 **Claim No: [. . . . .]**

Name of Court

IN THE HIGH COURT OF JUSTICE

BUSINESS AND PROPERTY COURTS [OF ENGLAND AND WALES or IN [*insert name of regional Business and Property Courts District Registry, e.g. Birmingham Manchester*]]

[*insert name of list, e.g. Business List / Competition List / Financial List / Insolvency and Companies List / Intellectual Property List / Property, Trusts and Probate List / Revenue List*] **(ChD)**

or

IN THE HIGH COURT OF JUSTICE

IN THE [*insert name of Chancery District Registry*] **DISTRICT REGISTRY CHANCERY DIVISION]**

or

IN THE COUNTY COURT AT [*insert*]

CHANCERY BUSINESS/BUSINESS AND PROPERTY LIST

*** Name of Judge and date of order***

Before [*insert the level and name of the Judge who made the order, e.g. His/Her Honour Judge xxxxxx or Master xxxxxx*] **sitting in private**

[*insert date of order*]

BETWEEN:

[*insert anonymised name of Claimant(s)*][2]

Intended Claimant/Applicant(s)

- and -

(1) [*insert anonymised name(s) of Defendant(s)*]

(2) [ ] NEWSPAPERS LIMITED

(3) THE PERSON OR PERSONS UNKNOWN

who has or have appropriated, obtained and/or offered or intend to offer for sale and/or publication the material referred to in Confidential Schedule 2 to this Order

Intended Defendant/Respondent(s)

PENAL NOTICE

IF YOU THE RESPONDENT DISOBEY THIS ORDER YOU MAY BE HELD TO BE IN CONTEMPT OF COURT AND MAY BE IMPRISONED (IN THE CASE OF [THE FIRST AND THIRD DEFENDANTS]) OR FINED OR HAVE YOUR ASSETS SEIZED.

ANY PERSON WHO KNOWS OF THIS ORDER AND DISOBEYS THIS ORDER OR DOES ANYTHING WHICH HELPS OR PERMITS ANY PERSON TO WHOM THIS ORDER APPLIES TO BREACH THE TERMS OF THIS ORDER MAY BE HELD TO BE IN CONTEMPT OF COURT AND MAY BE IMPRISONED, FINED OR HAVE THEIR ASSETS SEIZED.

---

[1] This form of order is adapted from the model order supplied in *Practice Direction (Interim Non-disclosure Orders)* [2012] 1 WLR 1003, to which attention is drawn. See also Practice Guidance: Interim Non-Disclosure Orders. It contains detailed commentary on the model order. Further adaptation is likely to be necessary for any given case.

[2] Anonymized names, typically in letter form (e.g., "DEF" or "XYZ"). "A" or "X" etc. should be avoided.

NOTICE TO ANYONE WHO KNOWS OF THIS ORDER

You should read the terms of the Order and the *Practice Guidance (Interim Non-disclosure Orders [2012] 1 WLR 1003 very carefully. You are advised to consult a solicitor as soon as possible. This Order prohibits you from doing the acts set out in Paragraphs 6 [, 7] and 10 of the Order and obliges you to do the acts set out in Paragraphs 8, 9, and 11 of the Order. You have the right to ask the Court to vary or discharge the Order. If you disobey this Order you may be found guilty of contempt of court and you may be sent to prison or fined or your assets may be seized.*

ORDER

1. This is an Injunction [granted at a hearing at which the Court was satisfied that it was in the interests of justice to sit in private]. The injunction, with other orders as set out below, was made against the Defendant[s] on [insert date] by the Judge identified above ("the Judge") on the application ("the Application") of the Claimant[s]. The Judge:

(a) read the witness statements referred to in Schedule A at the end of this Order, as well as the witness statements referred to in Confidential Schedule 1 [or "was given information orally by Counsel on behalf of the Claimant[s]"];
(b) accepted the undertakings set out in Schedule B at the end of this Order; and
(c) considered the provisions of the Human Rights Act 1998 ("HRA"), section 12. 2.

2. This Order was made at a hearing without notice to those affected by it, the Court having considered section 12(2) HRA and being satisfied:

(a) that the Claimant[s] has taken all practicable steps to notify persons affected; and/or
(b) that there are compelling reasons for notice not being given, namely: [set out in full the Court's reasons for making the order without notice]. The Defendant[s] (and anyone served with or notified of this Order) have a right to apply to the Court to vary or discharge the Order (or so much of it as affects them): see clause 17 below.]

[*ONLY TO BE GRANTED IN AN EXCEPTIONAL CASE WHERE ANONYMITY IS STRICTLY NECESSARY*]

ANONYMITY

3. Pursuant to section 6 HRA, and/or CPR 39.2(4) the Judge, being satisfied that it is strictly necessary, ordered that:

(a) the Claimant[s] be permitted to issue these proceedings naming the Claimant[s] as ["DEF"] and giving an address c/o the Claimant[s]'s solicitors;
(b) the Claimant[s] be permitted to issue these proceedings naming the [First] Defendant as ["XYZ"] [and the Third Defendant as "Person or Persons Unknown" and, once it is known to the Claimant, notifying the Defendant's home address by filing the same in a sealed letter which must remain sealed and held with the Court office subject only to the further order of a Judge or the Chief Chancery Master];
(c) there be substituted for all purposes in these proceedings in place of references to the Claimant[s] by name, and whether orally or in writing, references to the letters ["DEF"] ; and
(d) if necessary, there be substituted for all purposes in these proceedings in place of references to the Defendant[s] by name once identified and whether orally or in writing, references to the letters ["XYZ"].

[*ONLY TO BE GRANTED IN AN EXCEPTIONAL CASE WHERE A RESTRICTION ON ACCESS TO DOCUMENTS IS STRICTLY NECESSARY*]

ACCESS TO DOCUMENTS

4. Upon the Judge being satisfied that it is strictly necessary:

(a) (i) no copies of the statements of case; and (ii) no copies of the witness statements and the applications, will be provided to a non-party without further order of the Court.
(b) Any non-party other than a person notified or served with this Order seeking access to, or copies of the abovementioned documents, must make an application to the Court, proper notice of which must be given to the other parties.

SERVICE OF CLAIM FORM WHERE DEFENDANT NOT KNOWN OR WHEREABOUTS NOT KNOWN

5.(a) The Claim Form should be served as soon as reasonably practicable and in any event by [. . . . .] at the latest, save that there shall be liberty for the Claimant[s] to apply to the Court in the event that an extension is necessary; and
(b) Any such application referred to in paragraph 5(a) must be supported by a witness statement. Such application may be made by letter, the Court having dispensed with the need for an application notice.

INJUNCTION

6. Until [. . . . .] (the return date) / the trial of this claim or further Order of the Court, the Defendant[s] must not:

(a) use, publish or communicate or disclose to any other person (other than (i) by way of disclosure to legal advisers instructed in relation to these proceedings ("the Defendant[s]'s legal advisers") for the purpose of obtaining legal advice in relation to these proceedings or (ii) for the purpose of carrying this Order into effect) all or any part of the information referred to in Confidential Schedule 2 to this Order (the Information);

(b) publish any information which is liable to or might identify the Claimant[s] as a party to the proceedings and/or as the subject of the Information or which otherwise contains material (including but not limited to the profession [or age or nationality of the Claimant[s]]) which is liable to, or might lead to, the Claimant[s]'s identification in any such respect, provided that nothing in this Order shall prevent the publication, disclosure or communication of any information which is contained in [this Order other than in the Confidential Schedules] or in the public judgments of the Court in this action given on [insert date].

[*ONLY TO BE GRANTED IN AN EXCEPTIONAL CASE WHERE A REPORTING RESTRICTION IS STRICTLY NECESSARY*]

REPORTING RESTRICTION

7. Until service of the Order/ the return date/ [*date*] the Defendant[s] must not use, publish or communicate or disclose to any other person the fact or existence of this Order or these proceedings and the Claimant's interest in them, other than:

(a) by way of disclosure to the Defendant[s]'s legal advisers for the purpose of obtaining legal advice in relation to these proceedings; or

(b) for the purpose of carrying this Order into effect.

INFORMATION TO BE DISCLOSED

8. The Defendant[s] shall within [24] hours of service of this Order disclose to the Claimant[s]'s solicitors the following:

(a) the identity of each and every journalist, press or media organisation, press agent or publicist or any other third party with a view to publication in the press or media, to whom the Defendants have disclosed all or any part of the Information [since [insert date]]; and

(b) the date upon which such disclosure took place and the nature of the information disclosed.

9. The Defendant[s] shall confirm the information supplied in paragraph 8 above in a witness statement containing a statement of truth within 7 days of complying with paragraph 8 and serve the same on the Claimant[s]'s solicitors and the other parties and file it at court.

PROTECTION OF HEARING PAPERS

10. The Defendant[s] [, and any third party given advance notice of the Application,] must not publish or communicate or disclose or copy or cause to be published or communicated or disclosed or copied any witness statements and any exhibits thereto and information contained therein that are made, or may subsequently be made, in support of the Application or the Claimant[s]'s solicitors' notes of the hearing of the Application (the Hearing Papers), provided that the Defendant[s] [, and any third party,] shall be permitted to copy, disclose and deliver the Hearing Papers to the Defendants' [and third party's/parties'] legal advisers for the purpose of these proceedings.

11. The Hearing Papers must be preserved in a secure place by the Defendant[s]'s [and third party's/parties'] legal advisers on the Defendant[s]'s [and third party's/parties'] behalf.

12. The Defendant[s] [, and any third party given advance notice of the Application,] shall be permitted to use the Hearing Papers for the purpose of these proceedings provided that the Defendant[s]'s [third party's/parties'] legal advisers shall first inform anyone, to whom the said documents are disclosed, of the terms of this Order and, so far as is practicable, obtain their written confirmation that they understand and accept that they are bound by the same.

PROVISION OF DOCUMENTS AND INFORMATION TO THIRD PARTIES

13. The Claimant[s] shall be required to provide the legal advisers of any third party [where unrepresented, the third party] served with advance notice of the application, or a copy of this Order promptly upon request, and receipt of their written irrevocable undertaking to the Court to use those documents and the information contained in those documents only for the purpose of these proceedings:

(a) a copy of any material read by the Judge, including material read after the hearing at the direction of the Judge or in compliance with this Order [save for the witness statements referred to in Confidential Schedule 1 at the end of this Order] [the witness statements]; and/or

(b) a copy of the Hearing Papers.

[*ONLY TO BE GRANTED IN AN EXCEPTIONAL CASE WHERE HEARING THE APPLICATION IN PRIVATE IS STRICTLY NECESSARY*]

HEARING IN PRIVATE

14. The Judge considered that it was strictly necessary, pursuant to CPR 39.2(3)(a),(c) and (g), to order that the hearing of the Application be in private and there shall be no reporting of the same. [Pursuant to CPR rule 39.2(5), in the interests of justice this order is not to be published on the judiciary website.][1]

PUBLIC DOMAIN

15. For the avoidance of doubt, nothing in this Order shall prevent the Defendants from publishing, communicating or disclosing such of the Information, or any part thereof, as was already in, or that thereafter comes into, the public domain in England and Wales [as a result of publication in the national media] (other than as a result of breach of this Order [or a breach of confidence or privacy]).

COSTS

16. The costs of and occasioned by the Application are reserved.

VARIATION OR DISCHARGE OF THIS ORDER

17. The Defendants or anyone affected by any of the restrictions in this Order may apply to the Court at any time to vary or discharge this Order (or so much of it as affects that person), but they must first give written notice to the Claimant's solicitors. If any evidence is to be relied upon in support of the application, the substance of it must be communicated in writing to the Claimant's solicitors in advance. The Defendants may agree with the Claimant's solicitors and any other person who is, or may be bound by this Order, that this Order should be varied or discharged, but any agreement must be in writing and be filed at court.

INTERPRETATION OF THIS ORDER

18. A Defendant who is an individual who is ordered not to do something must not do it himself or in any other way. He must not do it through others acting on his behalf or on his instructions or with his encouragement.

19. A Defendant which is not an individual which is ordered not to do something must not do it itself or by its directors, officers, partners, employees or agents or in any other way.

[*In the case of an Order the effect of which may extend outside the jurisdiction*]

PERSONS OUTSIDE ENGLAND AND WALES

20.(a) Except as provided in paragraph (2) below, the terms of this Order do not affect or concern anyone outside the jurisdiction of this Court.

(b) The terms of this Order will affect the following persons in a country or state outside the jurisdiction of this Court - (a) the Defendant or his officer or agent appointed by power of attorney; (b) any person who - (i) is subject to the jurisdiction of this Court; (ii) has been given written notice of this Order at his residence or place of business within the jurisdiction of this Court; and (iii) is able to prevent acts or omissions outside the jurisdiction of this Court which constitute or assist in a breach of the terms of this Order; and

(c) any other person, only to the extent that this Order is declared enforceable by or is enforced by a court in that country or state.

PARTIES OTHER THAN THE CLAIMANT AND THE DEFENDANT

21. Effect of this Order It is a contempt of court for any person notified of this Order knowingly to assist in or permit a breach of this Order. Any person doing so may be imprisoned, fined or have their assets seized.

NAME AND ADDRESS OF THE CLAIMANT[S]'S LEGAL REPRESENTATIVES

22. The Claimant[s]'s solicitors are - [Name, address, reference, fax and telephone numbers both in and out of office hours and e-mail]

---

[1] The Court will sit in private where satisfied under CPR rule 39.2 that it is necessary to do so. In such circumstances, it may also be necessary to dispense with publication of the order on the Judiciary website.

COMMUNICATIONS WITH THE COURT

23. All communications to the Court about this Order should be sent to: [insert details of appropriate court, e.g. Chancery Judges' Listing Ground Floor, Rolls Building, 7 Rolls Buildings, Fetter Lane, London, EC4A 1NL, quoting the case number. The telephone number is 02079476297. The email address is *ChanncerryJudgesListing@justice.gov.uk.* The offices are open between 10 a.m. and 4.30 p.m. Monday to Friday.

SERVICE OF THE ORDER

24. The Claimant[s] shall serve a sealed copy of the Order on the Defendant[s].
25. The court has sent a sealed copy of the order to the serving party at:
[. . . . .]

SCHEDULE A

The Claimant[s] relied on the following witness statements:
1. .... [*insert names of witness, number of statement and date on which statement was signed*]
2. ....

SCHEDULE B

UNDERTAKINGS GIVEN TO THE COURT BY THE CLAIMANT[S]

(1) If the Court later finds that this Order has caused loss to the Defendant[s], and decides that the Defendant[s] should be compensated for that loss, the Claimant[s] will comply with any order the Court may make.
(2) If the Court later finds that this Order has caused loss to any person or company (other than the Defendant[s]) to whom the Claimant[s] has given notice of this Order, and decides that such person should be compensated for that loss, the Claimant[s] will comply with any Order the Court may make.
(3) [By 4.30pm on [ ] the Claimant[s] will (a) issue a Claim Form and an Application Notice claiming the appropriate relief and
 (a) As soon as practicable provide the identified Defendants with a transcript of the hearing on [..........] if available or otherwise a full note of the hearing
 (b) Forthwith serve on the identified Defendants a copy of the hearing papers and the Claim Form and Application Notice
(4) [The Claimant[s] will use all reasonable endeavours to identify and serve the unidentified Defendant[s] within four months of the date of this Order and in any event will do so by [ ] at the latest. Once identified the Claimant[s] will serve upon the Defendant[s] together with this Order copies of the documents provided to the Court on the making of the Application and as soon as practicable the documents referred to in (3) above.]
(5) On the return date the Claimant[s] will inform the Court of the identity of all third parties that have been notified of this Order. The Claimant[s] will use all reasonable endeavours to keep such third parties informed of the progress of the action [insofar as it may affect them], including, but not limited to, advance notice of any applications, the outcome of which may affect the status of the Order.
(6) If this Order ceases to have effect or is varied, the Claimant[s] will immediately take all reasonable steps to inform in writing anyone to whom they have given notice of this Order, or who they have reasonable grounds for supposing may act upon this Order, that it has ceased to have effect in this form.

CONFIDENTIAL SCHEDULE 1

The Claimant[s] also relied on the following confidential witness statements:
1. ....
2. ....

CONFIDENTIAL SCHEDULE 2

INFORMATION REFERRED TO IN THE ORDER
Any information or purported information concerning:
(1) [Set out the material sought to be protected]
(2) [Any information liable to or which might lead to the identification of the Claimant[s] (whether directly or indirectly) as the subject of the proceedings or the material referred to above, [the fact that he has commenced these proceedings or made the application herein].]

APPENDIX X

PREPARATION OF BUNDLES

INTRODUCTION

1. Subject to paragraph 6 below, no hard copy bundles, only electronic bundles, should be filed with the court unless requested by the judge. The parties should seek to minimise their own and other participants' use of hard copy bundles and documents. **1A-367**

2. If it is not possible for a litigant in person to comply with the requirements on electronic bundles, a brief explanation of the reasons for this should be provided to the Chancery Judges' Listing Office, ICC Judges' Hearings or the Master (as appropriate) via CE-File, as far in advance of the hearing as possible.

3. The preparation of bundles requires a high level of co-operation. It is the duty of all parties and/or their legal representatives to co-operate to the necessary level. Any failure to comply with the provisions of this Appendix may lead to the court imposing sanctions on the party or parties in default.

CORE BUNDLE FOR TRIAL

4. Where the volume of documents needed to be included in the bundles, and the nature of the case, makes it sensible, a separate core bundle should be prepared for the trial, disposal hearing or any other type of final hearing, containing those documents likely to be referred to most frequently. In an appropriate case the court may have directed the preparation of a bundle of key documents and a narrative chronology. If it has done so these documents are likely to form part of any core bundle. **1A-368**

5. The core bundle should be separately paginated, but each page should also bear its main bundle and page number reference.

6. Unless the court directs otherwise, the core bundle should be filed as an electronic bundle and in hard copy. The hard copy and electronic versions must be identical.

GENERAL GUIDANCE ON BUNDLES

7. So far as possible, bundles for all hearings should be prepared in accordance with the principles set out in this section. These principles apply to all bundles, electronic and hard copy, except where it is apparent from the context that the reference is only to electronic bundles. Further guidance relating specifically to hard copy bundles is provided at paragraph 21 below. **1A-369**

8. Bundles should contain only documents and authorities that are necessary for the hearing. Large electronic files can be slow to transmit and unwieldy to use and therefore should be avoided. The sensible selection (limitation) of the material reproduced in hearing bundles is as important as the quality of bundle preparation.

9. Each bundle should be given a concise title (see paragraph 12 (c) and 21 (f)) identifying its contents by type, which should be prominent and before identifying the case and any bundle number/letter as appropriate.

10. After a hearing is completed (and judgment has been handed down), an electronic bundle provided to the court and the parties through, for example, a data room, should be disabled (switched off) promptly and at a time agreed by the parties, noting that the bundle may need to be preserved in some format pending determination of any appeal. Any hard copy bundles should be removed from the court promptly.

11. Bundle Contents:

(a) statements of case should be assembled in 'chapter' form, i.e. claim form followed by particulars of claim, followed by further information (if any), followed by defence, etc. Redundant documents, e.g. particulars of claim overtaken by amendments, requests for further information recited in the responses to those requests and backsheets, should generally be excluded;

(b) where there are witness statements, affidavits and/or expert reports from two or more parties, each party's witness statements etc should, in large cases, be contained in separate bundles; any exhibits of contemporaneous documents should be excluded from these bundles and their contents instead included with other contemporaneous documents;

(c) documents should normally be placed in chronological order with clear cross referencing to statements of case, witness evidence, affidavits or expert evidence as provided for at paragraph 14 below. In some cases it may be appropriate to group some types of documents together in a separate bundle and consideration should always be given to whether to group landscape documents together rather than in a general documents bundle.

(d) inter-solicitor correspondence should normally be placed in a separate bundle. Only those letters which are likely to be referred to should be included (it will rarely be necessary to include all inter-solicitor correspondence in the bundle);

(e) documents in manuscript, or not fully legible, should be transcribed. The transcription should be marked and placed adjacent to the document transcribed; and

(f) documents in a foreign language should be translated; the translation should be marked and placed adjacent to the document transcribed; the translation should be agreed, or, if it cannot be agreed, each party's proposed translation should be included.

12. Bundle Format:

(a) where possible, the hearing bundles other than the core bundle and the authorities bundle(s) should be combined into one .pdf file, but in larger cases it may be sensible to combine separate categories of bundle into separate .pdf files. Where the hearing bundles have been separated into more than one .pdf file, the parties must have particular regard to the rules on pagination set out below;

(b) any authorities bundle(s) should always be provided separately, where possible combined as a single .pdf file;

(c) the file name for each .pdf file containing or constituting a bundle or bundles should contain a short version of the name of the case and an indication of the content (for example statements of case) and the number/letter of the bundle(s), and end with the hearing date.

(d) all significant documents and all sections in electronic bundles should be bookmarked for ease of navigation, with an appropriate description as the bookmark. The bookmark should contain the page number of the document;

(e) all individual bundles should be indexed (and, where the bundle is electronic, the index should if possible be searchable), except that chronological bundles of contemporaneous correspondence need not be indexed if an index is unlikely to be useful;

(f) a separate index or table of contents for the hearing bundles should also be provided, if possible hyperlinked to the indexed documents;

(g) no more than one copy of any one document should be included, unless there is good reason for doing otherwise;

(h) contemporaneous documents, and correspondence, should be included in chronological order, starting with the earliest document; however, where a contract or similar document is central to the case it may be included in a separate place but a page should be inserted in the chronological run of documents to indicate:

  i. the place the contract or similar document would have appeared had it appeared chronologically; and
  ii. where it may be found instead;

(i) all bundles should be paginated in the bottom right hand corner in a form that can be distinguished easily from any other pagination on the document and does not mask relevant document content;

(j) the pagination of electronic bundles must correspond to the pages of the .pdf file. This means that:

  i. every page in the electronic bundle, including any title page, index or contents page, must be paginated;
  ii. where the hearing bundle has been split into more than one .pdf file (which should be avoided to the extent possible, as set out at paragraph 15 and paragraph 16 below), the pagination must begin afresh in each file;
  iii. where possible, and in order to aid searching, pagination should include a preceding letter or number which clearly identifies the relevant volume of the bundle;
  iv. care should be taken to ensure that any additions to or deletions from a bundle do not cause the pagination to cease to match the page number of the .pdf file (see further paragraph 19 below).

13. Document Format:

(a) electronic documents, where possible, should be the subject of OCR (optical character recognition) to ensure that the text in the documents can be read as text and the document is word-searchable;

(b) documents should generally appear in portrait mode. Where there are only occasional documents that in the original were in landscape they should be oriented in the bundle in portrait but so as to be capable of being read with a 90-degree rotation clockwise. Where there are more numerous landscape documents it may be appropriate to order the documents so that all or the majority or the landscape documents can be collected together in a bundle that is in landscape mode. This may be useful for example where there are numerous spreadsheets, presentations or plans.

(c) For a CMC / CCMC the parties should prepare a separate bundle for landscape-format documents which should include the DRDs and/or costs budgeting documents;

(d) the default view for all pages in electronic bundles should be 100 per cent;

(e) meta data in electronic documents should be removed;

(f) if practicable scanned document resolution should not be greater than 300 dpi to avoid slow scrolling or rendering;

(g) in electronic bundles of authorities: (a) a .pdf copy of the original report, with headnote, should be included for reported decisions (and see Chapter 12 paragraph 12.58 to 12.60 and *Practice Direction (Citation of Authorities)* [2012] 1 WLR 780 on the correct sources to use); and (b) a .pdf copy of the official transcript should be used, where available, for unreported decisions.

14. Cross-referencing:
(a) where copy documents are taken from the disclosure of more than one party, then unless clearly unnecessary, the documents should be marked in a convenient way to show from which party's disclosure the copy document has been taken;
(b) where there is a reference in a statement of case, affidavit or witness statement to a document which is contained in the bundles, any copy of the statement of case, affidavit or witness statement in a bundle should be marked in a convenient way to identify where the document is to be found. Unless otherwise agreed it is the responsibility of the party that served the statement of case or witness statement to provide a cross-referenced copy for this purpose as part of its co-operation in the preparation of the hearing bundles; and
(c) where the method of cross-referencing used in (b) above has the effect of altering the format or length of the statement of case, affidavit or witness statement as compared to the signed originals to which a statement of truth was applied, then a solicitor responsible for the production of the bundles should add to the cross-referenced copy a short, signed certification that the content is unaltered from the signed originals except for the addition of the cross-referencing.

DELIVERY OF BUNDLES TO COURT

15. All electronic bundles should be delivered to the court: **1A-370**
(a) by upload to CE-File, if possible (which may depend on file sizes);
(b) by letter to the judge on CE-File giving access to a secure download site;
(c) by email to the judge's clerk (where applicable) either (i) attaching the bundle(s) or (ii) giving access to a secure download site; or
(d) by providing the judge with personal secure and confidential access to a shared digital workspace hosting the case materials, if such a workspace is being used by the parties.

16. Where file sizes are large, parties should avoid breaking down sensibly bundled documents into smaller bundles just for the purpose of ease of transmission and parties should consider (b), (c)(ii) or (d) above as preferred methods.

17. Where an original document is required to be filed, by order of the court or by provision of the Civil Procedure Rules ('CPR') or the Insolvency Rules 1986 or 2016, such original document cannot be filed electronically and must instead be physically filed with the court (See Appendix E for further guidance).

18. If bundles are transmitted by email the email subject line should provide the following detail:
(a) case number;
(b) case name (shortest comprehensible version);
(c) hearing date;
(d) judge name (if known); and
(e) the words in capitals 'REMOTE HEARING' where applicable.

19. If pages are to be added to or removed from a bundle after it has been transmitted to the judge it should not be assumed that a substitute bundle will be accepted, because the judge may have started to mark up the original. Absent a particular direction, a substitute bundle should be made available, but any pages to be added should also be provided separately, in a separate file, with pages appropriately sub-numbered, or a separate list should be provided of the pages to be removed (as the case may be).

20. This does not apply if a shared digital workspace is being used to host the bundles on which they may be amended without disturbing the judge's markings or notes. However, the judge should still be notified of any additions, substitutions or removals within the workspace so that they are aware of any new documents whether by letter filed on CE-File and emailed to the judge's clerk or by some electronic notification within the digital workspace.

ADDITIONAL GUIDANCE FOR HARD COPY BUNDLES

21. As indicated above, and subject to the rule on core bundles, only electronic bundles should be filed with the court unless one or more hard copy bundles are specifically requested, and the parties are encouraged to minimise their own use of hard copy bundles. Where hard copy bundles are used, the following requirements also apply: **1A-371**
(a) where possible, documents should be in A4;
(b) bundles should be printed/copied double-sided;
(c) bundles should not be overfilled, and should allow sufficient room for later insertions. Subject to this and to (iv) below, the size of file used should not be a size that is larger than necessary for the present and anticipated contents;
(d) in any event, each bundle should not contain more than 300 sheets of paper (i.e. 600 double-sided pages) and binders and files must be strong enough to withstand heavy use;

(e) dividers or tabs within bundles may assist in the organisation and use of a bundle, but they should not be overused (for example to divide each individual page or piece of correspondence);
(f) bundles should be paginated electronically and not by hand, and should be named on the spine, the outside of the front cover and on the inside front cover, the label to include the short title of the case and a short description of the content (for example statements of case) and the number/letter of the bundle, where relevant and the date of the hearing;
(g) documents should generally appear in portrait mode but if there are occasional documents which have to be read across rather than down the page (for example a single spreadsheet or plan), it should be orientated in the bundle to ensure that the top of the text is nearest the spine. Where there are more numerous landscape documents it may be appropriate to order the documents so that all or the majority or the landscape documents can be collected together in a bundle that is in landscape mode. This may be useful for example where there are numerous spreadsheets, presentations or plans.
(h) for a CMC / CCMC the parties should prepare a separate bundle for landscape-format documents, including any DRD and/or costs budgeting documents which should be orientated in the bundle to ensure that the top of the text is nearest the spine;
(i) where any marking or writing in colour on a document is important, for example on a conveyancing plan, the document must be copied in colour or marked up correctly in colour;
(j) large documents, such as plans, should be placed in an easily accessible file; and
(k) all staples, metal clips etc should be removed.

APPENDIX Y

SKELETON ARGUMENTS

GENERAL

1A-372 **1.** Where this Appendix is not complied with the costs of preparation of the skeleton argument may be disallowed in whole or in part.

2. The general rule is that the parties should prepare skeleton arguments for all hearings. The exceptions to this general rule are where the hearing is of an application and a skeleton argument is not warranted, for example because the hearing is likely to be short, (e.g. less than an hour) and uncontroversial, or where the application is so urgent that preparation of a skeleton argument is impracticable.

3. In an appropriate case the court may direct sequential rather than simultaneous delivery of skeleton arguments.

CONTENT OF SKELETON ARGUMENTS

1A-373 **4.** A skeleton argument is intended to identify both for the parties and the court those points which are, and are not, in issue and the nature of the argument in relation to those points that are in issue.

5. A skeleton argument is not a speaking note or a substitute for oral argument.

6. Skeleton arguments must therefore:
(a) make clear what is sought;
(b) identify concisely:
  i. the nature of the case generally and the background facts only insofar as they are relevant to the particular matter before the court;
  ii. the propositions of law relied on with references only to the necessary relevant authorities. More than one authority should not be cited for any proposition; and
  iii. the submissions of fact to be made with references to the evidence.

7. The following should be avoided in all skeleton arguments:
(a) arguing the case at length;
(b) lengthy quotation from, or other duplication of, the evidence; and
(c) lengthy quotation from authorities, citations from which should be: (i) as brief as possible; and (ii) confined to passages to which it is intended to take the court in oral argument to establish the proposition(s) for which the authority in question has been cited.

8. As regards format and presentation, a skeleton argument must:
(a) be in numbered paragraphs;
(b) state the name of the advocate(s) who prepared it, their professional address and their email address or telephone number;
(c) be prepared in a format which is easily legible - no skeleton should be served in a font smaller than 12 point and with line spacing of less than 1.5;
(d) comply with the limits on length to be found in this Guide or as ordered; and
(e) be provided to the court as a Word document (whether or not also provided in any other format, for example as a .pdf file).

DELIVERY TO COURT

9. All skeleton arguments for hearings in the Rolls Building should be filed by CE-File and where appropriate by email as follows: **1A-374**

(a) if the name of the High Court Judge ('HCJ'), is known, the Judge's clerk. A list of judges in the Chancery Division and the names and email addresses of their clerks is at *https://www.gov.uk/guidance/chancery-judges* and Appendix B;

(b) for hearings before a HCJ where the HCJ's name is not yet known, a Section 9 Judge or a Deputy HCJ, the Chancery Judges' Listing Office at *ChanceryJudgesListing@justice.gov.uk*;

(c) for hearings before Insolvency and Companies Court Judges *rolls.icl.hearings1@justice.gov.uk*; and

(d) for hearings before Masters, *Chancery.MastersAppointments@justice.gov.uk.*

10. All emails should have the following in their subject line, in the following order: the name of the case (in short form) and case number; the name of the judge (if known); and the date of the hearing if known or the hearing window where it is not.

11. In the Judges' Applications List (see Chapter 15) a fresh skeleton should be CE-Filed and emailed in respect of any adjourned hearing even if it has not changed in form since the earlier hearing; and it should be clearly re-dated.

12. If a supplemental or amended skeleton is lodged, it should be filed on CE-File and, where appropriate, the attention of the relevant judge's clerk should be drawn to that filing (preferably by direct email) so that it is not overlooked.

13. Unless the court directs otherwise, no hard copy of any skeleton argument should be lodged at court.

14. The above email boxes will be cleared of all skeletons over 14 days old at any given time.

APPENDIX Z

REMOTE AND HYBRID HEARINGS PROTOCOL

INTRODUCTION TO THIS PROTOCOL

1. This Protocol contains guidance on preparing for and conducting Remote and Hybrid Hearings in the Business and Property Courts. It is relevant to hearings of all kinds, including but not limited to trials, applications and those in which litigants in person are involved. It does not set out the circumstances in which the Court may consider it appropriate to order a Remote or Hybrid Hearing. **1A-375**

2. The Protocol is intended to assist judges and court users but it should be applied flexibly. It remains the case that the manner in which all hearings are conducted is a matter for individual judges, acting in accordance with applicable law, the Civil Procedure Rules (the 'CPR') and Practice Directions. Nothing in this Protocol derogates from the judge's duty to determine all issues that arise in the case judicially and in accordance with normal principles. A hearing conducted in accordance with this Protocol should, however, be treated for all other purposes as a hearing in accordance with the CPR.

3. The following defined terms are used in this Protocol:

(a) A 'Hybrid Hearing' is a hearing in which some Participants, together with the judge(s), are physically present in a courtroom, while other Participants attend the hearing by telephone or video link.

(b) A 'Remote Hearing' is a hearing in which all Participants, and the judge(s), attend the hearing from separate locations by telephone or video link, instead of gathering physically in a courtroom.

(c) A "Participant" means a party to the proceedings (meaning, in the case of corporate entities, a representative of the entity), a legal representative of a party, any person or entity instructed for the purposes of the hearing by a party, a witness, or an expert.

(d) A "Speaker" means a legal representative of a party, a witness, an expert and any other attendee who is required to present, respond, and/or give oral evidence at a Remote or Hybrid Hearing.

(e) A "Working Day" means every day except weekends and public holidays in England and Wales.

4. The general rule is that all court hearings, including Remote and Hybrid Hearings, are in public. This can be achieved in a number of ways. These include, without limitation, the court directing that: (a) the audio and (if available) video of the hearing be relayed to an open courtroom, (b) a media representative be allowed to access the Remote or Hybrid Hearing, and/or (c) the hearing be live-streamed over the internet, where such a broadcast is authorised in legislation (such as s85A of the Courts Act 2003).

5. Where this is not practicable, the court may direct that a Remote Hearing must take place in private where this is necessary to secure the proper administration of justice (CPR Practice Direction 51Y). This is in addition to the requirement that a hearing (howsoever conducted) be held in private where the court is satisfied that it is necessary in order to secure the proper administration of justice (CPR 39.2(3)(g)).

6. The unauthorised recording or transmission of a hearing is an offence. The taking of photographs (including screen shots) or the recording or transmission of someone taking part in a Remote Hearing is also prohibited. However, Remote and Hybrid Hearings will be recorded by the court, unless a recording has been dispensed with under CPR 39.9(1).

PREPARING FOR A REMOTE OR HYBRID HEARING

GENERAL POINTS

1A-376 **7.** In order to function effectively, Remote Hearings and, in particular, Hybrid Hearings require a high degree of preparation and co-operation between the parties and the court.

8. Whether a hearing will take place as a Remote Hearing or a Hybrid Hearing is a decision for the court. The court will provide guidance from time to time on which types of hearing will be remote hearings and which will be in person hearings by default. Where a party believes that a Remote or Hybrid Hearing would be appropriate, whether for an application, CMC / CCMC, directions hearing, PTR, and/ or part or all of a final hearing or trial, they should discuss and if possible agree the question with the other parties and then raise it with the court:

(a) at or in advance of a CMC / CCMC or directions hearing being listed
(b) when an application is issued and/or in advance of it being listed
(c) at or in advance of the PTR, if there is one; or
(d) where no PTR has been fixed, in correspondence in good time before the final hearing or trial.

9. At the time a Remote or Hybrid Hearing is requested, the parties should co-operate with each other in order to inform the court of any matters which they wish the court to reflect in any directions it may give, including (without limitation):

(a) any support or adjustments which any Participant would require in order to participate in and/or attend a Remote or Hybrid Hearing; and
(b) any proposal to instruct a third party provider to facilitate the Remote or Hybrid Hearing (see the section on 'Third party providers' below for more guidance).

10. The court may order a Remote or Hybrid Hearing and give directions for its conduct in whatever manner appears to it appropriate including at any PTR, at a short case management conference convened for the purpose, or on paper. In any event, Judges' Listing, Masters' Appointments, ICC Judges' Hearings, the relevant court's listing office and/or the judge's clerk will seek to contact the parties and/or their legal representatives in advance of a Remote or Hybrid Hearing to inform them of the time and date for the hearing as well as the format and the platform for the hearing.

11. Where a Hybrid Hearing is ordered, parties and/or their legal representatives should liaise with the Judges' Listing, Masters' Appointments, ICC Judges' Hearings, the relevant Court's listing office and/or the judge's clerk in advance of the hearing as to: (i) the number of courtrooms that will be available for the hearing and their capacity; and (ii) what extra equipment and preparation will be required to facilitate the Hybrid Hearing.

12. Judges' Listing, Masters' Appointments, ICC Judges' Hearings, the relevant Court's listing office and/or the judge's clerk will seek to ensure that the parties are informed, as far in advance as possible, of the identity of the judge(s) hearing the case.

ATTENDANCE

1A-377 **13.** Subject to applicable law, it is for the court to determine who may attend a Remote or Hybrid Hearing and to set such conditions for their attendance as it may consider appropriate. No person may access a Remote or Hybrid Hearing remotely without the court's permission. For additional guidance see the Practice Guidance on Remote Observation of Hearings. Unauthorised access may constitute an offence under section 41 of the Criminal Justice Act 1925 and section 9 of the Contempt of Court Act 1981.

14. In all cases, parties must inform the court in advance of whom they wish to attend the hearing, following the procedure set out in the following paragraphs.

15. The court may permit a person outside England and Wales to attend a Remote Hearing as a Participant where it considers that appropriate. The court has no express power to allow the broadcasting of a Hybrid Hearing to persons outside England and Wales. However, that does not prevent the court permitting Participants to attend such a hearing from outside England and Wales. The onus is on the relevant Participant to ensure that such attendance is not in breach of any local laws or regulations and that, if permission is required from the local court or other authority in the foreign jurisdiction, such permission has been obtained (and see paragraph 33 below in relation to witnesses attending a hearing from abroad).

16. The parties or their legal representatives should, before the Remote or Hybrid Hearing, provide the Judges' Listing, Masters' Appointments, ICC Judges' Hearings, the relevant Court's listing office and/or the judge's clerk with the following details for each Participant who wishes to attend:

(a) name;
(b) organisation;

(c) email address;
(d) the location, including country, from which they would be joining the hearing (if not England and Wales) (in this regard, parties should note paragraph 15 above); and
(e) whether it is proposed that the person in question be a Speaker.

In the ordinary course, the parties should provide the information sought in this paragraph no later than 10.30am two working days before the hearing.

17. In addition, each party should nominate one of its proposed Participants as its 'Primary Contact', being the person who should be contacted in accordance with the lost connections procedure set out at paragraph 30 below.

18. A member of the public or media representative who wishes to attend a Remote or Hybrid Hearing must notify the court by email of the details set out in subsections (a) to (d) of paragraph 16 above using the contact details set out in the Daily Cause List, Appendix B and Appendix C or the Hearing Notice.

19. If the court is satisfied that the requirements of paragraph 16 have been met in relation to any person, it will seek to facilitate attendance by that person at the Remote or Hybrid Hearing. However: (a) there is no absolute right to attend a Remote or Hybrid Hearing; (b) failure to give timely notice of a wish to attend may mean that attendance cannot be facilitated; and (c) access cannot in any event be guaranteed; the needs of other litigants, the limits on resources and the need to monitor the identities of those who view the proceedings may mean that the court is not able to provide access.

20. For hearings conducted by audio link:
(a) the court (or a third party provider authorised by the court) will call the parties at the time of the hearing or the parties should dial in to the hearing using the information provided in the invitation to join the remote hearing. In order to attend and/or participate in a telephone hearing, Participants will require access to a telephone with any relevant call barring services switched off; or
(b) the court will notify the parties that they are to dial in to the hearing on a video or audio conferencing platform, in which case the court will, wherever possible, no later than one working day before the hearing, provide the relevant telephone number and access code.

21. For hearings conducted by video link, the Judges' Listing, Masters' Appointments, ICC Judges' Hearings, the relevant Court's listing office and/or the judge's clerk will wherever possible send the parties information about the video hearing, including a link to access the hearing and any sign in details, no later than one working day before the hearing. In order to attend and/or participate in a hearing conducted by video link, Participants will require access to a device with internet access, which enables audio and video transmission.

22. A link provided to a Participant is for their own use. No-one who is provided with a link may forward it to any other person without the court's permission.

23. Available platforms for Remote and Hybrid Hearings conducted via telephone conference include (non-exhaustively): BT conference call, BT MeetMe, Microsoft Teams and ordinary telephone call. Available methods for videoconferences include (non-exhaustively): Microsoft Teams, Cloud Video Platform (CVP), Video Hearing Service (VHS), court video link, and Zoom. But any communication method available to the Participants can be considered if appropriate.

24. For video conferences, it is usually possible for the parties and/or their representatives to contact the Judges' Listing, Masters' Appointments, ICC Judges' Hearings, the relevant Court's listing office and/or the judge's clerk to arrange a test call. The test call should be conducted with a maximum of 10 users. In any event, Participants are advised to test their own devices and ensure they are able to access the relevant platform in advance of the hearing. Any technological issues should be made known to the Judges' Listing, Masters' Appointments, ICC Judges' Hearings, the relevant Court's listing office and/or the judge's clerk in advance of the hearing.

25. Parties and/or their legal representatives should notify the Judges' Listing, Masters' Appointments, ICC Judges' Hearings, the relevant Court's listing office and/or the judge's clerk no later than two working days before the video hearing if telephone dial-in facilities are required for Participants without internet access.

CONDUCT OF THE HEARING

26. Participants should join the hearing no later than 15 minutes before the set start time. **1A-378**

27. Remote and Hybrid Hearings should resemble courtroom hearings as closely as practicable. This means maintaining the same level of formality as is expected in the courtroom.

28. Subject to any contrary or more detailed direction of the court, Participants should observe the following etiquette:
(a) All persons who are not Speakers should keep their microphones muted and cameras switched off throughout the hearing.
(b) Speakers should keep their cameras turned on and mute their microphones when they are not speaking.
(c) A Participant, who is not a Speaker, may not address the court without the court's prior permission.
(d) Where possible, Speakers should ensure their cameras are at eye level and should maintain

a reasonable distance from the camera (with a plain background behind them) in order to ensure their head and upper body are clearly visible. Speakers may wear headsets if they wish.

(e) Speakers should try to attend the hearing from a quiet place from which privacy and minimal noise disruptions can be ensured.

(f) Reasonable and proportionate and noise-free use of devices to enable communication between team members or legal representatives and their clients is permitted during the hearing, provided that this does not interfere with the hearing; in particular, Participants must ensure that all notifications are set to silent for the duration of the hearing. However, Participants are reminded that witnesses must not communicate with anyone else about their evidence until their testimony is concluded. See the section below titled 'Witnesses, experts and other third parties' for further guidance.

29. It is the responsibility of each party and/or their legal representatives to inform those attending the Remote or Hybrid Hearing (including any person or entity engaged to provide technical support or assistance) of the strict prohibitions against any unauthorised dissemination of the hearing and the making of any sound or video recording of it (and of any other restrictions outlined in the relevant court order), in addition to the other obligations set out in this section.

30. In the event of an internet or phone line disconnecting or degrading to an unusable degree during the Remote or Hybrid Hearing, the Judges' Listing, Masters' Appointments, ICC Judges' Hearings, the relevant Court's listing office and/or the judge's clerk will contact the Primary Contact for each party to discuss whether a continuation is possible or whether an adjournment of the hearing is required.

WITNESSES, EXPERTS AND OTHER THIRD PARTIES

1A-379 **31.** Where a witness gives evidence by video or audio link in a Remote or Hybrid Hearing, the objective should be to make the process as close as possible to the usual practice in an in-person hearing where evidence is taken in open court.

32. In such cases, guidance should be taken from Annex 3 to Practice Direction 32 which addresses videoconferencing.

33. In particular, parties should be aware that where evidence is to be taken from a witness located outside the jurisdiction, permission may be required from the local court or other authority in the foreign jurisdiction. It is for the party calling the witness to ensure that such permission, if required, is obtained in good time for the hearing at which the witness is to give evidence and to inform the court that such permission has been obtained. For further guidance on the required timing for such permission in cases assigned to the fast track or the multi-track, please see this High Court Practice Note.

34. If a party wishes one or more of its witnesses to give their evidence from the offices of a legal representative, video conference centre or similar venue, that party should notify the other parties at the earliest opportunity, with a view to permitting a representative of the other parties to attend or making arrangements to ensure that the court can ascertain that the witness is not communicating with any other person or otherwise receiving assistance or impermissibly making reference to notes during the course of their evidence.

35. In cases where one or more of the witnesses is to give their evidence from a more informal venue than the type described in paragraph 34, it may be appropriate to arrange to have more than one camera available in the location from which the witness is giving their evidence. This is to ensure that the court can ascertain that the witness is not communicating with any other person or otherwise receiving assistance during the course of their evidence or impermissibly making reference to notes during the course of their evidence.

36. Witnesses must only have access to a device on which they access and participate in the hearing, the hearing bundle and their statement(s) and exhibit (either in electronic or hard copy, or both). The court will expect the parties to have made efforts to ensure that each witness has access to these materials in a format which is convenient and accessible to the witness. In some cases it may be more appropriate for a witness to have access to a hard copy bundle whether they are participating remotely or in person.

37. Where a witness has access to the hearing bundle only in electronic form, and the witness is asked a question about a document appearing in the bundle, the court and the advocates should ensure that the witness is given a proper opportunity to orientate or familiarise themselves with the document (for instance by being shown the front page, or the pages before/after the section they are being asked about) before answering.

38. Parties and/or their legal representatives should ensure that witnesses decide in good time before the hearing whether they prefer to swear an oath on a holy book/scripture or to make an affirmation. The relevant holy book/scripture and/or text of the oath or affirmation should be made available to the witness in advance of the hearing.

39. Parties are reminded that it will be for the parties to provide the necessary facilities to enable the witness to access the hearing bundle in electronic format even if the hearing takes place in a court room.

BUNDLES / DOCUMENTS FOR THE HEARING

40. The claimant should, if necessary, prepare an electronic bundle of documents and an electronic bundle of authorities for each Remote or Hybrid Hearing. Each electronic bundle should be compiled, formatted and delivered in accordance with the relevant court's guide. See Appendix X as necessary for further guidance. **1A-380**

41. To the greatest extent practicable, all bundles should be electronic, not hard copy (subject to paragraph 36). However, parties or their legal representatives should liaise with the court in advance of the hearing to determine the judge's preferences in the matter.

THIRD PARTY PROVIDERS

TRANSCRIBERS

42. Hearings in the B&PCs are tape-recorded or digitally-recorded by the court unless the judge directs otherwise (CPR 39.9(1)). A party may, after a hearing, require a transcript to be produced by a court-approved transcriber. Form EX107 should be completed and submitted to the court. The Guidance Notes to Form EX107 set out the procedure to be followed, a list of approved transcribers and the relevant charges. **1A-381**

43. Parties may, with the prior permission of the court, engage court-approved transcribers to prepare a real-time transcript of a hearing. The court's permission will be recorded in an Order which may also, without limitation, regulate the dissemination of the real-time transcript. The requesting party and the transcriber they wish to instruct must also submit to the court a completed Form EX107 OFC. A copy of the court's Order must be provided to the transcribers.

HEARING SUPPORT SERVICES

44. The scale or logistical complexity of some Remote or Hybrid Hearings may lead the parties to consider engaging a specialist third party to provide technical support services. These services can include the selection and operation of hardware and/or software necessary to support the hearing itself and/or electronic document management. **1A-382**

45. Permission to engage such third-party providers must be sought from the court in advance of the hearing. The parties and/or their legal representatives bear the responsibility of informing the relevant representatives from the third-party provider of any requirements and/or prohibitions set out in the relevant court order, in addition to the strict prohibition against making any unauthorised dissemination or recording of the hearing by any electronic means and that failure to comply could result in them being found in contempt of court and liable to criminal penalties.

INTERPRETERS

46. Where a Participant or Participants require an interpreter, a request should be made to the court in advance of the hearing. Parties or their legal representatives should provide the court with the details in paragraph 16 for the interpreter as relevant. If possible, parties or their legal representatives should try to arrange a test call with the interpreter and relevant witness in advance of the hearing. All Participants are reminded that using remote interpretation services may cause delays and/or technical difficulties and are encouraged to be mindful of this. **1A-383**

47. Where a witness is to give evidence remotely by an interpreter, consideration should be given as to where the interpreter should be located.

SECTION 1B KING'S BENCH GUIDE

The Queen's Bench Guide has been renamed as The King's Bench Guide. Additional changes are referenced below.

KING'S BENCH GUIDE

All references to Queen, QB, QBD and Her Majesty have been amended to King, KB, KBD and His Majesty, respectively.

ANNEX 2 –

CONTACTS LIST

1B-232 *Replace the first table in Annex 2 with:*

KB Masters, Listing, Asbestos and Childrens Funds, KB Judges listing

1B-232

Senior Master Fontaine Seniormaster.fontaine@ejudiciary.net	Jonathan.Eves@justice.gov.uk	
Master Eastman Master.eastman@ejudiciary.net	Rosie.Reid@justice.gov.uk	
Master McCloud Master.McCloud@ejudiciary.net	Agnes.Elsayed@justice.gov.uk	
Master Cook Master.Cook@ejudiciary.net	Ilaria.Capanni@justice.gov.uk	
Master Davison Master.Davison@ejudiciary.net	Sujen.Subenthiran@justice.gov.uk	
Master Thornett Master.thornett@ejudiciary.net	Mihaela.Baditoiu@justice.gov.uk	
Master Gidden Master.gidden@ejudiciary.net	Sheila.Anirudhan@justice.gov.uk	
Master Brown Master.brown@ejudiciary.net	Stephen.Keith@justice.gov.uk	
Master Sullivan Master.Sullivan@ejudiciary.net	Khurram.Mahmud@justice.gov.uk	
Master Dagnall Master.dagnall@ejudiciary.net	Beverley.Henningham@justice.gov.uk	
Master Stevens Master.Stevens@ejudciary.net	Ian.Ang1@justice.gov.uk	
Deputy Master Yoxall Deputymaster.yoxall@ejudiciary.net	Stephen.Keith@justice.gov.uk	
Deputy Master Bard Deputymaster.bard@ejudiciary.net	Stephen.Keith@justice.gov.uk	
Deputy Master Bagot QC Recorder.bagot.QC@ejudiciary.net	Stephen.Keith@justice.gov.uk	
Deputy Master Toogood Deputymaster.Toogood@ejudiciary.net	Stephen.Keith@justice.gov.uk	
Deputy Master Grimshaw Deputymaster.grimshaw@ejudiciary.net	Stephen.Keith@justice.gov.uk	
Deputy Master Fine Deputymaster.fine@ejudiciary.net	Stephen.Keith@justice.gov.uk	
KB Masters Listing	kbmasterslisting@justice.gov.uk	0203 936 8957 option 4
KB Asbestos	kb.asbestos@justice.gov.uk	0203 936 8957 option 4
KB Childrens Funds	kbchildrensfunds@justice.gov.uk	0203 936 8957 option 8
KB Judges Listing	KBJudgesListingOffice@Justice.gov.uk	0203 936 8957 option 5

Change the third table in Annex 2 with:

KB Issue & Enquiries and Enforcement Sections

KB Issue & Enquiries	KBEnquiries@justice.gov.uk
KB Enforcement Section	kbenforcement@Justice.gov.uk

	The general number is 0203 936 8957 and choose the appropriate option to the desired office. Enforcement Team is option 3 and Issues & Enquiries are at option 2.

Forums

Replace the sixth table in Annex 2 with:

KB Masters Court User Group	Elaine Harbert, (PA to The Senior Master) Elaine.harbert1@justice.gov.uk Tel: 020-7947-6911
Media & Communications List User Group (MACLUG)	Daniel Mendonca, Clerk to The Hon. Mr Justice Nicklin Daniel.mendonca@justice.gov.uk Tel: 020-7073-6217

ANNEX 6 -

MASTERS LISTING DIRECTIONS

Obtaining Transcripts of Hearings

Replace paragraph with:

Requests for transcripts of a Master's judgment should be sent to KBmasterslisting@justice. gov.uk **1B-236**

Contacting the Court

Replace the table with:

Master	***Clerk & email***
Senior Master Fontaine	Jonathan Eves Jonathan.Eves@justice.gov.uk
Master Eastman	Rosie Reid Rosie.Reid@justice.gov.uk
Master McCloud	Agnes Elsayed Agnes.Elsayed@justice.gov.uk
Master Cook	Ilaria Capanni Ilaria.Capanni@justice.gov.uk
Master Davison	Sujen Subenthiran Sujen.Subenthiran@justice.gov.uk
Master Thornett	Mihaela Baditoiu Mihaela.Baditoiu@justice.gov.uk
Master Gidden	Sheila Anirudhan Sheila.Anirudhan@justice.gov.uk
Master Sullivan	Khurram Mahmud Khurram.Mahmud@justice.gov.uk
Master Dagnall	Beverley Henningham beverley.henningham@Justice.gov.uk
Master Stevens	Ian Ang Ian.Ang1@justice.gov.uk
Master Brown & Deputy Masters	Stephen Keith stephen.keith@Justice.gov.uk

SECTION 1BA ADMINISTRATIVE COURT JUDICIAL REVIEW GUIDE

Replace the Administrative Court Judicial Review Guide with:

THE ADMINISTRATIVE COURT JUDICIAL REVIEW GUIDE

CONTENTS

FOREWORD TO THE 2022 EDITION

1BA-1 This is the seventh edition of the Judicial Review Guide, which has become a valuable resource for all who are involved in proceedings before the Administrative Court. It covers all the stages of a claim for judicial review. Good practice is identified and pitfalls foreshadowed. It is required reading for all those who conduct judicial review cases (whether or not they are lawyers).

The production of the Guide is dependent on the work of many judges, lawyers and the staff of the Court. I am particularly indebted to Mr Justice Swift (Judge in Charge of the Court) and Mr Justice Chamberlain (the editor of the sixth and seventh editions) for their valuable contributions. Their work was ably assisted by Laura McMullan, the Administrative Court Office lawyer who marshalled the amendments and Christine Sorrell, the Clerk to Mr Justice Chamberlain, who assisted with the production of the Guide. A number of other judges and Court staff have also contributed. I am grateful to all those who have given their time to produce this valuable Guide to such an important part of the High Court's work.

The Rt Hon Dame Victoria Sharp DBE
President of the Queen's Bench Division

PREFACE TO THE 2022 EDITION

1BA-2 This Guide provides a general explanation of the work and practice of the Administrative Court. It is designed to assist parties to conduct judicial review claims in the Administrative Court, by drawing together into one place the relevant statutory provisions, rules of procedure, practice directions and case law on procedural aspects of judicial review. It provides general guidance as to how litigation in the Administrative Court should be conducted in order to achieve the overriding objective of dealing with cases justly and at proportionate cost.

The Guide has been prepared with all Court users in mind, whether they are persons who lack legal representation (known as "litigants in person") or persons who have legal representation. All Court users are expected to follow this Guide when they prepare and present their cases.

The Guide refers readers to the relevant sections of the Civil Procedure Rules and associated Practice Directions. In recent years, the Administrative Court has become one of the busiest specialist courts within the High Court. It is imperative that everyone who is a party to judicial review proceedings is aware of and follows the Civil Procedure Rules and Practice Directions so that Court resources (including the time of the judges who sit in the Administrative Court) are used efficiently. That has not uniformly been the case in the past. The Court has experienced problems. To name a few: applications claiming unnecessary urgency; over-long written arguments and bundles of documents; authorities and skeleton arguments being filed very late and in the wrong format. The Court has had occasion to restate the importance of considering carefully whether urgency is required in *R (DVP) v Secretary of State for the Home Department* [2021] EWHC 606 (Admin). The Court has also emphasised the importance of concision in statements of case and skeleton arguments. On these and other topics, the Guide sets out in clear terms what is expected. Parties and/or their legal representatives may be subject to sanctions if they fail to comply.

The Upper Tribunal continues to undertake a significant number of judicial review cases. Annex 6 contains important information about its jurisdiction, with a particular emphasis on immigration cases.

We are grateful to all those who provided constructive feedback on the 2021 Guide, which we have reflected in the present edition. We continue to welcome feedback, which should be sent by email to *GuideFeedback@administrativecourtoffice.justice.gov.uk.* We plan to update this Guide from time to time, as appropriate.

The Honourable Mr Justice Swift, Judge in Charge of the Administrative Court
The Honourable Mr Justice Chamberlain
Royal Courts of Justice, July 2022

PART A:—PRELIMINARY MATTERS

1 INTRODUCTION

1.1 THE JUDICIAL REVIEW GUIDE

1.1.1 This Guide has been prepared under the direction of the Judge in Charge of the Administrative Court. It explains the practice and procedures of the Administrative Court in judicial review cases. It is designed to make it easier for parties to conduct such cases. It is not intended to address the substance of administrative law, or public law more generally. For this, reference should be made to the many academic and practitioner texts on the subject. **1BA-3**

1.1.2 The Guide must be read with the Civil Procedure Rules ("CPR") and the supporting Practice Directions. The Practice Directions accompanying Part 54 of the CPR have been amended with effect from 31 May 2021. Litigants and their advisers must acquaint themselves with the CPR and Practice Directions.

1.1.3 The Guide does not have the force of law, but is "essential reading for all those who practice in the Administrative Court".[1] All those engaged in proceedings in the Administrative Court should have regard to it.[2] However, where relevant, parties should draw the Court's attention to a particular rule or case and not merely rely on this Guide. The Guide applies to cases heard in the Administrative Court wherever it is sitting and in the Administrative Court Offices ("ACOs") across England and Wales.

1.1.4 The contents of the Guide, including any websites, email addresses, telephone numbers and addresses, are correct at the time of publication. The Guide will be updated from time to time.

1.1.5 Where possible, referenced documents are hyperlinked in the electronic version of this document, available at Administrative Court judicial review guide - GOV.UK (*www.gov.uk*)

1.2 THE CIVIL PROCEDURE RULES

1.2.1 The overriding objective set out in CPR 1.1(1) is central to all civil proceedings, including judicial review claims. It requires the parties and the Court to deal with cases justly and proportionately, including at proportionate cost. **1BA-4**

1.2.2 The CPR are divided into Parts. A Part is referred to in the form: "CPR Part 54". A rule (and paragraph) within a Part is referred to in the form: "CPR 54.12(2)". The current CPR can be viewed on the Government's website at *www.justice.gov.uk/courts/procedure-rules/civil/rules.*

1.2.3 The judicial review procedure is mainly (but not exclusively) governed by CPR Part 54 and the associated Practice Directions. These are required reading for any litigant considering judicial proceedings. More details on these provisions will be given throughout this Guide.

1.3 PRACTICE DIRECTIONS

1.3.1 Most Parts of the CPR have an accompanying Practice Direction or Practice Directions, and other Practice Directions deal with matters such as the Pre-Action Protocols. **1BA-5**

1.3.2 The Practice Directions are made pursuant to statute and have the same authority as the CPR themselves. However, in case of any conflict between a rule and a Practice Direction, the rule will prevail. Each Practice Direction is referred to in the Guide with the number of any Part that it supplements preceding it. For example, Practice Direction A supplementing CPR Part 54 is referred to as CPR 54A PD. A particular sub-paragraph of a Practice Direction will be referred to, for example, as CPR 54A PD para 5.1.

1.3.3 The key Practice Directions associated with CPR Part 54 are CPR 54A PD (Judicial Review), CPR 54B PD (Urgent applications and other applications for interim relief), CPR 54C PD (Administrative Court (Venue)) and CPR 54D PD (Planning Court Claims).

1.3.4 These Practice Directions are required reading for any litigant considering judicial review proceedings.

1.4 FORMS

1.4.1 CPR 4 PD lists the forms generally required to be used under the CPR. **1BA-6**

1.4.2 Annex A lists the Administrative Court forms that are referred to and required by the CPR and the Practice Directions. Other forms may be provided by the ACO and are not available online.

---

[1] *R (DVP) v Secretary of State for the Home Department* [2021] EWHC 606 (Admin), [8].
[2] *R (AB) v Chief Constable of Hampshire Constabulary & Others* [2019] EWHC 3461 (Admin), [108].

1.4.3 The relevant N forms that are most used in judicial review proceedings are:

N461	Judicial Review claim form
N461 PC	Judicial Review claim form (Planning Court)
N462	Judicial Review acknowledgment of service
N462 PC	Judicial Review acknowledgment of service (Planning Court)
N463	Judicial Review - application for urgent consideration
N463 PC	Judicial Review - application for urgent consideration (Planning Court)
N464	Application for directions as to venue for administration and determination
N464 PC	Application for directions as to venue for administration and determination (Planning Court)

1.4.4 The following general N forms are also required in a judicial review application:

N215	Certificate of service
N244	Application notice
N260	Statement of costs (Summary Assessment)
N279	Notice of discontinuance
N434	Notice of change of legal representative

1.4.5 The forms contained in CPR 4 PD are available on the ACO website: *www.gov.uk/government/collections/administrative-court-forms*

1.4.6 There are a few forms which are not set out in the rules that practitioners must use. Two important ones are Form QBD OHA, which is used for out of hours applications (see para 17.8 of this Guide), and Form 86b which is used to request an oral hearing where permission to apply for judicial review is refused on the papers (see para 9.2 of this Guide).

1.5 FEES

1BA-7 **1.5.1** By virtue of the Civil Proceedings (Fees) Order 2008 No. 1053 (L.5) (as amended), the ACO is required to charge fees at certain stages in proceedings or when a party requests an order from the Court. The relevant fees (at the time of publication) are outlined in Annex 2.[1] Current fees can also be checked at the Administrative Court website at *https://www.gov.uk/government/publications/fees-in-the-civil-and-family-courts-full-list-ex50a.*

1.5.2 Some litigants may be entitled to the remission of fees.[2] Guidance on whether a party may be entitled to fee remission can be found on form EX160A and litigants can apply online at *https://www.gov.uk/get-help-with-court-fees.* Litigants should be aware that fee remission is potentially available for all fees save for copying charges (except for vexatious litigants and persons subject to Civil Restraint Orders, where different rules apply: see para 5.1.6 of this Guide).

1.5.3 Court fees should not be confused with costs between parties, which can be considerably more than Court fees. Costs are discussed in this Guide in Chapter 25.

1.5.4 A litigant in person will be expected to comply with the requirements to use the right form and to pay fees, just like a represented litigant. Litigants in person should therefore make themselves familiar with those parts of this Guide which are relevant to their claim and with the applicable requirements.

1.6 CALCULATING TIME LIMITS

1BA-8 **1.6.1** Unless the period specified is 5 days or less, references to days in the CPR, Practice Directions or this Guide are to clear, calendar days, which include weekends and bank holidays.[3]

1.6.2 The date of service of a document is not the date when the document is actually received. Where service is by post, the date of service is the second working day after the day that the document was sent.[4]

---

[1] The fees are set out in the Civil Proceedings (Fees) Order 2008, Schedule 1 (as amended).

[2] The fee remission provisions are set out in Civil Proceedings (Fees) Order 2008, Schedule 2 (as amended).

[3] See CPR 2.8 for more detail and examples.

[4] CPR 6.14 and CPR 6.26.

1.7 THE ADMINISTRATIVE COURT

1.7.1 The Administrative Court is part of the Queen's Bench Division of the High Court (one of the 3 divisions of the High Court, together with the Chancery Division and Family Division). The Administrative Court hears applications for judicial review[1] and some statutory appeals and applications which fall outside the remit of this Guide. **1BA-9**

1.7.2 Judicial review is the procedure by which an individual, company or organisation can challenge the lawfulness of a decision or other conduct of a person or body whose powers are governed by public law. Persons and bodies who are amenable to judicial review are referred to here as "public bodies".

1.7.3 The Rt Hon Dame Victoria Sharp DBE is the President of the Queen's Bench Division ("the President"). Mr Justice Swift is the Judge in Charge of the Administrative Court ("Judge in Charge"). Mrs Justice Steyn DBE is the liaison judge for the Midlands and Wales and South West. Mr Justice Fordham is the liaison judge for the North and North East.

1.7.4 Most cases in the Administrative Court are heard by a single High Court Judge or by another judge or deputy judge authorised to sit in the Administrative Court.

1.7.5 Judicial review claims which challenge planning decisions are heard in the specialist Planning Court, which is part of the Administrative Court.

1.7.6 Some cases in the Administrative Court are heard by a Divisional Court, usually consisting of one Lord or Lady Justice of Appeal (or the President) and one High Court Judge.

1.7.7 If a party considers that their case should be heard by a High Court Judge (rather than by another judge), or by a Divisional Court, the ACO should be informed as soon as possible, and reasons should be given.

1.8 THE ADMINISTRATIVE COURT OFFICE

1.8.1 The management of judicial review cases in the Administrative Court is dealt with by the ACO. All documentation must be filed with the ACO and all enquiries on cases must be directed to the ACO (not sent directly to the judiciary). **1BA-10**

1.8.2 The ACO and its staff are a part of Her Majesty's Courts and Tribunals Service ("HMCTS"), which in turn is an executive agency of the Ministry of Justice ("MOJ"). There are ACOs in Birmingham Civil Justice Centre, Cardiff Civil Justice Centre, Leeds Combined Court Centre, Manchester Civil Justice Centre, and in the Royal Courts of Justice in London. Contact details for the ACOs can be found in Annex 1 and Annex 8 to this Guide.

1.8.3 The ACO is open for business from 10am to 4.30pm (10 am to 4pm for the out of London ACOs) on every day of the year except:[2]

1.8.3.1 Saturdays and Sundays;
1.8.3.2 Good Friday;
1.8.3.3 Christmas Day;
1.8.3.4 one further day over the Christmas period determined in accordance with the table annexed to CPR 2A PD. This will depend on which day of the week Christmas Day falls on;
1.8.3.5 bank holidays in England and Wales;
1.8.3.6 such other days as the Lord Chancellor, with the concurrence of the senior judiciary, may direct.

1.9 THE JUDICIARY AND THE MASTER

1.9.1 The judiciary in the Administrative Court consists of the High Court Judges (who are styled "The Honourable Mr/Mrs Justice...") and other judges and deputy judges who have been authorised to sit in the Administrative Court. When this Guide refers to a judge or judges, it includes all of these. All judges are addressed in Court as "My Lord" or "My Lady". **1BA-11**

1.9.2 In the Royal Courts of Justice there is also a Master of the Administrative Court, currently Master Gidden. He generally deals with interim and pre-action applications and is addressed in Court as "Master".

2 PROCEDURAL RIGOUR

2.1 THE NEED TO OBSERVE THE RULES

2.1.1 Judicial review proceedings are different from private law proceedings because the interests in play are typically not just those of the parties to the litigation. Depending on the context, the proceedings may affect third parties. It may also be necessary to consider the public interest. **1BA-12**

2.1.2 However, this does not mean that the Court will overlook or tolerate breaches of direc-

---

[1] See paras 6.5, 6.6 and 6.7 of this Guide, where the exceptions are discussed.
[2] CPR 2A PD para 2.

tions made by the Court or of obligations imposed by the CPR or Practice Directions or by this Guide. The appellate Courts have emphasised the need for procedural rigour in judicial review.[1]

2.1.3 The importance of procedural rigour is reflected in a number of sections of this Guide. In particular, attention is drawn to the need for legal professionals and litigants in person:

2.1.3.1 to consider carefully who are the proper parties to any claim (see para 3.2 of this Guide);

2.1.3.2 to comply rigorously with the duty of candour, at all times, but especially when making applications for urgent consideration (see para 17.3.3 of this Guide);

2.1.3.3 to ensure that applications are made at the earliest stage possible and not left to the last minute (for example, see para 13.7 for applications to extend time; para 23.2 for applications to adduce expert evidence);

2.1.3.4 to comply with deadlines set by Court direction, the CPR, or a Practice Direction and to apply for relief from sanctions where documents are filed late (see paras 13.7.7, and 13.9 of this Guide);

2.1.3.5 to file documents and authorities in hard copy and electronic form in the correct format (see paras 20.3, 21.4 and 22.4).

2.2 SANCTIONS

1BA-13 **2.2.1** If parties or their legal representatives fail to comply with the procedural requirements imposed by the CPR, Practice Directions or this Guide, the Court has a range of sanctions at its disposal, including the powers:

2.2.1.1 to decline to accept documents filed in the wrong format (see paras 7.3.9, 20.4.5, 21.4.5, 21.7.1 and 22.6.1 of this Guide) or late (see paras 20.4.5, 21.2.5, 21.7.1 and 22.6.1 of this Guide);

2.2.1.2 to impose adverse costs orders against a party (see para 24.1 of this Guide) or a wasted cost order against a legal representative (see para 25.13 of this Guide); and

2.2.1.3 to refer a legal representative to the relevant professional regulator (see Chapter 18 of this Guide).

3 THE PARTIES

3.1 IDENTIFYING THE PARTIES

1BA-14 **3.1.1** This part of the Guide is intended to give guidance on who should be the parties in a judicial review claim. Identifying the parties correctly ensures that pre-action discussions take place between the proper persons (see reference to the pre-action Protocol at para 6.2 of this Guide). It also ensures that the proper parties are referred to on any Court documents.

3.2 THE PARTIES

1BA-15 **3.2.1** Claimant(s)

3.2.1.1 Claimants are those persons who wish to challenge the conduct of a public body in the Administrative Court (for more detail about "standing", see para 6.3.2 of this Guide).

3.2.1.2 The claimant can be any individual or incorporated company (also known as a corporation). Partnerships can bring proceedings in the name of the partnership.

3.2.1.3 The Court may allow unincorporated associations (which do not have legal personality) to bring judicial review proceedings in their own name.[2] But it is sensible, and the Court may require, that proceedings are brought in the name of one or more individuals, such as an officeholder or member of the association, or by a private limited company formed by individuals. Costs orders may be made against the party or parties named as claimant(s).

3.2.1.4 Public bodies can be claimants in judicial review proceedings. The Attorney General has a common law power to bring proceedings. Local authorities may bring proceedings under s.222 of the Local Government Act 1972.

3.2.2 Defendant(s)

3.2.2.1 The defendant is the public body whose conduct is under challenge, not the individual decision-maker within that public body.

3.2.2.2 Where the decision is made by a Government Department, it is the relevant Secretary of State who is the defendant. Therefore, even if the decision challenged is that of a civil servant

---

[1] *R (Spahiu) v Secretary of State for the Home Department* [2018] EWCA Civ 2604, [2019] 1WLR 1297, [2]; *R (Talpada) v Secretary of State for the Home Department* [2018] EWCA Civ 841, [67]; *R (Dolan) v Secretary of State for Health and Social Care* [2020] EWCA Civ 1605, [2021] 1 WLR 2326, [116]-[120]; and *R (AB) Chief Constable of Hampshire Constabulary* [2019] EWHC 3461 (Admin), [108].

[2] *Aireborough Neighbourhood Development Forum v Leeds City Council* [2020] EWHC 45 (Admin), [29].

working in, for example, the Home Office, the defendant would be the Secretary of State for the Home Department.[1]

3.2.2.3 Where the conduct challenged is that of a court or tribunal, it is the court or tribunal which must be named as defendant. The opposing party in the underlying case is named as an "interested party" (see below at 3.2.3.2.).

3.2.3 Interested parties

3.2.3.1 An interested party is any person (including a corporation or partnership), other than the claimant or defendant, who is "directly affected" by the claim.[2]"Directly affected" means "affected without the intervention of any intermediate agency".[3] For example, where a claimant challenges the decision of a defendant local authority to grant planning permission to a third party, the third party is directly affected by the claim because the relief sought would affect his or her legal rights, so he or she must be named as an interested party.

3.2.3.2 Where the defendant is a court or tribunal, any opposing party in the lower court or tribunal must be named as an interested party in the judicial review claim.[4]

3.2.3.3 Interested parties must be included in pre-action correspondence and named in the Claim Form. Interested parties must also be served with the Claim Form.[5]

3.2.4 Interveners

3.2.4.1 In judicial review proceedings, the Court has an express power to receive evidence and submissions from persons who are not parties. Any person can apply under CPR 54.17 for permission to make representations or file evidence. The application must be made by filing an Application Notice. This must be done promptly.[6] There are costs considerations (see para 25.7 of this Guide).

3.2.4.2 Potential interveners should ensure that all parties are made aware of the intended application from the earliest stage.

3.2.4.3 The Application Notice should explain who the applicant is and indicate why and in what form the applicant wants to participate in the hearing (e.g. by written submissions only or by making written submissions and filing evidence).

3.2.4.4 The application should include a summary of the representations that the potential intervener proposes to make at the hearing and a copy of any evidence the potential intervener proposes to file and serve, with an explanation of the relevance of that evidence to the issues in the proceedings.

3.2.4.5 If the applicant to intervene seeks an order as to costs which departs from the provisions made by section 87 of the Criminal Justice and Courts Act 2015, the application must include a copy of the order sought and grounds on which it is sought.

3.3 MULTIPLE CLAIMANTS / DEFENDANTS / INTERESTED PARTIES

3.3.1 A claim for judicial review may be brought by one claimant or, in appropriate circumstances, by more than one claimant. It may, for example, be appropriate for the claim to be brought by more than one claimant where a number of different individuals are affected by the decision challenged. However, parties should bear in mind the need to ensure that claimants are limited to those best placed to bring the claim. It is not appropriate to add parties simply to raise the profile of the litigation or to make it easier to raise funds. The Court may decline to accord standing to such additional parties.[7] **1BA-16**

3.3.2 A claim may be brought against one defendant or, in appropriate circumstances, against two or more defendants. This may, for example, be appropriate where two or more bodies are responsible for the conduct under challenge.

3.3.3 There may, exceptionally, be circumstances in which a number of different challenges by different claimants against different defendants can be combined in one single claim for judicial review. This will generally only be appropriate if the different challenges can be conveniently dealt with together.

3.3.4 If a claimant considers that any person is directly affected by the claim, the claimant must identify that person as an interested party and serve the Claim Form on him or her.[8] A defendant must also identify in the Acknowledgment of Service any person who the defendant considers is an

---

[1] The whole system of departmental organisation and administration is based on the notion that the decision of a government official is constitutionally that of the Minister, who alone is answerable to Parliament. This is called the Carltona principle: see *Carltona Ltd v Commissioners of Works* [1943] 2 All ER 560.

[2] CPR 54.1(2)(f).

[3] *R v Rent Officer Service ex p. Muldoon* [1996] 1 WLR 1103, 1105.

[4] CPR 54A PD para 4.6(2).

[5] CPR 54.7(b).

[6] CPR 54.17(2).

[7] See para 6.3.2 of this Guide.

[8] CPR 54.6 and 54.7.

interested party because the person is directly affected by the decision challenged[1] and the Court will consider making that person an interested party when determining the application for permission to apply for judicial review.

3.3.5 Where a person who is a potential defendant or interested party has not been named or served with the Claim Form, the Court may direct that he or she be added as a party and that the claim be served on him or her. When this happens, the interested party may make representations or lodge an Acknowledgment of Service.[2]

3.4 CASE TITLES

1BA-17 **3.4.1** In judicial review proceedings, the case title differs from other civil proceedings to reflect the fact that judicial review is the modern version of a historic procedure in which Her Majesty's judiciary acted in a supervisory capacity to ensure that public powers were properly exercised. The case title reflects this:[3]

"The Queen (on the application of X) v Y", where X is the Claimant and Y is the Defendant.

3.4.2 The case title is often written as follows, with R (for Regina) denoting The Queen:

R (on the application of X) v Y & Ors; or R (X) v Y.

3.4.3 The Crown will not involve itself in any way in the claim on behalf of the claimant. The inclusion of The Queen in the title is purely nominal.[4]

4 LITIGANTS IN PERSON

4.1 GENERAL

1BA-18 **4.1.1** Many cases in the Administrative Court are now conducted by parties who do not have professional legal representation and who represent themselves. These are known as "litigants in person". The rules of procedure and practice apply to litigants in person in the same way as to parties represented by lawyers. Many forms of help are available for individuals who wish to seek legal advice before bringing claims for judicial review. In addition, the Court will, where appropriate, have regard to the fact that a party is unrepresented and will ensure that unrepresented parties are treated fairly.

4.1.2 Represented parties must treat litigants in person with consideration at all times during the conduct of the litigation. Represented parties are reminded of the guidance published by the Bar Council, CILEx and the Law Society: see *https://www.lawsociety.org.uk/topics/civil-litigation/litigants-in-person-guidelines-for-lawyers.*

4.1.3 Litigants in person must show consideration and respect to their opponents (whether legally represented or not), their opponents' representatives and the Court.

4.1.4 A litigant in person must give an address for service in England or Wales in the Claim Form. It is essential that any change of address is notified in writing to the ACO and to all other parties to the case, otherwise important communications such as notices of hearing dates may not arrive.

4.2 OBLIGATION TO COMPLY WITH PROCEDURAL RULES

1BA-19 **4.2.1** A litigant in person will be expected to comply with the CPR and Practice Directions and the provisions of this Guide apply to them. Litigants in person may be penalised if they do not comply with the rules.

4.2.2 Litigants in person should therefore make themselves familiar with those parts of this Guide which are relevant to their claim and also with the applicable provisions of the CPR and Practice Directions.[5] These are examples of things to consider:

4.2.2.1 The requirement to set out grounds of challenge in a coherent and well-ordered way (see para 7.3.1 of this Guide) applies to litigants in person in the same way as it applies to litigants with representation.

4.2.2.2 The requirement to provide all relevant information and facts to the Court and to the other parties to the claim (described at para 15.1 of this Guide under the heading "Duty of candour and cooperation with the Court") applies to all litigants. This includes a requirement that parties disclose to each other and to the Court documents and facts which are relevant to the is-

---

[1] CPR 54.8(4)(ii).

[2] CPR 19.2(2) & CPR 19.2(4). In an appropriate case, ACO lawyers would have power to make such an order under CPR 54.1A. For the requirement to serve the papers on a new party, see CPR 5A PD para 3.1. For removal of parties, see CPR 19.2(3). In an appropriate case, ACO lawyers would have powers to make such an order under CPR 54.1A.

[3] This form of the case title is stipulated in *Practice Direction (Administrative Court: Establishment)* [2000] 1 WLR 1654.

[4] *R (Ben-Abdelaziz) v Haringey LBC* [2001] EWCA Civ 803, [2001] 1 WLR 1485, [29].

[5] *Barton v Wright Hassall LLP* [2018] UKSC 12, [2018] 1 WLR 1119, [18].

sues, even if they are unfavourable to their own case. This duty is of particular importance when an application is made to the Court without the other party being present or notified in advance (usually in cases of urgency). Here, the litigant is under a duty specifically to draw the Court's attention to such matters.

4.2.2.3 It is the duty of all parties to litigation, whether represented or not, to bring relevant matters to the attention of the Court and not to mislead the Court. This means, for example, that parties must not misrepresent the law and must therefore inform the Court of any relevant legislation or previous Court decisions which are applicable to their case and of which they are aware (whether favourable or not to their case).

4.3 THE HEARING

4.3.1 Litigants in person must give copies of any written document (known as a "skeleton argument") which sets out the arguments they intend to rely on and any other material in support of their arguments (for example, reports of cases) to the Court and to their opponents in good time before the hearing. Litigants in person should familiarise themselves with the rules about skeleton arguments in Chapter 20 of this Guide. If they do not follow these rules, the Court may refuse to hear the case, or may adjourn the case to allow the other party or parties proper time to consider and respond to the late skeleton or material. If the court does this, it may order the litigant in person to pay the defendant's costs occasioned by the adjournment. **1BA-20**

4.3.2 Litigants in person should identify in advance of the hearing what they consider to be their strongest points. They should put these points first in their skeleton argument and in any oral submissions to the Court.

4.3.3 At the hearing, litigant in persons will be asked to give their name(s) to the usher or in-court support staff if they have not already done so.

4.3.4 The case name will be called out by the Court staff. The hearing will then begin.

4.3.5 At the hearing, the claimant usually speaks first, then the defendant. Finally, the claimant has an opportunity to comment on what the defendant has said. Sometimes the judge may think it is sensible, depending on the circumstances, to vary that order and, for example, let the defendant speak first.

4.3.6 At the hearing, the judge may make allowances for any litigant in person, recognising the difficulties that person faces in presenting his or her own claim. The judge will allow the litigant in person to explain his or her case in a way that is fair to that person. The judge may ask questions. Any other party in Court, represented or not, will also have an opportunity to make submissions to the judge. At the end of the hearing, the judge will either give a ruling or judgment orally or "reserve judgment" (i.e. adjourn to produce a written judgment). If an order is being made at the hearing, the judge will normally explain the effect of the order. Representatives for other parties should also do so after the hearing if the litigant in person wants further explanation.

4.4 PRACTICAL ASSISTANCE FOR LITIGANTS IN PERSON

4.4.1 Neither the Court staff nor the judges are in a position to give advice about the conduct of a claim. There is, however, a great deal of practical help available. **1BA-21**

4.4.2 Support Through Court is a free and independent service based in a number of court buildings which supports litigants in person. It does not give legal advice and will not represent a litigant, but will assist by taking notes, discussing the workings of the court process, and providing assistance with forms. Support Through Court operates in each of the Court centres in which the majority of judicial reviews are heard (Birmingham Civil Justice Centre, Bristol Civil Justice Centre, Cardiff Civil Justice Centre, Leeds Combined Court Centre, Manchester Civil Justice Centre, and the Royal Courts of Justice in London) as well as some other Court buildings. For more information see *www.supportthroughcourt.org*.

4.4.3 Citizens Advice provides advice on a wide range of issues at drop-in centres, by telephone and online (see *www.citizensadvice.org.uk*).

4.4.4 There is a Citizens Advice service at the Royal Courts of Justice which may be able to offer some advice. It is situated on the ground floor, on the left-hand side of the main hall (see *www.rcjadvice.org.uk*).

4.4.5 There are guides available designed to help litigants in person, including: the Bar Council Guide to representing yourself in Court
(*www.thejusticegap.com/wp-content/uploads/2013/07/Bar-Council-guide.pdf*).

4.5 LEGAL REPRESENTATION AND FUNDING

4.5.1 Legal representation can be provided in a number of ways, including fee-paid representation, legal aid, and pro bono (i.e. free) representation. **1BA-22**

4.5.2 Fee-paid representation

4.5.2.1 Legal representatives will act for a party who pays their fees directly. Fee-paid representation is generally conducted at an agreed hourly rate or by agreeing a fixed fee in advance.

4.5.2.2 Some legal representatives will agree to act for a party under a conditional fee agreement ("CFA"), commonly known as a "no win, no fee" agreement. Individual firm or barristers will be able to confirm the basis on which they will act.

4.5.2.3 Some lawyers will agree to undertake a specific piece of work, without representing the client for the whole case. For example, a lawyer may be prepared to draft a skeleton argument, which the litigant can then use for the hearing, or may appear at a particular hearing. This is sometimes called "unbundled" work.

4.5.3 Legal aid (civil cases)

4.5.3.1 Individual legal representatives will be able to confirm whether they can work on a legal aid basis and whether a particular claimant will be entitled to apply for legal aid and, if so, the terms on which legal aid may be granted.

4.5.4 Legal aid (criminal cases)

4.5.4.1 Judicial review proceedings are not incidental to lower court proceedings and thus any representation order granted in the lower Court will not cover judicial review proceedings.[1] A representation order may not be granted by the Administrative Court itself, although legal aid may be available from the Legal Aid Agency.

4.5.5 Pro bono advice and representation

4.5.5.1 Some solicitors and barristers will offer limited pro bono (i.e. free) legal advice on the prospects of a claim. Individual solicitors or barristers will be able to confirm if they are prepared to give advice on such terms.

4.5.5.2 There are some specialist organisations that arrange for free advice and representation. The largest are: The National Pro-Bono Centre (*www.nationalprobonocentre. org.uk*); Advocate (formerly known as the Bar Pro Bono Unit) (*www.weareadvocate.org.uk*); and Law Works (*www.lawworks.org.uk*).

4.5.5.3 Potential litigants should note that the resources usually available to pro bono organisations are limited. This means that they are not able to offer assistance to everyone who asks for it. The application process can be lengthy. The Administrative Court is unlikely to stay a claim or grant an extension of time to file a claim to await the outcome of an application for pro bono advice or representation.

4.6 MCKENZIE FRIENDS

1BA-23 **4.6.1** A litigant in person may have the assistance of a non-legally qualified person, known as a "McKenzie Friend". Where a McKenzie Friend assists, the litigant in person must be present at the hearing and will be responsible for the conduct of his or her case at that hearing, but the McKenzie Friend may provide some assistance.

4.6.2 Guidance on McKenzie Friends was given in *Practice Guidance (McKenzie Friends: Civil and Family Courts)*,[2] which established that a McKenzie Friend may:

4.6.2.1 provide moral support for litigant(s) in person;

4.6.2.2 take notes;

4.6.2.3 help with case papers; and

4.6.2.4 quietly give advice on any aspect of the conduct of the case.

4.6.3 The Practice Note also established that a McKenzie Friend may not:

4.6.3.1 act as the litigant's agent in relation to the proceedings;

4.6.3.2 manage litigants' cases outside Court, for example by signing Court documents; or

4.6.3.3 address the Court, make oral submissions or examine witnesses on behalf of the litigant in person.

4.6.4 The Court can give permission to a person who is not a party and who has no rights of audience to address the Court. This is only done in exceptional cases, if an application is made, and where it is shown to be in the interests of justice.

4.6.5 A litigant in person who wishes to attend a hearing with the assistance of a McKenzie Friend should inform the Court as soon as possible, indicating who the McKenzie Friend will be. The proposed McKenzie Friend should produce a short curriculum vitae or other statement setting out relevant experience, confirming that he or she has no interest in the case and that he or she understands the role and the duty of confidentiality.

4.6.6 The litigant in person and the McKenzie Friend must tell the Court if the McKenzie Friend is being paid for his or her assistance and be ready to give details of that remuneration. The Court may stop a McKenzie Friend from assisting if the Court believes there is good reason to do so in any individual case. It is unlawful for a person who is not authorised to do so to give paid or unpaid legal advice or representation in respect of immigration matters.[3]

4.6.7 If the Court considers that a person is abusing the right to be a McKenzie Friend (for example, by attending in numerous claims to the detriment of the litigant(s) and/or the Court) and

---

[1] Criminal Legal Aid (General) Regulations 2013, reg. 20(2)(a).

[2] [2010] 1 WLR 1881, [2010] 4 All ER 272, and see *https://www.judiciary.uk/publications/mckenzie-friends/*

[3] s.84 Immigration and Asylum Act 1999.

this abuse amounts to an interference with the proper processes of the administration of justice, the Court may make an order restricting or preventing a person from acting as a McKenzie Friend.[1]

5 CIVIL RESTRAINT ORDERS AND CIVIL PROCEEDINGS ORDERS

5.1 GENERAL

5.1.1 The Court has power to make a civil restraint order ("CRO") under CPR 3C PD in relation to any person who has brought claims or made applications considered to be "totally without merit". Under section 42 of the Senior Courts Act 1981 the Court may make a civil proceedings order ("CPO") in respect of a person who has used litigation vexatiously. **1BA-24**

5.1.2 The effect of either of those orders is that persons subject to them must obtain the permission of the Court before they may start a judicial review claim.

5.1.3 The application to start proceedings is distinct from the application for permission to apply for judicial review.

5.1.4 If a person who is subject to a CRO or CPO files a claim or makes an application to the Court without first making an application for permission to start proceedings and receiving permission to do so, the claim or application will not be issued. The Court may also consider the filing of the claim or application to be a contempt of court.

5.1.5 The application for permission to start proceedings must be made by filing an application notice (N244)[2] with the ACO with the relevant fee.

5.1.6 The fee is not subject to fee remission and must be paid. If permission to start proceedings is later granted and the applicant is able to claim fee remission, the fee can be refunded.[3]

5.2 CIVIL RESTRAINT ORDERS

5.2.1 Prior to making an application for permission to start proceedings or an application for permission to apply for amendment or discharge of the CRO, a party who is subject to a CRO must set out the nature and grounds of the application and give the other party at least 7 days to respond.[4] **1BA-25**

5.2.2 An application for permission to start proceedings or for permission to apply for amendment or discharge of the CRO must:[5]

5.2.2.1 be made in writing; and
5.2.2.2 include the other party's written response, if any, to the notice served.

5.2.3 Such an application will be determined without a hearing.

5.2.4 There is a right of appeal (see Chapter 26 of this Guide), unless the Court has ordered that the decision to dismiss the application will be final.[6]

5.3 CIVIL PROCEEDINGS ORDERS

5.3.1 The application notice for a person who is subject to a CPO must state:[7] **1BA-26**

5.3.1.1 the title and reference number of the proceedings in which the order was made;
5.3.1.2 the full name of the litigant and his/her address;
5.3.1.3 what the litigant wants permission to do (e.g. start a claim for judicial review or apply for an interim or pre-action order);
5.3.1.4 (briefly) why the applicant is seeking the order; and
5.3.1.5 the previous occasions on which the litigant has made an application for permission.[8]

5.3.2 The application notice must be filed together with any written evidence on which the litigant relies in support of his/her application.[9] Generally, this should be a copy of the claim papers which the litigant is requesting permission to file.

---

[1] *Noueiri v Paragon Finance plc* [2001] EWCA Civ 1402, [2001] 1 WLR 2357.
[2] CPR 3A PD para 7.2, CPR 3C PD paras 2.6, 3.6 and 4.6.
[3] Civil Proceedings (Fees) Order 2008, Sch. 2, para 19(3) (as amended).
[4] CPR 3C PD paras 2.5, 3.5 and 4.5.
[5] CPR 3C PD paras 2.6, 3.6 and 4.6
[6] CPR 3C PD paras 2.3(2), 2.6(3), 3.3(2), 3.6(3), 4.3(2) and 4.6(3). For the conditions under which an extended civil restraint order may be discharged, see *Middlesbrough Football & Athletic Co v Earth Energy Investments LLP and Millinder* [2019] EWHC 226 (Ch).
[7] CPR 3A PD para 7.3.
[8] CPR 3A PD para 7.5.
[9] CPR 3A PD para 7.4.

5.3.3 There is no requirement to serve the application on any other intended litigants unless directed by the Court,[1] but it is good practice to do so.

5.3.4 The application will be placed before a judge who may, without the attendance of the litigant:[2]

5.3.4.1 make an order giving the permission sought;

5.3.4.2 give directions for further written evidence to be supplied by the litigant before an order is made on the application;

5.3.4.3 make an order dismissing the application without a hearing; or

5.3.4.4 give directions for the hearing of the application.

5.3.5 The Court will dismiss the application unless satisfied that it is not an abuse of process and there are reasonable grounds for bringing it.[3]

5.3.6 For a person who is subject to a CPO, an order dismissing the application, with or without a hearing, is final and may not be subject to reconsideration or appeal.[4]

6 BEFORE STARTING THE CLAIM

6.1 GENERAL CONSIDERATIONS

1BA-27 **6.1.1** This section outlines the practical steps to be taken before bringing a claim, including the pre-action procedure, factors which may make bringing a claim inappropriate, costs protection, the timescales in which proceedings should be started and the duties of the parties concerning the disclosure of documents.

6.1.2 Any prospective claimant should think carefully about the implications of commencing a claim. A litigant acting in person faces a heavier burden in terms of time and effort than a litigant who is legally represented, but all litigation calls for a high level of commitment from the parties. This should not be underestimated.

6.1.3 The overriding objective of the CPR is to deal with cases justly and at proportionate cost. In almost all proceedings there are winners and losers. The loser is generally ordered to pay the costs of the winner and the costs of litigation can be large (see Chapter 25 of this Guide for further guidance about costs).

6.2 THE JUDICIAL REVIEW PRE-ACTION PROTOCOL

1BA-28 **6.2.1** So far as reasonably possible, an intending claimant should try to resolve the claim without litigation. Starting litigation should be a last resort.

6.2.2 The steps that should be taken before proceedings are commenced are set out in the Judicial Review Pre-action Protocol ("the Protocol"). The Protocol can be accessed on the Government's website at *https://www.justice.gov.uk/courts/procedure-rules/civil/protocol/prot_jrv.*

6.2.3 It is very important to follow the Protocol before commencing a claim, for two reasons: first, it may serve to resolve the issue without need of litigation or at least to narrow the issues in the litigation; secondly, if the Protocol has not been followed the party or parties responsible may be subject to costs sanctions.

6.2.4 A judicial review claim must be brought within the time limits fixed by the CPR. The Protocol process does not affect these time limits (see para 6.4 of this Guide). The fact that a party is following the steps set out in the Protocol would not, of itself, be likely to justify a failure to bring a claim within the time limits set by the CPR, nor would it provide a reason to extend time. So, a party considering applying for judicial review should act quickly to comply with the Protocol but note the time limits for issue if the claim remains unresolved.

6.2.5 If the case is urgent (e.g. where there is an urgent need for an interim order), it may not be possible to follow the Protocol in its entirety. However, even in urgent cases, the parties should attempt to comply with the Protocol to the fullest extent possible. The Court will not apply costs sanctions for non-compliance where it is satisfied that it was not possible to comply because of the urgency of the matter.

6.2.6 Stage one of the Protocol requires the parties to consider whether a method of alternative dispute resolution ("ADR") would be more appropriate. The Protocol mentions discussion and negotiation, referral to the Ombudsman and mediation (a form of facilitated negotiation assisted by an independent neutral party).

6.2.7 Stage two is to send the defendant a pre-action letter. The letter should be in the format outlined in Annex A to the Protocol. The letter should contain the date and details of the act or omission being challenged and a clear summary of the facts on which the claim is based. It should also contain details of any relevant information the claimant is seeking and an explanation of why it is relevant.

---

[1] CPR 3A PD para 7.7.

[2] CPR 3A PD para 7.7.

[3] s. 42(3) of the Senior Courts Act 1981.

[4] s. 42(4) of the Senior Courts Act 1981.

6.2.8 The defendant should normally be given 14 days to respond to the pre-action letter and must do so in the format outlined in Annex B to the Protocol. Where necessary, the defendant may ask for additional time to respond. The claimant should allow the defendant a reasonable time to respond, where that is possible in the circumstances of the case and without putting the time limits for starting the case in jeopardy.

6.3 SITUATIONS WHERE A CLAIM FOR JUDICIAL REVIEW MAY BE INAPPROPRIATE

6.3.1 There are situations in which judicial review will not be appropriate or possible. These should be considered at the outset. Litigants should refer to the CPR and to the commentary in academic works on administrative law. The following are some of those situations in outline: **1BA-29**

6.3.2 Lack of standing (or locus standi)

6.3.2.1 A person may not bring an application for judicial review unless he or she has a "sufficient interest" in the matter to which the claim relates.[1] This is known as the requirement for "standing" or (in Latin) locus standi.

6.3.2.2 Any issue about standing will usually be determined when considering the application for permission to apply for judicial review, but it may also be raised and determined at a later stage.

6.3.2.3 Neither the parties nor the Court can agree that a case should continue where the claimant does not have standing.[2] A party must have standing in order to bring a claim.

6.3.2.4 In general, persons whose legal rights and obligations are directly and adversely affected by a public body's conduct will have standing to challenge it. However, in some cases, a claimant whose legal rights and obligations are not affected (such as an association or non-governmental organisation), but has a particular expertise in the subject matter of the claim, may be considered to have sufficient standing if the claim is brought in the public interest.[3] An association or non-governmental organisation claiming standing on this basis will normally have to demonstrate genuine involvement in a specific subject area. The court will not necessarily accept that a corporate entity with very widely drawn objects will have standing to pursue claims in every case whose subject matter falls within those objects.[4]

6.3.2.5 What counts as a sufficient interest depends on the circumstances of the particular claim.[5] In some contexts a narrower test of standing applies.[6] A claimant who alleges that a public authority has acted in a way which is made unlawful by s. 6(1) of the Human Rights Act 1998 or who relies on a right under the European Convention of Human Rights must be a "victim" of the unlawful act.[7]

6.3.2.6 An individual who lacks the relevant expertise or is not representing the public interest may lack standing if he or she would not be personally affected by the relief sought. This is judged at the time when the Court considers whether to grant permission to apply for judicial review.[8]

6.3.2.7 If one or more claimants are directly affected or otherwise well placed to bring the claim that may mean that others who are not directly affected, or are less well-placed to bring the claim, will lack standing.[9]

6.3.2.8 It is not appropriate to add parties (particularly politicians or other public figures) simply in order to raise the profile of the litigation or assist in raising funds.[10]

6.3.3 Adequate alternative remedy

---

[1] s.31(3) of the Senior Courts Act 1981.

[2] This principle has been confirmed in a number of other cases, e.g. *R v Secretary of State for Social Services ex parte Child Poverty Action Group* [1990] 2 QB 540, 556.

[3] See e.g. *R v Secretary of State for Foreign and Commonwealth Affairs ex p. World Development Movement* [1994] EWHC Admin 1, [1995] 1 WLR 386, 392-396; *R (McCourt) v Parole Board* [2020] EWHC 2320 (Admin), [31]-[32].

[4] See *R (Good Law Project Ltd) v Prime Minister* [2022] EWHC 298 (Admin), [53]-[59].

[5] *Inland Revenue Commissioners v National Federation of Self-Employed and Small Businesses Ltd* [1982] AC 617.

[6] As to standing in procurement cases, see *R (Good Law Project Ltd) v Secretary of State for Health and Social Care* [2021] EWHC 346 (Admin), [2021] PTSR 1251. But see also *R (Good Law Project Ltd) v Minister for the Cabinet Office* [2022] EWCA Civ 21, [6].

[7] s. 7(1) of the Human Rights Act 1998. By s. 7(7), a person is a victim of an unlawful act only if he would be a victim for the purposes of Article 34 of the Convention if proceedings were brought in the European Court of Human Rights in respect of that act. The "victim" requirement is discussed in *R (Pitt) v General Pharmaceutical Council* [2017] EWHC 809 (Admin), (2017) 156 BMLR 222, [52]-[67].

[8] See e.g. *R (JS) v Secretary of State for the Home Department* [2021] EWHC 234 (Admin), [33].

[9] See e.g. *R (Jones) v Commissioner of Police of the Metropolis* [2019] EWHC 2957 (Admin), [2020] 1 WLR 519, [62]; *R (Good Law Project Ltd) v Prime Minister* [2022] EWHC 298 (Admin), [59].

[10] See e.g. *R (Good Law Project) v Secretary of State for Health and Social Care* [2021] EWHC 346 (Admin), [2021] PTSR 1251, [106]-[108].

6.3.3.1 Judicial review is a remedy of last resort.[1] If there is another route by which the decision can be challenged, which provides an adequate remedy for the claimant, that alternative remedy should generally be used before applying for judicial review.

6.3.3.2 Examples of alternative remedies include internal complaints procedures, review mechanisms and appeals (statutory or non-statutory).

6.3.3.3 If the Court finds that the claimant has (or had) an adequate alternative remedy, it will generally refuse permission to apply for judicial review.

6.3.4 The claim is academic

6.3.4.1 Where a claim is academic, i.e. there is no longer a case to be decided which will directly affect the rights and obligations of the parties to the claim,[2] it will generally not be appropriate to bring judicial review proceedings. An example is the situation where the defendant has agreed to reconsider the decision challenged. Where the claim has become academic since it was issued, it is generally inappropriate to pursue the claim.

6.3.4.2 In exceptional circumstances, the Court may decide to proceed with a claim even though the outcome has become academic for the claimant. The Court may do so if, for example, a large number of similar cases exist or are anticipated, or at least some other similar cases exist or are anticipated and the decision will not be fact-sensitive.[3]

6.3.5 The error is highly unlikely to make a substantial difference to the outcome

6.3.5.1 Section 31(3C)-(3F) of the Senior Court Act 1981 provides that the Court must refuse permission to apply for judicial review if it appears to the Court to be highly likely that the outcome for the claimant would not have been substantially different even if the conduct complained of had not occurred.

6.3.5.2 The conduct complained of is the conduct (or alleged conduct) of the defendant that the applicant claims justifies the High Court in granting relief.

6.3.5.3 Where this threshold is reached, the Court has a discretion to allow the claim to proceed if there is an exceptional public interest in doing so.

6.3.6 The claim challenges a superior court decision that is not subject to judicial review

6.3.6.1 Decisions of the High Court,[4] the Court of Appeal and the Supreme Court cannot be challenged by judicial review.

6.3.6.2 Where the Crown Court is dealing with a trial on indictment, its conduct is not subject to judicial review.[5] Otherwise, decisions of the Crown Court are subject to judicial review.

6.4 TIME LIMITS

1BA-30 **6.4.1** Claims for judicial review must be started promptly and in any event not later than 3 months after the grounds for making the claim first arose.[6] Claims are started by filing a Claim Form that meets the requirements set out in CPR Part 54. The primary requirement is to start the claim promptly. Even if the claim has been commenced within 3 months from the date of the conduct challenged, it may still be out of time if the claimant did not start the claim promptly.[7]

6.4.2 When considering whether a claim is within time a claimant should also be aware of two important points:

6.4.2.1 The time limit may not be extended by agreement between the parties.[8] However, it can be extended by the Court in its discretion and a prior agreement not to take a time point can be relevant to the exercise of that discretion.[9] For further detail on applications for extensions of time, see paras 6.4.4 and 7.3.1.5 of this Guide.

6.4.2.2 Where the claim challenges a decision, the time limit begins to run from the date the decision to be challenged was made (not the date when the claimant was informed about the decision).[10]

6.4.3 There are exceptions to the general time limit rule discussed above. These include the following:

---

[1] See e.g. *R (Archer) v Commissioner for Her Majesty's Revenue and Customs* [2019] EWCA Civ 1021, [2019] 1 WLR 6355, [68].

[2] *R v Secretary of State for the Home Department ex parte Salem* [1999] 1 AC 450; *R (L) v Devon County Council* [2021] EWCA Civ 358, [38] and [64].

[3] *R (Zoolife International Ltd) v The Secretary of State for Environment, Food and Rural Affairs* [2007] EWHC 2995 (Admin), [2008] ACD 44, [36].

[4] This includes a refusal to grant permission to appeal by the Court of Protection: *SM v The Court of Protection & Anor* [2021] EWHC 2046 (Admin).

[5] s. 29(3), and 46(1) of the Senior Courts Act 1981.

[6] CPR 54.5(1).

[7] See e.g. *R v Cotswold District Council ex parte Barrington Parish Council* [1998] 75 P & CR 515.

[8] CPR 54.5(2).

[9] See e.g. *R (Zahid) v The University Of Manchester* [2017] EWHC 188 (Admin), [73]-[78].

[10] *R v Department of Transport ex parte Presvac Engineering* [1992] 4 Admin LR 121.

6.4.3.1 Planning cases:[1] Where the claim relates to a decision made under planning legislation the claim must be filed not later than six weeks after the decision. Planning legislation means the Town and Country Planning Act 1990, the Planning (Listed Buildings and Conservation Areas) Act 1990, the Planning (Hazardous Substances) Act 1990 and the Planning (Consequential Provisions) Act 1990. The six week period starts from the date of the decision (for example, the grant of planning permission), not the date on which the claimant came to know of the decision.

6.4.3.2 In addition, statutory reviews and appeal (and some judicial review procedures) in planning cases are subject to strict and short time limits for starting proceedings. In some cases, the relevant legislation does not permit the period to be extended. Claimants need to check the provisions in relevant statutes with care.

6.4.3.3 Public contract cases:[2]The Public Contracts Regulations 2015 (SI 2015/102) govern the procedure by which public bodies may outsource public services (sometimes referred to as "procurement"). Where the claim relates to a decision under these Regulations, the claim must be started within the time specified by Regulation 92, currently 30 days from the date when the claimant first knew or ought to have known that grounds for starting the proceedings had arisen. Note that this time limit begins to run from the date of knowledge, in contrast to the general rule where the relevant date is the decision date itself. An additional time limit applies if the contract has already been entered into but the claimant seeks a declaration ineffectiveness (i.e., a declaration that the contract is ineffective for the future). Such a claim must be brought within six months beginning with the date when the contract was entered into: see Regulation 92.

6.4.3.4 Utilities Contracts: Similar provisions apply where the challenge is made under The Utilities Contracts Regulations 2016 (SI 2016/274) or The Concession Contracts Regulations 2016 (SI 2016/273). However, note that these time limits do not apply to private law claims for damages in respect of public procurement exercises that are not governed by these Regulations.[3] For further guidance on Public Contract Judicial Reviews, see para 6.7 of this Guide.

6.4.3.5 Judicial Review of the Upper Tribunal:[4] Where the defendant is the Upper Tribunal the claim must be started no later than 16 days after the date on which notice of the Upper Tribunal's decision was sent to the applicant. Again, note the difference from the general rule: here the time limit is calculated from the date the decision was sent, not the date it was made.

6.4.3.6 Judicial Review of a decision of a Minister in relation to a public inquiry, or a member of an inquiry panel.[5] The time limit for these challenges is 14 days unless extended by the Court. That shorter time limit does not apply to any challenge to the contents of the inquiry report, or to a decision of which the claimant could not have become aware until publication of the report.[6]

6.4.4 Extensions of time

6.4.4.1 CPR 3.1(2)(a) allows the Court to extend or shorten the time limit even if the time for compliance has already expired. Where the time limit has already expired, the claimant must apply for an extension of time. The application must be set out in section 9 of the Claim Form (Form N461). The application for an extension of time will be considered by the judge at the same time as deciding whether to grant permission to apply for judicial review.

6.4.4.2 In considering whether to grant an extension of time the Court will consider all the circumstances, including whether an adequate explanation has been given for the delay and whether an extension will cause substantial hardship or prejudice to the defendant or any other party or be detrimental to good administration.[7]

6.4.4.3 In certain types of planning cases (para 6.4.3.1 of this Guide) and public contract cases (para 6.4.3.3), extensions of time cannot be granted.

6.5 JUDICIAL REVIEW OF IMMIGRATION DECISIONS AND DECISIONS ON CLAIMS FOR ASYLUM

6.5.1 Since 1 November 2013, the Upper Tribunal (Immigration and Asylum Chamber) ("UTIAC"), and not the Administrative Court, has been the appropriate jurisdiction for starting a judicial review in the majority of decisions relating to immigration and asylum (see Annex 1 for UTIAC contact details). **1BA-31**

---

[1] CPR 54.5(5).

[2] CPR 54.5(6).

[3] *Secretary of State for Transport v Arriva Rail East Midlands Ltd* [2019] EWCA Civ 2259.

[4] CPR 54.7A(3).

[5] s. 38(1) of the Inquiries Act 2005.

[6] s. 38(3) of the Inquiries Act 2005.

[7] See *Maharaj v National Energy Corporation of Trinidad and Tobago* [2019] UKPC 5, [38]: "Here it is important to emphasise that the statutory test is not one of good reason for delay but the broader test of good reason for extending time. This will be likely to bring in many considerations beyond those relevant to an objectively good reason for the delay, including the importance of the issues, the prospect of success, the presence or absence of prejudice or detriment to good administration, and the public interest."

6.5.2 The Lord Chief Justice's Direction[1] requires that any application for permission to apply for judicial review and any substantive application for judicial review must be started in UTIAC (or if started in the Administrative Court must be transferred to UTIAC) if it challenges:

6.5.2.1 a decision made under the Immigration Acts or any instrument having effect, whether wholly or partly, under an enactment within the Immigration Acts, or otherwise relating to leave to enter or remain in the UK. The Immigration Acts are Immigration Act 1971, Immigration Act 1988, Asylum and Immigration Appeals Act 1993, Asylum and Immigration Act 1996, Immigration and Asylum Act 1999, Nationality, Immigration and Asylum Act 2002, Asylum and Immigration (Treatment of Claimants, etc.) Act 2004, Immigration, Asylum and Nationality Act 2006, UK Borders Act 2007, Immigration Act 2014 and Immigration Act 2016; or

6.5.2.2 a decision of the Immigration and Asylum Chamber of the First-tier Tribunal, from which no appeal lies to the Upper Tribunal.

6.5.3 All other immigration and asylum matters remain within the jurisdiction of the Administrative Court.[2] Further, even where an application comes within the classes of claim outlined at para 6.5.2 above, an application which comprises or includes any of the following must be brought in the Administrative Court:

6.5.3.1 a challenge to the validity of primary or subordinate legislation (or of immigration rules);
6.5.3.2 a challenge to the lawfulness of detention;
6.5.3.3 a challenge to a decision concerning inclusion on the register of licensed Sponsors maintained by the UKBA;
6.5.3.4 a challenge to a decision which determines British citizenship;
6.5.3.5 a challenge to a decision relating to asylum support or accommodation;
6.5.3.6 a challenge to the decision of the Upper Tribunal;
6.5.3.7 a challenge to a decision of the Special Immigration Appeals Commission;
6.5.3.8 an application for a declaration of incompatibility under s.4 of the Human Rights Act 1998; and
6.5.3.9 a challenge to a decision which is certified (or otherwise stated in writing) to have been taken by the Secretary of State wholly or partly in reliance on information which it is considered should not be made public in the interests of national security.

6.5.4 Challenges to decisions made under the National Referral Mechanism for identifying victims of human trafficking or modern slavery[3] are not immigration decisions. They fall within the jurisdiction of the Administrative Court.

6.5.5 Annex 6 contains further information about judicial review in the Upper Tribunal and the UTIAC in particular.

6.5.6 Whether, pursuant to the Direction made by the Lord Chief Justice, a claim falls within the jurisdiction of UTIAC or the Administrative Court is determined as a matter of substance, not form. For example, issuing a claim in the Administrative Court on the basis that it falls within the unlawful detention exception to UTIAC's jurisdiction may amount to an abuse of process where there is no obvious merit to the detention claim.[4]

6.6 JUDICIAL REVIEW OF FIRST-TIER TRIBUNAL DECISIONS

1BA-32 **6.6.1** Since 3 November 2008, the Upper Tribunal (Administrative Appeals Chamber) ("UTAAC"), not the Administrative Court, has been the appropriate jurisdiction for starting a judicial review that challenges certain decisions of the First-tier Tribunal (see Annex 1 for UTAAC contact details).

6.6.2 The Lord Chief Justice's Direction[5] requires filing in, or mandatory transfer to, the UTAAC of any application for permission to apply for judicial review and any substantive application for judicial review if it calls into question the following:

6.6.2.1 any decision of the First-tier Tribunal on an appeal made in the exercise of a right conferred by the Criminal Injuries Compensation Scheme in compliance with s.5(1) of the Criminal Injuries Compensation Act 1995 (appeals against decisions on reviews); and
6.6.2.2 any decision of the First-tier Tribunal where there is no right of appeal to the Upper Tribunal and that decision is not an excluded decision within para (b), (c), or (f) of s.11(5) of the 2007 Act (appeals against national security certificates).

---

[1] *https://www.judiciary.uk/publications/lord-chief-justices-direction-regarding-the-transfer-of-immigration-and-asylum-judicial-review-cases-to-the-upper-tribunal-immigration-and-asylum-chamber/*

[2] See para 6.5.4 of this Guide for an example.

[3] See Home Office guidance: *https://www.gov.uk/government/publications/human-trafficking-victims-referral-and-assessment-forms/guidance-on-the-national-referral-mechanism-for-potential-adult-victims-of-modern-slavery-england-and-wales*

[4] See *R (Ashraf) v Secretary of State for the Home Department* [2013] EWHC 4028 (Admin).

[5] Lord Chief Justice's Direction Upper Tribunal: Judicial Review Jurisdiction, pursuant to s.18(6) of the Tribunals, Courts and Enforcement Act 2007.

6.6.3 The direction does not have effect where a claimant seeks a declaration of incompatibility. In that case, the Administrative Court retains jurisdiction to hear the claim.

6.7 JUDICIAL REVIEW OF DECISIONS TAKEN UNDER THE PUBLIC CONTRACT REGULATIONS

6.7.1 Where a decision made under The Public Contract Regulations 2015 is challenged, claimants may consider it necessary to bring proceedings for judicial review in the Administrative Court as well as issuing a claim in the Technology and Construction Court ("TCC"). Where this happens, the claim will, unless otherwise directed by the Judge in Charge of the Administrative Court or the Judge in Charge of the TCC, proceed in the TCC before a judge who is also authorised to sit both in the TCC and in the Administrative Court. **1BA-33**

6.7.2 If this occurs, the claimant must:

6.7.2.1 at the time of issuing the Claim Form in the ACO, by letter to the ACO, copied to the Judge in Charge of the Administrative Court and of the TCC respectively, request transfer of the judicial review claim to the TCC;

6.7.2.2 mark that letter clearly: "URGENT REQUEST FOR TRANSFER OF A PUBLIC PROCUREMENT CLAIM TO THE TCC";

6.7.2.3 if not notified within 3 days of the issue of the Claim Form that the case will be transferred to the TCC, contact the ACO and thereafter keep the TCC informed of its position.

6.7.3 This procedure applies only when claim forms are issued by the same claimant against the same defendant in both the Administrative Court and the TCC simultaneously (i.e. within 48 hours of each other).

6.7.4 When the papers are transferred to the TCC by the ACO under this procedure, the Judge in Charge of the TCC will review the papers as soon as reasonably practicable and notify the claimant and the ACO whether the two claims should be case managed and/or heard together in the TCC.

6.7.5 If so, the claim for judicial review will be case managed and determined in the TCC.

6.7.6 If the Judge in Charge of the TCC decides that the judicial review claim should not proceed in the TCC, the judicial review claim will be transferred back to the Administrative Court. Reasons will be given. The claim for judicial review will then be case managed and determined in the Administrative Court.

PART B:—THE CLAIM

7 STARTING THE CLAIM

7.1 OVERVIEW OF JUDICIAL REVIEW PROCEDURE

7.1.1 Judicial review is a two-stage process. The first stage is that the claimant must obtain permission (formerly referred to as "leave"[1]) to apply for judicial review from the Court. If permission is granted, the second stage is the substantive determination of the claim. **1BA-34**

7.1.2 Unlike a number of other civil and criminal proceedings, the judicial review process does not automatically incorporate a case management hearing (although one may be ordered by a judge if considered necessary). The Court expects the parties to liaise with each other and the ACO to ensure that the claim is ready for determination by the Court. An open dialogue between the parties and the staff of the ACO is essential to the smooth running of any case.

7.1.3 The flow diagram on the next page may be used as a quick guide to the judicial review process. The flow diagram depicts stages in the High Court: the Court of Appeal's jurisdiction in relation to the permission stage is discussed later in this guide. Full details of each stage are outlined later in this Guide.

7.2 FILING THE CLAIM FORM

7.2.1 All judicial review claims must be started by filing a Claim Form in the ACO. The date of filing, usually written on the Claim Form in manuscript by the ACO staff when the Claim Form is received at the ACO, is to be distinguished from the date of issue which is the date shown by the Court seal which is applied when the Claim Form is issued by the ACO. A claim for judicial review is made on the date on which it is filed. **1BA-35**

7.2.2 The claimant is required to apply for permission to apply for judicial review in the Claim Form: see section 4 of the Form. The claimant must also specify the judicial review remedies sought (see Chapter 12 of this Guide). There is space for this in the Claim Form at section 8.

7.2.3 If the claimant has filed the claim in the ACO in Cardiff, the claim may be lodged in Welsh or English.

---

[1] "Leave" is still used in s. 31 of the Senior Courts Act 1981.

7.2.4 When the Claim Form is filed, it must be accompanied by the relevant fee. If the relevant fee is not paid, the Claim Form will be returned unissued together with any accompanying documentation.

7.2.5 The claimant must file one copy of the completed judicial review Claim Form to be retained by the ACO. (If the claim is later listed before a Divisional Court, a second/third copy will be required.) The claimant must also file an additional copy of the Claim Form for every defendant and interested party in the claim. The additional copies will be sealed and returned to the claimant to serve on the defendant(s) and interested parties (see para 7.9 of this Guide for guidance about service and Annex 3 for addresses for service on government departments).

7.2.6 On the Claim Form and/or in a document accompanying the Claim Form (see below) the claimant should refer to any statutory provision which excludes the jurisdiction of the Court to entertain the application, or to grant the relief sought, and any alternative appeal mechanism that could be or could have been used prior to seeking judicial review.[1]

7.2.7 Any person who is an interested party must be named in and served with the Claim Form. For further guidance as to who is an interested party, see para 3.2.3 of this Guide.

Judicial Review Process

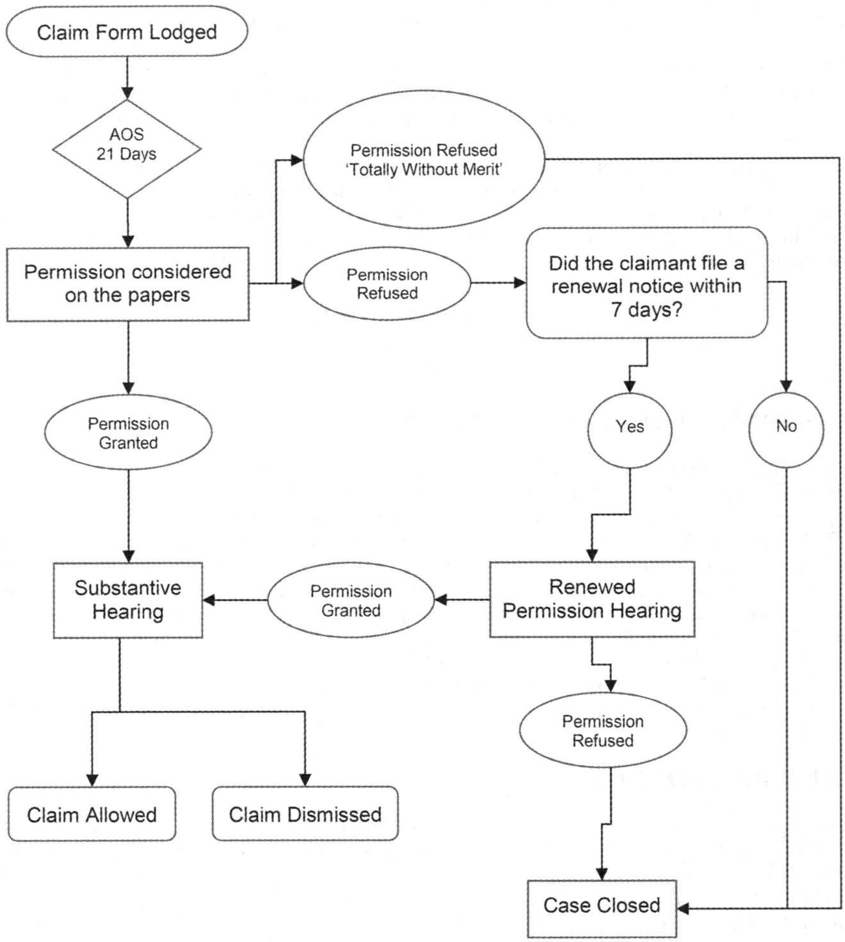

© David Gardner, reproduced with kind permission of The University of Wales Press from *Administrative Law and the Administrative Court in Wales* (2016).

[1] CPR 54A PD para 4.1(2).

7.3 REQUIRED DOCUMENTATION

7.3.1 When the Claim Form is filed, certain particulars must be provided.[1] These can be included in the Claim Form itself or on a separate document or documents accompanying it. The required particulars are: **1BA-36**

7.3.1.1 a statement of the facts relied on, set out in numbered paras (in section 5 of the Claim Form or a separate document);

7.3.1.2 a clear and concise[2] statement of the grounds for bringing the claim, again set out in numbered paras (in section 6 of the Claim Form or a separate document);

7.3.1.3 where the claim includes a claim for damages under the Human Rights Act 1998, the claim for damages must be properly pleaded and particularised (in section 4 of the Claim Form or on a separate document);[3]

7.3.1.4 where the claimant intends to raise a devolution issue, the claimant must identify the relevant provisions of the Government of Wales Act 2006, the Northern Ireland Act 1998 or the Scotland Act 1998; and the Claim Form must contain a summary of the facts, circumstances and legal points which give rise to the devolution issue;

7.3.1.5 any application for an extension of time for filing the Claim Form (which can be made in section 9 of the Claim Form or in an attached document);

7.3.1.6 any application for directions (which can be made in section 9 of the Claim Form or in an attached document).

7.3.2 The statement of material facts and the statement of the grounds for bringing the claim can be included in a single document called a "Statement of Facts and Grounds",[4] which can also be used to give details of any claim for damages, set out any devolution issues and provide grounds for any application made.

7.3.3 The statement of facts and the statement of grounds, taken together, must not exceed 40 pages.[5] In many cases the Court will expect the documents to be significantly shorter. The Court may grant permission to exceed the 40-page limit, an application for such permission should be made either before the document is filed, or at the latest at the same time as it is filed. However, parties should bear in mind that the Court of Appeal has noted that "excessively long documents conceal rather than illuminate the essence of the case being advanced" and "make the task of the court more difficult".[6] The purpose of the Statement of Facts and Grounds is to provide a clear and concise statement of the facts relied on in support of the claim and of the grounds on which the claim is brought. The grounds should explain the claimant's case succinctly by reference to the facts relied on.[7]

7.3.4 The statement of grounds should identify each ground of challenge; identify the relevant provision or principle of law said to have been breached; and concisely provide sufficient detail of the alleged breach to enable the parties and the Court to identify the essential issues.[8] Each ground should raise a distinct issue in relation to the decision under challenge.[9] Arguments and submissions in support of the grounds should be set out separately in relation to each ground.

7.3.5 Certain other documents must also be filed with the Claim Form:[10]

7.3.5.1 written evidence in support of the claim and (if applicable) any other application contained in the Claim Form;

7.3.5.2 a copy of any decision letter or order that the claimant challenges in the claim;

7.3.5.3 where the claim challenges a decision of a Court or tribunal, an approved copy of the reasons of the Court or tribunal for reaching the decision;

7.3.5.4 where the claim challenges the decision of any other public authority, a copy of any record of the decision;

7.3.5.5 copies of any documents on which the claimant proposes to rely;

7.3.5.6 copies of any relevant statutory material; and

---

[1] CPR 54A PD paras 4.2 - 4.3.

[2] For the importance of concision, see *R (Dolan) v Secretary of State for Health and Social Care* [2020] EWCA Civ 1605, [119]-[120].

[3] *R (Nazem Fayad) v Secretary of State for the Home Department* [2018] EWCA Civ 54, [54]-[56]. Claims for damages that are not adequately particularised may have costs consequences for the claimant.

[4] CPR 54A PD para. 4.2(2).

[5] CPR 54A PD para. 4.2(3).

[6] *R (Dolan) v Secretary of State for Health and Social Care* [2020] EWCA Civ 1605, [120].

[7] *R (SSE Generation Ltd) v Competition and Markets Authority* [2022] EWHC 865 (Admin), [75].

[8] CPR 54A PD para. 4.2(1)(b).

[9] *R (Talpada) v Secretary of State for the Home Department* [2018] EWCA Civ 841 emphasised the need for a clear and succinct statement of the grounds, in the context of appeals, [68]. See also *Hickey v Secretary of State for Work and Pensions* [2018] EWCA Civ 851, [74].

[10] CPR 54A PD para. 4.4.

7.3.5.7 a list of essential documents for advance reading by the Court (with page references to the passages relied on).

7.3.6 The documentation must be provided in an indexed and paginated claim bundle. (Where the claim is to be heard by a Divisional Court, one hard copy claim bundle is required for each judge.) An electronic version of the bundle must also be prepared in accordance with the Guidance at Annex 7 of this Guide. Both the hard copy and electronic copy bundles must be lodged with the Court (unless otherwise requested by the Court).[1]

7.3.7 One copy of the claim bundle must be provided to be retained by the Court.

7.3.8 The ACO retains one copy of the Claim Form, claim bundle and any other documentation filed with the Claim Form. This copy of the claim documentation cannot be returned after the claim has finished. The parties should ensure they have made their own copies of the claim documentation for their reference. The exception to this is where a party has been required to file an original document (such as a deed or identification document). When returning this document, the ACO may copy the document before returning it and retain the copy on the court file.

7.3.9 Where it is not possible to file all of the documents outlined at para 7.3.5 above, the claimant must indicate which documents have not been filed and the reasons why they are not currently available.[2] If the Claim Form is not accompanied by the required documentation without explanation as to why and detail of when it will be provided, the ACO may return the Claim Form without issuing it.

7.3.10 If the Claim Form is returned in accordance with para 7.3.9 above, it is not considered to have been filed for the purposes of the judicial review time limits (see para 6.4 of this Guide).

7.3.11 If the documentation required as outlined at para 7.3.1 above is not filed with the Claim Form, but at a later date, it will have been filed out of time. It must therefore be accompanied by an application to extend time to file the documentation. Such an application must be made in an Application Notice with the relevant fee (see para 13.7 of this Guide).

7.4 DUTY OF INQUIRY

1BA-37 **7.4.1** A claimant must make proper and necessary inquiries before seeking permission to apply for judicial review, urgent consideration or interim relief to ensure so far as reasonably possible that all relevant facts are known.[3]

7.5 DUTY OF CANDOUR AND COOPERATION WITH THE COURT

1BA-38 **7.5.1** There is a special duty - the duty of candour and cooperation with the Court - which applies to all parties to judicial review claims. Parties are obliged to ensure that all relevant information and all material facts are put before the Court. This means that parties must disclose relevant information or material facts which either support or undermine their case. The duty of candour may require a party to disclose a document rather than simply summarising it.

7.5.2 It is very important that parties comply with the duty of candour. The duty is explained in more detail below at para 15.1 of this Guide.

7.6 DISCLOSURE

1BA-39 **7.6.1** The duty of candour ensures that all relevant information is before the Court. The general rules governing the disclosure of documents in civil claims do not apply to judicial review claims.

7.6.2 An application for disclosure of specific documents or documents of a particular class or type may be made in the course of a judicial review claim. Under CPR 31.12(1), the Court may order disclosure of documents where this is necessary to deal fairly and justly with a particular issue.[4] An application under CPR 31.12(1) is made in accordance with the principles discussed in para 13.7 of this Guide.

7.6.3 In practice, orders for disclosure of documents are rarely necessary in judicial review claims. The disclosure of documents may not be necessary to allow the Court to consider a particular issue. Furthermore, a defendant may have disclosed the relevant documents either before the beginning of proceedings or as part of its evidence provided during proceedings: see para 15.1 of this Guide on the duty of candour.

---

[1] CPR 54A PD para. 4.5.

[2] CPR 54A PD para. 4.4(2).

[3] CPR 54A PD para. 4.1(1).

[4] See *R v Secretary of State for Foreign and Commonwealth Affairs ex p. World Development Movement Ltd* [1994] EWHC Admin 1, [1995] 1 WLR 386, [396]-[397]. This also applies to applications for disclosure from non-parties: *R (AB) v Secretary of State for Health and Social Care* [2022] EWHC 87 (Admin), [7]-[11].

7.7 WHERE TO FILE THE CLAIM (APPROPRIATE VENUE)

7.7.1 There are 5 ACOs in England and Wales where a claim may be filed. They are at the Birmingham Civil Justice Centre, the Cardiff Civil Justice Centre, the Leeds Combined Court Centre, the Manchester Civil Justice Centre, and in the Royal Courts of Justice in London. Contact details for the ACOs can be found in Annex 1 and Annex 8 to this Guide. **1BA-40**

7.7.2 Where a claim seeks to challenge the lawfulness of a Welsh public body's decision, it must be issued in the Cardiff ACO and all hearings will take place in Wales.[1]

7.7.3 In addition to the above, the general expectation is that proceedings will be administered and determined in the region with which the claim has the closest connection.[2] The claim should therefore be filed in the ACO with which the claim has the closest connection. Where the claim has the closest connection to the area covered by the Western Circuit it should be issued in the ACO in Cardiff Civil Justice Centre. The administration of the claim will take place in Cardiff, but all hearings will (unless there are exceptional circumstances) take place at Courts on the Western Circuit (principally in Bristol).

7.7.4 Any claim started in Birmingham will normally be determined at an appropriate Court in the Midlands; in Cardiff, a Court either in Wales or on the Western Circuit; in Leeds, a Court in the North-East of England; in Manchester, at a Court in the North-West of England; and in London, at the Royal Courts of Justice. Although this is not encouraged, the claimant may issue a claim in a different region from the one with which he/she has the closest connection. The claimant should outline why the claim has been lodged in a different region in section 4 of the Claim Form. The decision should be justified in accordance with the following considerations:[3]

7.7.4.1 any reason expressed by any party for preferring a particular venue;

7.7.4.2 the ease and cost of travel to a hearing;

7.7.4.3 the availability and suitability of alternative means of attending a hearing (for example, by video-link);

7.7.4.4 the extent and nature of any public interest that the proceedings be heard in any particular locality;

7.7.4.5 the time within which it is appropriate for the proceedings to be determined;

7.7.4.6 whether it is desirable to administer or determine the claim in another region in the light of the volume of claims issued at, and the capacity, resources and workload of, the Court at which it is issued;

7.7.4.7 whether the claim raises issues sufficiently similar to those in another outstanding claim to make it desirable that it should be determined together with, or immediately following, that other claim;

7.7.4.8 whether the claim raises devolution issues and for that reason whether it should more appropriately be determined in London or Cardiff; and

7.7.4.9 the region in which the legal representative of the parties are based.

7.7.5 If the claim is issued in an ACO considered not to be the most appropriate, it may be transferred by judicial order. The Court will usually invite the views of the parties before transferring a claim.[4] If the defendant or any interested party considers that the claim has been commenced in the wrong ACO, and the Court has not raised the point of its own motion, he or she may raise the issue of venue in their summary grounds of defence.

7.8 FILING DOCUMENTS WITH THE COURT

7.8.1 The London ACO counters remain closed to the public, save for the Fees Office Counter, which is open by appointment only. The Cardiff and Manchester counters are open by appointment only. The Leeds and Birmingham counters are open. **1BA-41**

7.8.2 In London, hard copy documents may be filed by leaving them in the drop box in the main hall of the Royal Courts of Justice, marked "Administrative Court" (Monday to Friday only). The drop box is emptied each day at 9.30am and 2.30pm. Documents deposited after 2.30pm will not be collected until the next day. If a document needs to be collected urgently (for example, because it is needed for a hearing), parties should email the Administrative Court general office at generaloffice@administrativecourtoffice.justice.gov.uk to make arrangements for the document to be retrieved. Mark your email as high priority and put "Urgent" in the subject line.

7.8.3 Functions previously dealt with at the counters are now being dealt with electronically, including filing documents with the Court. The process for electronic filing is set out in the Administrative Court: Information For Court Users, reproduced at Annex 7 to this Guide. The Court expects all parties to familiarise themselves with the guidance and to follow it.

---

[1] CPR 7.1A.

[2] CPR 54C PD paras 2.1 and 2.5.

[3] CPR 54C PD para 2.5.

[4] For examples of a decision transferring a claim to an ACO outside London, see *R (Fortt) v Financial Services Compensation Scheme Ltd* [2022] EWHC 152 (Admin) and *R (Khyam) v Secretary of State for Justice* [2022] EWHC 993 (Admin).

7.8.4 The ACO will accept the service of documents by email provided that:

7.8.4.1 the document being filed either does not require a fee, or is accompanied with a PBA number, receipt of payment by debit/credit card or a fee remission certificate;

7.8.4.2 the document, including attachments, does not exceed the maximum which the appropriate court office has indicated it can accept by email;[1]

7.8.4.3 the email, including any attachments, is under 10MB in size.

7.8.5 Where a document may be emailed it must be emailed to the appropriate ACO general inbox (see the contacts list at Annex 1 and Annex 8).[2] Any party filing a document by email should not also file a hard copy unless instructed to do so.

7.8.6 A document may be filed by fax where it needs to be filed urgently. Hearing bundles and/ or documents which require a fee should only be faxed in an emergency and must be accompanied by an undertaking to pay the fee. Any party filing a document by fax should not also file a hard copy unless instructed.[3] If any party intends to file documents by fax, that party should first telephone the relevant ACO to ensure that the fax machine is available and there is someone present to receive the document.

7.8.7 Skeleton arguments must be sent to the dedicated skeleton arguments email address for the relevant ACO (see the contacts list at Annex 1 and Annex 8). See Chapter 20 of this Guide on skeleton arguments generally.

7.8.8 Any document filed by fax or email after 4pm will be treated as filed on the next day on which the ACO is open.[4]

7.8.9 An email sent to the Court must include the name, telephone number and address or email address for contacting the sender and it (including attachments) must be in plain or rich text format rather than HTML. Where proceedings have been started, it must also clearly state the Court's reference number for the case, the names of the parties and the date and time of any hearing to which the email relates.

7.8.10 The ACO or a judge may give instructions or order that a document is to be filed by email or fax in circumstances other than those outlined above.

7.8.11 It is anticipated that the CE-File electronic file system will be applied to the Administrative Court during 2023. Further information as to start date and details will be published on the Judiciary website in due course. It is likely that a Practice Direction will be issued to coincide with the introduction of the CE-File system.

7.9 SERVING THE CLAIM FORM

1BA-42 **7.9.1** The claimant must serve a sealed copy of the Claim Form together with a copy of the bundle of the documentation filed with it, on the defendant(s) and any interested parties within 7 days of the claim being issued. This must be actual, not deemed, service.[5] In the event that the claim form has not been served within 7 days, an application must be made for an extension of time for service (see para 13.7 of this guide).[6]

7.9.2 All Government Departments should be served at the office as stipulated under the Crown Proceedings Act 1947 (reproduced at Annex 3 of this Guide).[7] Local authorities should be served at their main offices with a note that papers should be directed to the authority's legal department.

7.9.3 If the party to be served is outside the UK or the claimant wishes to apply to dispense with service of the Claim Form, there are separate provisions governing service. The claimant should consider CPR 6.16 (for dispensing with service) and CPR 6.30-6.34, CPR 6.36-6.37, and CPR 6B PD (for serving outside the UK).

7.9.4 Once the claimant has served the papers on the defendant(s) and any interested party or parties, the claimant must confirm this with the ACO by filing a certificate of service (Form N215) within 21 days of service of the Claim Form. If, after 28 days from lodging the Claim Form, the ACO has not received a certificate of service or an acknowledgment of service from the defendant, the case will be closed.

7.9.5 If a claim is closed because the claimant fails to file a certificate of service within time, the claim will only be reopened by judicial order. An application for such an order must be made in an application notice, which must be filed with the relevant fee (see para 13.7 of this Guide). In

---

[1] In many instances, 50 pages, but parties should check with the appropriate court office.

[2] CPR 5B PD para 2.1 and 2.2.

[3] CPR 5A PD para 5.3.

[4] CPR 5A PD para 5.3.(6) and CPR 5B PD para 4.2

[5] *R (Good Law Project Ltd) v Secretary of State for Health and Social Care)* [2022] EWCA Civ 355, [24].

[6] CPR 7.6 does not apply to extensions of time for service of a judicial review claim form, but its principles should be followed on an application under CPR 3.1(2)(a) to extend time for service of a judicial review claim. Therefore, unless a claimant had taken all reasonable steps to comply with CPR 54.7 but had been unable to do so, time for service should not be extended: ibid, [85]

[7] CPR 54A PD para 5.2(b).

the application the claimant must explain why the certificate of service was not filed in time and whether the failure caused any prejudice to any party or any delay to the judicial review process and outline the reasons why the claim should be reopened.

7.9.6 CPR 39.8 provides that any communication between a party to proceedings and the Court must be disclosed to, and if in writing (whether in paper or electronic format) copied to, the other party or parties or their representatives (with some exceptions). If a party fails to comply with the rule, the Court may impose sanctions or return the communication to the sender without consideration of its content.

7.10 ADDITIONAL PROVISIONS FOR PERSONS SUBJECT TO A CIVIL PROCEEDINGS ORDER OR A CIVIL RESTRAINT ORDER

7.10.1 If a claimant is subject to a civil proceedings order made under s. 42 of the Senior Courts Act 1981 or is subject to a civil restraint order made under CPR 3.11, the claimant must apply for permission to start proceedings before he or she files an application for permission to apply or judicial review. **1BA-43**

7.10.2 Such an application must be made on Form N244 and be accompanied by the relevant fee. This fee is not subject to fee remission, but it can be refunded if permission to start proceedings is granted.

7.10.3 The requirements for persons subject to a civil proceedings order or a civil restraint order are discussed in greater detail in Chapter 5 of this Guide.

7.11 AMENDING THE CLAIM OR GROUNDS FOR JUDICIAL REVIEW BEFORE THE COURT CONSIDERS PERMISSION

7.11.1 If the claimant wishes to file further evidence, amend or substitute the Claim Form or claim bundle, or rely on further grounds after they have been served, he or she must apply for an order allowing them to do so.[1] The interim applications procedure discussed at para 13.7 of this Guide applies. **1BA-44**

7.11.2 The Court has a discretion whether to permit amendments and will take into account any prejudice that would be caused to the other parties or to good administration.

7.11.3 Where the defendant has agreed to reconsider the original decision challenged (thus effectively agreeing to withdraw the decision challenged without the intervention of the Court), it may be more appropriate to end the claim (see Chapter 24 of this Guide), rather than to stay or seek to amend it. One exception is where the case raises a point of general public importance and the point which was at issue in relation to the original decision remains an important issue in relation to the subsequent decision.[2]

7.11.4 If the defendant has made a new decision superseding the decision under challenge, and the claimant wishes to challenge the fresh decision, in most cases the appropriate course will be to end the claim and file a new one. Although there is no hard and fast rule, it will usually be better for all parties if judicial review proceedings are not treated as "rolling" or "evolving".[3]

7.11.5 If an application is made to amend to challenge a later decision, there are a number of matters to note:[4]

7.11.5.1 The Court can impose a condition requiring the re-formulation of the claim and the re-preparation of any bundles of material, so as to eliminate any irrelevant surplus material and to work from a single set of papers. Any draft order or draft consent order seeking amendment of the claim in these circumstances should typically include a provision allowing for a new, amended claim bundle to be filed or, ideally, be accompanied by a copy of the proposed amended claim bundle.

7.11.5.2 The Court has a discretion to permit amendments and may make an assessment that the proper conduct of proceedings will best be promoted by refusing permission to amend and requiring a fresh claim to be brought.

7.11.5.3 The Court will be astute to check that a claimant is not seeking to avoid complying with any time limits by seeking to amend rather than commence a fresh claim.

7.11.5.4 A claimant seeking permission to amend will also be expected to have given proper notice to all relevant persons, including interested parties.

---

[1] See CPR 54A PD paras 11.1-11.4 for amendment of grounds. See *R (AB) Chief Constable of Hampshire Constabulary* [2019] EWHC 3461 (Admin), [112]-[114].

[2] *R (Bhatti) v Bury Metropolitan Borough Council* [2013] EWHC 3093 and *R (Yousuf) v Secretary of State for the Home Department* [2016] EWHC 663 (Admin).

[3] *R (Dolan) v Secretary of State for Health and Social Care* [2020] EWCA Civ 1605, [2021] 1 WLR 2326, [118]; *R (Spahiu) v Secretary of State for the Home Department* [2018] EWCA Civ 2604, [2019] 1 WLR 1297, [62]-[63].

[4] *R (Hussain) v Secretary of State for Justice* [2016] EWCA Civ 1111, [2017] 1 WLR 761.

8 THE ACKNOWLEDGMENT OF SERVICE

8.1 FILING AN ACKNOWLEDGMENT OF SERVICE

1BA-45 **8.1.1** Any defendant or interested party served with the Claim Form who wishes to take part in the permission stage of the judicial review claim must file and serve an Acknowledgment of Service.[1]

8.1.2 Form N462 must be used. If the claim was started in or has been transferred to the ACO in Cardiff, the Acknowledgment of Service and any evidence may be lodged in Welsh or English.

8.1.3 It is wise for any defendant or interested party to file an Acknowledgment of Service. It lets the Court know whether a defendant or interested party wishes to contest the claim. The filing of an Acknowledgment of Service is not however, mandatory unless ordered by the Court.

8.1.4 If a party fails to file an Acknowledgment of Service within the relevant time limit (see para 8.2 below), this will have 3 consequences:

8.1.4.1 the papers will be sent to a judge to consider whether to grant permission to apply for judicial review without any indication of the party's position;

8.1.4.2 if the judge directs that permission is to be considered at an oral hearing (see para 9.2.1.4 of this Guide) or if the judge refuses permission and the claimant applies for reconsideration at an oral hearing (see para 9.4 of this Guide), the party may not take part in the permission hearing without the permission of the Court;[2] and

8.1.4.3 the judge may take into account the failure to file an Acknowledgment of Service when considering costs (see Chapter 25 of this Guide).[3]

8.1.5 If a party does not file an Acknowledgment of Service and permission is subsequently granted, that party may still take part in the substantive determination of the claim for judicial review (see para 9.2.1.1 and Chapter 11 of this Guide).[4]

8.2 TIME FOR FILING THE ACKNOWLEDGMENT OF SERVICE

1BA-46 **8.2.1** The Acknowledgment of Service must be filed at the ACO within 21 days after service of the Claim Form.[5] The 21-day period may be extended or shortened by judicial order. A judge may also consider permission to apply for judicial review without waiting for an Acknowledgment of Service to be filed.

8.2.2 The parties cannot agree between themselves to extend the time for filing;[6] an order of the Court is required. An application for an extension of time must be made in accordance with the interim applications procedure and on payment of the relevant fee (see para 13.7 of this Guide). Alternatively, the application can be made retrospectively in the Acknowledgment of Service in section D, provided that the decision on the application for permission to apply for judicial review has not already been made.

8.2.3 The Acknowledgment of Service must be served on all other parties no later than 7 days after it was filed with the ACO.

8.2.4 As soon as an Acknowledgment of Service has been filed by each party to the claim, or upon the expiry of the permitted time, the papers may be sent to a judge to consider whether to grant permission to apply for judicial review by considering the papers alone (see Chapter 9 of this Guide).

8.3 CONTENTS OF THE ACKNOWLEDGMENT OF SERVICE

1BA-47 **8.3.1** The Acknowledgment of Service must:

8.3.1.1 set out the summary grounds for contesting the claim (or summary grounds of defence), the legal basis of the defendant's response to the claimant's case and any relevant facts (including any material matters of factual dispute), if the party does contest it. The summary grounds should provide a brief summary of the reasoning underlying the decision or conduct challenged, or reasons why the application for permission can be determined without that information.[7] The summary grounds may be set out in section C of the Acknowledgment of Service or attached in a separate document;

8.3.1.2 be as concise as possible and not exceed 30 pages. In many cases the Court will expect the summary grounds to be significantly shorter. The Court may grant permission to exceed the

---

1 CPR 54.8(2).
2 CPR 54.9(1)(a).
3 CPR 54.9(2).
4 CPR 54.9(1)(b).
5 CPR 54.8(2)(a).
6 CPR 54.8(3).
7 CPR 54.8(4)(a)(i); CPR 54A PD para 6.2.

30-page limit. This requires an application, which should be made before the document is filed, or at the latest at the same time as it is filed;[1]

8.3.1.3 state by ticking the appropriate box in Section A if the party is intending to contest the application for permission on the basis that it is highly likely that the outcome for the claimant would not have been substantially different if the conduct complained of had not occurred. If so, the summary grounds must explain why;[2]

8.3.1.4 state in section B the name and address of any person believed to be an interested party;[3]

8.3.1.5 state in section E if the party contests the claimant's application for an automatic costs limit under the Aarhus Convention (see para 25.15 of this Guide), if such an application was made.

8.3.2 Evidence may be filed with the Acknowledgment of Service but it is not generally required.

8.3.3 Where a party does not intend to contest the claim, it should be made clear in section C of the Acknowledgment of Service whether the party intends to remain neutral or would in principle agree to the decision being quashed. This information will allow the Court to manage the claim properly. If the party does agree in principle to the decision being quashed, the parties should attempt to agree settlement of the claim at the earliest opportunity.

8.3.4 The purpose of the Acknowledgment of Service (and in particular the summary grounds of defence) is to assist the Court in deciding whether permission to apply for judicial review should be granted and, if so, on what terms. Defendants and interested parties must not oppose permission reflexively or unthinkingly. In appropriate cases, they can and should assist the Court by indicating in the Acknowledgment of Service that permission is not opposed.

8.4 DEFENDANT'S APPLICATIONS

8.4.1 When lodging the Acknowledgment of Service, a defendant or interested party may request further directions or an interim order from the Court in section D.[4] Examples of applications that may be made at this stage are for the party's costs of preparing the acknowledgment of service and for the discharge of any previously made injunctions. **1BA-48**

8.5 PERMISSION STAGE REPLY

8.5.1 The CPR and Practice Directions do not make provision for the claimant to respond to the Acknowledgment of Service during the paper application process. Replies are rarely necessary and are not encouraged. The ACO will not delay consideration of permission on the basis that the claimant wishes to reply. If the claimant considers that there is something in the Acknowledgement of Service to which a reply is essential, a document should be drafted which is concise and confined to true reply points. This should be accompanied by an application for permission to file a reply and should be filed promptly. Any reply received before the case is sent to a judge to consider permission will be put before the judge. Whether to take it into account it is a matter for the judge to decide.[5] **1BA-49**

9 THE PERMISSION STAGE OF THE JUDICIAL REVIEW PROCEDURE

9.1 THE APPLICATION

9.1.1 The claimant must obtain permission from the Court to apply for judicial review. If permission is granted on some or all of the grounds advanced, the claim will usually proceed to a full hearing on those grounds for which permission has been granted. (This is referred to as the substantive hearing - see Chapter 11 of this Guide.) **1BA-50**

9.1.2 In the first instance, the claim papers (comprising the papers filed by the claimant, any Acknowledgment of Service and any reply received by the time the papers are collated) are sent to a judge. The judge will then consider the papers and determine whether to grant permission to apply for judicial review.

(The judge can make other orders before determining permission: see paras 9.2.1.4 - 9.2.1.6 of this Guide.)

9.1.3 The judge will refuse permission to apply for judicial review unless satisfied that there is an arguable ground for judicial review which has a realistic prospect of success.[6]

---

[1] CPR 54A PD para. 6.2.

[2] CPR 54.8(4)(a)(ia).

[3] CPR 54.8(4)(a)(ii). For more detail on who is an interested party, see para 3.2.3 of this Guide.

[4] CPR 54.8(4)(b).

[5] *R (Wingfield) v Canterbury City Council* [2019] EWHC 1975 (Admin), [80]-[81].

[6] See *Sharma v Brown-Antoine* [2006] UKPC 57, [2007] 1 WLR 780, [14(4)]; *Attorney General of Trinidad and Tobago v Ayers-Caesar* [2019] UKPC 44, [2]; *Maharaj v Petroleum Company of Trinidad and Tobago Ltd* [2019] UKPC 21; *Simone v Chancellor of the Exchequer* [2019] EWHC 2609 (Admin),

9.1.4 Even if a claim is arguable, the judge must refuse permission:

9.1.4.1 unless he or she considers that the applicant has a sufficient interest in the matter to which the application relates (see para 6.3.2 of this Guide); and

9.1.4.2 if it appears to be highly likely that the outcome for the claimant would not have been substantially different if the conduct complained of had not occurred.[1]

9.1.5 If the Court considers that there has been undue delay in bringing the claim, the Court may refuse permission.[2] Delay is discussed further at para 6.4 of this Guide.

9.1.6 Other reasons for refusing permission include an adequate alternative remedy (para 6.3.3) and that the claim is or has become academic (para 6.3.4).

9.2 COURT ORDERS AT THE PERMISSION STAGE

1BA-51 **9.2.1** A number of different orders may be made following consideration of the papers. The following are the most common.

9.2.1.1 Permission granted

The judge has determined that there is an arguable case on all grounds. The case will proceed to a substantive hearing. In this event, the judge will usually give directions for the substantive hearing.

9.2.1.2 Permission refused

The judge has determined that none of the grounds advanced by the claimant are arguable, so the claim should not proceed to a substantive hearing. The judge will record brief reasons in the order.[3] The claimant may be ordered to pay the defendant's costs of preparing the Acknowledgment of Service (see para 25.4 of this Guide).

9.2.1.3 Permission granted in part

In some cases, the judge may decide that some of the grounds advanced by the claimant are suitable for permission but others are not. The judge will direct the matter to proceed to a substantive hearing only on the grounds for which permission has been granted. The claimant can request that the application for permission on the refused grounds is reconsidered at an oral hearing (see para 9.4 of this Guide). The claimant may not raise or renew grounds at the substantive hearing where permission has not already been granted unless (unusually) the Court allows it.[4]

9.2.1.4 Permission adjourned to an oral hearing on notice

The judge has made no determination on the application for permission. Instead, the application for permission will be considered at an oral hearing with the claimant and any other parties who wish to make representations attending. The form of the hearing will be similar to a renewed permission hearing (see para 9.4 of this Guide).

9.2.1.5 Permission adjourned to a "rolled-up" hearing

The judge has made no determination on the application for permission. Instead the application for permission will be considered in Court with the substantive hearing to follow immediately if permission is granted. At the rolled-up hearing, the judge is likely to hear argument on permission and the substance together, and give a single judgment, but the procedure adopted at the hearing is a matter for the judge.

When preparing documentation for a rolled-up hearing, the parties should follow the same rules as apply when preparing for a substantive hearing (see Chapter 11 of this Guide). The documentation before the Court should be the same as if the hearing was the substantive hearing.

Where a rolled-up hearing is ordered the claimant will be asked by the ACO to sign an undertaking to pay the fee for the substantive application for judicial review which would then become payable if the judge later grants permission.

9.2.1.6 Application for permission to be resubmitted

The judge has made no determination on the application for permission. Instead the judge will request the parties perform some act (such as file additional documents or representations) or await some other event (such as the outcome of a similar case). Once the act or event has been performed, or when the time limit for doing so has expired, the papers will be resubmitted to the judge to consider permission on the papers.

9.3 TOTALLY WITHOUT MERIT ORDERS

1BA-52 **9.3.1** If the judge considers that the application for permission is totally without merit then he/she may refuse permission and record the claim as being totally without merit.

9.3.2 The term "totally without merit" applies to a case that is bound to fail; the case does not have to be abusive or vexatious.[5]

---

[112].

[1] s.31(3C)-(3F) of the Senior Courts Act 1981.

[2] s.31(6)(a) of the Senior Courts Act 1981.

[3] CPR 54.12(2).

[4] *R (Talpada) v SSHD* [2018] EWCA Civ 841, [23] and [68].

[5] *R (Wasif) v Secretary of State for the Home Department (Practice Note)* [2016] EWCA Civ 82, [2016]

9.3.3 Where a case is certified as totally without merit, there is no right to a renewed oral hearing[1] (see para 9.4 of this Guide) and the claim is concluded in the Administrative Court, although there is a right of appeal (see para 26.3 of this Guide).

9.4 RECONSIDERATION AT AN ORAL HEARING

9.4.1 If permission is refused the claimant should consider the judge's reasons for refusing permission on the papers before taking any further action. **1BA-53**

9.4.2 If the claimant takes no further action, 7 days after service of the order refusing permission, the ACO will close the case. If the Court has directed the parties to file written submissions on costs or has given directions in relation to any other aspect of the case, the claim will remain open until the costs or that other aspect is resolved. If there is an interim costs order in place at that time, and unless the Court has directed otherwise, it will continue in effect (even though the case is closed administratively) and the parties will have to apply to set aside that order (see para 13.7 of this Guide).

9.4.3 If, having considered the reasons, the claimant wishes to continue to contest the matter, there is no appeal, but there is a right to request that the application for permission to apply for judicial review be reconsidered at an oral hearing (often referred to as a renewal hearing).[2]

9.4.4 When the ACO serves an order refusing permission to apply for judicial review on the papers it will also include a renewal notice (Form 86b). If the claimant wishes to have their application for permission to apply for judicial review reconsidered at an oral hearing he or she must complete and send this form back to the ACO within 7 days[3] of the date upon which it is served. A fee is payable. The claimant should send a copy of the Form 86b to any party that filed an Acknowledgment of Service.

9.4.5 The claimant must provide grounds for renewing the application for permission and must in those grounds address the judge's reasons for refusing permission by explaining in brief terms why the claimant maintains those reasons are wrong.[4] It is not sufficient simply to state that renewal is sought on the original grounds, without seeking to explain the scope of the renewed application and the asserted error in the refusing judge's reasons. If the refusing judge's reasons are not addressed, the judge may make a costs order against the claimant at the renewal hearing and/or impose any other sanction which he or she considers to be appropriate.

9.4.6 On receipt of the renewal notice the ACO will list an oral hearing (see para 14.2.1 of this Guide on listing). Absent a judicial order, the hearing cannot take place without all parties being given at least two days' notice of the hearing.[5] The ACO will send notice to all parties of the date of the hearing.

9.4.7 The renewal hearing is normally a public hearing that anyone may attend and observe and will usually take place in Court.

9.5 TIME ESTIMATE FOR RENEWED APPLICATION

9.5.1 Renewal hearings are expected to be short, with the parties making succinct submissions. The standard time estimate for a renewed permission application is 30 minutes. This includes the time needed for the judge to give an oral judgment, if appropriate, at the end of the hearing. **1BA-54**

9.5.2 Any request for a longer listing must be included in the application. If any party believes the renewed application is likely to last more than 30 minutes, he or she must inform the ACO as soon as possible. In any event, within 7 days following the date when the application was filed, the parties must tell the Court the agreed time estimate for the hearing.[6]

9.5.3 Failure to inform the ACO may result in the hearing having to be adjourned on the hearing day for lack of Court time, in which event the Court will consider making a costs order against the party or parties who should have notified the Court of the longer time estimate.

9.5.4 Even where a party informs the Court that the renewed application is likely to take more than 30 minutes, the Court will only allocate such Court time as it considers appropriate, bearing in mind the pressure on Court time from other cases. In any event, it is rare that permission hearings will be allocated more than two hours.

---

1 WLR 2793.

[1] CPR 54.12(7).

[2] CPR 54.12(3).

[3] CPR 54.12(4).

[4] CPR 54A PD para 7.6.

[5] CPR 54.12(5).

[6] CPR 54A PD para 7.7.

9.6 PROCEDURE AT RENEWAL HEARINGS

1BA-55 **9.6.1** The defendant and/or any interested party may attend the oral hearing. Unless the Court directs otherwise, there is no need to attend.[1] If an Acknowledgment of Service has not been filed, there will be no right to be heard, though the Court may permit the party to make representations (see para 8.1.4 of this Guide).[2]

9.6.2 Where there are a number of cases listed before a judge in any day, a time marking may be given for each case. This may be shown on the daily cause list or the judge's clerk may contact the parties and/or their representatives. Alternatively, at the start of the day's list, the judge may release the parties and/or their representatives until a specific time later in the day.

9.6.3 The judge has a discretion as to how the hearing will proceed. Generally, and subject to the judge's discretion, hearings follow a set pattern:

9.6.3.1 The claimant will speak first setting out their grounds and why those grounds are arguable.

9.6.3.2 The defendant(s) will speak second setting out why the grounds are not arguable or other reasons why permission should not be granted.

9.6.3.3 Any interested parties will speak third to support or contest the application for permission.

9.6.3.4 The claimant is given the opportunity to reply briefly.

9.6.3.5 The decision refusing or granting permission, and, if appropriate, making any further directions or orders will usually be announced after the hearing.

9.6.4 In a hearing in the Administrative Court in Wales, any party has the right to speak Welsh or English.[3] The guidance outlined at para 10.3 of this Guide also applies to permission hearings.

9.6.5 The test for granting permission at an oral hearing is the same as the one applied by the judge considering permission on the papers (see para 9.1.3 of this Guide).

9.6.6 If permission is refused at the renewal hearing, the claim ends (subject to any appeal - see para 26.3 of this Guide). If permission is granted on one or more grounds, the case proceeds to the substantive hearing, which will take place on a later date (unless the hearing was "rolled up", in which case the substantive hearing will follow immediately: see para 9.2.1.5 of this Guide). The date for the hearing may be set by the judge or left to be determined by the ACO (see para 14.2.3 of this Guide for listing).

9.7 PROCEDURE WHERE THE UPPER TRIBUNAL IS THE DEFENDANT

1BA-56 **9.7.1** In most cases, decisions of the Upper Tribunal are subject to appeal. Decisions subject to appeal should not be challenged in judicial review proceedings because the appeal is an adequate alternative remedy. However, where the Upper Tribunal decision is one refusing permission to appeal from the First tier Tribunal, there is no further right of appeal. In that case, the only route of challenge is by judicial review, naming the Upper Tribunal as defendant and there is a special procedure for judicial review in CPR 54.7A.

9.7.2 A party seeking to challenge a decision of the Upper Tribunal should consider whether the decision was taken before or after 14 July 2022, the date on which s. 2 of the Judicial Review and Courts Act 2022 was commenced:

9.7.2.1 Where the Upper Tribunal's decision was taken before 14 July 2022, the Court will only grant permission to apply for judicial review if it considers that:

> there is an arguable case which has a reasonable prospect of success that both the decision of the Upper Tribunal
> refusing permission to appeal and the decision of the First Tier Tribunal against which permission to appeal was sought are wrong in law; and
> either the claim raises an important point of principle or practice or there is some other compelling reason to hear the claim.[4]

9.7.2.2 Where the Upper Tribunal's decision was taken on or after 14 July 2022, parties should bear in mind in addition that the High Court's judicial review jurisdiction is ousted except "so far as the decision involves or gives rise to any question as to whether—

(a) the Upper Tribunal has or had a valid application before it under section 11(4)(b),
(b) the Upper Tribunal is or was properly constituted for the purpose of dealing with the application, or
(c) the Upper Tribunal is acting or has acted—
  (i) in bad faith, or

---

[1] CPR 54A PD para 7.4.

[2] CPR 54.9(1)(a).

[3] Any party, or their legal representative, intending to use the Welsh language (orally or in written form) must inform the Court of that fact so that appropriate arrangements can be made for the management and listing of the case: Practice Direction relating to the use of the Welsh language in the civil courts in or having a connection with Wales, para 1.3.

[4] CPR 54.7A(7).

(ii) in such a procedurally defective way as amounts to a fundamental breach of the principles of natural justice."[1]

9.7.3 The general procedure in CPR Part 54 will apply with the following modifications:

9.7.3.1 The application for permission to apply for judicial review may not include any other claim, whether against the Upper Tribunal or not, and any such other claim must be the subject of a separate application.[2]

9.7.3.2 The Claim Form and the supporting documents must be filed no later than 16 days after the date on which notice of the Upper Tribunal's decision was sent to the applicant, not the normal 3 months.[3]

9.7.3.3 If the application for permission is refused on paper, there is no right to a renewed oral hearing (see para 9.4 of this Guide), though appeal rights do apply (see para 26.3 of this Guide).[4]

9.7.3.4 If permission to apply for judicial review is granted and the Upper Tribunal or any interested party seeks a hearing of the substantive application, it must make a request no later than 14 days after service of the order granting permission, in which case the ACO will list a substantive hearing. If no request is made within that period, the Court will make a final order quashing the Upper Tribunal's decision without a hearing.[5] The case will then return to the Upper Tribunal to consider permission to appeal again.

9.7.4 In claims against the Upper Tribunal, CPR 54.7A(4) requires certain documents to be filed with the claim. If these documents are not provided with the Claim Form the Court is unlikely to allow additional time for them to be submitted and may refuse permission to apply for judicial review on the grounds that it does not have sufficient information to properly consider the claim. The Court is very unlikely to order additional time to submit the documents in the absence of an application for extension of time to file the required documents. (Such applications, whilst not encouraged, should be made on the Claim Form, or by way of separate application, see para 13.7 of this Guide for details).

9.7.5 The documents required by CPR 54.7A are:

9.7.5.1 the decision of the Upper Tribunal to which the judicial review claim relates and any documents giving reasons for the decision;

9.7.5.2 the grounds of appeal to the Upper Tribunal and any documents sent with them;

9.7.5.3 the decision of the First-tier Tribunal, the application to that Tribunal for permission to appeal and its reasons for refusing permission to appeal; and

9.7.5.4 any other documents essential to the claim.

9.8 JUDICIAL REVIEW COSTS CAPPING ORDERS: GENERAL

9.8.1 A judicial review costs capping order ("CCO")[6] may take a number of forms. Usually, the order will specify a limit on the amount that a claimant can be ordered to pay in respect of other side's costs if the claimant loses (e.g. the claimant's liability for costs will be capped at £5,000). Where a CCO is granted, the order must be coupled with an order placing a limit on the amount that a claimant who is successful can recover from a defendant if the claimant ultimately wins the case (sometimes called a reciprocal costs capping order).[7] There is no requirement that the reciprocal cap should be set at the same level as the costs liability of the claimant.[8] **1BA-57**

9.8.2 A CCO may only be granted after permission to apply for judicial review has been granted.[9]

9.8.3 An application for a CCO may only be made by a claimant, not a defendant, interested party, or intervener.[10]

9.8.4 The Court may only make a CCO if it is satisfied that:[11]

9.8.4.1 the proceedings are public interest proceedings; and

9.8.4.2 in the absence of the order, the claimant would discontinue the application for judicial review or cease to participate in the proceedings; and

---

[1] s. 11A(1)-(4) of the Tribunals, Courts and Enforcement Act 2007, as inserted by s. 2 of the Judicial Review and Courts Act 2022.

[2] CPR 54.7A(2).

[3] CPR 54.7A(3).

[4] CPR 54.7A(8).

[5] CPR 54.7A(9).

[6] Defined in s.88(2) of the Criminal Justice and Courts Act 2015 as "an order limiting or removing the liability of a party to judicial review proceedings to pay another party's costs in connection with any stage of the proceedings". See *R (Elan-Cane) v Secretary of State for the Home Department* [2020] EWCA Civ 363.

[7] s.89(2) of the Criminal Justice and Courts Act 2015.

[8] *R (Elan-Cane) v Secretary of State for the Home Department* [2020] EWCA Civ 363. For a summary of the principles applicable when setting the reciprocal cap, see *R (Western Sahara Campaign UK) v Secretary of State for International Trade* [2021] EWHC 1756 (Admin), [43].

[9] s.88(3) of the Criminal Justice and Courts Act 2015.

[10] s.88(4) of the Criminal Justice and Courts Act 2015.

[11] s.88(6) of the Criminal Justice and Courts Act 2015.

9.8.4.3 it would be reasonable to do so.

9.8.5 Public interest proceedings are those where:[1]

9.8.5.1 the subject of the proceedings is of general public importance;

9.8.5.2 the public interest requires the issue to be resolved; and

9.8.5.3 the proceedings are likely to provide an appropriate means of resolving it.

9.8.6 When determining whether proceedings are public interest proceedings, the Court must have regard to:[2]

9.8.6.1 the number of people likely to be directly affected if relief is granted;

9.8.6.2 how significant the effect on those people is likely to be; and

9.8.6.3 whether the proceedings involve consideration of a point of law of general public importance.

9.8.7 When considering whether to make a CCO, the Court must have regard to:[3]

9.8.7.1 the financial resources of the parties to the proceedings, including the financial resources of any person who provides, or may provide, financial support to the parties;

9.8.7.2 the extent to which the claimant is likely to benefit if relief is granted;

9.8.7.3 the extent to which any person who has provided, or may provide, the applicant with financial support is likely to benefit if relief is granted;

9.8.7.4 whether legal representatives for the applicant for the order are acting free of charge; and

9.8.7.5 whether the claimant is an appropriate person to represent the interests of other persons or the public interest generally

9.9 CCOS: PROCEDURE[4]

1BA-58 **9.9.1** An application for a CCO must normally be contained in the Claim Form at section 8 or in a separate document accompanying the Claim Form.[5]

9.9.2 The application must be supported by evidence setting out:[6]

9.9.2.1 why a CCO should be made, having regard, in particular, to the matters at paras 9.8.4 – 9.8.7 above;

9.9.2.2 a summary of the claimant's financial resources, unless the Court has dispensed with this requirement;[7]

9.9.2.3 the costs (and disbursements) which the claimant considers the parties are likely to incur in the future conduct of the proceedings;

9.9.2.4 if the claimant is a body corporate, whether it is able to demonstrate that it is likely to have financial resources available to meet liabilities arising in connection with the proceedings. Where it cannot, the Court must consider giving directions for the provision of information about the body's members and their ability to provide financial support for the purpose of the proceedings.[8]

9.9.3 If the defendant wishes to resist the making of the CCO, the reasons should be set out in the Acknowledgment of Service. Similarly, any representations in support of a reciprocal costs capping order (capping both parties' costs) should be made in the Acknowledgment of Service.

9.9.4 The claimant will usually be liable for the costs incurred by the defendant in successfully resisting an application for a CCO, but it would normally be expected that it would be proportionate to incur no more than £1,000 in doing so.[9]

9.9.5 If permission to apply for judicial review is granted on the papers, the judge will normally consider at the same time whether to make the CCO and if so, in what terms. If permission to apply for judicial review is not granted, the judge cannot make a CCO (see para 9.8.2 above)

9.9.6 If the judge grants permission to apply for judicial review, but refuses to grant the CCO,

---

[1] s.88(7) of the Criminal Justice and Courts Act 2015.

[2] s.89(1) of the Criminal Justice and Courts Act 2015.

[3] s.88(8) of the Criminal Justice and Courts Act 2015. These are not "determining criteria", but "criteria which have to be considered": *R (Beety) v Nursing and Midwifery Council* [2017] EWHC 3579 (Admin), [8]; *R (Good Law Project Ltd) v Minister for the Cabinet Office* [2021] EWHC 1083 (TCC), [9].

[4] The relevant procedure in this section of the Guide is found in the Criminal Justice and Courts Act 2015 and supplemented where appropriate by the guidance on protective costs order procedure in *R (Corner House Research) v Trade and Industry Secretary* [2005] EWCA civ 192, [2005] 1 WLR 2600 and *R (Buglife) v Thurrock Thames Gateway Development Corp* [2008] EWCA Civ 1209, [2009] CP Rep 8 at [29]-[31].

[5] CPR 46 PD para. 10.2 and *R (Corner House Research) v Trade and Industry Secretary* [2005] EWCA civ 192, [2005] 1 WLR 2600, [78].

[6] CPR 46.17(1)(b).

[7] CPR 46.17(3).

[8] CPR 46.18.

[9] *R (Corner House Research) v Trade and Industry Secretary* [2005] EWCA Civ 193, [2005] 1 WLR 2600, [78].

and the claimant requests that the decision is reconsidered at a hearing, that hearing should generally be limited to an hour and the claimant will face liability for costs if the CCO is again refused.

9.9.7 When the Court reconsiders at a hearing whether or not to make a CCO, the paper decision should only be revisited in exceptional circumstances.[1]

9.9.8 An application for a CCO should normally be made in the Claim Form (see para 9.9.1 of this Guide). If it is necessary to make the application at some other time, the procedure outlined at para 13.7 of this Guide should be used. Any application for a CCO must, however, be made as soon as it becomes clear that a CCO is required.

10 After Permission

10.1 DIRECTIONS FOR SUBSTANTIVE HEARING

10.1.1 When permission to apply for judicial review is granted, the claim will proceed to the substantive hearing on a later date. **1BA-59**

10.1.2 Unless the judge orders a particular date for the hearing, the ACO will list the substantive hearing as soon as practicable (see para 14.2 of this Guide for listing; see also Annex 4 for the Administrative Court Listing Policy).

10.1.3 When granting permission, a judge will usually give directions as to how the case will progress to the substantive hearing, including:

10.1.3.1 the time within which the defendant or interested party or parties should file detailed grounds of resistance and any evidence on which it is intended to rely at the hearing;

10.1.3.2 which kind of judge should hear the case, and specifically whether it is suitable to be heard by a deputy judge or should be heard by a Divisional Court (a court with two or more judges), as to which see para 14.3 of this Guide;

10.1.3.3 other case management directions including a timetable for skeleton arguments, trial bundles and authorities bundles to be lodged.

10.1.4 Judicial directions will supersede any standard directions. If the judge does not make any directions, the following standard directions apply:

10.1.4.1 The claimant must pay the relevant fee to continue the application for judicial review. Failure to do so within 7 days of permission being granted will result in the ACO sending the claimant a notice requiring payment within a set time frame (normally 7 more days). Further failure will result in the claim being struck out without further order.[2]

10.1.4.2 Any party who wishes to contest or support the claim must file and serve any Detailed Grounds and any written evidence or documents not already filed in a paginated and indexed bundle (in both hard copy and electronic copy)[3] within 35 days of permission being granted.[4] Detailed Grounds should be as concise as possible and must not exceed 40 pages without the Court's permission.[5] The fact that the claimant's Statement of Facts and Grounds is prolix is not necessarily a good reason for the defendant's Detailed Grounds to exceed the 40-page limit.[6]

10.1.4.3 If all relevant matters have already been addressed in the Summary Grounds, a party may elect not to file separate Detailed Grounds and instead inform the court and the parties that the Summary Grounds are to stand as Detailed Grounds.[7] However, before doing so, the party should consider carefully whether the material in the Summary Grounds is sufficient to discharge the duty of candour and cooperation with the court. In this regard, it is important to note that what is required to discharge that duty at the substantive stage may be more extensive than what is required before permission has been granted (see para 15.3.2 of this Guide).

10.1.4.4 The claimant must file and serve a skeleton argument no less than 21 days before the substantive hearing (see para 20.2 of this Guide for the contents of the skeleton argument).[8]

10.1.4.5 The defendant and any other party wishing to make representations at the substantive hearing must file and serve a skeleton argument no less than 14 days before the substantive hearing.[9]

10.1.4.6 The parties must agree the contents of a paginated and indexed bundle containing all relevant documents required for the hearing of the judicial review. This bundle must be lodged

---

[1] *R (Buglife) v Thurrock Thames Gateway Development Corp* [2008] EWCA Civ 1209, [2009] CP Rep 8, [31].

[2] CPR 3.7(1)(d), (2), (3) & (4).

[3] CPR 54A PD para 9.1(3) and 9.2.

[4] CPR 54.14(1).

[5] CPR 54A PD para 9.1(2).

[6] *R (SSE Generation Ltd) v Competition and Markets Authority* [2022] EWHC 865 (Admin).

[7] CPR 54A PD para. 9.1(1).

[8] Previous versions of the PDs required skeleton arguments to be filed 21 working days before the date of the hearing. The new CPR 54A PD para 14.5 refers simply to "21 days before the date of the hearing". This means "calendar" days: see CPR 2.8.

[9] CPR 54A PD para 14.6. "14 days" means 14 calendar days.

with the Court in both electronic and hard copy form by the parties not less than 21 days before the date of hearing unless judicial order provides otherwise.[1]

10.1.4.7 The parties must agree the contents of a bundle containing the authorities to be referred to at the hearing. This bundle must be lodged by the parties with the Court in both electronic and hard copy form no later than 7 days before the date of hearing.[2]

10.1.4.8 In Divisional Court cases, one set of the hearing bundle and one set of the authorities bundle should be provided for each judge hearing the case. See paras 21.2.4 and 22.2.1 of this Guide for further details.

10.2 AMENDING THE CLAIM

1BA-60 **10.2.1** The Claim Form and Statement of Grounds may be amended at any time before it has been served on any other party. However, once the Statement of Grounds has been served, amendment requires the permission of the Court in accordance with CPR Part 23.[3]

10.2.2 The application to amend must be made promptly and should include, or be accompanied by, a draft of the amended grounds and be supported by evidence explaining the need for the proposed amendment and any delay in making the application. The application, proposed additional grounds and any written evidence, must be served on the defendant and any interested party named in the Claim Form or Acknowledgment of Service.[4]

10.2.3 The Court may deal with an application without a hearing if the parties agree to the terms of the order sought, the parties agree that the Court should dispose of the application without a hearing or the Court does not consider that a hearing would be appropriate.[5]

10.2.4 Where permission to rely on additional grounds is given, the Court may give directions as to amendments to be made to the defendant's Grounds or Detailed Grounds and/or such other case management directions as appropriate.[6] A party may apply to the Court for an order disallowing an amendment within 14 days of service of a copy of an amended statement of case.[7]

10.2.4.1 If the claimant wishes to file further evidence, he or she must ask for the Court's permission to do so.[8] To seek permission, the claimant must make an application in accordance with the interim applications procedure discussed at para 13.7 of this Guide.[9]

10.2.4.2 This rule also applies to other parties who are filing documents. Outside the 35-day time limit (see para 10.1.4.2 of this Guide).

10.2.4.3 The position where the defendant intends to reconsider the original decision challenged is discussed at para 7.11.3 of this Guide. The position where the defendant has made a new decision which the claimant seeks to challenge is discussed at para 7.11.4.

10.3 ACTION IF AN INTERPRETER IS REQUIRED

1BA-61 **10.3.1** If a party or witness requires an interpreter, it is generally the responsibility of that party or the party calling the witness to arrange for the attendance of and to pay for the interpreter.

10.3.2 The ACO can arrange for an interpreter to attend free of charge to the party seeking an interpreter's assistance where:

10.3.2.1 the party is a litigant in person who cannot address the Court in English (or Welsh if the case is proceeding in Wales) and the party cannot afford to pay for an interpreter, does not qualify for legal aid and does not have a friend or family member who the judge agrees can act as an interpreter; and

10.3.2.2 the judge agrees that an interpreter should be arranged free of charge to that party; or

10.3.2.3 this has been ordered by the Court.

10.3.3 It is the responsibility of any party requesting an interpreter free of charge to make the request in writing as soon as it becomes clear that a hearing will have to be listed and an interpreter is required.

10.3.4 The party requesting an interpreter free of charge must inform the ACO in writing that an interpreter is required and which language is required.

10.3.5 Where the party does not notify the Court that an interpreter is required and a hearing has to be adjourned to arrange for an interpreter to attend on another occasion, the Court may make a costs order against the party requiring an interpreter (see para 25.1 of this Guide).

---

[1] CPR 54A PD paras 15.1, 15.2 and 15.3.

[2] CPR 54A PD paras 15.4 and 15.5.

[3] CPR 54A PD para 11.1.

[4] CPR 54A PD paras 11.2 and 11.3. See *R (AB) v Chief Constable of Hampshire Constabulary* [2019] EWHC 3461 (Admin) [112]-[114].

[5] CPR 23.8.

[6] CPR 54A PD para 11.4.

[7] CPR 17.2(2).

[8] CPR 54.16(2).

[9] See *Hickey v Secretary of State for Work and Pensions* [2018] EWCA CIV 851, [73]-[74].

10.4 RESPONSIBILITY FOR PRODUCTION OF SERVING PRISONERS AND DETAINED PERSONS

10.4.1 Where a serving prisoner or a detained person is represented by counsel it is generally not expected that the serving prisoner or detained person will be produced at Court, unless the Court orders otherwise. **1BA-62**

10.4.2 A serving prisoner or detained person acting without legal representation must request the prison or detention centre authorities to produce him or her at Court or to arrange a video-link between the Court and prison or detention centre. The serving prisoner or detained person must make the request as soon as he or she receives notice of the hearing. The prison or detention centre authorities are responsible for considering requests for production, arranging production of a detained person at Court and arranging video-links.

11 SUBSTANTIVE HEARING

11.1 FORMAT OF THE HEARING

11.1.1 The general rule is that hearings are held in public, unless the court makes a specific direction under CPR 39.2 that the hearing should take place in private. Where a hearing takes place in public, any member of the public may attend and observe. (Different rules apply to hearings in cases where a declaration under s. 6 of the Justice and Security Act 2013 is sought or has been made: see para 19.3 of this Guide.) **1BA-63**

11.1.2 The Court will decide how the hearing should proceed. Most hearings follow the following sequence:

11.1.2.1 The claimant speaks first, setting out the arguments in support of the grounds of claim.

11.1.2.2 The defendant speaks second, setting out the arguments in support of the grounds of defence.

11.1.2.3 Any interested parties and/or interveners speak third to support, contest, or clarify anything that has been said.

11.1.2.4 The claimant will have a right to reply to the other parties' submissions.

11.1.3 When there is a danger of an important and difficult point of law being decided without the Court hearing relevant argument on one or more aspects of the law, the Attorney General may be invited by the Court to appoint an Advocate to the Court (previously known as an amicus curiae).[1] In cases where an Advocate to the Court is appointed, the Court will hear submissions from the Advocate at an appropriate point in the hearing.

11.2 EVIDENCE

11.2.1 Evidence before the Court will nearly always be given exclusively in writing. **1BA-64**

11.2.2 The Court has an inherent power to hear from witnesses orally.[2] If a party seeks to call or cross-examine a witness, an application should be made using the interim applications procedure outlined in para 13.7 of this Guide. Oral evidence is permitted at a judicial review hearing only exceptionally. Permission will be given only where oral evidence is necessary to dispose of the claim fairly and justly.[3]

11.3 USE OF THE WELSH LANGUAGE

11.3.1 Under section 22 of the Welsh Language Act 1993, any person addressing the Court may exercise their right to speak in Welsh. This right applies only to hearings in Wales. If a party seeks to exercise this right, the claim should be started in the ACO in Cardiff or the party should seek transfer of the claim to the ACO in Cardiff. **1BA-65**

11.3.2 Under the Practice Direction Relating to the Use of the Welsh Language in Cases in the Civil Courts in Wales, the Court may hear any person in Welsh without notice, providing all parties consent.[4]

11.3.3 The parties should, however, inform the Court as soon as possible, preferably when lodging the claim papers, if any person intends to speak in Welsh. This allows the Court to make proper directions and the ACO in Cardiff to make practical arrangements.

---

[1] See CPR 3G PD.

[2] See the comments of Munby J in *R (PG) v London Borough of Ealing* [2002] EWHC 250 (Admin), [20]-[21].

[3] *R (Bancoult) v Secretary of State for Foreign and Commonwealth Affairs* [2012] EWHC 2115, [14]. An example of permission for cross-examination being given is *Jedwell v Denbighshire CC v DH and Dr Jones* [2015] EWCA Civ 1232. The Court of Appeal has since reaffirmed that this should be viewed as an exceptional course: see *R (Talpada) v Secretary of State for the Home Department* [2018] EWCA Civ 841, [2] and [54].

[4] Para 1.2 of the Practice Direction Relating to the Use of the Welsh Language in Cases in the Civil Courts in Wales.

11.3.4 There are bilingual judges who can consider claims and hold hearings in Welsh. However, it is likely that an order will be made for simultaneous interpretation, where an interpreter appears in Court interpreting into English and Welsh.[1]

11.4 JUDICIAL REVIEW WITHOUT A HEARING

1BA-66 **11.4.1** If all parties agree, the substantive consideration may take place without a hearing and the judge will decide the claim by considering the papers alone.[2] The parties should inform the ACO in writing if all parties have agreed to this course of action. On consideration of the papers, the judge may refuse to make a decision on the papers and order an oral hearing. The open justice principle applies to a determination made on the papers and the court may have to give consideration to the question whether there should be public access to documents.[3]

11.5 THRESHOLD FOR RELIEF

1BA-67 **11.5.1** To succeed in the claim, the claimant must show that the defendant's conduct is unlawful.

11.5.2 Even if a claimant establishes that the defendant's conduct is unlawful, the Court has a discretion whether to grant a remedy or not: see para 12.9 and para 12.10 below.

11.6 JUDGMENT AND ORDERS

1BA-68 **11.6.1** When the hearing is concluded, the Court will usually give judgment either:

11.6.1.1 orally, straight away or after a short adjournment (an ex tempore judgment); or

11.6.1.2 in writing, sometime after the hearing (a reserved judgment).

11.6.2 A reserved judgment will be "handed down" by the Court at a later date. The procedure is governed by CPR 40E PD. Unless the Court otherwise directs, at least two working days before the hand down date the judge will provide a draft of the judgment to legal representatives in the case.[4] The sole purpose of doing so is to enable the parties to make suggestions for the correction of errors, prepare submissions on consequential matters and to prepare themselves for the publication of the judgment.[5]

11.6.3 A copy of the judgment may be supplied, in confidence, to the parties, provided that (a) neither the draft judgment nor its substance is disclosed to any other person or used in the public domain; and (b) no action is taken (other than internally) in response to the draft judgment, before the judgment is handed down.[6]

11.6.4 Legal representatives receiving draft judgments must be aware of the limited purposes for which the draft had been transmitted to them. It is not appropriate for draft judgments or summaries of them to be given to persons in clerks' rooms or offices of barristers' chambers. Drafting press releases is not a legitimate activity to undertake within the embargo. It should be sufficient for a single named clerk to provide the link between the court and the barrister(s). Nobody else in chambers should need access to the draft judgment or any document created in relation to it without there being a good reason connected to one of the permitted purposes. Counsel and solicitors are personally responsible for ensuring that reasonable steps are taken for maintaining the confidentiality of the draft judgment and for explaining the confidentiality obligations to their clients.[7]

11.6.5 If a party to whom a copy of the draft judgment is supplied is a partnership, company, government department, local authority or other organisation of a similar nature, additional copies may be distributed in confidence within the organisation, provided that all reasonable steps are taken to preserve its confidential nature and the requirements set out in para 11.6.3 are adhered to.[8] This is not a licence to distribute the draft judgment beyond those who need to see it for the purposes for which it has been distributed in draft.[9]

11.6.6 Where the party receiving a draft judgment is a Minister responsible for a government department, the judgment may be shown in confidence to other Ministers and officials in the same department. If the Minister wishes to show the draft judgment to Ministers or officials outside the department, the written permission of the judge must be sought, identifying (normally by name) the Ministers or officials to whom the draft judgment is to be shown and the reason why those individuals need to see it.

---

[1] This was the format ordered in *R (Welsh Language Commissioner) v National Savings and Investments* [2014] PTSR D8.

[2] CPR 54.18.

[3] *UXA v Merseycare NHS Foundation Trust* [2021] EWHC 3455, [2022] 4 WLR 30.

[4] CPR 40E PD para 2.3.

[5] *R (Counsel General for Wales) v Secretary of State for Business, Energy and Industrial Strategy* [2022] EWCA Civ 181, [18] & [24].

[6] CPR 40E PD para. 2.4.

[7] *R (Counsel General for Wales) v Secretary of State for Business, Energy and Industrial Strategy* [2022] EWCA Civ 181, [25]-[28].

[8] CPR 40E PD para 2.6.

[9] *R (Counsel General for Wales) v Secretary of State for Business, Energy and Industrial Strategy* [2022] EWCA Civ 181, [23].

11.6.7 If in doubt about whether a draft judgment may be disclosed to any person, it is best to seek the permission of the judge.[1]

11.6.8 Breach of the confidentiality obligations or restrictions in para 11.6.3 or failure to take reasonable steps as required in para 11.6.4 may be treated as a contempt of court.[2] In future, those who break embargos can expect to find themselves the subject of contempt proceedings.[3]

11.6.9 Unless the parties or their legal representatives are told otherwise when the draft judgment is circulated, any proposed corrections to the draft judgment should be sent to the clerk of the judge who prepared the draft with a copy to any other party.[4]

11.6.10 The circulation of a draft judgment should not be taken as a pretext to reargue the case. The corrections which may be appropriate are generally typographical and other minor corrections. Parties and their legal representatives should go beyond this only in the most exceptional circumstances.[5]

11.6.11 The parties must seek to agree the form of the final order and any consequential orders[6] (usually costs and permission to appeal - see Chapters 25 and 26 of this Guide). The parties should submit any agreed order, which should include the terms of any orders made by the judge in Court and the terms of any agreed consequential orders, by 12 noon on the working day before handing down.[7]

11.6.12 Most judgments are now handed down without a hearing by email circulation of the approved judgment to the parties or their representatives and release to the National Archives. If the judge decides that the judgment should be handed down in open court, there will be a short hearing (normally lasting about 5 minutes), at which the judge makes the final copy of the judgment available and endorses it. The judge will not read the judgment verbatim. If the judge decides to hold such a hearing, the judge's clerk or ACO will inform the parties or their representatives whether attendance is required. If the judgment is being handed down at a hearing and the parties agree the terms of the order, the parties need not attend the hand down hearing.[8]

11.6.13 If consequential matters cannot be agreed, the Court will decide them by considering representations. This may be done:

11.6.13.1 by written representations in advance of the time at which the judgment is handed down (in which case the Court may give reasons for resolving the consequential matters in the handed-down judgment or in the order made at the time of hand-down);

11.6.13.2 by the parties attending Court on the date of handing down and making representations orally; or

11.6.13.3 by the parties agreeing a final order that allows them to make written representations on consequential orders within a set time period.

11.6.14 If there is a hand-down hearing, and the parties wish to attend to make oral submissions, they should inform the ACO as soon as possible, as time will need to be allocated for the judge to hear representations. Such a hearing would usually last for 30 minutes. The judge will normally make a decision on consequential matters there and then.

11.6.15 If there are no oral submissions, and the parties make submissions in writing, the Court will consider these at a later date, decide what orders to make and give notice of the decision in writing.

11.6.16 The Judge in Charge of the Administrative Court has approved the arrangements for handing down judgments in Wales at Annex 5 of this Guide, which should be followed.

11.6.17 The ACO will send sealed copies of any orders approved by the judge to the parties. Until an order has been approved and sealed the parties should not assume that any agreed orders are approved. It is the order (not the judgment) that gives rise to legal effects and it is the order that can be enforced if a party fails to comply with its terms.

11.6.18 All judgments following substantive hearings and some judgments made on interlocutory applications are made publicly available at *https://caselaw.nationalarchives.gov.uk/*. Judgments are also available at *https://www.bailii.org/*. These sites do not charge for access.

12 REMEDIES

12.1 INTRODUCTION

12.1.1 A claimant must state in section 7 of the Claim Form what remedy is sought in the event that the claim succeeds. This section of the Guide discusses the remedies available. **1BA-69**

[1] CPR 40E PD para. 2.7.
[2] CPR 40E PD para 2.8.
[3] *R (Counsel General for Wales) v Secretary of State for Business, Energy and Industrial Strategy* [2022] EWCA Civ 181, [31].
[4] CPR 40E PD para. 3.1.
[5] *Michael Wilson & Partners Ltd v Sinclair* [2020] EWHC 1017 (QB), [12].
[6] CPR 40E PD para 4.1.
[7] CPR 40E PD para 4.2.
[8] CPR 40E PD para 5.1.

12.2 MANDATORY ORDER

1BA-70 **12.2.1** A mandatory order is an order the Court can make to compel a public body to act in a particular way.

12.3 QUASHING ORDER

1BA-71 **12.3.1** In proceedings commenced before 14 July 2022, only one form of quashing order is available. The effect of this is the same as the old prerogative remedy of certiorari. It quashes, or sets aside, a challenged decision. The consequence of a quashing order is that the challenged decision does not have legal force or effect. It is also treated as if it never had such force or effect. It is sometimes said that a quashed decision is void ab initio (i.e. from the beginning).

12.3.2 After making a quashing order the Court will generally remit the matter to the public body decision maker and direct it to reconsider the matter and reach a fresh decision in accordance with the judgment of the Court.[1]

12.3.3 The Court has power to substitute its own decision for the decision which has been quashed. But this power applies only where (a) the decision in question was made by a Court or tribunal, (b) the decision is quashed on the ground that there has been an error of law and (c) without the error there would have been only one decision which the Court or tribunal could have reached.[2]

12.3.4 In proceedings commenced on or after 14 July 2022, a quashing order may include provision (a) for the quashing not to take effect until a date specified in the order, or (b) removing or limiting any retrospective effect of the quashing.[3] In either case, the provision may be subject to conditions.[4]

12.3.5 Where provision is made for the quashing not to take effect until a specified date, the impugned act is (subject to any conditions imposed) upheld (i.e. treated for all purposes as if its validity and force were, and always had been, unimpaired by the relevant defect) until the quashing takes effect.[5] However, once the quashing takes effect, the impugned act is treated as if it never had force or effect.[6]

12.3.6 Where provision is made for removing or limiting any retrospective effect of the quashing, the impugned act is (subject to any conditions imposed) upheld (i.e. treated for all purposes as if its validity and force were, and always had been, unimpaired by the relevant defect) in any respect in which the provision prevents it from being quashed.[7]

12.3.7 In deciding whether to exercise the power to make the provision described in para 12.3.4 above, the Court must have regard to:

"(a) the nature and circumstances of the relevant defect;
(b) any detriment to good administration that would result from exercising or failing to exercise the power;
(c) the interests or expectations of persons who would benefit from the quashing of the impugned act;
(d) the interests or expectations of persons who have relied on the impugned act;
(e) so far as appears to the court to be relevant, any action taken or proposed to be taken, or undertaking given, by a person with responsibility in connection with the impugned act;
(f) any other matter that appears to the court to be relevant."[8]

12.4 PROHIBITING ORDER

1BA-72 **12.4.1** A prohibiting order prohibits a public body from doing something that the public body has indicated an intention to do but has not yet done.

12.5 DECLARATION

1BA-73 **12.5.1** A declaration is a statement by the Court about how the law applies in a particular case or class of case. It is one way in which the Court can authoritatively declare the conduct or proposed conduct of a public body lawful or unlawful.

---

[1] See s. 31(5)(a) of the Senior Courts Act 1981 and CPR 54.19(2)(a).
[2] See s. 31(5)(b) and 31(5A) of the Senior Courts Act 1981 and CPR 54.19(2)(b).
[3] s. 29A(1) of the Senior Courts Act 1981, as inserted by s. 1 of the Judicial Review and Courts Act 2022.
[4] s. 29A(2) of the Senior Courts Act 1981.
[5] s. 29A(3) and (5) of the Senior Courts Act 1981.
[6] s. 29A(6) of the Senior Courts Act 1981.
[7] s. 29A(4) and (5) of the Senior Courts Act 1981.
[8] s. 29A(8) of the Senior Courts Act 1981.

12.5.2 A declaration does not have any coercive effect. This means that it cannot be enforced. Failure to comply with the law as set out in a declaration is not a contempt of court. Public bodies are, however, expected to comply with the law as declared by the Court.

12.5.3 A declaration can be a remedy on its own,[1] or can be granted in combination with other remedies.

12.5.4 A declaration will generally not be granted where the question under consideration is hypothetical, nor where the person seeking the declaration has no real interest in it, nor where the declaration is sought without proper argument (e.g. in default of defence or on admissions or by consent).[2]

12.6 DECLARATION OF INCOMPATIBILITY

12.6.1 If the Court determines that a provision in an Act of Parliament is incompatible with a Convention right, i.e. one of the rights from the European Convention of Human Rights scheduled to the Human Rights Act 1998, it may make a declaration of incompatibility.[3] **1BA-74**

12.6.2 A declaration of incompatibility may be made in relation to other kinds of primary legislation[4] and subordinate legislation (for example an order, rules or regulations made under an Act of Parliament) if the Court is satisfied that (disregarding any possibility of revocation) the Act of Parliament concerned prevents removal of the incompatibility.[5]

12.6.3 The principles that relate to ordinary declarations (see para 12.5 of this Guide above), such as the requirement that a declaration will not be made in hypothetical circumstances, apply.[6]

12.6.4 A declaration of incompatibility does not affect the validity, continuing operation or enforcement of the provision in respect of which it is given and it is not binding on the parties to the proceedings in which it is made.[7] The declaration informs Parliament of the incompatibility of that provision with a Convention right.

12.6.5 The claimant must state in the remedies section of the Claim Form (section 7) if he or she is applying for a declaration of incompatibility, giving precise details of the Convention right said to have been infringed and the domestic law provision said to be incompatible with that right.[8]

12.6.6 The claimant should also ensure that the relevant Secretary of State (representing the Crown) is named as an interested party if a declaration of incompatibility is sought. In any event, where an application for a declaration of incompatibility has been made the Court may order that notice should be given to the Crown.[9] If the Court is considering making a declaration of incompatibility and the Crown is not already a party, the Court must inform the relevant Secretary of State and allow at least 21 days[10] to permit the Secretary of State to consider whether to intervene and make representations.[11]

12.7 INJUNCTION

12.7.1 Injunctions are available in many different types of proceedings. In judicial review proceedings, an injunction is an order requiring a public body to act in a particular way (a positive or "mandatory" injunction) or prohibiting it from acting in a particular way (a negative or "prohibitory" injunction). **1BA-75**

12.8 DAMAGES

12.8.1 The Administrative Court has power to award damages and other monetary remedies (restitution and money due as a debt).[12] But this power can only be exercised if: **1BA-76**

12.8.1.1 the claimant is also seeking another remedy;[13] and

12.8.1.2 the Court is satisfied that such an award would have been made if the claim had been made in an action begun by the applicant at the time of making the application.[14]

12.8.2 This latter condition reflects the principle that there is no general right to a monetary remedy flowing from unlawful conduct by a public body. A claimant who seeks a monetary remedy

---

[1] CPR 40.20.
[2] *Re F* [1990] 2 AC 1.
[3] s.4(1) and 4(2) of the Human Rights Act 1998.
[4] This is defined in s.21(1) of the Human Rights Act 1998.
[5] s.4(3) and 4(4) of the Human Rights Act 1998.
[6] See, for example, *Taylor v Lancashire County Council* [2005] 1 WLR 2668.
[7] s. 4(6) of the Human Rights Act 1998.
[8] CPR 54A PD para 4.7; CPR 16 PD para 15.
[9] CPR 54A PD para 7.2; CPR 19A PD para 6.1.
[10] CPR 19.4A (1).
[11] s.5(1) of the Human Rights Act 1998.
[12] s.31(4) of the Senior Courts Act 1981.
[13] CPR 54.3(2).
[14] s.31(4)(b) of the Senior Courts Act 1981.

must identify a legal basis for that remedy (known as a "cause of action") in addition to establishing that the conduct challenged is unlawful. Causes of action commonly relied on in judicial review proceedings include false imprisonment, breach of statutory duty, restitution of money paid pursuant to an unlawful statutory demand and damages under the Human Rights Act 1998.

12.8.3 Where the claim includes a claim for damages under the Human Rights Act 1998 it must be properly pleaded and particularised.[1]

12.8.4 Where the assessment and award of damages is likely to be a lengthy procedure, the general practice of the Court is to determine the judicial review claim, award the other remedy sought (if appropriate) and then transfer the claim either to the County Court or to an appropriate division of the High Court to determine the question of damages. All parties must address their minds to the possibility of transfer as soon as it becomes apparent that issues other than damages have been resolved.[2]

12.9 THE GRANT OF REMEDIES

1BA-77 **12.9.1** Remedies in judicial review proceedings are in the discretion of the Court.

12.9.2 Even where a claimant shows that a defendant has acted unlawfully, the Court may refuse to grant a remedy, in particular where:[3]

12.9.2.1 the claimant has delayed in filing the application for judicial review and the Court considers that the granting of the remedy sought would be likely to cause substantial hardship to, or would substantially prejudice the rights of any person, or would be detrimental to good administration;[4]

12.9.2.2 the error of law made by the public body was immaterial to its decision;

12.9.2.3 the remedy would serve no useful practical purpose; or

12.9.2.4 the claimant has suffered no harm or prejudice.

12.9.3 Whether damages or other monetary remedies are awarded can give rise to different considerations.

12.9.4 The Court may grant more than one remedy where appropriate.

12.10 REMEDIES WHERE THE OUTCOME WOULD NOT HAVE BEEN SUBSTANTIALLY DIFFERENT IF THE CONDUCT COMPLAINED OF HAD NOT OCCURRED

1BA-78 **12.10.1** If the claimant is successful in judicial review proceedings, but the Court considers that it is highly likely that the outcome for the claimant would not have been substantially different if the conduct complained of had not occurred, then the Court must refuse to grant any form of relief, and may not award damages, unless the Court considers it appropriate to do so for reasons of exceptional public interest.[5]

13 CASE MANAGEMENT

13.1 CASE MANAGEMENT IN THE ADMINISTRATIVE COURT

1BA-79 **13.1.1** All proceedings in the Administrative Court are conducted in accordance with the principles listed in the overriding objective at CPR 1.1.

13.1.2 The overriding objective requires all cases to be dealt with justly and at proportionate cost. Dealing with a case justly and at proportionate cost includes:[6]

13.1.2.1 ensuring that the parties are on an equal footing;

13.1.2.2 saving expense;

13.1.2.3 dealing with it in ways which are proportionate to the amount of money involved, to the importance of the case, to the complexity of the issues and to the financial position of each party;

13.1.2.4 ensuring that it is dealt with expeditiously and fairly;

13.1.2.5 allotting to it an appropriate share of the Court's resources, while taking into account the need to allot resources to other cases; and

13.1.2.6 ensuring compliance with rules, Practice Directions and orders.

---

[1] *R (Nazem Fayad) v Secretary of State for the Home Department* [2018] EWCA Civ 54, [54]-[56]. Claims for damages that are not adequately particularised may have costs consequences for the claimant.

[2] See e.g. *R (ZA (Pakistan)) v Secretary of State for the Home Department* [2020] EWCA Civ 146, [72].

[3] See *R (Baker) v Police Appeals Tribunal* [2013] EWHC 718 (Admin).

[4] s.31(6)(b) of the Senior Courts Act 1981.

[5] s.31(2A) and (2B) Senior Courts Act 1981.

[6] CPR 1.1(2).

13.1.3 In ensuring that the overriding objective is complied with, the Court must actively manage cases,[1] which includes (but is not limited to) the following:

13.1.3.1 encouraging the parties to co-operate with each other in the conduct of the proceedings;

13.1.3.2 identifying the issues at an early stage;

13.1.3.3 deciding promptly which issues need full investigation and trial and accordingly disposing summarily of the others;

13.1.3.4 deciding the order in which issues are to be resolved;

13.1.3.5 encouraging the parties to use an alternative dispute resolution use of such procedure;

13.1.3.6 helping the parties to settle the whole or part of the case;

13.1.3.7 fixing timetables or otherwise controlling the progress of the case;

13.1.3.8 considering whether the likely benefits of taking a particular step justify the cost of taking it;

13.1.3.9 dealing with as many aspects of the case as it can on the same occasion;

13.1.3.10 dealing with the case without the parties needing to attend at Court;

13.1.3.11 making use of technology; and

13.1.3.12 giving directions to ensure that the trial of a case proceeds quickly and efficiently.

13.1.4 The parties are required to help the Court to further the overriding objective.[2]

13.1.5 This Chapter of the Guide is intended to provide more detail on what is expected from the Court, the ACO, and the parties in order to further the overriding objective.

13.2 DUTIES OF THE PARTIES

13.2.1 The parties must make efforts to settle the claim without requiring the intervention of the Court. It is preferable to settle the claim before it is started. However, even after the claim has started, the parties must continue to evaluate their positions, especially after any indication from the Court (such as the refusal or grant of permission to apply for judicial review). The parties should consider using alternative dispute resolution (for example, mediation) to explore settlement of the case, or at least to narrow the issues in the case. **1BA-80**

13.2.2 CPR Part 54 does not provide for a formal case management hearing in judicial review proceedings. However, the parties may apply for an interim order or the Court may make case management orders with or without a hearing. It is not uncommon that the first time the parties appear in Court before the judge is at the final hearing of the claim. The parties therefore have a duty to ensure that they maintain effective, constructive and regular communication with each other and with the ACO.

13.2.3 The parties must comply with the procedural provisions in the CPR, the relevant Practice Directions and orders of the Court (including orders by ACO lawyers). If a party knows he that or she will not be able to comply with directions or orders the ACO and the other parties should be informed as soon as possible. An application to extend time for any particular step to be taken should be made as soon as it becomes apparent that the extension is required. The application should be made in accordance with the interim applications procedure in para 13.7 of this Guide.

13.2.4 If a party is aware that there may be a need to apply for an interim order, the agreement of the other parties to the claim should be sought. In default of agreement, the ACO should be informed. The application should then be made as quickly as possible. Delay in making an application, especially where it requires urgent consideration, is a factor which may weigh against the granting of the order sought.

13.2.5 If the parties are able to agree the form of any case management order and/or interim relief, an agreed draft order (known as a draft consent order) should be filed, which will be subject to the Court's approval. A fee is payable when submitting a draft consent order and the reasons for requesting the order should be included in an accompanying application notice (N244). A draft order (even if is agreed by the parties) does not have the status of an order until it has been approved by the Court.

13.2.6 The parties should also comply with any requests from ACO staff members (such as requests for documents or information). Whilst these requests do not have the force of an order of the Court, failure to comply with such a request may be a factor considered by a judge or ACO lawyer that weighs against granting an interim order, permission to apply for judicial review, substantive relief or costs.

13.2.7 If the parties are aware that a case is likely to settle without the further involvement of the Court the ACO should be informed as soon as possible.

13.3 ROLE OF THE ADMINISTRATIVE COURT OFFICE STAFF

13.3.1 The staff members in the ACO handle the day to day running of cases. **1BA-81**

13.3.2 ACO staff members are not legally qualified and cannot give legal advice on the merits

---

[1] CPR 1.4.

[2] CPR 1.3.

of the claim. Staff members may be able to assist with the basic judicial review procedure. However, any advice from a member of staff as to procedure must not be considered to circumvent any legal provision (be that provision in statute, case law, the CPR, or a Court order) or the provisions of this Guide. Parties and the Court are responsible for the conduct of proceedings and the parties will not be able to rely on advice from the ACO as a reason for not complying with legal provisions.

13.3.3 ACO staff may contact the parties to request information or specific documents if that information or document is required under the CPR or is thought to be necessary to allow the Court to properly consider or case manage the claim. The parties should comply with any requests unless they are unable to do so, when written reasons should be given for the failure.

13.3.4 ACO staff have a duty to ensure that cases are being conducted by the parties in accordance with the overriding objective. Where it appears that a case is not being conducted in accordance with the overriding objective they have a duty to either make enquiries of the parties to establish the proper further course of action and/or to refer the case to an ACO lawyer or judge to consider further case management.

13.4 ROLE OF THE ADMINISTRATIVE COURT OFFICE LAWYERS

1BA-82 **13.4.1** An ACO lawyer must be a qualified solicitor or barrister or a Fellow of the Chartered Institute of Legal Executives.

13.4.2 ACO lawyers are independent of the parties. They do not give advice on the merits of the claim. An ACO lawyer may draw the parties' attention to provisions or precedents that may have an impact on the claim. If this is done the parties should consider what is said, but this should not be considered to be formal legal advice or a determination on the law. The parties have responsibility for the conduct of their own claim and the decision on the law is the preserve of the judge who considers the claim.

13.4.3 The role of the ACO lawyer is to provide advice on practice and procedure in the Administrative Court to whoever requires it; be that judges, ACO staff, practitioners, or litigants; to undertake legal research for the judges of the Administrative Court; and to communicate with the parties and exercise delegated judicial powers to ensure that cases in the Administrative Court are managed properly.

13.4.4 An ACO lawyer has a duty to ensure that the case is managed in accordance with the overriding objective and may enter into discussions with the parties or make case management orders (when applied for, when a case is referred to them by an ACO staff member, or of his/her own volition) to further the overriding objective and properly manage the case. Any order of an ACO lawyer will always be made after consideration of the papers without a hearing.

13.4.5 The specific powers that the ACO lawyer may exercise are delegated by the President of the Queen's Bench Division[1] and include:

13.4.5.1 determining when an urgent application should be referred to a judge;

13.4.5.2 adding, removing, or correcting parties other than interveners;

13.4.5.3 extending or abridging the time for the filing of any document required by the CPR, Practice Direction or court order;

13.4.5.4 extending the time of any procedural step required of a party;

13.4.5.5 directing the filing of any document required for the proper disposal of the case;

13.4.5.6 dismissing a claim or application when a party has failed to comply with any order, rule or Practice Direction;

13.4.5.7 determining applications for relief from sanctions;

13.4.5.8 determining applications to stay proceedings by consent or otherwise;

13.4.5.9 mandatory transfer of claims to the Upper Tribunal;

13.4.5.10 order that the Court is minded to transfer the claim to a different region, which order will result in transfer if no objection is received;[2]

13.4.5.11 determining applications by solicitors to come off record;

13.4.5.12 determining applications to vacate or adjourn hearings;

13.4.5.13 determining any application for an agreed judgment or order for the disposal of the proceedings.[3]

13.4.6 If a party is not content with an order of the ACO lawyer the party may request that the order is reviewed by a judge.[4] The review may take place on the papers or, if the party requesting the review asks for one, by way of an oral hearing.[5] The request for a review must be made by fil-

---

[1] CPR 54.1A(1).

[2] Where an objection is received the final decision on transfer will be taken by a judge.

[3] ACO lawyers will only be able to approve if permission has already been granted as they are subject to the restriction under CPR 54.1A(3)(a).

[4] CPR 54.1A(5).

[5] CPR 54.1A(5)-(6).

ing the request in writing (a letter or application notice may be used) within 7 days of the date on which the party was served with the ACO lawyer's order.[1] If the request is filed in time, there is no fee. If not, an application notice (N244) must be filed with the relevant fee.

13.5 THE MASTER OF THE ADMINISTRATIVE COURT

13.5.1 The Master has the power to make any order unless the CPR provides otherwise. In judicial review proceedings this means that the Master may deal with interim applications that do not come within the powers delegated to the ACO lawyers. This includes determining liability for costs and making summary assessments of costs (see Chapter 25 of this Guide for costs). The Master may make orders with or without a hearing.[2] **1BA-83**

13.5.2 Any challenge to the terms of an order made by the Master without a hearing must be made by applying for reconsideration of the order at an oral hearing.[3] The application must be made on Form N244 and the relevant fee is payable. The hearing will be listed before a judge.

13.5.3 A challenge to an order made by the Master at an oral hearing must be made by appealing to a High Court judge (see para 26.5 of this Guide).[4]

13.6 ROLE OF THE JUDICIARY

13.6.1 Judges of the Administrative Court have all the powers of the High Court under statute, the CPR and the inherent jurisdiction of the Court. **1BA-84**

13.6.2 Case management orders made without a hearing can (on the application of a party) be reconsidered at oral hearings (see para 16.7 of this Guide). If a party wishes to challenge an order made following an oral hearing, the challenge is made by appeal to the Court of Appeal (see para 26.4 of this Guide).

13.7 APPLICATIONS ONCE A CLAIM HAS COMMENCED

13.7.1 An application for directions or an interim order can be made at any time after commencement of the claim.[5] For pre-commencement applications, see para 16.2 of this Guide. For applications for interim relief, see Chapter 16 of this Guide. **1BA-85**

13.7.2 To make such an application:

13.7.2.1 the application must be filed with the ACO on an application notice. If the application needs to be decided within seven days, it should be made on Form N463. Any other application should be made on Form N244;

13.7.2.2 the application must be accompanied by payment of the relevant fee;

13.7.2.3 the application must be accompanied by evidence stating why the direction or order is required; and

13.7.2.4 a draft order should be enclosed with the application.

13.7.3 A copy of the application, evidence and accompanying draft order should be sent to the other parties to the claim to give them notice that the application is being made. Where the application has been made without giving notice to the other parties, the evidence supporting the application should explain why.

13.7.4 In the application notice the applicant may request that the application be considered at a hearing or by a judge on the papers. In either case, the ACO will send the papers to a judge, Master, or ACO lawyer to consider in the first instance. An order may be made on the papers alone if a hearing is not appropriate. Otherwise, a hearing may be listed, usually at short notice (see para 14.2.2 of this Guide).

13.7.5 It is the responsibility of each party to indicate a time estimate for any hearing to determine the application. This should include time for giving judgment.

13.7.6 The parties should agree any case management order if possible. If so, the application may be made by consent, although the Court has a discretion whether to grant or refuse or vary the agreed order. Applications made by consent in this way are made in accordance with the procedure outlined at para 24.4 of this Guide. (This deals with consent orders to end the claim, but the procedure is identical.)

13.7.7 Where a rule or court order expressly states that the parties may make an "application" (e.g. "the claimant may make an application for permission to adduce further evidence within 21 days"), the procedure outlined in this paragraph will be applicable:

13.7.7.1 If the application is made within any applicable time limit, the relief from sanction principles (see para 13.9 of this Guide) do not apply.

---

[1] CPR 54.1A(7).

[2] CPR 23.8.

[3] *R (MD (Afghanistan)) v Secretary of State for the Home Department* [2012] EWCA Civ 194, 1 WLR 2422.

[4] CPR 52A PD para 4.3.

[5] CPR Part 23.

13.7.7.2 Where a rule or court order allows for "representations" (for example, "the claimant may make representations on costs within 7 days"), it is permissible to file the written representations without the need for a formal application.

13.7.7.3 If they are emailed, the representations should be in the form of an attached Word document.

13.7.7.4 If the representations are not received within any applicable time limit then an application must be made, in accordance with this paragraph and para 13.9, to extend the time limit.

13.7.7.5 The Court may make an order of its own initiative, without hearing the parties or giving them an opportunity to make representations.[1] Where the Court makes such an order, a party may apply to have it set aside, varied or stayed.[2]

13.8 APPLICATIONS FOR A CLAIM TO BE STAYED

1BA-86 **13.8.1** If any party wishes to stay a claim (i.e. to suspend or freeze the progress of the claim), an application must be made to the Court (see para 13.7 of this Guide for the procedure). Save in exceptional circumstances, the party should seek the agreement of other parties to a stay and the application should be made on notice to them.

13.8.2 The duration of the proposed stay must be made clear in the application notice. Usually, a stay is sought pending the outcome of a particular event (for example, the conclusion of a related Tribunal appeal or a lead case in the Court of Appeal) or for a specific period of time (not usually exceeding a few weeks or months).

13.8.3 A stay will not normally be permitted to enable the defendant to reconsider the decision under challenge in the claim. Where the defendant agrees to reconsider, the judicial review claim should generally be withdrawn. A fresh claim can then be brought if the claimant wishes to challenge the reconsideration.[3] In any event, the Court's permission will be required to amend the Claim Form in light of any subsequent decision: see paras 7.11 (pre-permission) and 10.2 (post-permission) of this Guide for further guidance on this principle).

13.9 RELIEF FROM SANCTIONS

1BA-87 **13.9.1** Where a party has failed to comply with a provision under the CPR, a Practice Direction or an order of the Court which specifies a sanction for noncompliance, or a sanction can otherwise be implied, and the party wishes to set aside the sanction, that party must apply for relief from sanction.[4] If this is not done, the Court may refuse to consider that party's case[5] and/or make an adverse costs order against the party.[6] An implied sanction is a sanction that is not expressly imposed by a rule or direction but the consequence of a failure to comply would be the same as if the rule expressly imposed a sanction for non-compliance (for example, if a party fails to file an appeal notice or renewal notice within the relevant time period, and does not obtain an extension of time from the Court, the claim cannot proceed; the implied sanction is therefore one of striking out).[7]

13.9.2 An application for relief from sanction must be made using the interim applications procedure (see para 13.7 of this Guide). The application for relief from sanction may be considered by an ACO lawyer, the Master, or a judge.

13.9.3 When considering whether to grant an application for relief from sanction, the ACO lawyer, the Master, or a judge, must consider the principles outlined in *Denton v T.H. White Ltd* [2014] EWCA Civ 906, [2014] 1 WLR 3926. The three stages set out in Denton at [25]-[38] should be considered if making such an application.

---

[1] CPR 3.3(4).

[2] CPR 3.3(5).

[3] See *R (Bhatti) v Bury Metropolitan Borough Council* [2013] EWHC 3093, and *R (Yousuf) v Secretary of State for the Home Department* [2016] EWHC 663 (Admin).

[4] CPR 3.8(1) and *R (Hysaj) v Secretary of State for the Home Department* [2014] EWCA Civ 1633. In *Hysaj* a failure to file an appellant's notice in time required an application to extend time to file the notice retrospectively or the appeal could not progress. The Court of Appeal held that the relief from sanctions provisions applied as the lack of ability to appeal unless an extension of time was granted was an implied sanction. In *R (Fayad) v SSHD* [2018] EWCA Civ 54 where the Court of Appeal confirmed at [22] that the approach to be adopted to applications for extension of time in judicial review cases was that set out in *Denton v TH White Ltd* [2014] EWCA Civ 906, citing *Hysaj*. See also *R (Liberty) v SSHD and SSFCO (Procedural Matters)* [2018] EWHC 976 (Admin), [3].

[5] CPR 3.4(2)(c).

[6] CPR 44.2(4)(a), CPR 44.2(5)(c) and CPR 44.4(3)(a)(i).

[7] See *Sayers v Clarke Walker* [2002] EWCA Civ 645 and *Altomart Ltd v Salford Estates (No.2) Ltd* [2014] EWCA Civ 1408.

13.10 ABUSE OF THE COURT'S PROCESS

13.10.1 The Court will ensure that its process is not abused. If a party, a legal representative, or any other person acts in a way thought to be inappropriate the Court may: **1BA-88**

13.10.1.1 strike out a statement of case;[1]

13.10.1.2 make an adverse costs order requiring the person to pay a party's costs (see para 25.1 of this Guide);[2]

13.10.1.3 make a wasted costs order requiring a legal representative to pay a party's costs (see para 25.13 of this Guide);[3]

13.10.1.4 refer a legal representative to their regulatory body to consider further sanctions (see Chapter 18 of this Guide);[4]

13.10.1.5 make a civil restraint order (see Chapter 5 of this Guide).[5]

13.10.2 Before making any of these orders, the Court will usually give the relevant party, legal representative, or third party the opportunity to make representations.

13.10.3 Abuse of process includes (but is not limited to) acting in bad faith or with an improper purpose, attempting to re-litigate a decided issue and/or persistent failure to comply with rules or orders of the Court.[6]

13.11 COMMUNICATIONS WHICH ARE ABUSIVE OR OTHERWISE IMPROPER

13.11.1 The ACO is generally in a position to communicate with the parties in person at the public counter, by telephone, email, or post (see Annex 1 and Annex 8 for details) and will respond to communications if the communication so requires. The exception is where a person is subject to a notification of restricted communication. **1BA-89**

13.11.2 Such a notification will be sent by the manager of the ACO if it is considered that the person has been communicating with the ACO in a manner which is:

13.11.2.1 aggressive, intimidating, or harassing; or

13.11.2.2 persistent, time-consuming, and without proper purpose.

13.11.3 Its purpose is to inform the person that the form in which communication with the ACO is permitted is restricted to the manner outlined in the notice, that all other forms of communication will be ignored and that a communication in the permitted form will be responded to only if the communication raises a new issue that requires a response from the ACO.

13.11.4 Notifications of restricted communication will be sent in writing to the last known address for the person subject to the notification.

13.11.5 The person subject to the notification may request in writing at any time that the ACO manager rescinds the notification at his/her discretion. Such a request should include reasons for the request and will be responded to in writing.

13.11.6 A notification of restricted communication is made by the manager of the ACO as an employee of HMCTS. Any complaint against such a notification must be made in accordance with the HMCTS complaints policy.

13.11.7 The Court, under its inherent jurisdiction to control its own proceedings, may also make, rescind, or vary a notification of restricted communication.

13.11.8 Communications with the Court in which any representation is made on a matter of substance or procedure - and which is not purely routine, uncontentious or administrative - must, absent an identified compelling reason, be copied to all other parties and their representatives.[7]

14 LISTING

14.1 LISTING POLICY

14.1.1 The Administrative Court Listing Policy is at Annex 4 to this Guide. This section of the Guide will summarise the procedure in the policy, but the policy itself should be referred to for full details. **1BA-90**

14.1.2 The policy is intended to be applied flexibly. The ACO may, where it considers it appropriate to do so, list cases otherwise than in accordance with the policy.

14.1.3 A particular case may be listed in a particular way by reason of a judicial order.

---

[1] CPR 3.4(2).

[2] CPR 44.2(4)(a), CPR 44.2(5) and CPR 44.4(3)(a)(i).

[3] s. 51(6) of the Senior Courts Act 1981 and CPR 46.8.

[4] *R (Hamid) v SSHD* [2012] EWHC 3070 (Admin).

[5] CPR 3.11, CPR 3C PD, and CPR 23.12.

[6] Examples taken from *Halsbury's Laws of England*, Vol.11 Civil Procedure (2015), Part 19, §1044, and from *R (Ashraf) v Secretary of State for the Home Department* [2013] EWHC 4028 (Admin).

[7] CPR 39.8.

14.2 LISTING PROCEDURE

1BA-91 **14.2.1** Permission hearings will usually be fixed for a date without seeking the views of representatives. Several weeks' notice of the hearing will normally be given.

14.2.2 Interim relief hearings are usually listed in the same way as permission hearings. If interim relief is required urgently the hearing may be listed at short notice with little or no consultation as to the availability of the parties. The application will usually be fixed on the basis that it will take no longer than 30 minutes to hear, unless a different time estimate is required by a judge, master, or ACO lawyer. If a party considers that the application will require a longer hearing, the suggested time estimate must be confirmed as soon as possible, in writing with reasons, and is subject to the Court's approval.

14.2.3 For substantive hearings, the ACO will usually attempt to agree a suitable date for the hearing. In cases where counsel is involved, this will generally occur in one of two ways:

14.2.3.1 In the ACO in London, the ACO will telephone or email counsel's clerks and/or solicitors to arrange an appointment to fix the hearing. Five working days' notice will be given of the appointment. At the appointment, if parties are unable to agree a date that is also acceptable to the Court, the ACO will list the matter for first available date convenient to the Court.

14.2.3.2 In ACOs outside London, the ACO will either email or telephone counsel's clerks or solicitors for all sides to request the dates of availability for counsel on the Court record (that is to say the Court has been informed counsel is/are acting). Unless availability is provided over the telephone at the time of the initial contact the clerk will be informed that details of availability must be provided within 48 hours, otherwise the ACO will list the matter for first available date convenient to the Court. If the availability of all counsel corresponds, the ACO will check for judicial availability and list accordingly; alternatively, if parties are unable to agree a date that is also acceptable to the Court, the ACO will list the matter for first available date convenient to the Court.

14.2.4 In some planning cases, it may be necessary for dates to be imposed so that cases are heard within an appropriate timescale.[1]

14.2.5 Due to limited judicial time the ACO is unable routinely to take into account the availability of instructing solicitors.

14.2.6 If there are good reasons why a litigant in person is unable to attend on particular dates, the ACO will take this into account when listing.

14.2.7 A substantive hearing will be allocated a hearing time estimate either by the judge granting permission or by the ACO. If a party considers that the application will require a longer hearing, the suggested time estimate must be confirmed as soon as possible, in writing with reasons, and is subject to the Court's approval.

14.2.8 Once the hearing has been listed, all parties will be sent a listing notice by the ACO which confirms the date, location, and time estimate for the hearing. The start time of the hearing will not be in the listing notice. Generally, Administrative Court hearings start at 10.30 am, but this may be changed up to 2 pm on the day before the hearing. The parties should check the start time on the day before the hearing by telephoning the ACO or visiting *https://www.gov.uk/government/collections/royal-courts-of-justice-and-rolls-building-daily-court-lists.*

14.3 DIVISIONAL COURTS

1BA-92 **14.3.1** A Divisional Court consists of two or more judges sitting together.

14.3.2 Divisional Courts may be convened for any case in the High Court.[2] They are generally convened for cases that raise issues of general public importance or criminal cases where there is no right of appeal to the Court of Appeal[3] which are not straightforward or are likely to set a precedent. A direction that the substantive hearing will be before a Divisional Court may be given by the judge granting permission[4] or at any time thereafter.

14.3.3 If a judicial review claim is allocated to the Divisional Court, the listing arrangements may differ, particularly if the case is urgent. The ACO will not be able to offer as many available dates for a hearing and will not generally take account of the availability of counsel when listing the hearing.

14.4 APPLYING TO ADJOURN A HEARING THAT HAS BEEN LISTED

1BA-93 **14.4.1** If a party wishes to apply to adjourn a listed hearing the application must be made in one of the following ways:

14.4.1.1 By agreeing with all other parties that the hearing should be adjourned and filing a

---

[1] *Westminster City Council v Secretary of State for Housing, Communities and Local Government* [2020] EWHC 1472 (Admin), [61].

[2] s. 66 of the Senior Courts Act 1981.

[3] See para 25.7 of this Guide.

[4] CPR 54.10(2)(b).

draft consent order for the approval of the Court.[1] The order must be signed by all parties and accompanied by the relevant fee (although see para 14.4.1.2 below). The parties may also include further directions in such a draft order. The parties should not assume that a hearing has been adjourned unless they have been informed by the ACO that the consent order has been approved. Reasons for the hearing being adjourned should be provided.

14.4.1.2 If the parties agree a consent order to adjourn the hearing, which does not seek other directions, and they file the draft consent order with the ACO more than 14 days before the hearing, then no fee is payable. The request should be made on form AC001. The other provisions noted at paras 14.4.1.1 and 24.4 of this Guide will still apply.

14.4.1.3 If the parties cannot agree a consent order, a party may make an application to adjourn the hearing (see the interim applications procedure at para 13.7 of this Guide). Such an application must be made on Form N244 and be accompanied by the relevant fee. The application notice should include the reasons for the request, any attempts made to agree the request with the other parties and any responses from the other parties to that request. A draft of the order sought should also be attached to the application.

14.4.2 The decision to adjourn a listed hearing is made by a judge, not the ACO. Even if all parties agree, an adjournment will not be granted without good reason. Where the sole reason is the unavailability of counsel, the application is unlikely to be granted.

PART C:—SPECIFIC PRACTICE POINTS

15 THE DUTY OF CANDOUR AND CO-OPERATION WITH THE COURT

15.1 THE DUTY

15.1.1 In most civil claims, the parties are required to give standard disclosure pursuant to CPR Part 31. In judicial review claims, disclosure is not required unless the Court orders otherwise.[2] **1BA-94**

15.1.2 However, in judicial review proceedings there is a special duty which applies to all parties: the "duty of candour". This requires the parties to assist the Court by ensuring that information relevant to the issues in the claim is drawn to the Court's attention, whether it supports or undermines their case.

15.1.3 Where a party relies on a document, it will be good practice to disclose the document rather than merely summarise it, because the document is the best evidence of what it says.[3] The same will be true in other situations where the precise terms of a document are relevant to an issue in the case. In such situations, it may in practice be difficult to comply with the duty of candour without disclosing the document.

15.1.4 However, this may not be enough. The duty of candour may also require the party in its statements of case to identify and explain the significance of information and/or documents adverse to that party's case.[4]

15.2 THE DUTY AS IT APPLIES TO CLAIMANTS AND THEIR REPRESENTATIVES

15.2.1 A claimant is under a duty to make full disclosure to the Court of material facts and known impediments to the claim (e.g. alternative remedy, delay, adverse case law, statutory ouster, change of circumstances).[5] This duty is a continuing one: it applies throughout the judicial review procedure. **1BA-95**

15.2.2 The fact that a defendant has a right to file an Acknowledgment of Service and summary grounds of defence does not justify a claimant in taking a more relaxed view of the duty of candour.[6]

15.2.3 The duty of candour applies to all claims and applications. However, it applies with particular force to applications made in circumstances where the other party or parties will not have the opportunity to respond (such as urgent applications). In this context, the claimant must:[7]

---

[1] See para 24.4 of this Guide for the procedure for filing a consent order in the context of ending a claim - the procedure is identical.

[2] CPR 54A PD para. 10.2.

[3] *Tweed v Parades Commission for Northern Ireland* [2006] UKHL 53, [2007] 1 AC, 650, [4] and [39].

[4] See e.g. *R (Hoareau) v Secretary of State for Foreign and Commonwealth Affairs* [2018] EWHC 1508 (Admin), [19]-[20]; *R (Citizens UK) v Secretary of State for the Home Department* [2018] EWCA Civ 1812, [2018] 4 WLR 123, [105]-[106].

[5] See Sir Michael Fordham, *Judicial Review Handbook* (7th ed., 2020), §10.3. The equivalent passage in a previous edition was approved by Sedley LJ in *R (Khan) v Secretary of State for the Home Department* [2008] EWHC 1367 (Admin), [12].

[6] *R (Khan) v Secretary of State for the Home Department* [2016] EWCA Civ 416, [35]-[36].

[7] *R (DVP) v Secretary of State for the Home Department* [2021] EWHC 606 (Admin), [8]-[9], approv-

15.2.3.1 disclose any fact (whether it supports or undermines the application) which it is material for the Court to know when dealing with the application, including (for example) any fact which is relevant to the degree of urgency;

15.2.3.2 make the Court aware of the issues that are likely to arise and the possible difficulties in the application or underlying claim; and

15.2.3.3 present the information in a fair and even-handed manner, and in a way which is not designed simply to promote his own case.

15.2.4 The duty of co-operation with the Court means that claimants and their representatives must reassess the viability and propriety of a challenge, and review the claimant's continued compliance with the duty of candour, as the claim progresses and in particular:

15.2.4.1 in light of the defendant's Acknowledgment of Service and summary grounds of defence;[1]

15.2.4.2 in the light of the detailed grounds of defence and evidence;[2] and

15.2.4.3 in the light of any material change of circumstances.[3]

15.3 THE DUTY AS IT APPLIES TO DEFENDANT PUBLIC AUTHORITIES AND THEIR REPRESENTATIVES

1BA-96 **15.3.1** A public authority's duty of candour and co-operation with the Court is "self policing". There is a particular obligation on solicitors and barristers acting for public authorities to ensure that it is fulfilled. The duty arises because public authorities are engaged in a common enterprise with the Court to fulfil the public interest in upholding the rule of law. They are accordingly required to assist the Court with full and accurate explanations of all the facts relevant to the issues which the Court must decide.[4]

15.3.2 The duty of candour has been recognised as applying at, or even before, the permission stage as well as at the substantive stage. However, what is required to discharge the duty at the substantive stage will be more extensive than what is required before permission has been granted.[5]

15.3.3 At the permission stage, the Summary Grounds should identify any material facts, highlight any material matters of factual dispute and provide a brief summary of the reasoning underlying the measures in respect of which permission to apply for judicial review is sought (unless the defendant gives reasons why the application for permission can be determined without that information).[6]

15.3.4 At the substantive stage, the duty requires a defendant in the detailed grounds of defence or evidence to identify any relevant facts and the reasoning underlying the measure in respect of which permission to apply for judicial review has been granted.[7] The duty of candour is a continuing one[8] and applies after detailed grounds and evidence have been filed and served.

15.3.5 The duty of candour means that:

15.3.5.1 the process of preparing statements of case and evidence must be Conducted "with all the cards face upwards on the table";[9] public authorities must not be selective in their disclosure;[10]

15.3.5.2 pleadings and evidence must be drafted in clear, unambiguous language, must not deliberately or unintentionally obscure areas of central relevance and must not be ambiguous or economical with the truth or contain "spin";[11] and

15.3.5.3 pleadings and evidence must not mislead by omission, for example by non-disclosure

---

ing the 2020 edition of this section of the Guide.

[1] *R (Ben Hoare Bell Solicitors) v Lord Chancellor* [2015] EWHC 523 (Admin), [43].

[2] *R (Bateman) v Legal Services Commission* [2001] EWHC 797 (Admin), [21].

[3] *R v Horseferry Road Magistrates' Court ex p. Prophet* [1995] Env LR 104, 112; *R (Ben Hoare Bell Solicitors) v Lord Chancellor* [2015] EWHC 523 (Admin), [43].

[4] *R (Hoareau) v Secretary of State for Foreign and Commonwealth Affairs* [2018] EWHC 1508 (Admin), [18]-[20]; *R (Citizens UK) v Secretary of State for the Home Department* [2018] EWCA Civ 1812, [2018] 4 WLR 123, [105]-[106].

[5] *R (Terra Services Ltd) v National Crime Agency* [2019] EWHC 1933 (Admin), [9], [14].

[6] CPR 54A PD, para 6.2(2).

[7] CPR 54A PD para. 10.1.

[8] *R (Legard) v Royal London Borough of Kensington and Chelsea* [2018] EWHC 32 (Admin), [174].

[9] *R v Lancashire County Council ex p. Huddleston* [1986] 2 All ER 941, 945; *R (Hoareau) v Secretary of State for Foreign and Commonwealth Affairs* [2018] EWHC 1508 (Admin), [16].

[10] *Lancashire County Council v Taylor* [2005] 1 WLR 2668, [60]; *R (National Association of Health Stores) v Secretary of State for Health* [2005] EWCA Civ 154, [47]; *R (Hoareau) v Secretary of State for Foreign and Commonwealth Affairs* [2018] EWHC 1508 (Admin), [21].

[11] *In the Matter of an Application by Brenda Downes for Judicial Review* [2006] NIQB 77, [31]; *R (Hoareau) v Secretary of State for Foreign and Commonwealth Affairs* [2018] EWHC 1508 (Admin), [22]; *R (Citizens UK) v Secretary of State for the Home Department* [2018] EWCA Civ 1812, [2018] 4 WLR 123, [106(4)].

of a material document or fact or by failing to identify the significance of a document or fact.[1]

15.3.6 The duty of co-operation with the Court means that defendants and their representatives have an ongoing duty to consider whether their defence remains viable, particularly after the grant of permission.[2]

15.4 INTERESTED PARTIES

15.4.1 The duty of candour applies to interested parties.[3] The same is true of the duty to co-operate with the Court. **1BA-97**

15.5 REDACTIONS

15.5.1 Parts of a document which otherwise fall to be disclosed under the duty of candour may be redacted if those parts: **1BA-98**

15.5.1.1 are confidential and irrelevant to the issues in the case;

15.5.1.2 attract legal professional privilege;

15.5.1.3 are subject to a statutory restriction on their disclosure; or

15.5.1.4 attract public interest immunity (see Chapter 19 of this Guide).

15.5.2 However, the fact that information in a document is exempt from disclosure under the Freedom of Information Act 2000 does not, in and of itself, mean that the information is subject to a statutory restriction on its disclosure or can be properly withheld from disclosure in legal proceedings. Where a redacted or edited document is included in evidence, the fact that redactions have been made, and the reasons for them, should be made clear, preferably on the face of the redacted document. Documents should never be filed or served in an edited form without making clear that they have been edited.[4]

15.5.3 Closed material proceedings are considered separately in Chapter 19.E

16 INTERIM RELIEF

16.1 WHEN IS INTERIM RELIEF APPROPRIATE?

16.1.1 A party (usually the claimant) may request an interim remedy. Examples include: **1BA-99**

16.1.1.1 an interim injunction prohibiting the defendant from taking some action that he or she plans to take (e.g. preventing the Secretary of State for the Home Department from removing a claimant from the UK);[5] and

16.1.1.2 an interim injunction requiring the defendant to act in a certain way (e.g. requiring a local authority to provide the claimant with accommodation).

16.1.2 Interim relief is usually requested in the Claim Form, but an application for it can be made at any stage of proceedings.

16.1.3 Exceptionally, an application for interim relief may be made before starting judicial review proceedings: see para 16.2 below. The Court may only grant an interim order before the claim has been issued where the matter is urgent or it is otherwise necessary to do so in the interests of justice.[6]

16.2 INTERIM RELIEF APPLICATIONS BEFORE STARTING PROCEEDINGS

16.2.1 Careful thought should be given to whether it is appropriate to make an application for interim relief before starting proceedings. It is normally better to apply for interim relief at the same time as lodging the claim papers. This makes it easier for the Court to understand the issues and is likely to save costs. **1BA-100**

16.2.2 If it is necessary to make an application before starting the claim, and no short term compromise can be reached, the applicant should file an application notice with the ACO (on Form

---

[1] *R (Citizens UK) v Secretary of State for the Home Department* [2018] EWCA Civ 1812, [2018] 4 WLR 123, [106(5)].

[2] See the observations about the analogous duty on parties to appeal proceedings in *R (N) v North Tyneside Borough Council* [2010] EWCA Civ 135, [2010] ELR 312, [18].

[3] *Belize Alliance of Conservation Non-Governmental Organisations v Department of the Environment* [2004] UKPC 6, [87]; *R (Qualter) v Preston Crown Court* [2019] EWHC 906 (Admin), [32].

[4] *R (GA) v Secretary of State for the Home Department* [2021] EWHC 868 (Admin), [19].

[5] Note that, where UTIAC has jurisdiction, it is the proper forum for such an application: see para 6.5 of this Guide.

[6] CPR 25.2(2)(b).

N244 or, if the application needs to be decided within 7 days, Form N463).[1] This must be accompanied by the relevant fee and supported by evidence establishing why the order is required[2] and a copy of the draft order should be enclosed.

16.2.3 Where possible, a copy of the application, evidence, and draft order should be sent to the proposed defendants and interested parties to give them notice that the application is being made.[3] Where the application has been made without giving notice to the other parties, the evidence supporting the application should explain why the application has been made without giving notice.[4]

16.2.4 The claimant will generally be required to undertake to file a Claim Form and grounds of claim, usually within a short period, or, if no satisfactory undertaking is offered, will be directed by the Court to do so.

16.3 INTERIM APPLICATIONS MADE WHEN THE CLAIM IS FILED

1BA-101 **16.3.1** Applications for interim relief are normally made when the claim is filed. In this case, the application should be set out in section 8 of the Claim Form (Form N461).

16.3.2 The application for interim relief will be considered by the judge on the papers, usually at the same time as the application for permission to apply for judicial review. If the application is considered at this time, no additional fee is required. The judge considering the application for interim relief alongside permission may either make an order based on the papers alone or order that the application for interim relief be dealt with at a hearing in Court: see para 14.2.2 of this Guide.

16.4 INTERIM RELIEF APPLICATIONS MADE AFTER PROCEEDINGS HAVE BEEN COMMENCED

1BA-102 **16.4.1** If it becomes necessary to make an application for interim relief after the claim has been commenced, the applicant should issue an application. If the application is time-sensitive but does not require a decision within seven days, the party should make that clear in the Application Notice (Form N244) and any covering letter and state the period within which the Court is requested to consider the application. The application must be served on all the other parties. The Court will only rarely consider the application if the opposing party has not been given an opportunity to respond in writing. If the application needs to be decided within seven days, it should be made on Form N463.

16.5 PROCEDURE FOR DETERMINING APPLICATIONS FOR INTERIM RELIEF

1BA-103 **16.5.1** The Court will rarely grant any form of interim relief without establishing what the other parties to the claim say in respect of the application. The Court will usually permit other parties the opportunity to respond to the application. In an urgent case, the time allowed for response may be short.

16.5.2 If time does not permit the defendant to be heard, then the Court will consider granting interim relief without a hearing for a very short period until other parties have been able to make submissions (either in writing or at a hearing).

16.6 CRITERIA FOR DECIDING APPLICATIONS FOR INTERIM RELIEF

1BA-104 **16.6.1** When considering whether to grant interim relief while a judicial review claim is pending, the judge will consider whether there is a real issue to be tried and whether the balance of convenience lies in favour of granting the interim order.[5] This involves balancing the harm to the claimant that would be caused if interim relief is not granted and the claim later succeeds against the harm to the defendant, any third parties and the public interest that would be caused if interim relief is granted and the claim later fails.

16.6.2 The strength of the public interest in permitting a public authority's decision to remain in force will depend on all the circumstances. Where interim relief is sought to prevent the enforcement of primary legislation, there is a strong public interest in allowing the public authority to

---

[1] CPR 23.3(1).
[2] CPR 25.3(2).
[3] CPR 23.4(1).
[4] CPR 25.3(3).
[5] *R (Medical Justice) v Secretary of State for the Home Department* [2010] EWHC 1425 (Admin), [6]-[13], applying *American Cyanamid Company v Ethicon Limited* [1975] AC 396.

continue to enforce an apparently authentic law pending the determination of the challenge.[1] Where subordinate legislation[2] or policy is challenged,[3] the public interest weighing against interim relief may also be strong, albeit less so than where the target is primary legislation.

16.6.3 Where a claimant seeks to restrain publication of information by a public authority which is obliged or empowered to do so, the Court must consider the rights of those who would otherwise be entitled to receive the information. These rights are protected by Article 10 ECHR and s. 12 of the Human Rights Act 1998. This means that interim relief will only be granted for "the most compelling reasons" or in "exceptional circumstances".[4]

16.6.4 In all cases the procedure for dealing with applications for interim relief will be controlled by the Court, and will be such as the Court deems appropriate to achieve a fair determination of issues. For example, sometimes, the Court may respond to an application for interim relief by ordering expedition of the substantive claim instead of hearing the application for interim relief separately.

16.7 CHALLENGING A DECISION ON AN APPLICATION FOR INTERIM RELIEF

16.7.1 If an application for an interim order has been decided without a hearing (and the parties did not consent to the application being determined without a hearing), either party has the right to apply to have the order set aside, varied or stayed.[5] **1BA-105**

16.7.2 The application must be made by Application Notice (Form N244), which must be issue within 7 days of service of the order challenged (unless the order specifies a different period).[6]

16.7.3 If a hearing of the application is required within a particular period, the application must make that clear. This point should also be made in any covering letter. The application must be served on all other parties.

16.7.4 The application will be determined at a hearing. Where there is an urgent need for a hearing, and the matter cannot wait until the Court's sitting hours, the application can be made by a party's legal representative to the out of hours judge in accordance with para 17.8 of this Guide. In such circumstances the practitioner will be asked to undertake to pay the relevant fee on the next working day.

16.7.5 If the parties have consented to a decision on interim relief on the papers, or if an order has been made following a hearing, then the order will be final (subject to any appeal). A party who wishes to challenge a decision made without a hearing must apply to have it set aside, varied or stayed in the Administrative Court before an appeal can be lodged. Any appeal must be commenced within 21 days of the date on which the order appealed was made.[7] See Chapter 26 of this Guide for appeals.

16.8 REMOVAL CASES

16.8.1 Particular rules apply where a decision by UK Visas and Immigration ("UKVI") to remove a person from the jurisdiction is challenged before the removal takes effect. These are set out in Section II of CPR 54A PD. Such challenges generally fall within the jurisdiction of UTIAC: see para 6.5 of this Guide. **1BA-106**

16.8.2 A person who makes an application for permission to apply for judicial review of such a decision must:

16.8.2.1 file a Claim Form and a copy at Court;[8] and

16.8.2.2 indicate on the face of the Claim Form that Section II of CPR 54A PD applies (which can be done by ticking the relevant box in section 4 of the Claim Form).[9]

16.8.3 The Claim Form must:

16.8.3.1 be accompanied by a copy of the removal directions, the decision to which the application relates and any document served with the removal directions (including any document which contains UK Visas and Immigration's ("UKVI") factual summary of the case);[10]

---

[1] *R v Secretary of State for Transport ex p. Factortame* [1991] 1 AC 603, 674C-D; *R (Medical Justice) v Secretary of State for the Home Department* [2010] EWHC 1425 (Admin), [12]-[13].

[2] *R v HM Treasury ex p. British Telecommunications plc* [1994] 1 CMLR 621, [41].

[3] *R (Medical Justice) v Secretary of State for the Home Department* [2010] EWHC 1425 (Admin), [13].

[4] *R (Barking and Dagenham College) v Office for Students* [2019] EWHC 2667 (Admin), [30]-[39]; *R (Governing Body of X School) v Office for Standards in Education* [2020] EWCA Civ 594, [2020] EMLR 22, [77]-[79].

[5] CPR 3.3(5).

[6] CPR 3.3(6).

[7] *R (Nolson) v Stevenage Borough Council* [2020] EWCA Civ 379, [2021] HLR 2, [18].

[8] CPR 54A PD para 17.2(1).

[9] CPR 54A PD para 17.2(1)(a).

[10] CPR 54A PD para 17.2(1)(b).

16.8.3.2 contain or be accompanied by a clear and concise statement of the claimant's grounds for bringing the claim for judicial review;[1]

16.8.3.3 state the claimant's Home Office reference number.[2]

16.8.4 If the claimant is unable to comply with any of the requirements in para 16.8.3, the Claim Form must contain or be accompanied by a statement of the reasons why.[3]

16.8.5 Immediately upon issue, copies of the issued Claim Form and accompanying documents must be sent to the address specified by UKVI.[4] It must also be served on the defendant within 7 days of the date of issue.[5]

16.8.6 The Court has set out certain principles to be applied when such applications are made.[6] In particular:

16.8.6.1 steps to challenge removal should be taken as early as possible, and should be taken promptly after receipt of notice of a removal window; and

16.8.6.2 applications to the Court for interim relief should be made with as much notice to the Secretary of State as is practicably feasible.

17 URGENT CASES

17.1 GENERAL

1BA-107 **17.1.1** The Court has procedures to deal with cases that have to be considered urgently. This is an important part of the Court's work in the public interest. However, some litigants and practitioners have misused or abused these procedures. This can mean that claimants with genuinely urgent cases wait longer than they should. The Divisional Court has addressed this issue and given guidance about applications for urgent consideration.[7] This section of the Guide reflects that guidance.

17.2 ASSESSING WHETHER A CASE IS URGENT AND, IF SO, HOW URGENT

1BA-108 **17.2.1** It will very often be possible to point to a reason why the claimant's interests would be better served if an application for interim relief or permission to apply for judicial review were determined quickly. However, this is not enough to justify using the Court's procedures for urgent consideration. Those procedures are made available only for urgent cases where there is a genuine need for the application to be considered urgently.

17.2.2 Such a need may arise where:

17.2.2.1 the claimant seeks an interim order preventing a defendant from doing something with irreparable consequences which may be done imminently or requiring the defendant to do something immediately or within a very short period (see Chapter 16 of this Guide); or

17.2.2.2 no interim relief is sought, but there are compelling reasons for applying for abridgement of time for service of the Acknowledgment of Service or other procedural directions and, if the directions are to be effective, it is necessary for the application to be considered urgently.

17.2.3 Litigants and their representatives should consider carefully the period within which their application needs to be considered. It is not acceptable to request consideration in a period shorter than genuinely required: see para 16.1.1 of this Guide.

17.2.4 In cases where there is a genuine need for the application to be considered urgently within 7 days after it is filed, Form N463 (Judicial Review: Application for Urgent Consideration) should be used.

17.2.5 In cases where the application needs to be considered quickly, but not in less than 7 days from filing, Form N244 should be used, with a cover letter explaining the required timescale for consideration by reference to the Administrative Court Listing Policy set out at Annex 4.

17.3 THE APPLICATION FOR URGENT CONSIDERATION

1BA-109 **17.3.1** Any application for urgent consideration using Form N463 must clearly set out:[8]

17.3.1.1 the circumstances giving rise to the urgency. If the representative was instructed late, or the form is filed only shortly before the end of the working day, it is necessary to explain why;

17.3.1.2 the timescale sought for the consideration of the application;

---

[1] CPR 54A PD para 17.2(1)(c).

[2] CPR 54A PD para 17.2(1)(d).

[3] CPR 54A PD para.17.2(1).

[4] CPR 54A PD para.17.2(2).

[5] CPR 54.7.

[6] *R (Madan) v Secretary of State for the Home Department (Practice Note)* [2007] EWCA Civ 770, [2007] 1 WLR 2891, endorsed in *R (SB (Afghanistan)) v Secretary of State for the Home Department* [2018] EWCA Civ 215, [2018] 1 WLR 4457, [55]-[56].

[7] *R (DVP & Others) v SSHD* [2021] EWHC 606 (Admin).

[8] CPR 54B PD para. 1.2.

17.3.1.3 the date by which any substantive hearing should take place;

17.3.1.4 that the defendant and any interested parties were put on notice of the application for urgent consideration (or if not, why not, and the efforts made to give notice to them).

17.3.2 This information must be set out on the face of the form. It is not sufficient to cross-refer to other documents.[1] All boxes must be completed. All relevant facts must be include. The beneficiary (or beneficiaries) of the intended relief and the terms of any proposed injunction must be clearly identified.[2]

17.3.3 All parties to judicial review proceedings must comply with their duty of candour and co-operation with the Court. The duty applies with particular force to applicants for urgent consideration, because their applications are likely to be made on limited notice to the defendant and may have to be determined without giving the respondent an opportunity to respond: see para 15.2.3 of this Guide.

17.3.4 Form N463 must be signed by the Claimant's advocate and be supported by a Statement of Truth. If time is so pressing such that it is impossible to obtain full instructions, legal representatives must alert the Court to any limitations in the evidence in order to allow a proper assessment of its probative value.

17.4 THE DOCUMENTS THAT MUST ACCOMPANY THE APPLICATION

17.4.1 In almost all cases, Form N463 is filed together with a Claim Form and full claim papers **1BA-110**
(including supporting documentation).[3] If an urgent application is made after proceeding shave been commenced and Form N461 has already been served on the other parties, there is no need to serve From N461 with Form N463.

17.4.2 However, in some exceptionally urgent cases, it may be filed with an Application Notice (Form N244) prior to issue of the Claim Form: see para 16.2 of this Guide.

17.4.3 The application for urgent consideration must be accompanied by an indexed and paginated bundle ("the application bundle") containing:

17.4.3.1 if the application is being filed together with the Claim Form, the Claim Form and full claim papers;

17.4.3.2 if the application is being filed before issue of the claim, the Application Notice and any accompanying documents;

17.4.3.3 in any case, the pre-action communications concerning the claim and all communications with the defendant concerning the application for urgent consideration;[4] and

17.4.3.4 a draft of the order sought.

17.5 HOW TO FILE THE APPLICATION AND APPLICATION BUNDLE

17.5.1 Applications for urgent consideration in London may be made in the Administrative **1BA-111**
Court on any working day between 10 am and 4.30 pm. During these times:

17.5.1.1 a High Court Judge authorised to sit in the Administrative Court ("the immediates judge") is available to deal with applications on paper;

17.5.1.2 accordingly, applications for interim orders should not generally be made to the Queen's Bench Division interim applications judge, nor to any other part of the High Court.

17.5.2 If a matter is brought before the Queen's Bench interim applications judge (or any inappropriate Court) between 10am and 4.30pm on a working day, the judge may refuse to deal with the application and direct that the application or proceedings be filed in the ACO.

17.5.3 On working days outside the hours of 10am to 4.30pm, and on non-working days, applications for interim orders should be directed to the Queen's Bench Division out of hours judge:[5] see para 17.8 of this Guide.

17.5.4 Urgent applications may be filed with the Court in London by email to *immediates@administrativecourtoffice.justice.gov.uk*. A size restriction of 20 MB applies. They may also be filed by delivery to the Administrative Court Office at the Royal Courts of Justice, Strand, London WC2A 2LL.[6]

17.5.5 Where an urgent application needs to be made to the Administrative Court outside London, the application must be made to the relevant Office and to the appropriate email address: see CPR 54C PD and Annex 1.[7]

---

[1] *R (DVP & Others) v SSHD* [2021] EWHC 606 (Admin), [15]-[17], [59]-[64].
[2] *R (KMI) v SSHD* [2021] EWHC 477 (Admin), [39].
[3] *Practice Statement (Administrative Court: Listing and Urgent Cases)* [2002] 1 WLR 810.
[4] CPR 54B PD para. 1.3.
[5] CPR 54B PD para. 1.1.
[6] CPR 54B PD para. 1.4.
[7] CPR 54B PD para 1.5.

17.6 SERVICE OF THE APPLICATION

1BA-112 **17.6.1** The application for urgent consideration, together with the application bundle, must be served on the defendant and interested parties, advising them that the application has been made and of their right to make representations. This must be done either (a) before the application is filed with the Court, or if that is not possible (b) when the application is filed with the Court.[1]

17.7 CONSIDERATION OF THE APPLICATION BY THE COURT

1BA-113 **17.7.1** Once the application has been filed, it will be referred to the immediates judge or another judge. The Court will consider the application within the time requested wherever possible.[2]

17.7.2 If possible, the Court will give the defendant and any interested party the opportunity to make representations before making any order. It may be necessary to set a very tight deadline for representations. Where it is not possible for a defendant to respond by the deadline, the Court is likely to proceed to consider the application without representations from the defendant.

17.7.3 The Court will normally deal with the application on paper. It may make procedural directions only (e.g. an order abridging time for the defendant to file an Acknowledgment of Service), but defendants should be aware that the order may alternatively (or in addition) include a prohibitory or mandatory injunction.

17.7.4 Prohibitory or mandatory injunctions granted on paper against a public authority do not generally contain a penal notice. However, that does not detract from their binding effect. Breach of such an injunction can result in proceedings for contempt of court.[3] Public authorities should ensure that they have in place proper arrangements to identify promptly and act upon injunction orders made on paper by the Administrative Court.

17.7.5 In some cases, the Court may decide that the application should be heard orally within a specified time. If so, the ACO will liaise with the parties to fix the hearing date. It may not be possible to accommodate all counsels' availability dates.

17.7.6 The judge dealing with the application may conclude that the application was not urgent and is suitable for disposal according to the Court's ordinary procedures. If so, the judge will refuse to deal with the matter on an urgent basis, and may:

17.7.6.1 make an adverse costs order against the applicant or his legal representatives (see para 25.1 on costs); and/or

17.7.6.2 refer the papers to the Hamid judge to consider whether any legal representative should be referred to the relevant professional regulator: see Chapter 18 of this Guide.

17.7.7 If an urgent application is refused on the papers, the applicant may request that the decision be reconsidered at an oral hearing (see para 16.7 of this Guide for the procedure). The application must be made by filing the application notice with the ACO, not by applying to the Queen's Bench Division interim applications judge, or any other Court.

17.8 OUT OF HOURS APPLICATIONS

1BA-114 **17.8.1** The out of hours service is not available to litigants in person.

17.8.2 Legal representatives must consider carefully whether an out of hours application is required. They should make such an application only if the matter cannot wait until the next working day.

17.8.3 If it is necessary to make an out of hours application, the application should be made to the Queen's Bench Division out of hours judge. The barrister or solicitor acting should telephone 020 7947 6000[4] and speak to the Queen's Bench Division out of hours duty clerk.

17.8.4 The out of hours duty clerk will require the practitioner to complete the out of hours form, which can be downloaded from the Government website *https://www.gov.uk/government/publications/form-qbd-oha-out-of-hours-application-queens-bench-division* and emailed to *DutyClerkQB@justice.gov.uk.* (Please do not send emails to this address unless invited to do so by the out of hours duty clerk.)

17.8.5 The judge may deal with the application on paper. Alternatively, arrangements may be made to hear the application by telephone or remotely. The judge may telephone any other party to the application if appropriate. (This is often done in immigration cases where the application seeks a stay on removal.)

17.8.6 The duty of candour assumes added significance when a judge is asked to make an order in a short time frame and without any (or any substantial) opportunity for the defendant to make representations: see para 15.2.3 of this Guide.

---

[1] CPR 54B PD para 1.7

[2] CPR 54B PD para 1.8

[3] *R (JM) v Croydon London Borough Council (Practice Note)* [2009] EWHC 2474 (Admin); *R (Mohammad) v Secretary of State for the Home Department* [2021] EWHC 240 (Admin), [23] and [26]; *R (KMI) v Secretary of State for the Home Department* [2021] EWHC 477 (Admin), [39].

[4] As required by CPR 54B PD para 1.1 and CPR 25A PD para 4.5.

18 ACTION AGAINST PROFESSIONAL REPRESENTATIVES FOR ABUSE OF THE COURT'S PROCEDURES

18.1 THE HAMID JURISDICTION: GENERAL

18.1.1 The Court's powers to prevent abuse of its procedures are set out at para 13.10 of this Guide. **1BA-115**

18.1.2 The Hamid jurisdiction is a facet of the Court's jurisdiction to regulate its own procedures and to enforce the overriding duties owed to it by legal professionals. Although the case in which the jurisdiction was first identified[1] was an immigration case, it is not confined to immigration or even to public law cases.[2]

18.1.3 Where the Court identifies a possible abuse of its procedures in a case in which legal representatives are involved, it may refer the matter to a designated judge ("the Hamid judge"), currently Mrs Justice Tipples.

18.1.4 The Hamid judge may send the legal representative(s) a letter inviting them to show cause why there should not be a referral to the relevant professional regulator (a "show cause" letter).

18.1.5 Having considered the legal representative's response, the Court may summon the representative(s) to explain their actions at a hearing in open court.

18.1.6 If the Court concludes that its procedures have been abused, it may decide to refer the legal representative(s) concerned to the relevant professional regulator(s) to consider disciplinary proceedings. It may also, or alternatively, consider making a wasted costs order against the legal representative(s).

18.1.7 Any orders made may be published and placed in the public domain. Any such publication will include the explanation provided by the legal representative.

18.2 THE HAMID JURISDICTION: ABUSE OF THE URGENT CONSIDERATION PROCEDURE

18.2.1 Abuse of the urgent consideration procedure has caused the Court to invoke the Hamid jurisdiction on a number of occasions. Practitioners should ensure that they read carefully and comply strictly with their obligations to the Court when using the urgent consideration procedure (see Chapters 16 and 17 of this Guide). **1BA-116**

18.2.2 The following are examples of conduct which has given rise to invocation of the Hamid procedure:

18.2.2.1 The claimant's solicitor had delayed making the urgent application until the last minute and had not disclosed the full facts of the case in an attempt to use the urgent process to prevent his client's removal from the UK.[3]

18.2.2.2 The claimant's solicitor requested urgent interim relief in respect of a decision that had been made 3 years earlier.[4]

18.2.2.3 A practitioner advanced arguments that his client was suicidal and psychotic which was known or ought to have been known were false and/ or inconsistent with their own medical evidence.[5]

18.2.2.4 A practitioner lodged an application with grounds that were opaque and brief and failed to set out any of the claimant's history of criminality.[6]

18.2.2.5 The claimants' legal team applied for interim relief to prevent the use of particular accommodation to house asylum seekers in circumstances where the defendant had already transferred the individual claimants into alternative accommodation; and the Form N463 did not make this clear.[7]

18.2.2.6 Form N463 was used to seek case management directions providing for a reply and for an expedited consideration of permission on the papers; and the Court was invited to make these directions within 48 hours.[8]

18.2.3 Practitioners should also bear in mind the guidance at para 16.8.6 of this Guide. The Hamid jurisdiction may be invoked in cases where that guidance is not complied with.[9]

---

[1] *R (Hamid) v Secretary of State for the Home Department* [2012] EWHC 3070 (Admin).

[2] *R (DVP) v Secretary of State for the Home Department* [2021] EWHC 606 (Admin), [2].

[3] *R (Hamid) v Secretary of State for the Home Department* [2012] EWHC 3070 (Admin).

[4] *R (Butt) v Secretary of State for the Home Department* [2014] EWHC 264 (Admin).

[5] *R (Okondu) v Secretary of State for the Home Department (wasted costs; SRA referrals; Hamid) IJR* [2014] UKUT 377 (IAC).

[6] *R (Okondu) v Secretary of State for the Home Department (wasted costs; SRA referrals; Hamid) IJR* [2014] UKUT 377 (IAC).

[7] *R (DVP & Ors) v Secretary of State for the Home Department* [2021] EWHC 606 (Admin).

[8] *In the matter of the Court's exercise of the Hamid jurisdiction* [2021] EWHC 1895 (Admin).

[9] See also *R (SB (Afghanistan) v Secretary of State for the Home Department* [2018] EWCA Civ 215 at [54]-[56].

18.3 ACTION BY PROFESSIONAL REGULATORS

1BA-117 **18.3.1** Making abusive applications in judicial review claims can result in severe disciplinary sanctions, including striking off.[1]

19 CLOSED MATERIAL

19.1 INTRODUCTION

1BA-118 **19.1.1** CLOSED material is material that is relevant to an issue before the Court which one party claims to be entitled to withhold from the other party or parties because its disclosure would be contrary to the public interest.

19.1.2 The fact that material is confidential does not, on its own, supply a ground for not disclosing it. However, parts of a document which otherwise falls to be disclosed may be redacted if they are both confidential and irrelevant to any issue (see para 15.5 of this Guide).

19.1.3 There are three situations in which the Administrative Court may have to consider CLOSED material:

19.1.3.1 Material may be withheld from disclosure if it attracts public interest immunity (PII). It is for the Court to decide whether to uphold a claim for PII. If so, the material covered by the claim is in general inadmissible (subject to para 19.1.3.3 below). Para 19.2 of this Guide sets out the procedure for making a PII claim in the Administrative Court.

19.1.3.2 Under the Justice and Security Act 2013 (JSA), the Court is empowered to hold a closed material procedure (CMP) where it has made a declaration under s. 6 that a closed material application may be made. This can be done only if there is relevant material whose disclosure would be damaging to the interests of national security. The rules governing proceedings under the JSA are in CPR Part 82. Para 19.3 below summarises the law and procedure in the Administrative Court.

19.1.3.3 Following the Supreme Court's decision in *Haralambous v St Albans Crown Court* [2018] UKSC 1, [2018] AC 236, where a judicial review claim challenges the issue of a search warrant granted ex parte on the basis of CLOSED material, the High Court may consider the CLOSED material and take it into account in reaching its decision on the claim. Para 19.4 below sets out the procedure for claims in the Administrative Court challenging search warrants under the Haralambous jurisdiction.

19.2 PUBLIC INTEREST IMMUNITY

1BA-119 **19.2.1** Where the claim for PII is made by a Government Department, it should include a certificate made personally by a Minister or a senior official.[2] Where the claim is made by a police force, the certificate should be given by the chief police officer or other senior officer.

19.2.2 The proper approach to PII involves a three-stage test:[3]

19.2.2.1 The person giving the PII certificate (or their lawyers) must decide whether the documentary material in question is relevant to the proceedings in question i.e., that the material should, in the absence of PII considerations, be disclosed in the normal way.

19.2.2.2 The person giving the certificate must consider whether there is a real risk that it would harm the public interest if the material was placed in the public domain.

19.2.2.3 The person giving the certificate must balance the public interests for and against disclosure (i.e. consider whether the damage to the public interest that would be caused by disclosure outweighs the damage to the public interest in the administration of justice that would be caused by non-disclosure). If the balance comes down against disclosure, then the PII certificate must state that, in the view of the author, it is in the public interest that the material be withheld.

19.2.3 When answering the second question, the person giving the certificate should consider whether any damage to the public interest can be prevented by disclosing part of a document or a

---

[1] See e.g. *Vay Sui IP v Solicitors Regulation Authority* [2018] EWHC 957 (Admin), where a Divisional Court upheld the sanction of striking off a solicitor for making repeated abusive applications for injunctions or stays to prevent the removal of claimants.

[2] In *R (Charles) v Secretary of State for Foreign and Commonwealth Affairs* [2020] EWHC 3010 (Admin), the Divisional Court rejected the submission that a PII certificate made by the Permanent Under-Secretary of the Foreign and Commonwealth Office (the most senior civil servant in that department) carried less weight than one given by a Minister. However, in that case, the certificate was given by a senior official (rather than a Minister) because the documents to which it related had been produced under a previous administration: [18(1)-(2)].

[3] *Al Rawi v Security Service* [2010] EWCA Civ 482, [2012] 1 AC 531, [24] (Lord Neuberger MR in the Court of Appeal).

gist (a summary) of it or disclosing it on a restricted basis.[1] A claim for PII should only be made in respect of those parts of the material which it is necessary to withhold in the public interest.[2]

19.2.4 Where the balance comes down against disclosure, claiming public interest immunity is a duty, rather than the exercise of an administrative discretion.[3]

19.2.5 A claim for PII should be considered as soon as it becomes clear that a party has in their possession material which does or will fall to be disclosed, but whose disclosure would be damaging to the public interest.

19.2.6 What is required to discharge the duty of candour at the substantive stage may be more extensive than what is required before permission is granted (see para 15.3.2 of this Guide). Thus:

19.2.6.1 In some circumstances, a defendant may properly conclude that (even leaving aside any damage to the public interest which its disclosure would cause) PII material would not fall to be disclosed at the permission stage. If so, a claim for PII can be left until permission is granted.

19.2.6.2 However, if (leaving aside any damage to the public interest) the duty of candour would require disclosure of the PII material at the permission stage, the party must make a claim for PII at that stage.

19.2.7 Where, at whatever stage of proceedings, a party makes a claim for PII:

19.2.7.1 The fact that such a claim is being made should be clearly indicated in a letter to the ACO, with the title "PUBLIC INTEREST IMMUNITY CLAIM". The letter should explain whether, in the view of the party, the claim can be properly considered without the assistance of a special counsel or special advocate.

19.2.7.2 The Court will then give directions for the determination of the claim for PII (including considering whether to invite the Attorney General to appoint a special counsel or special advocate).[4]

19.2.8 It is for the Court to determine whether a claim for PII should be upheld. The Court must decide for itself whether the public interest would be damaged by disclosure of the material to which the claim relates and, if so, whether that damage outweighs any damage to the public interest in the administration of justice which non-disclosure would cause.[5]

19.2.9 If the claim for PII is upheld, the material cannot in any circumstances be admitted; it is not open to either party or to the Court to do so. If the claim for PII is not upheld, the material must be disclosed if it remains relevant to an issue in dispute.[6]

19.2.10 In almost all cases, the consequence of a decision to uphold a claim for PII is that the proceedings continue without taking into account the inadmissible material covered by the claim. However, where the material is so central to the issues that it would not be fair for the proceedings to continue, the Court may strike out the claim.[7]

19.3 CLOSED MATERIAL PROCEEDINGS UNDER THE JUSTICE AND SECURITY ACT 2013

19.3.1 The Justice and Security Act 2013 (JSA) authorises the High Court to hold a closed mate- **1BA-120**
rial procedure (CMP). A CMP differs fundamentally from proceedings in which a claim for PII has been upheld. In a CMP, one party is entitled to rely on material not disclosed to the other party or parties (CLOSED material) and the Court can base its decision on such material.[8]

19.3.2 A CMP is available under the JSA only where the Court makes a declaration under s. 6(2) of that Act. This may be made on the application of the Secretary of State (whether or not the Secretary of State is a party to the proceedings) or any party to the proceedings, or of the Court's own motion.

19.3.3 The Court may only make a declaration if two conditions are met.

19.3.4 The first condition is that:[9]

"(a) a party to the proceedings would be required to disclose sensitive material in the course

---

[1] *R v Chief Constable of West Midlands Police ex p. Wiley* [1995] 1 AC 274, 306-7.

[2] *R (Charles) v Secretary of State for Foreign and Commonwealth Affairs* [2020] EWHC 3010 (Admin), [10(4)].

[3] *R v Chief Constable of West Midlands Police ex p. Wiley* [1995] 1 AC 274, 295G-H; *Rawlinson & Hunter Trustees SA v Director of the Serious Fraud Office (No. 2)* [2015] 1 WLR 797, [30].

[4] *Al Rawi v Security Service* [2010] EWCA Civ 482, [2012] 1 AC 531, [26] (Lord Neuberger MR in the Court of Appeal).

[5] *R v Chief Constable of West Midlands Police ex p. Wiley* [1995] 1 AC 274, 295-6; *Al Rawi v Security Service* [2010] EWCA Civ 482, [2012] 1 AC 531, [25] (Lord Neuberger MR in the Court of Appeal).

[6] *R v Lewes Justice ex p. Secretary of State for the Home Department* [1973] AC 388, 407; *Al Rawi v Security Service* [2011] UKSC 34, [2012] 1 AC 531, [41] (Lord Dyson in the Supreme Court).

[7] *Carnduff v Rock* [2001] 1 WLR 1786, *Al Rawi v Security Service* [2011] UKSC 34, [2012] 1 AC 531, [15] (Lord Dyson in the Supreme Court).

[8] *Al Rawi v Security Service* [2011] UKSC 34, [2012] 1 AC 531, [41] (Lord Dyson in the Supreme Court).

[9] Justice and Security Act 2013, s. 6(4).

of the proceedings to another person (whether or not another party to the proceedings), or

(b) a party to the proceedings would be required to make such a disclosure were it not for one or more of the following–
 (i) the possibility of a claim for public interest immunity in relation to the material,
 (ii) the fact that there would be no requirement to disclose if the party chose not to rely on the material,
 (iii) section 17(1) of the Regulation of Investigatory Powers Act 2000 (exclusion for intercept material),
 (iv) any other enactment that would prevent the party from disclosing the material but would not do so if the proceedings were proceedings in relation to which there was a declaration under this section."

19.3.5 The second condition is that "it is in the interests of the fair and effective administration of justice in the proceedings to make a declaration".[1]

19.3.6 The Court must not consider an application by the Secretary of State under s. 6(2) unless satisfied that the Secretary of State has, before making the application, considered whether to make, or advise another person to make, a claim for PII in relation to the material on which the application is based (see s. 6(7)).

19.3.7 For these purposes "sensitive material" means "material the disclosure of which would be damaging to the interests of national security".[2] Thus, a CMP under the JSA is not available in respect of material whose disclosure would only be damaging to another public interest (such as the international relations of the UK or the prevention and detection of crime).

19.3.8 Where the Secretary of State is not a party to proceedings and it appears to a party, or to the Court, that the party may be required to disclose material the disclosure of which would be damaging to the interests of national security, there is a requirement to notify the Secretary of State and the material must not be disclosed pending the Secretary of State's response.[3]

19.3.9 A person who intends to make an application for a declaration under s. 6 must, at least 14 days before making the application, serve written notice of that intention on the Court and on every other party to the proceedings and on the Secretary of State (if not a party); and may apply to the Court to the proceedings to be stayed pending the application or the person's consideration whether to make it.[4] The Court may stay the proceedings and may make the stay subject to conditions.[5]

19.3.10 An application for a declaration under s. 6 requires the applicant to file with the Court: (a) a statement of reasons to support the application and any additional written submissions; (b) material in relation to which the Court is asked to find that the first condition in s. 6 is met; and (c) the details of any special advocate already appointed.[6] The statement of reasons must include the Secretary of State's reasons for not making, or not advising another person to make, a claim for PII.[7]

19.3.11 Where the Secretary of State decides to make an application for a declaration under s. 6 or receives notice that another party intends to make such an application, the Secretary of State must immediately give notice of the proceedings to the Attorney General (who has power under s. 9 of the JSA to appoint a special advocate).[8] Unless a special advocate is appointed a relevant person (i.e. a person who would otherwise be required to disclose sensitive material) may not rely on sensitive material at a hearing on notice.[9]

19.3.12 The functions of the special advocate are to represent the interests of the "specially represented party" (i.e. a party from whom sensitive material is withheld) by: (a) making submissions to the Court at any hearing or part of a hearing from which the specially represented party and their legal representatives are excluded; (b) adducing evidence and cross-examining witnesses at any such hearing or part of a hearing; (c) making applications to the Court or seeking directions from the Court; (d) making written submissions to the Court.[10]

19.3.13 The special advocate is restricted from communicating with any person about any matter connected with the proceedings once sensitive material is served on him or her.[11]

19.3.14 Once an application for a declaration under s. 6 has been made, the Court will serve notice of the application on all other parties, the Secretary of State (if not a party), the legal

[1] Justice and Security Act 2013, s. 6(5).
[2] Justice and Security Act 2013, s. 6(11)
[3] CPR 82.20.
[4] CPR 82.21(1).
[5] CPR 82.21(2) & (3).
[6] CPR 82.22(1).
[7] CPR 82.22(2).
[8] CPR 82.9.
[9] CPR 82.13(1)(b).
[10] CPR 82.10.
[11] CPR 82.11.

representatives of all parties and the special advocate. The Court will fix a directions hearing unless it considers the application can be determined on the papers.[1] Any directions hearing will involve the party applying for the declaration, the Secretary of State (if not the applicant) and the special advocate, but not the specially represented party and their representatives.[2]

19.3.15 If the Court makes a declaration under s. 6 it must then give directions (or fix a hearing at which such directions are to be given) for a hearing of a closed material application.[3]

19.3.16 The procedure for the making and determination of a closed material application is set out in CPR 82.13 - 82.14. Essentially:

19.3.16.1 The relevant person (the person who would be required to disclose the sensitive material) applies to withhold the sensitive material, filing with the Court: (a) the sensitive material; (b) a statement of the reasons for withholding it.[4]

19.3.16.2 The Court fixes a hearing, unless the conditions in CPR 82.14(2) are met. One situation in which a hearing is not required is where the special advocate gives notice that the application is not challenged and the Court is satisfied that it would be just to give permission without a hearing.

19.3.16.3 The relevant person and the special advocate file with the Court a schedule of the issues that cannot be agreed between them, giving brief reasons for their contentions and setting out any proposals for the Court to resolve them.[5]

19.3.16.4 The hearing takes place in the absence of the specially represented party and their representatives.[6]

19.3.16.5 Where the Court gives permission to the relevant person to rely on sensitive material, it must consider whether to direct the relevant person to serve a summary of that material on the specially represented party and their representative, but must ensure that the summary does not contain material the disclosure of which would be damaging to national security.[7]

19.3.16.6 Where the Court has not given permission to the relevant person to withhold sensitive material, or has directed the service of a summary, the relevant person may elect not to serve the material or summary. In that case, the Court can do one of two things. If it considers the sensitive material might adversely affect the relevant person's case or support the case of another party, it can direct the relevant person not to rely on specified points, or to make specified concessions or take specified steps. In any other case, the Court can direct the relevant person not to rely on the material or on what is required to be summarised.[8]

19.3.16.7 CPR 82.14(10) imposes an absolute duty on the Court to give permission to the relevant person to withhold sensitive material where it considers that disclosure of the material would be contrary to the interests of national security. It may, however, be contended that in certain circumstances this duty should be "read down" to comply with Article 6 ECHR.[9]

19.3.17 Substantive hearings in cases where a declaration under s. 6 has been made will typically involve OPEN and CLOSED parts. The parties, their legal representatives and special advocates can attend the OPEN part. Only the Secretary of State and relevant person (and their legal representatives) and the special advocate can attend the CLOSED part.

19.3.18 There is a presumption that every OPEN hearing will take place in public. An OPEN hearing may not take place in private, even if the parties consent, unless and to the extent that the Court decides that it must be held in private.[10] It will be held in private if, and only to the extent that, the Court is satisfied of one or more of a list of specified matters and that it is necessary to sit in private to secure the proper administration of justice. The specified matters include that (a) publicity would defeat the object of the hearing, (b) it involves matters of national security or (c) it involves confidential information and publicity would damage that confidentiality.[11] Even where (b) is relied upon, clear and cogent evidence is required to displace the presumption that OPEN hearings take place in public.[12]

19.3.19 In proceedings in which a declaration under s. 6 has been made, the Court may, and

---

[1] CPR 82.23(1)

[2] CPR 82.23(2) & (4).

[3] CPR 82.26.

[4] CPR 82.13.

[5] CPR 82.14(4).

[6] CPR 82.14(5).

[7] CPR 82.14(7).

[8] CPR 82.14(9).

[9] See e.g. *R (K) v Secretary of State for Defence* [2016] EWCA Civ 1149, [2017] 1 WLR 1671, [21]; see also *R (Reprieve) v Prime Minister* [2021] EWCA Civ 972, [2022] 2 WLR 1.

[10] CPR 39.2(1).

[11] CPR 39.2(3).

[12] *Attorney General v British Broadcasting Corporation* [2022] EWHC 380 (QB).

almost always will, give two judgments - one OPEN judgment, which is generally made public in the normal way and one CLOSED judgment, which is provided only to the relevant person, the Secretary of State and the special advocate.[1]

19.3.20 Before providing the draft OPEN judgment to the specially represented party, the draft judgment is sent for security checking to the Secretary of State and the relevant person.[2] The Secretary of State or relevant person may, within 5 days of being served notice, apply to the Court to reconsider the terms of the judgment.[3] Where such an application is made, a copy of the judgment and application must be sent to the special advocate.[4] The procedure in CPR 82.14 (with the exception of paras (6)-(8)) then applies.[5]

19.3.21 Unless the Court otherwise directs, CPR 5.4 (a publicly accessible register of claims), 5.4B (the ability of a party to obtain court records) and 5.4C (the ability of a non-party to obtain court records) do not apply to proceedings in which a declaration under s. 6 has been made.[6]

19.4 THE HARALAMBOUS JURISDICTION

1BA-121 **19.4.1** In *R (Haralambous) v St Albans Crown Court*,[7] the Supreme Court considered whether a CMP is available in the High Court on a claim for judicial review of a decision to issue a search warrant, where the warrant was issued on an ex parte application relying on CLOSED material. The Supreme Court held that a CMP is in principle available. This enables the Court to consider all the material that was before the judicial authority which granted the warrant and to rely on that material when reaching its decision.

19.4.2 In *R (Jordan) v Chief Constable of Merseyside Police*, it was said that the procedure to be adopted in a claim invoking the Haralambous jurisdiction is as follows:[8]

19.4.2.1 Where the Court grants permission to apply for judicial review in a challenge to a warrant, and it is clear that the defendant or interested party has claimed or will claim PII over material relevant to the challenge, it should also give directions for: (i) a hearing to determine whether to uphold the PII claim; and (ii) a substantive hearing to determine the application for judicial review.

19.4.2.2 If possible, these two hearings should be listed before the same judge. It may be sensible for the listing of the second hearing to be left to be decided at the first hearing.

19.4.2.3 At the first hearing, if the PII claim is upheld in whole or in part, the Court should give directions dealing with: (i) the time within which the defendant must disclose and the claimant must respond to any new material; (ii) whether the case is sufficiently exceptional that it is necessary to invite the Attorney General to appoint a special advocate to represent the interests of the claimant in the CMP;[9] and (iii) in the light of these matters, the listing of the substantive hearing.

19.4.2.4 At the substantive hearing, the OPEN hearing should take place first, with the CLOSED hearing following. The claimant's representatives should be available to return for a short further OPEN hearing in case anything emerges from the CLOSED hearing on which it is necessary to invite further OPEN submissions.

19.4.2.5 Especially where, as in most cases, there is no special advocate to represent the interests of the claimant, counsel for the public authority has a special obligation to assist the Court by identifying any points arising from the CLOSED material which might arguably support the claimant or undermine the defence. The obligation is similar to that which arises when seeking an ex parte order. Counsel seeking such an order "must put on his defence hat and ask himself what, if he were representing the defendant or a third-party with the relevant interest, he would be saying to the judge, and, having answered that question, that is what he must tell the judge".[10] The same goes, mutatis mutandis, for counsel representing a defendant in any CMP held in a judicial review claim challenging a warrant.

19.4.2.6 After the substantive hearing, OPEN and CLOSED judgments should be prepared. To the extent possible, care should be taken to identify in the OPEN judgment every conclusion that has been reached in whole or in part on the basis of evidence referred to in the CLOSED judgment.[11]

---

1 CPR 82.16.
2 CPR 82.17(1).
3 CPR 82.17(2).
4 CPR 82.17(3).
5 CPR 82.17(4).
6 CPR 82.18.
7 [2018] UKSC 1, [2018] AC 236.
8 [2020] EWHC 2274 (Admin), [35].
9 *Competition and Markets Authority v Concordia International RX (UK)* [2018] EWCA Civ 1881, [2018] Bus LR 2452, [75].
10 *In re Stanford International Bank Ltd* [2011] Ch 33, [191].
11 *Bank Mellat v HM Treasury (No. 2)* [2013] UKSC 39, [2014] AC 700, [68].

20 SKELETON ARGUMENTS AND OTHER REQUIRED DOCUMENTS

20.1 GENERAL

20.1.1 The purpose of a skeleton argument is to assist the Court by setting out as concisely as practicable the arguments upon which a party intends to rely.[1] **1BA-122**

20.1.2 The claimant, the defendant and any party who wishes to make representations must prepare a skeleton argument before any substantive hearing.[2]

20.1.3 Parties should also prepare skeleton arguments before any interlocutory hearing (for example, any renewed permission or hearing for interim relief or directions), even if the issue is straightforward.

20.2 CONTENT OF SKELETON ARGUMENTS

20.2.1 A skeleton argument must be as concise as possible.[3] **1BA-123**

20.2.2 A skeleton argument should both define and confine the areas of controversy; be cross-referenced to any relevant document in the bundle; be self-contained and not incorporate by reference material from previous skeleton arguments or pleadings; and should not include extensive quotations from documents or authorities.[4]

20.2.3 It should not be left to other parties to infer from omissions in skeleton arguments what grounds of claim have been abandoned. If a party no longer pursues a ground of claim, that ought to be made clear to the court and to the other parties.[5]

20.2.4 Where it is necessary to refer to an authority, a skeleton argument must state the proposition of law for which the authority is cited and identify the parts of the authority that establish the proposition. Where the authority has paragraph numbers, these should be given. Otherwise, references to the page numbers of the report should be given. If more than one authority is cited in support of a given proposition, the skeleton argument must make clear why.[6]

20.2.5 It is important that:

20.2.5.1 the decision or other conduct under challenge is clearly identified;

20.2.5.2 the relevant facts, including any relevant change of circumstances since the Claim Form and supporting documentation were lodged, are set out;

20.2.5.3 the grounds for seeking judicial review (or interim relief, or any other order) are set out under numbered headings. The grounds must be stated shortly and numbered in sequence. Each ground should raise a distinct issue in relation to the decision under challenge;[7]

20.2.5.4 arguments and submissions in support of the grounds are set out separately in relation to each ground;

20.2.5.5 relevant legal principles are set out. Lengthy extracts from statutory or international materials, case law and other sources should be avoided unless it is considered that this will materially speed up the Court's pre-reading, the presentation of the oral argument or the preparation of judgment;

20.2.5.6 the remedy sought is identified;

20.2.5.7 any urgency or other matter relevant to the timing of the case is explained;

20.2.5.8 any other relevant point, such as delay, alternative remedy or any other bar to relief, is identified and addressed.

20.3 LENGTH AND FORMAT OF SKELETON ARGUMENTS

20.3.1 A skeleton argument must not exceed 25 pages. The Court may grant permission to exceed the 25-page limit.[8] Such an application should be made to a judge as soon as it is anticipated that one will be required. It is expected that this will be shortly after the Detailed Grounds of Defence are served.[9] **1BA-124**

20.3.2 Skeleton arguments should be as short as possible. In most cases, there should be no need for the skeleton argument to exceed 20 pages.

---

[1] CPR 54A PD para 14.1.

[2] CPR 54A PD paras 14.5 and 14.6.

[3] *R (Dolan) v Secretary of State for Health and Social Care* [2020] EWCA Civ 1605, [119]-[120].

[4] CPR 54A PD para 14.2(1).

[5] *R (All The Citizens) v Secretary of State for Culture, Media and Sport* [2022] EWHC 960 (Admin), [17].

[6] CPR 54A PD para 4.2(2).

[7] The Court emphasised the need for a clear and succinct statement of the grounds, in the context of appeals: *R (Talpada) v Secretary of State for the Home Department* [2018] EWCA Civ 841, [68]. See also *Hickey v Secretary of State for Work and Pensions* [2018] EWCA Civ 851, [74].

[8] CPR 54A PD para 14.3.

[9] *R (Palmer) v Northern Derbyshire Magistrates' Court* [2021] EWHC 3013 (Admin), [11].

20.3.3 A skeleton argument should be clearly typed and properly spaced. A font size of not less than 12-point should be used. Lines should be reasonably spaced (1.5 or double spacing is ideal).

20.3.4 Paragraphs should be numbered sequentially. Pages should also be numbered.

20.3.5 Skeleton arguments filed and served by email should be sent as Word documents, not PDF or any other format and not included in the body of the email.

20.3.6 Any skeleton argument that does not comply with the requirements at paras 20.2.2, 20.2.3 or 20.3.1 of this Guide may be returned to its author by the ACO and may not be re-filed unless and until it complies with those requirements. The Court may disallow the cost of preparing a skeleton argument which does not comply with these requirements.[1]

20.4 FILING AND SERVING SKELETON ARGUMENTS

1BA-125 **20.4.1** Absent a specific judicial direction, the time limits for filing and serving skeleton arguments before a substantive hearing are:

20.4.1.1 for the claimant, not less than 21 calendar days before the hearing or warned date;[2] and

20.4.1.2 for the defendant or any other party wishing to make representations at the hearing, not less than 14 calendar days before the hearing or warned date.[3]

20.4.2 Skeleton arguments should always be served on the other party or parties to the case, whether or not that party is in a position to provide a skeleton by way of exchange.

20.4.3 For all other hearings (for example, hearings for renewal of permission), and in the absence of specific directions, skeleton arguments should be served at least two working days before the hearing is listed. If there is or may be a problem with compliance with that deadline, the ACO should be alerted as soon as possible.

20.4.4 Skeleton arguments should not be handed to the Court on the day of the hearing.

20.4.5 If the skeleton argument does not comply with this guidance, or is served late, the Court may refuse to permit the party in default to rely on the skeleton; alternatively, the Court may make an adverse costs order against the party in default (see para 25.1 of this Guide on costs).[4]

20.5 OTHER REQUIRED DOCUMENTS

1BA-126 **20.5.1** In addition to the skeleton arguments, not less than 7 days before a substantive hearing, the parties must file:[5]

20.5.1.1 an agreed list of issues;

20.5.1.2 an agreed chronology of events (with page references to the hearing bundle); and

20.5.1.3 an agreed list of essential documents for the advanced reading for the Court (with page references in the hearing bundle to the passages relied on) and a time estimate for that reading.

20.5.2 These are important documents, designed to assist the Court in preparing for the case and in understanding the scope of the dispute and the dates of the key material events.

20.5.3 Because these documents must be agreed by all parties, the parties should liaise in good time before the deadline to decide who will produce the first drafts; the date by which this will be done; and the date by which the other party or parties will communicate their comments on the drafts. Parties are expected to approach this task in a spirit of co-operation. The issues and events in the chronology should be described neutrally. Tendentious descriptions should be avoided.

21 DOCUMENTS

21.1 BUNDLES: GENERAL

1BA-127 **21.1.1** A bundle is a paginated and indexed set of the documents (or extracts from them) which the parties consider it is necessary for the judge to consider at a particular hearing. Documents in a bundle should generally be presented in chronological order (i.e. starting with the oldest document and ending with the most recent document). Correspondence between the parties should only be included in the bundle if it serves a particular purpose of relevance to the issues in dispute at the hearing for which the bundle is being prepared.

---

[1] CPR 54A PD para 14.4. Advocates should expect that this practice will be followed: *R (SSE Generation Ltd) v Competition and Markets Authority* [2022] EWHC 865 (Admin).

[2] CPR 54A PD para 14.5.

[3] CPR 54A PD para 14.6.

[4] See e.g. *R (National Council of Civil Liberties) v Secretary of State for the Home Department (Procedural Matters)* [2018] EWHC 976 (Admin), [17].

[5] CPR 54A PD para. 14.7.

21.2 THE HEARING BUNDLE

21.2.1 The bundle prepared for a substantive hearing is known as the hearing bundle. The parties must agree its contents. If the hearing bundle is over 400 pages, there must also be a core bundle. This is a paginated and indexed bundle including the pleadings, a copy of the decision and/or measure challenged in the proceedings and such further documents (or extract from them) as the parties consider essential for the purposes of the hearing. Each party (or the party's solicitor) must certify that the hearing bundle and any core bundle meet these requirements.[1] **1BA-128**

21.2.2 The Court will not adjudicate disputes about which documents should be in the hearing bundle or core bundle. The parties should approach the task of agreeing their content in a spirit of co-operation. If one party considers that a document should be included and another party disagrees on the basis that the document is irrelevant or inadmissible, the document should be included, but the dispute as to its relevance or admissibility should be flagged in the index.

21.2.3 An electronic version of the hearing bundle and any core bundle must be prepared in accordance with the guidance at Annex 7.[2]

21.2.4 Sometimes the order granting permission, or another order, will include a direction about when the hearing bundles are to be lodged. Absent such a direction, the hearing bundle and any core bundle must be lodged, in hard copy and electronic form, not less than 21 days before the hearing date or warned date. For Divisional Court cases, one hard copy bundle must be lodged for each judge hearing the case.[3]

21.2.5 If it is necessary to lodge bundles late, the bundles should be accompanied by a letter making clear that the bundle relate to an imminent hearing and explaining the reasons why it was not possible to lodged the bundles on time. If this is not done, the bundles may not be placed before the judge hearing the case.

21.2.6 The Court does not expect to have documents handed up during the course of the hearing, although in exceptional circumstances it may give permission to adduce evidence or submit documents in that way.

21.3 OTHER HEARINGS

21.3.1 Sometimes (for example, when an urgent interlocutory application is made), there may be no directions about bundles. The party making the application must still ensure that all documents relevant to the application are before the Court by preparing an application bundle, in hard copy and electronic form, containing these documents. The bundle must be filed at Court and served on the other parties in good time before the hearing. **1BA-129**

21.3.2 This means that the application bundle must be served at least 3 clear days before the hearing or, in cases where the urgency of the application makes this impossible, no later than 1pm on the day before the hearing.

21.4 FORMAT OF BUNDLES

21.4.1 The Court always requires both hard copy and electronic bundles to be provided, subject to any order to the contrary. **1BA-130**

21.4.2 Hard copy bundles should be secured in a ring or lever arch binder or binders which can comfortably accommodate the documents contained in them. The binders must open and close properly. The bundle's spine must be clearly marked with the reference number of the case and name of the parties. Documents should be copied double-sided and in portrait format (not landscape). Copies must be legible.

21.4.3 Electronic bundles (or e-bundles) must be prepared as follows:

21.4.3.1 Each bundle filed in support of an urgent application must be contained in a single PDF file not exceeding 20 MB in size, which is suitable for use with all of Adobe Acrobat Reader, PDF Expert and PDF Xchange Editor. If the papers in support of any claim or non-urgent application exceed 20MB a core bundle no larger than 20MB should be filed in a PDF file with a further PDF file bundle containing the remaining bundles.

21.4.3.2 An index or table of contents of the documents should be prepared. The index must be hyperlinked to the pages or document it refers to. Each document within the bundle must be identified in the sidebar list of contents/bookmarks, by date and description (e.g., "email 11.9.21 from [x] to [y]"). The sidebar list must also show the bundle page number of the document.

21.4.3.3 All pages of the document (including index pages) must be numbered in ascending order, preferably by computer generation or at least in typed form and not numbered by hand. Pagination should not mask relevant detail on the original document. The Court will expect references to be made to the bundle page numbers, not the original (or internal) page numbers on the documents.

---

[1] CPR 54A PD para 15.1.
[2] CPR 54A PD para 15.2.
[3] CPR 54A PD para 15.3.

21.4.3.4 The default display view size of all pages must be 100%.

21.4.3.5 All documents should appear in portrait orientation. If an original document is in landscape orientation, it should be inserted so that it can be read with a 90 degree rotation clockwise. No document should appear upside down.

21.4.3.6 All bundles must be text based, not a scan of a hard copy bundle. If documents within a bundle have been scanned, optical character recognition should be undertaken so that the text is word searchable and comments and highlights can be imposed.

21.4.3.7 All significant documents and all sections in bundles must be bookmarked for ease of navigation. Bookmarks must be labelled indicating what documents they are referring to (it is best to have the same name or title as the actual document) and also display the relevant page numbers.

21.4.3.8 The resolution of the document must be reduced to about 200-300 DPI to prevent delays whilst scrolling from one page to another.

21.4.3.9 All PDF files must contain a short version of the name of the case and an indication of the number/letter of the bundle, and end with the hearing date. For example: "R (Joe Bloggs) v Secretary of State, Bundle B, 1-1-21" or "R (Joe Bloggs) v Secretary of State, Correspondence, 1-1-21". They must not be labelled just "Correspondence" or "Bundle B".

21.4.4 If it is necessary to prepare an updated electronic bundle after the original bundle has been sent to the judge, it should not be assumed that the judge will accept it as a complete replacement. The judge may already have started to mark up the original. Inquiries should be made of the judge as to their preference. Absent a particular direction, a substitute bundle should be made available, but any additional pages should also be provided in a separate supplementary bundle with those pages appropriately numbered and/or sub-numbered (143.1, 143.2 etc).

21.4.5 The judge may refuse to read a bundle which does not comply with these requirements, or direct that a revised bundle is submitted which does comply, in which event the judge may disallow the costs or make another adverse costs order.

21.5 HOW TO LODGE ELECTRONIC BUNDLES

1BA-131 **21.5.1** Hearing e-bundles for non-urgent judicial review claims and interlocutory applications should be lodged by email as follows:

21.5.1.1 Send a request by email to these addresses:

For cases in the London High Court: *DUC@administrativecourtoffice.justice.gov.uk*
For cases in the Birmingham High Court: *Birmingham@administrativecourtoffice.justice.gov.uk*
For cases in Wales and the Western Circuit: *Cardiff@administrativecourtoffice.justice.gov.uk*
For cases in the Leeds High Court: *Leeds@administrativecourtoffice.justice.gov.uk*
For cases in the Manchester High Court: *Manchester@administrativecourtoffice.justice.gov.uk*

21.5.1.2 The email will be answered with an invitation from an ejudiciary.net email address to upload the documents.

21.5.1.3 There is a maximum size of attached files which can be received by a justice.gov address (36MB in aggregate) and ejudiciary.net address (150MB in aggregate). Where those limits cause a problem, the solution may be to transmit bundles by separate emails. The temptation to break sensibly bundled documents into small bundles just for the purpose of transmission should be avoided, unless absolutely necessary. These limits do not apply when uploading documents to the Document Upload Centre.

21.5.1.4 The email subject line should provide the following detail: (a) case number (once issued); (b) case name (shortest comprehensible version); (c) hearing date (once listed); and (d) judge name (if known).

21.5.2 Application e-bundles accompanying applications for urgent consideration must be filed as indicated in para 17.5.4 of this Guide.

21.5.3 Parties and their legal representatives should only use the addresses set out above or another email address directed by the Court. Sending the same document to multiple email addresses risks it being overlooked and left unread.

21.5.4 Litigants in person who do not have access to email should contact the ACO by telephone (only to be used in an emergency) so that alternatives arrangements can be made if permitted by the Senior Legal Managers or a judge. The following telephone numbers are to be used:

For cases in the High Court in London: 020 7947 6158.
For cases in the High Court in Birmingham: 0121 681 4441.
For cases in Wales or the Western Circuit: 02920 376460.
For cases in the High Court in Leeds: 0113 306 2578.
For cases in the High Court in Manchester: 0161 240 5313.

21.5.5 For more information on electronic filing and fee payment see Administrative Court: Information for Court Users, 27 June 2022 (Annex 7 to this Guide).

21.6 LITIGANTS IN PERSON

1BA-132 **21.6.1** The general rule is that litigants in person must comply with the requirements in this Guide. If it is not possible for a litigant in person to comply with the rules on electronic bundles, the Court must be given a brief explanation of the reasons for this as far in advance of the hearing as possible. Where possible, a practical way of overcoming the problem should be identified. Where a litigant in person is the claimant or applicant and another party has legal representation, the legal representatives for that party should consider offering to prepare the e-bundle.

21.7 SANCTION FOR NON-COMPLIANCE

21.7.1 If the hearing bundle or application bundle of documents does not comply with this guidance, or is served late, the Court may refuse to allow the party in default to rely on the bundle of documents. Alternatively, it may make an adverse costs order against the party in default (see para 25.1 of this Guide). **1BA-133**

22 AUTHORITIES

22.1 GENERAL

22.1.1 Authorities are the source materials on which the Court relies to identify, interpret and apply the law. They include legislative provisions, reports or transcripts of decided cases, international legal materials, legal textbook extracts and legal journal articles. **1BA-134**

22.1.2 An authorities bundle is an indexed set of the authorities which the parties consider the Court will need to read at a particular hearing. It should contain only those authorities to which it is necessary to refer for the fair disposal of the issues at the hearing. It need not contain every authority referred to in the statements of case or skeleton arguments. It should not contain authorities for propositions which are not in dispute. In most cases, it is unnecessary to refer to more than 10 authorities. In some cases, fewer than that (or none at all) will be required.

22.1.3 Where large numbers of authorities are cited, it is preferable to agree a core bundle of authorities, itself not exceeding 10 authorities.

22.1.4 Where a decided case is reported in a set of law reports, the report (rather than a transcript of the judgment) should be cited. Where a case is reported in the Official Law Reports (AC, QB, Ch, Fam), that version should be used in preference to any other.[1] Copies of reported authorities printed from websites or databases should be in the same format as the hard-copy printed version of the report where possible.

22.2 SUBSTANTIVE HEARINGS

22.2.1 For substantive hearings, the parties are required to lodge the agreed authorities bundles no less than 7 days before the hearing date or warned date. For Divisional Court cases, one set of hard copy bundles will be required for each judge hearing the case.[2] If one party considers that an authority should be included, it should generally be included. **1BA-135**

22.2.2 Some of the authorities which it is necessary for the Court to see at the hearing may already have been filed at Court with the Claim Form, Acknowledgment of Service or Detailed Grounds. These should still be included in the authorities bundle, as the Court will not necessarily have the earlier bundles before it.

22.3 OTHER HEARINGS

22.3.1 For other hearings (including oral permission hearings, interim relief and other interlocutory hearings), there may be no directions about bundles. Even so, authorities bundles must be prepared if the Court will need to see authorities. The bundles should be agreed in the same way as for substantive hearings (see para 22.2 of this Guide). **1BA-136**

22.3.2 As with application bundles, authorities bundles must be lodged at Court and served on the other parties in good time before the hearing.

22.3.3 This means that the authorities bundles must be served at least 3 clear days before the hearing or, in cases where the urgency of the application makes this impossible, no later than 1pm on the day before the hearing.

22.4 FORMAT OF AUTHORITIES BUNDLES

22.4.1 Whenever they are required, authorities bundles should be provided both in hard copy and in electronic form, subject to any order to the contrary. **1BA-137**

22.4.2 Hard copy bundles must be indexed and tabbed. They may also be sequentially paginated. They must be secured in a ring or lever arch binder or binders which can comfortably accommodate the authorities contained in them. The binders must open and close properly. The bundle's spine must be clearly marked with the reference number of the case and name of the parties. Documents should be copied double-sided and in portrait format (not landscape). Copies must be legible.

---

[1] *Practice Direction - Citation of Authorities* [2012] 1 WLR 780.

[2] CPR 54A PD para 15.5

22.4.3 Electronic authorities bundles must be prepared in the same way as electronic hearing and application bundles (see para 21.4.3 of this Guide).

22.5 LITIGANTS IN PERSON

1BA-138 **22.5.1** The general rule is that litigants in person must comply with the requirements in this Guide. However, where a litigant in person is the claimant or applicant and another party has legal representation, the legal representatives for that party should generally prepare the authorities bundles.

22.6 SANCTIONS

1BA-139 **22.6.1** If the authorities bundle does not comply with this guidance, or is lodged late, the Court may refuse to allow the party in default to rely on those authorities, require the bundle to be adjusted to meet the Court's requirements, and/or make an adverse costs order against the party in default (see para 25.1 of this Guide).

23 EVIDENCE

23.1 WITNESS EVIDENCE

1BA-140 **23.1.1** A witness statement must be headed with the title of the proceedings.[1]

23.1.2 At the top right hand corner of the first page, there should be clearly written:[2]

23.1.2.1 the party on whose behalf the statement is made;

23.1.2.2 the initials and surname of the witness;

23.1.2.3 the number of the statement in relation to that witness;

23.1.2.4 the identifying initials and number of each exhibit referred to;

23.1.2.5 the date the statement was made; and

23.1.2.6 the date of any translation.

23.1.3 A witness statement must, if practicable, be in the witness's own words and must in any event be drafted in the witness's own language, expressed in the first person and should also state:[3]

23.1.3.1 the full name of the witness;

23.1.3.2 his place of residence or, if he is making the statement in his professional, business or other occupational capacity, the address at which he works, the position he holds and the name of his firm or employer;

23.1.3.3 his occupation, or if he has none, his description;

23.1.3.4 the fact that he is a party to the proceedings or is the employee of such a party (if it be the case); and

23.1.3.5 the process by which it has been prepared, for example, face-to-face, over the telephone, and/or through an interpreter.

23.1.4 A witness statement must state which of the statements in it are made from the witness's own knowledge, and which are matters of information or belief; and the source of matters of information or belief.[4] Where the maker of a witness statement is relying on evidence provided by an incorporated entity, and the source of the information is an officer or employee of that entity (rather than documents seen by the witness themselves), the person must be identified.[5] This applies also where the entity concerned is a government department.[6] Failure to comply strictly with this requirement may not render evidence inadmissible, but may affect the weight which can be attached to it.[7]

23.1.5 Each exhibit should be verified and identified by the witness and remain separate from the witness statement.[8] The statement should have pages numbered consecutively and be divided into numbered paragraphs.[9] It is usually convenient to follow the chronological sequence of the events or matters dealt with.[10]

23.1.6 A witness statement must include a statement of truth in the following terms:[11]

"I believe that the facts stated in this witness statement are true. I understand that proceed-

---

[1] CPR 32 PD para. 17.1.

[2] CPR 32 PD para 17.2.

[3] CPR 32 PD para 18.1.

[4] CPR 32 PD para 18.2.

[5] *Punjab National Bank (International) Ltd v Techtrek India Ltd* [2020] EWHC 539 (Ch), [20] (Chief Master Marsh).

[6] *Attorney General v British Broadcasting Corporation* [2022] EWHC 380 (QB), [30].

[7] *R (Gardner) v Secretary of State for Health and Social Care* [2022] EWHC 967 (Admin), [258].

[8] CPR 32 PD para 18.3.

[9] CPR 32 PD para 19.1.

[10] CPR 32 PD para 19.2.

[11] CPR 32 PD para 20.2.

ings for contempt of court may be brought against anyone who makes, or causes to be made, a false statement in a document verified by a statement of truth without an honest belief in its truth."

23.1.7 The witness must not sign that statement of truth unless he or she holds an honest belief in the truth of the statements made in the witness statement. Proceedings for contempt of court may be brought against a person if, without an honest belief in its truth, he or she makes or causes to be made a false statement in a document verified by a statement of truth.[1]

23.1.8 It is rare for a witness to be called to give oral evidence in judicial review proceedings: see para 11.2 of this Guide.

23.2 EXPERT EVIDENCE

23.2.1 A party wishing to rely on expert evidence must obtain the Court's permission to do so.[2] **1BA-141**
Permission will be given only where expert evidence is reasonably required to resolve the proceedings.[3] There is no special dispensation from compliance with these rules in public law cases. The rules must be observed.[4]

23.2.2 In judicial review proceedings, the Court's function is to determine whether the decision or conduct challenged was a lawful exercise of a public function, not to assess the merits of the decision or conduct under challenge. It is therefore seldom necessary or appropriate to consider any evidence going beyond what was before the decision-maker and evidence about the process by which the decision was taken - let alone any expert evidence.[5]

23.2.3 The situations in which evidence other than of the decision under challenge is admissible in judicial review proceedings are limited. They include (a) evidence showing what material was before or available to the decision maker; (b) evidence relevant to the determination of a question of fact on which the jurisdiction of the decision-maker depended; (c) evidence relevant in determining whether a proper procedure was followed; and (d) evidence relied on to prove an allegation of bias or other misconduct on the part of the decision-maker.[6]

23.2.4 Expert evidence not falling into these categories will be admissible only rarely. However, it may be admissible:

23.2.4.1 to explain technical matters, where an understanding of such matters is needed to enable the Court to understand the reasons relied on in making the decision in the context of a challenge to its rationality;[7]

23.2.4.2 where it is alleged that the challenged decision was reached by a process which involved a serious - and incontrovertible - technical error which is not obvious to an untutored lay person but can be demonstrated by a person with the relevant technical expertise;[8] and

23.2.4.3 where it is alleged that a process was unfair because of the failure to disclose information, expert evidence may assist in showing the importance of the information not disclosed, the submissions that would have been made in response to it and, therefore, the materiality of the failure.[9]

23.2.5 A claimant must give careful thought to whether to apply for permission to adduce expert evidence. Any application for permission to adduce expert evidence, and for appropriate consequential directions, must be made at the earliest possible opportunity.[10] Ideally, this should be done in the Claim Form or, if later, as soon as the need for it arises.

---

[1] CPR 32.14.

[2] CPR 35.4.

[3] CPR 35.1.

[4] *R (AB) v Chief Constable of Hampshire Constabulary* [2019] EWHC 3461 (Admin), [118].

[5] *R (Law Society) v Lord Chancellor* [2018] EWHC 2094 (Admin), [2019] 1 WLR 1649, [36]; *R (AB) v Chief Constable of Hampshire Constabulary* [2019] EWHC 3461 (Admin), [117].

[6] *R v Secretary of State for the Environment ex p. Powis* [1981] 1 WLR 584, 595; *R (Law Society) v Lord Chancellor* [2018] EWHC 2094 (Admin), [2019] 1 LR 1649, [37].

[7] *R (Lynch) v General Dental Council* [2003] EWHC 2987 (Admin), [2004] 1 All ER 1159, [22]; *R (Law Society) v Lord Chancellor* [2018] EWHC 2094 (Admin), [2019] 1 WLR 1649, [38].

[8] *R (Law Society) v Lord Chancellor* [2018] EWHC 2094 (Admin), [2019] 1 WLR 1649, [39]-[41]. The error must be incontrovertible, once the matter is explained by the expert. If the expert's evidence is contradicted by a rational opinion from another qualified expert, the justification for admitting it will fall away.

[9] *R (Law Society) v Lord Chancellor* [2018] EWHC 2094 (Admin), [2019] 1 WLR 1649, [42].

[10] *R (Law Society) v Lord Chancellor* [2018] EWHC 2094 (Admin), [2019] 1 WLR 1649, [44]; *R (AB) v Chief Constable of Hampshire Constabulary* [2019] EWHC 3461 (Admin), [118].

PART D:—ENDING THE CLAIM

24 ENDING A CLAIM

24.1 INTRODUCTION

1BA-142 **24.1.1** Cases are ended either by an order made by the Court (where the case is determined by the Court or settled by consent) or by notice of discontinuance.

24.2 CLAIM DETERMINED BY THE COURT

1BA-143 **24.2.1** Where the Court makes a final determination, and produces a Court order, the case will have concluded in the Administrative Court (subject only to an appeal to the Court of Appeal (see CPR Part 52 and Chapter 26 of this Guide).

24.2.2 A final determination will be made:

24.2.2.1 where permission to apply for judicial review is refused on the papers and the claim is declared to be totally without merit;

24.2.2.2 where permission to apply for judicial review is refused on the papers and reconsideration is not requested within 7 days;

24.2.2.3 where permission to apply for judicial review is refused after an oral hearing;

24.2.2.4 where the substantive claim is dismissed; or

24.2.2.5 where the substantive claim succeeds and a final order is made.

24.3 DISCONTINUANCE

1BA-144 **24.3.1** A case may be ended by discontinuing the claim, which may be done at any point in the proceedings.[1]

24.3.2 Discontinuance requires the claimant to file a notice of discontinuance (Form N279) and serve it on all parties.[2] There is no Court fee payable when discontinuing.

24.3.3 The claimant may discontinue the claim in relation to all or some of the parties.[3]

24.3.4 The Court's permission is required to discontinue where the claimant has obtained an interim injunction[4] or any party has given an undertaking to the Court.[5] This can be done by filing the notice of discontinuance, referring to the fact that permission is required, and the ACO will forward the notice to a judge to give permission without a hearing (unless the judge orders a hearing and representations). In other cases, permission is not required.

24.3.5 The discontinuance will take effect from the date on which the notice of discontinuance is served on the defendant(s).[6]

24.3.6 By filing a notice of discontinuance, the claimant accepts that he or she is liable for the defendant's costs up until that date[7] (unless the parties have agreed a different costs order) and a costs order will be deemed to have been made on the standard basis[8] (see para 25.2.3 of this Guide). The claimant may apply to reverse the general rule that he or she is liable for costs. Any such application must demonstrate a good reason for departing from the general rule. A good reason may exist if the defendant has behaved unreasonably. Any such application must be made in accordance with the interim applications procedure (see para 13.7 of this Guide).

24.4 CONSENT ORDERS AND UNCONTESTED PROCEEDINGS

1BA-145 **24.4.1** If the parties agree to end a claim, they must seek the approval of the Court. The parties must file 3 copies of a draft agreed order with the ACO, together with (a) a short statement of the matters relied on as justifying the proposed agreed order, and (b) copies of any authorities or statutory provisions relied on. Both the draft order and the agreed statement must be signed by all parties (including interested parties) to the claim. The relevant fee must also be paid.[9] The Court will only approve the order if it is satisfied that the order should be made; if not so satisfied, a hearing

---

[1] CPR 38.2(1).
[2] CPR 38.3(1).
[3] CPR 38.2(3).
[4] CPR 38.2(2)(i).
[5] CPR 38.2(2)(ii).
[6] CPR 38.5(1).
[7] CPR 38.6(1).
[8] CPR 44.9(1)(c).
[9] CPR 54A PD para 16. See Annex 2 of this Guide for the fee.

date may be set. The open justice principle applies to a determination made on the papers and the Court may have to give consideration to the question whether there should be public access to documents.[1]

24.4.2 The terms of the order can include anything that the parties wish the Court to approve, but will generally include the following:

24.4.2.1 an indication (often in the header to the order as well as in the recitals) that the order is made "By Consent";[2]

24.4.2.2 the signature of the legal representative for every party to the claim, or of the party themselves where he or she is acting in person;[3]

24.4.2.3 where the order will finally determine the claim, the manner of determination (e.g. that the claim is withdrawn or that the decision challenged is quashed).

24.4.3 Where the claim is withdrawn, this leaves the challenged decision in place (unless the defendant has voluntarily withdrawn the decision, thus removing the claimant's need to obtain the relief of the Court). Where the decision is quashed, it will be of no legal effect.

24.4.4 The consent order should make provision for determining costs, otherwise a deemed costs order will apply (see para 25.8 of this Guide for deemed costs orders). This is generally done in one of 3 ways:

24.4.4.1 by providing for an agreed, set sum to be paid between the parties;

24.4.4.2 by allowing the parties to agree the quantum of costs after the consent order has been finalised, with a fall-back option of applying for detailed assessment of costs. For example: the claimant is to pay the defendant's reasonable costs, to be subject to detailed assessment if not agreed (see para 25.3.4 of this Guide for detailed assessment);

24.4.4.3 by making provision for summary assessment of costs on the papers. Such a provision should follow the ACO Costs Guidance.

24.4.4.4 where the agreement relates to an order for costs only, the parties need only file a document signed by all the parties setting out the terms of the proposed order (a fee is payable).

24.5 SETTLEMENTS ON BEHALF OF CHILDREN AND PROTECTED PARTIES

24.5.1 Where a claim is made by or on behalf of, or against, a child or a protected party[4] no settlement, compromise or payment and no acceptance of money paid into Court shall be valid without the approval of the Court.[5] **1BA-146**

24.5.2 To obtain the Court's approval, an application must be made in accordance with the procedure described at para 13.7 of this Guide.

24.6 OTHER POINTS OF PRACTICE

24.6.1 The parties have an obligation to inform the Court if they believe that a case is likely to settle as soon as they become aware of the possibility of settlement.[6] Such information allows judges and staff to allocate preparation time and hearing time accordingly. Failure to do so may result in the Court making an adverse costs order against the parties (see para 25.1 of this Guide for costs). **1BA-147**

24.6.2 When a case is closed by the ACO the file may be immediately reduced in size for storage (or "broken up"). Particulars of claim and witness statements are retained on the closed file but all exhibits, written evidence, and authorities are destroyed. The reduced file is retained for 3 years after the case is closed. It is then destroyed.

25 COSTS

25.1 LIABILITY FOR COSTS

25.1.1 The Court has a discretion whether to order one party to pay the legal costs of another.[7] The discretion is governed by CPR Part 44. **1BA-148**

25.1.2 Where the Court decides to make an order for costs, the general rule is that the unsuccessful party will be ordered to pay the costs of the successful party.[8]

---

[1] See *UXA v Merseycare NHS Foundation Trust* [2021] EWHC 3455, [2022] 4 WLR 30.

[2] CPR 40.6(7)(b).

[3] CPR 54A PD para 16(1). "Party" for these purposes includes an interested party.

[4] CPR 21.1.

[5] CPR 21.10.

[6] *Yell Ltd v Garton* [2004] EWCA Civ 87, [6].

[7] s.51(1) of the Senior Courts Act 1981 and CPR 44.2(1).

[8] CPR 44.2(2)(a) and *R (M) v Croydon London Borough Council* [2012] EWCA Civ 595, [58]-[65]. The fact that one party is publicly funded is "not necessarily irrelevant" to the exercise of discretion on costs: *ZN (Afghanistan) v Secretary of State for the Home Department* [2018] EWCA Civ 1059, [91]-[92] and [106].

25.1.3 In deciding whether to make a different order, the Court must have regard to all the circumstances of the case, including the conduct of the parties.

25.1.4 The conduct of the parties includes (but is not limited to):[1]

25.1.4.1 conduct before as well as during the proceedings, and in particular the extent to which the parties followed the pre-action Protocol (see para 6.2 of this Guide);

25.1.4.2 whether it was reasonable for a party to raise, pursue or contest a particular allegation or issue;

25.1.4.3 the manner in which a party has pursued or defended their case or a particular allegation or issue; and

25.1.4.4 whether a claimant who has succeeded in the claim, in whole or in part, has exaggerated their claim.

25.1.5 Where a party has failed to comply with orders of the Court or other procedural rules (such as those outlined in this Guide) the Court may:

25.1.5.1 in a case where the party in default is the successful party, reduce the amount of costs to which he or she would normally be entitled; and

25.1.5.2 in a case where the party in default is the unsuccessful party, require that party to pay more than would otherwise be considered reasonable.

25.1.6 Where a party has succeeded on only part of its case a judge will ordinarily require the losing party to pay costs only insofar as they relate to the parts of the claim that have succeeded, or pay only a percentage of the winning party's costs.

25.2 REASONABLE COSTS AND THE BASIS OF THE ASSESSMENT

1BA-149 **25.2.1** The Court will not require payment of costs which have been unreasonably incurred or are unreasonable in amount.[2] In deciding whether costs are reasonable the Court will have regard to all the circumstances of the case.[3]

25.2.2 The amount payable is assessed (i.e. determined) either on the standard basis of assessment or on the indemnity basis of assessment.

25.2.3 Most costs orders are made on the standard basis. Where a Court order is silent as to the basis, the presumption is that the standard basis applies.[4]

25.2.4 Where the amount of costs is to be assessed on the standard basis, the Court will allow only those costs which are proportionate to the matters in issue. Where there is doubt as to whether costs were reasonable and proportionate in amount the Court will determine the question in favour of the paying party.[5] Costs incurred are proportionate if they bear a reasonable relationship to:[6]

25.2.4.1 the sums in issue in the proceedings;
25.2.4.2 the value of any non-monetary relief in issue in the proceedings;
25.2.4.3 the complexity of the litigation;
25.2.4.4 any additional work generated by the conduct of the paying party; and
25.2.4.5 any wider factors involved in the proceedings, such as reputation or public importance.

25.2.5 The Court will assess costs on the indemnity basis in cases where the losing party has acted unreasonably in bringing, maintaining or defending the claim or in any other way.

25.2.6 Where the amount of costs is to be assessed on an indemnity basis, the Court will resolve any doubt it may have as to whether costs were reasonably incurred or were reasonable in amount in favour of the receiving party. There is no requirement that the costs be proportionately incurred or proportionate in amount.[7]

25.3 SUMMARY AND DETAILED ASSESSMENT

1BA-150 **25.3.1** Where the Court orders a party to pay costs to another party, it may either assess those costs itself summarily (i.e. undertake a summary assessment), or order that a detailed assessment be undertaken by a Costs Judge.[8]

25.3.2 Where the Court does not make a summary assessment and does not mention the manner of assessment in a costs order, detailed assessment is presumed.[9]

25.3.3 The general rule is that the Court should make a summary assessment at the conclusion of any hearing which has lasted no more than one day, unless there is good reason not to do so. The Court may decide not to make a summary assessment if the paying party shows substantial grounds for disputing the sum claimed and the dispute is not suitable for summary determination.

---

[1] CPR 44.2(5).
[2] CPR 44.3(1).
[3] CPR 44.4(1).
[4] CPR 44.3(4)(a).
[5] CPR 44.3(2).
[6] CPR 44.3(5).
[7] CPR 44.3(3).
[8] CPR 44.6(1).
[9] CPR 44 PD para 8.2.

The costs covered by the summary assessment will be those of the application or matter to which the hearing related. If the hearing disposes of the whole claim, the order may deal with the costs of the whole claim.[1]

25.3.4 The procedure for summary assessment is as follows:

25.3.4.1 For any hearing which is listed to last for one day or less, each party who intends to claim costs must file and serve on the other parties a statement of costs. This must be done not less than 24 hours before the time fixed for the hearing (unless a judge has ordered a different timetable).[2]

25.3.4.2 The statement should follow as closely as possible Form N260 and must be signed by the party or the party's legal representative.[3]

25.3.4.3 Where an application is to be determined without a hearing, the statement of costs should be filed and served with the application papers.

25.3.4.4 The Court will not make a summary assessment of the costs of a receiving party who is an assisted person or a person for who civil legal services (within the meaning of Part 1 of the Legal Aid, Sentencing and Punishment of Offenders Act 2012) are provided under arrangements made for the purposes of that Part of that Act.[4]

25.3.4.5 The Court will not make a summary assessment of the costs of a receiving party who is a child or protected party within CPR Part 21 unless the legal representative acting for the child or protected party has waived the right to further costs. The Court may, however, make a summary assessment of the costs payable by a child or protected party.[5]

25.3.4.6 Unless a judge orders otherwise, any costs order must be complied with within 14 days of the costs order,[6] although the parties may vary this time limit and agree their own payment terms without seeking the agreement of the Court.

25.3.5 The procedure for detailed assessment is as follows:

25.3.5.1 Detailed guidance on the procedure for detailed assessment can be found in the Senior Courts Costs Office Guide, which can be found online at the following website: *www.gov.uk/government/publications/senior-courts-costs-office-guide.*

25.3.5.2 Where detailed assessment has been ordered by the Administrative Court in London, the application for detailed assessment of costs must be started at the Senior Courts Costs Office in London.

25.3.5.3 Where detailed assessment has been ordered by the Administrative Court sitting outside of London, the application for detailed assessment of costs must be made in the District Registry associated with the relevant ACO. For example, for a judicial review claim determined by the Administrative Court in Cardiff, the detailed costs assessment should be started in the District Registry in Cardiff, and so on. There is one exception: if the case is a Western Circuit case administered by the ACO in Cardiff but heard on the Western Circuit, any detailed cost assessment should be filed at the District Registry in Bristol.

25.3.5.4 It should be noted that detailed assessment proceedings are not Administrative Court proceedings and a new case number will be assigned to the proceedings. The ACO will not have any further involvement with the case.

25.4 COSTS ORDERS AT THE PERMISSION STAGE

25.4.1 If permission is granted, either on the papers or at an oral hearing, the claimant's costs are "costs in the case" (unless the Court make a different order). This means that whether the claimant will be able to recover the costs of the application for permission will depend on the outcome of the substantive hearing. **1BA-151**

25.4.2 If a defendant or interested party seeks their costs of responding to the application for permission to apply for judicial review an application should be included in Acknowledgment of Service, which should be accompanied by a schedule setting out the amount claimed (limited to the costs incurred in preparing the Acknowledgment of Service and the Summary Grounds of Defence).[7] If permission is refused on the papers, the judge will decide whether to award costs and, if so, will normally summarily assess them. This will be a final order unless the claimant makes representations in accordance with the directions contained in the judge's order.[8]

25.4.3 If the parties file costs representations outside the time permitted by the judge (usually 14 days) they must apply for an extension of time to file the costs submissions in accordance with the procedure at para 13.7 of this Guide.

---

[1] CPR 44 PD para 9.2.
[2] CPR 44 PD para 9.5(2) and (4)(b).
[3] CPR 44 PD para 9.5(3).
[4] CPR 44 PD para 9.8.
[5] CPR 44 PD para 9.9.
[6] CPR 44.7(1).
[7] *R (Ewing) v Office of the Deputy Prime Minister* [2005] EWCA Civ 1583, [2006] 1 WLR 1260, [47].
[8] *R (Jones) v Nottingham City Council* [2009] EWHC 271 (Admin).

25.4.4 If the claimant also seeks reconsideration of the refusal of permission at an oral hearing, any objections to costs that have been previously ordered may be considered at the renewal hearing. The Court may confirm or vary the earlier order as to costs.

25.4.5 If permission to apply for judicial review is refused at a hearing there are additional principles which the Court will generally apply:[1]

25.4.5.1 A successful defendant or other party at the permission stage who has filed an Acknowledgment of Service should generally recover the costs of doing so from the claimant, whether or not he or she attends any permission hearing.

25.4.5.2 A defendant or other party who attends and successfully resists the grant of permission at a renewal hearing will not usually recover from the claimant the costs of attending the hearing.[2]

25.4.5.3 A Court, in considering an award of costs against an unsuccessful claimant at a permission hearing, should only depart from the general principles above if it is considered that there are exceptional circumstances for doing so.

25.4.5.4 A Court considering costs at the permission stage should be allowed a broad discretion as to whether, on the facts of the case, there are exceptional circumstances justifying the award of costs against an unsuccessful claimant.

25.4.5.5 Exceptional circumstances may consist in the presence of one or more of the features in the following non-exhaustive list: (a) the hopelessness of the claim; (b) the persistence in it by the claimant after having been alerted to facts and/or of the law demonstrating its hopelessness; (c) the extent to which the Court considers that the claimant, in the pursuit of his application, has sought to abuse the process of judicial review; (d) whether, as a result of the deployment of full argument and documentary evidence by both sides at the hearing, the unsuccessful claimant has had, in effect, the advantage of an early substantive hearing of the claim; (e) whether the unsuccessful claimant has substantial resources which it has used to pursue the unfounded claim and which are available to meet an order for costs; (f) whether the permission was refused at a rolled-up hearing, in which event the defendant, who has prepared for a substantive hearing, may be awarded costs.

25.5 COSTS WHEN A CLAIM HAS BEEN SETTLED

1BA-152 **25.5.1** When a case is settled, parties should seek to agree costs through reasoned negotiation, mindful of the overriding objective and the amount of costs at stake. Only if they cannot agree should they apply to the Court for an order.

25.5.2 In their discussions on costs, the parties should bear in mind that the Court may already have decided the issue of costs of the application for permission. Where this decision amounts to a final order (see para 24.4.2 of this Guide), the Court must not be asked to revisit the decision in any submissions on costs.

25.5.3 Where a claim has settled (see para 24.4 of this Guide), but the parties have been unable to agree costs, the parties should follow the ACO Costs Guidance dated April 2016.

25.5.4 The Court will consider what order on costs to make in accordance with the principles contained in *M v Croydon London Borough Council* [2012] EWCA Civ 595, [2012] 1 WLR 2607 and *R (Tesfay) v Secretary of State for the Home Department* [2016] EWCA Civ 415, [2016] 1 WLR 4853.

25.6 INTERESTED PARTIES AND COSTS

1BA-153 **25.6.1** In cases where the claimant is unsuccessful at the substantive stage, the Court does not generally order an unsuccessful claimant to pay two sets of costs. However, it may do so where the defendant and the interested party have different interests which require separate representation.[3] If the claimant is acting in the public interest rather than out of personal gain then it is less likely that the Court will order the second set of costs.[4]

25.6.2 The Court may, however, and often does, order an unsuccessful claimant to pay two sets of costs of preparing Acknowledgments of Service at the permission stage.[5]

---

[1] *R (Mount Cook Ltd) v Westminster City Council* [2003] EWCA Civ 1346, [2004] CP Rep 12, [76].

[2] CPR 54A PD para 7.5.

[3] *Bolton MDC v Secretary of State for the Environment* [1995] 1 WLR 1176.

[4] *R (John Smeaton on behalf of Society for the Protection of Unborn Children) v Secretary of State for Health* [2002] EWHC 886 (Admin), [32]-[42]. See also *Campaign to Protect Rural England (Kent Branch) v Secretary of State for Communities and Local Government* [2019] EWCA Civ 1230.

[5] *R (Luton Borough Council) v Central Bedfordshire Council* [2014] EWHC 4325 (Admin), [221] - [226].

25.7 COSTS ORDERS IN FAVOUR OF AND AGAINST INTERVENERS

25.7.1 A person may apply to file evidence or make representations at a hearing[1] (see para 3.2.4 of this Guide). Such a person is commonly referred to as an intervener and there are specific rules governing whether an intervener can recover its costs or be ordered to pay costs, summarised below.[2] **1BA-154**

25.7.2 A claimant or defendant in substantive or permission judicial review proceedings,[3] cannot be ordered to pay an intervener's costs[4] unless there are exceptional circumstances that make such a costs order appropriate.[5]

25.7.3 Section 87 of the Criminal Justice and Courts Act 2015 sets out the conditions Under which the Court must order the intervener to pay any costs specified in an application by a claimant or defendant incurred by them as a result of the intervener's involvement in that stage of the proceedings. This applies where:[6]

25.7.3.1 the intervener has acted, in substance, as the sole or principal applicant or defendant; or

25.7.3.2 the intervener's evidence and representations, taken as a whole, have not been of significant assistance to the Court; or

25.7.3.3 a significant part of the intervener's evidence and representations relates to matters that it is not necessary for the Court to consider in order to resolve the issues that are the subject of the stage in the proceedings; or

25.7.3.4 the intervener has behaved unreasonably.

25.7.4 If the intervener becomes a party, the costs provisions above no longer apply and are treated as never having applied.[7]

25.8 ORDERS WHICH DO NOT MENTION COSTS

25.8.1 Where an order made by the Administrative Court does not mention costs: **1BA-155**

25.8.1.1 normally, the Court is deemed to have made no order as to costs;[8] but

25.8.1.2 in the case of an order granting permission to appeal, permission to apply for judicial review, or any other order or direction sought by a party on an application without notice, it is deemed to include an order that the applicant's costs are in the case (i.e. they will depend on the outcome of the claim).[9]

25.8.2 Any party may apply to vary a deemed costs order made in accordance with para 25.8.1.2 (but not para 25.8.1.1) of this Guide.[10] Such an application must be made in accordance with the interim orders procedure (see para 13.7 of this Guide).

25.9 APPLICATIONS TO SET ASIDE COSTS ORDERS

25.9.1 Save for deemed costs orders (see para 25.8 above), any costs order where the parties have had the opportunity to make representations before the order was made, whether made on the papers or after an oral hearing, is a final costs order.[11] The Administrative Court may not set it aside or reconsider the order at a hearing. If challenged, the order must be appealed (see Chapter 26 of this Guide). **1BA-156**

25.10 COSTS ORDERS WHEN THE PAYING PARTY IS IN RECEIPT OF LEGAL AID

25.10.1 Costs orders can be made against persons who have the benefit of legal aid (subject to the principles discussed earlier in this section of the Guide). Where the Court does make such an order it will order that the person with the benefit of legal aid must pay the costs of the requesting party and the Court may set the amount to be paid, but the Court will note that the person with the benefit of legal aid is subject to costs protection in accordance with s. 26 of the Legal Aid, Sentencing and Punishment of Offenders Act 2012. **1BA-157**

25.10.2 Costs protection means that the legally aided person is not automatically liable for the costs. If the person awarded costs wishes to require the legally aided person to pay those costs, he or she must apply for an order from the Senior Courts Costs Office or, where the costs order was made by an Administrative Court outside London, to the relevant associated District Registry.

---

1 CPR 54.17.
2 s.87 of the Criminal Justice and Courts Act 2015.
3 s.87(9) and (10) of the Criminal Justice and Courts Act 2015.
4 s.87(3) of the Criminal Justice and Courts Act 2015.
5 s.87(4) of the Criminal Justice and Courts Act 2015.
6 s.87(5) of the Criminal Justice and Courts Act 2015.
7 s.87(11) of the Criminal Justice and Courts Act 2015.
8 CPR 44.10(1)(a)(i).
9 CPR 44.10(2).
10 CPR 44.10(3).
11 *R (Jones) v Nottingham City Council* [2009] EWHC 271 (Admin), [2009] ACD 42; *R (Bahta) v Secretary of State for the Home Department* [2011] EWCA Civ 895, [2011] CP Rep 43.

25.11 ORDERS THAT COSTS BE PAID FROM CENTRAL FUNDS (CRIMINAL CASES ONLY)

1BA-158 **25.11.1** Where a claimant who was the defendant in a criminal court is successful in a judicial review claim relating to a criminal cause or matter, a Divisional Court may make a costs order, for payment out of central funds. In proceedings before a Divisional Court in respect of a summary offence, the court may order the payment out of central funds of such amount as the court considers reasonably sufficient to compensate a private prosecutor for any expenses properly incurred in the proceedings.[1] Where such an order is made, whether in favour of a defendant or a private prosecutor, the sum is paid by the Ministry of Justice.

25.11.2 The costs order is made in such amount as the Court considers reasonably sufficient to compensate for any expenses properly incurred in the proceedings, unless the Court considers that there are circumstances that make it inappropriate for the applicant to recover the full amount, in which case the Court may order a lesser amount that it considers just and reasonable.

25.11.3 The costs order may not require the payment out of central funds of an amount that includes legal costs unless those costs were incurred in proceedings in the Court below (Magistrates' Court or Crown Court on appeal against conviction or sentence).[2]

25.11.4 There is no power for a single judge to order costs be paid out of central funds. Where a claimant seeks an order for costs from central funds when appearing before a single judge, the judge will adjourn the matter to be considered on the papers by a Divisional Court, constituted by the single judge who heard the case and another judge.

25.11.5 When making the costs order, the Court will fix the amount to be paid out of central funds in the order if it considers it appropriate to do so.[3] Where the Court does not fix the amount to be paid out of central funds in the order it must describe in the order any reduction required and the amount must be fixed by means of a determination made by or on behalf of the Court by the Senior Courts Costs Office.[4]

25.11.6 If the claimant has the benefit of a representation order or a legal aid certificate there can be no claim for costs out of central funds.[5]

25.11.7 Where an order for costs from central funds has been made the claimant must forward the order to the Senior Courts Costs Office, which will arrange for payment of the amount specified.

25.12 COSTS ORDERS AGAINST COURTS, TRIBUNALS OR CORONERS

1BA-159 **25.12.1** Where judicial review proceedings are brought against a court, tribunal or coroner as defendant, and the defendant adopts a neutral position or attends to make submissions on procedure or law, the Administrative Court will generally not make a costs order against them.

25.12.2 In such cases, it may be appropriate for the Court to make a costs order against the interested party which took the underlying administrative decision which led to proceedings before the Court or tribunal. For example, in judicial review proceedings against the Upper Tribunal in immigration cases, the Court may make a costs order against the Secretary of State for the Home Department, who will generally be named as an interested party.[6]

25.12.3 Where a court, tribunal or coroner does contest the claim, it (or he or she) becomes liable for costs, subject to the principles discussed in this section of the Guide.

25.13 WASTED COSTS ORDERS

1BA-160 **25.13.1** In appropriate cases the Court has power to order that a legal representative should pay the costs of an opposing party or that a specified sum for costs is disallowed.[7] These orders are referred to as wasted costs orders.

25.13.2 A wasted costs order may be made against the receiving party's own legal representatives or against the representatives of the paying party.[8]

25.13.3 An application for a wasted costs order may be made by the party who suffered the wasted costs or may be ordered of the Court's own volition.

25.13.4 When considering whether to make a wasted costs order, the Court will consider 3 questions:[9]

25.13.4.1 Did the legal representative (or any employee of the representative) act improperly, unreasonably or negligently?

---

[1] s.16(6) and 17 of the Prosecution of Offences Act 1985. See *Lord Howard of Lympne v Director of Public Prosecutions* [2018] EWHC 100 (Admin).

[2] s.16A(1) and (4) of the Prosecution of Offences Act 1985.

[3] s.16(6C) of the Prosecution of Offences Act 1985.

[4] s.16(6D) of the Prosecution of Offences Act 1985.

[5] s.21(4A) of the Prosecution of Offences Act 1985.

[6] *R (Faqiri) v Upper Tribunal (Immigration and Asylum Chamber) v Secretary of State for the Home Department* [2019] EWCA Civ 151, [2019] 1 WLR 4497, [51].

[7] s.51(6) of the Senior Courts Act 1981 and CPR 46.8.

[8] *Brown v Bennett* [2002] 1 WLR 713.

[9] CPR 46 PD para 5.5 and *In Re A Barrister (Wasted Costs Order) (No 1 of 1991)* [1993] QB 293.

25.13.4.2 If so, did the conduct cause the party who incurred the costs to incur unnecessary costs or has the conduct caused costs incurred by a party prior to the conduct to be wasted?

25.13.4.3 If so, is it just in all the circumstances to order the legal representative to compensate the subject of the wasted costs for the whole or part of the relevant costs?

25.13.5 The Court will give the legal representative a reasonable opportunity to make written submissions or, if the legal representative prefers, to attend a hearing before it makes such an order.[1]

25.13.6 Wasted costs applications should generally be considered by the Court at the end of proceedings, unless there is good reason to consider them at another time.[2]

25.14 COSTS ORDERS WHERE A PARTY IS REPRESENTED PRO BONO

25.14.1 Section 194 of the Legal Services Act 2007 makes provision for the recovery of costs where the representation has been provided pro bono (free of charge to the represented party).[3] Where such an order is made, the costs awarded in favour of that party will not be payable to the party's legal representatives but to a charity, the Access to Justice Foundation. **1BA-161**

25.15 ENVIRONMENTAL LAW CLAIMS

25.15.1 There are limits on the amount of costs that a party may be ordered to pay in "Aarhus Convention claims" (i.e. certain claims involving environmental issues). The costs caps do not affect the application of the normal principles for ordering or assessing costs and are applied once those decisions are made.[4] **1BA-162**

25.15.2 The caps only apply where the claimant is a member of the public.[5] This includes natural persons, corporations and unincorporated associations,[6] but does not include public bodies.

25.15.3 An Aarhus Convention claim is a claim for judicial review or statutory review[7] which deals with subject matter within the scope of Articles 9(1), 9(2), or 9(3) of the Convention on Access to Information, Public Participation in Decision Making and Access to Justice in Environmental Matters (the Aarhus Convention).[8]

25.15.4 A claimant who believes that their claim is an Aarhus Convention claim and wishes to apply for a costs cap under these provisions must note that fact in Part 7 of the Claim Form[9] and file and serve with the Claim Form a schedule of their financial resources which is verified by a statement of truth and provides details of:[10]

25.15.4.1 the claimant's significant assets, liabilities, income and expenditure; and

25.15.4.2 in relation to any financial support which any person has provided or is likely to provide to the claimant, the aggregate amount which has been provided and which is likely to be provided.

25.15.5 If the claimant does not comply with para 25.15.4, the costs caps will not apply.[11]

25.15.6 Where the claimant complies with para 25.15.4, the costs limit is automatically in place.[12] The current costs limit is £5,000 where the claimant is claiming only as an individual and not as, or on behalf of, a business or other legal person. In all other cases the limit is £10,000. Where a defendant is ordered to pay costs, the limit is £35,000.[13]

25.15.7 The Court may vary or remove the limits outlined at para 25.15.6,[14] but only on an application[15] and only if satisfied that:

25.15.7.1 to do so would not make the costs of the proceedings prohibitively expensive for the claimant; and

25.15.7.2 in the case of a variation which would reduce a claimant's maximum costs liability or increase that of a defendant, without the variation the costs of the proceedings would be prohibitively expensive for the claimant.

---

[1] CPR 46.8(2).

[2] *Filmlab Systems International Ltd v Pennington* [1995] 1 WLR 673.

[3] CPR 46.7.

[4] *R (Campaign to Protect Rural England (Kent Branch) v Secretary of State for Communities and Local Government* [2019] EWCA Civ 1230, [2020] 1 WLR 352.

[5] CPR 45.41(2)(a).

[6] CPR 45.41(2)(a) and (b) and Article 2.4 of the Aarhus Convention

[7] Statutory review includes an appeal under s.289 of the Town and Country Planning Act 1990 or s. 65 of the Planning (Listed Buildings and Conservation Areas) Act 1990: see CPR 45.41(3).

[8] CPR 45.41(2)(a).

[9] CPR 45.42(1)(a).

[10] CPR 45.42(1)(b).

[11] CPR 45.42(1)-(2).

[12] CPR 45.42(1).

[13] CPR 45.43(2)-(3).

[14] CPR 45.44(1).

[15] The application must be made in accordance with CPR 45.44(5)-(7).

25.15.8 Proceedings are prohibitively expensive if the likely costs (including any court fees payable) either:[1] exceed the financial resources of the claimant; or are objectively unreasonable having regard to the six factors listed in CPR 45.44(3), namely:

25.15.8.1 the situation of the parties;
25.15.8.2 whether the claimant has a reasonable prospect of success;
25.15.8.3 the importance of what is at stake for the claimant;
25.15.8.4 the importance of what is at stake for the environment;
25.15.8.5 the complexity of the relevant law and procedure; and
25.15.8.6 whether the claim is frivolous.

25.15.9 When the Court considers the financial resources of the claimant for these purposes, it must have regard to any financial support which any person has provided or is likely to provide to the claimant.[2]

25.15.10 Where the defendant intends to challenge the assertion that the Aarhus Convention applies and, therefore, that the costs limit does not apply, the challenge should be made in the Acknowledgment of Service.[3] The Court will then determine the issue at the earliest opportunity.[4]

25.15.11 In any proceedings to determine whether the claim is an Aarhus Convention claim:[5]

25.15.11.1 if the Court holds that the claim is not an Aarhus Convention claim, it will normally make no order for costs in relation to those proceedings;

25.15.11.2 if the Court holds that the claim is an Aarhus Convention claim, it will normally order the defendant to pay the claimant's costs of those proceedings to be assessed on the standard basis. That order may be enforced even if this would increase the costs payable by the defendant beyond the amount stated at para 25.15.6 above or any variation of it.

26 APPEALS

26.1 APPEALS IN CIVIL CASES

1BA-163 **26.1.1** In civil cases, parties may seek to appeal to the Court of Appeal. Permission to appeal is required. The procedure is discussed between paras 26.2 and 26.6 of this Guide.

26.2 CHALLENGING A DECISION TO GRANT PERMISSION TO APPLY FOR JUDICIAL REVIEW

1BA-164 **26.2.1** Where permission to apply for judicial review has been granted neither the defendant nor any other person served with the Claim Form may apply to set aside the order granting permission to bring a judicial review.[6]

26.2.2 If the defendant or another interested party has not been served with the Claim Form, he or she may apply to the Administrative Court to set aside permission, but the power to set aside permission is exercised sparingly and only in a very clear case.[7]

26.3 APPEALS AGAINST THE REFUSAL TO GRANT PERMISSION TO APPLY FOR JUDICIAL REVIEW

1BA-165 **26.3.1** Where permission to apply for judicial review has been refused after a hearing in the Administrative Court, the claimant may apply for permission to appeal, but the application must be made directly to the Court of Appeal.[8]

26.3.2 Where the claim challenges a decision of the Upper Tribunal, or the application for permission to appeal for judicial review has been certified as totally without merit, there is no right to request reconsideration of that refusal at an oral hearing in the Administrative Court. In these cases, the applicant can apply to the Court of Appeal directly for permission to appeal.[9]

26.3.3 An appeal against the refusal of permission to apply for judicial review must be filed with the Court of Appeal within 7 days of the date of the decision, unless the Administrative Court

---

[1] CPR 45.44(2).
[2] CPR 45.44(3).
[3] CPR 45.45(1).
[4] CPR 45.45(2).
[5] CPR 45.45(3).
[6] CPR 54.13.
[7] See *R v Secretary of State ex p. Chinoy* (1992) 4 Admin L Rep 457.
[8] CPR 52.8(1); *Glencore Energy UK Ltd v Commissioners of HM Revenue and Customs* [2017] EWHC 1587 (Admin).
[9] CPR 52.8(2).

sets a different timetable.[1] In a case where the decision is made on paper and there is no right to reconsideration (para 26.3.2 of this Guide), the 7 days begins from the date of service of the order, not the date of the decision.[2]

26.3.4 The Court of Appeal may, instead of giving permission to appeal, give permission to apply for judicial review, in which event the case will proceed in the Administrative Court unless the Court of Appeal orders otherwise.[3]

26.4 APPEALS AGAINST CASE MANAGEMENT ORDERS

26.4.1 Before considering appealing against a case management order, parties should consider whether there is a right to apply for reconsideration of the order in the Administrative Court (see para 9.4 of this Guide). **1BA-166**

26.4.2 Where there is not, and the order is final, the time limit for appealing remains 21 days in civil cases, but the proceedings in the Administrative Court will not necessarily await the decision of the Court of Appeal. If the parties wish the Administrative Court proceedings to be stayed, they must make an application (see para 13.7 of this Guide).

26.4.3 Permission to appeal is generally granted more sparingly in appeals against case management orders. The Court of Appeal will consider not only whether the appeal would have a real prospect of success or there is some other compelling reason why the appeal should be heard, but also the significance of the decision, the costs involved in appealing, the delay or disruption likely to be caused to the Administrative Court proceedings, and whether the point would be better dealt with at or after the substantive hearing.

26.5 APPEALS AGAINST INTERIM ORDERS MADE BY A MASTER

26.5.1 An appeal against the order of the Master made at an oral hearing may be appealed to a High Court Judge. **1BA-167**

26.5.2 The application for permission to appeal must be filed on Form N161 and lodged with the ACO. The guidance above, save for any references to the Court of Appeal, equally apply to appeals against the Master's decisions.

26.6 APPEALS AGAINST DECISIONS MADE AT THE SUBSTANTIVE HEARING OF AN APPLICATION FOR JUDICIAL REVIEW

26.6.1 Where a party wishes to appeal against the Court's decision following a substantive hearing, permission to appeal is required. This can be granted by the Administrative Court or by the Court of Appeal. **1BA-168**

26.6.2 Applications for permission to the Administrative Court should be made at the hearing at which the decision to be appealed is made unless the Court directs the application to be made later.[4] The Court may adjourn the question of permission to appeal to another date or to be considered on written representations, but it must make an order doing so at the time of the hearing when the decision is made.

26.6.3 If permission to appeal is refused by the Administrative Court, a second application for permission to appeal may be made to the Court of Appeal by filing an Appellant's Notice (Form N161).[5]

26.6.4 Alternatively, a first application for permission to appeal can be made directly to the Court of Appeal. Any party seeking to appeal should submit grounds of appeal that are focused, clear and concise.[6] Parties must follow the relevant provisions of the CPR and Practice Directions on appeals.

26.6.5 In appeals against substantive decisions of the Administrative Court, the Appellant's Notice must be lodged with the Court of Appeal within 21 days of the date of the decision or within the time limit ordered by the Administrative Court.[7]

26.6.6 Permission to appeal will only be granted if the Court of Appeal finds that the appeal would have a real prospect of success or there is some other compelling reason why the appeal should be heard.[8]

26.6.7 Further information on appeals to the Court of Appeal can be provided by the Civil Appeals Office (see Annex 1 for contact details).

---

[1] CPR 52.8(3).
[2] CPR 52.8(4).
[3] CPR 52.8(5).
[4] CPR 52.3(2)(a).
[5] CPR 52.3(3) and CPR 52.12(1).
[6] *Hickey v Secretary of State for Work and Pensions* [2018] EWCA Civ 851, [2018] 4 WLR 71.
[7] CPR 52.12(2).
[8] CPR 52.6(1).

26.7 APPEALS IN CRIMINAL CAUSES OR MATTERS

1BA-169 **26.7.1** There is no right of appeal from the Administrative Court to the Court of Appeal in cases relating to any criminal cause or matter.[1] Whether an application for judicial review concerns a criminal cause or matter depends on the nature and character of the underlying litigation. The question is whether the direct outcome of the proceedings which underlay the proceedings in the High Court was that a person was placed in jeopardy of criminal trial and punishment for an alleged offence.[2]

26.7.2 In such cases, the only route of appeal from the Administrative Court is to the Supreme Court. An appeal to the Supreme Court is only possible where:

26.7.2.1 the Administrative Court certifies that the case raises a point of law of general public importance;[3] and

26.7.2.2 permission to appeal is granted (either by the Administrative Court or by the Supreme Court).

26.7.3 An application for permission to appeal to the Supreme Court and for a certificate that the case raises a point of law of general public importance must be made to the Administrative Court within 28 days of the decision challenged or the date when reasons for the decision are given.[4]

26.7.4 The application for a certificate of a point of law and for permission to appeal may be made in the same application. The procedure is the same as the interim applications procedure (see para 13.7 above). The Court may decide to grant the certificate even if it decides to refuse permission to appeal. The certificate will be used in any application to the Supreme Court for permission to appeal.

26.7.5 The right of appeal to the Supreme Court applies only to substantive decisions (i.e. there is no right of appeal for a refusal of permission to apply for judicial review).[5]

26.7.6 Further information on appeals to the Supreme Court can be obtained from the Supreme Court (see Annex 1 for contact details).

ANNEX 1

CONTACT DETAILS

THE ADMINISTRATIVE COURT OFFICES

Website

1BA-170 *www.gov.uk/courts-tribunals/administrative-court*

Birmingham

The Administrative Court Office Birmingham Civil and Family Justice Hearing Centre
Priory Courts
33 Bull Street
Birmingham
West Midlands B4 6DS
DX 01987 Birmingham 7

Telephone Number: 0121 250 6733
General Email: *Birmingham@administrativecourtoffice.justice.gov.uk*
Skeleton Arguments Email: *Birmingham.skeletonarguments@administrativecourtoffice.justice.gov.uk*

Leeds

The Administrative Court Office Leeds Combined Court Centre
The Courthouse
Oxford Row
Leeds

---

[1] s.18(1)(a) of the Senior Courts Act 1981.

[2] For the scope of what constitutes a criminal case, reference should be made to *Re McGuinness (Attorney General for Northern Ireland and others intervening)* [2020] UKSC 6 which confirmed the criteria in *Amand v Secretary of State for Home Affairs* [1943] AC 147. See also *R (Cleeland) v Criminal Cases Review Commission* [2022] EWCA Civ 5 in which it was decided that challenges to Criminal Cases Review Commission decisions do not involve a criminal cause or matter.

[3] s.1(2) of the Administration of Justice Act 1960.

[4] s.2(1) of the Administration of Justice Act 1960.

[5] *Re Poh* [1983] 1 All ER 287.

West Yorkshire LS1 3BG
DX: 703016 Leeds 6

Telephone Number: 0113 306 2578
General Email: *Leeds@administrativecourtoffice.justice.gov.uk*
Skeleton Arguments Email: *Leeds.skeletonarguments@administrativecourtoffice.justice.gov.uk*

London

The Administrative Court Office Royal Courts of Justice
The Strand
London WC2A 2LL
DX 44457 Strand

Telephone Number: 020 7947 6655
The Administrative Court public counter is open from 10am to 4:30pm.
From 3pm only urgent applications can be issued.
General Email: *generaloffice@administrativecourtoffice.justice.gov.uk*
Skeleton Arguments Email: *london.skeletonarguments@administrativecourtoffice.justice.gov.uk*
List Office Email: *listoffice@administrativecourtoffice.justice.gov.uk*
Case Progression Email: *caseprogression@administrativecourtoffice.justice.gov.uk*
Case Progression (Crime and Extradition only) Email: *crimex@administrativecourtoffice.justice.gov.uk*

Manchester

The Administrative Court Office Manchester Civil Justice Centre
1 Bridge Street West
Manchester M60 9DJ
DX 724783 Manchester 44

Telephone Number: 0161 240 5313
General Email: *Manchester@administrativecourtoffice.justice.gov.uk*
Skeleton Arguments Email: *Manchester.skeletonarguments@administrativecourtoffice.justice.gov.uk*

Wales and the Western Circuit

The Administrative Court Office Cardiff Civil Justice Centre
Park Street
Cardiff CF10 1ET
DX 99500 Cardiff 6

Telephone Number: 02920 376460
General Email: *Cardiff@administrativecourtoffice.justice.gov.uk Skeleton Arguments*
Email: *Cardiff.skeletonarguments@administrativecourtoffice.justice.gov.uk*

Upper Tribunal (Administrative Appeals Chamber)

Upper Tribunal (Administrative Appeals Chamber)
5th Floor, 7 Rolls Buildings
Fetter Lane
London EC4A 1NL
DX 160042 STRAND 4

Telephone Number: 020 7071 5662
Email *adminappeals@Justice.gov.uk*

Upper Tribunal (Immigration And Asylum Chamber)
For UTIAC – Judicial Reviews Only:
For London:

Upper Tribunal (Immigration and Asylum Chamber)
IA Field House, 15 Breams Buildings
London EC4A 1DZ

For UT(IAC) judicial reviews in Birmingham, Cardiff, Leeds, or Manchester, see the contact details for the Administrative Court Office in that area above.

For UTIAC - All non-judicial review cases:
Lodging Appeals:

Upper Tribunal (Immigration and Asylum Chamber)
IA Field House, 15 Breams Buildings,
London EC4A 1DZ

Unless advised otherwise, all other correspondence to:

Upper Tribunal (Immigration and Asylum Chamber)
Arnhem Support Centre, PO Box 6987
Leicester LE1 6ZX

Facsimile: 0116 249 4130
Customer Service Centre (Enquiry Unit) Telephone: 0300 123 171

Senior Courts Costs Office

Senior Courts Costs Office
Thomas More Building
Royal Courts of Justice
The Strand
London WC2A 2LL
DX 44454 Strand

Telephone Number: 020 7947 6469/ 6404 / 7818
Email: *SCCO@justice.gov.uk*
Website: *www.gov.uk/courts-tribunals/senior-courts-costs-office*

Court Of Appeal (Civil Division)

Civil Appeals Office, Room E307
Royal Courts of Justice
The Strand
London WC2A 2LL
DX: 44450 Strand

Telephone Number: 020 7947 7121/6533

Supreme Court

The Supreme Court
Parliament Square
London SW1P 3BD
DX 157230 Parliament Sq 4

Telephone Number: 020 7960 1500 or 1900

ANNEX 2

FORMS AND FEES

1BA-171

Act / Application	*Form**	*Fee***	*Ref***
Application for permission to apply for judicial review	N461 (Judicial Review Claim Form)	£154.00	1.9(a)
Reconsideration of permission at an oral hearing	86b	£385.00	1.9(b)
Continuing judicial review after permission has been granted Any fee paid under 1.9(aa) is deducted		£770.00	1.9(c)
Acknowledgment of Service	N462 (Judicial Review Acknowledgment of Service)	£0.00	-
Interim Application	N244 (Application Notice)	£275.00	2.4

Act / Application	*Form**	*Fee***	*Ref***
Consent Order	N244 (Application Notice) & Consent Order	£108.00	2.5
Discontinuance	N279 (Notice of Discontinuance)	£0.00	-
Urgent Consideration (within 48 hours of lodging claim)	N463 (Judicial Review Application for Urgent Consideration	£275.00 (unless made when lodging when the fee is £0.00)	2.4

* Current forms can be found at: *https://www.gov.uk/government/collections/administrative-court-forms*
** Schedule 1, Civil Proceedings Fees Order 2008 (as amended). The fees above were correct on 4 July 2022.

Annex 3

Addresses for Service of Central Government Departments[1]

Government Department	*Solicitor for Service*
Advisory, Conciliation and Arbitration Service Cabinet Office Commissioners for the Reduction of National Debt Crown Prosecution Service Department for Business, Energy and Industrial Strategy Department for Digital, Culture, Media and Sport Department for Education Department for Environment, Food and Rural Affairs Department for Health and Social Care Department for International Trade Department for Transport Export Credits Guarantee Department (UK Export Finance) Foreign, Commonwealth and Development Office Government Actuary's Department Health and Safety Executive	The Treasury Solicitor Government Legal Department 102 Petty France Westminster London SW1H 9GL
Her Majesty's Treasury Home Office Ministry of Defence Ministry of Housing, Communities and Local Government Ministry of Justice National Savings and Investments (NS&I) Northern Ireland Office Office for Budget Responsibility Office of the Secretary of State for Wales (Wales Office) Privy Council Office Public Works Loan Board Serious Fraud Office Statistics Board (UK Statistics Authority) The National Archives	The Treasury Solicitor Government Legal Department 102 Petty France Westminster London SW1H 9GL
Competition and Markets Authority	Director of Litigation Competition and Markets Authority 25 Cabot Square Canary Wharf London E14 4QZ
Department for Work and Pensions	Legal Director's Office Department for Work and Pensions Caxton House

1BA-172

[1] Addresses other than Government Legal Department are taken from published list by Penny Mordaunt, Paymaster General on 18 March 2021.

Government Department	*Solicitor for Service*
	Tothill Street London SW1H 9NA
Food Standards Agency	Head of Legal Services Food Standards Agency Floors 6 and 7 Clive House 70 Petty House London SW1H 9EX
Forestry Commission	Director of Estates Forestry Commission 620 Bristol Business Park Coldharbour Lane Bristol GL16 1EJ
Gas and Electricity Markets Authority (Ofgem)	General Counsel Office of Gas and Electricity Markets The Office of General Counsel 10 South Colonnade Canary Wharf London E14 4PU
Her Majesty's Revenue and Customs	General Counsel and Solicitor to Her Majesty's Revenue and Customs HM Revenue and Customs 14 Westfield Avenue South West Wing Stratford London E20 1HZ
National Crime Agency	Legal Adviser National Crime Agency Units 1-6 Citadel Place Tinworth Street London SE11 5EF
Office for Standards in Education, Children's Services and Skills (Ofsted)	Deputy Director, Legal Services Ofsted Clive House 70 Petty France Westminster London SW1H 9EX
Office of Qualifications and Examinations Regulations (Ofqual)	Legal Director Ofqual Earlsdon Park 53-55 Butts Road Coventry CV1 3BH
Office of Rail and Road (ORR)	General Counsel Office of Rail and Road 25 Cabot Square Canary Wharf London E14 4QZ
Water Services Regulation Authority (Ofwat)	General Counsel Water Services Regulation Authority (Ofwat) Centre City Tower 7 Hill Street Birmingham B5 4UA
Welsh Government	The Director of Legal Services to the Welsh Government Cathays Park Cardiff CF10 3NQ
Welsh Revenue Authority	Head of Legal Welsh Revenue Authority QED Centre Main Avenue Treforest Industrial Estate Pontypridd CF37 9EH

ANNEX 4

LISTING POLICY FOR THE ADMINISTRATIVE COURT

Administrative Court Listing Policy (All business except extradition appeals)

INTRODUCTION

This policy replaces the listing policy issued in June 2018. **1BA-173**

It provides guidance for officers when listing cases in the Administrative Court. It will be applied by the Administrative Court Office in the Royal Courts of Justice, London ("the London ACO") and by each of the Administrative Court Offices on circuit ("the circuit ACOs" - i.e. the Administrative Court Offices in Cardiff, Birmingham, Leeds and Manchester). The policy is intended to provide guidance for listing officers.

The policy concerns the listing of all hearings for claims and appeals brought in the Administrative Court, save for extradition appeals. (The practice followed when listing hearings in extradition appeals, including expedited appeals is stated in Criminal Practice Direction 50.)

The Honourable Mr Justice Swift
Judge in Charge of the Administrative Court
30 June 2021

PART A:—GENERAL

URGENT INTERIM APPLICATIONS

1 The following applies to urgent applications filed within working hours (i.e. Monday to Friday, London 9am to 4.30pm, out of London 9am to 4pm). Any out of hours urgent application should be directed to the Queen's Bench Division out of hours duty clerk (020 7947 6000).

2 Any urgent application made to the Administrative Court within working hours must be made using Form N463.

3 Urgent applications should be made by filing (a) Form N463 (properly completed see Practice Direction 54B at §1.2); together with (b) the required application bundle (see Practice Direction 54B at §1.3). Wherever possible, urgent applications and supporting documents should be filed by email. They may also be filed by post and DX. Litigants in person without access to email should contact the relevant Administrative Court office to discuss possible alternative arrangements.

4 The appropriate fee must be paid. Court users who wish to lodge an urgent application without payment of the court fee are required to follow the procedure at Annex 1.

5 Each urgent application will be reviewed by an ACO lawyer to ensure it meets the requirements in Practice Direction 54B as appropriate - i.e. Practice Direction 54B at §§1.2 - 1.3 and 1.7 (all applications); §§2.2 - 2.4 (applications for interim relief); and §§3.1 - 3.2 (applications for expedition). If the application meets the requirements in Practice Direction 54B and requires immediate attention, it will be sent to a judge the same day.

6 When considering the application, the judge will have regard to the matters at §1.8 of Practice Direction 54B.

7 If an oral hearing is required, it will be listed in accordance with directions given by the judge. The parties will be notified of any directions given by email. Hearings are likely to be listed without reference to the availability of the parties or their representatives.

8 If an application made on Form N463 does not require urgent attention it may either be refused, or be allocated for consideration by a judge as a non-urgent interim application - see at Paragraph 13) below.

PERMISSION HEARINGS: JUDICIAL REVIEW CLAIMS AND STATUTORY APPEALS.

9 A permission hearing will be listed on receipt of a Renewal Notice (Form 86B) and the relevant fee or a Judge's order adjourning a permission application into court.

10 The general expectation for cases in London is that the parties will be notified of the date for the hearing of the renewed application within 2 weeks, and that the hearing of the application take place between 3 and 8 weeks of the date the Renewal Notice was filed. The practice for listing renewal hearings by the circuit ACOs may differ. Hearings will usually be fixed at the Court's convenience; counsel's availability will not ordinarily be a relevant consideration.

11 Hearings will be listed with a time estimate of 30 minutes. If any party considers that a different time estimate is required, the court must be informed immediately - see Practice Direction 54A at §7.7.

NON-URGENT INTERIM APPLICATIONS

12 Non-urgent interim applications must be made using Form N244. The time within which the application needs to be decided (or any other information relevant to the time within which the application must be decided) must be included in Form N244 and in a covering letter. The application must include a draft order. If particular directions are sought for the purposes of determining the application, those directions must be stated in Form N244.

13 Applications will ordinarily be considered on paper, in the first instance. Any directions necessary for the determination of an application will be given by the court. Any hearing required will be listed in accordance with those directions.

FINAL HEARINGS (INCLUDING ROLLED-UP HEARINGS): JUDICIAL REVIEW, STATUTORY APPEALS/ APPLICATIONS AND CASE STATED APPEALS

14 Save as provided otherwise (see Part D below), final hearings in judicial review claims and statutory appeals will be listed within 9 months of the date of issue.

15 Once permission is granted, the claimant must pay the relevant fee for continuation within the statutory time limit. If the fee is not paid within the time permitted, the case will be closed and will not be listed. Where a rolled-up hearing has been ordered, the claimant must give an undertaking to pay the continuation fee if permission is ultimately granted. If the undertaking is not given, the case will be closed and will not be listed.

16 A case will enter the Warned List of the first day following time allowed by the CPR (or judicial order) for filing and service of documents (e.g. in an application for judicial review, the date for filing and service of Detailed Grounds of Defence and evidence). Once in the Warned List, the case will usually and subject always to any order to the contrary, be heard within 3 months ("the listing period").

17 When a case has entered the warned list, the listing office will email the parties (if represented, the representative) with details of the listing period. Parties will be told the date by which they must provide a list of dates to avoid. Parties are encouraged to seek to agree mutually convenient dates for the hearing (see further paragraph 20) below).

18 Cases will be listed for hearing in accordance with the following practice and principles.

19 Final hearings are usually only listed for hearing Tuesday to Thursday of each week in term time.

20 If the parties offer dates that (a) correspond; and (b) are within the listing period, every effort will be made to list the case for hearing on those dates.

21 If the available dates provided by the parties do not correspond, or the dates provided (even if they correspond) are unsuitable for the court, the case will be listed for hearing at the Court's convenience.

22 Where counsel or a solicitor advocate is instructed, the listing period will not be ordinarily be extended solely because of their availability.

23 A case allocated to any of the circuit offices will be listed for hearing on that circuit at the most geographically appropriate hearing centre, subject to judicial availability.

PART B:—DIVISIONAL COURTS

24 Where a party considers that a claim or application should be dealt with by a Divisional Court, then that party should notify the ACO in writing as soon as possible, i.e. usually in or with the claim form or application, or the acknowledgment of service or response to an application.

25 Although parties may make representations as to the suitability of a case to be heard before the Divisional Court, the decision whether a case should be listed before the Divisional Court and if so, the constitution of that Court, are matters for the Court.

26 The ACO will not be able to offer as many suitable available dates for a hearing and will not ordinarily take account of the availability of each party's counsel/solicitor advocate when listing the hearing.

PART C:—ADJOURNING/VACATING HEARINGS

27 If a hearing becomes unnecessary because a claim has been withdrawn or compromised, the parties must inform the court, as soon as possible.

28 A hearing will generally not be adjourned or vacated unless there are good reasons to do so, even where all parties agree that the hearing should be adjourned. An adjournment will rarely be granted if the only reason for the application is that counsel is unavailable.

29 Any application to adjourn or vacate a hearing must be made using either Form AC001 or Form N244 (see links on the Administrative Court website). The application notice should be filed with the court at least 3 days prior to the hearing (unless good reason is provided for the late filing of the application). A fee is payable save where the application is both made by consent and made more than 14 days before the date fixed for the hearing.

30 The application must set out the reasons in support of the application. Even when an application is made by consent, the application must set out the reasons why the hearing should be adjourned/vacated. A draft order must be provided.

31 Notwithstanding that an application to adjourn or vacate a hearing has been filed, parties should assume that the hearing remains listed until they are advised otherwise by the court.

32 A hearing may only be adjourned or vacated by judicial order. A decision whether to grant or refuse an application to adjourn can be taken by an ACO lawyer under delegated powers. If a party is not content with an order of the ACO lawyer, it may request that the order is reviewed by a judge. The review will be either on consideration of the papers or at a hearing. The request for a review must be made in writing (within 7 days of the date on which the party was served with the ACO lawyer's order). The request must include the original application; should address the reasons given by the ACO lawyer when refusing the application; and set out any further matters relied on. As long as the request is filed within 7 days (or such time as allowed by the order) no further fee is payable.

PART D:—PLANNING COURT

33 The Planning Court is a specialist list under the charge of the Planning Liaison Judge. The work covered by the Planning Court is defined in CPR 54.21. Claims in the Planning Court are heard by judges who have been nominated by the President of the Queen's Bench Division as specialist planning judges, some of whom are also nominated to hear "significant" cases: see CPR 54.22.

34 Cases in the Planning Court generally fall into four broad categories:-

(a) Planning Statutory Review claims under PD8C.[1] Permission to apply is required and an Acknowledgment of Service must be accompanied by summary grounds of defence;

(b) Planning Statutory Appeals (or Applications) under PD8A paragraph 222. Permission to apply is not required. A party intending to contest the claim is not required to file summary grounds of defence unless ordered by the Court to do so (under CPR PD 54D 3.5);

(c) Appeals under section 289 of TCPA 1990 against decisions on enforcement notice appeals and tree replacement orders (under section s.208) and appeals under section 65 of the Planning (Listed Buildings and Conservation Areas) Act 1990 on decisions against enforcement notice appeals, where permission is required (see PD 52D para 26);

(d) Planning judicial reviews where permission to apply and an Acknowledgment of Service are required (see CPR 54.4 and 54.8). These include challenges to decisions of local planning authorities, development consent orders (under s.118 of the Planning Act 2008) and neighbourhood plans (under s.61N of TCPA 1990).

35 The Planning Liaison Judge will designate cases as "significant" applying the criteria at paragraph 3.2 of Practice Direction 54D. Paragraph 3.4 of Practice Direction 54D sets the following target timescales for significant cases which will apply, save where the interests of justice require otherwise.

(a) Applications for permission to apply for judicial review or planning statutory review are to be determined within three weeks of the expiry of the time limit for filing of the acknowledgment of service.

(b) Oral renewals of applications for permission to apply for judicial review or planning statutory review are to be heard within one month of receipt of request for renewal.

(c) Applications for permission under section 289 of the Town and Country Planning Act 1990 are to be determined within one month of issue.

(d) Planning statutory reviews are to be heard within six months of issue.

Judicial reviews are to be heard within ten weeks of the expiry period for the submission of detailed grounds by the defendant or any other party as provided in CPR 54.14.

GENERAL

36 Subject to the points below, the listing policy at paragraphs 1 to 32 above applies equally to cases in the Planning Court.

NON-SIGNIFICANT CASES

37 Cases not designated as "significant" will be dealt with within the general timescales set out above for claims in the Administrative Court.

SIGNIFICANT CASES

PERMISSION HEARINGS

38 Hearings of renewed application for permission will usually be fixed at the Court's convenience; counsel's availability will not ordinarily be a relevant consideration. Hearings will be listed with a time estimate of 30 minutes. If any party considers that a different time estimate is required, the court must be informed immediately - see Practice Direction 54A at §7.7; see also the fixing letter, which states as follows

---

[1] Claims under section 287 or 288 of TCPA 1990, section 63 of the Planning (Listed Buildings and Conservation Areas) Act 1990, section 22 of the Planning (Hazardous Substances) Act 1990 and section 113 of the Planning and Compulsory Purchases Act 2004

"This application has been fixed in accordance with our listing policy and on the basis that it will take no longer than 30 minutes to hear. If you have already indicated that this application will require a hearing of longer than 30 minutes, I would be grateful if you could confirm this with the List Office, in writing. Otherwise on receipt of this letter you must confirm your current time estimate. This is a mandatory requirement. If it becomes necessary to adjourn because of a late increased time estimate, quite apart from any costs sanction, the solicitors and counsel involved may be required to appear before the Court to explain the failure to comply with the instruction above. Furthermore, the case will be re-listed for the earliest possible opportunity in accordance with the availability of a Judge and not the availability of counsel."

FINAL HEARINGS (INCLUDING ROLLED-UP HEARINGS)

39 Final hearings will be listed following the practice and principles above at paragraphs 19 – 23, and the following additional matters.

40 For cases to be heard in London, as soon as the Court fee required to continue the proceedings has been paid the List Office will inform the parties by email of a window of suitable dates, and encourage them to agree a mutually convenient date for the hearing.

41 The List Office will seek to offer the parties 3 dates, within the relevant timescale set in Practice Direction 54D. Hearing dates for significant cases are governed by the availability of a judge authorised to hear such cases. If parties are unable to agree one of the dates provided, the case will be listed for hearing without further reference to the parties. The appointment to fix procedure is used only when necessary.

42 The circuit offices generally apply the same policy.

ANNEX 1

URGENT APPLICATIONS: UNDERTAKINGS TO PAY THE REQUIRED FEE

43 Litigants are encouraged to use the HMCTS fee account facility to avoid unnecessary process and delay in issuing court proceedings.

To create an account please contact: *MiddleOffice.DDServices@liberata.gse.gov.uk*

44 Fees may be paid using a credit or debit card.

- For applications issued in London call 0203 936 8957 (10:00am and 16:00pm, Monday to Friday, not Bank Holidays) or email *RCJfeespayments@justice.gov.uk.*
- For applications issued out of London provide your phone number to the relevant circuit ACO office; the office will call you to take payment.

45 Litigants who need to lodge an urgent application but are unable to pay the fee either using an account or by credit or debit card, must follow the procedure set out below. This facility may be used only in exceptional circumstances as a result of unavoidable emergency, and only by solicitors/ barristers with rights to participate in litigation. The cut off time for using this procedure is 4.30pm for applications issued in London, 4pm for applications issued out of London.

Step 1

Email the required documents (set out below) to:
London *generaloffice@administrativecourtoffice.justice.gov.uk*
Tel: 020 7947 6655
Cardiff *cardiff@administrativecourtoffice.justice.gov.uk*
Tel: 02920 376 460
Birmingham *birmingham@administrativecourtoffice.justice.gov.uk*
Tel: 0121 681 4441
Leeds *leeds@administrativecourtoffice.justice.gov.uk*
Tel: 0113 306 2578
Manchester *manchester@administrativecourtoffice.justice.gov.uk*
Tel: 0161 240 5313

Step 2

Wait for the Court to process your application and email you a sealed claim form for service. Please note if you do not provide all of the documents required (see Practice Direction 54B) together with (a) the undertaking form EX160B3;[1] and (b) a covering letter explaining in full the emergency and why the required fee cannot be paid, your application will not be processed.

Step 3

Post the required fee to the Court. The undertaking requires that the fee must be received within 5 days. The Court reference must be clearly stated in the covering letter.

---

[1] The form can be found at *http://formfinder.hmctsformfinder.justice.gov.uk/ex160b-eng.pdf*

ANNEX 5

HANDING DOWN ADMINISTRATIVE COURT JUDGMENTS IN WALES

1 Pursuant to CPR 7.1A cases in which decisions of Welsh public bodies are challenged must be heard in Wales (unless required otherwise by any enactment, rule or practice direction). In addition, in accordance with the principles stated in CPR PD 54C, other public law claims that are closely connected with Wales will ordinarily be heard in Wales. **1BA-174**

2 When a case has been heard in Wales and judgment has been reserved, the judgment will be handed down in open court in the usual way if the judge is still sitting in Wales when the judgment is ready to hand down.

3 If when the reserved judgment is ready to be handed down, the judge is no longer sitting in Wales the practice will be as follows.

(a) If consequential matters are not agreed, and a hearing is required to determine them, the judge will return to Wales for that hearing.

(b) If all consequential matters are agreed, or the parties consent to determination of consequential matters on the basis of written submissions (so it is possible to hand down a judgment without the attendance of the parties), the judgment may be handed down either (i) by any judge sitting in a court in Wales, on behalf of the judge who conducted the hearing; or (ii) by listing the case on the Cause List ("Judgment, for hand down") and then publishing the judgment on Bailii at the specified time.

4 After the judgment has been handed down, copies of it will be available from the ACO in Cardiff.

5 Copies of the final judgment must be sent by the judge or judge's clerk to the ACO in Wales in advance of the hand-down to ensure that copies can be made available to any attendees at the hand-down. The ACO in Wales must ensure that so far as possible the embargo is respected, and the judgment is not made available until judgment has been formally handed down.

ANNEX 6

JUDICIAL REVIEW IN THE UPPER TRIBUNAL

A6.1 THE UPPER TRIBUNAL'S JUDICIAL REVIEW JURISDICTION

A6.1.1 The Upper Tribunal's judicial review jurisdiction is conferred by section 15 of the Tribunals, Courts and Enforcement Act 2007 ("TCEA"). The existence of the jurisdiction depends upon certain conditions being met, as explained in section 18 of the TCEA. **1BA-175**

A6.1.2 The UT has power to grant a mandatory, prohibiting or quashing order, a declaration and an injunction. Relief granted by the UT has the same effect as corresponding relief granted by the High Court and is enforceable as if it were relief granted by that Court. In deciding whether to grant relief the UT must apply the same principles that the High Court would apply in deciding whether to grant relief on an application for judicial review.

A6.1.3 Like the position in the High Court, section 16 of the TCEA provides that an application for judicial review may be made only if the applicant has obtained permission. Section 16 also contains provisions in the same terms as section 31(2A) of the Senior Courts Act 1981, restricting the grant of relief where the UT considers it highly likely the outcome would not have been substantially different even if the conduct complained of had not occurred.[1]

A6.2 TRANSFERS OF JUDICIAL REVIEW APPLICATIONS

A6.2.1 As explained at para 6.5 of the Guide, the effect of the Lord Chief Justice's Direction is that most applications for judicial review of immigration (and asylum) decisions are filed in the Upper Tribunal (Immigration and Asylum Chamber) ("UT(IAC)") and, if filed in the High Court, must be transferred to the UT(IAC). If an application is made to the UT(IAC) for judicial review of a decision that is not covered by the Direction, or which is specifically exempted by it (see 6.5.3), then, subject to what is said in the following para, the UT(IAC) must transfer the application to the High Court.[2]

A6.2.2 If certain conditions specified in section 31A(4) and (5) of the Senior Courts Act 1981 are met, the High Court may by order transfer [a judicial review application] to the Upper Tribunal if it appears to the High Court to be just and convenient to do so".[3] This power is routinely exercised in order to transfer to the UT(IAC) a judicial review made by a person who claims to be a minor from outside the United Kingdom, challenging a local authority's assessment of that person's age.

---

[1] See para 12.10 of this Guide.

[2] TCEA s. 18(3).

[3] Section 31A(3) of the Senior Courts Act 1981.

A6.2.3 The UT has power to permit or require an amendment which, if made, would give rise to an obligation to transfer the proceedings to the High Court. Except with the permission of the UT, additional grounds may not be advanced if they would give rise to an obligation to transfer. The UT therefore has power to decide whether to retain jurisdiction over the judicial review application. If the judicial review application has been transferred to the UT by the High Court under that Court's power of transfer, and the amendment or additional grounds would not have prevented the High Court from exercising that power, if the amendment or grounds had been in place prior to transfer, then the UT will transfer the application back to the High Court only if the UT considers it just and convenient to do so.[1]

A6.3 OUT OF HOURS APPLICATIONS

A6.3.1 The out of hours procedure described in para 17.1 of the Guide applies to urgent applications in immigration judicial review proceedings that cannot wait until the next working day. For this purpose, the out of hours High Court judge sits as a judge of the UT.

ANNEX 7

ADMINISTRATIVE COURT: INFORMATION FOR COURT USERS

1BA-176 **Effective date: 27 June 2022**

The following practical measures will remain in place until further notice, to assist the court to deal with its business as efficiently as possible.

Sections A and B apply to all Administrative Court claims. Compliance with Section A is required by Practice Directions 54A and 54B.

Sections C to H also apply to claims, appeals and applications administered by the Administrative Court; but where arrangements differ depending on which Administrative Court office is dealing with the matter, this is explained in the text below.

ARRANGEMENTS FOR ELECTRONIC WORKING

A. ELECTRONIC BUNDLES

(Practice Direction 54A, §§ 4.5 and 15; Practice Direction 54B, §1.3)

Electronic bundles must be prepared as follows and be suitable for use with all of Adobe Acrobat Reader and PDF Expert and PDF Xchange Editor.

1) A bundle must be a single PDF.
2) If the bundle is filed in support of an urgent application (i.e., an application made using Form N463) it must not exceed 20mb, and (unless the court requests otherwise) should be filed by email
3) If the papers in support of any claim or appeal or non-urgent application exceed 20mb, the party should file:
   (a) a core bundle (no larger than 20mb) including, as a minimum, the Claim Form and Grounds or Notice of Appeal and Grounds, or Application Notice and Grounds; documents regarded as essential to the claim, appeal, or application (for example the decision challenged, the letter before claim and the response, etc.); any witness statements (or primary witness statement) relied on in support of the claim, appeal or application; and a draft of the order the court is asked to make; and
   (b) a further bundle containing the remaining documents.

   Bundles should be filed using the Document Upload Centre.
4) All bundles must be paginated in ascending order from start to finish. The first page of the PDF will be numbered "1", and so on. (Any original page numbers of documents within the bundle are to be ignored.) Index pages must be numbered as part of the single PDF document, they are not to be skipped; they are part of the single PDF and must be numbered. If a hard copy of the bundle is produced, the pagination on the hard copy must correspond exactly to the pagination of the PDF.
5) Wherever possible pagination should be computer-generated; if this is not possible, pagination must be in typed form.
6) The index page must be hyperlinked to the pages or documents it refers to.
7) Each document within the bundle must be identified in the sidebar list of contents/bookmarks, by date and description (e.g., "email 11.9.21 from [x] to [y]"). The sidebar list must also show the bundle page number of the document.
8) All bundles must be text based, not a scan of a hard copy bundle. If documents within a bundle have been scanned, optical character recognition should be undertaken on the

[1] UT r 33A

bundle before it is lodged. (This is the process which turns the document from a mere picture of a document to one in which the text can be read as text so that the document becomes word-searchable, and words can be highlighted in the process of marking them up.) The text within the bundle must therefore be selectable as text, to facilitate highlighting and copying.

9) Any document in landscape format must be rotated so that it can be read from left to right.
10) The default display view size of all pages must always be 100%.
11) The resolution on the electronic bundle must be reduced to about 200 to 300dpi to prevent delays whilst scrolling from one page to another.
12) If a bundle is to be added to after the document has been filed, it should not be assumed the judge will accept a new replacement bundle because he/she may already have started to mark up the original. Inquiries should be made of the judge as to what the judge would like to do about it. Absent a particular direction, any pages to be added to the bundle as originally filed should be provided separately, in a separate document, with pages appropriately sub-numbered.

For guidance showing how to prepare an electronic bundle, see (as an example) this video prepared by St Philips Chambers, which explains how to create a bundle using Adobe Acrobat Pro *https://st-philips.com/creating-and-using-electronic-hearing-bundles/*

Any application filed by a legal representative that does not comply with the above rules on electronic bundles may not be considered by a Judge. If the application is filed by a litigant in person the electronic bundle must if at all possible, comply with the above rules. If it is not possible for a litigant in person to comply with the rules on electronic bundles, the application must include a brief explanation of the reasons why.

B. THE DOCUMENT UPLOAD CENTRE

Whenever possible, file documents electronically. This includes claims, responses, interlocutory applications, and hearing bundles. Unless stated otherwise below, file documents using the Document Upload Centre (DUC).

Requests to upload documents to the DUC should be sent to the email addresses referred to below in Sections D, E and F. After uploading a document, you must email the relevant court office to confirm the upload.

For guidance on how to use the DUC, see the HMCTS "Professional Users Guide" for detailed information about the Document Upload Centre[1], and the DUC video guide on YouTube[2].

ARRANGEMENTS FOR FILING AND RESPONDING TO CLAIMS, APPEALS AND APPLICATIONS

C. APPLICATIONS FOR URGENT CONSIDERATION

Administrative Court, London (Royal Courts of Justice)

Urgent applications (i.e. applications within the scope of Practice Direction 54B) should be filed either electronically (preferred wherever possible), or by post or DX. Until further notice, urgent applications may not be filed over the counter at the Royal Courts of Justice.

The process explained below should be used for any urgent interlocutory application that is filed electronically.

1) Applications must be filed by email to: *immediates@administrativecourtoffice.justice.gov.uk* accompanied with either a PBA number, receipt of payment by debit/credit card or a fee remission certificate (see below, Section G).
2) This inbox will be monitored Monday to Friday between the hours of 9:30am and 4:30pm. Outside of these hours the usual QB out of hours procedure should be used.
3) Your application must be accompanied by an electronic bundle containing only those documents which it will be necessary for the court to read for the purposes of determining the application - see Practice Direction 54B at §§1.3, and 2.2 - 2.3. The bundle must be prepared in accordance with the guidance at Section A; it must not exceed 20mb.
4) Any other urgent queries should be sent by email to: *generaloffice@ administrativecourtoffice.justice.gov.uk*, marked as high priority, and with 'URGENT' in the subject line. Any such emails will be dealt with as soon as possible.

If you are not legally represented and do not have access to email, you should contact the Administrative Court Office by telephone on 020 7947 6655 (option 6) so that details of your application may be taken by telephone and alternative arrangements made if permitted by the senior legal manager or the duty judge.

---

1 *https://assets.publishing.service.gov.uk/government/uploads/system/uploads/attachment_data/file/887109/Document_Upload_Centre_-_Professional_User.pdf*

2 *https://www.youtube.com/watch?v=rbYBhdPNr5E*

Other Administrative Court offices

Out of London, urgent applications may be filed between 10am and 4pm, Monday to Friday. Urgent applications may also be filed in person. If you wish to file in person, you should contact the relevant office by phone to arrange to attend the public counter. The phone numbers are as follows

Birmingham
0121 681 4441 - pick option 2 then option 5.
Cardiff
02920 376460
Leeds
0113 306 2578
Manchester 0161 240 5313

If filing an urgent application by email, the arrangements at 1 - 4 above apply, save that: (a) see Section H below for how to pay the application fee; and (b) please use the following email addresses.

Birmingham: *birmingham@administrativecourtoffice.justice.gov.uk*
Cardiff: *cardiff@administrativecourtoffice.justice.gov.uk*
Leeds: *leeds@administrativecourtoffice.justice.gov.uk*
Manchester: *manchester@administrativecourtoffice.justice.gov.uk*

D. NON-URGENT WORK: CIVIL CLAIMS AND APPEALS

All other civil business (i.e. non-urgent claims, appeals and applications) should be filed electronically (preferred wherever possible) or by post or DX. There may be a slight delay before claims/applications are issued, but the date the Claim Form or Notice of Appeal is received by the Administrative Court office will be recorded as the date of filing. It remains the responsibility of the party making an application or claim to ensure that it is filed within the applicable time limit.

If a decision on an interlocutory application is time-sensitive, please state (both in the Application Notice and in a covering letter) the date by which a decision on the application is required.

Filing claims, appeals and non-urgent applications

1) Wherever possible, claims for judicial review, statutory appeals, planning matters, and non-urgent interlocutory applications are to be filed electronically using the Document Upload Centre.
2) Requests to upload documents should be sent
   for London cases to: *DUC@administrativecourtoffice.justice.gov.uk*
   for other offices, use the appropriate email address at Section C above.

   You will receive an invitation by email to upload your documents. You should then upload the claim/appeal/application bundle (prepared in accordance with Section A).
3) If you are commencing a claim or appeal please upload a further PDF document comprising an additional copy of the Claim Form or Notice of Appeal and the decision document challenged. If filing in London include a PBA number or proof of payment by debit/credit card or a fee remission certificate (see Section H); if you are filing the claim at any office out of London, also see Section H.
4) Documents being uploaded must be in PDF format, no other format will be accepted by the system. If the papers in support of an application for judicial review or an appeal or an application exceed 20mb, the claimant/appellant/applicant should file:
   (a) a core bundle (no larger than 20mb) including, as a minimum, the Claim Form and Grounds or Notice of Appeal and Grounds, or Application Notice and Grounds; documents regarded as essential to the claim, appeal, or application (for example the decision challenged, the letter before claim and the response, etc.); any witness statements (or primary witness statement) relied on in support of the claim, appeal or application; and a draft of the order the court is asked to make; and
   (b) a further bundle containing the remaining documents.
5) All electronic bundles must be prepared/formatted in accordance with the guidance at Section A.
6) Once a claim or appeal has been issued, Administrative Court staff will provide the case reference number to the parties by email.
7) Interlocutory applications should be sent by email
   for London cases to: *generaloffice@administrativecourtoffice.justice.gov.uk*
   for other offices, use the appropriate email address at Section C above.

   If filing in London include a PBA number or receipt of payment by debit/credit card (see Section H); if filing at an office out of London, also see Section H.
8) If you are not legally represented and do not have access to email, contact the Administrative Court office by telephone so that alternative arrangements can be made. For London claims the number is 020 7947 6655 (option 6). For claims at other offices use the appropriate phone number at Section C above.

Responding to claims, appeals or application notices

1) Wherever possible, any response to a claim or appeal or application notice should be filed

electronically. This will include Acknowledgements of Service, Respondent's Notices, responses to interlocutory applications, and any supporting bundles.

2) File smaller documents (less than 50 pages or less than 10mb) by email. In London these should be sent to *caseprogression@administrativecourtoffice.justice.gov.uk*, for other offices use the appropriate email address at Section C above.

3) For all larger documents use the Document Upload Centre. Any request to upload documents must be made by the professional representative by email:
   for London cases to: *DUC@administrativecourtoffice.justice.gov.uk*
   for other offices, use the appropriate email address at Section C above.

4) The requirements for the preparation of bundles at Section A and Section D (filing claims) apply and must be followed. Please note the provisions on file size.

5) If you are not legally represented and do not have access to email, you should contact the Administrative Court office by telephone so that alternative arrangements can be made. For London claims the number is 020 7947 6655 (option 6). For claims at other offices use the appropriate phone number at Section C above.

E. NON-URGENT WORK: CLAIMS IN CRIMINAL CAUSES OR MATTERS, APPEALS BY CASE STATED

Filing claims and issuing applications and case stated appeals

1) Wherever possible, non-urgent claims for judicial review in criminal causes or matters and appeals by case stated are to be filed electronically using the Document Upload Centre.

2) Requests to upload documents should be sent
   for London cases to: *crimex@administrativecourtoffice.justice.gov.uk*
   for other offices, use the appropriate email address at Section C above.

3) You will receive an invitation by email to upload your documents. You should then upload the claim/appeal/application bundle (prepared in accordance with Section A). If you are commencing a claim or appeal please also upload a further PDF document comprising an additional copy of the Claim Form or Notice of Appeal and the decision document challenged. If filing in London include a PBA number or proof of payment by debit/credit card or a fee remission certificate (see Section H); if filing at any of the out of London offices, also see Section H.

4) Once a claim or appeal has been issued, Administrative Court staff will provide the case reference number to the parties by email.

5) Interlocutory applications should be sent by email
   for London cases to: *crimex@administrativecourtoffice.justice.gov.uk*
   for other offices, please use the appropriate email address referred to at Section B above.

   For London include a PBA number or receipt of payment by debit/credit card (see Section H); if you are filing the claim in one of the out of London offices, also see Section H.

6) The requirements for the preparation of bundles at Section A and Section D (filing claims) apply and must be followed. Please note the provisions on file size.

7) If you are not legally represented and do not have access to email, you should contact the Administrative Court office by telephone on 020 7947 6655 (option 6) so that alternative arrangements can be made.

Responding to claims and case stated appeals

1) Wherever possible, any response to a claim or appeal or application notice should be filed electronically. This includes Acknowledgements of Service, Respondent's Notices, responses to interlocutory applications, and any supporting bundles.

2) File smaller documents (less than 50 pages or less than 10mb) by email. In London, use *crimex@administrativecourtoffice.justice.gov.uk*, and for other offices use the appropriate email address at Section C above.

3) For all larger documents use the Document Upload Centre. Requests to upload documents should be sent
   for London cases to: *crimex@administrativecourtoffice.justice.gov.uk*
   for other offices, use the appropriate email address at Section C above.

4) The requirements the preparation of bundles at Section A and Section D apply and must be followed. Please note the provisions on file size.

5) If you are not legally represented and do not have access to email, you should contact the Administrative Court Office by telephone on 020 7947 6655 (Option 6) so that alternative arrangements can be made.

F. EXTRADITION APPEALS

Filing appeals and issuing Application Notices

1) Wherever possible, extradition appeals and interlocutory applications in extradition appeals must be sent electronically to: *crimex@administrativecourtoffice.justice.gov.uk*

Include a PBA number or proof of payment by debit/credit card (see Section H). If you are not legally represented and do not have access to email, you should contact the Administrative Court office by telephone 020 7947 6655 (Option 6) so that alternative arrangements can be made.

2) After the period for lodging amended grounds of appeal has expired the Appeal Bundle must be lodged. Please use the Document Upload Centre. Any request to upload documents must be made by the professional representative by email to: *crimex@administrativecourtoffice.justice.gov.uk*

Litigants in person without access to email should contact the Court to make alternative arrangements - see paragraph 1 above.

3) Any further bundles (whether for renewed application for permission to appeal or for the hearing of the appeal) shall also be lodged in by the methods stated at paragraph 2 above.

4) All bundles for the appeal or (if heard other than at the permission to appeal hearing or the appeal hearing), for any application in the appeal must be prepared in accordance with the requirements at Section A above. If the papers in support of an appeal or application exceed 20mb, the Appellant/Applicant should file:
   (a) a core bundle (no larger than 20mb) including, as a minimum, the Notice of Appeal and Grounds, or Application Notice and grounds; documents regarded as essential to the appeal, or application (for example the extradition request, the judgment of the District Judge, the Respondent's Notice etc.); any witness statements (or primary witness statement) relied on in support of the appeal or application; and a draft of the order the court is asked to make; and
   (b) a further bundle containing the remaining documents.

Responding to appeals and Application Notices

1) Wherever possible, responses to appeals and Application Notices should be filed electronically with the Administrative Court.
2) File smaller documents (less than 50 pages or less than 10mb) by email, to *Crimex@administrativecourtoffice.justice.gov.uk.*
3) Larger documents should be filed using the Document Upload Centre. Any request to upload documents must be made by email to *crimex@administrativecourtoffice.justice.gov.uk*
4) Litigants in person without access to email should contact the Administrative Court office by phone on 020 7947 6655 (Option 6) so that alternative arrangements can be made.
5) Any documents for the hearing of the appeal or application must be prepared in accordance with the requirements at Section A, and be lodged in the manner described above in the paragraphs concerning the filing of appeals.

OTHER ARRANGEMENTS

G. DETERMINATION OF CLAIMS

Paper applications

Applications for permission to apply for judicial review, applications for permission to appeal, and interlocutory applications will continue to be considered on the papers, as usual.

Orders

Orders will be served on all parties by email or, if service by email is not possible, they will be served by post.

Hearings

1) All matters for hearing will appear in the Daily Cause List. The list may be subject to change at short notice.
2) Hearings will ordinarily take place either in person (in court).
3) A judge may, on application by the parties, permit a different mode of hearing: either a hybrid hearing, or a remote hearing. A hybrid hearing is when some participants in court and others present by video. At a remote hearing all participants are present by video or phone. Hybrid hearings are conducted using the Cloud Video Platform (CVP) for persons attending by video. Remote hearings are by Cloud Video Platform (CVP) or Microsoft Teams (video), or BT Meet Me (phone). If a hearing takes place by video and/or phone, the arrangements will be made by the court.

   If an application is made that the hearing take place as a hybrid hearing or a remote hearing, the application will be determined by a judge who will decide whether it is in the interests of justice to grant the application. Whenever possible the judge will make this decision taking account of the views of the parties.
4) If it appears a hearing may need to be vacated (e.g. by reason of illness) or the arrangements for the hearing may need to be changed (e.g. because a party is required to self-isolate), please inform the court as soon as possible.

H. FEES (APPLIES TO ALL CLAIMS)

Payment by debit or credit card (by phone or email)

You can pay a court fee for a London claim by debit or credit card by contacting the Fees Office on 020 7073 4715 between the hours of 10:00am and 16:00pm, Monday to Friday (except bank holidays) or by emailing *RCJfeespayments@justice.gov.uk* Once the payment has been processed you will receive a receipt which you should submit with the claim form and/or application form.

Court fees for claims at other offices can also be paid by debit or credit card - please provide your contact telephone number in the email/letter that accompanies the claim or application, you will be contacted to make payment by phone.

Payment by PBA

If you have a PBA account, then you must include the reference number in a covering letter with any claim form and/or application you lodge so the fee can be deducted from this account.

Payment by cheque

Cheques should be made payable to HMCTS. The cheque should be sent together with the Claim Form or Application Notice, either by post or DX.

For London claims cheques can be sent via the drop box at the main entrance in the Royal Courts of Justice. For claims at other offices, if you have arranged to file the claim/application in person, you may bring the cheque with you.

Attending the Fees Office counter (Royal Courts of Justice, London only)

The Fees Office counter is open to the public Monday to Friday 10:00am to 4:30pm (except Bank Holidays). Access to the Fees Office counter is on an appointment only basis. There is no walk-in facility. To make an appointment to attend the counter contact the Fees Office, Monday to Friday 10.00am to 4.00pm (except Bank Holidays), by phone (020 7947 6527) or by email (*feesofficecounterbooking@justice.gov.uk*). Do not attend without a confirmed appointment.

Once the fee has been taken or the fee remission form completed the Claim Form, or Notice of Appeal or Application Notice may be sent and will be forwarded to the relevant Administrative Court office for processing.

Help with fees

To apply for fee remission, go to the Help with Fees website *www.gov.uk/get-help-with-court-fees* and complete the step-by-step application process.

If your claim is in London forward your 'HWF' reference to the Fees Office *feesrcj@justice.gov.uk* along with a copy of your Claim Form and/or application form. Please note, the number is confirmation of applying and is not confirmation of Remission entitlement. The Fees Office will process your application and contact you with the outcome of the Help with Fees application and will advise your next steps. For the out of London offices send your HWF reference along with the Claim Form and/or application form.

ANNEX 8

HOW TO CONTACT THE ADMINISTRATIVE COURT BY EMAIL

The Court receives a lot of emails each day. We will be able to deal with your email more quickly if you: **1BA-177**

- Only send your email to one of these addresses. If you send it to the wrong one, we will send it to the right one.
- Don't send your email to an individual. We will pass your email to the correct person.
- Include the hearing date in the subject line if it is soon
- If applicable, mark your email as High Priority and put the word 'URGENT' in the subject line
- Remember that emails sent after 4.30pm in London, and after 4pm in the regions, are unlikely to be seen until the next working day.

THE FOLLOWING EMAIL ADDRESSES ARE FOR LONDON CASES ONLY (see end for regional cases):

Email address	*Nature of correspondence*	*Please include in subject line*
immediates@administrativecourtoffice.justice.gov.uk	Emails filing (or asking questions about) urgent/ immediate applications **except CJA/DTA cases and Extradition cases**	Case number if you have one Proposed timeframe for urgent application to be considered

Email address	*Nature of correspondence*	*Please include in subject line*
generaloffice@administrativecourt-office.justice.gov.uk	Correspondence about issuing new cases New applications Sending proof of payment or PBA number where fee payable Filing Consent Orders and paying the fee by PBA in Civil cases Requesting initial DUC invitations to start a new case General enquiries about the Court	Case number if you have one Hearing date if your query or attachments relate to an imminent hearing The word 'URGENT' if the email or attachments need urgent attention
crimex@administrativecourtoffice.justice.gov.uk	Filing applications and short documents (other than those uploaded to the DUC) in Extradition or Criminal cases and CJA/DTA cases Case progression queries about Extradition and Criminal cases Filing applications for bail on behalf of the RP, or prosecution appeals against the grant of bail, in Extradition matters only Filing Consent Orders in Extradition and Criminal cases, and paying the fee by PBA Notifying the Court that you have uploaded a document to the DUC in an Extradition or Criminal case	Case number if you have one Hearing date if your query relates to an imminent hearing Indication that email is urgent, if applicable The word 'URGENT', if applicable
caseprogression@administrative-courtoffice.justice.gov.uk	Case progression queries in Civil cases Filing short documents in Civil cases (other than those uploaded to the DUC) Notifying the Court that you have uploaded a document to the DUC in a Civil case	Case number Hearing date if your query relates to an imminent hearing The word 'URGENT', if applicable
Listoffice@administrativecourtoffice.justice.gov.uk	Filing Renewal Notice Queries about hearings in London, including: Dates Method of hearing Attendees	Case number Hearing date if your query relates to an imminent hearing The word 'URGENT', if applicable
DUC@administrativecourtoffice.justice.gov.uk	Only to be used for ACO cases in London, to request DUC links in order to upload documents	Case number if you have one When uploading documents please enter Court's case reference number (if you have one) when prompted to do so Hearing date The word 'URGENT', if applicable
London.skeletonarguments@administrativecourtoffice.justice.gov.uk	Filing Skeleton Arguments for imminent hearing in London	Case number Hearing date The word 'URGENT', if applicable
If your case is not in London, please use the relevant email address from the list below:		

Email address	*Nature of correspondence*	*Please include in subject line*
Manchester.skeletonarguments@administrativecourtoffice.justice.gov.uk	Filing Skeleton Arguments for imminent hearing in Manchester, Leeds, Birmingham or Cardiff	Case number Hearing date
Leeds.skeletonarguments@administrativecourtoffice.justice.gov.uk		
Birmingham.skeletonarguments@administrativecourtoffice.justice.gov.uk		
Cardiff.skeletonarguments@administrativecourtoffice.justice.gov.uk		
Manchester@administrativecourtoffice.justice.gov.uk	All other queries regarding cases in the Administrative Court in Manchester, Leeds, Birmingham or Cardiff	Case number The word 'URGENT', if applicable
Leeds@administrativecourtoffice.justice.gov.uk		
Birmingham@administrativecourtoffice.justice.gov.uk		
Cardiff@administrativecourtoffice.justice.gov.uk		

Correct as at 4 July 2022

SECTION 2 SPECIALIST PROCEEDINGS

SECTION 2A COMMERCIAL COURT

PART 58—COMMERCIAL COURT

Impact of COVID-19: the conduct of hearings

Replace paragraph with:

The COVID-19 pandemic has, inevitably, had an impact on the conduct of hearings in the Commercial Court. At the time of writing, the default position is that hearings with an estimated length of under half a day are to be conducted remotely; the Court will only direct an oral hearing on application and where it considers an in-person hearing to be more appropriate. For trials and longer applications, whether a hearing is to be fully remote, fully in person or a hybrid will be determined by the judge on the facts of the case, but the expectation is that they will be held in person unless circumstances require otherwise. The parties will be asked in advance to express a preference to the Listing Office, supported by reasons. The default format for bundles is electronic for the foreseeable future; hard copy bundles are to be lodged only if the judge hearing the matter so requests. The current position is set out in guidance issued for the Business and Property Courts on 15 September 2021, here: *https://www.judiciary.uk/announcements/remote-hearings-guidance-to-help-the-business-and-property-courts/* [Accessed 28 October 2022]. See further (i) Practice Direction 51Y "Video or Audio Hearings During Coronavirus Pandemic" which came into force on 25 March 2020 (mostly now expired, but some provisions are still in effect); (ii) The Protocol regarding Remote Hearings, issued 26 March 2020 and updated 31 March 2020; (iii) *https://www.judiciary.uk/coronavirus-covid-19-advice-and-guidance/* [Accessed 28 October 2022], where any additional guidance is likely to be uploaded and (iv) the COMBAR guidance on remote hearings, 2nd edition, issued on 23 June 2020, at *https://www.combar.com/wp-content/uploads/2020/06/COMBAR-Guidance-Note-on-Remote-Hearings-2nd-edition-23-June-2020-002.pdf* [Accessed 28 October 2022]. The COMBAR guidance contains detailed provision as to the conduct of remote hearings, in particular as to technological arrangements and bundling (see further in relation to PDF bundles generally: *https://www.judiciary.uk/ announcements/general-guidance-on-electronic-court-bundles* [Accessed 28 October 2022]. Users are also encouraged to check regularly for updates in relation to the above. **2A-0**

Related sources

Replace list with:

- Part 62—Arbitration Claims (see para.2E-7 et seq.). **2A-3**

- The Commercial Court Guide, incorporating the Admiralty Court Guide (11th edition, published February 2022). See para.2A-36 and following and *https://www.gov.uk/government/publications/admiralty-and-commercial-courts-guide* [Accessed 28 October 2022].
- Practice Direction—Arbitrations (see para.2E-46 et seq.).
- Arbitration Act 1950 Pt II (see para.2E-58+ et seq.).
- Arbitration Act 1996 (see para.2E-84 et seq.).
- Civil Procedure Rules including CPR 1, 2, 6, 7, 8, 9, 10, 11, 12, 14, 15, 16, 17, 18, 20, 22, 23, 24, 25, 32, 34, 35, 43, 48, 70, 71, 72, 73 and 74.
- Practice Direction 57AC—Trial Witness Statements in the Business and Property Courts (see para.57ACPD.0.1).
- Practice Direction 57AD - Disclosure in the Business and Property Courts (replacing Practice Direction 51U, with effect from 1 October 2022). (See also section E of the Commercial Court Guide. For further guidance as to the correct approach to disclosure pursuant under the Disclosure Pilot, which was the predecessor of PD 57AD, see *McParland and Partners Ltd v Whitehead* [2020] EWHC 298 (Ch); [2020] W.L.R. (D) 91 (Vos C); *Lonestar Communications Corp LLC v Kaye* [2020] EWHC 1890 (Comm) (Mr P Macdonald Eggers QC), though cf *Revenue and Customs Commissioners v IGE USA Investments Ltd* [2020] EWHC 1716 (Ch); [2021] Bus.L.R. 424, at [59]).
- Practice Direction (CE-File): see Practice Direction 51O and Appendix 12 to the Guide.
- Cases which would benefit from being heard by judges with particular expertise in the financial markets or which raise issues of general importance to the financial markets may be assigned to the Financial List. See CPR Pt 63A and Practice Direction 63AA and the Guide at *https://assets.publishing.service.gov.uk/government/uploads/system/uploads/attachment_data/file/644030/financial-list-guide.pdf* [Accessed 28 October 2022]. Practice Direction 63AA includes provision for the Financial Markets Test Case Scheme, previously run as a pilot scheme under the now-repealed Practice Direction 51M. Under the Scheme, the Court has power to determine a matter which raises issues of general importance to the financial markets without the need for a present cause of action between the parties to the proceedings. To date, only one case has been heard using these provisions (*Financial Conduct Authority v Arch Insurance (UK) Ltd* [2020] EWHC 2448 (Comm); [2020] Lloyd's Rep. IR 527 (Flaux LJ and Butcher J; see also the leapfrog appeal to the Supreme Court [2021] UKSC 1; [2020] A.C. 649), relating to the applicability of business interruption insurance policy wordings in the context of the COVID pandemic).
- All claims and applications in the Commercial Court must be issued and all documents filed electronically via CE-File (*https://efile.cefile-app.com/login* [Accessed 28 October 2022]). It is no longer possible, unless one is a litigant in person, to issue claims or applications, or to file documents, on paper. Public access terminals and scanners are available in the Rolls Building reception area for those litigants with limited access to the necessary IT equipment. Staff are available to assist with any technical difficulties that may arise. Please see also: *https://www.gov.uk/guidance/ce-file-system-information-and-support-advice* [Accessed 28 October 2022].
- CPR Pt 57A and PD 57AB—Shorter and Flexible Trials Schemes: reference should also be made to this Practice Direction in relation to cases where the trial length is likely to be less than four days or where, because of the sums at stake or the nature of the issues, a bespoke procedure may be appropriate so as to reduce costs.
- Notice from the Judge in Charge of the Commercial Court on time estimates and conduct of hearings dated 29 March 2022, *https://www.judiciary.uk/wp-content/uploads/2022/03/Practice-Note-time-estimates-and-conduct-of-hearings-2022.pdf* [Accessed 28 October 2022], reminding parties to consider carefully the estimates for longer hearings, the number of points that can properly be made in oral argument and the number of authorities required in order to establish the propositions of law sought to be established, and identifying the consequences of any failure to do so.
- The Commercial Court's own website, on which many of the above sources can also be found: *http://www.commercialcourt.london* [Accessed 28 October 2022].

Editorial note

To the end of the paragraph, add:

2A-9.1 From 2022, all claims issued in the Commercial Court will be audited before a CMC is booked to ensure that the Court's resources can be given to cases which require its expertise and that smaller cases can benefit from shorter lead times in the Circuit Commercial Courts (see the Annual Report for the Court of 2020-21, *https://www.judiciary.uk/wp-content/uploads/2022/02/14.50_Commercial_Court_Annual_Report_2020_21_WEB.pdf* [Accessed 28 October 2022]).

Replace r.58.8 with:

Default judgment[1]

58.8—(1) If, in a Part 7 claim in the commercial list, a defendant fails to file an acknowledgment of service, the claimant need not serve particulars of claim before he may obtain or apply for default judgment in accordance with Part 12. **2A-13**

(2) Rule 12.7(1) applies with the modification that paragraph (a) shall be read as if it referred to the claim form instead of the particulars of claim.

Editorial note

To the end of the paragraph, add:

Paragraph (2) amended by the Civil Procedure (Amendment No.2) Rules 2022 (SI 2022/783) r.24, with effect from 1 October 2022 **2A-13.1**

COMMERCIAL COURT GUIDE

Editorial note

Replace the first paragraph with:

Following consultation with users and the setting up of a working group led by Mr Justice Andrew Baker, a new 11th edition of the Guide was published in February 2022, with immediate effect. Judges expect compliance with its provisions. Practitioners should note, in particular, the following changes to the Guide (in addition to those provisions identified in the earlier paragraphs of this section) which represent a significant departure from the previous edition. **2A-36**

- Section E (Disclosure) has been extensively updated to reflect the requirements of the Disclosure Pilot (enshrined in Practice Direction 57AD with effect from 1 October 2022) which applies to most cases in the Commercial Court. It also includes new provisions related to the ongoing review of evidence and to translations of documents.
- Section F (Applications) contains new and different provisions relating to the listing of applications, timetabling and time estimates, witness statement/affidavit evidence for the purposes of applications, expert evidence on applications, including evidence of foreign law and the citation of authorities.
- Section H (Evidence for Trial) reflects the changes to practice regarding witness statements brought about by Practice Direction 57AC (para.H1), and includes new provisions relating to expert evidence on foreign law (para.H3).
- Section J (Trial) includes new provisions relating to the use of information technology at trial (para.J3), reading lists for trial (para.J5) and written closing submissions at trial (para.J10).

To the end of the second paragraph, add:

(see also *https://www.judiciary.uk/announcements/general-guidance-on-electronic-court-bundles* [Accessed 28 October 2022])

SECTION 2B CIRCUIT COMMERCIAL COURTS

PART 59—CIRCUIT COMMERCIAL COURTS

Replace r.59.4 and add note paragraph: **2B-7**

Claim form and particulars of claim[2]

59.4—(1) If particulars of claim are not contained in or served with the claim form—

(a) the claim form must state that, if an acknowledgment of service is

[1] Introduced by the Civil Procedure (Amendment No.5) Rules 2001 (SI 2001/4015), and amended by the Civil Procedure (Amendment No.2) Rules 2022 (SI 2022/783) (effective from 1 October 2022).

[2] Amended by the Civil Procedure (Amendment No.2) Rules 2022 (SI 2022/783)

filed which indicates an intention to defend the claim, particulars of claim will follow;

(b) when the claim form is served, it must be accompanied by the documents specified in rule 7.8(1);

(c) the claimant must serve particulars of claim within 28 days of the filing of an acknowledgment of service which indicates an intention to defend; and

(d) rule 7.4(2) does not apply.

(2) If the claimant is claiming interest, he must—

(a) include a statement to that effect; and

(b) give the details set out in rule 16.4(2),

in both the claim form and the particulars of claim.

(3) Rules 12.7(1)(a) and 14.14(1)(a) apply with the modification that references to the particulars of claim shall be read as if they referred to the claim form.

2B-7.1 *Note* —Paragraph (3) amended by the Civil Procedure (Amendment No.2) Rules 2022 (SI 2022/783) r.25, with effect from 1 October 2022.

SECTION 2C PROCEEDINGS IN THE TECHNOLOGY AND CONSTRUCTION COURT

Replace the Technology and Construction Court Guide with:

TECHNOLOGY AND CONSTRUCTION COURT GUIDE

Contents

2C-35

Appendix H: TCC Guidance Note on Procedures for Public Procurement Cases
Appendix I: General Guidance on Statements of Case
Appendix J: General Guidance on Electronic Court Bundles
Appendix K: The BPC Protocol for Remote and Hybrid Hearings

Issued October 2022

SECTION 1 INTRODUCTION

1.1 PURPOSE OF GUIDE

1.1.1 The Technology and Construction Court ("TCC") Guide is intended to provide straightforward, practical guidance on the conduct of litigation in the TCC. Whilst it is intended to be comprehensive, it does not cover all the procedural points that may arise in litigation and should be seen as providing guidance, which should be adopted flexibly and adapted as appropriate to the particular case. This Guide does not substitue or override the Civil Procedural Rules ("CPR") or the relevant practice directions. It is not the function of the Guide to provide legal advice. **2C-36**

1.1.2 The TCC Guide is designed to ensure effective management of proceedings in the TCC. The parties, their solicitors and counsel are expected to cooperate, and to follow both the letter and spirit of the Guide. If parties act unreasonably or fail to comply with these requirements, the court may impose sanctions including orders for costs.

1.1.3 The parties and their advisors are expected to familiarise themselves with the CPR and, in particular, to understand the importance of the "overriding objective" set out at CPR 1.1. The TCC endeavours to ensure that all its cases are dealt with justly and at proportionate cost. This includes ensuring that the parties are on an equal footing; taking all practicable steps to save expenditure; dealing with the dispute in ways which are proportionate to the size of the claim and cross-claim and the importance of the case to the parties; and managing the case throughout in a way that takes proper account of its complexity and the different financial positions of the parties. The court will also endeavour to ensure expedition, and to allot to each case an appropriate share of the court's resources.

1.1.4 The Court expects the parties to observe the overriding objective and to conduct litigation efficiently, at proportionate cost and without rancour or aggressive correspondence: see *Gotch v Enelco* [2015] EWHC 1802 (TCC). Litigating parties are expected to give serious consideration to alternative dispute resolution ("ADR"). The Court may, in its discretion, require parties to explain why ADR has not been attempted and, in appropriate cases, will issue directions to facilitate dispute resolution.

1.1.5 The TCC Guide is published with the approval of the President of King's Bench Division. The TCC Guide has been prepared in consultation with the judges of the TCC in London, Cardiff, Birmingham, Manchester and Leeds, and with the advice and support of TECBAR, TeCSA, the Society for Construction Law, the Society for Computers and Law and the TCC Users' Committees in London, Cardiff, Birmingham, Manchester, Liverpool and Leeds.

1.1.6 Work has been done to seek to align the content of this Guide, the Commercial Court Guide and the Chancery Guide where practices in the TCC and those courts should be substantially the same, though there are many areas of practice that are different and where different guidance is appropriate.

1.1.7 The TCC Guide is published on the gov.uk website and the Judiciary website, and can also be found in the main procedural reference books. The Guide will be kept under review and amendments will be made from time to time as necessary. Suggestions for improvements to this Guide or the practice or procedure of the TCC are welcome, as are any corrections and comments on the text of the Guide. These should be addressed to the TCC Users' Committees.

1.2 THE CPR

1.2.1 Proceedings in the TCC are governed by the CPR and the supplementary Practice Directions. CPR Part 60 and its associated **Practice Direction** deal specifically with the practice and procedure of the TCC. **2C-37**

1.2.2 Other parts of the CPR that frequently arise in TCC cases include:

Part 1 (Overriding Objective);
Part 3 (Case Management Powers);
Part 6 (Service of Documents);
Part 7 (How to Start Proceedings–the Claim Form);
Part 8 (Alternative Procedure for Claims);
Parts 12 and 13 (Default Judgment and Setting Aside);
Part 16 (Statements of Case);
Part 17 (Amendments);
Part 19 (Parties and Group Litigation);
Part 20 (Counterclaims and Other Additional Claims);
Part 24 (Summary Judgment);

Part 25 (Interim Remedies and Security for Costs);
Part 26 (Case Management);
Part 32 (Evidence);
Part 35 (Experts and Assessors);
Part 44 (Costs);
Practice Directions: Practice Direction 51O (the Electronic Working Pilot Scheme); Practice Direction 57AD (Disclosure); Part 57A (Business and Property Courts); Practice Direction 57AA (Business and Property Courts); Practice Direction 57AB (Shorter and Flexible Trials Scheme); Practice Direction 57AC (Trial Witness Statements in the Business and Property Courts); and
Part 62 (Arbitration Claims).

1.3 THE TCC

1.3.1 TCC Claims

2C-38 CPR 60.1 (2) and (3) provide that a TCC claim is a claim which (i) involves technically complex issues or questions (or for which trial by a TCC judge is desirable) and (ii) has been issued in or transferred into the TCC specialist list. The following are examples of the types of claim which it may be appropriate to bring as TCC claims –

a) building or other construction disputes, including claims for the enforcement of the decisions of adjudicators under the Housing Grants, Construction and Regeneration Act 1996;
b) engineering disputes;
c) energy disputes, including claims concerning oil & gas pipelines and facilities, onshore and offshore windfarms, waste to energy plants and other renewables;
d) public procurement claims;
e) claims by and against engineers, architects, surveyors, accountants and other specialised advisors relating to the services they provide;
f) claims by and against local authorities relating to their statutory duties concerning the development of land or the construction of buildings;
g) claims relating to the design, supply and installation of computer systems, computer software and related network systems, including BIM systems;
h) claims relating to the quality of goods sold or hired, and work done, materials supplied or services rendered;
i) claims between landlord and tenant for breach of a repairing covenant;
j) claims between neighbours, owners and occupiers of land in trespass, nuisance, etc.
k) claims relating to the environment (for example, pollution cases);
l) claims arising out of fires;
m) claims involving taking of accounts where these are complicated; and
n) challenges to decisions of arbitrators in construction and engineering disputes including applications for permission to appeal and appeals.

This list is not exhaustive and many other types of claim might well be appropriate for resolution in the TCC.

1.3.2 Claim value guidance

With the exception of claims to enforce adjudicators' decisions or other claims with special features that justify a hearing before a High Court Judge, the **TCC at the Rolls Building in London** will not usually accept cases with a value of less than **£500,000** unless there is good reason for it to do so. A non-exhaustive list of special features which will usually justify listing the case in the High Court is:

a) Adjudication and arbitration cases of any value;
b) International cases of any value (international cases will generally involve one or more parties resident outside the UK and/or involve an overseas project or development);
c) Cases involving new or difficult points of law in TCC cases;
d) Any test case or case which will be joined with others which will be treated as test cases;
e) Public procurement cases;
f) Part 8 claims and other claims for declarations;
g) Complex nuisance claims brought by a number of parties, even where the sums claimed are small;
h) Claims which cannot readily be dealt with effectively in a County Court or Civil Justice centre by a designated TCC judge;
i) Claims for injunctions.

If a claimant issues lower value proceedings in the London High Court TCC, it should provide the court with an explanation of the reasons for doing so, whether falling within (a) to (i) above, or some other reason. For further guidance, see *West Country Renovations v McDowell* [2013] 1 WLR 416. It should be noted that the practice differs in the TCC courts outside London where the above claim valuation guidance does **not** apply.

1.3.3 TCC Judges

Both the High Court and the County Courts deal with TCC business. TCC business is conducted by TCC judges unless a TCC judge directs otherwise: see CPR 60.1(5)(ii).

TCC business in the High Court is conducted by TCC judges who are High Court judges, together with designated circuit judges, deputy high court judges and recorders who have been nominated by the Lord Chancellor pursuant to Section 68(1)(a) of the Senior Courts Act 1981 or are authorised to sit in the TCC as High Court judges under Section 9 of that Act.

TCC business in the County Court is conducted by TCC judges who include circuit judges, deputy High Court judges and recorders. TCC business may also be conducted by certain district judges ("TCC liaison district judges") provided that: (1) a TCC judge has so directed under CPR 60.1(5)(b)(ii); (2) the designated civil judge for the court has so directed in accordance with the Practice Direction at CPR 2BPD11.1(d).

It should be noted that those circuit judges who have been nominated pursuant to Section 68(1)(a) of the Senior Courts Act 1981 fall into two categories: "full time" TCC judges and "part time" TCC judges. "Full time" TCC judges spend most of their time dealing with TCC business, although they will do other work when there is no TCC business requiring their immediate attention. "Part time" TCC judges are circuit judges who are only available to sit in the TCC for part of their time. They have substantial responsibilities outside the TCC.

In respect of a court centre where there is no full time TCC judge, the term "principal TCC judge" is used in this Guide to denote the circuit judge who has principal responsibility for TCC work.

1.3.4 The Business & Property Courts

The Business & Property Courts ("BPCs") comprise the Chancery Division, the Commercial Court and Admiralty Court, and the TCC. The BPCs became operational on 2 October 2017. The Chancellor of the High Court (the 'Chancellor'), currently Sir Julian Flaux, has oversight of the day-to-day running of the BPCs in consultation with the President of the King's Bench Division.

The courts which deal with TCC claims are part of the King's Bench Division operating within the BPCs. When those courts are dealing with TCC business, CPR Part 60, **its accompanying Practice Direction and this Guide** govern the procedures of those courts.

The High Court judge in charge of the TCC ("the Judge in Charge"), although based principally in London, has overall responsibility for the judicial supervision of TCC business in those courts within and outside London.

1.3.5 The TCC in London

The principal centre for TCC High Court work in London is the Rolls Building, Fetter Lane, London, EC4 1NL. The Judge in Charge of the TCC sits principally at the Rolls Building together with other High Court judges who are TCC judges. Subject to Paragraph 3.7.1 below, any communication or enquiry concerning a TCC case, which is proceeding at the Rolls Building, should be directed to the clerk of the judge who is assigned to that case and, if by email, copied to the TCC Registry. The various contact details for the judges' clerks are set out in **Appendix D**.

Where TCC proceedings are commenced in the High Court in London, statements of case and applications should be headed:

> "In the High Court of Justice
> Business and Property Courts of England and Wales
> Technology and Construction Court (KBD)"

1.3.6 The TCC outside London

TCC claims can be brought in the High Court outside London in any District Registry, BPC District Registries have been established in **Birmingham, Bristol, Cardiff, Leeds, Liverpool, Manchester** and **Newcastle**, where full-time or part-time specialist TCC Judges sit. Contact details are set out in **Appendix D**. The TCC judges who are based at the Rolls Building will, when appropriate, sit in the BPCs outside London.

In a number of court centres outside London a "TCC liaison district judge" has been appointed. It is the function of the TCC liaison district judge:

a) to keep other district judges in that region well informed about the role and remit of the TCC (in order that appropriate cases may be transferred to the TCC at an early, rather than late, stage);
b) to deal with any queries from colleagues concerning the TCC or cases which might merit transfer to the TCC;
c) to deal with any subsidiary matter which a TCC judge directs should be determined by a district judge pursuant to CPR 60.1(5) (b)(ii);
d) to deal with urgent applications in TCC cases pursuant to Paragraph 7.2 of the Practice Direction (i.e. no TCC judge is available and the matter is of a kind that falls within the district judge's jurisdiction); and
e) to hear TCC cases when a TCC judge has so directed under CPR 60.1(5)(b)(ii) and when the designated civil judge for the court has so directed in accordance with the Practice Direction at CPR 2BPD11.1(d).

Where TCC proceedings are commenced in a district registry BPC, statements of case and applications should be headed:

"In the High Court of Justice
Business and Property Courts in [city]
Technology and Construction Court List (KBD)"

1.3.7 County Courts

TCC County Court cases in London are brought in (or transferred to) the specialist Business and Property List sitting at the Central London Civil Justice Centre, now located in the Royal Courts of Justice. TCC claims may also be brought in those county courts which are specified in the **Part 60 Practice Direction**. Contact details are again set out in **Appendix D**.

Where TCC proceedings are brought in a county court, statements of case and applications should be headed:

"In the County Court at [location]
Business and Property Courts List"

1.3.8 The division between High Court and County Court TCC cases

As a general rule TCC claims for more than £500,000 are brought in the High Court, whilst claims for lower sums are brought in the County Court. However, this is not a rigid dividing line (see paragraph 1.3.2 above). The monetary threshold for High Court TCC claims tends to be higher in London than in the other centres (as to which see below). Regard must also be had to the complexity of the case and all other circumstances.

Enforcement of adjudicator's decisions should ordinarily be commenced in the County Court when the sum is issue is less than £100,000. Where an enforcement action concerns significant points of principle or allegations of fraud, it may be more appropriate to commence it in the High Court.

1.3.9 In the BPC TCC outside London where High Court and County Court claims can be brought, the full range of cases dealt with by the TCC is undertaken, including claims to enforce an adjudicator's decision. Since in these centres the case will normally be tried by the same TCC judge regardless of whether the case is in the High Court or in the County Court, the practice is that whilst claims under £100,000 ought normally to be issued in the County Court, claims above £100,000 may be issued in the High Court, although the TCC judge retains the discretion: (1) to transfer cases to the County Court which ought more appropriately to be case managed and tried there; (2) to transfer cases out of the TCC in appropriate cases, such as where the claim value is under £50,000 and where there are no particular features which justify it proceeding in the TCC, such as arbitration claims, claims to enforce an adjudicator's decision or to obtain payment of an adjudicator's fees, and Party Wall Act appeals.

1.4 THE TCC USERS' COMMITTEES

2C-39 **1.4.1** The continuing ability of the TCC to meet the changing needs of all those involved in TCC litigation depends in large part upon a close working relationship between the TCC and its users.

1.4.2 London

The Judge in Charge chairs annual meetings of the London TCC Users' Committee. The judge's clerk acts as secretary to the Committee and takes the minutes of meetings. That Committee is made up of representatives of the London TCC judges together with two representatives of TECBAR, TECSA and the SCL. Approved Minutes will be published on the TeCSA, TECBAR and SCL websites.

1.4.3 Outside London

There are similar meetings of TCC Users' Committees in Birmingham, Manchester, Liverpool, Cardiff and Leeds. Each Users' Committee is chaired by the full time TCC judge or the principal TCC judge in that location.

1.4.4 The TCC regards these channels of communication as extremely important. Any suggestions or other correspondence raising matters for consideration by the Users' Committee should, in the first instance, be addressed to TECBAR/TECSA, or to the clerk to the Judge in Charge at the Rolls Building or to the clerk to the appropriate TCC judge outside London.

1.5 SPECIALIST ASSOCIATIONS

2C-40 **1.5.1** There are a number of associations of legal representatives which are represented on the Users' Committees and which also liaise closely with the Court. These contacts ensure that the Court remains responsive to the opinions and requirements of the professional users of the Court.

1.5.2 The relevant professional organisations are the TCC Bar Association ("TECBAR") and the TCC Solicitors Association ("TeCSA") and the Society of Construction Law (the "SCL"). Details of the relevant contacts at these organisations are set out on their respective websites, namely *www.tecbar.org*, *www.tecsa.org.uk* and *http://www.scl.org.uk*.

SECTION 2 PRE-ACTION PROTOCOL AND CONDUCT

2.1 INTRODUCTION

2.1.1 There is a Pre-Action Protocol for Construction and Engineering Disputes ("the Protocol"). Paragraph 1.1 provides that the Protocol applies to all construction and engineering disputes including professional negligence claims against architects, engineers or quantity surveyors. In professional negligence claims against such professionals and similar construction professionals, this Protocol prevails over the Professional Negligence Pre-Action Protocol: see also paragraphs 1.1 and 1.4 of the Protocol for Construction and Engineering Disputes and Paragraph A.1 of the Professional Negligence Pre-Action Protocol. The current version of the Construction and Engineering Pre-Action Protocol is set out in volume 1 of the *White Book* at **Section C5**. **2C-41**

2.1.2 The purpose of the Protocol is to encourage the frank and early exchange of information about the prospective claim and any defence to it; to enable parties to avoid litigation by agreeing a settlement of the claim before the commencement of proceedings; and to support the efficient management of proceedings where litigation cannot be avoided.

2.1.3 The overriding objective (CPR 1.1) applies to the pre-action period. The Protocol must not be used as a tactical device to secure advantage for one party or to generate unnecessary costs. In lower value TCC claims (such as those likely to proceed in the county court), the letter of claim and the response should be simple and the costs of both sides should be kept to a modest level. In all cases the costs incurred at the Protocol stage should be proportionate to the complexity of the case and the amount of money which is at stake. The Protocol does not impose a requirement on the parties to produce a detailed pleading as a letter of claim or response or to marshal and disclose all the supporting details and evidence or to provide witness statements or expert reports that may ultimately be required if the case proceeds to litigation. Where a party has serious concerns that the approach of the other party to the Pre-Action Protocol is not proportionate, then it is open for that party to issue a claim form and/or make an application (see paragraph 4.1.5 below) to seek the assistance of the Court.

2.2 APPLICATION OF THE PROTOCOL

2.2.1 The Court will expect all parties to have complied in substance with the provisions of the Protocol in all construction and engineering disputes. The only exceptions to this are identified in paragraph 2.3 below. **2C-42**

2.2.2 The Court regards the Protocol as setting out normal and reasonable pre-action conduct. Accordingly, whilst the Protocol is not mandatory for a number of the claims noted by way of example in paragraph 1.3.1 above, such as computer cases or dilapidations claims, the Court would, in the absence of a specific reason to the contrary, expect the Protocol generally to be followed in such cases prior to the commencement of proceedings in the TCC.

2.3 EXCEPTIONS

2.3.1 A claimant does not have to comply with the Protocol if the claim: **2C-43**

a) is to enforce the decision of an adjudicator;
b) is to seek an urgent declaration or injunction in relation to adjudication (whether ongoing or concluded);
c) includes a claim for interim injunctive relief;
d) will be the subject of a claim for summary judgment pursuant to Part 24 of the CPR; or
e) relates to the same or substantially the same issues as have been the subject of a recent adjudication or some other formal alternative dispute resolution procedure; or
f) relates to a public procurement dispute (for which there is a separate pre-action process as set out in **Appendix H**.

2.3.2 In addition, a claimant need not comply with any part of the Protocol if, by so doing, the claim may become time-barred under the Limitation Act 1980. In those circumstances, a claimant should commence proceedings without complying with the Protocol and must, at the same time, apply for directions as to the timetable and form of procedure to be adopted. The Court may order a stay of those proceedings pending completion of the steps set out in the Protocol.

2.4 ESSENTIAL INGREDIENTS OF THE PROTOCOL

2.4.1 The Letter of Claim

The letter of claim must comply with Section 3 of the Protocol. Amongst other things, it must contain a clear and concise summary of the facts on which each claim is based; the basis on which each claim is made; and details of the relief claimed, including a breakdown showing how any damages have been quantified. The claimant must also provide the names of experts already instructed and on whom reliance is intended. **2C-44**

2.4.2 The Defendant's Response

The defendant has 14 days to acknowledge the letter of claim and 28 days (from receipt of the letter of claim) either to take any jurisdictional objection or to respond in substance to the letter of claim. Paragraph 10.1 of the Protocol enables the parties to agree an extension of the 28 day period up to a maximum of 3 months. In any case of substance it is quite usual for an extension of time to be agreed for the defendant's response. The letter of response must comply with paragraph 8 of the Protocol. Amongst other things, it must state which claims are accepted, which claims are rejected and on what basis. It must set out any counterclaim to be advanced by the defendant. The defendant should also provide the names of experts who have been instructed and on whom reliance is intended. If the defendant fails either to acknowledge or to respond to the letter of claim in time, the claimant is entitled to commence proceedings.

2.4.3 Pre-action Meeting

The Construction and Engineering Protocol is the only Protocol under the CPR that generally requires the parties to meet, without prejudice, at least once, in order to identify the main issues and the root causes of their disagreement on those issues. The purpose of the meeting is to see whether, and if so how, those issues might be resolved without recourse to litigation or, if litigation is unavoidable, what steps should be taken to ensure that it is conducted in accordance with the overriding objective. At or as a result of the meeting, the parties should consider whether some form of alternative dispute resolution ("ADR") would be more suitable than litigation and if so, they should endeavour to agree which form of ADR to adopt. Although the meeting is "without prejudice", any party who attended the meeting is at liberty to disclose to the Court at a later stage that the meeting took place; who attended and who refused to attend, together with the grounds for their refusal; and any agreements concluded between the parties.

2.4.4 Proportionality

The Protocol does not contemplate an extended process and it should not be used as a tool of oppression. Thus, the letter of claim should be concise and it is usually sufficient to explain the proposed claim(s), identifying key dates, so as to enable the potential defendant to understand and to investigate the allegations. Only essential documents need be supplied, and the period specified for a response should not be longer than one month without good reason. In particular, where a claim is brought by a litigant based outside the UK it will generally be appropriate to confine the steps to the time limits provided by the Protocol and, in many cases, to dispense with the meeting referred to in paragraph 5.1 of the Protocol. In any event, such a meeting is not mandatory and may be dispensed with if it would involve disproportionate time and cost or it is clear that it would be unlikely to serve any useful purpose.

2.5 USE OF MATERIAL GENERATED BY THE PROTOCOL

2C-45 **2.5.1** The letter of claim, the defendant's response, and the information relating to attendance (or otherwise) at the meeting are not confidential or 'without prejudice' and can therefore be referred to by the parties in any subsequent litigation. The detail of any discussion at the meeting(s) and/or any note of the meeting cannot be referred to the Court unless all parties agree.

2.5.2 Normally the parties should include in the bundle for the first case management conference: (a) the letter of claim, (b) the response, and (c) if the parties agree, any agreed note of the pre-action meeting: see Section 5 below. The documents attached to or enclosed with the letter and the response should not be included in the bundle.

2.6 CONSEQUENCES OF NON-COMPLIANCE WITH THE PROTOCOL

2C-46 **2.6.1** There can often be a complaint that one or other party has not complied with the Protocol. The Court will consider any such complaints once proceedings have been commenced. If the Court finds that the claimant has not complied with one part of the Protocol, then the Court may stay the proceedings until the steps set out in the Protocol have been taken or impose such other conditions as the court thinks appropriate pursuant to CPR 3.1(2).

2.6.2 The Practice Direction in respect of Protocols (section C of volume 1 of the White Book) makes plain that the Court may make adverse costs orders against a party who has failed to comply with the Protocol. The Court will exercise any sanctions available with the object of placing the innocent party in a position no worse than if there had been compliance with the Protocol.

2.6.3 The court is unlikely to be concerned with minor infringements of the Protocol or to engage in lengthy debates as to the precise quality of the information provided by one party to the other during the Protocol stages. The court will principally be concerned to ensure that, as a result of the Protocol stage, each party to any subsequent litigation has a clear understanding of the nature of the case that it has to meet at the commencement of those proceedings.

2.7 COSTS OF COMPLIANCE WITH THE PROTOCOL.

2C-47 **2.7.1** If compliance with the Protocol results in settlement, the costs incurred will not be recoverable from the paying party, unless this is specifically agreed.

2.7.2 If compliance with the Protocol does not result in settlement, then the costs of the exercise cannot be recovered as costs, unless:

a) those costs fall within the principles stated by Sir Robert Megarry V-C in *Re Gibson's Settlement Trusts* [1981] Ch 179; or

b) the steps taken in compliance with the Protocol can properly be attributable to the conduct of the action: see the judgment of Coulson J in *Roundstone Nurseries v Stephenson* [2009] EWHC 1431 (TCC) where he held at [48]: "... as a matter of principle, it seems to me that costs incurred during the Pre-Action Protocol process may, in principle, be recoverable as costs incidental to the litigation: see *McGlinn v Waltham (No.1)* [2005] 3 All ER 1126".

Section 3 Commencement and transfer

3.1 CLAIM FORMS

3.1.1 All proceedings must be started using a claim form under CPR Part 7 or CPR Part 8 or an arbitration claim form under CPR Part 62: see Section 10 below. All claims allocated to the TCC are assigned to the Multi-Track: see CPR 60.6(1). **2C-48**

3.2 PART 7 CLAIMS

3.2.1 The Part 7 claim form must be marked "Business and Property Courts of England and Wales, Technology and Construction Court (KBD)" as explained in paragraphs 1.3.5, 1.3.6 and 1.3.7 above. **2C-49**

3.2.2 Particulars of Claim may be served with the claim form, but this is not a mandatory requirement. If the Particulars of Claim are not contained in or served with the claim form, they must be served within **14 days** after service of the claim form (CPR 7.4). Guidance as to the form and content of Particulars of Claim and other Statements of Case is set out in Appendix I.

3.2.3 A claim form, including any amendment to a claim form, must be verified by a statement of truth unless the Court otherwise orders (CPR 22.1).

3.3 PART 8 CLAIMS

3.3.1 The Part 8 claim form must be marked "Business and Property Courts of England and Wales, Technology and Construction Court (KBD)" as explained in paragraphs 1.3.5, 1.3.6 and 1.3.7 above. **2C-50**

3.3.2 A Part 8 claim form will normally be used where there is no substantial dispute of fact, such as the situation where the dispute turns on the construction of the contract or the interpretation of statute. Claims challenging the jurisdiction of an adjudicator or the validity of his decision are sometimes brought under Part 8, where the relevant primary facts are not in dispute. Part 8 claims will generally be disposed of on written evidence and oral submissions.

3.3.3 It is important that, where a claimant uses the Part 8 procedure, the claim form states that Part 8 applies and that the claimant wishes the claim to proceed under Part 8.

3.3.4 A statement of truth is required on a Part 8 claim form (CPR 22.1).

3.4 SERVICE

3.4.1 Claim forms issued in the TCC at the Rolls Building in London are to be served by the claimant, not by the Registry. In some other court centres claim forms are served by the court, unless the claimant specifically requests otherwise. **2C-51**

3.4.2 The different methods of service are set out in CPR Part 6 and the accompanying Practice Directions.

3.4.3 Applications for an extension of time in which to serve a claim form are governed by CPR 7.6 and there are only limited grounds on which such extensions of time are granted. The evidence required on an application for an extension of time is set out in paragraph 8.2 of Practice Direction A supplementing CPR Part 7 (7APD8.2).

3.4.4 Following service of the claim form, the claimant must file a certificate of service unless all defendants have filed acknowledgements of service: CPR 6.17(2). This is necessary if, for instance, the claimant wishes to obtain judgment in default (CPR Part 12).

3.4.5 Applications for permission to serve a claim form out of the jurisdiction are subject to CPR 6.30-6.47 inclusive. (Note that, following exit from the EU, changes have been effected to the regimes for service out of the jurisdiction). Further guidance can be found in Appendix 9 to the Commercial Court Guide.

3.5 ACKNOWLEDGMENT OF SERVICE

3.5.1 A defendant must file an acknowledgment of service in response to both Part 7 and Part 8 claims. Save in the special circumstances that arise when the claim form has been served out of the jurisdiction, or where the period is abridged for adjudication enforcement (see Section 9 below), the period for filing an acknowledgment of service is **14 days** after service of the claim form. **2C-52**

3.6 TRANSFER

3.6.1 Proceedings may be transferred from any Division of the High Court or from any specialist list to the TCC pursuant to CPR 30.5. The order made by the transferring court should be **2C-53**

expressed as being subject to the approval of a TCC judge. The decision whether to accept such a transfer must be made by a TCC judge: see CPR 30.5 (3). Many of these applications are uncontested, and may conveniently be dealt with on paper. Transfers from the TCC to other Divisions of the High Court or other specialist lists are also governed by CPR 30.5. In London there are sometimes transfers between the Chancery Division, the Commercial Court and the TCC, in order to ensure that cases are dealt with by the most appropriate judge. Outside London there are quite often transfers between the TCC and the circuit commercial list and chancery lists. It should be noted that transfers between divisions may be subject to the permission of the material heads of Division.

3.6.2 A TCC claim may be transferred from the High Court to a County Court or a County Court hearing centre, and from any County Court or County Court hearing centre to the High Court, if the criteria stated in CPR 30.3 are satisfied. In ordinary circumstances, proceedings will be transferred from the TCC in the High Court to the TCC in an appropriate County Court if the amount of the claim does not exceed £500,000.

3.6.3 Where no TCC judge is available to deal with a TCC claim which has been issued in a district registry or one of the county courts noted above, the claim may be transferred to another district registry or county court or to the High Court TCC in London (depending upon which court is appropriate).

3.6.4 On an application to transfer the case to the TCC from another court or Division of the High Court, there are a number of relevant considerations:

a) Is the claim broadly one of the types of claim identified in paragraph 2.1 of the Part 60 Practice Direction?
b) Is the financial value of the claim and/or its complexity such that, in accordance with the overriding objective, the case should be transferred into the TCC?
c) What effect would transfer have on the likely costs, the speed with which the matter can be resolved, and any other broader questions of convenience for the parties?

3.6.5 On an application to transfer into the TCC, when considering the relative appropriateness of different courts or divisions, the judge will ascertain where and in what areas of judicial expertise and experience the bulk or preponderance of the issues may lie. If there was little significant difference between the appropriateness of the two venues, and the claimant, having started in one court or division, was anxious to remain there, then the application to transfer in by another party is likely to be unsuccessful.

3.6.6 Where a TCC Claim is proceeding in a BPC outside London and it becomes apparent that the case would merit case management or trial before a High Court judge, the matter should be raised with the TCC judge at the District Registry BPC who will consult the Judge in Charge: see paragraph 3.7.4 below. If the case does merit the involvement of a High Court judge it is not necessary for the case to be transferred to London but rather a High Court judge can in appropriate cases sit outside London to deal with the case in the District Registry BPC.

3.7 ASSIGNMENT

2C-54 **3.7.1** Where a claim has been issued at or transferred to the TCC in London, the Judge in Charge of the TCC ("the Judge in Charge") shall assign it to a particular TCC judge.

3.7.2 In general the assigned TCC judge who case manages a case will also try that case. Although this continuity of judge is regarded as important, it is sometimes necessary for there to be a change of assigned judge to case manage or try a case because all High Court Judges in the King's Bench Division have other judicial duties.

3.7.3a) When a TCC case has been assigned to a named High Court judge, all communications about case management should be made to the assigned High Court judge's clerk with email communications copied to the TCC Registry at *tcc.issue@registry.justice.gov.uk.*

b) All communications in respect of the issue of claims or applications and all communications about fees, however, should be sent to the TCC Registry.

c) All statements of case and applications should be marked with the name of the assigned judge.

3.7.4 There are currently full time TCC judges at Birmingham, Manchester and Leeds. There are principal TCC judges at other court centres outside London. TCC cases at these court centres are assigned to judges either (a) by direction of the full time or principal TCC judge or (b) by operation of a rota. It will not generally be appropriate for the Judge in Charge (who is based in London) to consider TCC cases which are commenced in, or transferred to, court centres outside London. Nevertheless, if any TCC case brought in a court centre outside London appears to require management and trial by a High Court judge, then the full time or principal TCC judge at that court centre should refer the case to the Judge in Charge for a decision as to its future management and trial.

3.7.5 When a TCC case has been assigned to a named circuit judge at a court centre other than in London, all communications to the court about the case (save for communications in respect of fees) shall be made to that judge's clerk. All communications in respect of fees should be sent to the relevant registry. All statements of case and applications should be marked with the name of the assigned judge.

3.8 ELECTRONIC WORKING

3.8.1 The TCC in and outside London uses the CE-filing system and PD 51O applies. For a party who is legally represented, Electronic Working must be used by that party to start and/or continue any relevant claims or applications. For a party who is not legally represented, Electronic Working may be used by that party to start and/or continue any relevant claims or applications. **2C-55**

3.8.2 Accordingly, applications can and should be made electronically and documents may be uploaded to CE-file. Users should be aware that, when an application or document is uploaded, further action is required by a member of the court staff before the document comes to the attention of a judge. For example, a member of court staff will allocate an application to a judge and place it before a judge by way of an electronic alert, identifying an indicative due date for the application to be dealt with. The CE-filing system does not have the functionality to alert the judge automatically to any updates to the electronic file. If a hearing is imminent and the document needs to be seen urgently, or before the hearing, the parties should contact the judge's clerk and provide the document by e-mail.

3.8.3 Where a party to proceedings files an application for an order or other relief using Electronic Working and a hearing is required, the party filing the application shall lodge an application bundle with the Court. The application bundle shall be lodged in electronic format in accordance with the **General Guidance on Electronic Court Bundles** (see Appendix J). Hard copy bundles should not be lodged unless they have been requested by the judge hearing the case. In a hearing involving substantial volumes of documentation, the parties should check with the assigned judge's clerk whether the bundle, or any part of the bundle, is required to be filed in paper format

3.8.4 Where elsewhere in this Guide there is reference to the filing of skeleton arguments and submissions and statements of costs for hearings, these should be provided electronically to the judge's clerk (and, if requested by the judge's clerk, in hard copy) by the time directed for service and filing. Skeleton argument and submissions need not be filed on CE-file - the parties may wish to use this facility but it is not a substitute for provision to the judge's clerk. The parties should also note that skeleton submissions and statements of costs, if filed through CE file shortly before a hearing, are unlikely to be seen by the judge. Therefore, they should be sent by email or delivered in hard copy directly to the court. Further guidance on preparation of bundles for hearings is given Section 6 below.

SECTION 4 ACCESS TO THE COURT

4.1 GENERAL APPROACH

4.1.1 There may be a number of stages during the case management phase when the parties will make applications to the court for particular orders: see Section 6 below. There will also be the need for the court to give or vary directions, so as to enable the case to progress to trial. **2C-56**

4.1.2 The court is acutely aware of the costs that may be incurred when both parties prepare for an oral hearing in respect of such interlocutory matters and is always prepared to consider alternative, and less expensive, ways in which the parties may seek the court's assistance.

4.1.3 There are certain stages in the case management phase when it will generally be better for the parties to appear before the assigned judge, by in person, remote or hybrid hearing. Those are identified at Section 4.2 below. But there are other stages, and/or particular applications which a party may wish to make, which could conveniently be dealt with by way of a telephone hearing (Section 4.4 below) or by way of an electronic application through CE-file (Section 4.5 below).

4.1.4 A party may need access to the Court prior to the issue of proceedings, for example, applications for pre-action disclosure, taking samples or injunctive relief. Where the intended claim is a TCC claim, paragraph 4.1 of the Practice Direction supplementing CPR Part 60 provides that any pre-action application must be issued in the TCC.

4.2 HEARINGS IN COURT

4.2.1 First Case Management Conference

The court will normally require the parties to attend an oral hearing for the purposes of the first Case Management Conference, whether in person, remotely or by hybrid hearing. This is because there may be matters which the judge would wish to raise with the parties arising out of the answers to the case management information sheets and the parties' proposed directions: see Section 5.4 below. Even in circumstances where the directions and the case management timetable may be capable of being agreed by the parties and the court, the assigned judge may still wish to consider a range of case management matters with the parties, including cost budgeting and ADR. For these reasons CPR 29.4 may be applied more sparingly in the TCC. **2C-57**

4.2.2 Pre-trial Review

It will normally be helpful for the parties to attend before the judge on a Pre-trial Review ("PTR"). It is always preferable for Counsel or other advocates who will be appearing at the trial to attend the PTR. Again, even if the parties can agree beforehand any outstanding directions and the detailed requirements for the management of the trial, it is still of assistance for the judge to raise matters of detailed trial management with the parties at an oral hearing. In appropriate cases, e.g. where the amount in issue is disproportionate to the costs of a full trial, the judge may wish to consider with the parties whether there are other ways in which the dispute might be resolved. See Section 14 below for detailed provisions relating to the PTR.

4.2.3 Interim Applications

Whether or not other interim applications require an oral hearing will depend on the nature and effect of the application being made. Disputed applications for interim payments, summary judgment and security for costs will almost always require an oral hearing. Likewise, the resolution of a contested application to enforce an adjudicator's decision will normally be heard orally. At the other end of the scale, applications for extensions of time for the service of pleadings or to comply with other orders of the court can almost always be dealt with by way of an electronic application in writing and, indeed, orders sometimes expressly provide for this.

4.3 MODE OF HEARING

2C-58 **4.3.1** While the mode of hearing is ultimately a judicial decision, the default position for all hearings under half a day will be for such hearings to take place remotely. The Court will consider a live hearing in such cases only if there is a particular reason why an in-person hearing is more appropriate. Such remote hearings include:

a) the Friday applications lists; and
b) adjudication enforcement hearings.

4.3.2 The approach in relation to longer application hearings and trials will be a matter for decision by a judge on the facts of each case.

a) Parties will be asked by the Listing Office to express a preference (supported by reasons), with the final decision as to the appropriate mode of hearing being referred to a judge.
b) The decision on whether to make any such direction will always be a discretionary judicial decision. The overall criterion must be the interests of justice in all the circumstances of the case. This criterion will produce a range of different answers in different cases.
c) Remote and hybrid hearings may cover a full menu of options, from proceedings that are fully remote and accessible live to anyone who is in possession of a link, down to proceedings to which remote access is afforded to a single participant, everyone else being in court.

4.3.3 The BPC protocol for remote and hybrid hearings applies to all such hearings (see Appendix K).

4.4 TELEPHONE HEARINGS

2C-59 **4.4.1** Depending on the nature of the application and the extent of any dispute between the parties, the Court may be prepared to deal with short case management matters and other interlocutory applications by way of a telephone conference.

4.4.2 Whilst it is not possible to lay down mandatory rules as to what applications should be dealt with in this way (rather than by way of an in person, remote or hybrid hearing in court), it may be helpful to identify certain situations which commonly arise and which can conveniently be dealt with by way of a telephone conference.

If the parties are broadly agreed on the orders to be made by the court, but they are in dispute in respect of one or two particular matters, then a telephone hearing is a convenient way in which those outstanding matters can be dealt with by the parties and the assigned judge.

Similarly, specific arguments about costs, once a substantive application has been disposed of, or arguments consequential on a particular judgment or order having been handed down, may also conveniently be dealt with by way of telephone hearing.

4.4.3 Telephone hearings are not generally suitable for matters which are likely to last for more than an hour (although the judge may be prepared, in an appropriate case, to list a longer application for a telephone hearing) or which require extensive reference to documents.

4.4.4 Telephone hearings can be listed at any time between 8.30 a.m. and 5.30 pm, subject to the convenience of the parties and the availability of the judge. It is not essential that all parties are on the telephone when those that are not find it more convenient to come to court. Any party, who wishes to have an application dealt with by telephone, should make such request by letter or e-mail to the judge's clerk, sending copies to all other parties. Except in cases of urgency, the judge will allow a period of two working days for the other parties to comment upon that request before deciding whether to deal with the application by telephone.

4.4.5 If permission is given for a telephone hearing, the court will normally indicate which party is to make all the necessary arrangements. In most cases, it will be the applicant. The procedure to be followed in setting up and holding a telephone hearing is generally that set out in Section 6 of the Practice Direction 23A supplementing CPR Part 23 and the TCC in London and at Regional Centres are "telephone conference enabled courts" for the purposes of that section. The party making arrangements for the telephone hearing must ensure that all parties and the judge have a bundle for that hearing with identical pagination.

4.4.6 It is vital that the judge has all the necessary papers, in good time before the telephone conference, in order that it can be conducted efficiently and effectively. Save in very simple cases involving no or only minimal amounts of documentation, it is usually essential that any bundle provided be paginated for a telephone hearing, failing which the judge may cancel it.

4.5 ELECTRONIC APPLICATIONS

4.5.1 CPR 23.8 and paragraphs 11.1–11.2 of Practice Direction 23A enable certain applications to be dealt with in writing through CE-file. Parties in a TCC case are encouraged to deal with applications in writing, whenever practicable. Applications for abridgments of time, extensions of time and to reduce the trial time estimate can generally be dealt with in writing, as well as all other variations to existing directions which are wholly or largely agreed. Disputes over particular aspects of disclosure and evidence may also be capable of being resolved in this way. **2C-60**

4.5.2 If a party wishes to make an application to the court, it should ask itself the question: "Can this application be conveniently dealt with in writing?" Save for urgent applications, before issuing an application:

a) The applicant should send a draft of the application to the other party/ parties, inviting a response within 3 days or other reasonable, specified time.

b) The responding party/parties should indicate whether they consent to the application; whether they agree to the application being dealt with on paper; and, if it is agreed that the application can be dealt with on paper, whether they wish to serve any evidence or submissions in response.

c) If the application is agreed, a draft consent order can be filed.

d) If the application is not opposed, the application can be filed as such.

e) If the application is opposed, the parties should discuss and, if possible, agree whether it is suitable for determination on paper or by hearing, the timetable for exchange of submissions and evidence, and an estimate for any hearing.

4.5.3 Only then should the application be filed and served. The party making the application should file its short written submissions and should include an explanation of the responding party's/ parties' position, the agreed procedure, or, if not agreed, what it submits the Court should do. The applicant must include a draft of the precise order sought.

4.5.4 There are some paper applications which can be made without notice to the other party or parties so that this guidance does not apply: see CPR 23.4(2), 23.9 and 23.10.

4.5.5 In default of any agreed procedure or further direction of the court, the party against whom the application is made, and any other interested party, should respond within **3 days** of service dealing both with the substantive application and the request for it to be dealt with in writing.

4.5.6 The court can then decide whether or not to deal with the application in writing. If the parties are agreed that the court should deal with it in writing, it will be rare for the court to take a different view. If the parties disagree as to whether or not the application should be dealt with in writing, the court can decide that issue and, if it decides to deal with it in writing, can go on to resolve the substantive point on the basis of the parties' written submissions.

4.5.7 Further guidance in respect of electronic applications is set out in Section 6.7 below.

4.5.8 It is important for the parties to ensure that all documents provided to the court are also provided to all the other parties, so as to ensure that both the court and the parties are working on the basis of the same documentation. The pagination of any bundle which is provided to the court and the parties must be identical.

4.6 E-MAIL COMMUNICATIONS

4.6.1 The judges' clerks all have e-mail addresses identified in Appendix D. They welcome communication from the parties electronically. In addition, it is also possible to provide documents to the Court electronically by e-mail to the judge's clerk. However, it should be noted that HM Court Service imposes a restriction on the size of any e-mail, including attachments, so that other methods of delivering large electronic bundles may be appropriate. **2C-61**

4.6.2 Depending on the particular circumstances of an individual trial, the assigned judge may ask for an e-mail contact address for each of the parties and may send e-mail communications to that address. In addition, the judge may provide a direct contact e-mail address so that the parties can communicate directly with the judge out of court hours. In such circumstances, the judge and the parties should agree the times at which the respective e-mail addresses can be used.

4.6.3 Every e-mail communication to and from the Court or a judge must be copied simultaneously to all the other parties. The subject line of every e-mail should include the name of the case (abbreviated if necessary) and the claim number.

4.7 URGENT APPLICATIONS

4.7.1 If an application is urgent, the applicant should contact listings to discuss judicial availability and to fix a provisional date and time for the hearing. If an urgent application is on notice, the applicant should liaise with the respondent to agree the bundle, timing of skeletons and time estimate. **2C-62**

4.8 CONTACTING THE COURT OUT OF HOURS

2C-63 **4.8.1** Occasionally it is necessary to contact a TCC judge out of hours. For example, it may be necessary to apply for an injunction to prevent the commencement of building works which will damage adjoining property; or for an order to preserve evidence. A case may have settled and it may be necessary to inform the judge, before he/she spends an evening or a weekend reading the papers.

4.8.2 At the Rolls Building

RCJ Security has been provided with the telephone numbers and other contact information of all the clerks to the TCC judges based at the Rolls Building of the court manager. If contact is required with a judge out of hours, the initial approach should be to RCJ Security on 020-7947-6000. Security will then contact the judge's clerk and/or the court manager and pass on the message or other information. If direct contact with the judge or court manager is sought, RCJ Security must be provided with an appropriate contact number. This number will then be passed to the judge's clerk and/or the court manager, who will seek directions from the judge as to whether it is appropriate for the judge to speak directly with the contacting party. Particularly where a matter settles the evening before a hearing or over a weekend, the parties should contact the judge's clerk by e-mail. That is a practical approach but the parties should be aware that the judge's clerks are not expected to access e-mails outside court hours and may not, in any case, have access. If the judge's clerk has not responded within half an hour, other steps as indicated should be taken to contact the judge.

4.8.3 At other court centres

At the Central London Civil Justice Centre and at all court centres outside London there is a court officer who deals with out of hours applications.

4.9 LITIGANTS IN PERSON

2C-64 **4.9.1** An individual who exercises their right to conduct legal proceedings on their own behalf is known as a 'litigant in person'. It is important for litigants in person to be aware that the CPR (the rules of procedure and practice) apply to them in the same way as to lawyers. The court will however have regard to the fact that a party is unrepresented, so that the party is treated fairly.

4.9.2 Neither the court staff nor the judges can provide advice or assistance in relation to the conduct of a claim or defence. Litigants in person are encouraged to seek pro bono or other voluntary assistance, such as Support Through Court. The Bar Council of England and Wales publishes online, free of charge, a "Guide to Representing Yourself in Court". The RCJ Advice Bureau publishes, free of charge, a series of "Going to Court" Guides available online through the "Advicenow" website (*http://www.advicenow.org.uk*).

4.9.3 Litigants in person are not required to file or provide documents electronically, although they may do so. Enquiry should be made to the Listing Office for convenient alternative arrangements for filing or providing documents.

4.9.4 Where a litigant in person is involved in a case the Court will expect solicitors and counsel for other parties to do what they reasonably can to ensure that the litigant in person has a fair opportunity to prepare and put her or his case. The Court will expect solicitors and counsel for other parties to have regard to the "Litigants in Person: Guidelines for Lawyers" published jointly by the Bar Council, the Law Society and the Chartered Institute of Legal Executives in June 2015.

4.9.5 The duty of an advocate to ensure that the Court is informed of all relevant decisions and legislative provisions of which they are aware (whether favourable to the case of their client or not) and to bring any procedural irregularity to the attention of the Court during the hearing is of particular importance in a case where a litigant in person is involved.

4.9.6 Further, the Court will expect solicitors and counsel appearing for other parties to ensure that all necessary bundles are prepared and provided to the Court in accordance with the Guide, even where the litigant in person is unwilling or unable to participate. If the claimant is a litigant in person the Judge at the Case Management Conference will normally direct which of the parties is to have responsibility for the preparation and upkeep of the case management bundle.

4.9.7 Although CPR 39.6 allows a company or other corporation with the permission of the Court to be represented at trial by an employee, the complexity of most cases in the TCC generally makes that unsuitable. Accordingly, permission is likely to be given only in unusual circumstances, and is likely to require, at a minimum, clear evidence that the company or other corporation reasonably could not have been legally represented and that the employee has both the ability and familiarity with the case to be able to assist the court and also unfettered and unqualified authority to represent and bind the company or other corporation in dealings with the other parties to the litigation or with the Court.

SECTION 5 CASE MANAGEMENT IN THE TCC

5.1 GENERAL

5.1.1 The general approach of the TCC to case management is to give directions at the outset for the conduct of the case up to trial and then as necessary throughout the proceedings to serve the overriding objective of dealing with cases justly and at proportionate cost. Since the introduction of the disclosure pilot and costs management the control of disclosure and of costs will be important factors in how cases are managed from the outset: the parties must read this section in conjunction with Section 11 (disclosure) and Section 16 (costs management) The judge to whom the case has been assigned has wide case management powers, which will be exercised to ensure that: **2C-65**

- the real issues are identified early on and remain the focus of the ongoing proceedings;
- a realistic timetable is ordered which will allow for the fair and prompt resolution of the action;
- appropriate steps are taken to ensure that there is in place a suitable protocol for conducting e-disclosure (this should have been discussed by the parties at an early stage in the litigation and in addition to complying with the dislcosure pilot the parties may wish to use the TeCSA e-disclosure protocol (which can be found on its website).
- in document heavy cases the parties will be invited to consider the use of an electronic document management system; it is important that this is considered at an early stage because it will be closely linked to e-disclosure;
- costs are properly controlled and reflect the value of the issues to the parties and their respective financial positions. In claims below the value set by the relevant Practice Direction (£10 million), this will normally be done by way of Costs Management Orders and may be done, if the court considers it appropriate, in cases with a value of £10 million or above.

5.1.2 In order to assist the judge in the exercise of the court's costs and case management functions, the parties will be expected to co-operate with one another at all times - see CPR 1.3. Costs sanctions may be applied, if the judge concludes that one party is not reasonably cooperating with the other parties.

5.1.3 A hearing at which the judge gives general procedural directions is a case management conference ("CMC"). CMCs are relatively informal and business-like occasions. The judge and counsel will be unrobed. Representatives may sit when addressing the judge.

5.1.4 The following procedures apply in order to facilitate effective case management:

- Upon commencement of a case in the TCC, it is allocated automatically to the multi-track. The provisions of CPR Part 29 apply to all TCC cases (but see paragraph 4.2.1 above).
- The TCC encourages a structured exchange of proposals and submissions for CMCs in advance of the hearing, including compliance with the timetables set by the CPR as regards the completion of the disclosure review document, costs budgets and costs budget discussion reports, so as to enable the parties to respond on an informed basis to proposals made.
- The judges of the TCC operate pro-active case management. In order to avoid the parties being taken by surprise by any judicial initiative, the judge will consider giving prior notification of specific or unusual case management proposals to be raised at a case management conference.

5.1.5 The TCC's aim is to ensure that where possible the trial of each case takes place before the judge who has managed the case since the first CMC, although continuity of judge is not always possible, because of the need for High Court Judges to be deployed on other duties, or because cases can sometimes overrun their estimated length through no fault of the parties.

5.1.6 To ensure that costs are properly controlled the judge will consider at all stages of case management whether there are ways in which costs can be reduced. If the judge considers that any particular aspect has unnecessarily increased costs, such as prolix pleadings or witness statements, the judge may make a costs order disallowing costs or ordering costs to be paid, either on the basis of a summary assessment, or by giving a direction to the costs judge as to what costs should be disallowed or paid on a detailed assessment: see also paragraph 5.5.5 below.

5.2 THE FIXING OF THE FIRST CMC

5.2.1 Where a claim has been started in the TCC, or where it has been transferred into the TCC, paragraph 8.1 of the Part 60 Practice Direction requires the court within **14 days** of the earliest of: **2C-66**

- the filing by the defendant of an acknowledgement of service, or
- the filing by the defendant of the defence, or
- the date of the order transferring the case to the TCC

to fix the first CMC.

If some defendants but not others are served with proceedings, the claimant's solicitors should so inform the court and liaise about the fixing of the first CMC. See also paragraph 4.2.1 above.

5.2.2 The first CMC will usually be fixed sufficiently far ahead to allow the parties time to comply with the requirements of both the disclosure pilot and costs budgeting (although see paragraph 3.5 below as regards adjourning costs budgeting or disclosure in particular cases). If any of the parties wishes to delay the first CMC for any reason, it can write to the judge's clerk explaining why a delayed CMC is appropriate. Examples of good reasons for requesting a delay would include:

- the need for reasonable additional time to complete the exchange of statements of case;
- the need for reasonable additional time to comply with the disclosure pilot;
- the need to comply with the timetable for costs budgeting;
- the need for additional time to be allocated to the first CMC;
- the parties' wish to discuss transferring the case to the Capped Costs List or the Shorter or Flexible Trials Scheme (see paragraph 5.2.3) and
- the parties' wish to engage in ADR before the CMC.

The parties should consider and discuss this in good time before the time for the court to fix the first CMC, most obviously at the preaction meeting required under the Pre-Action Protocol (see Section 2.4).If such a request identifies a good reason and is agreed by the other party or parties, it is likely that the judge will grant the request. If such a request is made after the first CMC has already been listed an application will have to be made, by consent or, if not, on an opposed basis, which should normally be made as an electronic/ paper application (see Section 4.5).

5.2.3 The judge will consider in appropriate cases whether the case is suitable for transfer into the Capped Costs List or the Shorter or Flexible Trials Scheme. The parties are encouraged to consider these options in appropriate cases before proceedings are commenced, again most obviously at the pre-action meeting, but if they have not done so they should consider them in good time before the CMC since if the case is to be transferred into the Capped Costs List or into the Shorter or Flexible Trials Scheme there is no need to comply with the disclosure pilot and costs management will not apply.

5.3 THE CASE MANAGEMENT INFORMATION SHEET AND OTHER DOCUMENTS

2C-67 **5.3.1** All parties are expected to complete a detailed response to the case management information sheet sent out by the the listing office when the case is commenced/transferred. A copy of a blank case management information sheet is attached as Appendix A. It is important that all parts of the form are completed, particularly those sections that enable the judge to give directions in accordance with the overriding objective.

5.3.2 The the listing office will also send out a blank standard directions form to each party. A copy is attached at Appendix B (and is also available online). This provides an example of the usual directions made on the first CMC. The parties may either fill it in (manually), indicating the directions and timetable sought, or, preferably, provide draft directions in a similar format, revised as appropriate to suit the circumstances of the particular case. The standard directions contain references to the relevant sections of this Guide to assist those completing the standard directions form in a way which is consistent with the contents of this Guide.

5.3.3 The parties should return both the questionnaire and the proposed directions to the court, so that the areas (if any) of potential debate at the CMC can be identified. The parties are encouraged to exchange proposals for directions and the timetable sought, with a view to agreeing the same before the CMC for consideration by the court. Although Practice Direction 60.8.3 provides that the completed questionnaire and proposed directions should be filed not less than 2 (clear) days before the CMC, experience has shown that the parties will need to have produced and exchanged their drafts in good time beforehand to allow meaningful discussions and agreement where possible and that it is preferable to return the completed questionnaire and proposed directions at least four clear days before the CMC.

5.3.4 The parties should note that the Practice Direction 57AD requires the parties no less than 14 days before the first CMC to file the completed disclosure review document and that CPR 3.13 requires the parties to file and exchange costs budgets not later than 21 days before the CMC and to file budget discussion reports no later than 7 days before the CMC. Failure to file a budget may result in a party's recoverable costs being limited to the applicable court fees.

5.3.5 The claim value of a case may be such that costs management does not apply unless the Court so orders. Further, there may be cases where the particular directions sought by one or more parties may have such an impact on costs budgeting that it would be impracticable or unduly burdensome for the parties to have to prepare to deal with costs budgeting at the first CMC. In such cases, it is open to a party or to the parties to apply, by consent or on an opposed basis, for a direction that costs budgeting should not be dealt with at the first CMC and that the steps required by CPR 3.13 should not be required to be taken. The Court has discretion to dispense with costs management where appropriate or extend time for filing cost budgets. Likewise, there may also be cases where the particular directions or disclosure sought by one or more parties may have such an impact on the nature and scope of any disclosure order to be made that it would be impracticable or unduly burdensome for the parties to have to prepare to deal with disclosure in full compliance with the disclosure pilot at the first CMC. Any such application should normally be made as an electronic application (see Section 4.5).

5.3.6 The claimant's solicitor is responsible for ensuring that a Permanent Case Management Bundle containing the required documents identified in paragraph 5.11 below is produced and provided not less than 2 working days before the hearing of the first CMC. The bundle for the first CMC must be provided to the court in electronic format unless the court otherwise directs.

5.3.7 If the case is proceeding in the High Court, the advocates should prepare a Note to be exchanged and provided to the judge at the latest by 4 pm two clear working days before the CMC which can address the issues in the case, the suggested directions, and the principal areas of dispute between the parties, so as to enable the other parties to have a reasonable opportunity to consider and respond at the CMC to any points raised and to enable the judge to prepare for the CMC in good time. The advocates should also exchange and provide at the same time a skeleton argument for any applications as required by paragraphs 6.5.4 and 6.5.5.

5.3.8 In cases proceeding in the County Court, the advocates should prepare a Note for the CMC, to be provided at the latest by 4pm one clear working day before the CMC.

5.4 CHECKLIST OF MATTERS LIKELY TO BE CONSIDERED AT THE FIRST CMC

5.4.1 The following checklist identifies the matters which the judge is likely to want to consider **2C-68**
at the first CMC, although it is not exhaustive:

- The need for, and content of, any further statements of case to be served. This is dealt with in paragraph 5.5 below.
- The outcome of the Protocol process, and the possible further need for ADR. ADR is dealt with in Section 7 below.
- In an appropriate case, whether the case is suitable for transfer into the Capped Costs List (if the parties all agree) or for transfer into the Shorter Trials or the Flexible Trials Schemes.
- The desirability of dealing with particular disputes by way of a Preliminary Issue hearing. This is dealt with in Section 8 below.
- The court will require a list of issues to be provided and updated during the course of the procedural steps. This is dealt with in paragraph 5.6 below. Note that the list of the issues for determination at trial is likely to be different from the list of issues for disclosure as required by the disclosure pilot.
- Whether the trial should be in stages (e.g. stage 1 liability and causation, stage 2 quantum). In very heavy cases this may be necessary in order to make the trial manageable. In more modest cases, where the quantum evidence will be extensive, a staged trial may be in the interest of all parties.
- The appropriate orders in respect of the disclosure of documents and for a protocol to manage e-disclosure. This is dealt with in Section 11 below.
- The appropriate orders as to the exchange of written witness statements. This is dealt with in Section 12 below. It should be noted that, although it is normal for evidence-in-chief to be given by way of the written statements in the TCC, the judge may direct that evidence about particular disputes (such as what was said at an important meeting) should be given orally without reference to such statements.
- Whether it is appropriate for the parties to rely on expert evidence and, if so, what disciplines of experts should give evidence, on what issues, and whether any issues can be conveniently dealt with by single joint experts. This may be coupled with an order relating to the carrying out of inspections, the obtaining of samples, the conducting of experiments, or the performance of calculations. Considerations relating to expert evidence are dealt with in Section 13 below. The parties must be aware that, in accordance with the overriding objective, the judge will only give the parties permission to rely on expert evidence if it is both necessary and appropriate, and, even then, will wish to ensure that the scope of any such evidence is limited as far as possible.
- Review of the parties' costs budgets and the making of a Costs Management Order (subject to any financial threshold relevant to the case). In certain cases there is the possibility of making a costs capping order. See paragraph 16.3 below.
- Whether there will be any additional claims under Part 20. See paragraph 5.5.4 below.
- The appropriate timetable for the taking of the various interim steps noted above, and the fixing of dates for both the PTR and the trial itself (subject to paragraph 5.4.2 below). The parties will therefore need to provide the judge with an estimate for the length of the trial, including judicial reading time, assuming all issues remain in dispute. Unless there is good reason not to, the trial date will generally be fixed at the first CMC (although this may be more difficult at court centres with only one TCC judge). Therefore, to the extent that there are any relevant concerns as to availability of either witnesses or legal representatives, they need to be brought to the attention of the court on that occasion. The length of time fixed for the trial will depend on the parties' estimates, and also the judge's own view, and will in most cases also need to provide for judicial pre-reading as well as, in substantial and complex cases, time for preparation and pre-reading of written closing submissions before delivery of oral closing submissions. In such cases the parties should give consideration to, and the court may fix, a date for the exchange of written closing submissions and a further hearing for oral closing submissions. If the parties' estimate of trial length (including pre-

reading) subsequently changes, they should inform the clerk of the assigned judge immediately.

5.4.2 The fixing of the trial date at the CMC is, unless the contrary is specified, a firm date and will not be vacated or re-arranged save for good reason and with the consent of the judge. However, the trial fee is payable in accordance with section 2.1 in Schedule 1 to the Civil Proceedings Fees Order 2008, usually 2 months prior to the trial date. It should be noted that if the trial fee is not paid on or before the trial fee payment date then the claim will be automatically struck out: see CPR 3.7A1 and 3.7AA.

5.4.3 Essentially, the judge's aim at the first CMC is to set down a detailed timetable which, in the majority of cases, will ensure that the parties need not return to court until the PTR.

5.5 FURTHER STATEMENTS OF CASE

5.5.1 Defence

2C-69 If no defence has been served prior to the first CMC, then (except in cases where judgment in default is appropriate) the court will usually make an order for service of the defence within a specified period. The defendant must plead its positive case. Bare denials and non-admissions are, save in exceptional circumstances, unacceptable.

5.5.2 Further Information

If any party wants to request further information any other party's statement of case, the request should, if possible, be formulated prior to the first CMC, so that it can be considered on that occasion. All requests for further information should be kept within reasonable limits, and concentrate on the important parts of the case. The requests and the replies should always be set out in one composite document, with each reply appearing immediately after each request.

5.5.3 Reply

A reply to the defence is not always necessary. However, where the defendant has raised a positive defence on a particular issue, it may be appropriate for the claimant to set out in a reply how it answers such a defence. CPR 60.5 provides that the time for filing of the reply is 21 days after service of the defence. If no reply has been filed by the time of the CMC, the court may fix a different period or extend time for filing. If the defendant makes a counterclaim, the claimant's defence to counterclaim and its reply (if any) should be in the same document.

5.5.4 Additional or Part 20 Claims

The defendant should, at the first CMC, indicate (so far as possible) any additional (Part 20) claims that it is proposing to make, whether against the claimant or any other party. Additional (Part 20) claims are required to be pleaded in the same detail as the original claim. They are a very common feature of TCC cases, because the widespread use of sub-contractors in the UK construction industry often makes it necessary to pass claims down a contractual chain. Defendants are encouraged to start any necessary Part 20 proceedings to join additional parties as soon as possible. It is undesirable for applications to join additional defendants to be made late in the proceedings.

5.5.5 Costs

If at any stage the judge considers that the way in which the case has been pleaded, particularly through the inclusion of extensive irrelevant material or obscurity, is likely to lead or has led to inefficiency in the conduct of the proceedings or to unnecessary time or costs being spent, the judge may order that the party should re-plead the whole or part of the case and may make a costs order disallowing costs or ordering costs to be paid, either on the basis of a summary assessment or by giving a direction to the costs judge as to what costs should be disallowed or paid on a detailed assessment: see also paragraph 5.1.6 above and paragraph 12.1.4 below.

5.5.6 List of Issues

After service of the defence and prior to the CMC the claimant should circulate a list of the key issues of fact and law in the case in electronic format. This should be a succinct neutral document, intended to assist efficient case management, which begins by summarising what is common ground and then fairly identifies the main issues by reference to the statements of case. It should not cover every detail or rehearse every possible argument. Since it does not supersede the statements of case no party will be disadvantaged by any errors or omissions in the list of issues and the court will firmly discourage and, if appropriate, penalise in costs any unnecessary disputes as to its precise terms. There should be no need for the defendant to produce a separate list but, if necessary, it may include any comments and any amendments with a view to reaching agreement. If there are additional claims, then the claimants in those claims should add to the list of issues so that one composite list of issues is produced. The list or lists of issues should be provided to the judge in advance of the CMC and then kept under review by the parties.

5.6 SCOTT SCHEDULES

2C-70 **5.6.1** It can sometimes be appropriate for elements of the claim, or any additional (Part 20) claim, to be set out by way of a Scott Schedule (i.e. by a table, often in landscape format, in which the Claimant's case on liability and quantum is set out item by item in the first few columns and the Defendant's response is set out in the adjacent columns). For example, claims involving a final account or numerous alleged defects or items of disrepair, may be best formulated in this way, which then allows for a detailed response from the defendant. Sometimes, even where all the damage has been caused by one event, such as a fire, it can be helpful for the individual items of loss and damage to be set out in a Scott Schedule. The secret of an effective Scott Schedule lies in the information that is to be provided and its brevity: excessive repetition is to be avoided. This is defined by the column headings. The judge may give directions for the relevant column headings for any Schedule ordered by the court. It is important that the defendant's responses to any such Schedule are as detailed as possible. Each party's entries on a Scott Schedule should be supported by a statement of truth.

5.6.2 Nevertheless, before any order is made or agreement is reached for the preparation of a Scott Schedule, both the parties and the court should consider whether this course (a) will genuinely lead to a saving of cost and time or (b) will lead to a wastage of costs and effort (because the Scott Schedule will simply be duplicating earlier schedules, pleadings or expert reports). A Scott Schedule should only be ordered by the court, or agreed by the parties, in those cases where it is appropriate and proportionate.

5.6.3 When a Scott Schedule is ordered by the court or agreed by the parties, the format must always be specified. The parties must cooperate in the physical task of preparation. Electronic transfer between the parties of their respective entries in the columns will enable a clear and user-friendly Scott Schedule to be prepared, for the benefit of all involved in the trial.

5.7 AGREEMENT BETWEEN THE PARTIES

5.7.1 Many, perhaps most, of the required directions at the first CMC may be agreed by the parties. If so, the Court will endeavour to make orders in the terms which have been agreed pursuant to CPR 29.4, unless the judge considers that the agreed terms fail to take into account important features of the case as a whole, or the principles of the CPR. The agreed terms will always, at the very least, form the starting-point of the judge's consideration of the orders to be made at the CMC. If the agreed terms are submitted to the judge 3 days in advance of the hearing date, it may be possible to avoid the need for a hearing altogether, although it is normally necessary for the Court to consider the case with the parties (either at an oral hearing or by way of a telephone conference) in any event. **2C-71**

5.7.2 The approach outlined in paragraph 5.7.1 above is equally applicable to all other occasions when the parties come before the court with a draft order that is wholly or partly agreed.

5.8 ATTENDANCE AND REPRESENTATION

5.8.1 Clients need not attend a CMC unless the Court otherwise directs. A representative who has conduct of the case must attend from each firm of solicitors instructed. At least one of the advocates instructed in the case on behalf of each party should attend. Where a party has engaged more than one advocate (eg. leading and junior counsel), there is no requirement that all attend. The experience of the court is that on many case management issues, junior advocates within a team may be well placed to assist the court. Parties should consider in every case (a) whether attendance by the more (or most) senior advocates instructed in the case is reasonably required and (b) whether, even where that is the position, at least some of the matters arising may appropriately be dealt with by the more (or most) junior advocates. **2C-72**

5.9 DRAWING UP OF ORDERS

5.9.1 Unless the Court itself draws up the order, it may direct one party (usually the claimant or applicant) to do so within a specified time. If no such direction is given, then the advocate appearing for the Claimant (or applicant) must prepare and seek to agree a draft order and submit it for the judge's approval within 7 days of the conclusion of the hearing. This is to ensure that the draft is presented to the court whilst the case is still fresh in the judge's mind and so that the draft can be checked for accuracy and to ensure that it reflects the intended order. The party charged with drawing up the order must draw up the order and lodge it with the court for approval. Once approved, the order will be stamped by the Court and returned to that party for service upon all other parties. The order should refer to the date on which the order was made by stating "Date order made: [date]". Orders should be referred to by this date, rather than later dates which reflect the process of submission of the draft order, approval by the judge and sealing by the Court. **2C-73**

5.9.2 In exceptional cases where the parties cannot agree a minute of order (whether within the specified time or at all), then the party with carriage of the order should submit the order, so far as it has been agreed, to the judge together with a summary of those elements of those parts of the order which are not agreed, and setting out any rival wording proposed by the other side, within the specified time. That communication must be in an agreed form as far as possible stating neutrally the other parties' objections, and it must be copied to the other parties when it is submitted to the court. The Court heavily discourages extended satellite correspondence over the precise form of order. If, exceptionally, the judge wishes to hear further submissions on the draft form of order before it is approved those submissions can be requested. Unilateral further submissions to the Court as to the order are only to be made in exceptional circumstances (e.g. where a party considers that there is a real risk that the Court is being misled or its position is being seriously misrepresented). Parties who unreasonably refuse to agree a minute of order, or who take up court time arguing over the precise form of minute can expect to have costs orders made against them.

5.9.3 It is often the case that the parties, after the hearing, decide that it is sensible to include other directions in the draft order by consent, or to vary the timetable to accommodate such matters. Any such agreement must be clearly indicated in both the draft order (e.g. by adding in the matters under a separate heading stating that such matters are being made "By Consent") and in an explanatory note for the judge submitted with the proposed order.

5.10 FURTHER CMC

2C-74 **5.10.1** In an appropriate case, the judge will fix a review CMC, to take place part way through the timetable that has been set down, in order to allow the Court to review progress, and to allow the parties to raise any matters arising out of the steps that have been taken up to that point. However, this will not be ordered automatically and will be confined to cases of significant complexity.

5.10.2 Each party will be required to give notice in writing to the other parties and the Court of any directions which it will be seeking at the review CMC, two days in advance of the hearing.

5.11 THE PERMANENT CASE MANAGEMENT BUNDLE

2C-75 **5.11.1** In conjunction with the judge's clerk, the claimant's solicitor is responsible for ensuring that, for the first CMC and at all times thereafter, there is a permanent electronic bundle of documents available to the judge, which contains:

- any relevant documents resulting from the Pre-Action Protocol;
- the claim form and all statements of case;
- all orders;
- all completed case management information sheets;
- all costs budgets;
- any proposed protocol for e-disclosure (if agreed);
- Disclosure Review Documents and Disclosure Issues as required by PD 57AD.

5.11.2 The permanent case management bundle can then be supplemented by the specific documents relevant to any particular application that may be made. Whether these supplementary documents should (a) become a permanent addition to the case management bundle or (b) be set on one side, will depend upon their nature. The permanent case management bundle, whether electronic or hard copy, will usually not be retained by the judge after the hearing once the agreed order has been drawn up, approved and sealed, unless needed for a further imminent hearing or as agreed with the parties.

SECTION 6 APPLICATIONS AFTER THE FIRST CMC

6.1 RELEVANT PARTS OF THE CPR

2C-76 **6.1.1** The basic rules relating to all applications that any party may wish to make are set out in CPR Part 23 and its accompanying Practice Directions.

6.1.2 **Part 7** of the **Practice Direction** accompanying CPR Part 60, PD51O and the guidance in paragraph 3.8 in respect of electronic working are also of particular relevance.

6.2 APPLICATION NOTICE

2C-77 **6.2.1** As a general rule, any party to proceedings in the TCC wishing to make an application of any sort must file an application notice (CPR 23.3) and serve that application notice on all relevant parties as soon as practicable after it has been filed (CPR 23.4). Application notices should be served by the parties, unless (as happens in some court centres outside London) service is undertaken by the court. Where the circumstances may justify an application being made without notice, see paragraph 6.10 below.

6.2.2 The application notice must set out in clear terms what order is sought and, more briefly, the reasons for seeking that order: seeCPR 23.6.

6.2.3 The application notice must be served at least **3 days** before the hearing at which the Court deals with the application: CPR 23.7 (1). Such a short notice period is only appropriate for the most straight-forward type of application.

6.2.4 Most applications, in particular applications for summary judgment under CPR Part 24 or to strike out a statement of case underCPR 3.4, will necessitate a much longer notice period than **3 days**. In such cases, it is imperative that the applicant obtain a suitable date and time for the hearing of the application before the application notice is issued. When providing a time estimate, the applicant should give some thought as to the reading time required by the Judge in advance of the hearing; if longer than 1-2 hours, the applicant should notif y the court of this requirement when fixing the date so that reading time can be put in the diary. The applicant must serve the application notice and evidence in support sufficiently far ahead of the date fixed for the hearing of the application for there to be time to enable the respondent to serve evidence in response. Save in exceptional circumstances, there should be a minimum period of **10 working days** between the service of the notice (and supporting evidence) and the hearing date. If any party considers that there is insufficient time before the hearing of the application or if the time estimate for the application itself is too short, that party must notify the court and the hearing may then be refixed by agreement.

6.2.5 When considering the application notice, the judge may give directions in writing as to the dates for the provision or exchange of evidence and any written submissions or skeleton arguments for the hearing.

6.2.6 In cases of great urgency applications may be made without formal notice to the other party, but that party should (save in exceptional cases) be informed of the hearing sufficiently in advance to enable him to instruct a representative to attend.

6.3 EVIDENCE IN SUPPORT

6.3.1 The application notice when it is served must be accompanied by all evidence in support: **2C-78** CPR 23.7 (2).

6.3.2 Unless the CPR expressly requires otherwise, evidence will be given by way of witness statements. Such statements must be verified by a statement of truth signed by the maker of the statement: CPR 22.1.

6.4 EVIDENCE IN OPPOSITION AND EVIDENCE IN REPLY

6.4.1 Likewise, any evidence in opposition to the application should, unless the rules expressly **2C-79** provide otherwise, be given by way of witness statement verified by a statement of truth.

6.4.2 It is important to ensure that the evidence in opposition to the application is served in good time before the hearing so as to enable:

- the court to read and note up the evidence;
- the applicant to put in any further evidence in reply that may be considered necessary.

Such evidence should be served at least **5 working days** before the hearing.

6.4.3 Any evidence in reply should be served not less than **3 working days** before the hearing. Again, if there are disputes as to the time taken or to be taken for the preparation of evidence prior to a hearing, or any other matters in respect of a suitable timetable for that hearing, the Court will consider the written positions of both parties and decide such disputes on paper. It will not normally be necessary for either a separate application to be issued or a hearing to be held for such a purpose.

6.4.4 If the hearing of an application has to be adjourned because of delays by one or other of the parties in serving evidence, the Court is likely to order that party to pay the costs straight away, and to make a summary assessment of those costs.

6.5 APPLICATION BUNDLE

6.5.1 The bundle for the hearing of anything other than the most simple and straightforward **2C-80** application should consist of:

- the permanent case management bundle (see paragraph 5.8 above);
- the witness statements provided in support of the application, together with any exhibits;
- the witness statements provided in opposition to the application together with exhibits;
- any witness statements in reply, together with exhibits.

6.5.2 The permanent case management bundle should be provided to the court in electronic form not less than **2 working days** before the hearing. In any event, a paginated bundle in electronic form containing any material specific to the application should also be provided to the court not less than **2 working days** before the hearing, unless otherwise directed by the judge. A failure to comply with this deadline may result in the adjournment of the hearing, and the costs thrown away being paid by the defaulting party. The further guidance on electronic bundles in Appendix J applies.

6.5.3 If the bundle is requested by the judge in hard copy, PD32, paragraph 27.15 now provides that the default position is that application bundles should be provided in double-sided printing unless the Court otherwise directs. In the TCC, bundles for applications and short trials (such as a one day Part 8 hearing or a 2 day preliminary issue hearing) should be provided in single-sided printing (unless the Court otherwise directs).

6.5.4 In all but the simplest applications, the Court will expect the parties to provide skeleton arguments and copies of any authorities to be relied on. The form and content of the skeleton argument is principally a matter for the author, although the judge will expect it to identify the issues that arise on the application, the important parts of the evidence relied on, and the applicable legal principles. For detailed guidance as to the form, content and length of skeleton arguments, please see the relevant provisions of the King's Bench Guide, the Chancery Guide and the Commercial Court Guide.

6.5.5 For an application that is estimated to last half a day or less, the skeleton should be provided no later than **4pm one clear working day before the hearing**. It should be accompanied by an electronic bundle of the authorities relied on (preferably in the form of a common agreed bundle). An electronic copy of each skeleton argument (in Microsoft Word compatible format) should be sent to the clerk of the judge hearing the application: if a party is reluctant for other parties to be provided with its skeleton argument in Word, it may serve it in pdf (or other readable) form provided that it certifies that the version sent to the judge is identical in content to that served on the other parties.

6.5.6 For an application that is estimated to last more than half a day, the skeleton should be provided no later than **4 pm two clear working days before the hearing**. It should be accompanied by an electronic bundle of the authorities relied on (again, preferably in the form of a common agreed bundle).

6.5.7 The time limits at paragraphs 6.5.5 and 6.5.6 above will be regarded as the latest times by which such skeletons should be provided to the court. Save in exceptional circumstances, no extension to these periods will be permitted. **If the application bundle or skeleton argument is not provided by the time specified, the application may be stood out of the list without further warning and there may be cost consequences.**

6.5.8 Pagination

It is generally necessary for there to be a paginated bundle for the hearing. Where the parties have produced skeleton arguments, these should be cross-referred to the bundle page numbers. Where possible bundles should be paginated right through, but this may be dispensed with where a document within a discrete section of the bundle has its own internal pagination.

6.6 HEARINGS

2C-81 **6.6.1** Arbitration applications may be heard in private: see CPR 62.10. All other applications will be heard in public in accordance with CPR 39.2, save where otherwise ordered.

6.6.2 Provided that the application bundle and the skeletons have been lodged in accordance with the time limits set out above, the parties can assume that the court will have a good understanding of the points in issue. However, the Court will expect to be taken to particular documents relied on by the parties and will also expect to be addressed on any important legal principles that arise. If the parties have failed to comply with the guidance in paragraph 6.2.4 in respect of time estimates for pre-reading or have given an inadequate time estimate, the parties should be aware that that may affect the conduct of the hearing and the time estimate for hearing and that the judge may, as a result, adjourn the hearing.

6.6.3 It is important that the parties ensure that every application is dealt with in the estimated time period. Since many applications are dealt with on Fridays, it causes major disruption if application hearings are not disposed of within the estimated period. If the parties take too long in making their submissions, the application may be adjourned, part heard, and the Court may impose appropriate costs sanctions.

6.6.4 If, in the light of the evidence served in respect of an application, it becomes apparent to either party that the time estimate given is likely to be inadequate, the parties should notify the Court as soon as possible. It may be possible for the Court to accommodate a longer hearing but, if the Court is unaware of the likely longer hearing, this can cause real difficulties, inhibit the giving of an ex tempore judgment, and delay reserved judgments. If the Court is unable to offer a longer hearing, the parties are expected to co-operate to re-list the hearing as soon as possible.

6.6.5 At the conclusion of the hearing, unless the Court itself draws up the order, it will direct the applicant to do so within a specified period.

6.6.6 If a party is likely to require a transcript of either the hearing or any judgment or ruling, it should notify the judge's clerk straight away: see paragraph 15.9.2. If, by that time, the judge has returned the papers, the party seeking the transcript should retain a set of all papers used at the hearing in hard copy and/or electronic form and should inform the judge's clerk that they can be provided should the judge require them in order to correct and approve a form of judgment. Alternatively, the judge may seek the assistance of the parties in correcting proper names, citations, quotations and the like.

6.6.7 If an application settles the evening before a hearing or over a weekend, the parties should have regard to the guidance at paragraph 4.7.2 above.

6.7 ELECTRONIC APPLICATIONS

2C-82 **6.7.1** As noted in Section 4 above some applications may be suitable for determination on written submissions and documents under the procedure set out in paragraph 4.5 above.

6.7.2 In addition, certain simple applications (particularly in lower value cases) arising out of the management of the proceedings may be capable of being dealt with by correspondence without the need for any formal application or order of the Court. This is particularly true of applications to vary procedural orders, which variations are wholly or largely agreed, or proposals to vary the estimated length of the trial. In such cases, the applicant should write to the other parties indicating the nature of its application and to seek their agreement to it. If, however, it emerges that there is an issue to be resolved by the Court, then a formal application must be issued and dealt with as a paper application or, possibly, at an oral hearing.

6.7.3 It is essential that any communication by a party to the judge or the Court is copied to all other parties, subject to paragraph 6.10 below (applications without notice).

6.8 CONSENT ORDERS

6.8.1 Consent Orders may be submitted to the Court in draft for approval without the need for attendance. **2C-83**

6.8.2 Two copies of the draft order should be lodged, at least one of which should be signed. The copies should be undated as the Court will set out the date the order is made: see paragraph 5.8.1 above.

6.8.3 As noted elsewhere, whilst the parties can agree between themselves the orders to be made either at the Case Management Conference or the Pre-Trial Review, it is normally necessary for the Court to consider the case with the parties (either at an oral hearing or by way of a telephone conference) on those occasions in any event.

6.8.4 Generally, when giving directions, the Court will endeavour to identify the date by which the relevant step must be taken, and will not simply provide a period during which that task should be performed. The parties should therefore ensure that any proposed consent order also identifies particular dates, rather than periods, by which the relevant steps must be taken.

6.9 COSTS

6.9.1 Costs are dealt with generally at Section 16 below. **2C-84**

6.9.2 The costs of any application which took a day or less to be heard and disposed of will be dealt with summarily, unless there is a good reason for the court not to exercise its powers as to the summary assessment of costs.

6.9.3 Accordingly, it is necessary for parties to provide to the Court and to one another their draft statements of costs no later than **24 hours** before the start of the application hearing. Any costs which are incurred after these draft statements have been prepared, but which have not been allowed for (e.g. because the hearing has exceeded its anticipated length), can be mentioned at the hearing.

6.10 APPLICATIONS WITHOUT NOTICE

6.10.1 All applications should be made on notice, even if that notice has to be short, unless: **2C-85**

- any rule or Practice Direction provides that the application may be made without notice; or
- there are good reasons for making the application without notice, for example, because notice might defeat the object of the application.

6.10.2 If the application is urgent, the TCC Listing Office should be given a clear explanation in writing, certified by the legal representatives of the applicant if they are represented, of the degree of and reasons for the urgency. It is important to remember that urgency is separate from, and additional to, the question whether it is appropriate to make the application without notice. Once the application documents have been submitted, the application and the explanation for urgency will go before a Judge who will decide if the application is urgent, and if so the degree of urgency.

6.10.3 Where an application without notice does not involve giving undertakings to the Court, it will normally be made and dealt with on the documents, as, for example, applications for permission to serve the claim form out of the jurisdiction, and applications for an extension of time in which to serve a claim form. Any application for an interim injunction or similar remedy will usually require an oral hearing.

6.10.4 A party wishing to make an application without notice which requires an oral hearing before a judge should contact the TCC Listing Office at the earliest opportunity.

6.10.5 If a party wishes to make an application without notice at a time when no TCC judge is available, the application should be made to the King's Bench Judge in Chambers.

6.10.6 On all applications without notice it is the duty of the applicant and those representing him:

- to make full and frank disclosure of all matters relevant to the application;
- to ensure that a note of the hearing of the without notice application, the evidence and skeleton argument in support and any order made all be served with the order or as soon as possible thereafter.

6.10.7 The papers lodged on the application should include two copies of a draft of the order sought. Save in exceptional circumstances, all the evidence relied upon in support of the application and any other relevant documents must be lodged in advance with the TCC Listing Office. If the application is urgent, the Listing Office should be informed of the fact and of the reasons for the urgency. Counsel's estimate of reading time likely to be required by the court should also be provided.

6.11 INTERIM INJUNCTIONS

2C-86 **6.11.1** Applications for interim injunctions are governed by CPR 25.

6.11.2 Applications must be made on notice in accordance with CPR 23 unless there are good reasons for proceeding without notice.

6.11.3 A party who wishes to make an application for an interim injunction must give the TCC Listing Office as much notice as possible, indicating the type of application likely to be made, the anticipated time requirement for reading and a hearing, and when it is expected that papers will be ready for submission to a judge.

6.11.4 Except where there is such urgency as to make this impracticable, the applicant must issue a claim form and obtain the evidence on which it wishes to rely before making the application and should provide the Court with a skeleton argument in good time for the judge to read it before any hearing.

6.11.5 An affidavit, and not a witness statement, is required on an application for a freezing order: PD25A paragraph 3.1.

6.11.6 Where the applicant for an interim remedy is not able to show sufficient assets within the jurisdiction of the Court to provide substance for any undertakings given, it may be required to provide security in such form as the judge decides is appropriate.

6.11.7 An interim remedy expressed to remain in force until judgment, or further order, remains in force until the delivery of a final judgment (unless some other order is made in the meantime). If an interim remedy after judgment is required, an application to that effect must be made.

6.11.8 An order for an interim remedy should generally provide that acts which would otherwise be a breach of the order are permitted, if done with the written consent of the solicitor of the other party or parties, to reduce the need to come back to the Court with further applications.

6.11.9 Standard forms of wording for freezing injunctions, with important explanatory footnotes, are set out in Appendix 11 to the Commercial Court Guide. The standard wording may be modified but any modifications proposed by an applicant should be:

a) shown using tracked changes on a copy of the draft order provided to the Court;
b) identified and explained individually in any skeleton argument for the application; and
c) drawn to the judge's attention expressly at the application hearing.

6.11.10 Freezing injunctions made on an application without notice will provide for a return date unless the judge otherwise orders: PD25 paragraph 5.1(3).

However:

a) if, after service with notification of the injunction, one or more of the parties considers that the time allowed for the return date hearing will be insufficient to deal with the matter, the Listing Office should be informed forthwith and in any event not later than 4:00 pm one clear day before the return date;
b) if the parties agree to postpone the return date to a later date, an agreed form of order continuing the injunction to the postponed return date should be submitted for consideration by the judge; if the proposed order is approved, the parties do not need to attend on the original return date and the respondent, and any other interested party, will continue to have liberty to apply to vary or set aside the order;
c) a provision for the respondent to give notice of any application to discharge or vary the order is usually included as a matter of convenience in the order but it is not proper to attempt to fetter the right of the respondent to apply without notice or on short notice if necessary;
d) any bank or third parties served with, notified of, or affected by a freezing injunction may apply to the Court without notice to any party for directions, or notify the Court in writing without notice to any party, in the event that the order affects or may affect the position of the bank or third party under legislation, regulations or procedures aimed at preventing money laundering.

6.11.11 Applications to discharge or very freezing injunctions are treated as matters of urgency for listing purposes. Those representing applicants for discharge or variation should ascertain before a date is fixed for the hearing whether, having regard to the evidence which they wish to adduce, the other parties would wish to adduce further evidence; if so, all reasonable steps must be taken to agree the earliest practicable date at which the parties can be ready for a hearing, to avoid vacating a fixed date at the last minute. In cases of difficulty the matter should be referred to a judge.

6.11.12 If a freezing injunction is discharged on an application to discharge or vary, or on the return date, the judge will consider whether it is appropriate to assess damages forthwith and direct immediate payment by the applicant. Where a hearing in connection with the cross undertaking of damages or the assessment of damages is directed but postponed to a future date, case management directions will be given.

SECTION 7 ADR

7.1 GENERAL

7.1.1 The court will provide encouragement to the parties to use alternative dispute resolution ("ADR") and will, whenever appropriate, facilitate the use of such a procedure. In this Guide, ADR is taken to mean any process through which the parties attempt to resolve their dispute, which is voluntary. In most cases, ADR takes the form of inter-party negotiations or a mediation conducted by a neutral mediator. Alternative forms of ADR include early neutral evaluation either by a judge or some other neutral person who receives a concise presentation from each party and then provides his or her own evaluation of the case. **2C-87**

7.1.2 Although the TCC is an appropriate forum for the resolution of all IT and construction/ engineering disputes, the use of ADR can lead to a significant saving of costs and may result in a settlement which is satisfactory to all parties.

7.1.3 Legal representatives in all TCC cases should ensure that their clients are fully aware of the benefits of ADR and that the use of ADR has been carefully considered prior to the first CMC.

7.2 TIMING

7.2.1 ADR may be appropriate before the proceedings have begun or at any subsequent stage. However the later ADR takes place, the more the costs which will have been incurred, often unnecessarily. The timing of ADR needs careful consideration. **2C-88**

7.2.2 The TCC Pre-Action Protocol (Section 2 above) itself provides for a type of ADR because it requires there to be at least one face-to-face meeting between the parties before the commencement of proceedings. At this meeting, there should be sufficient time to discuss and resolve the dispute. As a result of this procedure having taken place, the court will not necessarily grant a stay of proceedings upon demand and it will always need to be satisfied that an adjournment is actually necessary to enable ADR to take place.

7.2.3 However, at the first CMC, the court will want to be addressed on the parties' views as to the likely efficacy of ADR, the appropriate timing of ADR, and the advantages and disadvantages of a short stay of proceedings to allow ADR to take place. Having considered the representations of the parties, the court may order a short stay to facilitate ADR at that stage. Alternatively, the court may simply encourage the parties to seek ADR and allow for it to occur within the timetable for the resolution of the proceedings set down by the court.

7.2.4 At any stage after the first CMC and prior to the commencement of the trial, the court, will, either on its own initiative or if requested to do so by one or both of the parties, consider afresh the likely efficacy of ADR and whether or not a short stay of the proceedings should be granted, in order to facilitate ADR.

7.3 PROCEDURE

7.3.1 In an appropriate case, the court may indicate the type of ADR that it considers suitable, but the decision in this regard must be made by the parties. In most cases, the appropriate ADR procedure will be mediation. **2C-89**

7.3.2 If at any stage in the proceedings the court considers it appropriate, an ADR order in the terms of Appendix E may be made. If such an order is made at the first CMC, the court may go on to give directions for the conduct of the action up to trial (in the event that the ADR fails). Such directions may include provision for a review CMC.

7.3.3 The court will not ordinarily recommend any individual or body to act as mediator or to perform any other ADR procedure. In the event that the parties fail to agree the identity of a mediator or other neutral person pursuant to an order in the terms of Appendix E, the court may select such a person from the lists provided by the parties. To facilitate this process, the court would also need to be furnished with the CVs of each of the individuals on the lists.

7.3.4 Information as to the types of ADR procedures available and the individuals able to undertake such procedures is available from TeCSA, TECBAR, the Civil Mediation Council, and from some TCC court centres outside London.

7.4 NON-COOPERATION

7.4.1 Generally

At the end of the trial, there may be costs arguments on the basis that one or more parties unreasonably refused to take part in ADR. The court will determine such issues having regard to all the circumstances of the particular case. In *Halsey v Milton Keynes General NHS Trust* [2004] EWCA Civ 576; [2004] 1 W.L.R. 3002, the Court of Appeal identified six factors that may be relevant to any such consideration: **2C-90**

a) the nature of the dispute;
b) the merits of the case;
c) the extent to which other settlement methods have been attempted;
d) whether the costs of the ADR would be disproportionately high;

e) whether any delay in setting up and attending the ADR would have been prejudicial;
f) whether the ADR had a reasonable prospect of success.

This case and later authority is the subject of extensive discussion in Civil Procedure, Volume 2, at Section 14. The parties' attention is also drawn to paragraph 1.1.6 of this Guide.

7.4.2 If an ADR Order Has Been Made

The court will expect each party to co-operate fully with any ADR procedure which takes place following an order of the court. If any other party considers that there has not been proper co-operation in relation to arrangements for mediation or any other ADR Procedure, the complaint will be considered by the court and cost orders and/or other sanctions may be ordered against the defaulting party in consequence. However, nothing in this paragraph should be understood as modifying the rights of all parties to a mediation or any other ADR Procedure to keep confidential all that is said or done in the course of that ADR Procedure.

7.5 EARLY NEUTRAL EVALUATION

2C-91 **7.5.1** An early neutral evaluation ("ENE") may be carried out by any appropriately qualified person, whose opinion is likely to be respected by the parties. In an appropriate case, and with the consent of all parties, a TCC judge may provide an early neutral evaluation either in respect of the full case or of particular issues arising within it. Unless the parties otherwise agree the ENE will be produced in writing and will set out conclusions and brief reasons. Such an ENE will not, save with the agreement of the parties, be binding on the parties.

7.5.2 If the parties would like an ENE to be carried out by the court, then they can seek an appropriate order from the assigned judge either at the first CMC or at any time prior to the commencement of the trial.

7.5.3 The assigned judge may choose to do the ENE. In such instance, the judge will take no further part in the proceedings once he has produced the ENE, unless the parties expressly agree otherwise. Alternatively, the assigned judge will select another available TCC judge to undertake the ENE.

7.5.4 The judge undertaking the ENE will give appropriate directions for the preparation and conduct of the ENE. These directions will generally be agreed by the parties and may include:

- a stay of the substantive proceedings whilst the ENE is carried out;
- a direction that the ENE is to be carried out entirely on paper with dates for the exchange of submissions;
- a direction that particular documents or information should be provided by a party.
- a direction that there will be an oral hearing (either with or without evidence), with dates for all the necessary steps for submissions, witness statements and expert evidence leading to that hearing; if there is an oral hearing the ENE will generally not last more than one day;
- a statement that the parties agree or do not agree that the ENE procedure and the documents, submissions or evidence produced in relation to the ENE are to be without prejudice, or, alternatively, that the whole or part of those items are not without prejudice and can be referred to at any subsequent trial or hearing;
- a statement whether the parties agree that the judge's evaluation after the ENE process will be binding on the parties or binding in certain circumstances (e.g. if not disputed within a period) or temporarily binding subject to a final decision in arbitration, litigation or final agreement.

7.6 COURT SETTLEMENT PROCESS

2C-92 **7.6.1** The Court Settlement Process is a form of mediation carried out by TCC judges. Whilst mediation may be carried out by any appropriately qualified person, in an appropriate case, and with the consent of all parties, a TCC judge may act as a Settlement Judge pursuant to a Court Settlement Order in the terms set out in **Appendix G**. This has proved to be successful in many cases.

7.6.2 If the parties would like to consider the use of the Court Settlement Process or would like further information, they should contact the TCC Registry in London or the TCC Liaison District Judges in the court centres outside London.

7.6.3 Where, following a request from the parties, the assigned TCC judge considers that the parties might be able to achieve an amicable settlement and that a TCC judge is particularly able to assist in achieving that settlement, that judge or another TCC judge, with the agreement of the parties, will make a Court Settlement Order (**Appendix G**) embodying the parties' agreement and fixing a date for the Court Settlement Conference to take place with an estimated duration proportionate to the issues in the case.

7.6.4 The TCC judge appointed as the Settlement Judge will then conduct the Court Settlement Process in accordance with that Court Settlement Order in a similar manner to that of a mediator. If no settlement is achieved then the case would proceed but, if the assigned judge carried out the Court Settlement Process, then the case would be assigned to another TCC judge. In any event, the Settlement Judge would take no further part in the court proceedings.

SECTION 8 PRELIMINARY ISSUES

8.1 GENERAL

8.1.1 The hearing of Preliminary Issues ("PI"), at which the Court considers and delivers a binding judgment on particular issues in advance of the main trial, can be an extremely cost-effective and efficient way of narrowing the issues between the parties and, in certain cases, of resolving disputes altogether. **2C-93**

8.1.2 Some cases listed in the TCC lend themselves particularly well to this procedure. A PI hearing can address particular points which may be decisive of the whole proceedings; even if that is not the position, it is often possible for a PI hearing to cut down significantly on the scope (and therefore the costs) of the main trial.

8.1.3 At the first CMC the Court will expect to be addressed on whether or not there are matters which should be taken by way of Preliminary Issues in advance of the main trial. Subject to paragraph 8.5 below, it is not generally appropriate for the Court to make an order for the trial of preliminary issues until after the defence has been served. After the first CMC, and at any time during the litigation, any party is at liberty to raise with any other party the possibility of a PI hearing and the Court will consider any application for the hearing of such Preliminary Issues. In many cases, although not invariably, a PI order will be made with the support of all parties.

8.1.4 Whilst, for obvious reasons, it is not possible to set out hard and fast rules for what is and what is not suitable for a PI hearing, the criteria set out in paragraph 8.2 below should assist the parties in deciding whether or not some or all of the disputes between them will be suitable for a PI hearing.

8.1.5 Drawbacks of preliminary issues in inappropriate cases

If preliminary issues are ordered inappropriately, they can have adverse effects:

a) evidence may be duplicated;
b) the same witnesses may give evidence before different judges, in the event that there is a switch of assigned judge;
c) findings may be made at the PI hearing, which are affected by evidence subsequently called at the main hearing;
d) the prospect of a PI hearing may delay the commencement of ADR or settlement negotiations; and
e) two trials are more expensive than one.

For all these reasons, any proposal for preliminary issues needs to be examined carefully, so that the benefits and drawbacks can be evaluated. The Court will give due weight to the views of the parties when deciding whether a PI hearing would be beneficial.

8.1.6 Staged trials

The breaking down of a long trial into stages should be differentiated from the trial of preliminary issues. Sometimes it is sensible for liability (including causation) to be tried before quantum of damages. Occasionally the subject matter of the litigation is so extensive that for reasons of case management the trial needs to be broken down into separate stages.

8.2 GUIDELINES

8.2.1 The Significance of the Preliminary Issues

The court would expect that any issue proposed as a suitable PI would, if decided in a particular way, be capable of: **2C-94**

- resolving the whole proceedings or a significant element of the proceedings; or
- significantly reducing the scope, and therefore the costs, of the main trial; or
- significantly improving the possibility of a settlement of the whole proceedings.

8.2.2 Oral Evidence

The court would ordinarily expect that, if issues are to be dealt with by way of a PI hearing, there would be either no or relatively limited oral evidence. If extensive oral evidence was required on any proposed PI, then it may not be suitable for a PI hearing. Although it is difficult to give specific guidance on this point, it is generally considered that a PI hearing in a smaller case should not take more than about 2 days, and in a larger and more complex case, should not take more than about 4 days.

8.3 COMMON TYPES OF PRELIMINARY ISSUE

The following are commonly resolved by way of a PI hearing: **2C-95**

a) Disputes as to whether or not there was a binding contract between the parties.
b) Disputes as to what documents make up or are incorporated within the contract between the parties and disputes as to the contents or relevance of any conversations relied on as having contractual status or effect.

c) Disputes as to the proper construction of the contract documents or the effect of an exclusion or similar clause.

d) Disputes as to the correct application of a statute or binding authority to a situation where there is little or no factual dispute.

8.4 OTHER POSSIBLE PRELIMINARY ISSUES

2C-96 The following can sometimes be resolved by way of a preliminary issue hearing, although a decision as to whether or not to have such a hearing will always depend on the facts of the individual case:

8.4.1 A Limitation Defence

It is often tempting to have limitation issues resolved in advance of the main trial. This can be appropriate in a suitable case—if a complex claim is statute-barred, a decision to that effect will lead to a significant saving of costs. However, there is also a risk that extensive evidence relevant to the limitation defence (relating to matters such as when the damage occurred or whether or not there has been deliberate concealment) may also be relevant to the liability issues within the main trial. In such a case, a preliminary issue hearing may lead to a) extensive duplication of evidence and therefore costs and b) give rise to difficulty if the main trial is heard by a different judge.

8.4.2 Causation and 'No Loss' Points

Causation and 'No Loss' points may be suitable for a PI hearing, but again their suitability will be diminished if it is necessary for the Court to resolve numerous factual disputes as part of the proposed PI hearing. The most appropriate disputes of this type for a PI hearing are those where the defendant contends that, even accepting all the facts alleged by the claimant, the claim must fail by reason of causation or the absence of recoverable loss.

8.4.3 'One-Off' Issues

Issues which do not fall into any obvious category, like economic duress, or misrepresentation, may be suitable for resolution by way of a PI hearing, particularly if the whole case can be shown to turn on them.

8.5 USE OF PI AS AN ADJUNCT TO ADR

2C-97 **8.5.1** Sometimes parties wish to resolve their dispute by ADR, but there is one major issue which is a sticking point in any negotiation or mediation. The parties may wish to obtain the Court's final decision on that single issue, in the expectation that after that they can resolve their differences without further litigation.

8.5.2 In such a situation the parties may wish to bring proceedings under CPR Part 8, in order to obtain the Court's decision on that issue. Such proceedings can be rapidly progressed. Alternatively, if the issue is not suitable for Part 8 proceedings, the parties may bring proceedings under Part 7 and then seek determination of the critical question as a preliminary issue. At the first CMC the position can be explained and the judge can be asked to order early trial of the proposed preliminary issue, possibly without the need for a defence or any further pleadings.

8.6 PRECISE WORDING OF PI

2C-98 **8.6.1** If a party wishes to seek a PI hearing, either at the first CMC or thereafter, that party must circulate a precise draft of the proposed preliminary issues to the other parties and to the Court well in advance of the relevant hearing.

8.6.2 If the Court orders a PI hearing, it is likely to make such an order only by reference to specific and formulated issues, in order to avoid later debate as to the precise scope of the issues that have been ordered. Of course, the parties are at liberty to propose amendments to the issues before the PI hearing itself, but if such later amendments are not agreed by all parties, they are unlikely to be ordered. In any event, any proposals of the parties, whether agreed or not, to amend the terms of the issue(s) ordered by the court require the approval of the Court which should be sought well in advance of the hearing.

8.7 APPEALS

2C-99 **8.7.1** When considering whether or not to order a PI hearing, the Court will take into account the effect of any possible appeal against the PI judgment, and the concomitant delay caused.

8.7.2 At the time of ordering preliminary issues, both the parties and the Court should specifically consider whether, in the event of an appeal against the PI judgment, it is desirable that the trial of the main action should (a) precede or (b) follow such appeal. It should be noted, however, that the first instance Court has no power to control the timetable for an appeal. The question whether an appeal should be (a) expedited or (b) stayed is entirely a matter for the Court of Appeal. Nevertheless, the Court of Appeal will take notice of any "indication" given by the lower court in this regard.

SECTION 9 ADJUDICATION BUSINESS

9.1 INTRODUCTION

9.1.1 The TCC is ordinarily the court in which the enforcement of an adjudicator's decision and any other business connected with adjudication is undertaken. Adjudicators' decisions predominantly arise out of adjudications which are governed by the mandatory provisions of the Housing Grants, Construction and Regeneration Act 1996 (as amended by the Local Democracy, Economic Development and Construction Act 2009 for contracts entered into on or after 1 October 2011) relating to the carrying out of construction operations in England and Wales ("HGCRA"). These provisions apply automatically to any construction contract as defined in the legislation. Some Adjudicators' decisions arise out of standard form contracts which contain adjudication provisions, and others arise from *ad hoc* agreements to adjudicate. The TCC enforcement procedure is the same for all kinds of adjudication. **2C-100**

9.1.2 In addition to enforcement applications, declaratory relief is sometimes sought in the TCC at the outset of or during an adjudication in respect of matters such as the jurisdiction of the adjudicator or the validity of the adjudication. This kind of application is dealt with in paragraph 9.4 below.

9.1.3 The HGCRA provides for a mandatory 28-day period within which the entire adjudication process must be completed, unless a) the referring party agrees to an additional 14 days, or b) both parties agree to a longer period. In consequence, the TCC has moulded a rapid procedure for enforcing an adjudication decision that has not been honoured. Other adjudication proceedings are ordinarily subject to similar rapidity.

9.2 PROCEDURE IN ENFORCEMENT PROCEEDINGS

9.2.1 Unlike arbitration business, there is neither a practice direction nor a claim form concerned with adjudication business. The enforcement proceedings normally seek a monetary judgment so that CPR Part 7 proceedings are usually appropriate. However, if the enforcement proceedings are known to raise a question which is unlikely to involve a substantial dispute of fact and no monetary judgment is sought, CPR Part 8 proceedings may be used instead. **2C-101**

9.2.2 The TCC has fashioned a procedure whereby enforcement applications are dealt with promptly. The details of this procedure are set out below.

9.2.3 The claim form should identify the construction contract, the jurisdiction of the adjudicator, the procedural rules under which the adjudication was conducted, the adjudicator's decision, the relief sought and the grounds for seeking that relief.

9.2.4 The claim form should be accompanied by an application notice that sets out the procedural directions that are sought. Commonly, the claimant's application will seek an abridgement of time for the various procedural steps, and summary judgment under CPR Part 24. The claim form and the application should be accompanied by a witness statement or statements setting out the evidence relied on in support of both the adjudication enforcement claim and the associated procedural application. This evidence should ordinarily include a copy of the Notice of Intention to Refer and the adjudicator's decisioı.. Further pleadings in the adjudication may be required where questions of the adjudicator's jurisdiction are being raised.

9.2.5 The claim form, application notice and accompanying documents should be lodged in the appropriate registry or court centre clearly marked as being a "Paper without notice adjudication enforcement claim and application for the urgent attention of a TCC judge". A TCC judge will ordinarily provide directions in connection with the procedural application within **3 working days** of the receipt of the application notice at the Listing Office.

9.2.6 The procedural application is dealt with by a TCC judge on the documents, without notice. The application and the consequent directions should deal with:

a) the abridged period of time in which the defendant is to file an acknowledgement of service;
b) the time for service by the defendant of any witness statement in opposition to the relief being sought;
c) an early return date for the hearing of the summary judgment application and a note of the time required or allowed for that hearing; and
d) identification of the judgment, order or other relief being sought at the hearing of the adjudication claim.

The order made at this stage will always give the defendant liberty to apply.

9.2.7 A direction providing that the claim form, supporting evidence and court order providing for the hearing are to be served on the defendant as soon as practicable, or sometimes by a particular date, will ordinarily also be given when the judge deals with the electronic procedural application.

9.2.8 The directions will ordinarily provide for an enforcement hearing within about **6** to **8 weeks** of the directions being made and for the defendant to be given at least **14 days** from the date of service for the serving of any evidence in opposition to the adjudication application. In more straightforward cases, the abridged periods may be less.

9.2.9 Draft standard directions of the kind commonly made by the court on a procedural application by the claimant in an action to enforce the decision of an adjudicator are attached as Appendix F.

9.2.10 The claimant should, with the application, provide an estimate of the time needed for the hearing of the application. This estimate will be taken into account by the judge when fixing the date and length of the hearing. Where no time estimate is given, the judge will commonly give a 2 hour estimate for the hearing. The parties should bear in mind that that is done when the court may have minimal information as to the issues that are likely to be raised by the defendant on enforcement. The parties should, if possible jointly, communicate any revised time estimate to the court promptly and the judge to whom the case has been allocated will consider whether to refix the hearing date or, as is commonly the case, to alter the time period that has been allocated for the hearing.

9.2.11 If the parties cannot agree on the date or time fixed for the hearing, an electronic application must be made to the judge to whom the hearing has been allocated for directions.

9.2.12 Parties seeking to enforce adjudication decisions are reminded that they might be able to obtain judgment in default of service of an acknowledgment of service or, if the other party does not file any evidence in response, they might be able to obtain an expedited hearing of the Part 24 application. Generally, it is preferable for a party to enter default judgment rather than seek an expedited hearing, because that reduces the costs involved (the terms of the order usually mention this explicitly).

9.3 THE ENFORCEMENT HEARING

2C-102 **9.3.1** Where there is any dispute to be resolved at the hearing, the judge should be provided with copies of the relevant sections of the HGCRA, the adjudication procedural rules under which the adjudication was conducted, the adjudicator's decision and copies of any adjudication provisions in the contract underlying the adjudication.

9.3.2 Subject to any more specific directions given by the court, the parties should lodge, **by 4.00 pm two clear working days before the hearing**, a bundle containing the documents that will be required at the hearing.

9.3.3 The parties should also file and serve short skeleton arguments and copies of any authorities which are to be relied on (preferably as an agreed joint bundle), summarising their respective contentions as to why the adjudicator's decision is or is not enforceable or as to any other relief being sought.

9.3.4 For a hearing that is expected to last half a day or less, the skeletons should be provided **no later than 4pm one clear working day before the hearing**.

9.3.5 For a hearing that is estimated to last more than half a day, the skeletons should be provided **no later than 4 pm two clear working days before the hearing**.

9.3.6 The parties should be ready to address the court on the limited grounds on which a defendant may resist an application seeking to enforce an adjudicator's decision or on which a court may provide any other relief to any party in relation to an adjudication or an adjudicator's decision.

9.4 OTHER PROCEEDINGS ARISING OUT OF ADJUDICATION

2C-103 **9.4.1** As noted above, the TCC will also hear any applications for declaratory relief arising out of the commencement of a disputed adjudication. Commonly, these will concern:

- Disputes over the jurisdiction of an adjudicator. It can sometimes be appropriate to seek a declaration as to jurisdiction at the outset of an adjudication, rather than both parties incurring considerable costs in the adjudication itself, only for the jurisdiction point to emerge again at the enforcement hearing.
- Disputes over whether there is a construction contract within the meaning of the Act (and, in older contracts, whether there was a written contract between the parties).
- Disputes over the permissible scope of the adjudication, and, in particular, whether the matters which the claimant seeks to raise in the adjudication are the subject of a pre-existing dispute between the parties.

9.4.2 Any such application will be immediately assigned to a named judge. In such circumstances, given the probable urgency of the application, the judge will usually require the parties to attend a directions hearing **within 2 working days** of the assignment of the case, and will then give the necessary directions to ensure the speedy resolution of the dispute.

9.4.3 Although not exclusive, the examples in paragraph 9.4.1 make it clear that not all applications that have some connection with an adjudication are ones where the TCC will hear applications for declaratory relief with the abbreviated timescales applied in the case of adjudication enforcement. The label of "an adjudication application" should not be used by parties to obtain an expedited hearing (for example of a Part 8 claim for declaratory relief) where there is no other justification for an expedited hearing. A judge may refuse to hear a claim or application which has been given this label in an attempt to jump the queue.

9.4.4 It sometimes happens that one party to an adjudication commences enforcement proceedings, whilst the other commences proceedings under Part 8, in order to challenge the validity of the adjudicator's award. This duplication of effort is unnecessary and it involves the parties in extra costs, especially if the two actions are commenced at different court centres. Accordingly, there should be sensible discussions between the parties or their lawyers, in order to agree the appropriate venue and also to agree who shall be claimant and who defendant. All the issues raised by each party can and should be raised in a single action.

9.4.5 However, in cases where an adjudicator has made a clear error (but has acted within his jurisdiction), it may on occasions be appropriate to bring proceedings under Part 8 for a declaration as a pre-emptive response to an anticipated application to enforce the decision. In the light of this guidance, a practice had grown up of applications to enforce an adjudicator's decision being met by an application for a declaration that the adjudicator had erred often without proceedings under Part 8 being commenced. This approach was disruptive and not in accordance with the spirit of the TCC's procedure for the enforcement of adjudicator's decisions. It is emphasised, therefore, that such cases are limited to those where:

a) there is a short and self-contained issue which arose in the adjudication and which the defendant continues to contest;
b) that issue requires no oral evidence, or any other elaboration beyond that which is capable of being provided during the interlocutory hearing for enforcement; and
c) the issue is one which, on a summary judgment application, it would be unconscionable for the court to ignore; and further that there should in all cases be proper proceedings for declaratory relief.

SECTION 10 ARBITRATION

10.1 ARBITRATION CLAIMS IN THE TCC

10.1.1 "Arbitration claims" are any application to the court under the Arbitration Act 1996 and any other claim concerned with an arbitration that is referred to in CPR 62.2(1). Common examples of arbitration claims are challenges to an award on grounds of jurisdiction under Section 67, challenges to an award for serious irregularity under Section 68 or appeals on points of law under Section 69 of the Arbitration Act 1996. Arbitration claims may be started in the TCC, as is provided for in paragraph 2.3 of the Practice Direction - Arbitration which supplements CPR Part 62. **2C-104**

10.1.2 In practice, arbitration claims arising out of or connected with a construction or engineering arbitration (or any other arbitration where the subject matter involved one or more of the categories of work set out in paragraph 1.3.1 above) should be started in the TCC. The only arbitration claims that must be started in the Commercial Court are those (increasingly rare) claims to which the old law (i.e. the pre-1996 Act provisions) apply: see CPR 62.12.

10.1.3 The TCC follows the practice and procedure for arbitration claims established by CPR Part 62 and (broadly) the practice of the Commercial Court as summarised by **Section O of the Admiralty and Commercial Court Guide**. In the absence of any specific directions given by the court, the automatic directions set out in section 6 of the Practice Direction supplementing CPR Part 62 govern the procedures to be followed in any arbitration claim from the date of service up to the substantive hearing.

10.2 LEAVE TO APPEAL

10.2.1 Where a party is seeking to appeal a question of law arising out of an award pursuant to Section 69 of the Arbitration Act 1996 and the parties have not in their underlying contract agreed that such an appeal may be brought, the party seeking to appeal must apply for leave to appeal pursuant to Sections 69(2), 69(3) and 69(4) of that Act. That application must be included in the arbitration claim form as explained in paragraph 12 of PD62. **2C-105**

10.2.2 In conformity with the practice of the Commercial Court, the TCC will normally consider any application for permission to appeal on paper after the defendant has had an appropriate opportunity to answer in writing the application being raised.

10.2.3 The claimant must include within the claim form an application for permission to appeal. No separate application notice is required.

10.2.4 The claim form and supporting documents must be served on the defendant. The judge will not consider the merits of the application for permission to appeal until (a) a certificate of service has been filed at the appropriate TCC registry or court centre and (b), subject to any order for specific directions, a further **28 days** have elapsed, so as to enable the defendant to file written evidence in opposition. Save in exceptional circumstances, the only material admissible on an application for permission to appeal is (a) the award itself and any documents annexed to or necessary to understand the award and (b) evidence relevant to the issue whether any identified question of law is of general public importance: see the requirements of paragraph 12 of the PD62.

10.2.5 If necessary, the judge dealing with the application will direct an oral hearing with a date for the hearing. That hearing will, ordinarily, consist of brief submissions by each party. The judge dealing with the application will announce his decision in writing or, if a hearing has been directed, at the conclusion of the hearing with brief reasons if the application is refused.

10.2.6 Where the permission has been allowed in part and refused in part:

a) Only those questions for which permission has been granted may be raised at the hearing of the appeal.

b) Brief reasons will be given for refusing permission in respect of the other questions.

10.2.7 If the application is granted, the judge will fix the date for the appeal, and direct whether the same judge or a different judge shall hear the appeal.

10.3 APPEALS WHERE LEAVE TO APPEAL IS NOT REQUIRED

2C-106 **10.3.1** Parties to a construction contract should check whether they have agreed in the underlying contract that an appeal may be brought without leave, since some construction and engineering standard forms of contract so provide. If that is the case, the appeal may be set down for a substantive hearing without leave being sought. The arbitration claim form should set out the clause or provision which it is contended provides for such agreement and the claim form should be marked "Arbitration Appeal - Leave not required"

10.3.2 Where leave is not required, the claimant should identify each question of law that it is contended arises out of the award and which it seeks to raise in an appeal under Section 69. If the defendant does not accept that the questions thus identified are questions of law or maintains that they do not arise out of the award or that the appeal on those questions may not be brought for any other reason, then the defendant should notify the claimant and the court of its contentions and apply for a directions hearing before the judge nominated to hear the appeal on a date prior to the date fixed for the hearing of the appeal. Unless the judge hearing the appeal otherwise directs, the appeal will be confined to the questions of law identified in the arbitration claim form.

10.3.3 In an appropriate case, the judge may direct that the question of law to be raised and decided on the appeal should be reworded, so as to identify more accurately the real legal issue between the parties.

10.4 THE HEARING OF THE APPEAL

2C-107 **10.4.1** Parties should ensure that the court is provided only with material that is relevant and admissible to the point of law. This will usually be limited to the award and any documents annexed to the award: see *Hok Sport Ltd v Aintree Racecourse Ltd* [2003] BLR 155 at 160. However, the court should also receive any document referred to in the award, which the court needs to read in order to determine a question of law arising out of the award: see *Kershaw Mechanical Services Ltd v Kendrick Construction Ltd* [2006] EWHC 727 (TCC).

10.4.2 On receiving notice of permission being granted, or on issuing an arbitration claim form in a case where leave to appeal is not required, the parties should notify the court of their joint estimate or differing estimates of the time needed for the hearing of the appeal.

10.4.3 The hearing of the appeal is in open court unless an application (with notice) has previously been made that the hearing should be wholly or in part held in private and the court has directed that this course should be followed.

10.5 SECTION 68 APPLICATIONS—SERIOUS IRREGULARITY

2C-108 **10.5.1** In some arbitration claims arising out of construction and engineering arbitrations, a party will seek to appeal a question of law and, at the same time, seek to challenge the award under Section 68 of the Arbitration Act 1996 on the grounds of serious irregularity. This raises questions of procedure, since material may be admissible in a Section 68 application which is inadmissible on an application or appeal under Section 69. Similarly, it may not be appropriate for all applications to be heard together. A decision is needed as to the order in which the applications should be heard, whether there should be one or more separate hearings to deal with them and whether or not the same judge should deal with all applications. Where a party intends to raise applications under both sections of the Arbitration Act 1996, they should be issued in the same arbitration claim form or in separate claim forms issued together. The court should be informed that separate applications are intended and asked for directions as to how to proceed.

10.5.2 The court will give directions as to how the Section 68 and Section 69 applications will be dealt with before hearing or determining any application. These directions will normally be given in writing but, where necessary or if such is applied for by a party, the court will hold a directions hearing at which directions will be given. The directions will be given following the service of any documentation by the defendant in answer to all applications raised by the claimant.

10.6 SUCCESSIVE AWARDS AND SUCCESSIVE APPLICATIONS

2C-109 **10.6.1** Some construction and engineering arbitrations give rise to two or more separate awards issued at different times. Where arbitration applications arise under more than one of these awards, any second or subsequent application, whether arising from the same or a different award, should be referred to the same judge who has heard previous applications. Where more than one judge has heard previous applications, the court should be asked to direct to which judge any subsequent application is to be referred.

10.7 OTHER APPLICATIONS AND ENFORCEMENT

10.7.1 All other arbitration claims, and any other matter arising in an appeal or an application concerning alleged serious irregularity, will be dealt with by the TCC in the same manner as is provided for in CPR Part 62, Practice Direction - Arbitration and Section O of the Commercial Court Guide. **2C-110**

10.7.2 All applications for permission to enforce arbitration awards are governed by Section III of Part 62 (Rules 62.17-62.19).

10.7.3 An application for permission to enforce an award in the same manner as a judgment or order of the court may be made in an arbitration claim form without notice and must be supported by written evidence in accordance withCPR 62.18(6). Two copies of the draft order must accompany the application, and the form of the order sought must correspond to the terms of the award.

10.7.4 An order made without notice giving permission to enforce the award:

- must give the defendant 14 days after service of the order (or longer, if the order is to be served outside the jurisdiction) to apply to set it aside;
- must state that it may not be enforced until after the expiry of the 14 days (or any longer period specified) or until any application to set aside the order has been finally disposed of: CPR 62.18(9) and (10).

10.7.5 On considering an application to enforce without notice, the judge may direct that, instead, the arbitration claim form must be served on specified parties, with the result that the application will then continue as an arbitration claim in accordance with the procedure set out in **Section I of Part 62**: see CPR 62.18(1)-(3).

Section 11 Disclosure

11.1 GENERAL

11.1.1 Disclosure in the TCC generally is subject to the disclosure rules set out in Practice Direction 57AD. **2C-111**

11.1.2 However, there are some exceptions of relevance to the TCC, as stated in section 1.4 of the Disclosure Pilot, namely: (1) Public Procurement claims; (2) proceedings within the Shorter and Flexible Trials Scheme; (3) proceedings within a fixed costs regime.

11.1.3 The provisions of CPR 31 and the Practice Directions supplementing it continue to apply to Public Procurement claims, as modified by the particular considerations applicable to such cases, as to which see Appendix H of this Guide. In relation to electronic disclosure, attention is drawn to the relevant provisions in CPR Part 31 and Practice Direction 31B: Disclosure of Electronic Documents. A protocol for e-disclosure prepared by TeCSA, TECBAR and the Society for Computers and Law was launched on 1 November 2013 which provides a procedure and guidance in relation to these matters. The protocol was developed in consultation with the judges of the TCC and is likely to be ordered by the court if the parties have not agreed on any alternative by the time of the first CMC. It is available on the TeCSA website.

11.1.4 Specific provisions in relation to disclosure are made in relation to proceedings in the Shorter and Flexible Trials Scheme and the Capped Costs List Pilot Scheme, to which reference should be made.

11.1.5 It is not intended to provide detailed guidance in relation to the Disclosure Pilot in this Guide. It will be necessary for parties and their legal representatives to familiarise themselves with its contents before and during the course of proceedings to which the Disclosure Pilot applies. The Chancellor of the High Court said in *UTB v Sheffield United* [2019] EWHC 914 (ChD) at [75] that the Disclosure Pilot is intended to effect a culture change, which operates along different lines to the CPR and is driven by reasonableness and proportionality. The Chancellor has also given clear guidance as to the operation of the Disclosure Pilot in *McParland v Whitebread* [2020] EWHC 298 (Ch).

11.1.6 The parties and their legal representatives should ensure that they are aware in particular of the duties which they are under in relation to disclosure under paragraph 3 of the Disclosure Pilot, of the requirement to provide Initial Disclosure under paragraph 5 of the Disclosure Pilot with their statements of case, and of the requirement to complete the Disclosure Review Document pursuant to paragraphs 7 and following of the Disclosure Pilot in advance of the first CMC.

11.1.7 When preparing for the first CMC the parties and their legal representatives should note that the blank standard directions form includes provision for disclosure to be given by reference to the Disclosure Review Document as agreed by the parties and approved by the court and/or as determined by the court in case of any disagreement.

11.1.8 The order made at the CMC will state the time for complying with any order for Extended Disclosure. If any party has a justified concern that another party may not be ready to comply with that order on the date specified it may apply to the court for an order permitting or requiring the parties to file their Disclosure certificates and Extended Disclosure Lists of Documents instead of serving such documents and producing the documents disclosed as required by paragraph 12.1 of the Disclosure Pilot. In such a case the application may include a request for such documents to be filed as a confidential document in the Electronic Working Case File in accordance with paragraph 5.2A of PD 51O.

SECTION 12 WITNESS STATEMENTS AND FACTUAL EVIDENCE FOR USE AT TRIAL

12.1 WITNESS STATEMENTS

2C-112 **12.1.1** Witness statements should be prepared generally in accordance with CPR Part 22.1 (documents verified by a statement of truth) and CPR Part 32 (provisions governing the evidence of witnesses) and their practice directions and particularly Practice Direction PD57AC and the Appendix to PD57AC.

12.1.2 A trial witness statement should contain only:

a) evidence as to matters of fact that need to be proved at trial by the evidence of witnesses in relation to one or more of the issues of fact to be decided at trial; and

b) the evidence as to such matters that the witness would be asked by the relevant party to give, and the witness would be allowed to give, in evidence in chief if they were called to give oral evidence at trial.

12.1.3 The witness statement must set out only matters of fact of which the witness has personal knowledge that are relevant to the case, and must identify by list what documents, if any, the witness has referred to or been referred to for the purpose of providing the evidence set out in their trial witness statement. Unless otherwise directed by the court, witness statements should not have annexed to them copies of other documents, save where a specific document needs to be annexed to the statement in order to make that statement reasonably intelligible.

12.1.4 The witness statement should be as concise as possible without omitting anything of significance, refer to documents only where necessary and should not:

- quote at any length from any document to which reference is made;
- seek to argue the case, either generally or on particular points;
- take the court through the documents in the case or set out a narrative derived from the documents, those being matters for argument; or
- include commentary on other evidence in the case (either documents or the evidence of other witnesses).

12.1.5 Even when prepared by a legal representative or other professional, the witness statement should be, so far as practicable, in the witness's own words.

12.1.6 The witness statement should indicate which matters are within the witness's own knowledge and which are matters of information and belief. Where the witness is stating matters of hearsay or of either information or belief, the source of that evidence should also be stated.

12.1.7 The witness must verify the statement by a statement of truth and confirm compliance with PD57AC.

12.1.8 The witness statement must be endorsed by a certificate of compliance by the legal representative, confirming compliance with PD57AC.

12.1.9 Sanctions for non-compliance include an order to produce a fresh witness statement, adverse cost orders and exclusion of the witness statement from evidence.

12.1.10 The order made at the CMC will state the time for complying with any order for exchange of witness statements. If any party has a justified concern that another party may not be ready to comply with that order on the date specified it may apply to the court for an order permitting or requiring the parties to file their witness statements instead of serving such documents. In such a case the application may include a request for such documents to be filed as a confidential document in the Electronic Working Case File in accordance with paragraph 5.2A of PD 51O.

12.2 OTHER MATTERS CONCERNED WITH WITNESS STATEMENTS

12.2.1 Foreign language

2C-113 If a witness is not sufficiently fluent in English to give his or her evidence in English, the witness statement should be in his or her own language and an authenticated translation provided. Where the witness is not confident in the use of English, the statement may be drafted by others so as to express the witness's evidence as accurately as possible. In that situation, however, the witness statement should indicate that this process of interpolation has occurred and also should explain the extent of the witness's command of English and how and to what parts of the witness statement the process of interpolation has occurred.

12.2.2 Reluctant witness

Sometimes a witness is unwilling or not permitted or is unavailable to provide a witness statement before the trial. The party seeking to adduce this evidence should comply with the provisions of CPR 32.9 concerned with the provision of witness summaries.

12.2.3 Hearsay

Parties should keep in mind the need to give appropriate notice of their intention to rely on hearsay evidence or the contents of documents without serving a witness statement from their maker or from the originator of the evidence contained in those documents. The appropriate procedure is contained in CPR 33.1 - 33.5.

12.2.4 Supplementary Witness Statements

The general principle is that a witness should set out in their witness statement their complete evidence relevant to the issues in the case. The witness statement should not include evidence on the basis that it might be needed depending on what the other party's witnesses might say. The correct procedure in such cases is for the witness to provide a supplementary witness statement or, as necessary, for a new witness to provide a witness statement limited to responding to particular matters contained in the other party's witness statement and to seek permission accordingly. In some cases it might be appropriate for the court to provide for the service of supplementary witness statements as part of the order at the first case management conference.

12.2.5 Supplementary Evidence in Chief

The relevant witness evidence should be contained in the witness statements, or if appropriate witness summaries, served in advance of the hearing. Where, for whatever reason, this has not happened and the witness has relevant important evidence to give, particularly where the need for such evidence has only become apparent during the trial, the judge has a discretion to permit supplementary evidence in chief.

12.3 CROSS-REFERENCING

12.3.1 Where a substantial number of documents will be adduced in evidence or contained in the trial bundles, it is of considerable assistance to the court and to all concerned if the relevant page references are annotated in the margins of the copy witness statements. It is accepted that this is a time-consuming exercise, the need for which will be considered at the PTR, and it will only be ordered where it is both appropriate and proportionate to do so. See further paragraphs 14.5.1 and 15.2.3 below. **2C-114**

12.4 VIDEO LINK

12.4.1 If any witness (whose witness statement has been served and who is required to give oral evidence) is located outside England and Wales or would find a journey to court inconvenient or impracticable, such evidence may be given via a video link with the Court's permission. Thought should be given before the PTR to the question whether this course would be appropriate and proportionate. Such evidence is regularly received by the TCC and facilities for its reception, whether in appropriate court premises or at a convenient venue outside the court building, are now readily available. **2C-115**

12.4.2 Any application for a video link direction and any question relating to the manner in which such evidence is to be given should be dealt with at the PTR. Attention is drawn to the Video-conferencing Protocol set out at Annex 3 to the Practice Direction supplementing CPR Part 32 - Evidence. The procedure described in Annex 3 together with the guidance in Appendix K is followed by the TCC.

SECTION 13 EXPERT EVIDENCE

13.1 NATURE OF EXPERT EVIDENCE

13.1.1 Expert evidence is evidence as to matters of a technical or scientific nature and will generally include the opinions of the expert. The quality and reliability of expert evidence will depend upon (a) the experience and the technical or scientific qualifications of the expert and (b) the accuracy of the factual material that is used by the expert for his assessment. Expert evidence is dealt with in detail in CPR Part 35 ("Experts and Assessors") and in the Practice Direction supplementing Part 35. Particular attention should be paid to all these provisions, given the detailed reliance on expert evidence in most TCC actions. Particular attention should also be paid to the "Protocol for the instruction of experts to give evidence in civil claims" annexed to Practice Direction 35 – Experts and Assessors (it should be noted that this Protocol is expected to be replaced at some point with the "Guidance for the instruction of experts to give evidence in Civil claims"). **2C-116**

13.1.2 The attention of the parties is drawn to the specific requirements in relation to the terms of the expert's declaration at the conclusion of the report.

13.1.3 The provisions in CPR Part 35 are concerned with the terms upon which the court may receive expert evidence. These provisions are principally applicable to independently instructed expert witnesses. In cases where a party is a professional or a professional has played a significant part in the subject matter of the action, opinion evidence will almost inevitably be included in the witness statements. Any points arising from such evidence (if they cannot be resolved by agreement) can be dealt with by the judge on an application or at the PTR.

13.2 CONTROL OF EXPERT EVIDENCE

13.2.1 Expert evidence is frequently needed and used in TCC cases. Experts are often appointed at an early stage. Most types of case heard in the TCC involve more than one expertise and some, even when the dispute is concerned with relatively small sums, involve several different **2C-117**

experts. Such disputes include those concerned with building failures and defects, delay and disruption, dilapidations, subsidence caused by tree roots and the supply of software systems. However, given the cost of preparing such evidence, the parties and the court must, from the earliest pre-action phase of a dispute until the conclusion of the trial, seek to make effective and proportionate use of experts. The scope of any expert evidence must be limited to what is necessary for the requirements of the particular case.

13.2.2 At the first CMC, or thereafter, the court may be asked to determine whether the cost of instructing experts is proportionate to the amount at issue in the proceedings, and the importance of the case to the parties. When considering an application for permission to call an expert, the court is to be provided with estimates of the experts' costs: see CPR 35.4(2). The permission may limit the issues to be considered by the experts: see CPR 35.4(3). This should ordinarily be linked to the party's costs budget.

13.2.3 The parties should also be aware that the court has the power to limit the amount of the expert's fees that a party may recover from another party pursuant to **CPR 35.4 (4)**. Thus, where the costs of an expert are payable by one party to another, the amount recovered by the receiving party may be less than full costs reasonably incurred.

When exercising its discretion as to costs, the court must have regard to all the circumstances, including the conduct of all the parties (CPR 44.2(4)(a)). In this context, the "conduct of the parties" could include the unreasonable raising and pursuing of issues requiring expert evidence and any failure to comply with any pre-action protocol relating to such evidence (CPR 44.2(5)). Note also CPR 44.4 (factors to be taken into account in deciding amount of costs.) If parties instruct experts without waiting for the court to give permission they are at risk as to recovering the costs if the court subsequently decides that expert evidence is not necessary, see *Coker v Barkland Cleaning Ltd* 6 December 1999, unrep., CA. Parties should ensure that the costs of experts are proportionate, see *Kranidiotes v Paschali* [2001] EWCA Civ 357; [2001] C.P. Rep. 81, CA.

13.3 PRIOR TO AND AT THE FIRST CMC

2C-118 **13.3.1** There is an unresolved tension arising from the need for parties to instruct and rely on expert opinions from an early pre-action stage and the need for the court to seek, wherever possible, to reduce the cost of expert evidence by dispensing with it altogether or by encouraging the appointment of jointly instructed experts. This tension arises because the court can only consider directing joint appointments or limiting expert evidence long after a party may have incurred the cost of obtaining expert evidence and have already relied on it. Parties should be aware of this tension. So far as possible, the parties should avoid incurring the costs of expert evidence on uncontroversial matters or matters of the kind referred to in Section 13.4.3 below, before the first CMC has been held.

13.3.2 In cases where it is not appropriate for the court to order a single joint expert, it is imperative that, wherever possible, the parties' experts co-operate fully with one another. This is particularly important where tests, surveys, investigations, sample gathering or other technical methods of obtaining primary factual evidence are needed. It is often critical to ensure that any laboratory testing or experiments are carried out by the experts together, pursuant to an agreed procedure. Alternatively, the respective experts may agree that a particular firm or laboratory shall carry out specified tests or analyses on behalf of all parties.

13.3.3 Parties should, where possible, disclose initial or preliminary reports to opposing parties prior to any pre-action protocol meeting, if only on a without prejudice basis. Such early disclosure will assist in early settlement or mediation discussions and in helping the parties to define and confine the issues in dispute with a corresponding saving in costs.

13.3.4 Before and at the first CMC and at each subsequent pre-trial stage of the action, the parties should give careful thought to the following matters:

- The number, disciplines and identity of the expert witnesses they are considering instructing as their own experts or as single joint experts.
- The precise issues which each expert is to address in his/her reports, to discuss without prejudice with opposing parties' experts and give evidence about at the trial.
- The timing of any meeting, agreed statement or report.
- Any appropriate or necessary tests, inspections, sampling or investigations that could be undertaken jointly or in collaboration with other experts. Any such measures should be preceded by a meeting of relevant experts at which an appropriate testing or other protocol is devised. This would cover (i) all matters connected with the process in question and its recording and (ii) the sharing and agreement of any resulting data or evidence.
- Any common method of analysis, investigation or reporting where it is appropriate or proportionate that such should be adopted by all relevant experts. An example of this would be an agreement as to the method to be used to analyse the cause and extent of any relevant period of delay in a construction project, where such is in issue in the case.
- The availability and length of time that experts will realistically require to complete the tasks assigned to them.

(Note that the amendment toCPR 35.4(3) permits the order granting permission to specify the issues which the expert evidence should address.)

13.3.5 In so far as the matters set out in the previous paragraph cannot be agreed, the court will give appropriate directions. In giving permission for the reception of any expert evidence, the court will ordinarily order the exchange of such evidence, with a definition of the expert's area of expertise and a clear description of the issues about which that expert is permitted to give evidence. It is preferable that, at the first CMC or as soon as possible thereafter, the parties should provide the court with the name(s) of their expert(s).

13.4 SINGLE JOINT EXPERTS

13.4.1 An order may be made, at the first CMC or thereafter, that a single joint expert should address particular issues between the parties. Such an order would be made pursuant to CPR Parts 35.7 and **35.8**. **2C-119**

13.4.2 Single joint experts are not usually appropriate for the principal liability disputes in a large case, or in a case where considerable sums have been spent on an expert in the pre-action stage. They are generally inappropriate where the issue involves questions of risk assessment or professional competence.

13.4.3 On the other hand, single joint experts can often be appropriate:

- in low value cases, where technical evidence is required but the cost of adversarial expert evidence may be prohibitive;
- where the topic with which the single joint expert's report deals is a separate and self-contained part of the case, such as the valuation of particular heads of claim;
- where there is a subsidiary issue, which requires particular expertise of a relatively uncontroversial nature to resolve;
- where testing or analysis is required, and this can conveniently be done by one laboratory or firm on behalf of all parties.

13.4.4 Where a single joint expert is to be appointed or is to be directed by the court, the parties should attempt to devise a protocol covering all relevant aspects of the appointment (save for those matters specifically provided for by CPR 35.6, 35.7 and 35.8).

13.4.5 The matters to be considered should include: any ceiling on fees and disbursements that are to be charged and payable by the parties; how, when and by whom fees will be paid to the expert on an interim basis pending any costs order in the proceedings; how the expert's fees will be secured; how the terms of reference are to be agreed; what is to happen if terms of reference cannot be agreed; how and to whom the jointly appointed expert may address further enquiries and from whom he should seek further information and documents; the timetable for preparing any report or for undertaking any other preparatory step; the possible effect on such timetable of any supplementary or further instructions. Where these matters cannot be agreed, an application to the court, which may often be capable of being dealt with as a paper application, will be necessary.

13.4.6 The usual procedure for a single joint expert will involve:

- The preparation of the expert's instructions. These instructions should clearly identify those issues or matters where the parties are in conflict, whether on the facts or on matters of opinion. If the parties can agree joint instructions, then a single set of instructions should be delivered to the expert. However, CPR 35.8 expressly permits separate instructions and these are necessary where joint instructions cannot be agreed.
- The preparation of the agreed bundle, which is to be provided to the expert. This bundle must include CPR 35, the Practice Direction PD 35 and Section 13 of the TCC Guide.
- The preparation and production of the expert's report.
- The provision to the expert of any written questions from the parties, which the expert must answer in writing.

13.4.7 In most cases the single joint expert's report, supplemented by any written answers to questions from the parties, will be sufficient for the purposes of the trial. Sometimes, however, it is necessary for a single joint expert to be called to give oral evidence. In those circumstances, the usual practice is for the judge to call the expert and then allow each party the opportunity to cross-examine. Such cross-examination should be conducted with appropriate restraint, since the witness has been instructed by the parties. Where the expert's report is strongly in favour of one party's position, it may be appropriate to allow only the other party to cross-examine.

13.5 MEETINGS OF EXPERTS

13.5.1 The desirability of holding without prejudice meetings between experts at all stages of the pre-trial preparation should be kept in mind. The desired outcome of such meetings is to produce a document whose contents are agreed and which defines common positions or each expert's differing position. The purpose of such meetings includes the following: **2C-120**

- to provide to the expert any written questions from the parties, which the expert must answer in writing;
- to define a party's technical case and to inform opposing parties of the details of that case;
- to clear up confusion and to remedy any lack of information or understanding of a party's technical case in the minds of opposing experts;
- to identify the issues about which any expert is to give evidence;

- to narrow differences and to reach agreement on as many "expert" issues as possible; and
- to assist in providing an agenda for the trial and for cross examination of expert witnesses, and to limit the scope and length of the trial as much as possible.

13.5.2 In many cases it will be helpful for the parties' respective legal advisors to provide assistance as to the agenda and topics to be discussed at an experts' meeting. However, (save in exceptional circumstances and with the permission of the judge) the legal advisors must not attend the meeting. They must not attempt to dictate what the experts say at the meeting.

13.5.3 Experts' meetings can sometimes usefully take place at the site of the dispute. Thought is needed as to who is to make the necessary arrangements for access, particularly where the site is occupied or in the control of a non-party. Expert meetings are often more productive, if (a) the expert of one party (usually the claimant) is appointed as chairman and (b) the experts exchange in advance agendas listing the topics each wishes to raise and identifying any relevant material which they intend to introduce or rely on during the meeting.

13.5.4 It is generally sensible for the experts to meet at least once before they exchange their reports.

13.6 EXPERTS' JOINT STATEMENTS

2C-121 **13.6.1** Following the experts' meetings, and pursuant to CPR 35.12 (3), the judge will almost always require the experts to produce a signed statement setting out the issues which have been agreed, and those issues which have not been agreed, together with a short summary of the reasons for their disagreement. In any TCC case in which expert evidence has an important role to play, this statement is a critical document and it must be as clear as possible.

13.6.2 It should be noted that, even where experts have been unable to agree very much, it is of considerable importance that the statement sets out their disagreements and the reasons for them. Such disagreements as formulated in the joint statement are likely to form an important element of the agenda for the trial of the action.

13.6.3 Whilst the parties' legal advisors may assist in identifying issues which the statement should address, those legal advisors must not be involved in either negotiating or drafting the experts' joint statement. Legal advisors should only invite the experts to consider amending any draft joint statement in exceptional circumstances where there are serious concerns that the court may misunderstand or be misled by the terms of that joint statement. Any such concerns should be raised with all experts involved in the joint statement.

13.7 EXPERTS' REPORTS

2C-122 **13.7.1** It is the duty of an expert to help the court on matters within his expertise. This duty overrides any duty to his client: CPR 35.3. Each expert's report must be independent and unbiased. The Pre-Action Protocol for Construction and Engineering Disputes contain provisions as to experts in TCC cases and accordingly Annex C to the Practice Direction—Pre-Action Conduct does not apply: see The Practice Direction—Pre-Action Conduct.

13.7.2 The parties must identify the issues with which each expert should deal in his or her report. Thereafter, it is for the expert to draft and decide upon the detailed contents and format of the report, so as to conform to the Practice Direction supplementing CPR Part 35 and the Protocol for the Instruction of Experts to give Evidence in Civil Claims. It is appropriate, however, for the party instructing an expert to indicate that the report (a) should be as short as is reasonably possible; (b) should not set out copious extracts from other documents; (c) should identify the source of any opinion or data relied upon; and (d) should not annex or exhibit more than is reasonably necessary to support the opinions expressed in the report. In addition, as set out in paragraph 15.2 of the Protocol for the Instruction of Experts to give Evidence in Civil Claims, legal advisors may also invite experts to consider amendments to their reports to ensure accuracy, internal consistency, completeness, relevance to the issues or clarity of reports.

13.8 PRESENTATION OF EXPERT EVIDENCE

2C-123 **13.8.1** The purpose of expert evidence is to assist the court on matters of a technical or scientific nature. Particularly in large and complex cases where the evidence has developed through a number of experts' joint statements and reports, it is often helpful for the expert at the commencement of his or her evidence to provide the court with a summary of their views on the main issues. This can be done orally or by way of a PowerPoint or similar presentation. The purpose is not to introduce new evidence but to explain the existing evidence.

13.8.2 The way in which expert evidence is given is a matter to be considered at the PTR. However, where there are a number of experts of different disciplines the court will consider the best way for the expert evidence to be given. It is now quite usual for all expert evidence to follow the completion of the witness evidence from all parties. At that stage there are a number of possible ways of presenting evidence including:

- For one party to call all its expert evidence, followed by each party calling all of its expert evidence.
- For one party to call its expert in a particular discipline, followed by the other parties call-

ing their experts in that discipline. This process would then be repeated for the experts of all disciplines.

- For one party to call its expert or experts to deal with a particular issue, followed by the other parties calling their expert or experts to deal with that issues. This process would then be repeated for all the expert issues.
- For the experts for all parties to be called to give concurrent evidence, colloquially referred to as "hot-tubbing". When this method is adopted there is generally a need for experts to be cross-examined on general matters and key issues before they are invited to give evidence concurrently on particular issues. Procedures vary but, for instance, a party may ask its expert to explain his or her view on an issue, then ask the other party's expert for his or her view on that issue and then return to that party's expert for a comment on that view. Alternatively, or in addition, questions may be asked by the judge or the experts themselves may each ask the other questions. The process is often most useful where there are a large number of items to be dealt with and the procedure allows the court to have the evidence on each item dealt with on the same occasion rather than having the evidence divided with the inability to have each expert's views expressed clearly. Frequently, it allows the extent of agreement and reason for disagreement to be seen more clearly. The giving of concurrent evidence may be consented to by the parties and the judge will consider whether, in the absence of consent, any modification is required to the procedure for giving concurrent evidence set out in the CPR (at PD35, paragraph 11).

SECTION 14 THE PRE-TRIAL REVIEW

14.1 TIMING AND ATTENDANCE

14.1.1 The Pre-Trial Review ("PTR") will usually be fixed for a date that is 4–6 weeks in advance of the commencement of the trial itself. It is vital that the advocates, who are going to conduct the trial, should attend the PTR and every effort should be made to achieve this. It is usually appropriate for the PTR to be conducted by way of an oral hearing (in person, remote or hybrid hearing) or, at the very least, a telephone conference, so that the judge may raise matters of trial management even if the parties can agree beforehand any outstanding directions and the detailed requirements for the management of the trial. In appropriate cases, e.g. where the amount in issue is disproportionate to the costs of a full trial, the judge may wish to consider with the parties whether there are other ways in which the dispute might be resolved. However there may be some cases where the judge is prepared to dispense with the need for a PTR so long as a request is made in sufficiently good time before the PTR to enable a decision to be made. **2C-124**

14.2 DOCUMENTS

14.2.1 The parties must complete the PTR Questionnaire (a copy of which is at Appendix C attached) and return it in good time to the court. In addition, the judge may order the parties to provide other documents for the particular purposes of the PTR. **2C-125**

14.2.2 In all cases, the advocates for each party should each prepare a Note for the PTR, which:

- addresses any outstanding directions or interlocutory steps still to be taken;
- explains the issues for determination at the trial and the evidence that will be required to determine those issues;
- addresses the most efficient way in which those issues might be dealt with at the trial, including all questions of timetabling of witnesses and speeches.

In any case proceeding in the High Court, the Notes should be exchanged and provided to the court at the latest by 4pm two clear working days before the PTR to enable the other parties to have a reasonable opportunity to deal with any points raised at the PTR itself.

In cases proceeding in the County Court the Notes should be exchanged and provided to the court at the latest by 4 pm one clear working day before the PTR.

14.2.3 The parties should also ensure that, for the PTR, the court has an up-to-date permanent case management bundle, together with a bundle of the evidence (factual and expert) that has been exchanged. This Bundle should also be made available to the court **by 4 pm one clear day before the PTR** .

14.3 OUTSTANDING DIRECTIONS

14.3.1 It can sometimes be the case that there are still outstanding interlocutory steps to be taken at the time of the PTR. That will usually mean that one, or more, of the parties has not complied with an earlier direction of the court. In that event, the court is likely to require prompt compliance, and may make costs orders to reflect the delays. **2C-126**

14.3.2 Sometimes a party will wish to make an application to be heard at the same time as the PTR. Such a practice is unsatisfactory, because it uses up time allocated for the PTR, and it gives rise to potential uncertainty close to the trial date. It is always better for a party, if it possibly can, to make all necessary applications well in advance of the PTR. If that is not practicable, the court should be asked to allocate additional time for the PTR, in order to accommodate specific applications. If additional time is not available, such applications will not generally be entertained.

14.4 ISSUES

2C-127 **14.4.1** The parties should provide the judge at the PTR with an updated list of the main issues for the forthcoming trial, agreed if possible. It should include, where appropriate, a separate list of technical issues to be covered by the experts. As with the list of issues to be provided for the CMC, the list of issues should not be extensive and should focus on the key issues. It is provided as a working document to assist in the management of the trial and not as a substitute for the pleadings.

14.4.2 If the parties are unable to agree the precise formulation of the issues, they should provide to the court their respective formulations. Because the list of issues should focus on the key issues the opportunity for disagreement should be minimised. The judge will note the parties' formulations, but, because the issues are those which arise on the pleadings, is unlikely to give a ruling on this matter at the PTR unless the different formulations show that there is a dispute as to the pleaded case.

14.5 TIMETABLING AND TRIAL LOGISTICS

2C-128 **14.5.1** Much of the PTR will be devoted to a consideration of the appropriate timetable for the trial, and other logistical matters. These will commonly include:

- Directions (or the revisiting of directions already given at the CMC) in respect of the timing and format of the oral and written openings and closings and any necessary reading time for the judge.
- Sequence of oral evidence; for example, whether as is the usual practice in the TCC all the factual evidence should be called before the expert evidence.
- Timetabling of oral evidence. To facilitate this exercise, the advocates should, after discussing the matter and whether some evidence can be agreed, provide a draft timetable indicating which witnesses need to be cross-examined and the periods during it is proposed that they should attend. Such timetables are working documents.
- The manner in which expert evidence is to be presented: see paragraph 13.8 above.
- Whether any form of time limits should be imposed. (Since the purpose of time limits is to ensure that that the costs incurred and the resources devoted to the trial are proportionate, this is for the benefit of the parties. The judge will endeavour to secure agreement to any time limits imposed.)
- Directions in respect of the trial bundle: when it should be agreed and lodged; the contents and structure of the bundle; avoidance of duplication; whether witness statements and/or expert reports should be annotated with cross references to page numbers in the main bundle (see paragraph 12.3 above); and similar matters.
- If there is a hard copy bundle, the normal practice will be that pleadings, witness statements and the body of the experts' reports will be printed single-sided. Annexes to reports, contracts, chronological documents and other documents may be printed single-sided or double-sided depending on the use likely to be made of the documents at trial. For example, letters and e-mails are likely to be easier to read and annotate if singlesided but technical specifications from which only one or two pages will be referred to may conveniently be printed doublesided. Where there is an electronic bundle, the court may wish to have some key documents in hard copy.
- Whether there should be a core bundle; if so how it should be prepared and what it should contain. (The court will order a core bundle in any case where (a) there is substantial documentation and (b) having regard to the issues it is appropriate and proportionate to put the parties to cost of preparing a core bundle). A typical core bundle will contain dividers representing each chronological bundle in which copies of key documents will be placed (keeping their original pagination).
- Rules governing any email communication during trial between the parties and the court.
- Any directions relating to the use of electronic document management systems at trial (this subject to agreement between the parties). The judge may request an electronic pdf copy of the trial bundle even if no document management system is being used and may also request copies of certain documents such as openings, statements of case, witness statements and expert reports in electronic word format to assist in preparation for trial and for the production of a written judgment.
- Any directions relating to the use of simultaneous transcription at trial (this subject to agreement between the parties).
- Whether there should be a view by the judge.
- The form and timing of closing submissions including, in substantial and complex cases, time for preparation and pre-reading of written closing submissions before delivery of oral closing submissions.
- Whether there is a need for a special court (because of the number of parties or any particular facilities required).
- Whether there is need for evidence by video link.

- Any applications for review or variation of costs budgets.

14.5.2 The topics identified in paragraph 14.5.1 are discussed in greater detail in section 15 below.

SECTION 15 THE TRIAL

15.1 ARRANGEMENTS PRIOR TO THE TRIAL—WITNESSES

15.1.1 Prior to the trial the parties' legal representatives should seek to agree on the following matters, in so far as they have not been resolved at the PTR: the order in which witnesses are to be called to give evidence; which witnesses are not required for cross examination and whose evidence in consequence may be adduced entirely from their witness statements; the timetable for the trial and the length of time each advocate is to be allowed for a brief opening speech. When planning the timetable, it should be noted that trials normally take place on Mondays to Thursdays, since Fridays are reserved for applications. **2C-129**

15.1.2 The witnesses should be notified in advance of the trial as to: (a) when each is required to attend court and (b) the approximate period of time for which he or she will be required to attend.

15.1.3 It is the parties' responsibility to ensure that their respective witnesses are ready to attend court at the appropriate time. It is never satisfactory for witnesses to be interposed, out of their proper place, and without good reason and, even where it is unavoidable, the relevant party must notify the other side and the Court as soon as they become aware of the issue. It would require exceptional circumstances for the trial to be adjourned for any period of time because of the unavailability of a witness.

15.2 OPENING NOTES, TRIAL BUNDLE AND ORAL OPENINGS

15.2.1 Opening notes

Unless the court has ordered otherwise, each party's advocate should provide an opening note, which outlines that party's case in relation to each of the issues identified at the PTR, including, where relevant, issues of law. Each opening note should indicate which documents (giving their page numbers in the trial bundle) that party considers that the judge should pre-read and, where relevant, the key paragraphs. The claimant's opening note should include a neutral summary of the background facts, as well as, where it will be of assistance, a neutral chronology and cast list. The other parties' opening notes should usually be shorter and should assume familiarity with the factual background. In general terms, all opening notes should be of modest length and proportionate to the size and complexity of the case. Subject to any specific directions at the PTR, all opening notes must be served two clear working days before the start of the trial. If the opening notes are served and exchanged in pdf or equivalent format, each party should also provide a Word version to the judge's clerk for the benefit and use of the judge. **2C-130**

15.2.2 Trial bundles

Subject to any specific directions at the PTR, the trial bundles should be delivered to court at least three working days before the hearing. It is helpful for the party delivering the trial bundles to liaise in advance with the judge's clerk, in order to discuss practical arrangements, particularly when a large number of bundles are to be delivered. The parties should provide for the court an agreed index of all trial bundles. There should also be an index at the front of each bundle. This should be a helpful guide to the contents of that bundle. (An interminable list, itemising every letter or sheet of paper is not a helpful guide; nor are bland descriptions, such as "exhibit "JT3", of much help to the bundle user.) The spines and inside covers of any hard copy bundles should be clearly labelled with the bundle number set out in a large prominent format and a brief description.

15.2.3 As a general rule the trial bundles should be clearly divided between statements of case, orders, contracts, witness statements, expert reports and correspondence/minutes of meetings, along with an agreed authorities bundle. The correspondence/minutes of meetings should be in a separate bundle or bundles and in chronological order. Documents should only be included if they are relevant to the issues in the case or helpful as background material. There is no need to include every disclosed document in the chronological bundle and parties should seek to agree a chronological bundle of documents likely to be referred to or required for context. Documents should not be duplicated, and unnecessary duplication of e-mail threads should be avoided where possible. Exhibits to witness statements should generally be omitted, since the documents to which the witnesses are referring will be found elsewhere in the bundles. References within witness statements to exhibits should be updated to reflect the location of the exhibit in the trial bundle. This can be done by hand or typed insert into the margin of the statement. The bundles of contract documents and correspondence/minutes of meetings should be paginated, so that every page has a discrete number. If this stretches to many lever arch files, it is likely to be more accessible if each file has its own internal numbering, rather than there being continuous pagination across thousands of documents. The other bundles could be dealt with in one of two ways:

- The statements of case, witness statements and expert reports could be placed in bundles and continuously paginated.
- Alternatively, the statements of case, witness statements and expert reports could be placed behind tabbed divider cards, and then the internal numbering of each such document can be used at trial. If the latter course is adopted, it is vital that the internal page numbering of each expert report continues sequentially through the appendices to that report.

The court encourages the parties to provide original copies of expert reports in this way so that any photographs, plans or charts are legible in their original size and, where appropriate, in colour. In such cases sequential numbering of every page including appendices is essential.

The ultimate objective is to create trial bundles which are user friendly and in which any page can be identified with clarity and brevity (e.g. "bundle G page 273" or "defence page 3" or "Dr Smith page 12"). The core bundle, if there is one (as to which see paragraph 14.5.1 above), will be a separate bundle with its own pagination or contain documents from other bundles retaining the original bundle number behind a divider marked with the bundle number.

15.2.4 In document heavy cases the parties should consider the use of an electronic document management system that can be used at the trial. In order for the most effective use to be made of such a system, it is a matter that may require consideration at an early stage in the litigation. If there is an electronic trial bundle, this should be made available to the judge in advance of the trial and should form part of the arrangements made with the judge's clerk as referred to in paragraph 15.2.2 above.

15.2.5 Opening speeches

Subject to any directions made at the PTR, each party will be permitted to make an opening speech. These speeches should be prepared and presented on the basis that the judge will have pre-read the opening notes and the documents identified by the parties for pre-reading. The claimant's advocate may wish to highlight the main features of the claimant's case and/or to deal with matters raised in the other parties' opening notes. The other parties' advocates will then make shorter opening speeches, emphasising the main features of their own cases and/or responding to matters raised in the claimant's opening speech.

15.2.6 It is not usually necessary or desirable to embark upon legal argument during opening speeches. It is, however, helpful to foreshadow those legal arguments which (a) explain the relevance of particular parts of the evidence or (b) will assist the judge in following a party's case that is to be presented during the trial. In some cases, the legal issues are at the heart of the dispute, in which case it may then be appropriate for a more in-depth legal analysis to be included within an opening speech.

15.2.7 Narrowing of issues

Experience shows that often the issues between the parties progressively narrow as the trial advances. Sometimes this process begins during the course of opening speeches. Weaker contentions may be abandoned and responses to those contentions may become irrelevant. The advocates will co-operate in focussing their submissions and the evidence on the true issues between the parties, as those issues are thrown into sharper relief by the adversarial process.

15.3 SIMULTANEOUS TRANSCRIPTION

2C-131 **15.3.1** Many trials in the TCC, including the great majority of the longer trials, are conducted with simultaneous transcripts of the evidence being provided. There are a number of transcribing systems available. It is now common for a system to be used involving simultaneous transcription onto screens situated in court. However, systems involving the production of the transcript in hard or electronic form at the end of the day or even after a longer period of time are also used. The parties must make the necessary arrangements with one of the companies who provide this service. The court can provide a list, on request, of all companies who offer such a service.

15.3.2 In long trials or those which involve any significant amount of detailed or technical evidence, simultaneous transcripts are helpful. Furthermore, they enable all but the shortest trials to be conducted so as to reduce the overall length of the trial appreciably, since the judge does not have to note the evidence or submissions in longhand as the trial proceeds. Finally, a simultaneous transcript makes the task of summarising a case in closing submissions and preparing the judgment somewhat easier. It reduces both the risk of error or omission and the amount of time needed to prepare a reserved judgment.

15.3.3 If possible, the parties should have agreed at or before the PTR whether a simultaneous transcript is to be employed. It is usual for parties to agree to share the cost of a simultaneous transcript as an interim measure pending the assessment or agreement of costs, when this cost is assessable and payable as part of the costs in the case. Sometimes, a party cannot or will not agree to an interim cost sharing arrangement. If so, it is permissible for one party to bear the cost, but the court cannot be provided with a transcript unless all parties have equal access to the transcript. Unlike transcripts for use during an appeal, there is no available means of obtaining from public funds the cost of a transcript for use at the trial.

15.4 TIME LIMITS

15.4.1 Generally trials in the TCC are conducted under some form of time limit arrangement. Several variants of time limit arrangements are available, but the TCC has developed the practice of imposing flexible guidelines in the form of directions as to the sharing of the time allotted for the trial. These are not mandatory but an advocate should ordinarily be expected to comply with them. **2C-132**

15.4.2 The practice is, in the usual case, for the court to fix, or for the parties to agree, at the PTR or before trial an overall length of time for the trial and overall lengths of time within that period for the evidence and submissions. The part of those overall lengths of time that will be allocated to each party must then be agreed or directed.

15.4.3 The amount of time to be allotted to each party will not usually be the same. The guide is that each party should have as much time as is reasonably needed for it to present its case and to test and cross examine any opposing case, but no longer.

15.4.4 Before the trial, the parties should agree a running order of the witnesses and the approximate length of time required for each witness. A trial timetable should be provided to the court when the trial starts and, in long trials, regularly updated.

15.4.5 The practice of imposing a strict guillotine on the examination or cross examination of witnesses, is not normally appropriate. Flexibility is encouraged, but the agreed or directed time limits should not ordinarily be exceeded without good reason. It is unfair on a party, if that party's advocate has confined cross-examination to the agreed time limits, but an opposing party then greatly exceeds the corresponding time limits that it has been allocated.

15.4.6 An alternative form of time limit, which is sometimes agreed between the parties and approved by the court, is the "chess clock arrangement". The available time is divided equally between the parties, to be used by the parties as they see fit. Thus each side has X hours. One representative on each side operates the chess clock. The judge has discretion "to stop the clock" in exceptional circumstances. A chess clock arrangement is only practicable in a two-party case, but a similar system could be adopted for multi-party disputes.

15.5 ORAL EVIDENCE

15.5.1 Evidence in chief is ordinarily adduced by the witness confirming on oath the truth and accuracy of the previously served witness statement or statements. A limited number of supplementary oral questions will usually be allowed (a) to give the witness an opportunity to become familiar with the procedure and (b) to cover points omitted by mistake from the witness statement or which have arisen subsequent to its preparation. **2C-133**

15.5.2 In some cases, particularly those involving allegations of dishonest, disreputable or culpable conduct or where significant disputes of fact are not documented or evidenced in writing, it is desirable that the core elements of a witness's evidence-in-chief are given orally. The giving of such evidence orally will often assist the court in assessing the credibility or reliability of a witness.

15.5.3 If any party wishes such evidence to be given orally, a direction should be sought either at the PTR or during the openings to that effect. Where evidence in chief is given orally, the rules relating to the use of witness statements in cross-examination and to the adducing of the statement in evidence at any subsequent stage of the trial remain in force and may be relied on by any party.

15.5.4 It is usual for all evidence of fact from all parties to be adduced before expert evidence and for the experts to give evidence in groups with all experts in a particular discipline giving their evidence in sequence: see paragraph 13.8.2 above for ways for expert evidence to be given. Usually, but not invariably, the order of witnesses will be such that the claimant's witnesses give their evidence first, followed by all the witnesses for each of the other parties in turn. If a party wishes a different order of witnesses to that normally followed, the agreement of the parties or a direction from the judge must be obtained in advance.

15.5.5 In a multi-party case, attention should be given (when the timetable is being discussed) to the order of cross-examination and to the extent to which particular topics will be covered by particular cross-examiners. Where these matters cannot be agreed, the order of cross-examination will (subject to any direction of the judge) follow the order in which the parties are set out in the pleadings. The judge will seek to limit cross examination on a topic which has been covered in detail by a preceding cross examination.

15.5.6 In preparing witness statements and in ascertaining what evidence a witness might give in an original or supplementary witness statement or as supplementary evidence-in-chief, lawyers may discuss the evidence to be given by a witness with that witness. The coaching of witnesses or the suggestion of answers that may be given, either in the preparation of witness statements or before a witness starts to give evidence, is not permitted. In relation to the process of giving evidence, witness familiarisation is permissible, but witness coaching is not. The boundary between witness familiarisation and witness coaching is discussed in the context of criminal proceedings by the Court of Appeal in *R v Momodou* [2005] EWCA Crim 177 at [61] - [62]. Once a witness has started giving evidence, that witness cannot discuss the case or their evidence either with the lawyers or with anyone else until they have finally left the witness box. Occasionally a dispensation is needed (for example, an expert may need to participate in an experts' meeting about some new development). In those circumstances the necessary dispensation will either be agreed between the advocates or ordered by the judge.

15.5.7 Where a party is represented by more than one advocate at the trial, the advocates may share the oral advocacy including submissions and examination of witnesses. The court encourages oral advocacy to be undertaken by junior advocates. However, the permission of the court is required for more than one advocate for a party to cross-examine the same witness.

15.6 SUBMISSIONS DURING THE TRIAL

2C-134 **15.6.1** Submissions and legal argument should be kept to a minimum during the course of the trial. Where these are necessary, (a) they should, where possible, take place when a witness is not giving evidence and (b) the judge should be given forewarning of the need for submissions or legal argument. Where possible, the judge will fix a time for these submissions outside the agreed timetable for the evidence.

15.7 CLOSING SUBMISSIONS

2C-135 **15.7.1** The appropriate form of closing submissions may have already been addressed at the PTR, but, if not, that will be determined during the course of the trial. Those submissions may take the form of (a) oral closing speeches or (b) written submission alone or (c) written submissions supplemented by oral closing speeches. In shorter or lower value cases, oral closing speeches immediately after the evidence may be the most cost effective way to proceed. Alternatively, if the evidence finishes in the late afternoon, a direction for written closing submissions to be delivered by specified (early) dates may avoid the cost of a further day's court hearing. In longer and heavier cases the judge may (in consultation with the advocates) set a timetable for the subsequent exchange of written submissions (alternatively, by sequential submissions) followed by an oral hearing. In giving directions for oral and/or written closing submissions, the judge will have regard to the circumstances of the case and the overriding objective.

15.7.2 It is helpful if, in advance of preparing closing submissions, the parties can agree on the principal topics or issues that are to be covered. It is also helpful for the written and oral submissions of each party to be structured so as to cover those topics in the same order.

15.7.3 It is both customary and helpful for the judge to be provided with electronic or hard copies of each authority and statutory provision that is to be cited in closing submissions.

15.8 VIEWS

2C-136 **15.8.1** It is sometimes necessary or desirable for the judge to be taken to view the subject-matter of the case. In normal circumstances, such a view is best arranged to take place immediately after the openings and before the evidence is called. However, if the subject matter of the case is going to be covered up or altered prior to the trial, the view must be arranged earlier. In that event, it becomes particularly important to avoid a change of judge. Accordingly, the court staff will note on the trial diary the fact that the assigned judge has attended a view. In all subsequent communications between the parties and court concerning trial date, the need to avoid a change of judge must be borne firmly in mind.

15.8.2 The matters viewed by the judge form part of the evidence that is received and may be relied on in deciding the case. However, nothing said during the view to (or in the earshot of) the judge, has any evidential status, unless there has been an agreement or order to that effect.

15.8.3 The parties should agree the arrangements for the view and then make those arrangements themselves. The judge will ordinarily travel to the view unaccompanied and, save in exceptional circumstances when the cost will be shared by all parties, will not require any travelling costs to be met by the parties.

15.9 JUDGMENTS

2C-137 **15.9.1** Depending on the length and complexity of the trial, the judge may (a) give judgment orally immediately after closing speeches; (b) give judgment orally on the following day or soon afterwards; or (c) deliver a reserved judgment in writing at a later date.

15.9.2 If a party wishes to obtain a transcript of an oral judgment, it should notify the judge's clerk so that any notes made by the judge can be retained in order to assist the judge when correcting the transcript.

15.9.3 Where judgment is reserved

The judge will normally indicate at the conclusion of the trial what arrangements will be followed in relation to (a) the making available of any draft reserved judgment and (b) the handing down of the reserved judgment in open court. If a judgment is reserved, it will be handed down as soon as possible. The judge will normally provide any reserved judgment in draft and will endeavour to do so within 3 months of the conclusion of the trial. Any enquiries as to the progress of a reserved judgment should be addressed in the first instance to the judge's clerk, with notice of that enquiry being given to other parties. If concerns remain following the judge's response to the parties, further enquiries or communication should be addressed to the judge in charge of the TCC.

15.9.4 If, as is usual, the judge releases a draft judgment in advance of the formal hand down, this draft judgment will be confidential to the parties and their legal advisers and subject to an embargo as set out on the front page of the draft:

"This is a draft judgment to which CPR Practice Direction 40E applies. The judgment will be handed down electronically, in accordance with the Practice Guidance dated 16 December 2021 on [date] at [time].

This draft is confidential to the parties and their legal representatives. Neither the draft itself nor its substance may be disclosed to any other person or made public in any way. The parties must take all reasonable steps to ensure that it is kept confidential. As explained in *Counsel General v. BEIS (No. 2)* [2022] EWCA Civ 181, the draft judgment is only to be used to enable the parties to make suggestions for the correction of errors, prepare submissions on consequential matters and draft orders and to prepare themselves for the publication of the judgment. A breach of any of these obligations may be treated as a contempt of court.

The parties' lawyers should by [time] on [date] submit to the clerk to [judge's name] at [clerk's email address] any typing corrections and other obvious errors (nil returns are required). The official version of the judgment will be available from the clerk after hand down."

Solicitors and counsel on each side should send to the judge a note (if possible, agreed) of any clerical errors or slips which they note in the judgment. However, this is not to be taken as an opportunity to re-argue the issues in the case.

15.9.5 Written judgments are handed down remotely and published through the National Archives, available online at **Find Case Law**.

15.10 DISPOSAL OF JUDGE'S BUNDLE AFTER CONCLUSION OF THE CASE

15.10.1 The judge will have made notes and annotations on any hard copy bundle during the **2C-138**
course of the trial. Accordingly, the normal practice is that the entire contents of the judge's bundle are disposed of as confidential waste. The empty ring files can be recovered by arrangement with the judge's clerk.

15.10.2 If any party wishes to retrieve from the judge's bundle any particular items of value which it has supplied (e.g. plans or photographs), a request for these items should be made to the judge's clerk promptly at the conclusion of the case. If the judge has not made annotations on those particular items, they will be released to the requesting party.

SECTION 16 COSTS AND COSTS MANAGEMENT

16.1 GENERAL

16.1.1 All disputes as to costs will be resolved in accordance with CPR Part 44, and in particular **2C-139**
CPR 44.2.

16.1.2 The judge's usual approach will be to determine which party can be properly described as 'the successful party', and then to investigate whether there are any good reasons why that party should be deprived of some or all of their costs.

16.1.3 It should be noted that, in view of the complex nature of TCC cases, a consideration of the outcome on particular issues or areas of dispute can sometimes be an appropriate starting point for any decision on costs.

16.1.4 As set out in paragraphs 5.1.6, 5.5.5 and 12.1.4 above, if the judge considers that any particular aspect is likely to or has led to unnecessarily increased costs, the judge may make a costs order disallowing costs or ordering costs to be paid, either on the basis of a summary assessment, or by giving a direction to the costs judge as to what costs should be disallowed or paid on a detailed assessment.

16.2 SUMMARY ASSESSMENT OF COSTS

16.2.1 Interlocutory hearings that last one day or less will usually be the subject of a summary **2C-140**
assessment of costs in accordance with CPR 44.6 and paragraph 9 of PD 44. The parties must ensure that their statements of costs, on which the summary assessment will be based, are provided to each other party, and the Court, no later than **24 hours** before the hearing in question: see paragraph 6.9.3 above.

16.2.2 The Senior Courts Costs Office ("SCCO") Guide to the Summary Assessment of Costs sets out clear advice and guidance as to the principles to be followed in any summary assessment. Generally summary assessment proceeds on the standard basis. In making an assessment on the standard basis, the court will only allow a reasonable amount in respect of costs reasonably incurred and any doubts must be resolved in favour of the paying party.

16.2.3 In arguments about the hourly rates claimed, the judge will have regard to the principles set out by the Court of Appeal in *Wraith v Sheffield Forgemasters Ltd* [1998] 1 W.L.R. 132: ie. the judge will consider whether the successful party acted reasonably in employing the solicitors who had been instructed and whether the costs they charged were reasonable compared with the broad average of charges made by similar firms practising in the same area.

16.2.4 When considering hourly rates, the judge in the TCC may have regard to any relevant guideline rates.

16.2.5 The court will also consider whether unnecessary work was done or an unnecessary amount of time was spent on the work.

16.2.6 It may be that, because of pressures of time, and/or the nature and extent of the disputes about the level of costs incurred, the court is unable to carry out a satisfactory summary assessment of the costs. In those circumstances, the court will direct that costs be assessed on the standard (or indemnity) basis and will usually order an amount to be paid on account of costs under CPR 44.3 (8).

16.3 COSTS MANAGEMENT

2C-141 **16.3.1** The rules concerning cost budgeting are set out in CPR 3 Section II and in CPR Practice Direction 3E. The rules concerning the filing of Precedent H Cost Budgets (21 days before the first CMC) and Precedent R Cost Budget Discussion Reports (7 days before the first CMC) are referred to in Section 5 above relating to the preparation for the first CMC. Parties should take care to ensure that the times for service of these documents are complied with, failing which they are at risk of having their costs limited to the court fees unless the court orders otherwise or grants relief from sanction (see *Denton v TH White Ltd* [2014] EWCA Civ 906).

16.3.2 Save for in cases which are set out in CPR 3.12 (including cases where the value of the case is above £10 million), the rules require each party to file a costs budget in the prescribed form at the outset of the litigation (before the first CMC). Precedent H is the form for a costs budget. This divides the litigation into different phases, and the court will consider the amount of the fees and disbursements for each phase separately. Costs budgets are to be supported by a statement of truth (see CPR 3EPD.2). The parties are required to then serve Budget Discussion Reports setting out the figures which are agreed, which are not agreed, and a brief summary of the grounds of dispute. The parties are encouraged to do so within the provided Precedent R (see CPR 3EPD.3). The parties are encouraged to continue to discuss cost issues between them so as to try and narrow or remove any outstanding issues.

16.3.3 At the first CMC the court will consider the costs budgets. If the estimated future costs are agreed, the court will make an order recording the extent to which the budgets have been agreed: see CPR 3.15(2)(a).

16.3.4 Where a budget or parts of a budget for estimated future costs are not agreed, the court will consider the budget and make such revisions as it thinks fit. These will then be recorded in a Costs Management Order: see CPR 3.15(2)(b).

16.3.5 Precedent H is the form for a costs budget. This divides the litigation into different phases, and the court will consider the amount of the fees and disbursements for each phase separately. Costs budgets are to be supported by a statement of truth (see CPR3EPD.4).

16.3.6 Once approved, the costs shown in each phase of the costs budget will usually be recoverable on a detailed assessment if they have been incurred. Recovery will not usually be permitted where a party has overspent its budget for a particular phase, even though it may have underspent on another phase. The court will not depart from the approved figure in the budget unless satisfied that there is good reason to do so: see CPR 3.18.

16.3.7 Precedent H allows a party to provide an allowance for certain contingencies, but these must be set out in the budget and the reason for them given. It is open to a party to apply to the court to amend its costs budget if there is good reason to do so.

16.4 COSTS CAPPING ORDERS

2C-142 **16.4.1** In exercising case management powers, the judge may make costs cap orders which, in normal circumstances, will be prospective only. New rules are set out in CPR 3, Section III. The judge should only do so, however, where:

- it is in the interests of justice to do so;
- there is a substantial risk that without such an order costs will be disproportionately incurred; and
- the court is not satisfied that the risk can be adequately controlled by case management and detailed assessment of costs after a trial.

See CPR 3 Section III "Costs Capping"

16.4.2 The possibility of a costs cap order should be considered at the first CMC. The later such an order is sought, the more difficult it may be to impose an effective costs cap.

16.4.3 The procedure for making an application for a costs capping order are set out in CPR 3.20 and PD3F Costs Capping (these include a new requirement that parties must file a costs budget rather than an estimate of costs with any application for a costs capping order).

16.5 COSTS: MISCELLANEOUS

2C-143 **16.5.1** Pursuant to CPR 44.8 and CPR 44PD.10, solicitors have a duty to tell their clients within 7 days if an order for costs was made against the clients and they were not present at the hearing, explaining how the order came to be made. They must also give the same information to anyone else who has instructed them to act on the case or who is liable to pay their fees.

SECTION 17 ENFORCEMENT

17.1 GENERAL

17.1.1 The TCC is concerned with the enforcement of judgments and orders given by the TCC and with the enforcement of adjudicators' decisions and arbitrators' awards. Adjudication and arbitration enforcement have been dealt with in, respectively, Sections 9 and 10 above. **2C-144**

17.2 HIGH COURT

17.2.1 London

A party wishing to make use of any provision of the CPR concerned with the enforcement of judgments and orders made in the TCC in London can use the TCC in London or any other convenient TCC BPC listed in Appendix D. **2C-145**

17.2.2 Outside London

Where the judgment or order in respect of which enforcement is sought was made by a judge of the TCC out of London, the party seeking enforcement should use the TCC BPC in which the judgment or order was made.

17.2.3 Where orders are required or sought to support enforcement of a TCC judgment or order, a judge of the TCC is the appropriate judge for that purpose. If available, the judge who gave the relevant judgment or made the relevant order is the appropriate judge to whom all applications should be addressed.

17.3 COUNTY COURT

17.3.1 A TCC County Court judgment (like any other County Court judgment): **2C-146**

- if for less than £600, must be enforced in the County Court;
- if for between £600 and £5000, can be enforced in either the County Court or the High Court, at the option of the judgment creditor;
- if for more than £5,000, must be enforced in the High Court.

17.3.2 If a judgment creditor in a TCC County Court wishes to transfer any enforcement proceedings to any other County Court hearing centre (whether a TCC County Court or not), he must make a written request to do so pursuant to section 2 of the Practice Direction supplementing Part 70. Alternatively, at the end of the trial the successful party may make an oral application to the trial judge to transfer the proceedings to some other specified County Court or County Court hearing centre for the purposes of enforcement.

17.4 ELECTRONIC ENFORCEMENT

17.4.1 Where the application or order is unopposed or does not involve any substantial dispute, the necessary order should be sought by way of an electronic application through CE-file. **2C-147**

17.5 CHARGING ORDERS AND ORDERS FOR SALE

17.5.1 One of the most common methods of enforcement involves the making of a charging order over the judgment debtor's property. There are three stages in the process. **2C-148**

17.5.2 The judgment creditor can apply to the TCC for a charging order pursuant to CPR 73.3 and 73.4. The application is in Form N379 in which the judgment creditor must identify the relevant judgment and the property in question. The application is initially dealt with by the judge without a hearing, and he may make an interim charging order imposing a charge over the judgment debtor's interest in the property and fixing a hearing to consider whether or not to make the charging order final.

17.5.3 The interim charging order must be served in accordance with CPR 73.7. If the judgment debtor or any other person objects to the making of a final charging order, then he must set out his objection in accordance with CPR 73.10. There will then be a hearing at which the court will decide whether or not to make the charging order final.

17.5.4 Ultimately, if the judgment remains unsatisfied, the party who has obtained the final charging order may seek an order for the sale of the property in accordance with CPR 73.10C. Although paragraph 4.2 of PD 73 might suggest that a claim for an order for sale to enforce a charging order must be started in the Chancery Division, there is no such restriction in the rule itself and practical difficulties have arisen for parties who have obtained a judgment, an interim charging order and a final charging order in the TCC and who do not want to have to transfer or commence fresh proceedings in another division in order to obtain an order for sale. The TCC will, in appropriate circumstances, in accordance with the overriding objective, make orders for sale in such circumstances, particularly if the parties are agreed that is the most convenient cost-effective course: see *Packman Lucas Limited v Mentmore Towers Ltd* [2010] EWHC 1037 (TCC).

17.5.5 In deciding whether or not to make an order for sale, the court will consider, amongst other things, the size of the debt, and the value of the property relative to that debt, the conduct of the parties and the absence of any other enforcement option on the part of the judgment creditor.

SECTION 18 THE TCC JUDGE AS ARBITRATOR

18.1 GENERAL

2C-149 **18.1.1** Section 93(1) of the Arbitration Act 1996 ("the 1996 Act") provides that a judge of the TCC (previously an Official Referee) may "if in all the circumstances he thinks fit, accept appointment as a sole arbitrator or as an umpire by or by virtue of an arbitration agreement." Judges of the TCC may accept appointments as sole arbitrators or umpires pursuant to these statutory provisions. The 1996 Act does not limit the appointments to arbitrations with the seat in England and Wales.

18.1.2 However, a TCC judge cannot accept such an appointment unless the Lord Chief Justice "has informed him that, having regard to the state of (TCC) business, he can be made available": see Section 93(3) of the 1996 Act. In exceptional cases a judge of the TCC may also accept an appointment as a member of a three-member panel of arbitrators if the Lord Chief Justice consents but such arbitrations cannot be under Section 93 of the 1996 Act because Section 93(6) of the 1996 Act modifies the provisions of the 1996 Act where there is a judge-arbitrator and this could not apply to arbitral tribunals with three arbitrators, one of whom was a judge-arbitrator.

18.1.3 Application should be made in the first instance to the judge whose acceptance of the appointment is sought. If the judge is willing to accept the appointment, he will make an application on behalf of the appointing party or parties, through the judge in charge of the TCC, to the Lord Chief Justice for his necessary approval. He will inform the party or parties applying for his appointment once the consent or refusal of consent has been obtained.

18.1.4 Subject to the workload of the court and the consent of the Lord Chief Justice, the TCC judges will generally be willing to accept such requests, particularly in short cases or where an important principle or point of law is concerned. Particular advantages have been noted by both TECBAR and TeCSA in the appointment of a TCC judge to act as arbitrator where the dispute centres on the proper interpretation of a clause or clauses within one of the standard forms of building and engineering contracts.

18.2 ARBITRATION MANAGEMENT AND FEES

2C-150 **18.2.1** Following the appointment of the judge-arbitrator, the rules governing the arbitration will be decided upon, or directed, at the First Preliminary Meeting, when other appropriate directions will be given. The judge-arbitrator will manage the reference to arbitration in a similar way to a TCC case.

18.2.2 The judge sitting as an arbitrator will sit in a TCC court room (suitably rearranged) unless the parties and the judge-arbitrator agree to some other arrangement.

18.2.3 Fees are payable to the Court Service for the judge-arbitrator's services and for any accommodation provided. The appropriate fee for the judge-arbitrator, being a daily rate, is published in the Fees Order and should be paid through the TCC Registry.

18.3 MODIFICATIONS TO THE ARBITRATION ACT 1996 FOR JUDGE-ARBITRATORS

2C-151 **18.3.1** As Section 93 envisages that appointments of judge-arbitrators will be in arbitrations where the seat of the arbitration is in England and Wales, Schedule 2 of the 1996 Act modifies the provisions of the Act which apply to arbitrations where the seat is in England and Wales.

18.3.2 In relation to arbitrations before judge-arbitrators, **paragraph 2 of Schedule 2 to the Arbitration Act 1996** provides that references in Part I of the 1996 Act to "the court" shall be construed in relation to a judge-arbitrator, or in relation to the appointment of a judge-arbitrator, as references to "the Court of Appeal". This means that, for instance, any appeal from a judge-arbitrator under Section 69 of the 1996 Act is therefore heard, in the first instance, by the Court of Appeal.

APPENDIX A

CASE MANAGEMENT INFORMATION SHEET

2C-152 This Appendix is the same as Appendix A to the Part 60 Practice Direction.

APPENDIX B

CASE MANAGEMENT DIRECTIONS FORM

2C-153 *[Delete or amend the following directions, as appropriate to the circumstances of the case]*

Claim No: HT-[*yyyy*]-

[*nnnnnn*]

[Title]

Dated [*dd*] *[mm] [yyyy] [Date on which the order was actually made]*

[Delete or amend the following directions, as appropriate to the circumstances of the case]

DIRECTIONS ORDER ON CASE MANAGEMENT CONFERENCE[1]

Warning: you must comply with the terms imposed upon you by this order otherwise your case is liable to be struck out or some other sanction imposed. If you cannot comply you are expected to make formal application to the court before any deadline imposed upon you expires.

[Delete or amend the following directions, as appropriate to the circumstances of the case]

FURTHER HEARINGS[2]

1. The trial [*Where required:* of all issues / of the following issues, namely ... (*complete as required, if lengthy by reference to an Appendix to the order)*] shall take place as follows, subject to any further directions to be given at the pre-trial review:

1.1 Reading day(s) (at which the parties are not required to attend): .....

1.2 Trial day 1: ...

1.3 Length of trial (excluding reading day(s) and Fridays[3]): ...

1.4 Any other trial directions: (*... Where appropriate, including any directions for provisional trial timetable, and for time for preparation of written closing submissions and for delivery of oral closing submissions in substantial and/or complex cases)*]

2. *Where required:* A review case management conference / further hearing *(specify which)* for the following purposes, namely ... *(complete as required)* shall be held on ... at ...am / pm.

Time allowed ...

3. The pre-trial review[4] shall be held on ... at ... am / pm. Time allowed ...

GENERAL MATTERS

4. *Where required:* The following directions shall apply only in relation to the preliminary issues directed above (save where expressly stated to the contrary).

5. This action is to be (consolidated / managed and tried with action no ... *(specify which)*). The lead action shall be ... All directions given in the lead action shall apply to both actions, unless otherwise stated.

6. At all stages the parties must consider settling this litigation by any means of Alternative Dispute Resolution (including Mediation); any party not engaging in any such means proposed by another must serve a witness statement giving reasons within 21 days of that proposal; such witness statement must not be shown to the trial judge until questions of costs arise. [*Where required:* The action is stayed for such purpose from ... to ... / the court is satisfied that the parties can engage in Alternative Dispute Resolution within the timetable set for these directions without the need for a stay *(specify which)*]

FURTHER STATEMENTS OF CASE AND LIST OF ISSUES AND SCOTT SCHEDULE

7. *Where required:* Further statements of case shall be filed and served as follows *(complete as required)*:

7.1 Defence and any counterclaim by 4 pm on ...

7.2 Reply (if any) and Defence to counterclaim (if any) by 4 pm on ...

7.3 Replies to the Requests for Further Information served by the ... by 4pm on ...

8. *Where required:* Permission to the ... to amend the ... in accordance with the draft (identify), as to which the following directions shall apply.

8.1 (*Specify which:* The ... shall file and serve the amended ..., verified by statement of truth, by 4pm on ... / re-service is dispensed with.)

8.2 The ... shall file and serve an amended ... consequential upon the amendments to the ..., by 4pm on ...

---

[1] See section 5 of the TCC Guide for general guidance in relation to case management conferences. Refer to the relevant sections of the TCC Guide in relation to the further hearings / steps set out below.

[2] It may not always be possible to fix dates at the CMC itself but dates will be fixed in time for the Order to be drawn up

[3] In London the practice is that non-trial business is listed on Fridays. Outside London the practice may differ.

[4] Pre-trial reviews are usually ordered but may be dispensed with if unnecessary. The TCC Guide makes provision for the parties to agree and to seek the court's agreement to vacate a PTR if it transpires at the time to be unnecessary.

8.3 *(Provision for any further consequential amendments, if required)*
8.4 The costs of and occasioned by the amendments shall be paid by the ... in any event.

9. *(If required include any directions which may be required in relation to the list of issues)*
10. (*If required:*There shall be a Scott Schedule in respect of the following issues ... *(specify, for example defects / items of damage / remedial costs)* as to which the following directions shall apply
10.1 The column headings shall be (as follows ... *(complete)* / agreed following liaison between the parties, with any dispute to be referred to and resolved by the judge *(specify which)*)
10.2 ... to serve the Scott Schedule, populated with its comments in the required column headings, in electronic format by 5 pm on ...
10.3 ... to respond to the Scott Schedule, populated with its comments in the required column headings, in electronic format by 5 pm on ...
10.4 (... to serve its reply, populated with its comments in the required column headings, in electronic format by 5 pm on ... *(if required)*)
10.5 The format for the Scott Schedule shall be as follows shall be (as follows ... *(e.g. whether word or excel, A4 or A3, portrait or landscape)* / agreed following liaison between the parties, with any dispute to be referred to and resolved by the judge *(specify which)*)
10.6 The party producing the final version of the Scott Schedule shall file an electronic copy at court.

DISCLOSURE

11. Disclosure is to be given by each party in accordance with Practice Direction 57AD – Disclosure for the Business and Property Courts and the Disclosure Review Document for the Business and Property Courts and the Disclosure Review Document (as agreed by the parties / as agreed by the parties and as determined by the judge at the hearing, an amended version of which, to include such amendments, shall be filed and served by the Claimant's solicitors within 7 days of the hearing *(specify which)*. Further:
1) The time for compliance with any order for Extended Disclosure in accordance with paragraph 12 of the Practice Direction shall be (specify date or dates).
2) When complying with an order for Extended Disclosure the parties should have regard to the guidance set out in Section 3 of the Disclosure Review Document.[1]
3) *Where required:* In relation to the matters recorded in the schedule left over for further discussion and agreement, if no agreement is reached by (specify date) the parties must issue an application notice to fix a Disclosure Guidance Hearing[2].
4) *Where required:* The question of which party bears the costs of disclosure is to be given separate consideration at ... *(specify later stage)*.[3]
5) ... *(any further specific directions as required)*]

WITNESS STATEMENTS

12. Signed statements of witnesses of fact (and any witness summaries or other notices relating to evidence) to be mutually exchanged by 5 pm on ...
13. *Where required:* Supplementary statements of witnesses of fact, limited to matters raised in the witness statements served by the other party and not already covered in the principal witness statements, to be mutually exchanged by 5 pm on ...

EXPERT EVIDENCE

14. *Where separate experts are permitted:* The parties each have permission to call the expert witnesses specified below in respect of the following issues:
14.1 [Party] [Name of witness] [Discipline] [Issues to be addressed]

15. In respect of any expert evidence permitted under paragraph 14:
15.1 *Where required:* Directions for carrying out inspections/ taking samples/ conducting experiments/ performance of calculations shall be ... *(complete as appropriate)*
15.2 Experts in like fields to hold discussions in accordance with rule 35.12 by ...
15.3 Experts' statements in accordance with rule 35.12 (3) to be prepared and filed by 5 pm on ...
15.4 Experts' reports to be served by 5 pm on ...
15.5 *Where required:* If the experts in like fields consider it appropriate, they shall be permitted to hold further discussions upon sight of reports served by the other experts with a view to reaching further agreement or narrowing or clarifying the issues in dispute and to prepare and file supplemental statements by 5pm on ....
15.6 (The experts shall attend trial if they are not in substantial agreement on all material mat-

---

[1] See paragraph 9.8 of the Disclosure Practice Direction.
[2] See paragraph 11 of the Disclosure Practice Direction.
[3] See paragraph 9.9 of the Disclosure Practice Direction.

ters / Any application for the experts to attend trial shall be made by ... *(specify which))*.

16. *Where a single joint expert is permitted:* A single joint expert shall be appointed by the parties to report on the following issue(s)

16.1 [Name of witness] [Discipline] [Issues to be addressed]

17. The following directions shall govern the appointment of the single joint expert:

17.1 *(complete as appropriate, including a timetable for agreeing the identity of the expert or referring any disagreement to the court, for agreeing and sending a letter of instruction or in default of agreement letters of instruction, for production of the report, for submitting questions, for applying or permission for the expert to attend court for cross-examination)*

The single joint expert shall be entitled to request a reasonable sum on account of reasonable fees and disbursements before beginning work. Such sum shall be paid in equal proportions by the instructing parties, subject to any final costs order made following judgment.

COSTS MANAGEMENT

18. Costs Management *(complete as appropriate)*

18.1 It is recorded that the parties have agreed the respective costs budgets dated ...

18.2 The costs budgets filed by the parties are approved (or)

18.3 The costs budget filed by the ... *(complete)* is approved, and

18.4 The costs budgets filed by the ... *(complete)* are approved subject to the following revisions:

The parties shall file amended costs budgets giving effect to such revisions by ...

EXTENSIONS OF TIME

19. The above dates and time limits may be extended by agreement between the parties. Nevertheless:

The dates and time limits specified above may not be extended by more than [14] days without the permission of the court.

The dates specified in paragraphs 1 (trial), 2 (further hearing) and paragraph 3 (pretrial review) cannot be varied without the permission of the court.

COSTS

20. The costs of the case management conference are ... *(specify, usually costs in the case, include any other particular costs order made)*.

DATED ...

APPENDIX C

PRE-TRIAL REVIEW QUESTIONNAIRE

This Appendix is the same as Appendix C to the Part 60 Practice Direction. **2C-154**

APPENDIX D

CONTACT DETAILS FOR TECHNOLOGY AND CONSTRUCTION COURT

THE HIGH COURT OF JUSTICE, KING'S BENCH DIVISION, TECHNOLOGY AND CONSTRUCTION COURT

Business and Property Courts sitting at:

The Rolls Building, 7 Rolls Buildings, Fetter Lane, London EC4A 1NL **2C-155**

Management

Court Manager: Mr Wilf Lusty
Email: wilf.lusty@justice.gov.uk

TCC Listings

Senior Listing Officer: Mr Michael Tame
Email: michael.tame@justice.gov.uk

Listing Officer: Ms Gina Hitchman

Email: tcc.listing@justice.gov.uk

General TCC listing enquiries - Email: tcc.listing@justice.gov.uk

Registry Tel: 020 7947 7591

TCC Judges

Mrs Justice O'Farrell DBE (Judge in Charge of the TCC)
Clerk: Samia Nur (samia.nur@justice.gov.uk)
Tel: 020 7073 1670

Mr Justice Fraser
Clerk: Madeleine Collins (madeleine.collins@justice.gov.uk)
Manizja Latifi (manizja.latifi@justice.gov.uk)
Tel: 020 7974 6124

Mrs Justice Jefford DBE
Clerk: Sam Taylor (sam.taylor1@justice.gov.uk)
Tel: 020 7947 7205

The following High Court Judges may be available, when necessary and by arrangement with the President of the King's Bench Division, to sit in the TCC:

Mrs Justice Cockerill DBE
Clerk: Laura Hope (laura.hope@justice.gov.uk)
Tel: 020 7947 6231

Mr Justice Waksman
Clerk: Lucius Allen lucius.allen@justice.gov.uk)
Tel: 020 7947 6104

Mr Justice Pepperall
Clerk: Chelsea Fincham (Chelsea.Fincham@justice.gov.uk)
Tel: 020 7947 6117

Mr Justice Kerr
Clerk: Mandy Torrens (Mandy.Torrens@Justice.gov.uk)
Tel: 020 7947 6143

Mr Justice Choudhury
Clerk: Katherine Stent (katherine.stent@justice.gov.uk)
Tel: 020 7947 7056

Mr Justice Eyre
Clerk: Rebecca Murphy (Rebecca.murphy4@justice.gov.uk)
Tel: 020 7947 7855

Mrs Justice Joanna Smith DBE
Clerk: Caroline Reid (caroline.reid@Justice.gov.uk)
Tel: 020 7071 5619

Business and Property Courts based in the Birmingham Civil Justice Centre at:

33 Bull Street, Birmingham, West Midlands B4 6DS

TCC listing enquiries: *ClerktoHHJWatson@justice.gov.uk*
Clerk: Susan Thomas (ClerktoHHJWatson@justice.gov.uk)
Tel: 012 1681 3181

TCC Judges

- Her Honour Judge Sarah Watson (Principal TCC Judge)

The following judges at Birmingham are nominated to deal with TCC business:

- HHJ David Worster
- HHJ Richard Williams
- HHJ Brian Rawlings

- HHJ James Tindal (from September 2022)

Business and Property Courts based at Bristol Civil Justice Centre at:

2 Redcliff Street, Bristol BS1 6GR

TCC Listing

TCC Listing Officer: Debbie Greenwood
Tel: 011 7366 4860 (hub)
Email: bristoltcclisting@justice.gov.uk

TCC Judges

- His Honour Judge Russen KC (Principal TCC judge)
  District Judges Tony Woodburn and Matthew Wales

Business and Property Courts in Wales based at Cardiff Civil and Family Justice Centre at:

2 Park Street, Cardiff, CF10 1ET

Main switchboard: 029 2037 6400

Listing office:

Tel: 029 2037 6430
Listings Email: bpc.cardiff@justice.gov.uk

Listing Manager: Matthew Solomons
Email: matthew.solomons1@justice.gov.uk
Tel: 029 2037 6430

Specialist Listing Clerk: Amanda Barrago
Email: amanda.barrago@justice.gov.uk
Tel: 029 2037 6430

TCC Judges

- His Honour Judge Keyser KC (Principal TCC Judge)
- His Honour Judge Jarman KC

Central London Civil Justice Centre, based at:
Thomas More Building, Royal Courts of Justice, Strand, London WC2 2LL

TCC Listing Enquiries

Tel: 030 0123 5577
Email: Enquiries.centrallondon.countycourt@justice.gov.uk & Leslie.Alfonso@justice.gov.uk

TCC Judges

- His Honour Judge Nick Parfitt
- His Honour Judge Alan Johns KC

Business and Property Courts based at Leeds Combined Court Centre at:
The Courthouse, Oxford Row, Leeds LS1 3BG

Listing Enquiries:

TCC Listing Officer: Sandie Umarji
Email: TCC.Leeds@justice.gov.uk
Tel: 011 3306 2460/2461

TCC Judges

- Her Honour Judge Siobhan Kelly (Principal/Lead TCC Judge)
- His Honour Judge Jonathan Klein
- His Honour Judge Malcolm Davis-White KC
- Her Honour Judge Claire Jackson

Business and Property Courts based at Liverpool Civil Justice Centre at:
35 Vernon Street, Liverpool, L2 2BX

TCC Listings:

TCC listing officer: Kevin Fitzmaurice
Email: Kevin.Fitzmaurice@justice.gov.uk

TCC Clerk: Steve Christiansen
Email: steve.christiansen@justice.gov.uk

Tel: 0151 296 2483

TCC Judges

- His Honour Judge Cadwallader (Principal TCC Judge)
- His Honour Judge Graham Wood KC
- District Judge Baldwin

Business and Property Courts based at Manchester Civil Justice Centre, at:
1 Bridge Street West, Manchester M60 9DJ
TCC Clerk: Samantha Samkange (BPC section team leader)
Tel: 016 1240 5307
Fax: 012 6478 5034

Listings:
BPC.Manchester@justice.gov.uk

TCC Judges

- His Honour Judge Stephen Davies (Principal TCC judge)

The following judges at Manchester are nominated to deal with TCC business:

- HHJ David Hodge KC
- HHJ Nigel Bird
- HHJ Richard Pearce
- HHJ Mark Halliwell
- HHJ Cawson

Business and Property Courts based at Newcastle upon Tyne Court/District Registry, at:
The Civil and Family Courts and Tribunal Centre, Barras Bridge, Newcastle upon Tyne NE1 8QF, DX 336901 Newcastle upon Tyne 55

Listings:

Listing Team
Email: Helen Tait (Clerk to HH Judge Kramer) & NewcastleBPC@justice.gov.uk
Tel: 0191 205 8751/8752/8753/8754/8755

TCC Judges
His Honour Judge Kramer (Principal TCC judge)

APPENDIX E

DRAFT ADR ORDER

2C-156 **1.** By [date/time] the parties shall exchange lists of three neutral individuals who have indicated their availability to conduct a mediation or ENE or other form of ADR in this case prior to [date].

2. By [date/time] the parties shall agree an individual from the exchanged lists to conduct the mediation or ENE or other form of ADR by [date]. If the parties are unable to agree on the neutral individual, they will apply to the Court in writing by [date/time] and the Court will choose one of the listed individuals to conduct the mediation or ENE or other form of ADR.

3. There will be a stay of the proceedings until [date/time] to allow the mediation or ENE or other form of ADR to take place. On or before that date, the Court shall be informed as to whether or not the case has been finally settled. If it has not been finally settled, the parties will:

a) comply with all outstanding directions made by the Court;
b) attend for a review CMC on [date/time].

DATED ...

APPENDIX F

DRAFT DIRECTIONS ORDER IN ADJUDICATION ENFORCEMENT PROCEEDINGS

Before **[Judge-in-Charge]** sitting in the High Court of Justice, Business and Property Courts of England and Wales, Technology and Construction Court (KBD) at the Rolls Building, 7 Rolls Buildings, London EC4A 1NL on **[date of order]** **2C-157**

UPON READING the Claimant's application for enforcement of an adjudication decision and supporting evidence

AND UPON the Court having considered matters on the papers

AND OF THE COURT'S OWN MOTION

IT IS ORDERED THAT:

REMOTE HEARING

1. The Claimant shall as soon as practicable after receipt of this Order serve this application upon the Defendant together with:

1) the Claim Form, Response Pack and any statement relied upon;
2) this Order.

2. The time for the Defendant to file its Acknowledgement of Service is abridged to four (4) working days. The Defendant is advised that failure to comply with the requirement to file this Acknowledgment can lead to judgment in default being entered against it. The Claimant is reminded that if there is such failure, serious consideration should be given to entering judgment in default as a cheaper option than taking the matter through to a hearing.

3. Any further evidence shall be served and filed:

1) By the Defendant, on or by [**date**];
2) By the Claimant, in response to that of the Defendant, on or by [**date**]; and in either case no later than 4.00 pm that day.

4. The Claimant has permission to issue an application for summary judgment prior to service by the Defendant of either an Acknowledgment of Service or a Defence, pursuant to CPR Rule 24.4(1). The period of notice to be given to the Defendant is abridged to four (4) working days.

5. There shall be a remote hearing of the Claimant's summary judgment application on **[date]** at **[time]** with a time estimate of 2 hours for the hearing (this time may be varied at short notice to accommodate the listing requirements of the court.

THIS HEARING SHALL TAKE PLACE BY REMOTE HEARING.

6. If and to the extent that such hearing cannot take place in public, then the hearing is to take place in private pursuant to CPR 39.2(3)(g) and Practice Direction 51Y.

NOTIFICATION OF ATTENDANCE

7. By no later than 10:00am on **[date - 2 days before the hearing]**, each party must file by email to **[the Judge's clerk]** the identity of each person attending the hearing, the capacity in which they will attend, their email and telephone contact details.

PROVISION OF DOCUMENTS FOR THE HEARING

8. The parties shall co-operate in ensuring that all documents necessary for the Court to determine the application or trial are made available in electronic form in good time before the hearing.

9. The Claimant shall serve and file an indexed and paginated electronic bundle comprising all relevant documents, including pleadings, statements, reports and other material by 1.00pm on **[date]**.

1) Electronic bundles should contain only documents that are essential to the remote hearing. Please note that large electronic files can be slow to transmit and unwieldy to use.
2) Electronic bundles can be prepared in .pdf or another format and should facilitate electronic annotation. Where possible, the electronic bundles should be sent to the court by link to an online data room or delivered to the court on a USB stick. If that is not possible, they must be filed through CE-file or sent by email to the Judge's clerk.

10. Any skeleton arguments should be prepared and sent to the Judge's clerk by email by 1.00pm on **[date – 2 days before the hearing]**.

11. Any authorities relied upon (an agreed bundle if possible) should be provided by electronic bundle to the judge's clerk and to all other representatives and parties by 1.00pm on **[date – 1 day before the hearing]**.

THE HEARING

12. The vehicle for the remote hearing shall be Microsoft Teams.

13. Invitations to join the meeting will be sent by email to all persons who have notified the Court as attending the remote hearing. Any person who has so notified the Court but not received an invitation to the hearing by 2:00pm on **[the day before the hearing]** should contact **[the Judge's clerk or listings]**.

14. Thirty (30) minutes before the hearing, the Claimant's legal representative will sign in and all attendees are obliged to attempt to sign in shortly thereafter, so that any issues with the connection can be addressed before the hearing is due to begin. Issues should be raised with **[the Judge's clerk]**.

15. The hearing will be recorded by the Judge's clerk. Although the hearing is being conducted remotely, the hearing remains a court hearing. The usual rules and formalities continue to apply. In particular, it is not permitted for any other party to record these proceedings, and breach of this rule amounts to a contempt of court.

LIBERTY TO APPLY

16. The parties have permission to apply to set aside or vary these directions on two (2) working days' written notice to the other.

REASONS

1. I have considered the papers in this matter and can see no reason why the application cannot fairly be disposed of by way of a remote hearing.

2. However, remote hearings bring with them added complexity, in terms of:

i) Ensuring the presence of all relevant parties; and

ii) Ensuring that all material documents are before the Court in a manner that all parties can easily identify and reference.

The order seeks to anticipate and deal with these issues.

REMOTE HEARING ATTENDANCE FORM

Case No	
Case Name	
Claimant	
Defendant	
Hearing date and time	
Party filing this document	

ALL PERSONS ATTENDING ON BEHALF OF THIS PARTY				
Name	**Email**	**Direct phone**	**Capacity attending**	**Speaking Y/N**

Appendix G

Draft Court Settlement Order

COURT SETTLEMENT

2C-158 **1.** The Court Settlement Process under this Order is a confidential, voluntary and non-binding dispute resolution process in which the Settlement Judge assists the Parties in reaching an amicable settlement at a Court Settlement Conference.

2. This Order provides for the process by which the Court assists in the resolution of the disputes in the Proceedings. This Order is made by consent of the Parties with a view to achieving the amicable settlement of such disputes. It is agreed that the Settlement Judge may vary this Order at any time as he thinks appropriate or in accordance with the agreement of the Parties.

3. The following definitions shall apply:

1) The Parties shall be [names]
2) The Proceedings are [identify]
3) The Settlement Judge is [name]

THE COURT SETTLEMENT PROCESS

4. The Settlement Judge may conduct the Court Settlement Process in such manner, as the Judge considers appropriate, taking into account the circumstances of the case, the wishes of the Parties and the overriding objective in Part 1 of the Civil Procedure Rules. A Preliminary Court Settlement Conference shall be held, either in person or in some other convenient manner, at which the Parties and the Settlement Judge shall determine, in general terms, the procedure to be adopted for the Court Settlement Process, the venue of the Court Settlement Conference, the estimated duration of the Court Settlement Conference and the material which will be read by the Settlement Judge in advance of the Court Settlement Conference.

5. Unless the Parties otherwise agree, during the Court Settlement Conference the Settlement Judge may communicate with the Parties together or with any Party separately, including private meetings at which the Settlement Judge may express views on the disputes. Each Party shall cooperate with the Settlement Judge. A Party may request a private meeting with the Settlement Judge at any time during the Court Settlement Conference. The Parties shall give full assistance to enable the Court Settlement Conference to proceed and be concluded within the time stipulated by the Settlement Judge.

6. In advance of the Court Settlement Conference, each Party shall notify the Settlement Judge and the other Party or Parties of the names and the role of all persons involved in the Court Settlement Conference. Each Party shall nominate a person having full authority to settle the disputes.

7. No offers or promises or agreements shall have any legal effect unless and until they are included in a written agreement signed by representatives of all Parties (the "Settlement Agreement").

8. If the Court Settlement Conference does not lead to a Settlement Agreement, the Settlement Judge may, if requested by the Parties, send the Parties such assessment setting out his views on such matters as the Parties shall request, which may include, for instance, his views on the disputes, his views on prospects of success on individual issues, the likely outcome of the case and what would be an appropriate settlement. Such assessment shall be confidential to the parties and may not be used or referred to in any subsequent proceedings.

TERMINATION OF THE SETTLEMENT PROCESS

9. The Court Settlement Process shall come to end upon the signing of a Settlement Agreement by the Parties in respect of the disputes or when the Settlement Judge so directs or upon written notification by any Party at any time to the Settlement Judge and the other Party or Parties that the Court Settlement Process is terminated.

CONFIDENTIALITY

10. The Court Settlement Process is private and confidential. Every document, communication or other form of information disclosed, made or produced by any Party specifically for the purpose of the Court Settlement Process shall be treated as being disclosed on a privileged and without prejudice basis and no privilege or confidentiality shall be waived by such disclosure.

11. Nothing said or done during the course of the Court Settlement Process is intended to or shall in any way affect the rights or prejudice the position of the Parties to the dispute in the Proceedings or any subsequent arbitration, adjudication or litigation. If the Settlement Judge is told by a Party that information is being provided to the Settlement Judge in confidence, the Settlement Judge will not disclose that information to any other Party in the course of the Court Settlement Process or to any other person at any time.

COSTS

12. Unless otherwise agreed, each Party shall bear its own costs and shall share equally the Court costs of the Court Settlement Process.

SETTLEMENT JUDGE'S ROLE IN SUBSEQUENT PROCEEDINGS

13. The Settlement Judge shall from the date of this Order not take any further part in the Proceedings nor in any subsequent proceedings arising out of the Court Settlement Process and no party shall be entitled to call the Settlement Judge as a witness in any subsequent adjudication, arbitration or judicial proceedings arising out of or connected with the Court Settlement Process.

EXCLUSION OF LIABILITY

14. For the avoidance of doubt, the Parties agree that the Settlement Judge shall have the same immunity from suit in relation to a Court Settlement Process as the Settlement Judge would have if acting otherwise as a Judge in the Proceedings.

PARTICULAR DIRECTIONS

15. A Court Settlement Conference shall take place on [date] at [place] commencing at [time].

16. If by [date] the Parties have not concluded a settlement agreement, the matter shall be listed on the first available date before an appropriate judge who shall be allocated for the future management and trial of the Proceedings.

17. The Court Settlement Process shall proceed on the basis of such documents as might be determined at the Preliminary Court Settlement Conference and which may include the documents filed in the court proceedings and further documents critical to the understanding of the issues in the dispute and the positions of the Parties.

Dated this ...

APPENDIX H

TCC GUIDANCE NOTE ON PROCEDURES FOR PUBLIC PROCUREMENT CASES

INTRODUCTION

2C-159 **1.** This protocol provides guidance on the management of public procurement claims. This is a rapidly developing area of law; while this guide should assist, practitioners must ensure that they are aware of the most recent relevant case law.

2. Public procurement cases, particularly those involving claims which seek to set aside the decision to award the contract in question, raise singular procedural issues and difficulties. The claimant commonly feels that it has insufficient evidence or documentation fully to particularise its case or otherwise prepare for trial, while the short limitation and mandatory standstill periods mean that proceedings are necessarily issued hastily. The provision of pleadings and documentation on disclosure often gives rise to serious difficulties in connection with confidentiality, particularly where there is a real risk that there will have to be a re-tendering process. Confidentiality rings will often need to be set up by agreement or order.

3. The issue and notice of proceedings challenging a contract award decision before the contract has been entered into, results in automatic suspension of the conclusion of the contract with the successful tenderer. The latter has a particular interest in the protection of the confidential information in its documents, many of which will be in the possession of the contracting authority and may wish to make representations in relation to confidentiality and other matters.[1] It is therefore not unusual for the successful tenderer to make an application to be joined in the proceedings or to have its interests protected by some other means.

PRE-ACTION PROCESS AND ADR

4. Given the short limitation period, the time for any pre-action process is limited. As the mandatory standstill period is only 10 days, a potential claimant may need to commence proceedings without delay to obtain automatic suspension of the award of the contract. Whilst a claimant is not bound to comply with the Protocol, it aims to enable parties to settle the issues between them without the need to start proceedings, by encouraging the parties to exchange information about the claim, and to consider using Alternative Dispute Resolution (ADR) to resolve cases before or during proceedings. Litigation should always be a last resort. Therefore, to the extent that this is practical and does not make it unreasonably difficult to issue and serve proceedings within the limitation period, the parties are encouraged to use a pre-action process.

5. The pre-action process which is recommended is as follows:

1) The potential claimant will send a letter before claim to the contracting authority. This should identify the procurement process to which the claim relates; the grounds then known for the claim (both factual and legal); any information sought from the authority; the remedy required, and any request for an extension of the standstill period and/or a request not to enter into the contract for a specific period of time and/or not to do so without a specified period of notice to the potential claimant. The letter should propose an appropriate, short, time limit for a response.
2) The authority should promptly acknowledge receipt of the letter before claim, notify its solicitors' details and (if requested) indicate whether the standstill period will be extended and if so, by how long. The authority should then provide any information to which the claimant may be entitled as soon as possible, and send a substantive response within the timescale proposed by the claimant, or as soon as practical thereafter.
3) Having exchanged correspondence and information, the parties should continue to make appropriate and proportionate efforts to resolve the dispute without the need to commence proceedings.

---

[1] This protocol refers to contracting authorities, but the same issues arise in relation to utilities under the relevant Utilities Contracts Regulations.

6. The parties should act co-operatively and reasonably in dealing with all aspects of the litigation, including requests for extensions of time, taking into account the expiry of the standstill period and/or any limitation periods. The parties should also act co-operatively and reasonably in dealing with all aspects of the litigation, including amendments following further disclosure.

7. The parties should also act reasonably and proportionately in providing one another with information, taking into account any genuine concerns with regard to confidentiality, whether their own, or those of third parties. The parties should consider the use of confidentiality rings and undertakings to support resolution of the dispute prior to the issue of proceedings (as to confidentiality rings and undertakings see below). The aim should be to avoid the need to issue proceedings simply to obtain early specific disclosure. The authority is strongly encouraged to disclose the key decision materials at an early stage where relevant to the complaint made[1].

8. ADR processes are encouraged, both before and during proceedings. The Court may order a stay of proceedings, direct a window in the timetable leading up to trial to enable mediation or other ADR to take place, or make an ADR order in the terms of Appendix E (see paragraph 7.3.2) particularly if (due to the claim being or becoming limited to damages) there is less urgency in fixing an early trial date.

INSTITUTION OF PROCEEDINGS

SERVICE OF THE CLAIM FORM

9. The Claim Form must be served on the Defendant within 7 days after the date of issue, the first day of the 7 being the day following the day on which the Court seals the Claim Form: accordingly, a claim form issued on Wednesday must be served no later than the following Wednesday. "Service" for the purposes of the regulations requires the claimant to complete the step constituting service under CPR 7.5(1) within 7 days of issuing the Claim Form[2].

SERVICE OF THE PARTICULARS OF CLAIM

10. Parties should be aware of the provisions of CPR 7.4 (1) and (2). CPR 7.4(2) requires that the Particulars of Claim be served no later than the latest time for serving the Claim Form.

11. If the Particulars of Claim (or other pleadings) contain confidential information, the party serving the pleading should lodge with the Court (a) a non-confidential version of the pleading redacted so as to preserve confidential information and (b) an unredacted version marked as confidential and sealed in an envelope also marked as confidential and seek an order by letter, copied to the other party and any relevant third parties, that the access to the Court file be restricted. Wherever possible, confidential information should be contained in a self-contained schedule or annex. Where a pleading is served electronically, the party serving it should ensure that redaction is effective and should give consideration to methods of protecting confidentiality, such as password protection. The continued arrangements to protect confidentiality should be addressed at the first CMC pursuant to paragraph 22 below.

JUDICIAL REVIEW

12. Sometimes claimants find it necessary to bring proceedings for Judicial Review in the Administrative Court as well as issuing a claim under the Regulations in the TCC. This usually happens where the claimant's right to bring a claim under the Regulations is or may be disputed, but there may be other reasons.

13. Where this happens the claim for Judicial Review will, unless otherwise ordered by the Judge in Charge of either the Administrative Court or the TCC, be heard and case managed together with the related claim in the TCC before a TCC judge who is also a designated judge of the Administrative Court.

14. In this situation claimants are to take the following steps:

1) At the time of issuing the claim form in the Administrative Court the claimant's solicitors are to write to the Administrative Court Office, with a copy to the Judges in Charge of both the Administrative Court and the TCC, to request that the claim be heard alongside the related claim in the TCC.
2) The letter is to be clearly marked

   "URGENT REQUEST FOR THE HEARING OF A PUBLIC PROCUREMENT CLAIM BY A JUDGE OF THE TCC WHO IS A DESIGNATED JUDGE OF THE ADMINISTRATIVE COURT"
3) If they are not notified within 3 days of the issue of the claim form that the papers will be transferred to the TCC, the claimant's solicitors should contact the Administrative Court Office and thereafter keep the TCC informed of the position.

15. This procedure is to apply only when claim forms are issued by the same claimant against the same defendant in both the Administrative Court and the TCC almost simultaneously (in other words, within 48 hours of each other, excluding non-working days).

---

[1] *Roche Diagnostics Limited v the Mid Yorkshire Hospitals NHS Trust* [2013] EWHC 933

[2] *Heron Bros. Ltd. V Central Bedfordshire Borough Council* [2015] EWHC 604 (TCC)

16. When the papers are transferred to the TCC by the Administrative Court Office the Judge in Charge of the TCC will review the papers immediately to ensure that it is appropriate for the two claims to be case managed and/or heard together by a judge of the Administrative Court who is also a judge of the TCC.

17. The Judge in Charge of the TCC will then notify the claimants and the Administrative Court Office whether or not both claims should proceed in the TCC. If it appears that the claim for Judicial Review should not be heard by a judge of the TCC, the Judge in Charge of the TCC will, after consultation with the Judge in Charge of the Administrative Court, transfer the case back to the Administrative Court and give his/her reasons for doing so.

18. If it is directed that the claim for Judicial Review should be heard by a judge of the TCC, the Judge in Charge of the TCC will ensure that the application for permission to apply for Judicial Review is determined at the earliest opportunity by a judge of the TCC who is also a designated judge of the Administrative Court.

19. If permission is granted, the claim will be case managed and heard by a TCC judge who is a designated judge of the Administrative Court, save that routine directions may, if it is appropriate and expedient to do so, be given by a judge of the TCC who is not a designated charge of the Administrative Court.

20. At all stages of the proceedings the titles of all documents filed in the JR proceedings are to bear the Administrative Court title and case number and are to state that the claim is being heard and managed together with TCC Case No HT-[]-[].

CMC

21. An early CMC may be appropriate, so that the Court may assess the urgency and fix appropriate dates for trial, specific anticipated applications (such as applications for lifting the statutory suspension, or applications for specific disclosure or expedited trial) and other stages of trial or other matters such as disclosure, witness statements and expert reports (the deployment of expert evidence will require clear justification). Either party may request the Court to fix the first CMC and the Court will endeavour to accommodate such requests.

22. The parties should be aware of the pilot scheme for Shorter and Flexible Trial Procedures and Practice Direction 51N and to address their minds to the question of whether either scheme might be appropriate for their case. These issues should be addressed at the first CMC.

COST BUDGETING

23. The provisions in the CPR about preparation of costs budgets (CPR Part 3.13 and Practice Direction 3E) and electronic disclosure (Practice Direction 31B) apply. However, if there is uncertainty as to the course the proceedings may take so that it is not possible to prepare a realistic costs budget, or if the speed at which proceedings are being pursued is such that there is insufficient time for the parties to prepare and file sensible costs budgets or to take the steps required in connection with electronic disclosure in time for the CMC fixed by the Court, it is recommended that the claimant apply to the Court in writing, either before or at the same time as applying to fix the CMC, for an urgent order that the parties do not have to serve costs budgets 7 days before the CMC or dis-applying the provisions of 31BPD.4 in relation to disclosure of electronic documents. Unless one party objects, the Court will deal with such applications on paper.

SPECIFIC AND EARLY DISCLOSURE

24. Early disclosure may be justified to enable the claimant to plead its case properly or to secure finalised pleadings if and when expedited trials are ordered.

25. Contracting authorities are encouraged to provide their key decision making materials at a very early stage of proceedings or during any pre-action correspondence. This may include the documentation referred to in Regulation 84 of the Public Contracts Regulations 2015 ("the 2015 Regulations").

26. The question of disclosure will be considered at the first CMC. Applications which are likely to be contested should be brought on promptly; early hearings can be fixed if required. The parties' attention is drawn to the general provisions on disclosure in this Guide at Section 11 and to the protocol for e-disclosure prepared by TeCSA of 9 January 2015.

CONFIDENTIALITY GENERALLY

27. Public procurement claims frequently involve the disclosure of, and reliance upon, confidential information. Confidentiality is not a bar to disclosure.[1] However, the need to protect confidential information needs to be balanced by the basic principle of open justice. Managing the use of confidential information in the proceedings tends to increase both the cost and complexity of the litigation. The Court will seek to manage the proceedings so that confidentiality is protected where genuinely necessary but ensuring that the issue of confidentiality does not give rise to unnecessary cost or complexity. Assertions of confidentiality should only be made where properly warranted.

---

[1] *Science Research Council v Nasse* [1980] AC 1028.

28. Once a case has been allocated to a particular TCC judge, papers and communications, particularly those which are to be treated as confidential, should generally be passed through the relevant Judge's Clerk to limit the risk of inadvertent disclosure.

29. Papers delivered to and communications with the Court and the Judge's Clerk should be marked as "Confidential" if they are confidential.

30. It is recommended that documents containing confidential material are provided on coloured paper so that their confidential status is immediately apparent (practitioners are asked to take care that the print remains legible when printed on a coloured background). Where relevant, the level of confidentiality should be identified either by a stamp or mark (e.g. "Confidential 1st Tier") or by a particular colour of paper.[1]

31. Where necessary to protect confidential information the Court may, if requested, make an order restricting inspection of the Court files. Requests to restrict inspection should only be made where necessary. Any member of the public may seek an order from the Court varying any such restrictions. Consideration should be given to providing appropriately redacted pleadings for the Court file so as to permit public access to them. As to the management of confidential information in pleadings generally, see paragraph 11 above.

REDACTIONS

32. Redaction of disclosed documents, statements or pleadings can be justified on the grounds that the redactions cover privileged and/or confidential material. In the latter case, redactions may be justified to enable documents to be more widely disclosable to people outside any confidentiality rings. In such cases, a schedule should be prepared which explains the justification for the redactions. The schedule should list the information in respect of which confidential treatment is claimed and the reasons for the claim for confidentiality. The schedule should contain two columns: the first giving the relevant page and paragraph reference (a line number should be added if there are a number of pieces of confidential information in one paragraph in the document concerned); and the second setting out the reasons for asserting confidentiality. For example:

Document Title	
Location in Document	***Reason for assertion of confidentiality***
Page 15, paragraph 4.2	The deleted material relates to ABC Limited's confidential costs and prices The information is in the nature of a business secret

33. Save in exceptional circumstances or where redacted material is irrelevant, the Court should, at the appropriate stage, be provided with the redacted documents also in unredacted form with the redactions highlighted in a prominent colour which does not obscure the information beneath it, together with the schedule of redactions. This can be important on specific disclosure applications as well as at trial. Each page of the document must include the header "CONTAINS CONFIDENTIAL INFORMATION".

CONFIDENTIALITY RINGS AND UNDERTAKINGS

34. Confidentiality rings may be established where necessary to facilitate the disclosure of confidential information. A confidentiality ring comprises persons to whom documents containing confidential information may be disclosed on the basis of their undertakings to preserve confidentiality.

35. It is highly desirable that any confidentiality ring is established as early as feasible. Agreements or proposals for confidentiality rings, their scope and limitations should be put before the Court at the first CMC or application for specific disclosure, whichever is earlier, with explanations as to why they are justified. The Court may make orders implementing, approving or amending the parties' agreements or proposals.

36. The terms of any confidentiality ring will depend on the circumstances of the particular case, including the matters in dispute and the nature of the material to be disclosed. Generally, however, it will be necessary to determine (1) who should be admitted to the ring and (2) the terms of the undertakings which any members of the ring may be required to give.

37. As to personnel, a party's external legal advisors (solicitors and counsel) will need to be admitted to any ring that is established.

38. Parties, and in particular the claimant, may also wish to include certain of their own employees in the ring, who may be in house lawyers or other personnel. This will usually be for the purpose of understanding material disclosed into the ring and/or for giving instructions to external lawyers.

39. Where a party proposes to admit an employee representative, and the ring contains material

[1] As to the use of tiers in confidentiality rings see paragraphs 41 and 42

which is confidential to a commercial competitor of that party, relevant factors are likely to include that party's right to pursue its claim, the principle of open justice, the confidential nature of the document and the need to avoid distortions of competition and/or the creation of unfair advantages in the market (including any retender) as a result of disclosure.

40. In considering whether a particular person should be admitted to the ring, the Court will take account of his/her role and responsibilities within the organisation; the extent of the risk that competition will be distorted as a result of disclosure to them; the extent to which that risk can be avoided or controlled by restrictions on the terms of disclosure; and the impact that any proposed restrictions would have on that individual (for example by prohibiting them from participating in a re-tender or future tenders for a period of time).

41. In order to manage these risks employee representatives may be admitted to a confidentiality ring on different terms from external representatives. Employee representatives may also have access to some but not all of the material disclosed into the ring (for example, technical material but not pricing information). This is sometimes referred to as a "two tier" ring.

42. Under an alternative form of two tier ring, the external representatives of a party in the first tier may apply for an employee representative in the second tier to have access to a particular document or documents, whether in open form or partly redacted. One way of dealing with this is for notice to be given to any person affected by the proposed disclosure, identifying the document, the form in which its disclosure to members of the second tier is sought, and the reasons why disclosure to the second tier is sought, and for the person affected to consent or object within a fixed time. The person or persons affected may be the contracting authority and/or the owner of the confidential information. In cases subject to expedition the period for response may be short and, in appropriate cases, less than a working day. Two tier rings necessarily introduce additional cost and complexity and will need to be justified in the circumstances.

43. Other specialist advisors (such as accountants or those with other expertise) may also be admitted to the ring if that is demonstrated to be necessary, either in lieu of or in addition to employee representatives.[1]

44. As to the terms of disclosure, the Court will order that confidential documents, information or pleadings are only to be provided to members of the ring if undertakings are given to the Court. Such undertakings will preclude the use of the relevant material other than for the purposes of the proceedings and prevent disclosure outside the ring. They will also contain provisions controlling the terms on which confidential information must be stored and the making of copies, and requiring the receiving person to either return or destroy the documents in question, or render them practically inaccessible, at the conclusion of the proceedings.

45. Additional undertakings may be required, particularly where there are concerns that disclosure could have an impact on competition and/or any subsequent procurement. These may include terms:

1) Preventing employee representatives from holding copies of documents at their place of work and requiring them to inspect the material at a defined location (such as the offices of their external lawyers);
2) Limiting the involvement of a recipient of a document in any re-procurement of the contract which is the subject of the litigation;
3) Limiting the role which a recipient can play in competitions for other similar contracts for a fixed period of time in a defined geographic area; and/or
4) Preventing the recipient from advising on or having any involvement in certain matters, again for a fixed period of time.

46. Whilst the Court will give weight to the need to protect competition in the market, the more onerous the proposed restriction is, the more clearly it will need to be justified. Further, the terms of the ring will need to be workable taking account of the timetable for the litigation, including any order for expedition.

47. Confidentiality rings will also contain provisions which establish how confidential information is to be identified as such, and how claims to confidentiality may be challenged.

48. Where documents are disclosed into the ring in confidential form, further non-confidential versions of those documents should also be disclosed with necessary redactions.

SUSPENSION LIFTING APPLICATIONS

49. The Court can lift the statutory suspension that prevents the contracting authority from entering into the contract in question. The timing of the application is a matter for the applicant but, if urgency in placing the contract is to form part of any balance of convenience test, the application needs to be brought on expeditiously. However, enough time needs to be provided for the respondent to submit evidence and for there to be any evidence in reply before any hearing.

50. If the Court orders that the suspension is to be lifted a stay of such an order will only be granted when it is appropriate to do so. The Court, if it considers that a stay is appropriate, and particularly when it has refused permission to appeal, will give consideration to a short stay of 1-2

[1] The provision of such advice is to be distinguished from acting as an expert witness.

working days to enable the applicant to seek expedited permission and to enable the Court of Appeal to set a timetable; such a stay will often be accompanied by a requirement that any application for permission or for an extended stay should be on notice to the other party, to enable it to make representations to the Court of Appeal.

INTERESTED PARTIES

51. Procurement claims frequently engage the interests of parties other than the claimant and the contracting authority ("interested parties"; in this protocol the term "interested party" is given a wider meaning than in CPR Part 54).

52. In particular, the successful bidder may be affected by the relief sought in a procurement claim, which typically claims an order setting aside the award decision in his favour. The successful bidder may also be affected by the disclosure of confidential information contained in his bid, as may other unsuccessful bidders.

53. Whilst an interested party may apply to become a full party to the proceedings, its interests can usually be considered and addressed by the Court without that being necessary.

54. The claimant and the defendant should take steps to ensure that an interested party is on notice of matters which affect its interests. It will often be appropriate for the defendant to ensure that other bidding parties are given such notice. However, particularly where applications are made as a matter of urgency, it may be appropriate for the claimant to ensure that the interested party has been given appropriate notice.

55. In order to allow an interested party to consider its position, it may be necessary to provide it with copies of any pleadings, redacted if necessary, any relevant application, supporting evidence and/or other relevant documentation.

56. An interested party needs to apply to be represented (if it so wishes) as soon as practicable. A written application, which may take the form of a letter to the Court, should be sent to the Court and served on all litigation parties (and any other interested parties). The application should clearly indicate the scope of the interested party's proposed involvement. If the interested party's involvement is agreed with the litigation parties, then that should be made clear in the application. In general, the Court will expect to hear from interested parties who are affected by an application or claim.

57. The Court may direct that an interested party is to be treated as a respondent to an application (CPR 23.1) but a direction to this effect is not essential, particularly in cases of urgency. The Court may order that an interested party is permitted or entitled to participate in particular applications, hearings or issues and/or may order that the involvement of the interested party is to be limited in defined respects.

58. If expedition so demands, the application for the interested party to be represented may be heard immediately before the relevant substantive application. However, earlier resolution is preferable to allow orderly preparation for hearings and the preparation of relevant evidence or submissions.

59. Attention is drawn to the requirement under Regulation 47F(3) of the Public Contracts Regulations (As Amended) 2006 and Regulation 94(3) of the Public Contracts Regulations 2015 to the requirement to give notice to the party to whom the contract was awarded in relation to claims for ineffectiveness.

60. Other interested parties who may express interest in procurement claims include sector regulators, competition authorities and/or sub-contractors, and the Court will give directions in relation to their involvement as appropriate.

61. An interested party can recover or be required to pay costs.[1]

EXPEDITION

62. Article 1 of Directive 89/665/EC (as amended by Article 1 of Directive 2007/66/EC) requires member states to ensure that decisions taken by contracting authorities may be reviewed "as rapidly as possible". Particularly in cases where the automatic suspension has been maintained, and subject to the principles set out in paragraph 1.1.4 of this Guide, the TCC is likely to support (and in appropriate cases may impose) rapid progress to a trial as early as is practicable. An expedited trial may in particular be appropriate where it will enable the contracting authority to enter into the contract without undue disruption to its timetable, or where the automatic suspension is maintained following an application for its termination.

63. In considering whether the trial should be expedited, it will be necessary to consider how the required procedural steps will be accomplished within the abbreviated timetable. In particular, adequate time will be required for disclosure and for the hearing of any interim applications which are expected. The Court may use its powers to control and define the scope of disclosure in cases where expedition is ordered.

64. The party applying for an expedited trial should do so on notice and at as early a stage as is

---

[1] See e.g. Section 51(3) of the Senior Courts Act 1981 and *Bolton Metropolitan District Council v The Secretary of State for the Environment* [995] 1 W.L.R. 1176.

practicable. The party applying should set out the reasons why expedited trial is appropriate and the party's proposals for the management of procedural steps. The Court should be provided with details of any third parties affected and third parties (in particular the successful tenderer) should be put on notice of the application. Where appropriate it will be part of the agenda for the first CMC.

TRIAL

65. Consideration needs to be given to confidentiality in terms of what may be reported, whether there should be restricted access to the Court recording of the proceedings and who can be present in the courtroom. The Court will as a matter of generality require as much of the trial as possible to be open to all who wish to attend and limit restrictions to those which are legitimate, fair and proportionate.

JUDGMENTS

66. Judgments in procurement cases will be handed down as open documents, save in the most exceptional circumstances (for instance in cases involving Official Secrets). Any confidential information will usually be contained in a separate schedule to the judgment (or such other form as appropriate) which will not be available more widely than the membership of any confidentiality ring (if applicable) without an order of the Court. Counsel should co-operate through the Judge's Clerk to agree what may be made publicly available.

APPENDIX I

GENERAL GUIDANCE ON STATEMENTS OF CASE

2C-160 **1.** The following principles apply to all statements of case. They should, as far as possible, also be observed when drafting a Part 8 claim form.

a) The document must be as concise as possible.
b) The document must be set out in separate consecutively numbered paragraphs and sub-paragraphs.
c) The document must deal with the case on a point by point basis to allow a point by point response. In particular, each separate cause of action, or defence, should be pleaded separately wherever possible.
d) So far as possible each paragraph or sub-paragraph should contain no more than one allegation.
e) Special care should be taken to set out (with proper particulars) only those factual allegations which are necessary to establish the cause of action, defence, or point of reply being advanced ("primary allegations"), to enable the other party to know what case it has to meet. Evidence should not be included, and a general factual narrative is neither required nor helpful (and is likely to contravene paragraphs (f), (h) and/or (k) below).
f) Particulars of primary allegations should be stated as particulars and not appear as if they are primary allegations.
(g) A party wishing to advance a positive case must set that case out; and reasons must be set out for any denial of an allegation.
h) Where particulars are given of any allegation or reasons are given for a denial, the allegation or denial should be stated first and the particulars or reasons for it listed one by one in separate numbered sub-paragraphs.
i) Where they will assist:
   i) headings should be used; and
   ii) abbreviations and definitions should be established and used, and a glossary annexed.
j) Contentious headings, abbreviations and definitions should not be used. Every effort should be made to ensure that headings, abbreviations and definitions are in a form that will enable them to be adopted without issue by the other parties.
k) Where it is necessary to give lengthy particulars of an allegation, these should be set out in schedules or appendices.
l) A response to particulars set out in a schedule should be set out in a corresponding schedule.
m) Where it is necessary for the proper understanding of the statement of case to include substantial parts of a lengthy document the passages in question should be set out in a schedule rather than in the body of the statement of case.
n) Contentious paraphrasing should be avoided.
o) The document must be signed by the individual person or persons who drafted it, not, in the case of a solicitor, in the name of the firm alone.

2. There is no general rule or maximum length for statements of case. It is recognised that some TCC cases by their nature require more detailed particulars of allegations than other cases.

Where practicable, consideration should be given to the use of schedules and appendices to ensure that excessive detail does not detract from an understanding of the essential facts necessary for the purpose of formulating a complete cause of action set out in the body of the pleading.

3. Particulars of Claim, the Defence (and Counterclaim) and any Reply must comply with the provisions of CPR 16.4 and 16.5.

4. Where the Disclosure Practice Direction (PD57AD) applies, Initial Disclosure must accompany each statement of case in accordance with paragraph 5.1 of PF57AD unless the parties have agreed to dispense with it or the court has ordered that it is not required.

5. If the Disclosure Pilot does not apply or Initial Disclosure under it has been dispensed with by agreement or order, then:

a) if any documents are to be served at the same time as a statement of case they should normally be served separately from rather than attached to the statement of case;

b) only those documents which are of central importance and necessary for a proper understanding of the statement of case should be attached to or served with it; and

c) the statement of case must itself refer to the fact that documents are attached to or served with it.

6. Particulars of claim, a defence and any reply must be verified by a statement of truth, as must any amendment, unless the Court otherwise orders: CPR 22.1.

APPENDIX J

GENERAL GUIDANCE ON ELECTRONIC COURT BUNDLES

This general guidance is intended to ensure a level of consistency in the provision of electronic bundles ("e-bundles") for court hearings (but not tribunal hearings) in a format that promotes the efficient preparation for, and management of, a hearing. It is subject to any specific guidance by particular courts or directions given for individual cases. It updates and replaces previous guidance published in May 2020. **2C-161**

1. E-bundles must be provided in pdf format.

2. All pages in an e-bundle must be numbered by computer-generated numbering, not by hand. The numbering should start at page 1 for the first page of the bundle (whether or not that is part of an index) and the numbering must follow sequentially to the last page of the bundle, so that the pagination matches the pdf numbering. If a hard copy of the bundle is produced, the pagination must match the e-bundle.

3. Each entry in the index must be hyperlinked to the indexed document. All significant documents and all sections in bundles must be bookmarked for ease of navigation, with a short description as the bookmark. The bookmark should contain the page number of the document.

4. All pages in an e-bundle that contain typed text must be subject to OCR (optical character recognition) if they have not been created directly as electronic text documents. This makes it easier to search for text, to highlight parts of a page, and to copy text from the bundle.

5. Any page that has been created in landscape orientation should appear in that orientation so that it can be read from left to right. No page should appear upside down.

6. The default view for all pages should be 100%.

7. If a core bundle is required, then a PDF core bundle should be produced complying with the same requirements as a paper bundle.

8. Thought should be given to the number of bundles required. It is usually better to have a single hearing e-bundle and (where appropriate) a separate single authorities e-bundle (compiled in accordance with these requirements), rather than multiple bundles (and follow any applicable court specific guidance - see eg CPR PD52C Section VII).

9. The resolution of the bundle should not be greater than 300 dpi, in order to avoid slow scrolling or rendering. The bundle should be electronically optimised so as to ensure that the file size is not larger than necessary.

10. If a bundle is to be added to after it has been transmitted to the judge, then new pages should be added at the end of the bundle (and paginated accordingly). An enquiry should be made of the court as to the best way of providing the additional material. Subject to any different direction, the judge should be provided with both (a) the new section and, separately, (b) the revised bundle. This is because the judge may have already marked up the original bundle.

DELIVERING E-BUNDLES

Filename:

The filename for a bundle must contain the case reference and a short version of the name of the case and an indication of the content of the bundle - eg "CO12342021 Carpenters v Adventurers Hearing Bundle" or "CO12342021 Carpenters v Adventurers Authorities Bundle".

Email:

If the bundle is to be sent by email, please ensure the file size is not too large. For justice.gov e-mail addresses the maximum size of email and attachments is 36Mb in aggregate. Anything larger will be rejected. The subject line of the email should contain the case number, short form case name, hearing date and name of judge (if known).

Uploading bundles:

Bundles should be sent to the court in accordance with the court's directions. Where the bundle would otherwise be sent by email (rather than being uploaded to a portal) but is too large to be sent under cover of a single email then it may be be sent to the Document Upload Centre by prior arrangement with the court - for instructions see the Professional Users Guide.

UNREPRESENTED LITIGANTS

Ordinarily the applicant is responsible for preparing the court bundles. If the applicant is unrepresented then the bundles must still if at all possible, comply with the above requirements. If it is not possible for an unrepresented litigant to comply with the requirements then a brief explanation of the reasons for this should be provided to the court as far in advance of the hearing as possible. Where possible the litigant in person should suggest a practical way of overcoming the problem. If the other party is represented then that party should consider offering to prepare the bundle.

OTHER INTERNET GUIDANCE

There is guidance available freely available on the internet on how to use software to create bundles.

APPENDIX K

THE BPC PROTOCOL FOR REMOTE AND HYBRID HEARINGS

INTRODUCTION TO THIS PROTOCOL

2C-162 **1.** This Protocol contains guidance on preparing for and conducting Remote and Hybrid Hearings in the Business and Property Courts. It is relevant to hearings of all kinds, including but not limited to trials, applications and those in which litigants in person are involved. It does not set out the circumstances in which the Court may consider it appropriate to order a Remote or Hybrid Hearing.

2. The Protocol is intended to assist judges and court users but it should be applied flexibly. It remains the case that the manner in which all hearings are conducted is a matter for individual judges, acting in accordance with applicable law, the Civil Procedure Rules (the 'CPR') and Practice Directions. Nothing in this Protocol derogates from the judge's duty to determine all issues that arise in the case judicially and in accordance with normal principles. A hearing conducted in accordance with this Protocol should, however, be treated for all other purposes as a hearing in accordance with the CPR.

3. The following defined terms are used in this Protocol:

a) A 'Hybrid Hearing' is a hearing in which some Participants, together with the judge(s), are physically present in a courtroom, while other Participants attend the hearing by telephone or video link.

b) A 'Remote Hearing' is a hearing in which all Participants, and the judge(s), attend the hearing from separate locations by telephone or video link, instead of gathering physically in a courtroom.

c) A 'Participant' means a party to the proceedings (meaning, in the case of corporate entities, a representative of the entity), a legal representative of a party, any person or entity instructed for the purposes of the hearing by a party, a witness, or an expert.

d) A 'Speaker' means a legal representative of a party, a witness, an expert and any other attendee who is required to present, respond, and/or give oral evidence at a Remote or Hybrid Hearing.

e) A 'Working Day' means every day except weekends and public holidays in England and Wales.

4. The general rule is that all court hearings, including Remote and Hybrid Hearings, are in public. This can be achieved in a number of ways. These include, without limitation, the Court directing that:

a) the audio and (if available) video of the hearing be relayed to an open courtroom,

b) a media representative be allowed to access the Remote or Hybrid Hearing, and/or

c) the hearing be live-streamed over the internet, where such a broadcast is authorised in legislation (such as s85A of the Courts Act 2003).

5. Where this is not practicable, the Court may direct that a Remote Hearing must take place in private where this is necessary to secure the proper administration of justice (CPR Practice Direction 51Y). This is in addition to the requirement that a hearing (howsoever conducted) be held in private where the Court is satisfied that it is necessary in order to secure the proper administration of justice (CPR 39.2(3)(g)).

6. The unauthorised recording or transmission of a hearing is an offence. The taking of photographs (including screen shots) or the recording or transmission of someone taking part in a Remote Hearing is also prohibited. However, Remote and Hybrid Hearings will be recorded by the Court, unless a recording has been dispensed with under CPR 39.9(1).

PREPARING FOR A REMOTE OF HYBRID HEARING

GENERAL POINTS

7. In order to function effectively, Remote Hearings and, in particular, Hybrid Hearings require a high degree of preparation and co-operation between the parties and the Court.

8. Whether a hearing will take place as a Remote Hearing or a Hybrid Hearing is a decision for the Court. Where a party believes that a Remote or Hybrid Hearing would be appropriate, they should discuss and if possible agree the question with the other parties and then raise it with the Court:

a) at or in advance of the PTR, if there is one; or
b) where no PTR has been fixed, in correspondence in good time before the hearing.

9. At the time a Remote or Hybrid Hearing is requested, the parties should co-perate with each other in order to inform the Court of any matters which they wish the Court to reflect in any directions it may give, including (without limitation):

a) any support or adjustments which any Participant would require in order to participate in and/or attend a Remote or Hybrid Hearing; and
b) any proposal to instruct a third party provider to facilitate the Remote or Hybrid Hearing (see the section on 'Third party providers' below for more guidance).

10. The Court may order a Remote or Hybrid Hearing and give directions for its conduct in whatever manner appears to it appropriate including at any PTR, at a short case management conference convened for the purpose, or on paper. In any event, the Court's listing office or judge's clerk will seek to contact the parties and/or their legal representatives in advance of a Remote or Hybrid Hearing to inform them of the time and date for the hearing as well as the format and the platform for the hearing.

11. Where a Hybrid Hearings is ordered, parties and/or their legal representatives should liaise with the Court's listing office or judge's clerk in advance of the hearing as to:

i) the number of courtrooms that will be available for the hearing and their capacity; and
ii) what extra equipment and preparation will be required to facilitate the Hybrid Hearing.

12. The Court's listing office or judge's clerk will seek to ensure that the parties are informed, as far in advance as possible, of the identity of the judge(s) hearing the case.

ATTENDANCE

13. Subject to applicable law, it is for the Court to determine who may attend a Remote or Hybrid Hearing and to set such conditions for their attendance as it may consider appropriate. No person may access a Remote or Hybrid Hearing remotely without the Court's permission. Unauthorised access may constitute an offence under section 41 of the Criminal Justice Act 1925 and section 9 of the Contempt of Court Act 1981.

14. In all cases, parties must inform the Court in advance of whom they wish to attend the hearing, following the procedure set out in the following paragraphs.

15. The Court may permit a person outside England and Wales to attend a Remote Hearing as a Participant where it considers that appropriate. The Court has no express power to allow the broadcasting of a Hybrid Hearing to persons outside England and Wales. However, that does not prevent the Court permitting Participants to attend such a hearing from outside England and Wales. The onus is on the relevant Participant to ensure that such attendance is not in breach of any local laws or regulations and that, if permission is required from the local court or other authority in the foreign jurisdiction, such permission has been obtained (and see paragraph 34 below in relation to witnesses attending a hearing from abroad).

16. The parties or their legal representatives should, before the Remote or Hybrid Hearing, provide the Court's listing office or judge's clerk with the following details for each Participant who wishes to attend:

a) name;
b) organisation;
c) email address;
d) the location, including country, from which they would be joining the hearing (in this regard, parties should note paragraph 15 above); and
e) whether it is proposed that the person in question be a Speaker.

In the ordinary course, the parties should provide the information sought in this paragraph no later than 10.30am two working days before the hearing.

17. In addition, each party should nominate one of its proposed Participants as its 'Primary Contact', being the person who should be contacted in accordance with the lost connections procedure set out at paragraph 31 below.

18. A member of the public or media representative who wishes to attend a Remote or Hybrid Hearing must notify the Court by email of the details set out in subsections (a) to (d) of paragraph 16 above using the contact details set out in the Daily Cause List or the Hearing Notice.

19. If the Court is satisfied that the requirements of paragraph 16 have been met in relation to any person, it will seek to facilitate attendance by that person at the Remote or Hybrid Hearing. However:

a) there is no absolute right to attend a Remote or Hybrid Hearing;
b) failure to give timely notice of a wish to attend may mean that attendance cannot be facilitated; and
c) access cannot in any event be guaranteed; the needs of other litigants, the limits on resources and the need to monitor the identities of those who view the proceedings may mean that the Court is not able to provide access.

20. For hearings conducted by audio link:

a) either the Court (or a third party provider authorised by the Court) will call the parties at the time of the hearing or the parties should dial in to the hearing using the information provided in the invitation to join the remote hearing. In order to attend and/or participate in a telephone hearing, Participants will require access to a telephone with any relevant call barring services switched off; or
b) the Court will notify the parties that they are to dial in to the hearing on a video or audio conferencing platform, in which case the Court will, no later than two working days before the hearing, provide the relevant telephone number and access code.

21. For hearings conducted by video link, the Court's listing office or judge's clerk will send the parties information about the video hearing, including a link to access the hearing and any sign in details, no later than one working day before the hearing. In order to attend and/or participate in a hearing conducted by video link, Participants will require access to a device with internet access, which enables audio and video transmission.

22. A link provided to a Participant is for their own use. No-one who is provided with a link may forward it to any other person without the Court's permission.

23. Available platforms for Remote and Hybrid Hearings conducted via telephone conference include (non-exhaustively): BT conference call, BT MeetMe, Microsoft Teams and ordinary telephone call. Available methods for videoconferences include (non-exhaustively): Microsoft Teams, Cloud Video Platform (CVP), Video Hearing Service (VHS), court video link, and Zoom. But any communication method available to the Participants can be considered if appropriate.

24. For video conferences, it is usually possible for the parties and/or their representatives to contact the Court's listing office or judge's clerk to arrange a test call. The test call should be conducted with a maximum of 10 users. In any event, Participants are advised to test their own devices and ensure they are able to access the relevant platform in advance of the hearing. Any technological issues should be made known to the Court's listing office or judge's clerk in advance of the hearing.

25. Parties and/or their legal representatives should notify the Court's listing office or judge's clerk no later than two working days before the video hearing if telephone dial-in facilities are required for Participants without internet access.

CONDUCT OF THE HEARING

26. Participants should join the hearing no later than 15 minutes before the set start time.

27. Remote and Hybrid Hearings should resemble courtroom hearings as closely as practicable. This means maintaining the same level of formality as is expected in the courtroom.

28. Subject to any contrary or more detailed direction of the Court, Participants should observe the following etiquette:

a) All persons who are not Speakers should keep their microphones muted and cameras switched off throughout the hearing.
b) Speakers should keep their cameras turned on and mute their microphones when they are not speaking.
c) A Participant who is not a Speaker may not address the Court without the Court's prior permission.
d) Where possible, Speakers should ensure their cameras are at eye level and should maintain a reasonable distance from the camera (with a plain background behind them) in order to ensure their head and upper body are clearly visible. Speakers may wear headsets if they wish.
e) Speakers should try to attend the hearing from a quiet place from which privacy and minimal noise disruptions can be ensured.
f) Reasonable and proportionate and noise-free use of devices to enable communication between team members or legal representatives and their clients is permitted during the hearing, provided that this does not interfere with the hearing; in particular, Participants

must ensure that all notifications are set to silent for the duration of the hearing. However, Participants are reminded that witnesses must not communicate with anyone else about their evidence until their testimony is concluded. See the section below titled 'Witnesses, experts and other third parties' for further guidance.

29. It is the responsibility of each party and/or their legal representatives to inform those attending the Remote or Hybrid Hearing (including any person or entity engaged to provide technical support or assistance) of the strict prohibitions against any unauthorised dissemination of the hearing and the making of any sound or video recording of it (and of any other restrictions outlined in the relevant court order), in addition to the other obligations set out in this section.

30. In the event of an internet or phone line disconnection or degrading to an unusable degree during the Remote or Hybrid Hearing, the Court's listing office or judge's clerk will contact the Primary Contact for each party to discuss whether a continuation is possible or whether an adjournment of the hearing is required.

WITNESSES, EXPERTS AND OTHER THIRD PARTIES

31. Where a witness gives evidence by video or audio link in a Remote or Hybrid Hearing, the objective should be to make the process as close as possible to the usual practice in an in-person hearing where evidence is taken in open court.

32. In such cases, guidance should be taken from **Annex 3 to Practice Direction 32** which addresses videoconferencing.

33. In particular, parties should be aware that where evidence is to be taken from a witness located outside the jurisdiction, permission may be required from the local court or other authority in the foreign jurisdiction. It is for the party calling the witness to ensure that such permission, if required, is obtained in good time for the hearing at which the witness is to give evidence and to inform the Court that such permission has been obtained.

34. If a party wishes one or more of its witnesses to give their evidence from the offices of a legal representative, that party should notify the other parties at the earliest opportunity, with a view to permitting a representative of the other parties to attend or making arrangements to ensure that the Court can ascertain that the witness is not communicating with any other person or otherwise receiving assistance during the course of their evidence.

35. In some cases, it may be appropriate to arrange to have more than one camera available in the location from which the witness is giving their evidence to ensure that impermissible reference to notes, prompting etc. is not taking place.

36. Witnesses must only have access to a device on which they access and participate in the hearing, the hearing bundle and their statement(s) and exhibit (either in electronic or hard copy, or both). The Court will expect the parties to have made efforts to ensure that each witness has access to these materials in a format which is convenient and accessible to the witness. In some cases it may be more appropriate for a witness to have access to a hard copy bundle whether they are participating remotely or in person.

37. Where a witness has access to the hearing bundle only in electronic form, and the witness is asked a question about a document appearing in the bundle, the Court and the advocates should ensure that the witness is given a proper opportunity to orientate or familiarise themselves with the document (for instance by being shown the front page, or the pages before/after the section they are being asked about) before answering.

38. Parties and/or their legal representatives should ensure that witnesses decide in good time before the hearing whether they prefer to swear an oath on a holy book/scripture or to make an affirmation. The relevant holy book/scripture or text of the affirmation should be made available to the witness in advance of the hearing.

39. Parties are reminded that it will be for the parties to provide the necessary facilities to enable the witness to access the hearing bundle in electronic format even if the hearing takes place in a court room.

BUNDLES / DOCUMENTS FOR THE HEARING

40. The claimant should, if necessary, prepare an electronic bundle of documents and an electronic bundle of authorities for each Remote or Hybrid Hearing. Each electronic bundle should be compiled, formatted and delivered in accordance with the relevant court's guide.

41. To the greatest extent practicable, all bundles should be electronic, not hard copy (subject to paragraph 37). However, parties or their legal representatives should liaise with the Court in advance of the hearing to determine whether the Judge's preferences in the matter.

THIRD PARTY PROVIDERS

TRANSCRIBERS

42. Hearings in the Business and Property Courts are tape-recorded or digitallyrecorded by the Court unless the judge directs otherwise (CPR 39.9(1)). A party may, after a hearing, require a transcript to be produced by a court-approved transcriber. Form **EX107** should be completed and submitted to the Court. The **Guidance Notes to Form EX107** set out the procedure to be followed, a list of approved transcribers and the relevant charges.

43. Parties may, with the prior permission of the Court, engage court-approved transcribers to prepare a real-time transcript of a hearing. The Court's permission will be recorded in an Order which may also, without limitation, regulate the dissemination of the real-time transcript. The requesting party and the transcriber they wish to instruct must also submit to the Court a completed Form **EX107** OFC. A copy of the Court's Order must be provided to the transcribers.

HEARING SUPPORT SERVICES

44. The scale or logistical complexity of some Remote or Hybrid Hearings may lead the parties to consider engaging a specialist third party to provide technical support services. These services can include the selection and operation of hardware and/or software necessary to support the hearing itself and/or electronic document management.

45. Permission to engage such third-party providers must be sought from the Court in advance of the hearing. The parties and/or their legal representatives bear the responsibility of informing the relevant representatives from the third-party provider of any requirements and/or prohibitions set out in the relevant Court order, in addition to the strict prohibition against making any unauthorised dissemination or recording of the hearing by any electronic means and that failure to comply could result in them being found in contempt of court and liable to criminal penalties.

INTERPRETERS

46. Where a Participant or Participants require an interpreter, a request should be made to the Court in advance of the hearing. Parties or their legal representatives should provide the Court with the details in paragraph 17 for the interpreter as relevant. If possible, parties or their legal representatives should try to arrange a test call with the interpreter and relevant witness in advance of the hearing. All Participants are reminded that using remote interpretation services may cause delays and/or technical difficulties and are encouraged to be mindful of this.

47. Where a witness is to give evidence remotely by an interpreter, consideration should be given as to where the interpreter should be located.

SECTION 2D ADMIRALTY JURISDICTION AND PROCEEDINGS

PART 61—ADMIRALTY CLAIMS

Restrictions on Admiralty jurisdiction

Add new paragraph 2D-23.1:

2D-23.1 *Personal injury claims wrongly commenced in the County Court*—In *Linton v Seaprecius Shipping Ltd* Claim (8 April 2022)(unrep.)—a decision on an application under Limitation Act 1980 s.33 to disapply the limitation period in a personal injury claim - the Admiralty Court expressed its disagreement with the County Court's decision in *Meek v BP Shipping & Fyffes* (2018)(unrep.). A District Judge had held that because a noise deafness claim arising out of the claimant's employment on ships had not been commenced in the Admiralty Court, he had no jurisdiction of any kind (including the jurisdiction to transfer up) and no option other than to strike the case out. That reasoning appeared to the Admiralty Court to be incorrect. The County Court could deal with a personal injury claim under the tort and contract jurisdiction conferred by s.15 of the County Courts Act 1984 and its predecessors. It was correct that the case also fell within the Admiralty Court's jurisdiction pursuant to s.20(2)(f) of the Senior Courts Act 1981. But that section did not establish an exclusive jurisdiction and nor did it oust the County Court's tort and contract jurisdiction. It was CPR 61.2(1)(a)(v) (not s.20(2)(f)) which mandated that a personal injury claim arising out of a defect in the management of a ship had to be commenced in the Admiralty Court. The proper (and normal) remedy for a failure to comply with that rule was to transfer the claim up, not to strike it out. Further, even if the County Court had lacked a substantive jurisdiction, (which it had not), that was not a reason to refuse to transfer up under s.42 of the County Courts Act 1984. Such a construction defeated the whole object of the section.

Replace r.61.4 with:

Special provisions relating to collision claims[1]

61.4—(1) This rule applies to collision claims. 2D-29

(2) A claim form should not contain or be followed by particulars of claim and rule 7.4 does not apply.

(3) An acknowledgment of service must be filed.

(4) A party who wishes to dispute the court's jurisdiction must make an application under Part 11 within 2 months after filing his acknowledgment of service.

(4A) Every party must—

(a) within 21 days after the defendant files their acknowledgment of service; or

(b) where the defendant applies under Part 11, within 21 days after the defendant files their further acknowledgment of service,

disclose any electronic track data which is or has been in its control, in accordance with Part 31, and, where every party has electronic track data in its control, each must provide copies, or permit inspection, of that electronic track data within 7 days of a request by another party to do so.

(5) Every party must—

(a) within 2 months after the defendant files the acknowledgment of service; or

(b) where the defendant applies under Part 11 within 2 months after the defendant files the further acknowledgment of service,

file at the court a completed collision statement of case in the form specified in Practice Direction 61.

(6) A collision statement of case must be—

(a) in the form set out in Practice Direction 61; and

(b) verified by a statement of truth.

(7) A claim form in a collision claim in personam may not be served out of the jurisdiction unless—

(a) the case falls within section 22(2)(a), (b) or (c) of the Senior Courts Act 1981; or

(b) the defendant has submitted to or agreed to submit to the jurisdiction; and

the court gives permission in accordance with Section IV of Part 6; or

(c) rule 6.33 applies.

(8) Where permission to serve a claim form out of the jurisdiction is given, the court will specify the period within which the defendant may file an acknowledgment of service and, where appropriate, a collision statement of case.

(9) Where, in a collision claim in rem ("the original claim")—

(a) (i) a counterclaim; or

(ii) a cross-claim in rem

arising out of the same collision or occurrence is made; and

(b) (i) the party bringing the original claim has caused the arrest of a ship or has obtained security in order to prevent such arrest; and

(ii) the party bringing the counterclaim or cross claim is unable to arrest a ship or otherwise obtain security,

the party bringing the counterclaim or cross claim may apply to the court to

---

[1] Amended by the Civil Procedure (Amendment No.5) Rules 2001 (SI 2001/4015), the Civil Procedure (Amendment) Rules 2008 (SI 2008/2178), the Civil Procedure (Amendment No.2) Rules 2009 (SI 2009/3390), Civil Procedure (Amendment) Rules 2017 (SI 2017/95), the Civil Procedure (Amendment) Rules 2019 (SI 2019/342), and the Civil Procedure (Amendment No.2) Rules 2022 (SI 2022/783).

stay the original claim until sufficient security is given to satisfy any judgment that may be given in favour of that party.

(10) The consequences set out in paragraph (11) apply where a party to a claim to establish liability for a collision claim (other than a claim for loss of life or personal injury)—

- **(a) makes an offer to settle in the form set out in paragraph (12) not less than 21 days before the start of the trial;**
- **(b) that offer is not accepted; and**
- **(c) the maker of the offer obtains at trial an apportionment equal to or more favourable than his offer.**

(11) Where paragraph (10) applies the parties will, unless the court considers it unjust, be entitled to the following costs—

- **(a) the maker of the offer will be entitled to—**
  - **(i) all his costs from 21 days after the offer was made; and**
  - **(ii) his costs before then in accordance with the apportionment found at trial; and**
- **(b) all other parties to whom the offer was made—**
  - **(i) will be entitled to their costs up to 21 days after the offer was made in accordance with the apportionment found at trial; but**
  - **(ii) will not be entitled to their costs thereafter.**

(12) An offer under paragraph (10) must be in writing and must contain—

- **(a) an offer to settle liability at stated percentages;**
- **(b) an offer to pay costs in accordance with the same percentages;**
- **(c) a term that the offer remain open for 21 days after the date it is made; and**
- **(d) a term that, unless the court orders otherwise, on expiry of that period the offer remains open on the same terms except that the offeree should pay all the costs from that date until acceptance.**

Note

To the end of the paragraph, add:

2D-29.1 Paragraph (2) amended by the Civil Procedure (Amendment No.2) Rules 2022 (SI 2022/783) r.26(1), with effect from 1 October 2022

Costs

Add new paragraph at end:

2D-33.1 In *Nautical Challenge Ltd v Evergreen Marine (UK) Ltd (Rev 2)* [2022] EWHC 830 (Admlty) Sir Nigel Teare, sitting as Judge of the High Court, considered the code for offers to settle set out in CPR 61.4 (10)-(12) in the context of the appeals to the Court of Appeal and the Supreme Court, (the costs of which had been remitted to him for determination). The owners of EVER SMART were unsuccessful in the Court of Appeal but successful in the Supreme Court. The owners of ALEXANDRA 1 had made an offer to settle apportionment 60:40 in their favour prior to the first trial. The offer was repeated prior to the appeal to the Supreme Court. Sir Nigel Teare held that it would be "just" to order that the offer (which was not beaten at the second trial where the apportionment was 70:30) should take effect so far as the costs of the appeal to the Supreme Court were concerned. But in relation to the appeal to the Court of Appeal, he held that he should follow *East West Corp v DKBS 1912* [2003] 1 Lloyd's Rep. 239 and that, given that there had been no specific offer regarding the costs of the appeal to the Court of Appeal, they were to reflect the issues on which each party won and lost. He awarded the Owners of the EVER SMART 40% of their costs of this appeal.

Replace r.61.9 with:

Judgment in default[1]

2D-58 **61.9—(1) In an admiralty claim the claimant may obtain judgment in**

[1] Amended by the Civil Procedure (Amendment No.5) Rules 2001 (SI 2001/4015); the Civil

default of–

(a) an acknowledgment of service only if at the date on which judgment is entered–

(i) the defendant has not filed an acknowledgment of service; and

(ii) the relevant time limit for doing so has expired;

(b) defence only if at the date on which judgment is entered–

(i) a defence has not been filed; and

(ii) the relevant time limit for doing so has expired.

(2) In a collision claim, a party who has filed a collision statement of case within the time specified by rule 61.4(5) may obtain judgment in default of a collision statement of case only if at the date on which judgment is entered–

(a) the party against whom judgment is sought has not filed a collision statement of case; and

(b) the time for doing so set out in rule 61.4(5) has expired.

(3) An application for judgment in default–

(a) in a claim in rem must be made by filing–

(i) an application notice as set out in Practice Direction 61;

(ii) a certificate proving service of the claim form; and

(iii) evidence proving the claim to the satisfaction of the court; and

(b) in a claim in personam must be made in accordance with Part 12 with any necessary modifications.

(4) An application notice seeking judgment in default and, unless the court orders otherwise, all evidence in support, must be served on all persons who have entered cautions against release on the Register.

(5) The court may set aside or vary any judgment in default entered under this rule.

(6) The claimant may apply to the court for judgment against a party at whose instance a notice against arrest was entered where–

(a) the claim form has been served on that party;

(b) the sum claimed in the claim form does not exceed the amount specified in the undertaking given by that party in accordance with rule 61.7(2)(a)(ii); and

(c) that party has not fulfilled that undertaking within 14 days after service on him of the claim form.

Add new paragraph 2D-58.1:

Note

Paragraphs (1), (9) amended by the Civil Procedure (Amendment No.2) Rules 2022 (SI 2022/783) r.26(1), with effect from 1 October 2022. **2D-58.1**

SECTION 2E ARBITRATION PROCEEDINGS

PART 62—ARBITRATION CLAIMS

Family Court claims

Replace "Haley v Haley [2020] EWCA Civ 1369; [2021] 2 W.L.R. 357; [2020] 1 F.L.R. 1429" with:

Haley v Haley [2020] EWCA Civ 1369; [2021] Fam 317; [2021] 2 W.L.R. 357 **2E-6**

Procedure (Amendment No.2) Rules 2009 (SI 2009/3390), the Civil Procedure (Amendment) Rules 2021 (SI 2021/117), with effect from 6 April 2021; and the Civil Procedure (Amendment No.2) Rules 2022 (2022/783).

I. Claims under the 1996 Act

Replace r.62.5 with:

Service out of the jurisdiction[1]

2E-12 **62.5—(1) Subject to paragraph (2A), the court may give permission to serve an arbitration claim form out of the jurisdiction if—**

(a) the claimant seeks to—

(i) challenge; or

(ii) appeal on a question of law arising out of,

an arbitration award made within the jurisdiction;

(The place where an award is treated as made is determined by section 53 of the 1996 Act).

(b) the claim is for an order under section 44 of the 1996 Act; or

(c) the claimant—

(i) seeks some other remedy or requires a question to be decided by the court affecting an arbitration (whether started or not), an arbitration agreement or an arbitration award; and

(ii) the seat of the arbitration is or will be within the jurisdiction or the conditions in section 2(4) of the 1996 Act are satisfied.

(2) An application for permission under paragraph (1) must be supported by written evidence—

(a) stating the grounds on which the application is made; and

(b) showing in what place or country the person to be served is, or probably may be found.

(2A) An arbitration claim form falling within (1)(a) to (c) above may be served out of the jurisdiction without permission if—

(a) the seat of the arbitration is or will be in England and Wales; and

(b) the respondent is party to the arbitration agreement in question.

(3) Rules 6.34, 6.35 and 6.40 to 6.46 apply to the service of an arbitration claim form under paragraph (1) or (2A).

(4) An order giving permission to serve an arbitration claim form out of the jurisdiction must specify the period within which the defendant may file an acknowledgment of service.

Add new paragraph 2E-12.1:

Note

2E-12.1 Paragraphs (1), (3) were amended and para.(2A) was inserted by the Civil Procedure (Amendment No.2) Rules 2022 (SI 2022/783) r.27, with effect from 1 October 2022.

Editorial note

Replace the penultimate paragraph (where case citations have been updated) with:

2E-19 See too *Emmott v Michael Wilson & Partners* [2008] EWCA Civ 184, [2008] 1 Lloyd's Rep. 616, CA, where the paramountcy of privacy in arbitration and the associated obligation of confidentiality and the exceptions thereto are reviewed. See also para.31.22.1, above. Public interest in the dispute, or the fact that information relating to it has been released into the public domain in breach of the arbitration agreement, does not justify a departure from the default position that the hearing of an arbitration claim should be in private: *Newcastle United Football Co Ltd v Football Association Premier League Ltd* [2021] EWHC 349 (Comm) (HHJ Pelling QC). However, it may nonetheless be appropriate to order publication of any judgment, even if both parties are opposed to publication, bearing in mind the principle of open justice: *Manchester City Football Club Ltd v The*

[1] Amended by the Civil Procedure (Amendment No.5) Rules 2001 (SI 2001/4015), the Civil Procedure (Amendment) Rules 2008 (SI 2008/2178) and the Civil Procedure (Amendment No.2) Rules 2022 (SI 2022/783) (effective from 1 October 2022).

Football Association Premier League Ltd [2021] EWCA Civ 1110; [2021] 1 W.L.R. 5513. Where a claim is connected with an arbitration but is not an arbitration claim falling within r.62.2, the principles set out in this paragraph do not apply, and instead any application for the claim to be heard in private must be made under r.39.2: *CDE v NOP* [2021] EWCA Civ 1908; [2022] 4 W.L.R. 6.

III. Enforcement

Service of enforcement proceedings

Replace "General Dynamics United Kingdom Ltd v Libya [2021] UKSC 22; [2021] 3 W.L.R. 231; [2021] 4 All E.R. 55" with:

General Dynamics United Kingdom Ltd v Libya [2022] A.C. 318; [2021] UKSC 22; [2021] 4 All E.R. 55 **2E-40.1**

Court's power to determine disputed issues of fact

Replace "Selevision Saudi Co v BeIN Media Group LLC [2021] EWHC 2802 (Comm)" with:

Selevision Saudi Co v BeIN Media Group LLC [2021] EWHC 2802 (Comm); [2021] Bus L.R. 1772 **2E-40.2**

Arbitration Act 1996

A party to an arbitration agreement

In the last paragraph, replace "Mozambique v Credit Suisse International [2021] EWCA Civ 329" with:

Mozambique v Credit Suisse International [2021] EWCA Civ 329; [2022] 1 All E.R. (Comm) 235 **2E-107**

Add new paragraph at end:

In *Lifestyle Equities CV v Hornby Street (MCR) Ltd* [2022] EWCA Civ 51; [2022] W.L.R. (D) 60; [2022] Bus. L.R. 619, the Court of Appeal, by a majority, considered that the proper law of the arbitration agreement (there, Californian law) was to be applied to determine whether a non-party to the arbitration agreement was bound by it. On the basis that under Californian law the non-party was bound by the arbitration agreement, a stay was granted under s.9.

"... or after he has taken any step in those proceedings to answer the substantive claim"

To the end of the first paragraph, add:

; though *c.f. Fairpark Estates Ltd v Heals Property Developments Ltd* [2022] EWHC 496 (Ch), where **2E-111** the seeking of a second extension of time, in circumstances where the possibility of a stay to arbitration had previously been canvassed, was held to constitute a step in the proceedings

Onus of showing that claim should proceed

Replace the first paragraph with:

It rests on the claimant to show that the dispute ought not to be referred to arbitration (*Hodgson* **2E-112** *v Ry. Passengers Assn. Co* (1882) 9 Q.B.D. 188; and see *Vawdrey v Simpson* [1896] 1 Ch. 166). The section provides for two jurisdictional thresholds which are to be decided by the court before a stay could be granted: first, whether there is a concluded arbitration agreement; and secondly whether the issue in the proceedings is a matter which under the arbitration agreement is to be referred to arbitration. The question of whether an arbitration agreement had been effectively superseded in respect of a particular matter by a subsequent consensual contractual process formed part of the second jurisdictional question: *China Export and Credit Insurance Corp v Emerald Energy Resources Ltd* [2018] EWHC 1503 (Comm); [2018] 2 Lloyd's Rep. 179 (Sir Richard Field). The standard of proof is the balance of probabilities: *JSC Aeroflot Russian Airlines v Berezovsky* [2013] EWCA Civ 784; [2013] 2 Lloyd's Rep 242, Aikens LJ at [72]-[74].

Add new paragraph at end:

Whilst the Court should not grant a stay if it is satisfied that the arbitration agreement is null and void, inoperative, or incapable of being performed (s.9(4)), it does not follow that, on a s.9 application, the Court must determine whether the agreement is in fact null and void, etc. It has a discretion to decide the matter summarily, to order a trial of the issue, or to refer the point to the arbitral tribunal for it to decide: see *Aeroflot v Berezovsky* (above), *Golden Ocean Group Ltd v Humpuss Intermoda Transportasi Tbk Ltd* [2013] EWHC 1240 (Comm) and *Soleymani v Nifty Gateway LLC* [2022] EWHC 773 (Comm); [2022] Bus LR 521.

Inoperative

Replace "An arbitration agreement is" with:

An arbitration agreement was **2E-113**

"... when one party serves ... a notice in writing requiring him ... to appoint an arbitrator ..."

To the end of the paragraph, add:

2E-126 Under the LCIA Rules, and other similar institutional rules, it is generally not permissible to seek to commence multiple arbitrations under different arbitration agreements by a single notice (*A v B* [2018] Bus L.R. 778; [2017] EWHC 3417 (Comm)), but a single notice may otherwise be sufficient to commence more than one arbitration, so long as the language used is sufficiently clear (*LLC Agronefteprodukt v Ameropa AG* [2021] EWHC 3474 (Comm)).

Add new paragraph 2E-130.1:

Editorial note

2E-130.1 Normally, an arbitrator will have been effectively appointed where there has been a clear and unconditional communication of acceptance of the appointment by the arbitrator which is then notified to the other party, or communication of an unconditional willingness by the arbitrator to accept the appointment, which the appointing party then acts upon by communicating the appointment to the appointee and the other party: *ARI v WXJ* [2022] EWHC 1543 (Comm) (Foxton J).

Exercise of court's powers

Replace paragraph with:

2E-137 In a case under s.10 of the 1950 Act it was held that the court had power to appoint a single arbitrator in respect of two arbitrations, and it is highly desirable to do so to avoid the danger of inconsistent findings, where disputes involve interrelated and also separate issues of fact and law in both arbitrations (see *Abu Dhabi Gas Liquefaction Co Ltd v Eastern Bechtel Corp* [1982] Com.L.R. 215; [1982] 2 Lloyd's Rep. 425, CA). In *Shagang South-Asia (Hong Kong) Trading Co Ltd v Daewoo Logistics* [2015] EWHC 194 (Comm); [2015] 1 All E.R. (Comm) 545; [2015] 1 Lloyd's Rep. 504 Hamblen J held that where an arbitrator had been appointed without any attempt to follow the procedures set out in s.16(3) and without recourse to the court under this section, the appointment made was invalid. In *Silver Dry Bulk Co Ltd v Homer Hulbert Maritime Co Ltd* [2017] EWHC 44 (Comm); [2017] 1 Lloyd's Rep. 154; [2017] 1 C.L.C. 1 Males J held that the court had no power to make a direction under the Arbitration Act 1996 s.18(3) concerning the appointment of an arbitrator where an arbitration clause agreed between the parties had operated as intended, albeit that one of the parties had failed to cooperate; the clause had made provision for non-cooperation. On an application under this section, it is sufficient for the applicant to show that there is a good arguable case that an arbitration has been commenced and that the tribunal has jurisdiction to determine the claims, and the court will not normally decide issues going to jurisdiction on such an application: *London Steam-ship Owners' Mutual Insurance Association Ltd v Spain* [2021] EWCA Civ 1589; [2022] 1 W.L.R. 3434.

Substantive jurisdiction

Replace "NWA v FSY [2021] EWHC 2666 (Comm)" with:

2E-161.1 *NWA v FSY* [2021] EWHC 2666 (Comm); [2021] Bus. L.R. 1788

Editorial note

Add new paragraph at end:

2E-228 The effect of s.58is not to confine the scope of any issue estoppel to successors in title to the parties or those engaged in the derivative exercise of the relevant contractual right, but any attempt to establish the preclusive effect of an award against anyone except the parties or their contractual privies will be extremely challenging:*PJSC National Bank Trust v Mints* [2022] EWHC 871 (Comm).

"By leave of the Court"

To the end of the last paragraph add:

2E-243 For the approach which the Court should adopt in relation to the enforcement under s.66 of an award for declaratory relief, see *Sodzawiczny v McNally* [2021] EWHC 3384 (Comm).

"On the ground of serious irregularity"

After the third paragraph, add new paragraph:

2E-262 As to whether a s.68(1)(a) application can be founded on the overlooking of evidence by the arbitrators, see *Livian GmbH v Elekta Ltd* [2022] EWHC 757 (Comm), noting that in *UMS Holding Ltd v Great Station Properties SA* [2017] EWHC 2398 (Comm); [2017] 2 Lloyd's Rep 421 it was concluded that it could not, whereas the question was left open in *Sonatrach v Statoil* [2014] EWHC 875 (Comm); [2014] 2 Lloyd's Rep 252. However, even if such a failure can ground a s.68(1)(a) application, it is necessary for the claimant to show that had the irregularity not occurred, the tribunal might well have reached a different view and produced a significantly different outcome, a test that was not satisfied in *Livian*.

The court's approach

Replace "CVLC Three Carrier Corp v Arab Maritime Petroleum Transport Co [2021] EWHC 551 (Comm)" with:

CVLC Three Carrier Corp v Arab Maritime Petroleum Transport Co [2021] EWHC 551 (Comm); [2022] 1 All E.R. (Comm) 839 **2E-267.1**

Editorial note

Add new paragraph at end:

The fact that an arbitrator has been appointed by the court under s.18 of the Act does not preclude a non-participating party from making an application under s.72: *National Investment Bank Ltd v Eland International (Thailand) Co Ltd* [2022] EWHC 1168 (Comm) (Foxton J). **2E-278**

"... be enforced ... as a judgment" s.101(2)

Replace "General Dynamics United Kingdom Ltd v Libya [2021] UKSC 22; [2021] 3 W.L.R. 231; [2021] 4 All E.R. 55" with:

General Dynamics United Kingdom Ltd v Libya [2021] UKSC 22; [2022] A.C. 318; [2021] 4 All E.R. 55 **2E-353**

Grounds of refusal

In the fifth paragraph, replace "Kabab-Ji S.A.L. (Lebanon) v Kout Food Group (Kuwait) [2021] UKSC 48" with:

Kabab-Ji S.A.L. (Lebanon) v Kout Food Group (Kuwait) [2021] UKSC 48; [2021] Bus LR 1717; [2022] All ER (Comm) 773 **2E-360**

Subsection (5)

Replace "Kabab-Ji S.A.L. (Lebanon) v Kout Food Group (Kuwait) [2021] UKSC 48" with:

Kabab-Ji S.A.L. (Lebanon) v Kout Food Group (Kuwait) [2021] UKSC 48; [2021] Bus LR 1717; [2022] All ER (Comm) 773 **2E-361**

SECTION 2F INTELLECTUAL PROPERTY PROCEEDINGS

PART 63—INTELLECTUAL PROPERTY CLAIMS

V. Intellectual Property Enterprise Court

Replace r.63.26 with:

Costs[1]

63.26—(1) Subject to paragraph (2), the court will reserve the costs of an application to the conclusion of the trial when they will be subject to summary assessment. **2F-17.19**

(2) Where a party has behaved unreasonably the court may make an order for costs at the conclusion of the hearing.

(3) Where the court makes a summary assessment of costs, it will do so in accordance with Section VII of Part 46.

[1] Amended by the Civil Procedure (Amendment No.7) Rules 2013 (SI 2013/1974), and the Civil Procedure (Amendment No.2) Rules 2022 (SI 2022/783).

Add new paragraph 2F-17.19.0:

Note

2F-17.19.0 Paragraph (3) was amended by the Civil Procedure (Amendment No.2) Rules 2022 (SI 2022/783) r.28(1), with effect from 1 October 2022.

2F-17.20 *Replace r.63.27 and add note paragraph 2F-17.20.1:*

Allocation to the small claims track[1]

63.27—(1) A claim started in or transferred to the Intellectual Property Enterprise Court will be allocated to the small claims track if—

- **(a) rule 63.13, but not rule 63.2, applies to the claim;**
- **(b) the value of the claim is not more than £10,000;**
- **(c) it is stated in the particulars of claim that the claimant wishes the claim to be allocated to the small claims track; and**
- **(d) no objection to the claim being allocated to the small claims track is raised by the defendant in the defence.**

(2) [Omitted]

(3) If either—

- **(a) the requirements of rule 63.27(1)(a), (b) and (c) are satisfied, but in the defence the defendant objects to the claim being allocated to the small claims track; or**
- **(b) the requirements of rule 63.27(1)(a) and (b) are satisfied, but not (c), and in the defence the defendant requests that the claim be allocated to the small claims track,**

the court will allocate the claim to the small claims track or the multi-track in accordance with Part 26 (case management — preliminary stage). For that purpose the court will send the parties a directions questionnaire and require them to file completed directions questionnaires and to serve them on all other parties within 14 days.

(4) Part 27 (small claims track) shall apply to claims allocated to the small claims track in the Intellectual Property Enterprise Court with the modification to rule 27.2(1)(a) that Part 25 (interim remedies) shall not apply to such claims at all. Section VII of Part 46 (scale costs for claims in the Intellectual Property Enterprise Court) shall not apply to claims allocated to the small claims track in the Intellectual Property Enterprise Court.

2F-17.20.1 *Note* —Paragraph (4) was amended by the Civil Procedure (Amendment No.2) Rules 2022 (SI 2022/783) r.28(2), with effect from 1 October 2022.

Scope and application of Small Claims in the Intellectual Property Enterprise Court

Replace the first paragraph list (sixth bullet point has been updated) with:

2F-17.21.2

- The claimant requests allocation to the small claims track in the particulars of claim; there is no directions questionnaire (save where set out below).
- A claim will be automatically allocated to the small claims track if each of the conditions set out in r.63.27(1) apply.
- If either condition r.63.27(1)(c) or (d) does not apply (i.e. either the Claimant or Defendant has not indicated that the claim should be so allocated (or objects)), the court will send out directions questionnaires, then the Court will allocate the claim in accordance with its case management powers at an early stage (r.63.27(3)). If the allocation decision is in dispute this will normally be dealt with without a hearing (please see para.5 of the Guide for more detail about disputes on allocation).
- The court's decision on allocation will take account of the value of the claim, the type of intellectual property rights the case relates to, likely complexity and the number of witnesses. Cases involving validity of trade marks (rather than infringement of trade marks) are unlikely to be suitable for the small claims track (para.5 of the Guide).

---

[1] Introduced by the Civil Procedure (Amendment No.2) Rules 2012 (SI 2012/2208). Amended by the Civil Procedure (Amendment) Rules 2013 (SI 2013/262), the Civil Procedure (Amendment No.7) Rules 2013 (SI 2013/1974), and the Civil Procedure (Amendment No.2) Rules 2022 (SI 2022/783).

- It is not possible to apply for an interim injunction in small claims actions which are also intellectual property proceedings. Where a party seeks such relief (an interim injunction, a search or seizure order or a freezing order) they should not use the small claims procedure; these orders are available in the Intellectual Property Enterprise Courts where cases are not allocated to the small claims track (r.63.27(4)).
- Claim can now be issued electronically, and can be issued in the IPEC in London or in the Business and Property Courts in Birmingham, Bristol, Cardiff, Leeds, Liverpool, Manchester or Newcastle. Small claims dealt with in London remain technically in the IPEC, but will be dealt with by specialist district judges who sit in the County Court at Central London.
- The general principle that an unsuccessful party will pay the costs of the successful party does not apply in the small claims track (see para.8 of the Guide for those limited costs that are recoverable, which cross refer to CPR r.27.14. Note that the sum in PD 27 para.7.3(1) is now £95 per day).
- Rule 63.28 sets out the parts of r.63 which do apply to small claims in the Intellectual Property Enterprise Court, namely:
    r.63.1 (Scope and interpretation);
    r.63.13 (Allocation);
    r.63.18 (Transfer of Proceedings);
    r.63.20 (Statements of Case);
    r.63.21 (Statement of Truth);
    r.63.22 (Defence and Reply);
    r.63.25 (Applications);
    r.63.26(1) and (2) (Costs);
    r.63.27 (Allocation to the Small Claims Track).
- PD 63.32 sets out those provisions of the PD 63 which apply to the Intellectual Property Enterprise Court small claims.

INTELLECTUAL PROPERTY ENTERPRISE COURT GUIDE

1. GENERAL

1.1 Introduction

Replace paragraph 1.1 with:

This is the Guide to the Intellectual Property Enterprise Court (IPEC). It primarily concerns the IPEC multi-track (explained further below, see section 1.2). There is a separate Guide for the IPEC's small claims track, available at **2F-149**
http://www.gov.uk/government/publications/intellectual-property-enterprise-court-a-guide-to-small-claims

The Guide is written for all users of IPEC, whether a litigant in person (i.e. a litigant who acts on their own behalf without professional representation) or a specialist intellectual property litigator. It explains how the court's procedures work and provides guidelines where appropriate.

IPEC is part of the High Court. It is a specialist list of the Chancery Division within the Business and Property Courts of England and Wales. It hears only cases concerning intellectual property.

IPEC aims to provide a procedure for intellectual property litigation which is speedier and less costly than is the case in the rest of the High Court. It is also designed to safeguard parties from the risk of paying large sums in costs to the opposing party at the conclusion of the proceedings. The intention is to ensure that parties without the benefit of large financial resources are not deterred from seeking access to justice because of the high cost of litigation.

1.2 Multi-track and small claims track

Replace paragraph 1.2 with:

IPEC has two sets of procedures or 'tracks'. They are known as the 'IPEC multi-track' and the 'IPEC small claims track'. They differ in that the small claims track deals with cases of a simpler nature with a claim for a lower level of damages.

The IPEC multi-track

In the IPEC multi-track, litigants may claim up to £500,000 in compensation for infringement of their rights. This cap on compensation may be waived by agreement of the parties.

At the end of the trial the losing party may be required to pay the winning party's legal costs, but with very limited exceptions such costs will not exceed £60,000 in the IPEC multi-track. The procedure not only caps the overall costs which a losing party will have to pay, it also limits costs payable for each stage of the proceedings. These 'costs caps' - limiting the extent of any adverse order on costs - form a significant feature of IPEC.

The IPEC small claims track

The IPEC small claims track is for suitable claims in which the compensation sought is no more than £10,000. Generally, at the end of the case the losing party will be required to pay little or none of the winning party's legal costs. There is thus even greater protection from an adverse order on costs in the event that a party is not successful. The procedure in the small claims track is shorter and less formal than in the multi-track and the court fees are lower.

Small claims cases are heard by specialist district judges who sit in London and in Business and Property Court centres out of London, namely Birmingham, Bristol, Leeds, Liverpool, Manchester, Newcastle and Wales (Cardiff). Matters to be heard outside London can be issued using the Business and Property Courts' electronic filing system (see Annex A).

Guidance is given below as to whether the multi-track or small claims track is likely to be the more appropriate forum for a dispute (see section 3.3).

Unless stated otherwise, the remainder of this Guide concerns only the IPEC multi-track.

1.3 Intellectual property cases

Replace paragraph 1.3 with:

IPEC hears intellectual property cases of any kind. For the most part this means cases concerning patents, registered designs, unregistered designs, trade marks, passing off, copyright, database rights, performance protection rights, trade libel and breach of confidence. There are other intellectual property rights less often relied on, such as moral rights, semiconductor topography rights and the protection of plant varieties, and all of these may also be litigated in IPEC. IPEC deals with disputes which involve matters other than intellectual property, such as contractual claims, but only if associated with an intellectual property claim.

Since the end of the Brexit transition period on 31 December 2020, EU registered and unregistered intellectual property rights ceased to be enforceable in the courts of England and Wales. Proceedings for enforcement of such rights started before that date will still be heard and enforced.

1.4 Remedies

Replace paragraph 1.4 with:

All the remedies available elsewhere in the High Court can be claimed in IPEC. These include preliminary and final injunctions, orders for the payment of damages or an account of profits, the latter being an order that a defendant found to infringe should disclose and pay over the profits made from the infringement. Search and seizure orders, asset freezing orders and orders requiring the dissemination of a judgment (such as publication on a website) may also be granted in IPEC.

1.5 The judges

Replace paragraph 1.5 with:

The Presiding Judge of IPEC is a specialist circuit judge. Nominated barristers and solicitors, all experienced in intellectual property law, sit as deputy IPEC judges. Judges who sit in the Patents Court also sit in IPEC when the need arises.

Replace paragraph 1.6 (including the title) with:

1.6 Trials outside London or heard by video link

IPEC trials can be heard outside London and this will happen in particular where it saves costs. If the parties wish the trial to be heard at a place other than London, they should contact the clerk of the Presiding IPEC Judge as soon as possible and in any event no later than the case management conference (see below) so that arrangements can be put in place well before the date of the proposed hearing. (Contact details are given at the end of this Guide.) Before making such an approach, the parties should discuss this between themselves.

Alternatively, trials may be heard remotely, i.e. by video link using software such as Teams or Skype.

If any party has a view as to where a trial should be heard or whether it should be heard remotely, the matter should be raised at the case management conference (see below). If the circumstances of a party alter after the case management conference, the matter can be raised by an application to the court.

The default arrangement for all interim applications, including case management conferences, is that a hearing will be conducted remotely. Any party can apply to the court for the hearing to be held in a courtroom, although subject to very unusual circumstances IPEC judges will not sit outside London for interim applications because hearings are too short to make this practical. Parties can also apply for a hearing to be conducted by telephone.

1.7 Representation

Replace the first and second paragraphs with:

A person may represent themselves in litigation in IPEC as a litigant in person. However, intellectual property disputes can be complex and litigants will often benefit from the assistance of a professional representative.

Solicitors and Patent and trade mark attorneys [1] are all entitled to represent clients in IPEC. These professionals may additionally instruct barristers to help prepare the case and/or to argue the case in court. In some instances, a barrister may accept instructions directly from the public.

IP Pro Bono

Replace paragraph with:

Where a person bringing or defending a case in IPEC cannot afford to pay for their own legal representative, they may be eligible to seek free or 'pro bono' advice. A scheme has been set up which provides free professional assistance for those involved in intellectual property litigation who do not have the resources to pay for advice. The IP Pro Bono scheme was organized with IPEC particularly in mind. It has a website at which explains how the scheme works and how a party may obtain free assistance from a professional adviser experienced in the relevant area of intellectual property law. Those who wish to use the scheme should apply as soon as is reasonably possible.

2. CIVIL PROCEDURE RULES

2.1 The CPR

Replace paragraph 2.1 with:

Like all proceedings in the High Court, procedure in IPEC is governed by the Civil Procedure Rules ('the CPR') which can be found at: *www.justice.gov.uk/courts/procedure-rules/civil/rules.* **2F-150**

It would be unwise for a litigant to navigate the rules in detail without informed advice. Users of IPEC should be aware that this Guide cannot and does not attempt to cover every issue which may arise in the course of litigation. However, the rules which are most relevant to litigants in IPEC are referred to in the course of explaining how IPEC works.

Replace paragraph 2.3 (including the title) with:

2.3 Rules of particular relevance to IPEC

- Part 63 applies to all intellectual property claims. It includes rules specific to intellectual property cases and also modifies some Parts of the CPR which would otherwise apply generally to all claims.
- Practice Direction 63 (PD 63) supplements Part 63.
- Attention is drawn to two other parts of the CPR which contain provisions specific to IPEC:
  - Part 30 and in particular PD 30 paras. 9.1 and 9.2. These apply to the transfer of proceedings to and from IPEC. Part 30 rule 5, when applied to IPEC transfers, is modified by Part 63 rule 18.
  - Part 46 Section VII and PD 46 paragraph 11.1 relate to costs in IPEC.

3. THE COURT IN WHICH TO BRING PROCEEDINGS

3.1 The options

Replace paragraph 3.1 with:

A litigant wishing to start an intellectual property claim must decide on the court in which to bring the proceedings. First, should the claim be brought in IPEC or elsewhere in the High Court? **2F-151**

If the case is to be brought in IPEC there is a second decision to be made: should it be started in the IPEC multi-track or the IPEC small claims track?

Replace paragraph 3.2 (including the title) with:

3.2 IPEC or elsewhere in the High Court

The following guidelines are provided to assist users in determining whether a case is suitable for IPEC:

- The financial resources of the parties. A party may have limited financial resources and may therefore require the lower cost of litigating in IPEC and the protection of costs caps in order to gain access to justice. If this can be shown, it is likely to be treated as a strong

---

[1] The rights of patent attorneys and trade mark attorneys to conduct litigation and appear in IPEC are determined by the Intellectual Property Regulation Board (IPREG) (*www.ipreg.org.uk*). Attorneys with an Intellectual Property Litigation Certificate may conduct litigation and appear in IPEC.

(though not overriding) reason to have the case heard in IPEC. This will be particularly the case if the court reaches the view that there is a risk of a better funded opponent being able to bring unfair financial pressure to bear should the case be heard outside IPEC. That said, a party wishing for the proceedings to be in IPEC remains under an obligation to tailor their case to ensure that all the issues in the proceedings will not give rise to a trial lasting more than 2 days, or at the most 3 days.

- The overall complexity of the claim. Where the claim is such that it will require a trial of more than 2 days, it is unlikely to be suitable for IPEC. Exceptionally, a trial of 3 days may be permitted. A litigant with a complex claim or a complex defence and/or counterclaim who wishes the case to be heard in IPEC, should give strong consideration to pruning their case down to the essentials. A failure to do so may result in the action being heard elsewhere in the High Court purely because there are too many issues for a 2 or 3 day trial.
- The nature of the evidence. If it is anticipated that a large number of witnesses will be required on either or both sides, all to be cross-examined, there may be a significant risk that the limit of a 2 or 3 day trial will be exceeded.
- The value of the claim. The value of the claim, though relevant, is generally not a major factor in the evaluation of whether a case is suitable for IPEC, in part because it is often difficult to give an accurate estimate of the overall value. The value of a claim is not necessarily the same as the amount of compensation claimed since it may include the value of an injunction.

A defendant sued in the Patents Court or in the general Chancery Division is entitled to apply to have the case transferred to IPEC, and vice versa. This should be raised in correspondence first. If the parties agree that the case should be transferred it still requires the approval of a judge in the court in which the case is currently listed, but is likely to happen. If there is no agreement, an application to transfer must be made. This should be done at the latest at the case management conference (see below).

Parties may take the joint view that a case which would not normally be suitable for IPEC should nonetheless be heard there. They are also free to agree that the £500,000 limit on compensation for infringement will be waived. In such a case the court will usually accommodate the parties' wish provided that the trial will not take excessively longer than is usual for an IPEC trial.

3.3 The IPEC multi-track or small claims track

Replace the first paragraph with:

Where a claimant has decided to bring their case in IPEC, consideration should be given to whether it should be in the IPEC multi-track or small claims track.

2F-152 *Change title of section 4:*

4. PROCEDURE IN IPEC

4.1 Before starting proceedings

Replace the text after the quote with:

This practice direction, including paragraph 6, was drafted to apply generally in civil litigation, not just in IPEC. In the context of IPEC proceedings there is no 'relevant pre-action protocol' as mentioned in the first sentence, so the remainder of the paragraph applies. With regard to 6(b), defendants in an IPEC case are expected to respond within 14 days save in exceptional circumstances.

4.2 Starting proceedings

Replace paragraph 4.2 with:

Proceedings are started when the court issues a claim form. To have this done, the intended claimant must complete Form **N1** (the Claim Form) and send it to the court. The Claim Form and notes for completing it can be found at *www.gov.uk/government/publications/form-n1-claim-form-cpr-part-7.*

The Claim Form and any other document can be filed with the court online, see Section 5 of this Guide 'General Arrangements' below. It may be filed in London or in any of the Business and Property Court Centres outside London at Birmingham, Bristol, Leeds, Liverpool, Manchester, Newcastle or Wales (Cardiff). Alternatively, the Claim Form may be posted to, or presented at the public counter at any of the foregoing centres.

The Rolls Building is a court building in London which contains IPEC. Its address, which is also the address of IPEC in London is given in Annex A at the end of this Guide. Annex A also provides the addresses of the Business and Property Court Centres outside London.

4.3 Service of the claim form

In paragraph 4.3, replace the last paragraph with:

It is good practice for a claimant to serve their Particulars of Claim with the claim form, but see Section 4.5(b) of this Guide for details of timing.

4.4 Response by the defendant

In paragraph 4.4, replace the second paragraph with:

CPR Part 10 rule 3 sets out the period for filing an Acknowledgment of Service. The CPR only requires the Acknowledgement of Service to be filed with the Court, although subsequent documents, such as the Defence, must both be filed with the Court and served on the other parties (see Part 15 rule 6). It is always helpful to send a copy of any document filed with the court to the other party to ensure that those documents are received by the other party in a timely manner.

4.5 Statements of Case

(a) Introduction

Replace the second paragraph with:

Part 63 rule 20(1) requires that a statement of case in IPEC must set out concisely all the facts and arguments upon which the party serving the statement relies. This is sometimes misunderstood. All relevant facts and arguments must be stated. But they should not be set out in a manner which includes every detail. There will be an opportunity by the time of the trial to explain to the court everything that matters. A good approach is to make the statement of case as concise as is possible, while considering whether any argument to be run at trial, or matter to be relied on, will come as a surprise to an opponent who has read the statement of case. If not, the statement of case has probably been drafted in sufficient detail.

(b) Time limits for filing and serving statements of case

Replace the first and second paragraphs with:

The relevant time limits are dispersed across different Parts of the CPR. The following is a summary guide.

The better practice is for a claimant to file and serve the Particulars of Claim with the court together with the claim form. However, the Particulars of Claim can be served up to 14 days later (Part 7 rule 4(1)) or, if the time for service of the claim form is due to expire in less than 14 days (see Part 7 rule 5) no later than the latest time for serving the claim form (Part 7 rule 4(2)). The Particulars of Claim must be filed with the court no later than 7 days after service on the defendant (Part 7 rule 4(3)).

Replace the fourth paragraph with:

The Defence (or Defence and Counterclaim) must be served on every other party (Part 15 rule 6). This should be done at the same time as filing the Defence.

Replace the last paragraph with:

Some time limits are stricter than others in IPEC. The parties are not at liberty to extend the time limits set out in Part 63 rule 22 without the prior consent of the judge. An application for an extension of time must be made before the expiry of the relevant period and set out good reasons why the extension is required. Such applications are almost always dealt with without a hearing.

(d) Statements of truth

Replace the first paragraph with:

Attention is drawn to Part 63 rule 21, which modifies Part 22 in its application to IPEC. The statement of truth must be made by a person with knowledge of the facts alleged (or by persons who between them have such knowledge). If more than one person signs the statement of truth, the individuals should indicate in some suitable manner which parts of the statement of case they are verifying. The knowledge of the person signing the statement of truth should be direct knowledge, so it will seldom be appropriate for that person to be a legal advisor.

4.6 Case management

(b) The application for the case management conference

Replace the first paragraph with:

The claimant should apply for a CMC within 14 days after all defendants who intend to file and serve a Defence have done so. Where a case has been transferred from another court, the claimant should apply for a CMC within 14 days of the transfer. However, any party may apply for a CMC at any point if there is good reason. If the claimant has failed to apply for a CMC within 14 days of service of the Defence, the defendant should do so.

(c) Preparation for the CMC

Replace the second paragraph with:

The CMC is a particularly important part of IPEC procedure. No material may be filed in the case by way of evidence, disclosure or written submissions unless permission is given by the judge. The first and last opportunity to obtain such permission is likely to be at the CMC. Save in exceptional circumstances the court will not permit a party to submit material in addition to that ordered at the CMC (Part 63 rule 23(2)). A cost-benefit test is applied to the filing of material in support of a case, see PD 63 para 29.2(2).

Disclosure

Replace paragraph with:

Whether disclosure of documents by the opposing side will be required and if so, which documents and why. Only specific disclosure is available in IPEC, i.e. disclosure of either particular documents or particular classes of documents, often identified by reference to one or more of the list of issues. Usually, whether or not other disclosure is ordered, the parties will be expected to disclose any 'known adverse documents' within the meaning of paragraph 2 of PD 51U (which can be found at *www.justice.gov.uk/courts/procedure-rules/civil/rules/practice-direction-51u-disclosure-pilot-for-the-business-and-property-courts#2*).

The disclosure pilot scheme in operation in other Business and Property Courts does not apply to IPEC.

(e) Amendments to a statement of case

Replace paragraph with:

On occasion a party may wish to amend its statement of case. If the other parties agree then generally no difficulties arise. If not, permission to amend may be sought at or before the CMC. Amending a statement of case after the CMC is difficult under IPEC procedure, so parties must be sure by the time of the CMC that their pleadings are in final form.

(i) Expression of a preliminary, non-binding opinion on the merits

Replace paragraph with:

If it is likely to assist the parties in reaching a settlement, IPEC is willing to express a preliminary and non-binding opinion on the merits of the case. This is often called an 'early neutral evaluation'. The court will almost certainly not take this course unless agreed by both sides. If there is agreement, the request to give the non-binding opinion should be made in advance of the CMC so that the court may consider whether it is appropriate. It is unlikely to be appropriate, for example, if the outcome of the proceedings will largely depend on unpredictable evidence that may emerge at trial.

Add new sub-paragraph (j):

(j) Expedited trial

In a suitable case, the court may order that the trial will be heard sooner than would normally happen. Such an order has the effect of jumping the queue of other litigants, so will not be ordered unless a good reason for expedition is shown. An application for an expedited trial is best made at the CMC but may be made at any time.

4.7 Applications

Replace the second and third paragraphs with:

With the exception of applications made at the CMC, once the application notice is received by the party on whom it is served - the respondent - the respondent to the application must file and serve a response on all relevant parties within 5 working days of service of the application notice, see Part 63 rule 25(2). This rule is specific to IPEC and is significant. If 5 working days elapse and the respondent has done nothing, the applicant is entitled to ask the court to make the order sought without further delay. It is therefore imperative that there is a response as soon as possible. Usually it is sufficient to contact the applicant and state the respondent's position with regard to the application. If a resolution cannot be agreed, the applicant will contact the court and arrange a hearing.

An applicant should take care to serve the application notice on the respondent. If the applicant notifies the court that 5 working days have elapsed without a response, they should also inform the court of the date on which the application notice was served and how this was done. Unless the court is shown that 5 working days have undoubtedly elapsed since service of the application notice, no action will be taken by the court.

4.8 Urgent applications

Replace paragraph with:

An application for an interim injunction or other urgent relief, should be made by filing an application notice in the usual way (save in cases of extreme urgency, discussed below). Once the application notice has been served, the applicant should contact the judge's clerk (see Annex A). The clerk will find a date for the hearing which is appropriate to the urgency of the matter and, if possible, is convenient to all parties. In the meantime, the parties should make every effort to agree a timetable for evidence to be filed and served in relation to the application and any question of relief pending the hearing. Failing agreement, the judge's clerk should be informed. The court will then finalise the timetable and deal with any application for relief pending the hearing. This may be done on paper, by a video application, or in a short hearing, as appropriate.

In cases of extreme urgency, an application may be made without an application notice. This is done by contacting the clerk to IPEC. No such application will be entertained unless the judge is given very good reason why the matter is extremely urgent.

The court will always fix a date and time for hearings appropriate to the urgency of the application. This may mean that the application will be heard by a judge other than the Presiding Judge of IPEC. The convenience of the parties and their advisors will be taken into account but will not be of paramount importance.

4.10 Costs

Replace the first five paragraphs with:

There is no requirement for costs budgets in IPEC.

Costs are subject to the cap provided by Part 46 rules 46.20 to 22. With certain limited exceptions the court will not order a party to pay total costs of more than £60,000 on the final determination of a claim in relation to liability and no more than £30,000 on an inquiry as to damages or account of profits.

Tables A and B of PD 46 paragraph 11.1 sets out the maximum amount of scale costs which the court will award for each stage of a claim.

There are exceptions: court fees, costs relating to enforcement of an order and wasted costs are excluded from the costs cap (Part 46 rule 46.21(5)). Any recoverable VAT is not included in the capped stage costs (Part 46 rule 46.21(6)) but the overall caps of £60,000 and £30,000 are inclusive of VAT For further details, see *Response Clothing Ltd v The Edinburgh Woollen Mill Ltd* [2020] EWHC 721 (IPEC).

In IPEC all costs are assessed summarily (Part 46 rule 46.20(3)). To enable the court to assess costs, the parties should prepare a statement of costs in advance of any hearing in which costs will be claimed. It is essential that the statement of costs breaks down the costs by reference to the stage of the claim in which they were incurred, see Table A and B of PD 46 paragraph 11.1.

The foregoing provisions regarding costs came into force on 1 October 2022. Proceedings started before that date will continue to be governed by the earlier cost cap rules (see the previous IPEC Guide for details.)

4.11 Alternative dispute resolution

Replace the first paragraph with:

Settlement of a dispute by alternative dispute resolution (ADR) has many advantages. It can result in significant saving of costs. It also has the potential to provide the parties with a wider range of solutions than can be offered by litigation. While the solution to litigation is usually limited to 'win/lose' on the issues put in front of the court, ADR may provide a creative 'win/win' solution, as some forms of ADR can explore other ways for the parties to co-operate. ADR can also explore settlement in several countries at the same time.

Delete the last paragraph.

5. GENERAL ARRANGEMENTS

5.1 Filing documents with the court

(c) Filing in person

Replace paragraph with:

Documents may also be filed by presenting them at the public counter of the Rolls Building, the court building in which IPEC is located. The address is given at Annex A below. **2F-152.1**

5.5 Documents bundles and skeletons for the trial and applications

Replace the last paragraph with:

In the case of trials, the deadline for filing skeleton arguments will be stated in the order following the CMC. The court will frequently be assisted by a chronology of relevant facts in the trial skeleton It should be included unless the chronology is short enough to be self-evident or would contribute nothing of value.

Delete paragraph 5.6, "Telephone applications" and renumber paragraphs 5.7 to 5.13 as paragraphs 5.6 to 5.12.

5.6 Consent Orders

Replace the newly numbered paragraph 5.6 with:

The court will usually make orders proposed with the consent of all parties without the need for the parties to attend. A draft of the agreed order and the written consent of all the parties or their respective legal representatives should be supplied to the judge's clerk. Unless the judge assigned to hear the application considers a hearing is needed, he or she will make the order in the agreed terms. It will be drawn up accordingly and sent to the parties.

5.8 Draft judgment

Replace the newly numbered paragraph 5.8 with:

Some judgments, almost always those after a trial, will be reserved and handed down at a later date. Usually the parties' legal representatives (or litigants in person) will be provided with a copy of the draft judgment in advance of the date of handing down so that they may notify the court of typographical and obvious errors (if any). The text may be shown, in confidence, to the parties, but only for the purpose of obtaining instructions and on the strict understanding that the judgment, and its effect, are not to be disclosed to any other person or used in the public domain, and that no action is taken (other than internally) in response to the judgment.

5.11 Appeals

In the newly numbered paragraph 5.11, replace the first and second paragraphs with:

An order of an IPEC judge may be appealed. This applies equally to orders made following a trial and those made in response to an application to the court. All appeals go the Court of Appeal, see PD52A, Section 3, Table 1. No party has an absolute right to appeal, permission must be obtained. Permission to appeal may and generally should be sought from the judge who made the order. If the judge refuses to give permission, the party may instead seek permission from the Court of Appeal.

NOTE THAT this does not apply to appeals from decisions in the IPEC Small Claims Track. All appeals from the IPEC Small Claims Track go to an Enterprise Judge, i.e. a judge of the IPEC multi-track, see CPR 63.19(3).

5.12 Information available on the Internet

In the newly numbered paragraph 5.12, replace the first paragraph with:

A link to 'Intellectual Property Enterprise Court' (and links to other courts) can be found at: *www.gov.uk/courts-tribunals*. It contains links to copies of this Guide and the Guide to the Intellectual Property Enterprise Court Small Claims Track.

Replace the penultimate paragraph with:

www.justice.gov.uk/courts/court-lists provides links to two useful sites. The first is 'Intellectual Property Enterprise Court Diary'which provides the diary for trials (but not applications) to be heard in IPEC and a record of past trials. The second is 'Business and Property Courts Rolls Building Cause List'. The link there to 'Intellectual Property List (ChD)' provides a list of all IP court hearings, including those heard in IPEC. After about 2pm the website shows the hearings for the following day.

Replace the last paragraph with:

IPEC judgments are available at the National Archive website and may be searched for by name at *http://www.caselaw.nationalarchives.gov.uk*.

ANNEX A

CONTACT DETAILS

THE INTELLECTUAL PROPERTY ENTERPRISE COURT

Replace section with:

2F-152.2 The home of IPEC is in the Rolls Building at this address:

The Rolls Building
7 Rolls Building
Fetter Lane

London
EC4A 1NL
DX160040 Strand 4

IPEC is presided over by a specialist circuit judge, at present His Honour Judge Hacon.

The judge's clerk and clerk to the Intellectual Property Enterprise Court is at present Francine Kouassi. Her contact details are:

Francine.Kouassi1@justice.gov.uk

Tel: 020 7947 6265

IP PRO BONO

Replace paragraph with:

A person with limited financial resources (including firms and companies if they qualify) may be entitled to free professional advice regarding any IP matter, whether concerning IPEC or not. The IP Pro Bono scheme is designed to help such persons. It may be contacted at:

www.ipprobono.org.uk.

INTELLECTUAL PROPERTY ENTERPRISE COURT USERS COMMITTEE

Replace the first paragraph with:

IPEC has a Users' Committee which considers the problems and concerns of intellectual property litigators in IPEC. Membership of the committee includes the judges of the Intellectual Property Enterprise Court and of the Patents Court, representatives of each of the Intellectual Property Office, European Patent Office, Intellectual Property Bar Association, IP Chambers Clerks, the Intellectual Property Lawyers Association, the Chartered Institute of Patent Attorneys, the Institute of Trade Mark Attorneys, the IP Federation, the British Copyright Council, the Pro Bono Committees and IP Academics.

ANNEX B

EXAMPLE CMC ORDER

EVIDENCE

After paragraph 14, add new paragraph 15: **2F-152.3**

15. Any party intending to rely on a cross-examination bundle shall give the relevant witness adequate notice of the bundle and must at the same time inform the court and the other parties (unless the court gives permission not to notify the other parties) of the exceptional reasons which are said to justify the late introduction of new documents into the case.

TRIAL

Renumber paragraphs 15 to 22 as paragraphs 16 to 23.

Replace the newly numbered paragraph 23 with:

23. Judgment in the action shall be handed down on [date]. The parties shall make themselves available for a hearing on that date to determine any matters consequential on the judgment, should it not be possible to agree a final order.

COSTS

Renumber paragraph 23 as paragraph 24.

ANNEX C

GUIDELINES ON BUNDLES

PAGINATION OF A BUNDLE FOR A TRIAL

Replace paragraph 8 with:

8. These page numbers should be inserted in a form, such as a colour or bold format, that can **2F-152.4**
clearly be distinguished from any other pagination on the document.

Add "Practice Statement: Listing of Cases for Trial in the Patents Court" and commentary:

PRACTICE STATEMENT: LISTING OF CASES FOR TRIAL IN THE PATENTS COURT

2F-154 The Patents Court endeavours bring patent cases on for trial where possible within 12 months of the claim being issued. To this end, the following procedure will be adopted.

1. The parties will be expected (a) to start to consider potential trial dates as soon as is reasonable practicable after the service of the proceedings and (b) to discuss and attempt to agree trial dates with each other when seeking to agree directions for trial.

2. The starting point for listing trials is the current applicable Trial Window advertised by the Chancery List Office. Patent cases will be listed on the basis that the Trial Windows are divided as follows: estimated hearing time (excluding pre-reading and preparation of closing submissions) up to 5 days; estimated hearing time (excluding pre-reading and preparation of closing submissions) 6 to 10 days; and estimated hearing (excluding pre-reading and preparation of closing submissions) over 10 days.

3. Where it will enable a case to be tried within 12 months, or shortly thereafter, the Court may list a trial up to one month earlier than the applicable Trial Window without the need for any application for expedition.

4. The Court will use its case management powers in a more active manner than hitherto, with a view to dealing with cases justly and at proportionate cost in accordance with CPR rule 1.1. This may have the effect of setting limits on hearing times that enable cases to be listed promptly. For example, the Court may direct that a case estimated at 6 days will be heard in 5 days, and may allocate time between the parties in a manner which enables that to be achieved.

5. Where it makes a significant difference to the time which cases must wait to be listed for trial and it will not cause significant prejudice to any party, cases may be listed without reference to the availability of counsel instructed by the parties.

These steps do not exclude the possibility of cases being expedited where expedition is warranted. Nor do they exclude the possibility of the parties opting to use the streamlined procedure or the Shorter Trial pilot scheme or the Flexible Trial pilot scheme.

This Practice Statement is issued with the concurrence of the Chancellor of the High Court. It supersedes the Practice Statement issued on 28 January 2015.

Arnold J
Judge in Charge of the Patents Court
7 December 2015

Editorial note

2F-154.1 The Practice Statement: Listing of Cases for Trial in the Patents Court was issued by the Judge in Charge of the Patents Court in December 2015. It was retained by the Chancery Practice Note 2022, issued by the Chancellor in July 2022.

SECTION 2FA FINANCIAL LIST

PART 63A—FINANCIAL LIST

Effect of rule

The Financial List judges

Replace Chancery Division list with:

2FA-5.1 The Chancellor of the High Court, currently Sir Julian Flaux;

Mr Justice Hildyard;
Mr Justice Marcus Smith;
Mrs Justice Falk; and
Mr Justice Zacaroli.

PRACTICE DIRECTION 63AA—FINANCIAL LIST

Editorial note

Qualifying claim

In the second and fifth paragraphs, replace "Financial Conduct Authority v Arch Insurance (UK) Ltd [2020] UKSC 1" with:

Financial Conduct Authority v Arch Insurance (UK) Ltd [2021] UKSC 1 **2FA-12.1**

SECTION 2G COMPANIES ACT PROCEEDINGS

Companies Act 2006

Editorial note

Replace paragraph with:

The court procedure relating to the conduct of derivative claims is set out in Pt 19.9 of the Civil Procedure Rules. A full commentary can be found in Vol.1 under that rule. Note the guidance recently given by the Supreme Court on the "rule against reflective loss" in the case of *Sevilleja v Marex Financial Ltd* [2020] UKSC 31. On the correct approach to the rule against reflective loss when the Contracts (Rights of Third Parties) Act 1999 is engaged, see *Broadcasting Investment Group Ltd v Smith* [2021] EWCA Civ 912 **2G-6.1**

PRACTICE DIRECTION 49A—APPLICATIONS UNDER THE COMPANIES ACTS AND RELATED LEGISLATION

Companies Court

Impact of COVID-19: the conduct of hearings

Replace "With the easing of restrictions, many" with:

With the lifting of restrictions, most **2G-39**

Urgent applications

In the second sentence, replace "capital reduction claims and cross-border merger" with:

and capital reduction **2G-42**

Schemes, reductions and similar proceedings

Replace the first paragraph with:

Arrangements for hearings of schemes and reductions (as well as those under the Financial Services and Markets Act 2000) in the Royal Courts of Justice should be made with the Companies Court case manager, Rolls Building, Fetter Lane, London EC4A 1NL, to whom inquiries may also be made by telephone (020 7947 6727). Papers should be lodged *at least* five working days before the hearing. **2G-43**

Applications to extend time for registering a charge or to rectify an omission or mis-statement

In the fifth paragraph, replace "During COVID-19, these applications are generally dealt with remotely; users" with:

Users **2G-45**

Unfair prejudice applications (2006 Act Pt 30)

To the end of the fifth paragraph (beginning with "The petition must specify"), add:

On the scope of allegations which may properly be pleaded and relied upon within the context **2G-46.1** of unfair prejudice proceedings, see the helpful guidance given by Snowden LJ (Nugee and Green LJJ concurring) in *Re Kings Solutions Ltd* [2021] EWCA Civ 1943

Replace the paragraph after the second list with:

Practitioners should note that the Disclosure Pilot set out in PD 51U, which as from 1 October 2022 became PD57AD, applies to Unfair Prejudice petitions: see *Message from the Chief Insolvency and Companies Court Judge* dated 6 February 2019 (see para.57ADPN.2). The automatic directions on Unfair Prejudice petitions were initially updated to make reference to PD51U and will shortly be updated again, to make reference to PD57AD. On the approach to be adopted to the Disclosure Pilot (and now PD57AD), see generally In the *UTB LLC v Sheffield United Ltd (Re Blades Leisure Ltd)* [2019] EWHC 914 (Ch), [11]-[25], [65], and [75]-[80] and the commentary to PD57AD.

Delete the penultimate paragraph.

PRACTICE DIRECTION 49B—ORDER UNDER SECTION 127 INSOLVENCY ACT 1986

Editorial note

To the end of the paragraph, add:

2G-53.1 PD49B—Order under Section 127 of the Insolvency Act 1986 was omitted from the CPR by CPR Update 149 (July 2022) as from 1 October 2022.

PRACTICE NOTE: COMPANIES COURT—COMPANY RESTORATION

Add new paragraph 2G-54.1:

Editorial introduction

2G-54.1 This Practice Note was originally issued in 2012. It was retained by the Chancery Practice Note 2022, issued by the Chancellor in July 2022.

SECTION 3 OTHER PROCEEDINGS
SECTION 3A HOUSING

Rent Act 1977

The Debt Respite Scheme

To the end of the paragraph, add:

3A-199.1 For examples of the operation of the scheme, see *Axnoller Events Ltd v Brake* [2021] EWHC 2308 (Ch) and *Lees v Kaye* [2022] EWHC 1151 (QB).

Replace s.2 with:

SCHEDULES

SECTIONS 2 AND 3

SCHEDULE 1

STATUTORY TENANCIES

PART I

STATUTORY TENANTS BY SUCCESSION

3A-236 2.—(1) The surviving spouse, or civil partner, (if any) of the original tenant, if residing in the dwelling-house immediately before the death of the original tenant, shall after the death be the statutory tenant if and so long as he or she occupies the dwelling-house as his or her residence.

(2) For the purposes of this paragraph, a person who was living with the original tenant as if they were a married couple or civil partners is to be treated as the spouse or civil partner of the original tenant.

(3) If, immediately after the death of the original tenant, there is, by virtue of sub-paragraph (2) above, more than one person who fulfils the conditions in sub-paragraph (1) above, such one of them as may be decided by agreement or, in default of agreement, by the county court shall for the purposes of this paragraph be treated as the tenant's spouse, or civil partner.

Note

To the end of the paragraph, add:
and by the Civil Partnership (Opposite-sex Couples) Regulations 2019 (SI 2019/1458). **3A-237**

Housing Act 1985

Housing associations and the Human Rights Act 1998

Replace paragraph with:
In determining whether a housing association is a functional public authority within the meaning of the Human Rights Act 1998 s.6(1), courts should adopt a "factor based approach". This requires them to have regard to all the features or factors which may cast light on whether the particular function under consideration is a public function or not, and weigh them in the round. If a body is a core public authority, all its functions are public functions, as are all acts pursuant to those functions. A body is a hybrid authority if only some of its functions are public functions. Even then, the particular act is not subject to convention principles if it is a private act (Human Rights Act 1998 s.6(5)). The character of an act is likely to take its colour from the character of the function of which it forms part. In *R. (Weaver) v London & Quadrant Housing Trust* [2009] EWCA Civ 587; [2010] 1 W.L.R. 363 the Court of Appeal held, by a majority, that the provision of social housing was a public function. Elias LJ found that seeking the termination of a social housing tenancy was not a private act. **3A-321**

> "[T]he act of termination is so bound up with the provision of social housing that once the latter is seen, in the context of this particular body, as the exercise of a public function, then acts which are necessarily involved in the regulation of the function must also be public acts. The grant of a tenancy and its subsequent termination are part and parcel of determining who should be allowed to take advantage of this public benefit. This is not an act which is purely incidental or supplementary to the principal function ..."

(para.76). See too *R. (McIntyre) v Gentoo Group Ltd* [2010] EWHC 5 (Admin) (a decision relating to the mutual exchange of social housing tenancies) and *R. (TRX) v Network Homes Ltd* [2022] EWHC 456 (Admin) (a refusal to grant an application for a management transfer following threats of domestic abuse). Such decisions and policies are likely to involve the exercise of a public function and so be amenable to judicial review and, by extension, subject to the Equality Act 2010 s.29.

The Debt Respite Scheme

To the end of the paragraph, add:
For examples of the operation of the scheme, see *Axnoller Events Ltd v Brake* [2021] EWHC 2308 (Ch) and *Lees v Kaye* [2022] EWHC 1151 (QB). **3A-359**

Equality Act 2010

Replace "Metropolitan Housing Trust Ltd v TM (A Protected Party) [2021] EWCA Civ 1890" with:
Metropolitan Housing Trust Ltd v TM (A Protected Party) [2021] EWCA Civ 1890; [2022] H.L.R. 16 **3A-378**

At the end of the paragraph, replace "J) and T.M. v Metropolitan Housing Trust Ltd [2020] EWHC 311 (QB)." with:
J).

Editorial introduction

Replace paragraph with:
A tenant who wishes to dispute the landlord's claim for possession under the absolute ground contained in s.84A must request a review of the landlord's decision to seek an order for possession within seven days beginning with the day on which the s.83ZA notice was served. In those circumstances, the landlord must review its decision. A local authority has no power to agree to accept an out of time request for a s.85ZA review or to waive compliance with the statutory time limit following service of a notice seeking possession served in accordance with s.83ZA. A request is only "duly" made in accordance with s.85ZA(3) if it is made within the specified period. A tenant who requests a statutory review outside the seven-day period laid down by s.85ZA(2) is not entitled to a statutory review and the landlord has no obligation or power to conduct one (*Hounslow LBC v Harris* [2017] EWCA Civ 1476 and *R. (Kalonga) v Croydon LBC* [2022] EWCA Civ 670). The procedure **3A-389.6**

to be followed on any such review is contained in the Absolute Ground for Possession for Anti-social Behaviour (Review Procedure) (England) Regulations (SI 2014/2554). An application for a review must include:

(a) the applicant's name and address;
(b) a description of the original decision in respect of which the review is sought including the date on which the decision was made;
(c) a statement of the grounds on which the review is sought;
(d) a statement to the effect that the applicant does, or does not, require the review to be conducted by way of an oral hearing;
(e) a statement to the effect that the applicant does, or does not, agree to receive communications relating to the review by email, and if the former, the email address to which such communications should be sent.

The review must be conducted by a person of greater seniority than the person who made the original decision. After the review, the landlord must notify the tenant of its decision in writing, and, if it confirms its original decision, it must also give its reasons.

Replace s.86A(5), (6) and (7) with:

Persons qualified to succeed tenant: England

3A-395.1 (5) For the purposes of this section, a person who was living with the tenant as if they were a married couple or civil partners is to be treated as the tenant's spouse or civil partner.

(6) Subsection (7) applies if, on the death of the tenant, there is by virtue of subsection (5) more than one person who fulfils the condition in subsection (1)(b).

(7) Such one of those persons as may be agreed between them or as may, where there is no such agreement, be selected by the landlord is for the purpose of this section to be treated as the tenant's spouse or civil partner.

Note

To the end of the first paragraph, add:

3A-395.2 Amended by the Civil Partnership (Opposite-sex Couples) Regulations 2019 (SI 2019/1458).

Replace the second paragraph with:

Tenancies which commenced before this section came into force on 1 April 2012 are still governed by the former, unamended version of s.87. See e.g. *Civil Procedure* 2010 Vol.2 para.3A-396 and the commentary thereto.

Editorial introduction

Replace the fourth paragraph with:

3A-440.7 Landlords cannot terminate flexible tenancies before the end of any fixed term unless the tenancy agreement contains a break clause or a proviso for forfeiture. If a flexible tenancy does not contain any express provision for early termination, then it does not fall within the ambit of s.82(1)(b) and, irrespective of any breach committed by the tenant, the landlord is unable to determine the tenancy agreement until after the expiry of the fixed term under s.107D (*Croydon LBC v Kalonga* [2022] UKSC 7; [2022] 2 W.L.R. 592). If there is a proviso for forfeiture, then, where applicable, a Law of Property Act 1925 s.146 notice must be served.

3A-449 *Replace s.113(1)(a) with:*

(a) he is the spouse or civil partner of that person, or he and that person live together as if they were a married couple or

Note

To the end of the paragraph, add:

3A-450 and by the Civil Partnership (Opposite-sex Couples) Regulations 2019 (SI 2019/1458)

Replace paragraph with:

SCHEDULE 2

PART I

GROUNDS ON WHICH COURT MAY ORDER POSSESSION IF IT CONSIDERS IT REASONABLE

Ground 2A

The dwelling-house was occupied (whether alone or with others) by a married couple, a couple who are civil partners of each other, or a couple living together as if they were a married couple or civil partners and— **3A-506**

(a) one or both of the partners is a tenant of the dwelling-house,

(b) one partner has left because of violence or threats of violence by the other towards—

(i) that partner, or

(ii) a member of the family of that partner who was residing with that partner immediately before the partner left, and

(c) the court is satisfied that the partner who has left is unlikely to return.

This Ground applies only in relation to dwelling-houses in England.

Note

To the end of the paragraph, add:

Ground 2A was amended by the Civil Partnership (Opposite-sex Couples) Regulations 2019 (SI 2019/1458) **3A-524**

Landlord and Tenant Act 1985

Damages

Replace the sixth paragraph with:

On the other hand, in *Earle v Charalambous* [2006] EWCA Civ 1090; [2007] H.L.R. 8; it was said: **3A-559**

> "A long-lease of a residential property is not only a home, but is also a valuable property asset. Distress and inconvenience caused by disrepair are not freestanding heads of claim, but are symptomatic of interference with the lessee's enjoyment of that asset. If the lessor's breach of covenant has the effect of depriving the lessee of that enjoyment, wholly or partially, for a significant period, a notional judgment of the resulting reduction in rental value is likely to be the most appropriate starting point for assessment of damages. Generally, this reduction will not be capable of precise estimation; ... it will be a matter for the judgment for the court, rather than for expert valuation evidence."

Claims for breach of repairing obligations fall squarely within the primary purpose of *Simmons v Castle* [2012] EWCA Civ 1288; [2013] 1 W.L.R. 1239 and so a 10% increase in damages should be added to awards to compensate successful claimants for being deprived of the right which they had enjoyed since 2000 to recover success fees from defendants where they were funding the legal costs of pursuing their claims by CFAs (*Khan v Mehmood* [2022] EWCA Civ 791).

Housing Act 1988

Equality Act 2010

Replace "Metropolitan Housing Trust Ltd v TM (A Protected Party) [2021] EWCA Civ 1890" with:

Metropolitan Housing Trust Ltd v TM (A Protected Party) [2021] EWCA Civ 1890; [2022] H.L.R. 16 **3A-778**

The Debt Respite Scheme

To the end of the paragraph, add:

For examples of the operation of the scheme, see *Axnoller Events Ltd v Brake* [2021] EWHC 2308 (Ch) and *Lees v Kaye* [2022] EWHC 1151 (QB). **3A-791.1**

Service of section 8 notices

After the first paragraph, add new paragraph:

Section 8 does not require that the landlord sign the notice. A landlord complies with s.8 if an agent serves notice on its behalf, even if the agent signs the notice in the landlord's name. In addition, the prescribed form explicitly allows notice to be given by and signed by an agent for the landlord (*Cooke v Northwood (Solihull) Ltd* [2022] EWCA Civ 40; [2022] H.L.R. 22). **3A-792**

Replace s.17 with:

MISCELLANEOUS

Succession to assured tenancy by spouse

3A-856 **17.**—(1) Subject to subsection (1D), in any case where—

(a) the sole tenant under an assured periodic tenancy dies, and

(b) immediately before the death, the tenant's spouse or civil partner was occupying the dwelling-house as his or her only or principal home,

then, on the death, the tenancy vests by virtue of this section in the spouse or civil partner (and, accordingly, does not devolve under the tenant's will or intestacy).

(1A) Subject to subsection (1D), in any case where—

(a) there is an assured periodic tenancy of a dwelling-house in England under which—

(i) the landlord is a private registered provider of social housing, and

(ii) the tenant is a sole tenant,

(b) the tenant under the tenancy dies,

(c) immediately before the death, the dwelling-house was not occupied by a spouse or civil partner of the tenant as his or her only or principal home,

(d) an express term of the tenancy makes provision for a person other than such a spouse or civil partner of the tenant to succeed to the tenancy, and

(e) there is a person whose succession is in accordance with that term,

then, on the death, the tenancy vests by virtue of this section in that person (and, accordingly, does not devolve under the tenant's will or intestacy).

(1B) Subject to subsection (1D), in any case where—

(a) there is an assured tenancy of a dwelling-house in England for a fixed term of not less than two years under which—

(i) the landlord is a private registered provider of social housing, and

(ii) the tenant is a sole tenant,

(b) the tenant under the tenancy dies, and

(c) immediately before the death, the tenant's spouse or civil partner was occupying the dwelling-house as his or her only or principal home,

then, on the death, the tenancy vests by virtue of this section in the spouse or civil partner (and, accordingly, does not devolve under the tenant's will or intestacy).

(1C) Subject to subsection (1D), in any case where—

(a) there is an assured tenancy of a dwelling-house in England for a fixed term of not less than two years under which—

(i) the landlord is a private registered provider of social housing, and

(ii) the tenant is a sole tenant,

(b) the tenant under the tenancy dies,

(c) immediately before the death, the dwelling-house was not occupied by a spouse or civil partner of the tenant as his or her only or principal home,

(d) an express term of the tenancy makes provision for a person other than such a spouse or civil partner of the tenant to succeed to the tenancy, and

(e) there is a person whose succession is in accordance with that term, then, on the death, the tenancy vests by virtue of this section in that person (and accordingly does not devolve under the tenant's will or intestacy).

(1D) Subsection (1), (1A), (1B) or (1C) does not apply if the tenant was himself a successor as defined in subsection (2) or subsection (3).

(1E) In such a case, on the death, the tenancy vests by virtue of this section in a person ("P") (and, accordingly, does not devolve under the tenant's will or intestacy) if, and only if—

(a) (in a case within subsection (1)) the tenancy is of a dwelling-house in England under which the landlord is a private registered provider of social housing,

(b) an express term of the tenancy makes provision for a person to succeed a successor to the tenancy, and

(c) P's succession is in accordance with that term.

(2) For the purposes of this section, a tenant is a successor in relation to a tenancy if—

(a) the tenancy became vested in him either by virtue of this section or under the will or intestacy of a previous tenant; or

(b) at some time before the tenant's death the tenancy was a joint tenancy held by himself and one or more other persons and, prior to his death, he became the sole tenant by survivorship; or

(c) he became entitled to the tenancy as mentioned in section 39(5) below.

(3) For the purposes of this section, a tenant is also a successor in relation to a tenancy (in this subsection referred to as "the new tenancy") which was granted to him (alone or jointly with others) if—

(a) at some time before the grant of the new tenancy, he was, by virtue of subsection (2) above, a successor in relation to an earlier tenancy of the same or substantially the same dwelling-house as is let under the new tenancy; and

(b) at all times since he became such a successor he has been a tenant (alone or jointly with others) of the dwelling-house which is let under the new tenancy or of a dwelling-house which is substantially the same as that dwelling-house.

(4) For the purposes of this section, a person who was living with the tenant as if they were a married couple or civil partners is to be treated as the tenant's spouse or civil partner.

(5) If, on the death of the tenant, there is, by virtue of subsection (4) above, more than one person who fulfils the condition in subsection (1)(b) or (1B)(c) above, such one of them as may be decided by agreement or, in default of agreement, by the county court shall for the purposes of this section be treated as the tenant's spouse, or if that person is the same sex as the tenant, and falls within subsection (4)(b), as the tenant's civil partner.

(6) If, on the death of the tenant, there is more than one person in whom the tenancy would otherwise vest by virtue of subsection (1A), (1C) or (1E), the tenancy vests in such one of them as may be agreed between them or, in default of agreement, as is determined by the county court.

(7) This section does not apply to a fixed term assured tenancy that is a lease of a dwelling-house—

(a) granted on payment of a premium calculated by reference to a percentage of the value of the dwelling-house or of the cost of providing it, or

(b) under which the lessee (or the lessee's personal representatives) will or may be entitled to a sum calculated by reference, directly or indirectly, to the value of the dwelling-house.

Note

To the end of the paragraph, add:

3A-857 and by the Civil Partnership (Opposite-sex Couples) Regulations 2019 (SI 2019/1458)

spouse

Replace "Clarion Housing Association Ltd v Carter [2021] EWHC 2890 (QB)" with:

3A-860.2 *Clarion Housing Association Ltd v Carter* [2021] EWHC 2890 (QB); [2022] H.L.R. 10

3A-971 *Replace paragraph with:*

Grounds on Which Court may Order Possession

Ground 14A

The dwelling-house was occupied (whether alone or with others) by a married couple, a couple who are civil partners of each other, or a couple living together as if they were a married couple or civil partners and—

(a) one or both of the partners is a tenant of the dwelling-house,

(b) the landlord who is seeking possession is a non-profit registered provider of social housing, a registered social landlord or a charitable housing trust, or, where the dwelling-house is social housing within the meaning of Part 2 of the Housing and Regeneration Act 2008, a profit-making registered provider of social housing,

(c) one partner has left the dwelling-house because of violence or threats of violence by the other towards—

  (i) that partner, or

  (ii) children of the partnership.

(d) the court is satisfied that the partner who has left is unlikely to return.

For the purposes of this ground "registered social landlord" and "member of the family" have the same meaning as in Part I of the Housing Act 1996 and "charitable housing trust" means a housing trust, within the meaning of the Housing Associations Act 1985, which is a charity within the meaning of the Charities Act 1993.

Note

Add new paragraph at end:

3A-991 Ground 14A amended (subject to transitional and saving provisions in Sch.3 thereof) by the Housing and Regeneration Act 2008 (Consequential Provisions) Order 2010 (SI 2010/866) Sch.2 para.74(3), with effect from 1 April 2010. Further amended by the Civil Partnership (Opposite-sex Couples) Regulations 2019 (SI 2019/1458).

Housing Act 1996

3A-1115 *Replace s.140(1)(a) with:*

(a) he is the spouse or civil partner of that person, or he and that person live together as if they were a married couple, or

Note

To the end of the paragraph, add:

3A-1116 and by the Civil Partnership (Opposite-sex Couples) Regulations 2019 (SI 2019/1458)

"reasonable to continue to occupy"

Replace the last paragraph with:

3A-1251 For the interaction between the public sector equality duty and Housing Act 1996 s.177, see *Lomax v Gosport BC* [2018] EWCA Civ 1846; [2018] H.L.R. 40, *Kannan v Newham LBC* [2019] EWCA Civ 57; [2019] H.L.R. 22 and *Biden v Waverley BC* [2022] EWCA Civ 442. See too *London and Quadrant Housing Trust v Patrick* [2019] EWHC 1263 (QB); [2020] H.L.R. 3 and *Metropolitan Housing Trust Ltd v TM (A Protected Party)* [2021] EWCA Civ 1890; [2022] H.L.R. 16.

Inquiry into cases of homelessness or threatened homelessness

Replace "Ciftci v Haringey LBC [2021] EWCA Civ 1772" with:

3A-1288 *Ciftci v Haringey LBC* [2021] EWCA Civ 1772; [2022] H.L.R. 9

Persons from abroad not eligible for housing assistance

Replace the second paragraph with:

Both these provisions are subject to exceptions contained in the Allocation of Housing and Homelessness (Eligibility) (England) Regulations 2006 (SI 2006/1294) and the Allocation of Housing and Homelessness (Miscellaneous Provisions) (England) Regulations 2006 (SI 2006/2527), as amended by the Allocation of Housing and Homelessness (Eligibility) (England) (Amendment) (No.2) Regulations 2006 (SI 2006/3340), the Allocation of Housing and Homelessness (Eligibility) (England) (Amendment) Regulations 2013 (SI 2013/1467), the Allocation of Housing and Homelessness (Eligibility) (England) (Amendment) Regulations 2016 (SI 2016/965), the Allocation of Housing and Homelessness (Eligibility) (England) (Amendment) Regulations 2021 (SI 2021/665), the Allocation of Housing and Homelessness (Eligibility) (England) and Persons subject to Immigration Control (Housing Authority Accommodation and Homelessness) (Amendment) Regulations (SI 2021/1045), the Allocation of Housing and Homelessness (Eligibility) (England) and Persons subject to Immigration Control (Housing Authority Accommodation and Homelessness) (Amendment) Regulations 2022 (SI 2022/339) and the Allocation of Housing and Homelessness (Eligibility) (England) and Persons Subject to Immigration Control (Housing Authority Accommodation and Homelessness) (Amendment) (No.2) Regulations 2022 (SI 2022/601). **3A-1296**

Vulnerability, disability and the Equality Act

Replace "Lomax v Gosport BC [2018] EWCA Civ 1846; [2018] H.L.R. 40 and Kannan v Newham LBC [2019] EWCA Civ 57; [2019] H.L.R. 22." with:

Lomax v Gosport BC [2018] EWCA Civ 1846; [2018] H.L.R. 40, *Kannan v Newham LBC* [2019] EWCA Civ 57; [2019] H.L.R. 22 and *Biden v Waverley BC* [2022] EWCA Civ 442. **3A-1324.1**

Eviction following arrears

To the end of the first paragraph, add:

and *Baptie v Kingston upon Thames RLBC* [2022] EWCA Civ 888. **3A-1339**

They are satisfied that the accommodation is suitable (s.193(7F) and s.206)

Replace paragraph with:

See s.210 below, the Homelessness (Suitability of Accommodation) (England) Order 2012 (SI 2012/2601), the Homelessness (Suitability of Accommodation) (England) Order 2003 (SI 2003/3326), as amended by the Homelessness (Suitability of Accommodation) (Amendment) (England) Order 2022 (SI 2022/521), and the commentary at para.3A-1470. **3A-1373**

Duty to persons with priority need who are not homeless intentionally

Replace list item "(b)" with:

(b) secure that suitable accommodation is made available for occupation (Housing Act 1996 ss.193(2) and 206). Once the conditions in s.193(1) are met, the duty to accommodate is triggered and it is unlawful to impose "any further hurdle or proviso before accepting that the duty arises" (e.g. service of notice to quit in relation to joint tenancy). See *R. (Hammia) v Wandsworth LBC* [2005] EWHC 1127; [2005] H.L.R. 45. Where housing authorities accept that they owe the main duty under s.193(2) to provide accommodation and make decisions that existing accommodation is not "suitable", they are automatically in breach of duty if they leave applicants in the existing accommodation, even for a short period. The law does not provide for a reasonable time in which to secure suitable alternative accommodation (*R. (M) v Newham LBC* [2020] EWHC 327 (Admin); [2021] H.L.R. 1 and *R. (Elkundi) v Birmingham CC*[2021] EWHC 1024 (Admin); [2021] 1 W.L.R. 4031 where it was held that placing such applicants on a waiting list was unlawful); or **3A-1374**

A fresh application

Replace list with:

- an authority has to accept and consider a second application if it is not factually "identical" to the earlier one; **3A-1377.1**
- this test of "exactly the same facts" was harder for an authority to use to refuse an application than the "material change of circumstances" approach;
- any new facts raised in the second approach to a council (provided not trivial or fanciful) require that it be treated as a fresh application (see too *Minott v Cambridge CC* [2022] EWCA Civ 15);
- the question is whether the facts as presented are "new" and comparison has to be made by contrasting the material put forward on the new approach with the facts as they had stood when the earlier application was "disposed of" by an initial or review decision (as opposed to the date that the earlier application had been made);

- that question does not involve any "inquiries" by an authority, nor any investigation as to whether the asserted new facts are accurate (per Neuberger and Keene LJJ). The issue is simply whether, in the purported new application, the applicant has put forward facts which are different and the differences are neither fanciful nor trivial. A safeguard against applicants "inventing" new facts is the possibility of criminal prosecution. Pill LJ, however, considered that "some inquiry" might be necessary to establish (a) what matters are now relied upon and (b) whether they are the same matters or new matters. As to the absence of "new facts", see *R. (Kensington and Chelsea RLBC) v Ealing LBC* [2017] EWHC 24 (Admin); [2017] H.L.R. 13.

Replace "R. (Ibrahim) v Westminster CC [2021] EWHC 2616 (Admin)" with:
R. (Ibrahim) v Westminster CC [2021] EWHC 2616 (Admin); [2022] H.L.R. 11

Referral of case to another local housing authority

3A-1402 *Delete the last paragraph.*

Suitability of accommodation

In the sixth paragraph, replace "Hajjaj v City of Westminster [2021] EWCA Civ 1688" with:
3A-1470 *Hajjaj v City of Westminster* [2021] EWCA Civ 1688; [2022] H.L.R. 12

Replace the ninth paragraph with:
The question of whether the accommodation offered is "suitable" for the applicant and each member of their household clearly requires the local authority to have regard to the need to safeguard and promote the welfare of any children in their household (Children Act 2004 s.11). Its suitability to meet their needs is a key component in its suitability generally. It is not enough for the decision-maker simply to ask whether any of the children are approaching GCSE or other externally assessed examinations. Disruption to their education and other support networks may be actively harmful to their social and educational development, but the authority also has to have regard to the need to promote, as well as to safeguard, their welfare. The decision maker should identify the principal needs of the children, both individually and collectively, and have regard to the need to safeguard and promote them when making the decision (*Nzolameso v Westminster CC* [2015] UKSC 22; [2015] 2 All E.R. 942). In *R. v Newham LBC Ex p. Khan* (2001) 33 H.L.R. 29, QBD Collins J held that the decision to "split" a family who had lived together prior to homelessness was unlawful. The statutory test may be satisfied by a single unit of accommodation in which a family can live together, but it may also be satisfied by two units of accommodation if they are so located that they enable the family to live "together" in practical terms (*Sharif v Camden LBC* [2013] UKSC 10; [2013] H.L.R. 16; [2013] 2 All E.R. 309). Cf. *R. (on the application of Abo-Ragheef) v Westminster City Council* [2000] 11 WLUK 799, 27 November 2001, QBD Admin Ct. As to affordability of accommodation, see *Paley v Waltham Forest LBC* [2022] EWCA Civ 112; [2022] H.L.R. 24.

Replace the tenth paragraph with:
As to the provision of out-of-area accommodation, see *Nzolameso v City of Westminster* [2015] UKSC 22; [2015] 2 All E.R. 942. Housing authorities have a statutory duty to accommodate within their area so far as this is reasonably practicable. "Reasonable practicability" imports a stronger duty than simply being reasonable. But if it is not reasonably practicable to accommodate "in borough", they must generally, and where possible, try to place the household as close as possible to where they were previously living. There will be some cases where this does not apply, for example where there are clear benefits in placing the applicant outside the district, because of domestic violence or to break links with negative influences within the district, and others where the applicant does not mind where they go or actively want to move out of the area. The combined effect of the Homelessness (Suitability of Accommodation) (England) Order 2012 (SI 2012/2601), as amended by the Homelessness (Suitability of Accommodation) (Amendment) (England) Order 2022 (SI 2022/521), and the Supplementary Guidance was meant to change the legal landscape as it was when previous cases dealing with an "out of borough" placement policy, such as *R. (Yumsak) v Enfield LBC* [2002] EWHC 280 (Admin); [2003] H.L.R. 1, and *R. (Calgin) v Enfield LBC* [2005] EWHC 1716 (Admin); [2006] H.L.R. 58, were decided. See though *Alibkhiet v Brent LBC; Adam v City of Westminster* [2018] EWCA Civ 2742; [2019] H.L.R. 15 where decisions to make offers to accommodate homeless persons outside their respective districts were upheld. The authorities were entitled to take account of the resources available, the difficulties of procuring sufficient units of temporary accommodation at affordable prices in their area, and the practicalities of procuring accommodation in nearby boroughs. An offer can only discharge the main housing duty under s.193(7F) if the authority is satisfied both that the accommodation is suitable and that it would be reasonable for the applicant to accept the offer. The particular needs of the applicant, for example to be protected from domestic violence and to be located near support networks, are relevant when considering suitability but that does not mean that those matters are material only to suitability. The submission that if premises were suitable it had to follow that it was reasonable to accept them

was rejected in *Slater v Lewisham LBC* [2006] EWCA Civ 394; [2006] H.L.R. 37. There may be circumstances in which it is reasonable to refuse accommodation that is objectively suitable.

Remove "Housing Act 1985 (Amendment of Schedule 2A) (Serious Offences) (Wales) Order 2016" (paras 3A-3107.2+ to 3A-3108+) and insert note:

Housing Act 1985 (Amendment of Schedule 2A) (Serious Offences) (Wales) Order 2016

(SI 2016/173(W. 74))

ARRANGEMENT OF

Note

The Housing Act 1985 (Amendment of Schedule 2A) (Serious Offences) (Wales) Order 2016 (SI 2016/173) was revoked by the Renting Homes (Wales) Act 2016 (Consequential Amendments to Secondary Legislation) Regulations 2022 (SI 2022/907) Sch.2 para.1, with effect from 1 December 2022. **3A-3107.2**

SECTION 3B BUSINESS TENANCIES

Landlord and Tenant Act 1954

Coronavirus pandemic

Replace paragraph with:

For the purposes of determining whether or not a landlord has made out the ground mentioned in s.30(1)(b) of the 1954 Act (persistent delay in paying rent) any failure to pay a "protected rent debt" due under that tenancy during the "moratorium period" as defined in the Commercial Rent (Coronavirus) Act 2022 is disregarded (see sch.2, para.5(3) of that Act at para.3B-315). **3B-178.1**

Replace the Coronavirus Act s.82 and commentary (paras 3B-315 to 3B-323) with the new Commercial Rent (Coronavirus) Act 2022 ss.1-6, 23-24 and Schs 2 and 3:

Commercial Rent (Coronavirus) Act 2022

(2022 c.12)

PART 1

INTRODUCTORY PROVISIONS

Overview

1.–(1) This Act enables the matter of relief from payment of protected rent debts due from the tenant to the landlord under a business tenancy to be resolved by arbitration (if not resolved by agreement). **3B-315**

(2) In this Act–

(a) sections 2 to 6 define for the purposes of this Act the terms "protected rent debt", "the matter of relief from payment" and other key terms used in this Act;

(b) Part 2 provides for statutory arbitration between the landlord and the tenant under a business tenancy in relation to the matter of relief from payment of a protected rent debt;

(c) Part 3 provides for temporary restrictions on the availability of certain remedies and insolvency arrangements that would otherwise be available in relation to a protected rent debt.

(3) Nothing in this Act is to be taken as—
   (a) affecting the capacity of the parties to a business tenancy to resolve by agreement, at any time, the matter of relief from payment of a protected rent debt (or any other matter relating to the tenancy), or
   (b) preventing an agreement resolving the matter of relief from payment of a protected rent debt from having effect or being enforced.

"Rent" and "business tenancy"

3B-316 **2.**—(1) "Rent", in relation to a business tenancy, means an amount consisting of one or more of the following—
   (a) an amount payable by the tenant to the landlord under the tenancy for possession and use of the premises comprised in the tenancy (whether described as rent or otherwise);
   (b) an amount payable by the tenant to the landlord under the tenancy as a service charge;
   (c) interest on an unpaid amount within paragraph (a) or (b).

(2) In subsection (1)—
   (a) a reference to an amount includes any VAT chargeable on that amount;
   (b) a reference to the landlord includes a person acting for the landlord (such as a managing agent);
   (c) "service charge" means an amount—
      (i) which is payable (directly or indirectly) for services, repairs, maintenance, improvements, insurance costs or the landlord's management costs (including management costs of a superior landlord which the landlord is required to pay), and
      (ii) which is a fixed amount or an amount that varies or may vary according to the relevant costs (or a combination of the two).

(3) In subsection (2)(c)—
   (a) "insurance costs" includes costs incurred by the landlord in connection with insuring against loss of rent or in complying with obligations under the tenancy either to insure the whole or any part of—
      (i) the premises comprised in the tenancy, and
      (ii) any common parts of a property which includes those premises,

   or to pay the costs of such insurance incurred by any superior landlord;
   (b) "the relevant costs" means the costs or estimated costs incurred or to be incurred by or on behalf of the landlord in connection with the matter for which the service charge is payable, and for this purpose—
      (i) "costs" includes overheads, and
      (ii) costs are relevant costs in relation to a service charge whether they are incurred, or to be incurred, in the period for which the service charge is payable or in an earlier or later period.

(4) An amount drawn down by the landlord from a tenancy deposit to meet the whole or part of a rent debt is to be treated as unpaid rent due from the tenant to the landlord (and such rent is "paid" where the tenant makes good any shortfall in the deposit).

(5) "Business tenancy" means a tenancy to which Part 2 of the Landlord and Tenant Act 1954 applies.

(6) "English business tenancy" means a business tenancy comprising premises in England.

(7) "Welsh business tenancy" means a business tenancy comprising premises in Wales.

"Protected rent debt"

3.—(1) A "protected rent debt" is a debt under a business tenancy consisting of unpaid protected rent. **3B-317**

(2) Rent due under the tenancy is "protected rent" if—

(a) the tenancy was adversely affected by coronavirus (see section 4), and

(b) the rent is attributable to a period of occupation by the tenant for, or for a period within, the protected period applying to the tenancy (see section 5).

(3) Rent consisting of interest on an unpaid amount within section 2(1)(a) or (b) is to be regarded for the purposes of subsection (2)(b) as attributable to the same period of occupation by the tenant as that unpaid amount.

(4) A period of occupation by the tenant that began, or ended, at a time during a particular day is to be treated as including the whole of that day.

(5) If any rent due under the tenancy is attributable to a period of occupation by the tenant of which only part is of the description in subsection (2)(b), then so much of the rent as can be reasonably attributed to that part of the period is protected rent.

(6) An amount treated by section 2(4) as unpaid rent is to be regarded as unpaid protected rent if the rent debt that was satisfied (in whole or part) by drawing it down from the tenancy deposit would otherwise have been a protected rent debt.

"Adversely affected by coronavirus"

4.—(1) A business tenancy was "adversely affected by coronavirus" for the purposes of section 3(2)(a) if, for any relevant period— **3B-318**

(a) the whole or part of the business carried on by the tenant at or from the premises comprised in the tenancy, or

(b) the whole or part of those premises,

was of a description subject to a closure requirement.

(2) For this purpose—

(a) "closure requirement" means a requirement imposed by coronavirus regulations which is expressed as an obligation—

(i) to close businesses, or parts of businesses, of a specified description, or

(ii) to close premises, or parts of premises, of a specified description; and

(b) "relevant period" means a period beginning at or after 2 p.m. on 21 March 2020 and ending at or before—

(i) 11.55 p.m. on 18 July 2021, for English business tenancies, or

(ii) 6 a.m. on 7 August 2021, for Welsh business tenancies.

(3) A requirement expressed as an obligation to close businesses or premises of a specified description, or parts of businesses or premises of a specified description, every day at particular times is to be regarded for the purposes of subsection (2)(a) as a closure requirement.

(4) It is immaterial for the purposes of subsection (2)(a) that specific limited activities were (as an exception) allowed by the regulations to be carried on despite the obligation to close (and accordingly the fact they were permitted or carried on is to be disregarded in determining whether the tenancy was adversely affected by coronavirus).

(5) Where the premises comprised in the tenancy were occupied by the tenant for the purposes of a business not carried on solely at or from those premises, the reference in subsection (1)(a) to the business carried on at or from the premises is to so much of the business as was carried on at or from the premises.

(6) In this section "coronavirus regulations" means regulations—
(a) made under section 45C of the Public Health (Control of Disease) Act 1984 (whether or not also made under any other power), and
(b) expressed to be made in response to the threat to public health posed by the incidence or spread of coronavirus.

"Protected period"

3B-319 **5.**—(1) The "protected period", in relation to a business tenancy adversely affected by coronavirus, is the period beginning with 21 March 2020 and ending with—
(a) where the business tenancy comprises premises in England—
(i) if subsection (2) identifies a day earlier than 18 July 2021, that day, or
(ii) in any other case, 18 July 2021;
(b) where the business tenancy comprises premises in Wales—
(i) if subsection (2) identifies a day earlier than 7 August 2021, that day, or
(ii) in any other case, 7 August 2021.

(2) The relevant day for the purposes of subsection (1)(a)(i) or (b)(i) is the last day on which (or for part of which)—
(a) the whole or part of the business carried on by the tenant at or from the premises, or
(b) the whole or part of those premises,
was of a description subject to either a closure requirement or a specific coronavirus restriction.

(3) In subsection (2) "specific coronavirus restriction" means a restriction or requirement (other than a closure requirement) imposed by coronavirus regulations which regulated any aspect of—
(a) the way a business, or a part of a business, of any specified description was to be carried on, or
(b) the way any premises, or any part of premises, of a specified description were or was to be used.

(4) But for the purposes of subsection (3)—
(a) requirements to display or provide information on premises (or parts of premises), and
(b) restrictions applying more generally than to specific descriptions of businesses or premises (or parts of businesses or premises),
are not specific coronavirus restrictions.

(5) In this section "closure requirement" and "coronavirus regulations" have the same meaning as in section 4 .

"The matter of relief from payment"

3B-320 **6.**—(1) References to the matter of relief from payment of a protected rent debt are to all issues relating to the questions—
(a) whether there is a protected rent debt of any amount, and
(b) if so, whether the tenant should be given relief from payment of that debt and, if so, what relief.

(2) "Relief from payment", in relation to a protected rent debt, means any one or more of the following—
(a) writing off the whole or any part of the debt;
(b) giving time to pay the whole or any part of the debt, including by allowing the whole or any part of the debt to be paid by instalments;
(c) reducing (including to zero) any interest otherwise payable by the tenant under the terms of the tenancy in relation to the whole or any part of the debt.

Temporary moratorium on enforcement of protected rent debts

23.—(1) Schedule 2 contains— 3B-321

(a) provision preventing a landlord who is owed a protected rent debt from using the following remedies in relation to (or on the basis of) the debt during the moratorium period—

(i) making a debt claim in civil proceedings;

(ii) using the commercial rent arrears recovery power;

(iii) enforcing a right of re-entry or forfeiture;

(iv) using a tenant's deposit;

(b) retrospective provision in relation to certain debt claims made by such a landlord before the start of the moratorium period for the protected rent debt;

(c) provision relating to the right of such a landlord during the moratorium period to appropriate any rent paid by the tenant;

(d) retrospective provision in relation to the right of such a landlord to appropriate any rent paid by the tenant before the start of the moratorium period for the protected rent debt;

(e) provision connected with certain things mentioned in paragraphs (a) to (d).

(2) In this section "the moratorium period", in relation to a protected rent debt, is the period—

(a) beginning with the day on which this Act is passed, and

(b) ending—

(i) where the matter of relief from payment of the protected rent debt is not referred to arbitration within the period of six months beginning with that day, with the last day of that period, or

(ii) where that matter is referred to arbitration, with the day on which the arbitration concludes.

(3) Subsection (2) is subject to any extension of the period mentioned in paragraph (b)(i) that—

(a) is made by or by virtue of section 24, and

(b) has effect in relation to the protected rent debt.

(4) For the purposes of subsection (2)(b) an arbitration concludes when—

(a) the arbitration proceedings are abandoned or withdrawn by the parties,

(b) the time period for appealing expires without an appeal being brought, or

(c) any appeal brought within that period is finally determined, abandoned or withdrawn.

(5) In this section "arbitration" means arbitration under Part 2 .

Alteration of moratorium period

24.—(1) In this section "extension regulations" means regulations under section 9(3) extending the period allowed by section 9(2) for making references to arbitration. 3B-322

(2) Where extension regulations made by virtue of section 9(3)(a) or (c) extend that period in the case of English business tenancies, the period specified in section 23(2)(b)(i), so far as it applies in the case of a protected rent debt under an English business tenancy, is extended for the same period of time.

(3) Subsection (4) below applies where extension regulations made by virtue of section 9(3)(b) or (c) extend that period in the case of Welsh business tenancies.

(4) The Secretary of State may by regulations made by statutory instrument extend the period specified in section 23(2)(b)(i), so far as it applies in the case

of a protected rent debt under a Welsh business tenancy, for the same period of time.

(5) Regulations under subsection (4) must provide for the extension referred to in that subsection—

(a) to have effect for the purposes of this Part including the purposes of Schedule 2, or

(b) to have effect for the purposes of this Part other than the purposes of Schedule 2.

(6) The power to make the provision referred to in subsection (5)(a) is exercisable only with the consent of the Welsh Ministers to the extension having effect for the purposes of Schedule 2 other than the purposes of paragraph 3(6) and (7).

(7) A statutory instrument containing regulations under subsection (4) is subject to annulment in pursuance of a resolution of either House of Parliament.

SECTION 23

SCHEDULE 2

TEMPORARY MORATORIUM ON ENFORCEMENT OF PROTECTED RENT DEBTS

Preliminary: interpretation

3B-323 1.—(1) This Schedule applies in relation to a protected rent debt under a business tenancy.

(2) In this Schedule—

(a) references to "the protected debt" or "the debt" are to the whole or any part of that protected rent debt;

(b) "the business tenancy" is the business tenancy under which the protected debt arose;

(c) "the landlord" and "the tenant" refer respectively to the landlord and the tenant under that tenancy;

(d) "the moratorium period", in relation to the protected debt, has the meaning given by section 23(2) ;

(e) a reference to doing something "in relation to" the protected debt includes, where appropriate, its being done on the basis of the debt.

Making a debt claim

2.—(1) The landlord may not, during the moratorium period for the debt, make a debt claim to enforce the protected debt.

(2) In this paragraph "debt claim" means a claim to enforce a debt in civil proceedings (including by a counterclaim or any other way of claiming payment of a debt in such proceedings).

Debt claims made before the day on which this Act is passed

3.—(1) This paragraph applies to proceedings on a debt claim which—

(a) is made on or after 10 November 2021 but before the day on which this Act is passed,

(b) is made by the landlord against the tenant, and

(c) relates to, or to debts which include, the protected rent debt.

(2) Either of the parties to the business tenancy may apply to the court for the proceedings on the debt claim to be stayed in order to enable the matter of payment of the protected rent debt to be resolved (whether by arbitration or otherwise).

(3) Where such an application is made in respect of proceedings on a debt claim the court must stay the proceedings (unless it is satisfied that they are not proceedings to which this paragraph applies).

(4) Sub-paragraphs (5) to (7) apply if judgment on the debt claim is given in favour of the landlord during the period described in sub-paragraph (1)(a).

(5) So long as the judgment debt so far as relating to the protected rent debt, or any interest on it, is unpaid, then—

(a) the matter of relief from payment of the judgment debt so far as relating to the protected rent debt, or any interest on it, may be resolved by arbitration under Part 2 of this Act or by agreement (as if that part of the judgment debt and any interest on it were a protected rent debt), despite the judgment having been given,

(b) the judgment debt, so far as relating to the protected rent debt or any interest on it, may not be enforced or relied on by the landlord before the end of the moratorium period for the protected rent debt, and

(c) if relief from payment is awarded or agreed, the effect of the judgment debt is to be taken as altered in accordance with the award or agreement.

(6) Where it comes to the attention of the officer of the court in which the judgment is entered that–

(a) the judgment relates solely to the protected rent debt,

(b) relief from payment of the protected rent debt has been awarded under Part 2 of this Act or agreed, and

(c) the moratorium period for the protected rent debt has ended,

the officer must send a request to the registrar to cancel the entry in the register of judgments under section 98 of the Courts Act 2003 .

(7) Following receipt of a request under sub-paragraph (6), the registrar must cancel the entry.

(8) In this paragraph–

"debt claim" has the same meaning as in paragraph 2 ;

"tenant" includes–

(a) a person who has guaranteed the obligations of the tenant under a business tenancy,

(b) a person other than the tenant who is liable on an indemnity basis for the payment of rent under a business tenancy, and

(c) a former tenant who is liable for the payment of rent under a business tenancy.

Using CRAR (the commercial rent arrears recovery power)

4.–(1) The landlord may not, during the moratorium period for the protected debt, use CRAR in relation to the debt.

(2) This means that during that period–

(a) an authorisation to exercise CRAR on behalf of the landlord in relation to the protected debt may not be given,

(b) a notice of enforcement may not be given in relation to the protected debt on behalf of the landlord, and

(c) the protected debt is to be disregarded in calculating the net unpaid rent for the purposes of section 77 of the Tribunals, Courts and Enforcement Act 2007 (the rent recoverable using CRAR).

(3) In this paragraph "CRAR" and "notice of enforcement" have the same meaning as in Chapter 2 of Part 3 of that Act.

(4) In section 77 of that Act, after paragraph (b) of subsection (1) insert

";

(c) it is not excluded from recovery using CRAR by paragraph 4 of Schedule 2 to the Commercial Rent (Coronavirus) Act 2022 (temporary moratorium on enforcement of protected rent debts)."

Enforcing a right of re-entry or forfeiture

5.–(1) The landlord may not, during the moratorium period for the protected debt, enforce, by action or otherwise, a right of re-entry or forfeiture for non-payment of the debt.

(2) No conduct by or on behalf of the landlord during the moratorium period, other than giving an express waiver in writing, is to be regarded as waiving a right of re-entry or forfeiture, under the business tenancy, for non-payment of the debt.

(3) For the purposes of determining whether the ground mentioned in section 30(1)(b) of the Landlord and Tenant Act 1954 (persistent delay in paying rent which has become due) is established in relation to the business tenancy, any failure to pay the debt during the moratorium period is to be disregarded.

6.–(1) This paragraph applies where–

(a) a superior landlord enforces, by action or otherwise, a right of re-entry or forfeiture in relation to a superior tenancy during the moratorium period, and

(b) the tenant applies for relief from forfeiture in relation to its interest in the property comprised in the tenancy.

(2) For the purposes of determining whether to grant the tenant relief from forfeiture and, if so, the terms of such relief, the court must disregard any failure to pay the protected rent debt.

Using landlord's right to appropriate rent

7.–(1) This paragraph applies in relation to a payment of rent under a business tenancy which is paid during the moratorium period for the debt at a time when–

(a) the tenant owes the landlord an unprotected rent debt in addition to the debt, and

(b) the tenant has not exercised the tenant's right to appropriate the payment to any particular rent debt owed to the landlord.

(2) The landlord's right to appropriate the payment must be used to apply the payment to meet the unprotected rent debt before it is applied to the protected rent debt.

(3) In this paragraph an "unprotected rent debt" is a debt consisting of–

(a) rent that is not protected rent, or

(b) interest on rent that is not protected rent.

8.—(1) This paragraph applies in relation to any payment of rent under a business tenancy which was paid during the period mentioned in sub-paragraph (2) at a time when—

(a) the tenant owed the landlord an unprotected rent debt in addition to the debt, and

(b) the tenant had not exercised the tenant's right to appropriate the payment to any particular rent debt.

(2) The period relevant for the purposes of sub-paragraph (1) is the period—

(a) beginning with the day after the last day of the protected period for the debt, and

(b) ending with the day before the first day of the moratorium period for the debt.

(3) During the moratorium period for the debt, the landlord's right to appropriate the payment must be used to apply the payment to meet the unprotected rent debt before it is applied to the protected rent debt.

(4) If the landlord used that right during the period mentioned in sub-paragraph (2) to appropriate the rent to the debt, then—

(a) the appropriation of the payment to the debt is ineffective to the extent of the unprotected rent debt, and

(b) the payment is to be treated for all purposes as having been appropriated to the unprotected rent debt first.

(5) In this paragraph "unprotected rent debt" has the same meaning as in paragraph 7 .

Using tenant's deposit to apply towards unpaid rent debt

9.—(1) This paragraph applies where a tenancy deposit is available to the landlord for the purpose of applying towards an unpaid rent debt.

(2) The landlord may not, during the moratorium period for the debt, recover the debt from the tenancy deposit.

(3) If the landlord has lawfully recovered the debt from the tenancy deposit before the beginning of the moratorium period, the tenant is not required to make good any shortfall in the deposit before the end of that period.

SCHEDULE 3

WINDING-UP AND BANKRUPTCY PETITIONS

Prohibition on presenting a winding-up petition solely in relation to a protected rent debt

3B-324 **1.**—(1) This paragraph applies where a landlord under a business tenancy is owed a protected rent debt and the tenant is a company.

(2) The landlord may not, during the moratorium period for the debt, present a petition for the winding up of the company under section 124 of the Insolvency Act 1986 on a ground specified—

(a) in the case of a registered company, in section 122(1)(f) of that Act, or

(b) in the case of an unregistered company, in section 221(5)(b) of that Act,

unless the landlord is owed a debt by the company which is not a protected rent debt.

(3) In this paragraph—

"the moratorium period", in relation to a protected rent debt, has the same meaning as in section 23 ;

"registered company" means a company registered under the Companies Act 2006 in England and Wales or Scotland;

"unregistered company" has the same meaning as in Part 5 of the Insolvency Act 1986 .

(4) This paragraph, so far as relating to registered companies, applies to limited liability partnerships.

Prohibition on presenting a bankruptcy order petition in relation to a protected rent debt

2.—(1) This paragraph (and paragraph 3) applies where the landlord under a business tenancy is owed a protected rent debt and the tenant is an individual.

(2) The landlord may not present a petition for a bankruptcy order against the tenant on a ground specified in section 268(1)(a) or (2) of the Insolvency Act 1986 where the demand referred to in those provisions related to any protected rent debt and was served during the relevant period.

(3) The landlord may not present a petition for a bankruptcy order against the tenant on a ground specified in section 268(1)(b) of that Act where the judgment or order referred to in that provision related to any protected rent debt and the claim for that debt was issued during the relevant period.

(4) If a petition mentioned in sub-paragraph (2) or (3) is presented, the court may make such order or give such directions as it thinks appropriate to restore the position to what it would have been if the petition had not been presented.

(5) If it appears to the interim receiver or special manager that the petition is one mentioned in sub-paragraph (2) or (3), the interim receiver or special manager must refer the matter to the court to determine whether to make an order or give directions under sub-paragraph (4).

(6) Neither the interim receiver or special manager is liable in any civil or criminal proceedings for anything done pursuant to an order made under section 286 or 370 of the Insolvency Act 1986 in relation to a petition that relates to any protected rent debt.

(7) The "relevant period" is the period which begins on 10 November 2021 and ends with the day mentioned in section 23(2)(b) .

(8) In this paragraph "claim" includes a counterclaim or any other way of claiming payment of a debt in civil proceedings.

(9) This paragraph is to be regarded as having come into force on 10 November 2021.

Bankruptcy orders made before the day on which this Act is passed

3.—(1) This paragraph applies where—

(a) a court makes a bankruptcy order against the tenant on a petition from the landlord under section 267 of the Insolvency Act 1986 ,

(b) the order was made on or after 10 November 2021 but before the day on which this Schedule comes into force, and

(c) the order was not one which the court would have made had this Schedule been in force at the time.

(2) The court is to be regarded as having had no power to make the order (and, accordingly, the order is to be regarded as void).

(3) Neither the trustee, official receiver, interim receiver or special manager is liable in any civil or criminal proceedings for anything done pursuant to the order.

(4) The court may make such order or give such directions as it thinks appropriate to restore the position to what it was immediately before the petition was presented.

(5) If at any time it appears to the trustee, official receiver, interim receiver or special manager that—

(a) a bankruptcy order made by the court is void by virtue of sub-paragraph (2), and

(b) it might be appropriate for the court to make an order or give directions under sub-paragraph (4),

the trustee, official receiver, interim receiver or special manager must refer the matter to the court to determine whether to make such an order or give such directions.

Interpretation

4.—(1) In this Schedule—

"interim receiver" means a person appointed under section 286 of the Insolvency Act 1986 ;

"special manager" means a person appointed under section 370 of that Act;

"trustee" means the trustee of a bankrupt's estate.

(2) In this Schedule, references to the "tenant" include—

(a) a person who has guaranteed the obligations of the tenant under a business tenancy,

(b) a person other than the tenant who is liable on an indemnity basis for the payment of rent under a business tenancy, and

(c) a former tenant who is liable for the payment of rent under a business tenancy.

Introduction—restrictions on landlord's remedies re: "protected rent debt"

The Commercial Rent (Coronavirus) Act 2022 came into force on 24 March 2022. The Act places a "temporary moratorium" on landlord's remedies during the "moratorium period" for recovery of a "protected rent debt" due from a tenant under a "business tenancy". The Act is designed to function with the Commercial rent code of practice following the COVID-19 pandemic, 7 April 2022. **3B-325**

Amongst the remedies restricted during the "moratorium period" a landlord may not forfeit the lease by court proceedings or peaceable re-entry for failure to pay the "protected rent debt". For more detail see: para.3B-332 below.

Absent agreement between landlord and tenant as to how the "protected rent debt" should be dealt with, either party may refer the matter to statutory arbitration as provided in the Act.

- If the rent debt owed from the tenant is not a "protected rent debt" the landlord is free to pursue its remedies;
- If at the end of the "moratorium period" the matter has not been referred to arbitration, the landlord is free to pursue its remedies.

Business tenancy

A relevant business tenancy is defined under s.2(4) as "a tenancy to which Pt 2 of the Landlord and Tenant Act 1954 applies". A so-called "contracted-out tenancy" is still a tenancy to which Pt 2 of the 1954 Act applies (ss.23, 38 and 38A of the 1954 Act; paras 3B-94, 3B-233 and 3B-234). **3B-326**

Rent

The definition of "rent" is wide. Section 2 defines it to include "an amount payable by the tenant to the landlord under the tenancy for possession and use of the premises comprised in the tenancy (whether described as rent or otherwise)". The definition specifically includes service charges (which are further defined under s.2(2)(c) and which may include insurance costs if the lease so provides), VAT and interest. and 3B-234). **3B-327**

Protected rent debt

Section 3 defines this as rent which is "attributable to a period of occupation by the tenant for, or for a period within, the protected period applying to the tenancy" and where "the tenancy was adversely affected by coronavirus". **3B-328**

Adversely affected by coronavirus

3B-329 Section 4 defines a business tenancy as "adversely affected by coronavirus" where it was subject to a "closure requirement" that was "imposed by coronavirus regulations" (as defined in s.2(6)) between 2pm on 21 March 2020 and no later than 11.55pm on 18 July 2021 (in England) and between 2pm on 21 March 2020 and no later than 6am on 7 August 2021 in Wales. Section 2(4) makes it clear that it is immaterial that during that period of closure "specific limited activities were (as an exception) allowed by the regulations to be carried on despite the obligation to close (and accordingly the fact they were permitted or carried on is to be disregarded in determining whether the tenancy was adversely affected by coronavirus)."

Protected period

3B-330 Section 5 defines "protected period" as beginning on 21 March 2020 and ending on the last day on which the tenant's business or premises (in whole or part) were "subject to either a closure requirement or a specific coronavirus restriction".

Moratorium period

3B-331 Landlord's remedies are restricted during the "moratorium period". Section 23(2) defines the temporary moratorium on enforcement of "protected rent debts" as starting on the day the Act was passed (24 March 2022) and ending on "the last day" for referring the matter of relief to arbitration which is 6 months from the date the Act was passed, so expiring on 23 September 2022, but extendable by the Secretary of State under s.9(3) (which power had not been exercised at the date this volume went to press) or, where the matter is in arbitration "the day on which the arbitration concludes". After that, the moratorium on landlord's remedies ends.

Temporary moratorium on enforcement of protected rent debts

3B-332 Section 23 and Sch.2 of the Act provide that during the "moratorium period" a landlord may not enforce a "protected rent debt" by making a debt claim in civil proceedings, exercising commercial rent arrears recovery, enforcing a right of re-entry by court proceedings or peaceable reentry, use a tenant's rent deposit.

In addition, any debt claim commenced after 10 November 2021 and before 24 March 2022 may be stayed on the application of the tenant or any guarantor (as defined in Sch.2 para.3) and any judgement given during that period may not be enforced to the extent that the proceedings or judgement relate to a "protected rent debt"; such debt may be referred to statutory arbitration under the Act.

The "temporary moratorium" on exercising commercial rent arrears recovery to recover the "protected rent debt" almost certainly means that notice under s.81 of the Tribunals, Courts and Enforcement Act 2007 cannot be validly served on a sub-tenant as s.81(1) specifically states that it only applies "where CRAR is exercisable by a landlord to recover rent due and payable from a tenant (the immediate tenant)".

In addition to restricting the landlord's right of re-entry in connection with the "protected rent debt", the Act provides that the landlord's conduct during the "moratorium period" shall not be considered waiver of the right to forfeit (Sch.2 para.5(2)). The Act also provides, in Sch.2 para.6, that where a head landlord still retains the right to forfeit, in the case of the sub-tenant owing a "protected rent debt" the court when determining whether to grant relief from forfeiture to the sub-tenant, and the terms of relief, must disregard any failure to pay the "protected rent debt".

Where the landlord has utilised the tenant's deposit to defray the "protected rent debt" prior to 24 March 2022, the tenant is not required to 'top-up' the deposit before the end of" the "moratorium period" that period.

Schedule 2 also provides (para.7) that where a landlord has the right to appropriate rent, this right can only be exercised in relation to non "protected rent debt".

The Act also contains restrictions on initiating voluntary arrangements and issuing a winding-up petition or a bankruptcy petition in relation to a "protected rent debt" in Pt 3 and in Sch.3.

SECTION 3C CONTEMPT OF COURT

A. An Outline of the Law of Contempt of Court

1. *Introduction*

(b) Criminal and civil contempt

Add a new penultimate paragraph:

3C-4 In *HM Attorney General v Dowie* [2022] EWFC 25, MacDonald J gave a detailed exposition of civil vs criminal contempt in relation to illicit recording of Children Act 1989 proceedings held in private (Contempt of Court Act 1981 s.9) as distinct from their publication (which engaged s.12 of the Administration of Justice Act 1960), and the relevance of s.1 of the 1981 Act to such publications.

3. *Jurisdiction*

(a) High Court

(ii) Supervisory jurisdiction (Administrative Court)

Replace the second paragraph with:

The jurisdiction of inferior courts to punish for contempt of court is not as extensive as that exercisable by the High Court. (As explained above, it includes power to deal with contempts "in the face of the court" and such other powers as may be conferred on the inferior court concerned by statute.) The general supervisory jurisdiction exercised by the High Court over inferior courts includes the power to deal with contempts of those courts. Thus, the High Court may punish contempts committed in connection with proceedings in an inferior court. Obviously, in a given case, the extent to which the High Court power overlaps and goes beyond the power of the inferior court concerned will depend upon the extent of the contempt power of the inferior court. Certain statutes have provision for contempts (or what would be contempts) in an inferior court or tribunal to be "certified" to a superior court or tribunal: see, for example, s.202 of the Data Protection Act 2018, and ss.54(4) and 61 of the Freedom of Information Act 2000, considered in *Moss v Kingston-Upon-Thames RLBC* [2022] 1 WLUK 515, (First-Tier Tribunal, NJ/2018/0007 promulgated 1 April 2022). **3C-29**

6. *Appeal in cases of contempt of court*

(a) Right of appeal

In the last paragraph, after the second sentence, add:

However, a Court will not normally exercise its inherent jurisdiction to strike a defendant from the Roll of Solicitors after committing for contempt, and may prefer to leave such matters to be determined by the Solicitors Disciplinary Tribunal: *Solicitors Regulatory Authority v Khan* [2022] EWHC 45 (Ch) at [68]-[72]. **3C-38**

(b) Route of appeal and permission to appeal

In the first paragraph, replace "HM Attorney General v Crosland (No.2) [2021] UKSC 58" with:

- *HM Attorney General v Crosland (No.2)* [2021] UKSC 58; [2022] 1 W.L.R. 367 **3C-39**

In the eighth paragraph (beginning "In this case"), replace "(Government of Sierra Leone v Davenport [2002] EWCA Civ 230; [2002] C.P.L.R. 236, CA)." with:

(*Government of Sierra Leone v Davenport* [2002] EWCA Civ 230; [2002] C.P.L.R. 236, CA; *Greetham v Greetham* [2022] EWCA Civ 49 at [5]-[8]).

Replace the ninth paragraph with:

As indicated above, s.13 countenances appeals, not only by contemnors (or alleged contemnors), but also by applicants in contempt proceedings. For example, an appeal by an applicant against a court's refusal to impose any sentence on a person in contempt of court (e.g. *JSC BTA Bank v Solodchenko (No.2)* [2011] EWCA Civ 1241; [2012] 1 W.L.R. 350, CA), or against the sentence imposed (where the applicant contends that it is inadequate) (e.g. *Wilson v Webster* [1998] 1 F.L.R. 1097, CA, *Wood v Collins* [2006] EWCA Civ 743 and under the new CPR Part 81, see the successful appeal for undue leniency in *AAA v CCC* [2022] EWCA Civ 479), or against an order discharging a contemnor (e.g. *Poole Borough Council v Hambridge* [2007] EWCA Civ 990). Such appeals may be made only with permission (because they are not appeals "against a committal order").

C. Contempt of Court Act 1981

Replace s.9 with:

Use of tape recorders

9.—(1) Subject to subsection (4) below, it is a contempt of court— **3C-67**

(a) to use in court, or bring into court for use, any tape recorder or other instrument for recording sound, except with the leave of the court;

(b) to publish a recording of legal proceedings made by means of any such instrument, or any recording derived directly or indirectly from it, by playing it in the hearing of the public or any section of the public, or to dispose of it or any recording so derived, with a view to such publication;

(c) to use any such recording in contravention of any conditions of leave granted under paragraph (a).

(d) to publish or dispose of any recording in contravention of any conditions of leave granted under subsection (1A).

(1A) In the case of a recording of Supreme Court proceedings, subsection (1)(b) does not apply to its publication or disposal with the leave of the Court.

(2) Leave under paragraph (a) of subsection (1), or under subsection (1A), may be granted or refused at the discretion of the court, and if granted—

(a) may, in the case of leave under subsection (1)(a), be granted subject to such conditions as the court thinks proper with respect to the use of any recording made pursuant to the leave; and

(b) may in the case of leave under subsection (1A), be granted subject to such conditions as the Supreme Court thinks proper with respect to publication or disposal of any recording to which the leave relates;

and where leave has been granted the court may at the like discretion withdraw or amend it either generally or in relation to any particular part of the proceedings.

(3) Without prejudice to any other power to deal with an act of contempt under paragraph (a) of subsection (1), the court may order the instrument, or any recording made with it, or both, to be forfeited; and any object so forfeited shall (unless the court otherwise determines on application by a person appearing to be the owner) be sold or otherwise disposed of in such manner as the court may direct.

(4) This section does not apply to the making or use of sound recordings for purposes of official transcripts of proceedings.

(4A) This section does not apply to anything done in accordance with a direction under section 85A of the Courts Act 2003 (remote observation and recording of court and tribunal proceedings).

(5) See section 32 of the Crime and Courts Act 2013 for power to provide for further exceptions.

Note

After the first paragraph add:

3C-67.1 Subsection (4A) inserted by the Police, Crime, Sentencing & Courts Act 2022 s.198(4).

SECTION 3D PROCEEDINGS UNDER THE HUMAN RIGHTS ACT 1998

Human Rights Act 1998

Section 1(1)

Replace the first paragraph with:

3D-3 *The Convention* here means "the Convention ... as it has effect for the time being in relation to the United Kingdom", as defined in s.21(1). A Convention right for these purposes is a Convention right as contained in Sch.1 to the Act, which will in principle be defined and interpreted by the domestic courts as having the same substantive content as the equivalent right under international law: see *R. (Ullah) v Special Adjudicator* [2004] UKHL 26; [2004] 2 A.C. 323 at [20]; *In re McQuillan* [2021] UKSC 55; [2022] 2 W.L.R. 49 at [113] and [155]-[157]; *R. (Elan-Cane) v Secretary of State for the Home Department* [2021] UKSC 56; [2022] 2 W.L.R. 133 at [86]-[88] and [94]-[107].

Replace paragraph:

Section 2(1)

This requires any court or tribunal determining a question which has arisen under any Act in connection with a Convention right to "take into account" the decisions of the Strasbourg organs, whenever made or given so far as, in the opinion of the court or tribunal, it is relevant to the proceedings in which that question has arisen. Section 2(1) HRA requires a court only to take a Strasbourg judgment into account, not to follow it: *R. v Horncastle* [2009] UKSC 14; [2010] 2 A.C. 373; [2010] 2 W.L.R. 47 (a seven-judge Court of Appeal); *R. (Haney) v Secretary of State for Justice* [2014] UKSC 66; [2015] A.C. 1344; [2015] 2 W.L.R. 76 at [18]-[23] and [30]-[37]; and *R. (Elan-Cane) v Secretary of State for the Home Department* [2021] UKSC 56; [2022] 2 W.L.R. 133 at [101]. However, the authority of a considered statement of the Grand Chamber is such that our courts ought to apply it absent highly unusual circumstances: see *R. (Anderson) v Secretary of State for the Home Department* [2002] UKHL 46; [2003] 1 A.C. 837; [2002] 3 W.L.R. 1800 at [18]; *AM (Zimbabwe) v Secretary of State for the Home Department* [2020] UKSC 17; [2021] A.C. 633 at [34] and *R. (Hallam) v Secretary of State for Justice* [2019] UKSC 2; [2020] A.C. 279 per Lord Mance at [29]-[35], Lord Sumption at [120]-[125]. In the absence of some special circumstance, a court should follow any clear and consistent jurisprudence of the European Court of Human Rights (ECtHR): *R. (Alconbury Development Ltd) v Secretary of State for Environment Transport and the Regions* [2001] UKHL 23; [2003] 2 A.C. 295; [2001] 2 W.L.R. 1389 at [26]; *Manchester City Council v Pinnock* [2010] UKSC 45; [2011] 2 A.C. 104; [2010] 3 W.L.R. 1441 per Lord Neuberger at [48]; It may be appropriate for a court to decline to follow the reasoning of the ECtHR if it is unpersuasive such as where it is founded on a factual or legal misunderstanding: see *R. v Spear* [2002] UKHL 31, [2003] 1 A.C. 734; [2002] 3 W.L.R. 437, HL at [12]-[13] and [65]-[66] and *R. v Lyons* [2002] UKHL 44; [2003] 1 A.C. 976; [2002] 3 W.L.R. 1562 at [46]. For an overview of caselaw on the approach, see *R. (Hicks) v Commissioner of Police for the Metropolis* [2014] EWCA Civ 3; [2014] 1 W.L.R. 2152 at [69]-[81] and upheld by the Supreme Court at [2017] UKSC 9; [2017] 1 A.C. 256; [2017] 2 W.L.R. 824. **3D-9**

The purpose of s.2 is to ensure that the same Convention rights are enforced under the HRA by courts within the United Kingdom as would be enforced by the ECtHR in Strasbourg. It is not intended to provide Convention rights with a domestically autonomous meaning: *R. (Elan-Cane) v Secretary of State for the Home Department* [2021] UKSC 56; [2022] 2 W.L.R. 133 at [86]-[89] and [101]. See also *R. (on the application of Al Jedda) v Secretary of State for Defence* [2007] UKHL 58; [2008] 1 A.C. 332; [2008] 2 W.L.R. 31. See too *R. (Quark Fishing Ltd) v Secretary of State for Foreign & Commonwealth Affairs* [2005] UKHL 57; [2006] 1 A.C. 529; [2005] 3 W.L.R. 837, *Aston Cantlow PCC v Wallbank* [2003] UKHL 37; [2004] 1 A.C. 546; [2003] 3 W.L.R. 283 at [6] and *R. (Greenfield) v Home Secretary* [2005] UKHL 14; [2005] 1 W.L.R. 673; [2005] 2 All E.R. 240 at [19] and *Breyer Group Plc v Department of Energy and Climate Change* [2015] EWCA Civ 408; [2015] W.L.R. (D) 192 at [42]-[49]. A national court should not, without strong reason, dilute or weaken the effect of Strasbourg case-law. Nor should the provision of more generous rights be the product of interpretation of the Convention by the national courts, since the meaning of the Convention should be uniform throughout the states party to it: *R. v Special Adjudicator Ex p. Ullah, sub nom. Doh v Secretary of State for the Home Department* [2004] UKHL 26, [2004] 2 A.C. 323; [2004] 3 W.L.R. 23 per Lord Bingham. Where the ECtHR has held that a Convention right is not breached on the basis that an issue falls within the State's margin of appreciation, it will not be open to the domestic courts to find a breach in that same situation: *R. (Elan-Cane) v Secretary of State for the Home Department* [2021] UKSC 56; [2022] 2 W.L.R. 133 at [68]-[108], departing from dicta of the House of Lords and Supreme Court in inter alia *In re G (Adoption: Unmarried Couple)* [2009] 1 A.C. 173 and *R. (Nicklinson) v Ministry of Justice* [2014] UKSC 38; [2015] A.C. 657. However, this does not mean that the domestic courts are unable to develop case law beyond the limits of existing Strasbourg case-law: in considering situations which have not yet come before the ECtHR, the domestic courts can and should aim to anticipate how the ECtHR might be expected to decide the case applying established principles: *R. (AB) v Secretary of State for Justice* [2021] UKSC 28; [2021] 3 W.L.R. 494 at [54]-[59]; *R. (Elan Cane) v Secretary of State for the Home Department* [2021] UKSC 56; [2022] 2 W.L.R. 133 at [101].

The principle of *stare decisis* compels domestic courts to follow the earlier decisions of higher courts, even if they conflict with later Strasbourg authority. See *Kay v Lambeth LBC* [2006] UKHL 10; [2006] 2 A.C. 465; [2006] 2 W.L.R. 570. See too *R. (Animal Defenders International) v Secretary of State for Culture, Media & Sport* [2008] UKHL 15; [2008] 1 A.C. 1312; [2008] 2 W.L.R. 781, and *R. (RJM) v Secretary of State for Work & Pensions* [2008] UKHL 63; [2009] 1 A.C. 311; [2008] 3 W.L.R. 1023 at 59-67; and *Doherty v Birmingham CC* [2008] UKHL 57; [2009] 1 A.C. 367; [2008] 3 W.L.R. 636. Even where bound to reject a claim, the judgment of a lower court may address obiter whether a claimant would succeed on the application of subsequent Strasbourg case-law: see e.g. *AM (Zimbabwe) v Secretary of State for the Home Department* [2018] EWCA Civ 64; [2018] 1 W.L.R. 2933, a decision reversed by the Supreme Court in [2020] UKSC 17; [2021] A.C. 633.

The Supreme Court is free to depart from its own previous decisions following a conflicting decision of the European Court of Human Rights: see e.g. *Catherine Smith v Ministry of Defence* [2013] UKSC 41; [2014] A.C. 52; [2013] 3 W.L.R. 69, *R. (Purdy) v DPP* [2009] UKHL 45; [2010] 1 A.C. 345; [2009] 3 W.L.R. 403, and *SSHD v AF (No.3)* [2009] UKHL 28; [2010] 2 A.C. 269; [2009] 3 W.L.R. 74.

Section 2(2)

Replace "para.8 of the Practice Direction–Miscellaneous Provisions Relating to Hearings: 39PD.8" with:

paras 8 and 9.3 of the Practice Direction to Miscellaneous Provisions Relating to Hearings: (Citation of Authorities) [2001] 1 W.L.R. 1001, CA **3D-13**

Section 2(3)

Replace the second paragraph with:

3D-14 For citation of authorities concerning human rights see CPR Practice Direction (Citation of Authorities) [2001] 1 W.L.R. 1001, CA supplementing r.39, paras 8.1 and 9.3.

Editorial note

In the fourth paragraph, to the end of the fourth sentence (finishing with "enacted the legislation") add:

3D-16 : *In Re United Nations Convention on the Rights of the Child (Incorporation)(Scotland) Bill* [2021] UKSC 42; [2021] 1 W.L.R. 5106 at [26].

In the eighth paragraph, replace "Re S (supra); Bellinger v Bellinger [2003] UKHL 21; [2003] 2 A.C. 467; [2003] 2 W.L.R. 1174." with:

Re S (supra); Bellinger v Bellinger [2003] UKHL 21; [2003] 2 A.C. 467; [2003] 2 W.L.R. 1174 and *Mercer v Alternative Future Group Ltd* [2022] EWCA Civ 379 at [77]–[81].

In the last paragraph, replace "RR v Secretary of State for Work and Pensions [2019] UKSC 52 at [29] and [32], the Supreme Court held" with:

RR v Secretary of State for Work and Pensions [2019] UKSC 52; [2019] W.L.R. 6430 at [18]–[32], the Supreme Court confirmed

Editorial note

Replace the first paragraph with:

3D-19 There is no strict requirement that a person who seeks a declaration of incompatibility is a "victim" within s.7, provided he or she has a sufficient interest and standing: *R. (on the application of Rusbridger) v Att-Gen* [2003] UKHL 38; [2004] 1 A.C. 357; [2003] 3 W.L.R. 232 para.21, per Lord Steyn; *Re Northern Ireland Human Rights Commission's Application for Judicial Review* [2018] UKSC 27; [2019] 1 All E.R. 173 at [62], [17] and [185]. Ordinarily, however, the court will only grant a declaration of incompatibility to a person who is a victim of an actual or proposed breach of a Convention right: *Re S (Care Order: Implementation of Care Plan)* [2002] 2 A.C. 291; [2002] 2 W.L.R. 720; [2002] 2 All E.R. 192 per Lord Nicholls; *Bellinger v Bellinger* [2003] UKHL 21; [2003] 2 A.C. 467; [2003] 2 W.L.R. 1174. In any event, a person cannot apply for a declaration of incompatibility on the basis of a hypothetical argument, nor unless they are adversely affected by the impugned measure: *Joseph Taylor v Lancashire CC and Secretary of State for the Environment, Food & Rural Affairs* [2005] EWCA Civ 284; [2005] 1 W.L.R. 2668; [2005] H.R.L.R. 17 paras 43–44, per Woolf, CJ.

In the third paragraph, after "per Lord Nicholls", add new case:

and *Mercer v Alternative Future Group Ltd* [2022] EWCA Civ 379 at [82]–[88].

Replace the fourth paragraph with:

Whether to make a declaration of incompatibility is a matter for the court's discretion. In *Steinfeld v Secretary of State for International Development* [2018] UKSC 32; [2020] A.C. 1; [2018] 3 W.L.R. 415, the Supreme Court affirmed (at [56]) that the power to make a declaration of incompatibility under s.4(2) HRA is discretionary; and (at [60]) that the making of a declaration of incompatibility does not require Parliament or the government to do anything. For a discussion of the exercise of discretion as to whether or not to make such a declaration see [56]–[61]. Such a declaration should only be made if the primary remedies under ss.6 and 3 cannot be used. See *Nasseri v Secretary of State for the Home Department* [2009] UKHL 23; [2010] 1 A.C. 1; [2009] 2 W.L.R. 1190 per Lord Hoffmann at [19] and *R. (F) v Secretary of State for the Home Department* [2010] UKSC 17; [2011] 1 A.C. 331; [2010] 2 W.L.R. 992. A declaration of incompatibility is a remedy of last resort: incompatibility must be avoided through interpretation unless it is plainly impossible to do so: *R. v A (No 2)* [2001] UKHL 25; [2002] 1 A.C. 45; [2001] 2 W.L.R. 1546 (see also commentary on s.3, above). Even where it is not possible to interpret a provision compatibly with the ECHR, the Court retains a discretion as to whether to grant a declaration, to be exercised according to the normal principles governing the grant of declarations. As to circumstances in which a declaration might be made, see *Wilson v First County Trust Ltd (No.2)* [2001] EWCA 633; [2002] Q.B. 74; [2001] 3 W.L.R. 42 (CA) (overruled on other grounds in *Wilson v first County Trust Ltd (No.2)* [2003] UKHL 40; [2004] 1 A.C. 816; [2003] 3 W.L.R. 568).

Replace the penultimate paragraph with:

Where the European Court of Human Rights (ECtHR) has held that a Convention right is not breached on the basis that an issue falls within the State's margin of appreciation, it will not be open to the domestic courts to find a breach in that same situation: *R. (Elan-Cane) v Secretary of State for the Home Department* [2021] UKSC 56; [2022] 2 W.L.R. 133 at [68]–[108], reversing dicta of the House of Lords/Supreme Court in inter alia *In re G (Adoption: Unmarried Couple)* [2009] 1 A.C. 173 and *R. (Nicklinson) v Ministry of Justice* [2014] UKSC 38; [2015] 1 A.C. 657. In such a situation, no question of making a declaration of incompatibility could arise. However, this does not mean that the domestic courts are not able to develop case law beyond the limits of existing case law of the ECtHR: in considering situations which have not yet come before the ECtHR, the domestic courts can and should aim to anticipate how the ECtHR might be expected to decide the case applying established principles: *R. (AB) v Secretary of State for Justice* [2021] UKSC 28; [2021] 3 W.L.R. 494 at [54]-[59]; *R. (Elan-Cane) v Secretary of State for the Home Department* [2021] UKSC 56; [2022] 2 W.L.R. 133 at [101].

Editorial note

After "No declaration may be made", delete "in private law proceedings". **3D-22**

Section 6(1)

After the first paragraph, add new paragraph:

For the limits of the Court's role in adjudicating on a claim for breach of s.6 see *R. (Richards) v Environment Agency* [2022] EWCA Civ 26 at [63]-[69]. **3D-24**

Replace the third paragraph with:

In *re McQuillan* [2021] UKSC 55; [2022] 2 W.L.R. 49 a seven judge Supreme Court reviewed the circumstances in which the s.6 duty, requiring a public authority not to act in a manner incompatible with Convention rights, could support a claim for breach of the investigative obligations under arts 2 and 3 of the ECHR triggered by events occurring at a point in time when the Act was not in force. The Supreme Court recalled that it was established law following *Brecknell v United Kingdom (32457/04)* [2007] 11 WLUK 675; (2008) 46 E.H.R.R. 42 that the arts 2 and 3 investigative duties can be revived if sufficiently weighty and compelling new evidence comes to light ([116]-[119]). However, it held that, where a triggering event preceded the coming into force of the Act, in order to engage the s.6 duty there must additionally be either: (a) a "genuine connection" between the triggering event and the date of the Act coming into force, including (i) a sufficiently close temporal connection, and (ii) that a major part of the investigation must have or ought to have been carried out after entry into force of the Act; or (b) exceptional circumstances satisfying the "Convention values" test i.e. a need to ensure protection of the guarantees and the underlying values of the Convention ([133]-[145] and [167]-[168]).

Section 6(2)

In the third paragraph, replace "RR v Secretary of State for Work and Pensions [2019] UKSC 52 at [27]-[32], the Supreme Court held" with:

RR v Secretary of State for Work and Pensions [2019] UKSC 52; [2019] 1 W.L.R. 6430 at [18]-[32], the Supreme Court confirmed **3D-26**

Section 7(1), 7(3) and 7(7) "victim"

Delete the last paragraph. **3D-30**

Practice Directions and Standard Orders Applicable to Civil Appeals and Practice Directions and Standing Orders Applicable to Criminal Appeals

Replace the fourth paragraph with:

The Investigatory Powers Tribunal is the appropriate tribunal in relation to matters under the Regulation of Investigatory Powers Act 2000: see *R. (A) v Director of Establishments of the Security Service* [2009] UKSC 12; [2010] 2 A.C. 1; [2010] 2 W.L.R. 1, SC. Decisions of the Investigatory Powers Tribunal are subject to the supervisory jurisdiction of the High Court notwithstanding s.67(8) of the 2000 Act: *R. (Privacy International) v Investigatory Powers Tribunal* [2019] UKSC 22; [2020] A.C. 491, applied in *R. (Privacy International) v Investigatory Powers Tribunal* [2022] EWHC 770 (QB). **3D-33**

Section 7(5)

Replace paragraph with:

See *Dunn v Parole Board* [2008] EWCA Civ 374; [2009] 1 W.L.R. 728; [2008] H.R.L.R. 32, CA and *Solaria Energy UK Ltd v Department for Business, Energy and Industrial Strategy* [2020] EWCA Civ 1625; [2021] 1 W.L.R. 2349. The defence under s.7(5) is a limitation defence in the ordinary sense and does not limit the jurisdiction of the court: see *M (A Child) v Ministry of Justice* [2009] EWCA Civ 419. It is likely that time starts to run from when the breach ended: see *A v Essex County Council* [2010] UKSC 33; [2011] 1 A.C. 280; [2010] 3 W.L.R. 509 at 113 per Baroness Hale. In *O'Connor v Bar Standards Board* [2017] UKSC 78; [2017] 1 W.L.R. 4833; [2018] 2 All E.R. 779, the Supreme Court held that in considering the limitation period for bringing a claim under the Human Rights Act 1998 s.7(5), the expression "the date on which the act complained of took place" could include **3D-34.1** a course of conduct and did not have to be interpreted as meaning an instantaneous act. The discretion to extend time is a broad one and can be exercised in a meritorious case: *Rabone v Pennine NHS Trust* [2012] UKSC 2; [2012] 2 A.C. 72; [2012] 2 W.L.R. 381. See application of *Rabone* in *C v Chief Constable of Northern Ireland* [2020] NIQB 3.

Section 7(6)(b)

3D-35 *Delete "As to the requirements of an appellant's notice see PD 52, paras 5.1A and 5.1B".*

Editorial note

Replace "RR v Secretary of State for Work and Pensions [2019] UKSC 52" with:

3D-39 *RR v Secretary of State for Work and Pensions* [2019] UKSC 52; [2019] 1 W.L.R. 6430

Sections 8(3) and 8(4)

In the second paragraph, after "Lord Bingham, para.11),", add:

3D-40 but see

Replace the fourth paragraph with:

Reported cases in which HRA damages have been awarded are now numerous, and include *R. (Bernard) v Enfield LBC* (above); *R. (KB) v Mental Health Review Tribunal* [2003] EWHC 193; [2004] Q.B. 936; [2003] 3 W.L.R. 185; *Van Colle v Chief Constable of Hertfordshire* [2006] EWHC 360; [2006] 3 All E.R. 963; [2006] 1 F.C.R. 755; [2007] EWCA Civ 325 though the *Van Colle* decision on liability was overturned by the House of Lords: see *Chief Constable of Hertfordshire v Van Colle* [2008] UKHL 50; [2009] 1 A.C. 225; [2008] 3 W.L.R. 593; *R. v Gas and Electricity Markets Authority* [2013] EWCA Civ 70; [2013] J.P.L. 1037 at [26]-[27]; *Rabone v Pennine Care NHS Foundation Trust* [2012] UKSC 2; [2012] 2 A.C. 72; [2012] 2 W.L.R. 381; and *D v Commissioner of Police of the Metropolis* [2014] EWHC 2493 (QB); [2015] 1 W.L.R. 1833; [2015] 2 All E.R. 272. In *Breyer Group Plc v Department of Energy and Climate Change* [2015] EWCA Civ 408; [2015] 1 W.L.R. 4559; [2016] 2 All E.R. 220 at [42]-[49], the Court of Appeal held (following the consistent approach of the European Court of Human Rights to the concept of "property" under Article 1 Protocol 1) that damages could not be claimed under the Convention for loss of expectation of future income unless it was in the form of capitalisable goodwill.

Section 9(1)

Replace paragraph with:

3D-43 In *Mazhar v Lord Chancellor* [2017] EWHC 2536 (Fam); [2018] Fam. 257; [2018] 2 W.L.R. 1304, it was held that the only forum for challenging the legality of a judicial act by a judge of the High Court, and for claiming damages against the Crown pursuant to s.9(3), was an appeal to the Court of Appeal. In the case of inferior courts, this can be achieved by exercising a right of appeal, judicial review (where applicable) or a claim to a judge of the High Court in accordance with CPR 7.11 or the FPR. Nothing in the HRA (taken together with either the CPR or the FPR) provides a power in a court or tribunal to make a declaration against the Crown in respect of a judicial act. Furthermore, the HRA has not modified the constitutional principle of judicial immunity. Likewise, the Crown is not to be held to vicariously liable for the acts of the judiciary with the consequence that a claim for a declaration against the Lord Chancellor that a high court judge had acted unlawfully was not justiciable.

Section 9(3)

Replace paragraph with:

3D-44.1 A claim for damages in respect of a good faith judicial act is only available where required by for breach of art.5(5) and not for any other judicial act violating another provision of the Convention. This applies also to a claim for costs: see *R v Director General of Fair Trading* [2001] EWCA Civ 1217; [2002] 1 W.L.R. 269; [2002] 1 All E.R. 853, CA, in which the court refused an application for costs because the first instance court lacked independence, on the basis of an interpretation of s.9(3) which precluded this. Where there is a claim for damages under s.9(3) against the Crown and the judicial act is that of a judge of the High Court, the claim cannot be determined by a court of co-ordinate jurisdiction, and so can only be made to the Court of Appeal as part of an appeal. In the case of inferior courts, the remedy created by ss.8 and 9(3) of the HRA is available by exercising a right of appeal, judicial review (where applicable) or a claim to a judge of the High Court in accordance with CPR 7.11 or the FPR: see *Mazhar v Lord Chancellor* [2017] EWHC 2536 (Fam); [2018] Fam. 257; [2018] 2 W.L.R. 1304. For a distillation of the restricted circumstances in which the entitlement to damages under art.5(5) ECHR will arise following an unlawful judicial order see *LL v Lord Chancellor* [2017] EWCA Civ 237; [2017] 4 W.L.R. 162; [2017] 2 F.L.R. 1429 at [88]-[89] and [104].

Editorial note

To the end of the paragraph, add:

A ministerial statement of compatibility is no more than a statement of opinion of the relevant minister and cannot be ascribed to Parliament: *R. (SC) v Secretary of State for Work and Pensions* [2021] UKSC 26; [2022] A.C. 223 at [170 **3D-64**

Section 22(4)

Before the last paragraph, add:

In *re McQuillan* [2021] UKSC 55; [2022] 2 W.L.R. 49 a seven judge Supreme Court reviewed the circumstances in which the s.6 duty requiring a public authority not to act in a manner incompatible with Convention rights could support a claim for breach of the investigative obligations under arts 2 and 3 of the ECHR triggered by events occurring at a point in time when the Act was not in force. The Supreme Court recalled that it was established law following *Brecknell v United Kingdom (32457/04)* [2007] 11 WLUK 675; (2008) 46 E.H.R.R. 42 that the arts 2 and 3 investigative duties can be revived if sufficiently weighty and compelling new evidence comes to light ([116]-[119]). However, it held that, where a triggering event preceded the coming into force of the Act, in order to engage the s.6 duty there must additionally be either: (a) a "genuine connection" between the triggering event and the date of the Act coming into force, including (i) a sufficiently close temporal connection, and (ii) that a major part of the investigation must have or ought to have been carried out after entry into force of the Act; or (b) exceptional circumstances satisfying the "Convention values" test i.e. a need to ensure protection of the guarantees and the underlying values of the Convention ([133]-[145] and [167]-[168]). **3D-71**

SECTION 3E INSOLVENCY PROCEEDINGS

INSOLVENCY PRACTICE DIRECTION RELATING TO THE CORPORATE INSOLVENCY AND GOVERNANCE ACT 2020

Editorial note

In the third paragraph, second sentence, replace "in the period 1 October 2021 to 31 March 2022. Petitions presented in the period 1 October 2021 to 31 March 2022" with:

on or after 1 October 2021. Petitions presented on or after 1 October 2021 **3E-21.1.0.10**

INSOLVENCY PROCEEDINGS: GENERAL

The "opening" of proceedings

In the sixth paragraph, replace "(currently 27 April 2020 to 30 September 2021), there is no "relation back"" with:

(27 April 2020 to 30 September 2021), there was no "relation back" **3E-23.2**

Procedure

Replace paragraph with:

Insolvency proceedings are governed primarily by the Insolvency Act 1986 (IA) (as most recently amended by the Corporate Insolvency and Governance Act 2020 and the Insolvency (Amendment) (EU Exit) Regulations 2019 (SI 2019/146)) and the Insolvency (England and Wales) Rules 2016 (SI 2016/1024)(IR), and not by the CPR. However, where the IA and the IR do not make provision for procedure, the CPR may be invoked (IR 2016 r.12.1). All insolvency proceedings are multi-track (Insolvency (England and Wales) Rules 2016 r.12.1(2) (formerly the Insolvency Rules 1986 r.7.51A(3))). On the impact of the Disclosure Pilot (Practice Direction 51U), which as from 1 October 2022 became PD57AD); see: *In the Matter of Blades Leisure Ltd* [2019] EWHC 914 (Ch), paras 11-25, 65 and 75-80. See too, "Message from the Chief Insolvency and Companies Court Judge" dated 6 February 2019 at para 57ADPN.2. **3E-24**

Urgent applications

At the start of the paragraph, replace "In normal (non-COVID 19) conditions, the" with:

The normal **3E-26**

Impact of COVID-19

Replace "easing of restrictions, more" with:
lifting of restrictions, most

Insolvency Express Trials

Replace paragraph with:
3E-27 From 6 April 2016 a new regime for insolvency cases began as a two year pilot in the ICC Judges' courts in the Chancery Division of the High Court at the Rolls Building. This Pilot has now concluded.

Corporate insolvency—The impact of CIGA 2020

Overview

Add new paragraph at end:
3E-31 Users should note that, save in relation to winding up petitions presented in the period 27 April 2020 to 31 March 2022, the temporary measures introduced by CIGA 2020 to protect businesses from winding up proceedings during the pandemic have now come to an end. In addition, the (twice-extended) temporary suspension of liability for wrongful trading introduced by CIGA 2020 s.12 ended on 30 June 2021.

Company Voluntary Arrangements

Replace the second paragraph with:
3E-34 For the rules relating to CVAs, see IR 2016 Pt 2 and rr.15.11, 15.14, 15.31, 15.34 and 15.35. A company in financial difficulties can agree a voluntary arrangement with its creditors if the requisite proportion of creditors (75 per cent calculated by value of debts) approve its proposals. Any challenge to the fairness or regularity of the decision process on a CVA proposal must usually be brought within 28 days: s.6 IA 1986. For recent examples of challenges in a retail context see *Discovery (Northampton) Ltd v Debenhams Retail Ltd* [2019] EWHC 2441 (Ch) and *Re Instant Cash Loans Ltd* [2019] EWHC 2795 (Ch). For an impressive overview of the law in this area, see *Re New Look Retailers Ltd* [2021] EWHC 1209 (Ch). For a case highlighting the shortcomings of the electronic voting procedure prescribed under IR 2016 in a CVA context, see *Re Nero Holdings Limited* [2021] EWHC 2600 (Ch).

Winding-up petitions (Parts IV and V Insolvency Act 1986)

Applications for relief from the effects of s.127

Replace the last sentence with:
3E-82 As to the procedure and principles governing such applications see para.9.11 of the 2018 Practice Direction and the guidance of the Court of Appeal in *Express Electrical Distributors Ltd v Beavis* [2016] EWCA Civ 765; [2016] 1 W.L.R. 4783. On the narrowed scope of the defence of change of position in this context, see *Re MKG Convenience Ltd (In Liquidation)* [2019] EWHC 1383 (Ch) and *Changtel Solutions UK Ltd* [2022] EWHC 694 (Ch).

SECTION 3G GENERAL DATA PROTECTION REGULATION

Introduction

Replace list item "(2)" with:
3G-1 (2) Part 3 DPA, with Schs 7–8, governs the processing of personal data by competent authorities for law enforcement purposes. It gives effect to the LED, although applies to law enforcement processing more generally even where it falls outside the scope of EU law. For discussion of the scope and scheme of Pt 3, see: *R. (M) v Chief Constable of Sussex Police* [2021] EWCA Civ 42; *R. (El Gizouli) v Secretary of State for the Home Department* [2020] UKSC 10; [2021] A.C. 937.

Brexit

In the second paragraph, after "Controllers in the UK must be aware that if", add:
3G-1.1 an adequacy decision ceases to be in place for the UK and

The General Data Protection Regulation 2016

Editorial note

Article 6

Replace the fifth paragraph with:

Article 6(1)(c) covers processing which is necessary to comply with a duty imposed on the controller by law. In accordance with *Cooper*, this can cover any form of legal obligation, including public law principles developed at common law. It must be read with art.6(3), which requires that the obligation be laid down by domestic law, as well as importing a clear requirement of proportionality. It is likely that this would be interpreted to include common law obligations, provided that they meet the requirements of legal certainty: see recitals (42) and (45). In *OT (C-184/20)*, the CJEU held that a Lithuanian public register of interests of heads of publicly-funded organisations exceeded the proportionality requirement inherent within art.6(1)(c), as read with art.6(3), insofar as it required publication of transaction data on the part of the official's spouse, partner and close family members (but not the official themselves **3G-7.4**

In the seventh paragraph, replace "Article 6(1)(e)" with:

Article 6(1)

Editorial note

In the second paragraph, after "Orange Romania SA (C-61/19)." add:

and *eprimo (C-102/20).* **3G-8.1**

Editorial note

In the second paragraph, after the third sentence (ending "of an offence."), add:

Although expressed in different terms, the CJEU came to much the same outcome in *OT (C-184/20)*, when it held that publication of transaction information by a spouse, partner or cohabitee of certain types of public officials indirectly disclosed that person's sexuality or sexual orientation data. A purposive and wide interpretation of the categories of special category data was required: indirect revelation is sufficient. **3G-9.4**

Editorial note

Exemptions

Replace the first paragraph with:

There are a range of exemptions from the individual rights. Article 23, as amended in the UK GDPR, provides that the Secretary of State may restrict the scope of the obligations and rights provided for in arts 12 to 22 when such a restriction respects the essence of the fundamental rights and freedoms and is a necessary and proportionate measure in a democratic society to safeguard a specified interests. Article 23(2) sets a series of matters which must be contained within, and addressed by, any exercise of the power in art.23(1). The UK has provided for exemptions from the rights and for modifications of the subject access right in Schs 2, 3, 4 and 5 of the DPA. The vast majority are contained in Sch.2. The aim appears to have been to reproduce, as far as possible, the exemptions and modifications applicable under the DPA 1998, with some amendments and additions. They do not, however, generally address the terms of art.23(2) (which did not apply in the DPA 1998 context). One notable new exemption is that in para.4 of Sch.2, covering prejudice to the maintenance of effective immigration control. A challenge to the inclusion of that exemption as contrary to art.23 GDPR, because of a failure to address the art.23(2) factors, was upheld in *R. (Open Rights Group) v Secretary of State for the Home Department* [2021] EWCA Civ 800; [2021] 1 W.L.R. 3611. That judgment emphasised that art.23 was a derogation from the rights afforded by the UK GDPR and so any exemption must satisfy a test of strict necessity. In a subsequent judgment, the Government was afforded until 31 January 2022 to remedy the exemption failing which it would be disapplied as incompatible with retained EU law: *R. (Open Rights Group) v Secretary of State for the Home Department* [2021] EWCA Civ 1573; [2022] Q.B. 166. Amendments were made with effect from 31 January 2022 by the Data Protection Act 2018 (Amendment of Schedule 2 Exemptions) Regulations 2022, which made alterations to the terms of para.4 and inserted new paras 4A and 4B. **3G-11**

Editorial note

Replace list with:

- if the third country or organisation has been designated by a decision of the Secretary of State as providing an adequate level of protection: art.45. (Decisions taken by the European Commission pre-Brexit remain in place); **3G-29.1**

- a legally binding and enforceable instrument between public authorities: art.46(2)(a);
- under binding corporate rules, governing intra-group transfers between linked companies and approved by a supervisory authority: arts 46(2)(b) and 47;
- under standard data protection clauses made by the Secretary of State and implemented in a contract between the controllers, or as between controller and processed: art.46(2)(c);
- under standard data protection clauses adopted by the Information Commissioner: art.46(2)(d), and see too DPA s.119A. On 21 March 2022, having been laid before Parliament by the Secretary of State, the international data transfer agreement, the international data transfer addendum to the European Commission's standard clauses, and transitional provisions, came into effect under s.119A and art.46(2)(d);
- under an approved code of conduct pursuant to art.40: art.46(2)(e). (There is no such approved code at present);
- under an approved certification mechanism pursuant to art.42: art.46(2)(f). (There is no such approved mechanism at present);
- if one of the specific and narrow derogations provided for in art.49 applies.

Editorial note

At the end of the paragraph, replace "Leighton v Information Commissioner (No.2) [2020] UKUT 23 (AAC) and Scranage v Information Commissioner [2020] UKUT 196 (AAC)." with:

3G-33.1 the judgment of the three-judge panel in *Killock v Information Commissioner* [2021] UKUT 299 (AAC).

Editorial note

In the second paragraph, replace "Lloyd v Google LLC [2021] UKSC 50" with:

3G-38.1 *Lloyd v Google LLC* [2021] UKSC 50; [2021] 3 W.L.R. 1268

In the fourth paragarph, after "There is no", add:

material

To the end of the last paragraph in the Editorial note, add:

The approach was applied in *Dudley v Phillips* [2022] EWHC 930 (QB), where the data protection breaches concerned harm to reputation, with compensation awarded in the sum of £10,000 (being the limit of the amount claimed)

In at least some cases, the courts have been prepared to strike out claims for compensation for one-off breaches of data protection law where the assertion of distress was unlikely or implausible, on the basis either of a de minimis principle or that no ordinary person in the modern age would be so affected as to warrant recovery even of modest sums: *Rolfe v Veale Wasbrough Vizards* [2021] EWHC 2809 (QB) and *Johnson v Eastlight Community Homes Ltd* [2021] EWHC 3069 (QB).

In *Underwood v Bounty UK Ltd* [2022] EWHC 888 (QB) the pleading of exemplary damages claims in data protection cases was deprecated as being available only in wholly exceptional cases.

SECTION 3H CONSUMER CREDIT AND CONSUMER LAW

Consumer Rights Act 2015

Replace paragraph 10 with:

SECTION 77

SCHEDULE 5

INVESTIGATORY POWERS ETC.

PART 2

THE ENFORCER'S LEGISLATION

Enforcer's legislation: duties and powers mentioned in paragraph 9(1)(a)

3H-1106 10. The duties and powers mentioned in paragraph 9(1)(a) are those arising under any of the following provisions—

section 26(1) or 40(1)(b) of the Trade Descriptions Act 1968 (including as applied by regulation 8(3) of the Crystal Glass (Descriptions) Regulations 1973 (SI 1973/1952) and regulation 10(2) of the Footwear (Indication of Composition) Labelling Regulations 1995 (SI 1995/2489));
section 9(1) or (6) of the Hallmarking Act 1973;
paragraph 6 of the Schedule to the Prices Act 1974 (including as read with paragraph 14(1) of that Schedule);
section 161(1) of the Consumer Credit Act 1974;
section 26(1) of the Estate Agents Act 1979;
Article 39 of the Weights and Measures (Northern Ireland) Order 1981 (SI 1981/231 (NI 10));
section 16A(1) or (4) of the Video Recordings Act 1984;
section 27(1) of the Consumer Protection Act 1987 (including as applied by section 12(1) of the Fireworks Act 2003 to fireworks regulations under that Act and by regulation 18 of the Standardised Packaging of Tobacco Products Regulations 2015 (SI 2015/829) to those Regulations);
section 215(1) of the Education Reform Act 1988;
section 107A(1) or (3) or 198A(1) or (3) of the Copyright, Designs and Patents Act 1988;
regulation 31 of the Package Travel and Linked Travel Arrangements Regulations 2018 (SI 2018/634);
section 30(4) or (7) or 31(4)(a) of the Clean Air Act 1993;
paragraph 1 of Schedule 2 to the Sunday Trading Act 1994;
section 93(1) or (3) of the Trade Marks Act 1994;
section 8A(1) or (3) of the Olympic Symbol etc (Protection) Act 1995;
regulation 5C(5) of the Motor Fuel (Composition and Content) Regulations 1999 (SI 1999/3107);
regulation 61 of the Medical Devices Regulations 2002 (S.I. 2002/618);
paragraph 1(a) of Schedule 10 to the Personal Protective Equipment Regulations 2002 (SI 2002/1144) so far as that paragraph remains in force by virtue of regulation 2(6) of the Personal Protective Equipment (Enforcement) Regulations 2018 (S.I. 2018/390);
section 3(1) of the Christmas Day Trading Act 2004;
the General Product Safety Regulations 2005 (SI 2005/1803), if they are duties and powers of an enforcement authority (within the meaning of regulation 2 of those Regulations);
regulation 10(1) of the Weights and Measures (Packaged Goods) Regulations 2006 (SI 2006/659);
regulation 13(1) or (1A) of the Business Protection from Misleading Marketing Regulations 2008 (SI 2008/1276);
regulation 19(1) or (1A) of the Consumer Protection from Unfair Trading Regulations 2008 (SI 2008/1277);
paragraph 2 or 5 of Schedule 5 to the Supply of Machinery (Safety) Regulations 2008 (SI 2008/1597);
section A11(7)(a) of the Apprenticeships, Skills, Children and Learning Act 2009;
regulation 32(2) or (3) of the Timeshare, Holiday Products, Resale and Exchange Contracts Regulations 2010 (SI 2010/2960);
regulation 10(1) of the Weights and Measures (Packaged Goods) Regulations (Northern Ireland) 2011 (SR 2011/331);
regulation 11 of the Textile Products (Labelling and Fibre Composition) Regulations 2012 (SI 2012/1102);
regulation 6(1) of the Cosmetic Products Enforcement Regulations 2013 (SI 2013/1478);
regulation 23(1) of the Consumer Contracts (Information, Cancellation and Additional Charges) Regulations 2013 (SI 2013/3134);
section 87(1) of this Act;
section 93(1) or (2) of this Act;
regulation 7(1) of the Packaging (Essential Requirements) Regulations 2015;
regulation 53 of the Tobacco and Related Products Regulations 2016 (SI 2016/507);
regulation 52(1)(a)(ii) or (b)(ii) of the Electromagnetic Compatibility Regulations 2016 (SI 2016/1091);
regulation 55(1) or (2) of the Simple Pressure Vessels (Safety) Regulations 2016 (SI 2016/1092);
regulation 61(1) or (2) of the Lifts Regulations 2016 (SI 2016/1093);
regulation 41(1) or (2) of the Electrical Equipment (Safety) Regulations 2016 (SI 2016/1101);
regulation 67(1) or (2) of the Pressure Equipment (Safety) Regulations 2016 (SI 2016/1105);
regulation 62 of the Non-automatic Weighing Instruments Regulations 2016 (SI 2016/1152);
regulations 67 of the Measuring Instruments Regulations 2016 (SI 2016/1153);
regulation 66(1) or (2) of the Recreational Craft Regulations 2017 (SI 2017/737);
regulation 56(1)(a)(ii) or (b)(ii) or (2) of the Radio Equipment Regulations 2017 (S.I. 2017/1206);
section 6 of the Tenant Fees Act 2019;
section 7 of the Tenant Fees Act 2019;
section 26 of the Tenant Fees Act 2019;
regulation 4(1) and (2) of the Gas Appliances (Enforcement) and Miscellaneous Amendments Regulations 2018 (SI 2018/389);

regulation 4(1) and (2) of the Personal Protective Equipment (Enforcement) Regulations 2018 (SI 2018/390);
section 64 of the Offensive Weapons Act 2019
section 20(1) and (3) of the Birmingham Commonwealth Games Act 2020.
section 4 of the Botulinum Toxin and Cosmetic Fillers (Children) Act 2021.

Note

To the end of the sixth paragraph (beginning with "Schedule 5 para.10"), add:

3H-1111 ; and the Offensive Weapons Act 2019 s.64(5), with effect from 6 April 2022

SECTION 3I DISCRIMINATION

Equality Act 2010

Editorial note

Replace the first and second paragraphs with:

3I-76.1 The Equality Act 2010 creates a series of statutory torts and statutory duties relating to prescribed and defined "protected characteristics" and makes additional provision (see Pt 2 for "Key Concepts" and Pts 3–7) for the unlawful acts. The provisions in the Equality Act 2010 addressing enforcement are set out below. Assessors must be appointed in all claims under the Equality Act 2010 heard in the county courts save where "the judge is satisfied that there are good reasons for not doing so" (s.114(7)). This means that assessors will be routinely appointed in all discrimination claims in the county courts (as to the role of assessors in discrimination proceedings, see para.3I-93, below). The Practice Direction provides that r.35.15 of the CPR (which addresses the role of assessors) "has effect in relation to an assessor who is to be appointed" in proceedings under the Equality Act 2010 (see para.3I-3 above).

The Equality Act 2010 also enacts the Public Sector Equality Duty (s.149) which was brought into force in April 2011. This duty is enforceable by way of judicial review proceedings (see, for example, *R. (on the application of Elias) v Secretary of State for the Home Department* [2006] EWCA Civ 1293; 1 W.L.R. 3213, *R. (on the application of Hajrula) v London Councils* [2011] EWHC 448 (Admin); [2011] Eq. L.R. 612, *R. (Rahman) v Birmingham City Council* [2011] EWHC 944 (Admin); [2011] Eq. L.R. 705). Further, the EHRC has power to "assess" the extent to which or manner in which a public authority has complied with the Public Sector Equality Duty or a specific duty enacted under the Equality Act 2010 s.153 (Equality Act 2010 s.31 and Sch.2). The EHRC also has power to issue compliance notices in respect of a breach of the Public Sector Equality Duty and the specific equality duties (but only after an "assessment" has been carried out and only where the notice relates to the results of the "assessment") (Equality Act 2006 s.32). For a summary of the applicable principles, see, *Bracking v Secretary of State for Work and Pensions* [2013] EWCA Civ 1345; [2014] EqLR 60 at [26], per McCombe LJ. And see, *Hotak v Southwark London Borough Council (Equality and Human Rights Commission and others intervening); Kanu v Southwark London Borough Council (Equality and Human Rights Commission and others intervening); Johnson v Solihull Metropolitan Borough Council (Equality and Human Rights Commission and others intervening)* [2015] UKSC 30; [2016] A.C. 811, at [73]–[76] and *R. (on the application of Bridges) v Chief Constable of South Wales* [2020] EWCA Civ 1058; [2020] 1 W.L.R. 5037 at [174]–[176].

Replace the fourth paragraph with:

By s.14(1) of the Equality Act 2006 (as amended), the EHRC may "issue a code of practice in connection with any matter addressed by the Equality Act 2010" (for the admissibility and weight to be afforded such Codes, see the Equality Act 2006 s.15(4) and para.3I-96 below): see, Code of Practice on Disability Discrimination for Trade Organisations etc ((Disability Discrimination Code of Practice (Trade Organisations, Qualifications Bodies and General Qualifications Bodies (Commencement) Order 2008 (SI 2008/1335)) and Code of Practice on Services, Public Functions and Associations Equality Act 2010 Codes of Practice (Services, Public Functions and Associations, Employment, and Equal Pay) Order 2011 (SI 2011/857)).

Note

To the end of the paragraph, add:

3I-79.1 and the Higher Education and Research Act 2017 s.89(6)

Notes on Parts 9 and 11 of the Equality Act 2010

Jurisdiction and proceedings

Replace "Metropolitan Housing Trust Ltd v TM (A protected party) [2021] EWCA Civ 1890" with:

Metropolitan Housing Trust Ltd v TM (A protected party) [2021] EWCA Civ 1890; [2022] H.L.R. 16 **3I-93**

Time limits

Replace the second paragraph with:

The question whether an act might be said to "extend over a period" for the purposes of the time limits has proved problematic and controversial. A policy, rule or practice, in accordance with which decisions are taken from time to time, might constitute a "continuing act" for these purposes, even where such policy is unwritten and informal (*Owusu v London Fire and Civil Defence Authority* [1995] I.R.L.R. 574, EAT; *Cast v Croydon College* [1998] I.C.R. 500, CA; *Pennine Acute Hospitals NHS Trust v Power* [2011] 2 WLUK 786, EAT). Likewise a continuing state of affairs may constitute a continuing act for these purposes (*Hendricks v MPC* [2003] I.C.R. 530, even where the individual acts relied upon are done by different persons and are done at different places). In addition, in each case, a claim may be considered notwithstanding that it has been instituted outside of the time limit where it would be "just and equitable" to do so (Equality Act 2010 s.118(1)(b)); as to the factors which are likely to be relevant, see *British Coal Corporation v Keeble* [1997] I.R.L.R. 336, EAT, at 338, and *London Borough of Southwark v Afolabi* [2003] I.C.R. 800, presented nearly nine years after the expiry of the statutory time limit and *Adedeji v University Hospitals NHS Foundation Trust* [2021] EWCA Civ 23). The discretion is "wide" and each case is likely to turn very much on its own facts: *Chief Constable of Lincolnshire Police v Caston* [2010] I.R.L.R. 327. **3I-94**

Enforcement and remedies

Replace "Harris (suing as personal representative of Andrews (Deceased)) v Lewisham and Guy's Mental Health NHS Trust [2000] 3 All E.R. 769" with:

Harris (suing as personal representative of Andrews (Deceased)) v Lewisham and Guy's Mental Health NHS Trust [2000] 3 All E.R. 769; 2000 I.R.L.R. 320 **3I-95**

Replace the second paragraph with:

As to remedies under the Equality Act 2010, the county courts may make any order as would be available in the High Court in proceedings in tort or on a claim for judicial review (s.119(2)). In particular, a court may award compensation, including for injury to feelings (*Vento v Chief Constable of West Yorkshire Police* [2002] EWCA Civ 1871; [2003] I.C.R. 318; *Da'Bell v National Society for the Prevention of Cruelty to Children* [2010] I.R.L.R. 19; *Taylor v XLN Telecom Ltd* [2010] I.R.L.R. 499) aggravated and exemplary damages (*Ministry of Defence v Fletcher* [2010] I.R.L.R. 25) and "stigma" damages (*Chagger v Abbey National plc* [2010] I.R.L.R. 47). General damages should be uplifted by 10% following *Simmons v Castle* [2012] EWCA Civ 1039 (see, *Summers v Bundy* [2016] EWCA Civ 126 and *Pereira de Souza v Vinci Construction UK Ltd* [2017] EWCA Civ 879; [2017] I.R.L.R. 844; see also *Presidential Guidance; Employment Tribunal Awards for Injury to Feelings and Psychiatric Injury following De Souza v Vinci Construction*, 5 September 2017). In determining whether any particular losses are recoverable the test to be applied is whether such losses are caused by (or arise naturally and directly from) the discrimination found proved. There is no requirement of foreseeabilty (*Essa v Laing Ltd* [2004] EWCA Civ 2; [2004] I.C.R. 746, CA). In claims of indirect discrimination (Equality Act 2010 s.19), a county court or sheriff court must not make an award of damages unless it first considers whether to make any other disposal in cases where it is satisfied that the provision, criterion or practice was not applied with the intention of discriminating against the claimant (Equality Act 2010 s.119(5) and (6)). However, there is nothing in the wording of the provision that prioritises or emphasises one remedy over another (*Wisbey v Commissioner of the City of London Police* [2021] EWCA Civ 650; [2021] I.C.R. 1485). Further, a court may infer that a defendant had the requisite intention where he knew when he applied the offending requirement or condition that the discriminatory consequences would follow (*London Underground Ltd v Edwards* [1995] I.R.L.R. 355, EAT; *JH Walker Ltd v Hussain* [1996] I.C.R. 291, EAT).

SECTION 3K CIVIL RECOVERY PROCEEDINGS

PRACTICE DIRECTION—CIVIL RECOVERY PROCEEDINGS

Scope and Interpretation

Add sub-paragraph (13A) to paragraph 1.5:

3K-7 **1.5**

(13A) "responsible officer" has the meaning set out in section 362A(8) of the Act;

Section IV—Further Provisions about Specific Applications under Part 8 of the Act or Part 1 of the 2013 Order

Unexplained wealth order

Replace paragraph 18.1 with:

18.1

3K-28.1 (1) The application notice must name as a respondent the person who is required to be specified under section 362A(2)(b) of the Act.

(2) In a case where the respondent is not an individual, the application notice may also name a person who is specified as a responsible officer of the respondent, pursuant to section 362(2A) of the Act.

Replace paragraph 18.2 with:

18.2 The application notice must–

(1) state the matters required by section 362A(2) and, if applicable, section 362A(2A) of the Act; and

(2) specify what other information in connection with the property is sought (see section 362A(3)(d) of the Act) and what documents are sought (see section 362A(5));

(3) specify whether the respondent is a politically exposed person in accordance with section 362B(4)(a) of the Act, or whether there are reasonable grounds to suspect that the respondent is, or has been, involved in serious crime in accordance with section 362B(4)(b) of the Act.

(4) give details of–

(a) the nature of the Order sought in respect of the matters set out in section 362A(4) of the Act);

(b) the period within which compliance with the unexplained wealth order is sought (see section 362A(6) of the Act);

(c) (i) the known sources of the respondent's lawfully obtained income (see section 362B(3) of the Act).

(ii) the unlawful conduct through which it is suspected that the property has been obtained (see section 362B(3)(b) of the Act).

Replace paragraph 18.3 with:

18.3 An unexplained wealth order must–

(1) state the person and the property to which it applies;

(2) specify the matters set out in section 362A(3), including in particular what other information in connection with the property is to be provided (see section 362A(3)(d);

(3) specify the matters set out in section 362A(4);

(4) state the period within which the respondent or, if applicable, the specified responsible officer must comply with the order (see section 362A(6) of the Act);

(5) contain a statement of the offences relating to unexplained wealth orders under section 362E of the Act.

Interim freezing order

Replace paragraph 18.10 with:

18.10 The court shall have regard to the following when setting the period for which an interim freezing order has effect— **3K-28.2**

(1) the period set under section 362A(6) for the respondent or, if applicable, the specified responsible officer to comply with the unexplained wealth order which applies to the property to which interim freezing order relates; and

(2) the period allocated to the enforcement agency under section 362D(2) to (4) to determine what enforcement or investigatory provisions it considers are to be taken in relation to the property ("the determination period").

Add new paragraph 18.10A:

18.10A Application to extend the determination period

An application under section 362DA of the Act to extend the determination period must—

(a) be made to a High Court judge;

(b) be made in accordance with CPR Part 23; and

(c) explain, pursuant to section 362DA—

  (i) the work that the enforcement authority is undertaking towards making a determination under section 362D(2);

  (ii) why further time is needed for the authority to make that determination; and

  (iii) why it is reasonable in all the circumstances for the period to be extended.

(Section 362DA of the Act specifies the limits which apply to an extension of the determination period.)

Exclusions from interim freezing order for the purpose of meeting legal costs: general provisions

Replace paragraph 18.11 with:

18.11 Subject to paragraph 18.12 when the court makes an interim freezing order on an application without notice, it will normally make an initial exclusion from the order for the purpose of enabling the respondent or, if applicable, the specified responsible officer to meet their reasonable legal costs so that they may— **3K-28.3**

(1) take advice in relation to the order;

(2) prepare a statement of assets in accordance with paragraph 18.14; and

(3) if so advised, apply for the order to be varied or set aside.

The total amount specified in the initial exclusion will not normally exceed £3,000.

Replace paragraph 18.14 with:

18.14 A statement of assets is a witness statement which sets out all the property which a person owns, holds or controls, or in which the person has an interest, giving the value, location and details of all such property. Information given in a statement of assets under this practice direction will be used only for the purpose of the civil recovery proceedings or in support of an application for an exclusion from a property freezing order or interim receiving order for the purpose of enabling a person to meet their reasonable legal costs (see paragraph 7.3).

Replace paragraph 18.15 with:

18.15 If the court is satisfied that a person has property to which the interim freezing order does not apply and from which the person may meet their or, if applicable, the specified responsible officer's reasonable legal costs, it—

(1) will not make an exclusion for the purpose of enabling a person to meet those reasonable legal costs (including an initial exclusion under paragraph 18.11); and

(2) may set aside any exclusion which it has made for that purpose or reduce any amount specified in such an exclusion.

SECTION 3M PREVENTION OF TERRORISM PROCEEDINGS (CPR PTS 76, 79, 80 & 88)

PART 79—PROCEEDINGS UNDER THE COUNTER-TERRORISM ACT 2008, PART 1 OF THE TERRORIST ASSET-FREEZING ETC. ACT 2010 AND PART 1 OF THE SANCTIONS AND ANTI-MONEY LAUNDERING ACT 2018[1]

Editorial introduction

Replace the third paragraph with:

3M-52 The Part was further extended to cover sanctions-related decisions made under the Sanctions and Anti-Money Laundering Act 2018 (2018 Act). This was done via the Civil Procedure (Amendment) (EU Exit) Rules 2019 (SI 2019/147), which came into force on 1 March 2019, which were rules made under powers conferred by s.40 of the 2018 Act. The 2018 Act was passed in anticipation of the UK exiting the EU because the UK's implementation of UN and other multilateral sanctions regimes has hitherto largely relied on the European Communities Act 1972. When the UK left the EU it was no longer able to continue to use the European Communities Act 1972 to implement sanctions and would have been in breach of international law by being unable to implement UN sanctions and without power to implement sanctions which have not been put in place at UN level. The 2018 Act thus aims to create a domestic framework of relevant powers to remedy this problem. See generally the Explanatory Notes to the 2018 Act. Under the 2018 Act, sanctions regulations may be made where the Minister considers it appropriate to do so for either; (a) the purposes of compliance with a UN obligation; (b) the purposes of compliance with any other international obligation; or (c) for a purpose stated within s.1(2) of the Act, which include furthering the prevention of terrorism in the UK or elsewhere, the interest of national security, or of international peace and security and providing accountability for, or be a deterrent to, gross violations of human rights, or otherwise promote compliance with international human rights law or respect for human rights. All sanctions regulations made by the appropriate Minister must set out the purpose for which they are made (s.1(3)). There are additional requirements for regulations made for a purpose which is not compliance with a UN or other international obligation, and these additional requirements are detailed in s.2. Different types of sanction are set out in s.1(5), which are then explained further in ss.3–8 of the 2018 Act. Sections 23–25, 27–29 and 36–37 set out procedures for requests to the appropriate Minister to have a designation reviewed. Section 38 then provides that the appropriate person may apply to the High Court for a decision made under those sections to be set aside. Pursuant to s.38(4) and (5) the principles applicable on an application for judicial review apply to the determination of such an application and the judicial review remedies are available. Section 39 makes provision in relation to damages and s.40 provides that the closed material procedure provided for in the Counter-Terrorism Act 2008 may be used (with listed modifications) in respect of proceedings under s.38 and on a claim arising from any matter to which such an application relates.

In *R. (on the application of Youssef) v Secretary of State for Foreign, Commonwealth and Development Affairs* [2021] EWHC 3188 (Admin), the Court held that the procedures under ss.25 and 38 of the 2018 Act satisfy the modest level of scrutiny required by Art.6 and Art.8 ECHR to have the arbitrariness of the listing under UN sanctions reviewed by a court [89], [102].

PART 88—PROCEEDINGS UNDER THE COUNTER-TERRORISM AND SECURITY ACT 2015

Editorial introduction

Replace the first, second and third paragraphs with:

3M-146 The Counter-Terrorism and Security Act 2015 (c.6) received the Royal Assent on 12 February

[1] Amended by the Civil Procedure (Amendment) (EU Exit) Rules 2019 (SI 2019/147).

2015, and came into force on the following day. Chapter 2 of Part 1 of the Act (ss.2 to 15) gives the Secretary of State power, if certain conditions are met, to impose, on an individual who has a right of abode in the United Kingdom and who is reasonably suspected of involvement in terrorist activity abroad, a temporary exclusion order (TEO), requiring that individual not to return to the United Kingdom except in accordance with a permit to return (or as a result of deportation to the United Kingdom). Section 9 permits the Secretary of State to impose various permitted obligations on those subject to TEOs who have returned to the UK. Section 11 permits the individual affected to apply to the court for a review of the decision, in relation to which the court must apply the principles applicable on an application for judicial review (s.11(3)).

Section 3 (Temporary exclusion orders: prior permission of the court) makes provision for the role of the court in providing prior permission to the Secretary of State to impose a TEO. The prior permission of the court is required, except in circumstances of particular urgency, in which case the Secretary of State may impose a TEO but must refer the matter to the court immediately after doing so. An individual on whom a TEO has been imposed may also apply to the court to review the Secretary of State's decision that the conditions for the TEO were met, the decision to impose the TEO, or the decision to impose conditions on an individual after return. Where the principal place of residence of the individual is neither Scotland nor Northern Ireland, the statutory jurisdiction is exercisable by the High Court.

Section 3 also introduces Sch.2 (Urgent temporary exclusion orders: reference to the court etc). Section 12 (Temporary exclusion orders: proceedings and appeals against convictions) introduces Sch.3 (Temporary exclusion orders: proceedings) and Sch.4 (Temporary exclusion orders: appeals against convictions), which details the provisions that can be made by rules of court in relation to temporary exclusion order proceedings, and the provisions that must be made in relation to disclosure. Schedule 4 details the appeal proceedings available to an individual where a TEO or associated in-country measure under it is quashed or altered and the individual has already been convicted of an offence under s.10(1) or (3) of the Act in connection with the TEO or measure.

Part 88 contains rules about proceedings in relation to TEO proceedings generally, and particularly where sensitive material is in issue and it is necessary to ensure that such material is not disclosed where such disclosure would be contrary to the public interest. This includes modification of the application of other Parts of the CPR for the purposes of those proceedings). Rule 1.2 (Application by the court of the overriding objective) is modified (see r.88.2).

Replace the fifth paragraph with:

In *QX v Secretary of State for the Home Department* [2020] EWHC 1221 (Admin), the Court held that the imposition of a TEO under s.2 of the 2015 Act qualifies the right of abode of British citizens, and so falls "within the hard core of public-authority prerogatives" that does not attract the procedural protections of art.6 ECHR (paras 55-56). However, the court found that art.6 may apply in relation to a review under s.11 of obligations imposed under s.9 of the 2015 Act upon a person who is subject to a TEO upon return to the UK, subject to the question of whether the obligations in question engage art.8 (see paras 58-78 and the notes to r.88.6 below).

The Temporary Exclusion Orders (Notices) Regulations 2015 (SI 2015/438) make provision under s.13(1) and (2) of the 2015 Act for the giving of notice to a person on whom the Secretary of State has decided to impose a TEO under s.2 or obligations under s.9. These Regulations deal with the timing and method of giving notice and provide for notice to be deemed to have been given in prescribed circumstances.

II. Permission Applications, Reviews and References to the High Court Relating to Temporary Exclusion Orders

Editorial note

Replace paragraph with:

In *QX v Secretary of State for the Home Department* [2020] EWHC 1221 (Admin) (judgment of 15 May 2020 – the first of a series of judgments in this case referred to below), the Court considered whether art.6 ECHR applies to applications for review under s.11(2)(d) of the 2015 Act (i.e. a review of obligations imposed under s.9 of the 2015 Act on a person who returns to the UK subject to a TEO) and, if so, what level of disclosure is required to satisfy art.6. The Court held that post-return obligations are not (unlike the decision to impose a TEO in the first place) immigration measures raising questions of state prerogative, thus art.6 is capable of applying to review of such obligations. The Court held that the obligations imposed in the particular case amounted to an interference with the applicant's right to respect for private life under art.8 and so the review of them was a determination of a civil right engaging art.6 (however, the Court declined to decide whether art.8 will always be engaged in relation to such a review). The Court emphasised that the extent of the disclosure required by art.6 will depend on the facts of the particular case (the cases falling on a spectrum from cases of "actual or virtual imprisonment", where disclosure complying with the standard set down in *Secretary of State for the Home Department v F (No.3)* [2010] 2 A.C. 269 is required, to cases where "an outline of the grounds for decision coupled with the protections built into the closed material procedure will suffice" (*QX* at [82]). The Court applied the test set out at [59] of *F (No.3)*. See generally the principles discussed in the notes to Part 82 at para.82.0.3. **3M-152.1**

The court may conduct a review in respect of a TEO that has expired. In such a case, the court's function is to review the Secretary of State's decisions that the relevant conditions for the imposition of the TEO were met and continued to be met up until the date of expiry (*QX v Secretary of State for the Home Department* [2022] EWHC 836 (Admin), at [22].

The question of whether the TEO ought to have been imposed and questions relating to the obligations that may be imposed under s.9 of the 2015 Act were deliberately separated by Parliament in s.11 (*QX v Secretary of State for the Home Department* [2022] EWHC 836 (Admin), at [25]. A party is not permitted in the course of a review of section 9 obligations to challenge the imposition of a TEO through the "side-wind" of a review of section 9 obligations *QX* [2020] EWHC 2508 (Admin), at [25]; [2022] EWHC 836 (Admin), at [27]. This does not prevent the claimant challenging those aspects of the national security case that are relevant to the Secretary of State's assessment that the section 9 obligations are necessary and proportionate, which may mean there is an evidential or factual overlap between a review of the TEO and a review of the section 9 obligations (*QX* [2020] EWHC 2508 (Admin), at [25]; [2022] EWHC 836 (Admin), [28]-[29]). The evidence may be reviewed for different purposes and the court is not bound to apply the same procedures in carrying out what are different elements of its review function: different aspects of a s.11 review may give rise to different procedural rights if that is what is required to achieve fairness and compatibility with the claimant's human rights *QX* [2022] EWHC 836 (Admin), at [29].

Add new paragraph 3M-160.1:

Editorial note

3M-160.1 There is authority to suggest that the court has the power under CPR 3.1(2)(m) to hear oral evidence and to order cross-examination of witnesses in relation to a s.11 application if required to enable the court to comply with art.6, although this should only be done in the most exceptional case: see *QX v Secretary of State for the Home Department* [2022] EWHC 836 (Admin) at [67] and the summary of the authorities and principles as to when the court will exercise its discretion to hear oral evidence and cross-examination in relation to s.11 applications at [67]-[78] and [80]-[88].

Note that in that case, the court rejected a submission that the Secretary of State's national security witness evidence should be excluded solely because it is not in the form of a witness statement signed by an identified individual for or on behalf of the Secretary of State [64].

SECTION 3O EMPLOYMENT

Employment Tribunals Extension of Jurisdiction (England and Wales) Order 1994

Other areas of overlapping jurisdiction between courts and employment tribunals

Wages

To the end of the third paragraph, add:

3O-0.15 Nor can a claim be brought under Pt II for a quantum meruit payment, invoking the law of unjust enrichment, as this falls outside of the scope of contractual entitlement and the concept of wages: *Abellio East Midlands Ltd v Thomas* [2022] EAT 20; [2022] I.C.R. 802, 28 January 2022.

Employment Tribunals (Constitution and Rules of Procedure) Regulations 2013

Add new paragraph 3O-1.2:

3O-1.2 With effect from 28 June 2022 an Employment Tribunal may also make a costs order in respect of representation by a legal representative acting free of charge. This is provided for by a new s.194A of the Legal Services Act 2007, inserted by Judicial Review and Courts Act 2022 s.48. Such an order may be made where the Tribunal could have made an ordinary costs order under r.76. The award is payable to the Access to Justice Foundation, a prescribed charity supporting the provision of pro bono legal services.

Replace paragraph with:

The amount of a costs order

3O-5 **78.**—(1) A costs order may—

(a) order the paying party to pay the receiving party a specified amount, not exceeding £20,000, in respect of the costs of the receiving party;

(b) order the paying party to pay the receiving party the whole or a specified part of the costs of the receiving party, with the amount to be paid being determined, in England and Wales, by way of detailed assessment carried out either by a county court in accordance with the Civil Procedure Rules 1998, or by an Employment Judge applying the same principles; or, in Scotland, by way of taxation carried out either by the auditor of court in accordance with the Act of Sederunt (Taxation of Judicial Expenses Rules) 2019, or by an Employment Judge applying the same principles;

(c) order the paying party to pay the receiving party a specified amount as reimbursement of all or part of a Tribunal fee paid by the receiving party;

(d) order the paying party to pay another party or a witness, as appropriate, a specified amount in respect of necessary and reasonably incurred expenses (of the kind described in rule 75(1)(c)); or

(e) if the paying party and the receiving party agree as to the amount payable, be made in that amount.

(2) Where the costs order includes an amount in respect of fees charged by a lay representative, for the purposes of the calculation of the order, the hourly rate applicable for the fees of the lay representative shall be no higher than the rate under rule 79(2).

(3) For the avoidance of doubt, the amount of a costs order under sub-paragraphs (b) to (e) of paragraph (1) may exceed £20,000.

Add new paragraph 3O-5.0:

Note —Paragraph (1) amended by the Employment Tribunals (Constitution and Rules of Procedure) (Amendment) Regulations 2022 (SI 2022/1034) reg.3, with effect from 2 November 2022 (subject to transitional provision specified in SI 2022/1034 reg.4). **3O-5.0**

SECTION 4 SUPREME COURT OF THE UNITED KINGDOM AND JUDICIAL COMMITTEE OF THE PRIVY COUNCIL

SECTION 4A SUPREME COURT OF THE UNITED KINGDOM APPEALS

Jurisdiction of the Court

Replace the following case citations, which have been updated in paragraph 4A-0.4:

Re McGuinness's Application for Judicial Review [2020] UKSC 6; [2021] A.C. 392 and *HM Attorney General v Crosland* [2021] UKSC 58; [2022] 1 W.L.R. 367 **4A-0.4**

Doctrine of precedent

Replace "Austin v Southwark London Borough Council [2010] UKSC 28; [2010] 3 W.L.R. 14, SC" with:

Austin v Southwark London Borough Council [2010] UKSC 28; [2011] 1 A.C. 355 **4A-0.5**

Supreme Court Rules 2009

Effect of rule

Replace the second paragraph with:

In the only application made to date for committal for contempt—following a blatant breach of the embargo on publication of the draft judgment of the Court contrary to paras 6.8.3–6.8.5 of PD 6—a panel of three Justices sat to consider the Attorney General's application, found the contempt made out and imposed a fine of £5,000: *Attorney General v Crosland* [2021] UKSC 15; [2021] 4 W.L.R. 103. The Court sat in the Royal Courts of Justice, presumably lest they had needed to take advantage of the detention facilities there which the Supreme Court does not possess. The Supreme Court subsequently held that it had jurisdiction to hear an appeal from the first panel's ruling, although the appeal was dismissed: *Attorney General v Crosland* [2021] UKSC 58; [2022] 1 W.L.R. 367. **4A-9.1**

Effect of rules 46 to 53

In the second paragraph, replace "BPE Solicitors v Gabriel [2015] UKSC 39; [2015] 3 W.L.R. 1" with:

4A-46.1 *BPE Solicitors v Gabriel* [2015] UKSC 39; [2015] A.C. 1663

PRACTICE DIRECTION 10—DEVOLUTION JURISDICTION

General note

Replace paragraph 10.1.6 (footnote has been updated) with:

4A-192 **10.1.6** The forms set out in Annex 1 to Practice Direction 7 may be used for appeals and applications brought under the Court's devolution jurisdiction. In cases where a reference is made to the Court, the use of Form 1 is likely to be inappropriate and, in those circumstances, a document should be filed which contains the information set out in Annex 1 to this Practice Direction: see the Local Government Byelaws (Wales) Bill 2012—Reference by the Attorney General for England and Wales[1].

PRACTICE STATEMENT (JUDICIAL PRECEDENT) [1966] 1 W.L.R. 1234

Editorial introduction

Replace "Austin v Southwark LBC [2010] UKSC 28; [2010] 3 W.L.R. 14" with:

4A-272.1 *Austin v Southwark LBC* [2010] UKSC 28; [2011] 1 A.C. 355

Replace "Arrangements during the Coronavirus Pandemic for Michaelmas term" with new Practice Note at 4A-273:

PRACTICE NOTE MARCH 2022

4A-273 Lord Reed, as President of the Supreme Court and Chairman of the Judicial Committee, issued a Covid Practice Note in May and September 2020. The Covid Practice Note is now rescinded, and the guidance set out in this Practice Note should now be followed, together with the relevant Rules and Practice Directions.

Papers for filing

4A-274 All documents, forms and notices etc should be sent to the registry electronically. For the avoidance of doubt, paper copies are no longer required except where explicitly requested in the PD for appeal hearings, and filing should be done solely electronically where possible.

Papers under 10MB in size can be sent to the relevant Registry attached to an email. For documents over 10MB see SharePoint guidance in the Annexes to UKSC PD 14 and JCPC PD 9. Please email the relevant registry if you require a link to the upload area; registry@supremecourt.uk or registry@jcpc.uk.

Orders

4A-275 Orders which are signed by the Registrar may be issued electronically as usual but may not be sealed. Unsealed orders are to be treated as authentic and are to take effect as if they have been sealed.

Urgent applications (out of hours)

4A-276 Parties should contact the relevant registry if an application is genuinely urgent and requires action out of Court hours. The respondent should be copied into the email. Where possible advanced notice of an urgent application should be given during Court hours.

---

[1] Reported as *Attorney General v National Assembly for Wales* [2013] 1 A.C. 792

Hearings

Although WebEx may still be used, hearings will be in person unless there are exceptional reasons to justify a hybrid hearing. **4A-277**

Practice Directions

Updates to the Practice Directions may be published in due course. **4A-278**

Lord Reed of Allermuir
March 2022

SECTION 6 ADMINISTRATION OF FUNDS, PROPERTY AND AFFAIRS
SECTION 6A COURT FUNDS

Court Funds Rules 2011

Editorial note

To the end of the paragraph, add:

Please note that the reference to "defence of tender before claim" will be amended to "A defence that, before the claimant started proceedings, the defendant unconditionally offered to the claimant the amount due." in accordance with the Civil Procedure (Amendment No.4) Rules SI 2021/855 with the next amendment to the Court Funds Rules **6A-25**

Editorial note

To the end of the paragraph, add:

Please note that the reference to "defence of tender before claim" will be amended to "A defence that, before the claimant started proceedings, the defendant unconditionally offered to the claimant the amount due." in accordance with the Civil Procedure (Amendment No.4) Rules SI 2021/855 with the next amendment to the Court Funds Rules **6A-52**

INVESTMENTS ON BEHALF OF CHILDREN AND PROTECTED BENEFICIARIES

Orders of the High Court, county court and Court of Protection

Replace the first paragraph with:

For orders made by the court write to the court that originally dealt with the case. Contact details for specific courts including the Court of Protection are available from: *https://www.gov.uk/find-court-tribunal* [Accessed 28 October 2022]. **6A-212**

Queen's and Lord Treasurer's Remembrancer—coronavirus update

Delete paragraph. **6A-217.1**

Special and Basic rates from 1 October 1965

Replace the first table with: **6A-220**

High Court Special (formerly S.T.I.)			High Court Basic (formerly M.O.D.)		
Date	**Rate**	**SI**	**Date**	**Rate**	**SI**
1.11.88	12¼	Lord Chancellor's direction d/d 22.10.88	1.8.99	5¼	Lord Chancellor's direction d/d 14.7.99
			1.2.02	4	Lord Chancellor's direction d/d 7.1.02

High Court Special (formerly S.T.I.)			High Court Basic (formerly M.O.D.)		
Date	Rate	SI	Date	Rate	SI
1.1.89	13	Lord Chancellor's direction d/d 21.12.88	1.2.09	2	Lord Chancellor's direction d/d 8.12.08
1.11.89	14¼	Lord Chancellor's direction d/d 27.10.89	1.6.09	1	Lord Chancellor's direction d/d 2.2.09
1.4.91	12	Lord Chancellor's direction d/d 25.3.91	1.7.09	0.3	Lord Chancellor's direction d/d 3.6.09
1.10.91	10¼	Lord Chancellor's direction d/d 20.9.91	6.6.16	0.1	Approved with the concurrence of Treasury in May 2016
1.2.93	8	Lord Chancellor's direction d/d 27.1.93	1.6.20	0.05	Lord Chancellor's direction d/d 28.5.20
1.8.99	7	Lord Chancellor's direction d/d 14.7.99	29.4.22	0.323	Lord Chancellor's direction d/d 26.4.22
1.2.02	6	Lord Chancellor's direction d/d 7.1.02	5.7.22	0.94	Lord Chancellor's direction d/d 5.7.22
1.2.09	3	Lord Chancellor's direction d/d 8.12.08	2.9.22	1.313	Lord Chancellor's direction d/d 30.08.22
1.6.09	1.5	Lord Chancellor's direction d/d 2.2.09	25.10.22	1.688	Lord Chancellor's direction d/d 20.10.22
1.7.09	0.5	Lord Chancellor's direction d/d 3.6.09			
1.6.20	0.1	Lord Chancellor's direction d/d 28.5.20			
29.4.22	0.645	Lord Chancellor's direction d/d 26.4.22			
5.7.22	1.25	Lord Chancellor's direction d/d 5.7.22			
2.9.22	1.75	Lord Chancellor's direction d/d 30.8.22			
25.10.22	2.25	Lord Chancellor's direction d/d 20.10.22			

Replace the second table with:

County Court Special (formerly S.T.I.)			**County Court Basic (formerly M.O.D.)**		
Date	**Rate**	**SI**	**Date**	**Rate**	**SI**
1.10.65	5	65/1500	1.10.65	2½	65/1500
1.9.66	5½	66/875	1.3.71	3½	71/260
1.3.68	6	68/107	1.3.73	4	73/230
1.3.69	6½	69/204	1.3.77	5	76/2234
1.3.70	7	70/228	1.4.83	9½	83/291
1.3.71	7½	71/260	1.4.84	8	84/285
1.3.73	8	73/230	1.8.86	7½	86/1142
1.3.74	9	74/206	1.1.87	8½	86/2115
1.3.77	10	76/2234	1.12.87	8	Lord Chancellor's direction d/d 23.11.87
1.3.79	12½	79/105			
1.1.80	15	79/1619			
1.1.81	12½	80/1857	1.5.88	7½	Lord Chancellor's direction d/d 22.4.88
1.12.81	15	81/1588			
1.03.82	14	82/124			
1.7.82	13	82/786	1.8.88	9	Lord Chancellor's direction d/d 19.7.88
1.4.83	12½	83/291			
1.4.84	12	84/285			
1.8.86	11½	86/1142	1.11.88	10¼	Lord Chancellor's direction d/d 22.10.88
1.1.87	12¼	86/2115			
1.4.87	11¾	Lord Chancellor's direction d/d 30.3.87			
			1.1.89	10¾	Lord Chancellor's direction d/d 20.12.88
1.11.87	11¼	Lord Chancellor's direction d/d 19.10.87	1.11.89	11¼	Lord Chancellor's direction d/d 27.10.89
1.12.87	11	Lord Chancellor's direction d/d 23.11.87	1.4.91	9½	Lord Chancellor's direction d/d 25.3.91
1.5.88	9½	Lord Chancellor's direction d/d 22.4.88	1.10.91	8	Lord Chancellor's direction d/d 20.9.91
1.8.88	11	Lord Chancellor's direction d/d 19.7.88	1.2.93	6	Lord Chancellor's direction d/d 27.1.93
1.11.88	12¼	Lord Chancellor's direction d/d 22.10.88	1.8.99	5¼	Lord Chancellor's direction d/d 14.7.99
1.1.89	13	Lord Chancellor's direction d/d 21.12.88	1.2.02	4	Lord Chancellor's direction d/d 7.1.02

County Court Special (formerly S.T.I.)			County Court Basic (formerly M.O.D.)		
Date	Rate	SI	Date	Rate	SI
1.11.89	14¼	Lord Chancellor's direction d/d 27.10.89	1.2.09	2	Lord Chancellor's direction d/d 8.12.08
1.4.91	12	Lord Chancellor's direction d/d 25.3.91	1.6.09	1	Lord Chancellor's direction d/d 2.2.09
1.10.91	10¼	Lord Chancellor's direction d/d 20.9.91	1.7.09	0.3	Lord Chancellor's direction d/d 3.6.09
1.2.93	8	Lord Chancellor's direction d/d 27.1.93	6.6.16	0.1	Approved with the concurrence of Treasury in May 2016
1.8.99	7	Lord Chancellor's direction d/d 14.7.99	1.6.20	0.05	Lord Chancellor's direction d/d 28.5.20
1.2.02	6	Lord Chancellor's direction d/d 7.1.02	2.9.22	1.313	Lord Chancellor's direction d/d 30.8.22
1.2.09	3	Lord Chancellor's direction d/d 8.12.08	25.10.22	1.688	Lord Chancellor's direction d/d 20.10.22
1.6.09	1.5	d/d 2.2.09			
1.7.09	0.5	d/d 3.6.09			
1.6.20	0.1	d/d 28.5.20			
29.4.22	0.645	d/d 26.4.22			
5.7.22	1.25	d/d 5.7.22			
2.9.22	1.75	d/d 30.8.22			
25.10.22	2.25	d/d 20.10.22			

SECTION 7 LEGAL REPRESENTATIVES—COSTS AND LITIGATION FUNDING

SECTION 7A LITIGATION FUNDING AFTER 1 APRIL 2013

Courts and Legal Services Act 1990

Editorial note

Replace the first paragraph with:

7A-9 Damages-based agreements ("DBAs") are a type of contingency fee agreement under which a lawyer can recover a percentage of the client's damages if the case is won. Agreements that defendants will pay their lawyers a percentage of the sums or assets which they resist paying or transferring are not DBAs: *Candey v Tonstate Group Ltd* [2022] EWCA Civ 936. As first enacted, solicitors and barristers were not permitted to act under DBAs in civil litigation, but solicitors were permitted to act under DBAs in non-contentious business, including cases before employment tribunals. The Damages-Based Agreements Regulations 2010 (SI 2010/1206) were made by the Lord Chancellor in exercise of powers conferred by s.58AA.

SECTION 8 LIMITATION

Limitation Act 1980

Same cause of action

Replace paragraph with:

In *Sciortino v Beaumont* [2021] EWCA Civ 786, the Court of Appeal held in a claim for professional negligence where there are two allegedly negligent advices about the same or similar issues, there was no general principle of logic or common sense which required any sort of "relation back" whereby the limitation period was triggered by the first occasion on which the allegedly negligent advice was given, regardless of any subsequent breaches of duty. **8-5.1**

Notes on s.32

Replace the penultimate paragraph with:

In *Test Claimants in the Franked Investment Income Group Litigation v Revenue and Customs Commissioners* [2020] UKSC 47, the Supreme Court held that s.32(1)(c) applies to mistakes of law as well as mistakes of fact. Time begins to run under s.32(1)(c) when the claimant discovers, or could with reasonable diligence discover, their mistake in the sense of recognising that a worthwhile claim arises. In *Gemalto Holdings BV v Infineon Technologies AG* [2022] EWCA Civ 782 the Court of Appeal held that the Franked Investment test applied equally to cases of deliberate concealment which engaged s.32(1)(b). **8-85.1**

SECTION 9 JURISDICTIONAL AND PROCEDURAL LEGISLATION
SECTION 9A MAIN STATUTES

Senior Courts Act 1981

Replace s.9 with:

OTHER PROVISIONS

Assistance for transaction of judicial business [...]

9.—(1) A person within any entry in column 1 of the following Table may subject to the proviso at the end of that Table at any time, at the request of the appropriate authority, act— **9A-30**

(a) as a judge of a relevant court specified in the request; or

(b) if the request relates to a particular division of a relevant court so specified, as a judge of that court in that division.

	1 **Judge**	2 **Where competent to act on request**	
1.	A judge of the Court of Appeal.	The High Court, the family court, the county court and the Crown Court.	**9A-31**

	1 **Judge**	2 **Where competent to act on request**
[...]		
3.	A puisne judge of the High Court.	The Court of Appeal.
[...]		
4A.	The Senior President of Tribunals	The Court of Appeal and the High Court.
5.	A Circuit judge.	The High Court and the Court of Appeal.
6.	A Recorder or a person within subsection (1ZB).	The High Court.

The entry in column 2 specifying the Court of Appeal in relation to a Circuit judge only authorises such a judge to act as a judge of a court in the criminal division of the Court of Appeal.

(1ZA) The Senior President of Tribunals is to be treated as not being within any entry in column 1 of the Table other than entry 4A.

(1ZB) A person is within this subsection if the person—

(a) is a Chamber President, or a Deputy Chamber President, of a chamber of the Upper Tribunal or of a chamber of the First-tier Tribunal,

(b) is a judge of the Upper Tribunal by virtue of appointment under paragraph 1(1) of Schedule 3 to the Tribunals, Courts and Enforcement Act 2007,

(c) is a transferred-in judge of the Upper Tribunal (see section 31(2) of that Act),

(d) is a deputy judge of the Upper Tribunal (whether under paragraph 7 of Schedule 3 to, or section 31(2) of, that Act), or

(e) is the President of Employment Tribunals (England and Wales) or the President of Employment Tribunals (Scotland).

(1A) A person shall not act as a judge by virtue of subsection (1) after the day on which he attains the age of 75.

(2) In subsection (1)

"the appropriate authority"—

(a) the Lord Chief Justice or a judicial office holder (as defined in section 109(4) of the Constitutional Reform Act 2005) nominated by him to exercise his functions under this section, or

(b) at any time when the Lord Chief Justice or the nominated judicial office holder is unable to make such a request himself, or there is a vacancy in the office of Lord Chief Justice, the Master of the Rolls;

"relevant court", in the case of a person within any entry in column 1 of the Table, means a court specified in relation to that entry in column 2 of the Table.

(2A) The power of the appropriate authority to make a request under subsection (1) is subject to subsections (2B) to (2D).

(2B) The appropriate authority may make the request only after consulting the Lord Chancellor.

(2C) [...]

(2CA) In the case of a request to a person within entry 5 or 6 in column 1 of the Table to act as a judge of the High Court, the appropriate authority may make the request only if the person is a member of the pool for requests under subsection (1) to persons within that entry.

(2D) In the case of a request to a Circuit judge to act as a judge of the Court of Appeal, the appropriate authority may make the request only with the concurrence of the Judicial Appointments Commission.

(3) The person to whom a request is made under subsection (1) must comply with the request, but this does not apply to—

(a) [...]

(b) [...]

(c) a request made to the Senior President of Tribunals if the holder of that office is a judge of the Court of Session or of the High Court, or Court of Appeal, in Northern Ireland.

(4) Without prejudice to section 24 of the Courts Act 1971 (temporary appointment of deputy Circuit judges [...]), if it appears to the Lord Chief Justice, after consulting the Lord Chancellor, that it is expedient as a temporary measure to make an appointment under this subsection in order to facilitate the disposal of business in the High Court or the Crown Court or any other court or tribunal to which persons appointed under this subsection may be deployed, he may appoint a person qualified for appointment as a puisne judge of the High Court to be a deputy judge of the High Court during such period or on such occasions as the Lord Chief Justice, after consulting the Lord Chancellor, thinks fit; and during the period or on the occasions for which a person is appointed as a deputy judge under this subsection, he may act as a puisne judge of the High Court.

(4A) No appointment of a person as a deputy judge of the High Court shall be such as to extend beyond the day on which he attains the age of 75.

(5) Every person while acting under this section shall, subject to subsections (6) and (6A), be treated for all purposes as, and accordingly may perform any of the functions of, a judge of the court in which he is acting.

(6) A person shall not by virtue of subsection (5)—

(a) be treated as a judge of the court in which he is acting for the purposes of section 98(2) or of any statutory provision relating to—

(i) the appointment, retirement, removal or disqualification of judges of that court;

(ii) the tenure of office and oaths to be taken by such judges; or

(iii) the remuneration, allowances or pensions of such judges; or

(b) subject to section 27 of the Judicial Pensions and Retirement Act 1993, be treated as having been a judge of a court in which he has acted only under this section.

(6A) A Circuit judge, Recorder or person within subsection (1ZB) shall not by virtue of subsection (5) exercise any of the powers conferred on a single judge by sections 31, 31B, 31C and 44 of the Criminal Appeal Act 1968 (powers of single judge in connection with appeals to the Court of Appeal and appeals from the Court of Appeal to the Supreme Court).

(7) [...]

(8) Such remuneration and allowances as the Lord Chancellor may, with the concurrence of the Minister for the Civil Service, determine may be paid out of money provided by Parliament—

(a) [...]

(b) to any deputy judge of the High Court appointed under subsection (4).

(8A) A person may be removed from office as a deputy judge of the High Court—

(a) only by the Lord Chancellor with the agreement of the Lord Chief Justice, and

(b) only on—

(i) the ground of inability or misbehaviour, or

(ii) a ground specified in the person's terms of appointment.

(8B) Subject to the preceding provisions of this section, a person appointed under subsection (4) is to hold and vacate office as a deputy judge of the High Court in accordance with the terms of the person's appointment, which are to be such as the Lord Chancellor may determine.

(9) The Lord Chief Justice may nominate a senior judge (as defined in section 109(5) of the Constitutional Reform Act 2005) to exercise functions of the Lord Chief Justice under this section.

Note

Replace the first paragraph with:

9A-32 Amended by the Administration of Justice Act 1982 s.58; the Judicial Pensions and Retirement Act 1993 ss.26 and 31; Schs 6 and 9; the Criminal Justice and Public Order Act 1994 s.52; the Courts Act 2003 s.109(1), Sch.8, para.260; the Constitutional Reform Act 2005 s.15(1), Sch.4 para.121 by the 2005 Act, ss.40, 59, Sch.9 para.36(2), Sch.11 para.26, Sch.17 para.22(3), with effect from 1 October 2009 (SI 2009/1604); and (in relation to the first amendment in subs.(4)) with effect, subject to savings and transitional provisions, from 15 July 2013 (see SI 2013/1725), by the Crime and Courts Act 2013 Sch.13 para.89, (for savings and transitional provisions see Sch.8 of the 2013 Act) and with effect, subject to savings and transitional provisions, from 1 October 2013 (see SI 2013/2200), by the Crime and Courts Act 2013 Sch.13, para.52, Sch.14, paras 1, 2, (for savings and transitional provisions see Sch.8 of the 2013 Act); the Public Service Pensions and Judicial Offices Act 2022 Sch.1(1) para.16(2), with effect from 10 March 2022 (for transitional provisions see 2022 c.7 Sch.1 para.43); and the Public Service Pensions and Judicial Offices Act 2022 (c.7) Sch.4(1) para.5(2), with effect from 10 March 2022 (for the limited purpose of making subordinate legislation or giving directions, or as it otherwise relates to the exercise of a power to make subordinate legislation, or give directions, on or after 10 March 2022); 1 October 2022 (subject to savings and transitional provisions specified in SI 2022/1014 reg.3) (otherwise).

Replace s.18(1) with:

9A-62 (1) No appeal shall lie to the Court of Appeal—

- (a) except as provided by the Administration of Justice Act 1960, from any judgment of the High Court in any criminal cause or matter;
- (b) from any order of the High Court or any other court or tribunal allowing an extension of time for appealing from a judgment or order;
- (c) from any order, judgment or decision of the High Court or any other court or tribunal which, by virtue of any provision (however expressed) of this or any other Act, is final;
- (d) from a decree absolute or nullity of marriage, by a party who, having had time and opportunity to appeal from the decree nisi on which that decree was founded, has not appealed from the decree nisi;
- (da) from a divorce order or nullity of marriage order that has been made final, by a party who, having had time and opportunity to appeal from the conditional order on which that final order was founded, has not appealed from the conditional order;
- (dd) from a divorce order;
- (e) [...]
- (f) [...]
- (fa) from a dissolution order, nullity order or presumption of death order under Chapter 2 of Part 2 of the Civil Partnership Act 2004 that has been made final, by a party who, having had time and opportunity to appeal from the conditional order on which that final order was founded, has not appealed from the conditional order;
- (g) except as provided by Part I of the Arbitration Act 1996, from any decision of the High Court under that Part;
- (h) [...]

Note

To the end of the paragraph, add:

; and the Divorce, Dissolution and Separation Act 2020 Sch.1(3) para.46, with effect from 6 April 2022 **9A-63**

Add new s.29A and note paragraph: **9A-98.1**

Further provision in connection with quashing orders

29A.—(1) A quashing order may include provision—

(a) for the quashing not to take effect until a date specified in the order, or

(b) removing or limiting any retrospective effect of the quashing.

(2) Provision included in a quashing order under subsection (1) may be made subject to conditions.

(3) If a quashing order includes provision under subsection (1)(a), the impugned act is (subject to any conditions under subsection (2)) upheld until the quashing takes effect.

(4) If a quashing order includes provision under subsection (1)(b), the impugned act is (subject to any conditions under subsection (2)) upheld in any respect in which the provision under subsection (1)(b) prevents it from being quashed.

(5) Where (and to the extent that) an impugned act is upheld by virtue of subsection (3) or (4), it is to be treated for all purposes as if its validity and force were, and always had been, unimpaired by the relevant defect.

(6) Provision under subsection (1)(a) does not limit any retrospective effect of a quashing order once the quashing takes effect (including in relation to the period between the making of the order and the taking effect of the quashing); and subsections (3) and (5) are to be read accordingly.

(7) Section 29(2) does not prevent the court from varying a date specified under subsection (1)(a).

(8) In deciding whether to exercise a power in subsection (1), the court must have regard to—

(a) the nature and circumstances of the relevant defect;

(b) any detriment to good administration that would result from exercising or failing to exercise the power;

(c) the interests or expectations of persons who would benefit from the quashing of the impugned act;

(d) the interests or expectations of persons who have relied on the impugned act;

(e) so far as appears to the court to be relevant, any action taken or proposed to be taken, or undertaking given, by a person with responsibility in connection with the impugned act;

(f) any other matter that appears to the court to be relevant.

(9) In this section—

"impugned act" means the thing (or purported thing) being quashed by the quashing order;

"relevant defect" means the defect, failure or other matter on the ground of which the court is making the quashing order.

Note —Section 29A was inserted by the Judicial Review and Courts Act 2022 (c.35) s.1(1), with effect from 14 July 2022 (only in relation to proceedings commenced on or after 14 July 2022). **9A-98.2**

Replace s.31 with:

Application for judicial review.

31.—(1) An application to the High Court for one or more of the following forms of relief, namely— **9A-101**

(a) a mandatory, prohibiting or quashing order;
(b) a declaration or injunction under subsection (2); or
(c) an injunction under section 30 restraining a person not entitled to do so from acting in an office to which that section applies,

shall be made in accordance with rules of court by a procedure to be known as an application for judicial review.

(2) A declaration may be made or an injunction granted under this subsection in any case where an application for judicial review, seeking that relief, has been made and the High Court considers that, having regard to—

(a) the nature of the matters in respect of which relief may be granted by mandatory, prohibiting or quashing orders;
(b) the nature of the persons and bodies against whom relief may be granted by such orders; and
(c) all the circumstances of the case,

it would be just and convenient for the declaration to be made or the injunction to be granted, as the case may be.

(2A) The High Court—

(a) must refuse to grant relief on an application for judicial review, and
(b) may not make an award under subsection (4) on such an application,

if it appears to the court to be highly likely that the outcome for the applicant would not have been substantially different if the conduct complained of had not occurred.

(2B) The court may disregard the requirements in subsection (2A)(a) and (b) if it considers that it is appropriate to do so for reasons of exceptional public interest.

(2C) If the court grants relief or makes an award in reliance on subsection (2B), the court must certify that the condition in subsection (2B) is satisfied.

(3) No application for judicial review shall be made unless the leave of the High Court has been obtained in accordance with rules of court; and the court shall not grant leave to make such an application unless—

(a) it considers that the applicant has a sufficient interest in the matter to which the application relates, and
(b) the applicant has provided the court with any information about the financing of the application that is specified in rules of court for the purposes of this paragraph.

(3A) The information that may be specified for the purposes of subsection (3)(b) includes—

(a) information about the source, nature and extent of financial resources available, or likely to be available, to the applicant to meet liabilities arising in connection with the application, and
(b) if the applicant is a body corporate that is unable to demonstrate that it is likely to have financial resources available to meet such liabilities, information about its members and about their ability to provide financial support for the purposes of the application.

(3B) Rules of court under subsection (3)(b) that specify information identifying those who are, or are likely to be, sources of financial support must provide that only a person whose financial support (whether direct or indirect) exceeds, or is likely to exceed, a level set out in the rules has to be identified.

This subsection does not apply to rules that specify information described in subsection (3A)(b).

(3C) When considering whether to grant leave to make an application for judicial review, the High Court—

(a) may of its own motion consider whether the outcome for the applicant would have been substantially different if the conduct complained of had not occurred, and

(b) must consider that question if the defendant asks it to do so.

(3D) If, on considering that question, it appears to the High Court to be highly likely that the outcome for the applicant would not have been substantially different, the court must refuse to grant leave.

(3E) The court may disregard the requirement in subsection (3D) if it considers that it is appropriate to do so for reasons of exceptional public interest.

(3F) If the court grants leave in reliance on subsection (3E), the court must certify that the condition in subsection (3E) is satisfied.

(4) On an application for judicial review the High Court may award to the applicant damages, restitution or the recovery of a sum due if—

(a) the application includes a claim for such an award arising from any matter to which the application relates; and

(b) the court is satisfied that such an award would have been made if the claim had been made in an action begun by the applicant at the time of making the application.

(5) If, on an application for judicial review, the High Court makes a quashing order in respect of the decision to which the application relates, it may in addition—

(a) remit the matter to the court, tribunal or authority which made the decision, with a direction to reconsider the matter and reach a decision in accordance with the findings of the High Court, or

(b) substitute its own decision for the decision in question.

(5A) But the power conferred by subsection (5)(b) is exercisable only if—

(a) the decision in question was made by a court or tribunal,

(b) the quashing order is made on the ground that there has been an error of law, and

(c) without the error, there would have been only one decision which the court or tribunal could have reached.

(5B) Unless the High Court otherwise directs, a decision substituted by it under subsection (5)(b) has effect as if it were a decision of the relevant court or tribunal.

(6) Where the High Court considers that there has been undue delay in making an application for judicial review, the court may refuse to grant—

(a) leave for the making of the application; or

(b) any relief sought on the application,

if it considers that the granting of the relief sought would be likely to cause substantial hardship to, or substantially prejudice the rights of, any person or would be detrimental to good administration.

(7) Subsection (6) is without prejudice to any enactment or rule of court which has the effect of limiting the time within which an application for judicial review may be made.

(8) In this section "the conduct complained of", in relation to an application for judicial review, means the conduct (or alleged conduct) of the defendant that the applicant claims justifies the High Court in granting relief.

Note

To the end of the paragraph, add:

Subsections (5), (5A)(b) were amended by the Judicial Review and Courts Act 2022 (c.35) s.1(2), with effect from 14 July 2022 (only in relation to proceedings commenced on or after 14 July 2022). **9A-101.1**

Courts Act 2003

Add new Part 7ZA at paragraphs 9A-928.7.1 to 9A-928.7.3:

PART 7ZA

TRANSMISSION AND RECORDING OF COURT AND TRIBUNAL PROCEEDINGS

REMOTE OBSERVATION AND RECORDING

Remote observation and recording of proceedings by direction of a court or tribunal

9A-928.7.1 **85A.**—(1) This section applies (subject to subsections (12) and (13)) to proceedings in any court; and in this section "court" has the same meaning as in the Contempt of Court Act 1981 (see section 19 of that Act).

(2) If the proceedings are specified under subsection (8)(a), the court may direct that images or sounds of the proceedings are to be transmitted electronically for the purpose of enabling persons not taking part in the proceedings to watch or listen to the proceedings.

(3) A direction under subsection (2) may authorise only the following types of transmission—

(a) transmission to designated live-streaming premises, or

(b) transmission to which individuals are given access only having first identified themselves to the court (or to a person acting on behalf of the court).

(4) In subsection (3)(a), "designated live-streaming premises" means premises that are designated by the Lord Chancellor as premises that are made available for members of the public to watch or listen to proceedings in accordance with directions under subsection (2).

(5) A direction under subsection (2) may include further provision about—

(a) the manner of transmission, or

(b) the persons who are to be able to watch or listen to the transmission (including provision making that ability subject to conditions, or aimed at preventing persons who are not meant to watch or listen from being able to do so).

(6) If images or sounds of the proceedings are transmitted electronically (whether under a direction under subsection (2) or any other power), the court may direct that a recording of the transmission is to be made, in the manner specified in the direction, for the purpose of enabling the court to keep a record of the proceedings.

(7) A direction under subsection (2) or (6)—

(a) may relate to the whole, or to part, of the proceedings concerned, and

(b) may be varied or revoked.

(8) The Lord Chancellor may by regulations—

(a) specify proceedings (by reference to their type, the court in which they take place, or any other circumstance) in relation to which directions under subsection (2) may be made;

(b) specify matters of which the court must be satisfied before deciding to make such a direction;

(c) specify matters that the court must take into account when deciding whether, and on what terms, to make such a direction;

(d) require directions under subsection (2) to include certain provision under subsection (5).

(9) Before making regulations under subsection (8), the Lord Chancellor must determine whether the function of giving or withholding concurrence to the regulations would most appropriately be exercised by—
(a) the Lord Chief Justice of England and Wales,
(b) the Senior President of Tribunals, or
(c) both of them.

(10) Regulations under subsection (8) may be made only with the concurrence of the Lord Chief Justice of England and Wales, the Senior President of Tribunals, or both of them, as determined under subsection (9).

(11) Regulations under subsection (8) may make different provision for different purposes.

(12) This section does not apply to proceedings in the Supreme Court.

(13) This section does not apply to proceedings if provision regulating the procedure to be followed in those proceedings could be made by—
(a) an Act of the Scottish Parliament,
(b) an Act of Senedd Cymru (including one passed with the consent of a Minister of the Crown within the meaning of section 158(1) of the Government of Wales Act 2006), or
(c) an Act of the Northern Ireland Assembly passed without the consent of the Secretary of State.

Editorial note

The remote observation provisions are implemented by the Remote Observation and Recording (Courts and Tribunals) Regulations 2022 (SI 2022/705) (see para.9B-1499). Also see the Practice Guidance on Remote Observation of Hearings—New Powers (Vol.1 para.39PG.3). **9A-928.7.1.1**

OFFENCE OF RECORDING OR TRANSMISSION

Offence of recording or transmission in relation to remote proceedings

85B.—(1) It is an offence for a person to make, or attempt to make— **9A-928.7.2**
(a) an unauthorised recording, or
(b) an unauthorised transmission,
of an image or sound within subsection (2) or (3).

(2) An image or sound is within this subsection if it is an image or sound of court proceedings that is being transmitted to the place where the recording or transmission referred to in subsection (1) is made or attempted to be made.

(3) An image or sound is within this subsection if it is an image or sound of a person while that person is remotely attending court proceedings.

(4) A person is remotely attending court proceedings at any time when the person—
(a) is not in the same place as any member of the court, and
(b) is taking part in, watching or listening to the proceedings by way of a transmission.

(5) For the purposes of this section a recording or transmission is "unauthorised" unless it is—
(a) authorised (generally or specifically) by the court in which the proceedings concerned are being conducted, or
(b) authorised (generally or specifically) by the Lord Chancellor.

(6) It is a defence for a person charged with an offence under subsection (1) to prove that, at the time of the actual or attempted recording or transmission, the person—
(a) was not in designated live-streaming premises, and
(b) did not know that the image or sound concerned was of a sort within subsection (2) or (3).

(7) In subsection (6)(a), "designated live-streaming premises" has the meaning given by section 85A(4).

(8) A person guilty of an offence under subsection (1) is liable on summary conviction to a fine not exceeding level 3 on the standard scale.

(9) Conduct that amounts to an offence under subsection (1) is also a contempt of court.

But a person cannot, in respect of the same conduct, be both convicted of the offence and punished for the contempt.

(10) For the purposes of this section it does not matter whether a person making, or attempting to make, a recording or transmission intends the recording or transmission, or anything comprised in it, to be seen or heard by any other person.

(11) This section does not apply to proceedings in the Supreme Court.

(12) This section does not apply to court proceedings if provision regulating the procedure to be followed in those proceedings could be made by—

- (a) an Act of the Scottish Parliament,
- (b) an Act of Senedd Cymru (including one passed with the consent of a Minister of the Crown within the meaning of section 158(1) of the Government of Wales Act 2006), or
- (c) an Act of the Northern Ireland Assembly passed without the consent of the Secretary of State.

(13) In this section—

"court" has the same meaning as in the Contempt of Court Act 1981 (see section 19 of that Act);

"court proceedings" means proceedings in any court;

"recording" means a recording on any medium—

- (a) of a single image, a moving image or any sound, or
- (b) from which a single image, a moving image or any sound may be produced or reproduced;

"transmission" means any transmission by electronic means of a single image, a moving image or any sound (and "transmitted" is to be construed accordingly).

9A-928.7.3 *Note* —Part 7ZA inserted by ss.198 and 199 of the Police, Crime, Sentencing and Courts Act 2022. In force from 28 April 2022.

Tribunals, Courts and Enforcement Act 2007

9A-1011 *Replace s.17 and add note paragraph:*

Quashing orders under section 15(1): supplementary provision

17.—(A1) In cases arising under the law of England and Wales, section 29A of the Senior Courts Act 1981 applies in relation to a quashing order under section 15(1)(c) of this Act as it applies in relation to a quashing order under section 29 of that Act.

(1) If the Upper Tribunal makes a quashing order under section 15(1)(c) in respect of a decision, it may in addition—

- (a) remit the matter concerned to the court, tribunal or authority that made the decision, with a direction to reconsider the matter and reach a decision in accordance with the findings of the Upper Tribunal, or
- (b) substitute its own decision for the decision in question.

(2) The power conferred by subsection (1)(b) is exercisable only if—

- (a) the decision in question was made by a court or tribunal,
- (b) the quashing order is made on the ground that there has been an error of law, and
- (c) without the error, there would have been only one decision that the court or tribunal could have reached.

(3) Unless the Upper Tribunal otherwise directs, a decision substituted by it under subsection (1)(b) has effect as if it were a decision of the relevant court or tribunal.

Note —Subsection (A1) was inserted and subs.(2)(b) was amended by the Judicial Review and Courts Act 2022 (c.35) s.1(3), with effect from 14 July 2022 (only in relation to proceedings commenced on or after 14 July 2022). **9A-1011.1**

SECTION 9B OTHER STATUTES AND REGULATIONS

Legal Services Act 2007

Replace s.194 with:

PRO BONO REPRESENTATION

Payments in respect of pro bono representation: civil courts in England and Wales

194.—(1) This section applies to proceedings in a civil court in which— **9B-550**

(a) a party to the proceedings ("P") is or was represented by a legal representative ("R"), and

(b) R's representation of P is or was provided free of charge, in whole or in part.

(2) This section applies to such proceedings even if P is or was also represented by a legal representative not acting free of charge.

(3) The court may order any person to make a payment to the prescribed charity in respect of R's representation of P (or, if only part of R's representation of P was provided free of charge, in respect of that part).

(4) In considering whether to make such an order and the terms of such an order, the court must have regard to—

(a) whether, had R's representation of P not been provided free of charge, it would have ordered the person to make a payment to P in respect of the costs payable to R by P in respect of that representation, and

(b) if it would, what the terms of the order would have been.

(5) The court may not make an order under subsection (3) against a person represented in the proceedings if the person's representation was at all times within subsection (6).

(6) Representation is within this subsection if it is—

(a) provided by a legal representative acting free of charge, or

(b) provided under arrangements made for the purposes of Part 1 of the Legal Aid, Sentencing and Punishment of Offenders Act 2012.

(7) Rules of court may make further provision as to the making of orders under subsection (3), and may in particular—

(a) provide that such orders may not be made in civil proceedings of a description specified in the rules;

(b) make provision about the procedure to be followed in relation to such orders;

(c) specify matters (in addition to those mentioned in subsection (4)) to which the court must have regard in deciding whether to make such an order, and the terms of any order.

(8) "The prescribed charity" means the charity prescribed under section 194C.

(9) [Omitted]

(10) In this section—

"legal representative", in relation to a party to proceedings, means a person exercising a right of audience or conducting litigation on the party's behalf;

"civil court" means—

(a) [Omitted]

(b) the civil division of the Court of Appeal,

(c) the High Court, or

(ca) the family court,

(d) the county court;

"free of charge" means otherwise than for or in expectation of fee, gain or reward.

(11) The court may not make an order under subsection (3) in respect of representation if (or to the extent that) it is provided before this section comes into force.

Note

Add new paragraph at end:

9B-550.1 Further amended by s.48 of the Judicial Review and Courts Act 2022, with effect from 28 June 2022.

9B-550.2 *Add new ss.194A to 194C at paragraphs 9B-550.2 to 9B-550.7:*

Payments in respect of pro bono representation: tribunals

194A.—(1) This section applies to relevant tribunal proceedings in which—

(a) a party to the proceedings ("P") is or was represented by a legal representative ("R"), and

(b) R's representation of P is or was provided free of charge, in whole or in part.

(2) This section applies to such proceedings even if P is or was also represented by a legal representative not acting free of charge.

(3) The tribunal may make an order under this section against a person if the condition in subsection (5) is met in respect of that person (and if subsection (7) does not apply).

(4) An order under this section is an order for the person to make a payment to the prescribed charity in respect of R's representation of P (or, if only part of R's representation of P was provided free of charge, in respect of that part).

(5) The condition is that, had R's representation of P not been provided free of charge, the tribunal would have had the power to order the person to make a payment to P in respect of sums payable to R by P in respect of that representation.

(6) In considering whether to make an order under this section against a person, and the terms of such an order, the tribunal must have regard to—

(a) whether, had R's representation of P not been provided free of charge, it would have made an order against that person as described in subsection (5), and

(b) if it would, what the terms of the order would have been.

(7) The tribunal may not make an order under this section against a person represented in the proceedings if the person's representation was at all times within subsection (8).

(8) Representation is within this subsection if it is provided—

(a) by a legal representative acting free of charge, or

(b) by way of legal aid.

(9) For the purposes of subsection (8)(b), representation is provided by way of legal aid if it is—

(a) provided under arrangements made for the purposes of Part 1 of the Legal Aid, Sentencing and Punishment of Offenders Act 2012,

(b) made available under Part 2 or 3 of the Legal Aid (Scotland) Act 1986, or

(c) funded under Part 2 of the Access to Justice (Northern Ireland) Order 2003 (S.I. 2003/435 (N.I. 10)).

(10) Procedure rules may make further provision as to the making of orders under this section, and may in particular—

(a) provide that such orders may not be made in proceedings of a description specified in the rules;

(b) make provision about the procedure to be followed in relation to such orders;

(c) specify matters (in addition to those mentioned in subsection (6)) to which the tribunal must have regard in deciding whether to make such an order, and the terms of any order.

(11) In this section "relevant tribunal proceedings" means proceedings in

(a) the First-tier Tribunal,

(b) the Upper Tribunal,

(c) an employment tribunal,

(d) the Employment Appeal Tribunal, or

(e) the Competition Appeal Tribunal,

but does not include proceedings within devolved competence.

(12) For the purposes of subsection (11), proceedings are within devolved competence if provision regulating the procedure to be followed in those proceedings could be made by—

(a) an Act of the Scottish Parliament,

(b) an Act of Senedd Cymru (including one passed with the consent of a Minister of the Crown within the meaning of section 158(1) of the Government of Wales Act 2006), or

(c) an Act of the Northern Ireland Assembly the Bill for which would not require the consent of the Secretary of State.

(13) The Lord Chancellor may by regulations—

(a) amend subsection (11) so as to add a tribunal to the list in that subsection, and

(b) make consequential amendments of the definition of "procedure rules" in subsection (14).

(14) In this section—

"free of charge" means otherwise than for or in expectation of fee, gain or reward;

"legal representative" means a person who is—

(a) entitled in accordance with section 13 to carry on the activity of exercising a right of audience or conducting litigation,

(b) a solicitor enrolled in the roll of solicitors kept under section 7 of the Solicitors (Scotland) Act 1980,

(c) a member of the Faculty of Advocates in Scotland,

(d) a person having a right to conduct litigation, or a right of audience, by virtue of section 27 of the Law Reform (Miscellaneous Provisions) (Scotland) Act 1990,

(e) a member of the Bar of Northern Ireland, or

(f) a solicitor of the Court of Judicature of Northern Ireland,

irrespective of the capacity in which the person is acting in the proceedings concerned;

"prescribed charity" means the charity prescribed under section 194C;

"procedure rules" means—

(a) Tribunal Procedure Rules, in relation to proceedings in the First-tier Tribunal or the Upper Tribunal,
(b) Employment Tribunal Procedure Rules, in relation to proceedings in an employment tribunal or the Employment Appeal Tribunal, or
(c) rules under section 15 of the Enterprise Act 2002, in relation to proceedings in the Competition Appeal Tribunal;

"tribunal" does not include an ordinary court of law.

(15) An order under this section may not be made in respect of representation if (or to the extent that) it was provided before section 48 of the Judicial Review and Courts Act 2022 came into force.

9B-550.3 *Note* —Section 194A inserted by s.48 of the Judicial Review and Courts Act 2022, with effect from 28 June 2022.

Payments in respect of pro bono representation: Supreme Court

9B-550.4 **194B.—**(1) This section applies to proceedings in a relevant civil appeal to the Supreme Court in which—

(a) a party to the proceedings ("P") is or was represented by a legal representative ("R"), and
(b) R's representation of P is or was provided free of charge, in whole or in part.

(2) This section applies to such proceedings even if P is or was also represented by a legal representative not acting free of charge.

(3) The Court may make an order under this section against a person if the condition in subsection (5) is met in respect of that person (and if subsection (7) does not apply).

(4) An order under this section is an order for the person to make a payment to the prescribed charity in respect of R's representation of P (or, if only part of R's representation of P was provided free of charge, in respect of that part).

(5) The condition is that, had R's representation of P not been provided free of charge, the Court would have had the power to order the person to make a payment to P in respect of sums payable to R by P in respect of that representation.

(6) In considering whether to make an order under this section against a person, and the terms of such an order, the Court must have regard to—

(a) whether, had R's representation of P not been provided free of charge, it would have made an order against that person as described in subsection (5), and
(b) if it would, what the terms of the order would have been.

(7) The Court may not make an order under this section against a person represented in the proceedings if the person's representation was at all times within subsection (8).

(8) Representation is within this subsection if it is—

(a) provided by a legal representative acting free of charge, or
(b) provided by way of legal aid.

(9) For the purposes of subsection (8)(b), representation is provided by way of legal aid if it is—

(a) provided under arrangements made for the purposes of Part 1 of the Legal Aid, Sentencing and Punishment of Offenders Act 2012, or
(b) funded under Part 2 of the Access to Justice (Northern Ireland) Order 2003 (S.I. 2003/435 (N.I. 10)).

(10) Supreme Court Rules may make further provision as to the making of orders under this section, and may in particular—

(a) provide that such orders may not be made in proceedings of a description specified in the Rules;

(b) make provision about the procedure to be followed in relation to such orders;

(c) specify matters (in addition to those mentioned in subsection (6)) to which the Court must have regard in deciding whether to make such an order, and the terms of any order.

(11) In this section -

"free of charge" means otherwise than for or in expectation of fee, gain or reward;

"legal representative", in relation to a party to proceedings, means—

(a) a person exercising a right of audience, or conducting litigation, on the party's behalf pursuant to an entitlement under section 13, or

(b) a member of the Bar of Northern Ireland, or a solicitor of the Court of Judicature of Northern Ireland, practising or acting as such on the party's behalf;

"prescribed charity" means the charity prescribed under section 194C;

"relevant civil appeal" means an appeal—

(a) from the High Court under Part 2 of the Administration of Justice Act 1969,

(b) from the Upper Tribunal under section 14B(4) of the Tribunals, Courts and Enforcement Act 2007,

(c) from the Court of Appeal under section 40(2) of the Constitutional Reform Act 2005 or section 42 of the Judicature (Northern Ireland) Act 1978, or

(d) under section 13 of the Administration of Justice Act 1960 (appeal in cases of contempt of court), other than an appeal from an order or decision made in the exercise of jurisdiction to punish for criminal contempt of court.

(12) An order under this section may not be made in respect of representation in proceedings in a relevant civil appeal—

(a) from a court in Northern Ireland, or

(b) from the Upper Tribunal under section 14B(4) of the Tribunals, Courts and Enforcement Act 2007,

if (or to the extent that) the representation was provided before section 48 of the Judicial Review and Courts Act 2022 came into force.

Note —Section 194B inserted by s.48 of the Judicial Review and Courts Act 2022, with effect from 28 June 2022. **9B-550.5**

Sections 194 to 194B: the prescribed charity

194C.—(1) The Lord Chancellor may by order prescribe a registered charity for the purposes of sections 194 to 194B. **9B-550.6**

(2) The charity must be one which provides financial support to persons who provide, or organise or facilitate the provision of, legal advice or assistance (by way of representation or otherwise) which is free of charge.

(3) In this section—

"free of charge" means otherwise than for or in expectation of fee, gain or reward;

"registered charity" means a charity registered in accordance with—

(a) section 30 of the Charities Act 2011,

(b) section 3 of the Charities and Trustee Investment (Scotland) Act 2005 (asp 10), or

(c) section 16 of the Charities Act (Northern Ireland) 2008 (c. 12 (N.I.)).

(4) An order under section 194(8) that was in force immediately before section 48 of the Judicial Review and Courts Act 2022 came into force—

(a) remains in force despite the amendment by that section of section 194(8),
(b) has effect as if its prescription of a charity for the purposes of section 194 were the prescription of that charity under this section for the purposes of sections 194 to 194B, and
(c) may be amended or revoked by an order under this section.

9B-550.7 *Note* —Section 194C inserted by s.48 of the Judicial Review and Courts Act 2022, with effect from 28 June 2022.

High Court and County Courts Jurisdiction Order 1991

Replace s.8A with:

Enforcement of traffic penalties

9B-943 **8A.**—(1) Proceedings for the recovery of—
(a) increased penalty charges provided for in charge certificates issued under—
(i) paragraph 6 of Schedule 6 to the 1991 Act;
(ii) paragraph 8 of Schedule 1 to the London Local Authorities Act 1996
(iii) regulation 17 of the Road User Charging (Enforcement and Adjudication) (London) Regulations 2001;
(iv) regulation 21 of the Civil Enforcement of Parking Contraventions (England) General Regulations 2007; and
(v) regulation 13 of the Civil Enforcement of Parking Contraventions (Penalty Charge Notices, Enforcement and Adjudication) (Wales) Regulations 2008;
(b) amounts payable by a person other than a local authority under an adjudication of a parking adjudicator pursuant to section 73 of the 1991 Act
(c) amounts payable by a person other than a local authority under an adjudication pursuant to—
(i) the Road User Charging (Enforcement and Adjudication) (London) Regulations 2001;
(ii) the Civil Enforcement of Road Traffic Contraventions (Representations and Appeals) (England) Regulations 2022; and
(iii) the Civil Enforcement of Parking Contraventions (Representations and Appeals) (Wales) Regulations 2008; and
(d) increased fixed penalties referred to in—
(i) regulation 17(6) of the Road Traffic (Vehicle Emissions) (Fixed Penalty) (England) Regulations 2002; and
(ii) regulation 17(6) of the Road Traffic (Vehicle Emissions) (Fixed Penalty) (Wales) Regulations 2003,

shall be taken in the County Court

(2) In this article, "the 1991 Act" means the Road Traffic Act 1991.

(3) In this article, "a local authority" means—
(a) in England, a London borough council, the Common Council of the City of London, Transport for London,, a county or district council or the Council of the Isles of Scilly; and
(b) in Wales, a county or county borough council.

Note

Replace paragraph with:

Amended by the High Court and County Courts Jurisdiction (Amendment) Order 1993 (SI 1993/1407), the High Court and County Courts Jurisdiction (Amendment) Order 1995 (SI 1995/205), the High Court and County Courts Jurisdiction (Amendment) Order 2001 (SI 2001/1387); (in relation to proceedings issued on or after 6 April 2009) the High Court and County Courts Jurisdiction (Amendment) Order 2009 (SI 2009/577); the High Court and County Court Jurisdiction (Amendment) Order 2014 (SI 2014/821) with effect from 22 April 2014; and the Civil Enforcement of Road Traffic Contraventions (Representations and Appeals) (England) Regulations 2022 (SI 2022/576) Sch.2 para.1, with effect from 31 May 2022. **9B-944**

Add "Remote Observation and Recording (Courts and Tribunals) Regulations 2022":

Remote Observation and Recording (Courts and Tribunals) Regulations 2022

(SI 2022/705)

Citation, commencement, interpretation and extent

1.—(1) These Regulations may be cited as the Remote Observation and Recording (Courts and Tribunals) Regulations 2022 and come into force on 28th June 2022. **9B-1499**

(2) In these Regulations, "section 85A" means section 85A of the Courts Act 2003 .

(3) These Regulations extend to England and Wales, Scotland and Northern Ireland.

Specified proceedings

2. Directions under section 85A(2) may be given in relation to proceedings, of any type and in any court to which section 85A applies, which are— **9B-1500**

(a) in public; or

(b) proceedings at which the general public is not entitled to be present but specific categories of person, or specific individuals, who are not taking part in the proceedings are entitled to be present by virtue of provision made by or under any enactment or of being authorised by the court.

Matters of which the court must be satisfied

3. Before making a direction under section 85A(2), the court must be satisfied that— **9B-1501**

(a) it would be in the interests of justice to make the direction; and

(b) there is capacity and technological capability to enable transmission, and giving effect to the direction would not create an unreasonable administrative burden.

Matters that the court must take into account

4. Before deciding whether, and on what terms, to make a direction under section 85A(2), the court must take into account— **9B-1502**

(a) the need for the administration of justice to be, as far as possible, open and transparent;

(b) the timing of any request or application to the court or tribunal to make a direction, and its impact on the business of the court or tribunal;

(c) the extent to which the technical, human and other resources necessary to facilitate effective remote observation are or can be made available;

(d) any limitation imposed by or under any enactment on the persons who are entitled to be present at the proceedings;

(e) any issues which might arise if persons who are outside the United

Kingdom are among those watching or listening to the transmission;
(f) any impact which the making or withholding of such a direction, or the terms of the direction, might have upon—
(i) the content or quality of the evidence to be put before the court or tribunal;
(ii) public understanding of the law and the administration of justice;
(iii) the ability of the public, including the media, to observe and scrutinise the proceedings;
(iv) the safety and right to privacy of any person involved with the proceedings.

Provision which must be included in a direction

9B-1503 **5.**—(1) A direction under section 85A(2) made in relation to proceedings specified in regulation 2(b) must include provision which has the effect of—
(a) prohibiting any person other than a person entitled to be present at those proceedings from watching or listening to the transmission; and
(b) requiring any person so entitled to demonstrate, in such manner as specified in the direction, the capacity in which that person is so entitled.

(2) A direction under section 85A(2) made in relation to any proceedings must, except where the direction is for transmission to designated live-streaming premises, include provision which has the effect—
(a) that no person will be able to watch or listen to the transmission without first, when identifying themselves to the court, providing their full name and their email address, unless the court dispenses with this requirement;
(b) of requiring as a condition of continued access that any person given access will during the transmission conduct themselves appropriately and in particular in accordance with any requirements of the direction or instructions of the judge for persons observing the proceedings.

SECTION 10 COURT FEES

Civil Proceedings Fees Order 2008

10-3.2.2 *Add article 3B and note paragraph:*

(3B) Fees 2.4(a) (on an application on notice where no other fee is specified) and 2.5(a) (on an application by consent or without notice where no other fee is specified) in Schedule 1 (fees to be taken) are not payable in respect of any application made by reference to sections 85F-K of the Courts Act 2003[1]
for an order or direction of the court relating to cross-examination in person of a party to or witness in the proceedings.

10-3.2.3 *Note* —Article 3B inserted by the Civil and Family Proceedings Fees (Amendment) Order 2022 (SI 2022/540) art.2, with effect from 21 July 2022.

[1] 2003 c. 39. There are no relevant amendments. Sections 85F-K were inserted by s.66 of the Domestic Abuse Act 2021 .

SECTION 13 RIGHTS OF AUDIENCE

D. Person Assisting in the Conduct of Litigation or Engaged in Legal Employment

Replace the second paragraph with:

Some unqualified persons who offer advocacy services describe themselves as "solicitor's agents". **13-10** This is a misleading term in this context as it implies an authority which does not exist. "Solicitor's agent" is not a term used in the 2007 Act. Such persons are generally self-employed and obtain work through an agency. Being unqualified they are not subject to the disciplinary process of any profession. Importantly, they are not "authorised persons" within s.18 of the 2007 Act nor "exempt persons" within s.19 and Sch.3 para.1(7) states that a right of audience accrues to such a person when they are: assisting in the conduct of litigation (see Sch.2 para.4(1), *Agassi v Robinson* [2006] 1 W.L.R. 2126, CA, paras 54-5); acting under the instructions and supervision of an authorised litigator e.g., a solicitor; acting in proceedings that are not being heard in chambers and which are not reserved family proceedings (see s.67 Senior Courts Act 1981 and CPR r.39.2). There is, unfortunately, a lack of clarity within the CPR as to what amounts to a hearing in 'chambers'. It is however, apparent, that a hearing 'in chambers' is not a hearing 'in private', but rather one held in a judge's chambers rather than a court room; *Hodgson v Imperial Tobacco Ltd* [1998] 1 W.L.R. 1056, CA, at 1069 and following, and see *R v Bow County Court* [1999] 1 W.L.R. 1807, CA, at 1813. Furthermore, there has yet to be authoritative general guidance on the application of Sch.3 para.1(7). Two County Court decisions concerning the application of the provision are illustrative of the need for a court to consider each aspect of the provision: *McShane v Lincoln*, 28 June 2016, unrep., County Court at Birkenhead (DJ Peake); *Ellis v Larson* 20 September 2016, unrep., County Court at Manchester (DDJ Hampson). Where the criteria in Sch.3 para.1(7) are satisfied, the court retains no discretion to refuse a right of audience (see *In re HS (Minors) (Chambers Proceedings: Right of Audience)* [1998] 1 F.L.R. 868, CA, in respect of the position under statutory predecessor to the current provision, s.27(2)(e) of the 1990 Act).

SECTION 14 ALTERNATIVE DISPUTE RESOLUTION

1. Introduction to ADR and its promotion

Introduction

Replace the third paragraph with:

The following summer saw another step towards mandatory mediation with publication of **14-1** Government consultation paper on proposals for automatically referring parties in small claims track to a free session with an HMCTS mediator. There may be exemptions for some case types. Further, the paper speaks of a future ambition to extend the requirement to mediate to all County Court claims. *https://consult.justice.gov.uk/dispute-resolution/increasing-the-use-of-mediation/supporting_documents/mediationconsultationweb.pdf* [Accessed 28 October 2022]

Given the facts that the Ministry of Justice and the senior judiciary have both welcomed the centrality of what have previously been regarded as "alternative" methods of dispute resolution and the role of ADR as an integral part of the developing online processes, while Halsey remains good law for the time being its future influence is likely to be one of terminal decline until it is formally set aside either by the Rule Committee or the Court of Appeal. The changes arising from this significant policy shift will take time to implement but the Master of the Rolls' leadership has seen the beginning of a change in culture: "I intend to try to make sure that the provision of ADR is at the heart of all parts of the civil justice firmament." (*https://www.judiciary.uk/announcements/speech-by-sir-geoffrey-voss-master-of-the-rolls-speech-to-hull-university* [Accessed 28 October 2022]. On the broader development of ADR, and particularly the integration of online dispute resolution into civil procedure as part of the HMCTS reform project, see: Ministry of Justice, Dispute Resolution in England and Wales: Call for Evidence (August 2021) (*https://assets.publishing.service.gov.uk/government/uploads/system/uploads/attachment_data/file/1008487/dispute-resolution-in-england-and-wales-call-for-evidence.pdf* [Accessed 28 October 2022]). See also mediated interventions within the Court Dispute Resolution Process (*https://www.judiciary.uk/wp-content/uploads/2021/10/Master-of-the-Rolls-GEMME-Mediated-interventions-within-the-Court-Dis-*

pute-Resolution-Process.pdf [Accessed 28 October 2022]), How Judges Work: a Reappraisal for the 21st Century Justice (*https://www.judiciary.uk/wp-content/uploads/2021/11/Master-of-the-Rolls-How-Judges-Work-A-Reappraisal-for-the-21st-Century.pdf* [Accessed 28 October 2022]), The Future for Dispute Resolution—Horizon Scanning (*https://www.judiciary.uk/wp-content/uploads/2022/03/MR-to-SCL-Sir-Brain-Neill-Lecture-2022-The-Future-for-Dispute-Resolution-Horizon-Scannings-.pdf* [Accessed 28 October 2022]) and "Mandating mediation: the digital solution" *https://www.judiciary.uk/announcements/speech-by-the-master-of-the-rolls-ciarb-roebuck-lecture* [Accessed 28 October 2022]. The term "ADR" may become anachronistic and be replaced by "Dispute Resolution" or "DR".

ADR in pre-action protocols

Replace the last paragraph with:

14-3 Reference to ADR can be found in the several protocols as follows (for complete texts, see Vol.1, Section C (Pre-Action Protocols)):

- Pre-Action Protocol for Personal Injury Claims, para.9;
- Pre-Action Protocol for the Resolution of Clinical Disputes, para.5;
- Pre-Action Protocol for Construction and Engineering Disputes, paras 5.1 to 5.7;
- Pre-Action Protocol for Defamation, paras 3.7 to 3.9;
- Pre-Action Protocol for Professional Negligence, para.12;
- Pre-Action Protocol for Judicial Review, para.9;
- Pre-action Protocols for Disease and Illness Claims, paras 2A.1 to 2A.4;
- Pre-Action Protocol for Housing Disrepair Claims, para.4;
- Pre-Action Protocol for Possession Claims by Social Landlords, para.2.10.

ADR in Court Guides and Handbooks

Replace list item "Chancery Guide, Ch.17 (Alternative Dispute Resolution) paras 17.1 to 17.6;" with:

14-4
- Chancery Guide 2022, Ch.10 (Alternative Dispute Resolution) paras 17.1 to 17.6, Appendix K and L;

2. ADR and Case Management

Active case management in relation to ADR after the introduction of the CPR

In the first sentence, replace "This section should be read in the context of para.14-1 above." with:

14-6 This section should be read in the context of recent developments and the move towards mandatory mediation referred to in para.14-1

In the penultimate paragraph, after the quote (ending "be of benefit"), add:

The passage immediately above was referred to by one of the parties in the Grenfell Tower Litigation in support of a submission for a stay for ADR [2022] EWHC 2006 (QB) at [54].

Add new paragraph at end:

See also *Newcastle Upon Tyne Hospitals NHS Foundation Trust v H (A Child)* [2022] EWCOP 14 (Hayden J, p.25)

> "The availability of such a (mediation) service strikes me as having invaluable potential, even where it doesn't achieve its stated objectives. It may for example, establish a greater respect for and understanding of different views. This in turn may defuse some distress and anger and benefit the parties in the court process that follows."

ADR, Halsey and the prohibition on compulsory mediation

In the ninth paragraph, replace the second quote with:

14-7
> "24. I think it is no longer enough to leave the parties the opportunity to mediate and to warn of costs consequences if the opportunity is not taken. In boundary and neighbour disputes the opportunities are not being taken and the warnings are not being heeded, and those embroiled in them need saving from themselves. The Court cannot oblige truly unwilling parties to submit their disputes to mediation: but I do not see why, in the notorious case of boundary and neighbour disputes, directing the parties to take (over a short defined period) all reasonable steps to resolve the dispute by mediation before preparing for a trial should be regarded as an unacceptable obstruction on the right of access to justice." (See also, regarding right of way and boundary disputes, *Oliver v Symons* [2012] EWCA Civ 267 (Elias LJ at [1] and Ward LJ at [53]); *Bramwell v Robinson* [2016] 10 WLUK 495, 21 October 2016, unrep., (Behrens HHJ at [1]) and, regarding domestic property renovation building contract disputes, *The Sky's the Limit Transformations Ltd v Mirza* [2022] EWHC 29 (TCC) (HHJ Stephen Davies at [6]-[9]).

Replace the last line in the last paragraph, with:

See also the findings of the Civil Justice Council Report "Compulsory Mediation" para.14-1

Add new paragraph at end:

See *The Sky's the Limit Transformations Ltd v Mirza* [2022] EWHC 29 (TCC) for a suggestion that in some circumstances the court may now be willing to order mediation (HHJ Stephen Davies at [6]–[9]).

Case management: facilitation of ADR procedures and criteria for referral to ADR

Replace paragraph with:

The overriding objective in the CPR, which is to enable "...the court to deal with cases justly and at proportionate cost" (r1.1(1)), requires the court to encourage the use of an ADR procedure, in appropriate cases, and to facilitate the use of such procedure, as one of the elements of active case management (r.1.4(2)(e)). The concept of proportionality reinforces the need for the court to keep the potential of ADR procedures under review whenever it deals with any aspect of case management. It should be noted, when considering case management, that although ADR, and mediation in particular, often leads to settlement of the entire action, there is the potential to use an ADR process to attempt settlement or agreement of discrete issues. This can be particularly useful in multi-party cases; see, for example *Supershield Ltd v Siemens Building Technologies FE Ltd* [2010] EWCA Civ 7; [2010] 2 All E.R. (Comm) 1185; [2010] 1 Lloyd's Rep. 349 and *Mouchel Ltd v Van Oord (UK) Ltd* [2011] EWHC 72 (TCC); 135 Con. L.R. 183. The report on Senior Master Fontaine's case management of the Grenfell Tower Litigation at [2022] EWHC 2006 (QB) illustrates many facets of how ADR can be deployed during the case management of a multi-party case and that both the court and lawyers now demonstrate a sophisticated grasp of how to interweave an ADR process in with the litigation process of a complex action. Master Fontaine said (at para.105): **14-9**

> "I consider that the ADR process being established is the obviously appropriate course to attempt before proceeding with litigation involving more than 1,000 Claimants and multiple Defendants. Although it may be that not all issues will be capable of settlement, it is highly likely that there will be a sufficient number of settlements and/or narrowing of issues so that when the stay is lifted more efficient progress to resolution of these claims can be made in the litigation."

The manner in which the court may facilitate the use of an ADR procedure includes the following:

(i) by ensuring that the opportunity to explore ADR prospects is not prejudiced by the rigours of case management procedures generally. (For example, see *Electrical Waste Recycling Group Ltd v Philips Electronics UK Ltd* [2012] EWHC 38 (Ch) where the court considered how ordering a split trial might impact on the prospects of mediating the matter.) In *CIP Properties (AIPT) Ltd v Galliford Try Infrastructure Ltd* [2014] EWHC 3546 (TCC); [2015] 1 All E.R. (Comm) 765; 156 Con. L.R. 202 Coulson J suggested "A timetable for trial that allows the parties to take part in ADR along the way is a sensible case management tool";

(ii) by acting as a source of information about professional and commercial bodies providing ADR services (for example, see *http://www.civilmediation.justice.gov.uk* [Accessed 28 October 2022];

(iii) by verbally encouraging the parties to consider ADR at a hearing or telephone conference, such as a case management conference or a pre-trial review;

(iv) by ordering a stay of the whole or part of the proceedings, for mediation or some other ADR procedure, pursuant to the application of the parties or one of them (r.3.1(2)(f) and r.3.3(1) (see the Grenfell Tower Litigation at [2022] EWHC 2006 (QB));

(v) by ordering such a stay of its own initiative (r.3.1(2)(f) and r.3.3(1)). An appropriate time to make such an order might be upon perusal of the parties' statements about ADR in their directions questionnaires;

(vi) by ordering such a stay upon the written request of a party or of its own initiative when considering completed directions questionnaires (r.26.4). (See also Standard Directions Model Paragraph B05-stay for settlement which provides:

> "1. ...
> 2. The claim is stayed until xxxx, during which period the parties will attempt to settle the matter or to narrow the issues.
> 3. By 4pm on xxxx the Claimant must notify the court in writing of the outcome of negotiations (without disclosing any matters which remain subject to "without prejudice" terms) and what, if any, further directions are sought. Failure to comply with this direction or to engage properly in negotiations may result in the application of sanctions. If settlement has been reached, the parties must file a consent order signed by all of them." (See *https://www.justice.gov.uk/courts/procedure-rules/civil/standard-directions/list-of-cases-of-common-occurrence/menu-of-sd-paragraphs* (B05-ADR.doc) [Accessed 28 October 2022]).

(vii) By ordering the parties to consider ADR (including Mediation) using, for example a direction in the form of *Standard Directions Model Paragraph A03-ADR.doc*, whether at the time of giving standard directions or otherwise as follows:

> "1. ...
> 2. At all stages the parties must consider settling this litigation by any means of Alternative Dispute Resolution (including Mediation); any party not engaging in any such means proposed by another must serve a witness statement giving reasons within 21 days of that proposal; such witness statement must not be shown to the trial judge until questions of costs arise.

3. '21 days' can be altered manually. The words 'and not less than 28 days before trial' can always be added after the word 'proposal' by the managing judge if appropriate. Not necessary for every Order." (See *https://www.justice.gov.uk/courts/procedure-rules/civil/standard-directions/list-of-cases-of-common-occurrence/menu-of-sd-paragraphs* (A03-ADR.doc) [Accessed 28 October 2022]). It might be particularly appropriate to consider directions of the type referred to immediately above when considering cost budgets and proportionality during the costs management and case management process. Such directions might be combined with directions designed to facilitate the holding of an immediate mediation. For example, provision could be made for early disclosure of a particular category of documents that would facilitate a mediation prior to full disclosure. See *Mann v Mann* [2014] EWHC 537 (Fam); [2014] 1 W.L.R. 2807; [2014] 2 F.L.R. 928 at [525]. In respect of directions for a stay in boundary disputes see the observations about *Bradley v Heslin* [2014] EWHC 3267 (Ch); [2014] 10 WLUK 287 in para.14-7 above.

(viii) By making an order, whether on directions for allocation or a later stage, of the type referred to in the Multi-Track Practice Direction (sometimes referred to as an "Ungley Order") (29PD4.10(9).

(ix) By making an ADR order on the basis of the draft in App.7 to the Admiralty and Commercial Courts Guide. The draft order includes the following paragraph: "4. The parties shall take such serious steps as they may be advised to resolve their disputes by ADR procedures before the neutral individual or panel so chosen by no later than [*]."

(x) By making an ADR order on the basis of the draft order in App.E to and Section 7 of the Technology and Construction Court Guide. Although these Guides refer to their particular courts there appears to be no reason why the type of ADR orders made in these courts could not be made, where appropriate, in other courts.

(xi) By ordering Early Neutral Evaluation. See CPR r.3.1(2)(m) and *Lomax v Lomax* [2019] EWCA Civ 1467; [2019] 1 W.L.R. 6527.

(xii) By arranging, in the Admiralty and Commercial Court or the Technology and Construction Court, for the court to provide Early Neutral Evaluation. Further, in the Technology and Construction Court the court can provide a judge to act as a mediator. (See *http://www.justice.gov.uk/downloads/courts/tech-court/tech-con-court-guide.pdf* [Accessed 28 October 2022].)

(xiii) By, in a case which is suitable to be resolved by an ADR procedure except for one sticking point, ordering the hearing of that point as a preliminary issue with a view to the case then being referred to ADR (see s.8 of the Technology and Construction Court Guide, again there is no reason why the approach taken by the Technology and Construction Court cannot be taken by other courts, where appropriate).

(xiv) By, ordering a stay for mediation followed, if necessary, by either an order for mediation or for compulsory early neutral evaluation. Such a tiered approach was suggested by HHJ Stephen Davies as part of a streamlined proportionate procedure for domestic property renovation building contract disputes in the *Sky's the Limit Transformations Ltd v Mirza* [2022] EWHC 29 (TCC).

(xv) By referring a small claim to the Small Claims Mediation Service.

(xvi) By making an appropriate costs order (or advising that such an order might be made in the future) in respect of failure to give adequate consideration to ADR prior to the commencement of proceedings.

(xvii) By providing information about Practice Direction 36V regarding the Family Mediation Voucher Scheme, which is designed to offer a financial contribution of £500 towards mediation costs for eligible cases. Family Procedure Rules 2010 (SI 2010/2955) r.36.2

(xviii) By refusing a party's application to the court unless and until ADR is attempted. See *Hussain v Chowdhury* [2020] EWHC 790 (Ch) at [18] where HHJ Jarman QC refused to give permission to commence charity proceedings until the parties "engaged in a meaningful way in mediation with a professional mediator." See also *Jaffer v Jaffer* [2021] EWHC 1329 (Ch). Another example is *Wilmington Trust SP Services (Dublin) Ltd v Spicejet Ltd* [2021] EWHC 1117 (Comm) where the court considered (at [74]):

"that the course most conducive to the furtherance of the overriding objective and the interests of justice (was) to give judgment for the First Claimant's undisputed claims but to stay execution. In that way, the entire dispute can be brought within the ambit of any ADR procedures that the parties may choose to adopt."

Case management: where a public authority is a party

Add new paragraph at end:

14-11 In *JR138's Application for Judicial Review* [2022] NIQB 46, an application in Northern Ireland, the court identified the case as an example of litigation coming before the court with increasing frequency. This was where a person in need contends that a health and social care trust is not providing them with the services to which they are entitled and which they desperately need. The court analysed (at [39]) why it was often unable to be of significant assistance in such matters and urged parties dealing with these issues to give serious consideration to mediation.

3. ADR and Costs

Cost sanctions and ADR

Before the penultimate paragraph, add new paragraph:

In *Richards v Speechly Bircham Llp* [2022] EWHC 1512 (Comm) HHJ Russen (sitting as a High Court judge) refused an application for indemnity costs notwithstanding that the defendants had been unreasonable in failing to mediate. He found that, in the circumstances of the case, this was only one aspect of the conduct to be considered in the exercise of the discretion under CPR 44.2. and such a such refusal did not automatically lead to costs penalties. Masood Ahmed, University of Leicester, has analysed the judgment in a Law Society Gazette article at *https://www.lawgazette.co.uk/legal-updates/unreasonable-refusal-to-engage-with-adr/5113250.article* [Accessed 28 October 2022] **14-13**

After the penultimate paragraph, add new paragraph:

See also *Benyatov v Credit Suisse Securities (Europe) Ltd* [2022] EWHC 528 (QB) (Freedman J, pp.29–34) and *Huntsworth Wine Co Ltd v London City Bond Ltd* [2022] EWHC 97 (Comm).

Costs where ADR declined

To the end of the fourteenth paragraph (after citation for "Wales (t/a Selective Investment Services) v CBRE Managed Services Ltd"), add:

and *Geoquip Marine Operations AG v Tower Resources Cameroon SA* [2022] EWHC 1408 (Comm) **14-14**

In the sixth last paragraph, replace "Courtwell Properties Ltd v Greencore PF (UK) Ltd [2014] EWHC 184 (TCC); [2014] 2 Costs L.O. 289; [2014] C.I.L.L. 3481, but contrast this with" with:

Courtwell Properties Ltd v Greencore PF (UK) Ltd [2014] EWHC 184 (TCC); [2014] 2 Costs L.O. 289; [2014] C.I.L.L. 3481 and in *Richards v Speechly Bircham LLP* [2022] EWHC 1512 (Comm), but contrast these cases with

4. ADR, confidentiality, without prejudice and "mediation privilege" in relation to mediation

Without prejudice

In the seventh paragraph, replace "Chantry Vellacott v Convergence Group [2007] EWHC 1774 and Carleton (Earl of Malmesbury) v Strutt & Parker (A Partnership) [2008] EWHC 424 (QB); 118 Con. L.R. 68; [2008] 5 Costs L.R. 736. In the latter case" with:

Chantry Vellacott v Convergence Group [2007] EWHC 1774, *Carleton (Earl of Malmesbury) v Strutt & Parker (A Partnership)* [2008] EWHC 424 (QB) and *Pedriks v Grimaux* [2021] EWHC 3448 (QB) (at [13]). In *Carleton,* **14-19**

To the end of the last paragraph, add:

An example of a case where the court refused to permit a party relying on matters that took place at a mediation is *E (A Child) (Mediation Privilege), Re* [2020] EWHC 3379 (Fam)

Without prejudice—threats

To the end of the paragraph, add:

See also *Interactive Technology Corporation Ltd v Ferster* [2015] EWHC 3895 (Ch) **14-20**

Mediation privilege

In the third paragraph, replace "Mr Justice Briggs" with:

Mr Justice Briggs, as he then was, **14-22**

Miscellaneous matters

To the end of the penultimate paragraph, add:

See also *Pedriks v Grimaux* [2021] EWHC 3448 (QB) where the court considered alleged breaches of a mediation settlement agreement in a commercial dispute relating to fiduciary relationships and estoppel by representation **14-25**

SECTION 15 INTERIM REMEDIES

A. Interim Injunctions

10. Interim Injunctions in Particular Proceedings

(a) Restricting freedom of expression, assembly or association

(i) The rights to freedom of expression, assembly and association

Add new paragraph at end:

15-41 The usual case will involve a balancing exercise between art.8 and art.10. Where the case engages rights under art.2 or art.3, there is conflicting first-instance authority as to whether such rights fall to be balanced against art.10. See the discussion in *HM Attorney General for England and Wales v BBC* [2022] EWHC 826 (QB), Chamberlain J of *RXG v Ministry of Justice* [2019] EWHC 2026 (QB); [2020] Q.B. 703 (Sharp P & Nicklin J), *A v Persons Unknown* [2016] EWHC 3295 (Ch);]2017] E.M.L.R. 11 (Vos C), and *Re Al Makhtoum (Reporting Restrictions)* [2020] EWHC 702 (Fam); [2020] E.M.L.R. 17 (McFarlane P).

12. Injunctions Against Persons Unknown

Replace the sixth paragraph with:

15-53.1 In *Barking and Dagenham LBC v Persons Unknown* [2022] EWCA Civ 13, the Court of Appeal clarified that injunctions against persons unknown, whether interim or final, can bind newcomers who become aware of the order made and "make themselves" a party by violating such order. Statements to the contrary in *Canada Goose UK Retail Ltd v Persons Unknown* [2020] EWCA Civ 303; [2020] 1 W.L.R. 2802, at [89]-[92], were inconsistent with earlier decisions of the Court of Appeal and were not to be regarded as good law.

APPENDIX 1 COURTS DIRECTORY

County Court Directory

Editorial note

Replace paragraph with:

AP-7 The County Court Directory was set out in the Schedule to PD 2C—Starting Proceedings in the County Court. It is retained at AP-9 for information.

County Court Directory

Delete paragraph AP-8.

INDEX

LEGAL TAXONOMY
FROM SWEET & MAXWELL

This index has been prepared using Sweet & Maxwell's Legal Taxonomy. Main index entries conform to keywords provided by the Legal Taxonomy except where references to specific documents or non-standard terms (denoted by quotation marks) have been included. These keywords provide a means of identifying similar concepts in other Sweet & Maxwell publications and online services to which keywords from the Legal Taxonomy have been applied. Readers may find some minor differences between terms used in the text and those which appear in the index. Suggestions to *sweetandmaxwell.taxonomy@tr.com.*

(All references are to paragraph numbers)

Paragraph numbers marked "+" denote online/CD content; those within [...] refer to Volume 2

Paragraph numbers marked "+" denote online/CD content; those within [...] refer to Volume 2

Paragraph numbers marked "+" denote online/CD content; those within [...] refer to Volume 2

Paragraph numbers marked "+" denote online/CD content; those within [...] refer to Volume 2